Compton, W. M., Thomas, Y. F., Stinson, F. S., & Grant, B. F. (2007). Prevalence, correlates, disability, and comorbidity of DSM-IV drug abuse and dependence in the United States. *Archives of General Psychiatry, 64,* 566–576. (Ch. 15)

Curry, D. T., Eisenstein, R. D., & Walsh, J. K. (2006). Pharmacologic management of insomnia: Past, present, and future. *Psychiatric Clinics of North America, 29,* 871–893. (Ch. 9)

Dapretto, M., Davies, M. S., Pfeifer, J. H., Scott, A. A., Sigman, M., Bookheimer, S. Y., et al. (2006). Understanding emotions in others: Mirror neuron dysfunction in children with autism spectrum disorders. *Nature Neuroscience, 9,* 28–30. (Ch. 3)

Deary, I. J., Strand, S., Smith, P., & Fernandes, C. (2007). Intelligence and educational achievement. *Intelligence, 35,* 13–21. (Ch. 10)

Deshpande, D. M., Kim, Y. S., Martinez, T., Carmen, J., Dike, S., Shats, I., et al. (2006). Recovery from paralysis in adult rats using embryonic stem cells. *Annals of Neurology, 60,* 32–44. (Ch. 3)

Di Milia, L. (2006). Shift work, sleepiness, and long distance driving. *Transportation Research, 9,* 278–285. (Ch. 9)

Ebstein, R. B. (2006). The molecular genetic architecture of human personality: Beyond self-report questionnaires. *Molecular Psychiatry, 11,* 427–445. (Ch. 14)

Feingold, L., & Flamm, B. L. (2006). Magnet therapy: Extraordinary claims, but no proved benefits. *British Medical Journal, 332,* 4. (Ch. 2)

Ford, M. T., Heinen, B. A., & Langkamer, K. L. (2007). Work and family satisfaction and conflict: A meta-analysis of cross-domain relations. *Journal of Applied Psychology, 92,* 57–80. (Ch. 20)

Foti, R. J., & Hauenstein, N. M. A. (2007). Pattern and variable approaches in leadership emergence and effectiveness. *Journal of Applied Psychology, 92,* 347–355. (Ch. 18)

Freitag, C. M. (2007). The genetics of autistic disorders and its clinical significance: A review of the literature. *Molecular Psychiatry, 12,* 2–22. (Ch. 15)

Gais, S., Lucas, B., & Born, J. (2006). Sleep after learning aids memory recall. *Learning & Memory, 13,* 259–262. (Ch. 9)

Galotti, K. M. (2007). Decision structuring in important real-life choices. *Psychological Science, 18,* 320–325. (Ch. 8)

Gangestad, S. W., Garver-Apgar, C. E., Simpson, J. A., & Cousins, A. J. (2007). Changes in women's mate preferences across the ovulatory cycle. *Journal of Personality and Social Psychology, 92,* 151–163. (Ch. 11)

Gilbert, D. T. (2006). *Stumbling on happiness.* New York: Knopf. (Ch. 11)

Gillham, J. E., Reivich, K. J., Freres, D. R., Chaplin, T. M., Shatté, A. J., Samuels, B., et al. (2007). School-based prevention of depressive symptoms: A randomized controlled study of the effectiveness and specificity of the Penn Resiliency Program. *Journal of Consulting and Clinical Psychology, 75,* 9–19. (Ch. 16)

Hamilton, L. H., & Robson, B. (2006). Performing arts consultation: Developing expertise in this domain. *Professional Psychology: Research and Practice, 37,* 254–259. (Ch. 1)

Hardesty, D. E., & Sackeim, H. A. (2007). Deep brain stimulation in movement and psychiatric disorders. *Biological Psychiatry, 61,* 831–835. (Ch. 16)

Harmison, R. J. (2006). Peak performance in sport: Identifying ideal performance states and developing athletes' psychological skills. *Professional Psychology: Research and Practice, 37,* 233–243. (Ch. 1)

Harvey, S. B., Stanton, B. R., & David, A. S. (2006). Conversion disorder: Towards a neurobiological understanding. *Neuropsychiatric Disease and Treatment, 2,* 13–20. (Ch. 15)

Haut, K. M., & Barch, D. M. (2006). Sex influences on material-sensitive functional lateralization in working and episodic memory: Men and women are not all that different. *NeuroImage, 32,* 411–422. (Ch. 3)

Heiss, W. D., & Teasel, R. W. (2006). Brain recovery and rehabilitation. *Stroke, 37*(2), 314–316. (Ch. 19)

Hershcovis, M. S., Turner, N., Barling, J., Arnold, K. A., Dupré, K. E., Inness, M., LeBlanc, M. M., & Sivanathan, N. (2007). Predicting workplace aggression: A meta-analysis. *Journal of Applied Psychology, 92,* 228–238. (Ch. 20)

Herzog, T. A., & Blagg, C. O. (2007). Are most precontemplators contemplating smoking cessation? Assessing the validity of the stages of change. *Health Psychology, 26,* 222–231. (Ch. 3)

Higuchi, S., Matsushita, S., & Kashima, H. (2006). New findings on the genetic influences on alcohol use and dependence. *Current Opinion in Psychiatry, 19,* 253–265. (Ch. 15)

Hochberg, L. R., Serruya, M. D., Friehs, G. M., Mukand, J. A., Saleh, M., Caplan, A. H., et al. (2006). Neuronal ensemble control of prosthetic devices by a human with tetraplegia. *Nature, 442,* 164–171. (Ch. 3)

Hughes, B. M. (2006). Lies, damned lies, and pseudoscience: The selling of eye movement desensitization and reprocessing (EMDR). *PsycCritiques, 51,* 10. (Ch. 2)

Hyman, S. E., Malenka, R. C., & Nestler, E. J. (2006). Neural mechanisms of addiction: The role of reward-related learning and memory. *Annual Review of Neuroscience, 29,* 565–598. (Ch. 3)

Jacoby, L. L., & Rhodes, M. G. (2006). False remembering in the aged. *Current Directions in Psychological Science, 15,* 49–53. (Ch. 12)

Keyes, C. L. M. (2007). Promoting and protecting mental health as flourishing: A complementary strategy for improving national mental health. *American Psychologist, 62,* 95–108. (Ch. 15)

Kitayama, S., Duffy, S., & Uchida, Y. (2007). Self as cultural mode of being. In S. Kitayama & D. Cohen (Eds.), *Handbook of cultural psychology.* New York: Guilford Press. (Ch. 14)

Klump, K. L., & Culbert, K. M. (2007). Molecular genetic studies of eating disorders: Current status and future directions. *Current Directions in Psychological Science, 16,* 37–41. (Ch. 11)

Kounios, J., Frymiare, J. L., Bowden, E. M., Fleck, J. I., Subramaniam, K., Parrish, T. B., & Jung-Beeman, M. (2006). The prepared mind: Neural activity prior to problem presentation predicts subsequent solution by sudden insight. *Psychological Science, 17,* 882–890. (Ch. 6)

Lamm, C., Batson, C. D., & Decety, J. (2007). The neural basis of human empathy—Effects of perspective-taking and cognitive appraisal: An event-related fMRI study. *Journal of Cognitive Neuroscience, 19,* 42–58. (Ch. 17)

Langens, T. A., & Schüler, J. (2007). Effects of written emotional expression: the role of positive expectancies. *Health Psychology, 26,* 174–182. (Ch. 1)

Lapierre, L. M., & Allen, T. D. (2006). Work-supportive family, family-supportive supervision, use of organizational benefits, and problem-focused coping: Implications for work-family conflict and employee well-being. *Journal of Occupational Health Psychology, 11,* 169–181. (Ch. 20)

Laurenceau, J.-P., Hayes, A. M., & Feldman, G. C. (2007). Some methodological and statistical issues in the study of change processes in psychotherapy. *Clinical Psychology Review, 27,* 682–695. (Ch. 16)

Li, M. D. (2006). The genetics of nicotine dependence. *Current Psychiatry Reports, 8,* 158–164. (Ch. 9)

Lilienfeld, S. O. (2007). Psychological treatments that cause harm. *Perspectives on Psychological Science, 2,* 53–70. (Ch. 16)

Lucas, R. E. (2007). Adaptation and the set-point model of subjective well-being: Does happiness change after major life events? *Current Directions in Psychological Science, 16,* 75–79. (Ch. 11)

Lynn, R., & Mikk, J. (2007). National differences in intelligence and educational attainment. *Intelligence, 35,* 115–121. (Ch. 10)

Manini, T. M., Everhart, J. E., Patel, K. V., Schoeller, D. A., Colbert, L. H., Visser, M., et al. (2006). Daily activity energy expenditure and mortality among older adults. *Journal of the American Medical Association, 296,* 171–179. (Ch. 12)

Marin, S., Vinaixa, M., Brezmes, J., Llobet, E., Vilanova, X., Correig, X., et al. (2007). Use of a MS-electronic nose for prediction of early fungal spoilage of bakery products. *International Journal of Food Microbiology, 114,* 10–16. (Ch. 4)

Maton, K., Kohout, J. L., Wicherski, M., Leary, G. E., & Vinokurov, A. (2006). Minority students of color in the psychology graduate pipeline: Disquieting and encouraging trends, 1989–2003. *American Psychologist, 61,* 117–131. (Ch. 1)

McGarvey, C., McDonnell, M., Hamilton, K., O'Regan, M., & Matthews, T. (2006). An 8-year study of risk factors for SIDS: Bed-sharing versus non-bed-sharing. *Archives of Disease in Childhood, 91,* 318–323. (Ch. 9)

Miller, P., Slawinski, J., Blessing, J., & Schwartz, S. (2006). Gender differences in high-school students' views about science. *International Journal of Science Education, 28,* 363–381. (Ch. 12)

NICHD Early Child Care Research Network. (2007). Are there long-term effects of early child care? *Child Development, 78,* 681–701. (Ch. 2)

Nichols, D. F. (2006). Tell me a story: MMPI responses and personal biography in the case of a serial killer. *Journal of Personality Assessment, 86,* 242–262. (Ch. 14)

Oberman, L. M., & Ramachandran, V. S. (2007). The simulating social mind: The role of the mirror neuron system and simulation in the social and communicative deficits of autism spectrum disorders. *Psychological Bulletin, 133,* 310–327. (Ch. 3)

Olson, I. R., Rao, H., Moore, K. S., Wang, J., Detre, J. A., & Aguirre, G. K. (2006). Using perfusion fMRI to measure continuous changes in neural activity with learning. *Brain and Cognition, 60,* 262–271. (Ch. 7)

Patterson, D. R., Hoffman, H. G., Palacios, A. G., & Jensen, M. J. (2006). Analgesic effects of posthypnotic suggestions and virtual reality distraction on thermal pain. *Journal of Abnormal Psychology, 115,* 834–841. (Ch. 4)

Peterson, C. (2006). *A primer in positive psychology.* New York: Oxford University Press. (Ch. 1)

Peterson, C. (2006). The Values in Action (VIA) Classification of Strengths: The un-DSM and the real DSM. In M. Csikszentmihalyi & I. Csikszentmihalyi (Eds.), *A life worth living: Contributions to positive psychology* (pp. 29–48). New York: Oxford University Press. (Ch. 14)

Pronin, E., Wegner, D. M., McCarthy, K., & Rodriguez, S. (2006). Everyday magical powers: The role of apparent causation in the overestimation of personal influence. *Journal of Personality and Social Psychology, 91,* 218–231. (Ch. 6)

Rains, G. C., Utley, S. L., & Lewis, W. J. (2006). Behavioral monitoring of trained insects for chemical detection. *Biotechnology Progress, 22,* 2–8. (Ch. 6)

Reyna, V. F., & Farley, F. (2006). Risk and rationality in adolescent decision making: Implications for theory, practice, and public policy. *Psychological Science in the Public Interest, 7,* 1–44. (Ch. 8)

Roediger, H. L., III, & Karpicke, J. D. (2006). Test-enhanced learning: Taking memory tests improve long-term retention. *Psychological Science, 17,* 249–255. (Ch. 7)

Roediger, H. L., III, McDaniel, M., & McDermott, K. (2006). Test enhanced learning. *APS Observer, 19,* 28. (Ch. 6)

Roisman, G. I. (2007). The psychophysiology of adult attachment relationships: Autonomic reactivity in marital and premarital interactions. *Developmental Psychology, 43,* 39–53. (Ch. 12)

Schnurr, P. P., Friedman, M. J., Engel, C. C., Foa, E. B., Shea, T., Chow, B. K., et al. (2007). Cognitive behavior therapy for posttraumatic stress disorder in women: A randomized controlled trial. *Journal of the American Medical Association, 297,* 820–830. (Ch. 16)

Schultz, P. W., Nolan, J. M., Cialdini, R. B., Goldstein, N. J. & Griskevicius, V. (2007). The constructive, destructive, and reconstructive power of social norms. *Psychological Science, 18,* 429–434. (Ch. 18)

Sharot, T., Martorella, E. A., Delgado, M. R., & Phelps, E. A. (2006). How personal experience modulates the neural circuitry of memories of September 11. *Proceedings of the National Academy of Sciences, 104,* 389–394. (Ch. 7)

Snyder, C. R., & Lopez, S. J. (2006). *Handbook of positive psychology.* New York: Oxford University Press. (Ch. 14)

Snyder, C. R., & Lopez, S. J. (2007). *Positive psychology: The scientific and practical explorations of human strengths.* New York: Sage. (Ch. 1)

Spano, M. S., Ellgren, M., Wang, X., & Hurd, Y. L. (2007). Prenatal cannabis exposure increases heroin seeking with allostatic changes in limbic enkephalin systems in adulthood. *Biological Psychiatry, 61,* 554–563. (Ch. 9)

Steinberg, L. (2007). Risk taking in adolescence: New perspectives from brain and behavioral science. *Current Directions in Psychological Science, 16,* 55–59. (Ch. 12)

Stewart, S. E., Platko, J., Fagerness, J., Birns, J., Jenike, E., Smoller, J. W., et al. (2007). A genetic family-based association study of OLIG2 in obsessive-compulsive disorder. *Archives of General Psychiatry, 64,* 209–214. (Ch. 15)

Strayer, D. L., & Drews, F. A. (2006). Multi-tasking in the automobile. In A. Kramer, D. Wiegmann, & A. Kirlik (Eds.), *Applied attention: From theory to practice* (pp. 121–133). New York: Oxford University Press. (Ch. 5)

Tabert, M. H., Manly, J. J., Liu, X., Pelton, G. H., Rosenbaum, S., Jacobs, M., et al. (2006). Neuropsychological prediction of conversion to Alzheimer disease in patients with mild cognitive impairment. *Archives of General Psychiatry, 63,* 916–924. (Ch. 19)

Tankersley, D., Stowe, C. J., & Huettel, S. A. (2007). Altruism is associated with an increased neural response to agency. *Nature Neuroscience, 10,* 150–151. (Ch. 17)

Tetlock, P. E. (2006). *Expert political judgment: How good is it? How can we know?* Princeton, NJ: Princeton University Press. (Ch. 8)

Thomas, J. A., & Walton, D. (2007). Measuring perceived risk: Self-reported and actual hand positions of SUV and car drivers. *Traffic Psychology and Behavior, 10,* 201–207. (Ch. 8)

Tippmann-Piekert, M., Park, J. G., Boeve, B. F., Shepard, J. W., & Silber, M. H. (2007). Pathologic gambling in patients with restless legs syndrome treated with dopaminergic agonists. *Neurology, 68,* 301–303. (Ch. 3)

Törnros, J. E., & Bolling, A. K. (2006). Mobile phone use: Effects of conversation on mental workload and driving speed in rural and urban environments. *Transportation Research Part F: Traffic Psychology and Behaviour, 9,* 298–306. (Ch. 5)

van Goozen, S. H. M., Fairchild, G., Snoek, H., & Harold, G. T. (2007). The evidence for a neurobiological model of childhood antisocial behavior. *Psychological Bulletin, 133,* 149–182. (Ch. 15)

Wagner, U., Hallschmid, M., Rasch, B., & Born, J. (2006). Brief sleep after learning keeps emotional memories alive for years. *Biological Psychiatry, 60,* 788–790. (Ch. 9)

Ward, J., & Mattingley, J. B. (2006). Synaesthesia: An overview of contemporary findings and controversies. *Cortex, 42,* 129–136. (Ch. 4)

Wells, G. L., Memon, A., & Penrod, S. D. (2006). Eyewitness evidence: Improving its probative value. *Psychological Science in the Public Interest, 7,* 45–75. (Ch. 7)

Williams, R. J., & Connolly, D. (2006). Does learning about the mathematics of gambling change gambling behavior? *Psychology of Addictive Behavior, 20,* 62–68. (Ch. 8)

Willis, J., & Todorov, A. (2006). First impressions: Making up your mind after a 100-ms exposure to a face. *Psychological Science, 17,* 592–598 (Ch. 17)

Wilson, K., & French, C. C. (2006). The relationship between susceptibility to false memories, dissociativity, and paranormal belief and experience. *Personality and Individual Differences, 41,* 1493–1502. (Ch. 7)

Wolf, M., Sander van Doorn, G., Leimar, O., & Weissing, F. J. (2007). Life-history trade-offs favour the evolution of animal personalities. *Nature, 447,* 581–584. (Ch. 14)

Zaccarco, S. J. (2007). Trait-based perspectives of leadership. *American Psychologist, 62,* 6–16. (Ch. 20)

PSYCHOLOGY

EIGHTH EDITION • *EXPANDED VERSION*

DOUGLAS A. BERNSTEIN
UNIVERSITY OF SOUTH FLORIDA
UNIVERSITY OF SOUTHAMPTON

LOUIS A. PENNER
WAYNE STATE UNIVERSITY
UNIVERSITY OF MICHIGAN

ALISON CLARKE-STEWART
UNIVERSITY OF CALIFORNIA, IRVINE

EDWARD J. ROY
UNIVERSITY OF ILLINOIS AT URBANA-CHAMPAIGN

WITH

JOEL I. SHENKER

AND

PAUL E. SPECTOR

HOUGHTON MIFFLIN COMPANY   BOSTON   NEW YORK

Editor-in-Chief/Publisher: George Hoffman
Sponsoring Editor: Jane Potter
Marketing Manager: Amy Whitaker
Senior Development Editor: Laura Hildebrand
Senior Project Editor: Aileen Mason
Senior Art and Design Coordinator: Jill Haber Atkins
Photo Editor: Jennifer Meyer Dare
Composition Buyer: Chuck Dutton
New Title Project Manager: James Lonergan
Editorial Associate: Henry Cheek
Marketing Assistant: Samantha Abrams
Editorial Assistant: Paola Moll

For permission to use copyrighted materials, grateful acknowledgment is made to the copyright holders listed on page C-1, which is hereby considered an extension of the copyright page.

Custom Publishing Editor: Dan Luciano
Custom Publishing Production Manager: Christina Battista
Project Coordinator: Jen Feltri

Cover Image: PhotoDisc

This book contains select works from existing Houghton Mifflin Company resources and was produced by Houghton Mifflin Custom Publishing for collegiate use. As such, those adopting and/or contributing to this work are responsible for editorial content, accuracy, continuity and completeness.

Printed in the United States of America.

ISBN-13: 978-0-547-07870-0
ISBN-10: 0-547-07870-6
1042256

1 2 3 4 5 6 7 8 9 – AB – 09 08 07

 Houghton Mifflin
Custom Publishing

222 Berkeley Street • Boston, MA 02116

Address all correspondence and order information to the above address.

BRIEF CONTENTS

CONTENTS

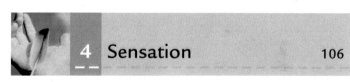

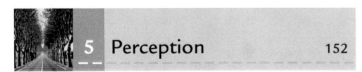

5 Perception 152

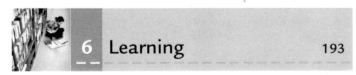

6 Learning 193

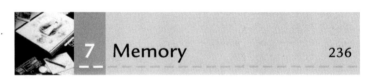

7 Memory 236

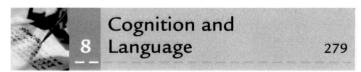

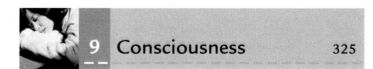

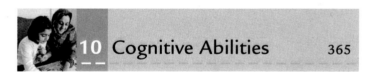

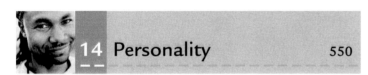

14 Personality 550

15 Psychological Disorders 587

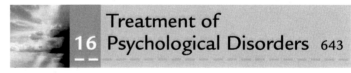

16 Treatment of Psychological Disorders 643

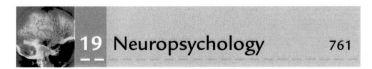
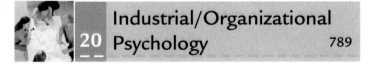

FEATURES

PREFACE

In revising *Psychology* we have rededicated ourselves to the goals we pursued in the first seven editions:

● To explore the full range of psychology, from cell to society, in an eclectic manner as free as possible of theoretical bias.

● To balance our need to explain the content of psychology with an emphasis on the doing of psychology, through a blend of conceptual discussion and description of research studies.

● To foster scientific attitudes and to help students learn to think critically by examining the ways that psychologists have solved, or failed to solve, fascinating puzzles of behavior and mental processes.

● To produce a text that, without oversimplifying psychology, is clear, accessible, and enjoyable to read.

● To demonstrate that, in spite of its breadth and diversity, psychology is an integrated discipline in which each subfield is linked to other subfields by common interests and overarching research questions. The productive cross-fertilization among social, clinical, and biological psychologists in researching health and illness is just one example of how different types of psychologists benefit from and build on one another's work.

Preparing the Eighth Edition provided us with new ways to do justice to our goals. We sought to respond to the needs of instructors who wanted us to reduce or expand coverage of various topics. For example, many instructors asked us to increase the amount of material on applied psychology without losing the book's emphasis on basic research in psychology. As a result, we have added material relating to applied areas such as industrial/organizational psychology, neuropsychology, and forensic psychology throughout the book, wherever appropriate. As always, we sought to strike an ideal balance between classic and current research. The important historic findings of psychological research are here, but so is coverage of much recent work. Approximately twenty percent of the research citations are new to the Eighth Edition, and we have added the latest information on such topics as

● Methods for evaluating claims for the effectiveness of eye movement desensitization (Chapter 2)

● Techniques for studying the brain (Chapter 3)

● The interaction of senses in synesthesia (Chapter 4)

● Perceptual grouping principles such as synchrony and connectedness (Chapter 5)

● Applying learning principles to help diagnose Alzheimer's disease (Chapter 6)

● Biological bases of memory (Chapter 7)

● Locating brain areas involved in analogical thinking (Chapter 8)

● The controversy over using marijuana for medical purposes (Chapter 9)

● How anxiety over ethnic stereotypes can affect cognitive test performance (Chapter 10)

● Achievement and happiness (Chapter 11)

● The challenges facing adults in twenty-first-century families (Chapter 12)

● Psychological reactions to stress (Chapter 13)

● Gray's Approach-Inhibition Theory (Chapter 14)

● The biopsychosocial model of psychological disorder (Chapter 15)

● Empirically supported therapies (Chapter 16)

● Terror management theory and social cognitive neuroscience (Chapter 17)

● Obedience and social power (Chapter 18)

The Eighth Edition also contains substantial material on culture and human diversity. Throughout the text students will encounter recent research on multicultural phenomena occurring in North America and around the world. We introduce this multicultural emphasis in Chapter 1, and we follow up on it in other chapters through such topics as

● Selecting human participants for research (Chapter 2)

● Culture, experience, and perception (Chapter 5)

● Classrooms across cultures (Chapter 6)

● Culture, language, and thought (Chapter 8)

● Ethnic differences in IQ (Chapter 10)

● Flavor, cultural learning, and food selection (Chapter 11)

● Social and cultural factors in sexuality (Chapter 11)

● Cultural and gender differences in achievement motivation (Chapter 11)

● Cultural aspects of emotional expression (Chapter 11)

● Culture and cognitive development (Chapter 12)

● Sociocultural factors in adult development (Chapter 12)

● Cultural background and heart disease (Chapter 13)

● Personality, culture, and human development (Chapter 14)

● Ethnic bias in psychodiagnosis (Chapter 15)

● Sociocultural factors in psychological disorders (Chapter 15)

- Gender and cultural differences in depression and suicide (Chapter 15)

- Cultural factors in psychotherapy (Chapter 16)

- Ethnic differences in responses to drug treatment (Chapter 16)

- Cultural differences in attribution (Chapter 17)

- The roots of ethnic stereotyping and prejudice (Chapter 17)

- Cultural factors and love (Chapter 17)

- Cultural factors in social norms (Chapter 18)

- Culture and conformity (Chapter 18)

- Culture and social loafing (Chapter 18)

- Cultural factors in aggression (Chapter 18)

We also have updated our coverage of behavioral genetics and evolutionary psychology. These topics are introduced in Chapters 1 and 2, and in the online behavioral genetics appendix. They are also explored wherever appropriate—for example, when we discuss

- Gene manipulation research on the causes of Alzheimer's disease (Chapter 3)

- Biopreparedness for learning (Chapter 6)

- Genetic components of intelligence (Chapter 10)

- Genetic components of sexual orientation (Chapter 11)

- Evolutionary explanations of mate selection (Chapter 11)

- Innate expressions of emotion (Chapter 11)

- The genetics of prenatal development (Chapter 12)

- The heritability of personality (Chapter 14)

- Genetic factors in psychological disorders (Chapter 15)

- Evolutionary/genetic explanations for aggression, helping, and altruism (Chapter 18)

We have also emphasized in the Eighth Edition the significant new developments and research occurring in the field of *positive psychology*. This emphasis appears in the introductory chapter, where we first describe positive psychology, as well as in coverage of positive psychology perspectives on and research in topics such as high achievement (Chapter 6), character strengths (Chapter 14), rounded approaches to diagnosing mental disorders (Chapter 15), exploiting strengths and promoting positive emotion in psychotherapy, and teaching skills that enhance well-being and resilience in the face of stress (Chapter 16).

Chapter Organization

As always, we have refrained from grouping the book's eighteen chapters into more general sections. We designed each chapter to be a freestanding unit so that you may assign chapters in any order you wish. For example, many instructors prefer to teach the material on human development relatively late in the course, which is why it appears as Chapter 12 in the Eighth Edition. But that chapter can be comfortably assigned earlier in the course as well.

For the Eighth Edition, we have added an "optional" nineteenth chapter on **Neuropsychology**, coauthored by Doug Bernstein and Joel Shenker, a diplomate of the American Board of Neurology and Psychiatry who specializes in memory loss, dementia, and neuro-cognitive behavioral impairments. We also offer an "optional" twentieth chapter on **Industrial/Organizational Psychology**, contributed by Paul Spector, University of South Florida. Either (or both) chapter(s) may be included in the textbook upon request, and most ancillaries contain supporting material for these chapters. Note that end-of-book materials for these chapters—such as references, credits, name index, and the combined subject index/glossary—are printed in those sections in blue.

Special Features

Psychology contains a number of special features designed to promote efficient learning and students' mastery of the material. These features include the following.

Linkages

In our experience, most students enter the introductory course thinking that psychology concerns itself mainly with personality, psychological testing, mental disorders, psychotherapy, and other aspects of clinical psychology. They have little or no idea of how broad and multifaceted psychology is. Many students are surprised, therefore, when we ask them to read about neuroanatomy, neural communication, the endocrine system, sensory and perceptual processes and principles, prenatal risk factors, and many other topics that they tend to associate with disciplines other than psychology.

We have found that students are better able to appreciate the scope of psychology when they see it not as a laundry list of separate topics but as an interrelated set of subfields, each of which contributes to and benefits from the work going on in all of the others. To help students see these relationships, we have built into the book an integrating tool called "Linkages." There are four elements in the Linkages program:

1. Beginning with Chapter 2, a Linkages diagram presents a set of questions that illustrate three of the ways in which material in the chapter is related to other chapters in the book. For example, the Linkages diagram in Chapter 3, Biological Aspects of Psychology, contains questions about how biological psychology is related to consciousness ("Does the brain shut down when we

sleep?"), human development ("How do our brains change over a lifetime?"), and treatment of psychological disorders ("How do drugs help people who suffer from schizophrenia?").

2. The Linkages diagrams are placed at the end of each chapter so that students will be more familiar with the material to which each linkage refers when they encounter this feature. To help students notice the Linkages diagrams and appreciate their purpose, we provide an explanatory caption with each.

3. The page numbers following each question in the Linkages diagram direct the student to pages that carry further discussion of that question. The relevant material is marked by a Linkages logo in the margin next to the discussion.

4. One of the questions in each chapter's Linkages diagram is treated more fully in a special section within the chapter, titled—appropriately enough—Linkages. A full list of topics appears on p. xi.

The Linkages elements combine with the text narrative to highlight the network of relationships among psychology's subfields. This Linkages program is designed to help students see the "big picture" that is psychology—no matter how many chapters their instructor assigns or in what sequence.

Thinking Critically

We try throughout the book to describe research on psychological phenomena in a way that reveals the logic of the scientific enterprise, that identifies possible flaws in design or interpretation, and that leaves room for more questions and further research. In other words, we try to display critical thinking processes. The "Thinking Critically" sections in each chapter are designed to make these processes more explicit and accessible by providing a framework for analyzing evidence before drawing conclusions. The framework is built around five questions that the reader should find useful in analyzing not only studies in psychology but other forms of communication as well. These questions, first introduced when we discuss the importance of critical thinking in Chapter 2, are

1. What am I being asked to believe or accept?

2. What evidence is available to support the assertion?

3. Are there alternative ways of interpreting the evidence?

4. What additional evidence would help to evaluate the alternatives?

5. What conclusions are most reasonable?

All the Thinking Critically sections retained from the Seventh Edition have been revised and updated. A full list of topics appears on p. xi.

Focus on Research Methods

This feature, appearing in Chapters 3 through 20, examines the ways in which the research methods described in Chapter 2, Research in Psychology, have been applied to help advance our understanding of some aspect of behavior and mental processes. To make this feature more accessible, it is organized around the following questions:

1. What was the researcher's question?

2. How did the researcher answer the question?

3. What did the researcher find?

4. What do the results mean?

5. What do we still need to know?

Examples of these Focus on Research Methods sections include the use of experiments to study attention (Chapter 5, Perception), learned helplessness (Chapter 6, Learning), the use of neuroimaging technology to locate areas of the brain involved in analogical thinking (Chapter 8, Cognition and Language), the development of physical knowledge (Chapter 12, Human Development), and self-esteem (Chapter 17, Social Cognition). Other sections illustrate the use of survey, longitudinal, and laboratory analogue designs. All of the Focus on Research Methods sections retained from the Seventh Edition were revised and updated. A full list of topics appears on p. xi.

An Emphasis on Active Learning

To help students become active learners, not just passive readers, we continue to develop new online tutorials, available on the *student web site* and within our course cartridges. These tutorials walk students through some of the most difficult concepts encountered in their text. Topics such as reinforcement, opponent-process theory, drive-reduction theory, and priming—among others—are brought to life in an interactive format with an opportunity for self-testing to confirm understanding. We have also created an Active Learning booklet, filled with activities that allow students to be hands-on with the key concepts covered in the text. An annotated instructor version of the booklet provides instructors with tips for assigning the activities and for ensuring that students derive the full benefit from these activities.

We have also retained in each chapter of the Eighth Edition "Try This" features that encourage students to become more deeply involved with the material:

● Dozens of figure and photo captions that help students understand and remember a psychological principle or phenomenon by suggesting ways in which they can demonstrate it for themselves. In Chapter 7, Memory, for example, a photo caption suggests that students show the photo to a friend and then ask the friend questions about it to illustrate the operation of constructive memory. These captions are all identified with a "Try This" symbol.

● Placement of "Try This" symbols in page margins at the many places throughout the book where active learning opportunities are encouraged in the narrative. At these points, we ask students to stop reading and try doing something to illustrate or highlight the psychological principle or phenomenon under discussion. For example, in Chapter 5, Perception, we ask the student to focus attention on various targets as a way of appreciating the difference between overt and covert shifts in attention.

Online Behavioral Genetics Appendix

This feature is designed to amplify the coverage of behavioral genetics methodology that is introduced in Chapter 2, Research in Psychology. The appendix includes a discussion of the impact of the Human Genome Project, a section on the basic principles of genetics and heredity, a brief history of genetic research in psychology, a discussion of what it means to say that genes influence behavior, and an analysis of what behavioral genetics research can—and cannot—tell us about the origins of such human attributes as intelligence, personality, and mental disorders. This appendix is available online on the *student web site,* which can be accessed via **college .hmco.com/pic/bernstein8e.** Note that the end-of-book materials for this appendix (as well as the online Statistics in Psychological Research appendix)—such as references, credits, name index, and the combined subject index/glossary—are printed in those sections in blue.

In Review Charts

In Review charts summarize information in a convenient tabular format. We have placed two or three In Review charts strategically in each chapter to help students synthesize and assimilate large chunks of information—for example, on drug effects, key elements of personality theories, and stress responses and mediators.

Key Terms

As in the Seventh Edition, key terms and their definitions appear in the margin of the Eighth Edition where the terms are first used and in the subject index/glossary at the end of the book.

Teaching and Learning Support Package

Many useful materials have been developed to support *Psychology,* emphasizing its role as an integrated teaching and learning experience for instructors, teaching assistants, and students alike. These materials are well integrated with the text and include some of the latest technologies. Several components are new to this edition.

For the Instructor

The *Test Bank, Instructor's Resource Manual,* and *Media Integration Guide* were prepared by Doug Bernstein and a number of colleagues who have worked with him over the years at the University of Illinois psychology department. You will find an especially high level of coordination between the textbook and these supplements. Note that two new chapters have been included in each to support the optional chapters Neuropsychology and Industrial/Organizational Psychology. The ancillaries are unified by a shared set of learning objectives and have been revised and enhanced for the Eighth Edition.

ONLINE MEDIA INTEGRATION GUIDE. The *Media Integration Guide* for instructors was introduced for the Seventh Edition by David B. Daniel (University of Northern Colorado). It has been revised for the Eighth Edition and outlines all the multimedia offered with this text, as well as strategies on how to use them all effectively in conjunction with the objectives of this text and your course.

ONLINE INSTRUCTOR'S RESOURCE MANUAL. The *Online Instructor's Resource Manual* by lead author Linda Lebie (Lake Land College, Mattoon, Illinois), Missa Murry Eaton (The Pennsylvania State University, Shenango Campus), Suzanne E. Juraska (Personnel Decisions Research Institutes, Inc.), Valeri A. Werpetinski and Sandra Goss Lucas (both at the University of Illinois Urbana-Champaign), and Douglas A. Bernstein, contains for each chapter a complete set of learning objectives, detailed chapter outlines, suggested readings, and numerous specific teaching aids—including ideas for discussion, class activities, focus on research sections, and the accompanying handouts. It also contains sections on pedagogical strategies, as well as material geared toward teachers of large introductory courses, including a section on classroom management and another on the administration of multisection courses. Please note that the Eighth Edition *Online Instructor's Manual* now contains supporting material for the two optional chapters—Chapter 19, Neuropsychology, and Chapter 20, Industrial/Organizational Psychology. As noted earlier, either or both of these chapters can be included in your text upon request—see your Houghton Mifflin sales representative for details. The *Online Instructor's Resource Manual* is available on the *instructor web site.*

ONLINE TEST BANK. The *Online Test Bank,* by Chris Armstrong (University of Illinois) and Douglas A. Bernstein, contains 165 multiple-choice items plus three essay questions per chapter. All multiple-choice items are keyed to pages in the textbook and to the learning objectives that appear in the *Instructor's Resource Manual* and *Study Guide.* Each question is identified by whether it tests simple factual recall or deeper conceptual understanding. More than 2,100 questions have been class-tested with between 500 and 2,500 students, and a statistical performance analysis is provided for those items. An additional 100 multiple-choice test questions and three essay questions have been added to the Eighth Edition for each of the two optional chapters (Chapter 19, Neuropsychology, and Chapter 20, Industrial/Organizational Psychology) that may be bundled with the text. The test bank is available on the *HM Testing CD-ROM*.

HM TESTING CD-ROM (0-547-01627-1).
HM Testing (powered by Diploma) is a flexible testing program that allows instructors to create, edit, customize, and deliver multiple types of tests via print, network server, or the web on either the MAC or WIN platform. The test bank contains over 3,200 multiple-choice and essay questions, including 100 questions for each of the two optional chapters (these chapters may be packaged with your text upon request). More than 2,100 questions have been class-tested with between 500 and 2,500 students, and the test item analysis—including a quintile graph for each of these items—is included within the testing program. The *Online Test Bank* Word files are also included on the CD-ROM for easy reference.

NEW! ENHANCED POWERPOINT PRESENTATIONS.
An enhanced set of *PowerPoint® presentations* consists of lecture sequences, tables, figures, and photos from the main text. **New** to this edition are hyperlinks to interactive tutorials that help to enliven lecture content and illuminate specific topics ranging from action potentials to classical conditioning. The slides are available on the *instructor web site*.

NEW! CLASSROOM RESPONSE SYSTEM (CRS).
Classroom Response System (CRS) content allows instructors to perform "on-the-spot" assessments, deliver quick quizzes, gauge students' understanding of a particular question or concept, conduct anonymous polling for class discussion purposes, and take their class roster easily. Students receive immediate feedback on how well they understand concepts covered in the text and where they need to improve. Answer slides provide the correct answer and an explanation of why the answer is correct. CRS content is available on the *instructor web site*.

HM CLASSPRESENT.
ClassPresent includes over 45 animations that project effectively in a lecture hall. The CD also has an easy-to-navigate interface, with searchable thumbnail images organized by topic. These animations can be easily inserted into PowerPoint presentations or projected directly from the ClassPresent CD-ROM.

NEW! ACTIVE LEARNING AND CRITICAL THINKING BOOKLETS.
The *Active Learning* and *Critical Thinking booklets* build on the pedagogy of the main text by offering a wealth of interesting exercises that help students apply key concepts to their own experiences and develop important critical thinking skills. Active Learning exercises range from visiting libraries and toy stores to observe and record differential gender roles (Activity 9.2, Gender Roles), to popping balloons in front of a friend to create a classically condi-

tioned response (Activity 5.1, Classical Conditioning). Critical Thinking activities range from assessing the impact of legislation (Activity 1.1) and evaluating the utility of multitasking (Activity 3.2) to analyzing the purpose of dreams (Activity 4.2) and forming an opinion about whether computers are beneficial in the classroom (Activity 5.3). The annotated instructor versions of these booklets contain additional tips for helping students derive the full benefit from these activities™ and, where applicable, include suggested answers to questions raised by some of the activities. Both instructor booklets are available on the *instructor web site*. Students can access their version of these booklets via the *student web site* by using the passkey access card, which comes packaged with all new texts.

NEW! NEUROPSYCHOLOGY AND INDUSTRIAL/ORGANIZATIONAL PSYCHOLOGY CHAPTERS.
The optional Neuropsychology and Industrial/Organizational Psychology chapters are available for inclusion in the main text, via the custom group. Supporting material for these chapters is available in all of the print supplements and in the HM Testing (computerized testing) program. Please consult your sales representative for details.

INSTRUCTOR WEB SITE (0-5470-1621-2).
The *instructor web site* (**college.hmco.com/pic/bernstein8e**) that accompanies *Psychology*, Eighth Edition, is a comprehensive gallery of online teaching resources that gives you one central place to access all of your teaching preparation tools. It includes the complete *Instructor's Resource Manual*, PowerPoint presentations, CRS content, downloadable PDFs of the overhead transparencies, and selected art from the textbook. **New** to this edition is a comprehensive image gallery of over 300 additional pieces of art from other Houghton resources. Also included are media integration, video, transition, and tabbing guides, as well as ideas for encouraging critical thinking and active learning. Premium content on the *student web site* may be accessed with the passkey access card, which comes packaged with all new texts. Please see your sales representative for details.

EDUSPACE.
Eduspace® is a powerful course management system that enables instructors to create all or part of their courses online using the widely recognized tools of Blackboard™ and text-specific content from Bernstein, *Psychology*, Eighth Edition. Instructors and students have access to automatically graded online homework, *Psych in Film* video clips with quizzes, and tutorials with accompanying pedagogy. Instructor presentation tools include PowerPoint presentations, CRS content, downloadable PDFs of overhead transparencies and select art from the textbook. **New** content includes *self-assessment quizzes* that provide scoring, explanation of correct and incorrect answers, and remediation back to specific sections of the text; Online Concept Maps, and an Online Multimedia eBook. The Homework exercises have been thoroughly revised and

reorganized to correlate to main headings in *Psychology*, Eighth Edition, to make it easier to assign. This homework now also includes—for every question—references back to every section in the main text, so students can study concepts they initially get wrong during quizzing.

CONTENT FOR COURSE MANAGEMENT SOFTWARE.
Blackboard and *Web CT* course cartridges are available with *Psychology*, Eighth Edition, allowing instructors to use text-specific material to create an online course on their own campus course management system. These cartridges feature all of the content in the Eduspace course described above.

NEW! EDUSPACE® ONLINE MULTIMEDIA eBook.
Available in an interactive PDF format, this eBook offers an online alternative to the print text, complete with embedded links to multimedia assets such as animations, video, and self-practice exercises. Students can access *tutorial activities* that expand upon and reinforce main concepts in the text. Electronic *Flashcards* provide an interactive study tool to review key terms and concepts. And students can link to *Psych in Film* videos and quizzes that engage their interest by connecting textbook material to current films that students recognize.

HOUGHTON MIFFLIN PSYCH IN FILM® DVD.
Houghton Mifflin's Psych in Film DVD contains 35 clips from Universal Studios films illustrating key concepts in psychology. Clips from films such as *Schindler's List, Snow Falling on Cedars,* and many others are combined with commentary and discussion questions to help bring psychology alive for students and demonstrate its relevance to contemporary life and culture. Teaching tips are correlated to specific text chapters and concepts, and are available on the *instructor web site*.

HOUGHTON MIFFLIN'S LECTURE STARTER CD-ROM.
This CD-ROM contains 40 clips, with an accompanying guide available on the *instructor web site*. (Note that Lecture Starter material is also available for child development, abnormal, and social psychology. Please consult your sales representative for further details.)

INTRODUCTORY PSYCHOLOGY READERS.
Psychology in Context: Voices and Perspectives, Second Edition, by David N. Sattler and Virginia Shabatay, contains engaging first-person narratives and essays keyed to major psychological concepts. Two additional readers by Laura Freberg, *Perspectives: Introductory Psychology* and *Stand! Introductory Psychology*, contain articles that explore contending ideas and opinions relating to fundamental issues in introductory psychology courses. Please consult your sales representative for further details.

For the Student

NEW! RESEARCH COMPANION FOR INTRODUCTORY PSYCHOLOGY.
The *Research Companion for Introductory Psychology*, by Mary Inman (Hope College), gives students firsthand experience as researchers. The book opens with a clear explanation of the research process: It describes how psychologists design studies and offers strategies for productive teamwork. Several specific investigations into different topics of psychology make up the second half of the book. Each investigation gives you the necessary background information and step-by-step instructions to set up an ethical study, conduct actual research, analyze data using SPSS, and prepare your findings as an APA-style paper or conference poster. Instructors can tailor the instructions to have their students engage in some or all of these activities. Sample teaching assignments and grading rubrics are included.

NEW! ACTIVE LEARNING AND CRITICAL THINKING BOOKLETS.
These booklets provide a wealth of fun and interesting exercises that help you to apply key concepts to your own experiences and develop important critical thinking skills. Both of these booklets may be accessed from the *student web site* via the passkey card that came with the new copy of your textbook.

NEW! INTERACTIVE TUTORIALS.
These tutorials walk you through some of the more difficult concepts in the text by bringing them to life through creative game scenarios, simulated research, and video. Accompanying quizzes test your understanding of the material. These tutorials are available within the Eduspace, Web CT, and Blackboard course cartridges and on the *student web site*.

NEW! ONLINE CONCEPT MAPS.
These concept maps present diagrams that show the relationships between concepts discussed in a given chapter. They are available within Eduspace, Web CT, and Blackboard course cartridges, and the *student web site* by using the passkey access card that came with the new copy of your textbook.

STUDY GUIDE.
The *Study Guide*, written by Kelly Bouas Henry (Missouri Western State College) and Douglas A. Bernstein, employs numerous techniques that help you to learn. Each chapter—including the optional Neuropsychology and Industrial/Organizational Psychology chapters—contains a detailed outline, a key terms section that presents fresh examples and aids to remembering, plus a fill-in-the-blank test, learning objectives (shared by the instructor's *Test Bank* and *Instructor's Resource Manual*). Also included is a concepts and exercises section that shows you how to apply your knowledge of psychology to everyday issues and concerns, a critical thinking exercise, and personal learning activities. In addition, each chapter concludes with a two-part self-quiz consisting of forty multiple-choice questions. An answer key tells you not only which response is correct but also why each of the other choices is wrong, and quiz analysis tables enable you to track patterns to your wrong answers, either by topic or by type of question—definition, comprehension, or application.

STUDENT WEB SITE (0-5470-1621-2). The *student web site* (college.hmco.com/pic/bernstein8e) contains additional study aids including ACE practice tests, interactive tutorials and flashcards—all designed to help you get a better grade. Premium online study tools that include the **ACE+ practice tests, Active Learning** and **Critical Thinking Booklets, Study Skills Video Modules, Online Concept Maps,** and **Self-Assessment quizzes** can be accessed with the passkey card that came with the new copy of your textbook. If you purchased a used textbook, the card is available for purchase through your bookstore or through Houghton Mifflin's eCommerce site (go to **college.hmco.com/pic/ bernstein8e** and click on the Purchase Product link for the passkey).

DOWNLOADABLE eBOOK. Purchase a downloadable PDF version of the student text directly from our eCommerce site. Please go to **college.hmco.com/pic/bernstein8e** for further details.

OUR COMMITMENT TO YOU. We are committed to the highest standards of customer support and service. Please contact us with any questions or comments you may have.

For technical questions related to web site access and CDs, including HM Testing and HM Class Present, please call Houghton Mifflin's Software Support line at (800) 732-3223 (Monday through Thursday 9 A.M. to 8 P.M. EST, Friday 9 A.M. to 5 P.M. EST) or go to **college.hmco.com/how/how_tech-supp.html** to submit an online help form. To learn more about Eduspace, please go to **www.eduspace.com**. To contact your sales representative, use our Sales Representative Locator at **college.hmco.com/instructors/index.html**.

Acknowledgments

Many people provided us with the help, criticism, and encouragement we needed to create the Eighth Edition.

Once again we must thank Katie Steele, who got the project off the ground in 1983 by encouraging us to stop talking about this book and start writing it.

We are indebted to a number of our colleagues for their expert help and advice on the revisions of a number of chapters for the Eighth Edition. These colleagues include, for Chapters 4, 9, and the optional Chapter 19 (Neuropsychology), Joel Shenker (University of Missouri School of Medicine); for Chapter 5, Eric Stephens (University of the Cumberlands); for Chapter 6, Doug Williams (University of Winnipeg); for Chapter 7, Elizabeth Marsh (Duke University); for Chapter 8, Paul Whitney (Washington State University); for Chapter 10, Douglas K. Detterman (Case Western Reserve University); for Chapter 11, Nancy Dess (Occidental College); for Chapter 13, Catherine Stoney (National Institutes of Health); for Chapter 15, Geoff Kramer (Grand Valley State University); for Chapter 16, Brian Burke (Fort Lewis College); for the optional Chapter 20 (Industrial/Organizational Psychology), Kim Schneider (Illinois State University), and

for the positive psychology content, Chris Peterson (University of Michigan).

We also owe an enormous debt to the colleagues who provided prerevision evaluations of, or reviewed the manuscript for, the Eighth Edition as it was being developed:

Dave Barkmeier, *Northeastern University*

Scott Bates, *Utah State*

James Becker, *Pulaski Technical College*

Bernardo Carducci, *Indiana University Southeast*

Jill Coleman, *Middlebury College*

Steve Drigotas, *Johns Hopkins University*

Todd Nelson, *California State University, Stanislaus*

Juan Salinas, *University of Texas-Austin*

Amy Sweetman, *Los Angeles City College*

Alena Yastchenko, *Central Washington University*

Their advice and suggestions for improvement were responsible for many of the good qualities you will find in the book. If you have any criticisms, they probably involve areas these people warned us about. We especially want to thank Sandra Goss Lucas (University of Illinois at Urbana-Champaign), David Buss (University of Texas), and Edward Donnerstein (University of Arizona), for their help.

We owe an enormous debt as well to the colleagues listed next for their invaluable contributions to the text over the life of many editions:

Gregory F. Ball, *Johns Hopkins University*

David R. Barkmeier, *Northeastern University*

James L. Becker, *Pulaski Technical College*

Edward Bernat, *University of Minnesota*

Ramesh Bhatt, *University of Kentucky*

Joseph Bilotta, *Western Kentucky University*

James F. Calhoun, *University of Georgia*

Julie Feldman, *University of Arizona*

Oney D. Fitzpatrick, *Lamar University*

Anastasia Houndoumadi, *Deree College, Athens*

Robert Krueger, *University of Minnesota*

David Lohman, *University of Iowa*

Kathleen McDermott, *Washington University*

Connie Meinholdt, *Ferris State University*

J. Bruce Overmier, *University of Minnesota*

Frank Penedo, *University of Miami*

Brett Roark, *Oklahoma Baptist University*

Doug Rohrer, *University of South Florida*

Jana S. Spain, *High Point University*

Paul Spector, *University of South Florida*

Matt Traxler, *University of California, Davis*

Eric Vanman, *Georgia State University*

Paul Whitney, *Washington State University*

Jun Zhang, *University of Michigan*

A special word of thanks to our very creative and dedicated ancillary team who have worked on the program both past and present: Sandra Goss Lucas, William Altman, Jill Shultz, Chris Armstrong, Linda Lebie, Kelly Bouas Henry, Kent Korek, Chris Thomas, Jamie Goldenberg, Mark Laumakis, Billa Reiss, Lora Harpster, Valeri Werpetinski, Missa Murry Eaton, Suzanne E. Juraska, and David B. Daniel.

The process of creating the Eighth Edition was greatly facilitated by the work of many dedicated people in the College Division at Houghton Mifflin Company. From the sales representatives and sales managers who told us of faculty members' suggestions for improvement to the marketing staff who developed innovative ways of telling our colleagues about the changes we have made, it seems that everyone in the division had a hand in shaping and improving the Eighth Edition. Several people deserve special thanks, however. Psychology Sponsoring Editor Jane Potter gave us invaluable advice about structural, pedagogical, and content changes for the new edition. Discipline Product Manager Damaris Curran and Media Producers Lynne Blaszak, Dustin Brant, and Adnan Virk were instrumental in implementing the integrated technology plan for this edition. Senior Developmental Editors Laura Hildebrand and Rita Lombard applied their collective editorial expertise and disciplined approach to helping us create this manuscript. Aileen Mason, our Senior Project Editor, again contributed her considerable organizational skills and a dedication to excellence that was matched by a wonderfully helpful and cooperative demeanor. Editorial Assistant Paola Moll lent a very capable hand to various aspects of the project. Thomas Finn, Developmental Editor, helped enormously by coordinating a wide range of tasks including those related to the *Test Bank, Study Guide,* and *Instructor's Manual*. Special thanks to Marketing Manager Amy Whitaker and Marketing Assistant Samantha Abrams for their continued stellar efforts in marketing this text. We also thank Jessyca Broekman for her outstanding work in the creation and updating of the art program for the Eighth Edition and Naomi Kornhauser for her creativity in developing new photo ideas and for her diligence in selecting and locating them. A big thank-you goes to Laurie McGee for her dedication and expertise in copyediting the manuscript. Thanks also to Lisa Goodman, who checked page proof to ensure its typographical accuracy, and Bernice Eisen, who tackled the monumental task of creating the indexes. Without these people, and those who worked with them, this revision simply could not have happened.

Finally, we want to express our deepest appreciation to our families and friends. Once again, their love saw us through an exhilarating but demanding period of our lives. They endured our hours at the computer, missed meals, postponed vacations, and occasional irritability during the creation of the First Edition of this book, and they had to suffer all over again during the lengthy process of revising it once more. Their faith in us is more important than they realize, and we will cherish it forever.

D. A. B.

L. A. P.

A. C.-S.

E. J. R.

PSYCHOLOGY EIGHTH EDITION

An Integrated Pedagogical System

HELPING STUDENTS TO THINK CRITICALLY

THINKING CRITICALLY **Do Violent Video Games Make People More Aggressive?**

A lot of research has been conducted on the impact of violent television on aggressiveness, but what about other forms of violent entertainment, such as video games? When these games first appeared in the late 1970s they contained little or no violence, but by the 1990s violent versions such as *Mortal Kombat* and *Street Fighter* had become extremely popular, and the current flood of graphically violent games remain the favorites of young game-players. For example, one survey of fourth-graders found that 59 percent of girls and 73 percent of boys preferred violent video games over nonviolent ones. In response to complaints from parents groups, the video-game industry devised a rating system designed to keep the most violent games out of the hands of preteens and young teenagers, but many of the games that the system deems appropriate for these groups still contain considerable violent content (Funk et al., 1999). Further, fewer than 1 percent of young teenagers in one survey said that their parents had ever stopped them from buying a video game because of its violence rating (Walsh, 2000). In other words, children in the United States have essentially unrestricted access to violent video games. If they can't buy a violent game in a store, they can always download it from the Internet.

THINKING CRITICALLY

A dedicated section in each chapter helps improve this vital skill.

Structured around five questions, these sections encourage students to analyze material before drawing conclusions:

❶ What am I being asked to believe or accept?

❷ Is there evidence available to support the claim?

❸ Can that evidence be interpreted another way?

❹ What evidence would help to evaluate the alternatives?

❺ What conclusions are most reasonable?

Fostering Scientific Attitudes

FOCUS ON RESEARCH

Highlighting a particular study, these sections emphasize the value of research and the creativity with which it is often conducted.

These sections are organized around five questions:

1 What was the researcher's question?

2 How did the researcher answer the question?

3 What did the researcher find?

4 What do the results mean?

5 What do we still need to know?

FOCUS ON
RESEARCH METHODS

Manipulating Genes in Animal Models of Human Disease

Alzheimer's disease is named for Alois Alzheimer, a German neurologist. Almost a century ago, Alzheimer examined the brain of a woman who had died after years of progressive mental deterioration and dementia. In looking for the cause of her disorder, he found that cells in her cerebral cortex and hippocampus were bunched up like a rope tied in knots and that cellular debris had collected around the affected nerves. These features came to be known as tangles and plaques. *Tangles* are twisted fibers within neurons; their main protein component is called *tau*. *Plaques* are deposits of protein and parts of dead cells found between neurons. The major component of plaques was found to be a small protein called *beta-amyloid*, which is made from a larger protein called *amyloid precursor protein*. Accumulation of beta-amyloid plaques can now be visualized in living people through the use of PET scans (Klunk et al., 2005; see Figure 3.15).

■ **What was the researchers' question?**

Ever since Alzheimer described plaques and tangles, researchers have been trying to learn about the role they play. One specific question that researchers have addressed is whether the proteins found in plaques and tangles actually *cause* Alzheimer's disease. They are certainly correlated with Alzheimer's, but as emphasized in the chapter on research in psychology, we can't confirm a causal relationship from a correlation alone. To discover if beta-amyloid and tau cause the death of neurons seen in Alzheimer's disease, researchers knew that controlled experiments would be necessary. This means

Demonstrating an Integrated Discipline

The *Linkages* feature reflects the relationships among the subfields of psychology.

Every chapter explores one linkage in depth.

Wherever a linkage is discussed in the text, a marginal callout directs students to further discussion.

 LINKAGES | **Emotionality and the Measurement of Cognitive Abilities**

 LINKAGES (a link to Motivation and Emotion, p. 409)

Emotional arousal is one of the most important noncognitive factors that can potentially influence scores on cognitive ability tests. As described in the chapter on motivation and emotion, people tend to perform best when their arousal level is moderate. Too much arousal, or even too little, tends to result in decreased performance. People whose overarousal impairs their ability to do well in testing situations are said to suffer from *test anxiety*.

As noted in the chapter on introducing psychology, all of psychology's many subfields are related to one another. Our discussion of treating psychological disorders through the use of psychoactive drugs illustrates just one way in which the topic of this chapter, the treatment of psychological disorders, is linked to the subfield of biological psychology (see the chapter on biological aspects of psychology). The Linkages diagram shows ties to two other subfields as well, and there are many more ties throughout the book. Looking for linkages among subfields will help you see how they all fit together and better appreciate the big picture that is psychology.

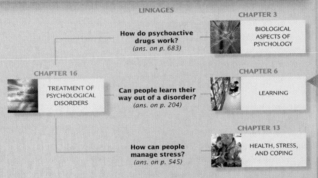

LINKAGES

CHAPTER 3 — BIOLOGICAL ASPECTS OF PSYCHOLOGY

How do psychoactive drugs work? (ans. on p. 683)

CHAPTER 16 — TREATMENT OF PSYCHOLOGICAL DISORDERS

CHAPTER 6 — LEARNING

Can people learn their way out of a disorder? (ans. on p. 204)

CHAPTER 13 — HEALTH, STRESS, AND COPING

How can people manage stress? (ans. on p. 545)

At the end of each chapter, a Linkages diagram presents three questions to illustrate how material in that chapter is related to other areas of psychology.

INSTRUCTOR RESOURCES

Eduspace®

Eduspace is a powerful course management system that enables instructors to create all or part of their courses online using the widely recognized tools of Blackboard™ and text-specific content from Bernstein, *Psychology*, Eighth Edition. Instructors and students have access to automatically graded online homework, *Psych in Film* video clips with quizzes, and tutorials with accompanying pedagogy. Instructor presentation tools include PowerPoint Presentations, CRS content, and downloadable PDFs of overhead transparencies and select art from the textbook. **New** content includes *self-assessment quizzes* that provide scoring, explanation of correct and incorrect answers, and remediation back to specific sections of the text; Online Concept Maps; and an Online Multimedia eBook.

Psych in Film®

This DVD/VHS contains 35 clips from Universal Studios films illustrating key concepts in psychology. Clips from films such as *Apollo 13*, *Schindler's List*, *Snow Falling on Cedars* and many others are combined with commentary, discussion questions, and teaching tips helping to make psychology come alive for students.

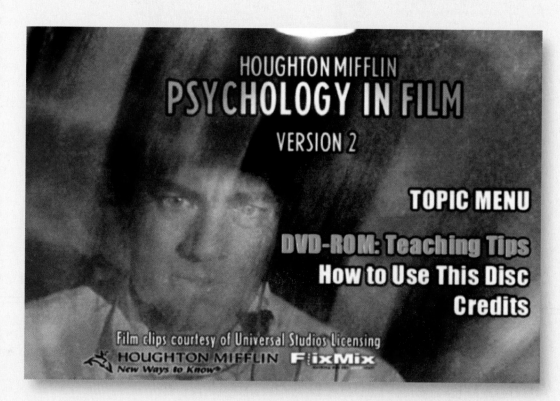

*Two optional chapters on **Neuropsychology** and **Industrial/Organizational Psychology** can be packaged with the text upon request. Please consult your sales representative for further details.*

Presentation Made Easy

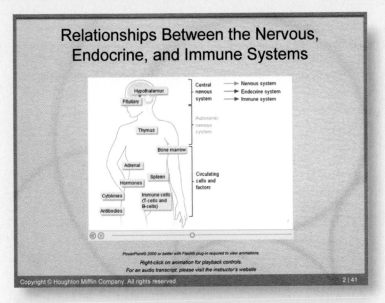

Enhanced PowerPoint® Presentations

Include lecture outlines, tables and figures from the text and hyperlinks to interactive tutorials.

Classroom Response System (CRS) Clicker Content

An additional set of PowerPoint slides for use with a CRS system gives you the flexibility to perform "on-the-spot" assessments, deliver quick quizzes, gauge students' understanding of a question or concept, conduct anonymous polling, and take the class roster.

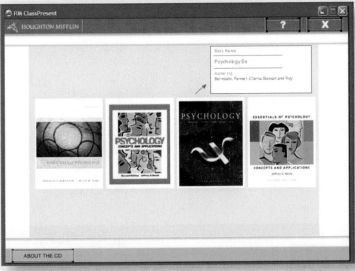

HM ClassPresent

Includes over 45 animations that project effectively in a lecture hall. Easy to navigate and searchable by thumbnail images organized by topic. Export the animations to your own computer or simply use them for presentation directly from the CD.

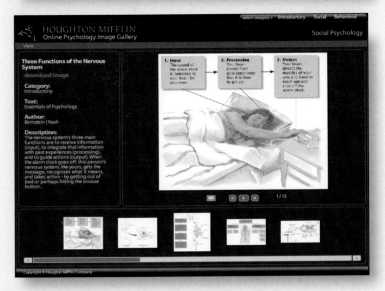

HMCO's Psychology Image Gallery

Includes over 250 images from the text as well as other sources, which can be downloaded for inclusion in your classroom presentations. The intuitive interface displays thumbnail images that make identifying images easy.

STUDENT RESOURCES

New! Eduspace® Online Multimedia eBook

Available in an interactive PDF format, this eBook offers an online alternative to the print text, complete with embedded links to multimedia assets such as animations, video, and self-practice exercises. Students can access **tutorial activities** that expand upon and reinforce main concepts in the text. Electronic **Flashcards** provide an interactive study tool to review key terms and concepts. And students can link to **Psych in Film** videos and quizzes that engage their interest by connecting textbook material to current films that students recognize. A downloadable static eBook is also available separately for purchase.

Research Companion

The **Research Companion for Introductory Psychology** gives students firsthand experience as researchers. It opens with a clear explanation of the research process, and the second half of the book includes several specific investigations into different topics of psychology.

Student Web Site

This offers additional study aids including ACE practice tests, interactive tutorials and flashcards. A passkey gives you access to premium online study tools that include **ACE+**, **Active Learning and Critical Thinking Booklets**, **Study Skills Video Modules**, **Online Concept Maps**, and **Self-Assessment quizzes**.

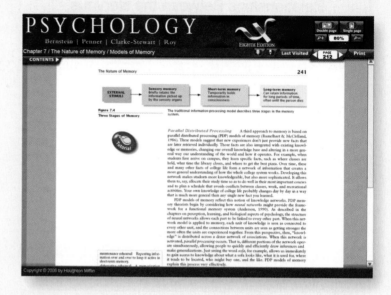

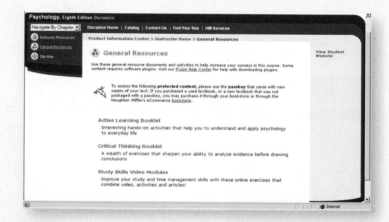

Introducing Psychology

Our goal in this opening chapter is to give you an overview of psychology and its subfields and to show how psychology's subfields are linked to one another and to other subjects, such as economics and medicine. We then tell the story of how psychology came to be and the various ways in which psychologists approach their work. We have organized the chapter as follows:

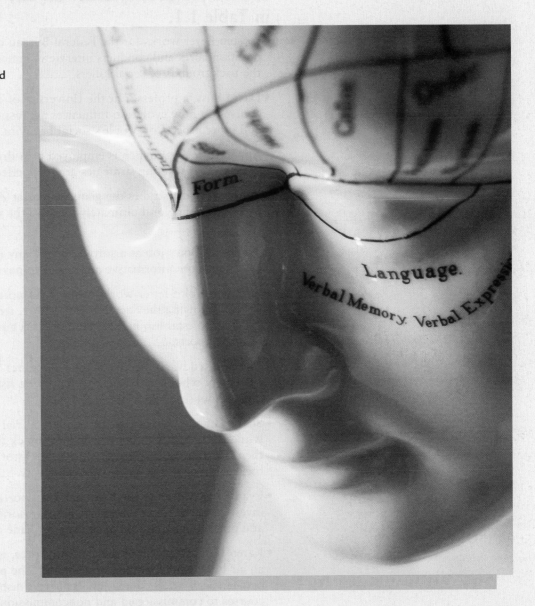

The people described next all hold truly interesting jobs. What do you think they studied to qualify for those jobs? See if you can fill in the blank next to each job description with one of the fields of study listed in Table 1.1.

- Kristen Beyer works for the Federal Bureau of Investigation, where she develops questionnaires and conducts interviews aimed at identifying common features in the backgrounds of serial killers. _____

- David Buss, a professor at the University of Texas, conducts research and teaches courses on how evolution influences aggression, the choice of sexual partners, and other aspects of people's social behavior. _____

- Anne Marie Apanovitch is employed by a drug company to study which of the company's marketing strategies are most effective in promoting sales. _____

- Rebecca Snyder studies the giant pandas at Zoo Atlanta in an effort to promote captive breeding and ultimately increase the wild population of this endangered species. _____

- Michael Moon's job at a software company is to find new ways to make Internet web sites more informative and easier to navigate. _____

- Elizabeth Kolmstetter works at the Transportation Security Administration, where, following the September 11, 2001, terrorist attacks, she took charge of a program to establish higher standards for hiring and training security screeners at U.S. airports. _____

- Marissa Reddy, codirector of the U.S. Secret Service's Safe Schools initiative, tries to prevent school shootings by identifying risk factors for violent behavior in high school students. _____

- Sharon Lundgren, founder of Lundgren Trial Consulting, Inc., helps prepare witnesses to testify in court, conducts mock trials in which attorneys rehearse their questioning strategies, and teaches attorneys how to present themselves and their evidence in the most convincing way. _____

- Evan Byrne works at the National Transportation Safety Board, where he investigates the role of memory lapses, disorientation, errors in using equipment, and other human factors in causing airplane crashes. _____

- Karen Orts, a captain in the U.S. Air Force, is chief of mental health services at an air base, where, among other things, she provides psychotherapy to military personnel suffering combat-related stress disorders and teaches leadership courses to commissioned and noncommissioned officers. _____

Because Captain Orts offers psychotherapy, you probably guessed that she is a psychologist, but what academic field did you associate with Rebecca Snyder, who studies giant pandas? It would have been perfectly reasonable to assume that she is a zoologist, but she, too, is a psychologist. So is Evan Byrne, whose work on web site design might suggest that he was a computer science major. And although Sharon Lundgren spends her time working with witnesses and conducting mock trials, she is a psychologist, not a lawyer. The fact is that *all* these people are psychologists! They may not all fit your image of what psychologists do, but as you will see in this chapter and throughout this book, psychology is much broader and more diverse than you might have expected.

TABLE 1.1	**What's My Line?**	
TRY THIS ⚙ Try matching educational backgrounds with the people described at the beginning of the chapter by writing the correct field of study next to each person's job description.	A. Engineering B. Criminal Justice C. Computer Science D. Law E. Psychology	F. Advertising G. Biology H. Education I. Zoology J. Business Administration

In other words, there are many different kinds of psychologists, doing all sorts of fascinating work in one or more of psychology's many specialty areas, or *subfields*. Most of these people took their first psychology course without realizing how many of these subfields there are or how many different kinds of jobs are open to psychologists. But like the people we have just described, they found something in psychology—perhaps something unexpected—that captured their interest, and they were hooked. And who knows? By the time you have finished this book and this course, you may have found some aspect of psychology so compelling that you will want to make it your life's work, too. Or not. At the very least, we hope you enjoy learning about psychology, about the work of psychologists, and about how that work benefits people everywhere.

The World of Psychology: An Overview

Psychology is the science that seeks to understand behavior and mental processes and to apply that understanding in the service of human welfare. It is a science that covers a lot of territory, as illustrated by the vastly different jobs that occupy the ten psychologists we described. They are all psychologists because they are all involved in studying, predicting, improving, or explaining some aspect of behavior and mental processes.

TRY THIS ➤ ⚙ To begin to appreciate all the things that are included under the umbrella of *behavior* and *mental processes*, take a moment to think about how you would answer this question: Who are you? Would you describe your personality, your 20/20 vision, your interests and goals, your skills and accomplishments, your IQ, your cultural background, or perhaps a physical or emotional problem that bothers you? You could have listed these and dozens of other things about yourself, and every one of them would reflect some aspect of what psychologists mean by behavior and mental processes. It is no wonder, then, that this book's table of contents includes so many different topics, including some—such as vision and hearing—that you might not have expected to see in a book about psychology. The topics have to be diverse in order to capture the full range of behaviors and mental processes that make you who you are and that come together in other ways in people of every culture around the world.

Some of the world's half-million psychologists focus on what can go wrong in behavior and mental processes—on psychological disorders, problems in childhood development, stress-related illnesses, and the like—while others study what goes right. They explore, for example, the factors that lead people to be happy and satisfied with their lives, to achieve at a high level, to be creative, to help others, and to develop their full potential as human beings. This focus on what goes right, on the things that make life most worth living, has become known as **positive psychology** (e.g., Peterson, 2006; Seligman & Csikszentmihalyi, 2000; Snyder & Lopez, 2007), and you will see many examples of it in the research described throughout this book.

● **psychology** The science of behavior and mental processes.

● **positive psychology** A field of research that focuses on people's positive experiences and characteristics, such as happiness, optimism, and resilience.

● Subfields of Psychology

When psychologists choose to focus their attention on certain aspects of behavior and mental processes, they enter one of psychology's subfields. Let's take a quick look at the typical interests and activities of psychologists in each subfield. We will describe their work in more detail in later chapters.

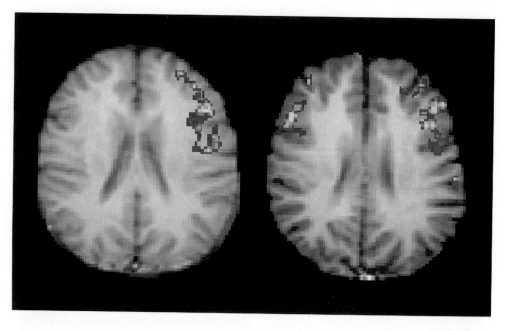

FIGURE 1.1

Visualizing Brain Activity

Magnetic resonance imaging (MRI) techniques allow biological psychologists to study the brain activity accompanying various mental processes. This study found that males (left) and females (right) show different patterns of brain activity (indicated by the brightly colored areas) while reading (Shaywitz et al., 1995).

● **Biological Psychology** Biological psychologists, also called *physiological psychologists*, use high-tech scanning devices and other methods to study how biological processes in the brain and other organs affect, and are affected by, behavior and mental processes (see Figure 1.1). Have you ever experienced *déjà vu*, the feeling that a new experience, such as entering an unfamiliar house, has actually happened to you before? Biological psychologists studying this illusion suggest that it may be due to a temporary malfunction in the brain's ability to combine incoming information from the senses, creating the impression of two "copies" of a single event (Brown, 2004). In the chapter on biological aspects of psychology, we describe biological psychologists' research on many other topics, such as how your brain controls your movements and speech and what organs help you to cope with stress and fight disease.

● **Developmental Psychology** Developmental psychologists describe the changes in behavior and mental processes that occur from birth through old age and try to understand the causes and effects of those changes (see Figure 1.2). Their research on the development of memory and other mental abilities, for example, is used by judges and attorneys in deciding how old a child has to be in order to serve

FIGURE 1.2

Where Would You Put a Third Eye?

In a study of how thinking processes develop, children were asked to show where they would place a third eye, if they could have one. Nine-year-old children, who were still in an early stage of mental development, drew the extra eye between their existing eyes, "as a spare." Having developed more advanced thinking abilities, eleven-year-olds drew the third eye in more creative places, such as the palm of the hand "so I can see around corners" (Shaffer, 1973).

Drawing by a nine-year-old   Drawing by an eleven-year-old

biological psychologists Psychologists who analyze the biological factors influencing behavior and mental processes.

as a reliable witness in court or to responsibly choose which divorcing parent to live with. The chapter on human development describes other research by developmental psychologists and how it is being applied in areas such as parenting, evaluating day care, and preserving mental capacity in elderly people.

● **Cognitive Psychology** Stop reading for a moment and look left and right. Your ability to follow this suggestion, to recognize whatever you saw, and to understand the words you are reading right now are the result of mental, or *cognitive*, abilities. Those abilities allow you to receive information from the outside world, understand it, and act on it. **Cognitive psychologists** (some of whom prefer to be called *experimental psychologists*) study mental abilities such as sensation and perception, learning and memory, thinking, consciousness, intelligence, and creativity. Cognitive psychologists have found, for example, that we don't just receive incoming information—we mentally manipulate it. Notice that the drawing in Figure 1.3 stays physically the same, but two different versions emerge, depending on which of its features *you* emphasize.

Applications of cognitive psychologists' research are all around you. Research by those whose special interest is **engineering psychology**—also known as *human factors*—has helped designers create computer keyboards, mobile phones, Internet web sites, aircraft instrument panels, nuclear power plant controls, and even TV remotes that are more logical, easier to use, and less likely to cause errors. You will read more about human factors research and many other aspects of cognitive psychology in several chapters of this book.

● **Personality Psychology** **Personality psychologists** study similarities and differences among people. Some of them use tests, interviews, and other measures to

FIGURE **1.3**

Husband and Father-in-Law

TRY THIS This figure is called "Husband and Father-in-Law" (Botwinick, 1961) because you can see an old man or a young man, depending upon how you mentally organize its features. The elderly father-in-law faces to your right and is turned slightly toward you. He has a large nose, and the dark areas represent his coat pulled up to his protruding chin. However, the tip of his nose can also be seen as the tip of a younger man's chin; the younger man is in profile, also looking to your right, but away from you. The old man's mouth is the young man's neckband. Both men are wearing a broad-brimmed hat.

● **developmental psychologists** Psychologists who seek to understand, describe, and explore how behavior and mental processes change over a lifetime.

● **cognitive psychologists** Psychologists who study the mental processes underlying judgment, decision making, problem solving, imagining, and other aspects of human thought or cognition. Also called *experimental psychologists*.

● **engineering psychology** A field in which psychologists study human factors in the use of equipment and help designers create better versions of that equipment.

● **personality psychologists** Psychologists who study the characteristics that make individuals similar to, or different from, one another.

A Bad Design Consultation by human factors psychologists would surely have improved the design of this self-service gasoline pump. The pump will not operate until you press the red "start" button under the yellow "push to" label (see enlargement at the upper right). The button is difficult to locate among all the other signs and stickers. Such user-unfriendly designs are all too common these days (e.g., Cooper, 2004; visit www.baddesigns.com for some amazing examples).

Photograph courtesy of www.baddesigns.com.

Getting Ready for Surgery Health psychologists have learned that when patients are mentally prepared for a surgical procedure, they are less stressed by it and recover more rapidly. Their research is now routinely applied in hospitals through programs in which children and adults are given more information about what to expect before, during, and after their operations.

compare individuals on characteristics such as openness to experience, emotionality, reliability, agreeableness, and sociability. Personality psychologists also study the characteristics of people who are prejudiced against others, who tend to be pessimistic or depressed, or even who claim to have been abducted by space aliens. As described in the personality chapter, their research has been applied in the diagnosis of mental disorders, and in the identification of people who are most likely to develop stress-related health problems. On the positive side, research by personality psychologists is helping to identify, understand, and encourage personality characteristics, such as optimism, that are associated with the resilience that allows some people to survive, and even thrive in the face of stress and to find happiness in life (Linley & Joseph, 2004; Snyder & Lopez, 2006, 2007).

● **Clinical, Counseling, Community, and Health Psychology** Clinical psychologists and counseling psychologists conduct research on the causes of mental disorders and offer services to help troubled people overcome those disorders. They have found, for example, that many irrational fears, called *phobias*, are learned through the bad experiences people have with dogs, public speaking, or whatever, and that fearful people can literally be taught to overcome their fears. Research by other clinical psychologists has resulted in a listing of treatment methods that are most effective with particular kinds of disorders.

Community psychologists work to ensure that psychological services reach the homeless and others who need help but tend not to seek it. They also try to *prevent* psychological disorders by promoting people's resilience and other personal strengths, and by working with community leaders and neighborhood organizations to improve local schools and reduce the crime, poverty, and other stressful conditions that so often lead to disorders. Health psychologists study the effects of behavior on health, as well as the effects that illness has on people's behavior and emotions. Their research is applied in programs that help people to cope effectively with illness, as well as to reduce the risk of cancer, heart disease, and stroke by giving up smoking, eating a healthy diet, and exercising more. You can read more about the work of clinical, counseling, community, and health psychologists in the chapters on health, stress, and coping; psychological disorders; and treatment of psychological disorders.

● **clinical and counseling psychologists** Psychologists who seek to assess, understand, and change abnormal behavior.

● **community psychologists** Psychologists who work to obtain psychological services for people in need of help and to prevent psychological disorders by working for changes in social systems.

● **health psychologists** Psychologists who study the effects of behavior and mental processes on health and illness, and vice versa.

● **educational psychologists** Psychologists who study methods by which instructors teach and students learn and who apply their results to improving those methods.

● **Educational and School Psychology** Educational psychologists conduct research and develop theories about teaching and learning. The results of their work are applied in programs designed to improve teacher training, refine school curricula, reduce dropout rates, and help students learn more efficiently. For example, they have supported the use of the "jigsaw" technique, a type of classroom activity, described in the social cognition chapter, in which children from various ethnic groups must work together to complete a task or solve a problem. These cooperative experiences appear to promote learning, generate mutual respect, and reduce intergroup prejudice (Aronson, 2004).

School psychologists traditionally specialized in IQ testing, diagnosing learning disabilities and other academic problems, and setting up programs to improve students' achievement and satisfaction in school. Today, however, they are also involved in activities such as early detection of students' mental health problems and crisis intervention following school violence (Benjamin & Baker, 2004; Elliot, Reynolds, & Kratochwill, 2006).

● **Social Psychology** Social psychologists study the ways that people think about themselves and others and how people influence one another. Their research on social persuasion has been applied to public health campaigns aimed at preventing the spread of AIDS and promoting the use of seat belts, not to mention the creation of compelling advertisements. Social psychologists also explore how peer pressure affects us, what determines whom we like (or even love), and why and how prejudice forms. They have found that although we may pride ourselves on not being prejudiced, we may actually hold unconscious negative beliefs about certain groups that affect the way we relate to people from those groups (Vanman et al., 2004). The chapters on social cognition and social influence describe these and many other examples of research in social psychology.

● **Industrial/Organizational Psychology** Industrial/organizational psychologists study leadership, stress, competition, pay scales, and other factors that affect the efficiency, productivity, and satisfaction of workers and the organizations that employ them. They conduct research on topics such as increasing the motivation of current employees and helping companies select the best new workers. They also explore the ways in which businesses and industrial organizations work—or fail to

school psychologists Psychologists who test IQs, diagnose students' academic problems, and set up programs to improve students' achievement.

social psychologists Psychologists who study how people influence one another's behavior and mental processes, individually and in groups.

industrial/organizational psychologists Psychologists who study ways to improve efficiency, productivity, and satisfaction among workers and the organizations that employ them.

Got a Match? Some commercial dating and matchmaking services apply social psychologists' research on interpersonal attraction in an effort to pair up people whose characteristics are most likely to be compatible.

Working Underground Before moving its data-processing center to the basement of a new office building, executives of a large corporation consulted an environmental psychologist. They wanted to know how the employees' performance and morale might be affected by working in a windowless space. The psychologist described the possible negative effects and, to combat those effects, recommended that architects create shafts that let in natural light. He also suggested that the area should include plants and artwork depicting nature's beauty (Sommer, 1999).

work—and they make recommendations for helping them to work better (Spector, 2003). Companies all over the world are applying research by industrial/organizational psychologists to foster the development of *positive organizational behavior* (Luthans, 2003; Wright, 2003) through more effective employee training programs, ambitious but realistic goal-setting procedures, fair and reasonable evaluation tools, and incentive systems that motivate and reward outstanding performance.

● **Quantitative Psychology** Quantitative psychologists develop and use statistical tools to analyze vast amounts of data collected by their colleagues in many other subfields (e.g., Keselman et al., 2004). These tools help to evaluate the reliability and validity of psychological tests, to trace the relationships between childhood experiences and adult behaviors, and even to estimate the relative contributions of heredity and environment in determining intelligence. To what extent are people born smart—or not so smart—and to what extent are their mental abilities created by their environments? This is one of the hottest topics in psychology today, and quantitative psychologists are right in the middle of it.

● **Other Subfields** Our list of psychology's subfields is still not complete. There are **sport psychologists**, who use visualization and relaxation training programs, for example, to help athletes reduce excessive anxiety, focus attention, and make other changes that let them perform at their best. **Forensic psychologists** assist in jury selection, evaluate defendants' mental competence to stand trial, and deal with other issues involving psychology and the law. And **environmental psychologists** study the effects of the environment on people's behavior and mental processes. The results of their research are applied by architects and interior designers as they plan or remodel residence halls, shopping malls, auditoriums, hospitals, prisons, offices, and other spaces to make them more comfortable and functional for the people who will occupy them. There are also neuropsychologists, military psychologists, consumer psychologists, rehabilitation psychologists, and more.

Further information about the subfields we have mentioned and some that we haven't is available in books (e.g., Stec & Bernstein, 1999; Super & Super, 2001), as well as on web sites of the American Psychological Association (**www.apa.org**) and the Association for Psychological Science (**www.psychologicalscience.org**).

Where do the psychologists in all these subfields work? Table 1.2 contains the latest figures on where the approximately 160,000 psychologists in the United States find employment, as well as the kinds of things they typically do in each setting.

quantitative psychologists Psychologists who develop and use statistical tools to analyze research data.

sport psychologists Psychologists who explore the relationships between athletic performance and such psychological variables as motivation and emotion.

forensic psychologists Psychologists who assist in jury selection, evaluate defendants' mental competence to stand trial, and deal with other issues involving psychology and the law.

environmental psychologists Psychologists who study the effects of the physical environment on behavior and mental processes.

TABLE 1.2   Typical Activities and Work Settings for Psychologists

The fact that psychologists can work in such a wide variety of settings and do so many interesting—and often well-paying—jobs helps account for the popularity of psychology as an undergraduate major (Fogg, Harrington, & Harrington, 2005; National Center for Education Statistics, 2003). Psychology courses also provide excellent background for students planning to enter medicine, law, business, and many other fields.

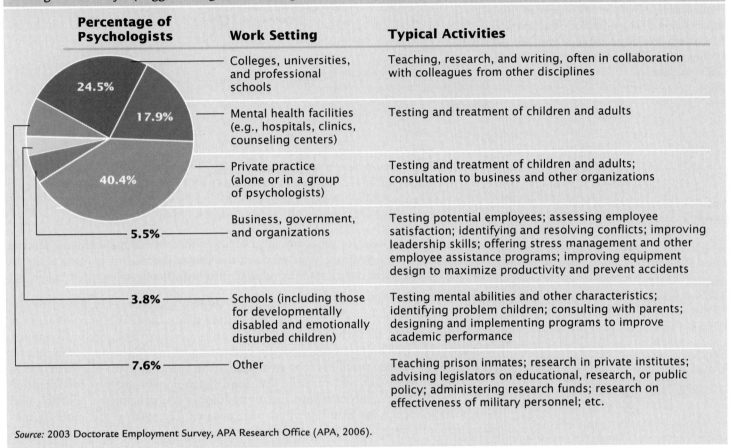

Percentage of Psychologists	Work Setting	Typical Activities
24.5%	Colleges, universities, and professional schools	Teaching, research, and writing, often in collaboration with colleagues from other disciplines
17.9%	Mental health facilities (e.g., hospitals, clinics, counseling centers)	Testing and treatment of children and adults
40.4%	Private practice (alone or in a group of psychologists)	Testing and treatment of children and adults; consultation to business and other organizations
5.5%	Business, government, and organizations	Testing potential employees; assessing employee satisfaction; identifying and resolving conflicts; improving leadership skills; offering stress management and other employee assistance programs; improving equipment design to maximize productivity and prevent accidents
3.8%	Schools (including those for developmentally disabled and emotionally disturbed children)	Testing mental abilities and other characteristics; identifying problem children; consulting with parents; designing and implementing programs to improve academic performance
7.6%	Other	Teaching prison inmates; research in private institutes; advising legislators on educational, research, or public policy; administering research funds; research on effectiveness of military personnel; etc.

Source: 2003 Doctorate Employment Survey, APA Research Office (APA, 2006).

● Linkages Within Psychology and Beyond

We have listed psychology's subfields as though they were separate, but they often overlap, and so do the activities of the psychologists working in them. When developmental psychologists study the changes in children's thinking skills, for example, their research is linked to the research of cognitive psychologists. Similarly, biological psychologists have one foot in clinical psychology when they look at how chemicals in the brain affect the symptoms of depression. And when social psychologists apply their research on cooperation to promote group learning activities in the classroom, they are linking up with educational psychology. Even when psychologists work mainly in one subfield, they are still likely to draw on, and contribute to, knowledge in other subfields.

So if you want to understand psychology as a whole, you have to understand the linkages among its subfields. To help you recognize these linkages, we highlight three of them in a Linkages diagram at the end of each chapter—similar to the one shown here. Each linkage is represented by a question that connects two subfields, and the page numbers in parentheses tell you where you can read more about each question. We pay particular attention to one question in each diagram by discussing it in a special Linkages section. If you look at the Linkages diagrams and follow the links where they lead, the relationships among psychology's many subfields will become much clearer. We hope you find this kind of detective work to be interesting and that

LINKAGES

By staying alert to the many linkages among psychology's subfields as you read this book, you will come away not only with threads of knowledge about each subfield but also with an appreciation of the fabric of psychology as a whole. We discuss one linkage in detail in each chapter in a special Linkages section.

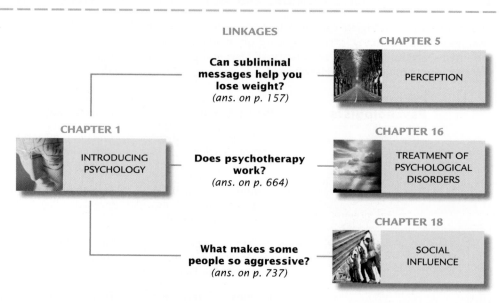

LINKAGES

Can subliminal messages help you lose weight?
(ans. on p. 157)

CHAPTER 5
PERCEPTION

CHAPTER 1
INTRODUCING PSYCHOLOGY

Does psychotherapy work?
(ans. on p. 664)

CHAPTER 16
TREATMENT OF PSYCHOLOGICAL DISORDERS

What makes some people so aggressive?
(ans. on p. 737)

CHAPTER 18
SOCIAL INFLUENCE

it will lead you to look for the many other linkages that we did not mention. Tracing linkages might even improve your grade in the course, because it is often easier to remember material in one chapter by relating it to linked material in other chapters.

● **Links to Other Fields**   Much as psychology's subfields are linked to one another, psychology itself is linked to many other fields. Some of these linkages are based on interests that psychologists share with researchers from other disciplines. For example, psychologists are working with computer scientists and engineers on artificial-intelligence machines that rival humans in their ability to recognize voices and images, to reason, and to make decisions. Psychologists are also collaborating with specialists in neuroanatomy, neurophysiology, neurochemistry, genetics, and other disciplines in the field known as *neuroscience*. The goal of this multidisciplinary research enterprise is to examine the structure and function of the nervous system in animals and humans at levels ranging from the individual cell to overt behavior. Someday, biological psychologists, like the colleagues with whom they work, may be known simply as "neuroscientists."

Many of the links between psychology and other disciplines appear when research conducted in one field is applied in the other. For example, biological psychologists are learning about the brain with scanning devices developed by computer scientists, physicists, and engineers. Economists are using research by psychologists to better understand the thought processes that influence people's decisions about investments and other financial matters. In fact, one psychologist, Daniel Kahneman, recently won a Nobel Prize in economics for his work in this area. Other psychologists' research on memory has influenced how lineups are displayed to eyewitnesses attempting to identify criminals, how attorneys question eyewitnesses in court, and how lawyers and judges question witnesses and instruct juries (Memon, Vrij, & Bull, 2004). And psychological studies of the effect of brain disorders on elderly patients' mental abilities is shaping doctors' recommendations about when those patients should stop driving cars (Reger et al., 2004). This book is filled with examples of other ways in which psychological theories and research have been applied to health care, law, business, engineering, architecture, aviation, public health, and sports, to name just a few.

Research: The Foundation of Psychology

The knowledge that psychologists share across subfields and with other disciplines stems from the research they conduct on many aspects of behavior and mental

Linking Psychology and Law
Cognitive psychologists' research on the quirks of human memory has led to revised guidelines for police and prosecutors when dealing with crime witnesses (U.S. Department of Justice, 1999). These guidelines warn that asking witnesses leading questions (e.g., "Do you remember seeing a gun?") can distort their memories and that false accusations are less likely if witnesses are told that the real criminal might not be in a lineup or in a group of photos (Doyle, 2005).

processes. So instead of just speculating about why, for example, people eat too much or too little, psychologists look for answers by using the methods of science. This means that they perform experiments and other scientific procedures to systematically gather and analyze information about behavior and mental processes and then base their conclusions—and their next questions—on the results of those procedures.

To take just one example related to eating, let's consider a fascinating study conducted by Paul Rozin and his associates (Rozin et al., 1998) on what causes people to begin and end a meal. Suppose you have just finished a big lunch at your favorite restaurant when a server gets mixed up and brings you another plate of the same food that was meant for someone else. You would almost certainly send it away, but why? Decisions to start eating or stop eating are affected by many biological factors, including signals from your blood that tell your brain how much "fuel" you have available. Rozin was interested in how these decisions are affected by psychological factors, such as being aware that you have already eaten. For example, what if you didn't remember that you just had lunch? Would you have started eating that second plate of food?

To explore this question, Rozin conducted a series of tests with R. H. and B. R., two men who had suffered a kind of brain damage that left them unable to remember anything for more than a few minutes. (You can read more about this condition, called *anterograde amnesia*, in the memory chapter.) The men were tested individually, on three different days, in a private room where they sat with a researcher at lunchtime and were served a tray of their favorite food. Before and after eating, they were asked to rate their hunger on a scale from 1 (extremely full) to 9 (extremely hungry). Once lunch was over, the tray was removed, and the researcher continued chatting, making sure that each man drank enough water to clear his mouth of food residue. After ten to thirty minutes, a hospital attendant reentered with an identical meal tray and announced "Here's lunch." These men had no memory of having eaten lunch already, but would signals from their stomachs or their blood be enough to keep them from eating another one?

Apparently not. Table 1.3 shows that, in every test session, R. H. and B. R. ate all or part of the second meal and, in all but one session, ate at least part of a third lunch that was offered to them ten to thirty minutes after the second one. Rozin

TABLE 1.3	The Role of Memory in Deciding When to Eat			

Here are the results of a study in which brain-damaged people were offered a meal shortly after having eaten an identical meal. Their hunger ratings (1–9, where 9 = extremely hungry) before and after eating are shown in parentheses. B. R. and R. H. had a kind of brain damage that left them unable to remember recent events (anterograde amnesia); J. C. and T. A. had normal memory. These results suggest that the decision to start eating is determined partly by knowing when we last ate. Notice that hunger ratings, too, were more consistently affected by eating for the people who remembered having eaten.

Session	B. R. (Amnesia)	R. H. (Amnesia)	J. C.	T. A.
One				
Meal 1	Finished (7/8)	Partially eaten (7/6)	Finished (5/2)	Finished (5/4)
Meal 2	Finished (2/5)	Partially eaten (7/7)	Rejected (0)	Rejected (3)
Meal 3	Rejected (3)	Partially eaten (7/7)	—	—
Two				
Meal 1	Finished (6/5)	Partially eaten (7/6)	Finished (7/2)	Finished (7/3)
Meal 2	Finished (5/3)	Partially eaten (7/6)	Rejected (1)	Rejected (3)
Meal 3	Partially eaten (5)[a]	Partially eaten (7/6)	—	—
Three				
Meal 1	Finished (7/3)	Partially eaten (7/6)	—	—
Meal 2	Finished (2/3)	Partially eaten (7/6.5)	—	—
Meal 3	Partially eaten (5/3)	Partially eaten (7.5)	—	—

[a]B. R. began eating his third meal but was stopped by the researcher, presumably to avoid illness.

Source: Adapted from Rozin et al. (1998).

conducted similar tests with J. C. and T. A., a woman and a man who had also suffered brain damage but who still had normal memory for recent events. In each of two test sessions, these people finished their lunch but refused the opportunity to eat a second one. These results suggest that the memory of when we last ate can indeed be a factor in guiding decisions about when to eat again. They also support a conclusion described in the motivation and emotion chapter, namely that eating is controlled by a complex combination of biological, social, cultural, and psychological factors. As a result, we may eat when we *think* it is time to eat, regardless of what our bodies tell us about our physical need to eat.

Rozin's study illustrates the fact that although psychologists often begin with speculation about behavior and mental processes, they take additional steps toward understanding those processes. Using scientific methods to test their ideas, they reach informed conclusions and generate new questions. Even psychologists who don't conduct research still benefit from it. They are constantly applying the results of their colleagues' studies to improve the quality, accuracy, and effectiveness of their teaching, writing, or service to clients and organizations. In the developing field of *performance psychology*, for example, practicing clinical psychologists are combining their psychotherapy skills with research from cognitive, industrial/organizational, and sport psychology to help business executives, performing artists, and athletes to excel (Berman & Bradt, 2006; Hamilton & Robson, 2006; Harmison, 2006).

The rules and methods of science that guide psychologists in their research are summarized in the chapter on research in psychology. We have placed that chapter early in the book to highlight the fact that without scientific research methods and the foundation of evidence they provide, psychologists' statements and recommendations about behavior and mental processes would carry no more weight than those of astrologers, psychics, or tabloid journalists. Accordingly, we will be relying on the results of psychologists' scientific research when we tell you what they have discovered so far about behavior and mental processes and also when we evaluate their efforts to apply that knowledge to improve the quality of human life.

● A Brief History of Psychology

The birth date of modern psychology is usually given as 1879, the year that Wilhelm Wundt (pronounced "voont") established the first formal psychology research laboratory at the University of Leipzig, Germany (Benjamin, 2000). However, the roots of psychology can be traced back through centuries of history in philosophy and science. Since at least the time of Socrates, Plato, and Aristotle in ancient Greece, there has been debate about where human knowledge comes from, the nature of the mind and soul, the relationship of the mind to the body, and whether it is possible to scientifically study such things (Wertheimer, 2000).

The philosophy of *empiricism* was particularly important to the development of scientific psychology. Beginning in the seventeenth century, proponents of empiricism—especially the British philosophers John Locke, George Berkeley, and David Hume—challenged the claim, made by philosophers as far back as Plato, that some knowledge is innate. Empiricists argued instead that what we know about the world comes to us through experience and observation, not through imagination or intuition. This view suggests that, at birth, our minds are like a blank slate (*tabula rasa*, in Latin) upon which our experiences write a lifelong story. For nearly 130 years now, empiricism has guided psychologists in seeking knowledge about behavior and mental processes through observations governed by the rules of science.

● Wundt and the Structuralism of Titchener   By the mid-1800s, a number of German physiologists, including Hermann von Helmholtz and Gustav Fechner (pronounced "FECK-ner"), were conducting scientific studies of the structure and function of vision, hearing, and the other sensory systems and perceptual processes that empiricism had identified as the channels through which human knowledge flows. Fechner's work was especially valuable because he realized that one could study these mental processes by observing people's reactions to changes in sensory stimuli. By exploring, for example, how much brighter a light must become before we see it as twice as bright, Fechner discovered complex, but predictable, relationships between changes in the *physical* characteristics of stimuli and changes in our *psychological experience* of them. Fechner's approach, which he called *psychophysics*, paved the way for much of the research described in the chapter on perception.

As a physiologist, Wundt, too, used the methods of laboratory science to study sensory-perceptual systems, but the focus of his work was *consciousness*, the mental experiences created by these systems. Wundt wanted to describe the basic elements of consciousness, how they are organized, and how they relate to one another (Schultz & Schultz, 2004). For example, he developed ingenious laboratory methods to study the speed of decision making and other mental events. And in an attempt to observe conscious experience, Wundt used the technique of *introspection*, which means "looking inward." After training research participants in this method, he repeatedly showed a light or made a sound and asked them to describe the sensations and feelings these stimuli created. Wundt concluded that "quality" (e.g., cold or blue) and "intensity" (e.g., brightness or loudness) are the two essential elements of any sensation and that feelings can be described in terms of pleasure-displeasure, tension-relaxation, and excitement-depression (Schultz & Schultz, 2004). In conducting this kind of research, Wundt began psychology's transformation from the *philosophy* of mental processes to the *science* of mental processes.

Wilhelm Wundt (1832–1920) In an early experiment on the speed of mental processes, Wundt (third from left) first measured how quickly people could respond to a light by releasing a button they had been holding down. He then measured how much longer the response took when they held down one button with each hand and had to decide—based on the color of the light—which one to release. Wundt reasoned that the additional response time reflected how long it took to perceive the color and decide which hand to move. As noted in the chapter on cognition and language, the logic behind this experiment remains a part of research on cognitive processes today.

Source: The Psychology Archive—The University of Akron

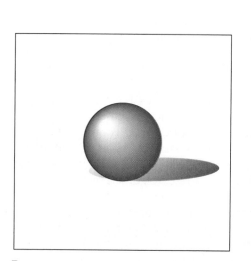

FIGURE 1.4

A Stimulus for Introspection

TRY THIS Look at this object and try to ignore what it is. Instead, try to describe only your conscious experience, such as redness, brightness, and roundness, and how intense and clear the sensations and images are. If you can do this, you would have been an excellent research assistant in Titchener's laboratory.

Edward Titchener, an Englishman who had been a student of Wundt's, used introspection in his own laboratory at Cornell University. He studied Wundt's basic elements of consciousness, as well as images and other aspects of conscious experience that are harder to quantify (see Figure 1.4). One result was that Titchener added "clearness" as an element of sensation (Schultz & Schultz, 2004). Titchener called his approach *structuralism* because he was trying to define the structure of consciousness.

Wundt was not alone in the scientific study of mental processes, nor was his work universally accepted. Some of his fellow German scientists, such as Hermann Ebbinghaus, believed that analyzing consciousness through introspection was not as important as exploring the capacities and limitations of mental processes such as learning and memory. Ebbinghaus's own laboratory experiments—in which he served as the only participant—formed the basis for some of what we know about memory today. Around 1912, other German colleagues, including Max Wertheimer, Kurt Koffka, and Wolfgang Köhler, argued against Wundt's efforts to break down human experience or consciousness into its component parts. They were called Gestalt psychologists because they pointed out that the whole (or *Gestalt*, in German) of conscious experience is not the same as the sum of its parts. Wertheimer noted, for example, that if a pair of lights goes on and off in just the right sequence, we experience not two flashing lights but a single light "jumping" back and forth. You have probably seen this *phi phenomenon* in action on advertising signs that create the impression of a series of lights racing around a display. Movies provide another example. Imagine how boring it would be to browse slowly through the thousands of still images that are printed on a reel of film. Yet when those same images are projected onto a screen at a particular rate, they combine to create a rich, emotional experience. In other words, said the Gestaltists, consciousness should be studied as a whole, not piece by piece.

● Freud and Psychoanalysis
While Wundt and his colleagues in Leipzig were conducting scientific research on consciousness, Sigmund Freud (1856–1939)

was in Vienna, Austria, beginning to explore the unconscious. As a physician, Freud had presumed that all behavior and mental processes have *physical* causes somewhere in the nervous system. He began to question that assumption in the late 1800s, however, after encountering several patients who displayed a variety of physical ailments that had no apparent physical cause. After interviewing these patients using hypnosis and other methods, Freud became convinced that the causes of these people's physical problems were not physical. The real causes, he said, were deep-seated problems that the patients had pushed out of consciousness (Friedman & Schustack, 2003). He eventually came to believe that all behavior—from everyday slips of the tongue to severe forms of mental disorder—is motivated by *psychological* processes, especially by mental conflicts that occur without our awareness, at an unconscious level. For nearly fifty years, Freud developed his ideas into a body of work known as *psychoanalysis*, which included a theory of personality and mental disorder, as well as a set of treatment methods. Partly because they were based on a small number of medical cases, not a long series of laboratory experiments, Freud's ideas are by no means universally accepted. Still, he was a groundbreaker whose theories have had a significant influence on psychology and many other fields.

● **William James and Functionalism**   Scientific research in psychology began in North America not long after Wundt started his work in Germany. William James founded a psychology laboratory at Harvard University in the late 1870s, though it was used mainly to conduct demonstrations for his students (Schultz & Schultz, 2004). It was not until 1883 that G. Stanley Hall at Johns Hopkins University established the first psychology research laboratory in the United States. The first Canadian psychology research laboratory was established in 1889 at the University of Toronto by James Mark Baldwin, Canada's first modern psychologist and a pioneer in research on child development.

Like the Gestalt psychologists, William James rejected both Wundt's approach and Titchener's structuralism. He saw no point in breaking consciousness into component parts that never operate on their own. Instead, in accordance with

William James's Lab   William James (1842–1910) established this psychology demonstration laboratory at Harvard University in the late 1870s. Like the Gestalt psychologists, James saw the approach used by Wundt and Titchener as a scientific dead end; he said that trying to understand consciousness by studying its components is like trying to understand a house by looking at individual bricks (James, 1884). He preferred instead to study the ways in which consciousness functions to help people adapt to their environments.

Charles Darwin's theory of evolution, James wanted to understand how images, sensations, memories, and the other mental events that make up our flowing "stream of consciousness" *function* to help us adapt to our environment (James, 1890, 1892). This idea was consistent with an approach to psychology called *functionalism*, which focused on the role of consciousness in guiding people's ability to make decisions, solve problems, and the like.

James's emphasis on the functions of mental processes encouraged North American psychologists to look not only at how those processes work to our advantage but also at how they differ from person to person. Some of these psychologists began to measure individual differences in learning, memory, and other mental processes associated with intelligence, made recommendations for improving educational practices in the schools, and even worked with teachers on programs tailored to children in need of special help (Bernstein, Kramer, & Phares, 2008).

● John B. Watson and Behaviorism

Besides fueling James's interest in the functions of consciousness, Darwin's theory of evolution led other psychologists—especially those in North America after 1900—to study animals as well as humans. If all species evolved in similar ways, perhaps the behavior and mental processes of all species followed the same, or similar, laws and we can learn something about people by studying animals. Psychologists could not expect cats or rats or pigeons to introspect, so they watched what animals did when confronted with laboratory tasks such as finding the correct path through a maze. From these observations, they made *inferences* about the animals' conscious experience and about the general laws of learning, memory, problem solving, and other mental processes that might apply to people as well as animals.

John B. Watson, a psychology professor at Johns Hopkins University, agreed that the observable behavior of animals and humans is the most important source of scientific information for psychology. However, Watson thought it was utterly unscientific to use behavior as the basis for making inferences about consciousness, as structuralists and functionalists did—let alone about the unconscious, as Freudians did. In 1913, Watson published an article called "Psychology As the Behaviorist Views It." In it, he argued that psychologists should ignore mental events and base psychology only on what they can actually see in overt behavior and in responses to various stimuli (Watson, 1913, 1919).

Watson's view, called *behaviorism*, recognized the existence of consciousness but did not consider it worth studying because it would always be private and therefore not observable by scientific methods. In fact, said Watson, preoccupation with consciousness would prevent psychology from ever being a true science. Watson believed that the most important determinant of behavior is *learning* and that it is through learning that animals and humans are able to adapt to their environments. He was famous for claiming that with enough control over the environment, he could create learning experiences that would turn any infant into a doctor, a lawyer, or even a criminal.

American psychologist B. F. Skinner was another early champion of behaviorism. From the 1930s until his death in 1990, Skinner worked on mapping out the details of how rewards and punishments shape, maintain, and change behavior through what he termed "operant conditioning." Through his *functional analysis of behavior*, he would explain, for example, how parents and teachers can unknowingly encourage children's tantrums by rewarding them with attention, and how a virtual addiction to gambling can result from the occasional and unpredictable rewards it brings.

Many psychologists were drawn to Watson's and Skinner's vision of psychology as the learning-based science of observable behavior. In fact, behaviorism dominated psychological research from the 1920s through the 1960s, while the study of consciousness received less attention, especially in the United States. ("In Review: The Development of Psychology" summarizes behaviorism and the other schools of thought that have influenced psychologists in the past century.)

in **review** The Development of Psychology			
School of Thought	**Early Advocates**	**Goals**	**Methods**
Structuralism	Edward Titchener, trained by Wilhelm Wundt	To study conscious experience and its structure	Experiments; introspection
Gestalt psychology	Max Wertheimer	To describe the organization of mental processes: "The whole is greater than the sum of its parts."	Observation of sensory/perceptual phenomena
Psychoanalysis	Sigmund Freud	To explain personality and behavior; to develop techniques for treating mental disorders	Study of individual cases
Functionalism	William James	To study how the mind works in allowing an organism to adapt to the environment	Naturalistic observation of animal and human behavior
Behaviorism	John B. Watson, B. F. Skinner	To study only observable behavior and explain behavior through learning principles	Observation of the relationship between environmental stimuli and behavioral responses

● **Psychology Today** Psychologists continue to study all kinds of overt behavior in humans and in animals. By the end of the 1960s, however, many had become dissatisfied with the limitations imposed by behaviorism (some, especially in Europe, had never accepted it in the first place). They grew uncomfortable about ignoring mental processes that might be important in more fully understanding behavior (e.g., Ericsson & Simon, 1994). The dawn of the computer age influenced these psychologists to think about mental activity in a new way—as information processing. Computers and rapid progress in computer-based biotechnology began to offer psychologists exciting new ways to study mental processes and the biological activity that underlies them. As shown in Figure 1.1, for example, it is now possible to literally see what is going on in the brain when, for example, a person thinks or makes decisions.

Armed with ever more sophisticated research tools, psychologists today are striving to do what Watson thought was impossible: to study mental processes with precision and scientific objectivity. In fact, there are probably now as many psychologists who study cognitive and biological processes as there are who study observable behaviors. So mainstream psychology has come full circle, once again accepting consciousness—in the form of cognitive processes—as a legitimate topic for scientific research and justifying the definition of psychology as the science of behavior and mental processes (Gallagher & Sørensen, 2006; Haynes & Rees, 2005).

Approaches to the Science of Psychology

As you can see, the history of psychology is partly the history of the different aspects of behavior and mental processes—such as conscious experiences, unconscious conflicts, or overt actions—that have been emphasized by different groups of psychologists. Why so much variation? Put yourself in their shoes. Suppose that you are a psychologist, and you want to know why some people stop to help a sick or injured stranger and others just keep walking. Where would you start? You could look for answers in people's brain cells and hormones, in their genetic background, in their personality traits, and in what they have learned from family, friends, and cultural traditions, to

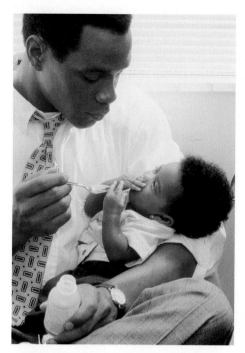

A Father's Love Mothers are solely responsible for the care and protection of their offspring in almost all species of mammals. These species survive without male involvement in parenting, so why are some human fathers so involved in child rearing? Do evolutionary forces make fathering more adaptive for humans? Is it a matter of learning to care? Is it a combination of both? Psychologists who take an evolutionary approach study these questions and others relating to the origins of both the positive and negative aspects of human social behavior (Buss, 2004a; Wright, 1994).

name just a few possibilities. With so many research directions available, you'd have to decide which sources of information were most likely to explain helping.

Psychologists have to make the same kinds of decisions, not only about where to focus their research but also about what kind of treatment methods to use, or what services to provide to schools, businesses, government agencies, or other clients. Their decisions are guided mainly by their overall *approach* to psychology—that is, by the assumptions, questions, and methods they believe will be most useful in their work. The approaches we described earlier as structuralism and functionalism are gone now, but the psychodynamic and behavioral approaches remain, along with others known as biological, evolutionary, cognitive, and humanistic approaches. Some psychologists adopt just one of these approaches, but most psychologists are *eclectic*. This means that they blend assumptions and methods from two or more approaches in an effort to more fully understand behavior and mental processes (e.g., Cacioppo et al., 2000). Some approaches to psychology are more influential than others these days, but we will review the main features of all of them to help you understand how they differ and how they have affected psychologists' work over the years.

The Biological Approach

As its name implies, the **biological approach** to psychology assumes that behavior and mental processes are largely shaped by biological processes. Psychologists who take this approach study the psychological effects of hormones, genes, and the activity of the nervous system, especially the brain. So if they are studying memory, they might try to identify the changes taking place in the brain as information is stored there (Figure 7.18, in the chapter on memory, shows an example of these changes). Or if they are studying thinking, they might look for patterns of brain activity associated with, say, making quick decisions or reading a foreign language.

Research discussed in nearly every chapter of this book reflects the enormous influence of the biological approach on psychology today. To help you better understand the terms and concepts used in that research, we have included an appendix on the principles of genetics and a chapter on biological aspects of psychology.

The Evolutionary Approach

Biological processes also figure prominently in an approach to psychology based on Charles Darwin's book, *The Origin of Species*. Darwin argued that the forms of life we see today are the result of *evolution*—of changes in life forms that occur over many generations. He said that evolution occurs through *natural selection*, which promotes the survival of the fittest individuals. Most evolutionists now see natural selection operating at the level of genes, but at either level, the process is the same. Genes that result in characteristics and behaviors that are adaptive and useful in a certain environment will enable the creatures that inherited them to survive and reproduce, thereby making it more likely that those genes will be passed on to the next generation. Genes that result in characteristics that are not adaptive in that environment are not passed on to subsequent generations, because the creatures possessing them don't survive to reproduce. So evolutionary theory says that many (but not all) of the genes we possess today are the result of natural selection.

The **evolutionary approach** to psychology assumes that the *behavior* of animals and humans today is also the result of evolution through natural selection. For example, psychologists who take this approach see cooperation as an adaptive survival strategy, aggression as a form of territory protection, and gender differences in mate-selection preferences as reflecting strategies that have been successful in previous generations. The evolutionary approach has generated a growing body of research (Buller, 2005; Buss, 2004a; Cosmides & Tooby, 2004); in later chapters, you will see how it is applied in relation to topics such as helping and altruism, mental disorders, temperament, and interpersonal attraction.

biological approach An approach to psychology in which behavior and behavior disorders are seen as the result of physical processes, especially those relating to the brain and to hormones and other chemicals.

evolutionary approach An approach to psychology that emphasizes the inherited, adaptive aspects of behavior and mental processes.

FIGURE 1.5

What Do You See?

TRY THIS Take a moment to jot down what you see in these clouds. According to the psychodynamic approach to psychology, what we see in cloud formations and other vague patterns reflects unconscious wishes, impulses, fears, and other mental processes. In the personality chapter, we discuss the value of personality tests based on this assumption.

● The Psychodynamic Approach

The **psychodynamic approach** to psychology offers a different slant on the role of inherited instincts and other biological forces in human behavior. Rooted in Freud's psychoanalysis, this approach assumes that our behavior and mental processes reflect constant, and mostly unconscious, psychological struggles within us (see Figure 1.5). Usually, these struggles involve conflict between the impulse to satisfy instincts (such as for food, sex, or aggression) and the need to follow the rules of civilized society. So psychologists taking the psychodynamic approach might see aggression, for example, as a case of primitive urges overcoming a person's defenses against expressing those urges. They would see anxiety, depression, or other disorders as overt signs of inner turmoil.

Freud's original theories are not as influential today as they once were (Mischel, 2004a), but you will encounter modern versions of the psychodynamic approach in other chapters when we discuss theories of personality, psychological disorders, and psychotherapy.

● The Behavioral Approach

The assumptions of the **behavioral approach** to psychology contrast sharply with those of the psychodynamic, biological, and evolutionary approaches. As founded by John Watson, behaviorism characterizes behavior as primarily the result of *learning*. From a strict behaviorist point of view, biological, genetic, and evolutionary factors simply provide "raw material," which is then shaped by learning experiences into what we see in each individual's actions. So strict behaviorists seek to understand all behavior—whether it is aggression or drug abuse, shyness or sociability, confidence or anxiety—by looking at the individual's learning history, especially the patterns of reward and punishment the person has experienced. They also believe that people can change all sorts of problematic behaviors, from overeating to criminality, by unlearning old habits and developing new ones.

Recall, though, that behaviorism was criticized precisely because it ignored everything but observable behavior. That criticism has had an impact on the many behaviorists who now apply their learning-based approach in an effort to understand thoughts, or cognitions, as well as observable behavior. Those who take this *cognitive-behavioral*, or *social-cognitive*, approach explore how learning affects the development

psychodynamic approach A view developed by Freud that emphasizes the interplay of unconscious mental processes in determining human thought, feelings, and behavior.

behavioral approach An approach to psychology emphasizing that human behavior is determined mainly by what a person has learned, especially from rewards and punishments.

Why Is He So Aggressive?
Psychologists who take the cognitive-behavioral approach suggest that children's aggressiveness is largely learned. They say this learning occurs partly through seeing family and friends acting aggressively, but also through hearing people talk about aggression as the only way to deal with threats, disagreements, and other conflict situations (e.g., Gifford-Smith et al., 2005).

of thoughts, attitudes, and beliefs and, in turn, how these learned cognitive patterns affect overt behavior.

● The Cognitive Approach

The growth of the cognitive-behavioral perspective reflects the influence of a broader cognitive approach to psychology. The **cognitive approach** focuses on how we take in, mentally represent, and store information; how we perceive and process that information; and how cognitive processes are related to our behavior. In other words, psychologists who take the cognitive approach study the rapid series of hidden mental events—including those taking place outside of awareness—that accompany the behavior they can see. Here is how a psychologist might use the cognitive approach to describe the information processing that occurs during an aggressive incident outside a movie theater: The aggressive person (1) *perceives* that someone has cut into the ticket line, (2) *recalls* information stored in memory about appropriate social behavior, (3) *decides* that the other person's action was inappropriate, (4) *labels* the person as rude and inconsiderate, (5) *considers* possible responses and their likely consequences, (6) *decides* that shoving the person is the best response, and (7) *executes* that response.

Psychologists who take a cognitive approach focus on these and other mental processes to understand many kinds of individual and social behaviors, from decision making and problem solving to interpersonal attraction and intelligence, to name but a few. In the situation we just described, for example, the person's aggression would be seen as the result of poor problem solving, because there were probably several better ways to deal with the problem of line-cutting. The cognitive approach is especially important in the field of *cognitive science,* in which researchers from psychology, computer science, biology, engineering, linguistics, and philosophy study intelligent systems in humans and computers. Together, they are trying to discover the building blocks of cognition and to determine how these components produce complex behaviors such as remembering a fact, naming an object, writing a word, or making a decision.

● The Humanistic Approach

Mental events play a different role in the **humanistic approach** to psychology (also known as the *phenomenological approach*). Psychologists who favor the humanistic perspective see behavior as determined primarily by each person's capacity to choose how to think and act. They don't see these choices as driven by instincts,

cognitive approach A way of looking at human behavior that emphasizes research on how the brain takes in information, creates perceptions, forms and retrieves memories, processes information, and generates integrated patterns of action.

humanistic approach An approach to psychology that views behavior as controlled by the decisions that people make about their lives based on their perceptions of the world.

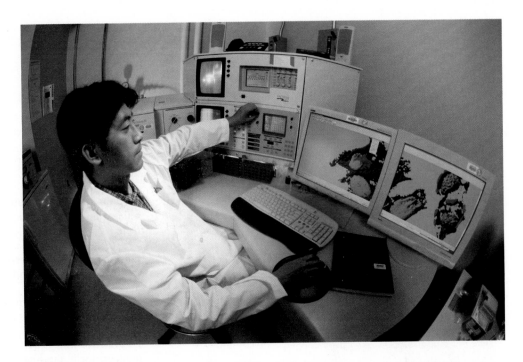

Cognitive Science at Work
Psychologists and other cognitive scientists are working on a "computational theory of the mind" in which they create computer programs that simulate how humans process information. In the chapter on cognition and language, we discuss their progress in creating "artificial intelligence" in computers that can help make medical diagnoses and perform other complex cognitive tasks.

biological processes, or rewards and punishments, but by each individual's unique perceptions of the world. So if you see the world as a friendly place, you are likely to be optimistic and secure. If you perceive it as full of hostile, threatening people, you will probably be defensive and fearful.

Like their cognitively oriented colleagues, psychologists who choose the humanistic approach would see aggression in a theater line as stemming from a perception that aggression is justified. But where the cognitive approach leads psychologists to search for laws governing *all* people's thoughts and actions, humanistic psychologists try to understand how each individual's unique experiences guide *that* person's thoughts and actions. In fact, many proponents of the humanistic approach say that behavior and mental processes can be fully understood only by understanding the perceptions and feelings of individuals. Humanistic psychologists also believe that people are essentially good, that they are in control of themselves, and that they have an innate tendency to grow toward their highest potential. Indeed, some of the roots of today's growing emphasis on positive psychology can be found in the writings of humanistic psychologists such as Abraham Maslow and Carl Rogers (Peterson & Seligman, 2004; Strümpfer, 2005).

The humanistic approach began to attract attention in North America in the 1940s through the writings of Rogers (1902–1987), a psychologist who had been trained in, but later rejected, the psychodynamic approach. We describe his views on personality and his psychotherapy methods in the chapters on personality and the treatment of psychological disorders. Maslow (1908–1970) also shaped and promoted the humanistic approach through his famous hierarchy-of-needs theory of motivation, which we describe in the chapters on motivation and emotion and personality. Today, however, the impact of the humanistic approach to psychology is limited, mainly because many psychologists find humanistic concepts and predictions too vague to be expressed and tested scientifically. (For a summary of the approaches we have discussed, see "In Review: Approaches to the Science of Psychology.")

Human Diversity and Psychology

Today, the diversity seen in psychologists' approaches to their work is matched by the diversity in their own backgrounds. This was not always the case. As in other academic disciplines in the early twentieth century, most psychologists were white,

in review · Approaches to the Science of Psychology

Approach	Characteristics
Biological	Emphasizes activity of the nervous system, especially of the brain; the action of hormones and other chemicals; and genetics.
Evolutionary	Emphasizes the ways in which behavior and mental processes are adaptive for survival.
Psychodynamic	Emphasizes internal conflicts, mostly unconscious, which usually pit sexual or aggressive instincts against environmental obstacles to their expression.
Behavioral	Emphasizes learning, especially each person's experience with rewards and punishments.
Cognitive	Emphasizes mechanisms through which people receive, store, retrieve, and otherwise process information.
Humanistic	Emphasizes individual potential for growth and the role of unique perceptions in guiding behavior and mental processes.

Mary Whiton Calkins (1863–1930)
Mary Whiton Calkins studied psychology at Harvard University, where William James described her as "brilliant." Because she was a woman, though, Harvard refused to grant her a doctoral degree unless she received it through Radcliffe, which was then an affiliated school for women. She refused, but went on to do research on memory and, in 1905, became the first woman president of the American Psychological Association. Margaret Washburn (1871–1939) encountered similar sex discrimination at Columbia University, so she transferred to Cornell and became the first woman to earn a doctorate in psychology. In 1921, she became the second woman president of the APA.

● **culture** The accumulation of values, rules of behavior, forms of expression, religious beliefs, occupational choices, and the like for a group of people who share a common language and environment.

middle-class men (Walker, 1991). Almost from the beginning, however, women and people of color were also part of the field (Schultz & Schultz, 2004). Throughout this book you will find the work of their modern counterparts, whose contributions to research, service, and teaching have all increased in tandem with their growing representation in psychology. In the United States, women now constitute about 48 percent of all psychologists holding doctoral degrees (National Science Foundation, 2004a). Women are also earning 75.7 percent of the new master's degrees and 73.4 percent of the new doctoral degrees awarded in psychology each year (American Psychological Association, 2006). Moreover, 18.3 percent of new doctoral degrees in psychology are being earned by members of ethnic minority groups (American Psychological Association, 2006; National Science Foundation, 2004b). These numbers reflect continuing efforts by psychological organizations and governmental bodies, especially in the United States and Canada, to promote the recruitment, graduation, and employment of women and ethnic minorities in psychology (Maton et al., 2006).

Another aspect of diversity in psychology lies in the wide range of people psychologists study and serve. This was not always the case, because most psychologists once assumed that all people are very much alike and that whatever principles emerged from research or treatment efforts with one group would apply to everyone, everywhere. They were partly right, because people around the world *are* alike in many ways. They tend to live in groups; have religious beliefs; and create rules, music, dances, and games. The principles of nerve cell activity or reactions to heat or a sour taste are the same in men and women everywhere, as is their recognition of a smile. But are all people's moral values, achievement motivation, or communication styles the same, too? Would the results of research on white male college students in the midwestern United States apply to African American women or to people in Greece, Korea, Argentina, or Egypt? Not always. These and many other aspects of behavior and mental processes are affected by *sociocultural factors*, including people's gender, ethnicity, social class, and the culture in which they grow up (Miller, 2002). These variables create many significant differences in behavior and mental processes, especially from one culture to another (e.g., Markus et al., 2006; Miyamoto, Nisbett, & Masuda, 2006).

Culture has been defined as the accumulation of values, rules of behavior, forms of expression, religious beliefs, occupational choices, and the like for a group of

TABLE 1.4   Some Characteristics of Behavior and Mental Processes Typical of Individualist vs. Collectivist Cultures

Psychologists and anthropologists have noticed that cultures can create certain general tendencies in behavior and mental processes among the people living in them (Bhagat et al., 2002). As shown here, individualist cultures tend to support the idea of placing one's personal goals before the goals of the extended family or workgroup, whereas collectivist cultures tend to encourage putting the goals of those groups ahead of personal goals. Remember, however, that these labels represent very rough categories. Cultures cannot be pigeonholed as being either entirely individualist or entirely collectivist, and not everyone raised in a particular culture always thinks or acts in exactly the same way (Oyserman, Coon, & Kemmelmeier, 2002).

Variable	Individualist	Collectivist
Personal identity	Separate from others	Connected to others
Major goals	Self-defined; be unique; realize your personal potential; compete with others	Defined by others; belong; occupy your proper place; meet your obligations to others; be like others
Criteria for self-esteem	Ability to express unique aspects of the self; ability to be self-assured	Ability to restrain the self and be part of a social unit; ability to be modest
Sources of success and failure	Success comes from personal effort; failure, from external factors	Success is due to help from others; failure is due to personal faults
Major frame of reference	Personal attitudes, traits, and goals	Family, work group

Gilbert Haven Jones (1883–1966)
When Gilbert Haven Jones graduated from the University of Jena in Germany in 1909, he became one of the first African Americans to earn a doctorate in psychology. Many others were to follow, including J. Henry Alston, who was the first African American to publish research in a major U.S. psychology journal (Alston, 1920).

people who share a common language and environment (Fiske et al., 1998). Culture is an organizing and stabilizing influence. It encourages or discourages particular behaviors and thoughts; it also allows people to understand and know what to expect from others in that culture. It is a kind of group adaptation, passed along by tradition and example rather than by genes from one generation to the next (Castro & Toro, 2004). Culture determines, for example, whether children's education will focus on skill at hunting or reading, how close people stand during a conversation, and whether or not they form lines in public places.

Psychologists and anthropologists have found that cultures can differ in many ways (Abi-Hashem, 2000; Gelfand, Nishii, & Raver, 2006; Triandis, 1998). They may have strict or loose rules governing social behavior. They might place great value on achievement or on self-awareness. Some seek dominance over nature; others seek harmony with it. Time is of great importance in some cultures, but not in others. Psychologists have tended to focus on the differences between cultures that can best be described as individualist or collectivist (Triandis & Trafimow, 2001). As shown in Table 1.4, many people in *individualist* cultures, such as those typical of North America and Western Europe, tend to value personal rather than group goals and achievement. Competitiveness to distinguish oneself from others is common in these cultures, as is a sense of isolation. By contrast, many people in *collectivist* cultures, such as Japan, tend to think of themselves mainly as part of family or work groups. Cooperative effort aimed at advancing the welfare of such groups is highly valued, and although loneliness is seldom a problem, fear of rejection by the group is common. Many aspects of U.S. culture—from self-reliant cowboy heroes and bonuses for "top" employees to the invitation to "help yourself" at a buffet table—reflect its tendency toward an individualist orientation (see Table 1.5).

A culture is often associated with a particular country, but most countries are actually *multicultural*; in other words, they host many *subcultures* within their borders. Often, these subcultures are formed by people of various ethnic origins. The population of the United States, for instance, includes African Americans, Hispanic Americans, Asian Americans, and American Indians, as well as European

TABLE 1.5   **Cultural Values in Advertising**

TRY THIS ⚙ The statements listed here appeared in advertisements in Korea and the United States. Those from Korea reflect collectivist values, whereas those from the United States emphasize a more individualist orientation (Han & Shavitt, 1994). See if you can tell which are which; then check the bottom of page 26 for the answers. You can follow up on this exercise by identifying cultural values in ads you see in newspapers and magazines, as well as on billboards and television. By surfing the Web or scanning international newspapers, you can compare the values conveyed by ads in your culture with those in ads from other cultures.

Source: Brehm, Kassin, & Fein (2005).

1. "She's got a style all her own."
2. "You, only better."
3. "A more exhilarating way to provide for your family."
4. "We have a way of bringing people closer together."
5. "Celebrating a half-century of partnership."
6. "How to protect the most personal part of the environment: Your skin."
7. "Our family agrees with this selection of home furnishings."
8. "A leader among leaders."
9. "Make your way through the crowd."
10. "Your business success: Harmonizing with (company name)."

Americans whose families came from Italy, Germany, Britain, Poland, Ireland, and many other places (see Figure 1.6). In each of these groups, the individuals who identify with their cultural heritage tend to share behaviors, values, and beliefs based on their culture of origin, thus forming a *subculture*.

Like fish unaware of the water in which they are immersed, people often fail to notice how their culture or subculture has shaped their thinking and behavior until they come in contact with people whose culture or subculture has shaped different patterns. Consider hand gestures, for example. The "thumbs-up" sign means that "everything is OK" to people in North America and Europe, but it is considered a rude gesture in Australia, Nigeria, and Bangladesh. And though in North America, making eye contact during social introductions is usually seen as a sign of interest or sincerity, it is likely to be considered rude in Japan. Even some of the misunderstandings that occur between men and women in the same culture can be traced to slight culturally influenced differences in their communication styles (Tannen, 1994).

FIGURE 1.6

Cultural Diversity in the United States

The people of the United States represent a wide array of cultural backgrounds. (These figures total more than 100 percent because many people see themselves belonging to two or more groups.) Most other countries are multicultural, too. Sadly, this fact becomes obvious to outsiders only when conflicts flare among a country's subcultures, as they have in Iraq, Afghanistan, Rwanda, Yemen, Bosnia, India, Pakistan, and Indonesia, to name a few.

Source: U.S. Census Bureau (2006).

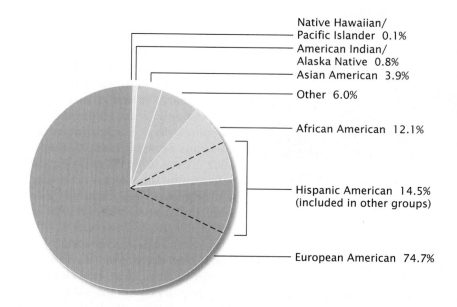

Native Hawaiian/ Pacific Islander 0.1%
American Indian/ Alaska Native 0.8%
Asian American 3.9%
Other 6.0%
African American 12.1%
Hispanic American 14.5% (included in other groups)
European American 74.7%

The Impact of Culture   Culture helps shape almost every aspect of our behavior and mental processes, from how we dress to how we think to what we believe is important. Because we grow up immersed in our culture, we may be unaware of its influence on our own thoughts and actions until—like these young women who immigrated from Africa to Denmark—they encounter people whose culture has shaped them in different ways (Nisbett & Masuda, 2003).

In the United States, for example, women's efforts to connect with others by talking are perceived by some men as "pointless" unless the discussion is aimed at solving a specific problem. As a result, women may feel frustrated and misunderstood by men who offer well-intentioned but unwanted advice instead of conversation.

For decades, the impact of culture on behavior and mental processes was of concern mainly to a relatively small group of researchers working in *cross-cultural psychology*. In the chapters to come, however, you will see that psychologists in almost every subfield are now looking at how ethnicity, gender, age, and many other sociocultural variables can influence behavior and mental processes. In short, psychology is striving to be the science of *all* behavior and mental processes, not just of those in the cultures where it began.

SUMMARY

Psychology is the science that seeks to understand behavior and mental processes and to apply that understanding in the service of human welfare.

The World of Psychology: An Overview

The concept of "behavior and mental processes" is a broad one, encompassing virtually all aspects of what it means to be a human being. Some psychologists study and seek to alleviate the problems that can plague human life, while those working in *positive psychology* focus their attention on understanding happiness, optimism, human strengths, and the like.

Subfields of Psychology   Because the subject matter of psychology is so diverse, most psychologists work in particular subfields within the discipline. For example, *biological psychologists*, also called physiological psychologists, study topics such as

the role played by the brain in regulating normal and disordered behavior. *Developmental psychologists* specialize in trying to understand the development of behavior and mental processes over a lifetime. *Cognitive psychologists*, some of whom prefer to be called *experimental psychologists*, focus on basic psychological processes such as learning, memory, and perception; they also study judgment, decision making, and problem solving. *Engineering psychology*, the study of human factors in the use of equipment, helps designers create better versions of that equipment. *Personality psychologists* focus on characteristics that set people apart from one another. *Clinical psychologists* and *counseling psychologists* provide direct service to troubled people and conduct research on abnormal behavior. *Community psychologists* work to prevent mental disorders and to extend mental health services to those who need them. *Health psychologists* study the relationship between behavior and health and help promote healthy lifestyles. *Educational psychologists* conduct and apply research on teaching and learning, whereas *school psychologists* specialize in assessing and alleviating children's academic problems. *Social psychologists* examine questions regarding how people influence one another. *Industrial/organizational psychologists* study ways to increase efficiency and productivity in the workplace. *Quantitative psychologists* develop ways to analyze research data from all subfields. *Sport psychologists*, *forensic psychologists*, and *environmental psychologists* exemplify some of psychology's many other subfields.

Linkages Within Psychology and Beyond Psychologists often work in more than one subfield and usually share knowledge with colleagues in many subfields. Psychologists also draw on, and contribute to, knowledge in other disciplines, such as computer science, economics, and law.

Research: The Foundation of Psychology Psychologists use the methods of science to conduct research. This means that they perform experiments and use other scientific procedures to systematically gather and analyze information about psychological phenomena.

A Brief History of Psychology The founding of modern psychology is usually marked as 1879, when Wilhelm Wundt established the first psychology research laboratory. Wundt studied consciousness in a manner that was expanded by Edward Titchener into an approach he called structuralism. It was in the late 1800s, too, that Freud, in Vienna, began his study of the unconscious, while in the United States, William James took the functionalist approach, suggesting that psychologists should study how consciousness helps us adapt to our environments. In 1913, John B. Watson founded behaviorism, arguing that to be scientific, psychologists should study only the behavior they can see, not private mental events. Behaviorism dominated psychology for decades, but psychologists are once again studying consciousness in the form of cognitive processes.

Approaches to the Science of Psychology

Psychologists differ in their approaches to psychology—that is, in their assumptions, questions, and research methods. Some adopt just one approach; many others combine features of two or more approaches. Those adopting a *biological approach* focus on how physiological processes shape behavior and mental processes. Psychologists who prefer the *evolutionary approach* emphasize the inherited, adaptive aspects of behavior and mental processes. In the *psychodynamic approach*, behavior and mental processes are seen as reflecting struggles to resolve conflicts between raw impulses and the rules of society that limit the expression of those impulses. Psychologists who take the *behavioral approach* view behavior as determined primarily by learning based on experiences with rewards and punishments. The *cognitive approach* assumes that behavior can be understood through analysis of the basic mental processes that underlie it. To those adopting the *humanistic approach*, behavior is controlled by the decisions that people make about their lives based on their perceptions of the world.

Human Diversity and Psychology

Psychologists are diverse in their backgrounds, and in their activities. Most of the prominent figures in psychology's early history were white males, but women and members of minority groups made important contributions from the start and continue to do so.

Psychologists are increasingly taking into account the influence of culture and other sociocultural variables such as gender and ethnicity in shaping human behavior and mental processes.

Answer key for Table 1.5: U.S. ads are numbers 1, 2, 6, 8, and 9.

Research in Psychology

Our goal in this chapter is to describe the research methods psychologists use to help answer their questions about behavior and mental processes. We will also describe the critical thinking processes that help psychologists to form those questions and to make sense of research results. We have organized our presentation as follows:

Francine Shapiro, a clinical psychologist in northern California, had an odd experience one day in 1987. She was taking a walk and thinking about some distressing events when she noticed that her emotional reaction to them was fading away (Shapiro, 1989a).

In trying to figure out why this should be, she realized that she had been moving her eyes from side to side. Could these eye movements have caused the change in her emotions? To test this possibility, she made more deliberate eye movements and found that the emotion-reducing effect was even stronger. Would the same thing happen to others? Curious, she first tested the effects of side-to-side eye movements with friends and colleagues, and then with clients who had suffered traumatic experiences such as sexual abuse, military combat, or rape. She asked these people to think about unpleasant experiences in their lives while keeping their eyes on her finger as she moved it rapidly back and forth in front of them. Like her, they found that during and after these eye movement sessions, their reactions to unpleasant thoughts faded away. Most notably, her clients reported that their emotional flashbacks, nightmares, fears, and other trauma-related problems had decreased dramatically (Shapiro, 1989a).

Based on the success of these cases, Shapiro developed a treatment method she calls *eye movement desensitization and reprocessing*, or EMDR (Shapiro, 1991, 2001; Shapiro & Forrest, 2004). She and her associates at EMDR Institute, Inc., have now trained more than 30,000 therapists in fifty-two countries to use EMDR in the treatment of an ever-widening range of anxiety-related problems in adults and children, from phobias and posttraumatic stress disorder to marital conflicts and skin rashes (Edmond & Rubin, 2004; Konuk et al., 2006; Madrid, Skolek, & Shapiro, 2006; Russell, 2006; Shapiro, 2005; Silver et al., 2005).

Suppose you had an anxiety-related problem. Would the growth of EMDR be enough to convince you to spend your own money on it? If not, what would you want to know about EMDR before deciding? As a cautious person, you would probably ask some of the same questions that have occurred to many scientists in psychology: Are the effects of EMDR caused by the treatment itself, or by the faith that clients might have in any new and impressive treatment? And are EMDR's effects faster, stronger, and longer lasting than those of other treatments?

Raising tough questions about cause and effect, quality, and value is part of the process of *critical thinking*. Whether you are choosing a therapy method or an Internet service, a college or a computer, a political candidate or a mobile phone plan, critical thinking can guide you to ask the kinds of questions that lead to informed decisions. But asking good questions is not enough; you also have to try answering them. Critical thinking helps here, too, by prompting you to do some research on each of your options. For most people, this means asking the advice of friends or relatives, reading *Consumer Reports*, surfing the Internet, studying a candidate's background, or the like. For psychologists, research means using scientific methods to gather information about behavior and mental processes.

In this chapter, we summarize five questions that emerge when thinking critically about behavior and mental processes. Then we describe the scientific methods psychologists use in their research and show how some of those methods have been applied in evaluating EMDR.

Thinking Critically About Psychology (or Anything Else)

TRY
THIS
⚙

Ask several friends and relatives if mental patients become more agitated when the moon is full, if psychics help the police solve crimes, and if people have suddenly burst into flames for no reason. They will probably agree with at least one of these statements, even though not one of them is true (see Table 2.1).

TABLE 2.1   Some Popular Myths

Many people believe in the statements listed here, but critical thinkers who take the time to investigate them will discover that they are not true.

Myth	Fact
Many children are injured each year in the United States when razor blades, needles, or poison is put in Halloween candy.	Reported cases are rare, most turn out to be hoaxes, and in the only documented case of a child dying from poisoned candy, the culprit was the child's own parent (Brunvald, 1989).
If your roommate commits suicide during the school term, you automatically get A's in all your classes for that term.	No college or university anywhere has ever had such a rule.
People have been known to burst into flames and die from fire erupting within their own bodies.	In rare cases, humans have been consumed by fires that caused little or no damage to the surrounding area. However, this phenomenon has been duplicated in a laboratory, and each alleged case of "spontaneous human combustion" has been traced to an external source of ignition (Benecke, 1999; Nienhuys, 2001).
Most big-city police departments rely on the advice of psychics to help them solve murders, kidnappings, and missing persons cases.	Only about 35% of urban police departments ever seek psychics' advice, and that advice is virtually never more helpful than other means of investigation (Nickell, 1997; Wiseman, West, & Stemman, 1996).
Murders, suicides, animal bites, and episodes of mental disorder are more likely to occur when the moon is full.	Records of crimes, dog bites, and mental hospital admissions do not support this common belief (Bickis, Kelly, & Byrnes, 1995; Chapman & Morrell, 2000; Rotton & Kelly, 1985).
You can't fool a lie detector.	Lie detectors can be helpful in solving crimes, but they are not perfect; their results can free a guilty person or send an innocent person to jail (see the chapter on motivation and emotion).
Viewers never see David Letterman walking to his desk after the opening monologue because his contract prohibits him from showing his backside on TV.	When questioned about this story on the air, Letterman denied it and, to prove his point, lifted his jacket and turned a full circle in front of the cameras and studio audience (Brunvald, 1989).
Psychics have special abilities to see into the future.	Even the most famous psychics are almost always wrong, as in these predictions for the years 2004 and 2005: "Colin Powell will be elected president," "Osama Bin Laden will be crushed by a comet," and "A tidal wave will wipe out Tokyo." No psychic's 2001 predictions included the September 11 terrorist attacks on New York and Washington. When psychics do appear to be correct, it is usually because their forecasts are either vague ("The Hollywood area is due for a colossal earthquake") or easy to predict without special powers ("Pope John Paul will pass away") (Emery, 2005; Farha, 2005).
If you are stopped for drunken driving, sucking on a penny will cause a police Breathalyzer test to show you are sober.	This is not true, nor can Breathalyzers be fooled by sucking on a nickel or a mint, or by eating garlic, peanuts, curry powder, or vitamin C tablets (Emery, 2004).

Uncritically accepting claims for the value of astrologers' predictions, "get-rich-quick" investment schemes, new therapies, or proposed government policies can be embarrassing, expensive, and dangerous. Critical thinkers carefully evaluate evidence for *and* against such claims before drawing a final conclusion.

DOONESBURY

Perhaps you already knew that, but don't feel too smug. At one time or another, we all accept things we are told simply because the information seems to come from a reliable source or because "everyone knows" it is true (Losh et al., 2003). If this were not the case, advertisers, politicians, salespeople, social activists, and others who seek our money, our votes, or our loyalty would not be as successful as they are. These people want you to believe their promises or claims without careful thought. In other words, they don't want you to think critically.

Often, they get their wish. Millions of people waste billions of dollars every year on worthless predictions by on-line and telephone "psychics"; on bogus cures for cancer, heart disease, and arthritis; on phony degrees offered by nonexistent Internet "universities"; and on "miracle" defrosting trays, eat-all-you-want weight-loss pills, "effortless" exercise gadgets, and other consumer products that simply don't work. Millions more are lost in investment scams and fraudulent charity appeals (Cassel & Bernstein, 2007).

Critical thinking is the process of assessing claims and making judgments on the basis of well-supported evidence (Wade, 1988). One way to apply critical thinking to EMDR—or to any other topic—is by asking the following five questions:

1. *What am I being asked to believe or accept?* In this case, the assertion to be examined is that EMDR reduces or eliminates anxiety-related problems.

2. *What evidence is available to support the assertion?* Shapiro experienced a reduction in her own emotional distress following certain kinds of eye movements. Later, she found the same effect in others.

3. *Are there alternative ways of interpreting the evidence?* The dramatic effects reported by Shapiro might not have been due to EMDR but to people's desire to overcome their problems or perhaps their desire to prove her right. And who knows? They might have eventually improved on their own, without any treatment. Even the most remarkable evidence can't automatically be accepted as proof of an assertion until other plausible alternatives such as these have been ruled out. The ruling-out process leads to the next step in critical thinking: conducting scientific research.

4. *What additional evidence would help to evaluate the alternatives?* The ideal method for collecting further evidence about the value of EMDR would be to identify three groups of people with anxiety-related problems who were alike in every way except for the anxiety treatment they received. One group would receive EMDR. A second group would get an equally motivating but useless treatment, and a third group would get no treatment at all. Now suppose the people in the EMDR group improved much more than those who got no treatment or the motivating, but useless, treatment. Results such as these would make it harder to explain away the improvements following EMDR as due to client motivation or the mere passage of time.

● **critical thinking** The process of assessing claims and making judgments on the basis of well-supported evidence.

Taking Your Life in Your Hands?
Does exposure to microwave radiation from mobile phone antennas cause brain tumors? Do the dangers of hormone replacement therapy (HRT) for postmenopausal women outweigh its benefits? And what about the value of herbal remedies, dietary supplements, and other controversial treatments for cancer, AIDS, and depression? These questions generate intense speculation, strong opinions, and a lot of wishful thinking, but the answers ultimately depend on scientific research based on critical thinking. So, even though there is no conclusive evidence that mobile phones cause tumors (Christensen et al., 2005; Hepworth et al., 2006; Schoemaker et al., 2005), some scientists suggest that there may be danger in long-term exposure (Lonn et al., 2004), and research continues. Evidence that HRT may be related to breast cancer and heart disease led to the cancellation of a large clinical trial in the United States (Kolata, 2003), and scientists have called for new research on the safety of the testosterone replacement therapy that about 250,000 U.S. men receive each year (Groopman, 2002; Kolata, 2002).

5. *What conclusions are most reasonable?* The research evidence collected so far has not yet ruled out alternative explanations for the effects of EMDR (e.g., Goldstein et al., 2000; Hertlein & Ricci, 2004; Hughes, 2006; Lohr et al., 2003). And although those effects are often greater than the effects of no treatment at all, they appear to be no stronger than those of several other kinds of treatment (Beriault & Larivee, 2005; Bradley et al., 2005; Ironson et al., 2002; Taylor et al., 2003). So the only reasonable conclusions to be drawn at this point are that (1) EMDR remains a controversial treatment, (2) it seems to have an impact on some clients, and (3) further research is needed in order to understand it.

Do these conclusions sound inconclusive? Critical thinking sometimes does seem to be indecisive thinking. Like the rest of us, scientists in psychology would love to find quick, clear, and final answers to their questions, but the conclusions they reach have to be supported by evidence. So if the evidence about EMDR is limited in some way, conclusions about whether and why the treatment works have to be limited, too. In the long run, though, critical thinking opens the way to understanding. To help you sharpen your own critical thinking skills, we include in each chapter to come a section called "Thinking Critically," in which we examine a particularly interesting issue in psychology by asking the same five questions we raised here about EMDR.

● Critical Thinking and Scientific Research

Scientific research often begins with questions born of curiosity, such as "Can eye movements reduce anxiety?" Like many seemingly simple questions, this one is more complex than it first appears. Are we talking about horizontal, vertical, or diagonal eye movements? How long do they continue in each session, and how many sessions should there be? What kind of anxiety is to be treated, and how will we measure improvement? In other words, scientists have to ask *specific* questions in order to get meaningful answers.

I Love It! When we want something—or someone—to be perfect, we may ignore all evidence to the contrary. This is one reason people end up in faulty used cars—or in bad relationships. Psychologists and other scientists use special procedures, such as the "double-blind" methods described in this chapter, to help keep confirmation bias from distorting the conclusions they draw from research evidence.

Psychologists and other scientists clarify their questions about behavior and mental processes by phrasing them in terms of a **hypothesis**—a specific, testable proposition about something they want to study. Hypotheses state in clear, precise words what researchers think may be true and how they will know if it is not. A hypothesis about EMDR might be: *EMDR treatment causes significant reduction in anxiety*. To make it easier to understand and evaluate their hypotheses, scientists employ **operational definitions**, which are descriptions of the exact operations or methods they will use in their research. In relation to our EMDR hypothesis, for example, "EMDR treatment" might be operationally defined as creating a certain number of side-to-side eye movements per second for a particular period of time. And "significant reduction in anxiety" might be operationally defined as a decline of 10 points or more on a test that measures clients' anxiety. The kind of treatment a client is given (say, EMDR versus no treatment) and the results of that treatment (the amount of anxiety reduction observed) are examples of research **variables**, the specific factors or characteristics that are manipulated and measured in research.

To determine whether a study's results provide support for a hypothesis, researchers look at the numbers or scores that represent client improvement or whatever other variables are of interest. This kind of evidence is called **data** (the plural of *datum*), or a *data set*. The data themselves are objective, and scientists try to be objective when interpreting them. But like all human beings, scientists may sometimes pay a little more attention to numbers or scores that confirm their hypotheses, especially if they expect or hope that those hypotheses are true. This *confirmation bias* is described in the chapter on cognition and language. Scientists have a special responsibility to combat confirmation bias by looking for evidence that contradicts their hypotheses, not just for evidence that supports them.

Scientists must also consider the value of the evidence they collect. They usually do this by evaluating its reliability and validity. *Reliability* is the degree to which the data are stable and consistent. The *validity* of data is the degree to which they accurately represent the topic being studied. For example, the first evidence for EMDR

hypothesis In scientific research, a prediction stated as a specific, testable proposition about a phenomenon.

operational definition A statement that defines the exact operations or methods used in research.

variable A factor or characteristic that is manipulated or measured in research.

data Numbers that represent research findings and provide the basis for research conclusions.

Theories of Prejudice It is all too easy these days to spot evidence of prejudice against almost any identifiable group, including Muslims, Jews, Protestants, Catholics, Blacks, Hispanics, Asians, gays and lesbians, and even teenagers and the elderly. But why does it occur? The chapter on social cognition describes several theories that researchers have proposed about the causes of prejudice—and how to prevent it. The testing of these theories is an example of how theory and research go hand in hand. Without research results, there would be nothing to explain; without explanatory theories, the results might never be organized in a useful way. The knowledge generated by psychologists over the past 130 years has been based on this constant interaction of theory and research.

was based on Shapiro's own experience with eye movements. If she had not been able to consistently repeat, or *replicate*, those initial effects in other people, she would have had to question the reliability of her data. And if her clients' reports of reduced anxiety were not supported by, say, their overt behavior or the reports of their close relatives, she would have had to doubt the validity of her data.

● The Role of Theories

After examining research evidence, scientists may begin to favor certain explanations as to why these results occurred. Sometimes they organize their explanations into a **theory**, which is a set of statements designed to account for, predict, and even suggest ways of controlling certain phenomena. Shapiro's theory about the effects of EMDR suggests that eye movements activate parts of the brain in which information about trauma or other unpleasant experiences has been stored but never fully processed. EMDR, she says, promotes the "adaptive information processing" required for the elimination of certain anxiety-related emotional and behavioral problems (Shapiro & Forrest, 2004). In the chapter on introducing psychology, we review broader and more famous examples of explanatory theories, including Charles Darwin's theory of evolution and Sigmund Freud's theory of psychoanalysis.

Theories are tentative explanations that must be subjected to scientific examination based on critical thinking. For example, Shapiro's theory about EMDR has been criticized as being vague, as lacking empirical support, and as being less plausible than other, simpler explanations (e.g., Carpenter, 2004; Gaudiano & Dalrymple, 2005; Herbert et al., 2000; Lohr et al., 2003). In other words, theories are based on research results, but they also generate hypotheses to be tested in further research. The predictions of one psychologist's theory will be evaluated by many other psychologists. If research does not support a theory, the theory will be revised or abandoned.

The process of creating, evaluating, and revising psychological theories does not always lead to a single "winner." You will discover in later chapters that there are several competing explanations for color vision, memory, sleep, aggression, prejudice, and many other behaviors and mental processes. As research on these topics continues, explanations become more complete, and, sometimes, they change. So the conclusions we offer are always based on what is known so far, and we always cite the need for additional research. We do this because research often raises at least as many questions as it answers. The results of one study might not apply to every situation or to all people. A treatment might be effective for mild depression in women, but it would have to be tested in more severe cases, and with both sexes,

theory An integrated set of propositions that can be used to account for, predict, and even suggest ways of controlling certain phenomena.

before drawing final conclusions about its value. Keep this point in mind the next time you hear a talk-show guest confidently offering simple solutions to complex problems such as obesity or anxiety, or presenting easy formulas for a happy marriage and perfect children. These self-proclaimed experts—called "pop" (for *popular*) psychologists by the scientific community—tend to oversimplify issues, to cite evidence for their views without concern for its reliability or validity, and to ignore good evidence that contradicts the pet theories that they promote for profit.

Psychological scientists are much more cautious. They don't offer conclusions and recommendations, especially about complex behaviors and mental processes, until they have enough high-quality data to support what they say. And their data have allowed them to say a lot. Research in psychology has created an enormous body of knowledge that is being put to good use in many ways. Psychologists in all subfields are using today's knowledge as the foundation for the research that will increase tomorrow's understanding of behavior and mental processes. Let's now look at the research methods they use and some of the pitfalls that lie in the path of progress toward their goals.

Research Methods in Psychology

Like other scientists, psychologists strive to achieve four main goals in their research: to *describe* behavior and mental processes, to make accurate *predictions* about them, to demonstrate some *control* over them, and ultimately to *explain* how and why behavior and mental processes occur. Consider depression, for example. Researchers in clinical psychology and other subfields have been involved in *describing* the nature, intensity, and duration of depressive symptoms, as well as the various kinds of depressive disorders that commonly appear in various cultures around the world. They are also studying the genetic characteristics, personality traits, life situations, and other factors that allow better *predictions* about those who are at the greatest risk for developing depressive disorders. In addition, clinical researchers have developed and tested a whole range of treatments designed to *control* depressive symptoms and even to prevent them. Finally, they have proposed a number of theories to *explain* depression, including why and how it occurs, why it is more common in women than in men, and why particular treatment methods are (or are not) likely to be effective.

Certain research methods are especially useful for reaching certain of these goals. For example, psychologists tend to use *naturalistic observation, case studies, surveys,* and *correlational studies* to describe and predict behavior and mental processes. They use *experiments* to control and explain behavior and mental processes. For example, Francine Shapiro initially used naturalistic observation to describe the effects of eye movements on her emotional state. She then conducted case studies to test her prediction that if the change in her emotions had something to do with eye movements, the same effects should occur in other people. Later we discuss an experiment in which she tried to more systematically control people's emotional reactions and to evaluate various explanations for EMDR's apparent effects. Let's take a closer look at how psychologists use these and other scientific research methods as they seek to describe, predict, control, and explain many kinds of behavior and mental processes.

● Naturalistic Observation: Watching Behavior

Sometimes, the best way to describe behavior is through **naturalistic observation**, which is the process of watching without interfering as behavior occurs in the natural environment (Hoyle, Harris, & Judd, 2002). This method is especially valuable when more intrusive methods might alter the behavior you want to study or create

naturalistic observation The process of watching without interfering as a phenomenon occurs in the natural environment.

Little Reminders If you asked this person what he needs to use various computer programs efficiently, he might not think to mention the notes on his monitor that list all his log-in names and passwords. Accordingly, researchers in human factors and industrial/organizational psychology usually arrange to watch employees at work rather than just ask them what they do, how they do it, and how they interact with machines and fellow employees.

false impressions about it. Suppose you wanted to know about people's fitness efforts. You could ask people to keep track of how often they exercise, but your request might prompt them to suddenly begin working out more than usual, thus providing an inaccurate picture of their typical behavior.

With proper permission, psychologists can observe people in many kinds of situations. For example, much of what we know about gender differences in how children play and communicate with each other has come from observations in classrooms and playgrounds. Live or video-taped observations of adults as they work on group problem-solving tasks, talk about current events, or discuss problems in their relationships have provided valuable insights into friendships, couple communication patterns, and even responses to terrorism (e.g., Mehl & Pennebaker, 2003). And to understand the problems people encounter in doing their jobs, human factors psychologists often find it helpful to observe employees as they work.

Although naturalistic observation can provide large amounts of useful research evidence, it is not problem free. For one thing, if people know they are being observed (and ethics usually requires that they do know), they tend to act differently than they otherwise would. Researchers usually combat this problem by observing long enough for participants to get used to the situation and begin behaving more naturally. Observational data can also be distorted if the observers expect to see certain behaviors. Suppose you were hired to watch videotapes of people who had just participated in a study of EMDR. Your job is to rate how anxious they appear to be, but if you knew which participants had received EMDR and which had not, you might tend to see the treated participants as less anxious, no matter how they actually behave. To get the most out of naturalistic observation, psychologists have to counteract problems such as these. So when conducting observational evaluations of treatment, for example, they don't tell the observers which participants have received treatment.

● Case Studies: Taking a Closer Look

Observations are often an important part of **case studies,** which are intensive examinations of behavior or mental processes in a particular individual, group, or situation. Case studies can also include tests; interviews; and the analysis of letters,

TRY
THIS **Translating Naturalistic Observation into Data**
It is easy to observe people in natural situations, but it is not so easy to translate the observations into meaningful data. To make this translation process easier and more consistent, psychologists create coding systems that tell observers how to categorize the various kinds of behavior that might occur during a live or videotaped observation session. Imagine that you are studying these children at play. Try creating your own coding system by making a list of the exact behaviors that you would count as "aggressive," "shy," "fearful," "cooperative," and "competitive."

● **case study** A research method involving the intensive examination of some phenomenon in a particular individual, group, or situation.

Learning from Rare Cases Dustin Hoffman's character in *Rain Man* was based on the case of "Joseph," an autistic man who can, for example, mentally multiply or divide six-digit numbers. Other case studies have described autistic *savants* who can correctly identify the day of the week for any date in the past or the future, or tell at a glance that, say, exactly 125 paper clips are scattered on the floor. By carefully studying such rare cases, cognitive psychologists are learning more about human mental capacities and how they might be maximized in everyone.

school transcripts, or other written records. Case studies are especially useful when studying something that is new, complex, or relatively rare. Shapiro's EMDR treatment, for example, first attracted psychologists' attention through case studies of its apparently remarkable effects on her clients.

In fact, case studies have a long tradition in clinical work. Freud's theory of psychoanalysis was largely developed from case studies of people whose paralysis or other physical symptoms disappeared when they were hypnotized or asleep. Case studies have also played a special role in *neuropsychology*, the study of the relationships among brain activity, thinking, and behavior. Consider the case of Dr. P., a patient described by neurologist Oliver Sacks (1985). A distinguished musician with superior intelligence, Dr. P. began to display odd symptoms, such as the inability to recognize familiar people or to distinguish between people and objects. During a visit to Sacks's office, Dr. P. mistook his foot for his shoe. When he rose to leave, he tried to lift off his wife's head—like a hat—and put it on his own. He could not name common objects when he looked at them, although he could describe them. When handed a glove, for example, he said, "A continuous surface, infolded on itself. It appears to have . . . five outpouchings, if this is the word. . . . A container of some sort." Only later, when he put it on his hand, did he exclaim, "My God, it's a glove!" (Sacks, 1985, p. 13). Case studies such as this one have helped pioneers in neuropsychology to describe the difficulties suffered by people with particular kinds of brain damage or disease. Eventually, neuropsychologists were able to tie specific disorders to certain types of injuries, tumors, poisons, and other causes (Banich, 2004). (Dr. P.'s symptoms may have been caused by a large brain tumor.)

Case studies are even used by industrial/organizational psychologists. For example, an I/O psychologist might review documents, make observations, and conduct interviews with an employee team in order to understand how its members handled a production problem, an interpersonal conflict, or a change in company policy. Such case studies would then help guide the psychologist's recommendations for how company executives might increase productivity, reduce stress, or improve communication with employees.

Case studies do have their limitations, however. They may contain only the evidence that a particular researcher considered important, and, of course, they are unlikely to be representative of people in general. Nonetheless, case studies can provide valuable raw material for further research. They can also be vital sources of information about particular people, and they serve as the testing ground for new treatments, training programs, and other applications of research (Tavris, 2004).

● Surveys: Looking at the Big Picture

In contrast to the individual close-ups provided by case studies, surveys provide wide-angle views of large groups. In **surveys,** researchers use interviews or questionnaires to ask people about their behavior, attitudes, beliefs, opinions, or intentions. Just as politicians and advertisers rely on opinion polls to test the popularity of policies or products, psychologists use surveys—conducted in person, through the mail, or on line—to gather descriptive data on just about anything related to behavior and mental processes, from parenting practices to sexual behavior.

However, the validity of survey data depends partly on whether the wording is clear and how questions are phrased (Bhopal et al., 2004). In one survey at a health clinic, patients were asked how often they experienced headaches, stomach pain, and other symptoms of illness (Schwarz & Scheuring, 1992). About 75 percent of the patients said that the weather affected their health when the wording suggested that this was a common phenomenon, but only 21 percent said so if the wording suggested that this was an uncommon phenomenon. Were the people in the first group actually sicker than the people in the second? Probably not. It is more likely that they reported more symptoms because of the way the question was worded.

A survey's validity also depends on who is included in it. If the particular people surveyed do not represent the views of the population you are interested in, it is easy to be misled by survey results (Gosling et al., 2004). If you were interested in Americans' views on the prevalence of religious prejudice, you would come to the wrong conclusion if you surveyed only Christians or only Muslims. To get a complete picture, you would have to survey people from all religious groups so that each group's opinions could be fairly represented.

TRY THIS ⚙ **Designing Survey Research** How do people feel about whether gay men and lesbians should have the right to legally marry? To appreciate the difficulties of survey research, try writing a question about this issue that you think is clear enough and neutral enough to generate valid data. Then ask some friends whether or not they agree it would be a good survey question and why.

● **survey** A research method that involves giving people questionnaires or special interviews designed to obtain descriptions of their attitudes, beliefs, opinions, and intentions.

Other limitations of the survey method are more difficult to avoid. For one thing, even if they can't be personally identified, people may be reluctant to admit undesirable or embarrassing things about themselves. Or they might say what they think they *should* say about an issue. The American Society for Microbiology (ASM) found that 95 percent of the U.S. adults it surveyed said that they wash their hands after using toilet facilities. However, naturalistic observations of thousands of people in public restrooms across the United States revealed that the figure is closer to 67 percent (ASM, 2000). So surveys that ask people to say whether they cheat on exams, use illegal drugs, drive while drunk, or engage in other forms of socially disapproved or dangerous behaviors will probably underestimate the frequency of these behaviors. Further, suppose you send out a questionnaire about raising local taxes. If those who are opposed to the tax increase are more likely to return their questionnaire, you will probably get an inaccurate view of public opinion. In other words, to the extent that there are response biases or data collection problems, survey results—and the conclusions drawn from them—can be distorted (Hoyle et al., 2002). Still, surveys provide an efficient way to gather large amounts of data about people's attitudes, beliefs, or other characteristics.

● Correlational Studies: Looking for Relationships

The data collected from naturalistic observations, case studies, and surveys provide valuable descriptions of behavior and mental processes, but they can do more than that. These data can also be examined to see what they reveal about the relationships, or correlations, between one research variable and another. For example, fear surveys show that most people have fears, but correlational analysis of those surveys also shows that the number of fears is related to age. Specifically, adults have fewer fears than children (e.g., Kleinknecht, 1991). **Correlational studies** examine relationships between variables in order to describe research data more fully, to test predictions, to evaluate theories, and to suggest new hypotheses about why people think and act as they do.

Consider the question of how aggression develops. One theory suggests that people learn to be aggressive by seeing aggressiveness in others. Psychologists have tested this theory through correlational studies that focus on the relationship between children's aggressiveness and the amount of aggression they see on television. Just as the theory predicts, those who watch a lot of televised violence do tend to be more aggressive than other children. Another theory asserts that sexual aggressiveness in adults can be triggered by viewing pornography. And in fact, correlational analyses of case studies and surveys show that sex criminals often view pornographic material just prior to committing their offenses. And correlational studies of observational data indicate that children in day care for more than thirty hours a week are more aggressive than those who stay at home with their mothers.

Do violent television, pornography, and separation from parents actually *cause* the various forms of aggressiveness with which they have been associated? They might, but psychologists must be careful about jumping to such conclusions. The most obvious explanation for the relationship found in a correlational study may not always be the correct one (see Table 2.2). Perhaps the correlation between aggression and violent television appears because children who were the most aggressive in the first place are also the ones who choose to watch the most violent television. Perhaps sex offenders exaggerate the role of pornography in their crimes because they hope to avoid taking responsibility for those crimes. And perhaps the aggressiveness seen among some children in day care might have something to do with the children themselves or with what happens to them in day care, not just with separation from their parents.

● **correlational study** A research method that examines relationships between variables in order to analyze trends in data, to test predictions, to evaluate theories, and to suggest new hypotheses.

TABLE 2.2   Correlation and Causation

TRY THIS   Look at the relationships described in the left-hand column, then ask yourself why the two variables in each case are correlated. Could one variable be causing an effect on the other? If so, which variable is the cause, and how might it exert its effect? Could the relationship between the two variables be caused by a third one? If so, what might that third variable be? We suggest some possible explanations in the right-hand column. Can you think of others?

Correlation	Possible Explanation
A survey found that the more sexual content that U.S. teenagers reported watching on television, the more likely they were to begin having sex themselves during the following year (Collins et al., 2004).	It might have been some teens' greater interest in sex that led them to watch more sexually oriented shows and also to become sexually active.
The number of drownings in the United States rises and falls during the year, along with the amount of ice cream sold each month.	This relationship probably reflects a third variable—time of year—that affects both ice cream consumption and the likelihood of swimming and boating.
In places where beer prices are raised, the number of new cases of sexually transmitted disease falls among young people living in those places.	If price increases cause less beer consumption, people might stay sober enough to remember to use condoms during sexual encounters. The relationship could also reflect coincidence, because prices do not always affect alcohol use. More research is required to understand this correlation.
A study found that the more antibiotics a woman has taken, and the longer she has taken them, the greater is her risk of breast cancer (Velicer et al., 2004).	Long-term antibiotic use might have impaired the women's immune systems, but the cancer risk might also have been increased by the diseases that were being treated with antibiotic drugs, not the drugs themselves. Obviously, much more research would be required before condemning the use of antibiotics.
Individuals and teams wearing red are more likely to win fights and other athletic contests than those wearing other colors (Hill & Barton, 2005).	Does red convey a signal of dominance that intimidates opponents? Possibly, but other research has found color-related outcome patterns when *neither* contestant wears red (Rowe, Harris, & Roberts, 2005), so other factors, including coincidence, might be at work.
The U.S. stock market rises during years in which a team from the National Football Conference wins the Super Bowl and falls during years in which an American Conference team wins.	The so-called Super Bowl Effect has occurred 30 times in 37 years; striking as this might seem, coincidence seems to be the most likely explanation.

One way psychologists evaluate hypotheses such as these is to conduct further correlational studies in which they look for trends in observational, case study, and survey data that support or conflict with those hypotheses. Further analysis of day-care research, for example, shows that the aggressiveness seen in preschoolers who spend a lot of time in day care is the exception, not the rule. Most children don't show any behavior problems, no matter how much time they have spent in day care. This more general trend suggests that whatever effects separation has, it may be different for different children in different settings, causing some to express aggressiveness, others to display fear, and still others to find enjoyment (see the chapter on human development). To explore this possibility, psychologists will have to conduct further studies to examine correlations between children's personality traits, qualities of different day-care programs, and reactions to day care (NICHD Early Child Care Research Network, 2007). Throughout this book you will see many more examples of how correlational studies help to shed light on a wide range of topics in psychology.

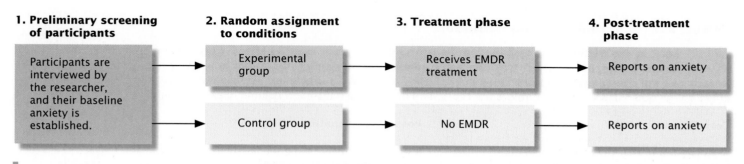

1. Preliminary screening of participants

Participants are interviewed by the researcher, and their baseline anxiety is established.

2. Random assignment to conditions

Experimental group

Control group

3. Treatment phase

Receives EMDR treatment

No EMDR

4. Post-treatment phase

Reports on anxiety

Reports on anxiety

FIGURE 2.1

A Simple Two-Group Experiment

Ideally, the only difference between the experimental and control groups in experiments such as this one is whether the participants receive the treatment the experimenter wishes to evaluate. Under such ideal circumstances, any difference in the two groups' reported levels of anxiety at the end of the experiment would be due only to whether or not they received treatment.

■ ● Experiments: Exploring Cause and Effect

Still, the surest way to test hypotheses and confirm cause-effect relationships between variables is to exert some control over those variables. This kind of research usually takes the form of an experiment. **Experiments** are situations in which the researcher manipulates one variable and then observes the effect of that manipulation on another variable, while holding all other variables constant.

Consider the experiment Francine Shapiro conducted in an attempt to better understand the effects of EMDR. As illustrated in Figure 2.1, she first identified twenty-two people who were suffering the ill effects of traumas such as rape or military combat. These were her research participants. She then assigned each of the participants to one of two groups. The first group received a single fifty-minute session of EMDR treatment; the second group focused on their unpleasant memories for eight minutes, but without moving their eyes back and forth (Shapiro, 1989b).

The group that receives an experimental treatment such as EMDR is called, naturally enough, the **experimental group**. The group that receives no treatment or some other treatment is called the **control group**. Control groups provide baselines against which to compare the performance of other groups. In Shapiro's experiment, having a control group allowed her to measure how much change in anxiety could be expected from exposure to bad memories without EMDR treatment. If everything about the two groups were exactly the same before the experiment, then any difference in anxiety between the groups afterward would have something to do with the EMDR treatment rather than with mere exposure to unpleasant memories.

Notice that Shapiro controlled one variable in her experiment, namely which kind of treatment her participants received. In an experiment, the variable controlled by the experimenter is called the **independent variable**. It is called *independent* because the experimenter is free to adjust it at will, offering one, two, or three kinds of treatment, for example, or perhaps setting the length of treatment at one, five, or ten sessions. Notice, too, that Shapiro looked for the effects of treatment by measuring a different variable, namely her clients' anxiety level. This second variable is called the **dependent variable** because it is affected by, or depends on, the independent variable. So in Shapiro's experiment, the presence or absence of treatment was the independent variable, because she manipulated it. Her participants' anxiety level was the dependent variable, because she measured it to see how it was affected by treatment. (Table 2.3 describes the independent and dependent variables in other experiments.)

The results of Shapiro's (1989b) experiment showed that participants who received EMDR treatment experienced a complete and nearly immediate reduction in anxiety related to their traumatic memories, whereas those in the control group showed no change. This difference suggests that EMDR caused the improvement.

● **experiment** A situation in which the researcher manipulates one variable and then observes the effect of that manipulation on another variable, while holding all other variables constant.

● **experimental group** In an experiment, the group that receives the experimental treatment.

● **control group** In an experiment, the group that receives no treatment or provides some other baseline against which to compare the performance or response of the experimental group.

● **independent variable** The variable manipulated by the researcher in an experiment.

● **dependent variable** In an experiment, the factor affected by the independent variable.

TABLE 2.3   Independent and Dependent Variables

TRY THIS Fill in the names of the independent and dependent variables in each of these experiments (the answers are listed at the bottom of page 42). Remember that the independent variable is manipulated by the experimenter. The dependent variable is measured to determine the effect of the independent variable. How did you do on this task?

1. Children's reading skill is measured after taking either a special reading class or a standard reading class.	The independent variable is _____. The dependent variable is _____.
2. College students' memory for German vocabulary words is tested after a normal night's sleep or a night of no sleep.	The independent variable is _____. The dependent variable is _____.
3. Experiment title: "The effect of a daily walking program on elderly people's lung capacity."	The independent variable is _____. The dependent variable is _____.
4. People's ability to avoid "accidents" in a driving simulator is tested before, during, and after talking on a cell phone.	The independent variable is _____. The dependent variable is _____.

But look again at the structure, or design, of the experiment. The EMDR group's session lasted about fifty minutes, but the control group focused on their memories for only eight minutes. Would the people in the control group have improved, too, if they had spent fifty minutes focusing on their memories? We don't know, because the experiment did not compare methods of equal duration.

Anyone who conducts or relies on research must be on guard for such flaws in experimental design. So before drawing conclusions from research, experimenters must consider factors that might confound, or confuse, the interpretation of results. Any factor, such as differences in the length of treatment, that might have affected the dependent variable along with or instead of the independent variable can become a **confounding variable**. When confounding variables are present, the experimenter cannot know whether the independent variable or the confounding variable produced the results. Let's examine three sources of confounding: random variables, participants' expectations, and experimenter bias.

●Random Variables

In an ideal research world, everything about the experimental and control groups would be the same except for their exposure to the independent variable (such as whether or not they received treatment). In reality, however, there are always other differences between the groups that reflect random variables. **Random variables** are uncontrolled, sometimes uncontrollable, factors such as the time of year when research takes place and differences in the participants' backgrounds, personalities, life experiences, and vulnerability to stress, for example.

In fact, there are so many ways in which participants might vary from each other that it is usually impossible to form groups that are matched on all of them. Instead, experimenters simply flip a coin or use some other random process to assign each research participant to experimental or control groups. These procedures—called **random assignment**—are presumed to distribute the impact of uncontrolled variables randomly (and probably about equally) across groups, thus minimizing the chance that these variables will distort the results of the experiment (Shadish, Cook, & Campbell, 2002).

●Participants' Expectations

After eight minutes of focusing on unpleasant memories, participants in the control group in Shapiro's (1989b) experiment were instructed to begin moving their eyes. At that point they, too, said they began to experience a reduction in anxiety. Was this improvement caused by the eye movements themselves, or could it be that the instructions made the participants feel

confounding variable In an experiment, any factor that affects the dependent variable, along with or instead of the independent variable.

random variable In an experiment, a confounding variable in which uncontrolled or uncontrollable factors affect the dependent variable, along with or instead of the independent variable.

random assignment The procedure by which random variables are evenly distributed in an experiment by putting participants into various groups through a random process.

They Are All the Same Scientists have succeeded in cloning mice, thus creating a population of genetically identical animals. These animals can be assigned to various experimental and control groups with no worries about the confounding effects that individual differences might have on the dependent variable. Laws and research ethics rule out creating a pool of cloned people, so the process of random assignment will remain a vital component of psychological research with human beings.

Ever Since I Started Wearing These Magnets . . . Placebo-controlled experiments are vital for establishing cause-effect relationships between treatment and outcome with human participants. For example, many people swear that magnets held against their joints relieve the pain of sports injuries and even arthritis. Some research supports this view (Harlow et al., 2004), but most experiments have found magnets to be no more effective than placebo treatment with an identical, but nonmagnetic, metal object (e.g., Collacott et al., 2000; Feingold & Flamm, 2006; Winemiller et al., 2003). Something other than magnets—wishful thinking, perhaps—appears to be causing the reported benefits.

more confident that they were now getting "real" treatment? This question illustrates a second source of confounding: differences in what people *think* about the experimental situation. If participants who receive an impressive treatment expect that it will help them, they may try harder to improve than those in a control group who receive no treatment or a less impressive treatment. When improvement is created by a participant's knowledge and expectations, it is called the *placebo effect*. A **placebo** (pronounced "pla-SEE-boe") is a treatment that contains nothing known to be helpful but that nevertheless produces benefits because a person believes it will be beneficial.

How can researchers measure the extent to which a result is caused by the independent variable or by a placebo effect? Usually, they include a special control group that receives *only* a placebo treatment. Then they compare results for the experimental group, the placebo group, and a no-treatment group. In one quit-smoking study, for example, participants in a placebo group took sugar pills described by the experimenter as "fast-acting tranquilizers" that would help them learn to endure the stress of giving up cigarettes (Bernstein, 1970). These people did far better at quitting than those who got no treatment; in fact, they did as well as participants in the experimental group, who received extensive treatment. These results suggested that the success of the experimental group may have been due largely to the participants' expectations, not to the treatment methods. Placebo effects may not be as strong as experimenters once assumed (Hrobjartsson & Gotzsche, 2001), but some people do improve after receiving medical or psychological treatment, not because of the treatment itself but because they believe that it will help them (e.g., Wager et al., 2004).

Research on EMDR treatment suggests that the eye movements themselves may not be responsible for improvement, inasmuch as staring, finger tapping, feeling vibrations or listening to rapid clicks or tones while focusing on traumatic memories has also produced benefits (e.g., Carrigan & Levis, 1999; Cusack & Spates,

Answer key to Table 2.3: The independent variable (IDV) in experiment 1 is the type of reading class; the dependent variable (DV) is reading skill. In experiment 2, the IDV is the amount of sleep; the DV is the score on a memory test. In experiment 3, the IDV is amount of exercise; the DV is lung capacity. In experiment 4, the IDV is using or not using a cell phone; the DV is performance on a simulated driving task.

placebo A physical or psychological treatment that contains no active ingredient but produces an effect because the person receiving it believes it will.

1999; Rosen, 1999; Seidler & Wagner, 2006; Servan-Schreiber et al., 2006). In fact, although EMDR appears to benefit some clients, it often fails to outperform impressive placebo treatments or other established anxiety treatment methods (e.g., Rothbaum, Astin, & Marsteller, 2005; Seidler & Wagner, 2006; Taylor, 2003). These results have led many researchers to conclude that EMDR should not be a first-choice treatment for anxiety-related disorders (Davison & Parker, 2001; Lohr et al., 2003; Taylor, 2004; Taylor et al., 2003).

●**Experimenter Bias**   Another potential confounding variable comes from **experimenter bias**, the unintentional effect that experimenters may exert on their results. Robert Rosenthal (1966) was one of the first to demonstrate one kind of experimenter bias, called *experimenter expectancies*. His research participants were laboratory assistants whose job was to place rats in a maze. Rosenthal told some of the assistants that their rats were "maze-bright"; he told the others that their rats were "maze-dull." In fact, both groups of rats were randomly drawn from the same population and had about equal maze-learning capabilities. But the "maze-bright" animals learned the maze significantly faster than the "maze-dull" rats. Why? Rosenthal concluded that the result had nothing to do with the rats and everything to do with the experimenters. He suggested that the assistants' expectations about their rats' supposedly superior (or inferior) capabilities caused them to slightly alter their training and handling techniques. These slight differences may have speeded (or slowed) the animals' learning. Similarly, when experimenters give different kinds of anxiety treatments to different groups of people, they might do a slightly better job with the treatment they believe to be the best. This slight, unintentional difference could improve the effects of that treatment compared with the others.

To prevent experimenter bias from confounding results, experimenters often use a **double-blind design**. In this arrangement, both the research participants and those giving the treatments are unaware of, or "blind" to, who is receiving a placebo, and they do not know what results are expected from various treatments. Only researchers who have no direct contact with participants have this information, and they do not reveal it until the experiment is over. The fact that double-blind studies

TRY THIS   **Keeping Experimenters "Blind"**   Suppose you are a sport psychologist conducting an experiment to evaluate two methods for reducing performance anxiety: standard coaching versus a new relaxation-based technique. How could you create a double-blind design in this experiment? If you could not, how would you at least try to keep coaches in the dark about which method is expected to produce the best results?

experimenter bias   A confounding variable that occurs when an experimenter unintentionally encourages participants to respond in a way that supports the hypothesis.

double-blind design   A research design in which neither the experimenter nor the participants know who is in the experimental group and who is in the control group.

To best control for participant expectancies and experimenter bias, neither experimenters nor participants should know who is getting the experimental treatment and who is getting placebo treatment. In practice, though, it is often difficult to establish and maintain experimenter "blindness" (Fergusson et al., 2004).

By permission of John L. Hart FLP and Creators Syndicate, Inc.

THE WIZARD OF ID — Brant parker and Johnny hart

of EMDR have not yet been conducted is another reason for caution in drawing conclusions about this treatment.

In short, experiments are vital tools for examining cause-effect relationships between variables, but like the other methods we have described (see "In Review: Methods of Psychological Research"), they are vulnerable to error. To maximize the value of their experiments, psychologists try to eliminate as many confounding variables as possible. Then they replicate their work to ensure consistent results and temper their interpretation of those results to take into account the limitations or problems that remain.

● Selecting Human Participants for Research

Visitors from outer space would be wildly mistaken if they tried to describe the typical earthling after meeting only, say, Arnold Schwarzenegger, Michael Jackson,

in **review** Methods of Psychological Research

Method	Features	Strengths	Pitfalls
Naturalistic observation	Observation of human or animal behavior in the environment in which it typically occurs	Provides descriptive data about behavior presumably uncontaminated by outside influences	Observer bias and participant self-consciousness can distort results
Case studies	Intensive examination of the behavior and mental processes associated with a specific person or situation	Provide detailed descriptive analyses of new, complex, or rare phenomena	May not provide representative picture of phenomena
Surveys	Standard sets of questions asked of a large number of participants	Gather large amounts of descriptive data relatively quickly and inexpensively	Sampling errors, poorly phrased questions, and response biases can distort results
Correlational studies	Examine relationships between research variables	Can test predictions, evaluate theories, and suggest new hypotheses	Cannot confirm causal relationships between variables
Experiments	Manipulation of an independent variable and measurement of its effects on a dependent variable	Can establish a cause-effect relationship between independent and dependent variables	Confounding variables may prevent valid conclusions

Shakira, and a trained seal. Likewise, the conclusions that psychologists draw from their observations, case studies, surveys, correlational studies, and experiments will be distorted if the participants they study are not typical of the people or animals they are interested in. Accordingly, the process of selecting participants for research, called **sampling,** is an extremely important step.

Suppose, for example, that you are conducting a survey of television viewing habits. Your research budget is small, so you restrict your survey to the residents of your apartment building, all of whom, by some strange coincidence, turn out to be male Asian American concert violinists. The responses you get from these people might be perfectly accurate, but their favorite shows might differ significantly from those of the general population. So sampling procedures can not only affect research results but also limit their meaning. In this case, your results would probably apply, or *generalize*, mainly to other male Asian American musicians. If that were the only group you want to draw conclusions about, then your limited sample might not be too problematic—assuming the men in your building were typical of other Asian American musicians. If they were all also ex-convicts, your results would be even more limited!

The main point is that if psychologists want to make scientific statements about the behavior and mental processes of any large group, they must select a **representative sample** of participants whose characteristics fairly reflect the characteristics of other people in that group. This point is important, because psychologists often study behavior or mental processes that are affected by age, gender, ethnicity, cultural background, socioeconomic status, sexual orientation, disability, or other participant characteristics. The more of these characteristics that are represented in a research sample, the broader can be the conclusions from research results.

In theory, psychologists could draw representative samples of people in general, of Canadians, of Florida college students, or of any other group by choosing them at random from the entire population of interest. To do this, though, they would first have to enter hundreds of thousands, perhaps millions, of names into a computer, then run a program to randomly select participants from this vast population, then track those people down and invite them to take part in the research. This method would result in a truly **random sample,** because every member of the population to be studied would have an equal chance of being chosen. Any selection procedure that does not offer this equal chance is said to result in a **biased sample.**

Unfortunately, not even a truly random sample will create a perfectly representative sample of Canadians, Florida college students, or the like. For one thing, the people who happen to be selected may be slightly different from the people who are not selected. In other words, the luck of the draw creates what psychologists call *sampling error*. Further, not everyone who is randomly selected for a research project will agree to participate, creating a problem called *nonresponse error*. These two kinds of errors help explain why the results of random surveys are not always accurate. Still, a group of individuals selected at random from a larger population will usually provide a reasonably representative sample of that population. The big problem, though, is that random sampling is often too expensive and time-consuming to be practical.

So in the real world of research, psychologists often draw their participants from the populations that are conveniently available. The populations from which these *convenience samples* are drawn depend to some extent on the size of the researcher's budget. They might include, for example, the students enrolled in a particular course, students enrolled on a local campus, the students who are willing to sign up for a study, or visitors to Internet web sites or chat rooms (e.g., Stone & Pennebaker, 2002). Ideally, this selection process will yield a sample that fairly represents the population from which it was drawn, but the researcher will check this by noting the age, gender, ethnicity, and other characteristics of the participants.

sampling The process of selecting participants who are members of the population that the researcher wishes to study.

representative sample A group of research participants whose characteristics fairly reflect the characteristics of the population from which they were selected.

random sample A group of research participants selected from a population whose members all had an equal chance of being chosen.

biased sample A group of research participants selected from a population each of whose members did not have an equal chance of being chosen.

 Selecting Research Participants Imagine that as a social psychologist, you want to study people's willingness to help each other. You have developed a method for testing helpfulness, but now you want a random sample of people to test. Take a minute to think about the steps necessary to select a truly random sample; then ask yourself how you might obtain a representative sample, instead. Remember that although the names are similar, *random sampling* is not the same as *random assignment*. Random sampling is used in many kinds of research to ensure that the people studied are representative of some larger group. Random assignment is used in experiments to distribute participant characteristics about evenly across various groups.

In all cases, scientific researchers are obliged to limit the conclusions they draw in light of the samples they draw (Kraut et al., 2004). Because of this obligation, psychologists often conduct additional studies to determine the extent to which their initial conclusions will apply to people who differ in important ways from their original sample (APA Office of Ethnic Minority Affairs, 2000; Case & Smith, 2000).

LINKAGES

 ## Psychological Research Methods and Behavioral Genetics

 LINKAGES (a link to Biological Aspects of Psychology, p. 59)

One of the most fascinating and difficult challenges in psychology is to find research methods that can help us understand the ways in which people's genetic inheritance (their biological *nature*) intertwines with environmental events and conditions before and after birth (often called *nurture*) to shape their behavior mental processes (Moffitt, Caspi, & Rutter, 2005). Consider Mark and John, identical twins who were both adopted at birth because their parents were too poor to care for them. John grew up with a married couple who made him feel secure and loved. Mark went from orphanage to foster home to hospital and, finally, back to his natural father's second wife. In other words, these genetically identical people had encountered quite different environments. Still, when they met for the first time at the age of twenty-four, they discovered similarities that went beyond physical appearance. They used the same aftershave lotion, smoked the same brand of cigarettes, used the same imported brand of toothpaste, and liked the same sports. They had joined the military within eight days of each other, and their IQ scores were nearly identical. How had genetic influences operated in two different environments to shape such similarities?

Exploring questions such as these has taken psychologists into the field of **behavioral genetics**, the study of how genes and environments work together to shape behavior. They have discovered that most behavioral tendencies are likely to be influenced by interactions between the environment and many different genes. Accordingly, research in behavioral genetics is designed to explore the relative roles of genetic and environmental factors in creating differences among people in personality, mental ability, mental disorders, and other phenomena. It also seeks to identify specific genes that contribute to hereditary influences.

Some behavioral genetics research takes the form of experiments, mainly on the selective breeding of animals (Suomi, 2004). For example, Stephen Suomi (1999) identified monkeys whose genes predisposed them to show strong or weak reactions to stress. He then mated strong reactors with other strong reactors and mated weak reactors with other weak reactors. Within a few generations, descendants of the strong-reactor pairs reacted much more strongly to stressors than did the descendants of the weak-reactor pairs. Selective-breeding experiments must be interpreted with caution, though, because animals do not inherit specific behaviors. What they inherit instead are differing sets of physical structures and capacities that make certain behaviors more likely or less likely. But these behavioral tendencies can be altered by the environment (Grigorenko, 2002; Parker et al., 2006). For example, when Suomi (1999) placed young, highly stress-reactive monkeys with unrelated "foster mothers," he discovered that the foster mothers' own stress reactivity amplified or dampened the youngsters' genetically influenced behavioral tendencies. If stress-reactive monkeys were placed with stress-reactive foster mothers, they tended to be fearful of exploring their environments and had strong reactions to stressors. But if equally stress-reactive young monkeys had calm, supportive foster mothers, they appeared eager to explore their environments and were much less upset by stressors than their peers with stress-reactive foster mothers.

Research on behavioral genetics in humans must be interpreted with even greater care. Legal, moral, and ethical considerations obviously prohibit experiments on the selective breeding of people, so research in human behavioral genetics depends on correlational studies. These usually take the form of family studies, twin studies, and adoption studies (Plomin et al., 2001). Let's consider the logic of these behavioral genetics research methods. (For more on the basic principles of genetics and heredity that underlie these methods, see the behavioral genetics appendix.)

In *family studies,* researchers look at whether close relatives are more likely than distant ones to show similar behavior and mental processes. If increasing similarity is associated with closer family ties, the similarities might be inherited. For example, family studies suggest a genetic basis for schizophrenia because this severe mental disorder appears much more often in the closest relatives of schizophrenics than in other people (see Figure 2.2). But remember that a correlation between variables does not guarantee that one is causing the other. The appearance of similar disorders in close relatives might be due to environmental factors instead of, or in addition to, genetic ones. After all, close relatives tend to share environments, as well as genes. So family studies alone cannot establish the role of genetic factors in mental disorders or other characteristics.

Twin studies explore the heredity-environment mix by comparing the similarities seen in identical twins with those of nonidentical pairs. Twins usually share the same family environment as they grow up, and they may also be treated very much the same by parents and others. So if identical twins (whose genes are exactly the same) are more alike on some characteristic than nonidentical twins (whose genes are no more similar than those of other siblings), that characteristic may have a significant genetic component. As we will see in later chapters, this pattern of results holds for a number of characteristics, including some measures of intelligence and some mental disorders. As shown in Figure 2.2, for example, if one member of an identical twin pair develops schizophrenia, the chances are about 45 percent that the other twin will, too. Those chances drop to about 17 percent if the twins are nonidentical.

● **behavioral genetics**   The study of how genes and environment work together to shape behavior.

FIGURE 2.2

Family and Twin Studies of Schizophrenia

The risk of developing schizophrenia, a severe mental disorder, is highest for the siblings and children of schizophrenia patients and lowest for those who are not genetically related to anyone with schizophrenia. Does this mean that schizophrenia is inherited? These results are consistent with that interpretation, but the question cannot be answered through family studies alone. Environmental factors, such as stressors that close relatives share, could also play an important role. Studies comparing identical and nonidentical twins also suggest genetic influence, but even twin studies do not eliminate the role of environmental influences.

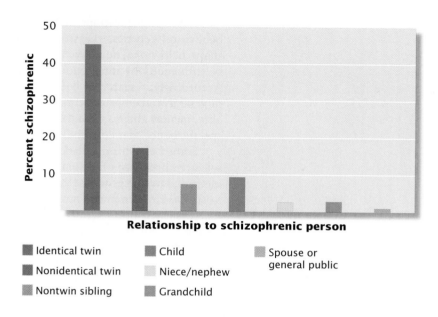

Relationship to schizophrenic person

- ■ Identical twin
- ■ Nonidentical twin
- ■ Nontwin sibling
- ■ Child
- ■ Niece/nephew
- ■ Grandchild
- ■ Spouse or general public

Adoption studies take scientific advantage of cases in which babies are adopted very early in life. The logic of these studies is that if adopted children's characteristics are more like those of their biological parents than of their adoptive parents, genetics probably plays a clear role in those characteristics. In fact, as described in the chapter on personality, the traits of young adults who were adopted at birth tend to be more like those of their biological parents than those of their adoptive parents. Adoption studies can be especially valuable when they focus on identical twins who, like Mark and John, were separated at or near birth. If identical twins show similar characteristics after years of living in very different environments, the role of heredity in those characteristics is highlighted. Adoption studies of intelligence tend to support the role of genetics in variations in mental ability, but they show the impact of environmental influences, too.

Family, twin, and adoption studies have played an important role in behavioral genetics research, but when you read in other chapters about the role of genes in personality, intelligence, mental disorders, and other characteristics, remember this important point: Research on human behavioral genetics can tell us about the relative roles of heredity and environment in creating differences *among* individuals, but it cannot determine the degree to which a *particular* person's behavior is due to

Research in Behavioral Genetics

Like other identical twins, each member of this pair has identical genes. Twin studies and adoption studies help to reveal the interaction of genetic and environmental influences in human behavior and mental processes. Cases in which identical twins who had been separated at birth are found to have similar interests, personality traits, and mental abilities suggest that these characteristics have a significant genetic component.

heredity or environment. The two factors are too closely entwined in an individual to be separated that way. In the future, though, behavioral genetics will also be shaped by research methods made possible by the Human Genome Project, which has now unlocked the genetic code contained in the DNA that makes each human being unique (International Human Genome Sequencing Consortium, 2001; see the behavioral genetics appendix). This achievement has allowed behavioral geneticists and other scientists to begin pinpointing some of the many genes that contribute to individual differences in disorders such as autism, learning disabilities, hyperactivity, and Alzheimer's disease, as well as to the normal variations in personality and cognitive abilities that we see all around us (Saudino, Ronald, & Plomin, 2005). Finding the DNA differences responsible for certain personal attributes and behaviors will eventually make it possible to understand exactly how heredity interacts with the environment as development unfolds. ■

Statistical Analysis of Research Results

The data gathered through naturalistic observations, case studies, surveys, correlational studies, and experiments usually take the form of numbers that represent research findings and provide the basis for conclusions about them. These data might represent scores on intelligence tests, levels of stress hormones in blood samples, tiny differences in the time required to detect visual signals, ratings of people's personality traits, or whatever else a psychologist might be studying.

Like other scientists, psychologists use descriptive and inferential *statistics* to summarize and analyze their data and interpret what they mean. As their name suggests, **descriptive statistics** describe data. **Inferential statistics** are mathematical procedures that help psychologists make inferences about what the data mean. Here, we describe a few statistical terms that you will encounter in later chapters; you can find more information about these terms in the statistics appendix.

● Descriptive Statistics

The three most important descriptive statistics are *measures of central tendency*, which describe the typical score (or value) in a set of data; *measures of variability*, which describe the spread, or dispersion, among the scores in a set of data; and *correlation coefficients*, which describe relationships between variables.

● Measures of Central Tendency
Suppose you wanted to test the effects of EMDR treatment on fear of the dark. Looking for participants, you collect the eleven self-ratings of anxiety listed on the left side of Table 2.4. What is the typical score, the central tendency, that best represents the anxiety level of this group of people? There are three measures designed to capture this typical score: the mode, the median, and the mean.

The **mode** is the value or score that occurs most frequently in a data set. You can find it by simply counting how many times each score appears. On the left side of Table 2.4, the mode is 50, because the score of 50 occurs more often than any other. Notice, however, that in this data set the mode is actually an extreme score. Sometimes, the mode acts like a microphone for a small but vocal minority that, though speaking loudest or most frequently, does not represent the views of the majority.

Unlike the mode, the median takes all of the scores into account. The **median** is the halfway point in a set of data. When scores are arranged from lowest to highest, half the scores fall above the median, and half fall below it. For the scores on the left side of Table 2.4, the halfway point—the median—is 45.

The third measure of central tendency is the **mean**, which is the *arithmetic average* of a set of scores. When people talk about the "average" in everyday conversation, they are usually referring to the mean. To find the mean, add the scores and

descriptive statistics Numbers that summarize a set of research data.

inferential statistics A set of mathematical procedures that help psychologists make inferences about what their research data mean.

mode A measure of central tendency that is the value or score that occurs most frequently in a data set.

median A measure of central tendency that is the halfway point in a set of data: Half the scores fall above the median, and half fall below it.

mean A measure of central tendency that is the arithmetic average of the scores in a set of data.

TABLE **2.4**	A Set of Pretreatment Anxiety Ratings		

Here are scores representing people's self-ratings, on a 1–100 scale, of their fear of the dark.

Data from 11 Participants		Data from 12 Participants	
Participant Number	Anxiety Rating	Participant Number	Anxiety Rating
1	20	1	20
2	22	2	22
3	28	3	28
4	35	4	35
5	40	5	40
6	45 (Median)	6	45 (Median = 46[a])
7	47	7	47
8	49	8	49
9	50	9	50
10	50	10	50
11	50	11	50
		12	100

Measures of central tendency
Mode = 50
Median = 45
Mean = 436/11 = 39.6

Measures of variability
Range = 30
Standard deviation = 11.064

Measures of central tendency
Mode = 50
Median = 46
Mean = 536/12 = 44.7

Measures of variability
Range = 80
Standard deviation = 19.763

[a]When there is an even number of scores, the exact middle of the list lies between two numbers. The median is the value halfway between those numbers.

divide by the number of scores. For the data on the left side of Table 2.4, the mean is 436/11 = 39.6.

Like the median (and unlike the mode), the mean reflects all the data to some degree, not just the most frequent data. Notice, however, that the mean reflects the actual values of all the scores, whereas the median gives each score equal weight, whatever its value. This distinction can have a big effect on how well the mean and median represent the scores in a particular set of data. Suppose, for example, that you add to your sample a twelfth participant, whose anxiety rating is 100. When you reanalyze the anxiety data (see the right side of Table 2.4), the median hardly changes, because the new participant counts as just one more score. However, when you compute the new mean, the actual *amount* of the new participant's rating is added to everyone else's ratings; as a result, the mean jumps five points. As this example shows, the median is sometimes a better measure of central tendency than the mean because the median is

Descriptive statistics are valuable for summarizing research results, but we must evaluate them carefully before drawing conclusions about what they mean. Given this executive's reputation for uncritical thinking, you can bet that Dogbert's impressive-sounding restatement of the definition of *median* will win him an extension of his pricey consulting contract.

© Scott Adams/Dist. by United Feature Syndicate, Inc.

TRY
THIS **The Effect of Variability**
Suppose that on your first day as a substitute teacher at a new school, you are offered either of two classes. The mean IQ score in both classes is 100, but the standard deviation (SD) of scores is 16 in one class and 32 in the other. Before you read the next sentence, ask yourself which class you would choose if you wanted an easy day's work or if you wanted a tough challenge. (Higher standard deviation means more variability, so students in the class with the SD of 32 will vary more in ability, thus creating a greater challenge for the teacher.)

less sensitive to extreme scores. But because the mean is more representative of the values of all the data, it is often the preferred measure of central tendency.

● **Measures of Variability**   The variability (also known as *spread* or *dispersion*) in a set of data is described by statistics known as the *range* and the *standard deviation*. The **range** is simply the difference between the highest and the lowest scores in a data set (it would be 30 for the data on the left side of Table 2.4 and 80 for the data on the right side). In contrast, the **standard deviation**, or **SD**, measures the average difference between each score and the mean of the data set. So the standard deviation tells us how much the scores in a data set vary, or differ, from one another. The more variable the data are, the higher the standard deviation will be. For example, the SD for the eleven participants on the left side of Table 2.4 is 11.064, but it rises to 19.763 once that very different twelfth score is added on the right side. In the statistics appendix, we show how to calculate the standard deviation.

● **Correlation and Correlation Coefficients**   When we described correlational studies on the relationship between media violence and aggression, we left out one important question: How do psychologists describe the correlation between these variables or between any other pair of variables?

Correlation means just what it says, "co-relation," and it refers both to how strongly one variable is related to another and to the direction of the relationship. A *positive correlation* means that two variables increase together or decrease together. A *negative correlation* means that the variables move in opposite directions: When one increases, the other decreases. For example, James Schaefer observed 4,500 customers in sixty-five bars and found that the tempo of jukebox music was negatively correlated with the rate at which the customers drank alcohol; the slower the tempo, the faster the drinking (Schaefer et al., 1988).

Does this mean that Schaefer could have worn a blindfold and predicted exactly how fast people were drinking by timing the music? Or could he have plugged his ears and determined the musical tempo by watching how fast people drink? No and no, because the accuracy of predictions about one variable from knowledge of another depends on the strength of the correlation. Only a perfect correlation between two variables would allow you to predict the exact value of one from a knowledge of the other. The weaker the correlation, the less one variable can tell you about the other.

● **range**   A measure of variability that is the difference between the highest and the lowest values in a data set.

● **standard deviation (SD)**   A measure of variability that is the average difference between each score and the mean of the data set.

● **correlation**   In research, the degree to which one variable is related to another.

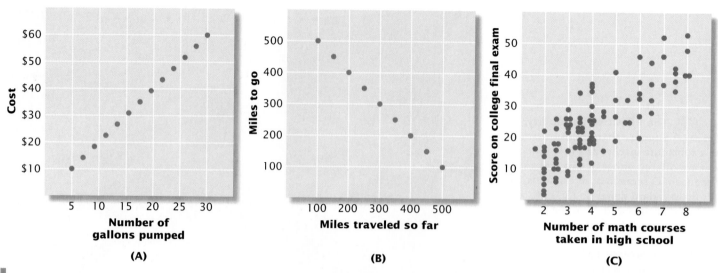

FIGURE 2.3

Three Correlations

The strength and direction of the correlation between variables can be seen in a graph called a *scatterplot*. Here are three examples. In Part A, we have plotted the cost of a gasoline purchase against the number of gallons pumped. The number of gallons is positively and perfectly correlated with their cost, so the scatterplot appears as a straight line, and you can predict the value of either variable from a knowledge of the other. Part B shows a perfect negative correlation between the number of miles you have traveled toward a destination and the distance remaining. Again, one variable can be exactly predicted from the other. Part C illustrates a correlation of +.81 between the number of math courses students had in high school and their scores on a college math exam; each dot represents one student (Hays, 1981). As correlations decrease, they are represented by less and less organization in the pattern of dots. A correlation of 0.00 would appear as a shapeless cloud.

Psychologists describe correlations using a statistic called the **correlation coefficient** (the statistics appendix shows how to calculate it). The correlation coefficient is given the symbol *r*, and it can vary from +1.00 to −1.00. The actual size of the correlation, such as .20 or .80, tells us how strong the correlation is. The higher the number, the stronger the correlation. The plus or minus sign tells us the direction of the correlation. A plus sign says the correlation is positive. A minus sign says the correlation is negative.

So an *r* of +.80 between people's height and weight would tell us that the correlation between these two variables is strong and positive: The taller people are, the more they tend to weigh. A correlation of +.01 between their shoe size and the age of their cars would indicate that there is almost no relationship between these two variables. An *r* of −1.00 describes a perfectly predictable, but negative, relationship between two variables (see part B of Figure 2.3). The variables that psychologists study are seldom perfectly correlated. Most of the correlational studies described in this book yield correlation coefficients in the .20 to .50 range, though some are as high as .90.

Remember, too, that even a strong correlation between two variables doesn't guarantee that one is *causing* an effect on the other. And even if one *does* affect the other, a correlation coefficient can't tell us which variable is influencing which. As mentioned earlier, correlations can reveal and describe relationships, but correlations alone cannot explain them.

● Inferential Statistics

correlation coefficient   A statistic, *r*, that summarizes the strength and direction of a relationship between two variables.

To help them interpret the meaning of correlations and the other descriptive statistics that flow from research results, psychologists rely on *inferential statistics*.

in review — Descriptive and Inferential Statistics

Statistic	Characteristics	Information Provided
Mode	Describes the central tendencies of a set of scores	The score that occurs most frequently in a data set
Median	Describes the central tendencies of a set of scores	The halfway point in a data set; half the scores fall above this score, half below
Mean	Describes the central tendencies of a set of scores	The arithmetic average of the scores in a data set
Range	Describes the variability of a set of scores	The difference between the highest and lowest scores in a data set
Standard deviation	Describes the variability of a set of scores	The average difference between each score and the mean of a data set
Correlation coefficient	Describes the relationship between two variables	How strongly the two variables are related and whether the relationship is positive (variables move in same direction) or negative (variables move in opposite directions)
Tests of significance	Help make inferences about the relationships between descriptive statistics	How likely it is that the difference between measures of central tendencies or the size of a correlation coefficient is due to chance alone

For example, it was on the basis of analyses using inferential statistics that many researchers concluded that the benefits of EMDR are not great enough when compared with other treatment options to recommend it as a first choice in cases of anxiety.

Inferential statistics use certain rules to evaluate whether a correlation or a difference between group means is a significant finding or might have occurred just by chance. Suppose, for example, that a group of people treated with EMDR showed a mean decrease of 10 points on a posttreatment anxiety test, whereas the scores of a no-treatment control group decreased by a mean of 7 points. Does this 3-point difference between the groups' means reflect the impact of EMDR, or could it have been caused by random factors that made EMDR appear more powerful than it actually is? Traditionally, psychologists have answered questions such as this by using tests of statistical significance to estimate how likely it is that an observed difference was due to chance alone (Krueger, 2001). When those tests show that a correlation coefficient or the difference between two means is larger than would be expected by chance alone, that correlation or difference is said to be **statistically significant**. In the statistics appendix, we describe some of these tests and discuss the factors that affect their results.

Positive outcomes on tests of statistical significance are important, but they do not necessarily prove that a difference is "real" or that a particular treatment is effective or ineffective. Accordingly, quantitative psychologists recommend that research findings be evaluated using other statistical analysis methods, too (e.g., Kileen, 2005; Kline, 2004; Krueger, 2001). Whatever the methods, though, psychological scientists are more confident in, and pay the most attention to, correlations or other research findings that statistical analyses suggest are robust and not flukes. (For a review of the statistical measures discussed in this section, see "In Review: Descriptive and Inferential Statistics.")

● **statistically significant** Referring to a correlation, or a difference between two groups, that is larger than would be expected by chance.

The Social Impact of Research
The impact of research in psychology depends partly on the quality of the results and partly on how people feel about those results. Despite negative results of controlled experiments on facilitated communication, the Facilitated Communication Institute's web site continues to announce training for the many professionals and relatives of autistic people who still believe in its value. The fact that some people ignore, or even attack, research results that challenge cherished beliefs reminds us that scientific research has always affected, and been affected by, the social and political values of the society in which it takes place (Lynn et al., 2003; Tavris, 2002).

Statistics and Research Methods as Tools in Critical Thinking

As you think critically about evidence for or against any hypothesis, remember that part of the process is to ask some tough questions. Does the evidence come from a study whose design is free of major confounds and other flaws? Have the results been subjected to careful statistical analysis? Have the results been replicated? Using your critical thinking skills to evaluate research designs and statistical methods becomes especially important when you encounter results that are dramatic or unexpected.

This point was well illustrated when Douglas Biklen (1990) began promoting a procedure called "facilitated communication (FC)" to help people with severe autistic disorder use language for the first time (autistic disorder is described in the chapter on psychological disorders). Biklen claimed that these people have language skills and coherent thoughts but no way to express them. He reported case studies in which autistic people were apparently able to answer questions and speak intelligently using a special keyboard, but only when assisted by a "facilitator" who physically supported their unsteady hands. Controlled experiments showed this claim to be groundless, however (Jacobson, Mulick, & Schwartz, 1995; Mostert, 2001; Wegner, Fuller, & Sparrow, 2003). The alleged communication abilities of these autistic people disappeared under conditions in which the facilitator (1) did not know the question being asked of the participant or (2) could not see the keyboard (Delmolino & Romanczyk, 1995). The discovery that facilitators were—perhaps inadvertently (Spitz, 1997)—guiding participants' hand movements has allowed those who work with autistic people to see FC in a different light.

The role of experiments and other scientific research methods in understanding behavior and mental processes is so important that in each chapter to come we include a special feature called "Focus on Research Methods." These features describe in detail the specific procedures used in one particularly interesting research project. Our hope is that by reading these sections, you will see how the research methods discussed in this chapter are applied in every subfield of psychology.

Ethical Guidelines for Psychologists

The obligation to analyze and report research fairly and accurately is one of the many ethical requirements that guide psychologists in their work. Preserving the welfare and dignity of research participants, both animal and human, is another. So although researchers *could* measure severe anxiety by putting a loaded gun to people's heads, or study marital conflicts by telling one partner that the other has been unfaithful, those methods might cause harm and are therefore unethical. Whatever their research topic, psychologists' first priority is to investigate it in accordance with the highest ethical standards. They must find ways to protect their participants from harm while still gathering data that will have potential benefits for everyone. So to measure anxiety a researcher might ask people to enter a situation that is anxiety provoking but not traumatic (e.g., approaching a feared animal, or sitting in a dark room). And research on marital conflict usually involves videotaping couples as they discuss problems in their relationship.

Psychologists take very seriously the obligation to minimize any immediate discomfort or risk for research participants, as well as the need to protect those participants from long-term harm. They are careful to inform prospective participants about every aspect of the study that might influence the decision to participate, and they ensure that each person's involvement is voluntary. But what if the purpose of the study is to measure people's emotional reactions to being insulted? Participants might not react normally if they know ahead of time that an "insult" will be part of the experiment. When deception is necessary to create certain experimental conditions, ethical standards require the researcher to "debrief" participants as soon as the study is over by revealing all relevant information about the research and correcting any misconceptions it created.

Laws in the United States, Canada, and many other countries require that any research involving human participants must be approved by an Institutional Review Board (IRB) whose members have no connection to the research. If a proposed study is likely to create risks or discomfort for participants, the IRB members weigh its potential benefits in terms of knowledge and human welfare against its potential for harm. Standards set by organizations such as the Association for the Accreditation of Human Research Protection Programs also help psychologists think through the ethical implications of any research that might have the slightest risk of harm to human participants.

The obligation to protect participants' welfare also extends to animals, which are used in 7 or 8 percent of psychological research studies (American Psychological Association Committee on Animal Research and Ethics, 2006; Plous, 1996). Psychologists study animals—mainly rats, mice, and pigeons—partly because their behavior is interesting and partly because research with animals can provide information that would be impossible or unethical to collect from humans. For example, researchers can randomly assign animals to live alone or with others and then look at how these conditions affect later social interactions. The same thing could not ethically be done with people, but animal studies such as this can provide clues about how social isolation might affect humans (see the chapter on motivation and emotion).

Contrary to the claims of some animal-rights activists, animals used in psychological research are not routinely subjected to extreme pain, starvation, or other inhumane conditions. Even in the small proportion of studies that require the use of electric shock, the discomfort created is mild, brief, and not harmful. High standards for the care and treatment of animal participants are outlined in the Animal Welfare Act, the National Institutes of Health's *Guide for the Care and Use of Laboratory Animals*, the National Institute of Mental Health's *Methods and Welfare Considerations in Behavioral Research with Animals*, the American

Caring for Animals in Research
Psychologists are careful to protect the welfare of animal participants in research. They do not wish to see animals suffer, and besides, undue stress on animals can create reactions that can act as confounding variables. For example, in a study of how learning is affected by food rewards, the researcher could starve animals to make them hungry enough to want rewards. But this would introduce discomfort, making it impossible to separate the effects of the rewards from the effects of starvation.

Psychological Association's *Principles on Animal Use*, and in other laws and regulations (APA Committee on Animal Research and Ethics, 2006). In those relatively rare studies that require animals to undergo short-lived pain or other forms of moderate stress, legal and ethical standards require that funding agencies—as well as local committees charged with monitoring animal research—first determine that the discomfort is justified by the expected benefits to human welfare.

The responsibility for conducting research in the most humane fashion is just one aspect of the *Ethical Principles of Psychologists and Code of Conduct* developed by the American Psychological Association (2002b). This document not only emphasizes the importance of ethical behavior but also describes specific ways in which psychologists can protect and promote the welfare of society and the particular people with whom they work in any capacity. So as teachers, psychologists should give students complete, accurate, and up-to-date coverage of each topic, not a narrow, biased point of view. Psychologists should perform only those services and use only those techniques for which they are adequately trained; a psychologist untrained in clinical methods, for example, should not try to offer psychotherapy. Except in the most unusual circumstances (discussed in the chapter on treatment of psychological disorders), psychologists should not reveal information obtained from clients or students. They should also avoid situations in which a conflict of interest might impair their judgment or harm someone else. They should not, for example, have sexual relations with their clients, their students, or their employees.

Despite these guidelines, doubt and controversy arise in some cases about whether a proposed experiment or a particular practice, such as deceiving participants, is ethical. The American Psychological Association has published a casebook to help psychologists resolve such issues (Nagy, 1999). The ethical principles themselves must continually be updated to deal with complex new questions—such as how to protect the confidentiality of e-mail communications—that psychologists face in their ever-expanding range of work (APA, 2002b; Hays, 2006; Pipes, Holstein, & Aguirre, 2005; Smith, 2003b).

LINKAGES

As noted in the chapter on introducing psychology, all of psychology's subfields are related to one another. Our discussion of behavioral genetics illustrates just one way in which the topic of this chapter, research in psychology, is linked to the subfield of biological psychology (see the chapter on biological aspects of psychology). The Linkages diagram shows ties to two other subfields as well, and there are many more ties throughout the book. Looking for linkages among subfields will help you see how they all fit together and help you better appreciate the big picture that is psychology.

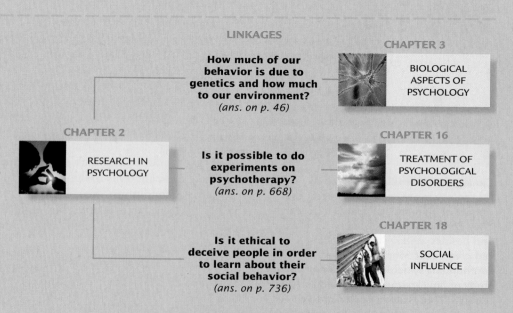

LINKAGES

CHAPTER 2
RESEARCH IN PSYCHOLOGY

How much of our behavior is due to genetics and how much to our environment?
(ans. on p. 46)

CHAPTER 3
BIOLOGICAL ASPECTS OF PSYCHOLOGY

Is it possible to do experiments on psychotherapy?
(ans. on p. 668)

CHAPTER 16
TREATMENT OF PSYCHOLOGICAL DISORDERS

Is it ethical to deceive people in order to learn about their social behavior?
(ans. on p. 736)

CHAPTER 18
SOCIAL INFLUENCE

SUMMARY

Thinking Critically About Psychology (or Anything Else)

Critical thinking is the process of assessing claims and making judgments on the basis of well-supported evidence.

Critical Thinking and Scientific Research Often, questions about behavior and mental processes are phrased in terms of *hypotheses* about *variables* that have been specified by *operational definitions*. Tests of hypotheses are based on objective, quantifiable evidence, or *data*, representing the variables of interest. If data are to be useful, they must be evaluated for reliability and validity.

The Role of Theories Explanations of phenomena often take the form of a *theory*, which is a set of statements that can be used to account for, predict, and even suggest ways of controlling certain phenomena. Theories must be subjected to careful evaluation.

Research Methods in Psychology

Research in psychology, as in other sciences, focuses on four main goals: description, prediction, control, and explanation.

Naturalistic Observation: Watching Behavior *Naturalistic observation* entails watching without interfering as behavior occurs in the natural environment. This method can be revealing, but care must be taken to ensure that observers are unbiased and do not alter the behavior being observed.

Case Studies: Taking a Closer Look *Case studies* are intensive examinations of a particular individual, group, or situation. They are useful for studying new or rare phenomena and for evaluating new treatments or training programs.

Surveys: Looking at the Big Picture *Surveys* ask questions, through interviews or questionnaires, about behavior, attitudes, beliefs, opinions, and intentions. They provide an efficient way to gather large amounts of data from many people at a relatively low cost, but their results can be distorted if questions are poorly phrased, if answers are not given honestly, or if respondents do not constitute a representative sample of the population whose views are of interest.

Correlational Studies: Looking for Relationships *Correlational studies* examine relationships between variables in order to describe research data, test predictions, evaluate theories, and suggest hypotheses. Correlational studies are an important part of psychological research. However, the reasons behind the relationships they reveal cannot be established by correlational studies alone.

Experiments: Exploring Cause and Effect In *experiments*, researchers manipulate an *independent variable* and observe the effect of that manipulation on a *dependent variable*. Participants receiving experimental treatment are called the *experimental group*; those in comparison conditions are called *control groups*. Experiments can reveal cause-effect relationships between variables, but only if researchers use *random assignment*, *placebo* conditions, *double-blind designs*, and other strategies to avoid being misled by *random variables*, participants' expectations, *experimenter bias*, and other *confounding variables*.

Selecting Human Participants for Research Psychologists' research can be limited if their *sampling* procedures do not give them a fair cross section of the population they want to study and about which they want to draw conclusions. Anything other than a *random sample* is said to be a *biased sample* of participants. In most cases, psychologists try to select representative samples of the populations that are available to them.

Statistical Analysis of Research Results

Psychologists use *descriptive statistics* and *inferential statistics* to summarize and analyze data.

Descriptive Statistics Descriptive statistics include measures of central tendency (such as the *mode, median,* and *mean*), measures of variability (such as the *range* and *standard deviation*, or SD), and *correlation coefficients*. Although valuable for describing relationships, *correlations* alone cannot establish that two variables are causally related, nor can they determine which variable might affect which, or why.

Inferential Statistics Psychologists employ inferential statistics to guide conclusions about data and, especially, to determine if correlations or differences between means are *statistically significant*—that is, larger than would be expected by chance alone.

Statistics and Research Methods as Tools in Critical Thinking Scientific evaluation of research requires the use of critical thinking to carefully assess the design and statistical analysis of even the most dramatic or desirable results.

Ethical Guidelines for Psychologists

Ethical guidelines promote the protection of humans and animals in psychological research. They also set the highest standards for behavior in all other aspects of psychologists' scientific and professional lives.

Biological Aspects of Psychology

Before you read the next sentence, close your eyes and touch your nose. This task is easy, but it is not simple. To get the job done, your brain used specific nerves to tell your eyelids to close. It used other nerves to tell your hand to extend a finger and then sent a series of messages that moved your arm in just the right direction until it received a message that your finger and your nose were in contact. This example illustrates that everything you do—including how you feel and think—is based on some kind of biological activity in your body, especially in your brain. This chapter tells the story of that activity, beginning with the neuron, one of the body's most basic biological units. We describe how neurons form systems capable of receiving and processing information and translate it into behavior, thoughts, and biochemical changes. We have organized our presentation as follows:

Do you drink coffee or cola? Do you like beer or wine? Are you still unable to quit smoking? If so, you know that caffeine, alcohol, and nicotine can change the way you feel. The effects of these substances are based largely on their ability to change the chemistry of your brain. There are many other examples of how our mental experiences, and our identity as individuals, are rooted in biological processes. Each year, millions of people who suffer anxiety, depression, and other psychological disorders take prescription drugs that alter brain chemistry in ways that relieve their distress. Millions of others have the resilience to bounce back, without drugs, from even the worst experiences life can throw at them, and find meaning and fulfillment in their lives. To what extent are these negative and positive reactions rooted in biological differences among people?

The importance and impact of biological processes stems from the fact that brain cells, hormones, genes, and other biological factors are related to everything you think and feel and do, from the fleeting memory you had a minute ago to the anxiety or excitement or fatigue you felt last night to the movements of your eyes as you read right now. In this chapter, we describe these biological factors in more detail. Reading it will take you into the realm of **biological psychology**, which is the study of the cells and organs of the body and the physical and chemical changes involved in behavior and mental processes. It is here that we begin to consider the relationship between your body and your mind, your brain and your behavior.

It is a complex relationship. Scientific psychologists are no doubt correct when they say that every thought, every feeling, and every action are represented somehow in the nervous system and that none of these events could occur without it. However, we must be careful not to oversimplify or overemphasize biological explanations in psychology. Many people assume, for example, that if a behavior or mental process has a strong biological basis, it is beyond our control—that "biology is destiny." Accordingly, many smokers don't even try to quit, simply because they are sure that their biological addiction to nicotine will doom them to failure. This is not necessarily true, as millions of ex-smokers can confirm. The fact that all behavior and mental processes are *based on* biological processes does not mean that they can be fully understood through the study of biological processes alone.

In fact, reducing all of psychology to the analysis of brain chemicals would seriously underestimate the complexity of the interactions between our biological selves and our psychological experiences, between our genes and our environments. Just as all behaviors and mental processes are influenced by biology, all biological processes are influenced by the environment. We will see later that the experiences we have can change our brain chemistry and even our brain anatomy—often by affecting whether certain aspects of our genetic makeup are expressed. Examples of experience-dependent gene expression are discussed in the appendix on behavioral genetics, but for now, just consider height. Your height is strongly influenced by genetics, but how tall you actually become depends heavily on nutrition and other environmental factors (Tanner, 1992). Hereditary and environmental influences also combine to determine intelligence, personality, mental disorders, and all our other characteristics.

In short, understanding behavior and mental processes requires that we combine information from many sources, ranging from the activity of cells and organ systems to the activity of individuals and groups in social contexts. This chapter focuses on the biological level, not because it reveals the whole story of psychology but because it tells an important part of that story.

biological psychology The psychological specialty focused on the physical and chemical changes that cause, and occur in response to, behavior and mental processes.

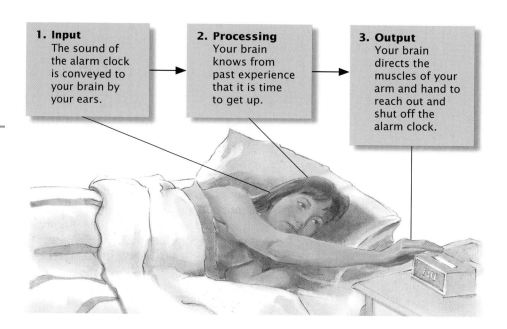

1. Input
The sound of the alarm clock is conveyed to your brain by your ears.

2. Processing
Your brain knows from past experience that it is time to get up.

3. Output
Your brain directs the muscles of your arm and hand to reach out and shut off the alarm clock.

FIGURE **3.1**

Three Functions of the Nervous System

The nervous system's three main functions are to receive information (input), integrate that information with past experiences (processing), and guide actions (output). When the alarm clock goes off, this person's nervous system, like yours, gets the message, recognizes what it means, decides what to do, and then takes action—by getting out of bed or perhaps hitting the snooze button.

We begin by considering the **nervous system**, the billions of cells that make up your brain, your spinal cord, and other nerve fibers. The combined activity of these cells tells you what is going on inside and outside your body and allows you to make appropriate responses. For example, if you are jabbed with a pin, your nervous system gets the message and immediately causes you to flinch. But your nervous system can do far more than detect information and execute responses. When information about the world reaches your brain, that information is *processed*—meaning that it is combined with information about past experiences and current wants and needs—so that you can make a decision about how to respond. The chosen action is then taken (see Figure 3.1). In other words, your nervous system displays the characteristics of an information-processing system: It has input, processing, and output capabilities.

The processing capabilities of the nervous system are especially important, not only because the brain interprets information, makes decisions, and guides action but also because the brain can actually adjust the impact of incoming information. This phenomenon helps explain why you can't tickle yourself. In one study, simply telling ticklish people that they were about to be touched on the bottom of their feet caused activation in the brain region that receives sensory information from the foot (Carlsson et al., 2000). The anticipation of being touched made these people all the more sensitive to that touch. However, when they were asked to touch the bottoms of their own feet, there was far less advance activation of this brain region, and they did not overreact to their touch. Why? The explanation is that when the brain plans a movement, it also predicts which of its own touch-detecting regions will be affected by that movement. So predictable, self-controlled touches, even in a normally "ticklish" spot, reduce activation of the sensory regions associated with that spot (Blakemore, Wolpert, & Frith, 2000).

The nervous system is able to do what it does partly because it is made up of cells that communicate with each other. Like all cells in the body—indeed, like all living cells—those in the nervous system can respond to various kinds of signals. Many of the signals that cells respond to come in the form of chemicals released by other cells. So even as various cells specialize during prenatal development to become skin, bone, hair, and other tissues, they still "stay in touch" through chemical signals. Bone cells, for example, add or lose calcium in response to hormones secreted in another part of the body. Cells in the bloodstream respond to viruses and other invaders by destroying them. We'll focus first on the cells of the nervous system, because their ability to communicate is the most efficient and complex.

● **nervous system** A complex combination of cells whose primary function is to allow an organism to gain information about what is going on inside and outside the body and to respond appropriately.

The Nervous System

We begin our exploration of the nervous system at the "bottom," with a description of the individual cells and molecules that compose it. Then we consider how these cells are organized to form the structures of the human nervous system.

● Cells of the Nervous System

Brain tissue appears to be a hopelessly complex web of interconnecting fibers, but about a hundred years ago, the great Spanish anatomist Ramon y Cajal (pronounced "ka-HALL) argued that the nervous system is made up of separate cells, called *neurons*. When the invention of the electron microscope allowed scientists to see individual neurons, and the gaps between them, Cajal's idea was confirmed. **Neurons** are cells that are specialized to rapidly respond to signals and to quickly send signals of their own. For many years communication in the nervous system was thought to take place only between neurons, but this *neuron doctrine* has turned out to be incorrect (Bullock et al., 2005). Non-neuronal cells perform important communication functions, too. These cells are called *glial cells* because *glial* means "glue," and scientists had long believed that they did no more than hold neurons together. However, we now know that **glial cells** also help neurons communicate by directing their growth, keeping their chemical environment stable, providing energy, and secreting chemicals to help restore damage (Fellin et al., 2004). So without glial cells, neurons could not function. Further, glial cells are capable of the signature functions of neurons, including releasing chemicals that influence neurons, responding to chemicals from neurons, and changing in response to experience (Auld & Robitaille, 2003; Ge et al., 2006). So the nervous system is actually made up of two major types of cells—neurons and glial cells—that, together, allow the system to carry out its complex signaling tasks so efficiently.

● Common Features of Neurons

Figure 3.2 shows three features that neurons share with almost every other kind of cell in the body. First, neurons have an *outer membrane* that acts like a fine screen, letting some substances pass in and out while blocking others. Second, nervous system cells have a *cell body,* which contains a *nucleus* (only red blood cells have no nucleus). The nucleus carries the genetic information that determines how a cell will function. Third, nervous system cells contain *mitochondria* (pronounced "my-toh-CON-dree-ah"), which are structures that turn oxygen and glucose into energy. This process is especially vital to brain cells. Although the brain accounts for only 2 percent of the body's weight, it consumes more than 20 percent of the body's oxygen (Sokoloff, 1981). All of this energy is required because brain cells transmit signals among themselves to an even greater extent than do cells in the rest of the body.

Besides being similar to other cells in the human body, neurons are also amazingly similar to the cells in all living organisms, from bacteria to plants to humans. For example, bacteria, plant cells, and brain cells all synthesize similar proteins when they are subjected to reduced oxygen or elevated temperatures. Because of this similarity, we can learn something about human brain cells by studying cells in much simpler organisms. For example, research on the cells in worms recently provided clues to the causes of Alzheimer's disease (Cohen et al., 2006).

● Special Features of Neurons

However, neurons have three special features that enable them to communicate signals efficiently. The first is their structure. Although neurons come in many shapes and sizes, they all have long, thin fibers that extend outward from the cell body (see Part A of Figure 3.2). When these fibers get close to other neurons, communication between the cells can occur. The intermixing

neuron Fundamental unit of the nervous system; nerve cell.

glial cells Cells in the nervous system that hold neurons together and help them communicate with one another.

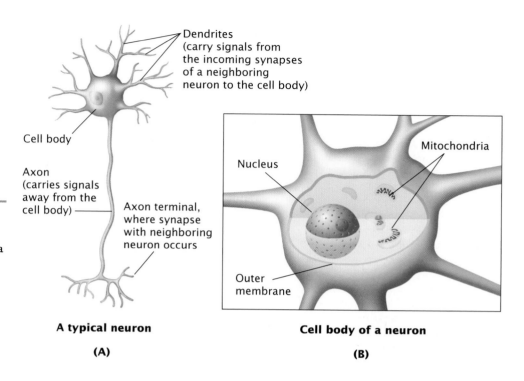

Dendrites (carry signals from the incoming synapses of a neighboring neuron to the cell body)

Cell body

Axon (carries signals away from the cell body)

Axon terminal, where synapse with neighboring neuron occurs

A typical neuron
(A)

Nucleus

Mitochondria

Outer membrane

Cell body of a neuron
(B)

FIGURE 3.2

The Neuron

Part A shows fibers extending outward from the cell body of a neuron, which is a nervous system cell. These fibers, called *axons* and *dendrites,* are among the features that make neurons unique. Part B shows an enlarged drawing of the neuron's cell body. The cell body of a neuron includes an outer membrane, a nucleus, and mitochondria.

axon   A fiber that carries signals from the body of a neuron out to where communication occurs with other neurons.

dendrite   A neuron fiber that receives signals from the axons of other neurons and carries those signals to the cell body.

synapse   The tiny gap between neurons across which they communicate.

of all these fibers with fibers from other neurons allows each neuron to be close to thousands or even hundreds of thousands of other neurons.

Two types of fibers extend from a neuron's cell body: axons and dendrites. **Axons** are the fibers that carry signals away from the cell body, out to where communication occurs with other neurons. Each neuron generally has only one axon leaving the cell body, but that one axon may have many branches. Axons can be very short or several feet long, like the axon that sends signals from your spinal cord all the way down to your big toe. **Dendrites** are the fibers that receive signals from the axons of other neurons and carry those signals to the cell body. A neuron can have many dendrites. Dendrites, too, usually have many branches. Remember that *axons* carry signals *away* from the cell body, whereas *dendrites detect* signals from other cells.

The neuron's ability to communicate efficiently also depends on two other features: the "excitable" surface membrane of some of its fibers and the tiny space between neurons, called a *synaptic gap*, or **synapse.** Let's consider how these features allow a signal to be sent rapidly from one end of a neuron to the other and from one neuron to another.

● Action Potentials

To understand how signals are sent in the nervous system, you first need to know something about nerve cell membranes and the chemicals within and outside these cells. The neuron's cell membrane is a *semipermeable* barrier, meaning that, as already mentioned, it lets some chemical molecules pass through but blocks others. Many of these molecules carry a positive or negative electrical charge. Normally, the cell pumps positively charged molecules out through its membrane, making the inside of the cell slightly more negative than the outside. In this state, the cell membrane is said to be *polarized.* Molecules with a positive charge are attracted to those with a negative charge. This attraction creates a force called an *electrochemical potential*, which drives the positively charged molecules toward the inside of the cell.

The cell membrane keeps out many of these positively charged molecules, but some are able to enter by passing through special openings, or *channels*, in the membrane. These channels are distributed along the axon and dendrites and act as gates

FIGURE 3.3

The Beginning of an Action Potential

This greatly simplified view of a polarized nerve cell shows the normally closed gates in the cell membrane. The electrochemical potential across the membrane is created because there are more positively charged molecules outside the membrane than inside. There are also more negatively charged molecules on the inside than on the outside. If stimulation causes depolarization near a particular gate, that gate may swing open, allowing positively charged molecules to rush in. This, in turn, depolarizes the neighboring region of membrane and stimulates the next gate to open, and so on down the axon. This wave of depolarization is called an *action potential*. Membrane gates allow action potentials to spread along dendrites in a similar fashion.

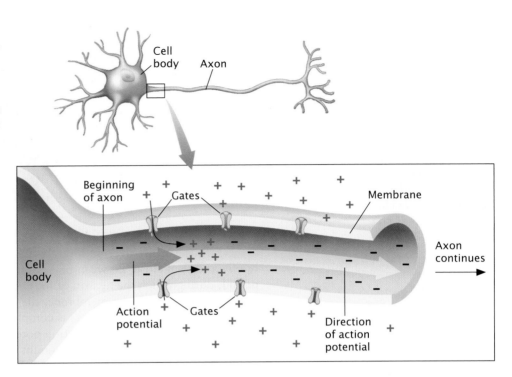

that can be opened or closed (see Figure 3.3). Normally the channels along the axon are closed, but changes in the environment around the cell can *depolarize* part of its membrane, causing the gates in that area to swing open and allowing positively charged molecules to rush in. When this happens, the next area of the axon becomes depolarized, causing the neighboring gate to open. This sequence continues, creating a wave of changes in electrochemical potential that spreads rapidly all the way down the axon.

This sudden wave of electrochemical changes in the axon is called an **action potential**. When an action potential shoots down an axon, the neuron is said to have "fired." This term is appropriate because action potentials in axons are like gunshots: The cell either fires at full strength or it does not fire at all. For many years, scientists believed that only axons are capable of generating action potentials. However, research has now revealed that action potentials also occur in dendrites (Magee & Johnston, 1997). In many neurons, action potentials beginning in the axon go in both directions—down the axon and also "backward" through the cell body and into the dendrites. Action potentials that spread into the dendrites from the cell body appear to reach some dendritic branches and not others, leading scientists to conclude that these messages may be important in strengthening particular connections between neurons that are important to learning and memory (Golding, Staff, & Spruston, 2002).

The speed of the action potential as it moves down an axon is constant for a particular cell, but in different cells that speed can range from 0.2 meters per second to 120 meters per second (about 260 miles per hour). The speed depends on the diameter of the axon—larger ones are faster—and on whether myelin is present. **Myelin** (pronounced "MY-a-lin") is a fatty substance that wraps around some axons and speeds action potentials. Larger, myelinated cells are usually found in parts of the nervous system that carry the most urgently needed information. For example, the neurons that receive information from the environment about oncoming cars, hot irons, and other dangers are fast-acting, myelinated cells. Multiple sclerosis (MS), a severe brain disorder that destroys myelin, may occur because some viruses and bacteria are very similar to components of myelin (Westall, 2006). When the MS victim's immune system attacks those pathogens, it destroys vital myelin as well, resulting in disruption of vision, speech, balance, and other important functions.

● **action potential** An abrupt wave of electrochemical changes traveling down an axon when a neuron becomes depolarized.

● **myelin** A fatty substance that wraps around some axons and increases the speed of action potentials.

FIGURE **3.4**

A Synapse

This photograph taken with an electron microscope shows part of a neural synapse magnified 50,000 times. The ending of the presynaptic cell's axon is shaded green; the green ovals are mitochondria. The red spots are neurotransmitter-containing vesicles. The synapse itself appears as the narrow gap between the presynaptic cell's axon and the dendrite of the postsynaptic cell, which is shaded blue.

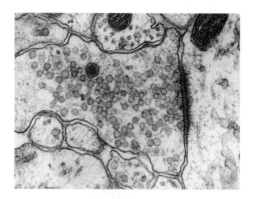

Neurons can fire over and over again because their membrane gates open only briefly and then close. Between firings there is a very short rest, called a **refractory period,** during which the neuron cannot fire. As the positively charged molecules are pumped back outside the membrane, the cell returns to its original polarized state. When this *repolarization* process is complete, the neuron can fire again. The rate of firing can vary from just a few action potentials per second to as many as 1,000 per second. Patterns of neuron firing amount to coded messages that, for example, tells us about the intensity of light or sound. We describe some of the codes used by the nervous system in the chapter on sensation.

● Synapses and Communication Between Neurons

How does an action potential fired by one neuron affect the activity of other neurons? For communication to occur between cells, a signal must be transmitted across the synapse, or gap, between neurons. Usually, the axon of one cell delivers its signals across a synapse to the dendrites of a second cell. Those dendrites, in turn, transmit the signal to their cell body, which may relay the signal down its axon to a third cell, and so on. But there can be other communication patterns, too. Axons can signal to other axons or even directly to the cell body of another neuron. And dendrites of one cell can send signals to the dendrites of other cells. These and other communication patterns allow the brain to conduct extremely complex information-processing tasks (Bullock et al., 2005).

● **Neurotransmitters** Communication between neurons across the synapse relies first on chemical messengers called **neurotransmitters.** These chemicals are usually stored in numerous little "bags," called *vesicles*, at the tips of axons (see Figure 3.4). When an action potential reaches the end of an axon, a neurotransmitter is released into the synapse, where it spreads to reach the next, or *postsynaptic*, cell (see Figure 3.5). (In the less common case of dendrite-to-dendrite communication, neurotransmitters are released by unknown mechanisms; Pape, Munsch, & Budde, 2004).

When they reach the membrane of the postsynaptic cell, neurotransmitters attach to proteins called **receptors.** Like a puzzle piece fitting into its proper place, a neurotransmitter snugly fits, or "binds" to, its own receptors but not to receptors for other neurotransmitters (again, see Figure 3.5). Although each receptor "recognizes" only one type of neurotransmitter, each neurotransmitter type can bind to several different receptor types. As a result, the same neurotransmitter can have different effects depending on the type of receptor to which it binds.

When a neurotransmitter binds to a receptor, it stimulates channels in the membrane of the postsynaptic cell to open, allowing charged molecules to flow in or out. The flow of these charged molecules into and out of the postsynaptic cell produces a change in its membrane potential. So the *chemical* signal that crosses the synapse creates an *electrochemical* signal in the postsynaptic cell.

● **refractory period** A short rest period between action potentials.

● **neurotransmitters** Chemicals that assist in the transfer of signals from one neuron to another.

● **receptors** Sites on the surface of a cell that allow only one type of neurotransmitter to fit into them, triggering a chemical response that may lead to an action potential.

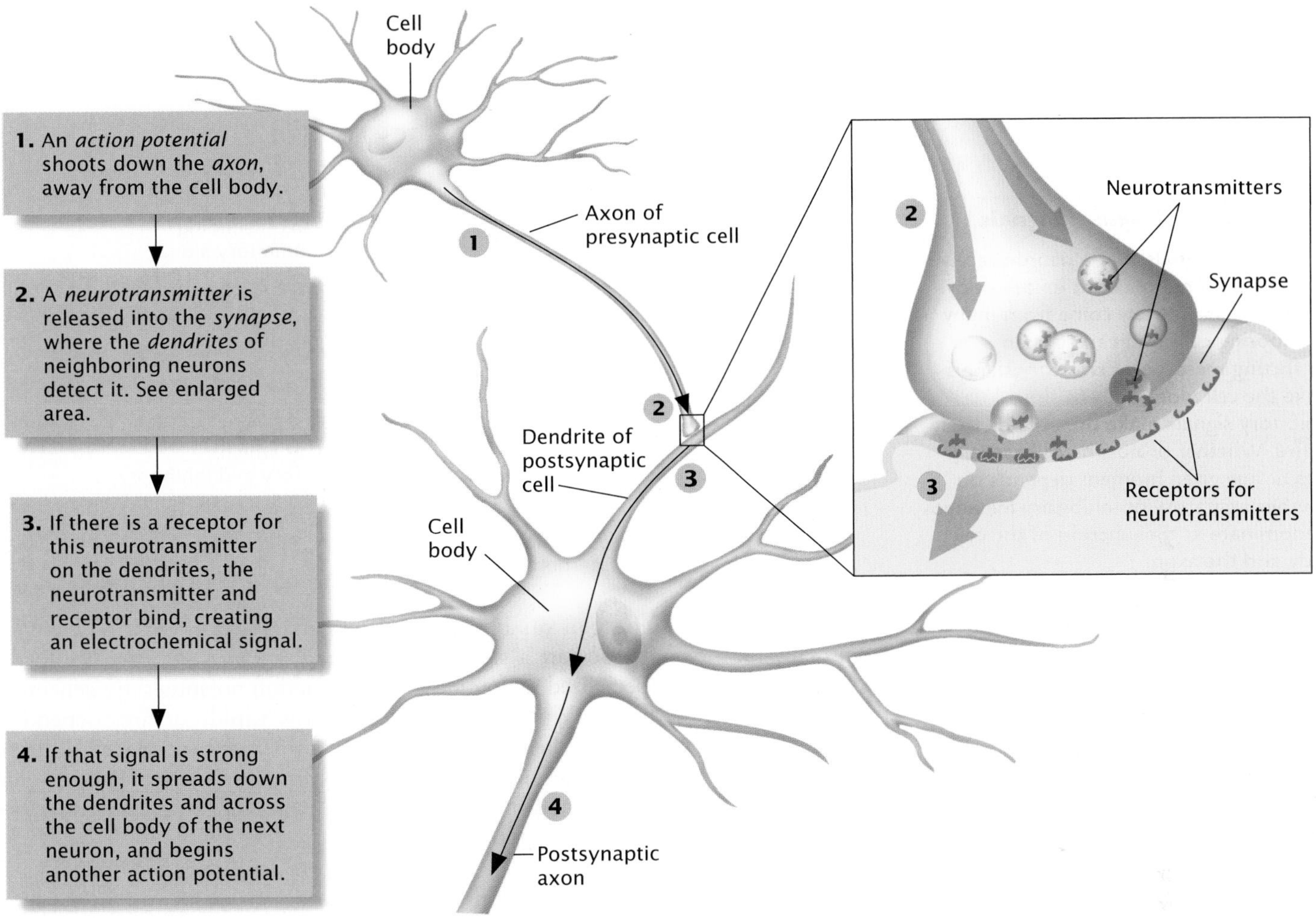

1. An *action potential* shoots down the *axon*, away from the cell body.

2. A *neurotransmitter* is released into the *synapse*, where the *dendrites* of neighboring neurons detect it. See enlarged area.

3. If there is a receptor for this neurotransmitter on the dendrites, the neurotransmitter and receptor bind, creating an electrochemical signal.

4. If that signal is strong enough, it spreads down the dendrites and across the cell body of the next neuron, and begins another action potential.

Cell body

Axon of presynaptic cell

Dendrite of postsynaptic cell

Cell body

Postsynaptic axon

Neurotransmitters

Synapse

Receptors for neurotransmitters

FIGURE 3.5
Communication Between Neurons

When a neuron fires, an action potential shoots to the end of its axon, triggering the release of a neurotransmitter into the synapse. Neurotransmitters influence neighboring cells by stimulating special receptors on the surface of those cells' membranes. Each type of receptor receives only one type of neurotransmitter; the two fit together like puzzle pieces or like a lock and its key. As shown here, when stimulated by their neurotransmitter, a cell's receptors can help generate a wave of depolarization in that cell's dendrites, making it more likely to fire. Later, we'll see that a cell's receptors can also receive signals that have the opposite effect, making the cell less likely to fire.

postsynaptic potential The change in the membrane potential of a neuron that has received stimulation from another neuron.

excitatory postsynaptic potential A postsynaptic potential that depolarizes the neuronal membrane, making the cell more likely to fire an action potential.

inhibitory postsynaptic potential A postsynaptic potential that hyperpolarizes the neuronal membrane, making a cell less likely to fire an action potential.

● **Excitatory and Inhibitory Signals** The change that takes place in the membrane potential of the postsynaptic cell is called the **postsynaptic potential**. The change can make the cell either more likely or less likely to fire. For example, if positively charged molecules of chemicals such as sodium or calcium flow *into* the neuron, it becomes slightly less polarized. Because this *depolarization* of the membrane can lead the neuron to fire an action potential, a depolarizing postsynaptic potential is called an **excitatory postsynaptic potential**, or EPSP. However, if positively charged molecules (such as potassium) flow *out* of the neuron, or if negatively charged molecules flow in, the neuron becomes slightly *more* polarized. This *hyperpolarization* makes it less likely that the neuron will fire an action potential. For this reason, a hyperpolarizing postsynaptic potential is called an **inhibitory postsynaptic potential**, or IPSP.

The postsynaptic potential spreads along the membrane of the postsynaptic cell. But unlike the action potential in an axon, which remains at a constant strength, the postsynaptic potential fades as it goes along. Usually, it is not strong enough to pass all the way along the dendrite and through the cell body to the axon, so a single EPSP will not cause a neuron to fire. However, each neuron is constantly receiving EPSPs and

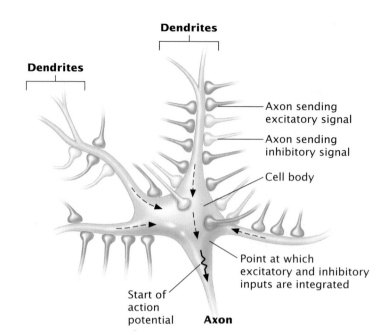

FIGURE 3.6

Integration of Neural Signals

Most of the signals that a neuron receives arrive at its dendrites or at its cell body. These signals typically come from many neighboring cells and can contain conflicting messages. Excitatory signals make the cell more likely to fire. Inhibitory signals make the cell less likely to fire. Whether or not the cell actually fires at any given moment depends on whether excitatory or inhibitory messages predominate at the junction of the cell body and the axon.

A Damaged Nervous System If axons, dendrites, or other components of the nervous system are damaged or disordered, serious problems can result. The spinal cord injury that this woman suffered in a car accident cut the neural communication lines that had allowed her to feel and move the lower part of her body.

IPSPs. The combined effect of rapidly repeated potentials—or of potentials coming from many locations—can create a signal strong enough to reach the junction of the axon and cell body, a specialized region in which new action potentials are generated.

Whether or not the postsynaptic cell fires and how rapidly it fires depend on whether, at a given moment, there are more excitatory ("fire") or more inhibitory ("don't fire") signals from other neurons at this junction (see Figure 3.6). So as neurotransmitters transfer information across many neurons, each neuron constantly integrates or processes this information.

Neurotransmitters are involved in every aspect of behavior and mental processes, as you will see later in this chapter and in other chapters, too. In the chapter on sensation, for example, we describe some of the neurotransmitters used in pathways that convey pain messages throughout the brain and spinal cord. In the consciousness chapter, we describe how neurotransmitters are affected by alcohol and illegal drugs. In the chapter on psychological disorders, we discuss the role that neurotransmitters play in schizophrenia and depression, and in the chapter on the treatment of psychological disorders, we consider how prescription drugs act on neurotransmitters to reduce the symptoms of those disorders. Neurotransmitters are affected by many other chemicals, too, from the nerve agents used in biological weapons to the Botox used in anti-wrinkle treatments.

● Organization and Functions of the Nervous System

Impressive as individual neurons are (see "In Review: Neurons, Neurotransmitters, and Receptors"), we can best understand their functions by looking at how they operate in groups. In the brain and spinal cord, neurons are organized into groups called **neural networks.** Many neurons in a network are closely connected, sending axons to the dendrites of many other neurons in the network. Signals from one network also go to other networks, and small networks are organized into bigger collections. By studying these networks, neuroscientists have begun to see that the nervous system conveys information not so much by the activity of single neurons sending single messages with a particular meaning but by the activity of groups of neurons firing together in varying combinations. So the same neurons may be involved in producing different patterns of behavior, depending on which combinations of them are active (Destexhe & Marder, 2004).

● **neural network** Neurons that operate together to perform complex functions.

in review — Neurons, Neurotransmitters, and Receptors

Part	Function	Type of Signal Carried
Axon	Carries signals away from the cell body	The action potential, an all-or-nothing electrochemical signal that shoots down the axon to vesicles at the tip of the axon, releasing neurotransmitters
Dendrite	Detects and carries signals to the cell body	The postsynaptic potential, an electrochemical signal moving toward the cell body
Synapse	Provides an area for the transfer of signals between neurons, usually between the axon of one cell and the dendrite of another	Chemicals that cross the synapse and reach receptors on another cell
Neurotransmitter	A chemical released by one cell that binds to the receptors on another cell	A chemical message telling the next cell to fire or not to fire its own action potential
Receptor	Protein on the cell membrane that receives chemical signals	Recognizes certain neurotransmitters, thus allowing it to begin a postsynaptic potential in the dendrite

The groups of neurons in the nervous system that provide information about the environment are known as the senses, or **sensory systems.** These systems—including hearing, vision, taste, smell, and touch—are described in the chapter on sensation. Integration and processing of information occur mainly in the brain. Output flows through **motor systems,** which are the parts of the nervous system that influence muscles and other organs to respond to the environment.

The nervous system has two major divisions, which work together: the peripheral nervous system and the central nervous system (see Figure 3.7). The **peripheral nervous system (PNS),** which includes all of the nervous system that is not housed in bone, carries out sensory and motor functions. The **central nervous system (CNS)** is the part encased in bone. It includes the brain, which is inside the skull, and the spinal cord, which is inside the spinal column (backbone). The CNS is often called the "central executive" of the body because information is usually sent to the CNS to be processed and acted on. Let's take a closer look at these divisions of the nervous system.

The Peripheral Nervous System: Keeping in Touch with the World

sensory systems The parts of the nervous system that provide information about the environment.

motor systems The parts of the nervous system that influence muscles and other organs to respond to the environment in some way.

peripheral nervous system The parts of the nervous system not housed in bone.

central nervous system The parts of the nervous system encased in bone, including the brain and the spinal cord.

somatic nervous system The subsystem of the peripheral nervous system that transmits information from the senses to the central nervous system and carries signals from the central nervous system to the muscles.

As shown in Figure 3.7, the peripheral nervous system has two components, each of which performs both sensory and motor functions.

● The Somatic Nervous System

The first of these components is the **somatic nervous system,** which transmits information from the senses to the CNS and carries signals from the CNS to the muscles that move the skeleton. *Sensory neurons* bring information into the brain. *Motor neurons* carry information from the brain to direct motion. For example, imagine that you are at the beach. You feel the warmth of the sun and smell the ocean because sensory neurons in your somatic nervous system take in these pieces of sensory information and send them to the central nervous system for processing. And when you decide it is time to turn over, sit up, or put on some more sunscreen, your brain sends movement instructions through motor neurons in the somatic nervous system. These motor neurons extend from your spinal cord to your muscles, where the release of a neurotransmitter onto them causes the muscles to contract.

Organization of the Nervous System

The brain and spinal cord make up the bone-encased central nervous system (CNS), the body's central information processor, decision maker, and director of actions. The peripheral nervous system, which is not housed in bone, functions mainly to carry messages. The somatic subsystem of the peripheral nervous system transmits information to the CNS from the outside world and conveys instructions from the CNS to the muscles. The autonomic subsystem conveys messages from the CNS that alter the activity of organs and glands, and it sends information about that activity back to the brain.

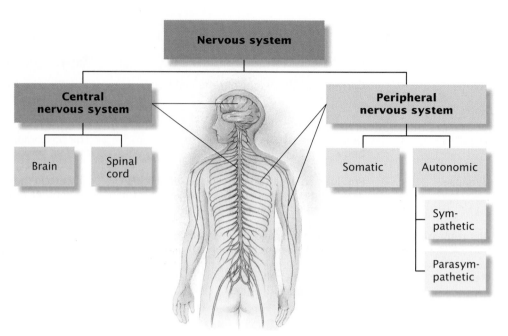

The Autonomic Nervous System

The second component of the peripheral nervous system, the **autonomic nervous system,** carries messages back and forth between the CNS and the heart, lungs, and other organs and glands. These messages increase or decrease the activity of the organs and glands to meet varying demands placed on the body. For example, neural connections from your liver to your brain influence how much fat you burn and how much you store (Uno et al., 2006). And as you lie on the beach, it is your autonomic nervous system that makes your heart beat a little faster when an attractive person walks by and smiles at you.

The name *autonomic* means "autonomous" and suggests independent operation. This term is appropriate because, although the autonomic nervous system is influenced by the brain, it controls activities that are normally outside of conscious control, such as digestion and perspiration (sweating). The autonomic nervous system exercises this control through its two divisions: the sympathetic and parasympathetic branches. Generally, the *sympathetic system* mobilizes the body for action in the face of stress. The responses that result from intense activity of the sympathetic system are collectively referred to as the *fight-or-flight syndrome.* The *parasympathetic system* regulates the body's energy-conserving functions. The two branches of the autonomic nervous system often create opposite effects. For example, the sympathetic nervous system can make your heart beat faster, whereas the parasympathetic nervous system can slow it down.

The functions of the autonomic nervous system may not get star billing, but you would miss them if they were gone. Just as a race-car driver is nothing without a good pit crew, the somatic nervous system depends on the autonomic nervous system to get its job done. For example, when you want to move your muscles, you create a demand for energy. The autonomic nervous system fills the bill by increasing sugar fuels in the bloodstream. If you decide to stand up, you need increased blood pressure so that your blood does not flow out of your brain and settle in your legs. Again, the autonomic nervous system makes the adjustment. Disorders of the autonomic nervous system can make people sweat uncontrollably or faint whenever they stand up; they can also lead

● **autonomic nervous system** A subsystem of the peripheral nervous system that carries messages between the central nervous system and the heart, lungs, and other organs and glands.

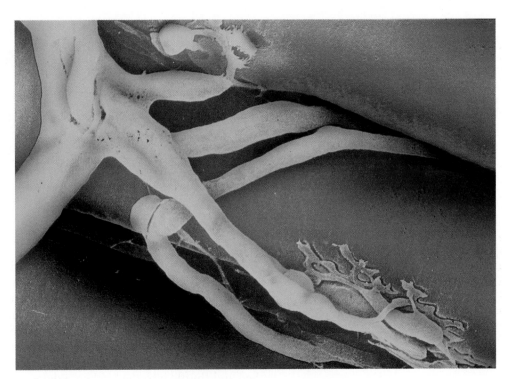

The Neuromuscular Junction When nerve cells (shown here as green fibers) release neurotransmitters onto muscle tissue, the muscle contracts. Much of what we know about neurotransmitters was discovered in laboratory studies of this "neuromuscular junction," especially in the hind legs of frogs. At the neuromuscular junction, the action of a neurotransmitter allows a quick response that can mean the difference between life and death, for a frog or any other animal, including humans.

to other problems, such as an inability to have sex. We examine the autonomic nervous system in more detail in the chapter on motivation and emotion.

The Central Nervous System: Making Sense of the World

The amazing speed and efficiency of the neural networks that make up the central nervous system—the brain and spinal cord—have prompted many people to compare it to the central processor in a computer. In fact, to better understand how human and other brains work and how they relate to sensory and motor systems, *computational neuroscientists* have created neural network models on computers (Koch & Davis, 1994). Figure 3.8 shows an example of how the three components of the nervous system (input, processing, and output) might be represented in a neural network model. Notice that input simultaneously activates several paths in the network, so information is processed in various places at the same time. Accordingly, the activity of these models is described as *parallel distributed processing*. In the chapters on sensation, perception, learning, and memory, we describe how parallel distributed processing often characterizes the activity of the brain.

Neural network models are neatly laid out like computer circuits or the carefully planned streets of a new suburb, but the flesh-and-blood central nervous system is far more difficult to follow. In fact, the CNS looks more like Boston or London, with distinct neighborhoods, winding back streets, and multilaned highways. Its "neighborhoods" are collections of neuronal cell bodies called **nuclei**. The "highways" of the central nervous system are made up of axons that travel together in bundles called **fiber tracts** or **pathways**. Like a freeway ramp, the axon from a given cell may merge with and leave fiber tracts, and it may send branches into other tracts. The pathways travel from one nucleus to other nuclei, and scientists have learned much about how the brain works by tracing the connections among nuclei. To begin our description of some of these nuclei and anatomical connections, let's consider a practical example of nervous system functioning.

nuclei Collections of nerve cell bodies in the central nervous system.

fiber tracts/pathways Axons in the central nervous system that travel together in bundles.

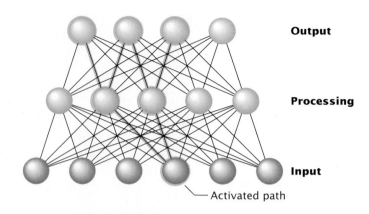

FIGURE **3.8**

A Neural Network Model

This simple computer-based neural network model includes an input layer, a processing layer, and an output layer. Notice that each element in each layer is connected to every other element in each of the other layers. As in the brain itself, these connections can be either excitatory or inhibitory, and the strength of the connections between elements can be modified depending on the results of the output. In other words, a computerized neural network model has the capacity to learn. We discuss examples of such "artificial intelligence" systems in the chapter on cognition and language.

At 6 A.M., your alarm goes off. The day begins innocently enough with what appears to be a simple case of information processing. Input in the form of sound from the alarm clock is received by your ears, which convert the sound into neural signals that reach your brain. Your brain compares these signals with previous experiences stored in memory and correctly associates the sound with "alarm clock." However, your output is somewhat impaired because your brain's activity has not yet reached the waking state. It directs your muscles poorly: You get out of bed and shuffle into the kitchen, where, in your drowsy condition, you touch a hot burner as you reach for the coffeepot. Now things get more lively. Heat energy activates sensory neurons in your fingers, and action potentials flash along fiber tracts going into the spinal cord.

The Spinal Cord

The **spinal cord** receives signals from the senses, including pain and touch from the fingertips, and relays those signals to the brain through fibers within the cord. Neurons in the spinal cord also carry signals downward, from the brain to the muscles. In addition, cells of the spinal cord can direct some simple behaviors without instructions from the brain. These behaviors are called **reflexes** because the response to an incoming signal is directly "reflected" back out (see Figure 3.9).

For example, when you touched that hot burner, impulses from sensory neurons in your fingers reflexively activated motor neurons, which caused muscles in your arm to contract and quickly withdraw your hand. Because spinal reflexes like this one include few time-consuming synaptic links, they are very fast. And because spinal reflexes occur without instructions from the brain, they are considered involuntary. Still, they do send action potentials along fiber tracts going to the brain. So you officially "know" you have been burned a fraction of a second after your reflex got you out of trouble.

The story does not end there, however. When a simple reflex set off by touching something hot causes one set of arm muscles to contract, an opposing set of muscles relaxes. If this did not happen, the arm would go rigid. Furthermore, muscles have receptors that send impulses to the spinal cord to let it know how extended they are, so that a reflex pathway can adjust the muscle contraction to allow smooth movement. This is an example of a *feedback system*, a series of processes in which information about the consequences of an action goes back to the source of the action so that adjustments can be made.

In the spinal cord, sensory neurons are called *afferent* neurons and motor neurons are called *efferent* neurons, because *afferent* means "coming toward" and *efferent* means "going away." To remember these terms, notice that *afferent* and *approach* both begin with *a; efferent* and *exit* both begin with *e.*

spinal cord The part of the central nervous system within the spinal column that relays signals from peripheral senses to the brain and conveys messages from the brain to the rest of the body.

reflex Involuntary, unlearned reaction in the form of swift, automatic, and finely coordinated movements in response to external stimuli.

FIGURE 3.9

A Reflex Pathway

TRY THIS ⚙ Sit on a chair, cross one leg over the other, and then use the handle of a butter knife or some other solid object to gently tap your top knee, just below the kneecap, until you get a "knee jerk" reaction. Tapping your knee at just the right spot sets off an almost instantaneous sequence of events that begins with stimulation of sensory neurons that respond to stretch. When those neurons fire, their axons, which end within the spinal cord, cause spinal neurons to fire. This, in turn, stimulates the firing of motor neurons with axons ending in your thigh muscles. The result is a contraction of those muscles and a kicking of the lower leg and foot. Information about the knee tap and about what the leg has done also goes to your cerebral cortex, but the reflex is completed without waiting for guidance from the brain.

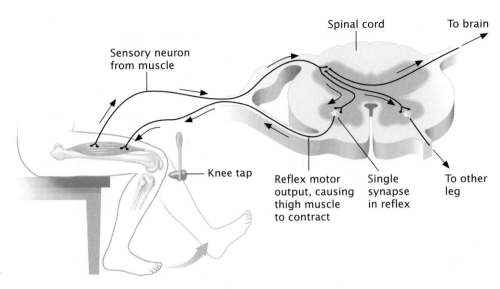

● The Brain

When pain messages from that hot burner reach your brain, you don't become aware just of being burned. You might also realize that you have burned yourself twice before in the past week and get annoyed at your own carelessness. The brain is the most complex element in the central nervous system, and it is your brain's astonishing capacity for information processing that allows you to have these thoughts and feelings. A variety of modern brain-scanning techniques, combined with some older ones, have allowed neuroscientists to learn more than ever before about the workings of the human brain (Miller, 2003; see Table 3.1).

Each technique can indirectly measure the activity of neurons firing, and each has different advantages and disadvantages. One of the earliest of these techniques, called the *electroencephalograph (EEG)*, measures general electrical activity of the brain. Electrodes are pasted on the scalp to detect the electrical fields resulting from the activity of billions of neurons. This tool can associate rapidly changing electrical activity with changes in the activity of the brain, but it cannot tell us exactly where the active cells are.

A newer technique, called the *PET scan*, can locate cell activity by recording where substances such as glucose or other cellular fuels become concentrated after being made radioactive and injected into the bloodstream. *PET* stands for *positron emission tomography*. It records images from the brain that indicate the location of the radioactivity as the brain performs various tasks. For instance, PET studies have revealed that specific brain regions are activated when we look at fearful facial expressions (Wharton et al., 2000) and which neurotransmitter receptors are stimulated when a smoker inhales on a cigarette (Brody et al., 2006). PET scans can tell us a lot about where changes in brain activity occur, but they reveal only crude information about the details of the brain's physical structure.

A detailed structural picture of the brain can be seen, however, using *magnetic resonance imaging*, or *MRI*. MRI exposes the brain to a magnetic field and measures the resulting radio frequency waves to get amazingly clear pictures of the brain's anatomical details (see Figure 3.10). *Functional MRI*, or *fMRI* (Figure 3.11), combines the advantages of PET and MRI and is capable of detecting changes in blood flow that reflect ongoing changes in the activity of neurons—providing a sort of "moving picture" of the brain. The newest techniques offer

TABLE **3.1**	Techniques for Studying Human Brain Function and Structure	
Technique	**What It Shows**	**Advantages (+) and Disadvantages (−)**
EEG (electroencephalograph) Multiple electrodes are pasted to the outside of the head	Lines that chart the summated electrical fields resulting from the activity of billions of neurons	+ Detects very rapid changes in electrical activity, allowing analysis of stages of cognitive processing − Provides poor spatial resolution of the source of electrical activity; EEG is sometimes combined with magnetoencephalography (MEG), which localizes electrical activity by measuring magnetic fields associated with it
PET (positron emission tomography) and SPECT (single-photon emission computed tomography) Positrons and photons are emissions from radioactive substances	An image of the amount and localization of any molecule that can be injected in radioactive form, such as neurotransmitters, drugs, or tracers for blood flow or glucose use (which indicates specific changes in neuronal activity)	+ Allows functional and biochemical studies + Provides visual image corresponding to anatomy − Requires exposure to low levels of radioactivity − Provides spatial resolution better than that of EEG but poorer than that of MRI − Cannot follow rapid changes (faster than 30 seconds)
MRI (magnetic resonance imaging) Exposes the brain to a magnetic field and measures radio frequency waves	Traditional MRI provides high-resolution image of brain anatomy. Functional MRI (fMRI) provides images of changes in blood flow (which indicate specific changes in neural activity). A new variant, diffusion tensor imaging (DTI), shows water flow in neural fibers, thus revealing the "wiring diagram" of neural connections in the brain.	+ Requires no exposure to radioactivity + Provides high spatial resolution of anatomical details (< 1 mm) + Provides high temporal resolution (< 1/10 second)
TMS (transcranial magnetic stimulation) Temporarily disrupts electrical activity of a small region of brain by exposing it to an intense magnetic field	Normal function of a particular brain region can be studied by observing changes after TMS is applied to a specific location.	+ Shows which brain regions are necessary for given tasks − Long-term safety not well established

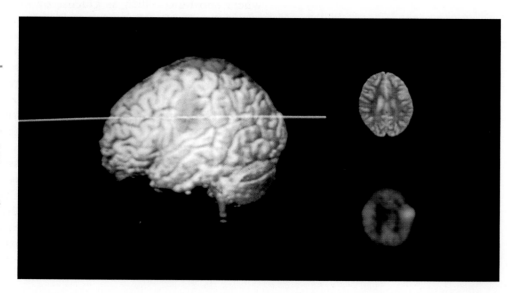

FIGURE **3.10**

Combining a PET Scan and Magnetic Resonance Imaging

Researchers have superimposed images from PET scans and MRI to construct a three-dimensional view of the living brain. Here you can see the brain of a young girl with epilepsy. The picture of the outer surface of the brain is from the MRI. The pink area is from the PET scan and shows the source of epileptic activity. The images at the right are the MRI and PET images at one plane, or "slice," through the brain (indicated by the line on the brain at the left).

FIGURE 3.11

Linking Eastern Medicine and Western Neuroscience Through Functional MRI

Scientists are using MRI to investigate the role of the brain in the effects of acupuncture (Cho et al., 1998), an ancient Asian medical practice in which physical disorders are treated by stimulating specific skin locations with needles. Most acupuncture points are far from the organ being treated. For example, vision problems are treated by inserting needles at "acupoints" in the foot. This may sound far-fetched, but MRI shows that visual information entering the eyes and needle stimulation of certain acupoints in the foot do activate similar areas of the brain. The MRI image on the left was produced by visual stimuli; the one on the right shows activation of the same brain area in response to acupuncture at a certain spot in the foot. Acupoints in the foot are located near nerves, but the pathways to specific parts of the brain have not been charted.

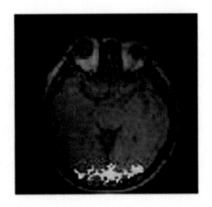
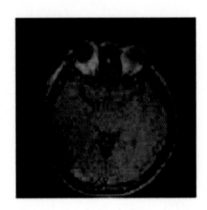

even deeper insight into brain activity, structure, and functioning. These techniques include a variant on fMRI called *diffusion tensor imaging (DTI)*, which traces activity of axon pathways, as well as a procedure called *transcranial magnetic stimulation (TMS)*, which temporarily disrupts the function of a particular part of the brain. TMS can be combined with MRI to further refine localization of brain activity, and it may also have unexpected value in the treatment of depression and migraine headaches (Rumi et al., 2005).

THINKING CRITICALLY What Can fMRI Tell Us About Behavior and Mental Processes?

A picture may be worth a thousand words, but the pictures of brain activity offered by fMRI are generating millions of them. As of 2007, more than 7,500 scientific articles have discussed the results of fMRI scans taken while people engaged in various kinds of thinking or experienced various emotions. Neuroscientists who use brain imaging techniques are now to be found in psychology departments around the world, and as described in other chapters, their work is changing the research landscape in cognitive, social, and abnormal psychology. Excitement over fMRI is not confined to scientists. Popular and scientific magazines routinely carry fMRI pictures that appear to "show" people's thoughts and feelings as they happen.

■ What am I being asked to believe or accept?

In the early 1800s, similar excitement surrounded *phrenology*, a technique that involved feeling bumps and depressions on the skull. It was claimed that these contours reflect the size of twenty-seven structures on the brain's surface that determine personality traits, mental abilities, talents, and other characteristics. Although wildly popular with the public (Benjamin & Baker, 2004), phrenology did not survive the critical thinking of nineteenth-century scientists, and the technique has long been discredited. Today, some scientists wonder whether fMRI is a twenty-first-century version of phrenology, at least in the sense that their colleagues might be accepting its value too readily. These scientists point out that although fMRI images can indicate where brain activity occurs as people think and experience emotion, there is no guarantee that this activity is actually *causing* the associated thoughts and feelings (Aldridge, 2005). Questions are also being raised about the assumption that particular thought processes or emotions occur in a particular brain structure, or set of structures. It is easy to talk about "thinking" or "attention," but these psychological terms might not correspond to specific biological processes that can be isolated and located by *any* technology. In short, critics claim that the results of fMRI scans can be misleading and that they don't necessarily tell us much about how the mind works (Uttal, 2003). Perhaps it would be better to focus on *how* the brain produces thoughts and feelings instead of searching for their locations.

■ Is there evidence available to support the claim?

When the participant in an fRMI experiment thinks or feels something, you can actually see the colors in the brain scan change, much like the color changes you see on weather radar as a rainstorm intensifies or weakens. Looking at an fMRI scan, you get a clear impression that the brain areas that "light up" when a person experiences an emotion or performs a mental task are the ones involved in that emotion or task (see Figure 1.1 in the chapter on introducing psychology).

These scans are not as precise as they seem, though, because fMRI doesn't directly measure brain cell activity. The colors seen in an fMRI scan reflect instead the flow of blood in the brain, and the amount of oxygen the blood is carrying. Changes in blood flow and blood oxygen are *related* to changes in the firing rates of neurons, but the relationship is complex and not yet fully understood (Buxton et al., 2004). Further, when brain cells process information, their firing rate may either increase or decrease (Gonsalves et al., 2005). If the increases and decreases in a particular brain region happen to cancel each other out, an fMRI scan will miss the neuronal activity taking place in that region. In fact, compared to the direct measurement of brain cell activity that can be done in research with animals, fMRI technology is still rather crude. It takes coordinated changes in millions of neurons to produce a detectible change in the fMRI signal.

Critics also argue that the results of fMRI research can depend too much on how experimenters choose to interpret them. In a typical fMRI experiment, participants are shown some kind of display, such as pairs of photos, and asked to perform various tasks. One task might be to press a button if the photos are exactly the same. A second task might be to press the button if objects in the photos are arranged in the same way. In this second task, a participant should press the button if one photo shows, say, a short man standing to the left of a tall woman, and the other photo shows a small dog standing to the left of a giraffe. Both versions of the task require the participant to compare two images, but only the second of them requires considering whether things that look different are actually similar in some way. The fMRI scans taken during these tasks might show certain brain areas "lighting up" only during the second task. If so, the researcher would suggest that those areas are involved in recognizing *analogies*, or the similarities between apparently different things (Wharton et al., 2000). The researcher would base this conclusion on a computer program that first compares fMRI scans taken during two tasks, then subtracts all the "lighted" areas that are the same in both scans, and keeps only those that are different. But what the computer classifies as "different" depends on a rule that is set by the experimenter. If the experimenter programs the computer to display only big differences between the scans, not many "lit up" areas will remain after the comparison process. But if even tiny differences are allowed to count as "different," many more "lighted" areas will remain after the subtraction process. In our example, then, there could be large or small areas apparently associated with recognizing analogies, all depending on a rule set by the researcher.

These problems aside, critics wonder what it really means when fMRI research shows that certain brain areas appear activated during certain kinds of tasks or experiences. Their concern focuses on studies such as one from the new field of *neuroeconomics* suggesting that excessive activity in a particular brain area leads to bad investment decisions (Kuhnen & Knutson, 2005). Another fMRI study claimed to show the "neural basis of romantic love." In this study, investigators scanned people's brains as they looked at pictures of their romantic partner and compared these

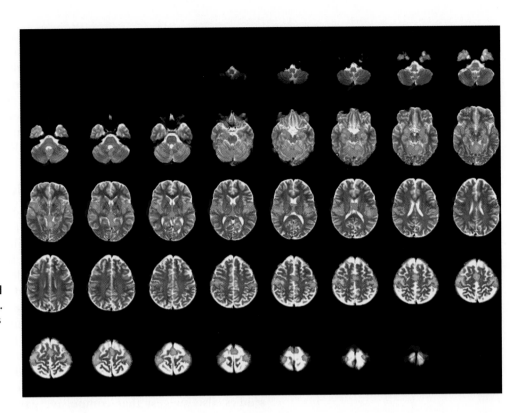

Exploring Brain Functions with fMRI
As a research participant performs a mental task, a functional magnetic resonance imaging scanner records blood flow and blood oxygen levels in her brain. The resulting computer analysis shows as "lit up" areas the parts of the brain that appear to be activated during the task, but critics doubt that fMRI scanning is as clear or accurate as its proponents suggest.

scans to those taken while the same people viewed a nonromantic friend (Bartels & Zeki, 2000). According to the "difference" rule established by the experimenters, four brain areas were more active when viewing a romantic loved one than when viewing a friend. But does this result tell us anything about how or why these areas became active, or what results this activity might have? In other words, do we now know more about love? Critics of fMRI would say no.

■ Can that evidence be interpreted another way?

Supporters of fMRI disagree. They believe that the colorful areas seen on fMRI scans can provide vital new information that will eventually allow scientists to answer important questions about behavior and mental processes. They would point, for example, to fMRI research on brain mechanisms that help us to appreciate what other people are feeling—that is, to experience empathy—and to learn by watching others.

These *mirror neuron mechanisms* were discovered accidentally by scientists who had been using surgical techniques to directly record the activity of neurons in monkeys' brains (Rizzolatti et al., 1996). They found that neurons in an area called F5 are activated not only when a monkey plans to reach for an object, such as a peanut, but also if the monkey sees *an experimenter* reach for a peanut! After fMRI scanning became available, researchers could begin looking for mirror mechanisms in the human brain. And in fact some of the mirror systems they found in humans correspond to the F5 region in monkeys (Rizzolatti & Arbib, 1998). One of them is called *Broca's area* and, as described later, is an important component of our ability to speak. It makes sense that Broca's area contains a mirror mechanism because language is a skill that we learn partly by imitation. The new fMRI findings suggest that Broca's area may also be important for many other skills that involve imitation. One recent study found that this area "lights up" when a guitar student learns chords by watching a professional guitarist (Buccino et al., 2004). Other fMRI research has found that mirror systems in other parts of the brain become active when a person sees someone experiencing emotion. For example, the brain area that is activated when you experience disgust (from the smell of rotten eggs, for example) is also activated if you see a video in which someone else reacts to a smell with disgust (Wicker et al., 2003).

So fMRI can be uniquely useful, say its defenders. Without it, research on mirror neurons in humans could not have taken place. And because of it, we have evidence that the experience of empathy comes about because seeing the actions and emotions of others activates the same brain regions that would be active if we were doing or feeling the same things ourselves. Some fMRI studies have also found that malfunctioning mirror mechanisms are associated with the impaired language development, imitative skills, and empathy seen in children diagnosed with autistic disorder (Dapretto et al., 2006; Oberman & Ramachandran, 2007; see the chapter on psychological disorders).

■ What evidence would help to evaluate the alternatives?

As technology continues to be refined, the quality of fMRI scans will continue to improve, giving us ever better images of where brain activity is taking place. But the value of this scanning technology will depend on a better understanding of what it can and cannot tell us about how brain activity is related to behavior and mental processes. We also need more evidence about correlation and causation in fMRI research. For example, a recent study conducted fMRI scans on compulsive gamblers as they played a simple guessing game (Reuter et al., 2005). When they won the game, these people showed an unusually small amount of activity in a brain area that is normally activated by the experience of rewards, or pleasure. Noting the correlation between compulsive gambling and lower-than-normal activity in the reward area, the researchers suggested that an abnormality in the brain's reward mechanisms might be responsible for gambling addiction. But case studies also suggest that compulsive gambling appears in people taking a prescription drug that *increases* activity in reward areas—and that the gambling stops when the drug is discontinued (Dodd et al., 2005; Tippmann-Piekert et al., 2007). As noted in the chapter on introducing psychology, correlation does not guarantee causation. Is the brain activity reflected in fMRI scans causing the thoughts and feelings taking place during the scanning process? Possibly, but those thoughts and feelings might themselves be caused *by* activity elsewhere in the brain that affects the areas being scanned.

Reaching an understanding about questions like these will require continuing debate and dialog between those who dismiss fMRI and those who sing its praises. To make this interaction easier, a group of government agencies and private foundations has recently funded an fMRI Data Center (**www.fmridc.org/f/fmridc**). This facility stores information from fMRI experiments and makes it available to both critics and supporters of fMRI, who can review the research data, conduct their own analyses, and offer their own interpretations. Having access to an ever-growing database such as this will no doubt help scientists get the most out of fMRI technology while also helping each other to avoid either overstating or underestimating the meaning of fMRI research.

■ What conclusions are most reasonable?

When the EEG was invented nearly a 100 years ago, scientists had their first glimpse of brain cell activity, as reflected in the "brain waves" traced on a long sheet of paper rolling from the EEG machine (see Figure 9.5). To many of these scientists, EEG must have seemed a golden gateway to an understanding of the brain and its relationship to behavior and mental processes. EEG has, in fact, helped to advance knowledge of the brain, but it certainly didn't solve all of its mysteries. When all is said and done, the same will probably be true of fMRI. It is an exciting new tool, and it offers previously undreamed of images of the structure and functioning of the brain, but it is unlikely on its own to explain just how the brain creates our behavior and mental processes. It seems reasonable to conclude, then, that those who question the use of fMRI to study psychological processes are right in calling for a careful analysis of the value of this important high-tech tool. ■

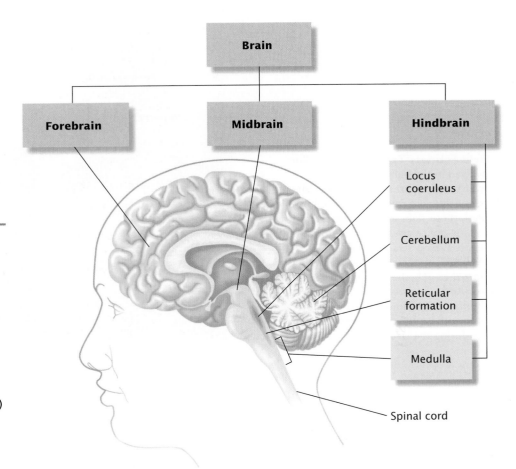

FIGURE 3.12

Major Structures of the Brain (with Hindbrain Highlighted)

This side view of a section cut down the middle of the human brain reveals the forebrain, midbrain, hindbrain, and spinal cord. Many of these subdivisions do not have clear-cut borders, because they are all interconnected by fiber tracts. The anatomy of the mammalian brain reflects its evolution over millions of years. Newer structures (such as the cerebral cortex, which is the outer surface of the forebrain) that handle higher mental functions were built on older ones (such as the medulla) that coordinate heart rate, breathing, and other more basic functions.

- **hindbrain**   An extension of the spinal cord contained inside the skull where nuclei control blood pressure, heart rate, breathing, and other vital functions.

- **medulla**   An area in the hindbrain that controls blood pressure, heart rate, breathing, and other vital functions.

- **reticular formation**   A network of cells and fibers threaded throughout the hindbrain and midbrain that alters the activity of the rest of the brain.

Although the meaning of fMRI data will remain a subject for debate, there is no doubt that brain scanning techniques in general have opened new frontiers for biological psychology, neuroscience, and medicine. Much of our growing understanding of how and why behavior and mental processes occur is coming from research with these techniques (Coltheart, 2006). Let's explore some of the structures they have highlighted, starting with the brain's three major subdivisions: the hindbrain, the midbrain, and the forebrain.

● **The Hindbrain**   As you can see in Figure 3.12, the **hindbrain** lies just inside the skull, and is actually a continuation of the spinal cord. So signals coming from the spinal cord reach the hindbrain first. Blood pressure, heart rate, breathing, and many other vital autonomic functions are controlled by nuclei in the hindbrain, particularly in an area called the **medulla**. Reflexes and feedback systems are important to the functioning of the hindbrain, just as they are in the spinal cord. If you stand up very quickly, your blood pressure can drop so suddenly that it produces lightheadedness until the hindbrain reflex "catches up." If the hindbrain does not activate autonomic nervous system mechanisms to increase blood pressure, you will faint.

Threading throughout the hindbrain and into the midbrain is a collection of cells that are not arranged in any well-defined nucleus. Because the collection resembles a net, it is called the **reticular formation** (*reticular* means "net-like"). This network is very important in altering the activity of the rest of the brain. It is involved, for example, in arousal and attention. If the fibers from the reticular system are disconnected from the rest of the brain, a person would enter a permanent coma. Some of the fibers carrying pain signals from the spinal cord make connections in the reticular formation, which immediately arouses the rest of the brain

A Field Sobriety Test The cerebellum is involved in the balance and coordination required for walking. When the cerebellum's activity is impaired by alcohol, these skills are disrupted, which is why the police ask suspected drunk drivers to walk a straight line. The cerebellum's importance is suggested by the fact that only the cerebral cortex is bigger. And compared with other species, the human cerebellum has grown more than any other part of the brain, tripling in size during the last million years.

from sleep. Within seconds, the hindbrain causes your heart rate and blood pressure to increase.

Activity of the reticular formation also leads to activity in a small nucleus within it called the **locus coeruleus** (pronounced "LO-kus seh-ROO-lee-us"), which means "blue spot" (see Figure 3.12). There are relatively few cells in the locus coeruleus—only about 30,000 of the 100 billion or so in the human brain (Foote, Bloom, & Aston-Jones, 1983)—but each sends out an axon that branches extensively, making contact with as many as 100,000 other cells. Studies of rats, monkeys, and humans suggest that the locus coeruleus is involved in directing attention. In humans, abnormalities in the locus coeruleus have been linked to depression, attention deficit hyperactivity disorder, sleep disorders, and posttraumatic stress disorder (Aston-Jones, 2005).

The hindbrain also includes the **cerebellum** (pronounced "sair-a-BELL-um"). Its primary function was long thought to be the coordination of movements, such as those involved in threading a needle. However, it may also be the storehouse for well-rehearsed movements, such as those associated with dancing, playing a musical instrument, and athletics (McCormick & Thompson, 1984). Brain imaging studies have led neuroscientists to believe that the cerebellum is involved, too, in many activities that are not directly related to physical movement, such as memory, impulse control, emotion, language, and other higher-order cognitive processes. For example, the cerebellum is important in timing (Xu et al., 2006). Timing, in turn, plays a vital role in normal speech, integrating moment-to-moment feedback about vocal sounds with a sequence of precise movements of the lips and tongue (Leiner, Leiner, & Dow, 1993). When this process of integration and sequencing is disrupted, stuttering can result. Even nonstutterers who hear their own speech with a slight delay begin to stutter. (This is why radio talk-show hosts ask callers to turn off their radios. A momentary gap occurs before the shows are actually broadcast, and listening to the delayed sound of their own voice on the radio can cause callers to stutter.) Surgery that affects the cerebellum sometimes results in a syndrome called *cerebellar mutism*, in which patients become unable to speak for periods ranging from a few days to several years (Gelabert-Gonzalez & Fernandez-Villa, 2001). In short, the cerebellum seems to be involved in both physical and cognitive agility.

● **The Midbrain** Above the hindbrain is the **midbrain**. In humans it is a small structure, but it serves some important functions. Certain types of automatic

locus coeruleus A small nucleus in the reticular formation that is involved in directing attention.

cerebellum The part of the hindbrain whose main functions include controlling finely coordinated movements and storing memories about movement, but which may also be involved in impulse control, emotion, and language.

midbrain A small structure between the hindbrain and forebrain that relays information from the eyes, ears, and skin and that controls certain types of automatic behaviors.

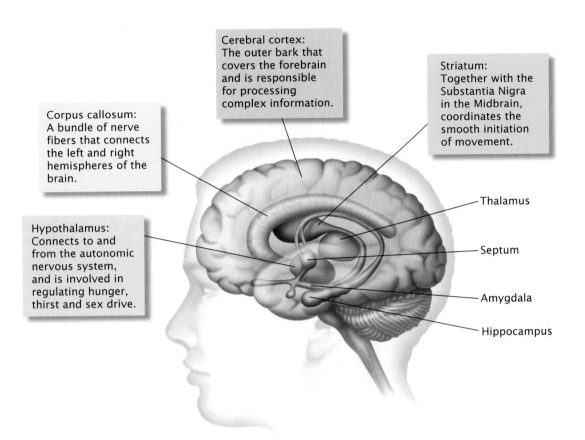

Corpus callosum: A bundle of nerve fibers that connects the left and right hemispheres of the brain.

Cerebral cortex: The outer bark that covers the forebrain and is responsible for processing complex information.

Striatum: Together with the Substantia Nigra in the Midbrain, coordinates the smooth initiation of movement.

Hypothalamus: Connects to and from the autonomic nervous system, and is involved in regulating hunger, thirst and sex drive.

Thalamus

Septum

Amygdala

Hippocampus

FIGURE 3.13

Major Structures of the Forebrain

The structures of the forebrain are covered by an outer "bark" known as the *cerebral cortex.* This diagram shows some of the structures that lie within the forebrain. The amygdala, the hippocampus, the hypothalamus, the septum, and portions of the cerebral cortex are all part of the limbic system.

behaviors that integrate simple movements with sensory input are controlled there. For example, when you move your head, midbrain circuits allow you to move your eyes smoothly in the opposite direction, so that you can keep your eyes focused on an object despite the head movement. And when a car backfires, causing you to turn your head reflexively and look in the direction of the sound, your midbrain circuits are at work.

One particularly important nucleus in the midbrain is the **substantia nigra,** meaning "black substance." This small area and its connections to the **striatum** (named for its "striped" appearance) in the forebrain are necessary in order to smoothly begin movements. Without them, you would find it difficult, if not impossible, to get up out of a chair, lift your hand to swat a fly, move your mouth to form words, or reach for that coffeepot at 6:00 A.M. Together, the midbrain and parts of the hindbrain other than the cerebellum are called the *brainstem.*

●**The Forebrain** Like the cerebellum, the human **forebrain** has grown out of proportion to the rest of the brain, so much so that it folds back over and completely covers the other parts. It is responsible for the most complex aspects of behavior and mental life. As Figure 3.13 shows, the forebrain includes a variety of structures.

Two of these structures lie deep within the brain. The first is the **thalamus,** which relays pain signals from the spinal cord, as well as signals from the eyes and most other sense organs, to upper levels in the brain. It also plays an

- **substantia nigra** An area of the midbrain involved in the smooth beginning of movement.

- **striatum** A structure within the forebrain that is involved in the smooth beginning of movement.

- **forebrain** The most highly developed part of the brain; it is responsible for the most complex aspects of behavior and mental life.

- **thalamus** A forebrain structure that relays signals from most sense organs to higher levels in the brain and plays an important role in processing and making sense out of this information.

important role in processing and making sense out of this information. The other is the **hypothalamus,** which lies under the thalamus (*hypo* means "under") and is involved in regulating hunger, thirst, and sex drives. It has many connections to and from the autonomic nervous system, as well as to other parts of the brain. Destruction of one section of the hypothalamus results in an overwhelming urge to eat (see the chapter on motivation and emotion). Damage to another area of a male's hypothalamus causes his sex organs to degenerate and his sex drive to decrease drastically. There is also a fascinating part of the hypothalamus that contains the brain's own timepiece: the **suprachiasmatic nuclei.** The suprachiasmatic (pronounced "soo-pra-kye-as-MAT-ik") nuclei keep an approximately twenty-four-hour clock that establishes your biological rhythms. We discuss these rhythms in the chapter on consciousness.

Two other forebrain structures, the **amygdala** (pronounced "ah-MIG-duh-luh") and the **hippocampus,** are part of the **limbic system.** The interconnected structures of this system, which also includes the hypothalamus and the septum, play important roles in regulating memory and emotion. For example, the amygdala associates features of stimuli from two different senses, as when we link the shape and feel of objects in memory (Murray & Mishkin, 1985). It is also involved in fear and other emotions (LeDoux, 1995). People suffering from post-traumatic stress disorder show unusual activity in the amygdala (Shin, Rauch, & Pitman, 2006; see the chapter on health, stress, and coping). The amygdala may even influence our sensitivity to other people (Corden et al., 2006).

The hippocampus is important in the formation of memories, as becomes evident in certain cases of brain damage. People with damage to the hippocampus may lose the ability to remember new events, a condition called *anterograde amnesia.* You may have seen the film *Memento,* in which the characters of Leonard Shelby and Sammy Jankis developed this condition as the result of head injury. In one real case, a patient known as R. B. had a stroke (an interruption of blood flow in the brain) that damaged only his hippocampus. Although tests indicated that his intelligence was above average and that he could still recall old memories, he was almost totally unable to build new ones (Squire, 1986). In the memory chapter, we describe H. M., who developed a similar condition following brain surgery, and has become the single most studied patient in all of neuropsychology (Corkin, 2002). The role of the hippocampus in memory is further supported by MRI studies of normal elderly people. These studies have found that memory ability is correlated with the size of the hippocampus (Golomb et al., 1996). In fact, a small hippocampus predicts the development of severe memory problems in the elderly (Devanand et al., 2007). Other studies suggest that some people's inborn response to stress includes a loss of neurons in the hippocampus (Caspi, Sugden, et al., 2003; Frodl et al., 2004). The smaller hippocampus sometimes seen in people who have suffered depression or post-traumatic stress disorder might help explain the memory problems some of these individuals experience (Bremner et al., 2003, 2004).

Although the hippocampus is vital in the creation of new memories, it doesn't keep them for long. Animal studies have shown that damage to the hippocampus within a day of a mildly painful experience erases memories of the experience but that removal of the hippocampus several days after the experience has no effect on the memory. So the memories must have been transferred elsewhere. As described in the chapter on memory, maintaining your storehouse of memories—and having the ability to recall them—depends on the coordinated activities of many parts of the brain.

One of the greatest threats to the brain's memory capacities comes from Alzheimer's disease. Alzheimer's is a major cause of *dementia,* the deterioration of cognitive capabilities often associated with aging. The symptoms of Alzheimer's disease stem from severe degeneration of neurons in specific regions of the hippocampus and other limbic and cortical structures (Small et al., 2002; see Figure 3.14).

● **hypothalamus** A structure in the forebrain that regulates hunger, thirst, and sex drives.

● **suprachiasmatic nuclei** Nuclei in the hypothalamus that generate biological rhythms.

● **amygdala** A structure in the forebrain that, among other things, associates features of stimuli from two sensory modalities.

● **hippocampus** A structure in the forebrain associated with the formation of new memories.

● **limbic system** A set of brain structures that play important roles in regulating emotion and memory.

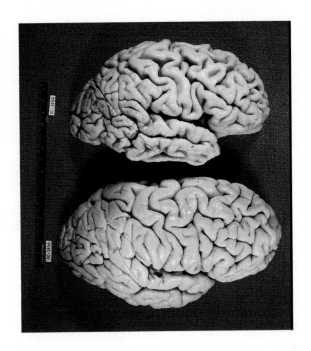

FIGURE **3.14**

Alzheimer's Disease and the Brain

These human brains were photographed after death. Notice that, compared to a normal brain (bottom), the brain of a person with Alzheimer's disease shows considerable degeneration in the cerebral cortex. The limbic system deteriorates, too (Callen et al., 2001). For example, the hippocampus of Alzheimer's patients is about 40 percent smaller than normal. In fact, a smaller than average hippocampus in the elderly predicts the onset of the disease (Jack et al., 1999).

About 10 percent of people over the age of sixty-five, and more than 47 percent of people over eighty-five, suffer from this disorder (Kukull et al., 2002; U.S. Department of Health and Human Services, 2001a). The financial cost of Alzheimer's disease in the United States alone is more than $100 billion a year (U.S. Department of Health and Human Services, 2001a). The cost in human suffering is incalculable. It is no wonder, then, that the search for its causes and cures has a high priority among researchers who study the brain.

FOCUS ON
RESEARCH METHODS **Manipulating Genes in Animal Models of Human Disease**

A lzheimer's disease is named for Alois Alzheimer, a German neurologist. Almost a century ago, Alzheimer examined the brain of a woman who had died after years of progressive mental deterioration and dementia. In looking for the cause of her disorder, he found that cells in her cerebral cortex and hippocampus were bunched up like a rope tied in knots and that cellular debris had collected around the affected nerves. These features came to be known as tangles and plaques. *Tangles* are twisted fibers within neurons; their main protein component is called *tau*. *Plaques* are deposits of protein and parts of dead cells found between neurons. The major component of plaques was found to be a small protein called *beta-amyloid*, which is made from a larger protein called *amyloid precursor protein*. Accumulation of beta-amyloid plaques can now be visualized in living people through the use of PET scans (Klunk et al., 2005; see Figure 3.15).

■ What was the researchers' question?

Ever since Alzheimer described plaques and tangles, researchers have been trying to learn about the role they play. One specific question that researchers have addressed is whether the proteins found in plaques and tangles actually *cause* Alzheimer's disease. They are certainly correlated with Alzheimer's, but as emphasized in the chapter on research in psychology, we can't confirm a causal relationship from a correlation alone. To discover if beta-amyloid and tau cause the death of neurons seen in Alzheimer's disease, researchers knew that controlled experiments would be necessary. This means

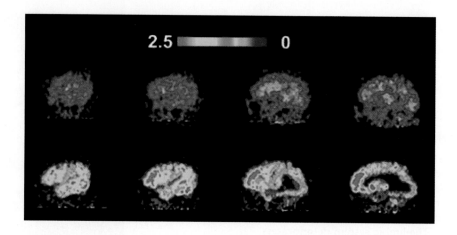

FIGURE 3.15

Diagnosing Alzheimer's Disease

A research team has recently developed a molecule that binds with beta-amyloid plaques and can be seen on a PET scan. As shown in the brightly colored areas of these scans, when the molecule was injected into Alzheimer's patients (bottom row), it became concentrated in the hippocampus and other regions where amyloid usually accumulates in Alzheimer's disease (Klunk et al., 2004, 2005). As shown by the darker colors in the upper row, the molecule does not build up in the brains of older people who do not have the disease. This procedure holds great promise as a tool for diagnosing Alzheimer's disease long before its symptoms appear, allowing treatment efforts to begin as early as possible.

manipulating an independent variable and measuring its effect on a dependent variable. In the case of Alzheimer's, the experiment would involve creating plaques and tangles (the independent variable) and looking for their effects on memory (the dependent variable). Such experiments cannot ethically be conducted on humans, so scientists began looking for Alzheimer's-like conditions in another species. Progress in finding the causes of Alzheimer's disease depended on their finding an "animal model" of the disease.

■ How did the researchers answer the question?

Previous studies of the genes of people with Alzheimer's disease had revealed that in some cases it is associated with a mutation, or error, in the beta-amyloid precursor protein. However, the mutations seen in many Alzheimer's patients appeared not in this protein but in other ones. Researchers called these other proteins *presenilins* because they are associated with senility. To determine whether these mutated proteins could actually cause the brain damage and memory impairment associated with Alzheimer's disease, they had to find a way to insert the proteins into the cells of animals. New genetic engineering tools allowed them to do just that. Genes can now be modified, eliminated, or added to cells, and if those cells give rise to sperm or eggs, the animals that result will have these altered genes in all their cells. Such animals are called "transgenic."

In their first attempts to create an animal model of Alzheimer's disease, researchers inserted into one group of mice a gene for a mutant form of beta-amyloid precursor protein. If Alzheimer's disease is, indeed, caused by faulty beta-amyloid precursor protein, inserting the gene for this faulty protein should cause deposits of beta-amyloid and the loss of neurons in the same brain structures that are affected in human Alzheimer's victims. No such changes should be observed in a control group of untreated animals.

■ What did the researchers find?

For more than a decade, scientists have been creating dozens of different transgenic mice with differing abnormalities in the proteins associated with tangles and plaques (McGowan, Eriksen, & Hutton, 2006). As a result of this work, most researchers believe that amyloid is somehow involved as a cause of Alzheimer's disease. When multiple abnormalities in amyloid are introduced into mice, the animals show memory impairments, and they develop plaques in the brain. However, they do not develop tangles. So it appears that the development of tangles and the loss of neurons are indirect effects of amyloid accumulation, interacting with other factors (McGowan et al., 2006). In other words, scientists are getting closer to a good animal model of Alzheimer's disease, but they still have a way to go.

Nevertheless, transgenic mice have paved the way for an exciting new possibility in the treatment of Alzheimer's disease: a vaccine against beta-amyloid. Mice given this vaccine have shown not only improved memory but also a reversal of beta-amyloid deposits in their brains (Morgan et al., 2000; Younkin, 2001). Early clinical trials of beta-amyloid vaccines in humans showed encouraging results, but a small percentage of patients developed fatal reactions, so the trials were stopped for a while (Broytman & Malter, 2004). Scientists believe that they now understand what caused these reactions, and new clinical trials of more specific vaccines have begun (Lemere et al., 2006).

■ What do the results mean?

Scientists will continue to use transgenic mice to evaluate the roles of mutations in beta-amyloid precursor protein, presenilins, tau, and other proteins in causing Alzheimer's disease. This research is important not only because it might eventually solve the mystery of this terrible disorder but also because it illustrates the power of experimental modification of animal genes for testing all kinds of hypotheses about biological factors influencing behavior.

Besides inserting new or modified genes into brain cells, scientists also can manipulate an independent variable by "knocking out" or disrupting specific genes, then looking at the effect on dependent variables (Feng et al., 2004). One research team has shown, for example, that knocking out a gene for a particular type of neurotransmitter receptor causes mice to become obese and to overeat even when given appetite-suppressant drugs (Tecott et al., 1995). Another team using protein-disrupting technology has found important clues to the neural basis of cocaine's addictive power (Chen et al., 2006).

■ What do we still need to know?

The scarcity of animal models of obesity, drug addiction, and other problems has slowed progress in finding biological treatments for them. As animal models for these conditions become more available through genetic engineering techniques, they will open the door to new types of animal studies that are directly relevant to human problems. The next challenge will be to use these animal models to develop and test treatments that can effectively be applied to humans. ■

● The Cerebral Cortex

So far, we have described some key structures *within* the forebrain; now we turn to a discussion of the structures on its surface. The outermost part of the brain appears rather round and has right and left halves that are similar in appearance. These halves are called the cerebral hemispheres. The outer part of the cerebral hemispheres, the cerebral cortex, has a surface area of one to two square feet—an area that is larger than it looks because of the folds that allow the cortex to fit inside the skull. The cerebral cortex is much larger in humans than in most other animals (dolphins are an exception). It is associated with the analysis of information from all the senses, control of voluntary movements, higher-order thought, and other complex aspects of our behavior and mental processes.

The left side of Figure 3.16 shows the *anatomical* or physical features of the cerebral cortex. The folds of the cortex give the surface of the human brain its wrinkled appearance—its ridges and valleys. The ridges are called *gyri* (pronounced "ji-rye"), and the valleys are called *sulci* (pronounced "sulk-eye") or *fissures*. As you can see in the figure, several deep sulci divide the cortex into four areas: the *frontal*, *parietal*, *occipital*, and *temporal* lobes. The right side of Figure 3.16 depicts the areas of the cerebral cortex in which various *functions* or activities occur. The functional areas do not exactly match the anatomical areas, because some functions occur in more than one area. Let's consider three of these functional areas—the sensory cortex, the motor cortex, and the association cortex.

● Sensory Cortex

The sensory cortex lies in the parietal, occipital, and temporal lobes and is the part of the cerebral cortex that receives information from our senses. Different regions of the sensory cortex receive information from different senses. Visual information is received by the *visual cortex*, made up of cells in the

cerebral hemispheres   The left and right halves of the rounded, outermost part of the brain.

cerebral cortex   The outer surface of the brain.

sensory cortex   The parts of the cerebral cortex that receive stimulus information from the senses.

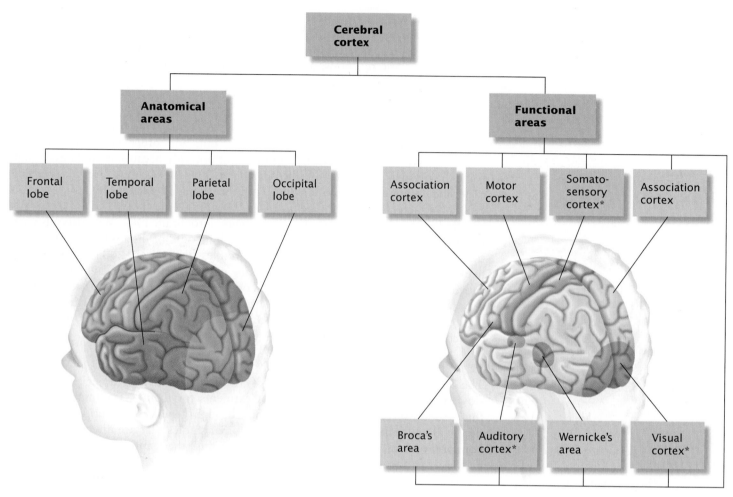

*Somatosensory cortex, auditory cortex, and visual cortex make up the Sensory Cortex.

FIGURE 3.16

The Cerebral Cortex (viewed from the left side)

The brain's ridges (gyri) and valleys (sulci) are landmarks that divide the cortex into four lobes: the frontal, parietal, occipital, and temporal. These terms describe where the regions are (the lobes are named for the skull bones that cover them), but the cortex is also divided in terms of function. These functional areas include the motor cortex (which controls movement), sensory cortex (including somatosensory, auditory, and visual areas that receive information from the senses), and association cortex (which integrates information). Also labeled are Wernicke's area and Broca's area, two regions that are found only on the left side of the cortex and that are vital to the interpretation and production of speech.

occipital lobe; auditory information is received by the *auditory cortex*, made up of cells in the temporal lobe; and information from the skin about touch, pain, and temperature is received in the *somatosensory cortex*, made up of cells in the parietal lobe (*soma* is Greek for "body").

Information about skin sensations from neighboring parts of the body comes to neighboring parts of the somatosensory cortex. As Figure 3.17 illustrates, the places on the cortex where information from each area of skin arrives can be represented by the figure of a tiny person, stretched out along the cortex. This figure is called the sensory *homunculus*, which is Latin for "little man." The links between skin locations and locations in somatosensory cortex have been demonstrated during brain surgery. If a surgeon stimulates a particular spot on the somatosensory cortex, the patient experiences a touch sensation at the place on the skin that normally

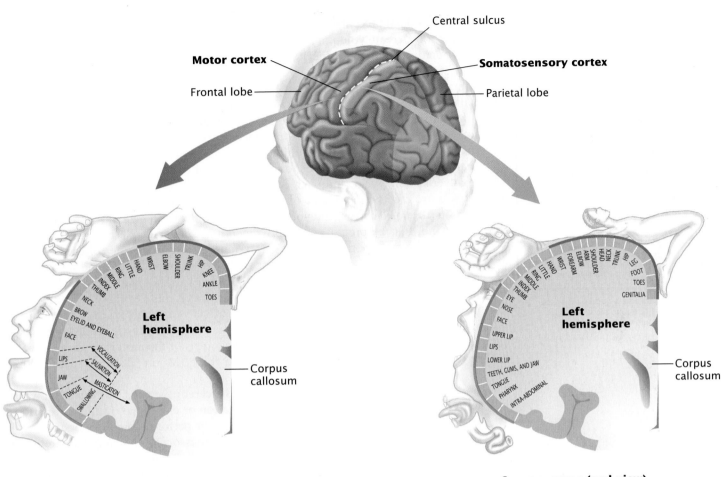

Motor areas (end view)

Sensory areas (end view)

FIGURE 3.17

Motor and Somatosensory Cortex

The areas of cortex that move parts of the body (motor cortex) and receive sensory input from body parts (somatosensory cortex) appear in both hemispheres of the brain. Here we show cross sections of only those on the left side, looking from the back of the brain toward the front. Areas receiving input from neighboring body parts, such as the lips and tongue, are near one another in the sensory cortex. Areas controlling movement of neighboring parts of the body, such as the foot and leg, occupy neighboring parts of the motor cortex. Notice that the size of these areas is uneven; the larger the area devoted to each body part, the larger that body part appears on the "homunculus."

Note: Did you notice the error in this classic drawing? (The figure shows the right side of the body, but the left hand and left side of the face.)
Source: Penfield & Rasmussen (1968).

sends information to that spot of cortex. It was long assumed that the organization of the homunculus remains the same throughout life, but recent research has shown that the amount of sensory cortex that responds to particular sensory inputs can be changed by experience (Pascual-Leone et al., 2005). So if a person loses a limb, the areas of somatosensory cortex that had been stimulated by that limb will eventually be stimulated by other regions of skin. Even practicing the violin can increase the number of neurons in somatosensory cortex that respond to finger touches (Candia et al., 2005). These changes appear to be coordinated partly by brain areas outside the cerebral cortex, which reassign more neurons to process particular sensory inputs. For example, activity in the basal nucleus of the forebrain can generate a massive reorganization of the sensory cortex involved in sound processing (Kilgard & Merzenich, 1998).

"Whoa! *That* was a good one! Try it, Hobbs—just poke his brain right where my finger is."

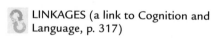

LINKAGES (a link to Cognition and Language, p. 317)

● **Motor Cortex**   Neurons in specific areas of the **motor cortex**, which is in the frontal lobe, create voluntary movements in specific parts of the body. Some control movement of the hand; others stimulate movement of the foot, the knee, the head, and so on. As you can see in Figure 3.17, the motor homunculus mirrors the somatosensory homunculus. That is, the parts of the motor cortex that control the hands, for instance, are near parts of the somatosensory cortex that receive sensory information from the hands. The specific muscles activated by these regions are linked not to specific neurons but, as mentioned earlier, to the patterned activity of many neurons. For example, some of the same neurons are active in moving more than one finger. In other words, different parts of the homunculus in the motor cortex overlap somewhat (Indovina & Sanes, 2001).

Controlling the movement of your body seems simple: You have a map of body parts in the motor cortex, and you activate cells in the hand region if you want to move your hand. But the process is actually much more complex. Recall again your sleepy reach for the coffeepot. The motor cortex must first translate the coffeepot's location in space into a location relative to your body. For example, your hand might have to be moved forward and a certain number of degrees to the right or to the left of your body. Next, the motor cortex must determine which muscles must be contracted to produce those movements. Populations of neurons work together to produce just the right combinations of direction and force in the particular muscle groups necessary to create the desired effects. Many interconnected areas of the motor cortex are involved in making these determinations (Graziano, Taylor, & Moore, 2002; Krauzlis, 2002).

● **Association Cortex**   The parts of the cerebral cortex not directly involved with either receiving specific sensory information or creating movement are referred to as **association cortex**. These are the areas that perform complex cognitive tasks, such as associating words with images. The term *association* is appropriate because these areas either receive information from more than one sense or combine sensory and motor information. Damage to association areas can create severe losses, or deficits, in all kinds of mental abilities.

One of the most devastating deficits, called *aphasia* (pronounced "a-FAY-zhuh"), causes difficulty in understanding or producing speech and can involve all the functions of the cerebral cortex. Language information comes from the auditory cortex (for spoken language) or from the visual cortex (for written language). Areas of the motor cortex produce speech (Geschwind, 1979). But language also involves activity in association cortex.

Scientists have long known that two areas of association cortex are involved in different aspects of language. In 1861, French surgeon Paul Broca described the difficulties that result from damage to the association cortex in the frontal lobe near motor areas that control facial muscles, an area now called *Broca's area* (see Figure 3.16). When Broca's area is damaged, the mental organization of speech suffers, a condition called *Broca's aphasia*. Victims have great difficulty speaking, and what they say is often grammatically incorrect. Each word comes slowly.

A different set of language problems result from damage to a portion of the association cortex first described in the 1870s by Carl Wernicke (pronounced "VER-nick-ee") and thus called *Wernicke's area*. As Figure 3.16 shows, it is located in the temporal lobe, near an area of the cortex that receives information from the ears and eyes. Wernicke's area is involved in the interpretation of both speech and written words. Damage to this area can leave a person able to speak, but it disrupts the ability to understand the meaning of words or to speak understandably.

Case studies illustrate the differing effects of damage to Broca's area versus Wernicke's area (Lapointe, 1990). In response to the request "Tell me what you do with a cigarette," a person with Broca's aphasia replied, "Uh . . . uh . . . cigarette (pause) smoke it." Though halting and ungrammatical, this speech was meaningful. In response to the same request, a person with Wernicke's aphasia replied, "This is a segment of a pegment. Soap a cigarette." Here, the speech is fluent, but without

● **motor cortex**   The part of the cerebral cortex whose neurons control voluntary movements in specific parts of the body.

● **association cortex**   Those parts of the cerebral cortex that receive information from more than one sense or that combine sensory and motor information to perform complex cognitive tasks.

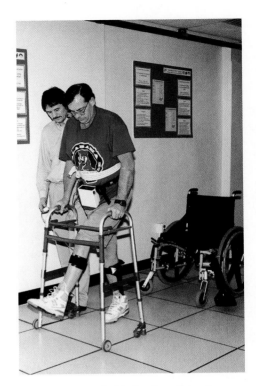

Movement and the Brain Scientists are trying to understand exactly how smooth movements are coordinated by neural activity in the brain and the spinal cord. The complexity of the processes involved presents a challenge to researchers working on devices to restore movement in paralyzed individuals. As shown here, delivering computer-controlled electrical stimulation to leg muscles allows walking movements to occur, though they are jerkier than the brain normally produces. It has also been possible to implant a device that records activity from the motor cortex of a completely paralyzed man. When data from the device was fed into a computer that controlled an artificial hand, the man was able to open and close the hand by imagining these movements (Hochberg et al., 2006). A video of this remarkable accomplishment is available at http://www.nature.com/nature/journal/v442/n7099/extref/nature04970-s7.mov.

meaning. A fascinating aspect of Broca's aphasia is that when a person with the disorder sings, the words come fluently and correctly. Indeed, PET scans show that words set to music are handled by a different part of the brain than spoken words (Jeffries, Fritz, & Braun, 2003). Capitalizing on this observation, "melodic intonation therapy" helps Broca's aphasia patients gain fluency in speaking by teaching them to speak in a "singsong" manner (Lapointe, 1990).

It appears that differing areas of association cortex are activated, depending on whether language is spoken or written and whether particular grammatical and conceptual categories are involved (Shapiro, Moo, & Caramazza, 2006). For example, consider the cases of two women—H. W. and S. J. D.—who, in 1985, had strokes that damaged different language-related parts of their association cortex (Caramazza & Hillis, 1991). Afterward, neither woman had difficulty speaking or writing nouns, but both have difficulty with verbs. H. W. can write verbs but cannot speak them: She has difficulty pronouncing *watch* when it is used as a verb in the sentence "I watch TV," but she speaks the same word easily when it appears as a noun in "My watch is slow." S. J. D. can speak verbs but has difficulty writing them. Another odd language abnormality following brain damage, known as "foreign accent syndrome," was illustrated by a thirty-two-year-old stroke victim whose native language was English. His speech was slurred immediately after the stroke, but as it improved, he began to speak with a Scandinavian accent, adding syllables to some words ("How are you today-ah?") and pronouncing *hill* as "heel." His normal accent did not fully return for four months (Takayama et al., 1993). Case studies of "foreign accent syndrome" suggest that specific regions of the brain are involved in the sound of language, whereas others are involved in various aspects of its meaning.

Other association areas in the front of the brain, called the *prefrontal cortex*, are involved in the complex processes necessary for the conscious control of thoughts and actions and for understanding the world (Fincham & Anderson, 2006; Powell & Voeller, 2004). For example, these areas of association cortex allow us to understand sarcasm or irony—that is, when someone says one thing but means the opposite. In one study, people with prefrontal cortex damage listened to sarcastic stories such as this: "Joe came to work, and instead of beginning to work, he sat down to rest. His boss noticed his behavior and said, 'Joe, don't work too hard.'" Normal people immediately understood what the boss really meant, but people with prefrontal damage had difficulty understanding that she was being sarcastic (Shamay-Tsoory & Tomer, 2005).

● The Divided Brain in a Unified Self

A striking idea emerged from observations of people with damage to the language areas of the brain. Researchers noticed that when damage was limited to areas of the left hemisphere, there were impairments in the ability to use or understand language. Damage to corresponding parts of the right hemisphere usually did not have these effects. Perhaps, they reasoned, the right and left halves of the brain serve different functions.

This concept was not entirely new. It had long been understood, for example, that most sensory and motor pathways cross over as they enter or leave the brain. As a result, the left hemisphere receives information from, and controls movements of, the right side of the body, whereas the right hemisphere receives input from and controls the left side of the body. However, both sides of the brain perform these functions. The fact that language centers, such as Broca's area and Wernicke's area, are found almost exclusively on the left side of the brain suggested that each hemisphere might be specialized to perform some functions almost independently of the other hemisphere (Stephan et al., 2003).

● **Split-Brain Studies** As far back as the late 1800s, scientists had wanted to test the hypothesis that the cerebral hemispheres might be specialized, but they had

TRY THIS **Language Areas of the Brain** Have you ever tried to write notes while you were talking to someone? Like this teacher, you can probably write and talk at the same time, because each of these language functions uses different areas of association cortex. However, stop reading for a moment, and try writing one word with your left hand and a different word with your right hand. If you had trouble, it is partly because you asked the same language area of your brain to do two things at once.

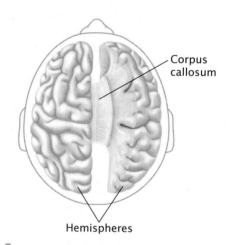

Corpus callosum

Hemispheres

FIGURE 3.18

The Brain's Left and Right Hemispheres

The brain's two hemispheres are joined by a core bundle of nerve fibers known as the *corpus callosum*. In this figure the hemispheres are separated to reveal the corpus callosum. The two cerebral hemispheres look nearly the same but perform somewhat different tasks. For one thing, the left hemisphere receives sensory input from, and controls movement on, the right side of the body. The right hemisphere senses and controls the left side of the body.

no techniques for doing so. Then, during the 1960s, Roger Sperry, Michael Gazzaniga, and their colleagues began to study *split-brain* patients—people who had undergone a surgical procedure in an attempt to control severe epilepsy. Before the surgery, their seizures began in one hemisphere and then spread to engulf the whole brain. As a last resort, surgeons isolated the two hemispheres from each other by severing the **corpus callosum,** a massive bundle of more than a million fibers that connects the two hemispheres (see Figure 3.18).

After the surgery, researchers used a special apparatus to present visual images to only one side of these patients' split brains (see Figure 3.19). They found that severing the tie between the hemispheres had dramatically affected the way these people thought about and dealt with the world. For example, when the image of a spoon was presented to the left, language-oriented side of one patient's split brain, she could say what the spoon was; but when the spoon was presented to the right side of her brain, she could not describe the spoon in words. She still knew what it was, however. Using her left hand (controlled by the right hemisphere), she could pick out the spoon from a group of other objects by its shape. But when asked what she had just grasped, she replied, "A pencil." The right hemisphere recognized the object, but the patient could not describe it because the left (language) half of her brain did not see or feel it (Sperry, 1968).

Although the right hemisphere has no control over spoken language in split-brain patients, it does have important capabilities, including some related to nonspoken language. For example, a split-brain patient's right hemisphere can guide the left hand in spelling out words with Scrabble tiles (Gazzaniga & LeDoux, 1978). Thanks to this ability, researchers discovered that the right hemisphere of split-brain patients has self-awareness and normal learning abilities. In addition, it is superior to the left hemisphere on tasks dealing with spatial relations (especially drawing three-dimensional shapes) and at recognizing human faces.

● **Lateralization of Normal Brains** Sperry (1974, p. 7) concluded from his studies that each hemisphere in the split-brain patient has its own "private sensations, perceptions, thoughts, and ideas all of which are cut off from the corresponding experiences in the opposite hemisphere. . . . In many respects each

FIGURE 3.19

Apparatus for Studying Split-Brain Patients

When the person stares at the dot on the screen, images briefly presented on one side of the dot go to only one side of the brain. For example, a picture of a spoon presented on the left side of the screen goes to the right side of the brain. The right side of the brain can find the spoon and direct the left hand to touch it. However, because the language areas on the left side of the brain did not see the spoon, the person is unable to say what it is.

- **corpus callosum** A massive bundle of fibers that connects the right and left cerebral hemispheres and allows them to communicate with each other.

- **lateralized** Referring to the tendency for one cerebral hemisphere to excel at a particular function or skill compared with the other hemisphere.

disconnected hemisphere appears to have a separate 'mind of its own.'" But what about people whose hemispheres are connected normally? Are certain of their functions, such as mathematical reasoning or language skills, lateralized? A **lateralized** task is one that is performed more efficiently by one hemisphere than by the other.

To find out, researchers presented images to just one hemisphere of people with normal brains and then measured how fast they could analyze information. If information is presented to one side of the brain, and if that side is specialized to analyze that type of information, a person's responses will be faster than if the information must first be transferred to the other hemisphere for analysis. These studies have confirmed that the left hemisphere has better logical and language abilities than the right, whereas the right hemisphere has better spatial, artistic, and musical abilities (Springer & Deutsch, 1989). Positron emission tomography (PET) scans of normal people receiving varying kinds of auditory stimulation also demonstrate these differences (see Figure 3.20). We know that the language abilities of the left hemisphere are not specifically related to auditory information, though, because people who are deaf also use the left hemisphere, Broca's area specifically, more than the right for sign language (Horwitz et al., 2003).

The precise nature and degree of lateralization vary quite a bit among individuals. Functional MRI studies show, for example, that one in ten people show activation of both hemispheres during language tasks, and the brains of another 10 percent appear to coordinate language in the right hemisphere (Fitzgerald, Brown, & Daskalakis, 2002). Both of these patterns are seen mostly in left-handed people (Knecht et al., 2002). Evidence of sex differences in brain laterality comes from studies of the cognitive abilities of normal men and women, of the effects of brain damage on cognitive function, and of anatomical differences between the sexes. Among normal individuals, there are sex differences in the ability to perform tasks that are known to be lateralized in the brain. For example, women tend to do better than men at perceptual fluency tasks, such as rapidly identifying matching items, and at arithmetic calculations. Men tend to be better at imagining the rotation of an object in space and tasks involving target-directed motor skills, such as guiding projectiles or intercepting them, in real or virtual-reality situations (Halperin, 1992; Waller, 2000). However, these sex differences tend to be quite small (Boles, 2005; Frost et al., 1999; Haut & Barch, 2006).

FIGURE 3.20

Lateralization of the Cerebral Hemispheres

These PET scans show overhead views of a section of a person's brain while the person was receiving different kinds of stimulation. At the upper left, the person was resting, with eyes open and ears plugged. Note that the greatest brain activity (as indicated by the red color) was in the visual cortex, which was receiving input from the eyes. As shown at the lower left, when the person listened to spoken language, the auditory cortex in the left temporal lobe became more active, but the right temporal lobe did not. When the person listened to music (lower right), there was intense activity in the right temporal lobe but little in the left. When the person heard both words and music, the temporal cortex on both sides of the brain became activated. Here is visual evidence of the involvement of each side of the brain in processing different kinds of information (Phelps & Mazziotta, 1985).

Reprinted by permission of the publisher from *The Postnatal Development of the Human Cerebral Cortex*, Vol. I–VIII by Jesse LeRoy Conel, Cambridge, Mass.: Harvard University Press, Copyright © 1939–1975 by the President and Fellows of Harvard College.

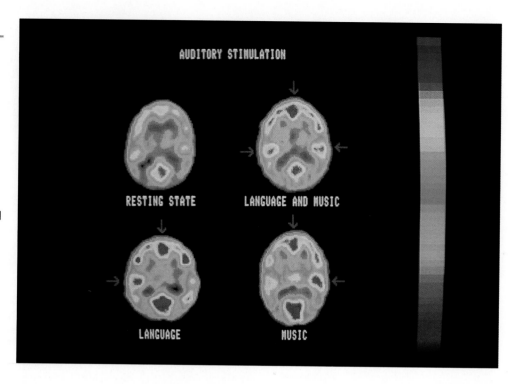

Damage to just one side of the brain is more disabling to men than to women. In particular, men show larger deficits in language ability than women when the left side is damaged (McGlone, 1980). This difference may reflect a wider distribution of language abilities in the brains of women compared with those of men. When participants in one study performed language tasks, such as thinking about whether particular words rhyme, MRI scans showed increased activity on the left side of the brain for men but on both sides for women (Shaywitz et al., 1995; see Figure 1.1 in the chapter on introducing psychology). Women appear to have proportionately more of their association cortex devoted to language tasks (Harasty et al., 1997).

Although humans and animals show definite sex differences in brain anatomy (Allen, Hines, et al., 1989; Gur et al., 1995; Juraska, 1998), no particular anatomical feature has been identified as underlying sex differences in lateralization. One study reported that the corpus callosum is larger in women than in men (de Lacoste-Utamsing & Holloway, 1982), but more than fifty attempts to replicate this finding have all failed (Morton & Rafto, 2006; Olivares, Michalland, & Aboitz, 2000). Despite the overwhelming evidence against it, the original report of a sex difference in the corpus callosum continues to be cited, suggesting that scientists are sometimes not entirely unbiased.

Having two somewhat specialized hemispheres allows the brain to more efficiently perform some tasks, particularly difficult ones, but the differences between the hemispheres should not be exaggerated. The corpus callosum usually integrates the functions of the "two brains," a role that is particularly important in tasks that require sustained attention (Rueckert et al., 1999). As a result, the hemispheres work so closely together, and each makes up so well for whatever lack of ability the other may have, that people are normally unaware that their brains are made up of two partially independent, somewhat specialized halves (Banich & Heller, 1998; Staudt et al., 2001).

Plasticity in the Central Nervous System

We mentioned earlier that the amount of somatosensory cortex devoted to finger touch changes as people practice a musical instrument. Such changes are possible because of **plasticity,** the remarkable ability of the central nervous system to strengthen neural connections at synapses, as well as to establish new connections (Tailby et al., 2005). Plasticity depends partly on neurons and partly on glial cells (Ullian et al., 2001), and it provides the basis for the learning and memory processes described in other chapters. The connections between brain cells are highly dynamic, changing from week to week (Stettler et al., 2006). Plasticity occurs throughout the central nervous system. Even the simplest reflex in the spinal cord can be modified by experience (Wolpaw & Chen, 2006).

Brain scanning technology allows researchers to directly observe the effects of plasticity. They have seen that, as blind people learn to read Braille, the amount of sensory cortex devoted to the "reading" fingertip increases dramatically (Pascual-Leone & Torres, 1993). They have seen, too, that as blind people read Braille, there is activity in the occipital lobe, a brain area that normally receives visual information (Chen, Cohen, & Hallett, 2002). MRI studies of individuals who were learning to juggle found an increase in the density of cortical regions associated with processing visual information about moving objects (Draganski et al., 2004). Motor cortex is "plastic," too. Musicians have a larger portion of cortex devoted to the movements of their hands than nonmusicians, and nonmusicians who practice making rhythmic finger movements increase the amount of cortex devoted to this task as they become better at it (Munte, Altenmuller, & Jancke, 2002). Even more amazing is the finding that merely *imagining* practicing these movements causes changes in the motor cortex (Pascual-Leone, 2001). Athletes have long engaged in exercises in which they visualize skilled sports movements; brain imaging research reveals that this "mental practice" can change the brain.

● **Repairing Brain Damage** Unfortunately, the power of plasticity is limited, especially when it comes to repairing damage to the brain and spinal cord. Unlike the skin or the liver, the adult central nervous system does not automatically replace damaged cells. Still, it does display a certain amount of self-healing. Undamaged neurons may take over for damaged ones, partly by changing their own function and partly by sprouting axons whose connections help neighboring regions take on new functions (Bareyre et al., 2004). These changes rarely result in complete restoration of lost functions, though, so most victims of severe stroke, Alzheimer's disease, spinal cord injury, or other central nervous system disorders are permanently disabled in some way.

Scientists are searching for ways to help a damaged central nervous system heal some of its own wounds. One approach has been to transplant, or graft, tissue from a still-developing fetal brain into the brain of an adult animal. If the receiving animal does not reject it, the graft sends axons out into the brain and makes some functional connections. This treatment has reversed animals' learning difficulties, movement disorders, and other results of brain damage (Noble, 2000). The technique has also been used to treat a small number of people with *Parkinson's disease*—a disorder characterized by tremors, rigidity of the arms and legs, difficulty in beginning movements, and poor balance (Lindvall & Hagell, 2001). The initial results were encouraging (Mendez et al., 2005). Some patients showed improvement for several years, though improvement faded for others, and some patients suffered serious side effects (Freed et al., 2001).

The brain-tissue transplant procedure is promising, but because its use with humans requires tissue from aborted fetuses, it has generated considerable controversy. As an alternative, some scientists have tried transplanting neural tissue from another species, such as the pig, into humans (Savitz et al., 2005). The difficulty with this approach is that the immune system rejects foreign tissue, even in the brain.

The most promising source for new neurons now appears to be an individual's own body, because these cells would not be rejected. This is a revolutionary idea, because it was long believed that once humans reached adulthood, the cells of the

plasticity   The ability to create new synapses and to change the strength of synapses.

FIGURE 3.21

Developmental Changes in the Cerebral Cortex

During childhood, the brain overproduces neural connections, establishes the usefulness of certain connections, and then "prunes" the extra ones. Overproduction of synapses, especially in the frontal cortex, may be essential for children to develop certain intellectual abilities. One research team used repeated MRI scans to track the thickness of the cerebral cortex in children of average and exceptionally high intelligence as they grew from age six to nineteen. There were no differences between groups at the beginning of the study, or at the end, but cortical thickness had reached a higher preadolescent peak in the bright youngsters. So adult cognitive ability was correlated not with the final thickness of cortex, but with how thick it had once been (Shaw, Greenstein, et al., 2006). As described in the chapter on cognitive abilities, the relationship between intelligence and brain development is not a simple one.

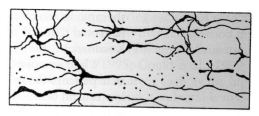

At birth

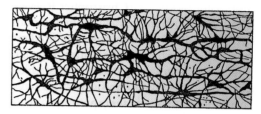

Six years old

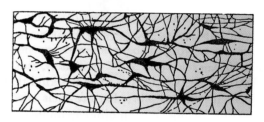

Fourteen years old

Kozorovitskiy et al., 2005). Our genes apparently determine the basic pattern of growth and the major lines of connections—the "highways" of the brain and its general architecture. (For a summary of this architecture, see "In Review: Organization of the Brain.") But the details of the connections depend on experience, including the amount of complexity and stimulation in the environment. For example, researchers have compared the brains of rats raised alone with only a boring view of the side of their cages to the brains of rats raised with interesting toys and stimulating playmates. The cerebral cortex of those from the enriched environment had more and longer dendrites, as well as more synapses and neurotrophic factors, than the cortex of animals from barren, individual housing (Klintsova & Greenough, 1999; Torasdotter et al., 1998). Furthermore, the number of cortical synapses increased when isolated animals were moved to an enriched environment. To the extent that these ideas and research findings apply to humans, they hold obvious implications for how people raise children and treat the elderly.

In any event, this line of research highlights the interaction of environmental and genetic factors. Some overproduced synapses may reflect genetically directed preparation for certain types of experiences. Generation of these synapses is an "experience-expectant" process, and it accounts for sensitive periods during development when certain things can be most easily learned (Hensch, 2005). But overproduction of synapses also occurs in response to totally new experiences; this process is "experience dependent" (Greenough, Black, & Wallace, 1987). Within constraints set by genetics, interactions with the world mold the brain itself (e.g., Chang & Merzenich, 2003; Holtmaat et al., 2006). ■

in review — Organization of the Brain

Major Division	Some Important Structures	Some Major Functions
Hindbrain	Medulla	Regulation of breathing, heart rate, and blood pressure
	Reticular formation (also extends into midbrain)	Regulation of arousal and attention
	Cerebellum	Control of fine movements and coordination of certain cognitive processes
Midbrain	Various nuclei	Relay of sensory signals to forebrain; creation of automatic responses to certain stimuli
	Substantia nigra	Smooth initiation of movement
Forebrain	Hypothalamus	Regulation of hunger, thirst, and sex drives
	Thalamus	Interpretation and relaying of sensory information
	Hippocampus	Formation of new memories
	Amygdala	Connection of sensations and emotions
	Cerebral cortex	Analysis of sensory information; control over voluntary movements, abstract thinking, and other complex cognitive activity
	Corpus callosum	Transfer of information between the two cerebral hemispheres

The Chemistry of Psychology

We have now described how the cells of the nervous system communicate by releasing neurotransmitters at their synapses, and we have outlined some of the basic structures of the nervous system and their functions. Let's now pull these topics together by considering which neurotransmitters occur in which structures, and how neurotransmitters affect behavior. As we mentioned earlier, different sets of neurons use different neurotransmitters; a group of neurons that communicates using the same neurotransmitter is called a **neurotransmitter system.** Certain neurotransmitter systems play a dominant role in particular functions, such as emotion or memory, and in particular problems, such as Alzheimer's disease.

Chemical neurotransmission was first demonstrated, in frogs, by Otto Loewi (pronounced "LOW-ee") in 1921. Since then more than a hundred different neurotransmitters have been identified. Some of the chemicals that act on receptors at synapses have been called *neuromodulators*, because they act slowly and often modify or "modulate" a cell's response to other neurotransmitters. The distinction between neurotransmitter and neuromodulator is not always clear, however. Depending on the type of receptor it acts on at a given synapse, the same substance can function as either a neuromodulator or a neurotransmitter.

● **neurotransmitter system** A group of neurons that communicates by using the same neurotransmitter.

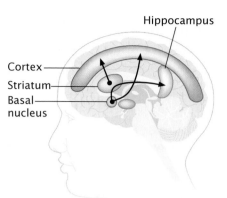

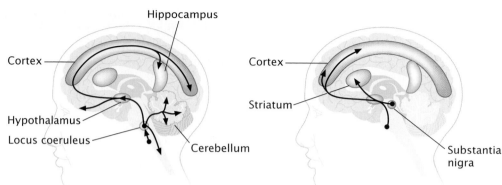

Acetylcholine   **Norepinephrine**   **Dopamine**

FIGURE 3.22

Some Neurotransmitter Pathways

Neurons that use a certain neurotransmitter may be concentrated in one particular region (indicated by dots) and send fibers into other regions with which they communicate (see arrows). Here are examples for three major neurotransmitters. *Psychoactive* drugs affect behavior and mental processes by altering these systems. In the consciousness chapter, we discuss how drugs of abuse, such as cocaine, affect neurotransmitters. The neurotransmitter effects of therapeutic drugs are described in the chapter on the treatment of psychological disorders.

● Three Classes of Neurotransmitters

The neurotransmitters used in the nervous system fall into three main categories, based on their chemical structure: *small molecules, peptides,* and *gases.* Let's consider some examples in each category.

● **Small Molecules** The *small-molecule* neurotransmitters were discovered first, partly because they occur in both the central nervous system and the peripheral nervous system. For example, **acetylcholine** (pronounced "a-see-tull-KO-leen") is used by neurons of the parasympathetic nervous system to slow the heartbeat and activate the digestive system and by neurons that make muscles contract. In the brain, neurons that use acetylcholine (called *cholinergic* neurons) are especially plentiful in the midbrain and striatum, where they occur in circuits that are important for movement (see Figure 3.22). Axons of cholinergic neurons also make up major pathways in the limbic system, including the hippocampus, and in other areas of the forebrain that are involved in memory. Drugs that interfere with acetylcholine prevent the formation of new memories. In Alzheimer's disease, there is a nearly complete loss of cholinergic neurons in a nucleus in the forebrain that sends fibers to the cerebral cortex and hippocampus—a nucleus that normally enhances plasticity in these regions (Kilgard & Merzenich, 1998).

Three other small-molecule neurotransmitters are known as *catecholamines* (pronounced "cat-ah-KO-lah-means"). They include *norepinephrine, serotonin,* and *dopamine.* **Norepinephrine** (pronounced "nor-eppa-NEF-rin"), also called *noradrenaline,* occurs in both the central and peripheral nervous systems. In both places, it contributes to arousal. Norepinephrine (and its close relative, epinephrine, or adrenaline) are the neurotransmitters used by the sympathetic nervous system to activate you and prepare you for action. Approximately half of the norepinephrine in the entire brain is contained in cells of the locus coeruleus, which is near the reticular formation in the hindbrain (see Figure 3.22). Because norepinephrine systems cover a lot of territory, it is logical that norepinephrine would affect several broad categories of behavior. Indeed, norepinephrine is

● **acetylcholine** A neurotransmitter used by neurons in the peripheral and central nervous systems in the control of functions ranging from muscle contraction and heart rate to digestion and memory.

● **norepinephrine** A neurotransmitter involved in arousal, as well as in learning and mood regulation.

involved in the appearance of wakefulness and sleep, in learning, and in the regulation of mood.

Serotonin is similar to norepinephrine in several ways. First, most of the cells that use it as a neurotransmitter occur in an area along the midline of the hindbrain. Second, axons from neurons that use serotonin send branches throughout the forebrain, including the hypothalamus, the hippocampus, and the cerebral cortex. Third, serotonin affects sleep and mood. Serotonin differs from norepinephrine, however, in that the brain can get one of the substances from which it is made, *tryptophan*, directly from food. So what you eat can affect the amount of serotonin in your brain. Carbohydrates increase the amount of tryptophan reaching the brain and therefore affect how much serotonin is made. A meal high in carbohydrates produces increased levels of serotonin, which normally causes a reduction in the desire for carbohydrates. Some researchers suspect that malfunctions in the serotonin feedback system are responsible for the disturbances of mood and appetite seen in certain types of obesity, premenstrual tension, and depression (Lira et al., 2003; Wurtman & Wurtman, 1995). Serotonin has also been implicated in aggression and impulse control. One of the most consistently observed relationships between a particular neurotransmitter system and a particular behavior is the low level of serotonin metabolites in the brains of suicide victims, who tend to show a combination of depressed mood, self-directed aggression, and impulsivity (Bach-Mizrachi et al., 2006; Oquendo & Mann, 2000).

Dopamine is the neurotransmitter used in the substantia nigra and striatum, which are important for movement. Malfunctioning of the dopamine-using (or *dopaminergic)* system in these regions contributes to movement disorders, including Parkinson's disease. As dopamine cells in the substantia nigra degenerate, Parkinson's disease victims experience severe shakiness and difficulty in beginning movements. Parkinson's disease is most common in elderly people, and it may result in part from sensitivity to environmental toxins. These toxins have not yet been identified, but there is evidence from animal studies that chemicals in some common garden pesticides damage dopaminergic neurons (Jenner, 2001). A prospective study with humans found that people exposed to pesticides have a 70 percent higher incidence of Parkinson's disease than those not exposed (Ascherio et al., 2006). Parkinson's disease has been treated, with partial success, using drugs that enable neurons to make more dopamine (Chase, 1998). Malfunctioning of a separate group of dopaminergic neurons whose axons go to the cerebral cortex may be partly responsible for schizophrenia, a severe disorder in which perception, emotional expression, and thought are severely distorted (Marenco & Weinberger, 2000).

Other dopaminergic systems that send axons from the midbrain to the forebrain are important in the experience of reward or pleasure (Wise & Rompre, 1989). Animals will work hard to receive a direct infusion of dopamine into their forebrains. These dopamine systems play a role in the rewarding properties of many drugs, including cocaine. In fact, current theories of addiction suggest that the normal mechanisms of reward-based learning are exploited by these drugs, and that dopaminergic systems play an important role in the process (Hyman, Malenka, & Nestler, 2006).

Two other small-molecule neurotransmitters—*GABA* and *glutamate*—are amino acids. Neurons in widespread regions of the brain use **GABA,** or gamma-amino butyric acid. GABA reduces the likelihood that postsynaptic neurons will fire an action potential. In fact, it is the major inhibitory neurotransmitter in the central nervous system. When you fall asleep, neurons that use GABA deserve part of the credit. Drugs that cause reduced neural activity often do so by amplifying the "braking" action of GABA. In the case of alcohol, for example, the result is an impairment of thinking, judgment, and motor skills.

● **serotonin**　A neurotransmitter used by cells in parts of the brain involved in the regulation of sleep, mood, and eating.

● **dopamine**　A neurotransmitter used in the parts of the brain involved in regulating movement and experiencing pleasure.

● **GABA**　A neurotransmitter that inhibits the firing of neurons.

Malfunctioning of GABA systems has been implicated in a variety of disorders, including severe anxiety and *Huntington's disease*, an inherited and incurable disorder in which the victim is plagued by uncontrollable jerky movement of the arms and legs, along with dementia. Huntington's disease results in the loss of many GABA-containing neurons in the striatum. Normally these GABA systems inhibit dopamine systems; so when they are lost through Huntington's disease, the dopamine systems may run wild, impairing many motor and cognitive functions. Because drugs that block GABA receptors produce intense repetitive electrical discharges, known as *seizures*, researchers suspect that malfunctioning GABA systems probably contribute to *epilepsy*, a brain disorder associated with seizures and convulsive movements. Repeated or sustained seizures can result in permanent brain damage. Drug treatments can reduce their frequency and severity, but completely effective drugs are not yet available.

Glutamate is the major excitatory neurotransmitter in the central nervous system. It is used by more neurons than any other neurotransmitter, and its synapses are especially plentiful in the cerebral cortex and the hippocampus. Glutamate is particularly important because it plays a major role in the ability of the brain to "strengthen" its synaptic connections—that is, to allow messages to cross the synapse more efficiently. This process is necessary for normal development and may be at the root of learning and memory (Bredt & Nicoll, 2003). At the same time, overactivity of glutamate synapses can cause neurons to die. In fact, this overactivity is the main cause of the brain damage that occurs when oxygen is cut off from neurons during a stroke. Glutamate can "excite neurons to death," so blocking glutamate receptors immediately after a brain trauma can prevent permanent brain damage (Colak et al., 2003). Recent studies have revealed that glutamate helps neurons and glial cells communicate with one another (Carmignoto & Fellin, 2006).

● **Peptides**   Hundreds of chemicals called *peptides* have been found to act as neurotransmitters. The first of these was discovered in the 1970s, when scientists were investigating *opiates*, such as heroin and morphine. Opiates can relieve pain, produce feelings of elation, and in high doses, bring on sleep. After marking morphine with a radioactive substance, researchers traced where it became concentrated in the brain. They found that opiates bind to receptors that were not associated with any known neurotransmitter. Because it was unlikely that the brain had developed opiate receptors just in case a person might want to use morphine or heroin, researchers reasoned that the body must already contain a substance similar to opiates. This hypothesis led to the search for a naturally occurring, or endogenous, morphine, which was called *endorphin* (short for endogenous morphine). As it turned out, there are many natural opiate-like compounds. So the term **endorphin** refers to any neurotransmitter that can bind to the same receptors stimulated by opiates. Neurons in several parts of the brain use endorphin, including neuronal pathways that modify pain signals to the brain.

● **Gases**   The concept of what neurotransmitters can be was radically altered following the recent discovery that *nitric oxide* and *carbon monoxide*—two toxic gases that contribute to air pollution—can act as neurotransmitters (Boehning & Snyder, 2003). When nitric oxide or carbon monoxide is released by a neuron, it spreads to nearby neurons, sending a signal that affects chemical reactions inside those neurons rather than binding to receptors on their surface. Nitric oxide is not stored in vesicles, as most other neurotransmitters are; it can be released from any part of the neuron. Nitric oxide appears to be one of the neurotransmitters responsible for such diverse functions as penile erection and the formation of memories—not at the same site, obviously. (For a summary of the main neurotransmitters and the consequences of malfunctioning neurotransmitter systems, see "In Review: Classes of Neurotransmitters.")

● **glutamate**   An excitatory neurotransmitter that helps strengthen synaptic connections between neurons.

● **endorphin**   One of a class of neurotransmitters that bind to opiate receptors and moderate pain.

in review · Classes of Neurotransmitters

Neurotransmitter Class	Normal Function	Disorder Associated with Malfunction
Small Molecules		
Acetylcholine	Memory, movement	Alzheimer's disease
Norepinephrine	Mood, sleep, learning	Depression
Serotonin	Mood, appetite, impulsivity	Depression
Dopamine	Movement, reward	Parkinson's disease, schizophrenia
GABA	Sleep, movement	Anxiety, Huntington's disease, epilepsy
Glutamate	Memory	Damage after stroke
Peptides		
Endorphins	Pain control	No established disorder
Gases		
Nitric oxide	Memory	No established disorder

The Endocrine System: Coordinating the Internal World

As we mentioned earlier, neurons are not the only cells that can use chemicals to communicate with one another in ways that affect behavior and mental processes. Another class of cells with this ability resides in the **endocrine system** (pronounced "EN-doh-krinn"), which regulates functions ranging from stress responses to physical growth. The cells of endocrine organs, or **glands,** communicate by secreting chemicals, much as neurons do. In the case of endocrine organs, the chemicals are called **hormones.** Figure 3.23 shows the location and functions of some of the major endocrine glands.

Hormones secreted from the endocrine organs are similar to neurotransmitters. In fact, many of these chemicals, including norepinephrine and the endorphins, act both as hormones and as neurotransmitters. However, whereas neurons release neurotransmitters into synapses, endocrine organs put their chemicals into the bloodstream, which carries them throughout the body. In this way, endocrine glands can stimulate cells with which they have no direct connection. But not all cells receive the hormonal message. Hormones, like neurotransmitters, can influence only those cells with receptors capable of receiving them. Organs whose cells have receptors for a hormone are called *target organs*.

Each hormone acts on many target organs, producing coordinated effects throughout the body. For example, when the sex hormone *estrogen* is secreted by a woman's ovaries, it activates her reproductive system. It causes the uterus to grow in preparation for nurturing an embryo; it enlarges the breasts to prepare them for nursing; it stimulates the brain to enhance interest in sexual activity; and it stimulates the pituitary gland to release another hormone that causes a mature egg to be released by the ovary for fertilization. Male sex organs, called the testes, secrete *androgens*, which are sex hormones such as testosterone. Androgens stimulate the maturation of sperm, increase a male's motivation for sexual activity, increase his aggressiveness, and affect his responses to social stimuli (Romeo, Richardson, & Sisk, 2002).

Can differences between hormones in men and women account for some of the differences between the sexes? During development and in adulthood, sex

endocrine system Cells that form organs called glands and that communicate with one another by secreting chemicals called hormones.

gland An organ that secretes hormones into the bloodstream.

hormones Chemicals secreted by a gland into the bloodstream, which carries them throughout the body.

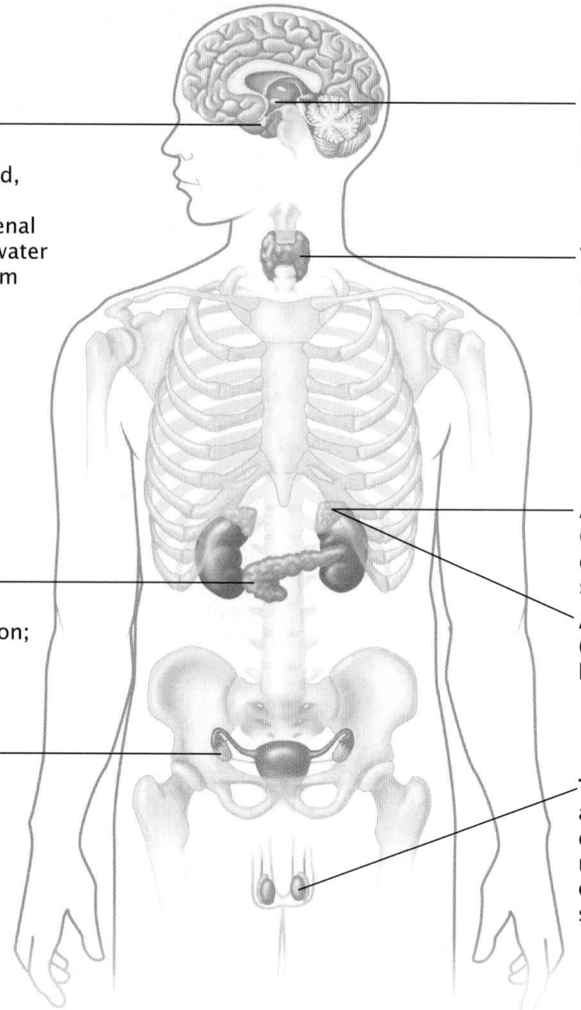

Pituitary — regulates growth; controls the thyroid, ovaries or testes, pancreas, and adrenal cortex; regulates water and salt metabolism

Hypothalamus — controls the pituitary gland

Thyroid — controls the metabolic rate

Pancreas — controls levels of insulin and glucagon; regulates sugar metabolism

Adrenal cortex — (shell) regulates carbohydrate and salt metabolism

Adrenal medulla — (core) prepares the body for action

Ovaries (female) — affect physical development, reproductive organs, and sexual behavior

Testes (male) — affect physical development, reproductive organs, and sexual behavior

FIGURE 3.23

Some Major Glands of the Endocrine System

Each of the glands shown releases its hormones into the bloodstream. Even the hypothalamus, a part of the brain, regulates the nearby pituitary gland by secreting hormones.

differences in hormones are relative rather than absolute. In other words, both men and women have androgens and estrogens, but men have relatively higher concentrations of androgens, whereas women have relatively higher concentrations of estrogens. There is plenty of evidence from animal studies that the presence of higher concentrations of androgens in males during development, at around the time of birth and at puberty, creates both structural sex differences in the brain and sex differences in adult behaviors (Gooren & Kruijver, 2002). Other animal studies suggest that estrogens might contribute to the development of the female brain (Bakker et al., 2003). Humans, too, may be affected by hormones early in development. For example, studies of girls who were exposed to high levels of androgens before birth found that they were later more aggressive than their sisters who had not had such exposure (Berenbaum & Resnick, 1997). Even the artwork of such girls is affected by exposure to androgens; they are more likely than nonexposed girls to draw pictures of cars, boats, and airplanes, for example (Iijima et al., 2001). And as shown in Figure 1.1, MRI studies have revealed specific brain regions that function differently in men and women. However, such sex differences may not be simple, inevitable, or caused by the actions of hormones alone. Most likely, the sex differences we see in behavior depend not only on hormones but also on complex interactions of biological and social forces, as described in the chapter on motivation and emotion.

Hormones at Work The appearance of a threat activates a pattern of hormonal secretions and other physiological responses that prepare humans and other animals to confront, or flee, the danger. This pattern is known as the "fight-or-flight syndrome."

The brain has ultimate control over the secretion of hormones. Through the hypothalamus, it controls the pituitary gland, which in turn controls endocrine organs in the body. The brain is also one of the target organs for most endocrine secretions. In fact, the brain creates some of the same hormones that are secreted in the endocrine system and uses them for neural communication (Compagnone & Mellon, 2000). In summary, the endocrine system typically involves four elements: the brain, the pituitary gland, an endocrine organ, and the target organs, which include the brain. Each element in the system uses hormones to signal to the next element, and the secretion of each hormone is stimulated or suppressed by other hormones (Dubrovsky, 2005).

For example, in stress-hormone systems, the brain controls the pituitary gland by signaling the hypothalamus to release hormones that stimulate receptors of the pituitary gland, which secretes another hormone, which stimulates another endocrine gland to secrete its hormones. More specifically, when the brain interprets a situation as threatening, the pituitary releases *adrenocorticotropic hormone (ACTH)*, which causes the adrenal glands to release the hormone *cortisol* into the bloodstream. These hormones, in turn, act on cells throughout the body, including the brain. One effect of cortisol, for example, is to activate the emotion-related limbic system, making it more likely that you will remember stressful or traumatic events (Cahill & McGaugh, 1998). The combined effects of the adrenal hormones and the activation of the sympathetic system result in a set of responses called the **fight-or-flight syndrome**, which, as mentioned earlier, prepares us for action in response to danger or other stress. With these hormones at high levels, the heart beats faster, the liver releases glucose into the bloodstream, fuels are mobilized from fat stores, and we usually enter a state of high arousal.

The hormones provide feedback to the brain, as well as to the pituitary gland. Just as a thermostat and furnace regulate heat, this feedback system regulates hormone secretion so as to keep it within a certain range. If a hormone rises above a certain level, feedback about this situation signals the brain and pituitary to stop stimulating that hormone's secretion. So after the immediate threat is over, feedback about cortisol's action in the brain and in the pituitary stops the secretion of ACTH and, in turn, cortisol. Because the feedback suppresses further action, this arrangement is called a *negative feedback system*.

fight-or-flight syndrome Physical reactions triggered by the sympathetic nervous system that prepare the body to fight or to run from a threatening situation.

The Immune System: Defending the Body

Like the nervous system and endocrine system, the **immune system** serves as both a sensory system and a security system. It monitors the internal state of the body and detects invading cells and toxic substances. It recognizes and remembers foreign substances, and it engulfs and destroys foreign cells, as well as cancer cells. Individuals whose immune system is impaired—AIDS patients, for example—face death from invading bacteria or malignant tumors. However, if the system becomes overactive, the results can be just as devastating: Many diseases, including arthritis, diabetes, and multiple sclerosis, are now recognized as **autoimmune disorders,** in which cells of the immune system attack normal cells of the body, including brain cells (Marrack, Kappler, & Kotzin, 2001).

The immune system is as complex as the nervous system, and it contains as many cells as the brain. Some of these cells are in organs such as the thymus and spleen, whereas others circulate in the bloodstream and enter tissues throughout the body (see Figure 3.24). In the chapter on health, stress, and coping, we describe a few of the immune system's many cell types and how they work.

The nervous system and the immune system were once thought of as separate (Ader, Felten, & Cohen, 1990). However, five lines of evidence suggest important interactions between the two. First, stress can alter the outcome of disease in animals,

FIGURE 3.24

The Nervous System, Endocrine System, and Immune System

All three systems interact and influence one another. The nervous system affects the endocrine system by controlling secretion of hormones via the pituitary gland. It also affects the immune system through the autonomic nervous system's action on the thymus gland. The thymus, spleen, and bone marrow are sites of generation and development of immune cells. Hormones of the pituitary gland and adrenal gland modulate immune cells. Immune cells secrete cytokines and antibodies to fight foreign invaders. Cytokines are blood-borne messengers that regulate the development of immune cells and also influence the central nervous system.

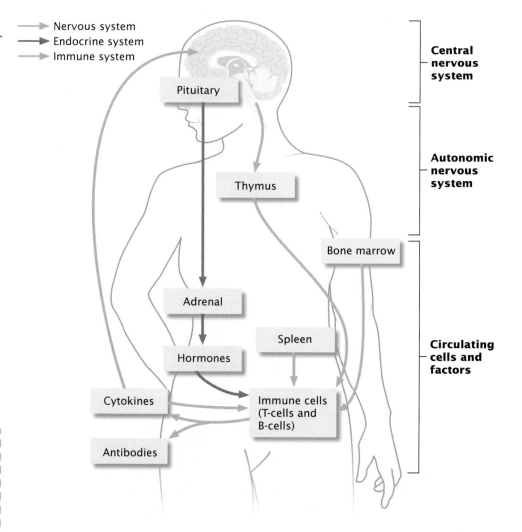

- **immune system** The body's system of defense against invading substances and microorganisms.

- **autoimmune disorders** Physical problems caused when cells of the body's immune system attack normal body cells as if they were foreign invaders.

The Common Cold   The interaction of the immune system and the nervous system can be seen in some of the symptoms associated with routine "sickness." Sleepiness, nausea, and fever are actually a result of chemicals released by immune cells called *cytokines,* which act directly on the brain through specific receptors (Pousset, 1994).

and as discussed in the chapter on health, stress, and coping, there is clear evidence that psychological stressors also affect disease processes in humans. Second, immune responses can be "taught" using some of the principles outlined in the chapter on learning. In one study with humans, for example, exposure to the taste of strawberry milk flavored with lavender was repeatedly associated with an injection of cyclosporin, which decreases immune system activity. Later, a decrease in immune system activity could be prompted by the taste of the flavored milk alone (Goebel et al., 2002). Third, animal studies have shown that stimulating or damaging specific parts of the hypothalamus, the cortex, or the brainstem that control the autonomic nervous system can enhance or impair immune functions (Felten et al., 1998). Fourth, activation of the immune system can produce changes in the electrical activity of the brain, in neurotransmitter activity, in hormonal secretion, and in behavior—including symptoms of illness (Kronfol & Remick, 2000). Finally, some of the same chemical messengers are found in both the brain and the immune system. For example, one way in which glial cells help to repair damaged neurons is by secreting "immune messengers" called *interleukins* (Parish et al., 2002).

These converging lines of evidence point to important relationships that illustrate the intertwining of biological and psychological functions, the interaction of body and mind. They highlight the ways in which the immune system, nervous system, and endocrine system—all systems of communication between and among cells—are integrated to form the biological basis for a smoothly functioning self that is filled with interacting thoughts, emotions, and memories and is capable of responding to life's challenges and opportunities with purposeful and adaptive behavior.

As noted in the chapter on introducing psychology, all of psychology's subfields are related to one another. Our discussion of developmental changes illustrates just one way in which the topic of this chapter, the biological aspects of psychology, is linked to the subfield of developmental psychology, which is described in the chapter on human development. The Linkages diagram shows ties to two other subfields as well, and there are many more ties throughout the book. Looking for linkages among subfields will help you see how they all fit together and help you better appreciate the big picture that is psychology.

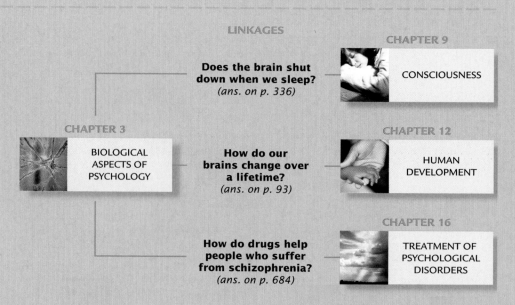

LINKAGES

CHAPTER 3
BIOLOGICAL ASPECTS OF PSYCHOLOGY

Does the brain shut down when we sleep? *(ans. on p. 336)*

CHAPTER 9
CONSCIOUSNESS

How do our brains change over a lifetime? *(ans. on p. 93)*

CHAPTER 12
HUMAN DEVELOPMENT

How do drugs help people who suffer from schizophrenia? *(ans. on p. 684)*

CHAPTER 16
TREATMENT OF PSYCHOLOGICAL DISORDERS

SUMMARY

Biological psychology focuses on the biological aspects of our being, including the nervous system, which provide the physical basis for behavior and mental processes. The *nervous system* is a system of cells that allows an organism to gain information about what is going on inside and outside the body and to respond appropriately.

The Nervous System

Much of our understanding of the biological aspects of psychology has stemmed from research on animal and human nervous systems at levels ranging from single cells to complex organizations of cells.

Cells of the Nervous System   The main units of the nervous system are cells called *neurons* and *glial cells*. Neurons are especially good at receiving signals from, and transmitting signals to, other neurons. Neurons have cell bodies and two types of fibers, called *axons* and *dendrites*. Axons usually carry signals away from the cell body, whereas dendrites usually carry signals to the cell body. Neurons can transmit signals because of the structure of these fibers, the excitable surface of some of the fibers, and the synapses, or gaps, between cells.

Action Potentials   The membranes of neurons normally keep the distribution of electrically charged molecules uneven between the inside of cells and the outside, creating an electrochemical force, or potential. The membrane surface of the axon can transmit a disturbance in this potential, called an *action potential*, from one end of the axon to the other. The speed of the action potential is fastest in neurons sheathed in *myelin*. Between firings there is a very brief rest, called a *refractory period*.

Synapses and Communication Between Neurons   When an action potential reaches the end of an axon, the axon releases a chemical called a *neurotransmitter*. This chemical crosses the synapse and interacts with the postsynaptic cell at special sites called *receptors*. This interaction creates a postsynaptic potential—either an *excitatory postsynaptic potential (EPSP)* or an *inhibitory postsynaptic potential (IPSP)*—that makes the postsynaptic cell more likely or less likely to fire an action potential of its own. So whereas communication within a neuron is electrochemical, communication between neurons is chemical. Because the fibers of neurons have many branches, each neuron can interact with thousands of other neurons. Each neuron constantly integrates signals received at its many synapses; the result of this integration determines how often the neuron fires an action potential.

Organization and Functions of the Nervous System   Neurons are organized in *neural networks* of closely connected cells. *Sensory systems* receive information from the environment, and *motor systems* influence the actions of muscles and other organs. The two major divisions of the nervous system are the *peripheral nervous system (PNS)* and the *central nervous system (CNS)*, which includes the brain and spinal cord.

The Peripheral Nervous System: Keeping in Touch with the World

The peripheral nervous system has two components: the somatic nervous system and the autonomic nervous system.

The Somatic Nervous System   The first component of the peripheral nervous system is the *somatic nervous system*, which transmits information from the senses to the CNS and carries signals from the CNS to the muscles that move the skeleton.

The Autonomic Nervous System   The second component of the peripheral nervous system is the *autonomic nervous system*. It carries messages back and forth between the CNS and the heart, lungs, and other organs and glands.

The Central Nervous System: Making Sense of the World

The CNS is laid out in interconnected groups of neuronal cell bodies, called *nuclei*, whose collections of axons travel together in *fiber tracts*, or *pathways*.

The Spinal Cord The *spinal cord* receives information from the peripheral senses and sends it to the brain; it also relays messages from the brain to the periphery. In addition, cells of the spinal cord can direct simple behaviors, called *reflexes*, without instructions from the brain.

The Brain The brain's major subdivisions are the *hindbrain, midbrain,* and *forebrain.* The hindbrain includes the *medulla,* the *cerebellum,* and the *locus coeruleus.* The midbrain includes the *substantia nigra.* The *reticular formation* is found in both the hindbrain and the midbrain. The forebrain is the largest and most highly developed part of the brain; it includes many structures, including the *hypothalamus* and *thalamus.* A part of the hypothalamus called the *suprachiasmatic nuclei* maintains a clock that determines biological rhythms. Other forebrain structures include the *striatum, hippocampus,* and *amygdala.* Several of these structures form the *limbic system,* which plays an important role in regulating emotion and memory.

The Cerebral Cortex The outer surface of the *cerebral hemispheres* is called the *cerebral cortex*; it is responsible for many of the higher functions of the brain, including speech and reasoning. The functional areas of the cortex include the *sensory cortex, motor cortex,* and *association cortex.*

The Divided Brain in a Unified Self The functions of the right and left hemispheres of the cerebral cortex are specialized to some degree. In most people, the left hemisphere is more active in language and logical tasks and the right hemisphere is more active in spatial, musical, and artistic tasks. A task that is performed more efficiently by one hemisphere than the other is said to be *lateralized.* The hemispheres are connected through the *corpus callosum,* allowing them to operate in a coordinated fashion.

Plasticity in the Central Nervous System *Plasticity* in the central nervous system, the ability to strengthen neural connections at its synapses as well as to establish new synapses, forms the basis for learning and memory. Scientists are searching for ways to increase plasticity following brain damage.

The Chemistry of Psychology

Neurons that use the same neurotransmitter form a *neurotransmitter system.*

Three Classes of Neurotransmitters There are three classes of neurotransmitters: small molecules, peptides, and gases. *Acetylcholine* systems in the brain influence memory processes and movement. *Norepinephrine* is released by neurons whose axons spread widely throughout the brain; it is involved in arousal, mood, and learning. *Serotonin,* another widespread neurotransmitter, is active in systems regulating mood and appetite. *Dopamine* systems are involved in movement, motivation, and higher cognitive activities. Both Parkinson's disease and schizophrenia involve a disturbance of dopamine systems. *GABA* is an inhibitory neurotransmitter involved in anxiety and epilepsy. *Glutamate* is the most common excitatory neurotransmitter. It is involved in learning and memory and, in excess, may cause neuronal death. *Endorphins* are peptide neurotransmitters that affect pain pathways. Nitric oxide and carbon monoxide are gases that function as neurotransmitters.

The Endocrine System: Coordinating the Internal World

Like nervous system cells, those of the *endocrine system* communicate by releasing a chemical that signals to other cells. However, the chemicals released by endocrine organs, or *glands,* are called *hormones* and are carried by the bloodstream to remote target organs. The target organs often produce a coordinated response to hormonal stimulation. One of these responses is the *fight-or-flight syndrome,* which is triggered by adrenal hormones that prepare for action in times of stress. Hormones also affect brain development, contributing to sex differences in the brain and behavior. Negative feedback systems are involved in the control of most endocrine functions. The brain is the main controller. Through the hypothalamus, it controls the pituitary gland, which in turn controls endocrine organs in the body. The brain is also a target organ for most endocrine secretions.

The Immune System: Defending the Body

The *immune system* serves both as a sensory system that monitors the internal state of the body and as a protective system for detecting and destroying invading cells and toxic substances. *Autoimmune disorders* result when cells of the immune system attack normal cells of the body. There are important interactions among the immune system, nervous system, and endocrine system.

Sensation

How do you know where you are right now? Your brain tells you, of course, but it must get its information from your eyes and ears and your other senses. In this chapter, we draw your attention to the amazing processes through which your senses work and to some of the problems that occur when they don't. We have organized our tour of the senses as follows:

Years ago, Fred Aryee lost his right arm below the elbow in a boating accident, yet he still "feels" his missing arm and hand (Shreeve, 1993). Like Fred, many people who have lost an arm or a leg continue to experience itching and other sensations from a "phantom limb." When asked to "move" it, they can feel it move, and some people feel intense pain when their missing hand suddenly seems to tighten into a fist, digging nonexistent fingernails into a phantom palm. Worse, they may be unable to "open" their hand to relieve the pain. In an effort to help these people, scientists have seated them at a table in front of a mirror, then angled the mirror to create the illusion that their amputated arm and hand have been restored. When these patients moved their real hands while looking in the mirror, they not only "felt" movement occurring in their phantom hands, but they could also "unclench" their phantom fists and stop their intense pain (Ramachandran & Rogers-Ramachandran, 2000). This clever strategy

TRY THIS

arose from research on how vision interacts with the sense of touch. To experience this kind of interaction yourself, sit across a table from someone and ask that person to stroke the tabletop while stroking your knee under the table in exactly the same way, in exactly the same direction. If you watch the person's hand stroking the table, you will soon experience the touch sensations coming from the table, not your knee! If the person's two hands do not move in synch, however, the illusion will not occur (Tsakiris & Haggard, 2005).

This illusion illustrates several points about our senses. It shows, first, that the streams of information coming from different senses can interact. Second, it reveals that experience can change the sensations we receive. Third, and most important, the illusion suggests that "reality" differs from person to person. This last point sounds silly if you assume that there is an objective reality that is the same for everyone. After all, the seat you sit on and the book you are reading are solid objects. You can see and feel them with your senses, so they must look and feel the same to you as they would to anyone else. But sensory psychologists tell us that reality is not that simple—that the senses do not reflect an objective reality. Just as people can feel a hand that is not actually "there," the senses of each individual actively shape information about the outside world to create a *personal reality*. The sensory experiences of different species—and individual humans—vary. You do not see the same world a fly sees, people from California may not hear music quite the same way as do people from Singapore, and different people experience color differently.

To understand how your own sensory systems create your own personal reality, you have to understand something about the senses themselves. A **sense** is a system that translates information from outside the nervous system into neural activity. For example, vision is the system through which the eyes convert light into neural activity. This neural activity tells the brain something about the source of the light (e.g., that it is bright) or about objects from which the light is reflected (e.g., that there is a round, red object out there). These messages from the senses, called **sensations,** provide a link between the self and the world outside the brain. This link is a vital one because what we see, hear, smell, taste, and touch shapes many aspects of behavior and mental processes and helps us to adapt and survive in our environment.

Traditionally, psychologists have distinguished between *sensation*—the initial message from the senses—and *perception*, the process through which messages from the senses are given meaning. They point out, for example, that you do not actually sense a cat lying on the sofa; you sense shapes and colors—visual sensations. You

sense A system that translates information from outside the nervous system into neural activity.

sensations Messages from the senses that make up the raw information that affects many kinds of behavior and mental processes.

then use your knowledge of the world to interpret, or perceive, these sensations as a cat. However, it is impossible to draw a clear line between sensation and perception, partly because the process of interpreting sensations begins in the sense organs themselves. For example, a frog's eye immediately interprets any small black object as "fly!"—thus enabling the frog to attack the fly with its tongue without waiting for its brain to process the sensory information (Lettvin et al., 1959).

This chapter covers the first steps of the sensation-perception process; the chapter on perception deals with the later steps. Together, these chapters illustrate how we human beings, with our sense organs and brains, create our own realities. In this chapter we explore how sensations are produced, received, and acted upon. First, we consider what sensations are and how they inform us about the world. Then we examine the physical and psychological mechanisms involved in the auditory, visual, and chemical senses. And finally, we turn to a discussion of the somatic senses, which enable us to feel things, to experience temperature and pain, and to know where our body parts are in relation to one another.

Sensory Systems

The senses gather information about the world by detecting various forms of energy, such as sound, light, heat, and physical pressure. The eyes detect light energy, the ears detect the energy of sound, and the skin detects the energy of heat and pressure. Humans depend primarily on vision, hearing, and the skin senses to gain information about the world; they depend less than other animals on smell and taste. To your brain, "the world" also includes the rest of your body, and there are sensory systems that provide information about its movement and position.

All of these senses detect incoming stimulus energy, encode it in the form of neural activity, and transfer this coded information to the brain. Figure 4.1 illustrates these basic steps in sensation. At each step, sensory information is "processed" in some way. So the information that arrives at one point in the system is not the same as the information that goes to the next step.

In some sensory systems, the first step in sensation involves **accessory structures,** which modify the energy created by something in the environment—such as a person talking or a flashing sign (Step 1 in Figure 4.1). The outer part of the ear is an accessory structure that collects sound; the lens of the eye is an accessory structure that changes incoming light by focusing it.

The second step in sensation is **transduction,** which is the process of converting incoming energy into neural activity (Step 2 in Figure 4.1). Just as a mobile phone receives energy and transduces it into sounds, the ears receive sound energy and transduce it into neural activity that people recognize as voices, music, and

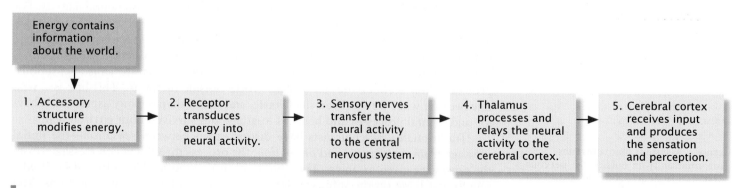

FIGURE 4.1

Elements of a Sensory System

In each sensory system, energy from the world is focused by accessory structures and detected by sensory receptors, which convert the energy into neural signals. These signals are then relayed through the brain, which processes them into perceptual experiences.

other auditory experiences. Transduction takes place at structures called **sensory receptors,** specialized cells that detect certain forms of energy. Sensory receptors are somewhat like the neurons that we describe in the chapter on biological aspects of psychology; they respond to incoming energy by firing an action potential and releasing neurotransmitters that send a signal to neighboring cells. (However, some sensory receptors do not have axons and dendrites, as neurons do.) Sensory receptors respond best to changes in energy (Graziano et al., 2002). A constant level of stimulation usually produces **adaptation,** a process through which responsiveness to an unchanging stimulus decreases over time. This is why the touch sensations you get from your glasses or wristwatch disappear shortly after you have put them on.

Next, sensory nerves carry the output from receptors to the central nervous system—the spinal cord and the brain (Step 3 in Figure 4.1). For all the senses except smell (Shepherd, 2005), sensory information entering the brain goes to the thalamus (Step 4). The thalamus does a preliminary analysis of each kind of information, then relays it to the appropriate sensory area of the cerebral cortex (Step 5). It is in the sensory cortex that the most complex processing occurs.

● The Problem of Coding

As sensory receptors transduce energy into patterns of nerve cell activity, they create a coded message that tells the brain about the physical properties of whatever stimulus has reached the receptors. The brain unscrambles this coded neural activity, allowing you to make sense of the stimulus—to decide, for example, whether you are looking at a cat, a dog, or a person. In other words, each psychological dimension of a sensation, such as the brightness or color of light, is based on its corresponding physical dimension, as coded by sensory receptors.

To better appreciate the problem of coding physical stimuli into neural activity, imagine that for your birthday you receive a Pet Brain. You are told that your Pet Brain is alive, but it does not respond when you open the box and talk to it. You remove it from the box and show it a hot-fudge sundae; no response. You show it pictures of other attractive brains; still no response. You are about to toss your Pet Brain in the trash when you suddenly realize that the two of you are not speaking the same language. As described in the chapter on biological aspects of psychology, the brain usually receives information from sensory neurons and responds by activating motor neurons. So if you want to communicate with your Pet Brain, you will have to send it messages by stimulating its sensory nerves. To read its responses you will have to record signals from its motor nerves.

After having this insight and setting up an electric stimulator and a recording device, you are faced with an awesome problem. How do you describe a hot-fudge sundae to sensory nerves so that they will pass on the correct information to the brain? This is the problem of **coding,** the translation of the physical properties of a stimulus into a pattern of neural activity that specifically identifies those properties.

If you want the brain to see the sundae, you should stimulate its optic nerve (the nerve from the eye to the brain) rather than its auditory nerve (the nerve from the ear to the brain). This idea is based on the **doctrine of specific nerve energies:** Stimulation of a particular sensory nerve provides codes for that one sense, no matter how the stimulation takes place. For example, if you apply gentle pressure to your eyeball, you will produce activity in the optic nerve and sense little spots of light. **TRY THIS**

Having chosen the optic nerve to send visual information, you must next develop a code for the specific attributes of the sundae: the soft white curves of the vanilla ice cream, the dark richness of the chocolate, the bright red roundness of the cherry on top. These dimensions must be coded in the language of neural activity—that is, in the firing of action potentials.

Some attributes of a stimulus are coded relatively simply. For example, certain neurons in the visual system fire faster in response to a bright light than to a dim light. This is called a **temporal code,** because it involves changes in the *timing*

● **accessory structures** Structures, such as the lens of the eye, that modify a stimulus.

● **transduction** The process of converting incoming energy into neural activity.

● **sensory receptors** Specialized cells that detect certain forms of energy.

● **adaptation** The process through which responsiveness to an unchanging stimulus decreases over time.

● **coding** Translating the physical properties of a stimulus into a pattern of neural activity that specifically identifies those properties.

● **doctrine of specific nerve energies** The discovery that stimulation of a particular sensory nerve provides codes for that sense, no matter how the stimulation takes place.

● **temporal codes** Coding attributes of a stimulus in terms of changes in the timing of neural firing.

pattern of nerve firing. Other temporal codes can be more complex. For example, a burst of firing followed by a slower firing rate means something different than does a steady rate of firing. Information about a stimulus can also take the form of a **spatial code,** which involves the *location* of neurons that are firing and those that are not. For example, different sensory neurons will fire depending on whether someone touches your hand or your foot. Sensory information can also be recoded at several relay points as it makes its way to, and through, the brain.

In summary, the problem of coding is solved by means of sensory systems, which allow the brain to receive detailed, accurate, and useful information about stimuli in its environment. If you succeed in creating the right coding system, your Pet Brain will finally know what a hot-fudge sundae looks like.

LINKAGES Sensation and Biological Aspects of Psychology

What Is It? In the split second before you recognized this stimulus as a hot-fudge sundae, sensory neurons in your visual system detected the light reflected off this page and transduced it into a neural code that your brain could interpret. The coding and decoding process occurs so quickly and efficiently in all our senses that we are seldom aware of it. Later in this chapter, we describe how this remarkable feat is accomplished.

● **spatial codes** Coding attributes of a stimulus in terms of the location of firing neurons relative to their neighbors.

LINKAGES (a link to Biological Aspects of Psychology, p. 84)

As sensory systems transfer information to the brain, they also organize that information. This organized information is called a *representation*. If you have read the chapter on biological aspects of psychology, you are already familiar with some characteristics of sensory representations. In humans, representations of vision, hearing, and the skin senses in the cerebral cortex share the following features:

1. The information from each of these senses reaches the cortex through the thalamus. (Figure 3.13 shows where this area of the brain is.)

2. Each side of the cerebral cortex builds a sensory representation of the opposite, or *contralateral*, side of the world. So the left side of the visual cortex "sees" the right side of the world, whereas the right side of that cortex "sees" the left side of the world. Similarly, the contralateral representation of skin senses occurs because most sensory nerve fibers from each side of the body cross over to the opposite side of the thalamus and go from there to the cerebral cortex.

3. The cortex contains maps, or *topographical representations*, of each sense. Accordingly, features that are next to each other in the world eventually stimulate neurons that are next to each other in the brain. For example, two notes that are similar in pitch activate neighboring neurons in the auditory cortex, and the neurons that respond to sensations in the elbow and in the forearm are relatively close to one another in the somatosensory cortex. There are multiple maps representing each sense, but the area that receives information directly from the thalamus is called the *primary cortex* for that sense.

4. The density of nerve fibers in a sense organ determines how extensively it is represented in the cortex. The skin on your fingertip, for example, has more touch receptors per square inch than the skin on your back does. So the area of cortex that represents your fingertip is larger than the area that represents your back.

5. Each region of primary sensory cortex is divided into columns of cells, each of which has a somewhat specialized role in sensory processing. For example, some columns of cells in the visual cortex respond most strongly to diagonal lines, whereas other columns respond most strongly to horizontal lines.

6. For each of the senses, regions of cortex other than the primary areas do additional processing of sensory information. As described in the chapter on biological aspects of psychology, these areas of *association cortex* may contain representations of more than one sense, thus setting the stage for the combining of sensory information that we described at the beginning of this chapter.

In summary, sensory systems convert various forms of physical energy into neural activity. (As described in Figure 4.1, the energy may first be modified by accessory structures.) The resulting pattern of neural activity encodes the physical properties of the energy. The codes are modified as the information is transferred to the brain and processed further. In the remainder of this chapter we describe how these processes take place in hearing, vision, and other sensory systems. ■

Hearing

In 1969, when Neil Armstrong became the first human to step onto the moon, millions of people back on the earth heard his radio transmission: "That's one small step for [a] man, one giant leap for mankind." But if Armstrong had taken off his space helmet and shouted, "Whoo-ee! I can moonwalk!" another astronaut, a foot away, would not have heard him. Why? Because Armstrong would have been speaking into airless, empty space. **Sound** is a repeated fluctuation, a rising and falling, in the pressure of air, water, or some other substance called a *medium*. On the moon, which has almost no atmospheric medium, sound cannot exist.

● Sound

Vibrations of an object produce the fluctuations in pressure that create sound. Each time the object moves outward, it increases the pressure in the medium around it. As the object moves back, the pressure drops. When you speak, for example, your vocal cords vibrate, producing fluctuations in air pressure that spread as waves. A *wave* is a repeated variation in pressure that spreads out in three dimensions. The wave can move great distances, but the air itself barely moves. Imagine a jam-packed line of people waiting to get into a movie. If someone at the rear of the line shoves the next person, a wave of people jostling against people may spread all the way to the front of the line, but the person who shoved first is still no closer to getting into the theater.

Noise Eliminators   Complex sound, including noise, can be analyzed into its component, simple sine waves by means of a mathematical process called *Fourier analysis*. Noise-eliminating headphones perform this waveform analysis, then use a sound synthesizer to produce exactly opposite waveforms. The opposing waves cancel each other out, and the amazing result is silence. Similar devices are being developed to treat chronic tinnitus, or "ringing in the ear."

● **Physical Characteristics of Sound**   Sound is represented graphically by waveforms like those in Figure 4.2. A *waveform* represents a wave in two dimensions, but remember that waves actually move through the air in all directions. This is the reason that, when people talk to each other in a movie theater or a lecture, others all around them are distracted by the conversation.

Three characteristics of the waveform are important in understanding sounds. First, the difference in air pressure from the baseline to the peak of the wave is the **amplitude** of the sound, or its intensity. Second, the distance from one wave peak to the next is called the **wavelength.** Third, a sound's **frequency** is the number of complete waveforms, or cycles, that pass by a given point each second. Frequency is described in a unit called *hertz*, abbreviated *Hz* (for Heinrich Hertz, a nineteenth-century physicist). One cycle per second is 1 Hz. Because the speed of sound is constant in a given medium, wavelength and frequency are related: The longer the wavelength, the lower the frequency; the shorter the wavelength, the higher the frequency. Most sounds are mixtures of many different frequencies and amplitudes. In contrast, a pure tone is made up of only one frequency and can be represented by what is known as a *sine wave* (Figure 4.2 shows such sine waves).

● **Psychological Dimensions of Sound**   The amplitude and frequency of sound waves determine the sounds that you hear. These physical characteristics of the waves produce the psychological dimensions of sound known as *loudness, pitch,* and *timbre.*

● **sound**   A repetitive fluctuation in the pressure of a medium, such as air.

● **amplitude**   The difference between the peak and the baseline of a waveform.

● **wavelength**   The distance from one peak to the next in a waveform.

● **frequency**   The number of complete waveforms, or cycles, that pass by a given point in space every second.

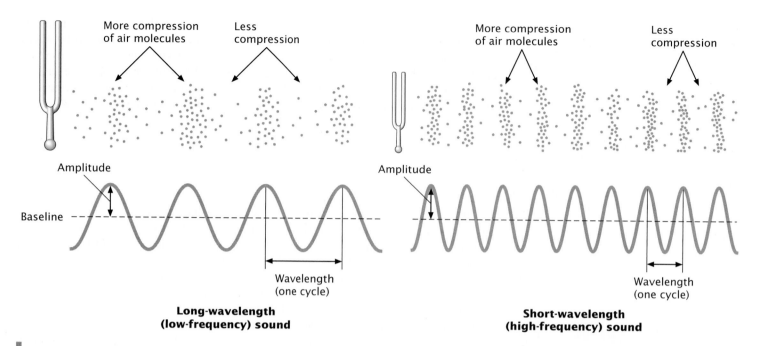

Long-wavelength (low-frequency) sound

Short-wavelength (high-frequency) sound

FIGURE 4.2

Sound Waves and Waveforms

Sound is created when objects, such as a tuning fork, vibrate. The vibrations create alternating regions of greater and lesser compression of air molecules, which can be represented as a waveform. The point of greatest compression is the peak of the graph. The lowest point, or trough, is where compression is least.

Loudness is determined by the amplitude of the sound wave; waves with greater amplitude produce sensations of louder sounds. Loudness is described in units called *decibels*, abbreviated *dB*. By definition, zero decibels is the minimum detectable sound for normal hearing. Table 4.1 gives examples of the loudness of a wide range of sounds.

Pitch, or how high or low a tone sounds, depends on the frequency of sound waves. High-frequency waves are sensed as sounds of high pitch. The highest note on a piano has a frequency of about 4000 Hz; the lowest note has a frequency of about 50 Hz. Humans can hear sounds ranging from about 20 Hz to about 20000 Hz.

TABLE 4.1   Intensity of Sound Sources

Sound intensity varies across an extremely wide range. A barely audible sound is, by definition, 0 decibels (dB). Every increase of 20 dB reflects a tenfold increase in the amplitude of sound waves. So the 40-dB sounds of an office are actually 10 times as intense as a 20-dB whisper, and traffic noise of 100 dB is 10,000 times as intense as that whisper.

Source	Sound Level (dB)
Spacecraft launch (from 45 m)	180
Loudest rock band on record	160
Pain threshold (approximate)	140
Large jet motor (at 22 m)	120
Loudest human shout on record	111
Heavy auto traffic	100
Conversation (at about 1 m)	60
Quiet office	40
Soft whisper	20
Threshold of hearing	0

An Accessory Structure Some animals, like Annie here, have a large pinna that can be rotated to help detect sounds and locate their source.

Almost everyone experiences relative pitch; that is, they can tell whether one note is higher than, lower than, or equal to another note. However, some people have *perfect pitch*, which means they can identify specific frequencies and the notes they represent. They can say, for example, that a 262-Hz tone is middle C. Perfect pitch appears to be an inborn trait (Bella & Peretz, 2003), but some children can improve their skill at pitch identification if given special training before about the age of six (Takeuchi & Hulse, 1993). About 4 percent of people appear to be "tone deaf," which means they are not good at discriminating among musical tones (Hyde et al., 2006), even though they can discriminate the pitches of nonmusical sounds (Hyde & Peretz, 2004).

Timbre (pronounced "tamber") is the quality of sound. It is determined by complex wave patterns that are added onto the lowest, or *fundamental*, frequency of a sound. The extra waves allow you to tell, for example, the difference between a note played on a flute and the same note played on a clarinet. Experiencing this dimension of sound appears to depend on specialized neurons in the auditory system; there are cases of brain injury in which timbre is no longer sensed even though all other aspects of hearing remain intact (Kohlmetz et al., 2003).

● The Ear

The human ear converts sound energy into neural activity through a series of accessory structures and transduction mechanisms.

● **Auditory Accessory Structures** Sound waves are collected in the outer ear, beginning with the *pinna*, the crumpled part of the ear visible on the side of the head. The pinna funnels sound down through the ear canal (see Figure 4.3). (People straining to hear a faint sound may cup a hand to their ear and bend the pinna forward, which enlarges the sound-collection area. Try this yourself, and you will notice a clear difference in how sounds sound.) At the end of the ear canal, the sound waves reach the middle ear, where they strike a tightly stretched membrane known as the *eardrum*, or **tympanic membrane**. The sound waves set up matching vibrations in the tympanic membrane.

TRY THIS ▸

Next, the vibrations of the tympanic membrane are passed on by a chain of three tiny bones: the *malleus*, or *hammer*; the *incus*, or *anvil*; and the *stapes* (pronounced "STAY-peez"), or *stirrup* (see Figure 4.3). These bones amplify the changes in pressure produced by the original sound waves, by focusing the vibrations of the tympanic membrane onto a smaller membrane, the *oval window*.

● **Auditory Transduction** When sound vibrations pass through the oval window, they enter the inner ear, reaching the **cochlea** (pronounced "COCK-lee-ah"), the structure in which transduction occurs. The cochlea is wrapped into a coiled spiral. (*Cochlea* is derived from the Greek word for "snail.") If you unwrapped the spiral, you would see that a fluid-filled tube runs down its length. The **basilar membrane** forms the floor of this long tube (see Figure 4.3). Whenever a sound wave passes through the fluid in the tube, it moves the basilar membrane, and this movement bends *hair cells* of the *organ of Corti*, a group of cells that rests on the membrane. These hair cells connect with fibers from the **auditory nerve**, a bundle of axons that goes into the brain. When the hair cells bend, they stimulate neurons in the auditory nerve to fire in a pattern that sends the brain a coded message about the amplitude and frequency of the incoming sound waves (Griesinger, Richards, & Ashmore, 2005). You sense this information as loudness and pitch.

● **Deafness** The middle and inner ear are among the most delicate structures in the body, and if they deteriorate or are damaged deafness can result. One form of deafness is caused by problems with the bones of the middle ear. Over time they can

- **loudness** A psychological dimension of sound determined by the amplitude of a sound wave.

- **pitch** How high or low a tone sounds.

- **timbre** The mixture of frequencies and amplitudes that make up the quality of sound.

- **tympanic membrane** A membrane in the middle ear that generates vibrations that match the sound waves striking it.

- **cochlea** A fluid-filled spiral structure in the ear in which auditory transduction occurs.

- **basilar membrane** The floor of the fluid-filled duct that runs through the cochlea.

- **auditory nerve** The bundle of axons that carries stimuli from the hair cells of the cochlea to the brain.

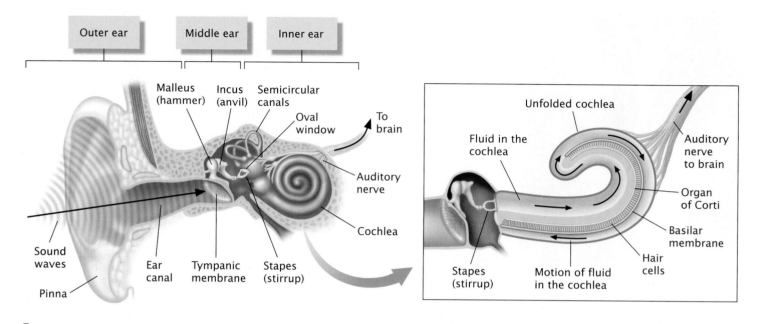

FIGURE 4.3

Structures of the Ear

The outer ear (pinna and ear canal) channels sounds into the middle ear, where the vibrations of the tympanic membrane are amplified by three delicate bones, creating vibrations in the fluid inside the cochlea in the inner ear. The coils of the cochlea are unfolded in this illustration to show the path of the fluid waves along the basilar membrane. Movements of the basilar membrane stimulate the hair cells of the organ of Corti, which transduce the vibrations into changes in neural firing patterns, which are sent along the auditory nerve to the brain.

fuse together, preventing accurate conduction of vibrations from one bone to the next. This condition, called *conduction deafness,* can be treated by surgery to break the bones apart or to replace the natural bones with plastic ones (Ayache et al., 2003). Hearing aids that amplify incoming sounds can also help.

A more common problem, called *nerve deafness,* results when the auditory nerve or, more commonly, the hair cells are damaged (Shepherd & McCreery, 2006). Hair cell damage occurs gradually with age, but it can also be caused by extended exposure to the noise of jet engines, industrial equipment, gunfire, intense rock music, and the like (Goldstein, 2002; see Figure 4.4).

For example, Stephen Stills, Pete Townshend, and other 1970s rock musicians have become partially deaf after many years of performing extremely loud music

FIGURE 4.4

Effects of Loud Sounds

High-intensity sounds can actually tear off the hair cells of the inner ear. Part (A) shows the organ of Corti of a normal guinea pig. Part (B) shows the damage caused by exposure to twenty-four hours of 2000 Hz sound at 120 decibels. Generally, any sound loud enough to produce tinnitus (ringing in the ears) causes some damage. In humans, small amounts of damage can accumulate over time to produce a significant hearing loss by middle age—as many middle-aged rock musicians can attest.

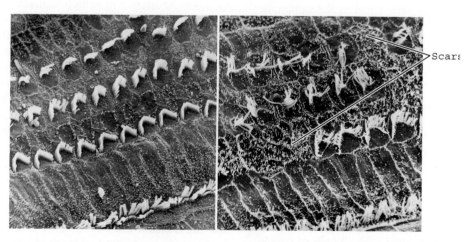

(A)　　　　　　　　　(B)

Shaping the Brain   The primary auditory cortex is larger in trained musicians than in people whose jobs are less focused on fine gradations of sound. How much larger this area becomes is correlated with how long the musicians have studied their art. This finding reminds us that, as described in the chapter on biological aspects of psychology, the brain can literally be shaped by experience and other environmental factors.

(Ackerman, 1995). In the United States and other industrialized countries, people born after World War II are experiencing hearing loss at a younger age than did those in earlier generations, possibly because noise pollution has increased during the past sixty years (Levine, 1999).

Although hair cells can regrow in chickens (who seldom listen to rock music), such regrowth was long believed impossible in mammals (Salvi et al., 1998). However, evidence that mammals can regenerate a related kind of inner-ear hair cell has fueled optimism about finding a way to stimulate regeneration of human auditory hair cells (Malgrange et al., 1999). This feat might be accomplished by treating damaged areas with growth factors similar to those used to repair damaged brain cells (Shepherd et al., 2005; see the chapter on biological aspects of psychology). Gene therapy offers another promising approach. In one study, researchers inserted into the inner ears of deaf guinea pigs the gene that normally guides prenatal development of hair cells in these animals. The result was regeneration of hair cells in the cochlea, and restoration of the animals' hearing (Izumikawa et al., 2005). Hair cell regeneration in humans could revolutionize the treatment of nerve deafness, which cannot be overcome by conventional hearing aids. Meanwhile, scientists have developed an electronic device that can be implanted in the inner ear to serve as an artificial cochlea. These *cochlear implants* can't eliminate deafness, but they provide enough coded stimulation of the auditory nerve to restore a useful degree of hearing in many patients (Seghier et al., 2005; Zeng, 2005).

● Auditory Pathways, Representations, and Experiences

Before sounds can be heard, the information coded in the activity of auditory nerve fibers must be sent to the brain and processed further. The auditory nerve, the bundle of axons that conveys this information, connects to structures in the brainstem, and from there to the thalamus. After preliminary processing in the thalamus, the sound information is relayed to the **primary auditory cortex**. As described in the chapter on biological aspects of psychology, this area lies in the brain's temporal lobe, close to the areas involved in language perception and production (see Figure 3.16). It is in the primary auditory cortex, and in these nearby areas, that information about sound is subjected to the most intense and complex analysis (Semple & Scott, 2003). The auditory cortex is also activated by imagined sounds, such as those occurring when people mentally rehearse a phone number, replay a song "in their heads," or in certain kinds of mental disorder, experience auditory hallucinations (Shergill et al., 2000).

Various aspects of sound are processed by different regions of the brain's auditory system. For example, information about the source of a sound and information about its frequency are processed in separate regions of the auditory cortex (Rauschecker, 1997). Further, cells in the cortex have similar *preferred frequencies*, meaning that they respond most vigorously to sounds of a particular frequency. The cells are arranged so as to create a frequency "map" in which cells with similar preferred frequencies are closer to each other than those with very different preferred frequencies. Each neuron in the auditory nerve, too, is most responsive to a certain frequency, though each also responds to some extent to a range of frequencies (Schnee et al., 2005). The auditory cortex must examine the pattern of activity of a number of neurons in order to determine the frequency of a sound.

Certain parts of the auditory cortex process certain types of sounds. One part, for example, specializes in responding to information coming from human voices (Belin, Zatorre, & Ahad, 2002); others are particularly responsive to sounds made by animals, sounds made by tools, or the sounds of musical instruments (Lewis et al., 2005; Zatorre, 2003). The primary auditory cortex receives information from other senses as well. It is activated, for example, when you watch someone say words (but not when the person makes other facial movements). This activity forms part of the biological basis for the lip reading that helps you to hear what people say (van Wassenhove, Grant, & Poeppel, 2005).

● **primary auditory cortex**   The area in the brain's temporal lobe that is first to receive information about sounds from the thalamus.

Processing Language As this student and teacher communicate using American Sign Language, the visual information they receive from each other's hand movements is processed by the same areas of their brains that allow hearing people to understand spoken language (Neville et al., 1998).

● **Sensing Pitch** The frequency of a sound determines its pitch, but sensing pitch is not as simple as you might expect. The reason is that most sounds are made up of mixtures of frequencies. The mixtures in musical chords and voices, for example, can produce sounds whose pitch is ambiguous, or open to interpretation. As a result, different people may experience the "same" sound as different pitches (Patel & Balaban, 2001). In fact, a sequence of chords can sound like a rising scale to one person and a falling scale to another. As mentioned earlier, pitch-recognition abilities are influenced by genetics (Drayna et al., 2001), but cultural factors are partly responsible for the way in which pitch is sensed (Cross, 2003). For instance, people in the United States tend to hear ambiguous musical scales as progressing in a direction that is opposite to the way they are heard by people from Canada and England (Dawe, Platt, & Welsh, 1998). This cross-cultural difference appears to be a reliable one, though researchers do not yet know exactly why it occurs.

● **Locating Sounds** Your brain analyzes the location of sound sources based partly on the very slight difference in the time at which a sound arrives at each of your ears (it reaches the closer ear slightly earlier). The brain also uses information about the difference in sound intensity at each ear (sounds from sources that are closer to one ear are slightly louder in that ear). As a result, you can be reasonably sure where a voice or other sound is coming from even when you can't see its source. To perform this feat, the brain must analyze the activities of groups of neurons that, individually, signal only a rough approximation of the location. It is the combined firing frequencies of these many neurons in the auditory cortex that creates a sort of "Morse code" that describes where a sound is coming from (Wright & Fitzgerald, 2001). Other codes tell the brain about the intensity and frequency of sounds. Let's consider those coding systems next.

● Coding Intensity and Frequency

People can hear an incredibly wide range of sound intensities. The faintest sound that can be heard moves the inner ear's hair cells less than the diameter of a single hydrogen atom (Hudspeth, 1997). Sounds more than a trillion times more intense can also be heard. Between these extremes, the auditory system codes intensity in a straightforward way: The more intense the sound, the more rapid the firing of a given neuron.

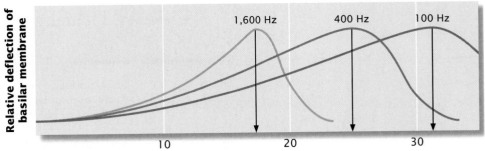

FIGURE 4.5

Movements of the Basilar Membrane

As waves of fluid in the cochlea spread along the basilar membrane, the membrane is bent and then recovers. As shown in these three examples, the point at which the bending of the basilar membrane reaches a maximum is different for each sound frequency. According to place theory, these are the locations at which the hair cells receive the greatest stimulation.

The range of sound frequencies that humans can hear is not as wide as the range which dogs and some other animals can detect. People are much better than most other mammals, though, at hearing slight differences between frequencies (Shera, Guinan, & Oxenham, 2002). How do people discriminate these differences? Frequency appears to be coded in two ways, which are described by place theory and frequency-matching theory.

● **Place Theory** Georg von Bekesy's pioneering experiments in the 1930s and 1940s were built on Hermann von Helmholtz's earlier research on how frequency is coded (Evans, 2003; von Bekesy, 1960). Studying human cadavers, von Bekesy created an opening in the cochlea in order to see the basilar membrane within. He then presented sounds of differing frequencies by vibrating a rubber membrane that was installed in place of the oval window. Using special optical instruments, von Bekesy observed ripples of waves moving down the basilar membrane. He noticed that the outline of the waves, called the *envelope*, grows and reaches a peak; then it quickly tapers off, much like an ocean wave that crests and then dissolves.

As shown in Figure 4.5, the critical feature of this wave is that the place on the basilar membrane where the envelope peaks depends on the frequency of the sound. High-frequency sounds produce a wave that peaks soon after it starts down the basilar membrane. Lower-frequency sounds produce a wave that peaks farther along the basilar membrane, farther from the oval window.

How does the location of the peak affect the coding of frequency? Helmholtz suggested an explanation. According to his **place theory**, later called the *traveling wave theory* by von Bekesy, the greatest response by hair cells occurs at the peak of the wave. Because the location of the peak varies with the frequency of the sound, it follows that hair cells at a particular place on the basilar membrane respond most to a particular frequency of sound, called a *characteristic frequency*. In other words, place theory describes a spatial, or place-related, code for frequency. When hair cells at a particular location respond to a sound, we sense a pitch that is at the characteristic frequency of those cells. One important result of this arrangement is that extended exposure to a very loud sound of a particular frequency can destroy hair cells at one spot on the basilar membrane, making it impossible to hear sounds of that frequency.

● **Frequency-Matching Theory** Place theory accounts for a great deal of data on hearing, but it cannot explain the coding of very low frequencies, such as that of a deep bass note. We know this because humans can hear frequencies as low as 20 Hz even though no auditory nerve fibers respond to very low characteristic frequencies. These low frequencies must be coded in some other way. The answer is provided by **frequency-matching theory**, which is based on the fact that the firing rate of a neuron in the auditory nerve can match the frequency of a sound wave. Frequency matching provides a *temporal*, or timing-related, code for frequency. For

● **place theory** A theory that hair cells at a particular place on the basilar membrane respond most to a particular frequency of sound.

● **frequency-matching theory** The view that some sounds are coded in terms of the frequency of neural firing.

in review Hearing

Aspect of Sensory System	Elements	Key Characteristics
Energy	Sound: pressure fluctuations of air produced by vibrations	The amplitude, frequency, and complexity of sound waves determine the loudness, pitch, and timbre of sounds.
Accessory structures	Ear: pinna, tympanic membrane, malleus, incus, stapes, oval window, basilar membrane	Changes in pressure produced by the original wave are amplified.
Transduction mechanism	Hair cells of the organ of Corti	Frequencies are coded by the location of the hair cells receiving the greatest stimulation (place theory) and by the firing rate of neurons (frequency-matching theory).
Pathways and representations	Auditory nerve to thalamus to primary auditory cortex	Neighboring cells in the auditory cortex have similar preferred frequencies, thus providing a map of sound frequencies.

example, one neuron might fire at every peak of a wave. So a sound of 20 Hz could be coded by a neuron that fires 20 times per second.

Frequency matching by individual neurons could apply up to about 1000 Hz, but no neuron can fire faster than 1000 times per second. A frequency matching code can be created for frequencies somewhat above 1000 Hz, though, through the combined activity of a group of neurons. Some neurons in the group might fire, for example, at every other wave peak, others at every fifth peak, and so on, producing a *volley* of firing at a combined frequency that is higher than any of these neurons could manage alone. Accordingly, frequency-matching theory is sometimes called the *volley theory* of frequency coding.

In summary, the nervous system uses more than one way to code the range of audible frequencies. The lowest sound frequencies are coded by frequency matching, whereby the frequency is matched by the firing rate of auditory nerve fibers. Low to moderate frequencies are coded by both frequency matching and the place on the basilar membrane at which the wave peaks. High frequencies are coded only by the place at which the wave peaks. (For a review of how changes in air pressure become signals in the brain that are perceived as sounds, see "In Review: Hearing.")

Vision

Soaring eagles have the incredible ability to see a mouse move in the grass from a mile away. Cats have special "reflectors" at the back of their eyes that help them to see even in very dim light. Nature has provided each species with a visual system uniquely adapted to its way of life. The human visual system is also adapted to do many things well: It combines great sensitivity and great sharpness, enabling us to see objects near and far, during the day and at night. Our night vision is not as good as that of some animals, but our color vision is excellent. This is not a bad tradeoff; being able to appreciate a sunset's splendor seems worth an occasional stumble in the dark. In this section, we consider the human visual sense and how it responds to light.

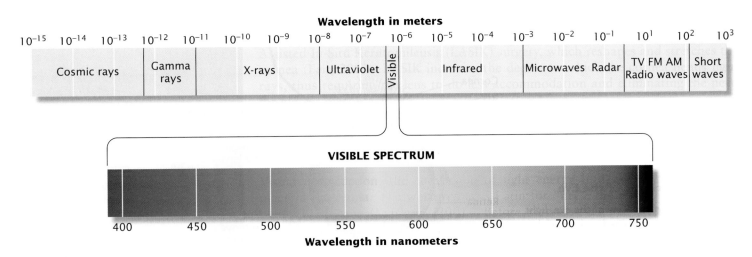

VISIBLE SPECTRUM

Wavelength in nanometers

FIGURE 4.6

The Spectrum of Electromagnetic Energy

The range of wavelengths that the human eye can see as visible light is limited to a band of only about 370 nanometers within the much wider spectrum of electromagnetic energy. To detect energy outside this range, we must rely on electronic instruments such as radios, TV sets, mobile phones, radar, and infrared night-vision scopes that can "see" this energy, just as the eye sees visible light.

● Light

Light is a form of energy known as *electromagnetic radiation*. Most electromagnetic radiation—including x-rays, radio waves, television signals, and radar is invisible to the human eye. In fact, as shown in Figure 4.6, the range, or spectrum, of **visible light** is just the tiny slice of electromagnetic radiation that has a wavelength from just under 400 nanometers (nm) to about 750 nanometers (a *nanometer* is one-billionth of a meter). Unlike sound, light does not need a medium to pass through. So, even on the airless moon, astronauts can see one another, even if they can't hear one another without radios. Light waves are like particles that pass through space, but they vibrate with a certain wavelength. In other words, light has some properties of waves and some properties of particles, and it is correct to refer to light as either *light waves* or *light rays*.

Sensations of light depend on two physical dimensions of light waves: intensity and wavelength. **Light intensity** refers to how much energy the light contains; it determines the brightness of light, much as the amplitude of sound waves determines the loudness of sound. What color you sense depends mainly on **light wavelength**. At a given intensity, different wavelengths produce sensations of different colors, much as different sound frequencies produce sensations of different pitch. For instance, 440-nm light appears violet blue, and 700-nm light appears orangish red.

● Focusing Light

Just as sound energy is converted to nerve cell activity in the ear, light energy is transduced into neural activity in the eye. The first step in this process occurs as accessory structures in the human eye modify incoming light rays. The light rays enter the eye by passing through the transparent, protective layer called the **cornea** (see Figure 4.7). Then the light passes through the **pupil,** the opening just behind the cornea. The **iris,** which gives the eye its color, adjusts the amount of light allowed into the eye by constricting to reduce the size of the pupil or relaxing to enlarge it. Directly behind the pupil is the **lens.** The cornea and the lens of the human eye are both curved so that, like the lens of a camera, they bend light rays. The light rays are focused into an image on the surface at the back of the eye; this surface is called the **retina.** Light

visible light Electromagnetic radiation that has a wavelength of about 400 nm to about 750 nm.

light intensity A physical dimension of light waves that refers to how much energy the light contains; it determines the brightness of light.

light wavelength The distance between peaks in light waves.

cornea The curved, transparent, protective layer through which light rays enter the eye.

pupil An opening in the eye, just behind the cornea, through which light passes.

iris The colorful part of the eye, which constricts or relaxes to adjust the amount of light entering the eye.

lens The part of the eye behind the pupil that bends light rays, focusing them on the retina.

retina The surface at the back of the eye onto which the lens focuses light rays.

TRY THIS **Rods and Cones** This electron microscope view of rods (blue) and cones (aqua) shows what your light receptors look like. Rods are more light sensitive, but they do not detect color. Cones can detect color, but they require more light in order to be activated. To experience the difference in how these cells work, look at an unfamiliar color photograph in a room where there is barely enough light to see. Even this dim light will activate your rods and allow you to make out images in the picture. But because there is not enough light to activate your cones, you will not be able to see colors in the photo.

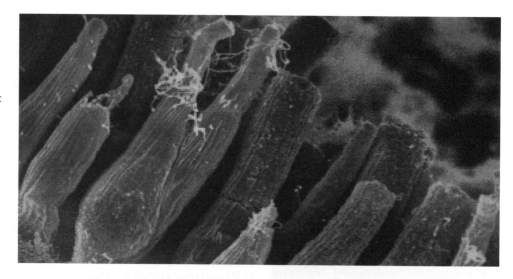

● **Interactions in the Retina** If the eye simply transferred to the brain the stimuli that are focused on the retina, we would experience images that are somewhat like a blurred TV picture. Instead, interactions among the cells of the retina allow the eye to actually sharpen visual images. As illustrated in Figure 4.9, the most direct connections from the photoreceptor cells to the brain go first to *bipolar cells* and then to *ganglion cells*. The axons of the ganglion cells extend out of the eye and into the brain.

However, this direct pathway is modified by interactions with other cells that change the information reaching the brain. These interactions enhance the sensation of contrast between areas of light and dark. Here's how it works: Most of the time, the amount of light reaching any two photoreceptors will differ slightly, because the edges and other specific features of objects create differing patterns of incoming light. When this happens, the receptor that is receiving more light inhibits, or

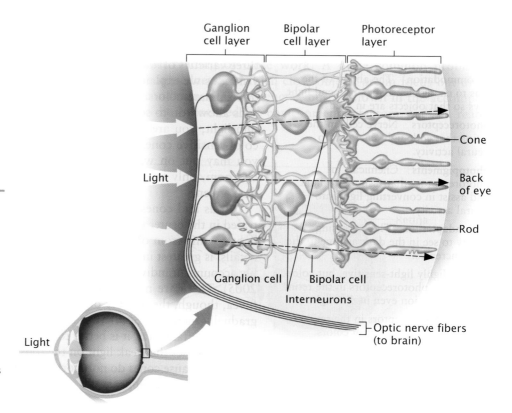

FIGURE 4.9

Cells in the Retina

Light rays actually pass through several layers of cells before striking photoreceptors, which are called rods and cones. Signals generated by the rods and cones then go back toward the surface of the retina, passing through bipolar cells and ganglion cells and on to the brain. Interconnections among interneurons, bipolar cells, and ganglion cells allow the eye to begin analyzing visual information and sharpening images even before the information leaves the retina.

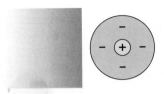

Uniform lighting produces moderate activity because the excitatory and inhibitory receptors cancel each other's effects.

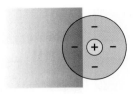

Higher activity when a region of light borders a darker region, because some inhibitory surround receptors are not activated.

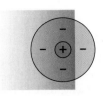

Low activity because light is only stimulating receptors in the inhibitory surround.

FIGURE 4.10

Center-Surround Receptive Fields of Ganglion Cells

Having center-surround receptive fields allows ganglion cells to act as edge detectors. As shown at the left, if an edge is outside the receptive field of a center-on ganglion cell, there will be a uniform amount of light on both the excitatory center and the inhibitory surround, creating some baseline level of activity. If, as shown in the middle drawing, the dark side of an edge covers part of the inhibitory surround but leaves light on the excitatory center, the output of the cell will increase, signaling an edge in its receptive field. If, as shown at right, a dark area covers both the center and the surround, the cell's activity will decrease, because neither segment of its receptive field is receiving much stimulation.

reduces, the activity of the nearby photoreceptor that is receiving less light. As a result, the brain gets the impression that there is even less light at that nearby cell's location than there really is. How can one photoreceptor suppress the output of its neighbor? The process is called **lateral inhibition**, and it is made possible by *interneurons*, which are cells that make sideways, or lateral, connections between photoreceptors (see Figure 4.9). In other words, the brain is always receiving *comparisons* of the light that is hitting neighboring photoreceptors. Because of lateral inhibition, any difference in the amount of light reaching these photoreceptors will be exaggerated. This exaggeration helps us to see more clearly. The image of the buttons on your mobile phone, for example, consists of lighter areas next to darker ones. Lateral inhibition in the retina amplifies these differences, creating greater contrast that sharpens the edges of the buttons and makes them more noticeable.

● **Ganglion Cells and Their Receptive Fields**   Photoreceptors (rods and cones) and bipolar cells communicate by releasing neurotransmitters. But as discussed in the chapter on biological aspects of psychology, neurotransmitters cause only small, graded changes in the membrane potential of the next cell, which cannot travel the distance from the eye to the brain. It is the **ganglion cells** in the retina that generate action potentials that are capable of traveling that distance along axons that extend out of the retina and into the brain.

As illustrated in Figure 4.9, ganglion cells each receive information from a certain group of photoreceptors. Accordingly, each ganglion cell can tell the brain about what is going on only in its own particular **receptive field**, which is the part of the retina and the corresponding part of the visual world to which the cell responds (Sekuler & Blake, 1994). So, depending on their location in the retina, some ganglion cells respond to light in, say, the upper right-hand side of the visual field, whereas others respond to light in the lower left-hand side, and so on. The receptive fields of most ganglion cells are shaped a bit like a doughnut, with a center and a surround. These *center-surround receptive fields* allow ganglion cells to compare the amount of light stimulating photoreceptors in the center of their receptive fields with the amount of light stimulating photoreceptors in the area around the center. Some ganglion cells are called *center-on cells* because they are activated by light in the center of their receptive fields and inhibited by light in the regions around the center (see Figure 4.10). *Center-off* ganglion cells work in just the opposite way. They are inhibited by light in the center of their receptive fields and activated by light in the surrounding areas.

lateral inhibition   A process in which lateral connections allow one photoreceptor to inhibit the responsiveness of its neighbor, thus enhancing the sensation of visual contrast.

ganglion cells   Cells in the retina that generate action potentials.

receptive field   The portion of the retina, and the visual world, that affects a given ganglion cell.

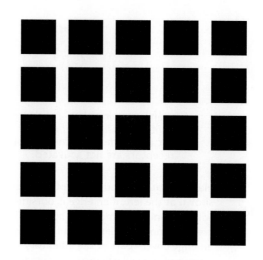

FIGURE 4.11

The Hermann Grid

Shadows appear at the intersections of this *Hermann grid*, until you look directly at them. To understand why, look at the smaller grid at right. The circles on that grid represent the receptive fields of two center-on ganglion cells in your retina. The cell whose receptive field includes the grid intersection has more whiteness shining on its inhibitory surround than the cell whose receptive field is just to the right of the intersection. So the output of the "intersection" cell will be lower than that of the one on the right, creating the impression of darkness at the intersection. Looking directly at an intersection projects its image onto your fovea, the area of the retina where ganglion cells have the smallest receptive fields. Now the whiteness of the intersection is stimulating the excitatory centers of several ganglion cells, creating a greater sensation of whiteness and making the shadow disappear.

The center-surround receptive fields of ganglion cells make it easier for you to see edges and, as illustrated in Figure 4.11, also create a sharper contrast between darker and lighter areas than actually exists. By enhancing the sensation of important features, the retina gives your brain an "improved" version of the visual world. As described next, the brain performs even more elaborate processing of visual information than does the retina.

● Visual Pathways

We have seen that visual information reaches the brain through the axons of ganglion cells, which leave the eye as a bundle of fibers called the **optic nerve** (see Figure 4.7). There can be no photoreceptors at the point where the optic nerve exits the eyeball, so you have a **blind spot** at that point, as Figure 4.12 shows.

After leaving the retina, about half the fibers of each eye's optic nerve cross over to the opposite side of the brain, creating a crisscross structure called the **optic chiasm**. (*Chiasm* means "cross" and is pronounced "KYE-az-um.") Fibers from the inside half of each eye, nearest to the nose, cross over; fibers from the outside half of each eye do not (see Figure 4.13). As a result of this arrangement, no matter where you look, information from the right half of your visual field goes to the left hemisphere of your brain and information from the left half of your visual field goes to the right hemisphere.

The optic chiasm lies on the bottom surface of the brain. Beyond the chiasm, optic fibers ascend into the brain itself. As shown in Figure 4.13, the axons from most of the retina's ganglion cells send their messages to a region of the thalamus

FIGURE 4.12

Finding Your Blind Spot

TRY THIS There is a blind spot where axons from the ganglion cells leave the eye. To "see" your blind spot, cover your left eye and stare at the cross inside the circle. Move the page closer and then farther away, and at some point the dot to the right should disappear. However, the vertical lines around the dot will probably look continuous, because the brain tends to fill in visual information at the blind spot (Spillmann et al., 2006). We are normally unaware of this "hole" in our vision because the blind spot of one eye is in the normal visual field of the other eye.

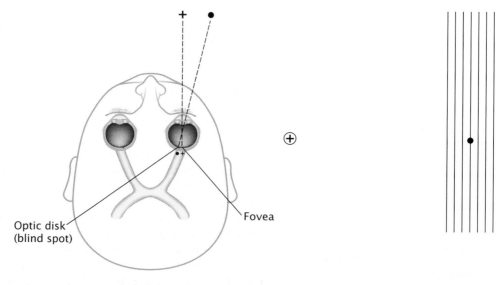

Optic disk (blind spot)

Fovea

FIGURE **4.13**

Pathways from the Ganglion Cells into the Brain

Light rays from the right side of the visual field (the right side of what you are looking at) end up on the left half of each retina (shown in red). Light rays from the left visual field end up on the right half of each retina (shown in blue). From the right eye, axons from the nasal side of the retina (the side nearer the nose, which receives information from the right visual field) cross over the midline and travel to the left side of the brain with those fibers from the left eye that also receive input from the right side of the visual world. A similar arrangement unites left visual-field information from both eyes in the right side of the brain.

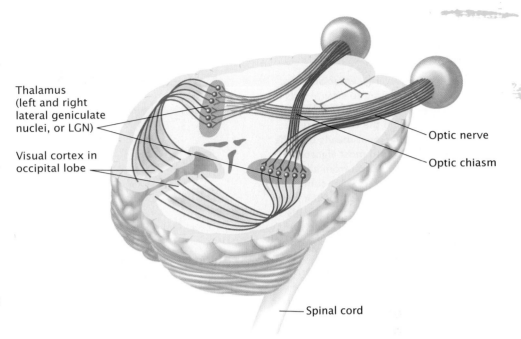

Thalamus (left and right lateral geniculate nuclei, or LGN)

Visual cortex in occipital lobe

Optic nerve

Optic chiasm

Spinal cord

called the **lateral geniculate nucleus (LGN)**. Neurons in the LGN then send the visual input to the **primary visual cortex**, which lies in the occipital lobe at the back of the brain. Visual information is also sent from the primary visual cortex for processing in many other areas of cortex. Studies of monkeys have identified thirty-two separate visual areas interconnected by more than three hundred pathways (Van Essen, Anderson, & Felleman, 1992).

The retina is organized to create a map of the visual world, such that neighboring points on the retina receive information from neighboring points in the visual world. A "copy" of this map is maintained in the LGN, in the primary visual cortex, and in each of the many other visual areas of the brain. Through this spatial coding system, neighboring points in the retina are represented in neighboring cells in the brain. Larger areas of cortex are devoted to the areas of the retina that have larger numbers of photoreceptors. For example, the fovea, which is densely packed with photoreceptors, is represented in an especially large segment of cortex.

● Visual Representations

So the apparently effortless experience of sight is based on a very complex system, in which visual information is transmitted from the retina through the thalamus and on to various cortical regions. We can appreciate the complexities of this system by considering just two of its more remarkable characteristics: *parallel processing of visual properties* and *hierarchical processing of visual information*.

● Parallel Processing of Visual Properties

Like ganglion cells, neurons of the LGN in the thalamus have center-surround receptive fields. However, the LGN is organized in several layers, and each layer contains a complete map of the retina. Further, neurons in different layers respond to particular aspects of visual stimuli. For example, the *form* of an object and its *color* are handled by one set of neurons (called the "what" system), whereas the *movement* of an object and *cues to its distance* are handled by another set (called the "where" system; Creem & Proffitt, 2001). These are called *parallel processing systems* because they allow the brain to conduct separate kinds of analysis on the same information at the same time (Livingstone & Hubel, 1987).

These parallel streams of visual information are sent to the cerebral cortex, but the question of how they are assembled into a unified conscious experience is still being debated (Derrington & Webb, 2004; Shafritz, Gore, & Marois, 2002). Some

- **optic nerve** A bundle of fibers composed of axons of ganglion cells that carries visual information to the brain.
- **blind spot** The light-insensitive point at which axons from all of the ganglion cells converge and exit the eyeball.
- **optic chiasm** Part of the bottom surface of the brain where half of each optic nerve's fibers cross over to the opposite side of the brain.
- **lateral geniculate nucleus (LGN)** A region of the thalamus in which axons from most of the ganglion cells in the retina end and form synapses.
- **primary visual cortex** An area at the back of the brain to which neurons in the lateral geniculate nucleus relay visual input.

FIGURE 4.14

Construction of a Feature Detector

This figure shows several center-on ganglion cells connecting to several cells in the lateral geniculate nucleus (LGN) that connect to one cell in the visual cortex. This "wiring" arrangement means that the cortical cell will respond most vigorously when it receives stimulation from all the LGN cells that feed into it. That combined LGN cell stimulation will occur when light falls on the center of the receptive fields of their ganglion cells. In this case, those receptive fields lie in a row, so it will take a bar-shaped feature at that same angle to stimulate all their centers. This cortical cell is called a feature detector because it responds best when a bar-shaped feature appears at a particular angle in its receptive field. If the bar were rotated to a different angle, this particular cortical cell would stop responding.

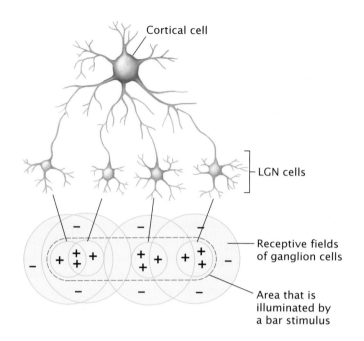

researchers argue that the separate streams of processing never actually converge in a single brain region (Engel et al., 1992). Instead, they say, cortical regions that process separate aspects of visual sensation are connected, allowing them to integrate their activity and create a distributed, but unified, experience of vision (Gilbert, 1992).

Positron emission tomography (PET) scans have provided evidence for the existence of separate processing channels. They have shown, for example, that one area of visual cortex is activated when a person views a colorful painting; a different area is activated by viewing black-and-white moving images (Zeki, 1992). Cases of brain damage have also helped to reveal these separate channels (Heilman & Valenstein, 2003). Damage in one area can leave a person unable to see colors or even remember them but still able to see and recognize objects. Damage in another area can leave a person able to see only stationary objects; as soon as an object moves, it disappears. People with brain damage in still other regions can see only moving objects, not stationary ones (Zeki, 1992). The same kinds of separate processing channels apparently operate even when we just imagine visual information. Some patients with brain damage can recall parts of a visual image, but not their correct spatial relationship. For example, they may be able to "see" a mental image of a bull's horns and ears but be unable to assemble them mentally to form a bull's head (Kosslyn, 1988).

● **Hierarchical Processing of Visual Information** Figure 4.14 shows that individual cells in the visual cortex receive input from several LGN neurons in the thalamus. The receptive fields of these cortical cells are more complex than the center-surround receptive fields of LGN cells. For example, a cell in the cortex might respond only to vertical edges that appear in its receptive field. One class of cells responds only to moving objects; a third class responds only to objects with corners, and so on. Because cortical cells respond to specific features of objects in the visual field, they have been described as **feature detectors** (Hubel & Wiesel, 1979).

Complex feature detectors can be built up out of more and more complex connections among simpler feature detectors (Hubel & Wiesel, 1979). For example, several center-surround cells might feed into one cortical cell to make a line detector, and several line detectors might feed into another cortical cell to make a cell that responds to a particular orientation in space, such as vertical. With further connections, a more complex "box detector," might be built from simpler line and corner detectors. Feature detectors illustrate that some of the cortical processing of visual information occurs in a *hierarchical*, or stepwise, fashion.

feature detectors Cells in the cortex that respond to a specific feature of an object.

in review Seeing

Aspect of Sensory System	Elements	Key Characteristics
Energy	Light: electromagnetic radiation from about 400 nm to about 750 nm	The intensity and wavelength of light waves determine the brightness and color of visual sensations.
Accessory structures	Eye: cornea, pupil, iris, lens	Light rays are bent to focus on the retina.
Transduction mechanism	Photoreceptors (rods and cones) in the retina	Rods are more sensitive to light than cones, but cones discriminate among colors. Sensations of color depend first on the cones, which respond differently to different light wavelengths. Interactions among cells of the retina exaggerate differences in the light stimuli reaching the photoreceptors, enhancing the sensation of contrast.
Pathways and representations	Optic nerve to optic chiasm to LGN of thalamus to primary visual cortex	Neighboring points in the visual world are represented at neighboring points in the LGN and primary visual cortex. Neurons there respond to particular aspects of the visual stimulus—such as color, movement, distance, or form.

Cells that respond to similar kinds of stimulation are organized into columns in the cortex. These columns are arranged at right angles to the surface of the cortex. For example, if you locate a cell that responds to diagonal lines at a particular spot in the visual field, most of the cells above and below that cell will also respond to diagonal lines. Other properties, too, are represented by whole columns of cells. For example, there are columns in which all of the cells are most sensitive to a particular color. Research has also revealed that individual neurons in the cortex perform several different tasks, allowing complex visual processing (Schiller, 1996). ("In Review: Seeing" summarizes how the nervous system gathers the information that allows us to see.)

● Seeing Color

Like beauty, color is in the eye of the beholder. Many animals see only shades of gray, even when they look at a rainbow, but for humans color is a major feature of vision. A marketer might tell you about the impact of color on buying preferences, a poet might tell you about the emotional power of color, but we will tell you about how you see colors—a process that is itself a thing of beauty and elegance.

● **Wavelengths and Color Sensations** We mentioned earlier that at a given intensity, each wavelength of light is sensed as a certain color (look again at Figure 4.6). However, the eye is seldom, if ever, exposed to pure light of a single wavelength. Sunlight, for example, is a mixture of all wavelengths of light. When sunlight passes through a droplet of water, each wavelength of light within it bends to a different extent, separating into a colorful rainbow. The spectrum of color found in the rainbow illustrates an important concept: The sensation produced by a mixture of different wavelengths of light is not the same as the sensations produced by separate wavelengths. So just as most sounds are a mixture of sound waves of different frequencies, most colors are a mixture of light of different wavelengths.

Three characteristics of this wavelength mixture determine the color sensation: hue, saturation, and brightness. These are *psychological* dimensions that correspond roughly to the physical properties of light. **Hue** is the essential "color," determined by the dominant wavelength in the mixture of the light striking the eye. For example, the

hue The essential "color," determined by the dominant wavelength of light.

FIGURE **4.15**

The Color Circle

Arranging colors according to their psychological similarities creates a color circle that predicts the result of additive mixing of two colored lights. The resulting color will be on a line between the two starting colors, the exact location on the line depending on the relative proportions of the two colors. For example, mixing equal amounts of pure green and pure red light will produce yellow, the color that lies at the midpoint of the line connecting red and green. (*Nm* stands for *nanometers*, the unit in which wavelengths are measured.)

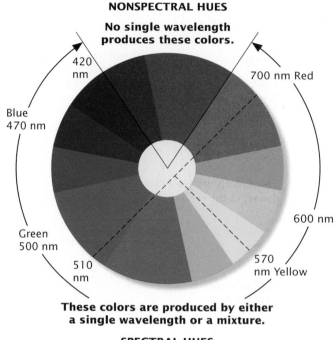

NONSPECTRAL HUES

No single wavelength produces these colors.

420 nm

700 nm Red

Blue 470 nm

600 nm

Green 500 nm

570 nm Yellow

510 nm

These colors are produced by either a single wavelength or a mixture.

SPECTRAL HUES

wavelength of yellow is about 570 nm and that of red is about 700 nm. Black, white, and gray are not considered hues, because no wavelength predominates in them. **Saturation** is related to the purity of a color. A color is more saturated and more pure if just one wavelength is relatively more intense—contains more energy—than other wavelengths. If many wavelengths are added to a pure hue, the color is said to be *desaturated*. For example, pastels are colors that have been desaturated by the addition of whiteness. **Brightness** refers to the overall intensity of all of the wavelengths in the incoming light.

The color circle shown in Figure 4.15 arranges hues according to their perceived similarities. If lights of two different wavelengths but of equal intensity are mixed, the color you sense is at the midpoint of a line drawn between the two original colors on the color circle. This process is known as *additive color mixing*, because the effects of the wavelengths from each light are added together. If you keep adding different colored lights, you eventually get white (the combination of all wavelengths).

You are probably more familiar with a different form of color mixing, called *subtractive color mixing*, which occurs when paints are combined. Like other physical objects, paints reflect certain wavelengths and absorb all others. For example, grass is green because it absorbs all wavelengths except wavelengths that are sensed as green. White objects are white because they reflect all wavelengths. Light reflected from paints or other colored objects is seldom a pure wavelength, so predicting the color resulting from mixing paint is not as easy as combining pure wavelengths of light. But if you keep combining different colored paints, all of the wavelengths will eventually be subtracted, resulting in black. (The discussion that follows refers to *additive color mixing*, the mixing of light.)

By mixing lights of just a few wavelengths, we can produce different color sensations. How many wavelengths are needed to create any possible color? Figure 4.16 illustrates an experiment that addresses this question. The results of such experiments helped lead scientists to an important theory of how people sense color—the trichromatic theory of color vision.

● **saturation**   The purity of a color.

● **brightness**   The overall intensity of all of the wavelengths that make up light.

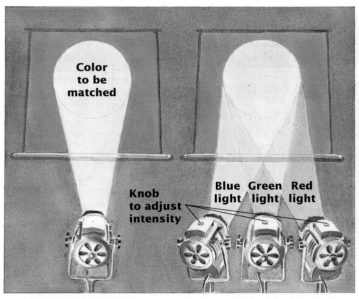 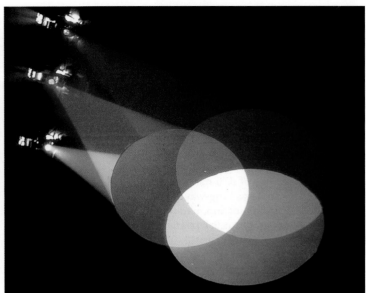

Mixture of many wavelengths

Each projector produces one pure-wavelength color

FIGURE **4.16**

Matching a Color by Mixing Lights of Pure Wavelengths

In this experiment, colored light is aimed at white paper, which reflects all wavelengths and therefore appears to be the color of the light shining on it. A target color is projected on the left-hand paper. The research participant's task is to adjust the intensity of different pure-wavelength lights until the resulting mixture looks exactly like the target color. It turns out that a large number of colors can be matched by mixing two pure-wavelength lights, but *any* color can be matched by mixing three pure-wavelength lights. Experiments such as this provided information that led to the trichromatic theory of color vision.

● **The Trichromatic Theory of Color Vision** Early in the 1800s, Thomas Young and, later, Hermann von Helmholtz demonstrated that they could match any color by mixing pure lights of only three wavelengths. For example, by mixing blue light (about 440 nm), green light (about 510 nm), and red light (about 700 nm) in different ratios, they could produce any other color. Young and Helmholtz interpreted this evidence to mean that there must be three types of visual elements in the eye, each of which is most sensitive to different wavelengths, and that information from these three elements combines to produce the sensation of color. This theory of color vision is called the *Young-Helmholtz theory*, or the **trichromatic theory**.

Support for the trichromatic theory has come from research on photoreceptor responses to particular wavelengths of light and on the activity of cones in the human eye (Schnapf, Kraft, & Baylor, 1987). This research reveals that there are three types of cones. Each type responds to a broad range of wavelengths, but is most sensitive to particular wavelengths. *Short-wavelength* cones respond most to light in the blue range. *Medium-wavelength* cones are most sensitive to light in the green range. *Long-wavelength* cones respond best to light in the reddish-yellow range (these have traditionally been called "red cones").

No single cone, by itself, can signal the color of a light. It is the *ratio* of the activities of the three types of cones that determines what color will be sensed. In other words, color vision is coded by the *pattern of activity* of the different cones. For example, a light is sensed as yellow if it has a pure wavelength of about 570 nm; this light stimulates both medium- and long-wavelength cones, as illustrated by arrow A in Figure 4.17. But yellow is also sensed whenever any mixture of other lights stimulates the same pattern of activity in these two types of cones. The trichromatic theory was applied in the creation of color television screens, which

trichromatic theory A theory of color vision identifying three types of visual elements, each of which is most sensitive to different wavelengths of light.

FIGURE **4.17**

Relative Responses of Three Cone Types to Different Wavelengths of Light

Each type of cone responds to a range of light wavelengths but responds more to some wavelengths than to others. Any combination of wavelengths that creates a particular pattern of cone activity will create a particular color sensation. For example, a pure light of 570 nanometers (see arrow A) stimulates long-wavelength cones at 1.0 relative units and medium-wavelength cones at about 0.7 relative units. This ratio of cone activity (1/0.7 = 1.4) gives the sensation of yellow. But any combination of wavelengths at the proper intensity that generates this same ratio of activity in these cone types will also produce the sensation of yellow.

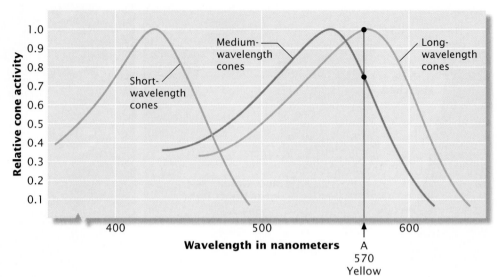

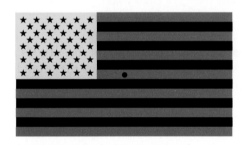

FIGURE **4.18**

Afterimages Produced by the Opponent-Process Nature of Color Vision

TRY THIS Stare at the black dot in the center of the flag for at least thirty seconds, then focus on the dot in the white space below it.

contain microscopic elements of red, green, and blue. A television broadcast excites these elements to varying degrees, mixing their colors to produce many other colors. You see color mixtures on the screen—not patterns of red, green, and blue dots—because the dots are too small and close together to be seen individually.

● **The Opponent-Process Theory of Color Vision** Brilliant as it is, the trichromatic theory alone cannot explain all aspects of color vision. For example, it cannot account for the fact that if you stare at the flag in Figure 4.18 for thirty seconds and then look at the dot in the blank white space below it, you will see a color afterimage. What was yellow in the original image will be blue in the afterimage, what was green before will appear red, and what was black will now appear white.

This type of phenomenon led Ewald Hering to offer an alternative to the trichromatic theory of color vision, called the **opponent-process theory.** According to this theory, the color-sensitive visual elements in the eye are grouped into three pairs, and the members of each pair oppose, or inhibit, each other. The three pairs are a *red-green element*, a *blue-yellow element*, and a *black-white element*. Each element signals one color or the other—red or green, for example—but never both. This theory explains color afterimages. When one part of an opponent pair is no longer stimulated, the other is activated. So, as in Figure 4.18, if the original image you look at is green, the afterimage will be red.

The opponent-process theory also explains the phenomenon of complementary colors. Two colors are *complementary* if a neutral color, such as gray, appears when lights of the two colors are mixed. (The neutral color can appear as anything from white to gray to black, depending on the intensity of the lights being mixed.) On the color circle shown in Figure 4.15, complementary colors are roughly opposite each other. Red and green lights are complementary, as are yellow and blue. Notice that complementary colors are *opponent* colors in Hering's theory. According to opponent-process theory, complementary colors stimulate the same visual element (e.g., red-green) in opposite directions, canceling each other out. This theory helps explain why mixing lights of complementary colors produces gray.

● **A Synthesis and an Update** The trichromatic and opponent-process theories seem quite different, but both are correct to some extent, and together they can explain most of what is known about color vision. Electrical recordings made from different types of cells in the retina has paved the way for a synthesis, or blending, of the two theories (Gegenfurtner & Kiper, 2003).

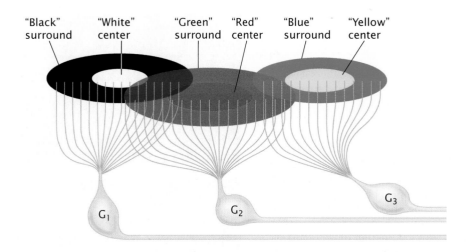

FIGURE 4.19

Color Coding and the Ganglion Cells

The center-surround receptive fields of ganglion cells form the basis for opponent colors. Some ganglion cells, like G_2, have a center whose photoreceptors respond best to red wavelengths and a surround whose photoreceptors respond best to green wavelengths. Other ganglion cells pair blue and yellow, whereas still others receive input from all types of photoreceptors.

At the level of the photoreceptors, a slightly revised version of the trichromatic theory is correct. As a general rule, there *are* three types of cones that have three different photopigments. However, molecular biologists who isolated the genes for cone pigments have found variations in the genes for the cones sensitive to middle-wavelength and long-wavelength light. These variants have slightly different sensitivities to different wavelengths of light. So a person can have two, three, or even four genes for long-wavelength pigments (Deeb, 2005). Individual differences in people's long-wavelength pigments become apparent in color-matching tasks. When asked to mix a red light and a green light to match a yellow light, a person with one kind of long-wavelength pigment will choose a different red-to-green ratio than someone with a different kind of long-wavelength pigment. Women are more likely than men to have four distinct photopigments, and people who do have them also have a richer experience of color. They can detect more shades of color than people with the more common three photopigments, but their experience of color pales in comparison to that of certain tropical shrimp. These shrimp live on colorful coral reefs and have twelve different photopigments, which allows them to see colors even in the ultraviolet range, which no human—male or female—can sense (Marshall & Oberwinkler, 1999).

Color vision works a little differently at the level of ganglion cells. As we mentioned earlier, information about light from many photoreceptors feeds into each ganglion cell, and the output from each ganglion cell goes to the brain. We also said that the receptive fields of most ganglion cells are arranged in center-surround patterns. It turns out that the center and the surround are color coded, as illustrated in Figure 4.19. The center responds best to one color, and the surround responds best to a different color. This color coding arises because varying proportions of the three cone types feed into the center and the surround of the ganglion cell.

When either the center or the surround of a ganglion cell's receptive field is stimulated, the other area is inhibited. In other words, the center and the surround of a given ganglion cell's receptive field are most responsive to opponent colors. Recordings from many ganglion cells show that three very common pairs of opponent colors are the ones predicted by Hering's opponent-process theory: red-green, blue-yellow, and black-white. Stimulating both the center and the surround of these cells' receptive fields cancels the effects of either light, producing gray. Black-white cells receive input from all types of cones, so it does not matter what color stimulates them. All this color information is further analyzed in the brain, where cells in specific regions of the visual cortex also respond in opponent pairs that are sensitive to the red-green and blue-yellow input coming from ganglion cells in the retina (Engel, Zhang, & Wandell, 1997; Heywood & Kentridge, 2003).

In summary, color vision is possible because three types of cones have different sensitivities to different wavelengths, as the trichromatic theory suggests. The sensation of

opponent-process theory   A theory of color vision stating that color-sensitive visual elements are grouped into red-green, blue-yellow, and black-white elements.

FIGURE 4.20

Are You Colorblind?

TRY THIS At the upper left is a photo as it appears to people who have all three cone photopigments. The other photos simulate how colors appear to people who are missing photopigments for short wavelengths (lower left), long wavelengths (upper right), or medium wavelengths (lower right). If any of these photos look to you just like the one at the upper left, you may have a form of colorblindness.

different colors results from stimulating the three cone types in different ratios. Because there are three types of cones, any color can be produced by mixing three different wavelengths of light. But the story does not end there. The output from cones is fed into ganglion cells whose receptive fields have centers and surrounds that respond to opponent colors and inhibit each other. This arrangement provides the basis for color afterimages. So the trichromatic theory describes the properties of the photoreceptors, whereas the opponent-process theory describes the properties of the ganglion cells. Both theories are needed to account for the complexity of visual sensations of color.

● **Colorblindness**   People who are born with cones containing only two of the three possible color-sensitive pigments are described as *colorblind* (Carroll et al., 2004; see Figure 4.20). They are not actually blind to all color; they simply discriminate fewer colors than other people. Two centuries ago, a colorblind chemist named John Dalton carefully described the colors he sensed—to him, a red ribbon appeared the same color as mud—and concluded that the fluid in his eyeball must be tinted blue. He instructed his doctor to examine the fluid after he died, but it turned out to be clear. His preserved retinas were examined recently by molecular biologists. The scientists were not surprised to find that, just as most colorblind people today lack the genes that code one or more of the pigments, Dalton had no gene for medium-wavelength pigments (Deeb & Kohl, 2003; Hunt et al., 1995).

● Interaction of the Senses: Synesthesia

At the beginning of this chapter, we gave examples of the interaction of two senses, namely, vision and touch, but there are many other interactions. For example, vision interacts with hearing. If a brief sound occurs just as lights are flashed, it can create the impression of more lights than there actually are (Shams, Kamitani, & Shimojo, 2000), and hearing a sound as objects collide can affect your perception of their motion (Watanabe & Shimojo, 2001). Sound can also improve your ability to see an object at the sound's source, which can help you avoid or respond to danger (McDonald, Teder-Salejarvi, & Hillyard, 2000). Hearing sounds can alter sensitivity to touch (Hötting & Röder, 2004), and there is even evidence that smells are more readily detected when accompanied by images related to them (Gottfried & Dolan, 2003). Such interactions occur in everyone, but some people also report **synesthesia** (pronounced "sin-ess-THEE-zhah"), a more unusual mixing of senses, or of dimensions

● **synesthesia**   A blending of sensory experience that causes some people to "see" sounds or "taste" colors, for example.

FIGURE 4.21

Synesthesia

In this experiment on synesthesia, a triangular pattern of H's was embedded in a background of other letters, as shown at left. Most people find it difficult to detect the triangle, but "J. C.", a person with synesthesia, picked it out immediately because, as simulated at right, he saw the H's as green, the F's as yellow, and the P's as red (Ramachandran & Hubbard, 2001).

Source: Figure 3 from Ramachandran & Hubbard (2001).

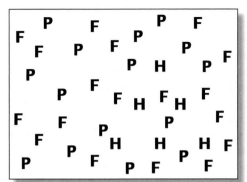 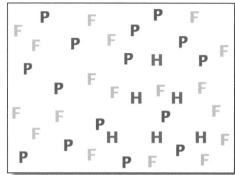

within senses. These people may say that they "feel" colors or sounds as touches, or that they "taste" shapes; others claim that they sense certain colors, such as red, when they hear certain sounds, such as a trumpet. Some report experiencing certain tastes, numbers, or letters as vivid visual patterns or as particular colors. These synesthetic experiences are so continuous and automatic that they are difficult to supress or ignore (Ward & Mattingley, 2006). In some cases, visual sensations triggered by touch or hearing persist even after a person has become blind (Steven, Hansen, & Blakemore, 2006).

Though once dismissed as poetic delusions, many claims of synesthesia have been supported by experiments (Mattingley et al., 2001; Ward & Mattingley, 2006; see Figure 4.21). In one case, a man reported that he always sees numbers in distinct colors, even when they are printed in black ink. To him, he said, the 2s look orange and the 5s look green. And in fact, when he was asked to pick out a 2 that was embedded in an array of 5s, he could do so much more rapidly than other people. To him, the 2 seemed to "pop out" of the array (Palmeri et al., 2002).

Researchers speculate that synesthesia occurs partly because brain areas that process colors are near areas that process letters and numbers and partly because the connections between these neighboring areas may be more extensive in people who experience synesthesia. Synesthesia experiences are also associated with unusually wide-ranging activity in brain regions that process different kinds of sensory information (Hubbard & Ramachandran, 2005). Studies of people who experience color sensations when they hear words, for example, show that hearing words activates both auditory cortex in the temporal lobes and visual cortex in the occipital lobe (Aleman et al., 2001; Nunn et al., 2002). Similar, but less extensive, connections in nonsynesthetic people may be partly responsible for their use of intersensory descriptions in which a shirt is "loud," a cheese is "sharp," or a wine is said to have "a light straw color with greenish hues" (Martino & Marks, 2001). Growing scientific interest in synesthesia is indicated by the fact that there are now standardized procedures for identifying people who experience these fascinating sensory phenomena (Eagleman et al., 2007).

The Chemical Senses: Smell and Taste

There are animals without vision, and there are animals without hearing, but there are no animals without some form of chemical sense. Chemical senses arise from the interaction of chemicals and receptors. **Olfaction** (our sense of smell) detects chemicals that are airborne, or volatile. **Gustation** (our sense of taste) detects chemicals in solution that come into contact with receptors inside the mouth.

● Olfaction

As in other senses, accessory structures shape sensations in the olfactory system. In humans, these accessory structures include the nose, the mouth, and the upper part of

● **olfaction**   The sense of smell.

● **gustation**   The sense of taste.

the throat, all of which help funnel odor molecules to receptors. So just as bending the ear's pinna forward can help collect sound waves, taping nasal dilator strips over the bridge of the nose intensifies food odors (Raudenbush & Meyer, 2002). Odor molecules can reach olfactory receptors in the nose either by entering the nostrils or by rising through an opening in the palate at the back of the mouth. This second route allows us to sample odors from food as we eat (see Figure 4.22). The olfactory receptors themselves are located on the dendrites of specialized neurons that extend into the moist lining of the nose, called the *mucous membrane*. Odor molecules bind to these receptors, causing depolarization of the dendrites' membrane, which in turn leads to changes in the firing rates of the neurons. A single molecule of an odorous substance can cause a change in the membrane potential of an olfactory neuron, but detection of the odor by a human normally requires about fifty such molecules (Reed, 2004). (A hot pizza generates lots more than that.) The number of molecules needed to trigger an olfactory sensation can vary, however. For example, women are more sensitive to odors during certain phases of their menstrual cycles (Navarrete-Palacios et al., 2003).

Olfactory neurons are repeatedly replaced with new ones, as each lives only about two months. Scientists are especially interested in this process because, as noted in the chapter on biological aspects of psychology, most neurons cannot divide to create new ones. An understanding of how new olfactory neurons are generated—and how they make appropriate connections in the brain—may someday be helpful in treating brain damage.

In contrast to vision, which uses only four basic receptor types (rods and three kinds of cones), the olfactory system employs about a thousand different types of receptors. In fact, up to 2 percent of the human genetic code is devoted to these olfactory receptors, perhaps because a good sense of smell helped humans to adapt and survive over thousands of years (Firestein, 2001). A given odor stimulates various olfactory receptors to varying degrees, and the particular patterns of stimulation create codes for particular odor sensations (Kajiya et al., 2001). So many stimulation patterns are possible that humans can discriminate tens of thousands of

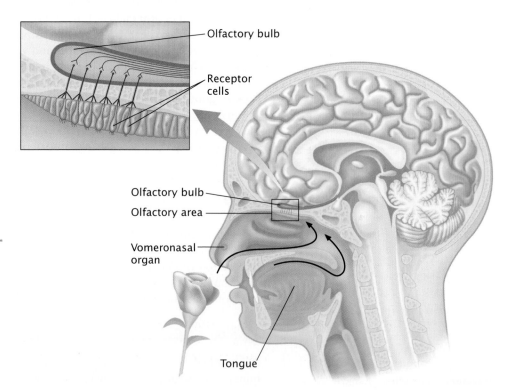

FIGURE 4.22

The Olfactory System

Airborne chemicals reach the olfactory area through the nostrils and through the back of the mouth. Fibers pass directly from the olfactory area to the olfactory bulb in the brain, and from there signals pass to areas such as the hypothalamus and amygdala, which are involved in emotion.

A "Mating Ball" Among snakes there is intense competition for females. Dozens of males will wrap themselves around a single female in a "mating ball." Snakes' forked tongues allow them to sample airborne chemicals at two different points as they follow an olfactory trail (Schwenk, 1994). Males with the best olfactory tracking abilities are the ones most likely to reach a female first, thus passing on their genes to the next generation.

olfactory bulb A brain structure that receives messages regarding olfaction.

pheromones Chemicals released by one animal and detected by another that shape the second animal's behavior or physiology.

vomeronasal organ A portion of the mammalian olfactory system that is sensitive to pheromones.

different odors (Kajiya et al., 2001; Zou & Buck, 2006). We know that substances with similar chemical structures tend to have similar odors, but exactly how olfactory receptors discriminate various smells and send coded messages about them to the brain is only now being determined (Kadohisa & Wilson, 2006; Reed, 2004).

The question of how smells are coded has been of special interest to governments and industries. Particularly since the September 11, 2001, terrorist attacks in the United States, researchers have accelerated their efforts to develop an "electronic nose" capable of detecting odorants associated with guns and explosives (Thaler, Kennedy, & Hanson, 2001). Versions of these devices are already in use at some airports. An "electronic nose" has also been developed that can detect the presence of diseases that might not be evident to an examining doctor (Machado et al., 2005), and other artificial olfactory devices are being used to examine the condition and composition of food products and the air we breathe (Marin et al., 2007).

Olfaction is the only sensory system that does not send its messages through the thalamus. Instead, axons from neurons in the nose extend through a bony plate and directly into the brain, reaching a structure called the **olfactory bulb**, where processing of olfactory information continues (Urban, 2002). Pathways from the olfactory bulb send the information on for further processing in several brain regions, including the frontal lobe and the amygdala, which is involved in emotional experience (Kareken et al., 2003; Zou et al., 2001).

These features of the olfactory system may account for the fact that losing the sense of smell can sometimes be an early sign of brain diseases that disrupt memory and emotion (Albers, Tabert, & Devanand, 2006). These same features may also help explain the strong relationship between olfaction, memory, and emotion (Stevenson & Boakes, 2003). For example, the associations between particular odors and particular experiences, especially emotional ones, do not weaken with time or later experiences (Lawless & Engen, 1977). So catching a whiff of the scent once worn by a lost loved one can reactivate intense feelings associated with that person. Odors can also bring back accurate memories of significant experiences linked with them, especially positive experiences (Mohr et al., 2001).

The mechanisms of olfaction are remarkably similar in species ranging from humans to worms. And all mammals, including humans, have brain systems for detecting the source of smells by comparing the strength of sensory inputs reaching the left and right nostrils (Porter et al., 2005). Different species vary considerably, however, in their sensitivity to smell, and in the degree to which they depend on it for survival. For example, humans have about 9 million olfactory neurons, whereas there are about 225 million such neurons in dogs, a species that is far more dependent on smell to identify food, territory, and receptive mates. In addition, dogs and many other species depend on an accessory olfactory system that is able to detect pheromones. **Pheromones** (pronounced "FAIR-o-mones") are chemicals that are released by one animal and that, when detected by another, can shape the second animal's behavior or physiology (Silvotti, Montanu, & Tirindelli, 2003). For example, when male snakes detect a chemical exuded on the skin of female snakes, they are stimulated to "court" the female.

In mammals, pheromones can be nonvolatile chemicals that, when licked by animals, are passed into a portion of the olfactory system called the **vomeronasal organ** (Witt & Wozniak, 2006). In female mice, for example, the vomeronasal organ detects chemicals in the male's urine. By this means, a male can cause a female to ovulate and become sexually receptive, and an unfamiliar male can cause a pregnant female to abort her pregnancy (Bruce, 1969).

The role of pheromones in humans is much less clear. At one extreme are perfume advertisers who want us to believe that their products contain sexual attractants that act as pheromones to subconsciously influence the behavior of desirable partners. At the other extreme are those who argue that in humans, the vomeronasal organ is an utterly nonfunctional vestige, like the appendix. In fact, it appears that not everybody even has one. A vomeronasal organ was identified in only 32 to 38 percent of adults in one study (Besli et al., 2004). The best current scientific evidence supports a more measured set of conclusions. For humans who have one, the vomeronasal organ is, in fact, capable of responding to certain hormonal substances and can influence certain hormonal secretions (Berliner et al., 1996). Further, whatever the anatomical basis, it is increasingly clear that humans do have some sort of pheromone-like system (Berglund, Lindström, & Savic, 2006; Savic, Berglund, & Lindström, 2005). For example, odorants that are not consciously detectable can nevertheless influence people's moods (Jacob & McClintock, 2000). Odorants can also alter activity in the cerebral cortex and other brain areas that are not directly involved in olfaction (Jacob et al., 2001). In one study, specific areas of the hypothalamus were activated in men and women when they were exposed to an odorless substance similar to the hormones—either estrogen or testosterone—that are associated with the opposite sex (Savic et al., 2001). A possible human gene for pheromone receptors has been found (Rodriguez et al., 2000), and pheromones have been shown to cause reproduction-related physiological changes in humans (Grammer, Fink, & Neave, 2005). Specifically, pheromonal signals secreted in the perspiration of a woman can shorten or prolong the menstrual cycle of other women nearby (Stern & McClintock, 1998). In such cases, pheromones are responsible for *menstrual synchrony*, the tendency of women living together to menstruate at the same time.

Despite the steamy perfume ads, though, there is still no solid evidence that humans, or even nonhuman primates, give off or can detect pheromones that act as sexual attractants. If a certain scent does enhance a person's readiness for sex, it is probably because the person has learned to associate that scent with previous sexual experiences. There are many other examples of people using olfactory information in social situations. For example, after just a few hours of contact, mothers can usually identify their newborn babies by the infants' smell (Porter, Cernich, & McLaughlin, 1983). And if infants are breastfed, they can discriminate their own mothers' odor from that of other breastfeeding women, and they appear to be comforted by it (Porter, 1991). In fact, individual mammals, including humans, have a distinct "odortype," which is determined by their immune cells and other inherited physiological factors (Beauchamp et al., 1995). During pregnancy, a woman's own odortype combines with the odortype of her fetus to form a third odortype. Each of these three odors is distinguishable, suggesting that recognition of odortypes may help establish the mother-infant bonds discussed in the chapter on human development.

■ ● Gustation

The chemical sense system in the mouth is gustation, or taste. The receptors for taste are in the taste buds, which are grouped together in structures called **papillae** (pronounced "pa-PILL-ee"). Normally, there are about 10,000 taste buds in a person's mouth, mostly on the tongue but also on the roof of the mouth and on the back of the throat.

In contrast to the olfactory system, which can discriminate thousands of different odors, the human taste system detects only a few elementary sensations. The most familiar of these are sweet, sour, bitter, and salty. Each taste bud responds best to one or two of these categories, but it also responds weakly to others (Zhang et al., 2003). The sensation of a particular substance appears to result from the responses of taste buds that are relatively sensitive to a specific category. Behavioral studies and electrical recordings from taste neurons have also established two additional taste sensations. One, called *umami* (which means "delicious" in Japanese), enhances other tastes and is produced by certain proteins, as well as by monosodium glutamate (MSG; DuBois, 2004). The other, called *astringent*, is the taste produced by tannins, which are found in tea, for example.

● **papillae** Structures on the tongue containing groups of taste receptors, or taste buds.

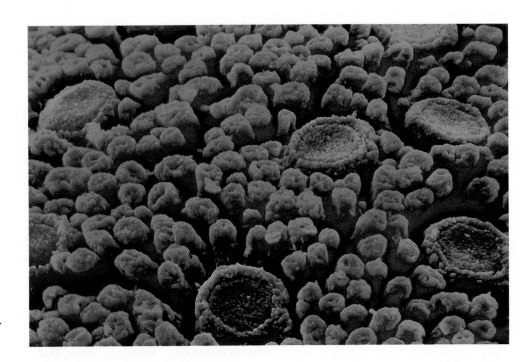

Taste Receptors Taste buds are grouped into structures called *papillae*. Two kinds of papillae are visible in this greatly enlarged photo of the surface of the human tongue.

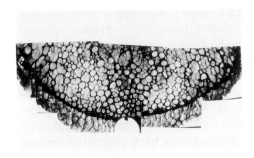

FIGURE 4.23

Are You a Supertaster?

TRY THIS This photo shows the large number of papillae on the tongue of a "supertaster." If you don't mind a temporary stain on your mouth and teeth, you can look at your own papillae by painting the front of your tongue with a cotton swab soaked in blue food coloring. Distribute the dye by moving your tongue around and swallowing; then look into a magnifying mirror as you shine a flashlight on your tongue. The pink circles you see against the blue background are papillae, each of which has about six taste buds buried in its surface. Get several friends to do this test, and you will see that genes create wide individual differences in taste bud density.

Different tastes are transduced into neural activity by different types of taste receptors and in different ways (Small et al., 2003; Stillman, 2002). For example, sweet and bitter are signaled when chemicals fit into specific receptor sites (Montmayeur et al., 2001), whereas sour and salty act through more direct effects on the ion channels in membranes of taste cells. Understanding the chemistry of sweetness is allowing scientists to design new chemicals that fit into sweetness receptors and taste thousands of times sweeter than sugar. Many of these substances are now being used to allow people more ways to enjoy low-calorie hot-fudge sundaes.

A taste component in its own right, saltiness also enhances the taste of food by suppressing bitterness (Breslin & Beauchamp, 1997). In animals, taste responses to salt are determined during early development, before and after birth. Research with animals has shown that if mothers are put on a low-salt diet, their offspring are less likely to prefer salt (Hill & Przekop, 1988). In humans, experiences with salty foods over the first four years of life may alter the sensory systems that detect salt and contribute to enduring preferences for salty foods (Hill & Mistretta, 1990).

There may be genetically determined differences in the ability to taste things. About 25 percent of the population are "supertasters"—individuals who have an especially large number of papillae on their tongues (Bartoshuk, 2000). Supertasters have thousands of taste buds, whereas "nontasters" have only hundreds of buds (see Figure 4.23). Most people fall between these extremes. Supertasters are more sensitive than other people to bitterness, as revealed in their reaction to foods such as broccoli, soy products, and grapefruit. Having different numbers of taste buds may help account for differences in people's food intake, as well as weight problems. For example, Linda Bartoshuk has found that compared with overweight people, thin people have many more taste buds (Duffy et al., 1999). Perhaps they do not have to eat as much to experience the good tastes of food.

● Smell, Taste, and Flavor

People with *anosmia* (pronounced "ay-NOSE-me-a") are unable to distinguish different smells. Some are born this way, but the condition can also result from brain damage (Hawkes, 2003; Leopold, 2002). Anosmic individuals also have trouble distinguishing different tastes, even though there is nothing wrong with their taste system. Why? For the same reason that, when you have a stuffy nose, everything tastes the same—usually like cardboard. Smell and taste act as two components of a single system, known as *flavor* (Rozin, 1982). Most of the properties that make food taste good are actually odors detected by the olfactory system, not activities of the taste system. The olfactory and gustatory pathways converge in the *orbitofrontal cortex* (de Araujo et al., 2003), where neurons also respond to the sight and texture of food. The responses of neurons in this "flavor cortex" are also influenced by conditions of hunger and satiety ("fullness").

Both tastes and odors prompt strong emotional responses. For tastes, the reaction to bitter or sweet flavors appears to be inborn (Mueller et al., 2005), but for most mammalian species, including humans, there are few other innate flavor preferences. Most of what we like to eat, and what we avoid, is based on the experiences we have had with various foods (Myers & Sclafani, 2006). Our emotional reactions to odors, too, are learned (Bartoshuk, 1991). In one study, for example, people were asked to sniff an air sample that was described as coming from either cheddar cheese or from body odor. Those who thought they were smelling body odor rated the air sample as more unpleasant than those who thought they were smelling cheese (de Araujo et al., 2005).

Variations in nutritional state can affect the taste, flavor, and pleasure associated with eating food, as well as the motivation to eat particular foods (Yeomans & Mobini, 2006). For example, being hungry or having a salt deficiency makes sweet or salty things taste better and more likely to be eaten. Influences on protein and fat intake are less direct. Protein and fat molecules have no particular taste or smell. So preferring or avoiding foods that contain these nutrients is based on associations between scent cues from other volatile substances in food and on the nutritional results of eating the foods (Bartoshuk, 1991; Schiffman et al., 1999).

Flavor includes other characteristics of food, too—including how it feels in your mouth and, especially, its temperature. Temperature does not alter saltiness, but warm foods are experienced as sweeter. In fact, simply warming a person's taste receptors creates a sensation of sweetness (Cruz & Green, 2000). Aromas released from warm food rise from the mouth into the nose and create more flavor sensations. This is why some people find hot pizza delicious and cold pizza disgusting. Spicy "hot" foods actually stimulate pain fibers in the mouth because they contain a substance called *capsaicin* (pronounced "kap-SAY-uh-sin"), which opens ion channels in pain neurons that are also opened by heat. As a result, these foods are experienced as physiologically "hot" (Caterina et al., 1997). Why do people eat spicy foods even though they stimulate pain? The practice may have originated because many "hot" spices have antibacterial properties. In fact, researchers have found a

in review   Smell and Taste

Aspect of Sensory System	Elements	Key Characteristics
Energy	Smell: volatile chemicals Taste: chemicals in solution	The amount, intensity, and location of the chemicals determine taste and smell sensations.
Structures of taste and smell	Smell: chemical receptors in the mucous membrane of the nose Taste: taste buds grouped in papillae in the mouth	Odor and taste molecules stimulate chemical receptors.
Pathways to the brain	Olfactory bulb and taste buds	Axons from the nose bypass the thalamus and extend directly to the olfactory bulb.

strong correlation between frequent use of antibacterial spices and living in climates that promote bacterial contamination (Billing & Sherman, 1998). Capsaicin also tends to create a sense of "fullness" (Westerterp-Plantenga, Smeets, & Lejeune, 2005), so perhaps eating spicy foods originally helped people to curb their hunger during times of famine.

In short, experiencing the flavor of the foods we eat is not just a process of sensing chemical signals coming from the tongue and the nose. It also involves temperature and texture, and it can be affected, too, by what we have learned (Verhagen, 2006). ("In Review: Smell and Taste" summarizes our discussion of these senses.)

Somatic Senses and the Vestibular System

Some senses are not located in a specific organ, such as the eye or the ear. These are the somatic senses, also called *somatosensory systems*, which are spread throughout the body. The **somatic senses** include the skin senses of touch, temperature, and pain, as well as kinesthesia, the sense that tells the brain where the parts of the body are. Closely related to kinesthesia is the vestibular system, which tells the brain about the position and movements of the head. Although not strictly a somatosensory system, the vestibular system will also be considered in this section.

● Touch and Temperature

Touch is crucial. People can function and prosper without vision, hearing, or smell, but a person without touch would have difficulty surviving. Without a sense of touch, you could not even swallow food, because you could not tell where it was in your mouth and throat.

● **Stimulus and Receptors for Touch**   The energy detected by the sense of touch is physical pressure on tissue, usually the skin, or hairs on the skin. The skin covers nearly two square yards of surface and weighs more than twenty pounds. The receptors that transduce pressure into neural activity are in, or just below, the skin.

Many nerve endings in the skin act as touch receptors. Some neurons come from the spinal cord, enter the skin, and simply end; these are called *free nerve endings*. Many other neurons end in a variety of elaborate, specialized structures. However, there is generally little relationship between the type of nerve ending and the type of sensory information carried by the neuron. Many types of nerve endings respond to mechanical stimuli, but the exact process through which they transduce mechanical energy is still unknown. These somatosensory neurons are unusual in that they have no dendrites. Their cell bodies are outside the spinal cord, and their axon splits and extends both to the skin and to the spinal cord. Action potentials travel from the nerve endings in the skin to the spinal cord, and onward from there into the brain.

Information from this touch system tells us what is happening to our bodies, but we do more than just passively respond. For humans, touch is also an active sense that is used for getting specific information. In much the same way that you can look as well as just see, you can also touch as well as feel. When people are involved in active sensing, they usually use the part of the sensory apparatus that has the greatest sensitivity. For vision, this is the eye's fovea; for touch, the fingertips. (The area of primary somatosensory cortex devoted to the fingertips is especially large.) Fingertip touch is the principal way people explore the textures of surfaces. It can be extremely sensitive, as evidenced by blind people who can read Braille as rapidly as 200 words per minute (Foulke, 1991) or by the ease with which sighted but blindfolded people can learn to to recognize faces by touching them (Kilgour & Lederman, 2002).

somatic senses   Senses of touch, temperature, pain, and kinesthesia.

● **Adaptation of Touch Receptors** Constant input from all your touch neurons would provide a lot of unnecessary information. Once you get dressed, for example, you do not need to be constantly reminded that you are wearing clothes. Thanks in part to the process of adaptation mentioned earlier, you do not continue to feel your clothes against your skin.

The most important sensory information involves *changes* in touch—as when a broken lace suddenly makes your shoe feel loose. The touch sense emphasizes these changes and filters out the excess information. How? Typically, a touch neuron responds with a burst of firing when a stimulus is applied, then quickly returns to its baseline firing rate, even though the stimulus may still be in contact with the skin. If the touch pressure increases, the neuron again responds with an increase in firing rate, but then slows down. Some neurons in the somatosensory cortex also stop firing if a tactile stimulus remains constant for some time (Graziano et al., 2002). A few touch neurons adapt more slowly, continuing to fire at an elevated rate as long as pressure is applied to the skin. By attending to this input, you can

TRY THIS → sense a constant stimulus (try doing this by focusing on sensations from your glasses or shoes).

● **Coding and Representation of Touch Information** The sense of touch codes information about two aspects of an object in contact with the skin: its weight and its location. The *intensity* of the stimulus—how heavy it is—is coded by both the firing rate of individual neurons and the number of neurons stimulated. A heavy object produces a higher rate of firing and stimulates more neurons than a light object. The *location* of touch is coded much as it is for vision: by the location of the neurons that are responding to the touch.

Touch information is organized such that signals from neighboring points on the skin stay next to one another, even as they travel from the skin through the spinal cord to the thalamus and on to the somatosensory cortex. So just as there is a map of the visual field in the brain, the area of cortex that receives touch information resembles a map of the surface of the body (see Figure 3.17). As with the other senses, these representations are contralateral; that is, input from the left side of the body goes to the right side of the brain, and vice versa. In nonhuman primates, however, touch information from each hand is sent to both sides of the brain. This arrangement appears to amplify information from manual exploration of objects and to improve feedback from hand movements (Iwamura, Iriki, & Tanaka, 1994).

● **Temperature** When you dig your toes into a sandy summer beach, the pleasant experience you get comes partly from the sensation of warmth. Touch and temperature seem to be separate senses, and to some extent they are; but the difference between the two senses is not always clear.

Some of the skin's sensory neurons respond to a change in temperature, but not to simple contact. There are "warm fibers," which are nerve fibers that increase their firing rates when the temperature changes in the range of about 95° to 115° F (35° to 47° C). Temperatures above this range are painful and stimulate different fibers. Other nerve fibers are "cold fibers"; they respond to a broad range of cool temperatures. However, many of the fibers that respond to temperature also respond to touch, so sensations of touch and temperature sometimes interact. For example, warm and cold objects can feel up to 250 percent heavier than body-temperature objects (Stevens & Hooper, 1982). Also, if you touch an object made up of alternating warm and cool bars, you will have the sensation of intense heat (Thunberg, 1896, cited in Craig & Bushnell, 1994).

Stimulation of the touch sense can have psychological and physiological effects. For example, premature infants gain weight 47 percent faster when they are given massages. (They do not eat more but, rather, they process their food more efficiently; Diego, Field, & Hernandez-Reif, 2005). Massage is also associated with reduced pain and lowered stress hormones in arthritic children (Field et al., 1997), and with reduced anxiety, increased alertness, and improved math performance in adults (Field et al., 1996; Simmons et al., 2004).

● Pain

The skin senses can convey a great deal of pleasure, but if you increase the intensity of the same kind of stimulation, you have a much different sensation: pain. Pain provides you with information about the impact of the world on your body. It can tell you, for example, that "A hammer just crushed your left thumb." Pain also has a distinctly negative emotional component. Researchers have focused on the information-carrying aspects of pain, its emotional components, and the various ways that the brain can adjust the amount of pain that reaches consciousness.

● Pain as an Information Sense   The information-carrying aspect of pain is very similar to that of touch and temperature. The receptors for pain are free nerve endings. As mentioned earlier, for example, capsaicin, the active ingredient in chili peppers, creates pain in the mouth by stimulating these pain nerve endings. Painful stimuli cause the release of chemicals that fit into specialized receptors in pain neurons, causing them to fire. The axons of pain-sensing neurons release neurotransmitters not only near the spinal cord, sending information to the brain, but also near the skin, causing local inflammation.

Two types of nerve fibers carry pain signals from the skin to the spinal cord. *A-delta fibers* carry sharp, pricking pain sensations. Their axons are coated with myelin, which speeds the transmission of these sharp pain messages. *C fibers* carry long-lasting, dull aches and burning sensations. So when you stub your toe, the immediate wave of sharp, intense pain is signaled by messages from A-delta fibers. That slightly delayed wave of gnawing, dull pain is signaled by messages from C fibers.

Both kinds of pain come from the same place, but the sensations follow separate pain fibers all the way to the brain, where they activate different brain regions (Ploner et al., 2002). Pain fibers enter the spinal cord, where they form synapses

A Life with No Pain   Ashlyn Blocker, shown here at age five being checked for injuries, was born with a rare genetic disorder that prevented the development of pain receptors. As a result, she feels no pain if she is cut or bruised, if she bites her tongue while eating, or even if she is burned by hot soup or a hot stove. She only knows she has been injured if she sees herself bleeding, so she will have to find ways to protect herself from danger without the vital information provided by the pain system. Ashlyn doesn't yet understand the seriousness of her condition, but her worried mother says "I would give anything for her to feel pain" (Associated Press, 2004).

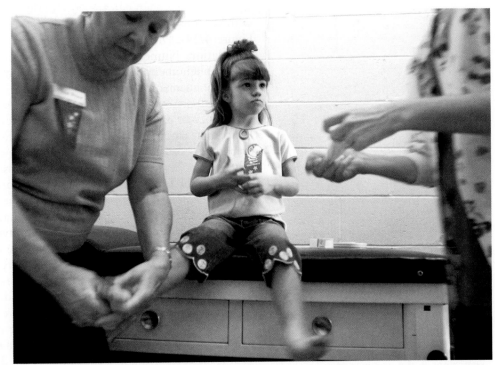

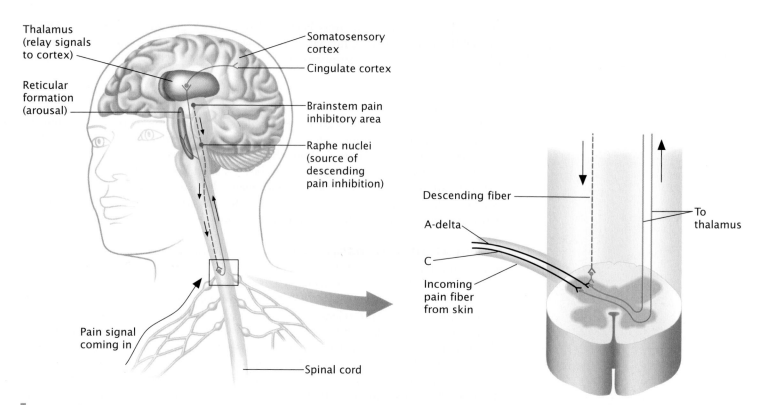

FIGURE 4.24

Pain Pathways

Pain messages are carried to the brain by way of the spinal cord. Myelinated *A-delta fibers* carry information about sharp pain. Unmyelinated *C fibers* carry several types of pain, including chronic, dull aches. Pain fibers make synapses in the reticular formation, causing arousal. They also project to the thalamus and from there to the cortex. Pain sensations can be intensified when activity in pain-carrying neurons stimulates activity in glial cells in the spinal cord (Watkins & Maier, 2003; see the chapter on biological aspects of psychology).

with neurons that carry pain signals to the thalamus and other parts of the brain (see Figure 4.24). Different pain neurons are activated by different degrees of painful stimulation. Numerous types of neurotransmitters are used by different pain neurons, a phenomenon that has allowed the development of a variety of new drugs for pain management.

Scientists once thought that the cerebral cortex played little or no role in the experience of pain, but several lines of evidence have now reversed that conclusion. Functional magnetic resonance imaging (fMRI) studies of healthy volunteers have compared cortical activity during pain experiences with cortical activity during other tasks (Tracey, 2005). These studies showed activation of the somatosensory cortex under both conditions and additional activity during pain in the *anterior cingulate cortex,* an evolutionarily primitive brain region thought to be important in emotions. Other studies have confirmed that the anterior cingulate cortex and other cortical regions are activated during painful stimulation (Mohr et al., 2005). Further, when hypnosis is used to increase or decrease the unpleasantness of pain, there are corresponding changes in the anterior cingulate cortex (Schulz-Stubner et al., 2004). Reductions in anterior cingulate cortex activity also occur in response to pain-reducing drugs and even to pain-reducing placebos (Petrovic et al., 2002). Finally, research suggests that pain can be experienced without any external stimulation of pain receptors. In such cases, the pain appears to originate in the activity of neurons within the thalamus and various regions of the cerebral cortex (Devulder, Crombez, & Mortier, 2002; Seghier et al., 2005).

● **gate control theory** A theory suggesting that a functional "gate" in the spinal cord can either let pain impulses travel upward to the brain or block their progress.

● **analgesia** The absence of pain sensations in the presence of a normally painful stimulus.

The Complex Nature of Pain If pain were based only on the nature of incoming stimuli, this participant in a purification ceremony in Singapore would be hurting. However, as described in the chapter on consciousness, the experience of pain is a complex phenomenon affected by psychological and biological variables that can make it more or, as in this case, less intense.

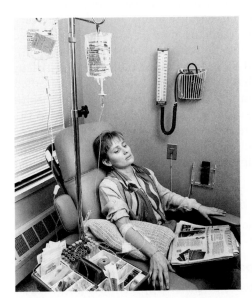

Easing Pain Candy containing capsaicin is sometimes given for the treatment of painful mouth sores associated with cancer chemotherapy (Berger et al., 1995). Capsaicin is what makes chili peppers "hot," but eating enough of it results in desensitization and a corresponding reduction in pain sensations (Bevan & Gepetti, 1994).

● **Emotional Aspects of Pain** All senses can have emotional components, most of which are learned responses. For example, the smell of baking cookies can make you feel good if it has been associated with happy childhood times. The emotional response to pain is more direct. Specific pathways carry an emotional component of the painful stimulus to areas of the hindbrain and reticular formation (see Figure 4.24), as well as to the cingulate cortex via the thalamus (Johansen, Fields, & Manning, 2001).

Nevertheless, the overall emotional response to pain depends greatly on cognitive factors, that is, on how we think about it (Spinhoven et al., 2005). For example, experimenters compared responses to a painful stimulus in people who were informed about the nature of the stimulus and when to expect it with responses in people who were not given this information. Knowing about pain seemed to make it less objectionable, even though the sensation was reported to be just as noticeable (Mayer & Price, 1982). Another factor affecting emotional responses to pain sensations is the use of pain-reducing cognitive strategies, such as focusing on distracting thoughts (Patterson et al., 2006). In one study, distraction created by a cognitively demanding task reduced both the unpleasantness of painful heat stimuli and activity in brain regions involved in processing pain sensations (Bantick et al., 2002).

● **Modulation of Pain: The Gate Control Theory** Pain is extremely useful, because in the long run it protects you from harm. However, there are times when enough is enough. Fortunately, the nervous system has several mechanisms for controlling the experience of pain.

One explanation of how the nervous system controls the amount of pain that reaches the brain is the **gate control theory** (Melzack & Wall, 1965). It proposes that there is a "gate" in the spinal cord that either lets pain impulses travel upward to the brain or blocks their progress. Many details of the original gate control theory turned out to be incorrect, but later work supported the idea that natural mechanisms can block pain sensations, so it remains the most comprehensive account of pain modulation (Stanton-Hicks & Salamon, 1997; Sufka & Price, 2002). According to gate control theory, input from other skin senses can come into the spinal cord at the same time the pain gets there and "take over" the pathways that the pain impulses would have used. This appears to be why rubbing the skin around a wound temporarily reduces pain from the wound, and why electrical stimulation of the skin around a painful spot relieves that pain. Gate control theory may also partially explain why scratching relieves itching, because itch sensations involve activity in fibers located close to pain fibers (Andrew & Craig, 2001).

The brain can also close the gate to pain impulses by sending signals down the spinal cord. The control of sensation by messages coming from the brain is a common aspect of sensory systems (Willis, 1988). In the case of pain, these messages from the brain block incoming pain signals at spinal cord synapses. The result is **analgesia**, the absence of the sensation of pain in the presence of a normally painful stimulus. For example, if part of a rat's hindbrain is electrically stimulated, pain signals generated in the skin never reach the brain (Reynolds, 1969). Permanently implanting electrodes that stimulate this same region of the human brain has reduced severe pain in some patients, but unfortunately it also produces a profound sense of impending doom (Hoffert, 1992).

● **Natural Analgesics** At least three substances play a role in the brain's ability to block pain signals: (1) the neurotransmitter *serotonin*, (2) natural opiates called *endorphins*, and (3) *endocannabinoids*, all of which are chemicals released by the body during stress (Hohmann et al., 2005). As described in the chapter on biological aspects of psychology, endorphins are natural painkillers that act as neurotransmitters at many levels of the pain pathway, including the spinal cord,

Natural Analgesia The stress of athletic exertion causes the release of endorphins, natural painkillers that have been associated with pleasant feelings known as "runner's high."

where they block the synapses of pain-carrying fibers. Endorphins may also relieve pain when secreted into the bloodstream as hormones by the adrenal and pituitary glands. The more endorphin receptors a person has inherited, the more pain tolerance that person has (Benjamin, Wilson, & Mogil, 1999).

Several conditions are known to cause the body to ease its own pain. For example, endorphins are released by immune cells that arrive at sites of inflammation (Cabot, 2001). And during the late stages of pregnancy, an endorphin system is activated that reduces the mother's labor pains (Dawson-Basoa & Gintzler, 1997). An endorphin system is also activated when people believe they are receiving a painkiller even though they are not (Zubieta et al., 2005). This phenomenon may be one of the mechanisms underlying the placebo effect, which is discussed in the chapter on research in psychology. Remarkably, the resulting pain inhibition is experienced in the part of the body where relief was expected to occur, but not elsewhere (Benedetti, Arduino, & Amanzio, 1999). Physical or psychological stress, too, can activate natural analgesic systems. Stress-induced release of natural analgesics may account for cases in which injured soldiers and athletes continue to perform in the heat of battle or competition with no apparent pain (Colloca & Benedetti, 2005).

There are also mechanisms for reactivating pain sensitivity once a crisis is past. Studies with animals show that they can learn that certain situations signal "safety" and that these safety signals trigger the release of a neurotransmitter that counteracts endorphins' analgesic effects (Wiertelak, Maier, & Watkins, 1992). Blocking these "safety signals" increases the painkilling effects brought on by a placebo (Benedetti & Amanzio, 1997).

THINKING CRITICALLY Does Acupuncture Relieve Pain?

*A*cupuncture is an ancient and widely used treatment in Asian medicine that is alleged to work many wonders, including curing epilepsy, speeding recovery from stroke, helping people quit smoking, reducing nausea from chemotherapy, and the like (Li, Jack, & Yang, 2006; Shouzhuang & Chao, 2006; Yongxia, 2006). Most notably, though, acupuncture is said to be capable of relieving pain (Ulett, 2003). The method is based on the idea that body energy flows along lines called *channels*. It is said that there are fourteen main channels and that a person's health depends on the balance of energy flowing in them. Inserting thin needles into the skin and twirling them is meant to stimulate these channels and restore a balanced flow of energy. The needles produce an aching and tingling sensation called *Teh-ch'i* at the site of stimulation, but they relieve pain at distant, seemingly unrelated parts of the body.

■ What am I being asked to believe or accept?

Acupuncturists assert that twirling a needle in the skin can relieve pain caused by everything from tooth extraction to cancer.

■ What evidence is available to support the assertion?

There is no scientific evidence for the existence of the energy channels proposed in the theory behind acupuncture. However, as described in the chapter on biological aspects of psychology, some acupuncture stimulation sites are near peripheral nerves, and evidence from functional MRI scans suggests that stimulating these sites changes activity in brain regions related to the targets of treatment (Yan et al., 2005).

What about the more specific assertions that acupuncture relieves pain and that it does so through direct physical mechanisms? Several studies have shown positive

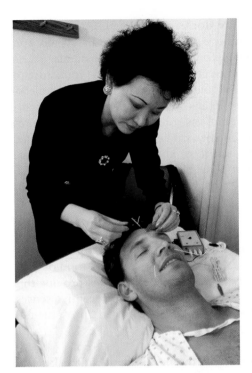

How Does Acupuncture Work? This acupuncturist is inserting fine needles in her patient's face in hopes of treating poor blood circulation in his hands and feet. Acupuncture treatments appear to alleviate a wide range of problems, including many kinds of pain, but the mechanisms through which it works are not yet determined.

results in 50 to 80 percent of patients treated with acupuncture for various kinds of pain (Brinkhaus et al., 2006; Manheimer et al., 2005; Witt et al., 2005). In one controlled study of headache pain, for example, 33 percent of the patients in a placebo group improved following mock electrical nerve stimulation (which is about the usual proportion of people who respond to a placebo), but 53 percent reported reduced pain following real acupuncture (Dowson, Lewith, & Machin, 1985). Another headache study found both acupuncture and drugs to be superior to a placebo. Each reduced the frequency of headaches, but the drugs were more effective than acupuncture at reducing the severity of headache pain (Hesse, Mogelvang, & Simonsen, 1994). Such well-controlled studies are rare, however, and their results are often contradictory (Ter Riet, Kleijnen, & Knipschild, 1990). Some studies of patients with back or neck pain, for example, have found acupuncture to be no better than a placebo or massage therapy (Assefi et al., 2005; Linde et al., 2005; Melchart et al., 2005); others have found that acupuncture benefits certain patients (Kvorning et al., 2004; Meng et al., 2003).

There is evidence that acupuncture activates the endorphin system. It is associated with the release of endorphins in the brain, and drugs that slow the breakdown of opiates also prolong the analgesia produced by acupuncture (He, 1987). Furthermore, the pain-reducing effects of acupuncture during electrical stimulation of a tooth can be reversed by naloxone, a substance that blocks the painkilling effects of endorphins and other opiate drugs. This finding suggests that acupuncture somehow activates the body's natural painkilling system. If acupuncture does activate endorphins, is the activation brought about only through the placebo effect? Probably not entirely, because acupuncture produces naloxone-reversible analgesia in monkeys and rats, who could not have developed positive expectancies by reading about acupuncture (Kishioka et al., 1994).

■ Are there alternative ways of interpreting the evidence?

Yes. Evidence about acupuncture might be interpreted as simply confirming that the body's painkilling system can be stimulated by external means. Acupuncture may merely provide one activating method (Pariente et al., 2005); there may be other, even more efficient ways of doing so (Petrovic et al., 2005; Ulett, 2003). We already know, for example, that successful placebo treatments for human pain appear to operate by activating the endorphin system.

■ What additional evidence would help to evaluate the alternatives?

More placebo-controlled studies of acupuncture are needed, but it is difficult to control for the placebo effect in acupuncture treatment, especially in double-blind fashion (Derry et al., 2006). (How could a therapist not know whether the treatment being given was acupuncture or not? And from the patient's perspective, what placebo treatment could look and feel like having a needle inserted and twirled in the skin?) Nevertheless, researchers have tried to separate the psychological and physical effects of acupuncture—for example, by using phony needles; by giving mock electrical nerve stimulation, in which electrodes are attached to the skin but no electricity is delivered; or by stimulating at pain-irrelevant locations (Kaptchuk et al., 2006; Park, White, & Ernst, 2001).

Researchers must also go beyond focusing on the effects of acupuncture to consider the general relationship between internal painkilling systems and external methods for stimulating them. Regarding acupuncture itself, scientists do not yet know what factors govern its ability to activate the endorphin system. Other important unknowns include the types of pain for which acupuncture is most effective, the types of patients who respond best, and the precise procedures that are most effective.

■ What conclusions are most reasonable?

Although acupuncture is not a cure-all, there seems little doubt that, in some circumstances, it does relieve pain and reduce nausea (British Medical Association,

2000; National Institutes of Health Consensus Conference, 1998). One study, for example, found that acupuncture before surgery reduced postoperative pain and nausea, decreased the need for pain-relieving drugs, and reduced patients' stress responses (Kotani et al., 2001). Another found electrical-stimulation acupuncture to be more effective than either drugs or mock stimulation at reducing nausea following major breast surgery; the acupuncture group also reported the least postoperative pain (Gan et al., 2004). So although some critics argue that further expenditures for acupuncture research are not warranted, further studies will probably continue. The quality of their methodology and the nature of their results will determine whether acupuncture finds a more prominent place in Western medicine. ■

● Proprioception: Sensing Body Position

Most sensory systems receive information from the external world, such as the light reflected from a flower or the feeling of cool water. But as far as the brain is concerned, the rest of the body is "out there," too. You know about the position of your body and what each of its parts is doing only because sensory systems provide this information to the brain. These sensory systems are called **proprioceptive senses** (*proprioceptive* means "received from one's own" and is pronounced "pro-pree-oh-SEP-tiv").

● **Vestibular Sense** The **vestibular sense** tells the brain about the position of the head (and hence the body) in space and about its general movements. It is a primary component of what people think of as the *sense of balance*. People usually become aware of the vestibular sense only when it is disrupted in some way, causing the sensation of dizziness.

The organs for the vestibular sense are two vestibular sacs and three semicircular canals in our inner ears. (You can see the semicircular canals in Figure 4.3; the vestibular sacs connect these canals and the cochlea.) The **vestibular sacs** are filled with a thick, oily fluid and contain small crystals called **otoliths** ("ear stones") that rest on hair endings. The **semicircular canals** are fluid-filled, arc-shaped tubes, with tiny hairs extending into the fluid. When your head moves, the otoliths shift in the vestibular sacs and the fluid moves in the semicircular canals, stimulating hair endings. This process activates neurons that travel with the auditory nerve, signaling the brain about the amount and direction of head movement.

The vestibular system has neural connections to several brain areas, including to the cerebellum, to the part of the autonomic nervous system (ANS) that affects the digestive system, and to the muscles of the eyes. The connections to the cerebellum help coordinate accurate body movements. The connections to the ANS are partly responsible for the nausea that sometimes follows intense stimulation of the vestibular system—on amusement park rides, for example. Finally, the connections to the eye muscles create *vestibular-ocular reflexes*. For instance, when your head moves in one direction, your eyes reflexively move in the opposite direction. This reflex allows your eyes to focus on a fixed point in space even if your head is moving—as when you track a ball in flight while running to catch it. You can experience this reflex by having a friend spin you around on a stool for a while. When you stop spinning, try to fix your gaze on one point in the room. You will be temporarily unable to do so, because the excitation of the vestibular system will cause your eyes to move repeatedly in the direction opposite to the spinning. Because vestibular reflexes adapt to the lack of gravity in outer space, astronauts returning to earth have postural and movement difficulties until their vestibular systems readjust to the effects of gravity (Paloski, 1998).

TRY THIS

● **Kinesthesia** Balance depends partly on **kinesthesia** (pronounced "kin-es-THEE-zha"), the sense that tells you where the parts of your body are with respect to one another. You probably do not think much about kinesthetic information,

---

proprioceptive senses The sensory systems that allow us to know about where we are and what each part of our body is doing.

vestibular sense The proprioceptive sense that provides information about the position of the head (and hence the body) in space and about its movements.

vestibular sacs Organs in the inner ear that connect the semicircular canals and the cochlea and contribute to the body's sense of balance.

otoliths Small crystals in the fluid-filled vestibular sacs of the inner ear that, when shifted by gravity, stimulate nerve cells that inform the brain of the position of the head.

semicircular canals Tubes in the inner ear whose fluid, when shifted by head movements, stimulates nerve cells that tell the brain about those movements.

kinesthesia The sense that tells you where the parts of your body are with respect to one another.

but you definitely use it, and you can demonstrate it for yourself. Close your eyes, hold your arms out in front of you, and try to touch your two index fingertips together. You probably did this easily because your kinesthetic sense told you where each finger was with respect to your body. You also depend on kinesthetic information to guide all your movements. Otherwise, it would be impossible to develop or improve any motor skill, from walking to complex athletic movements. These movement patterns become simple and fluid because with practice, the brain uses kinesthetic information automatically.

← TRY THIS

Kinesthetic information comes from special receptors in joints and muscles. Receptors in muscle fibers send information to the brain about the stretching of muscles (McCloskey, 1978). When the position of your bones changes, as when you move your arms and legs, receptors in the joints transduce this mechanical energy into neural activity, providing information about both the rate of change and the angle of the bones. This coded information goes to the spinal cord and is sent from there to the thalamus, along with sensory information from the skin. Eventually the information goes to the cerebellum and to the somatosensory cortex (see Figures 3.12 and 3.16), where it is used in the smooth coordination of movements.

Proprioception is a critical sense for success in physical therapy and rehabilitative medicine, especially for people who have to relearn how to move their muscles after strokes or other problems. Research in a branch of physics called *nonlinear dynamics* has been applied to problems in proprioception. For example, using the discovery that the right amount of random, background noise can improve the detection of signals, rehabilitation neurologists have added a small amount of vibration (or "noise") to muscle and joint sensations. This procedure dramatically increases patients' ability to detect joint movements and position (Glanz, 1997). (See "In Review: Body Senses" for a summary of our discussion of touch, temperature, pain, and kinesthesia.)

Balancing Act   The smooth coordination of all physical movement, from scratching your nose to complex feats of balance, depends on proprioception, the senses that provide information about the position of the head and body, their movements, and where each body part is in relation to all the others.

in review   Body Senses

Sense	Energy	Conversion of Physical Energy to Nerve Activity	Pathways and Characteristics
Touch	Mechanical deformation of skin	Skin receptors (may be stimulated by hair on the skin)	Nerve endings respond to changes in weight (intensity) and location of touch.
Temperature	Heat	Sensory neurons in the skin	Changes in temperature are detected by warm-sensing and cool-sensing fibers. Temperature interacts with touch.
Pain	Increases with intensity of touch or temperature	Free nerve endings in or near the skin surface	Changes in intensity cause the release of chemicals detected by receptors in pain neurons. Some fibers convey sharp pain; others convey dull aches and burning sensations.
Kinesthesia	Mechanical energy of joint and muscle movement	Receptors in muscle fibers	Information from muscle fibers is sent to the spinal cord, thalamus, cerebellum, and cortex.

**FOCUS ON
RESEARCH METHODS**

The Case of the Mysterious Spells

Early in this chapter we discussed the doctrine of specific nerve energies, which says that each sensory system can send information to the brain only about its own sense, regardless of how the stimulation occurs. So gently pressing on your closed eye will send touch sensations from the skin on your eyelid and visual sensations from your eye. This doctrine applies even when stimulation of sensory systems arises from within the brain itself. For example, *tinnitus*, a continuous "ringing in the ears," occurs as a result of spontaneous activation of nerve cells in auditory areas of the brain, not from any external sound source. The following case study illustrates a far less common example, in which spontaneous brain activity resulted in erotic sensations.

■ What was the researcher's question?

A thirty-one-year-old woman we'll call "Linda" reported that, for many years, she had been experiencing recurring "spells" that began with what seemed like sexual sensations (Janszky et al., 2002). These "orgasm-like euphoric erotic sensations" were followed by a staring, unresponsive state in which she lost consciousness. The spells, which occurred without warning and in response to no obvious trigger, interfered severely with her ability to function normally in everyday life. Linda was examined by József Janszky, a neurologist, who suspected that she might be suffering from epilepsy, a seizure disorder in which nerve cells in the brain suddenly start firing uncontrollably. The symptoms of an epileptic seizure depend on which brain areas are activated. Seizures that activate the motor area of the cerebral cortex will cause uncontrollable movements, seizures that activate visual cortex will create the sensation of images, and so on. Could there be a specific brain region that, when activated by a seizure, cause the sensations of orgasm that are normally brought on by external stimulation?

■ How did the researcher answer the question?

It is not easy to study the neurological basis of sexual sensations because most people are understandably reluctant to allow researchers to monitor their sexual activity. In the process of diagnosing Linda's problem, Janszky had a unique opportunity to learn something about the origin of orgasmic sensations without intruding on his patient's privacy. His approach exemplifies the *case study* method of research. As described in the chapter on research in psychology, case studies focus intensively on a particular individual, group, or situation. Sometimes they lead to important insights about clinical problems or other phenomena that occur so rarely that they cannot be studied through surveys or controlled experiments. In this case, Janszky decided to study Linda's brain activity while she was actually having a spell. He reasoned that if the spells were caused by seizures in a specific brain region, it might be possible to eliminate the problem through surgery.

■ What did the researcher find?

Linda's brain activity was recorded during five of her spells, using electroencephalography (EEG), a method described in more detail in the chapter on biological aspects of psychology. During each spell, the EEG showed that she was having seizures in the right temporal lobe of her brain. A subsequent MRI of her brain revealed a small area of abnormal tissue in the same area of the right temporal lobe. The organization of nerve cells in abnormal brain tissue can make it easier for seizures to occur, so Linda was advised to have some tissue surgically removed from the problem area. After the surgery, her seizures stopped.

■ What do the results mean?

Janszky concluded that Linda had been having "localization-related epilepsy," meaning that her spells were seizures coming from a specific brain location. This conclusion was supported by the fact that she had right temporal lobe seizures on the EEG each time she had a spell. Her MRI showed an abnormality in the same region that commonly gives rise to seizures, and her spells disappeared after the abnormality was removed. Linda's case also led Janszky to suggest that the right temporal lobe may play a special role in creating the sensory experience of orgasm.

■ What do we still need to know?

Janszky's suggestion might be correct, meaning that activation of the right temporal cortex may be sufficient for the sensory experience of orgasm. But at least one important question remains. How specific is the linkage between activity in this brain region and the sensory experiences of orgasm? Could seizures in other brain regions cause similar experiences, for example? Is right temporal cortex activity one of many ways to generate orgasm-like experiences, or is it necessary for these experiences? Answering this question would be easier if we knew whether Linda continued to experience orgasms during sexual activity. If she did, the implication would be that the area of right temporal lobe tissue that was removed was not necessary for the experience of orgasm. Unfortunately, Janszky's report is silent on this point, but future cases and further research will no doubt shed additional light on this fascinating sensory puzzle. ■

LINKAGES

As noted in the chapter on introducing psychology, all of psychology's many subfields are related to one another. Our discussion of the representation of sensory systems in the brain illustrates just one way in which the topic of this chapter, sensation, is linked to the subfield of biological psychology, which is the focus of the chapter on biological aspects of psychology. The Linkages diagram shows ties to two other subfields as well, and there are many more ties throughout the book. Looking for linkages among subfields will help you see how they all fit together and help you appreciate the big picture that is psychology.

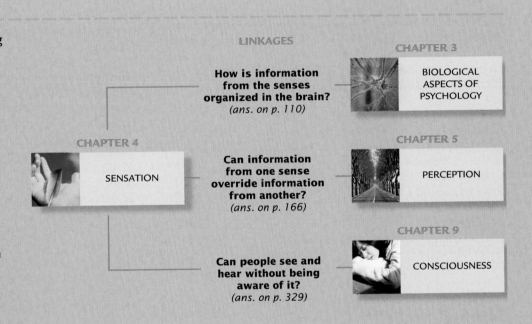

LINKAGES

How is information from the senses organized in the brain? (ans. on p. 110)

CHAPTER 3
BIOLOGICAL ASPECTS OF PSYCHOLOGY

CHAPTER 4
SENSATION

Can information from one sense override information from another? (ans. on p. 166)

CHAPTER 5
PERCEPTION

Can people see and hear without being aware of it? (ans. on p. 329)

CHAPTER 9
CONSCIOUSNESS

SUMMARY

A *sense* is a system that translates information from outside the nervous system into neural activity. Messages from the senses are called *sensations*.

Sensory Systems

The first step in sensation involves *accessory structures*, which collect and modify sensory stimuli. The second step is *transduction*, the process of converting incoming energy into neural activity; it is accomplished by *sensory receptors*, cells specialized to detect energy of some type. *Adaptation* takes place when receptors receive unchanging stimulation. Neural activity is transferred through the thalamus (except in the case of olfaction) and on to the cortex.

The Problem of Coding *Coding* is the translation of physical properties of a stimulus into a pattern of neural activity that specifically identifies those physical properties. It is the language the brain uses to describe sensations. Coding is characterized by the *doctrine of specific nerve energies*: Stimulation of a particular sensory nerve provides codes for that one sense, no matter how the stimulation takes place. There are two basic types of sensory codes: *temporal codes* and *spatial codes*.

Hearing

Sound is a repetitive fluctuation in the pressure of a medium such as air. It travels in waves.

Sound The *frequency* (which is related to *wavelength*) and *amplitude* of sound waves produce the psychological dimensions of *pitch* and *loudness*, respectively. *Timbre*, the quality of sound, depends on complex wave patterns added to the lowest frequency of the sound.

The Ear The energy from sound waves is collected and transmitted to the *cochlea* through a series of accessory structures, including the *tympanic membrane*. Transduction occurs when sound energy stimulates hair cells of the organ of Corti on the *basilar membrane* of the cochlea, which in turn stimulate the *auditory nerve*.

Auditory Pathways, Representations, and Experiences Auditory information is relayed through the thalamus to the *primary auditory cortex* and to other areas of auditory cortex. Sounds of similar frequency activate neighboring cells in the cortex, but loudness is coded temporally.

Coding Intensity and Frequency The intensity of a sound stimulus is coded by the firing rate of auditory neurons. *Place theory* describes the coding of higher frequencies: They are coded by the place on the basilar membrane where the wave envelope peaks. Each neuron in the auditory nerve is most sensitive to a specific frequency (its characteristic frequency). Very low frequencies are coded by frequency matching, which refers to the fact that the firing rate of a neuron matches the frequency of a sound wave. According to *frequency-matching theory*, or volley theory, some frequencies may be matched by the firing rate of a group of neurons. Low to moderate frequencies are coded through a combination of these methods.

Vision

Light *Visible light* is electromagnetic radiation with a wavelength of about 400 nm to about 750 nm. *Light intensity*, or the amount of energy in light, determines its brightness. Differing *light wavelengths* are sensed as different colors.

Focusing Light Accessory structures of the eye include the *cornea, pupil, iris,* and *lens*. Through *accommodation* and other means, these structures focus light rays on the *retina*, the netlike structure of cells at the back of the eye.

Converting Light into Images *Photoreceptors* in the retina—*rods* and *cones*—have *photopigments* and can transduce light into neural activity. Rods and cones differ in their shape, their sensitivity to light, their ability to discriminate colors, and their distribution across the retina. The *fovea*, the area of highest *acuity*, has only cones, which are color sensitive. Rods are more sensitive to light but do not discriminate colors; they are distributed in areas around the fovea. Both types of photoreceptors contribute to *dark adaptation*. From the photoreceptors, energy transduced from light is transferred to bipolar cells and then to *ganglion cells*, aided by lateral connections between photoreceptors, bipolar cells, and ganglion cells. Through *lateral inhibition*, the retina enhances the contrast between dark and light areas. Most ganglion cells, in effect, compare the amount of light falling on the center of their *receptive fields* with that falling on the surrounding area.

Visual Pathways The ganglion cells send action potentials out of the eye, at a point where a *blind spot* is created. Axons of ganglion cells leave the eye as a bundle of fibers called the *optic nerve*; half of these fibers cross over (creating the *optic chiasm*) and terminate in the *lateral geniculate nucleus* (LGN) of the thalamus. Neurons in the LGN send visual information on to the *primary visual cortex*.

Visual Representations Visual form, color, movement, and distance are processed by parallel systems. Complex *feature detectors* in the visual cortex are built in hierarchical fashion out of simpler units that detect and respond to features such as lines, edges, and orientations.

Seeing Color The color of an object depends on which of the wavelengths striking it are absorbed and which are reflected. The sensation of color has three psychological dimensions: *hue, saturation,* and *brightness*. According to the *trichromatic* (or Young-Helmholtz) *theory*, color vision results from the fact that the eye has three types of cones, each of which is most sensitive to short, medium, or long wavelengths of light. Information from these three cone types combines to produce the sensation of color. Individuals vary in the number and sensitivity of their cone pigments. According to the *opponent-process* (or Hering) *theory*, there are red-green, blue-yellow, and black-white visual elements in the eye. Members of each pair inhibit each other so that only one member of a pair may produce a signal at a time. This theory explains color afterimages, as well as the fact that lights of complementary colors cancel each other out and produce gray when mixed together.

Interaction of the Senses: Synesthesia Various dimensions of vision interact, and vision can also interact with hearing and other senses in a process known as *synesthesia*. For example, some people experience certain colors when stimulated by certain letters, numbers, or sounds.

The Chemical Senses: Smell and Taste

The chemical senses include olfaction (smell) and gustation (taste).

Olfaction   *Olfaction* detects volatile chemicals that come into contact with olfactory receptors in the nose. Olfactory signals are sent to the *olfactory bulb* in the brain without passing through the thalamus. *Pheromones* are odors from one animal that change the physiology or behavior of another animal; in mammals, pheromones act through the *vomeronasal organ*.

Gustation   *Gustation* detects chemicals that come into contact with taste receptors in *papillae* on the tongue. Elementary taste sensations are limited to sweet, sour, bitter, salty, umami, and astringent. The combined responses of many taste buds determine a taste sensation.

Smell, Taste, and Flavor   The senses of smell and taste interact to produce flavor.

Somatic Senses and the Vestibular System

The *somatic senses*, or somatosensory systems, include skin senses and proprioceptive senses. The skin senses include touch, temperature, and pain.

Touch and Temperature   Nerve endings in the skin generate touch sensations when they are stimulated. Some nerve endings are sensitive to temperature, and some respond to both temperature and touch. Signals from neighboring points on the skin stay next to one another all the way to the cortex.

Pain   Pain provides information about damaging stimuli. Sharp pain and dull, chronic pain are carried by different fibers—A-delta and C fibers, respectively. The emotional response to pain depends on how the painful stimulus is interpreted. According to the *gate control theory*, incoming pain signals can be blocked by a "gate" in the spinal cord. Messages sent down the spinal cord from the brain also can block pain signals, producing *analgesia*. Endorphins and other chemicals act at several levels of the pain systems to reduce sensations of pain.

Proprioception: Sensing Body Position   *Proprioceptive senses* provide information about the body. The *vestibular sense* provides information about the position of the head in space through the *otoliths* in *vestibular sacs* and the *semicircular canals*, and *kinesthesia* provides information about the positions of body parts with respect to one another.

Perception

You are using perception right now in order to understand this sentence. Perception allows you to translate the shapes and patterns of the letters you see here and turn them into meaningful words and sentences. Without perception, you could still see the letters, but they would make no more sense than if they were written in an unfamiliar language. In this chapter, we tell you more about the amazing perceptual systems that allow you to understand what you see and hear. We have organized our presentation as follows:

At a traffic circle in Scotland, fourteen fatal accidents occurred in a single year, partly because drivers failed to slow down as they approached the circle. When warning signs failed to solve the problem, Gordon Denton, a British psychologist, proposed an ingenious solution. White lines were painted across the road leading to the circle, spaced to form a pattern that looked something like this:

/   /   /   /   /   /   / / /////

If drivers crossed these progressively more closely spaced lines at a constant speed, they got the impression that they were going faster and faster, and their automatic response was to slow down (Denton, 1980). During the fourteen months after Denton's idea was put to use, there were only two fatalities at the traffic circle. The same striping is now being used to slow drivers on roads approaching small towns in many countries, including the United States. Denton's solution to this problem relied heavily on his knowledge of the principles of human perception.

Perception is the process through which sensations are interpreted, using knowledge and understanding of the world, so that they become meaningful experiences. Perception is not a passive process of simply absorbing and decoding incoming sensations. If it were, our experience of the environment would be a constantly changing, utterly confusing mishmash of light and color. Instead, our brains take sensations and create a coherent world, often by filling in missing information and using past experience to give meaning to what we see, hear, or touch. For example, the raw sensations coming to your eyes from Figure 5.1 convey only the information that there is a series of intersecting lines. But your perceptual system automatically interprets this image as a rectangle (or window frame) on its side.

Let's first consider these perceptual processes and the various approaches that psychologists have taken in trying to understand them. We will then explore how people detect incoming sensory stimuli, organize these sensations into stable patterns, and recognize those patterns. We'll also examine the role of attention in guiding the perceptual system to analyze some parts of the world more closely than others. Finally, we provide some examples of how research on perception has been applied to some practical problems.

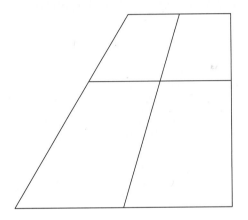

FIGURE 5.1

What Do You See?

The Perception Paradox

As in the case of drivers who find themselves slowing down in response to lines on the pavement, perception often takes place automatically, without conscious awareness. This quick and seemingly effortless aspect of perceptual processing suggests that perception is a rather simple affair. But perception contains a basic contradiction, or paradox: What is so easy for the perceiver to do has proven difficult for psychologists to understand and explain. The difficulty lies in the fact that to function so effectively and efficiently, our perceptual systems must be exceedingly complex.

To illustrate the workings of these complex systems, psychologists draw attention to *perceptual failures*, cases in which our perceptual experience of a stimulus differs from the actual characteristics of that stimulus. You can experience a perceptual failure for yourself by looking at Figure 5.2. Perceptual failures provide clues to the problems that our perception systems must solve and to the solutions they reach. Consider, for example, why the two lines in Figure 5.2 appear to differ in length. Part of the answer is that your visual system always tries to interpret stimuli as three-dimensional,

perception The process through which people take raw sensations from the environment and interpret them, using knowledge, experience, and understanding of the world, so that the sensations become meaningful experiences.

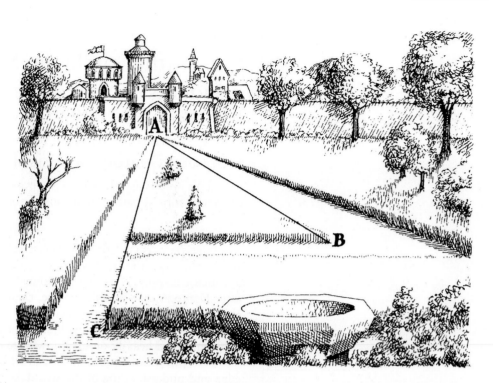

FIGURE 5.2

Misperceiving Reality

Which line is longer: Line A–C or Line A–B? They are exactly the same length, but you probably perceived A–C as longer. Understanding why our perceptual systems make this kind of error has helped psychologists understand the basic principles of perception.

even when they are not. A three-dimensional interpretation of the drawing would lead you to see the two lines as defining the edges of two parallel paths, one of which ends closer to you than the other. Because your eyes tell you that the two paths start at about the same point (the castle entrance), you solved the perceptual problem by assuming that the closer line must be the longer of the two. You can remove the three-dimensional cues by tracing the two intersecting lines onto a sheet of clear plastic and placing it on a white surface. In this more clearly two-dimensional display, the impression of unequal length will disappear.

Three Approaches to Perception

Psychologists have taken three main approaches in their efforts to understand human perception. The most recent of these is the **computational approach,** which tries to determine the calculations that a computer would have to perform to solve perceptual problems. Psychologists taking this approach believe that understanding these calculations will help them explain how complex computations within the nervous systems of humans and animals might turn raw sensory stimulation into a representation of the world. Computational theorists also hope that it might eventually be possible to build computerized robots capable of near-human levels of perceptual skill at jobs such as bomb detection, product inspection, and the like (Thaler, Kennedy, & Hanson, 2001). The computational approach owes much to two earlier, but still influential, views of perception: the constructivist approach and the ecological approach.

Psychologists who take the **constructivist approach** argue that our perceptual systems construct a representation of reality from fragments of sensory information. They are particularly interested in situations in which the same stimulus creates different perceptions in different people. As a case in point, the optical illusion you saw in Figure 5.2 occurs for people in many cultures but it may not occur for people whose cultural backgrounds do not include experience with the objects or linear perspectives shown in the drawing (Leibowitz et al., 1969). Constructivists emphasize that our perception is strongly influenced by what we have learned from our experiences and by the expectations and inferences that those experiences create (Rock, 1983). For example, a desk might prevent you from seeing the lower half of a person seated behind it,

computational approach An approach to perception that focuses on how computations by the nervous system translate raw sensory stimulation into an experience of reality.

constructivist approach A view of perception taken by those who argue that the perceptual system uses fragments of sensory information to construct an image of reality.

Is Anything Missing?   Because you know what animals look like, you perceive a whole cat in this picture even though its midsection is hidden. The constructivist approach to perception emphasizes our ability to use knowledge and expectations to fill in the gaps in incomplete objects and to perceive them as unified wholes, not disjointed parts.

but you still "see" the person as a complete human being. Experience tells you to expect that people remain intact even when parts of them are obscured.

Researchers influenced by the **ecological approach** to perception claim that most of our perceptual experience comes directly from the wealth of information contained in the stimuli coming to us from the environment rather than from our interpretations, inferences, and expectations. This ecological perspective has been summed up as follows: "Ask not what's inside your head, but what your head's inside of" (Mace, 1977). J. J. Gibson (1979), founder of the ecological approach, argued that the primary goal of perception is to support actions, such as walking, grasping, or driving, by "tuning in" to the part of the environmental stimulus array that is most important for performing those actions. So these researchers are less interested in our inferences about the person behind the desk than in how we would use visual information from that person, from the desk, and from other objects in the room to guide us as we walk toward a chair and sit down (Nakayama, 1994).

In summary: To explain perception, the *computational* approach focuses on the nervous system's manipulations of incoming signals, the *constructivist* approach emphasizes the inferences that people make about the environment, and the *ecological* approach emphasizes the information provided by the environment. Later, we discuss evidence in support of each of these approaches.

Psychophysics

ecological approach   An approach to perception maintaining that humans and other species are so well adapted to their natural environment that many aspects of the world are perceived without requiring higher-level analysis and inferences.

psychophysics   An area of research focusing on the relationship between the physical characteristics of environmental stimuli and the psychological experiences those stimuli produce.

How can psychologists measure perceptions when there is no way to get inside people's heads to experience what they are experiencing? One solution to this problem is to present people with lights, sounds, and other stimuli and ask them to report their perception of the stimuli. This method of studying perception, called **psychophysics**, describes the relationship between *physical energy* in the environment and our *psychological experience* of that energy (e.g., Purves et al., 2004).

● Absolute Thresholds: Is Something Out There?

How much stimulus energy is needed to trigger a conscious perceptual experience? Not much. Normal human vision can detect the light equivalent to a candle flame burning in the dark thirty miles away. The smallest amount of light, sound, pressure,

TABLE 5.1 Some Absolute Thresholds

Absolute thresholds can be amazingly low. Here are examples of stimulus equivalents at the absolute threshold for the five primary senses in humans. Set up the conditions for testing the absolute threshold for sound, and see if you can detect this minimal amount of auditory stimulation. If you can't hear it, the signal-detection theory we discuss later in this chapter may help explain why.

Source: Galanter (1962).

Human Sense	Absolute Threshold Is Equivalent to:
Vision	A candle flame seen at 30 miles on a clear night
Hearing	The tick of a watch under quiet conditions at 20 feet
Taste	1 teaspoon of sugar in 2 gallons of water
Smell	1 drop of perfume diffused into the entire volume of air in a 6-room apartment
Touch	The wing of a fly falling on your cheek from a distance of 1 centimeter

or other physical energy we can detect is called the **absolute threshold** (see Table 5.1). Stimuli below this threshold—stimuli that are too weak or too brief for us to notice—are traditionally referred to as **subliminal stimuli.** Stimuli above the absolute threshold—stimuli that are consistently perceived—are referred to as **supraliminal stimuli.**

If you were participating in a typical experiment to measure the absolute threshold for vision, you would sit in a darkened laboratory. After your eyes adapted to the darkness, you would be presented with a long series of brief flashes of light that varied in brightness. After each one, you would be asked if you saw a stimulus. If your absolute threshold were truly "absolute," your detection accuracy should jump from 0 to 100 percent at the exact level of brightness where your threshold is. This ideal absolute threshold is illustrated by the point at which the green line in Figure 5.3 suddenly rises. But research shows that the average of your responses over many trials would actually form a curve much like the purple line in that figure. In other words, the "absolute" threshold is not really an all-or-nothing phenomenon. Notice in Figure 5.3 that a flash whose brightness (intensity) is 3 is detected 20 percent of the time and missed 80 percent of the time. Is that stimulus *subliminal* or *supraliminal*? Psychologists have dealt with questions of this sort by redefining the absolute threshold as the minimum amount of stimulus energy that can be detected 50 percent of the time.

● **absolute threshold** The minimum amount of stimulus energy that can be detected 50 percent of the time.

● **subliminal stimuli** Stimuli that are too weak or brief to be perceived.

● **supraliminal stimuli** Stimuli that are strong enough to be consistently perceived.

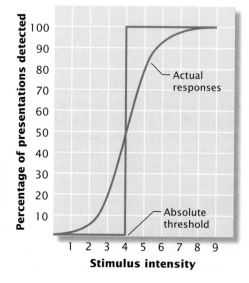

FIGURE 5.3

The Absolute Threshold

The curve shows the relationship between the intensity of a signal and the likelihood that it will be detected. If the absolute threshold were truly absolute, signals at or above a particular intensity would always be detected, and signals below that intensity would never be detected (see green line). But this response pattern almost never occurs, so the "absolute" threshold is defined as the intensity at which the signal is detected with 50 percent accuracy.

THINKING CRITICALLY   Can Subliminal Stimuli Influence Your Behavior?

LINKAGES (a link to Introducing Psychology, p. 10)

In 1957, an adman named James Vicary claimed that a New Jersey theater flashed messages such as "buy popcorn" and "drink Coke" on a movie screen, too briefly to be noticed, while customers watched the movie *Picnic*. He said that these subliminal messages caused a 15 percent rise in sales of Coca-Cola and a 58 percent increase in popcorn sales. Can such "mind control" really work? Many people seem to think so: They spend millions of dollars each year on audios and videos that promise subliminal help to lose weight, boost self-esteem, quit smoking, make more money, or achieve other goals.

■ What am I being asked to believe or accept?

Two types of claims have been made about subliminal stimuli. The more general claim is that subliminal stimuli can influence our behavior. The second, more specific assertion is that subliminal stimuli provide an effective means of changing people's buying habits, political opinions, self-confidence, and other complex attitudes and behaviors, with or without their awareness or consent.

■ What evidence is available to support the assertion?

Most evidence for the first claim—that subliminal stimuli can influence behavior in a general way—comes from research on visual perception. For example, using a method called *subliminal priming*, participants are shown clearly visible (supraliminal) stimuli, such as pictures of people, and then asked to make some sort of judgment about them. Unbeknownst to the participants, however, each of the visible pictures is preceded by other pictures or words flashed so briefly that the participants are unaware of them. The critical question is whether the information in the subliminal stimuli influences participants' responses to the visible stimuli that follow them.

In one subliminal priming study, visible pictures of individuals were preceded by subliminal pictures that were either "positive" (e.g., happy children) or "negative" (e.g., a monster). The participants in this study judged the people in the visible pictures as more likable, polite, friendly, successful, and reputable when their pictures had been preceded by a subliminal picture that was positive rather than negative (Krosnick et al., 1992). Researchers have also found that subliminally presented words can influence decisions about the meaning of words. For example, after being exposed to subliminal presentations of a man's name (e.g., "Tom"), participants were able to decide more rapidly whether a visible stimulus (e.g., "John") was a man's or woman's name. However, the impact of the subliminally presented name lasted for only about one-tenth of a second (Greenwald, Draine, & Abrams, 1996).

Other research shows that subliminal stimuli can lead to a change in people's physiological responses. In one study, participants were exposed to subliminal photos of snakes, spiders, flowers, and mushrooms while researchers recorded their *galvanic skin resistance (GSR)*, a measure of physiological arousal. Although the slides were flashed too quickly to be perceived consciously, participants who were afraid of snakes or spiders showed increased GSR measurements (and reported fear) in response to snake and spider photos (Öhman & Soares, 1994).

The results of studies such as these support the claim that subliminal information can have at least a temporary impact on judgment and emotion, but they say little or nothing about the effects of subliminal advertising or the value of subliminal self-help programs. In fact, there is no laboratory evidence to support the alleged effectiveness of such programs. Their promoters offer only testimonials from satisfied customers.

■ Are there alternative ways of interpreting the evidence?

Many claims for subliminal advertising—including those reported in the New Jersey theater case we mentioned—have turned out to be publicity stunts using phony data

(Haberstroh, 1995; Pratkanis, 1992). And testimonials from people who have purchased subliminal tapes and videos may be biased by what these people want to believe about the product they bought. This interpretation is supported by experiments that manipulate the beliefs of participants regarding the messages on subliminal audios or videos. In one study, half the participants were told that they would be hearing tapes containing subliminal messages that would improve their memory skills. The other half were told that the subliminal messages would improve their self-esteem. However, half the participants who expected self-esteem tapes actually received memory-improvement tapes, and half the participants who expected memory-improvement tapes actually received self-esteem tapes. Regardless of which tapes they actually heard, participants who thought they had heard memory-enhancement messages reported improved memory; those who thought they had heard self-esteem messages said that their self-esteem had improved (Pratkanis, Eskenazi, & Greenwald, 1994). In other words, the effects of the tapes were determined by the listeners' expectations—not by the tapes' subliminal content.

■ What additional evidence would help to evaluate the alternatives?

The effectiveness of self-help tapes and other subliminal products must be evaluated through further experiments—like the one just mentioned—that carefully control for expectations. Those who advocate subliminal influence methods are responsible for conducting those experiments, but as long as customers are willing to buy subliminal products on the basis of testimonials alone, any scientific evaluation efforts will probably come from those interested in consumer protection.

■ What conclusions are most reasonable?

Available scientific evidence suggests that subliminal perception does occur but that it has no potential for "mind control" (Greenwald, Klinger, & Schuh, 1995; Strahan, Spencer, & Zanna, 2005). Subliminal effects are usually small and short-lived, and they mainly affect simple judgments and general measures of overall arousal. Most researchers agree that subliminal messages have no special power to create major changes in people's needs, goals, skills, or actions (Pratkanis, 1992; Strahan et al., 2005). In fact, advertisements, political speeches, and other messages that people *can* perceive consciously have far stronger persuasive effects. ■

● Signal-Detection Theory

Look again at Figure 5.3. It shows that stimuli just above and just below the absolute threshold are sometimes detected and sometimes missed. For example, a stimulus at intensity level 3 appears to be subliminal, even though you will perceive it 20 percent of the time; a stimulus at level 5 is above threshold, but it will be missed 20 percent of the time. Why should the "absolute" threshold vary this way? The two most important reasons have to do with sensitivity and our response criterion.

Sensitivity refers to our ability to pick out a particular stimulus, or *signal*. Sensitivity is influenced by the *intensity of the signal* (stronger ones are easier to detect), the *capacity of sensory systems* (good vision or hearing makes us more sensitive), and the *amount of background stimulation*, or *noise*, arriving at the same time. Some noise comes from outside the person, as when electrical equipment hums or overhead lights flicker. There is also noise coming from the spontaneous, random firing of cells in our own nervous systems. Varying amounts of this *internal noise* is always occurring, whether or not we are stimulated by physical energy. You might think of it as a little like the "snow" on an unused television channel or static between radio stations.

The second source of variation in absolute threshold comes from the **response criterion**, which reflects our willingness to respond to a stimulus. Motivation—wants and needs—as well as expectancies affect the response criterion. Suppose, for example, that you work at an airport security checkpoint, where you spend hours looking at x-ray images of people's handbags, briefcases, and luggage. The signal to be detected in this situation is a weapon, whereas the "noise" consists

● **sensitivity** The ability to detect a stimulus.

● **response criterion** The internal rule a person uses to decide whether or not to report a stimulus.

Detecting Vital Signals According to signal-detection theory, the likelihood that airport security screeners will detect the outline of a bomb or other weapon in x-rays of a passenger's luggage depends partly on the sensitivity of their visual systems and partly on their response criterion. That criterion is affected by their expectations that weapons might appear and by how motivated they are to look carefully for them. To help keep inspectors' response criteria sufficiently low, airport security officials occasionally attempt to smuggle a simulated weapon through a checkpoint. This procedure serves to evaluate the inspectors, and it also helps keep them focused on their vital task (McCarley et al., 2004).

of harmless objects in a person's luggage, vague or distorted images on the viewing screen, and anything else that is not a weapon. If there has been a recent terrorist attack, or if the threat level has just been elevated, your airport will be on special alert. Accordingly, your response criterion will drop. That is, you will need to be less certain before saying that a questionable object on the x-ray image might be a weapon. In other words, expecting a stimulus makes it more likely that you will detect it than if it is unexpected.

Once researchers understood that detecting a signal depends on a combination of each person's sensitivity and response criterion, they realized that the measurement of absolute thresholds could never be more precise than the 50 percent rule mentioned earlier. So they abandoned the notion of absolute thresholds and focused instead on **signal-detection theory,** a mathematical model of how each person's sensitivity and response criterion combine to determine decisions about whether or not a near-threshold stimulus has occurred (Green & Swets, 1966).

As in a threshold experiment, a psychologist using signal-detection theory would analyze your responses to a series of trials on which lights (or sounds) may or may not be presented. The lights would be so faint that you would find it hard to tell whether a signal occurred, or whether there was only background "noise." Your response on each trial would be placed into one of four categories: a false alarm, a miss, a hit, or a correct rejection. A *false alarm* is an error that occurs when external or internal noise is high enough to make you report seeing a signal when no signal was presented. If a signal occurs but is so faint that it does not produce enough stimulation for you to detect it, you will have made an error known as a *miss*. A person with a more sensitive sensory system might have correctly detected that same stimulus when it occurred—which is called a *hit*. If no signal occurs and you don't report one, you will have made a *correct rejection*.

By analyzing the pattern of hits, misses, false alarms, and correct rejections, research based on signal-detection theory allows precise measurement of people's sensitivity to stimuli of any kind. It also provides a way to understand and predict people's responses in a wide range of situations (MacMillan & Creelman, 2004; Swets, 1996).

Consider tornado warnings. Signal-detection theory can help us understand why, even with the latest Doppler radar systems, weather forecasters sometimes fail to warn of a tornado that local residents can clearly see. The forecasters' task is not easy, because their radar systems are so sensitive that they don't just detect

● **signal-detection theory** A mathematical model of what determines a person's report that a near-threshold stimulus has or has not occurred.

FIGURE 5.4

Signal Detection

Part A shows the possible outcomes of examining a weather radar display: a *hit* (correctly detecting a tornado), a *miss* (failing to detect a tornado), a *correct rejection* (seeing no tornado when there is none), or a *false alarm* (reporting a tornado when none existed). The rest of the figure illustrates the impact of two different response criteria: Part B represents outcomes of a high response criterion, which would be set under conditions when tornadoes are expected only half the time; Part C represents outcomes of a low response criterion, which would be set under conditions when tornadoes are very likely to appear.

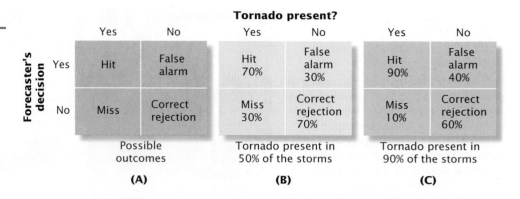

a tornado's spinning funnel but also harmless patterns created by swirling dust and swarming insects. So even a tornado's telltale radar "signature" will appear against a potentially confusing background of visual "noise." Whether or not that signature will be picked out and reported depends both on the forecaster's sensitivity to the signal and on the response criterion being used. In establishing the criterion for sounding a warning, the forecaster must consider the consequences. If the response criterion is too low, and warnings are issued at the slightest hint of a tornado, there would surely be false alarms that would unnecessarily disrupt people's lives, activate costly emergency plans, and even lead people to ignore future warnings. But setting the criterion too high, so that warnings occur only when the forecaster is certain of a tornado, could allow a dangerous storm to go unreported. Such a miss could cost many lives if it left a populated area with no warning of danger (see Figure 5.4A). In other words, there is a tradeoff. To minimize false alarms, the forecaster could set a very high response criterion, but doing so would also make misses more likely.

Let's examine how various kinds of expectations or assumptions can change the response criterion and how those changes might affect the accuracy of a forecaster's decisions. If a forecaster knows it's a time of year when tornadoes occur in only about 50 percent of the storm systems seen on radar, a rather high response criterion would be appropriate. That is, it will take relatively strong evidence to trigger a tornado warning. The hypothetical data in Figure 5.4B show that under these conditions, the forecaster correctly detected 70 percent of actual tornadoes but missed 30 percent of them. Also, 30 percent of the tornado reports were false alarms. Now suppose the forecaster learns that a different kind of storm system is on the way and that about 90 percent of such systems spawn tornadoes. This information is likely to increase the forecaster's expectation that a tornado signature will appear, thus lowering the response criterion. The forecaster will now require less evidence of a tornado before reporting one. Under these conditions, as shown in Figure 5.4C, the hit rate might rise from 70 percent to, say, 90 percent, but the false-alarm rate might also increase from 30 percent to 40 percent.

A forecaster's hit rate and false-alarm rate will also be affected by the forecaster's sensitivity to tornado signals. Those with greater sensitivity to these signals will have high hit rates and low false-alarm rates. Forecasters with less sensitivity are still likely to have high hit rates, but their false-alarm rates will be higher, too.

Psychologists' research on signal-detection theory helps us understand why people sometimes make mistakes at spotting tornadoes, inspecting luggage, diagnosing medical conditions, searching for oil, or looking for clues at a crime scene. That research is also being applied to improve people's performance on these kinds of signal-detection tasks (Wickens, 1992). For example, psychologists recommend that manufacturers occasionally place flawed items among a batch of objects to be inspected. This strategy increases inspectors' expectations of seeing flaws, thus lowering their response criterion and raising their hit rate.

Judging Differences: Has Anything Changed?

Sometimes our perceptual task is not to detect a faint stimulus but rather to notice small differences as a stimulus changes or to judge whether there are differences between two stimuli. For example, when tuning up, musicians must focus on whether the notes played by two instruments are the same or different. When evaluating a body shop's repair work, you must judge whether the color of the newly painted section matches the rest of your car. And you have to decide if your soup tastes any spicier after you have added some pepper.

Your ability to judge differences between stimuli depends partly on the strength of the stimuli you are dealing with. The weaker the stimuli are, the easier it is to detect small differences between them. For example, if you are comparing the weight of two envelopes, you will be able to detect a difference of as little as a fraction of an ounce. But if you are comparing two boxes weighing around fifty pounds each, you may not notice a difference unless it is a pound or more.

The smallest difference between stimuli that we can detect is called the **difference threshold** or **just-noticeable difference** (**JND**). How small is that difference? The size of a JND is described by one of the oldest laws in psychology. Named after the nineteenth-century German physiologist Ernst Weber (pronounced "VAY-ber"), **Weber's law** states that the smallest detectable difference in stimulus energy is a constant fraction of the intensity of the stimulus. This fraction, often called *Weber's constant* or Weber's fraction, is given the symbol K. As shown in Table 5.2, K is different for each of the senses. The smaller K is, the more sensitive a sense is to stimulus differences.

Specifically, Weber's law says that $JND = KI$, where K is the Weber's constant for a particular sense and I is the amount, or intensity, of the stimulus. To compute the JND for a particular stimulus, we must know its intensity and what sense it is stimulating. For example, as shown in Table 5.2, the value of K for weight is .02. If an object weighs 25 pounds (I), the JND is only half a pound (.02 × 25 pounds). So while carrying a 25-pound bag of groceries, you would have to add or remove a half a pound before you would be able to detect a change in its weight. But candy snatchers beware: It takes a change of only two-thirds of an ounce to determine that someone has been into a 2-pound box of chocolates!

Weber's constants vary somewhat among individuals, and as we get older we tend to become less sensitive to stimulus differences. There are exceptions to this rule, however. If you like candy, you will be happy to know that Weber's fraction for sweetness stays fairly constant throughout life (Gilmore & Murphy, 1989). Weber's law does not hold when stimuli are very intense or very weak, but it does apply to complex, as well as simple, stimuli. We all tend to have our own personal Weber's fractions that describe how much prices can increase before we notice or worry about the change. For example, if your Weber's fraction for cost is .10, then you would surely notice, and perhaps protest, a fifty-cent increase in a one-dollar bus fare. But the same fifty-cent increase in monthly rent would be less than a JND and thus unlikely to cause much notice or concern.

Magnitude Estimation: How Intense Is That?

How much would you have to turn up the volume on your stereo to make it sound twice as loud as your neighbor's? How much would you have to turn it down to make it sound only half as loud as it was before your neighbor complained? These are questions about *magnitude estimation*—about how our perception of stimulus intensity is related to the actual strength of the stimulus. In 1860, Gustav Fechner (pronounced "FECK-ner") used Weber's law to study the relationship between the physical magnitude of a stimulus and its *perceived* magnitude. He reasoned that if just-noticeable differences get progressively larger as stimulus magnitude increases, then the amount of change in the stimulus required to double or triple its perceived

Perfect! This chef's ability to taste the difference in his culinary creation before and after he has adjusted the spices depends on the same psychophysical laws that apply to judging differences in sights, sounds, and other sensory stimuli.

- **just-noticeable difference (JND)** The smallest detectable difference in stimulus energy.

- **Weber's law** A law stating that the smallest detectable difference in stimulus energy is a constant fraction of the intensity of the stimulus.

Stimulus	*K*
Pitch	.003
Brightness	.017
Weight	.02
Odor	.05
Loudness	.10
Pressure on skin	.14
Saltiness of taste	.20

intensity must get larger, too. He was right. For example, it takes only a small increase in volume to make a soft sound seem twice as loud, but imagine how much additional volume it would take to make a rock band seem twice as loud. To put it another way, constant increases in physical energy will produce progressively smaller increases in perceived magnitude. This observation, when expressed as a mathematical equation relating actual stimulus intensity to perceived intensity, became known as *Fechner's law*.

Fechner's law applies to most, but not all, stimuli. For example, it takes larger and larger increases in light or sound to create the same amount of change in perceived magnitude, but this is not the case for stimuli such as electric shock. It takes a relatively large increase in shock intensity to make a weak shock seem twice as intense, but if the shock is already painful, it takes only a small increase in intensity before you would perceive it as twice as strong. S. S. Stevens offered a formula (known as *Stevens's power law*) for magnitude estimation that works for a wider array of stimuli, including electric shock, temperature, and sound and light intensity. Stevens's law is still used today by psychologists who want to determine how much larger, louder, longer, or more intense a stimulus must be for people to perceive a specific difference or amount of change.

Overall, people do well at estimating differences between stimuli. For example, we are very good at estimating how much longer one line is than another. Yet as shown in Figure 5.2, this perceptual comparison process can be disrupted when the lines are embedded in more complex figures (Figure 5.5 offers some additional examples). The perceptual laws that we have discussed, and the exceptions to these laws, all emphasize a fundamental principle: Perception is a relative process. Our experience of one stimulus depends on its relationship to others. In the next section, on perceptual organization, we discuss what researchers have learned about the way in which our perceptual system relates one stimulus to another.

FIGURE 5.5

Length Illusions

People can usually estimate line lengths very accurately, but this ability can be impaired under certain conditions. The pairs of lines marked A and B are the same length in each drawing, but most people report that line A appears longer than line B. These optical illusions, like the one in Figure 5.2, occur partly because of our tendency to see two-dimensional figures as three-dimensional. With the exception of the top hat, all or part of line A in each drawing can easily be interpreted as being farther away than line B. When two equal-size objects appear to be at different distances, the visual system tends to infer that the more distant object must be larger.

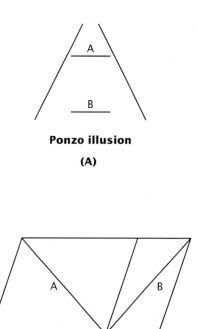

Ponzo illusion
(A)

Sanders illusion
(C)

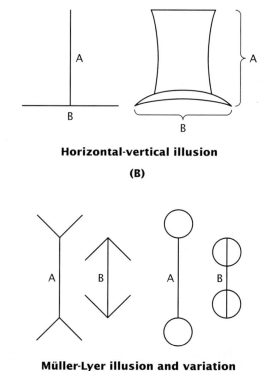

Horizontal-vertical illusion
(B)

Müller-Lyer illusion and variation
(D)

Organizing the Perceptual World

Suppose you are driving on a busy road while searching for Barney's Diner, an unfamiliar restaurant where you are supposed to meet a friend. The roadside is crammed with signs of all shapes and colors, some flashing and some rotating. If you are ever to recognize the sign that says "Barney's Diner," you must impose some sort of organization on this overwhelming array of visual information.

Perceptual organization is the task performed by the perceptual system to determine what edges and other stimuli go together to form an object (Peterson & Rhodes, 2003). In this case, the object would be the sign for Barney's Diner. It is perceptual organization, too, that makes it possible for you to separate the sign from its background of lights, colors, letters, and other competing stimuli. Figure 5.6 shows some of the ways in which your perceptual system can organize stimuli. The figure appears as a hollow cube, but notice that you can see it from two angles: either looking down at the top of the cube or looking up toward the bottom of the cube. Notice, too, that the "cube" is not really a cube at all but rather a series of unconnected arrows and Ys. Your perceptual system organizes these elements into a cube by creating imaginary connecting lines called *subjective contours*. That system can also change the apparent location of the cube. You probably first saw it as "floating" in front of a background of large black dots, but those dots can also become "holes" through which you see the cube against a solid black background "behind" the page. It may take a little time to see this second perceptual organization, but when you do, notice that the subjective contours you saw earlier are gone. They disappear because your perceptual system adjusts for the fact that when an object is partially obscured, we should not be able to see all of it.

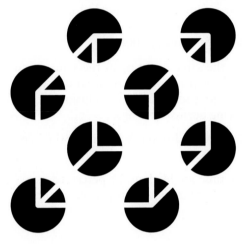

FIGURE 5.6

Organize This!

TRY THIS Psychologists have employed the principles of figure-ground organization and grouping to help explain how your visual system allows you to perceive these disconnected lines as a cube, to see it from above or below, and to see it as being either on the page or "behind" it.

● Basic Processes in Perceptual Organization

To explain phenomena such as these and to understand the way our perceptual systems organize more naturalistic scenes, psychologists have focused on two basic processes: *figure-ground organization* and *grouping*.

● **Figure-Ground Organization** When you look at a complex scene or listen to a noisy environment, your perceptual apparatus automatically emphasizes certain features, objects, or sounds; all other stimuli in that environment become the background. So as you drive toward an intersection, a stop sign stands out clearly against the background of trees, houses, and cars. This is an example of figure-ground organization. A *figure*, as the part of the visual field that has meaning, stands in front of the rest and always seems to include the contours or edges that separate it from the less relevant *ground*, or background. As described in the chapter on sensation, edges are one of the most basic features detected by our visual system; they combine to form figures.

To experience how your perceptual system creates figure and ground, look at the drawings in Figure 5.7. These drawings are called *reversible figures*, because you can repeatedly reverse your perceptual organization of what is figure and what is ground. Your ability to do this shows that perception is not only an active process but a categorical one as well. People usually organize sensory stimulation into one perceptual category or another, but rarely into both or into something in between. In Figure 5.7, for instance, you cannot easily see both faces and a vase, or the words *figure* and *ground,* at the same time.

● **Grouping** To distinguish figure from ground, our perceptual system must first identify stimulus elements in the environment, such as the edges of a stop sign or billboard, that belong together as figures. We tend to group certain elements together more or less automatically. In the early 1900s, several German psychologists began to study how this happens. They concluded that people perceive sights and sounds as

● **perceptual organization** The task of determining what edges and other stimuli go together to form an object.

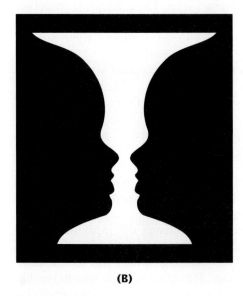

figure

(A)

(B)

FIGURE 5.7

Reversible Images

TRY THIS *Reversible images* can be organized by your perceptual system in two ways. If you perceive Part A as the word *figure*, the space around the letters becomes meaningless background. Now emphasize the word *ground*, and what had stood out a moment ago now becomes background. In Part B, when you emphasize the white vase, the two black profiles become background; if you organize the faces as the figure, what had been a vase now becomes background.

FIGURE 5.8

Gestalt Principles of Perceptual Grouping

We tend to perceive Part A as two groups of two circles plus two single circles, rather than as, say, six single circles. In Part B, we tend to see two columns of Xs and two columns of Os, not four rows of XOXO. We see the X in Part C as made out of two continuous lines, not a combination of the odd forms shown. We perceive the disconnected segments of Part D as a triangle and a circle. In Part E, we tend to pair up dots in the same oval even though they are far apart. Part F shows that connected objects are grouped together.

organized wholes. These wholes, they said, are different from, and more than, just the sum of individual sensations, much as water is something more than just an assortment of hydrogen and oxygen atoms. Because the German word meaning (roughly) "whole figure" is *Gestalt* (pronounced "ge-SHTALT"), these researchers became known as *Gestalt psychologists*. They proposed a number of principles, or "Gestalt laws," that describe how perceptual systems group stimuli into a world of shapes and objects (Kimchi, 2003). Some of the most enduring of these principles are the following:

1. *Proximity.* The closer objects or events are to one another, the more likely they are to be perceived as belonging together, as Figure 5.8A illustrates.

2. *Similarity.* Similar elements are perceived to be part of a group, as in Figure 5.8B.

3. *Continuity.* Sensations that appear to create a continuous form are perceived as belonging together, as in Figure 5.8C.

4. *Closure.* We tend to fill in missing contours to form a complete object, as in Figure 5.8D. The gaps are easy to see, but as illustrated in Figure 5.6, the tendency to fill in missing contours can be so strong that you may see faint connections that are not really there (Lleras & Moore, 2006).

5. *Common fate.* Objects that are moving in the same direction at the same speed are perceived together. Choreographers use the principle of common fate when they arrange for several dancers to move in unison, creating the illusion of waves of motion or of a single object moving across the stage.

Stephen Palmer (1999) has introduced three additional grouping principles, which include:

1. *Synchrony.* Stimuli that occur at the same time are likely to be perceived as belonging together. For example, if you see a car up ahead stop violently at the same instant you hear a crash, you will probably perceive these visual and auditory stimuli as part of the same event.

2. *Common region.* Elements located within some boundary tend to be grouped together. The boundary can be created by an enclosing perimeter, as in Figure 5.8E; a region of color; or other factors.

3. *Connectedness.* Elements that are connected by other elements tend to be grouped together. Figure 5.8F demonstrates how important this law is. The circles connected by dotted lines seem to go together even though they are farther apart than some pairs of unconnected circles. In this situation, the principle of connectedness appears more important than the principle of proximity.

Why do we organize the world according to these grouping principles? One answer is that they reflect the way stimuli are likely to be organized in the natural

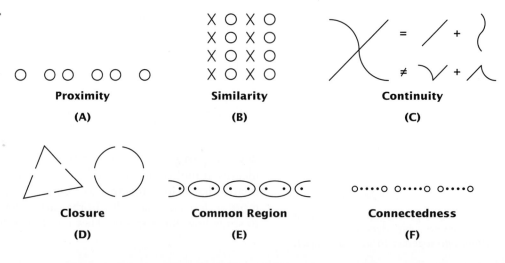

Proximity
(A)

Similarity
(B)

Continuity
(C)

Closure
(D)

Common Region
(E)

Connectedness
(F)

Common Fate   When a set of objects, such as a flock of birds, move together, we see them as a group or even as a single large object in the sky. Marching band directors put this perceptual grouping process to good use. By arranging for musicians to move together, they make it appear as though huge letters and other large "objects" are in motion on the field during half-time shows at college football games.

world. Nearby elements are, in fact, more likely than separated elements to be part of the same object. Stimulus elements moving in the same direction at the same rate are also likely to be part of the same object. Your initial impression of the cube in Figure 5.6 reflects this *likelihood principle* in action. At first glance, you probably saw the cube as being below you rather than above you. This tendency makes adaptive sense, because boxes and other cube-shaped objects are more likely to be on the ground than hanging in midair.

The likelihood principle is consistent with both the ecological and constructivist approaches to perception. From the ecological perspective, the likelihood principle evolved because it worked, giving our ancestors reliable information about how the world is likely to be organized, and thus increasing their chances of survival. Constructivists point out, however, that our personal experiences in the world also help determine the likelihood of interpreting a stimulus array in one way over another. The likelihood principle operates automatically and accurately most of the time. As shown in Figure 5.9, however, when we try using it to organize very *unlikely* stimuli, it can lead to frustrating misperceptions.

Complementing the likelihood principle is the *simplicity principle*, which says that we organize stimulus elements in a way that gives us the simplest possible perception (Palmer, 1999). Your visual system, for example, will group stimulus elements so as to reduce the amount of information that you must process. You can see the simplicity principle in action in Figure 5.6; it was simpler to see a single cube than an assortment of separate, unrelated arrows and Ys.

● Perception of Location and Distance

One of the most important perceptual tasks we face is to determine where objects and sound sources are located. This task involves knowing both their two-dimensional position (left or right, up or down) and their distance from us.

● **Two-Dimensional Location**   Determining whether an object is to your right or your left appears to be simple. All the perceptual system has to do, it seems, is determine where the object's image falls on the retina. If the image falls on the center of the retina, then the object must be straight ahead. But when an object is, say, far to your right, and you focus its image on the center of your retina by turning your head and eyes toward it, you do not assume it is straight ahead. According to the computational approach, your brain estimates the object's location by using an equation that takes information about where an image strikes the retina and adjusts it based on information about the movement of your eyes and head.

As mentioned in the chapter on sensation, localization of sounds depends on cues about differences in the information received by each of your ears. If a sound is continuous, sound waves coming toward the right side of your head will reach the right ear before reaching the left ear. Similarly, a sound coming toward the right side

FIGURE 5.9

Impossible Objects

TRY THIS   These objects can exist as two-dimensional drawings, but could they exist in three-dimensional space? When you try to use the likelihood principle to organize them as the three-dimensional objects you expect them to be, you'll discover that they are "impossible."

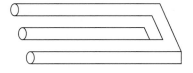

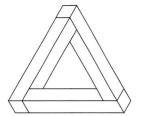

FIGURE 5.10

Stimulus Cues for Depth Perception

 **TRY THIS** See if you can identify the cues of relative size, interposition, linear perspective, height in the visual field, textural gradient, and shadows that combine to create a sense of three-dimensional depth in this photograph. Notice, too, that sidewalk artist Kurt Wenner has used some of these same cues to create a dramatic illusion of depth in his drawing. (You can see more of Wenner's amazing work at http://www.kurtwenner.com/street/.)

LINKAGES (a link to Sensation, p. 149)

of your head will seem a little bit louder to the right ear than to the left ear, because your head blocks some of the sound to the left ear. The brain uses these slight differences in the timing and the intensity of a sound as cues to locate its source. Visual cues are often integrated with auditory cues to determine the exact identity and location of the sound source. Most often, information from the eyes and the ears converges on the same likely sound source. However, there are times when the two senses produce conflicting impressions; in such cases, we tend to believe our eyes rather than our ears. This bias toward using visual information is known as *visual dominance*. The phenomenon is illustrated by our impression that the sound of a television program is coming from the screen rather than the speaker. Next **TRY THIS** time someone is talking on your TV, close your eyes. If your television has a single speaker below or to the side of the screen, you will notice that the sound no longer seems to be coming from the screen but from the speaker itself. As soon as you open your eyes, the false impression resumes; words once again seem to come from the obvious visual source of the sound—the person on the screen.

● **Depth Perception**   One of the oldest puzzles in psychology relates to **depth perception,** our ability to perceive distance. How are we able to experience the world in three-dimensional depth even though the visual information we receive from it is projected onto two-dimensional retinas? The answer lies in the many *depth cues* provided by the environment and by certain properties of our visual system (Anderson, 2004).

To some extent, people perceive depth through the same cues that artists use to create the impression of depth and distance on a two-dimensional canvas. Figure 5.10 illustrates several of these cues:

• One of the most important depth cues is **interposition,** or *occlusion*: Closer objects block the view of things farther away. This cue is illustrated in Figure 5.10 by the couple walking away from the camera. Because their bodies block out part of the buildings, we perceive them as being closer to us than the buildings are.

depth perception   The ability to perceive distance.

interposition   A depth cue whereby closer objects block one's view of things farther away.

A Case of Depth Misperception
The runner in this photo is actually farther away than the man on the pitcher's mound. But because he is lower, not higher, in the visual field—and because it is easy to misperceive his leg as being in front of, not behind, the pitcher's leg—the runner appears smaller than normal rather than farther away.

- You can see the principle of **relative size** operating in Figure 5.10 by measuring the image of that same couple and comparing it to the size of the man in the foreground. If two objects are assumed to be about the same size, the object producing a larger image on the retina is perceived as closer than the one producing a smaller image.

- Another cue comes from **height in the visual field:** On the ground, more distant objects are usually higher in the visual field than those nearby. Because the building in the center of Figure 5.10 is higher than the people in the restaurant, the building appears to be farther away from you. This is one reason why objects higher in the visual field are more likely to be interpreted as the background for objects that are lower in a scene (Vecera, Vogel, & Woodman, 2002).

- The tiny figures near the center of Figure 5.10 are seen as very far away because they are near a point where the buildings on each edge of the plaza, like all parallel lines that recede into the distance, appear to converge toward a single point. This apparent convergence provides a cue called **linear perspective.** The closer together two converging lines are, the greater the perceived distance. So objects that are nearer the point of convergence are seen as farther away.

- An additional depth cue comes from continuous changes across the visual field, called *gradients*. For example, a **texture gradient** is a graduated change in the texture, or "grain," of the visual field, as you can see in the plaza and the street in Figure 5.10. Texture appears finer and less detailed as distance increases. So, as the texture of a surface changes across the retinal image, you perceive a change in distance.

Still other depth cues depend on *clarity, color,* and *shadows*. Distant objects often appear hazier; notice that the street in Figure 5.10 fades into a hazy background. They also tend to take on a bluish tone, which is why art students are taught to add a little blue when mixing paint for distant background features. Light and shadow also contribute to the perception of depth. The buildings in Figure 5.10 are seen as three-dimensional, not flat, because of the shadows on some of their surfaces. Figure 5.11 offers a more dramatic example of shadows' effect on depth perception.

Texture Gradient The details of a scene fade gradually as distance increases. This texture gradient helps us to perceive the less detailed birds in this photo as being farther away.

- **relative size** A depth cue whereby larger objects are perceived as closer than smaller ones.

- **height in the visual field** A depth cue whereby objects higher in the visual field are perceived as more distant.

- **linear perspective** A depth cue whereby objects closer to the point at which two lines appear to converge are perceived as being at a greater distance.

- **texture gradient** A graduated change in the texture, or grain, of the visual field, whereby objects with finer, less detailed textures are perceived as more distant.

FIGURE **5.11**

Light, Shadow, and Depth Perception

TRY THIS The shadows cast by these protruding rivets and deep dents make it easy to see them in three dimensions. But if you turn the book upside down, the rivets now look like dents and the dents look like bumps. This reversal in depth perception occurs partly because we normally assume that illumination comes from above and interpret the pattern of light and shadow accordingly (Adams, Graf, & Ernst, 2004). With the picture upside down, light coming from the top would produce the observed pattern of shadows only if the circles were dents, not rivets.

An important visual depth cue that cannot be demonstrated in Figure 5.10, or in any other still image, comes from motion. You may have noticed, for example, that when you look out the side window of a moving car, objects nearer to you seem to speed across your visual field, whereas objects in the distance seem to move slowly, if at all. This difference in the apparent rate of movement is called **motion parallax,** and it provides cues to differences in the distance of various objects.

Several additional depth cues result from the way human eyes are built and positioned. As mentioned in the chapter on sensation, for example, the eye's lens changes shape, or *accommodates*, bending light rays and focusing images on the retina. To accomplish this task, muscles surrounding the lens either tighten, to make the lens more curved for focusing on close objects, or relax, to flatten the lens for focusing on more distant objects. Information about this muscle activity is relayed to the brain, providing an **accommodation** cue that helps create the perception of an object's distance.

The relative location of our two eyes produces two other depth cues. The first is called **convergence.** Because the eyes are located a short distance apart, they must converge, or rotate inward, to project an object's image on each retina. The brain receives information about this movement from the eye muscles and uses it to help calculate an object's distance. The closer the object, the more the eyes must converge, which sends more intense stimulation to the brain. Focusing on more distant objects requires less convergence and creates less feedback from the eye muscles. To experience feedback from your eye muscles, hold up a finger at arm's length and try to keep it in focus as you move it toward your nose.

TRY THIS

Second, because of their differing locations, each eye receives a slightly different view of the world. The difference between the two retinal images of an object is called **binocular disparity.** For any particular object, this difference gets smaller as distance increases. The brain combines the two images, processes information about the amount of disparity, and generates the impression of a single object having depth as well as height and width. This impression of depth is created by 3-D movies and some virtual reality systems by displaying to each eye a separate image of a scene, each viewed from a slightly different angle.

The wealth of depth cues available to us is consistent with the ecological approach to perception. However, researchers taking the constructivist and computational approaches argue that even when temporarily deprived of these depth cues, we can still move about and locate objects in an environment. In one study, for

● **motion parallax**   A depth cue whereby a difference in the apparent rate of movement of different objects provides information about the relative distance of those objects.

● **accommodation**   The ability of the lens of the eye to change its shape and bend light rays so that objects are in focus.

● **convergence**   A depth cue involving the rotation of the eyes to project the image of an object on each retina.

TRY THIS 🔆 **Binocular Disparity** The disparity, or difference, between each eye's view of an object is smaller for distant objects and greater for closer ones. These binocular disparity cues help to create our perception of distance. To see how distance affects binocular disparity, hold a pencil vertically about six inches in front of your nose; then close one eye and notice where the pencil is in relation to the background. Now open that eye, close the other one, and notice how much the pencil "shifts." These are the two different views your eyes have of the pencil. Repeat the procedure while holding the pencil at arm's length. There is now less disparity or "shift," because there is now less difference in the angles from which your two eyes see the pencil.

example, participants viewed an object from a particular place in a room. Then, with their eyes closed, they were guided to a point well to the side of the object and asked to walk toward it from this new position. The participants were amazingly accurate at this task, leading the researchers to suggest that seeing an object at a particular point in space creates a spatial model in our minds—a model that remains intact even when immediate depth cues are removed.

● Perception of Motion

Sometimes the most important thing about an object is not its size or shape or distance but its motion—how fast it is going and where it is heading. For example, a car in front of you may change speed or direction, requiring that you change your own speed or direction, often in a split second.

As with the detection of location and depth, your brain "tunes in" to a host of cues to perceive changes in motion. Many of these cues come from *optical flow*, or the changes in retinal images across the entire visual field. One particularly meaningful pattern of optical flow is known as **looming**, the rapid expansion in the size of an image so that it fills the retina. When an image looms, you tend to interpret it as an approaching stimulus. Your perceptual system quickly assesses whether the expansion on the retina is about equal in all directions or greater to one side than to the other. If it is greater to the right, for example, the approaching stimulus will miss you and pass to your right. If the retinal expansion is approximately equal in all directions, it means the object is coming straight for your eyes. In other words, you had better duck!

Two questions have been of particular interest to psychologists who study motion perception. First, how do we know whether the flow of images across the retina is due to the movement of objects in the environment or to our own movements? If changes in retinal images were the only factor contributing to motion perception, then moving your eyes would create the perception that everything in the visual field was moving. This is not the case, though, because, as noted earlier, the brain also receives and processes information about the motion of your eyes and head. If you look around right now, tables, chairs, and other stationary objects will not appear to move, because your brain determines that all the movement of images on your retinas is due to your eye and head movements (Goltz et al., 2003). But now close one eye, and wiggle your open eyeball by gently pushing your

TRY THIS

binocular disparity A depth cue based on the difference between two retinal images of the world.

looming A motion cue involving a rapid expansion in the size of an image so that it fills the retina.

lower eyelid. Because your brain receives no signals that your eye is being moved by its own muscles, everything around you will appear to move.

A second question about motion perception relates to the fact that there is a delay of about one-twentieth of a second between the moment when an image is registered on your retina and the moment when information about that image reaches your brain. In theory, each moment's perception of, say, a dog running toward you is actually a perception of where the dog was about one-twentieth of a second earlier. How does the perceptual system deal with this time lag so as to accurately interpret information about an object's motion and location? Psychologists have found that when a stimulus is moving along a relatively constant path, the brain corrects for the image delay by predicting where the stimulus should be one-twentieth of a second in the future (Nijhawan, 1997).

Motion perception is of special interest to sport psychologists. They try to understand, for example, why some individuals are so good at perceiving motion. One team of British psychologists discovered a number of cues and computations apparently used by "expert catchers." In catching a ball, these individuals seem to be especially sensitive to the angle between their "straight ahead" gaze (i.e., a position with the chin parallel to the ground) and the gaze used when looking up at a moving ball. Their task is to move the body continuously, and often quickly, to make sure that this "gaze angle" never becomes too small (such that the ball falls in front of them) or too large (such that the ball sails overhead). In other words, these catchers appear to unconsciously use a specific mathematical rule: "Keep the tangent of the angle of gaze elevation to zero" (McLeod, Reed, & Dienes, 2003).

LINKAGES (a link to Sensation, p. 114)

Sometimes, we perceive motion when there is none. Psychologists are interested in these motion illusions because they can tell us something about how the brain processes various kinds of movement-related information. When you accelerate in a car, for example, the experience of motion doesn't come just from the flow of visual information across your retinas. It also comes from touch information as you are pressed against the seat, and from vestibular information as your head tilts backward. If a visual flow suggests that you are moving but you don't receive appropriate sensations from other parts of your body, particularly the vestibular senses, you may experience a nauseating movement illusion. This explains why you might feel queasy while in a motion simulator or playing certain video games, especially those with virtual reality technology. The images suggest that you are moving through space when there is no real motion.

Other illusions of motion are much more enjoyable. The most important of these occurs when still images appear, one at a time, in rapid succession, as they do on films, videos, and DVDs. Because each image differs slightly from the preceding one,

Stroboscopic Motion If this series of still photographs of an athlete's handspring were presented to you, one at a time, in quick succession, an illusion called stroboscopic motion would cause you to perceive him to be moving.

FIGURE 5.12

A Size Illusion

The monster that is higher in the drawing probably appears larger than the other one, but they are actually the same size. Why does this illusion occur? The converging lines of the tunnel provide strong depth cues telling us that the higher monster is farther away, but because that monster casts an image on our retinas that is just as big as the "nearer" one, we assume that the more distant monster must be bigger. (Look again at Figure 5.5 for other examples of this illusion.)

● **stroboscopic motion** An illusion in which lights or images flashed in rapid succession are perceived as moving.

● **perceptual constancy** The perception of objects as constant in size, shape, color, and other properties despite changes in their retinal image.

the brain sees the people and objects in each image appearing in one place for only a fraction of a second before they disappear and then quickly reappear in a slightly different location. The entertaining result is **stroboscopic motion**, an illusion of motion created when objects disappear and then quickly reappear nearby. The same illusion occurs when flashing lights on a theater or casino sign appear to move around the sign. Stroboscopic motion is based on the organizing principles of likelihood and simplicity. Objects in the world do not usually disappear, only to be immediately replaced by a similar object nearby. Accordingly, your brain makes the simpler and more likely assumption that a disappearing and reappearing object has moved.

● Perceptual Constancy

Suppose that one sunny day you are watching someone walking toward you along a tree-lined sidewalk. The visual sensations produced by this person are actually rather strange. For one thing, the size of the image on your retinas keeps getting larger as the person gets closer. To see this for yourself, hold your hand out at **TRY THIS** arm's length and look at someone far away. The retinal image of that person will be so small that your hand can easily cover it. If you do the same when the person is three feet away, the retinal image will be much larger than your hand, but you will perceive the person as being closer now, not bigger. Similarly, if you watch people pass from bright sunshine through the shadows of trees, your retinas receive images that are darker, then lighter, then darker again. Still, you perceive individuals whose coloring remains the same.

These examples illustrate **perceptual constancy**, the perception of objects as constant in size, shape, color, and other properties despite changes in their retinal image. Without perceptual constancy, the world would be an Alice-in-Wonderland kind of place in which objects continuously changed their properties.

● **Size Constancy** Why do objects appear to remain about the same size, no matter what changes occur in the size of their retinal image? One explanation emphasizes the computational aspects of perception. It suggests that as objects move closer or farther away, our brains perceive the change in distance and automatically adjust our perception. This calculation can be expressed as a formula: The perceived size of an object is equal to the size of the retinal image multiplied by the perceived distance (Holway & Boring, 1941). As an object moves closer, its retinal image increases, but the perceived distance decreases at the same rate, so the perceived size remains constant. If, instead, a balloon is inflated in front of your eyes, perceived distance remains constant, and the perceived size (correctly) increases as the retinal image size increases.

The computational perspective is reasonably good at explaining most aspects of size constancy, but it cannot fully account for the fact that people are better at judging the true size (and distance) of familiar rather than unfamiliar objects. This phenomenon suggests that, in line with the constructivists' view, there is an additional, knowledge-based mechanism for size constancy: Our knowledge and experience tells us that most objects (aside from balloons) do not suddenly change size.

The perceptual system usually produces size constancy correctly and automatically, but it can sometimes fail, resulting in size illusions such as the one illustrated in Figure 5.12. Because this figure contains strong linear perspective cues (lines converging in the "distance"), and because objects nearer the point of convergence are interpreted as farther away, we perceive the monster near the top of the figure as the larger one, even though both are exactly the same size. Size illusions can have serious consequences when the objects involved are, say, moving automobiles. A small car produces a smaller retinal image than a large one at the same distance. As a result, the driver of a following vehicle can easily overestimate the distance to the small car (especially in dim light) and therefore fail to brake in time to avoid a collision. Size illusions may help explain why, in countries in which cars vary greatly in size, small cars have higher accident rates than large ones (Eberts & MacMillan, 1985). Size misjudgments illustrate the *inferential* nature of perception emphasized by constructivists: People make logical inferences or hypotheses about the world based on the available cues. Unfortunately, if the cues are misleading or the inferences are wrong, perceptual errors may occur.

● **Shape Constancy** The principles behind shape constancy are closely related to those of size constancy. To see shape constancy at work, remember what page you are on, close this book, and tilt it toward and away from you several times. The book will continue to look rectangular, even though the shape of its retinal image changes dramatically as you move it. The brain automatically integrates information about retinal images and distance as movement occurs. In this case, the distance information involves the difference in distance between the near and far edges of the book.

As with size constancy, much of the ability to judge shape constancy depends on automatic computational mechanisms in the nervous system, but expectations about the shape of objects also play a role. For example, in Western cultures, most corners are at right angles. Knowledge of this fact helps make "rectangle" the most likely interpretation of the retinal image shown in Figure 5.1. Sometimes, shape constancy

TRY
THIS ►

A Failure of Shape Constancy When certain stimuli are viewed from an extreme angle, the brain's ability to maintain shape constancy can break down. British traffic engineers have taken this phenomenon into account in the design of road markings. For example, the arrow in the top photo appears to be about the same height as the lettering below it, but it isn't. The arrow had to be greatly elongated, as shown in the side view, so that approaching drivers would see its shape clearly. If the arrow had been painted to match the height of the accompanying letters, it would appear "squashed" and only half as tall as the lettering.

FIGURE 5.13

Brightness Contrast

TRY THIS At first glance, the inner rectangle on the left probably looks lighter than the inner rectangle on the right. But carefully examine the inner rectangles alone by covering their surroundings. You will see that they are equally bright. The lighter border in the right-hand figure leads you to perceive its inner rectangle as relatively darker.

mechanisms are so good at creating perceptions of a stable world that they can keep us from seeing changes when they occur. In one study, for example, participants looking at a computer display of a person's head failed to notice that, as the head turned, it morphed gradually into the head of a different person (Wallis & Bülthoff, 2001).

● **Brightness Constancy** Even with dramatic changes in the amount of light striking an object, the object's perceived brightness remains relatively constant (MacEvoy & Paradiso, 2001). To see this for yourself, place a piece of charcoal in sunlight and a piece of white paper in nearby shade. The charcoal will look dark and the paper will look bright, even though a light meter would reveal much more light reflected from the sun-bathed coal than from the shaded paper. One reason the charcoal continues to look dark, no matter what the illumination, is that you *know* that charcoal is nearly black, illustrating once again the knowledge-based nature of perception. Another reason is that the charcoal is still the darkest object relative to its background in the sunlight, and the paper is the brightest object relative to its background in the shade. As shown in Figure 5.13, the brightness of an object is perceived in relation to its background.

For a summary of this discussion, see "In Review: Principles of Perceptual Organization and Constancy."

in review Principles of Perceptual Organization and Constancy

Principle	Description	Example
Figure-ground organization	Certain objects or sounds are automatically identified as figures, whereas others become meaningless background.	You see a person standing against a building, not a building with a person-shaped hole in it.
Grouping (Gestalt laws)	Properties of stimuli lead us to automatically group them together. These include proximity, similarity, continuity, closure, common fate, synchrony, common region, and connectedness.	People who are sitting together, or who are dressed similarly, are perceived as a group.
Perception of location and depth	Knowing an object's two-dimensional position (left and right, up and down) and distance enables us to locate it. The image on the retina and the orientation of the head provide information about the two-dimensional position of visual stimuli; auditory localization relies on differences in the information received by the ears. Depth or distance perception uses stimulus cues such as interposition, relative size, height in the visual field, texture gradients, linear perspective, clarity, color, and shadow.	Large, clear objects appear closer than small, hazy objects.
Perceptual constancy	Objects are perceived as constant in size, shape, brightness, color, and other properties, despite changes in their retinal images.	A train coming toward you is perceived as getting closer, not larger; a restaurant sign is perceived as rotating, not changing shape.

Recognizing the Perceptual World

In discussing how people organize the perceptual world, we have set the stage for addressing one of the most vital questions that perception researchers must answer: How do people recognize what objects are? If you are driving in search of Barney's Diner, exactly what happens when your eyes finally locate the pattern of light that spells out its name?

To know that you have finally found what you have been looking for, your brain must analyze incoming patterns of information and compare them with information stored in memory. If your brain finds a match, recognition takes place, and the stimulus is classified into a *perceptual category*. Once recognition occurs, your perception of a stimulus may never be the same again. Look at Figure 5.14. Do you see anything familiar? If not, look ahead to Figure 5.17, then look at Figure 5.14 again. You should now see it in an entirely new light. The difference between your "before" and "after" experiences of Figure 5.14 is the difference between the sensory world before and after a perceptual match occurs and recognition takes place.

Exactly how does such matching occur? Some aspects of recognition begin at the "top," guided by knowledge, expectations, and other psychological factors. This phenomenon is called **top-down processing,** because it involves higher-level, knowledge-based information. Other aspects of recognition begin at the "bottom," relying on specific, detailed information elements from the sensory receptors that are integrated and assembled into a whole. This phenomenon is called **bottom-up processing,** because it begins with basic information units that serve as a foundation for recognition. Let's consider the contributions of bottom-up and top-down processing to recognition, as well as the use of neural network models to understand both.

● Bottom-Up Processing

Research on the visual system is providing a detailed picture of how bottom-up processing works. As described in the chapter on sensation, all along the path from the eye to the brain, certain cells respond to certain features of a stimulus. So the stimulus is first analyzed into basic features before those features are recombined to create a perceptual experience.

FIGURE 5.14

Categorizing Perceptions

TRY THIS What do you see here? If you can't recognize this pattern of information as falling into any perceptual category, turn to Figure 5.17 for some help in doing so.

top-down processing Aspects of recognition that are guided by higher-level cognitive processes and psychological factors such as expectations.

bottom-up processing Aspects of recognition that depend first on the information about the stimulus that comes to the brain from the sensory receptors.

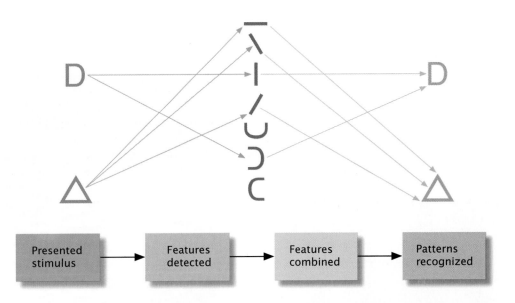

FIGURE 5.15

Feature Analysis

Feature detectors operating at lower levels of the visual system analyze incoming stimuli, such as the letter "D" or a triangle, into the corners and angles shown in the center of this figure. Later in the perceptual sequence, bottom-up processing recombines these features to aid in pattern recognition, as shown on the right.

What are these features? As also noted in the sensation chapter, certain cells specialize in responding to stimuli that have certain orientations in space (Hubel & Wiesel, 1979). For example, one cell in the cerebral cortex might fire only in response to a diagonal line, so it acts as a *feature detector* for diagonal lines. Figure 5.15 illustrates how the analysis by such feature detectors, early in the information-processing sequence, may contribute to recognition of letters or judgments of shape. Color, motion, and even corners are other sensory features that appear to be analyzed separately in different parts of the brain prior to full perceptual recognition (Beatty, 1995; Treisman, 1999).

Features such as color, motion, overall shape, and fine details can all contribute to our ability to recognize objects, but some carry more weight than others in various situations. In the case of face recognition, for example, not all features are equally weighted when we decide who it is that we are seeing (Sinha & Poggio, 1996). Take just a quick look at Figure 5.16, and see if you recognize the person on the left. If you are like most people, it will take a second look to realize that your first glance led you to an incorrect conclusion. Such recognition errors are evidence that, at least initially, we tend to rely on large-scale features, such as hair and head shape, to recognize people.

FIGURE 5.16

The Face Looks Familiar

Who are these people? Most people first see Dick Cheney and George W. Bush, but look more closely. The image on the left is actually a composite, combining the head shape and glasses of Cheney and the facial features of Bush. The tendency to identify this composite as Cheney suggests that large-scale features, such as overall shape, may be more important than eyes or other small-scale features in the initial recognition of people.

FIGURE 5.17

Another Version of Figure 5.14

Now that you can identify a dog in this figure, it should be much easier to recognize when you look back at the original version.

FIGURE 5.18

What Does it Look Like to You?

TRY THIS 🔧 Many people reported seeing a demonic face in the smoke pouring from New York's World Trade Center after terrorists attacked it on September 11, 2001. This perceptual categorization results from a combination of bottom-up and top-down recognition processes. Feature detectors automatically register the edges and colors of images, whereas knowledge and beliefs about the evil of the attack can create expectations that give meaning to these features. A person who does not expect to see a face in the smoke—or whose cultural background does not include the concept of "the devil"—might not see one until that interpretation is suggested. To check that possibility, show this photo to people from various religions and cultures who have not seen it before (don't tell them what to look for) and make a note of which individuals require prompting in order to identify a demonic face.

How do psychologists know that feature analysis is actually involved in pattern recognition? Recordings of brain activity indicate that the sensory features we have listed here cause particular sets of neurons to fire. In fact, scientists have shown that it may be possible to determine what category of object a person is looking at (e.g., a face vs. a house) based on the pattern of activity occurring in visual processing areas of the person's brain (Haxby et al., 2001). Further, as described in the chapter on sensation, people with certain kinds of brain damage show selective impairment in the ability to perceive certain sets of sensory features, such as an object's color or movement.

● Top-Down Processing

Bottom-up feature analysis can explain why you recognize the letters in a sign for Barney's Diner. But why is it that you can recognize the sign more easily if it appears where you were told to expect it rather than a block earlier? And why can you recognize it even if a few letters are missing from the sign? The answers are provided by top-down processing. Fo- ex-mp-e, y-u c-n r-ad -hi- se-te-ce -it- ev-ry -hi-d l-tt-r m-ss-ng. In top-down processing, people use their knowledge in making inferences or "educated guesses" to recognize objects, words, or melodies, especially when sensory information is vague or ambiguous. Once you knew that there was a dog in Figure 5.14, it became much easier for you to perceive it. Similarly, police officers find it easy to recognize familiar people on blurry security camera videos, but it is much more difficult for them to recognize strangers (Burton et al., 1999).

In hearing, too, top-down processing can compensate for ambiguous stimuli. In one experiment, participants heard strings of five words in meaningless order, such as "wet brought who socks some." There was so much background noise, however, that only about 75 percent of the words could be recognized (Miller, Heise, & Lichten, 1951). The words were then read to a second group of participants in a meaningful order (e.g., "who brought some wet socks"). The second group was able to recognize almost all of the words, even under the same noisy conditions. In fact, it took twice as much noise to reduce their performance to the level of the first group. Why? When the words were in meaningless order, only bottom-up processing was available. Recognizing one word was no help in identifying the next. Meaningful sentences, however, provided a more familiar context and allowed for

The Eye of the Beholder Top-down processing can affect our perception of people as well as objects. As noted in the chapter on social cognition, for example, if you expect everyone in a certain ethnic or social group to behave in a certain way, you may perceive a particular group member's behavior in line with this prejudice. And have you ever noticed that someone's physical attractiveness seemed to increase or decrease as you got to know the person better? This change in perception occurs largely because new information about the person alters your interpretation of the raw sensations you get from him or her.

some top-down processing. Hearing one word helped the listener make a reasonable guess (based on knowledge and experience) about the others.

Many aspects of perception can best be explained by higher-level cognitive influences, especially by expectancy and context (e.g., Kazanina, Phillips, & Idsardi, 2006). Consider again the two faces in Figure 5.16. Do you think that you'd have been as likely to mistakenly identify the man on the left as Dick Cheney if the person on the right had been, say, Mexico's president, Felipe Calderón or John Travolta? Probably not. Through bottom-up processing you correctly identified the combination of features on the right as George Bush. Then, your knowledge-based top-down processing led you to expect to see certain individuals at his side, such as Cheney. Your perceptual system made a quick "educated guess" that, in this case, turned out to be wrong.

Top-down processing is also involved in a phenomenon called *pareidolia* (pronounced "pare-eh-DOLE-ee-a"), the perception of a specific image in an ambiguous stimulus array. For example, look at Figure 5.18, which shows the World Trade Center under attack. Some people see an image of the devil in the smoke. This interpretation requires some knowledge of paintings and other representations of the devil. Expectancy plays a role, too. Many people who have not heard about the image do not see a demonic face in this photo.

These examples illustrate that top-down processing can have a strong influence on pattern recognition. Our experiences create **schemas**, which are mental representations of what we know and have come to expect about the world. Schemas can bias our perception toward one recognition or another by creating a *perceptual set*, a readiness or predisposition to perceive a stimulus in a certain way. A tragic example occurred several years ago in London when police shot a man who they were told was carrying a sawed-off shotgun. The object in his hand was actually a table leg, but it was dark, so when he raised his arm, they assumed he was about to fire at them.

Perceptual predispositions can be shaped by the context in which a stimulus occurs. For example, we know of a woman who saw a masked man in the darkened hallway of a house she was visiting. Her first perception was that the man who lived there was playing a joke, but in fact she had confronted a burglar. Context has biasing effects for sounds, too. A gunshot heard in a parking lot, for example, is often perceived as a firecracker or a car backfiring. At a shooting range, it would immediately be interpreted as gunfire. So top-down processing allows us to identify objects and sounds even before examination of features is complete, or even when features are missing, distorted, or ambiguous. As in Figure 5.16, though, it can sometimes lead us to jump to false conclusions.

Motivation is another aspect of top-down processing that can affect perception (Balcetis & Dunning, 2006). If you are extremely hungry, you might misperceive a sign for "Burger's Body Shop" as indicating a place to eat. Similarly, if you have ever watched sports, you can probably remember a time when an obviously incompetent referee incorrectly called a penalty on your favorite team. You knew the call was wrong because you clearly saw the other team's player at fault. But suppose you had been cheering for that other team. The chances are good that you would have seen the referee's call as the right one.

Motivation and other aspects of top-down processing can even affect elements of the brain's bottom-up processing. For example, cells in the visual cortex that fire in response to specific features of an object show higher levels of activity if that object is of particular importance at the moment (Li, Piëch, & Gilbert, 2004). So corner-detecting cells will show more intense firing in response to the corners of the Barney's Diner sign you are looking for than to the corners of other signs.

● Network Processing

Researchers taking a computational approach to perception have attempted to explain various aspects of object recognition in terms of both top-down and bottom-up processing. In one study, participants were asked to say whether a particular feature, like

● **schemas** Mental representations of what we know, and have come to expect, about the world.

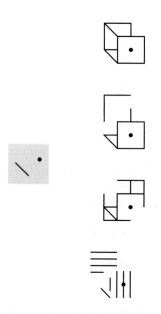

FIGURE 5.19

The Object Superiority Effect

When people are asked to say whether the feature at left appears in patterns briefly flashed on a computer screen, the feature is more likely to be detected when it appears in patterns like those at the top right, which most resemble three-dimensional objects. This "object superiority effect" supports the importance of network processing in perception.

Source: Reprinted with permission from figures by Weisstein & Harris, *Science,* 1974, *186,* 752–755. Copyright © 1974 by American Association of the Advancement of Science.

the dot and angled line on the left side of Figure 5.19, appeared within a pattern that was briefly flashed on a computer screen. The participants detected this feature faster when it was embedded in a pattern resembling a three-dimensional object than when it appeared within a random pattern of lines (Purcell & Stewart, 1991). This result is called the *object superiority effect*. There is also a *word superiority effect*: When strings of letters are briefly flashed on a screen, people's ability to detect target letters is better if the string forms a word than if it is a nonword (Prinzmetal, 1992).

Neural network models have been used to explain findings such as these. As described in the chapter on biological aspects of psychology, each element in these networks is connected to every other element, and each connection has a specific strength. Applying network processing models to pattern recognition involves focusing on the interactions among the various feature analyzers we have discussed. More specifically, some researchers explain recognition using **parallel distributed processing (PDP) models** (Rumelhart & McClelland, 1986). According to PDP models, the units in a network operate in parallel—simultaneously. Connections between units either excite or inhibit other units. If the connection is excitatory, activating one unit spreads the activation to connected units. Using a connection may strengthen it.

How does this process apply to recognition? According to PDP models, recognition occurs as a result of the simultaneous operation of connected units. Units are activated when matched by features in a stimulus. To the extent that features, such as the letters in a word or the angles in a box, have occurred together in the past, the links between them will be stronger, and detection of any of them will be made more likely by the presence of all the others. This appears to be what happens in the word and object superiority effects, and the same phenomenon is illustrated in Figure 5.20. PDP models, sometimes called *connectionist models*, clearly represent the computational approach to perception. Researchers have achieved many advances in theories of pattern recognition by programming computers to carry out the kinds of complex computations that neural networks are assumed to perform in the human perceptual system. These computers have "learned" to read, recognize faces, and process color in a manner that may turn out to be similar to the way humans learn and perform the same perceptual tasks (e.g. Behnke, 2003). (For a summary of our discussion of recognition processes, see "In Review: Mechanisms of Pattern Recognition.")

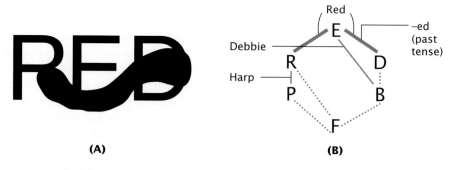

(A)   (B)

FIGURE 5.20

Recognizing a Word

You probably recognized the pattern shown in (A) as the word *RED*, even though the first letter of the word shown could be *R* or *P*, the second *E* or *F*, and the third *D* or *B*. According to PDP models, your recognition occurred because, together, the letters excite each other's correct interpretation. This mutual excitation process is illustrated in (B) by a set of letter "nodes" (corresponding to activity sites in the brain) and some of the words they might activate. These nodes will be activated if the feature they detect appears in the stimulus array. They will also be activated if nodes to which they are linked become active. All six letters shown in (B) will initially be excited when the stimulus in (A) is presented, but mutual excitement along the strongest links leads to perception of the word "red" (Rumelhart & McClelland, 1986).

Source: Rumelhart & McClelland (1986).

● **parallel distributed processing (PDP) model** An approach to understanding object recognition in which various elements of the object are thought to be simultaneously analyzed by a number of widely distributed, but connected, neural units in the brain.

in review | Mechanisms of Pattern Recognition

Mechanism	Description	Example
Bottom-up processing	Raw sensations from the eye or the ear are analyzed into basic features, such as form, color, or movement; these features are then recombined at higher brain centers, where they are compared with stored information about objects or sounds.	You recognize a dog as a dog because its features—four legs, barking, panting—match your perceptual category for "dog."
Top-down processing	Knowledge of the world and experience in perceiving allow people to make inferences about the identity of stimuli, even when the quality of raw sensory information is low.	On a dark night, what you see as a small, vague blob pulling on the end of a leash is recognized as a dog because the stimulus occurs at a location where you would expect a dog to be.
Network, or PDP, processing	Recognition depends on communication among feature-analysis systems operating simultaneously and enlightened by past experience.	A dog standing behind a picket fence will be recognized as a dog even though each disjointed "slice" of the stimulus may not look like a dog.

● Culture, Experience, and Perception

So far, we have talked as if all aspects of perception work or fail in the same way for everyone, everywhere. The truth is, though, that perception can vary if people's experiences have created differing expectations and other knowledge-based, top-down processes (Chua, Boland, & Nisbett, 2005; Kitayama et al., 2003). For example, researchers have compared responses to depth cues by people from cultures that do and do not use pictures and paintings to represent reality. The results suggest that people in cultures that provide little experience with pictorial representations, such as the Me'n or the Nuba in Africa, have a more difficult time judging distances shown in pictures (see Figure 5.21). These individuals also tend to have a harder time sorting pictures of three-dimensional objects into categories, even though they can easily sort the objects themselves (Derogowski, 1989).

Experience even teaches us when to ignore certain stimulus cues. To fully experience the depth portrayed in a painting, for example, you have to ignore ridges, scratches, dust, or other texture cues from the canvas that would remind you of its flatness. And the next time you are watching TV, notice the reflections of objects in the room that appear on the screen. You have learned to ignore these reflections, so it will take a little effort to perceive them and a lot of effort to focus on them for long. What if you hadn't had a chance to learn or practice these perceptual skills? One way to explore this question is through case studies of people who had been blind for decades and then had surgery that restored their sight. It turns out that these people can immediately recognize simple objects and perceive movement, but they usually have problems with other aspects of perception (Gregory, 2005). For example, M. M. had been blind from early childhood. When his vision was restored in his forties, he adjusted well overall, but he still has difficulty with depth perception and object recognition (Fine et al., 2003). Often, as people move toward or away from him, they appear to shrink or inflate. Identifying common objects can be difficult for him, and faces pose a particular challenge. To recognize individuals, he depends on features such as hair length or eyebrow shape. M. M. has trouble, too, distinguishing male faces from female ones and great difficulty recognizing the meaning of facial expressions. And like people from cultures that provide little or no experience with straight lines, he is unable to experience many of the perceptual illusions shown in this chapter.

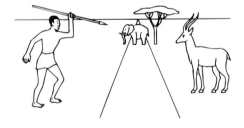

FIGURE 5.21

Culture and Depth Cues

Participants in various cultures were shown drawings like these and asked to judge which animal is closer to the hunter. People in cultures that provide lots of experience with pictured depth cues choose the antelope, which is at the same distance from the viewer as the hunter. Those in cultures less familiar with such cues may choose the elephant, which, though closer on the page, is more distant when depth cues are considered (Hudson, 1960).

LINKAGES Perception and Human Development

LINKAGES (a link to Human Development, p. 462)

Knowledge and experience play an important role in recognition, but are they also required for more basic aspects of perception? Which perceptual abilities are babies born with, and which do they develop by seeing, hearing, smelling, touching, and tasting things? How do their perceptions compare with those of adults? To learn about infants' perception, psychologists have studied two inborn patterns called *habituation* and *dishabituation*. For example, infants stop looking when they repeatedly see stimuli that are perceived to be the same. This is habituation. If a stimulus appears that is perceived to be different, infants resume looking. This is dishabituation. Researchers have used the habituation and dishabituation phenomena, along with measurements of brain activity, to study color perception in infants. They have found that newborns can perceive differences among stimuli showing different amounts of black-and-white contrast but that they are unable to distinguish differences between colors (Burr, Morrone, & Fiorentini, 1996). By three months of age, though, infants can discriminate among blue, green, yellow, and red (Adams, Courage, & Mercer, 1991). Other researchers have found that newborns can perceive differences in the angles of lines (Slater et al., 1991). These studies and others suggest that we are born with some of the basic components of feature detection.

Are we also born with the ability to combine features into perceptions of whole objects? This question generates lively debate among specialists in infant perception. Some research indicates that at one month of age, infants concentrate their gaze on one part of an object, such as the corner of a triangle (Goldstein, 2002). By two months, though, the eyes systematically scan all the edges of the object, suggesting that only then has the infant begun to perceive the pattern of the object, or its shape, rather than just its component features. However, other researchers have found that once newborns have become habituated to specific combinations of features, they show dishabituation (that is, they pay attention) when those features are combined in a new way. The implication is that even newborns notice, and keep track of, the way some features are put together (Slater et al., 1991).

There is evidence that infants may be innately tuned to perceive at least one important complex pattern—the human face. In one study of newborns, some less than an hour old, patterns such as those in Figure 5.22 were moved slowly past the infants' faces (Johnson et al., 1991). The infants moved their heads and eyes to follow these patterns, but they tracked the face-like pattern shown on the left side of Figure 5.22 significantly farther than any of the nonfaces. The difference in tracking indicates that the infants could discriminate between faces and nonfaces and were more interested in the faces, or at least in face-like patterns (Simion et al., 2003).

Infants also notice differences among faces. At first, this ability to discriminate applies to both human and nonhuman faces. So at the age of six months, infants are actually better than adults at discriminating among the faces of monkeys (Pascalis, de Haan, & Nelson, 2002). By about the age of nine months, however, face discrimination ability has become focused on human faces, the kind most babies see

FIGURE 5.22

Infants' Perceptions of Human Faces

Newborns show significantly greater interest in the face-like pattern at the far left than in any of the other patterns. Evidently, some aspects of face perception are innate.

Source: Johnson et al. (1991).

FIGURE 5.23

The Visual Cliff

The *visual cliff* is a glass-topped table that creates the impression of a sudden drop-off. A ten-month-old placed at what looks like the edge will calmly crawl across the shallow side to reach a parent but will hesitate and cry rather than crawl over the "cliff" (Gibson & Walk, 1960). Changes in heart rate show that infants too young to crawl also perceive the depth but are not frightened by it. Here again, nature and nurture interact adaptively: Depth perception appears shortly after birth, but fear and avoidance of dangerous depth do not develop until an infant is old enough to crawl into trouble.

most often. Researchers who take an evolutionary approach suggest that interest in faces, especially human faces, is adaptive because it helps newborns focus on their only source of food and care.

Other research on perceptual development suggests that our ability to use certain distance cues develops more slowly than our recognition of object shapes (see Figure 5.23). For example, infants' ability to use binocular disparity and relative motion cues to judge depth appears to develop some time after about three months of age (Yonas, Arterberry, & Granrud, 1987). Infants do not use texture gradients and linear perspective as cues about depth until they are three to seven months old (Arterberry, Yonas, & Bensen, 1989; Bhatt & Bertin, 2001).

In summary, there is little doubt that many of the basic building blocks of perception are present within the first few days after birth. The basics include organ-based cues to depth, such as accommodation and convergence. Maturation of the visual system adds to these basics as time goes by. For example, over the first few months after birth, the eye's fovea gradually develops the number of cone cells necessary for high visual acuity and perception of small differences in color (Goldstein, 2002). However, visual experience may also be necessary if the infant is to recognize some patterns and objects in frequently encountered stimuli, to interpret depth and distance cues, and to use these cues in moving safely through the world (Johnson, 2004; Quinn & Bhatt, 2005). In other words, like so many aspects of human psychology, perception is the result of a blending of heredity and environment. From infancy onward, the perceptual system creates a personal reality based in part on the experience that shapes each individual's feature-analysis networks and knowledge-based expectancies. ■

Attention

Believe it or not, you still haven't found Barney's Diner! By now, you understand *how* you will recognize the right sign when you perceive it, but how can you be sure you *will* perceive it? As you drive, the diner's sign will appear as just one small piece in a sensory puzzle that also includes road signs, traffic lights, sirens, talk radio, and dozens of other stimuli. You can't perceive all of them at once, so to find Barney's you are going to have to be sure that the information you select for perceptual processing includes the stimuli that will help you reach your goal. In other words, you are going to have to pay attention.

Attention is the process of directing and focusing certain psychological resources to enhance perception, performance, and mental experience. We use attention to *direct* our sensory and perceptual systems toward certain stimuli, to *select* specific information for further processing, to *ignore* or screen out unwanted stimuli, to *allocate* the mental energy required to process selected stimuli, and to *regulate* the flow of resources necessary for performing a task or coordinating several tasks at once (Wickens & Carswell, 2006).

Psychologists have discovered three important characteristics of attention. First, it *improves mental processing*; you often have to concentrate attention on a task to do your best at it. If your attentional system temporarily malfunctions, you might drive right past Barney's Diner. Second, attention takes *effort*. Prolonged concentration of attention can leave you feeling drained (McNay, McCarty, & Gold, 2001). And when you are already tired, focusing attention on anything becomes more difficult. Third, attentional resources are *limited*. If your attention is focused on reading this book, for example, you'll have less attention left over to listen to a conversation in the next room.

 TRY THIS To experience attention as a process, try "moving it around" a bit. When you finish reading this sentence, look at something behind you, then face forward and notice the next sound you hear, then visualize your best friend, and then focus on how your tongue feels. You just used attention to direct your perceptual systems toward different aspects of your external and internal environments. Sometimes, as when you looked behind you, shifting attention involves *overt orienting*—pointing sensory systems at a particular stimulus. But you were able to shift attention to an image of your friend's face without having to move a muscle. This is called *covert orienting*. (We've heard a rumor that students sometimes use covert orienting to shift their attention from their lecturer to thoughts that have nothing to do with the lecture.)

FOCUS ON RESEARCH METHODS An Experiment in "Mind Reading"

Everyone knows what it is like to covertly shift attention, but how can we tell when someone else is doing it? The study of covert attention requires the sort of "mind reading" that has been made possible by innovative experimental research methods. These techniques are helping psychologists to measure where a person's attention is focused.

■ What was the researchers' question?

Michael Posner and his colleagues were interested in finding out what changes in perceptual processing occur when people covertly shift their attention to a specific location in space (Posner, Nissen, & Ogden, 1978). Specifically, the researchers addressed the question of whether these attentional shifts lead to more sensitive processing of stimuli in the location to which attention is focused.

■ How did the researchers answer the question?

Posner and his colleagues took advantage of an important property of mental events: They take time. Moreover, the time taken by mental events can vary considerably, thus providing important clues about internal processes such as covert attention.

The researchers designed a study in which participants were asked to focus their eyes on a fixation point that appeared at the center of a computer screen. One second later, a tiny square appeared at either the right or left edge of the screen. The

● **attention** The process of directing and focusing psychological resources to enhance perception, performance, and mental experience.

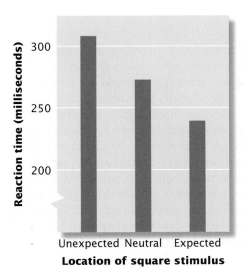

FIGURE 5.24

Measuring Covert Shifts in Attention

It took people less time (measured in thousandths of a second) to detect a square appearing at an expected location than at an unexpected one. This result suggests that, even though their eyes did not move, these research participants covertly shifted their attention to the expected location before the stimulus was presented.

participants were then asked to indicate, by pressing a key as quickly as possible, when they detected the square. Because their vision was focused on the fixation point, they could detect the square only out of the "corners" of their eyes.

On any given trial, a participant could never be sure where the square would appear. However, the researchers provided a cue, or "hint," at the start of some of the trials, in the form of an arrow at the fixation point. Sometimes, the arrow pointed to the right edge of the screen (→). This cue gave correct information 80 percent of the time. On other trials, the arrow pointed to the left edge of the screen (←). This cue was also correct 80 percent of the time. On still other trials, participants saw a plus sign (+) at the fixation point, which indicated that the square was equally likely to appear on the left or the right.

The researchers reasoned that when the plus sign appeared, the best strategy for quickly detecting the square would be to keep attention focused on the center of the screen and to shift it only after the square appeared. When one of the arrow cues appeared, though, the best strategy would be to covertly shift attention in the direction indicated by the arrow before the square appeared. If the participants were covertly shifting their attention in this way, they should be able to detect the square fastest when the cue provided accurate information about where the square would appear—even though they were not actually moving their eyes.

The dependent variable in this study was the speed of target detection, measured in milliseconds. The independent variable was the type of cue given: correct, incorrect, or neutral. Correct cues were arrows that accurately predicted the target location; incorrect ones were arrows that pointed the wrong way. Neutral cues gave no guidance.

■ What did the researchers find?

As shown in Figure 5.24, the target square was detected significantly faster when the cue gave correct information about where the square would appear. Incorrect cues resulted in a distinct drop in target detection speed: When participants were led to covertly shift their attention in the wrong direction, it took them longer to detect the square.

■ What do the results mean?

The data provide evidence that the participants used cues to shift their attention to the expected location. This shift readied their perceptual systems to detect information at that location. When a cue led them to shift their attention to the wrong location, they were less ready to detect information at the correct location, and their detection speed was slower. In short, attention can enhance the processing of information at one location, but it does so at the expense of processing information elsewhere.

■ What do we still need to know?

More recent research on the costs and benefits associated with perceptual expectancies has been generally consistent with the findings of Posner's pioneering team (e.g., Ball & Sekuler, 1992; Carrasco & McElree, 2001). However, there are still many unanswered questions about how covert attention actually operates. How quickly can we shift attention from one location to another? Estimates range from about a quarter of a second to as fast as a tenth of a second (Theeuwes, Godijn, & Pratt, 2004; Wolfe, 1998). And how quickly can we shift attention between sensory modalities—from watching to listening, for example? It will be difficult to find the methods necessary to address these questions, but they are fundamental to understanding our ability to deal with the potentially overwhelming load of stimuli that reaches our sensory receptors. Experiments designed to answer such questions not only expand our understanding of attention but also illustrate the possibility of measuring hidden mental events through observation of overt behavior (Wolfe, Alvarez, & Horowitz, 2000). ■

■ ● Directing Attention

As shown in Posner's experiment on "mind reading," attending to some stimuli leaves us less able to attend to others. In other words, attention is *selective*; it is like a spotlight that can illuminate only a part of the external or internal environment at any particular moment. How do you control, or allocate, your attention?

Control over attention can be voluntary or involuntary (Yantis, 1993). *Voluntary*, or goal-directed, control occurs when you purposely focus your attention in order to perform a task, such as listening for your name to be called in a noisy restaurant or watching for a friend in a crowd. Voluntary control reflects top-down processing, because attention is guided by intentions, beliefs, expectations, motivation, or other knowledge-based factors. As people learn certain skills, they voluntarily direct their attention to information they once ignored. For example, experienced drivers notice events taking place farther down the road than new drivers do. If you are watching a sports event, learning where to allocate your attention is important if you are to understand what is going on. And if you are a competing in a sport, the proper allocation of attention is absolutely essential for success.

When, in spite of these top-down factors, some aspect of the environment—such as a loud noise—diverts your attention, control is said to be *involuntary*. In such cases, attentional control is a bottom-up, or stimulus-driven, process. Stimulus characteristics that tend to capture attention include sudden changes in lighting or color (such as flashing signs), movement, and the appearance of unusual shapes. Research by human factors, or engineering, psychologists on the stimuli most likely to attract—and distract—attention has been used in the design of everything from Internet web sites to operator warning devices for airliners, nuclear power plants, and other complex systems (Clay, 2000; Laughery, 1999). Other psychologists use the results of attention research to help design advertisements, logos, and product packaging that "grab" potential customers' attention.

■ ● Ignoring Information

When the spotlight of your attention is voluntarily or involuntarily focused on one part of the environment, you may ignore, or be "blind" to, stimuli occurring in other parts. This phenomenon, called *inattentional blindness* (Mack, 2003; Mack & Rock, 1998), can be helpful when it allows us to ignore construction noise while we are taking an exam. But it can also endanger us if we ignore information—such as a stop sign—that we should be attending to. Inattentional blindness can cause us to miss some rather dramatic changes in our environment. In one study, a researcher asked a number of college students for directions to a campus building (Simons & Ambinder, 2005). During each conversation, two other researchers dressed as workmen passed between the first researcher and the student, carrying a large door. As the door hid the researcher from the student's view, one of the "workmen" took his place. This new person then resumed the conversation with the student as though nothing had happened. Amazing as it seems, only half of the students noticed that they were suddenly talking to a new person! The rest had apparently been paying so much attention to the researcher's question or to the map he was showing that they did not notice what he looked like. And half the participants in another study were so focused on their assigned task of counting the passes made during a videotaped basketball game that they did not notice that a woman in a gorilla suit walked in front of the camera, beat her chest, and walked away (Simons & Chabris, 1999). Magicians take advantage of inattentional blindness when they use sudden movements or other attention-grabbing stimuli to draw our attention away from the actions that lie behind their tricks. To experience a type of inattentional blindness known as "change blindness," take a look at the photos in Figure 5.25.

FIGURE 5.25

Change Blindness

TRY THIS These two photos are almost, but not exactly, the same. If you can't see the difference, or if it took you a while to see it, you may have been focusing your attention on the similarity of main features, resulting in blindness to one small, but obvious difference. (See page 186 for the answer).

● Divided Attention

People can sometimes divide their attention in ways that allow them to do more than one thing at a time, a skill sometimes called *multitasking*. You can drive a car, listen to the radio, sing along, and keep a beat by drumming on the steering wheel, all at the same time. In fact, as Figure 5.26 illustrates, it is sometimes difficult to stop dividing our attention and to stay focused on just one thing. However, your attention can't be divided beyond a certain point without a loss in performance and mental processing ability. For example, it is virtually impossible to read and talk at the

BLUE GREEN
GREEN ORANGE
PURPLE ORANGE
GREEN BLUE
RED RED
GRAY GRAY
RED BLUE
BLUE PURPLE

FIGURE 5.26

The Stroop Task

TRY THIS Look at these words and, as rapidly as possible, call out the *color of the ink* in which each word is printed. This Stroop task (Stroop, 1935) is not easy, because your brain automatically processes the *meaning* of each word, which then competes for attention with the response you are supposed to give. To do well, you must focus on the ink color and not allow your attention to be divided between color and meaning. Children just learning to read have less trouble with this task, because they do not yet process word meanings as automatically as experienced readers do.

same time. The reason is that attention is a limited resource. If you try to spread it over too many targets, or between certain kinds of tasks, you "run out" of attention.

Why is it sometimes so easy and at other times so difficult to do two things at once? When one task is so *automatic* that it requires little or no attention, it is usually easy to do something else at the same time, even if the other task takes some attention (Schneider, 1985). When two tasks both require attention, it may still be possible to perform them simultaneously, as long as each taps into different kinds of attentional resources (Wickens, 2002). For example, some attentional resources are devoted to perceiving incoming stimuli, whereas others handle making responses. This specialization of attention allows a skilled pianist to read musical notes and press keys simultaneously, even the first time through a piece. Apparently, the human brain has more than one type of attentional resource and more than one spotlight of attention (Wickens, 1989). This notion of different types of attention also helps explain why a driver can listen to the radio while steering safely and why voice control can be an effective way of performing a second task in an aircraft while the pilot's hands are busy with the controls (Wickens, 1992). If two tasks require the same kind of attention, however, performance on both tasks will suffer (Just et al., 2001).

● Attention and Automatic Processing

Your search for Barney's Diner will be helped by your ability to voluntarily allocate attention to a certain part of the environment, but it would be even easier if you knew that Barney's had the only bright red sign on that stretch of road (see "In Review: Attention"). Your search would not take much effort in this case because you could simply "set" your attention to filter out all signs except red ones. Actively ignoring certain information will help you find Barney's, but it will also continue to affect your perceptions for some time afterward. Suppose, for example, that while you are ignoring blue signs, you pass a billboard showing a giant blue palm tree. Researchers have found that your efforts to ignore certain stimuli may create *negative priming* (Rock & Gutman, 1981), making you slightly less able than before to identify palm trees of any color for several minutes, hours, or days (DeSchepper & Treisman, 1996).

in review Attention		
Characteristics	**Functions**	**Mechanisms**
Improves mental functioning	Directs sensory and perceptual systems toward stimuli	Overt orienting (e.g., cupping your ear to hear a whisper)
Requires effort		
Has limits	Selects specific information for further processing	Covert orienting (e.g., thinking about spring break while looking at the notes in front of you)
	Allows us to ignore some information	Voluntary control (e.g., purposefully looking for cars before crossing a street)
	Allocates mental energy to process information	Involuntary control (e.g., losing your train of thought when you're interrupted by a thunderclap)
	Regulates the flow of resources necessary for performing a task or coordinating multiple tasks	Automatic processing (e.g., no longer thinking about grammar rules as you become fluent in a foreign language)
		Divided attention (e.g., looking for an open teammate while you dribble a soccer ball down the field)

The difference between the photos in Figure 5.25 is that the top picture includes a clump of trees just to the left of the statue.

Our ability to search for targets rapidly and automatically is called *parallel processing*. It is as if you can examine all nearby locations at once (in parallel) and rapidly detect the target no matter where it appears. So if the sign you are looking for is bright red and twice as large as any other one on the road, you could conduct a parallel search, and it would quickly "pop out." The automatic, parallel processing that allows detection of color or size suggests that these features are analyzed before the point at which attention is required. However, if the target you seek shares many features with others nearby, you must conduct a slower, serial search, examining each item in turn (Treisman, 1988).

● Attention and the Brain

If directing attention to a task causes extra mental work to be done, there should be evidence of that work in brain activity. Such evidence has been provided by positron emission tomography (PET) and magnetic resonance imaging (MRI) scans, which reveal increased blood flow and greater neural activity in regions of the brain associated with the mental processing necessary for the task. In one study, for example, people were asked either to focus attention on reporting only the color of a stimulus or to divide attention in order to report its color, speed of motion, and shape (Corbetta et al., 1991). When attention was focused on color alone, increased blood flow appeared only in the part of the brain where that stimulus feature was analyzed; when attention was divided, the added supply of blood was shared between two locations. Similarly, increased neural activity occurs in two different areas of the brain when participants perform two different tasks, such as deciding whether sentences are true while also deciding whether two three-dimensional objects are the same or different (Just et al., 2001).

Because attention appears to be a linked set of resources that improve information processing at several levels and locations in the brain, it is not surprising that no single brain region has been identified as an "attention center" (Posner & Peterson, 1990; Sasaki et al., 2001). However, scientists have found regions in the brain that are involved in momentary lapses in attention, and in the *switching* of visual attention from one stimulus element or location to another (Posner & Raichle, 1994; Weissman et al., 2006).

Applications of Research on Perception

Throughout this chapter we have mentioned ways in which perceptual systems shape people's ability to handle tasks ranging from recognizing restaurant signs to detecting tornadoes. We have also seen how research on perception explains the principles behind movies and videos and affects the design of advertisements. In this section we examine three other areas in which perception research has been applied: aviation, human-computer interaction, and traffic safety.

● Aviation Psychology

To land an aircraft, pilots must make accurate judgments of how far they are from the ground, as well as how fast and from what angle they are approaching the runway. In this situation the visual environment provides many overlapping bottom-up perceptual cues (Gibson, 1979). Pilots can also use their experience-based expectations about the approaching ground surface, thus adding top-down processing to produce an accurate perception of reality. But suppose there are few depth cues because the landing occurs at night, and suppose the lay of the land differs from what the pilot normally experiences. With both bottom-up and top-down processing impaired, the pilot's interpretation of reality may be disastrously incorrect. If, for

Avoiding Perceptual Overload The pilot of a modern commercial jetliner is faced with a potentially overwhelming array of visual and auditory signals that must be correctly perceived and interpreted to ensure a safe flight. Engineering psychologists are helping to design instrument displays, warning systems, and communication links that make this task easier and make errors less likely.

example, the runway is much smaller than a pilot expects, it might be perceived as farther away than it actually is—especially at night—and thus may be approached too fast (O'Hare & Roscoe, 1991). (This illusion is similar to the one mentioned earlier in which drivers overestimate their distance from small cars.) Or if a pilot expects the runway to be perfectly flat but it actually slopes upward, the pilot might falsely perceive that the aircraft is too high. Misguided attempts to "correct" a plane's altitude under these circumstances have caused pilots to fly in too low, an error that resulted in a series of major nighttime crashes in the 1960s (Kraft, 1978).

Research on the perceptual processes—and possible perceptual failures—that occur while flying an airplane has made major contributions to aviation safety. For example, psychologists' analysis of the tragedies just described led to successful prevention of similar accidents. They recommended that airline pilot training programs emphasize the dangers of visual illusions and the importance of relying on their flight instruments during landings, especially at night.

Psychologists have also addressed problems related to the information those instruments provide. In a traditional aircraft cockpit, that information bears little resemblance to the perceptual world. Especially when visibility is poor, a pilot depending on flight instruments must do a lot of time-consuming and effortful serial processing to perceive and piece together the information necessary to understand the aircraft's position and movement. To ease this cognitive and attentional burden, engineering psychologists have helped to develop instrument displays that present a realistic three-dimensional image of the flight environment—similar in some ways to a video-game screen. This image more accurately captures the many cues for depth perception that the pilot needs.

Research on auditory perception has also contributed to aviation safety, both in the creation of warning signals that are most likely to catch the pilot's attention and in efforts to minimize communication errors. Air-traffic control communications use a special vocabulary and standardized phrases designed to avoid misunderstandings. But as a result, these communications are usually short, with little of the built-in redundancy that, in normal conversation, allows people to understand a sentence even if some words are missing. For example, if a pilot eager to depart on time perceives an expected message as "clear for takeoff" when the actual message is "hold for takeoff," the results can be catastrophic. Problems like these have been addressed "bottom up," through noise-canceling microphones and visual message displays, as well as through the use of slightly longer messages that aid top-down processing by providing more contextual cues.

● Human-Computer Interaction

The principles of perception are also being applied by human factors psychologists serving on design teams at computer and computer software companies. For example, in line with the ecological approach to perception, they have duplicated in the world of computer displays many of the depth cues that help people navigate in the physical world. The next time you visit a website or use a word-processing or spreadsheet program, you might notice that shading cues make certain "buttons" on the screen seem to protrude from their background, as real buttons would. Similarly, when you open several documents or spreadsheets, notice that interposition cues make them appear to be lying on top of one another.

The results of research on attention have even been applied to your cursor. It blinks to attract your attention, making it possible to do a quick parallel search rather than a slow serial search when you are looking for it amid all the other stimuli on the screen. Perceptual principles have also guided creation of the pictorial images, or icons, that are used to represent objects, processes, and commands in your computer programs. These icons speed your use of the computer if their features are easy to detect, recognize, and interpret (McDougall, de Bruijn, & Curry, 2000; Niemela & Saarinen, 2000). This is the reason a little trash-can icon is used in some programs to show you where to click when you want to delete a file. A tiny eraser or paper shredder might have worked, too, but its features might be harder to recognize. These are just a few of the ways in which psychologists are applying perception research to make computers easier to use.

● Traffic Safety

Research on perception is being applied in many ways to enhance traffic safety. For example, human factors psychologists are identifying features of automobile controls, instrument displays, road signs, and traffic signals that are likely to reduce older drivers' involvement in car accidents (Owsley et al., 1998; Vance et al., 2006). Others are studying ways of increasing drivers' perception of danger in various situations, including night driving (Pradhan et al. 2005; Wood, Tyrrell, & Carberry, 2005). Psychologists are also involved in the design of automotive night-vision displays that make it easier for drivers to see low-visibility targets, such as pedestrians dressed in dark clothing, or animals (Essock et al., 1999).

Further, research on divided attention is informing the debate over the use of mobile phones while driving. The demands of traffic safety groups and the examples set by many countries around the world have led Connecticut, New York, New Jersey, and the District of Columbia to outlaw drivers' use of hand-held mobile phones. Most other U.S. states are considering similar laws; some of these laws would ban even hands-free phone conversations while driving. Mobile phone manufacturers and network providers agree that using a phone while driving can be dangerous, but only because looking at the handset, pushing its buttons, and holding it in place during the call can distract the driver from steering and watching the road. They claim that hands-free phones and voice-controlled dialing eliminate any dangers associated with drivers' use of cell phones.

That argument is contradicted by research showing that drivers' ability to attend to visual cues is impaired simply by holding a phone to their ears, even if the phone is off (Oommen & Stahl, 2005). Other research shows that driving performance is impaired and the risk of accidents is increased while talking on *any* mobile phone, whether hand-held or hands-free (Beede & Kass, 2006; Dingus et al., 2006; McEvoy et al., 2005; Spence & Read, 2003; Strayer, Drews, & Johnston, 2003; Törnros & Bolling, 2005, 2006). This research suggests that the dangers of driving while using a phone do not stem simply from listening to someone speak or even from talking.

Driven to Distraction? Recent research shows that, at any given moment, about 10 percent of drivers in the United States are talking on a mobile telephone, and about 6 percent, or nearly one million of them are driving while using a hand-held model (Glassbrenner, 2005). Some cell phone manufacturers claim that hands-free models can eliminate any dangers associated with using a phone while driving, but perception research indicates that using any kind of phone can create inattentional blindness and distractions that impair driving performance and may contribute to accidents (e.g., Beede & Kass, 2006; Strayer, Drews, & Johnston, 2003).

The driving performance of research participants was not impaired by listening to books on tape or by repeating words that they heard. Performance *did* decline, though, when participants were asked to do more elaborate processing of auditory information, such as rephrasing what they heard. (You may have experienced similar effects if you have ever missed a turn or had a near-accident while deeply engaged in conversation with a passenger.) One study of people' performance on a driving simulator found that the accident-avoidance skills of sober drivers talking on mobile phones were impaired more than those of drivers who were legally drunk but not using phones (Strayer, Drews, & Crouch, 2003). These results suggest that using a mobile phone while driving is dangerous not only because it can take your eyes off the road and a hand off the wheel but also because the phone conversation competes for the cognitive/attentional resources you need to drive safely. Perception researchers suggest that this competition can actually create a form of inattentional blindness that is unlikely to be reduced by hands-free car phones (Just et al., 2001; Strayer & Drews, 2006; Strayer, Drews, & Johnston, 2003; Strayer et al., 2004).

LINKAGES

As noted in the chapter on introducing psychology, all of psychology's subfields are related to one another. Our discussion of how perceptual processes develop in infants illustrates just one way in which the topic of this chapter, perception, is linked to the subfield of developmental psychology (which is the topic of the chapter on human development). The Linkages diagram shows ties to two other subfields as well, and there are many more ties throughout the book. Looking for linkages among subfields will help you see how they all fit together and better appreciate the big picture that is psychology.

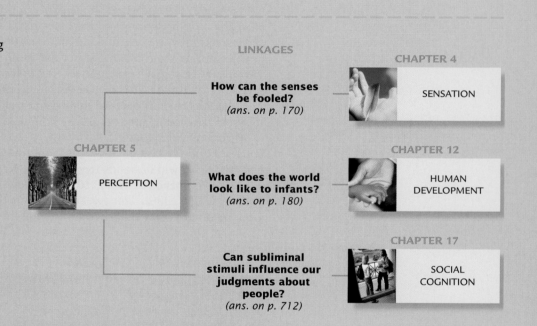

LINKAGES

CHAPTER 5 — PERCEPTION

How can the senses be fooled? (ans. on p. 170) — CHAPTER 4 SENSATION

What does the world look like to infants? (ans. on p. 180) — CHAPTER 12 HUMAN DEVELOPMENT

Can subliminal stimuli influence our judgments about people? (ans. on p. 712) — CHAPTER 17 SOCIAL COGNITION

SUMMARY

Perception is the process through which people actively use knowledge and understanding of the world to interpret sensations as meaningful experiences.

The Perception Paradox

Because perception often seems so rapid and effortless, it appears to be a rather simple operation; however, this is not the case. An enormous amount of processing is required to transform energy received by receptors into perceptual experience. The complexity of perception is revealed by various perceptual errors (e.g., illusions).

Three Approaches to Perception

The *computational approach* to perception emphasizes the computations performed by the nervous system. The *constructivist approach* suggests that the perceptual system constructs the experience of reality, making inferences and applying knowledge in order to interpret sensations. The *ecological approach* holds that the environment itself provides the cues that people use to form perceptions.

Psychophysics

Psychophysics is the study of the relationship between stimulus energy and the psychological experience of that energy.

Absolute Thresholds: Is Something Out There?
Psychophysics has traditionally been concerned with matters such as determining absolute thresholds for the detection of stimuli. Research shows that this threshold is not, in fact, absolute. The *absolute threshold* has been redefined as the minimum amount of stimulus energy that can be detected 50 percent of the time. *Supraliminal stimuli* fall above this threshold; *subliminal stimuli* fall below it.

Signal-Detection Theory *Signal-detection theory* describes how people respond to faint or ambiguous stimuli. Detection of a signal is affected by external and internal noise, *sensitivity*, and the *response criterion*. Signal-detection theory has been applied to understanding decision making and performance in areas such as the detection of tornadoes on radar.

Judging Differences: Has Anything Changed? *Weber's law* states that the minimum detectable amount of change in a stimulus—the *difference threshold*, or *just-noticeable difference (JND)*—increases in proportion to the initial amount of the stimulus. The less the initial stimulation, the smaller the change that will be detected.

Magnitude Estimation: How Intense Is That? Fechner's law and Stevens's power law describe the relationship between the magnitude of a stimulus and its perceived intensity.

Organizing the Perceptual World

Basic Processes in Perceptual Organization *Perceptual organization* is the process whereby order is imposed on the information received by your senses. The perceptual system automatically distinguishes figure from ground, and it groups stimuli into patterns. Gestalt psychologists and others identified laws or principles that guide such grouping: proximity, similarity, continuity, closure, common fate, synchrony, common region, and connectedness. These laws appear to ensure that perceptual organization creates interpretations of incoming information that are simple and most likely to be correct.

Perception of Location and Distance Visual localization requires information about the position of the body and eyes, as well as information about where a stimulus falls on the retinas. Auditory localization depends on detecting differences in the information that reaches the two ears, including differences in timing and intensity. Perception of distance, or *depth perception*, depends partly on stimulus cues and partly on the physical structure of the visual system. Some of the stimulus cues for depth perception are *interposition*, *relative size*, *height in the visual field*, *texture gradient*, *linear perspective*, and *motion parallax*. Cues based on the structure of the visual system include *accommodation* (the change in the shape of the lenses as objects are brought into focus), *convergence* (the fact that the eyes must move to focus on the same object), and *binocular disparity* (the fact that the eyes are set slightly apart).

Perception of Motion The perception of motion results, in part, from the movement of stimuli across the retinas. Expanding or *looming* stimulation is perceived as an approaching object. Movement of the retinal image is interpreted along with information about movement of the head, eyes, and other parts of the body so that one's own movement can be discriminated from the movement of external objects. *Stroboscopic motion* is an illusion that accounts for our ability to see smooth motion in films, videos, and DVDs.

Perceptual Constancy Because of *perceptual constancy*, the brightness, size, and shape of objects are seen to remain the same, even though the sensations received from those objects may change. Size constancy and shape constancy depend on the relationship between the retinal image of an object and the knowledge-based perception of its distance. Brightness constancy depends on the perceived relationship between the brightness of an object and its background.

Recognizing the Perceptual World

Both *bottom-up processing* and *top-down processing* contribute to recognition of the world. The ability to recognize objects is based on finding a match between the pattern of sensations organized by the perceptual system and a pattern that is stored in memory.

Bottom-Up Processing Bottom-up processing seems to be accomplished by the analysis of stimulus features or combinations of features, such as form, color, and motion.

Top-Down Processing Top-down processing is influenced by expectancy and motivation. *Schemas* based on past experience can create a perceptual set, the readiness or predisposition to perceive stimuli in certain ways. Expectancies can also be created by the context in which a stimulus appears.

Network Processing Research on pattern recognition has focused attention on network models, or *parallel distributed processing (PDP)* models, of perception. These emphasize the simultaneous activation and interaction of feature-analysis systems and the role of experience.

Culture, Experience, and Perception To the extent that the visual environments of people in different cultures differ, their perceptual experiences—as evidenced by their responses to perceptual illusions—may differ as well.

Attention

Attention is the process of focusing psychological resources to enhance perception, performance, and mental experience. We can shift attention overtly—by moving the eyes, for example—or covertly, without any movement of sensory systems.

Directing Attention Attention is selective; it is like a spotlight that illuminates different parts of the external environment or various mental processes. Control over attention can be voluntary and knowledge based or involuntary and driven by environmental stimuli.

Ignoring Information Sometimes attention can be so focused that it results in inattentional blindness, a failure to detect or identify normally noticeable stimuli.

Divided Attention Although there are limits to how well people can divide attention, they can sometimes attend to two tasks at once. For example, tasks that have become automatic can often be performed along with more demanding tasks, and tasks that require very different types of processing, such as gardening and talking, can be performed together because each task depends on a different supply of mental resources.

Attention and Automatic Processing Some information can be processed automatically, in parallel, whereas other situations demand focused attention and a serial search.

Attention and the Brain Although the brain plays a critical role in attention, no single brain region has been identified as the main attention center.

Applications of Research on Perception

Research on human perception has numerous practical applications.

Aviation Psychology Accurate size and distance judgments, top-down processing, and attention are all important to safety in aviation.

Human-Computer Interaction Perceptual principles relating to recognition, depth cues, and attention are being applied by psychologists who work with designers of computers and computer programs.

Traffic Safety Research on divided attention is being applied to help understand the potential dangers of driving while using various kinds of mobile phones.

Learning

Live and learn. This simple phrase captures the idea that learning is a lifelong process that affects our behavior every day. Understanding how learning takes place is an important part of understanding ourselves, and in this chapter, we explore the learning process and the factors that affect it. We have organized our presentation as follows:

Can you recall how you felt on your first day of kindergarten? Like many young children, you may have been bewildered, even frightened, as the comforting familiarity of home or day care was suddenly replaced by an environment filled with new names and faces, rules and events. But like most youngsters, you probably adjusted to this new situation within a few days, much as you did again when you started middle school, high school, and college.

Your adjustment, or *adaptation*, to these new environments occurred in many ways. Ringing bells, lunch lines, midterm grades, and other once-strange new school events not only became part of your expectations about the world but also began to serve as signals. You soon realized that if a note was delivered to your teacher during class, someone would be called to the main office. If a substitute teacher appeared, it meant an easy lesson or a chance to act up. And if your teacher arrived with a box of papers, you'd know the tests had been graded. Adapting to school also meant developing new knowledge about what behavior was appropriate and inappropriate in the new settings you encountered. Although your parents might have encouraged you to talk whenever you wanted to at home, perhaps you found that at school, you had to raise your hand first. And the messy finger painting that got you in trouble at home might have earned you praise in art class. You found, too, that there were things you could do—such as paying attention in class and getting to school on time—to reap rewards and avoid punishment. Finally, of course, you adapted to school by absorbing facts about the world and developing skills ranging from kickball and reading to writing and debating.

The entire process of development, from birth to death, involves a biological adaptation to increasingly complex, ever-changing environments, using continuously updated knowledge gained through experience. Although perhaps most highly developed in humans, the ability to adapt to changing environments appears to varying degrees in all species. According to the evolutionary approach to psychology, it is individual variability in the capacity to adapt that shapes the evolution of appearance and behavior in animals and humans. As Charles Darwin noted, individuals who don't adapt may not survive to reproduce.

Many forms of animal and human adaptation follow the principles of learning. **Learning** is the adaptive process through which experience modifies pre-existing behavior and understanding. The pre-existing behavior and understanding may have been present at birth, acquired automatically as we mature, or learned earlier. Learning plays a central role in the development of most aspects of human behavior. It allows us to build the motor skills we need to walk or tie a shoe, the language skills we use to communicate, and the object categories—such as "food," "vehicle," or "animal"—that help us organize our perceptions and think logically about the world. Sayings such as "Once burned, twice shy" and "Fool me once, shame on you; fool me twice, shame on me" reflect this vital learning process. If you want to know who you are and how you became the person you are today, examining what and how you have learned is a good place to start.

Humans and other animals learn primarily by experiencing events, observing relationships between those events, and noticing consistencies in the world around them. For example, when two events repeatedly take place together, we can predict the occurrence of one from knowledge of the other. We learn that a clear blue sky means dry weather, that too little sleep makes us irritable, that we can reach someone by typing a certain e-mail address, and that flattery motivates some people and annoys others. Some learning takes place consciously, as when we study for an

learning The modification through experience of pre-existing behavior and understanding.

habituation The process of adapting to stimuli that do not change.

exam, but, as mentioned later, we can also learn things without being aware we are doing so (Watanabe, Náñez, & Sasaki, 2001).

Psychological research on learning has been guided by three main questions: (1) Which events and relationships do people learn about? (2) What circumstances determine whether and how people learn? and (3) Is learning a slow process requiring lots of practice, or does it involve sudden flashes of insight? In this chapter we provide some of the answers to these questions.

We first consider the simplest forms of learning—learning about sights, sounds, and other individual stimuli. Then we examine the two major kinds of learning that involve *associations* between events—classical conditioning and operant conditioning. Next we consider the role of thinking, or cognition, in learning, and we conclude by discussing how research on learning might help people learn better.

Learning About Stimuli

In a changing world, people are constantly bombarded by stimuli. If we tried to pay attention to every sight and sound, our information-processing systems would be overloaded, and we would be unable to concentrate on anything. People appear to be genetically tuned to attend to certain kinds of events, such as loud sounds, special tastes, or pain. *Novel* stimuli—things we have not experienced before—also tend to attract our attention.

By contrast, our response to *unchanging* stimuli decreases over time. This aspect of adaptation is a simple form of learning called **habituation,** and it can occur in relation to sights, sounds, smells, tastes, or touches. Through habituation, you eventually fail to notice that you are wearing glasses or a watch. And after having been in a room for a while, you no longer smell that musty or flowery odor or hear that loudly ticking clock. Habituation is especially important for adapting to initially startling but harmless events such as the repeated popping of balloons, but it occurs in some degree to all kinds of stimuli and in all kinds of animals, from simple sea snails to humans (Gottfried, O'Doherty, & Dolan, 2003; Pinel, 1993). After our response to a stimulus has habituated, it may quickly return if the stimulus changes. So if that loudly ticking clock suddenly stops, you may become aware of it again because now, something in your environment has changed. This reappearance of your original response when a stimulus changes is called *dishabituation.* In the perception chapter, we describe how habituation and dishabituation processes have helped psychologists determine what babies notice, and fail to notice, as perceptual skills develop.

A second simple form of learning, called *sensitization,* appears as an increase in responsiveness to a stimulus. Sensitization occurs, for example, when people and animals show exaggerated responses to unexpected, potentially threatening sights or sounds, especially during periods of emotional arousal. So while breathlessly exploring a dark, spooky house, you might scream, run, or violently throw something in response to the unexpected creaking of a door.

Habituation and sensitization provide organisms with a useful way to adapt to their environments, but notice that these kinds of learning result from exposure to a single stimulus. It does not involve the association of one stimulus with another, as when we learn that, say, dark clouds signal rain. For this reason, habituation and sensitization are referred to as *nonassociative learning* (Barker, 1997).

Psychologists have been especially interested in how habituation occurs. According to Richard Solomon's (1980) *opponent process theory,* new stimulus events—especially those that arouse strong positive or negative emotions—disrupt the individual's physiological state of equilibrium, or homeostasis. This disruption triggers an opposite, or opponent, process that counteracts the disruption and eventually restores equilibrium. If the arousing event occurs repeatedly, this opponent process gets stronger and occurs more rapidly. It eventually becomes so quick

Learning to Live with It   People who move to a big city may at first be distracted by the din of traffic, low-flying aircraft, and other urban sounds, but after a while, the process of habituation makes all this noise far less noticeable.

Sensitization The documentary filmmakers portrayed in *The Blair Witch Project* demonstrated the simple learning process called *sensitization* as their behavioral reactions to sudden stimuli became more and more extreme. The next time you are watching a tense or "scary" film, look for similar examples of sensitization in the reactions of the audience, and perhaps in yourself, too!

and strong that it actually suppresses the initial response to the stimulus, creating habituation.

As described in the motivation and emotion chapter, the opponent-process theory of habituation may help explain why some people skydive and engage in other highly arousing activities. It may also help explain some of the dangers associated with certain drugs. Consider, for example, what happens as someone continues to use a drug such as heroin. The "high," or pleasurable reaction that follows a particular dose of the drug begins to decrease, or habituate, with repeated doses. Habituation occurs, Solomon says, because the initial, pleasurable reaction to the drug is followed by an unpleasant, increasingly rapid, opposing reaction that counteracts the drug's primary effects. As drug users become habituated, they must take progressively larger doses to get the same high. According to Solomon and other researchers, these opponent processes form the basis of drug tolerance and addiction (e.g., McDonald & Siegel, 2004).

It has been suggested that similar opponent processes may be partly responsible for some accidental drug overdoses. Suppose the unpleasant reaction that counteracts a drug's initial effects becomes associated with a particular room, person, or other stimulus that is normally present when the drug is taken. This stimulus may eventually come to trigger the counteracting process, allowing the user to tolerate larger drug doses. Now suppose that a person takes this larger drug dose in an environment in which this stimulus is not present. The strength of the drug's primary effect will remain the same, but without the familiar environmental stimulus, the counteracting process may be weaker. The net result may be a stronger-than-usual drug reaction, possibly leading to an overdose (Melchior, 1990; Siegel et al., 1982).

Notice that opponent process explanations of drug abuse and overdose are based not just on simple habituation and sensitization but also on a *learned association* between certain environmental stimuli and certain opponent responses. Indeed, the nonassociative processes of habituation and sensitization cannot, by themselves, explain many of the behaviors and mental processes that are the focus of psychology. To better understand how learning affects our thoughts and behaviors, we have to consider forms of learning that involve the building of associations between various stimuli, as well as between stimuli and responses. One major type of associative learning is called *classical conditioning*.

Classical Conditioning: Learning Signals and Associations

At the first notes of the national anthem, an athlete's heart may start pounding; those sounds signal that the game is about to begin. A flashing red light on the instrument panel may make your heart rate rise, too, because it means that something is wrong with your car. People are not born with these reactions. They learn them by observing relationships or *associations* between events in the world. The experimental study of this kind of learning was begun, almost by accident, by Ivan Petrovich Pavlov.

Pavlov's Discovery

Pavlov is one of the best-known figures in psychology, but he was not a psychologist. A Russian physiologist, Pavlov won a Nobel Prize in 1904 for his research on the digestive processes of dogs. In the course of this work, Pavlov noticed a strange phenomenon: The first stage of the digestive process—salivation, or drooling—sometimes occurred when no food was present. His dogs salivated, for example, when they saw the assistant who normally brought their food, even if the assistant was empty-handed.

Pavlov devised a simple experiment to determine why salivation occurred without an obvious physical cause. First he performed a simple operation to divert a dog's saliva into a container so that the amount of salivation could be measured precisely. He then placed the dog in an apparatus similar to the one shown in Figure 6.1. The experiment had three phases.

In the first phase of the experiment, Pavlov and his associates confirmed that when meat powder was placed on the dog's tongue, the dog salivated, but that it did not salivate in response to a neutral stimulus—a musical tone, for example. Thus the researchers had established the two basic components for Pavlov's experiment:

Pen recording on cylinder

FIGURE 6.1

Apparatus for Measuring Conditioned Responses

In this more elaborate version of Pavlov's original apparatus, the amount of saliva flowing from a dog's cheek is measured, then recorded on a slowly revolving drum of paper.

PHASE 1: Before conditioning has occurred

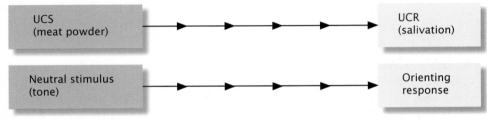

PHASE 2: The process of conditioning

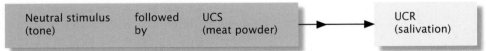

PHASE 3: After conditioning has occurred

FIGURE 6.2

Classical Conditioning

Before classical conditioning has occurred, meat powder on a dog's tongue produces salivation, but the sound of a tone—a neutral stimulus—brings only orienting responses such as turning toward the sound. During the process of conditioning, the tone is repeatedly paired with the meat powder. After classical conditioning has taken place, the sound of the tone alone acts as a conditioned stimulus, producing salivation.

classical conditioning A procedure in which a neutral stimulus is repeatedly paired with a stimulus that elicits a reflex or other response until the neutral stimulus alone comes to elicit a similar response.

unconditioned stimulus (UCS) A stimulus that elicits a response without conditioning.

unconditioned response (UCR) The automatic or unlearned reaction to a stimulus.

conditioned stimulus (CS) The originally neutral stimulus that, through pairing with the unconditioned stimulus, comes to elicit a conditioned response.

conditioned response (CR) The response that the conditioned stimulus elicits.

(1) a *reflex*, which is a quick, automatic response to a stimulus and (2) a *neutral stimulus* that does not trigger that reflex.

It was the second and third phases of the experiment that showed how one type of associative learning can occur. In the second phase, the tone sounded, and then a few seconds later meat powder was placed in the dog's mouth. The dog salivated. This *pairing*—the tone followed immediately by meat powder—was repeated several times. The tone predicted that the meat powder was coming, but the question remained: Would the animal learn that the tone signals the meat powder? The answer was yes. In the third phase of the experiment, the tone was sounded, and even though no meat powder was presented, the dog again salivated. In other words, the tone by itself now elicited salivation. You may have seen a similar process if you regularly open pet food with an electric can opener. The sound of the opener probably brings your pet running (and salivating) because that sound means that food is on its way.

Pavlov's experiment was the first laboratory demonstration of a basic form of associative learning. Today, it is called **classical conditioning**—a procedure in which a neutral stimulus is repeatedly paired with a stimulus that already triggers a reflexive response. As a result of this pairing, the previously neutral stimulus itself comes to trigger a response that is similar to that reflex. Figure 6.2 shows the basic elements of classical conditioning. The stimulus that elicits a response without conditioning, such as the meat powder in Pavlov's experiment, is called the **unconditioned stimulus (UCS)**. The automatic reaction to this stimulus is called the **unconditioned response (UCR)**. As the neutral stimulus is repeatedly paired with the unconditioned stimulus, it comes to be called the **conditioned stimulus (CS)**, and the response it comes to elicit is the **conditioned response (CR)**.

● Conditioned Responses over Time: Extinction and Spontaneous Recovery

Continued pairings of a conditioned stimulus with an unconditioned stimulus strengthen conditioned responses. The curve on the left side of Figure 6.3 shows an example: Repeated associations of a tone (CS) with meat powder (UCS) caused Pavlov's dogs to increase their salivation (CR) to the tone alone.

FIGURE 6.3

Changes over Time in the Strength of a Conditioned Response (CR)

As the conditioned stimulus (CS) and the unconditioned stimulus (UCS) are repeatedly paired during initial conditioning, the strength of the conditioned response (CR) increases. If the CS is repeatedly presented without the UCS, the CR weakens—and eventually disappears—through a process called *extinction*. However, after a brief period, the CR reappears if the CS is again presented. This phenomenon is called *spontaneous recovery*.

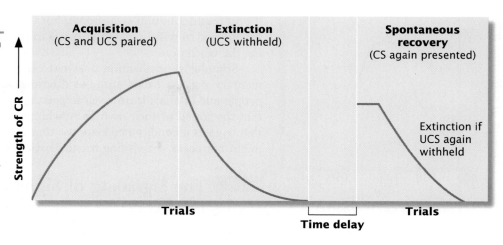

What if the meat powder is no longer given? In general, if the conditioned stimulus continues to occur without being followed at least occasionally by the unconditioned stimulus, the conditioned response will gradually disappear. This fading process is known as **extinction** (see the center section of Figure 6.3). If the conditioned stimulus and the unconditioned stimulus are again paired after the conditioned response has been extinguished, the conditioned response returns to its original strength very quickly, often after only one or two trials. This quick relearning of a conditioned response after extinction is called **reconditioning**. Because reconditioning takes much less time than the original conditioning, extinction must not have erased the original learned association. Instead, the original learning had been suppressed by a newly learned tendency to not respond (Bouton, 2002; Myers & Davis, 2007).

Additional evidence for this conclusion is illustrated on the right side of Figure 6.3: An extinguished conditioned response will temporarily reappear if, after some time delay, the conditioned stimulus is presented again—even without the unconditioned stimulus. This reappearance of the conditioned response after extinction (and without further CS-UCS pairings) is called **spontaneous recovery**. In general, the longer the time between extinction and the reoccurrence of the conditioned stimulus, the greater the recovered conditioned response. (However, unless the UCS is again paired with the CS, extinction rapidly occurs again.) In other words, even after they have been extinguished, associations may not be entirely forgotten. Spontaneous recovery may make them available even years later, as when a person hears a song or smells a scent associated with a long-lost lover or a departed relative and experiences a ripple of emotion—a conditioned response.

● Stimulus Generalization and Discrimination

After a conditioned response is learned, stimuli that are similar but not identical to the conditioned stimulus also elicit the response—but to a lesser degree. This phenomenon is called **stimulus generalization**. Usually the greater the similarity between a new stimulus and the conditioned stimulus, the stronger the conditioned response will be. So a person who was bitten by a small, curly-haired dog is likely to be most afraid of dogs that closely resemble it. Figure 6.4 shows another example involving sounds.

Stimulus generalization has obvious adaptive advantages. For example, it is important for survival that, if you get sick after drinking sour-smelling milk, you now avoid dairy products that have a similar odor. Generalization would be a problem, though, if it had no limits. Like most people, you would probably be frightened

extinction The gradual disappearance of a conditioned response when a conditioned stimulus is no longer followed by an unconditioned stimulus.

reconditioning The quick relearning of a conditioned response following extinction.

spontaneous recovery The reappearance of the conditioned response after extinction and without further pairings of the conditioned and unconditioned stimuli.

stimulus generalization A phenomenon in which a conditioned response is elicited by stimuli that are similar but not identical to the conditioned stimulus.

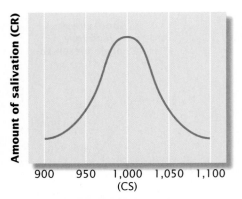

FIGURE 6.4

Stimulus Generalization

The strength of a conditioned response (CR) is greatest when the original conditioned stimulus (CS) occurs, but the CR also appears following stimuli that closely resemble the CS. Here, the CS is the sound of a buzzer at 1000 Hz (hertz), and the CR is salivation. Notice that the CR generalizes well to stimuli at 990 or 1010 Hz, but that it is weaker and weaker in response to stimuli that are less and less similar to the CS.

if you found a lion in your home, but imagine the disruption if your fear response generalized so widely that you were panicked by a picture of a lion, or even by reading the word *lion*.

Stimulus generalization does not run wild because it is balanced by a complementary process called **stimulus discrimination**. Through stimulus discrimination, people and animals learn to differentiate among similar stimuli. Many parents find that the sound of their own baby whimpering may become a conditioned stimulus that triggers a conditioned response that wakes them up. That conditioned response might not occur if a visiting friend's baby whimpers.

● The Signaling of Significant Events

Is classical conditioning entirely automatic? Pavlov's research suggested that it is—that classical conditioning involves nothing more than automatic associations that allow one stimulus (the conditioned stimulus, or CS) to substitute for another (the unconditioned stimulus, or UCS) in triggering an automatic, reflexive response. For years the study of classical conditioning focused mainly on its role in the control of such automatic, involuntary behavior, but this view has turned out to be too simplified. For example, a rat's unconditioned, reflexive response to a mild shock (UCS) will be flinching and jumping. But at the sound of a tone (CS) that always precedes shock, the animal's conditioned response will not be to flinch and jump but to freeze—much as it would if threatened by a predator (Domjan, 2005). In other words, classical conditioning involves more than the appearance of robot-like, reflexive responses.

Many psychologists now believe that organisms acquire conditioned responses when one event reliably predicts, or *signals*, the appearance of another. These psychologists also believe that instead of giving rise to simple reflexes, classical conditioning leads to responses based on the *information* provided by conditioned stimuli. As a result, animals and people develop *mental representations* of the relationships between important events in their environment and expectancies about when such events will occur (Rescorla, 1988; Shanks, 1995). These representations and expectancies aid adaptation and survival.

What determines whether and how a conditioned response is learned? Important factors include the timing, predictability, and strength of signals; the amount of attention they receive; and how easily the signals can be associated with other stimuli.

● **Timing** If your instructor always finishes class at 9:59 and a bell rings at 10:00, the bell comes too late to act as a signal for the end of the session. For the same reason, classical conditioning works best when the conditioned stimulus precedes the unconditioned stimulus. In this arrangement, known as *forward conditioning*, the conditioned stimulus signals that the unconditioned stimulus is coming.

There is also an arrangement, called *backward conditioning*, in which the conditioned stimulus *follows* the unconditioned stimulus. When this happens, however, a conditioned response develops very slowly, if at all. (Part of the explanation is that the CS in backward conditioning comes too late to signal the approach of the UCS. In fact, as described later, the CS signals the *absence* of the UCS and eventually triggers a response that is opposite to the conditioned response, thus inhibiting its development.)

Research shows that conditioning usually works best when there is an interval between the conditioned stimulus and the unconditioned stimulus. This interval can range from a fraction of a second to a few seconds to more than a minute, depending on the particular CS, UCS, and UCR involved (Longo, Klempay, & Bitterman, 1964; Ross & Ross, 1971). Classical conditioning will always be weaker if the interval between the CS and the UCS is longer than what is ideal for the stimuli and responses in a given situation. This makes adaptive sense. Normally, the appearance

● **stimulus discrimination** A process through which individuals learn to differentiate among similar stimuli and respond appropriately to each one.

Safety Signals Pavlov discovered that associating a tone (CS) with the appearance of food (UCS) creates conditioned salivation in response to the tone. He also found that if a CS is associated with the *absence* of food, the conditioned response (salivation) is inhibited, or reduced. The effect of this *inhibitory conditioning* can be seen in the adjustments sometimes made by people who suffer with agoraphobia and panic disorder (see the chapter on psychological disorders). These people are normally intensely afraid of leaving home, but some of them find that the presence of a trusted friend acts as a safety signal that inhibits their conditioned fear responses enough to let them venture out into the world (Schmidt et al., 2006).

of food, predators, or other significant events is most reliably predicted by smells, growls, or other stimuli that occur at varying intervals before those events. So it is logical that organisms are "wired" to form associations most easily between things that occur in a relatively tight time sequence.

● **Predictability** For classical conditioning to occur, though, it is not enough that the conditioned stimulus precede the unconditioned stimulus and that the two events are close together in time. Suppose you have two dogs, Moxie and Fang, each with different personalities. When Moxie growls, she sometimes bites, but sometimes she doesn't. Other times, she bites without growling first. Fang, however, growls *only* before biting. Your conditioned fear response to Moxie's growl will probably occur slowly, if at all, because her growl is a stimulus that does not reliably signal the danger of a bite. But you are likely to quickly develop a classically conditioned fear response to Fang's growl, because classical conditioning proceeds most rapidly when the conditioned stimulus *always* signals the unconditioned stimulus, and *only* the unconditioned stimulus. So even if both dogs provide the same number of pairings of the conditioned stimulus (growl) and the unconditioned stimulus (bite), it is only in Fang's case that the conditioned stimulus *reliably* predicts the unconditioned stimulus (Rescorla, 1968).

● **Signal Strength** A conditioned response will be greater if the unconditioned stimulus is strong than if it is weak. So a predictive signal associated with a strong UCS, such as an intense shock, will come to evoke more fear than one associated with a weak shock. As with timing and predictability, the effect of signal strength on classical conditioning makes adaptive sense. It is more important to be prepared for major events than for events that have little impact.

How quickly a conditioned response is learned also depends on the strength of the conditioned stimulus. As described in the chapter on perception, louder tones, brighter lights, or other, more intense stimuli tend to get attention, so they are most rapidly associated with an unconditioned stimulus—as long as they remain reliable predictive signals.

● **Attention** In the classical conditioning laboratory, a single neutral stimulus is presented, followed shortly by an unconditioned stimulus. In the natural environment, however, several stimuli might be present just before an unconditioned stimulus occurs. Suppose you are at the beach, sipping lemonade, reading a magazine, listening to a Beyoncé CD, and inhaling the scent of sunscreen, when you are stung by a wasp. Where your attention was focused at that moment can influence which potential conditioned stimulus—the taste of lemonade, the sight of the magazine, the sound of Beyoncé, or the smell of sunscreen—becomes associated with that painful unconditioned stimulus. The stimulus you were attending to most closely—and thus most fully perceiving—is the one likely to be more strongly associated with pain than any of the others (Hall, 1991).

● **Biopreparedness** After Pavlov's initial experiments, many psychologists believed that the associations formed through classical conditioning were like Velcro. Just as Velcro pieces of any size or shape can be attached with equal ease, some believed that any conditioned stimulus has an equal potential for becoming associated with any unconditioned stimulus, as long as the two stimuli occur in the right time sequence. This view, called *equipotentiality*, was later challenged by experiments showing that certain signals or events are especially likely to form associations with other events (Logue, 1985). This apparent natural tendency for certain events to become linked suggests that humans and animals are "biologically prepared" or "genetically tuned" to develop certain conditioned associations.

The most dramatic example of this *biopreparedness* is seen in conditioned taste aversions. Consider the results of a study in which rats were either shocked or made

Taste Aversions Humans can develop classically conditioned taste aversions, even to preferred foods. Ilene Bernstein (1978) gave one group of cancer patients Mapletoff ice cream an hour before they received nausea-provoking chemotherapy. A second group ate the same kind of ice cream on a day they did not receive chemotherapy. A third group got no ice cream. Five months later, the patients were asked to taste several ice cream flavors. Those who had never tasted Mapletoff and those who had not eaten it in association with chemotherapy chose it as their favorite. Those who had eaten Mapletoff before receiving chemotherapy found it very distasteful.

nauseous in the combined presence of a bright light, a loud buzzer, and saccharin-flavored water. Only certain conditioned associations were formed. Specifically, the animals that had been shocked developed a conditioned fear response to the light and the buzzer, but not to the flavored water. Those that had been made nauseous developed a conditioned aversion to the flavored water but showed no particular response to the light or buzzer (Garcia & Koelling, 1966). Notice that these associations are useful and adaptive: Nausea is more likely to be produced by something we eat or drink than by a noise or some other external stimulus. So nausea is more likely to become a conditioned response to an internal stimulus, such as a saccharine flavor, than to an external stimulus, such as a light or buzzer. In contrast, the sudden pain of a shock likely to have been caused by an external stimulus, so it makes evolutionary sense that organisms should be "tuned" to associate pain with external stimuli such as sights or sounds.

Conditioned taste aversion shows that for certain kinds of stimuli, classical conditioning can occur even when there is a long delay between the CS (taste) and the UCS (sickness). For example, the illness caused by poisons or other nauseating substances is usually delayed by minutes or hours, which is far longer than the intervals that normally produce conditioning. But for people who have experienced food poisoning or stomach flu after eating a certain kind of food, just the smell of it can make them queasy, and they may never eat that food again. Taste aversion makes sense in evolutionary terms, because organisms that are biologically prepared to link taste signals with illness, even if it occurs after a considerable delay, are more likely to survive than organisms not so prepared.

Evidence from several sources suggests other ways in which animals and people are innately prepared to learn aversions to certain stimuli. For example, experiments with animals suggest that they are prone to learn the type of associations that are most common in, or most relevant to, their environments (Wilcoxon, Dragoin, & Kral, 1971). Birds are strongly dependent upon their vision in searching for food and may develop taste aversions on the basis of visual stimuli. Coyotes and rats, more dependent on their sense of smell, tend to develop aversions related to odor. Humans are much more likely to develop a conditioned fear of harmless dogs or snakes than of potentially more dangerous objects, such as electrical outlets or knives (Öhman & Mineka, 2001, 2003). We are also particularly likely to learn fear responses to people who are "different," such as members of other ethnic groups (Olsson et al., 2005).

● **Second-Order Conditioning**   Once we learn that a conditioned stimulus (CS) signals the arrival of an unconditioned stimulus (UCS), the CS may operate as if it actually were that UCS. For instance, suppose that a child endures a painful medical procedure (UCS) at the doctor's office, and the pain becomes associated with the doctor's white coat. The white coat might then become a conditioned stimulus (CS) that can trigger a conditioned fear response. Once the white coat is able to set off a conditioned fear response, the coat may take on some properties of an unconditioned stimulus. So if the child later sees a white-coated pharmacist at the drugstore, that once-neutral store can become a conditioned stimulus for fear because it signals the appearance of a white coat, which in turn signals pain. When a conditioned stimulus (the white coat) acts like an unconditioned stimulus, creating conditioned stimuli (the drugstore) out of events associated with it, the process is called **second-order conditioning**.

Conditioned fear, along with the second-order conditioning that can be based on it, illustrates one of the most important adaptive characteristics of classical conditioning: the ability to prepare a person or an animal for threatening events—unconditioned stimuli—that are reliably signaled by a conditioned stimulus. Unfortunately, second-order conditioning can also cause problems. For example, the high blood pressure seen in medical patients known as *white-coat hypertensives* (Ugajin et al., 2005) doesn't reflect a physical disorder. It occurs simply because the

● **second-order conditioning** A phenomenon in which a conditioned stimulus acts like an unconditioned stimulus, creating conditioned stimuli out of events associated with it.

The Power of Second-Order Conditioning   Cancer patients may feel queasy when they enter a chemotherapy room because they have associated the room with treatment that causes nausea. Through second-order conditioning, almost anything associated with that *room* can also become a conditioned stimulus for nausea. One cancer patient, flying out of town on a business trip, became nauseated just by seeing her hospital from the air.

mere sight of a doctor or nurse has become a conditioned stimulus for fear. Medical staff must be alert to such cases in order not to give blood pressure medication to patients who don't need it.

● Some Applications of Classical Conditioning

"In Review: Basic Phenomena in Classical Conditioning" summarizes the principles of classical conditioning. These principles have been applied in many areas, including in overcoming fears, controlling predators, detecting explosives, and predicting Alzheimer's disease, to name just a few examples.

in review Basic Phenomena in Classical Conditioning

Process	Description	Example
Acquisition	A neutral stimulus and an unconditioned stimulus (UCS) are paired. The neutral stimulus becomes a conditioned stimulus (CS), eliciting a conditioned response (CR).	A child learns to fear (conditioned response) the doctor's office (conditioned stimulus) by associating it with the reflexive emotional reaction (unconditioned response) to a painful injection (unconditioned stimulus).
Stimulus generalization	A conditioned response is elicited not only by the conditioned stimulus but also by stimuli similar to the conditioned stimulus.	A child fears most doctors' offices and places that smell like them.
Stimulus discrimination	Generalization is limited so that some stimuli similar to the conditioned stimulus do not elicit the conditioned response.	A child learns that his mother's doctor's office is not associated with the unconditioned stimulus.
Extinction	The conditioned stimulus is presented alone, without the unconditioned stimulus. Eventually the conditioned stimulus no longer elicits the conditioned response.	A child visits the doctor's office several times for a checkup but does not receive an injection. Fear may eventually cease.

● **Phobias**   Classical conditioning can play a role in the development not only of mild fears (such as a child's fear of a doctor's white coat) but also of phobias (Bouton, Mineka, & Barlow, 2001). *Phobias* are extreme fears of objects or situations that either are not objectively dangerous—public speaking, for example—or are less dangerous than the phobic person's reaction suggests. In some instances, phobias can seriously disrupt a person's life. A child who is frightened by a large dog may learn a fear of that dog that is so intense and generalized that it creates a phobia of all dogs and avoidance of all situations in which dogs might be encountered. Classically conditioned fears can be very long-lasting, especially when they are based on experiences with strong unconditioned stimuli. Combat veterans and victims of violent crime, terrorism, or other traumatic events may show intense fear responses to trauma-related stimuli for many years afterward. As described in the chapter on health, stress, and coping, these symptoms, combined with others such as distressing dreams about the troubling events, characterize posttraumatic stress disorder (PTSD).

Classical conditioning procedures can be employed to treat phobias, and even PTSD. Joseph Wolpe (1958) pioneered the development of this methodology. Using techniques first developed with laboratory animals, Wolpe showed that irrational fears could be relieved through *systematic desensitization*, a procedure that associates a new response, such as relaxation, with a feared stimulus. To treat a thunderstorm phobia, for instance, a therapist might first teach the client to relax deeply and then associate that relaxation with increasingly intense sights and sounds of thunderstorms presented on videotape (Öst, 1978). Because, as Wolpe noted, a person cannot be relaxed and afraid at the same time, the new conditioned response (relaxation) to thunderstorms replaces the old one (fear). Desensitization is discussed in more detail in the chapter on the treatment of psychological disorders.

● **Predator Control**   The power of classically conditioned taste aversion has been put to work to help ranchers who are plagued by wolves and coyotes that kill and eat their sheep. To alleviate this problem without killing the predators, some ranchers have set out lithium-laced mutton for marauding wolves and coyotes to eat. The dizziness and nausea caused by the lithium becomes associated with the smell and taste of mutton, thus making sheep an undesirable meal for these predators and protecting the ranchers' livelihood (Garcia, Rusiniak, & Brett, 1977).

LINKAGES (a link to Treatment of Psychological Disorders, p. 654)

Using Classical Conditioning to Save People and Tigers   A program supported by the government of India has greatly reduced human deaths from tiger attacks, as well as the need to kill marauding tigers. Stuffed dummies—connected by hidden wires to a shock generator—are placed in areas in which tigers have attacked people. When the animals approach, they receive a shock (unconditioned stimulus), which they learn to associate with the human form. Humans thus become a conditioned stimulus for fear, and the tigers learn to avoid them (conditioned response). Other classical conditioning methods have helped ranchers in the western United States to prevent grazing horses and cattle from eating poisonous plants (Pfister et al., 2003).

● **Detecting Explosives**   Researchers are using classical conditioning to teach insects to help detect explosive material. In one project with wasps, the taste of sugar water is repeatedly paired with the smell of a chemical used in certain explosives. The wasps quickly develop a conditioned response to the smell alone. When several of these trained insects are placed in a plastic tube and brought near the target chemical, they display an immediate attraction to it (Rains, Utley, & Lewis, 2006). Researchers hope that it may someday be possible to use these so-called wasp hounds and other similar devices to detect explosives or drugs concealed in airline passengers' luggage.

● **Predicting Alzheimer's Disease**   A puff of air directed at your eye is an unconditioned stimulus that causes the reflexive unconditioned response we call an *eye blink*. If each air puff is preceded by a flash of light, the light will become a conditioned stimulus that can then cause an eye blink on its own. Research with animals has demonstrated that the hippocampus, a brain structure that is damaged in the early stages of Alzheimer's disease, is involved in the development of this type of conditioned response (Green & Woodruff-Pak, 2000). That research is now being applied to identify people who are at high risk for this devastating brain disorder. One study found that elderly people whose eye-blink conditioning was impaired were the ones most likely to develop Alzheimer's disease in the next two or three years (Downey-Lamb & Woodruff-Pak, 1999). Knowing who is at risk for Alzheimer's disease is important because it allows doctors to offer these people medication that can delay the emergence of the disease.

Operant Conditioning: Learning the Consequences of Behavior

Classical conditioning is an important kind of learning, but it can't explain most of what people learn on a daily basis. In classical conditioning, neutral and unconditioned stimuli are predictably paired, and the result is an association between the two. The association is shown by the conditioned response that occurs when the conditioned stimulus appears. Notice that both stimuli occur *before* or *along with* the conditioned response. But people also learn associations between their actions and the stimuli that *follow* them—in other words, between behavior and its consequences. A child learns to say "please" to get a piece of candy; a headache sufferer learns to take a pill to escape pain; a dog learns to "shake hands" to get a treat.

● From the Puzzle Box to the Skinner Box

Much of the groundwork for research on the consequences of behavior was done by Edward L. Thorndike, an American psychologist. While Pavlov was exploring classical conditioning in animals, Thorndike was studying animals' intelligence and ability to solve problems. He would place an animal, usually a hungry cat, in a *puzzle box*, where it had to learn some response—say, stepping on a pedal—in order to unlock the door and get to some food (see Figure 6.5). The animal would solve the puzzle, but very slowly. It did not appear to understand, or suddenly gain insight into, the problem (Thorndike, 1898).

So what were Thorndike's cats learning? Thorndike argued that any response (such as pressing the pedal) that produces a satisfying effect (such as access to food) gradually becomes stronger, whereas any response (such as pacing or meowing) that does not produce a satisfying effect gradually becomes weaker. The cats' learning, said Thorndike, is governed by the **law of effect**. According to this law, if a response made in the presence of a particular stimulus is followed by satisfaction (such as a reward), that response is more likely to be made the next time the stimulus is encountered. Responses that produce discomfort are less likely to be performed again. Thorndike described this kind of learning as *instrumental conditioning*, because responses are strengthened when they are instrumental in producing rewards (Thorndike, 1905).

law of effect   A law stating that if a response made in the presence of a particular stimulus is followed by satisfaction, that response is more likely next time the stimulus is encountered.

Thorndike's Puzzle Box

This drawing illustrates the kind of "puzzle box" used in Thorndike's research. His cats learned to open the door and reach food by stepping on the pedal, but the learning occurred gradually. Some cats actually took longer to get out of the box on one trial than on a previous trial.

About forty years after Thorndike published his work, B. F. Skinner extended and formalized many of Thorndike's ideas. Skinner (1938) emphasized that during instrumental conditioning, an organism learns a response by *operating on* the environment, so he called the process of learning these responses **operant conditioning.** His primary aim was to analyze how behavior is changed by its consequences. To study operant conditioning, Skinner devised a chamber that, despite his objections, became known as the *Skinner box.* This chamber differed from Thorndike's puzzle box in an important way: The puzzle box measured learning in terms of whether an animal successfully completed a trial (i.e., got out of the box) and how long it took to do so. The Skinner box measures learning in terms of how often an animal responds during a specified period of time (Barker, 1997).

● Basic Components of Operant Conditioning

The tools Skinner devised allowed him and other researchers to precisely arrange relationships between a response and its consequences and then to analyze how those consequences affected behavior over time. They found that the basic phenomena

Edward L. Thorndike (1874–1949) and B. F. Skinner (1904–1990)
Edward Thorndike (left) and B. F. Skinner (shown at right with a "Skinner box") studied instrumental and operant conditioning, respectively. Though similar in most respects, instrumental and operant conditioning differ in one way. In instrumental conditioning, the experimenter defines each opportunity for the organism to produce a response, and conditioning is usually measured by how long it takes for the response to appear. In operant conditioning, the organism can make responses at any time; conditioning is measured by the *rate* of responding. In this chapter, the term *operant conditioning* refers to both kinds of conditioning.

Edward Thorndike photo: Psychology Archives—The University of Akron

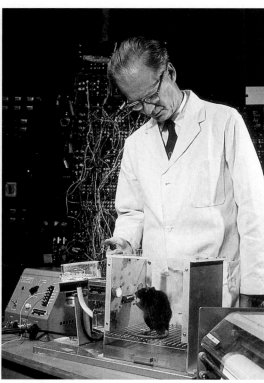

POSITIVE REINFORCEMENT

| **Behavior** You put coins into a vending machine. | → | **Presentation of a pleasant or positive stimulus** You receive a cold can of soda. | → | **Frequency of behavior increases** You put coins in vending machines in the future. |

NEGATIVE REINFORCEMENT

| **Behavior** In the middle of a boring date, you say you have a headache. | → | **Termination of an unpleasant stimulus** The date ends early. | → | **Frequency of behavior increases** You use the same tactic on future boring dates. |

FIGURE 6.6

Positive and Negative Reinforcement

TRY THIS ⚙ Remember that behavior is strengthened through *positive reinforcement* when something pleasant or desirable occurs following the behavior. Behavior is strengthened through *negative reinforcement* when the behavior results in the termination of something unpleasant. To see how these principles apply in your own life, list two examples of situations in which your behavior was affected by positive reinforcement and two in which you were affected by negative reinforcement.

operant conditioning A process through which an organism learns to respond to the environment in a way that produces positive consequences and avoids negative ones.

operant A response that has some effect on the world.

reinforcer A stimulus event that increases the probability that the response that immediately preceded it will occur again.

positive reinforcers Stimuli that strengthen a response if they follow that response.

negative reinforcers The removal of unpleasant stimuli, such as pain.

escape conditioning A type of learning in which an organism learns to make a particular response in order to terminate an aversive stimulus.

seen in classical conditioning—such as stimulus generalization, stimulus discrimination, extinction, and spontaneous recovery—also occur in operant conditioning. However, operant conditioning involves additional concepts and processes as well. Let's consider these now.

● **Operants and Reinforcers** Skinner introduced the term *operant* or *operant response* to distinguish the responses in operant conditioning from those in classical conditioning. Recall that in classical conditioning, the conditioned response doesn't affect whether or when a stimulus occurs. Dogs salivated when a tone sounded, but the salivation had no effect on the tone or on whether food was presented. In contrast, an **operant** is a response that has some effect on the world; it is a response that *operates on* the environment. For example, when a child says, "Momma, I'm hungry," and is then fed, the child has made an operant response that influences when food will appear.

A **reinforcer** increases the probability that an operant behavior will occur again. There are two main types of reinforcers: positive and negative. **Positive reinforcers** strengthen a response if they are experienced after that response occurs. They are roughly equivalent to rewards. The food given to a hungry pigeon after it pecks at a switch is a positive reinforcer; it increases the pigeon's switch pecking. For people, positive reinforcers can include food, smiles, money, and other desirable outcomes. The process of presenting a positive reinforcer after a response is called *positive reinforcement*. **Negative reinforcers** are the *removal* of unpleasant stimuli such as pain, noise, threats, or a disapproving frown. For example, the disappearance of headache pain after you take an aspirin is a negative reinforcer that makes you more likely to take that pain reliever in the future. When a response is strengthened by the removal of an unpleasant stimulus, the process is called *negative reinforcement*. So reinforcement can be presenting something pleasant or removing something unpleasant, but in either case it always *increases* the strength of the behavior that precedes it (see Figure 6.6).

● **Escape and Avoidance Conditioning** The effects of negative reinforcement can be seen in escape conditioning and avoidance conditioning. **Escape conditioning** occurs as a person or animal learns responses that stop an aversive stimulus. The left-hand panel of Figure 6.7 shows a laboratory example in which

Escape conditioning

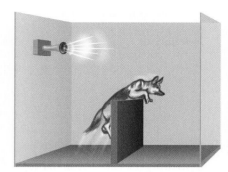

Avoidance conditioning

FIGURE 6.7

A Shuttle Box

A shuttle box has two sections, and its floor is an electric grid. The left-hand panel shows escape conditioning, in which an animal learns to get away from a mild shock by jumping over the barrier. The next two panels show avoidance conditioning. Here, the animal has learned to avoid shock by jumping over the barrier when it hears a warning buzzer just before shock occurs. Remember that in escape conditioning the learned response *stops* an aversive stimulus; in avoidance conditioning the learned response *prevents* the aversive stimulus from occurring in the first place.

Source: Adapted from Hintzman (1978).

dogs learn to jump over the barrier in a shuttle box to get away from a shock. In humans, escape conditioning appears not only when we learn to take pills to stop pain but also when parents learn to stop a child's annoying demands for a toy by agreeing to buy it. And television viewers learn to use the mute button to shut off obnoxious commercials.

When an animal or a person responds to a signal in a way that avoids an aversive stimulus that has not yet arrived, **avoidance conditioning** has occurred. Look at the right-hand sections of Figure 6.7 and imagine that a buzzer sounds a few seconds before one side of the shuttle box is electrified. The animal will soon learn to jump over the barrier when the warning buzzer sounds, thus avoiding the shock. Along with positive reinforcement, avoidance conditioning is one of the most important influences on everyday behavior. We go to work or school even when we would rather stay in bed, we stop at red lights even when we are in a hurry, and we apologize for our mistakes even before they are discovered. Each of these behaviors helps us avoid a negative consequence, such as lost pay, bad grades, a traffic ticket, or a scolding.

Notice that avoidance conditioning involves a marriage of classical and operant conditioning. In the shuttle box, for example, the buzzer signals that an unconditioned stimulus (shock) is about to occur. Through classical conditioning, this signal becomes a conditioned stimulus that triggers fear as a conditioned response. Like the shock itself, fear is unpleasant. Once the animal learns to jump over the barrier to avoid shock, this operant response is reinforced by its consequences—the reduction of fear. In short, avoidance conditioning takes place in two steps. The first step involves classical conditioning—a signal is repeatedly paired with shock. The second step involves operant conditioning—learning to make a response that reduces fear.

Once learned, avoidance is a difficult habit to break, because avoidance responses continue to be reinforced by fear reduction (Solomon, Kamin, & Wynne, 1953). So even if the shock is turned off in a shuttle box, animals may keep jumping when the buzzer sounds because they never discover that avoidance is no longer necessary. The same is often true of people. Those who fear and avoid, say, escalators never get a chance to find out that they are safe. And those with limited social skills may avoid potentially embarrassing social situations, but doing so also prevents them from learning how to be successful in those situations.

The study of avoidance conditioning has not only expanded our understanding of negative reinforcement but has also led psychologists to consider more complex cognitive processes in learning. They suggest, for example, that in order for people to learn to avoid an unpleasant event (such as getting fired or paying a fine), they

● **avoidance conditioning** A type of learning in which an organism responds to a signal in a way that prevents exposure to an aversive stimulus.

● **discriminative stimuli** Stimuli that signal whether reinforcement is available if a certain response is made.

"Oh, not bad. The light comes on, I press the bar, they write me a check. How about you?"

Although the artist may not have intended it, this cartoon nicely illustrates one way in which discriminative stimuli can affect behavior.

© The New Yorker Collection 1993 Tom Cheney from cartoonbank.com. All Rights Reserved.

must have established an expectancy or other mental representation of that event. The role of these mental representations is emphasized later in this chapter in our discussion of the cognitive factors involved in learning.

● **Discriminative Stimuli and Stimulus Control** The consequences of behavior can be different in different situations, so success in life often depends on the ability to identify and quickly adjust to changing environments. For example, if pigeons are reinforced with food for pecking at a switch when a red light is on but are not reinforced for pecking when a green light is on, they will soon learn to peck only when they see a red light. Their behavior demonstrates the effect of **discriminative stimuli,** which are stimuli that signal whether a reinforcer is available if a certain response is made. Most people, too, are sensitive to discriminative stimuli. They know that a flirtatious comment about someone's appearance may be welcomed on a date, but not at the office. And even if you have been repeatedly rewarded for telling jokes, you are not likely to do so at a funeral.

When an organism learns to make a particular response in the presence of one stimulus but not another, *stimulus discrimination* has occurred (see Figure 6.8).

FIGURE 6.8

Stimulus Discrimination

In this experiment the rat could jump from a stand through any of three doors. However, it was reinforced only if it jumped through the door that differed from the other two. The rat learned to do this quite well. On this trial, it discriminated vertical from horizontal stripes.

Getting the Hang of It Learning to eat with a spoon is, as you can see, a hit-and-miss process at first. However, this child will learn to hit the target more and more often as the food reward gradually shapes a more efficient, and far less messy, pattern of behavior.

Another way to say this is that the response is now under *stimulus control*. In general, stimulus discrimination allows people and animals to learn what is appropriate (reinforced) and inappropriate (not reinforced) in particular situations.

Stimulus generalization also occurs in operant conditioning. For example, a pigeon might peck when it sees an amber light because that light is similar to the red one that had previously signaled the availability of reinforcement. And as in classical conditioning, the more similar the new stimulus is to the old one, the more likely it is that the response will be performed. So if you had a wonderful dinner at "Captain Jack's," a restaurant that was decorated to look like the inside of a sailing ship, you might later choose to eat at places with similar names or interiors.

As in classical conditioning, stimulus discrimination and stimulus generalization often complement each other in operant conditioning. In one study, for example, pigeons received food for pecking at a switch, but only when they saw certain works of art (Watanabe, Sakamoto, & Wakita, 1995). As a result, these birds learned to discriminate the works of the impressionist painter Claude Monet from those of the cubist painter Pablo Picasso. Later, when the birds were shown new paintings by other impressionist and cubist artists, they were able to generalize from the original artists to other artists who painted in the same style. It was as if they had learned the conceptual categories of "impressionism" and "cubism." We humans learn to place people and things into even more finely detailed categories, such as "honest," "dangerous," or "tax deductible." We discriminate one stimulus from another and then, through generalization, respond similarly to all stimuli we perceive to be in a particular category. This ability to respond in a similar way to all members of a category can save us considerable time and effort, but it can also lead to the development of unwarranted prejudice against certain groups of people (see the chapter on social cognition).

● Forming and Strengthening Operant Behavior

Daily life is full of examples of operant conditioning. People go to movies, parties, classes, and jobs primarily because doing so brings reinforcers. Let's consider how operant behavior develops and how the type and timing of reinforcers affect the operant conditioning process.

● **Shaping** Imagine that you want to train your dog, Henry, to sit and to "shake hands." The basic method using positive reinforcement is obvious: Every time Henry sits and shakes hands, you give him a treat. But the problem is also obvious: Smart as Henry is, he may never make the desired response on his own, so you will never be able to give the reinforcer. Instead of your teaching and Henry's learning, the two of you will just stare at each other (and he'll probably wag his tail).

The way around this problem is to *shape* Henry's behavior. **Shaping** is accomplished by reinforcing *successive approximations*—that is, responses that come successively closer to the desired response. So you might first give Henry a treat whenever he sits down. Then you might reinforce him only when he sits and partially lifts a paw. Next, you might reinforce more complete paw lifting. Eventually, you would require that Henry perform the entire sit-lift-shake sequence before giving the treat. Shaping is an extremely powerful, widely used tool. Animal trainers use it to teach chimpanzees to roller-skate, dolphins to jump through hoops, and pigeons to play Ping-Pong (Coren, 1999).

● **Secondary Reinforcement** Often, operant conditioning begins with the use of **primary reinforcers**, events or stimuli—such as food or water—that are innately rewarding. But Henry's training will be slowed if he has to stop and eat every time he makes a correct response. Also, once he is full, food will no longer act as an effective reinforcer. To avoid these problems, animal trainers and others in the teaching business rely on the principle of secondary reinforcement.

shaping The process of reinforcing responses that come successively closer to the desired response.

primary reinforcers Reinforcers that meet an organism's basic needs, such as food and water.

Secondary Reinforcers A touch or a smile, words of praise or thanks, and a loving or approving look are just a few of the social stimuli that can serve as secondary reinforcers for humans. Parents have used these reinforcers for generations to shape the behavior of children in accordance with their cultural values.

A **secondary reinforcer** is a previously neutral stimulus that, when paired with a stimulus that is already reinforcing, will take on reinforcing properties. In other words, secondary reinforcers are rewards that people or animals learn to like. For example, if you say, "Good boy!" a moment before you give Henry each food reward, these words will become associated with the food and can then be used alone to reinforce Henry's behavior (as long as the words are again paired with food now and then). Does this remind you of classical conditioning? It should, because the primary reinforcer (food) is an unconditioned stimulus. If the sound of "Good boy!" predictably precedes, and thus signals, food, it becomes a conditioned stimulus. For this reason, secondary reinforcers are sometimes called *conditioned reinforcers*.

The power of operant conditioning can be greatly increased by using secondary reinforcers. Consider the secondary reinforcer we call money. Some people will do almost anything for it despite the fact that it tastes terrible and won't quench your thirst. Its reinforcing power lies in its association with the many rewards it can buy. Smiles and other forms of social approval (such as the words "Great work!") are also important secondary reinforcers for human beings. However, what becomes a secondary reinforcer can vary a great deal from person to person and culture to culture. For example, tickets to a rock concert are an effective secondary reinforcer for some people, but not everyone. And a ceremony honoring outstanding job performance might be highly reinforcing to most employees in individualist cultures, but it might be embarrassing for some employees from cultures in which group cooperation is valued more than personal distinction (Miller, 2001). Still, when chosen carefully, secondary reinforcers can build or maintain behavior even when primary reinforcement is absent for long periods.

● **Delay and Size of Reinforcement** Much of our behavior is learned and maintained because it is regularly reinforced. But many people overeat, smoke, drink too much, or procrastinate, even though they know these behaviors are bad for them. They may want to change, but they seem to lack "self-control." If behavior is controlled by its consequences, why do people do things that are ultimately harmful?

Part of the answer lies in the *timing* of reinforcers. In general, the effect of a reinforcer is stronger when it comes soon after a response occurs (Rachlin, 2000). The good feelings (positive reinforcers) that follow, say, drinking too much are immediate and strong. The hangovers and other negative consequences are usually delayed, so their effects on future drinking are weakened. Similarly, a dieter's efforts to eat less will eventually lead to weight loss, but because that positive reinforcer is delayed, it may have less impact than the immediate pleasure of eating a jelly donut. In fact, under some conditions, delaying a positive reinforcer for even a few seconds can decrease the effectiveness of positive reinforcement. (An advantage of praise or other secondary reinforcers is that they can easily be delivered immediately after a desired response occurs.)

The *size* of a reinforcer is also important. In general, operant conditioning creates more vigorous behavior when the reinforcer is large than when it is small. For example, a strong electrical shock will cause a faster escape or avoidance response than a weak one.

● **Schedules of Reinforcement** We flip a light switch, and the light comes on. We put money in a vending machine, and the item we want comes out. When a reinforcer is delivered every time a particular response occurs, the arrangement is called a **continuous reinforcement schedule**. This schedule can be helpful when teaching someone a new skill, but it can be impractical in the long run. Imagine how inefficient it would be, for example, if an employer had to deliver praise or pay following every little task employees performed all day long. So quite often, reinforcement is administered only some of the time, on a **partial reinforcement schedule**, also called an *intermittent reinforcement schedule*.

● **secondary reinforcer** A reward that people or animals learn to like.

● **continuous reinforcement schedule** A pattern in which a reinforcer is delivered every time a particular response occurs.

● **partial reinforcement schedule** A pattern in which a reinforcer is administered only some of the time after a particular response occurs.

Most partial reinforcement schedules can be described in terms of when and how reinforcers are given. "When" refers to the number of responses that have to occur, or the amount of time that must pass, before a reinforcer will occur. "How" refers to whether the reinforcer will be delivered in a predictable or unpredictable way. Accordingly, there are four basic types of intermittent reinforcement schedules:

1. *Fixed-ratio (FR) schedules* provide a reinforcer following a fixed number of responses. So rats might receive food after every tenth time they press the lever in a Skinner box (FR 10) or after every twentieth time (FR 20). Computer help desk technicians might be allowed to take a break after every fifth call they handle, or every tenth.

2. *Variable-ratio (VR) schedules* also provide a reinforcer after a given number of responses, but that number can vary. On these schedules, it is impossible to predict which particular response will bring reinforcement. A rat on a VR 30 schedule might sometimes be reinforced after ten lever presses, sometimes after fifty, and sometimes after five, but the *average* number of responses required to get a reinforcer would be thirty. Gambling offers humans a similar variable-ratio schedule. A slot machine, for example, pays off only after a frustratingly unpredictable number of lever pulls, averaging perhaps one in twenty.

3. *Fixed-interval (FI) schedules* provide a reinforcer for the first response that occurs after some fixed time has passed since the last reward, no matter how many responses have been made during that interval. For example, on an FI 60 schedule, the first response after sixty seconds have passed will be rewarded. Some radio stations create fixed-interval schedules by telling listeners who just won a prize that they are not eligible to win again for thirty days. Under these circumstances, there is no point in competing until that time has elapsed.

4. *Variable-interval (VI) schedules* reinforce the first response after some period of time, but the amount of time varies. On a VI 60 schedule, for example, the first response to occur after an *average* of 60 seconds is reinforced, but the actual time between reinforcements might vary from, say, 1 second to 120 seconds. Some teachers use VI schedules to help keep order in class by giving "points"—at unpredictably varying intervals—to children who are in their seats. A VI schedule has also been successfully used to encourage seat belt use: During a ten-week test in Illinois, police stopped drivers at random times and awarded prizes to those who were buckled up (Mortimer et al., 1988).

Different schedules of reinforcement produce different patterns of responding, as Figure 6.9 shows (Skinner, 1961). The figure illustrates two important points. First, both fixed-ratio and variable-ratio schedules produce high rates of behavior overall. The reason in both cases is that the frequency of the reward depends directly on the rate of responding. Industrial/organizational psychologists have applied this principle to help companies increase worker productivity and reduce absenteeism. Workers who are paid on the basis of the number of items they produce or the number of days they show up for work usually produce more items and miss fewer workdays (Muchinsky, 2003). Similarly, gamblers reinforced on a variable-ratio schedule for pulling a slot machine handle, rolling dice, or playing other games of chance tend to maintain a high rate of responding—some people may become virtually unable to stop.

The second important aspect of Figure 6.9 relates to the curves, or "scallops," shown in the fixed-interval schedule. Under this schedule, it does not matter how many responses are made during the time between rewards. As a result, the rate of responding typically drops dramatically immediately after a reinforcer occurs and then increases as the time for another reward approaches. When teachers schedule

TRY THIS **Reinforcement Schedules on the Job** Make a list of all the jobs you have ever held, along with the reinforcement schedule on which each employer paid you. Which of the four types of schedules (FR, FI, VR, VI) was most common, and which did you find most satisfying?

● **fixed-ratio (FR) schedule** A partial reinforcement schedule that provides reinforcement following a fixed number of responses.

● **variable-ratio (VR) schedule** A partial reinforcement schedule that provides reinforcement after a varying number of responses.

● **fixed-interval (FI) schedule** A partial reinforcement schedule that provides reinforcement for the first response that occurs after some fixed time has passed since the last reward.

● **variable-interval (VI) schedule** A partial reinforcement schedule that provides reinforcement for the first response after varying periods of time.

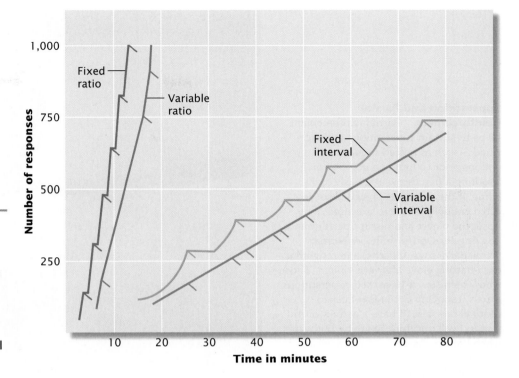

FIGURE 6.9

Schedules of Reinforcement

These curves illustrate the patterns of behavior typically seen under different reinforcement schedules. The steeper the curve, the faster the response rate. The thin diagonal lines crossing the curves show when reinforcement was given. In general, the rate of responding is higher under ratio schedules than under interval schedules.

all their quizzes in advance, for example, some students study just before each quiz and then virtually stop studying in that course until just before the next quiz. Behavior rewarded on variable-interval schedules looks quite different. The unpredictable timing of rewards typically generates slow, steady responding. So students whose teacher might give a pop quiz at any class session are more likely to study for that course almost every day (Kouyoumdjian, 2004).

● **Schedules and Extinction**   In the section on classical conditioning we saw that if a conditioned stimulus (CS) no longer predicts the appearance of an unconditioned stimulus, the conditioned response to that CS will weaken through the process called extinction. Similarly, if an operant response is no longer followed by a reinforcer, the response will occur less and less often and eventually may disappear, or *extinguish*. If lever pressing no longer brings food, a rat stops pressing; if repeated text messages to a friend are not answered, you eventually stop sending them. As in classical conditioning, extinction in operant conditioning does not totally erase learned relationships (Delamater, 2004). If a signaling stimulus reappears at some time after an operant response has been extinguished, that response may recur (spontaneously recover), and if it is again reinforced, it will be quickly return to its former level, as though extinction had never happened.

In general, behaviors learned under a partial reinforcement schedule are far more difficult to extinguish than those learned on a continuous reinforcement schedule. This phenomenon—called the **partial reinforcement extinction effect**—is easy to understand if you imagine yourself in a gambling casino, standing near a broken slot machine and a broken candy machine. You might put money in the broken candy machine once, but this behavior will probably stop (extinguish) very quickly. The candy machine should deliver its goodies on a continuous reinforcement schedule, so you can easily tell that it is not going to provide a reinforcer. But slot machines offer rewards on an unpredictable intermittent schedule, so you might put in coin after coin, unsure of whether the machine is broken or is simply not paying off at that particular moment.

---

extinction   The gradual disappearance of operant behavior due to elimination of rewards for that behavior.

partial reinforcement extinction effect   A phenomenon in which behaviors learned under a partial reinforcement schedule are more difficult to extinguish than behaviors learned on a continuous reinforcement schedule.

Superstition and Partial Reinforcement Partial reinforcement helps to sustain superstitious athletic rituals—such as a fixed sequence of actions prior to hitting a golf ball or shooting a free throw in a basketball game. If the ritual has preceded success often enough, failure to execute it may upset the player and disrupt performance. Los Angeles Dodger infielder Nomar Garciaparra tugs, loosens, and retightens each batting glove after every pitch. Those who watch sports have their superstitious rituals, too. One Green Bay Packers football fan said, "I have a certain outfit I wear. I will not drink anything but water when I'm watching. . . . And I have a touchdown dance I have to do or they won't score again" (Pearson, 2000).

Partial reinforcement also helps explain why superstitious behavior is so resistant to extinction (Vyse, 2000). Suppose you had been out for a run just before hearing that you passed an important exam. The run did nothing to cause this outcome; the reward followed it through sheer luck. Still, for some people, this *accidental reinforcement* can function like a partial reinforcement schedule, strengthening actions that preceded, and thus appeared to "cause," good news or other rewards or events (Pronin et al., 2006). Those people might then run "for luck" after every exam, or take exams only with their "lucky pen," or while wearing their "lucky shirt." Of course, the laws of chance dictate that doing such things is bound to be followed by something good every now and then, thus further strengthening the superstitious behavior on a sparse partial schedule (Vyse, 2000).

● Why Reinforcers Work

What makes reinforcers reinforcing? For primary reinforcers, at least, the reason could be that they satisfy hunger, thirst, and other needs that are basic to survival. This explanation is incomplete, however, because substances such as saccharin, which have no nutritional value, can have as much reinforcing power as sugar, which is nutritious. Further, addictive drugs are powerful reinforcers even though they threaten the health of people who use them.

Some psychologists have argued that reinforcement is based not on a stimulus itself but on the opportunity to engage in an activity that involves the stimulus. According to David Premack (1965), for example, at any moment each person maintains a list of behavioral preferences, ranked from most desirable to least desirable, like a kind of psychological "Top Ten." The higher on the list an activity is, the greater is its power as a reinforcer. This means that a preferred activity can serve as a reinforcer for any other activity that is less preferred at the moment. For example, when parents allow their teenage daughter to use the car in return for mowing the lawn, they are using something high on her preference list (driving) to reinforce an activity that is lower on the list (lawn mowing). This idea is known as the *Premack principle.*

Taking the Premack principle a step further, some psychologists have suggested that virtually any activity can become a reinforcer if a person or animal has not been allowed to perform that activity for a while (Timberlake & Farmer-Dougan, 1991). To understand how this *response deprivation hypothesis* works, suppose that you would rather study than work out at the gym. Now suppose that the gym has been closed for several weeks, and you have been unable to have a workout. According to the response deprivation hypothesis, because your opportunity to exercise has been held below its normal level, its value as a reinforcer has been raised. In fact, it might have become so preferred that it could be used to reinforce studying! In short, under certain circumstances, even activities that are normally not strongly preferred can become reinforcers for normally more preferred activities. The response deprivation hypothesis helps explain why money is such a powerful secondary reinforcer: It can be exchanged for whatever a person finds reinforcing at the moment. In fact, some researchers believe that the response deprivation hypothesis may provide a better overall explanation of why reinforcers work than the Premack principle does (Hergenhahn & Olson, 1997).

Research by biological psychologists suggests that the stimuli and activities we know as reinforcers may work by exerting particular effects within the brain. This possibility was raised decades ago when James Olds and Peter Milner (1954) discovered that mild electrical stimulation of certain areas of the hypothalamus can be such a powerful reinforcer that a hungry rat will ignore food in a Skinner box, preferring to spend hours pressing a lever that stimulates these "pleasure centers" in its brain (Olds, 1973). It is not yet clear whether physiological mechanisms underlie the power of all reinforcers, but evidence available so far suggests that these mechanisms are important components of the process (Waelti, Dickinson, & Schultz, 2001). For example, as mentioned in the chapter on biological aspects of psychology, activation of dopamine systems is associated with the pleasure of many stimuli, including food, music, sex, the uncertainty involved in gambling, and some addictive drugs, such as cocaine (Berns et al., 2001; Blood & Zatorre, 2001; Ciccocioppo, Sanna, & Weiss, 2001; Reuter et al., 2005; Tobler, Fiorillo, & Schultz, 2005). Indeed, it appears that complex and widespread patterns of brain activity are involved in our response to reinforcers, allowing us to enjoy them, to learn to want them, and to learn how to get them (Montague, Hyman, & Cohen, 2004; Pessiglione et al., 2006; Robinson et al., 2005).

● Punishment

So far, we have discussed positive and negative reinforcement, both of which *increase* the frequency of a response, either by presenting something pleasurable or by removing something unpleasant. In contrast, **punishment** *reduces* the frequency of an operant behavior by presenting an unpleasant stimulus or removing a pleasant one. Shouting "No!" and swatting your cat when she begins chewing on your plants illustrates the kind of punishment that presents an unpleasant stimulus following a response. Taking away a child's TV privileges because of rude behavior is a second kind of punishment—sometimes called *penalty*—that removes a positive stimulus (see Figure 6.10).

Punishment is often confused with negative reinforcement, but they are actually quite different. Reinforcement of any sort always *strengthens* behavior; punishment weakens it. If shock is *turned off* when a rat presses a lever, that is negative reinforcement. It increases the chances that the rat will press the lever when shock occurs again. But if shock is *turned on* when the rat presses the lever, that is punishment. The rat will be less likely to press the lever again.

Punishment can certainly alter behavior, but it has several potential drawbacks (Gershoff, 2002). First, it does not "erase" an undesirable habit; it merely suppresses it. This suppression usually occurs in the presence of stimuli (such as a parent or teacher) that were around at the time of punishment. In other words, people

● **punishment**   Presentation of an aversive stimulus or the removal of a pleasant stimulus.

FIGURE 6.10

Two Kinds of Punishment

In one form of punishment, a behavior is followed by an aversive or unpleasant stimulus. In a second form of punishment, sometimes called *penalty*, a pleasant stimulus is removed following a behavior. In either case, punishment reduces the chances that the behavior will occur in the future. When a toddler reaches toward an electric outlet and her father says "NO!" and gently taps her hand, is that punishment or negative reinforcement? (If you said "punishment," you are right, because it will *reduce* the likelihood of touching outlets in the future.)

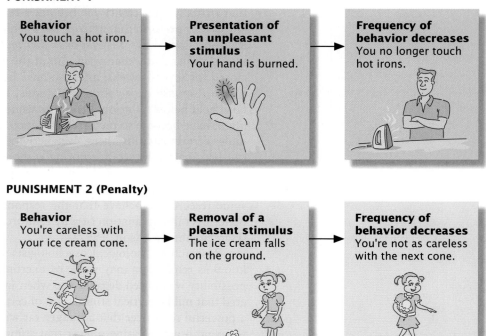

PUNISHMENT 1

Behavior
You touch a hot iron.

Presentation of an unpleasant stimulus
Your hand is burned.

Frequency of behavior decreases
You no longer touch hot irons.

PUNISHMENT 2 (Penalty)

Behavior
You're careless with your ice cream cone.

Removal of a pleasant stimulus
The ice cream falls on the ground.

Frequency of behavior decreases
You're not as careless with the next cone.

may repeat previously punished acts when they think they can avoid detection. This tendency is summed up in the adage "When the cat's away, the mice will play." Second, punishment sometimes produces unwanted side effects. For example, if you severely punish a child for swearing, the child may associate punishment with the punisher and end up fearing you. Third, punishment is often ineffective unless it is given immediately after the response and each time the response is made. This is especially true in relation to animals or young children. If a child gets into a cookie jar and enjoys a few cookies before being discovered and punished, the effect of the punishment will be greatly reduced. Similarly, if a child confesses to misbehavior and is then punished, the punishment may discourage honesty rather than eliminate undesirable behavior. Fourth, physical punishment can become aggression and even abuse if administered in anger. Fifth, because children tend to imitate what they see, children who are frequently punished may be more likely to behave aggressively themselves (Gilbert, 1997). Finally, although punishment signals that inappropriate behavior occurred, it does not specify what should be done instead. An F on a term paper says the assignment was poorly done, but the grade alone tells the student nothing about how to improve.

In the 1970s and 1980s, concerns over these drawbacks led many professionals to discourage parents from using spanking and other forms of punishment with their children (Rosellini, 1998). The debate about punishment has been reopened more recently by studies suggesting that spanking can be an effective way to control the behavior of children who are between three and thirteen years of age. These studies found that occasional spanking does not harm children's development, if used in combination with other disciplinary practices. These other practices include requiring that the children pay some penalty for their misdeeds, having them provide some sort of restitution to the victims of their actions, and making them aware of what they did wrong (Gunnoe & Mariner, 1997; Larzelere, 1996).

When used *properly*, then, punishment can be a valuable tool (Baumrind, Larzelere, & Cowan, 2002). Occasionally, it may be the only alternative. For example, some children suffer developmental disabilities in which they hit or mutilate themselves or display other potentially life-threatening behaviors. As shown in Figure 6.11, punishing these behaviors has sometimes proven to be the only effective treatment

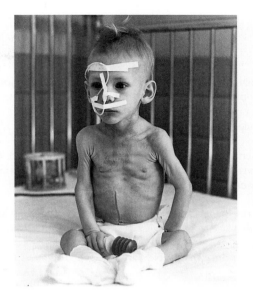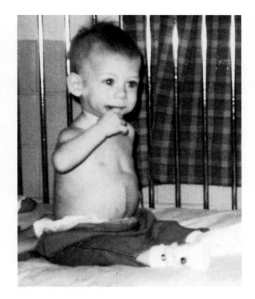

FIGURE 6.11

Lifesaving Punishment

This child suffered from chronic ruminative disorder, a condition in which he vomited everything he ate. At left, the boy was approximately one year old and had been vomiting for four months. At right is the same child thirteen days after punishment with electric shock had eliminated the vomiting behavior. His weight had increased 26 percent. He was physically and psychologically healthy when tested six months, one year, and two years later (Lang & Melamed, 1969).

Source: Lang & Melamed (1969).

(e.g., Flavell et al., 1982). Whatever the case, punishment is most effective when it is administered in accordance with several guidelines. First, the person giving punishment should specify why it is being given and that its purpose is to change the person's behavior, not to harm or demean the person. This step helps prevent a general fear of the punisher. Second, without being abusive, punishment should be immediate and noticeable enough to eliminate the undesirable behavior. A halfhearted "Quit it" may actually reinforce a child's misbehavior, because almost any attention is reinforcing to some children. Moreover, if children become habituated to very mild punishment, the parent may end up using substantially more severe punishment to stop inappropriate behavior than would have been necessary if a stern, but moderate, punishment had been used in the first place. (You may have witnessed this *escalation effect* in grocery stores or restaurants, where parents are often not initially firm enough in dealing with their children's misbehavior.) Finally, because punishment alone is usually not enough to change behavior in the long run, it is important also to identify what the person should do instead of the punished act and then to reinforce the appropriate behavior when it occurs. As the frequency of appropriate behavior increases through reinforcement, the frequency of undesirable responses (and the need for further punishment) should decline.

When these guidelines are not followed, the potentially beneficial effects of punishment may disappear or be only temporary. As illustrated in many countries' justice systems, punishment for criminal acts is typically administered long after the acts have occurred, and initial punishments are often relatively mild—as when offenders are repeatedly given probation. Even being sent to prison rarely leads to rehabilitation, because this punishment is usually not supplemented by efforts to teach and reinforce noncriminal lifestyles (Cassel & Bernstein, 2007). It is no wonder, then, that of the more than 2 million criminals in prison in the United States alone, about two-thirds are likely to be rearrested for serious crimes within three years of completing their sentences and that about 50 percent of them will return to prison (Cassel & Bernstein, 2007).

● Some Applications of Operant Conditioning

The principles of operant conditioning were originally developed with animals in the laboratory, but they are valuable for understanding human behavior in an endless variety of everyday situations. ("In Review: Reinforcement and Punishment" summarizes some key principles of operant conditioning.) The unscientific but effective use of rewards and punishments by parents, teachers, and peers is vital to helping

in review Reinforcement and Punishment

Concept	Description	Example or Comment
Positive reinforcement	Increasing the frequency of a behavior by following it with the presentation of a positive reinforcer—a pleasant, positive stimulus or experience	You say "Good job!" after someone works hard to perform a task.
Negative reinforcement	Increasing the frequency of a behavior by following it with the removal of an unpleasant stimulus or experience	You learn to use the "mute" button on the TV remote control to remove the sound of an obnoxious commercial.
Escape conditioning	Learning to make a response that removes an unpleasant stimulus	A little boy learns that crying will cut short the time that he must stay in his room.
Avoidance conditioning	Learning to make a response that avoids an unpleasant stimulus	You slow your car to the speed limit when you spot a police car, thus avoiding being stopped and reducing the fear of a fine; very resistant to extinction.
Punishment	Decreasing the frequency of a behavior by either presenting an unpleasant stimulus (punishment 1) or removing a pleasant one (punishment 2, or penalty)	You swat the dog after it steals food from the table, or you take a favorite toy away from a child who misbehaves. A number of cautions should be kept in mind before using punishment.

children learn what is and is not appropriate behavior at the dinner table, in the classroom, or at a birthday party. People learn how to be "civilized" in their own cultures partly through positive ("Good!") and negative ("Stop that!") responses from others. As described in the chapter on human development, differing patterns of rewards and punishments for boys and girls also underlie the development of behaviors that fit culturally approved *gender roles*.

The scientific study of operant conditioning has led to numerous treatment programs for modifying problematic behavior. These programs combine rewards for appropriate behaviors with extinction methods, or carefully administered punishment,

Speak Up!   Students are often reluctant to make comments or to ask or answer questions, especially in large classrooms. Some professors have used operant conditioning principles to help overcome this problem. In one introductory psychology course, classroom participation was reinforced with coin-like tokens that students could exchange for extra credit (Boniecki & Moore, 2003). The students responded faster to the professor's questions and offered many more comments and questions when this "token economy" was introduced. The frequency of student questions and comments dropped again when tokens were no longer given, but students continued their quick responses to the professor's questions. By that time, apparently, the professor's social reinforcement was enough to encourage this aspect of classroom participation.

for inappropriate behaviors. They have helped countless mental patients, mentally retarded or brain-damaged individuals, severely autistic children, and hard-to-manage preschoolers to develop the behaviors they need to live happier and more productive lives (e.g., Alberto, Troutman, & Feagin, 2002; Dickerson, Tenhula, & Green-Paden, 2005; Pear & Martin, 2002). These same methods have been used successfully to help keep former drug addicts drug free and to help patients with alcohol-related memory problems to recognize and remember new faces and names—including those of their own grandchildren (Hochhalter et al., 2001; Silverman et al., 2001). Many self-help books also incorporate principles of positive reinforcement, recommending self-reward following each small victory in efforts to lose weight, stop smoking, avoid procrastination, or reach other goals (e.g., Grant & Kim, 2002; Rachlin, 2000).

When people can't do anything about the consequences of a behavior, discriminative stimuli may hold the key to changing the behavior. For example, people trying to quit smoking often find it easier to do so if they stay away from bars and other places where there are discriminative stimuli for smoking. Stimulus control can also be applied in the treatment of insomnia. Insomniacs tend to use their beds for activities such as watching television, writing letters, reading magazines, worrying, and so on. Soon the bedroom becomes a discriminative stimulus for so many activities that relaxation and sleep become less and less likely. *Stimulus control therapy* encourages insomniacs to use their beds only for sleeping, and perhaps sex, making it more likely that they will sleep better when in bed (Edinger et al., 2001).

LINKAGES ⏀ Neural Networks and Learning

⏀ LINKAGES (a link to Perception, p. 178)

We have seen that associations between conditioned stimuli and reflexes or between responses and their consequences play an important role in learning. How are these associations actually stored in the brain? No one yet knows for sure, but neural network models provide a good way of thinking about the process. As suggested in the chapters on perception and memory, networks of neural connections in the brain are believed to play a critical role not only in recognizing objects, but also in storing and organizing information. These associative networks can be very complex. Consider the word *dog*. As shown in Figure 6.12, each person's experience builds many associations to this word, and the strength of each association will reflect the frequency with which *dog* has been mentally linked to the other objects, events, and ideas in that person's life.

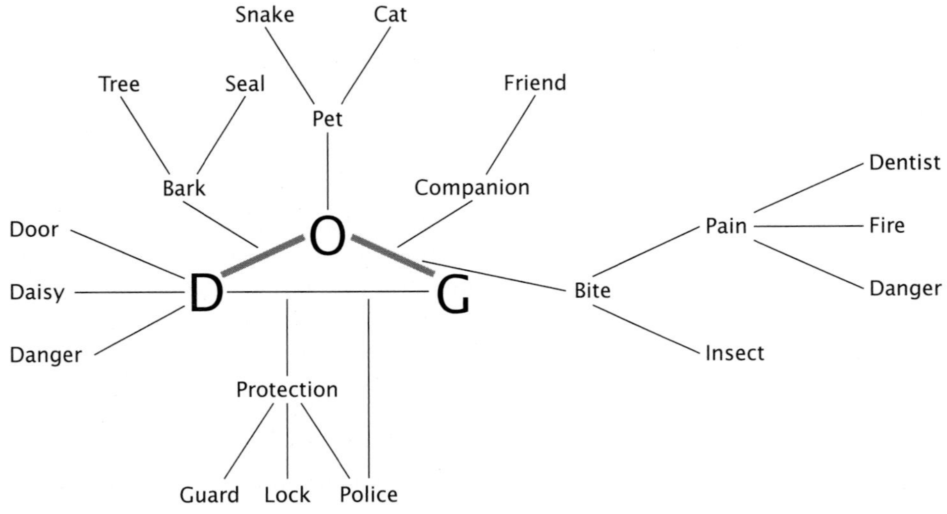

FIGURE 6.12

An Associative Network

Here is an example of a network of associations to the word *dog*. Network theorists suggest that the connections shown here represent patterns of neural connections in the brain.

Using what they know about the laws of learning and about the way neurons communicate and alter their synaptic connections, psychologists have been trying to develop models of how these associations are established (Messinger et al., 2001). We discuss some of their efforts in the chapters on perception and memory in terms of *neural networks* and *parallel distributed processing* models. An important feature of these models is the idea of distributed memory or distributed knowledge. They suggest, for example, that the knowledge of "dog" does not lie in a single location, or node, in your brain. Instead, knowledge is distributed throughout the network of associations that connect the letters *D*, *O*, and *G*, along with other dog-related experiences. In addition, as shown in Figure 6.12, each of the interconnected nodes that make up your knowledge of "dog" is connected to many other nodes as well. So the letter *D* will be connected to "Daisy," "Danger," and a host of other concepts. Networks of connections also appear to be the key to explaining how people come to understand the words and sentences they read (Wolman, van den Broek, & Lorch, 1997).

Neural network models of learning focus on how these connections are developed through experience (Hanson & Burr, 1990). For example, suppose you are learning a new word in a foreign language. Each time you read the word and associate it with its English equivalent, you strengthen the neural connections between the sight of the letters forming that word and all of the nodes activated when its English equivalent is brought to mind. Neural network, or *connectionist*, models of learning predict how much the strength of each linkage grows (in terms of the likelihood of neural communication between the two connected nodes) each time the two words are experienced together.

The details of various theories about how these connections grow are very complex, but a theme common to many of them is that the weaker the connection between two items, the greater the increase in connection strength when they are experienced together. So in a simple classical conditioning experiment, the connections between the nodes characterizing the conditioned stimulus and those characterizing the unconditioned stimulus will show the greatest increase in strength during the first few learning trials. Notice that this prediction nicely matches the typical learning curve shown in Figure 6.3 (Rescorla & Wagner, 1972).

Neural network models have yet to fully explain the learning of complex tasks, nor can they easily account for how people adapt when the "rules of the game" are suddenly changed and old habits must be unlearned and replaced. Nevertheless, a better understanding of what we mean by *associations* may very well lie in future research on neural network models (Boden, 2006; Houghton, 2005). ■

Cognitive Processes in Learning

During the first half of the twentieth century, psychologists in North America tended to look at classical and operant conditioning through the lens of behaviorism, the theoretical approach that was dominant in psychology at the time. As described in the chapter on introducing psychology, behaviorists tried to identify the stimuli, responses, and consequences that build and alter overt behavior. In other words, they saw learning as resulting from the automatic, unthinking formation or modification of associations between observable events. Behaviorists paid almost no attention to the role of conscious mental activity that might accompany the learning process.

This strictly behavioral view of classical and operant conditioning is challenged by the cognitive approach, which has become increasingly influential in recent decades. Cognitive psychologists see a common thread in these apparently different forms of learning (Blaisdell, Sawa, & Leising, 2006). To them, both classical and operant conditioning help animals and people to detect causality—to understand what causes what. They see both types of conditioning as the result not only of automatic associations but of more complex mental processes, including how people represent, store, and use information. It is these processes, they say, that underlie our ability to adapt to, and understand the world around us (Dickinson, 2001).

Cognitive psychologists have found, for example, that a classically conditioned response (such as fear) is more likely to develop if an unconditioned stimulus (such as electric shock) comes as a surprise than if it is expected (Kamin, 1969). Even the brain's reaction to a given stimulus can differ depending on whether that stimulus was expected or unexpected (Waelti, Dickinson, & Schultz, 2001). In other words, according to the cognitive view, learning is affected not only by the nature of the stimuli we experience but also by our expectations about them. Further, just as our perceptions depend on the meaning we attach to sensations (see the chapter on perception), learning can depend on the meaning we attach to events. So being praised by a boss we respect may be more reinforcing than getting the same good evaluation from a boss we hate.

Further evidence for the role of cognitive processes in learning comes from research on learned helplessness, latent learning, cognitive maps, insight, and observational learning.

● Learned Helplessness

Babies learn that crying attracts attention. Children learn which button turns on the TV, and adults learn what behaviors are rewarded (or punished) in the workplace. On the basis of this learning, people come to expect that certain actions on their part cause certain consequences. But sometimes events are beyond our control. What happens when behavior has no effects on events, and especially when escape or avoidance behaviors fail? If such ineffectiveness is prolonged, one result may be **learned helplessness,** a tendency to give up any effort to control the environment (Overmier, 2002; Seligman, 1975).

Learned helplessness was first demonstrated in animals. As described earlier, dogs placed in a shuttle box (see Figure 6.7) will normally learn to jump over a barrier to escape a shock. However, if these dogs first receive shocks that they cannot escape, they later do not even try to escape when a shock is turned on in the shuttle box (Overmier & Seligman, 1967). It is as if the animals had learned that "shock happens, and there is nothing I can do to control it."

**FOCUS ON
RESEARCH METHODS** **An Experiment on Human Helplessness**

The results of animal studies on learned helplessness led psychologists to wonder whether learned helplessness might play a role in human psychological problems. But they first had to deal with a more basic question: Does lack of control over the environment lead to helplessness in humans, as it does in other species?

■ What was the researcher's question?

Donald Hiroto (1974) conducted an experiment to test the hypothesis that people would develop learned helplessness after either experiencing lack of control or simply being told that their control was limited.

■ How did the researcher answer the question?

Hiroto assigned research participants to one of three groups. One group heard a series of thirty random bursts of loud, obnoxious noise and, like dogs receiving inescapable shock, they had no way to stop it. A second group could control the noise by pressing a button to turn it off. The third group heard no noise at all.

● **learned helplessness**   Learning that responses do not affect consequences, resulting in failure to try to exert control over the environment.

After this preliminary phase, all three groups were exposed to eighteen additional bursts of noise, each preceded by a red warning light. During this second phase, *all* participants could stop the noise by pushing a lever. However, they didn't know whether to push the lever to the left or the right on any given trial. Still, they could prevent the noise if they acted quickly enough.

Before these new trials began, the experimenter led half the participants in each group to expect that avoiding or escaping the noise depended on their skill. The other half were led to expect that their success would be a matter of chance. So in this experiment the dependent variable—the participants' efforts to control noise—could be affected by either or both of two independent variables: prior experience with noise (control, lack of control, or no noise) and expectation (skill or chance) about the ability to influence the noise.

■ What did the researcher find?

On the average, participants who had previously experienced lack of control now failed to control noise on almost four times as many trials (50 percent vs. 13 percent) as did participants who had earlier been in control. *Expectation* of control also had an effect on behavior. Regardless of whether participants had experienced control before, those who expected noise control to depend on their skill exerted control on significantly more trials than did those who expected chance to govern the outcome.

■ What do the results mean?

These results supported Hiroto's hypothesis that people, like other animals, tend to make less effort to control their environment when prior experience leads them to expect their efforts will be in vain. Unlike other animals, though, people can develop expectations of helplessness either by personally experiencing lack of control or by being *told* that they are powerless. Hiroto's (1974) results appear to reflect a general phenomenon: When people's prior experience leads them to *believe* that nothing they do can change their lives or control their destiny, they generally stop trying (Faulkner, 2001; LoLordo, 2001; Peterson, Maier, & Seligman, 1993). Instead, they tend to passively endure distressing situations.

■ What do we still need to know?

Further research is needed on when and how learned helplessness affects people's thoughts, feelings, and actions. For example, could learned helplessness explain why some battered women remain with abusive partners? We do know that learned-helplessness experiences are associated with the development of a generally pessimistic way of thinking that can produce depression and other disorders (Peterson & Seligman, 1984). People with this *pessimistic explanatory style* see the good things that happen to them as temporary and due to chance and the bad things as permanent and due to internal factors (e.g., lack of ability). This explanatory style has, in fact, been associated with poor grades, inadequate sales performance, health problems, and other negative outcomes (Bennett & Elliott, 2002; Seligman & Schulman, 1986; Taylor, 2002). The exact mechanisms responsible for this connection are still unknown, but understanding how pessimistic (or optimistic) explanatory styles can lead to negative (or positive) consequences remains an important focus of research (e.g., Brennan & Charnetski, 2000).

Does repeated success at controlling events create a sense of "learned mastery" or "learned resourcefulness" that supports efforts to exert control in new situations? Animal experiments suggest that this is the case (Volpicelli et al., 1983). Further, people with a history of successful control appear more likely than others to develop the *optimistic cognitive style*, hopefulness, and resilience that leads to even more success and healthier lives (Gillham, 2000; Zimmerman, 1990). (We discuss this cognitive style in the chapter on health, stress, and coping.) Accordingly, research is focusing on how best to minimize learned helplessness and maximize learned optimism in areas such as education, parenting, and psychotherapy (e.g., Jackson, Sellers, & Peterson, 2002). One option being evaluated at the moment is "resiliency training" for children at risk for depression (Cardemil, Reivich, & Seligman, 2002). Time will tell if such training leads to beneficial outcomes. ■

● Latent Learning and Cognitive Maps

The study of cognitive processes in learning goes back at least to the 1920s and Edward Tolman's research on maze learning in rats. The rats' task was to find the goal box of the maze, where food awaited them. The animals typically took lots of wrong turns, but over the course of many trials they made fewer and fewer mistakes. The strict behavioral interpretation of these results was that the rats learned a long chain of turning responses that were ultimately reinforced by the food. To Tolman, this interpretation was incomplete, and he offered evidence for the influence of cognitive processes in the animals' behavior.

In one study, for example, Tolman allowed rats to explore a maze once a day for several consecutive days (Tolman & Honzik, 1930). For rats in Group A, food was placed in the goal box on each trial. As shown in Figure 6.13, these rats gradually improved their performance so that by the end of the experiment, they made only one or two mistakes as they ran through the maze. For rats in Group B, there was never any food in their goal box. These animals continued to make many errors throughout the experiment. Neither of these results is surprising, and each is consistent with a behavioral view of learning as driven strictly by associating behavior with reward.

A third group of rats, Group C, was the critical one. For the first ten days, there was no food in their goal box, and like Group B, they continued to make many mistakes. But on the eleventh day, food was placed in their goal box for the first time. Figure 6.13 shows the surprising result: On day 12, the day after receiving their first positive reinforcement, these rats made almost no mistakes. In fact, their performance was as good as that of the rats that had been reinforced every day. In other words, for Group C the single reinforcement trial on day 11 produced a dramatic change in behavior the next day.

Tolman argued that these results supported two conclusions. First, the reinforcement on day 11 could not have significantly affected the rats' *learning* of the maze; it simply changed their subsequent *performance*. They must have learned the

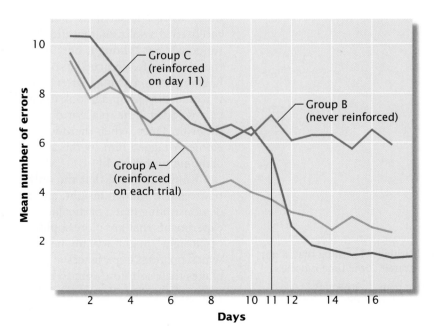

FIGURE 6.13

Latent Learning

Notice that when rats in Group C did not receive food reinforcement, they continued to make many errors in locating the goal box of a maze. The day after first finding food there, however, they took almost no wrong turns! The reinforcement, argued Tolman, affected only the rats' performance; they must have learned the maze earlier, without reinforcement.

maze earlier as they wandered around making mistakes on their way to the end of the maze. These rats demonstrated **latent learning**—learning that is not evident when it first occurs. (Latent learning occurs in humans, too; after years of experience in your neighborhood, you could probably tell a visitor that the corner drugstore is closed on Sundays, even if you had never tried to go there on a Sunday yourself.)

Second, the rats' improved performance immediately after the first reinforcement trial could have occurred only if the rats had already developed a **cognitive map**—that is, a mental representation of how the maze was arranged. Tolman concluded that cognitive maps develop naturally, and without the need for reinforcement, as people and animals gain experience with the world. Research on learning in the natural environment has supported this view. For example, we develop mental maps of shopping malls and city streets, even when we receive no direct reward for doing so (Tversky & Kahneman, 1991). Having such a map allows you to tell that visitor to your neighborhood exactly how to get to the corner drugstore from where you are standing.

● Insight and Learning

Wolfgang Köhler was a psychologist whose work on the cognitive aspects of learning came about almost by accident. He was visiting the island of Tenerife when World War I broke out in 1914. As a German in an area controlled by Germany's enemy, Britain, he was confined to the island for the duration of the war, and he devoted his time to studying problem solving by chimpanzees housed there (Köhler, 1924, 1976). For example, Köhler would put a chimpanzee in a cage and place a piece of fruit so that it was visible but out of the animal's reach. He sometimes hung the fruit from a string too high to reach or laid it on the ground too far outside the cage to be retrieved. Many of the chimps overcame these obstacles easily. If the fruit was out of reach on the ground outside the cage, some chimps looked around the cage and, finding a long stick, used it to rake in the fruit. Surprised that the chimpanzees could solve these problems, Köhler tried more difficult tasks. Again, the chimps proved very skilled, as Figure 6.14 illustrates.

Three aspects of Köhler's observations convinced him that animals' problem solving does not have to depend solely on trial and error and the gradual, automatic association of responses with consequences. First, once a chimpanzee solved a particular problem, it would immediately do the same thing in a similar situation. In other words, it acted as if it understood the problem. Second, the chimpanzees rarely tried a solution that didn't work. Apparently, the solution was not discovered randomly but "thought out" ahead of time and then acted out successfully. Third, the animals often reached a solution suddenly. When confronted with a piece of fruit hanging from a string, for example, a chimp might jump for it several times. Then it would stop jumping, look up, and pace back and forth. Finally it would run over to a wooden crate, place it directly under the fruit, and climb on top of it to reach the fruit. Once, when there were no other objects available, a chimp went over to Köhler, dragged him by the arm until he stood beneath the fruit, and then started climbing up his back!

Köhler believed that the only explanation for these results was that the chimpanzees had sudden **insight**, an understanding of the problem as a whole. However, demonstrating that a particular performance is the product of sudden insight requires experiments that are more sophisticated than those conducted by Köhler. Some cases of "insight" might actually be the result of a process known as *learning to learn*, in which previous experiences in problem solving are applied to new ones in a way that makes their solution seem to be instantaneous (Birch, 1945; Harlow, 1949). In fact, some psychologists argue that all known cases of "insight" include a long history of experience with the objects that are used to solve the problem (Epstein et al., 1984; Kounios et al., 2006; Wynne, 2004). Indeed, insight may actually result from a

● **latent learning** Learning that is not demonstrated at the time it occurs.

● **cognitive map** A mental representation of the environment.

● **insight** A sudden understanding about what is required to solve a problem.

FIGURE 6.14

Insight

Here are three impressive examples of problem solving by chimpanzees. At left, the animal fixed a fifteen-foot pole in the ground, climbed to the top, and dropped down after grabbing fruit that had been out of reach. In the center photo, the chimp stacked two boxes from different areas of the compound, climbed to the top, and used a pole to knock down the fruit. The chimp at right stacked three boxes and climbed them to reach the fruit.

"mental trial-and-error" process in which people (and some other animals) envision a course of action, mentally simulate its results, compare it with the imagined outcome of other alternatives, and settle on the course of action most likely to aid complex problem solving and decision making (Klein, 1993). So although Köhler's work helped establish the importance of cognitive processes in learning, questions remain about whether it demonstrated true insight.

● Observational Learning: Learning by Imitation

Research on the role of cognitive processes in learning has been further stimulated by the finding that learning can occur not only by doing but also by observing what others do, and what happens to them as a result. Learning by watching others—called **observational learning**, or *social learning*—is efficient and adaptive. For example, young chimpanzees learn how to use a stone to crack open nuts by watching their mothers do so (Inoue-Nakamura & Matsuzawa, 1997). And we don't have to find out for ourselves that a door is locked or an iron is hot if we have just seen someone else try the door or suffer a burn.

The biological basis for observational learning may lie partly in the operation of *mirror neurons* in the brain (Fogassi et al., 2005). As described in the chapter on biological aspects of psychology, mirror neurons fire not only when we do something or experience something, but also when we see someone do or experience the same thing. This mirrored pattern of activity in our own brains makes it almost as though we are actually performing the observed action or having the observed experience. Mirror neurons are active, for example, when we feel disgust upon seeing someone react to the taste of sour milk. They probably are firing, too,

observational learning Learning how to perform new behaviors by watching others.

Painful learning experiences.

Despite of the power of observational learning, some people just have to learn things the hard way.

when we are trying to imitate the correct pronunciation of foreign words, or to use an unfamiliar tool.

Children are particularly influenced by the adults and peers who act as models for appropriate behavior in various situations. In one classic experiment, Albert Bandura showed nursery school children a film featuring an adult and a large, inflatable, bottom-heavy "Bobo" doll (Bandura, 1965). The adult in the film punched the Bobo doll in the nose, kicked it, threw things at it, and hit its head with a hammer while saying things like "Sockeroo!" There were different endings to the film. Some children saw an ending in which the aggressive adult was called a "champion" by a second adult and rewarded with candy and soft drinks. Some saw the aggressor scolded and called a "bad person." Some saw a neutral ending in which there was neither reward nor punishment. After the film, each child was allowed to play alone with a Bobo doll. How the children played in this and similar studies led to some important conclusions about learning and about the role of cognitive factors in it.

Bandura found that children who saw the adult rewarded for aggression showed the most aggressive acts in play (see Figure 6.15). They had received **vicarious conditioning**, a kind of observational learning in which a person is influenced by seeing or hearing about the consequences of other people's behavior. Those who had seen the adult punished for aggressive acts showed less aggression, but they still learned something. When later offered rewards for all the aggressive acts they could perform, these children displayed just as many as the children who had watched the rewarded adult. Observational learning can occur even when there are no vicarious consequences; many children in the neutral condition also imitated the model's aggression.

Observational learning seems to be a powerful source of the *socialization* process through which children learn about which behaviors are—and are not—appropriate in their cultures (Bandura, 1999). Experiments show, for example, that children are more willing to help and share after seeing a demonstration of helping by a friendly, impressive model—even after some months have elapsed (Schroeder et al., 1995). Indeed, watching or even just hearing about the selfless or heroic acts of others can inspire us to seek higher goals in ourselves (Haidt, 2003).

TRY THIS **Learning by Imitation** Much of our behavior is learned by imitating others, especially those who serve as role models. To appreciate the impact of social learning in your life, list five examples of how your own actions, speech, mannerisms, or appearance have come to match those of a parent, a sibling, a friend, a teacher, or even a celebrity.

● **vicarious conditioning** Learning responses by watching what happens to others.

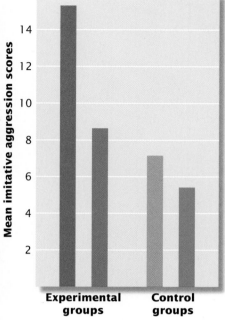

FIGURE 6.15

Observational Learning

Albert Bandura found that after observing an aggressive model, many children imitate the model's acts precisely, especially if the model's aggression was rewarded.

Source: Bandura, Ross, & Ross (1963).

■ Aggressive model rewarded
■ Aggressive model punished
■ Nonaggressive model
■ No model

THINKING CRITICALLY

Does Watching Violence on Television Make People More Violent?

I f observational learning is important, then surely television—and televised violence—must teach children a great deal. It is estimated that the average child in the United States spends about three hours each day watching television (Annenberg Public Policy Center, 2000). Much of what children see is violent. In addition to the real-life violence portrayed on the news (van der Molen, 2004), prime-time entertainment programs in the United States present an average of five acts of simulated violence per hour. Some Saturday-morning cartoons include more than twenty per hour (American Psychological Association, 1993; Gerbner, Morgan, & Signorielli, 1994). As a result, the average child will have witnessed at least 8,000 murders and more than 100,000 other acts of televised violence before finishing elementary school and twice that number by age eighteen (Annenberg Public Policy Center, 1999; Parents Television Council, 2006).

Psychologists have long speculated that watching so much violence might be emotionally arousing, making viewers more likely to react violently to frustration (Huston & Wright, 1989). In fact, there is evidence that exposure to media violence can trigger or amplify viewers' aggressive thoughts and feelings, thus increasing the likelihood that they will act aggressively (Anderson & Dill, 2000; Bushman, 1998). Televised violence might also provide models that viewers imitate, particularly if the violence is carried out by attractive, impressive models—the "good guys," for example (Huesmann et al., 2003). Finally, prolonged viewing of violent TV programs might "desensitize" viewers, making them less distressed when they see others suffer and less disturbed about inflicting pain on others (Aronson, 1999; Donnerstein,

Slaby, & Eron, 1995). Concern over the influence of violence on television led to the development of a violence-blocking V-Chip for new television sets in the United States.

■ What am I being asked to believe or accept?

Many have argued that through one or more of the mechanisms just listed, watching violence on television causes violent behavior in viewers (Anderson et al., 2003; Anderson & Bushman, 2002b; Bushman & Huesmann, 2000; Eron et al., 1996; Huesmann, 1998). A 1993 report by the National Academy of Sciences concluded that "overall, the vast majority of studies, whatever their methodology, showed that exposure to television violence resulted in increased aggressive behavior, both contemporaneously and over time" (Reiss & Roth, 1993, p. 371). An American Psychological Association Commission on Violence and Youth reached the same conclusion (American Psychological Association, 1993).

■ What evidence is available to support the assertion?

Three types of evidence support the claim that watching violent television programs increases violent behavior. First, there is evidence from anecdotes and case studies. Children have poked one another in the eye after watching the Three Stooges appear to do so on television, and adults have claimed that watching TV shows prompted them to commit murders or other violent acts matching those seen on the shows (Werner, 2003).

Second, many correlational studies have found a relationship between watching violent television programs and later acts of aggression and violence (Johnson, Cohen, et al., 2002). One such study tracked people from the time they were six or seven (in 1977) until they reached their early twenties (in 1992). Those who had watched more violent television as children were significantly more aggressive as adults (Huesmann et al., 1997; Huesmann et al., 2003) and more likely to engage in criminal activity (Huesmann, 1995). They were also more likely to use physical punishment on their own children, who themselves tended to be much more aggressive than average. These latter results have been found not only in the United States but also in Israel, Australia, Poland, the Netherlands, and even Finland, where the number of violent TV shows is very small (Centerwall, 1990; Huesmann & Eron, 1986).

Finally, the results of numerous experiments also support the view that TV violence increases aggression among viewers (American Psychological Association, 1993; Paik & Comstock, 1994; Reiss & Roth, 1993). In one study, groups of boys watched violent or nonviolent programs in a controlled setting and then played floor hockey (Josephson, 1987). Boys who had watched the violent shows were more likely than those who had watched nonviolent programs to behave aggressively on the hockey floor. This effect was greatest for those boys who had the most aggressive tendencies to begin with. More extensive experiments, in which children are exposed for long periods to carefully controlled types of television programs, also suggest that exposure to large amounts of violent activity on television results in aggressive behavior (Eron et al., 1996).

■ Are there alternative ways of interpreting the evidence?

To some, this evidence leaves no doubt that media violence causes increases in aggressive and violent behavior, especially in children (Anderson et al., 2003). Others suggest that the evidence is not conclusive and is open to some qualifications and alternative interpretations (e.g., Browne & Hamilton-Giachritsis, 2005; Freedman, 2002; Thakkar, Garrison, & Christakis, 2006). Anecdotal reports and case studies are particularly suspect. When people face imprisonment or execution for their violent acts, how much confidence can we place in their claims that these acts were triggered by television programs? And how many other people might say that the same programs made them *less* likely to be violent? Anecdotes alone do not provide a good basis for drawing solid scientific conclusions.

What about the correlational evidence from studies that followed children over time? As discussed in the chapter on research in psychology, a *correlation* between two variables does not necessarily mean that one is *causing* an effect on the other. Both might be affected by a third factor. Why, for example, are certain people watching so much violent television in the first place? This question suggests a possible third factor that might account for the observed relationship between watching TV violence and acting aggressively: People who tend to be aggressive may prefer to watch more violent TV programs *and* may behave aggressively toward others. In other words, personality may partly account for the observed correlations (e.g., Aluja-Fabregat & Torrubia-Beltri, 1998).

The results of controlled experiments on the effects of televised violence have been criticized as well (Freedman, 2002; Geen, 1998). The major objection is that both the independent and dependent variables in these experiments are artificial, so they may not apply beyond the laboratory or last very long (Browne & Hamilton-Giachristsis, 2005; Freedman, 2002). For example, the kinds of violent shows viewed by the participants during some of these experiments, as well as the ways in which their aggression has been measured, may not reflect what goes on in the real-world situations we most want to know about.

■ What additional evidence would help to evaluate the alternatives?

By their very nature, correlational studies of the role of TV violence in violent behavior can never be conclusive. As we've pointed out, a third, unidentified causal variable could always be responsible for the results. So it would be useful to have evidence from controlled experiments in which equivalent groups of people were exposed for years to differing "doses" of the violence actually portrayed on TV and in which the effects on their subsequent behavior were observed in real-world situations. Such experiments could also explore the circumstances under which different people (e.g., children vs. adults) were affected by various forms of violence. However, studies like these would create an ethical dilemma. If watching violent television programs really does cause violent behavior, are psychologists justified in creating conditions that might lead some people to be more violent? If such violence occurred, would the researchers be partly responsible to the victims and to society? Difficulty in answering questions such as these is partly responsible for the use of short-term experiments and correlational designs in this research area, as well as for some of the remaining uncertainty about the effects of television violence.

■ What conclusions are most reasonable?

The evidence collected so far makes it reasonable to conclude that watching TV violence may be one cause of violent behavior, especially in some children and especially in boys (Anderson & Bushman, 2002b; Bushman & Anderson, 2001; Browne & Hamilton-Giachristsis, 2005; Huesmann et al., 1997; Robinson et al., 2001; Smith & Donnerstein, 1998). Playing violent video games may be another (Anderson, 2004; Anderson & Bushman, 2001). But a cause-effect relationship between watching TV violence and acting violently is not inevitable and may not always be long-lasting (Browne & Hamilton-Giachristsis, 2005). Further, there are many circumstances in which the effect does not occur (Charleton, Gunter, & Coles, 1998; Freedman, 1992, 2002). Parents, peers, and other environmental influences, along with personality factors, may dampen or amplify the effect of watching televised violence. Indeed, not every viewer interprets violence in the same way, and not every viewer is equally vulnerable (Ferguson, 2002; Wood, Wong, & Chachere, 1991). The most vulnerable may be young boys, and especially those who are most aggressive or violence-prone in the first place, a trait that could well have been acquired by observing the behavior of parents or peers (Huesmann et al., 1997).

Still, the fact that violence on television *can* have a causal impact on violent behavior is reason for serious concern and continues to influence public debate about what should and should not be aired on television. ■

"I have HAD it with you two and your violent video games!"

The violence that may affect children's aggressive behavior may not be limited to what they see on television and in video games.

Using Research on Learning to Help People Learn

Teaching and training—explicit efforts to assist learners in mastering a specific skill or body of material—are major aspects of socialization in virtually every culture. So the study of how people learn has important implications for improved teaching in our schools (Bjork & Linn, 2006; Halpern & Hakel, 2003; Li, 2005) and for helping people develop skills ranging from typing to tennis.

● Classrooms Across Cultures

Many people are concerned that schools in the United States are not doing a very good job. The average performance of U.S. students on tests of reading, math, and other basic academic skills has tended to fall short of that of youngsters in other countries, especially some Asian countries (International Association for the Evaluation of Education Achievement, 1999; National Center for Education Statistics, 2002; Program for International Student Assessment, 2005). In one comparison study, Harold Stevenson (1992) followed a sample of pupils in Taiwan, Japan, and the United States from first grade, in 1980, to eleventh grade, in 1991. In first grade, the Asian students scored no higher than their U.S. peers on tests of mathematical aptitude and skills, nor did they enjoy math more. However, by fifth grade the U.S. students had fallen far behind. Corresponding differences were seen in reading skills.

Some possible causes of these differences were found in the classroom itself. In a typical U.S. classroom session, teachers talked to students as a group. The students then worked at their desks independently. Reinforcement or other feedback about performance on their work was usually delayed until the next day or, often, not provided at all. In contrast, the typical Japanese classroom placed greater emphasis on cooperative work among students (Kristof, 1997). Teachers provided more immediate feedback on a one-to-one basis. And there was an emphasis on creating teams of students with varying abilities, an arrangement in which faster learners help teach slower ones. However, before concluding that the differences in performance are the result of social factors alone, we must consider another important distinction: The Japanese children practiced more. They spent more days in school during the year and on average spent more hours doing homework.

Although the significance of these cultural differences in learning and teaching is not yet clear, the educational community in the United States is paying attention to them (e.g., Felder & Brent, 2001). Psychologists and educators are also considering how other principles of learning can be applied to improve education. Anecdotal and experimental evidence suggests that some of the most successful educational techniques are those that apply basic principles of operant conditioning, offering frequent testing, positive reinforcement for correct performance, and immediate corrective feedback following mistakes (Kass, 1999; Oppel, 2000; Roediger, McDaniel, & McDermott, 2006; Walberg, 1987).

Further, research in cognitive psychology (e.g., Bjork, 1999; Cepeda et al., 2006) also suggests that students are more likely to retain what they learn if they engage in numerous study sessions rather than in a single "cramming" session on the night before a quiz or exam. To encourage this more beneficial "distributed practice" pattern, researchers say, teachers should give enough exams and quizzes (some unannounced, perhaps) that students will be reading and studying more or less continuously. And because learning is aided by repeated opportunities to use new information, these exams and quizzes should cover material from throughout the term, not just from recent classes. Such recommendations are not necessarily popular with students, but there is good evidence that they promote long-term retention of course material (e.g., Bjork, 1999, 2001).

Reciprocal Teaching Ann Brown and her colleagues (Brown et al., 1992) demonstrated the success of reciprocal teaching, in which children take turns teaching each other. This technique is similar to the cooperative arrangements seen in Japanese education.

▨● Active Learning

The importance of cognitive processes in learning is apparent in instructional methods that emphasize *active learning* (Bonwell & Eison, 1991). These methods take many forms, such as small-group problem-solving tasks, discussion of "one-minute essays" written in class, use of "thumbs up" or "thumbs down" to indicate agreement or disagreement with the instructor's lecture, and multiple-choice questions that give students feedback about their understanding of the previous fifteen minutes of lecture (Goss Lucas & Bernstein, 2005). There is little doubt that for many students, the inclusion of active learning experiences makes classes more interesting and enjoyable (Moran, 2000; Murray, 2000). Active learning methods also provide immediate reinforcement and help students to go beyond memorizing isolated facts by encouraging them to think more deeply about new information, consider how it relates to what they already know, and apply it in new situations. The more elaborate mental processing associated with active learning makes new information not only more personally meaningful but also easier to remember. (The many *Try This* opportunities sprinkled throughout this book are designed to promote active learning and better retention.)

Active learning strategies have been found to be superior to passive teaching methods in a number of studies with children and adults. In one study, a fifth-grade science teacher spent some class periods calling on only those students whose hands were raised; the rest listened passively. On other days, all students were required to answer every question by holding up a card on which they had written their response. Scores on next-day quizzes and biweekly tests showed that students remembered more of the material covered on the active learning days than on the "passive" days (Gardner, Heward, & Grossi, 1994). Studies with students in high school, as well as with community college and university students, have found that active learning approaches result in better test performance and greater class participation compared with standard instructional techniques (e.g., Kellum, Carr, & Dozier, 2001). For example, students who passively listened to a physics lecture received significantly lower scores on a test of lecture content than did those who participated in a virtual reality lab that allowed them to "interact" actively with the physical forces covered in the lecture (Brelsford, 1993). Results

Active Learning Field trips provide students with firsthand opportunities to see and interact with the things they study in the classroom. Such experiences are just one example of the active learning exercises that can help students become more deeply involved in the learning process.

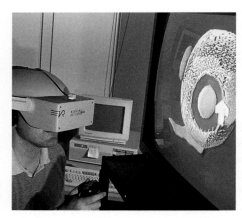

Virtual Surgery Using a virtual reality system called "Surgery in 3-D," this medical student can actively learn and practice eye surgery skills before working with real patients. Computer-based human body simulators are also giving new doctors active learning experience in emergency room diagnosis and treatment, in heart, lung, and abdominal surgery, and other medical skills (Groopman, 2005).

like these have fueled the development of other science education programs that place students in virtual laboratory environments where they can actively manipulate materials and test hypotheses (e.g., Horwitz & Christie, 2000). Despite the enthusiasm generated by active learning methods, rigorous experimental research is still needed to compare their short- and long-term effects with those of more traditional methods in teaching various kinds of course content (Moran, 2006).

● Skill Learning

The complex action sequences, or *skills*, that people learn to perform in everyday life—tying a shoe, opening a door, operating a computer, shooting a basketball, driving a car—develop through direct and vicarious learning processes involving imitation, instructions, reinforcement, and, of course, lots of practice. Some skills, such as those of a basketball player or violinist, demand exceptional perceptual-motor coordination. Others, such as those involved in scientific thinking, have a large cognitive component, requiring rapid understanding. In either case, the learning of skills usually involves practice and feedback.

Practice—the repeated performance of a skill—is the most critical component of skill learning (Howe, Davidson, & Sloboda, 1998). For perceptual-motor skills, both physical and mental practice are beneficial (Druckman & Bjork, 1994). To be most effective, practice should continue past the point of correct performance until the skill can be performed automatically, with little or no need for attention. As mentioned earlier, in learning many cognitive skills, what counts most seems to be practice in retrieving relevant information from memory. Trying to recall and write down facts that you have read, for example, is a more effective learning tool than simply reading the facts a second time.

Feedback about the correctness of responses is also necessary. As with any learning process, the feedback should come soon enough to be effective, but not so quickly that it interferes with the learner's efforts to learn independently. Large amounts of guidance may produce very good performance during practice, but too much guidance may impair later performance (Kluger & DeNisi, 1998; Wickens, 1992). Coaching students about correct responses in math, for example, may impair their ability later to retrieve the correct response from memory on their own. And

Try It This Way Good coaches provide enough guidance and performance feedback to help budding athletes develop their skills to the fullest, but not so much that the guidance interferes with the learning process. Striking this delicate balance is one of the greatest challenges faced by coaches and by teachers in general.

in coaching athletes, if feedback is given too soon after an action occurs or while it is still taking place, it may divert the learner's attention from understanding how that action was achieved and what it felt like to perform it (Schmidt & Bjork, 1992). Independent practice at retrieving previously learned responses or information requires more effort, but it is critical for skill development (Ericsson & Charness, 1994).

How do some people reach high levels of achievement in physical or cognitive skills? A number of researchers in the field of positive psychology are studying such people (e.g. Murray, 2003; Simonton, 2000). They have found that stellar accomplishments in the arts and sciences and athletics, for example, are associated with having worked very hard for a very long time, with having a helpful coach or mentor, with being optimistic about success, and also with being in the right place at the right time. This research suggests that, to reach your own highest potential, you should first identify your interests and skills, choose a field in which these are likely to fit well, then find a good mentor, put in lots of time and effort, stay optimistic even in the face of setbacks, and take advantage of every opportunity that presents itself (Peterson, 2006). There appears to be little or no evidence to support "sleep learning" or other schemes designed to make learning effortless (Druckman & Bjork, 1994; Phelps & Exum, 1992). In short, "no pain, no gain."

LINKAGES

As noted in the chapter on introducing psychology, all of psychology's many subfields are related to one another. Our discussion of neural networks as possible models of associative learning illustrates just one way in which the topic of this chapter, learning, is linked to the subfield of perception, which is covered in the chapter by that name. The Linkages diagram shows ties to two other subfields as well, and there are many more ties throughout the book. Looking for linkages among subfields will help you see how they all fit together and better appreciate the big picture that is psychology.

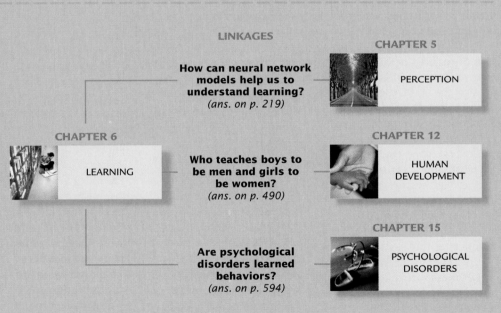

LINKAGES

CHAPTER 6
LEARNING

CHAPTER 5
PERCEPTION
How can neural network models help us to understand learning? (ans. on p. 219)

CHAPTER 12
HUMAN DEVELOPMENT
Who teaches boys to be men and girls to be women? (ans. on p. 490)

CHAPTER 15
PSYCHOLOGICAL DISORDERS
Are psychological disorders learned behaviors? (ans. on p. 594)

SUMMARY

Individuals adapt to changes in the environment through the process of *learning*, which is the modification through experience of pre-existing behavior and understanding.

Learning About Stimuli

One kind of learning is *habituation*, which is reduced responsiveness to a repeated stimulus. According to Richard Solomon's opponent-process theory, habituation results as two processes balance each other. The first process is a relatively automatic response to some stimulus. The second, or opponent, process follows and counteracts the first. This theory may help explain drug tolerance and some overdose cases.

Classical Conditioning: Learning Signals and Associations

Pavlov's Discovery One form of associative learning is *classical conditioning*. It occurs when a neutral stimulus (such as a tone), is repeatedly paired with an *unconditioned stimulus*, or *UCS* (such as meat powder on a dog's tongue), which naturally brings about an *unconditioned response*, or *UCR* (such as salivation). Through its association with the UCS, the neutral stimulus eventually becomes a *conditioned stimulus*, or *CS*, that will elicit a response, known as the *conditioned response*, or *CR*, even when the unconditioned stimulus is not presented.

Conditioned Responses over Time: Extinction and Spontaneous Recovery In general, the strength of a conditioned response grows as CS-UCS pairings continue. If the conditioned stimulus is repeatedly presented without being paired with the unconditioned stimulus, the conditioned response eventually disappears; this is *extinction*. Following extinction, the conditioned response often reappears if the conditioned stimulus is presented after some time; this is *spontaneous recovery*. In addition, if the conditioned and unconditioned stimuli are paired once or twice after extinction, *reconditioning* occurs. That is, the conditioned response regains its original strength.

Stimulus Generalization and Discrimination Because of *stimulus generalization*, conditioned responses are elicited by stimuli that are similar, but not identical, to conditioned stimuli. Generalization is limited by *stimulus discrimination*, which reduces conditioned responses to stimuli that are substantially different from the conditioned stimulus.

The Signaling of Significant Events Classical conditioning involves learning that the conditioned stimulus is an event that predicts the occurrence of another event, the unconditioned stimulus. The conditioned response is not just an automatic reflex but also a means through which animals and people develop mental models of the relationships between events. Classical conditioning works best when the conditioned stimulus precedes the unconditioned stimulus, an arrangement known as forward conditioning. Conditioned responses develop best when the conditioned stimulus precedes the unconditioned stimulus by intervals ranging from less than a second to a minute or more, depending on the stimuli involved. Conditioning is also more likely when the conditioned stimulus reliably signals the unconditioned stimulus.

In general, the strength of a conditioned response and the speed of conditioning increase as the intensity of the unconditioned stimulus increases. Stronger conditioned stimuli also speed conditioning. The particular conditioned stimulus likely to be linked to a subsequent unconditioned stimulus depends in part on which stimulus was being attended to when the unconditioned stimulus occurred. Some stimuli are easier to associate than others; organisms seem to be biologically prepared to learn certain associations, as exemplified by taste aversions. *Second-order conditioning* occurs when a conditioned stimulus becomes powerful enough to function as an unconditioned stimulus for another stimulus associated with it.

Some Applications of Classical Conditioning Classical conditioning principles are being applied in understanding the development and treatment of phobias, in the humane control of predators in the wild, in the detection of explosives, and in procedures for identifying people at risk for Alzheimer's disease.

Operant Conditioning: Learning the Consequences of Behavior

Learning occurs not only through associating stimuli but also through associating behavior with its consequences.

From the Puzzle Box to the Skinner Box Edward L. Thorndike's *law of effect* holds that any response that produces satisfaction becomes more likely to occur again when the same stimulus is encountered, and any response that produces discomfort becomes less likely to occur again. Thorndike called this type of learning instrumental conditioning. B. F. Skinner called the same basic process *operant conditioning*. In operant conditioning the organism is free to respond at any time, and conditioning is measured by the rate of responding.

Basic Components of Operant Conditioning An *operant* is a response that has some effect on the world. A *reinforcer* increases the probability that the operant preceding it will occur again. In other words, reinforcers strengthen behavior. There are two types of reinforcers: *positive reinforcers*, which are pleasant stimuli that strengthen a response if they are presented after that response occurs, and *negative reinforcers*, which are the removal of an unpleasant stimulus following some response. Both kinds of reinforcers strengthen the behaviors that precede them. *Escape conditioning* results when behavior terminates an aversive event. *Avoidance conditioning* results when behavior prevents or avoids an aversive stimulus; it reflects both classical and operant conditioning. Behaviors learned through avoidance conditioning are highly resistant to extinction. *Discriminative stimuli* indicate whether reinforcement is available for a particular behavior.

Forming and Strengthening Operant Behavior Complex responses can be learned through *shaping*, which involves reinforcing successive approximations of the desired response. *Primary reinforcers* are innately rewarding; *secondary reinforcers* are rewards that people or animals learn to like because of their association with primary reinforcers. In general, operant conditioning proceeds more quickly when the delay in receiving reinforcement is short rather than long and when the reinforcer is large rather than small. Reinforcement may be delivered on a *continuous reinforcement schedule* or on one of four types of *partial reinforcement schedules* (also called intermittent reinforcement schedules): *fixed-ratio (FR) schedules, variable-ratio (VR) schedules, fixed-interval (FI) schedules,* and *variable-interval (VI) schedules*. Ratio schedules lead to a rapid rate of responding. Behavior learned through partial reinforcement, particularly through variable schedules, is very resistant to extinction; this phenomenon is called the *partial reinforcement extinction effect*. Partial reinforcement is involved in superstitious behavior, which results when a response is coincidentally followed by a reinforcer.

Why Reinforcers Work   Research suggests that reinforcers are rewarding because they provide an organism with the opportunity to engage in desirable activities, which may change from one situation to the next. Another possibility is that activity in the brain's pleasure centers plays a role in reinforcement.

Punishment   The frequency of a behavior can be decreased through *punishment*, in which the behavior is followed by either an unpleasant stimulus or the removal of a pleasant stimulus. Punishment modifies behavior but has several drawbacks. It suppresses behavior without erasing it; fear of punishment may generalize to the person doing the punishing; it is ineffective when delayed; it can be physically harmful and may teach aggressiveness; and it teaches only what not to do, not what should be done to obtain reinforcement.

Some Applications of Operant Conditioning   The principles of operant conditioning have been used in many areas of life, including the teaching of everyday social skills, the treatment of sleep disorders, the development of self-control, and the improvement of classroom education.

Cognitive Processes in Learning

Cognitive processes—how people represent, store, and use information—play an important role in learning.

Learned Helplessness   *Learned helplessness* appears to result when people believe that their behavior has no effect on the world.

Latent Learning and Cognitive Maps   Humans and other animals display *latent learning*, learning that is not obvious at the time it occurs. They also form *cognitive maps* of their environments, even in the absence of any reinforcement for doing so.

Insight and Learning   Experiments on *insight* also support the idea that cognitive processes and learned strategies play an important role in learning, perhaps even by animals.

Observational Learning: Learning by Imitation   The process of learning by watching others is called *observational learning*, or social learning. Some observational learning occurs through *vicarious conditioning*, in which an individual is influenced by seeing or hearing about the consequences of others' behavior. Observational learning is more likely to occur when the person observed is rewarded for the observed behavior. Observational learning is a powerful source of socialization.

Using Research on Learning to Help People Learn

Research on how people learn has implications for improved teaching and for the development of a wide range of skills.

Classrooms Across Cultures   The degree to which immediate reinforcement and extended practice are used in teaching varies considerably from culture to culture, but research suggests that the application of these and other basic learning principles is important to promoting effective teaching and learning.

Active Learning   The importance of cognitive processes in learning is seen in active learning methods designed to encourage people to think deeply about and apply new information instead of just memorizing isolated facts.

Skill Learning   Observational learning, practice, and corrective feedback play important roles in the learning of skills.

Memory

Have you ever forgotten someone's name five seconds after you were introduced? What happened to that memory, and why you lost it, are just two of the many questions that memory researchers study. In this chapter, we'll review what they have discovered about memory so far, and we'll suggest some ideas for improving your own memory. Here's how we have organized our presentation:

Several years ago an air-traffic controller at Los Angeles International Airport cleared a US Airways flight to land on runway 24L. A couple of minutes later, the US Airways pilot radioed the control tower that he was on approach for runway 24L, but the controller did not reply because she was preoccupied by a conversation with another pilot. After finishing that conversation, the controller told a Sky West commuter pilot to taxi onto runway 24L for takeoff, completely forgetting about the US Airways plane that was about to land on the same runway. The US Airways jet hit the commuter plane, killing thirty-four people. The controller's forgetting was so complete that she assumed the fireball from the crash was an exploding bomb. How could her memory have failed her at such a crucial time?

Memory is full of contradictions. It is common, for example, for adults to remember the name of their first-grade teacher but not the phone number they just called. Like perception, memory is selective. So although we retain a great deal of information, we also lose a great deal. Consider Tatiana Cooley. She was the U.S. National Memory Champion for three years in a row, but says that she is so absent-minded that she relies on Post-it Notes to remember everyday errands (Schacter, 2001). Cases such as hers show that memory is made up of many abilities, some of which may operate much more effectively, or less effectively, than others.

Memory plays a critical role in your life. Without memory, you would not know how to shut off your alarm clock, take a shower, get dressed, or recognize objects. You would be unable to communicate with other people, because you would not remember what words mean, or even what you had just said. You would be unaware of your own likes and dislikes, and you would have no idea of who you are (Craik et al., 1999). In this chapter we describe what is known about both memory and forgetting. First, we discuss what memory is—the different kinds of memory and the different ways we remember things. Then we examine how new memories are formed and later recalled, and why they are sometimes forgotten. We continue with a discussion of the biological bases of memory, and we conclude with some practical advice for improving your memory and study skills.

The Nature of Memory

Mathematician John Griffith estimated that in an average lifetime, each of us will have stored roughly five hundred times as much information as can be found in all the volumes of the *Encyclopaedia Britannica* (Hunt, 1982). The impressive capacity of human memory depends on the operation of a complex mental system (Schacter, 1999).

Basic Memory Processes

In February 2002, prison warden James Smith lost his set of master keys to the Westville Correctional Facility. As a result, 2,559 inmates were kept under partial lockdown for eight days while the Indiana Department of Correction spent $53,000 to change locks in the affected areas. As it turned out, the warden had put the keys in his pocket when he went home, forgot he had done so, and reported the keys "missing" when they were not in their usual place in his office the next day (Associated Press, 2002). What went wrong? There are several possibilities. Memory

Encoding Code and put into memory	**Storage** Maintain in memory	**Retrieval** Recover from memory
Types of **memory codes** ▪ Acoustic ▪ Visual ▪ Semantic	**Types of long-** **term memory** ▪ Episodic ▪ Procedural ▪ Semantic	**Types of** **retrieval tests** ▪ Recall ▪ Recognition

FIGURE 7.1

Basic Memory Processes

Remembering something requires, first, that the item be encoded—put in a form that can be placed in memory. It must then be stored and, finally, retrieved, or brought into awareness. If any of these processes fails, forgetting will occur.

depends on three basic processes: encoding, storage, and retrieval (see Figure 7.1). Our absent-minded warden might have had problems with any one of these processes.

First, information must be put into memory, a step that requires **encoding**. Just as incoming sensory information must be coded so that it can be communicated to the brain, information to be remembered must be put in a form that the memory system can accept and use. Sensory information is put into various *memory codes*, which are mental representations of physical stimuli. Suppose you see a billboard that reads "Huey's Going-Out-of-Business Sale," and you want to remember it so you can take advantage of the sale later. If you encode the sound of the words as if they had been spoken, you are using **acoustic encoding**, and the information is represented in your memory as a sequence of sounds. If you encode the image of the letters as they were arranged on the sign, you are using **visual encoding**, and the information is represented in your memory as a picture. Finally, if you encode just the fact that you saw an ad for Huey's, you are using **semantic encoding**, and the information is represented in your memory by its general meaning. The type of encoding used can influence what is remembered. For example, semantic encoding might allow you to remember that a car was parked in your neighbors' driveway just before their house was robbed. If there was little or no other encoding, however, you might not be able to remember the make, model, or color of the car.

The second basic memory process is **storage**, which refers to keeping information in memory over time—often over a very long time. When you find that you can still use a pogo stick that you haven't played with since you were a child or that you can recall a vacation from many years ago, you are depending on the storage capacity of your memory.

The third process, **retrieval**, occurs when you locate information stored in memory and bring it into consciousness. Retrieving stored information such as your address or telephone number is usually so fast and effortless that it seems automatic. Only when you try to retrieve other kinds of information—such as the answer to a quiz question that you know but cannot quite recall at that moment—do you become aware of the searching process. Retrieval processes include both recall and recognition. To *recall* information, you have to retrieve it from memory without much help. This is what is required when you answer an essay test question or play *Jeopardy!* In *recognition*, retrieval is aided by clues, such as the response alternatives given on multiple-choice tests and the questions on *Who Wants to Be a Millionaire*. Accordingly, recognition tends to be easier than recall.

● Types of Memory

When was the last time you charged something on your credit card? Who was the first president of the United States? How do you keep your balance when you are skiing? To answer these questions, you must use your memory. However, each answer may require a different type of memory. To answer the first question, you

encoding The process of acquiring information and entering it into memory.

acoustic encoding The mental representation of information as a sequence of sounds.

visual encoding The mental representation of information as images.

semantic encoding The mental representation of an experience by its general meaning.

storage The process of maintaining information in memory over time.

retrieval The process of recalling information stored in memory.

TRY
THIS **How Does She Do That?** As she practices, this young violinist is developing procedural memories of how to play her instrument that will be difficult to put into words. To appreciate the special nature of procedural memory, try writing a step-by-step description of *exactly* how you tie a shoe.

must remember a particular event in your life. To answer the second one, you must recall a piece of general knowledge that is unlikely to be tied to a specific event. And the answer to the final question is difficult to put into words but appears in the form of remembered actions when you are on skis. How many types of memory are there? No one is sure, but most research suggests that there are at least three basic types. Each type is named for the kind of information it handles: episodic, semantic, and procedural (Roediger, Marsh, & Lee, 2002).

Memory of a specific event that happened while you were present—that is, during an "episode" in your life—is called **episodic memory** (Tulving, 2005). Remembering what you had for dinner yesterday, what you did last summer, or where you were last Friday night all require episodic memory. Generalized knowledge of the world that does not involve memory of a specific event is called **semantic memory.** For instance, you can answer a question such as "Are wrenches pets or tools?" without remembering any specific event in which you learned that wrenches are tools. As a general rule, people convey episodic memories by saying, "I remember when . . . ," whereas they convey semantic memories by saying, "I know that . . ." (Tulving, 2000). Finally, memory of how to do things, such as riding a bike or tying a shoelace, is called **procedural memory** (Cohen & Squire, 1980). Often, procedural memory consists of a complicated sequence of movements that cannot be described adequately in words. For example, a gymnast might find it impossible to describe the exact motions in a particular routine. As a result, teachers of music, dance, cooking, woodworking, and other skills usually prefer to first show their students what to do rather than describe how to do it.

Many activities require all three types of memory. Consider the game of tennis. Knowing the official rules or how many sets are needed to win a match involves semantic memory. Remembering which side served last requires episodic memory. Knowing how to lob or volley involves procedural memory.

● Explicit and Implicit Memory

Recalling these three kinds of memories can be either intentional or unintentional. For example, you make use of **explicit memory** when you intentionally try to remember something and are consciously aware of doing so (Masson & MacLeod, 1992). Suppose someone asks you about your last vacation. As you think about where you went, you are using explicit memory to recall this episode from your past. Similarly, when responding to an exam question, you use explicit memory to retrieve the information needed to give a correct answer. In contrast, **implicit memory** is the unintentional recognition and influence of prior experiences (McDermott, 2002; Nelson, 1999). For example, if you were to read this chapter a second time, implicit memories of its content would help you to read it more quickly than you did the first time. For the same reason, you can solve a puzzle faster if you have solved it in the past. This facilitation of performance (often called *priming*) is automatic, and it occurs without conscious effort. Have you ever found yourself disliking someone you just met, but you didn't know why? One explanation is that implicit memory may have been at work. Specifically, you may have reacted as you did because the person bore a resemblance to someone from your past who treated you badly. In such instances, people are usually unable to recall the person from the past and are unaware of any connection between the two individuals (Lewicki, 1992). Episodic, semantic, and procedural memories can be explicit or implicit, but procedural memory usually operates implicitly. This is the reason that, for example, you can skillfully ride a bike even though you cannot explicitly remember all the procedures necessary to do so.

It is not surprising that experience affects how people behave. The surprising thing is that they are often unaware that their actions have been influenced by previous events (see the chapter on consciousness). Because some influential events cannot be recalled even when people try to do so, implicit memory has been said to involve "retention without remembering" (Roediger, 1990).

● **episodic memory** Memory of an event that happened while one was present.

● **semantic memory** A type of memory containing generalized knowledge of the world.

● **procedural memory** A type of memory containing information about how to do things.

● **explicit memory** The process in which people intentionally try to remember something.

● **implicit memory** The unintentional influence of prior experiences.

Making Implicit Memories By the time they reach adulthood, these boys may have no explicit memories of the interactions they had in early childhood with friends from differing ethnic groups. Research suggests, however, that their implicit memories of such experiences could have an unconscious effect on their attitudes toward and judgments about members of those groups.

FOCUS ON RESEARCH METHODS | Measuring Explicit Versus Implicit Memory

In Canada, Endel Tulving and his colleagues undertook a series of experiments to map the differences between explicit and implicit memory (Tulving, Schacter, & Stark, 1982).

■ What was the researcher's question?

Tulving knew he could measure explicit memory by giving a recognition test. On such a test, participants are given a set of words and asked to say whether they remember seeing each of the words on a previous list. The question was, How would it be possible to measure implicit memory?

■ How did the researcher answer the question?

First, Tulving asked the participants in his experiment to study a long list of words—the "study list." An hour later, they took a recognition test involving explicit memory—saying which words on a new list had been on the original study list. Then, to test their implicit memory, Tulving asked them to perform a "fragment completion" task. In this task, participants were shown a "test list" of word fragments, such as *d _ l i _ _ u _*, and asked to complete the word (in this case, *delirium*). On the basis of priming studies such as those described in the chapter on consciousness, Tulving assumed that memory from a previous exposure to the correct word would improve the participants' ability to complete the fragment, even if they were unable to consciously recall having seen the word before. A week later, all participants took a second test of their explicit memory (recognition) and implicit memory (fragment completion) of the study list. Some of the words on this second test list had been on the original study list, but none had been used in the first set of memory tests. The independent variable in this experiment, then, was the amount of time that had elapsed since the participants read the study list (one hour versus one week), and the dependent variable was performance on each of the two types of memory tests, explicit and implicit.

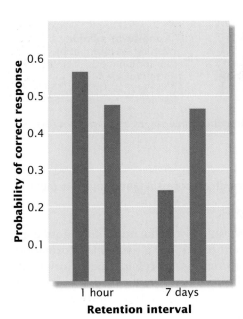

■ Recognition (explicit)
■ Fragment completion (implicit)

FIGURE 7.2

Measures of Explicit and Implicit Memory

This experiment showed that the passage of time greatly affected people's recognition (explicit memory) of a word list but left fragment completion (implicit memory) essentially intact. Results such as these suggest that explicit and implicit memory may be different memory systems.

Source: Tulving, Schacter, & Stark (1982).

■ What did the researcher find?

As shown in Figure 7.2, explicit memory for the study list decreased dramatically over time, but implicit memory (or priming) was virtually unchanged. Results from several other experiments also show that the passage of time affects explicit memory more than implicit memory (Komatsu & Naito, 1992; Mitchell, 1991). For example, it appears that the aging process has fewer negative effects on implicit memory than on explicit memory (Light, 1991).

■ What do the results mean?

The work of Tulving and others supports the idea of a dissociation, or independence, between explicit and implicit memory, suggesting that the two may operate on different principles (Gabrieli et al., 1995). In fact, some researchers believe that explicit and implicit memory may involve the activity of distinct neural systems in the brain (Squire, 1987; Tulving & Schacter, 1990). Others argue that the two types of memory are best described as requiring different cognitive processes (Nelson, McKinney, & Bennett, 1999; Roediger & McDermott, 1992).

■ What do we still need to know?

Psychologists have studied the role of implicit memory (and dissociations between explicit and implicit memory) in such important psychological phenomena as amnesia (Schacter, Church, & Treadwell, 1994; Tulving, 1993), depression (Elliott & Greene, 1992), posttraumatic stress disorder (McNally & Amir, 1996), problem solving (Jacoby, Marriott, & Collins, 1990), prejudice and stereotyping (Payne, Jacoby, & Lambert, 2004), the development of self-concept in childhood (Nelson, 1993), and even the power of ads to associate brand names with good feelings (Duke & Carlson, 1994). The results of these studies are helping to shed new light on implicit memory and how it operates in the real world.

For example, some social psychologists are trying to determine whether consciously held attitudes are independent of *implicit social cognitions*—past experiences that unconsciously influence a person's judgments about a group of people (Greenwald & Banaji, 1995). A case in point would be a person whose explicit thoughts about members of some ethnic group are positive but whose implicit thoughts are negative. Early work on implicit memory for stereotypes seemed to indicate that explicit and implicit stereotypes are independent (Devine, 1989), but more recent research suggests that they can be related, depending on how motivated people are to avoid expressing prejudice, and on how much control they have over their behavior at a particular time (Dunton & Fazio, 1997; Payne, 2001).

Further research is needed to determine what mechanisms are responsible for implicit versus explicit memory and how these two kinds of memory are related to one another (Lustig & Hasher, 2001; Nelson et al., 1998). That research will be facilitated by functional neuroimaging techniques. As described later, these techniques allow scientists to observe brain activity during various memory tasks and to determine which areas are associated with the explicit and implicit cognitive processes involved in these tasks (Buckner & Wheeler, 2001; McDermott, 2002; Schacter, Dobbins, & Schnyer, 2004). ■

● Models of Memory

We remember some information far better than other information. For example, suppose your friends throw a surprise party for you. When you enter the room, you might barely notice, and later fail to recall, the flash from a camera. And you might forget in a few seconds the name of a person you met at the party. But if you live to be a hundred, you will never forget where the party took place or how surprised and pleased you were. Why do some stimuli leave no more than a fleeting impression and others remain in memory forever? Each of five models of memory provides a somewhat different explanation. Let's see how the information-processing, levels-of-processing,

| EXTERNAL STIMULI | → | **Sensory memory** Briefly retains the information picked up by the sensory organs | → | **Short-term memory** Temporarily holds information in consciousness | → | **Long-term memory** Can retain information for long periods of time, often for life. |

FIGURE 7.3

Three Stages of Memory

The traditional information-processing model describes three stages in the memory system.

transfer-appropriate processing, parallel distributed processing, and multiple memory systems models look at memory.

● **Information Processing**   The earliest, most influential, and most comprehensive theories of memory have been based on a general **information-processing model** (Roediger, 1990). The information-processing model originally suggested that in order for information to become firmly embedded in memory, it must pass through three stages of mental processing: sensory memory, short-term memory, and long-term memory (Atkinson & Shiffrin, 1968; see Figure 7.3).

In *sensory memory,* information from the senses—sights or sounds, for example—is held for a very brief period of time, often for less than a second. This information might be attended to, analyzed, and encoded as a meaningful pattern. This is the process of perception, as discussed in the chapter on that topic. If the information in sensory memory is perceived, it can enter short-term memory. If nothing further is done, the information will disappear in less than twenty seconds. But if the information in short-term memory is processed further, it may be encoded into long-term memory, where it may remain indefinitely.

The act of reading illustrates all three stages of memory processing. As you read any sentence in this book, light energy reflected from the page reaches your eyes, where it is converted to neural activity and registered in your sensory memory. If you pay attention to these visual stimuli, your perception of the patterns of light can be held in short-term memory. This stage of memory holds the early parts of the sentence so that they can be integrated and understood as you read the rest of the sentence. As you read, you are constantly recognizing words by matching your perceptions of them with the patterns and meanings you have stored in long-term memory. In short, all three stages of memory are necessary for you to understand a sentence.

Today's versions of the information-processing model emphasize these constant interactions among sensory, short-term, and long-term memory. For example, sensory memory can be thought of as that part of your knowledge base (or long-term memory) that is momentarily activated by information sent to the brain via the sensory nerves. And short-term memory can be thought of as that part of your knowledge base that is the focus of attention at any given moment (Massaro & Cowan, 1993; Wagner, 1999). Like perception, memory is an active process, and what is already in long-term memory influences how new information is encoded (Cowan, 1988). To understand this interaction better, try the exercise in Figure 7.4.

● **Levels of Processing**   Early versions of information-processing models presumed that encoding, storage, and retrieval processes were all about equally important. In contrast, the **levels-of-processing model** suggests that the most important determinant of memory is how extensively information is encoded or processed when it is first received (Craik & Lockhart, 1972). Consider, for example, the task of remembering a phone number you just heard on the radio. If you were unable to write it down, you would probably repeat the number over and over to yourself until you could get to a phone. This repetition process is called **maintenance rehearsal.** It can be an effective way of remembering information temporarily, but what if you need to remember something for hours or months or years? In that case, you are

TRY THIS   **Sensory Memory at Work** In a darkened room, ask a friend to switch on a small flashlight and move it slowly in a circle. You will see a moving point of light. If it appears to have a "tail," like a comet, that is your sensory memory of the light before it fades away. Now ask your friend to speed up the movement. You should now see a complete circle of light, because as the light moves, its impression on your sensory memory does not have time to fade before the circle is completed. A similar process allows us to see "sparkler circles."

FIGURE 7.4

The Role of Memory in Comprehension

TRY THIS Read the paragraph shown here, then turn away and try to recall as much of it as possible. Then read the footnote on page 244 and reread the paragraph. The second reading probably made a lot more sense and was much easier to remember because knowing the title of the paragraph allowed you to retrieve from long-term memory your knowledge about the topic (Bransford & Johnson, 1972).

The procedure is actually quite simple. First, you arrange items into different groups. Of course, one pile may be sufficient, depending on how much there is to do. If you have to go somewhere else due to lack of facilities that is the next step; otherwise, you are pretty well set. It is important not to overdo things. That is, it is better to do too few things at once than too many. In the short run, this may not seem important, but complications can easily arise. A mistake can be expensive as well. At first, the whole procedure will seem complicated. Soon, however, it will become just another facet of life. It is difficult to foresee any end to the necessity for this task in the immediate future, but then, one never can tell. After the procedure is completed, one arranges the materials into different groups again. Then they can be put into their appropriate places. Eventually they will be used once more, and the whole cycle will then have to be repeated. However, that is part of life.

better off using **elaborative rehearsal,** which involves thinking about how new material relates to information already stored in memory. For example, instead of trying to remember a new person's name by simply repeating it to yourself, try thinking about how the name is related to something you already know. If you are introduced to a man named Jim Crews, for example, you might think, "He is as tall as my uncle Jim, who always wears a crew cut."

Study after study has shown that memory is improved when people use elaborative rehearsal rather than maintenance rehearsal (Jahnke & Nowaczyk, 1998). According to the levels-of-processing model, this improvement occurs because information is mentally processed to a greater degree or "depth" during elaborative rehearsal (Roediger, Gallo, & Geraci, 2002). The more you think about new information, organize it, and relate it to existing knowledge, the "deeper" the processing, and the better your memory of it becomes. Teachers use this idea when they ask their students not only to define a new word but also to use it in a sentence. Figuring out how to use the new word takes deeper processing than merely TRY THIS defining it. (The next time you come across an unfamiliar word in this book, don't just read its definition. Try using the word in a sentence by coming up with an example of the concept that relates to your knowledge and experience.)

information-processing model A model of memory in which information is seen as passing through sensory memory, short-term memory, and long-term memory.

levels-of-processing model A view stating that how well something is remembered depends on the degree to which incoming information is mentally processed.

maintenance rehearsal Repeating information over and over to keep it active in short-term memory.

elaborative rehearsal A memorization method that involves thinking about how new information relates to information already stored in long-term memory.

transfer-appropriate processing model A model of memory that suggests that a critical determinant of memory is how well the retrieval process matches the original encoding process.

parallel distributed processing (PDP) models Memory models in which new experiences change one's overall knowledge base.

● **Transfer-Appropriate Processing** The level of processing is not the only factor affecting what we remember (Baddeley, 1992). Another critical factor, suggested by the **transfer-appropriate processing model,** is how well the processes involved during retrieval match the way in which the information was originally encoded. Consider an experiment in which half the students in a class were told that an upcoming exam would contain multiple-choice questions. The rest were told to expect essay questions. Only half the students actually got the type of exam they expected, however. These students did much better on the exam than those who took an unexpected type of exam. Apparently, in studying for the exam, the two groups used encoding strategies that were most appropriate to the type of exam they expected. Those who tried to retrieve the information in a way that did not match their encoding method had a harder time (d'Ydewalle & Rosselle, 1978). Results such as these illustrate that the match between encoding and retrieval processes can be as important as depth of processing in memory.

● **Parallel Distributed Processing** A fourth approach to memory is based on **parallel distributed processing (PDP) models** of memory (Rumelhart & McClelland, 1986). These models suggest that new experiences don't just provide new facts that are later retrieved individually. Those facts are also integrated with existing knowledge or memories, changing our overall knowledge base and altering in a more general way our understanding of the world and how it operates. For example, when students first arrive on campus, they learn specific facts, such as where classes are held, what time the library closes, and where to get the best pizza.

Over time, these and many other facts of college life form a network of information that creates a more general understanding of how the whole college system works. Developing this network makes students more knowledgeable, but also more sophisticated. It allows them to, say, allocate their study time so as to do well in their most important courses and to plan a schedule that avoids conflicts between classes, work, and recreational activities. Your own knowledge of college life probably changes day by day in a way that is much more general than any single new fact you learned.

PDP models of memory reflect this notion of knowledge networks. PDP memory theorists begin by considering how *neural networks* might provide the framework for a functional memory system (Anderson, 2000). As described in the chapters on perception, learning, and biological aspects of psychology, the structure of neural networks allows each part to be linked to every other part. When this network model is applied to memory, each unit of knowledge is seen as connected to every other unit, and the connections between units are seen as getting stronger the more often the units are experienced together. From this perspective, then, "knowledge" is distributed across a dense network of associations. When this network is activated, *parallel processing* occurs. That is, different portions of the network operate simultaneously, allowing people to quickly and efficiently draw inferences and make generalizations. Just seeing the word *sofa*, for example, allows us immediately to gain access to knowledge about what a sofa looks like, what it is used for, where it tends to be located, who might buy one, and the like. PDP models of memory explain this process very effectively.

● **Multiple Memory Systems** The **multiple memory systems** approach suggests that the brain contains several relatively separate memory systems, each of which resides in a different area and each of which serves somewhat different purposes (Schacter & Tulving, 1994; Schacter, Wagner, & Buckner, 2000). As mentioned in the Focus on Research Methods section, for example, the fact that explicit and implicit memory appear to operate on different principles suggests that they are separate systems, each of which is supported by activity in different regions of the brain. Additional evidence for the multiple memory systems approach comes from case studies, such as that of H. M. (described later), in which damage to the brain's hippocampus impairs performance on tests of explicit memory, but not on implicit memory tests (e.g., Warrington & Weiskrantz, 1970). Other research shows that

in review Models of Memory

Model	Assumptions
Information processing	Information is processed in three stages: sensory, short-term, and long-term memory.
Levels of processing	The more deeply material is processed, the better the memory of it.
Transfer-appropriate processing	Retrieval is improved when we try to recall material in a way that matches how the material was encoded.
Parallel distributed processing (PDP)	New experiences add to and alter our overall knowledge base; they are not separate, unconnected facts. PDP networks allow us to draw inferences and make generalizations about the world.
Multiple memory systems	There are several separate memory systems, each in a different brain area and each serving different purposes.

● **multiple memory systems model** A model of memory that suggests that the brain contains several memory systems, each of which resides in a different area and each of which serves somewhat different purposes.

The title of the paragraph in Figure 7.4 is "Washing Clothes."

inactivating the hippocampus with drugs causes massive disruption of explicit, but not implicit, memory processes (Frank, O'Reilly, & Curran, 2006).

For a summary of the five models we have discussed, see "In Review: Models of Memory." Each of these models provides an explanation of why we remember some things and forget others. Which one offers the best explanation? The answer is that more than one model may be required to understand memory. Just as it is helpful for physicists to characterize light in terms of both waves and particles, psychologists find it useful to think of memory both in terms of cognitive processes, as suggested by the information-processing, levels-of-processing, and transfer-appropriate processing approaches, and in terms of underlying brain activity, as suggested by the parallel distributed processing and multiple memory systems approaches.

Storing New Memories

The storage of information is critical to memory, because we can retrieve only information that has been stored. According to the information-processing model, sensory, short-term, and long-term memory each provide a different type of storage system. Let's take a closer look at these three memory systems in order to better understand how they work—and sometimes fail.

Sensory Memory

To recognize incoming stimuli, the brain must analyze and compare them with what is already stored in long-term memory. Although this process is very quick, it still takes time. The major function of **sensory memory** is to hold information long enough for it to be processed further (Nairne, 2003). This maintenance is the job of the **sensory registers**, which act as temporary storage bins. There is a separate register for each of the five senses, and each register is capable of storing a nearly complete representation of sensory stimuli. Sensory memories are stored only briefly, often for less than one second, but this is long enough for stimulus identification to begin (Eysenck & Keane, 2005).

TRY THIS ➤ Sensory memory helps us experience a constant flow of information, even if that flow is interrupted. To appreciate this fact, turn your head slowly from left to right. It may seem as though your eyes are moving smoothly, like a movie camera scanning a scene, but that's not what is happening. Instead, your eyes fixate at one point for about one-fourth of a second and then rapidly jump to a new position. The sensation of smooth movement through the visual field occurs because you hold each scene in your visual sensory register until your eyes fixate again. Similarly, when you listen to someone speak, the auditory sensory register allows you to experience a smooth flow of information. Information persists for varying amounts of time in the five sensory registers. For example, information in the auditory sensory register lasts longer than information in the visual sensory register.

The fact that sensory memories quickly fade if they are not processed further is an adaptive characteristic of the memory system. You simply could not deal with all of the sights, sounds, odors, tastes, and touch sensations that reach your sense organs at any given moment. As mentioned in the chapter on perception, **selective attention** focuses mental resources on only part of the stimulus field, thus controlling what information is processed further. It is through the process of perception that the fleeting impressions of sensory memory are captured and transferred to short-term memory.

Short-Term Memory and Working Memory

The sensory registers allow your memory system to develop a representation of a stimulus. However, they can't perform the more thorough representation and

sensory memory A type of memory that holds large amounts of incoming information very briefly, but long enough to connect one impression to the next.

sensory registers Memory systems that hold incoming information long enough for it to be processed further.

selective attention The focusing of mental resources on only part of the stimulus field.

analysis that is needed if the information is going to be used in some way. These functions are accomplished by short-term memory and working memory.

Short-term memory (STM) is the part of your memory system that stores limited amounts of information for a limited amount of time. When you check the television listings for the channel number of a show you want to watch, and then switch to that channel, you are using short-term memory. **Working memory** is the part of the memory system that allows us to mentally work with, or manipulate, the information being held in short-term memory. When you mentally calculate what time you have to leave home in order to have lunch on campus, return a library book, and still get to class on time, you are using working memory.

So short-term memory is actually a component of working memory. Together, they enable us to do many kinds of mental work. Suppose you are buying something for 83 cents, and you go through your change and pick out two quarters, two dimes, two nickels, and three pennies. To do this, you use both short-term and working memory to remember the price, retrieve the rules of addition from long-term memory, *and* keep a running count of how much change you have so far. Now try to recall ⚙ ← TRY THIS how many windows there are on the front of the house or apartment where you grew up. In attempting to answer this question, you probably formed a mental image of the building, which required one kind of working-memory process, and then, while maintaining that image in short-term memory, you "worked" on it by counting the windows. So working memory has at least two components: *maintenance* (holding information in short-term memory) and *manipulation* (working on that information).

● Encoding in Short-Term Memory

The encoding of information in short-term memory is much more elaborative and varied than that in the sensory registers (Brandimonte, Hitch, & Bishop, 1992). *Acoustic encoding* (by sound) seems to dominate. Evidence for this assertion comes from analyzing the mistakes people make when encoding information in short-term memory. These mistakes tend to be acoustically related, which means that they involve the substitution of similar sounds. For example, Robert Conrad (1964) showed people strings of letters and asked them to repeat the letters immediately. Their mistakes tended to involve replacing the correct letter (say, C) with another that *sounded* like it (such as D, P, or T). These mistakes occurred even though the letters were presented visually, without any sound.

Evidence for acoustic coding in short-term memory also comes from studies showing that items are more difficult to remember if their spoken sounds are similar. For example, native English speakers do less well when asked to remember a string of letters such as *ECVTGB* (which all have similar sounds) than when asked to remember one like *KRLDQS* (which have distinct sounds). Encoding in short-term memory is not *always* acoustic, however. Visual codes are also used (Zhang & Simon, 1985), but information coded visually tends to fade much more quickly from short-term memory than information that is encoded acoustically (Cornoldi, DeBeni, & Baldi, 1989). There is also evidence for kinesthetic encoding, which involves physical movements (Best, 1999). In one study, deaf people were shown a list of words and then asked to immediately write them down from memory (Shand, 1982). When these people made errors, they wrote words that are expressed through similar *hand movements* in American Sign Language, rather than words that *sounded* similar to the correct words. Apparently, these individuals had encoded the words on the basis of the movements they would use when making the signs for them.

● Storage Capacity of Short-Term Memory

You can easily determine the capacity of short-term memory by conducting the simple experiment shown in Figure 7.5 (Howard, 1983). Your **immediate memory span** is the maximum number of items you are able to recall perfectly after one presentation. If your memory span is like most people's, you can repeat about six or seven items from the test in this figure. The interesting thing is that you should come up with about the same

● **short-term memory (STM)** The maintenance component of working memory, which holds unrehearsed information for a limited time.

● **working memory** The part of the memory system that allows us to mentally work with, or manipulate, information being held in short-term memory.

● **immediate memory span** The maximum number of items a person can recall perfectly after one presentation of the items.

```
9 2 5                        G  M  N
8 6 4 2                      S  L  R  R
3 7 6 5 4                    V  O  E  P  G
6 2 7 4 1 8                  X  W  D  X  Q  O
0 4 0 1 4 7 3                E  P  H  H  J  A  E
1 9 2 2 3 5 3 0              Z  D  O  F  W  D  S  V
4 8 6 8 5 4 3 3 2            D  T  Y  N  R  H  E  H  Q
2 5 3 1 9 7 1 7 6 8          K  H  W  D  A  G  R  O  F  Z
8 5 1 2 9 6 1 9 4 5 0        U  D  F  F  W  H  D  Q  D  G  E
9 1 8 5 4 6 9 4 2 9 3 7      Q  M  R  H  X  Z  D  P  R  R  E  H
```

CAT BOAT RUG
RUN BEACH PLANT LIGHT
SUIT WATCH CUT STAIRS CAR
JUNK LONE GAME CALL WOOD HEART
FRAME PATCH CROSS DRUG DESK HORSE LAW
CLOTHES CHOOSE GIFT DRIVE BOOK TREE HAIR THIS
DRESS CLERK FILM BASE SPEND SERVE BOOK LOW TIME
STONE ALL NAIL DOOR HOPE EARL FEEL BUY COPE GRAPE
AGE SOFT FALL STORE PUT TRUE SMALL FREE CHECK MAIL LEAF
LOG DAY TIME CHESS LAKE CUT BIRD SHEET YOUR SEE STREET WHEEL

FIGURE 7.5

Capacity of Short-Term Memory

TRY THIS Here is a test of your immediate memory span. Ask someone to read to you the numbers in the top row at the rate of about one per second. Then try to repeat them back in the same order. Do the same test on the next row, and the one after that, until you make a mistake. Your immediate memory span is the maximum number of items you can repeat back perfectly. Similar tests can be performed using the rows of letters and words.

number whether you estimate your immediate memory span with digits, letters, words, or virtually any type of unit. George Miller (1956) noticed that studies of a wide variety of tasks showed the same limit on the ability to process information. This "magic number," which is seven plus or minus two, appears to be the capacity of short-term memory. In addition, the "magic number" refers not only to discrete elements, such as words or digits, but also to meaningful *groupings* of information, called **chunks.**

TRY THIS To appreciate the difference between discrete elements and chunks, read the following letters to a friend, pausing at each dash: *FB-IAO-LM-TVI-BMB-MW.* The chances are very good that your friend will not be able to repeat this string of letters perfectly. Why? There are fifteen letters, which exceeds most people's immediate memory span. Now, give your friend the test again, but group the letters like this: *FBI-AOL-MTV-IBM-BMW.* Your friend will probably repeat that string easily because, even though the same fifteen letters are involved, they will be processed as only five meaningful chunks of information (Bower, 1975).

● **The Power of Chunking** Chunks of information can become very complex. If someone says, "The boy in the red shirt kicked his mother in the shin," you could probably repeat the sentence very easily. Yet it contains twelve words and forty-three letters. How can you repeat the sentence so effortlessly? The answer is that people can build bigger and bigger chunks of information (Ericsson & Staszewski, 1989). In this case, you might have represented "the boy in the red shirt" as one chunk of information rather than as six words or nineteen letters. Similarly, "kicked his mother" and "in the shin" could be represented as just two chunks of information.

Learning to use bigger and bigger chunks of information can enhance short-term memory. Children's memories improve partly because they gradually become able to hold as many as seven chunks in memory, but also because they get better at grouping information into chunks (Servan-Schreiber & Anderson, 1990). Adults, too, can greatly increase the capacity of their short-term memory by more appropriate chunking. One college student increased his immediate memory span from

● **chunks** Stimuli that are perceived as one unit or as a meaningful grouping of information.

Chunking in Action Those who provide instantaneous translation of speeches—such as this one at the United Nations—must store long, often complicated segments of speech in short-term memory while searching long-term memory for the equivalent second-language expressions. The task is made easier by chunking the speaker's words into phrases and sentences.

seven digits to eighty digits (Ericsson, Chase, & Faloon, 1980). In short, although the capacity of short-term memory is more or less constant—five to nine chunks of meaningful information—the size of those chunks can vary tremendously.

● **Duration of Short-Term Memory** Imagine how hard it would be to, say, mentally calculate the tip you should leave in a restaurant if your short-term memory was cluttered with every other bill you had ever paid, every phone number you had ever called, and every conversation you had ever heard. This problem doesn't come up because—unless you continue repeating information to yourself (maintenance rehearsal) or use elaborative rehearsal to transfer it to long-term memory—information in short-term memory is usually forgotten quickly. You may have experienced this adaptive, though sometimes inconvenient, phenomenon if you have ever been interrupted while repeating to yourself a new phone number you were about to call, and then couldn't remember the number.

How long does unrehearsed information remain in short-term memory? To answer this question, John Brown (1958) and Lloyd and Margaret Peterson (1959) devised the **Brown-Peterson procedure,** which is a method for preventing rehearsal. A person is presented with a group of three letters, such as GRB, and then counts backward by threes from some number until a signal is given. Counting prevents the person from rehearsing the letters. At the signal, the person stops counting and tries to recall the letters. By varying the number of seconds that the person counts backward, the experimenter can determine how much forgetting takes place over a certain amount of time. As you can see in Figure 7.6, information in short-term memory is forgotten gradually but rapidly: After eighteen seconds, participants can remember almost nothing. Evidence from these and other experiments suggests that unrehearsed information can be maintained in short-term memory for no more than about eighteen seconds. However, if the information is rehearsed or processed further, it may be encoded into long-term memory.

● Long-Term Memory

When people talk about memory, they are usually talking about **long-term memory (LTM),** the part of the memory system whose encoding and storage capabilities can produce memories that last a lifetime.

● **Brown-Peterson procedure** A method for determining how long unrehearsed information remains in short-term memory.

● **long-term memory (LTM)** A relatively long-lasting stage of memory whose capacity to store new information is believed to be unlimited.

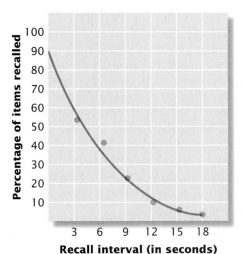

FIGURE 7.6

Forgetting in Short-Term Memory

This graph shows the percentage of items recalled after various intervals during which rehearsal was prevented. Notice that virtually complete forgetting occurred after a delay of eighteen seconds.

Source: Data from Peterson & Peterson (1959).

● **Encoding in Long-Term Memory** Some information is encoded into long-term memory without any conscious attempt to memorize it (Ellis, 1991). However, putting information into long-term memory is often the result of more elaborate and conscious processing, which usually involves some degree of *semantic encoding*. In other words, encoding in long-term memory often ignores details and instead encodes the general, underlying meaning of the information.

Jacqueline Sachs (1967) demonstrated the dominance of semantic encoding in long-term memory in a classic study. She first asked research participants to listen to tape recordings of people speaking. She then showed them sentences and asked them to say which contained the exact wording heard on the tape. People did very well when they were tested immediately (using mainly short-term memory). However, after only twenty-seven seconds, at which point the information had to be retrieved from long-term memory, they could not determine which of two sentences they had heard if both sentences expressed the same meaning. For example, they could not determine whether they had heard "He sent a letter about it to Galileo, the great Italian scientist" or "A letter about it was sent to Galileo, the great Italian scientist." In short, they remembered the general meaning of what they had heard, but not the exact wording.

Perhaps you are thinking, "So what?" After all, the two sentences mean the same thing. Unfortunately, when people encode the general meaning of information they hear or read, they can make mistakes about the details. This can be a problem when recalling exact words is important—such as in the courtroom, during business negotiations, and in discussions between students and teachers about previous agreements. Psychologists have found that when people encode the general meaning of information, they may make mistakes about the specifics of what they have heard (Brewer, 1977). For example, after listening to a list of words such as *cold, white, ice, winter, frosty, blizzard, frozen, drift, flurries, parka, shovel, skis, sled,* and *flakes,* people often remember having heard the related word *snow* even though it was not presented (Roediger & McDermott, 1995; Roediger & McDermott, 2000).

TRY THIS You can replicate this research by reading this list to five friends, then asking them to recall as many of its words as they can. Chances are that, like participants in laboratory experiments, several of them will be so certain that *snow* was on the list that they may not believe you when you tell them it wasn't! As discussed later in this chapter, these errors occur partly because people encode into long-term memory not only the general meaning of information but also what they think and assume about that information (McDermott & Chan, 2006). Those expectations and assumptions—such as that a list of "winter-related" words must have included *snow*—may alter what is recalled.

Counterfeiters depend on the fact that people encode only the general meaning of visual, as well as auditory, stimuli. For example, look at Figure 7.7, and find the correct drawing of the U.S. penny (Nickerson & Adams, 1979). Most people from the United States are unsuccessful at this task; people from other countries do just as poorly at recognizing their nation's coins (Jones, 1990). Research showing that people fail to remember specific details about visual information has prompted the

FIGURE 7.7

Encoding into Long-Term Memory

TRY THIS Which is the correct image of a U.S. penny? (See the footnote on page 250 for the answer.) Most people often cannot explicitly remember the specific details of information stored in long-term memory, but priming studies suggest that they do retain some implicit memory of them (e.g., Srinivas, 1993).

Source: Nickerson & Adams (1979).

(A) **(B)** **(C)** **(D)** **(E)**

U.S. Treasury to begin using more distinctive drawings on the paper currencies it distributes.

Although long-term memory normally involves semantic encoding, people can also use visual encoding to process images into long-term memory. In one study, people viewed 2,500 pictures. It took 16 hours just to present the stimuli, but the participants later correctly recognized more than 90 percent of the pictures on which they were tested (Standing, Conezio, & Haber, 1970). *Dual coding theory* suggests that pictures tend to be remembered better than words because pictures are represented in two codes—visual and verbal—rather than in only one (Paivio, 1986). This suggestion is supported by neuroimaging studies showing that when people are asked to memorize pictures, they tend to create a verbal label for the picture (e.g., *frog*), as well as to look at the drawing's visual features (Kelley et al., 1998).

● **Storage Capacity of Long-Term Memory**   Whereas the capacity of short-term memory is limited, the capacity of long-term memory is extremely large. In fact, most memory theorists believe it to be unlimited (Matlin, 1998). The unlimited capacity of long-term memory is impossible to prove, but there are no cases of people being unable to learn something new because they had too much information stored in long-term memory. We do know for sure that people store vast quantities of information in long-term memory and that they often remember it remarkably well for long periods of time. For example, people can recall the plot of a novel more than three years after having read it (Stanhope, Cohen, & Conway, 1993), and they are amazingly accurate at recognizing the faces of high school classmates they have not seen for over twenty-five years (Bruck, Cavanagh, & Ceci, 1991). They also do surprisingly well on tests of a foreign language or high school algebra fifty years after having formally studied these subjects (Bahrick & Hall, 1991; Bahrick et al., 1994). So you will probably retain some of what you learn in this psychology course a lot longer than you might expect (Conway, Cohen, & Stanhope, 1991).

However, long-term memories are also subject to distortion. In one study, college students were asked to recall their high school grades. Even though the students were motivated to be accurate, they correctly remembered 89 percent of their A grades but only 29 percent of their D grades. And you might not be surprised to learn that when they recalled grades incorrectly, the errors usually involved remembering grades as being higher than they actually were (Bahrick, Hall, & Berger, 1996). What about *flashbulb memories*—those vivid recollections of personally significant events that, like a snapshot, seem to preserve all the details of the moment (Brown & Kulik, 1997)? They, too, can be distorted, especially in people who are not actually present at such events (Sharot et al., 2006). For example, one group of students was asked to describe where they were and what they were doing when they heard about the verdict in the O. J. Simpson murder trial (Schmolck, Buffalo, & Squire, 2000). The students reported their recollections three times, first just three days after the verdict, and then again after fifteen months and thirty-two months. Only half the recollections reported at fifteen months were accurate, and 11 percent contained major errors or distortions. Among those reporting after thirty-two months, 71 percent of their recollections were inaccurate, and just over 40 percent contained major errors or distortions. For example, three days after the verdict, one student said he heard about it while in a campus lounge with other students. Thirty-two months later, the same student recalled hearing the news in the living room of his home with his father and sister. Do you remember where were you were and what you were doing when you heard

---

Drawing (A) shows the correct penny image in Figure 7.7.

Magnani's painting

Photo of the same scene

TRY THIS  **A Remarkable Memory** Using only his long-term memory, Franco Magnani created amazingly accurate paintings of his hometown in Italy even though he had not seen it for more than thirty years (Sacks, 1992). People like Magnani display *eidetic imagery,* commonly called *photographic memory.* It is not actually photographic, but it does create automatic, detailed, and vivid images of virtually everything they have ever seen. About 5 percent of school-age children have eidetic imagery, but it is extremely rare in adults (Haber, 1979). You can test yourself for eidetic imagery by drawing a detailed picture or map of a place that you know well but have not seen recently. How did you do?

about the 9/11 terrorist attacks on the United States? You may be quite sure that you do, but if you are like the students tested in one study, your flashbulb memories of 9/11 may not be entirely correct (Talarico & Rubin, 2003). Most of the students whose flashbulb memories had been substantially distorted over time were unaware that this distortion had occurred. In fact, they were very confident that their reports were accurate. Later, we will see that such overconfidence can also appear in courtroom testimony by eyewitnesses to crime.

● Distinguishing Between Short-Term and Long-Term Memory

Some psychologists claim that there is no need to distinguish between short-term and long-term memory. They say that what we call short-term (and working) memory is simply that part of memory that we happen to be thinking about at any particular time, whereas long-term memory is the part of memory that we are not thinking about at any given moment. ("In Review: Storing New Memories"

in **review** Storing New Memories			
Storage System	**Function**	**Capacity**	**Duration**
Sensory memory	Briefly holds representations of stimuli from each sense for further processing	Large: absorbs all sensory input from a particular stimulus	Less than 1 second
Short-term and working memory	Holds information in awareness and manipulates it to accomplish mental work	Five to nine distinct items or chunks of information	About 18 seconds
Long-term memory	Stores new information indefinitely	Unlimited	Unlimited

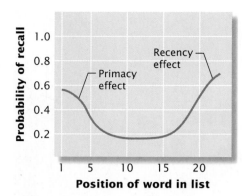

FIGURE 7.8

A Serial-Position Curve

The probability of recalling an item is plotted here as a function of its serial position in a list of items. Generally, the first several items and the last several items are most likely to be recalled.

summarizes the characteristics of these systems.) However, other psychologists argue that short-term and long-term memory are fundamentally different—that they obey different laws (Cowan, 1988; Talmi et al., 2005). Evidence that information is transferred from short-term memory to a distinct storage system comes from experiments on recall.

● **Experiments on Recall**   To conduct your own recall experiment, TRY THIS look at the following list of words for thirty seconds, then look away and write down as many of the words as you can, in any order: desk, chalk, pencil, chair, paperclip, book, eraser, folder, briefcase, essays. Which words you remember depends in part on their *serial position*—that is, where the words are in the list, as Figure 7.8 shows. This figure is a *serial-position curve*, which shows the chances of recalling words appearing in each position in a list. For the first two or three words in a list, recall tends to be very good—a characteristic that is called the **primacy effect.** The probability of recall decreases for words in the middle of the list and then rises dramatically for the last few words. The ease of recalling words near the end of a list is called the **recency effect.** It has been suggested that the primacy effect reflects rehearsal that puts early words into long-term memory, and that the recency effect occurs because the last few words are still in short-term memory when we try to recall the list (Glanzer & Cunitz, 1966; Koppenaal & Glanzer, 1990).

Retrieving Memories

Have you ever been unable to recall the name of an old television show or movie star, only to think of it the next day? Remembering something requires not only that it be appropriately encoded and stored but also that you have the ability to bring it into consciousness—in other words, to *retrieve* it.

Retrieval Cues and Encoding Specificity

Stimuli that help people retrieve information from long-term memory are called **retrieval cues.** They allow people to recall things that were once forgotten and help them to recognize information stored in memory. In general, recognition tasks are easier than recall tasks, because they contain more retrieval cues. As noted earlier, it is usually easier to recognize the correct alternative on a multiple-choice exam than to recall material for an essay test.

The effectiveness of cues in aiding retrieval depends on the degree to which they tap into information that was encoded at the time of learning (Tulving, 1983). This rule, known as the **encoding specificity principle,** is consistent with the transfer-appropriate processing model of memory. Because long-term memories are often encoded semantically, cues related to the *meaning* of the stored information tend to work best. For example, imagine you have learned a long list of sentences, one of which is either (1) "The man lifted the piano" or (2) "The man tuned the piano." Having the cue "something heavy" during a recall test would probably help you remember the first sentence, because you probably encoded something about the weight of a piano, but "something heavy" would probably not help you recall the second sentence. Similarly, the cue "makes nice sounds" would be likely to help you recall the second sentence, but not the first (Barclay et al., 1974).

Context and State Dependence

Have you ever revisited a place that you hadn't been to in a long time, and suddenly found yourself remembering events that happened there? In general, people

primacy effect   A characteristic of memory in which recall of the first two or three items in a list is particularly good.

recency effect   A characteristic of memory in which recall is particularly good for the last few items in a list.

retrieval cue   A stimulus that aids the recall or recognition of information stored in memory.

encoding specificity principle   A principle stating that the ability of a cue to aid retrieval depends on the degree to which it taps into information that was encoded at the time of the original learning.

Context-Dependent Memories Many people attending a reunion at their old high school find that being in the building again provides context cues that help bring back memories of their school days.

remember more of what they learned when the conditions during recall are the same as those during learning (Smith & Vela, 2001). This effect may appear because we tend to encode features of the environment in which the learning occurred, and these features may later serve as retrieval cues (Richardson-Klavehn & Bjork, 1988). In one experiment, people studied a series of photos while in the presence of a particular odor. Later, they reviewed a larger set of photos and tried to identify the ones they had seen earlier. Half of these people were tested in the presence of the original odor and half in the presence of a different odor. Those who smelled the same odor during learning and testing did significantly better on the recognition task than those who were tested in the presence of a different odor. The matching odor served as a powerful retrieval cue (Cann & Ross, 1989).

When memory is helped or hindered by the environment, it is called **context-dependent memory**. Police and prosecutors sometimes take advantage of context-dependent memory by asking eyewitnesses to revisit the scene of the crime they saw, either in person or by mentally reconstructing it during an interview. The goal is to reinstate retrieval cues that can improve the accuracy of eyewitness testimony (e.g., Campos & Alonso-Quecuty, 2006), but as we will see later, these techniques may not result in perfect retrieval.

Like the external environment, the internal environment can be encoded during learning, and thus it can act as a retrieval cue. When a person's internal state can aid or hamper retrieval, the person has what is called **state-dependent memory**. For example, if people learn new material while under the influence of a drug, they tend to recall it better if they are tested under the influence of that same drug (Eich et al., 1975). But don't get the wrong idea: Memory works best overall when people are drug-free during encoding and retrieval. Mood states, too, can affect memory (Eich & Macaulay, 2000). People tend to remember more positive incidents from their past when they are in a positive mood at the time of recall and more negative events when they are in a negative mood (Ehrlichman & Halpern, 1988; Lewinsohn & Rosenbaum, 1987). These *mood congruency effects* are strongest when people try to recall personally meaningful episodes, because such events were most likely to be colored by their moods (Eich & Metcalfe, 1989).

● **Retrieval from Semantic Memory**

All of the retrieval situations we have discussed so far are relevant to episodic memory. ("In Review: Factors Affecting Retrieval from Long-Term Memory"

● **context-dependent memory** Memory that can be helped or hindered by similarities or differences between the context in which it is learned and the context in which it is recalled.

● **state-dependent memory** Memory that is aided or impeded by a person's internal state.

in **review**	Factors Affecting Retrieval from Long-Term Memory	
Process	**Effect on Memory**	
Encoding specificity	Retrieval cues are effective only to the extent that they tap into information that was originally encoded.	
Context dependence	Retrieval is most successful when it occurs in the same environment in which the information was originally learned.	
State dependence	Retrieval is most successful when people are in the same physiological or psychological state as when they originally learned the information.	

summarizes this material.) But how do we retrieve information from semantic memory, in which our general knowledge about the world is stored? Researchers studying this process typically ask participants general-knowledge questions, such as (1) Are fish minerals? (2) Is a beagle a dog? (3) Do birds fly? and (4) Does a car have legs? As you might imagine, most people respond correctly to such questions. By measuring the amount of time people take to answer the questions, however, psychologists have found important clues about how semantic memory is organized and how we retrieve information from it.

● **Semantic Networks** *Semantic network theory* suggests that all the concepts we have learned are represented in a dense network of associations (Collins &

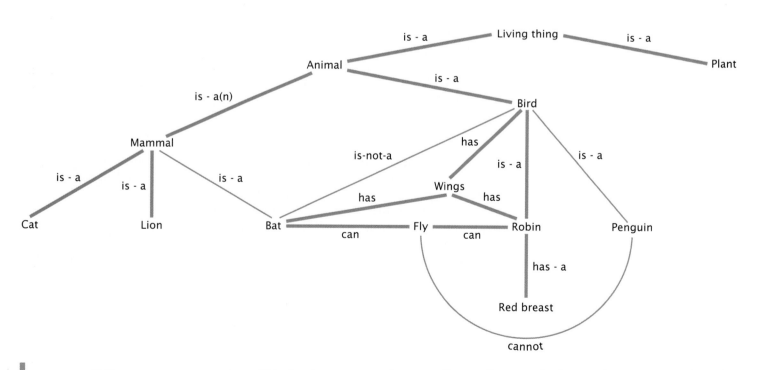

FIGURE 7.9

Semantic Networks

This drawing represents just a small part of a network of semantic associations. Semantic network theories of memory suggest that networks like these allow us to retrieve specific pieces of previously learned information, to draw conclusions about how concepts are related, and to make new inferences about the world.

Loftus, 1975). Figure 7.9 presents just a tiny part of what such a *semantic memory network* might look like. In general, semantic network theory suggests that information is retrieved from memory through **spreading activation** (Medin, Ross, & Markman, 2001). So whenever you think about some concept, that concept becomes activated in the network, and this activation—in the form of neural energy—begins to spread along all the paths related to it. For example, if a person is asked to say whether "A robin is a bird" is true or false, the concepts of both "robin" and "bird" will become activated, and the spreading activation from each will meet somewhere along the path between them. When they do, you know what answer to give.

Some associations within the network are stronger than others. Differing strengths are depicted by the varying thicknesses of the lines in Figure 7.9. Spreading activation travels faster along thick paths than along thin ones. For example, most people probably have a stronger association between "bat" and "can fly" or "has wings" than between "bat" and "is a mammal." Accordingly, most people respond more quickly to "Can a bat fly?" than to "Is a bat a mammal?"

Because of the tight organization of semantic networks and the speed at which activation spreads through them, we have quick and easy access to an enormous body of knowledge about the world. We can retrieve not only the facts we have learned directly but also the knowledge that allows us to infer or draw our own conclusions about other facts (Matlin, 1998). For example, imagine answering the following two questions: (1) Is a robin a bird? and (2) Is a robin a living thing? You can probably answer the first question "directly," because you probably learned this fact at some point in your life. However, you may never have consciously thought about the second question, so answering it requires you to make an inference. Figure 7.9 illustrates the path to that inference. Because you know that a robin is a bird, a bird is an animal, and animals are living things, you can infer that a robin must be a living thing. As you might expect, however, it takes slightly longer to answer the second question than the first.

● **Retrieving Incomplete Knowledge**   Figure 7.9 also shows that concepts such as "bird" are represented in semantic memory as collections of features or characteristics. When you can retrieve some features of a concept from your semantic network, but not enough of them to identify the concept, you are said to have retrieved *incomplete knowledge*. For example, you might know that there is an animal that is not a bird but that has wings and can fly. Yet you might be unable to retrieve its name (bat) at the moment.

You have probably experienced a particular example of incomplete knowledge called the *tip-of-the-tongue phenomenon*. In a typical experiment on this phenomenon, people listen to dictionary definitions of words and are then asked to name each defined word (Brown & McNeill, 1966). If they cannot recall a particular word, they are asked whether they can recall any feature of it, such as its first letter or how many syllables it has. People are surprisingly good at this task, indicating that they are able to retrieve at least some knowledge of the word (Brennen et al., 1990). Most people—especially older people—tend to experience the tip-of-the-tongue phenomenon about once a week (Brown & Nix, 1996).

Another example of retrieving incomplete knowledge is the *feeling-of-knowing experience*, which is often studied by asking people trivia questions (Reder & Ritter, 1992). When they cannot answer a question, they are asked to say how likely it is that they could recognize the correct answer among several options. Again, people are remarkably good at this task. Even though they cannot recall the answer, they can retrieve enough knowledge to determine whether the answer is actually stored in their memory (Costermans, Lories, & Ansay, 1992).

● **spreading activation**   A principle that explains how information is retrieved in semantic network theories of memory.

Constructing Memories

Our memories are affected by what we experience, but also by what we already know about the world (Schacter, Norman, & Koutstaal, 1998). We use that knowledge to organize new information as we receive it, and we fill in gaps in the information that we encode and retrieve (Sherman & Bessenoff, 1999). These processes are called *constructive memory*.

In one study of constructive memory, William Brewer and James Treyens (1981) asked undergraduates to wait for several minutes in the office of a graduate student. When later asked to recall everything that was in the office, most of the students mistakenly "remembered" that books were present, even though there were none. Apparently, the general knowledge that graduate students read many books influenced the participants' memory of what was in the room (Roediger, Meade, & Bergman, 2001). In another study, participants read one of two versions of a story about a man and woman at a ski lodge. One version ended with the man proposing marriage to the woman. The second version was identical until the end, when instead of proposing, the man sexually assaulted the woman. A few days after reading the story, all the participants were asked what they remembered from it. Those who had read the "proposal" version recalled nice things about the man, such as that he wanted the woman to meet his parents. Those who read the "assault" version recalled negative things, such as that the man liked to drink a lot. However, neither kind of information had actually been part of the original story. The participants had "recalled" memories of the man that they had constructed in accordance with their overall impression of him (Carli, 1999).

● **Relating Semantic and Episodic Memory: PDP Models**   Parallel distributed processing models offer one way of explaining how semantic and episodic information become integrated in constructive memories. As mentioned

TRY THIS   **Constructive Memory**   Ask a friend to examine this photo for a minute or so (cover the caption). Then close the book and ask whether each of the following items appeared in the photo: chair, wastebasket, bottle, typewriter, coffeepot, and book. If your friend reports having seen a wastebasket or book, you will have demonstrated constructive memory.

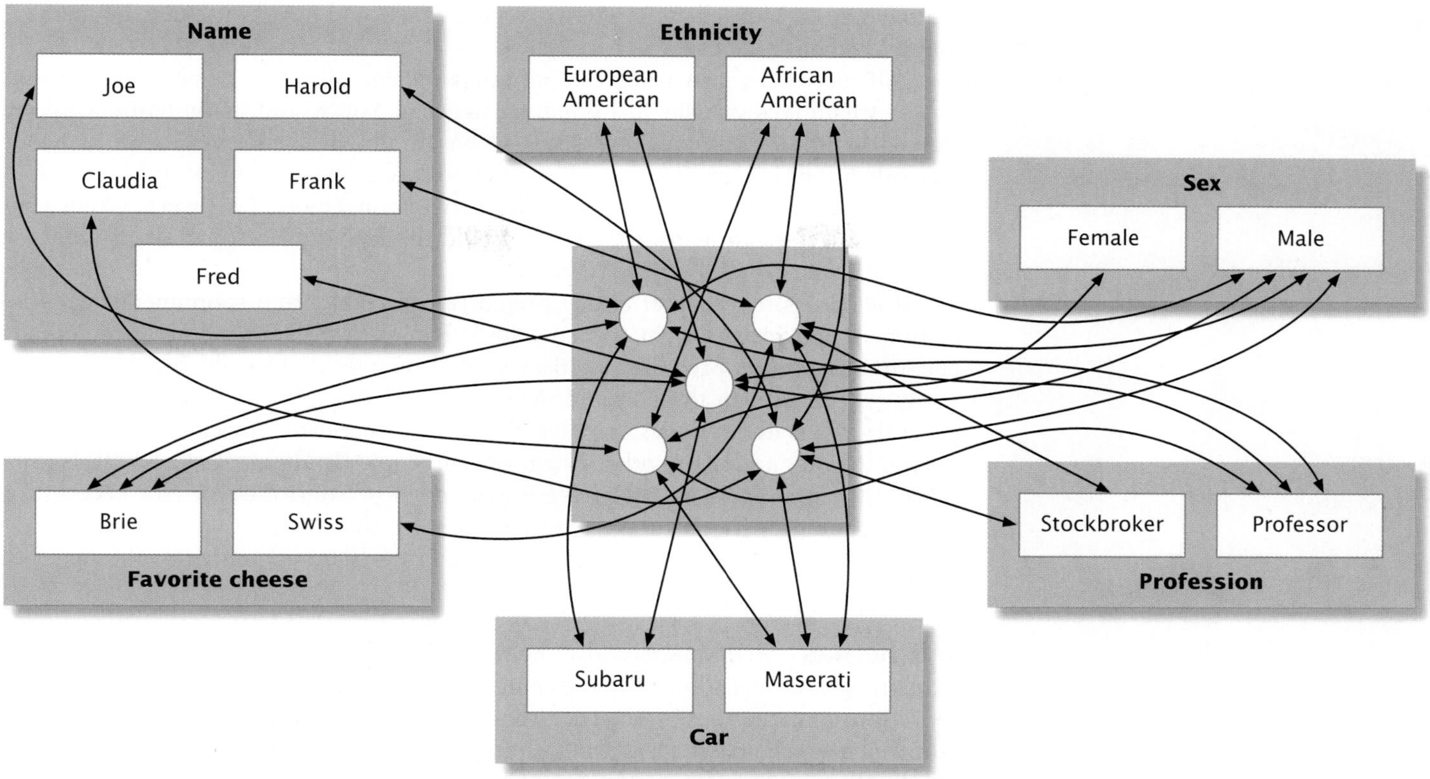

FIGURE 7.10

A PDP Network Model

This simple parallel distributed processing network model represents what someone knows about the characteristics of five people and how these characteristics are related to one another. Each arrow between a rectangle and a circle connects a characteristic with a person. More complex versions of such networks are capable of accounting not only for what people know but also for the inferences and generalizations they tend to make.

Source: From *Cognitive Psychology,* 1st Edition, by C. Martindale, © 1991. Reprinted with permission of Wadsworth Publishing, a division of International Thompson Publishing. Fax 800-730-2215.

earlier, PDP models suggest that newly learned facts alter our general knowledge of what the world is like. Figure 7.10 shows a simple PDP network model of just a tiny part of someone's knowledge of the world (Martindale, 1991). At its center lie the intersections of several learned associations between specific facts about five people, each of whom is represented by a circle. This network "knows" that Joe is a male European American professor who likes Brie cheese and drives a Subaru. It also "knows" that Claudia is a female African American professor who drives a Maserati. Notice that the network has never learned what type of cheese she prefers.

Suppose Figure 7.10 represents your memory, and you now think about Claudia. Because of the connections in the network, the facts that she is a female African American professor and drives a Maserati would be activated. You would automatically remember these facts about her. However, "likes Brie cheese" would also be activated to some extent, because it is linked to other professors in the network. If there were only a few such links, the activation for Brie cheese would be low, and the idea that Claudia likes Brie might be considered a hypothesis or an educated guess. But suppose every other professor you know likes Brie. In that case, the connection between "professors" and "likes Brie cheese" would be so strong that you would be confident that Claudia, too, likes Brie

PDP Models and Constructive Memory   If you hear that "our basketball team won last night," your schema about basketball might cause you to encode, and later retrieve, the fact that the players were men. Such spontaneous, though sometimes incorrect, generalizations associated with PDP models of memory help account for constructive memory.

(Rumelhart & McClelland, 1986). In short, you would have constructed a memory about Claudia.

PDP networks also produce spontaneous generalizations. For example, suppose a friend tells you she just bought a new car. You would know without asking that—like other cars you have seen—it has four wheels. However, spontaneous generalizations can create errors if the network is based on limited or biased experience with a class of objects. So if the network in Figure 7.10 were asked what European American males are like, it would think that all of them drive Japanese cars.

If it occurs to you that ethnic prejudice can result from spontaneous generalization errors, you are right (Greenwald & Banaji, 1995). Researchers are actually encouraged by this prejudicial aspect of PDP networks, though, because it accurately reflects human thought and memory. Virtually everyone makes spontaneous generalizations about males, females, European Americans, African Americans, the young, the old, and many other categories of people (Rudman et al., 1999). Is prejudice, then, a process that we have no choice in or control over? Not necessarily. Relatively unprejudiced people tend to recognize that they are making generalizations and consciously try to ignore or suppress them (Monteith, Sherman, & Devine, 1998).

● **Schemas**   PDP models also help us understand constructive memory by explaining the operation of the schemas that guide it. **Schemas** are mental representations of categories of objects, events, and people. For example, among people who have a schema for *baseball*, simply hearing the word is likely to activate whole clusters of information in long-term memory, including the rules of the game, images of players, bats, balls, a green field, summer days, and perhaps hot dogs and stadiums. The generalized knowledge contained in schemas provides a basis for making inferences about incoming information during the encoding stage. Suppose you hear that a baseball player was injured. Your schema about baseball might lead you to assume the incident was game related and to encode it that way, even though the cause was not mentioned. As a result, you are likely to recall the injury as having occurred during a game. Similarly, if your experience has created a schema that most world news comes through television, your flashbulb memory of how you heard about 9/11 might be that you were watching TV, even if you weren't (Neisser & Harsch, 1986; Wright, 1993; see Figure 7.11 for another example).

FIGURE **7.11**

The Effect of Schemas on Recall

In a classic experiment, participants were shown figures like these, along with labels designed to activate certain schemas (Carmichael, Hogan, & Walter, 1932). For example, when showing the top figure, the experimenter said either "This resembles eyeglasses" or "This resembles a dumbbell." When the participants were asked to copy the figures from memory, their drawings tended to resemble the items mentioned by the experimenter. In other words, the labels activated their schemas, and the schemas altered their memories.

Figure shown to participants	Group 1		Group 2	
	Label given	Figure drawn by participants	Label given	Figure drawn by participants
○—○	Eyeglasses	○○	Dumbbell	○—○
✕	Hourglass	✕	Table	✕
7	Seven	7	Four	4
⊳——	Gun	⊶	Broom	🧹

LINKAGES Memory, Perception, and Eyewitness Testimony

There are few situations in which accurate retrieval of memories is more important—and constructive memory is more dangerous—than when an eyewitness testifies in court about a crime. Eyewitnesses provide the most compelling evidence in many trials, but they can sometimes be mistaken (Loftus & Ketcham, 1991; Wells, Memon, & Penrod, 2006). In 1984, for example, a North Carolina college student, Jennifer Thompson, confidently identified Ronald Cotton as the man who had raped her at knifepoint. Mainly on the basis of Thompson's testimony, Cotton was convicted of rape and sentenced to life in prison. After eleven years behind bars, DNA evidence revealed that he was innocent (and it identified another man as the rapist). The eyewitness-victim's certainty had convinced a jury, but her memory had been faulty (O'Neill, 2000). Let's consider the accuracy of eyewitness memory and how it can be distorted.

Like the rest of us, eyewitnesses can remember only what they perceive, and they can perceive only what they attend to (Backman & Nilsson, 1991). As described in the perception chapter, perception is influenced by a combination of the stimulus features we find "out there" in the world and what we already know, expect, or want—that is, by both bottom-up and top-down processing.

Witnesses are asked to report exactly what they saw or heard; but no matter how hard they try to be accurate, there are limits to how faithful their reports can be (Kassin, Rigby, & Castillo, 1991). For one thing, as mentioned earlier, the semantic encoding typical of long-term memory can cause the loss of certain important details (Fahsing, Ask, & Granhag, 2004). Further, the appearance of new information, including information contained in questions posed by police or lawyers, can alter a witness's memory (Belli & Loftus, 1996). In one study, when witnesses were asked, "How fast were the cars going when they *smashed into* each other?" they were likely to recall a higher speed than when they were asked, "How fast were the cars going when they *hit* each other?" (Loftus & Palmer, 1974; see Figure 7.12). There is also evidence that an object mentioned during questioning about an incident is often mistakenly remembered as having been there during the incident (Dodson & Reisberg, 1991). So if a lawyer says that a screwdriver was lying on the ground (when it was not), witnesses often recall with great certainty having seen it (Ryan & Geiselman, 1991). This *misinformation effect* can occur in several ways

LINKAGES (a link to Perception, p. 174)

FIGURE 7.12

The Impact of Questioning on Eyewitness Memory

After seeing a filmed traffic accident, people were asked, "About how fast were the cars going when they (smashed into, hit, or contacted) each other?" As shown here, the witnesses' responses were influenced by the verb used in the question; "smashed" was associated with the highest average speed estimates. A week later, people who heard the "smashed" question remembered the accident as being more violent than did people in the other two groups (Loftus & Palmer, 1974).

Question	Verb	Estimated mph
About how fast were the cars going when they _____ each other?	smashed into	40.8
	hit	34.0
	contacted	30.8

Original information

External information

The "memory"

About how fast were the cars going when they SMASHED INTO each other?

schemas Mental representations of categories of objects, events, and people.

"Thank you, gentlemen—you may all leave except for No. 3."

This is exactly the sort of biased police lineup that *Eyewitness Evidence: A Guide for Law Enforcement* (U.S. Department of Justice, 1999) is designed to avoid. Based on research in memory and perception, the guide recommends that no one in a lineup should stand out from the others, that police should not suggest that the real criminal is in the lineup, and that witnesses should not be encouraged to guess when making an identification.

(Loftus & Hoffman, 1989). In some cases, hearing new information can make it harder to retrieve the original memory (Tversky & Tuchin, 1989). In others, the new information may be integrated into the old memory, making it impossible to distinguish the new information from what was originally seen (Loftus, 1992). In still others, an eyewitness report might be influenced by the person's assumption that if a lawyer or police officer says an object was there or that something happened, it must be true. A version of this phenomenon was illustrated in 2002 when, over a three-week period, snipers shot more than a dozen people in Maryland, Virginia, and Washington, DC. After early media reports suggested that the snipers might be driving a white van, eyewitnesses to later shootings recalled seeing a white van nearby. In truth, though, the snipers were driving a blue car.

A jury's belief in a witness's testimony often depends as much (or even more) on *how* the witness presents evidence as on the content or relevance of that evidence (Leippe, Manion, & Romanczyk, 1992). Many jurors are impressed, for example, by witnesses who give lots of details about what they saw or heard. Extremely detailed testimony from prosecution witnesses is especially likely to lead to guilty verdicts, even when the details reported are irrelevant (Bell & Loftus, 1989). When a witness gives highly detailed testimony, such as the exact time of the crime or the color of the criminal's shoes, jurors apparently assume that the witness paid especially close attention or has a particularly accurate memory. At first glance, these assumptions seem reasonable. However, as discussed in the chapter on perception, the ability to divide attention is limited. As a result, witnesses might be able to focus attention on the crime and the criminal, or on the surrounding details, but probably not on both—particularly if they were emotionally aroused and the crime happened quickly. So witnesses who accurately remember unimportant details of a crime scene may not accurately recall more important ones, such as the criminal's facial features (Backman & Nilsson, 1991).

Juries also tend to believe witnesses who are confident (Leippe et al. 1992). Unfortunately, research shows that witnesses' *confidence* in their testimony is often greater than the *accuracy* of their testimony (Devilly et al., 2007; Wells, Olson, & Charman, 2002). In some cases, repeated exposure to misinformation and the repeated recall of that misinformation can lead witnesses to feel certain about their testimony even when—as in the Jennifer Thompson case—it may not be correct (Lamb, 1998; Mitchell & Zaragoza, 1996; Roediger, Jacoby, & McDermott, 1996).

The weaknesses inherent in eyewitness memory can be amplified by the use of police lineups and certain other criminal identification procedures (Haw & Fisher, 2004; Wells et al., 2006). In one study, for example, participants watched a videotaped crime and then tried to identify the criminal from a set of photographs (Wells & Bradfield, 1999). None of the photos showed the person who had committed the crime, but some participants nevertheless identified one of them as the criminal they saw on tape. When these mistaken participants were led to believe that they had correctly identified the criminal, they became even more confident in the accuracy of their false identification (Semmler, Brewer, & Wells, 2004; Wells, Olson, & Charman, 2003). These incorrect, but confident, witnesses became more likely than other participants to claim that it had been easy for them to identify the criminal from the photos because they had had a good view of him and had paid careful attention to him.

Since 1973 at least 123 people, including Ronald Cotton, have been released from U.S. prisons after DNA tests or other evidence revealed that they had been falsely convicted—mostly on the basis of faulty eyewitness testimony (Death Penalty Information Center, 2007; Scheck, Neufeld, & Dwyer, 2000; Wells et al., 2000). DNA evidence freed Charles Fain, who had been convicted of murder and spent almost eighteen years on death row in Idaho (Bonner, 2001). Maryland officials approved $900,000 in compensation for Bernard Webster, who served twenty years in prison for rape before DNA revealed that he was innocent (Associated Press, 2003). Frank Lee Smith, too, would have been set free after the sole eyewitness at his murder trial retracted her testimony, but he had already died of cancer while awaiting execution in a Florida prison. Research on memory and perception helps explain how these miscarriages of justice can occur, and it is also guiding efforts to prevent such errors in the future. The U.S. Department of Justice has acknowledged the potential for errors in eyewitness evidence, as well as the dangers of asking witnesses to identify suspects from lineups and photo arrays. One result is *Eyewitness Evidence: A Guide for Law Enforcement* (U.S. Department of Justice, 1999), the first-ever guide for police and prosecutors who work with eyewitnesses. The guide warns these officials that asking leading questions about what witnesses saw can distort their memories. It also suggests that witnesses should examine photos of possible suspects one at a time and points out that false identifications are less likely if witnesses viewing suspects in a lineup are told that the real criminal might not be included (Beresford & Blades, 2006; Wells & Olson, 2003; Wells et al., 2000). ■

Forgetting

The frustrations of forgetting—where you left your keys, the answer to a test question, an anniversary—are apparent to most people nearly every day (Neisser, 2000). Let's look more closely at the nature of forgetting and at some of the mechanisms that are responsible for it.

● How Do We Forget?

In the late 1800s, Hermann Ebbinghaus, a German psychologist, began the systematic study of memory and forgetting by conducting research on his own memory. His aim was to study memory in its "pure" form, uncontaminated by emotional reactions and other pre-existing associations between new material and what was already in memory. To eliminate any such associations, Ebbinghaus created the *nonsense syllable*, a meaningless set of two consonants and a vowel, such as *POF, XEM,* and *QAL.* He read a list of nonsense syllables aloud at a constant rate and then tried to recall the syllables.

To measure forgetting, Ebbinghaus devised the **method of savings,** which involves computing the difference between the number of trials needed to learn a list

method of savings Measuring forgetting by computing the difference between the number of repetitions needed to learn and, after a delay, relearn the same material.

FIGURE 7.13

Ebbinghaus's Curve of Forgetting

TRY THIS Make a list of thirty words, chosen at random from a dictionary, and spend a few minutes memorizing them. After an hour, write down as many of these words as you can remember, but don't look at the original list again. Test yourself again eight hours later, a day later, and two days later. Then look at the original list, and see how well you did on each recall test. Ebbinghaus found that most forgetting occurs during the first nine hours after learning, and especially during the first hour. If this was not the case for you, why do you think your results were different?

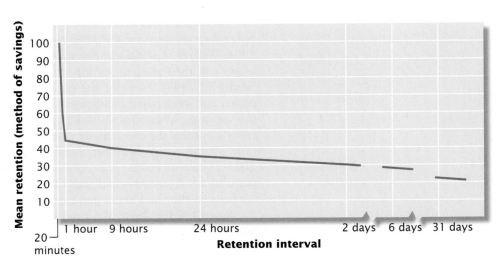

It's All Coming Back to Me   This grandfather hasn't fed an infant for decades, but his memory of how to do it is not entirely gone. He showed some "savings"; it took him less time to relearn the skill than it took him to learn it initially.

of items and the number of trials needed to learn it again after some time has passed. This difference is called the *savings*. If it took Ebbinghaus ten trials to learn a list and ten more trials to relearn it, there would be no savings, and forgetting would have been complete. If it took him ten trials to learn the list and only five trials to relearn it, there would be a savings of 50 percent.

As you can see in Figure 7.13, Ebbinghaus found a decline in savings (and a corresponding increase in forgetting) as time passes. However, the most dramatic drop in what people retain in long-term memory occurs during the first nine hours, especially in the first hour. After this initial decline, the rate of forgetting slows down considerably. In Ebbinghaus's study, some savings existed even thirty-one days after the original learning.

Ebbinghaus's research had some limitations, but it produced two lasting discoveries. One is the shape of the forgetting curve, shown in Figure 7.13. Psychologists have repeated some of his work, substituting words, sentences, and even stories for nonsense syllables. In virtually all cases the forgetting curve shows the same strong initial drop in memory, followed by a much more moderate decrease over time (Wixted, 2004). Of course, people remember sensible stories better than nonsense syllables, but the shape of the curve is the same no matter what type of material is involved (Davis & Moore, 1935). Even the forgetting of events from daily life tends to follow Ebbinghaus's forgetting curve (Thomson, 1982).

The second of Ebbinghaus's important discoveries is just how long-lasting savings in long-term memory can be. Psychologists now know from the method of savings that information about everything from algebra to bike riding is often retained for decades (Matlin, 1998). You may forget something you have learned if you do not use the information, but it is easy to relearn the material if the need arises, indicating that the forgetting was not complete (Hall & Bahrick, 1998).

● Why Do We Forget? The Roles of Decay and Interference

We have seen *how* forgetting occurs, but *why* does it happen? In principle, either of two processes can be responsible. One process is **decay**, the gradual disappearance of the mental representation of a stimulus. Decay occurs in memory much as the inscription engraved on a ring or bracelet wears away and becomes less visible over time. Forgetting might also occur because of **interference**, a process through which either the storage or retrieval of information is impaired by the presence of other

● **decay**   The gradual disappearance of the mental representation of a stimulus.

● **interference**   The process through which either the storage or the retrieval of information is impaired by the presence of other information.

PROACTIVE INTERFERENCE EXPERIMENT

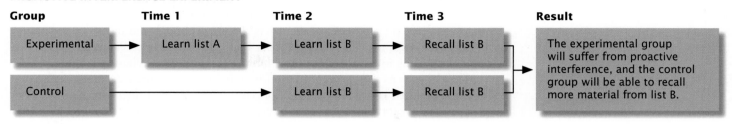

RETROACTIVE INTERFERENCE EXPERIMENT

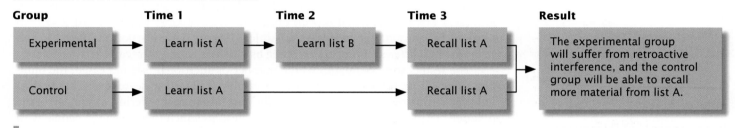

FIGURE **7.14**

Procedures for Studying Interference

To remember the two types of interference, keep in mind that the prefixes—*pro* and *retro*—indicate directions in time. *Pro* means "forward," and *retro* means "backward." In *pro*active interference, previously learned material "comes forward" to interfere with new learning. *Retro*active interference occurs when new information "goes back" to interfere with the recall of past learning.

information. Interference might occur either because one piece of information actually *displaces* other information, pushing it out of memory, or because one piece of information makes storing or recalling other information more difficult.

In the case of short-term memory, if an item is not rehearsed or elaborated, memory of it decreases consistently over the course of about eighteen seconds. So decay appears to play a prominent role in forgetting information in short-term memory. But interference through displacement can also produce forgetting from short-term memory. Like a desktop, short-term memory can hold only so much. When additional items are added, the old ones tend to "fall off" and are no longer available (Haberlandt, 1999). Displacement is one reason why the phone number you just looked up is likely to drop out of short-term memory if you read another number before making your call. Rehearsal prevents displacement by continually reentering the same information into short-term memory.

The cause of forgetting from long-term memory seems to be more directly tied to interference, but it is also more complicated because there can be two kinds of interference. In **retroactive interference**, learning of new information interferes with recall of older information. In **proactive interference**, old information interferes with learning or remembering new information. For example, retroactive interference would help explain why studying French vocabulary this term might make it more difficult to remember the Spanish words you learned last term. And because of proactive interference, the French words you are learning now might make it harder to learn German next term. Figure 7.14 outlines the types of experiments that are used to study the influence of each form of interference in long-term memory.

Suppose a person learns something and then, when tested on it after various intervals, remembers less and less as time passes. Is the forgetting due to decay or to interference? It is not easy to tell, because longer testing intervals produce both more decay and more retroactive interference from information the person is exposed to while waiting. To separate the effects of decay from those of interference, Karl Dallenbach created situations in which time passed but there was little or no accompanying interference. Evidence of forgetting in such situations would suggest that decay, not interference, was operating.

● **retroactive interference** A cause of forgetting in which new information placed in memory interferes with the ability to recall information already in memory.

● **proactive interference** A cause of forgetting in which information already in long-term memory interferes with the ability to remember new information.

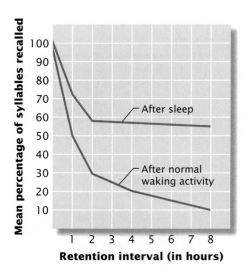

FIGURE 7.15

Interference and Forgetting

In this study, college students forgot more of what they had learned, and forgot it faster, if they engaged in normal activity after learning than if they spent the time asleep. These results suggest that interference is more important than decay in forgetting information in long-term memory.

In one of Dallenbach's studies, college students learned a list of nonsense syllables and then either continued with their usual routine or were sheltered from interference by going to sleep (Jenkins & Dallenbach, 1924). Although the delay (and thus the potential for decay) was held constant for both groups, the greater interference associated with being awake produced much more forgetting (see Figure 7.15).

Results such as these suggest that although decay sometimes occurs, interference is the major cause of forgetting from long-term memory. But does interference actually push the forgotten information out of memory, or does it just make the retrieval process more difficult? To find out, Endel Tulving and Joseph Psotka (1971) presented people with different numbers of word lists. Each list contained words from one of six categories, such as types of buildings (*hut, cottage, tent, hotel*) or geographical features (*cliff, river, hill, volcano*). Some people learned a list and then recalled as many of the words as possible. Other groups learned the first list and then learned different numbers of other lists before trying to recall the first one.

The results were dramatic. As the number of additional lists increased, the number of words that people could recall from the original list decreased. This finding reflected strong retroactive interference; the new lists were interfering with recall of the first one. Then the researchers gave a second test, in which they provided people with a *retrieval cue* by telling them the category of the words (such as "types of buildings") to be recalled. Now the number of intervening lists had almost no effect on the number of words recalled from the original list, as Figure 7.16 shows. These results indicate that the words were still in long-term memory. They had not been pushed out, but the participants had been unable to recall them without appropriate retrieval cues. In other words, the original forgetting was due to a failure in retrieval. So putting more and more information into long-term memory may be like putting more and more CDs into a storage cabinet. None of the CDs disappears, but it becomes increasingly difficult to find the one you are looking for.

Data such as these suggest to some memory theorists that all forgetting from long-term memory is due to some form of retrieval failure (Ratcliff & McKoon, 1989). Does this mean that everything in long-term memory remains there for life, even if you cannot always, or ever, recall it? No one knows for sure, but as described in the next section, this question lies at the heart of some highly controversial court cases.

THINKING CRITICALLY

 Can Traumatic Memories Be Repressed, Then Recovered?

LINKAGES (a link to Consciousness, p. 329)

In 1989, Eileen Franklin-Lipsker told police in California that when she looked into her young daughter's eyes one day, she suddenly remembered having seen her father kill her childhood friend more than twenty years earlier. Her father, George Franklin, Sr., was sent to prison for murder on the basis of her testimony about that memory (Loftus & Ketcham, 1994). This case sparked intense debate among psychologists, and in the North American legal system as well. The controversy centers on the validity of claims of recovered memory. Some psychologists accept the idea that it is possible for people to *repress*, or push into unconsciousness, memories of traumatic incidents and then recover these memories many years later. Other psychologists are skeptical about recovered memory claims.

■ What am I being asked to believe or accept?

The prosecution in the Franklin case successfully argued that Eileen had repressed, and then recovered, her memory of a murder. Similar arguments in a number of other cases in the early 1990s resulted in the imprisonment of other parents whose now-adult children claimed to have recovered childhood memories of being physically or sexually abused by them. The juries in these trials accepted the assertion that repression can keep all memory of shocking events out of awareness for decades, yet leave them potentially subject to accurate recollection

FIGURE 7.16

Retrieval Failures and Forgetting

Tulving and Psotka found that people's ability to recall a list of items was strongly affected by the number of other lists they learned before being tested on the first one. When retrieval cues were provided on a second test, however, retroactive interference from the intervening lists almost disappeared.

Source: Tulving & Psotka (1971).

(Hyman, 2000). Jurors are not the only believers in this phenomenon. A few years ago a major American news organization reported that the United States had illegally used nerve gas during the war in Vietnam. The story was based, in part, on a Vietnam veteran's account of recovered memories of having been subjected to a nerve gas attack.

■ What evidence is available to support the assertion?

Proponents of the recovered memory argument point to several lines of evidence to support their claims. First, as discussed in the chapter on consciousness, a substantial amount of mental activity occurs outside of conscious awareness (Kihlstrom, 1999). Second, research on implicit memory shows that information of which we are unaware can influence our behavior (Betch et al., 2003; Kouider & Dupoux, 2005; Schacter, Chiu, & Ochsner, 1993). Third, research on *motivated forgetting* suggests that people are able to willfully suppress information so that it is no longer accessible on a later memory test (Anderson & Green, 2001). Even suppressing one's emotional reactions to events can interfere with memories of those events (Richards & Gross, 2000). And people appear more likely to forget unpleasant rather than pleasant events (Erdelyi, 1985). In one study, a psychologist kept a detailed record of his daily life over a six-year period. When he later tried to recall those experiences, he remembered more than half of the positive ones, but only one-third of the negative ones. In another study, 38 percent of women who, as children, had been brought to a hospital because of sexual abuse did not report the incident as adults (Williams, 1994). Fourth, retrieval cues can help people recall memories that had previously been inaccessible to conscious awareness (Andrews et al., 2000; Landsdale & Laming, 1995). For example, these cues have helped soldiers remember for the first time the circumstances under which they had been wounded many years before (Karon & Widener, 1997). Finally, there is the confidence with which people report recovered memories; they say they are just too vivid to be anything but real.

■ Are there alternative ways of interpreting the evidence?

Those who are skeptical about recovered memories do not deny the operation of subconscious memory and retrieval processes (Kihlstrom, 1999). They also recognize that, sadly, child abuse and other traumas are all too common. But to these psychologists, the available evidence is not strong enough to support the conclusion that traumatic memories can be repressed and then accurately recalled. Any given "recovered" memory, they say, might actually be a distorted, or constructed, memory (Clancy et al., 2000; Loftus, 1998). As already mentioned, our recall of past events is affected by what happened at the time, what we knew beforehand, and everything we have experienced since. Without realizing it, the people described earlier who "remembered" nonexistent books in a graduate student's office used their prior knowledge to construct a memory for the books. Similarly, the "recovered memory" of the Vietnam veteran mentioned earlier appears to have no basis in fact. The news story about the alleged nerve gas attack was later retracted.

Research shows that *false memories*—distortions of actual events and the recall of events that didn't actually happen—can be at least as vivid as accurate ones and that people can be just as confident in them (Brainerd & Reyna, 2005; Brainerd et al., 2003; Loftus, 2004; Nourkova, Bernstein, & Loftus, 2004; Roediger & McDermott, 1995, 2000). Most of us have experienced everyday versions of false memories. It is not unusual for people to "remember" turning off the coffeepot or mailing the rent check, only to discover later that they did not. Researchers have demonstrated that false memories can occur in relation to more emotional events, too. In one case study, a teenager named Chris was given descriptions of four incidents from his childhood and asked to write about each of them every day for five days (Loftus, 1997a). One of those incidents—being lost in a shopping mall at age five—never really happened. Yet Chris not only eventually "remembered" this event but added many details about the mall and the stranger whose hand he was supposedly found holding. He also rated this (false) memory as being more vivid than two of the other three (real) incidents. Similar results occurred in about half of

Exploring Memory Processes
Elizabeth Loftus (at the far right) is shown here with her students and Alan Alda, who filmed a documentary about her research. She and other cognitive psychologists have demonstrated mechanisms through which false memories can be created. They have found, for example, that false memories appear even in research participants who are told about them and are asked to avoid them (McDermott & Roediger, 1998). Their work has helped to focus scientific scrutiny on reports of recovered memories, especially those arising from contact with therapists who assume that most people have repressed memories of abuse.

seventy-seven child participants in another set of case studies (Porter, Yuille, & Lehman, 1999).

The same pattern of results has appeared in formal experiments on the planting of emotion-laden false memories (Hyman & Pentland, 1996). Researchers have been able to create vivid and striking, but completely false, memories of events that people thought they experienced when they were one day old (DuBreuil, Garry, & Loftus, 1998). In other experiments, children who were repeatedly asked about a nonexistent trauma (getting a hand caught in a mousetrap) eventually developed a vivid and unshakable false memory of experiencing it (Ceci et al., 1994). Some people will even begin to avoid a certain food after researchers create in them a false memory of having been ill after eating that food as a child (Bernstein et al., 2005).

In other words, people sometimes have a difficult time distinguishing between what has happened to them and what they have only imagined, or have come to believe, has happened. Some studies have found that people who score high on tests of introversion, fantasy-proneness, and dissociation (which includes a tendency toward lapses of memory and attention) are more likely than others to develop false memories and may also be more likely to report the recovery of repressed memories (McNally, 2003, McNally et al., 2000a, 2000b, 2005; Porter et al., 2000; Wilson & French, 2006). Two other studies have found that women who have suffered physical or sexual abuse are more likely to falsely remember words on a laboratory recall test (Bremner, Shobe, & Kihlstrom, 2000; Zoellner et al., 2000). This tendency appears strongest among abused women who show signs of posttraumatic stress disorder (Bremner et al., 2000). Another study found that susceptibility to false memory in a word recall task was greater in women who reported recovered memories of sexual abuse than in nonabused women or in those who had always remembered the abuse they suffered (Clancy et al., 2000). False memories on this laboratory recall task are also more common among people who claim to have been abducted by space aliens than among other people (Clancy et al., 2002).

Why would anyone "remember" a traumatic event that did not actually occur? Elizabeth Loftus (1997b) suggests that, for one thing, popular books such as *The Courage to Heal* (Bass & Davis, 1994), *Secret Survivors* (Blume, 1998), and *Surviving Babylon* (Garson, 2006) may lead people to believe that anyone who experiences guilt, depression, low self-esteem, overemotionality, or any of a long list of other problems is harboring repressed memories of abuse. This message, says Loftus, tends to be reinforced and extended by therapists who specialize in using guided imagination, hypnosis, and other methods to "help" clients recover repressed memories (Lindsay et al., 2004; Pendergrast, 1996; Polusny & Follette, 1996; Poole et al., 1995). These therapists may influence people to construct false memories by encouraging them to imagine experiencing events that might never have actually occurred or that occurred only in a dream (Mazzoni & Loftus, 1996; Olio, 1994). As one client described her therapy, "I was rapidly losing the ability to differentiate between my imagination and my real memory" (Loftus & Ketcham, 1994, p. 25). To such therapists, a client's failure to recover memories of abuse or refusal to accept their existence is evidence of "denial" of the truth (Loftus, 1997a; Pendergrast, 1996; Tavris, 2003).

The possibility that recovered memories might actually be false memories has led to dismissed charges or not-guilty verdicts for defendants in some repressed memory cases. In others, previously convicted defendants have been set free. (George Franklin's conviction was overturned, but only after he served five years in prison.) Concern over the potential damage resulting from false memories led to the establishment of the False Memory Syndrome Foundation, a support group for families affected by abuse accusations stemming from allegedly repressed memories. More than a hundred of these families (including Franklin's family) have filed lawsuits against hospitals and therapists. In 1994, California winery executive Gary Ramona received $500,000 in damages from two therapists who had "helped" his daughter recall alleged sexual abuse at his hands. A more recent suit led to a $2 million judgment against a Minnesota therapist whose client realized that her "recovered" memories of childhood abuse were false. A similar case in Wisconsin brought a $5 million judgment against two therapists. And an Illinois case resulted in a $10.6 million settlement and a license suspension for the psychiatrist who had "found" his patient's "lost" memories (Loftus, 1998).

■ What additional evidence would help to evaluate the alternatives?

Evaluating reports of recovered memories would be easier if we had more information about whether it is possible for people to repress traumatic events. If it *is* possible, we also need to know how common it is and how accurate recovered memories might be. So far, we know that some people apparently do forget intense emotional experiences, but that most people's memories of them are vivid and long lasting, like the flashbulb memories we discussed earlier (McGaugh, 2003). In fact, many people who live through trauma are *unable* to forget it, though they wish they could (Henig, 2004). In the sexual abuse study mentioned earlier, for example (Williams, 1994), 62 percent of the abuse victims did recall their trauma. A similar study of a different group of adults found that 92 percent of them recalled their documented childhood abuse (Alexander et al., 2005; Goodman et al., 2003). The true recall figures might actually be higher in such studies, because some people who remember abuse may not wish to talk about it. In any case, more research such as this—research that tracks the fate of memories in known abuse cases—would not only help to estimate the prevalence of this kind of forgetting but also might offer clues as to the kinds of people and events most likely to be associated with it. It would also be valuable to know more about the processes through which repression might occur and how they are related to empirically established theories and models of human memory. Is there a mechanism that specifically pushes traumatic memories out of awareness, then keeps them at a subconscious level for long periods and allows them to be accurately recalled? Despite some suggestive results (Anderson & Green, 2001; Anderson et al., 2004; DePrince & Freyd, 2004), cognitive psychologists have so far not found reliable evidence for such a mechanism (Bulevich et al., 2006; Geraerts et al., 2006; Loftus, 1997a; McNally, 2003; McNally, Clancy, & Schacter, 2001; McNally et al., 2000a; Pope et al., 1998).

■ What conclusions are most reasonable?

An objective reading of the available research evidence supports the view that recovery of memories of trauma is at least possible, but that the implantation of false memories is also possible—and has been demonstrated experimentally. Accordingly, it is difficult, and sometimes impossible, to decide whether any particular case is an instance of recovered memory or false memory, especially in the absence of objective corroborating evidence.

The intense conflict between those who uncritically accept claims of recovered memories and those who are more wary about the accuracy of such claims reflects a fundamental disagreement about evidence (Tavris, 2003). Client reports constitute "proof" for therapists who deal daily with victims of sexual abuse and other traumas and who rely more on personal experiences than on scientific research findings. Those reports are viewed with far more skepticism by psychologists who engage in, or rely on, empirical research on the processes of memory and forgetting (Loftus, 2003, 2004; Pope, 1998). They are looking for additional sources of evidence, including brain activity "signatures" that might distinguish true memories from false ones (e.g., Cabeza et al., 2001; Slotnick & Schacter, 2004).

So whether or not you believe a claim of recovered memory may be determined by the relative weight you assign to personal experiences and intuition versus empirical evidence from controlled experiments. Still, the apparent ease with which false memories can be created should lead judges, juries, and the general public to exercise great caution before accepting as valid unverified memories of traumatic events. At the same time, we should not automatically and uncritically reject the claims of people who appear to have recovered memories. Perhaps the wisest course is to use all the scientific and circumstantial evidence available to carefully and critically examine such claims, while keeping in mind that constructive memory processes *might* have influenced them (Alison, Kebbell, & Lewis, 2006). This careful, scientific approach is vital if we are to protect the rights and welfare of those who report recovered memories, as well as of those who face accusations arising from them. ■

Biological Bases of Memory

Many psychologists who study memory focus on explicit and implicit mental processes (e.g., Schott et al., 2005). Others explore the physical, electrical, and chemical changes that take place in the brain when information is encoded, stored, and retrieved (Abraham, 2006; Fields, 2005; Touzani, Puthanveettil, & Kandel, 2007). The story of the scientific search for the biological bases of memory begins with the work of Karl Lashley and Donald Hebb, who spent many years studying how memory is related to brain structures and processes. Lashley (1950) taught rats new behaviors and then observed how damage to various parts of the rats' brains changed their ability to perform the tasks they had learned. Lashley hoped that his work would identify the brain area that contained the "engram"—the physical manifestation of memory in the brain. However, after many experiments, he concluded that memories are not localized in one specific region, but instead are distributed throughout large areas of brain tissue.

Hebb, who was a student of Lashley's, proposed another biological theory of memory. Hebb believed that each memory is represented by a group of interconnected neurons in the brain. These neurons, which he called a *cell assembly*, form a network in the cortex. The connections among these neurons are strengthened, he said, when the neurons are simultaneously stimulated through sensory experiences (Hebb, 1949). Though not correct in all its details, Hebb's theory stimulated research and contributed to an understanding of the physical basis of memory. His theory is also consistent, in many respects, with contemporary parallel distributed processing models of memory (Hergenhahn & Olson, 1997).

Let's consider more recent research on the biochemical mechanisms and brain structures that are most directly involved in memory processes.

▬ ● The Biochemistry of Memory

As described in the chapter on biological aspects of psychology, communication among brain cells takes place at the synapses between axons and dendrites, and it depends on chemicals, called *neurotransmitters*, released at the synapses. The formation and storage of new memories are associated with at least two kinds of changes in synapses.

The first kind of change occurs when stimulation from the environment promotes the formation of new synapses, thus increasing the complexity of the communication networks through which neurons receive information (Black & Greenough, 1991; Rosenzweig & Bennett, 1996). Scientists can now actually see this process occur. As shown in Figure 7.17, repeatedly sending signals across a particular synapse increases the number of special little branches, called *spines*, that appear on the receiving cell's dendrites (Lang et al., 2004; Toni et al., 1999).

The second kind of change occurs as new experiences alter the functioning of existing synapses. Researchers have discovered that when two neurons fire at the same time and together stimulate a third neuron, that third neuron will later be more responsive than before to stimulation by either neuron alone (Sejnowski, Chattarji, & Stanton, 1990). This process of "sensitizing" synapses is called *long-term potentiation* (Li, Cullen, et al., 2003). Changing patterns of electrical stimulation can also weaken synaptic connections, a process called *long-term depression* (Malenka, 1995). Such changes in sensitivity could account for the development of conditioned responses and other types of learning (Olson et al., 2006; Whitlock, Heynen, et al., 2006).

In the hippocampus (see Figure 7.18), these changes appear to occur at synapses that use the neurotransmitter glutamate (Malenka & Nicoll, 1999). Other neurotransmitters, such as acetylcholine, also play important roles in memory formation (e.g., Furey, Pietrini, & Haxby, 2000; Li, Cullen, et al., 2003). The memory problems seen in people with Alzheimer's disease are related to a deficiency in neurons that use acetylcholine and send fibers to the hippocampus and the cortex (Muir, 1997). Drugs that interfere with the action of acetylcholine impair memory, and drugs that increase the amount of acetylcholine in synapses improve memory in aging animals and humans (Pettit, Shao, & Yakel, 2001; Sirvio, 1999).

In short, research has shown that the formation of memories is associated with changes in many individual synapses that, together, strengthen and improve the communication in networks of neurons. These findings provide some support for the ideas formulated by Hebb many years ago.

FIGURE **7.17**

Building Memories

These models of synapses are based on electron microscope images of neurons in the brain. The model on the left shows that before signals were repeatedly sent across the synapse, just one spine (shown in white) appears on this part of the dendrite. Afterward, as shown in the other model, there are two spines, which helps improve communication across the synapse. The creation and changing of many individual synapses in the brain appears to underlie the formation and storage of new memories.

Source: Toni et al. (1999).

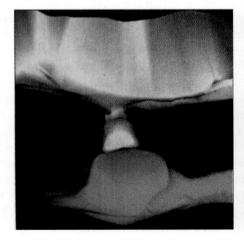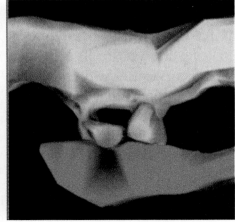

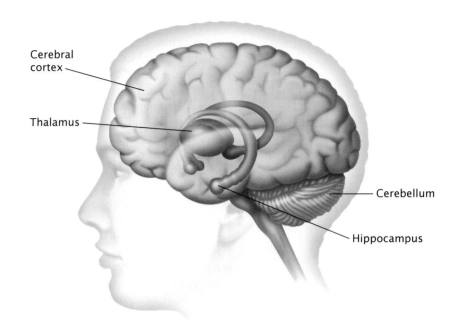

Cerebral cortex

Thalamus

Cerebellum

Hippocampus

LINKAGES (a link to Biological Aspects of Psychology, p. 80)

FIGURE 7.18

Some Brain Structures Involved in Memory

Combined neural activity in many parts of the brain allows us to encode, store, and retrieve memories. The complexity of the biological bases of these processes is underscored by research showing that different aspects of a memory—such as the sights and sounds associated with some event—are stored in different parts of the cerebral cortex.

Brain Structures and Memory

Are the biochemical processes involved in memory concentrated in certain regions, or are they distributed throughout the brain? The latest research suggests that memory involves both specialized regions for various types of memory formation and widespread areas for storage (Takashima et al., 2006). Several of the brain regions shown in Figure 7.18, including the hippocampus and nearby parts of the cortex and the thalamus, are vital to the formation of new memories. Evidence for the memory-related functions of these regions comes from two main sources. First, there are case studies of patients with brain injuries that allow neuropsychologists to determine how damage to specific brain areas is related to specific kinds of memory problems. Second, studies using PET scans, functional MRI, and other neuroimaging methods (described in the chapter on biological aspects of psychology) have allowed neuroscientists to observe where brain activity is concentrated as normal people perform various memory tasks (e.g., Wagner, Schacter, & Rotte, 1998). Data from these two sources are leading to an ever-growing understanding of how the brain encodes and retrieves memories.

● **The Impact of Brain Damage** Research has confirmed that the hippocampus, which is part of the limbic system, is among the brain regions involved in the formation of new memories. Damage to the hippocampus often results in **anterograde amnesia,** a loss of memory for any event occurring after the injury. The case of H. M. provides a striking example of anterograde amnesia (Milner, 1966). When H. M. was twenty-seven years old, part of his hippocampus was removed to end his severe epileptic seizures. Afterward, both his long-term and short-term memory appeared normal, but he had a severe problem. Two years after the operation, he still believed that he was twenty-seven. When his family moved into a new house, H. M. could not remember the new address or how to get there. When told that his uncle had died, he grieved in a normal way. But soon afterward, he began to ask why his uncle had not visited him. He had to be repeatedly reminded of the death, and each time, he became just as upset as when he was first told. The surgery had apparently destroyed the mechanism that transfers information from short-term to long-term memory. Now in his seventies, H. M. lives in a nursing home, where his only long-term memories are from fifty years ago, before the operation. He is still

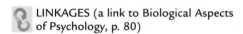

● **anterograde amnesia** A loss of memory for any event that occurs after a brain injury.

unable to recall events and facts he has experienced since then—not even the names of people he sees every day (Corkin, 2002; Hathaway, 2002).

Although patients with anterograde amnesia cannot form episodic memories following hippocampal damage, they may still be able to form implicit memories. For example, H. M. was presented with a complicated puzzle on which mistakes are common and performance gradually improves with practice. Over several days his performance steadily improved, just as it does with normal people, and eventually it became virtually perfect. But each time he tried the puzzle, he insisted that he had never seen it before (Cohen & Corkin, 1981; see Figure 9.4 for another example). A musician with a similar kind of brain damage was able to use his implicit memory to continue leading choral groups (Vattano, 2000). Other researchers, too, have found intact implicit memory in patients who have anterograde amnesia for new episodic material (Squire & McKee, 1992; Tulving, Hayman, & Macdonald, 1991). These patients are also able to keep information temporarily in working memory, which depends on the activity of dopamine neurons in the prefrontal cortex (Williams & Goldman-Rakic, 1995). So the hippocampus is crucial in the formation of new episodic memories, but implicit memory, procedural memory, and working memory appear to be governed by other regions of the brain (Schott et al., 2005; Touzani et al., 2007).

Retrograde amnesia involves a loss of memory for events that occurred *before* a brain injury. This condition is also consistent with the idea that memory processes are widely distributed. Often, a person with retrograde amnesia is unable to remember anything that took place in the months, or even years, before the injury (Kapur, 1999). In 1994, head injuries from a car crash left thirty-six-year-old Perlene Griffith-Barwell with retrograde amnesia so severe that she forgot virtually everything she had learned about everything and everybody over the previous twenty years. She thought she was still sixteen and did not recognize her husband, Malcolm, or her four children. She said, "The children were sweet, but they didn't seem like mine," and she "didn't feel anything" for Malcolm. Her memories of the twenty years before the accident have never fully returned. At last report, she was divorced, but still living with her children and working in a bank (Weinstein, 1999).

Unlike Perlene, most victims of retrograde amnesia gradually recover their memories (Riccio, Millin, & Gisquet-Verrier, 2003). The most distant events are recalled first, and the person gradually regains memory for events leading up to the injury. Recovery is seldom complete, however, and the person may never remember

A Famous Case of Retrograde Amnesia   After Ralf Schumacher slammed his race car into a wall during the United States Grand Prix in June of 2004, he sustained a severe concussion that left him with no memory of the crash. Retrograde amnesia is relatively common following concussions, so if you ride a motorcycle, wear that helmet!

● **retrograde amnesia**   A loss of memory for events prior to a brain injury.

the last few seconds before the injury. Cases of retrograde amnesia that covers the minutes or hours before a blow to the head have led researchers to suggest that as memories are transferred from short-term memory to long-term memory, they are initially unstable and therefore vulnerable to disruption (Dudai, 2004). It may take minutes, hours, or days before these memories are fully solidified, or *consolidated* (Donegan & Thompson, 1991).

This consolidation process appears to depend on movement of electrochemical impulses within clusters of neurons in the brain (Taubenfeld et al., 2001). Accordingly, conditions that suppress neural activity in the brain may also disrupt the transfer of information from short-term to long-term memory. These conditions include anesthetic drugs, poisoning by carbon monoxide or other toxins, and strong electrical impulses such as those in the electroconvulsive therapy that is sometimes used to treat cases of severe depression (see the chapter on treatment of psychological disorders).

An additional clue to the role of specific brain areas in memory comes from research on people with *Korsakoff's syndrome*, a disorder that usually occurs in chronic alcoholics. These people's brains become unable to use glucose as fuel, resulting in severe and widespread brain damage. Damage to the mediodorsal nucleus of the thalamus is particularly implicated in the memory problems typical of these patients, which can include both anterograde and retrograde amnesia (Squire, Amara, & Press, 1992). Moreover, like patients with hippocampal damage, Korsakoff's patients show impairments in the ability to form new episodic memories but retain some implicit memory abilities. Research has demonstrated that damage to the prefrontal cortex (also common in Korsakoff's patients) is related to disruptions in remembering the order in which events occur (Squire, 1992). Other studies have found that regions within the prefrontal cortex are involved in working memory in both animals and humans (D'Esposito et al., 1995; Smith, 2000; Touzani et al., 2007).

● **Multiple Storage Areas**   Obviously, the hippocampus does not permanently store long-term memories (Bayley, Hopkins, & Squire, 2003; Rosenbaum et al., 2000). (If it did, H. M. would not have retained memories from the years before part of his hippocampus was removed.) However, both the hippocampus and the thalamus send nerve fibers to the cerebral cortex. Memories are probably stored in and around the cortex—but not just in one place (Levy, Bayley, & Squire, 2004; Maviel et al., 2004).

As described in the chapters on biological aspects of psychology and on sensation, messages from different senses are represented in different regions of the cortex, so information about specific aspects of an experience is probably stored in or near these regions. This arrangement would explain why damage to the auditory cortex disrupts memory for sounds (Colombo et al., 1990). A memory, however, involves more than one sensory system. Even in the simple case of a rat remembering a maze, the experience of the maze includes vision, smell, movement, and emotions, each of which may be stored in different regions of the brain (Gallagher & Chiba, 1996). So memories are both localized and distributed; certain brain areas store specific aspects of each remembered event, but many brain regions are involved in experiencing a whole event (Brewer et al., 1998; Kensinger & Corkin, 2004). The cerebellum, for instance (see Figure 7.18), is involved in the storage of procedural memories, such as dance steps and other movements.

The memory problems observed in cases of damage to various brain areas are consistent with the view that short-term and long-term memory are distinct systems and that the problems result from an inability to transfer information from one system to the other. However, the precise physiological processes involved in this transfer are not yet clear. As mentioned earlier, it appears that a physiological trace that codes the experience must be gradually transformed and stabilized, or consolidated, if the memory is to endure.

What happens in the brain as we retrieve memories? Functional neuroimaging studies consistently show that the hippocampus, as well as regions of the parietal cortex and prefrontal cortex, are active during memory retrieval (Buckner & Wheeler,

2001; Cabeza & Nyberg, 2000; Eldridge et al., 2000; Davachi, Mitchell, & Wagner, 2003; McDermott & Buckner, 2002; Rugg & Wilding, 2000). There is also evidence to suggest that retrieving memories of certain experiences, such as a conversation or a tennis game, reactivates the sensory and motor regions of the brain that had been involved during the event itself (Nyberg et al., 2001). Research shows, too, that when animals recall an emotional (fear-related) memory, that memory may have to be stored again. During this biological restorage process, it may be open to distortion (Eisenberg et al., 2003; Lee, Everitt, & Thomas, 2004; Nader, Schafe, & Le Doux, 2000). Researchers are exploring the question of whether this *reconsolidation* process occurs in humans, too (Dudai, 2004; Walker et al., 2003). Cognitive neuroscientists are also trying to discover whether different patterns of brain activity are associated with the retrieval of accurate versus inaccurate memories (Cabeza et al., 2001; Gonsalves & Paller, 2000; Slotnick & Schacter, 2004). These lines of research will have obvious applications in areas such as lie detection, the understanding of false memory processes, and the evaluation of claims of recovered memories.

Applications of Memory Research

Some questions remain about what memory is and how it works, but the results of memory research offer many valuable guidelines to help people improve their memories and function more effectively (Neisser, 2000).

● Improving Your Memory

The most valuable memory enhancement strategies are based on the elaboration of incoming information, and especially on linking new information to what you already know.

● **Mnemonics**   Psychologists have found that people with normal memory skills, and even those with brain damage, can improve their memory through the use of *mnemonics* (pronounced "nee-MON-ix"). Named for Mnemosyne, the Greek goddess of memory, mnemonics are strategies for placing information into an organized context in order to remember it. For example, to remember the names of the Great Lakes, you might use the acronym HOMES (for Huron, Ontario, Michigan, Erie, and Superior). Verbal organization is the basis for many mnemonics. You can link items by weaving them into a story, a sentence, or a rhyme. To help customers remember where they have parked their cars, some large garages have replaced section designations such as "A1" or "G8" with labels that use colors, animal names, or months. Customers can then tie the location of their cars to information already in long-term memory—for example, "I parked in the month of my mother's birthday."

TRY
THIS →   One simple but powerful mnemonic is called the *method of loci* (pronounced "LOW-sigh"), or the method of places. To use this method, first think about a set of familiar locations—in your home, for example. You might imagine walking through the front door, around all four corners of the living room, and through each of the other rooms. Next, imagine that each item to be remembered is in one of these locations. Whenever you want to remember a list, use the same locations, in the same order. Creating vivid, unusual images of how these items appear in each location seems to be particularly effective (Kline & Groninger, 1991). For example, tomatoes smashed against the front door or bananas hanging from the bedroom ceiling might be helpful in recalling these items on a grocery list.

● **Guidelines for More Effective Studying**   The success of mnemonic strategies demonstrates again the importance of relating new information to knowledge already stored in memory. All mnemonic systems require that you have a well-learned body of knowledge (such as locations) that can be used to provide a context

mnemonics   Strategies for placing information in an organized context in order to remember it.

for organizing incoming information (Hilton, 1986). When you want to remember more complex material, such as a textbook chapter, the same principles apply (Palmisano & Herrmann, 1991). You can improve your memory for text material by first creating an outline or some other overall context for learning, rather than by just reading and rereading (Glover et al., 1990). Repetition may *seem* effective, because it keeps material in short-term memory; but for retaining information over long periods, repetition alone tends to be ineffective, no matter how much time you spend on it (Bjork, 1999; Bjorklund & Green, 1992). In short, "work smarter, not harder."

In addition, spend your time wisely. *Distributed practice* is much more effective than *massed practice* for learning new information. If you are going to spend ten hours studying for a test, you will be much better off studying for ten one-hour blocks (separated by periods of sleep and other activity) than "cramming" for one ten-hour block. By scheduling more study sessions, you will stay fresh and tend to think about the material from a new perspective at each session. This method will help you elaborate on the material (elaborative rehearsal) and remember it better.

You should also practice retrieving what you have learned by repeatedly testing yourself. For example, instead of simply rereading a section to help you remember it, close the book and try to jot down the section's main points from memory. You can test yourself on important vocabulary terms by creating a deck of flashcards, each of which has a key term on one side and its definition on the other. Then browse through the cards, trying to recall the definition of each term before turning the card over to give yourself feedback on your performance. To take advantage of the benefits of distributed practice, don't wait until the day before the test to write your flashcards. Create new ones after each study session and each lecture, and carry them around with you. That way, you can review them whenever you have a spare moment. Laboratory studies have found that students' later exam performance is significantly better after self-testing than after merely reading and rereading the material they are trying to learn (Roediger & Karpicke, 2006). These simple procedures can help you, too.

● **Reading a Textbook** More specific advice for remembering textbook material comes from a study that examined how successful and unsuccessful college students approach their reading (Whimbey, 1976). Unsuccessful students tend to read the material straight through. They do not slow down when they reach a difficult section, and they keep going even when they don't understand what they

Understand and Remember Research on memory suggests that students who simply read their textbooks will not remember as much as those who, like this woman, read for understanding using the PQ4R method. Further, memory for the material is likely to be better if you read and study it over a number of weeks rather than in one marathon session on the night before a test.

are reading. In contrast, successful college students monitor their understanding, reread difficult sections, and stop now and then to review what they have learned. (This book's *In Review* features are designed to help you do that.) In other words, effective learners engage in a deep level of processing. They are active learners, thinking of each new fact in relation to other material, and they develop a context in which many new facts can be organized effectively.

Research on memory suggests two specific guidelines for reading a textbook. First, make sure that you understand what you are reading before moving on (Herrmann & Searleman, 1992). Second, use the *PQ4R method* (Thomas & Robinson, 1972), which is one of the most successful strategies for remembering textbook material (Anderson, 2000; Chastain & Thurber, 1989). PQ4R stands for six activities to engage in when you read a chapter: *preview, question, read, reflect, recite,* and *review.* These activities are designed to increase the depth to which you process the information you read and should be done as follows:

1. *Preview.* First, take a few minutes to skim the chapter. Look at the section headings and any boldfaced or italicized terms. Get a general idea of what material will be discussed, the way it is organized, and how its topics relate to one another and to what you already know. Some students find it useful to survey the entire chapter once and then survey each major section a little more carefully before reading it.

2. *Question.* Before reading each section, ask yourself what content will be covered and what information you should be getting from it.

3. *Read.* Now read the text, but *think about* the material as you read. Are you understanding the material? Are the questions you raised earlier being answered?

4. *Reflect.* As you read, think of your own examples—and create visual images—of the concepts and phenomena you encounter. Ask yourself what the material means, and consider how each section relates to other sections in the chapter and to other chapters in the book (this book's *Linkages* features are designed to promote this kind of reflection).

5. *Recite.* At the end of each section, recite the major points. Resist the temptation to be passive and say, "Oh, I'll remember that." Be active. Put the ideas into your own words by reciting them aloud to yourself, or by summarizing the material in a minilecture to a friend or study partner. Recitation is another form of the important self-testing process we mentioned earlier.

6. *Review.* Finally, at the end of the chapter, review all the material. You should see connections not only within each section but also among sections. The objective is to see how the material is organized. Once you grasp the organization, the individual facts will be far easier to remember.

By following these procedures you will learn and remember the material better, and you will also save yourself considerable time.

● **Lecture Notes** Effective notetaking during lectures is a vital skill that can be learned and that improves with practice (Pauk, 2002). Research on memory suggests some simple strategies for taking and using notes effectively.

Realize first that in notetaking, more is not necessarily better. Taking detailed notes of everything you hear requires that you pay close attention to both important and unimportant content, leaving little time for thinking about the material. Note takers who concentrate on expressing the major ideas in relatively few words remember more than those who try to catch every detail (Pauk & Fiore, 2000). The best way to take notes is to think about what is being said, draw connections with other material in the lecture, and then summarize the major points clearly and concisely (Kiewra, 1989).

in review Improving Your Memory

Goal	Helpful Techniques
Remembering lists of items	Use mnemonics. Look for meaningful acronyms. Try the method of loci.
Remembering textbook material	Follow the PQ4R system. Allocate your time to allow for distributed practice. Read actively, not passively. Test yourself as you read.
Taking lecture notes	Take notes, but record only the main points. Think about the overall organization of the material. Review your notes as soon after the lecture as possible in order to fill in missing points.
Studying for exams	Write a detailed outline of your lecture notes rather than passively reading them. Do further self-testing; review key term flashcards.

Once you have a set of lecture notes, review them as soon as possible after the lecture so that you can fill in missing details and create flashcards for key terms. (Remember that most forgetting from long-term memory occurs within the first few hours after learning.) When the time comes for serious study, use your notes as if they were a chapter in a textbook. Write a detailed outline. Think about how various points are related. Once you have organized the material, the details will make more sense and will be much easier to remember. ("In Review: Improving Your Memory" summarizes tips for studying.)

● Design for Memory

The scientific study of memory has influenced the design of the electronic and mechanical devices that play an increasingly important role in our lives. Those who design computers, MP3 and DVD players, digital cameras, and even microwave ovens are faced with a choice: Either place the operating instructions on the devices themselves, or assume that users will remember how to operate them. Understanding the limits of both working memory and long-term memory has helped designers distinguish between information that is likely to be stored in (and easily retrieved from) the user's memory and information that should be presented in the form of labels, instructions, or other cues that reduce memory demands (Norman, 1988). Placing unfamiliar or hard-to-recall information in plain view makes it easier to use the device as intended and with less chance of errors (Segal & Suri, 1999).

Psychologists have influenced advertisers and designers to create many other "user-friendly" systems (Wickens et al., 2004). As a result, toll-free numbers are designed to take advantage of chunking, which, as mentioned earlier, provides an efficient way to maintain information in working memory. Which do you think would be easier to remember: 1-800-438-4357 or 1-800-GET-HELP? Obviously, the more meaningful "get help" number is more memorable (there are web sites that can help you translate any phone number into words or a phrase). In the automotive arena, designers ensure that navigation systems provide audible reminders about where to turn and that turn signals emit an audible cue when activated. Features such as these help reduce your memory load while driving and leave you with enough working memory capacity to keep in mind that there is a car in your "blind spot."

As ever more complex devices appear in the marketplace, it will be increasingly important that instructions about how to operate them are presented clearly and memorably. With guidance from research on memory, it should be possible for almost anyone to operate these devices efficiently.

LINKAGES

As noted in the chapter on introducing psychology, all of psychology's subfields are related to one another. Our discussion of the accuracy of eyewitnesses' memories illustrates just one way in which the topic of this chapter, memory, is linked to the subfield of perception (see the chapter on perception). The Linkages diagram shows ties to two other subfields as well, and there are many more ties throughout the book. Looking for linkages among subfields will help you see how they all fit together and help you better appreciate the big picture that is psychology.

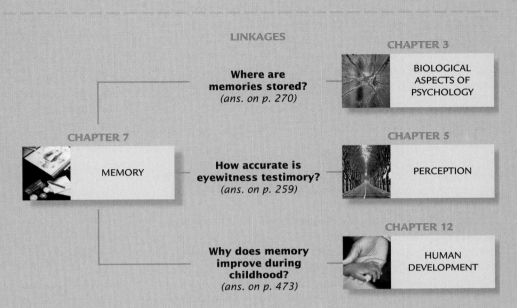

LINKAGES

CHAPTER 7

MEMORY

Where are memories stored? (ans. on p. 270) — CHAPTER 3 BIOLOGICAL ASPECTS OF PSYCHOLOGY

How accurate is eyewitness testimory? (ans. on p. 259) — CHAPTER 5 PERCEPTION

Why does memory improve during childhood? (ans. on p. 473) — CHAPTER 12 HUMAN DEVELOPMENT

SUMMARY

The Nature of Memory

Human memory depends on a complex mental system.

Basic Memory Processes There are three basic memory processes. *Encoding* transforms information into some type of mental representation. Encoding can be *acoustic* (by sound), *visual* (by appearance), or *semantic* (by meaning). *Storage* maintains information in the memory system over time. *Retrieval* is the process of gaining access to previously stored information.

Types of Memory Most psychologists agree that there are at least three types of memory. *Episodic memory* contains information about specific events in a person's life. *Semantic memory* contains generalized knowledge about the world. *Procedural memory* contains information about how to do various things.

Explicit and Implicit Memory Some research on memory concerns *explicit memory*, the processes through which people intentionally try to remember something. Psychologists also examine *implicit memory*, which refers to the unintentional influence of prior experiences.

Models of Memory Five theoretical models of memory have guided most research. The *information-processing model* suggests that in order for information to become firmly embedded in memory, it must pass through three stages of processing: sensory memory, short-term memory, and long-term memory. According to the *levels-of-processing model*, the most important determinant of memory is how extensively information is encoded or processed when it is first received. In general, *elaborative rehearsal* is more effective than *maintenance rehearsal* in learning new information, because it represents a deeper level of processing. According to the *transfer-appropriate processing model*, the critical determinant of memory is not how deeply information is encoded but whether processes used during retrieval match those used during encoding. *Parallel distributed processing (PDP) models* of memory suggest that new experiences not only provide specific information but also become part of, and alter, a whole network of associations. The *multiple memory systems* approach emphasizes the role of different brain areas in different aspects of memory encoding and retrieval.

Storing New Memories

Sensory Memory *Sensory memory* maintains incoming information in the *sensory registers* for a very brief time. *Selective attention*, which focuses mental resources on only part of the stimulus field, controls what information in the sensory registers is actually perceived and transferred to short-term and working memory.

Short-Term Memory and Working Memory *Working memory* is a system that allows us to store, organize, and manipulate information in order to think, solve problems, and make decisions. The storage, or maintenance, component of working memory is referred to as *short-term memory*. Remembering a phone number long enough to call it involves simple maintenance of the information in short-term memory.

Various memory codes can be used in short-term memory, but acoustic codes seem to dominate in most verbal tasks. Studies of the *immediate memory span* indicate that the storage capacity of short-term memory is approximately seven *chunks*, or meaningful groupings of information. Studies using the *Brown-Peterson procedure* show that information in short-term memory is usually forgotten within about eighteen seconds if it is not rehearsed.

Long-Term Memory *Long-term memory* normally involves semantic encoding, which means that people tend to encode the general meaning of information, not specific details, in long-term memory. The capacity of long-term memory to store new information is extremely large, and perhaps even unlimited.

Distinguishing Between Short-Term and Long-Term Memory According to some psychologists, there is no need to distinguish between short-term and long-term memory. Still, some evidence suggests that these systems are distinct. For example, the *primacy* and *recency effects* that occur when people try to recall a list of words may indicate the presence of two different systems.

Retrieving Memories

Retrieval Cues and Encoding Specificity *Retrieval cues* help people remember things that they would otherwise not be able to recall. The effectiveness of retrieval cues follows the *encoding specificity principle*: Cues help retrieval only if they match some feature of the information that was originally encoded.

Context and State Dependence All else being equal, memory may be better when one attempts to retrieve information in the same environment in which it was learned; this is called *context-dependent memory*. When a person's physiological or mood state can aid or impede retrieval, the person is said to have *state-dependent memory*.

Retrieval from Semantic Memory Researchers usually study retrieval from semantic memory by examining how long it takes people to answer general knowledge questions. It appears that ideas are represented as associations in a dense semantic memory network and that the retrieval of information occurs by a process of *spreading activation*. Each concept in the network is represented as a collection of features or attributes. The tip-of-the-tongue phenomenon and the feeling-of-knowing experience represent the retrieval of incomplete knowledge.

Constructing Memories In the process of constructive memory, people use their existing knowledge to fill in gaps in the information they encode and retrieve. Parallel distributed processing models provide one explanation of how people make spontaneous generalizations about the world. They also explain the *schemas* that shape the memories people construct.

Forgetting

How Do We Forget? In his research on long-term memory and forgetting, Hermann Ebbinghaus introduced the *method of savings*. He found that most forgetting from long-term memory occurs during the first several hours after learning and that savings can be extremely long lasting.

Why Do We Forget? The Roles of Decay and Interference *Decay* and *interference* are two mechanisms of forgetting. Although there is evidence of both decay and interference in short-term memory, it appears that most forgetting from long-term memory is due to either *retroactive interference* or *proactive interference*.

Biological Bases of Memory

The Biochemistry of Memory Research has shown that memory can result as new synapses are formed in the brain and as communication at existing synapses is improved. Several neurotransmitters appear to be involved in the strengthening that occurs at synapses.

Brain Structures and Memory Neuroimaging studies of normal people, as well as research with patients with *anterograde amnesia*, *retrograde amnesia*, Korsakoff's syndrome, and other memory problems, provide valuable information about the brain structures involved in memory. The hippocampus and thalamus are known to play a role in the formation of memories. These structures send nerve fibers to the cerebral cortex, in which memories are probably stored and which is activated during memory retrieval. Memories appear to be both localized and distributed throughout the brain.

Applications of Memory Research

Improving Your Memory Among the many applications of memory research are *mnemonics,* devices that are used to remember things better. One of the simplest but most powerful mnemonics is the method of loci. It is useful because it provides a context for organizing material more effectively. Guidelines for effective studying have also been derived from memory research. For example, the key to remembering textbook material is to read actively rather than passively. One of the most effective ways to do this is to follow the PQ4R method: preview, question, read, reflect, recite, and review. To take good lecture notes and to study them effectively, organize the points into a meaningful framework and think about how each main point relates to the others. When preparing for an exam, don't cram. Space your study sessions over time, and be sure to test yourself repeatedly.

Design for Memory Research on the limits of memory has helped product designers to create more user-friendly electronic and mechanical systems and devices.

Cognition and Language

hat are you thinking right now? This can actually be a hard question, because thoughts don't come to us in clear, complete sentences. We have to construct those sentences—using the language we've learned—from the words, images, ideas, and other mental materials in our minds. In this chapter, we explore what thoughts are, what language is, and how we translate one into the other as we reason, make decisions, and solve problems. Here's how we have organized the discussion:

Humans are animals, but we are different from other species in some very important ways. Most scientists agree that what sets us apart is our ability to reason logically, to solve complex problems, and to use language. We tend to take these abilities for granted, but the truth is that they are precious and fragile; they can be disrupted or even lost if our brains are damaged by injury or disease.

Consider "Elliot," an intelligent and successful young businessman who had a cancerous tumor removed from the frontal area of his brain. After the surgery, his normally sharp reasoning and decision-making abilities failed. On a simulated gambling task, for example, he made bets without regard for the risks of losing, and with real money he made a series of reckless, impulsive business moves that forced him into bankruptcy (Damasio, 1994). D. J., a bilingual physician, experienced very different problems when, in his early sixties, he suffered a stroke on the left side of his brain (Kohnert, 2004). Unlike Elliot, D. J. could think and reason as well as ever, and could still understand what people said in English or Spanish, but his ability to speak either language was severely impaired. It took great effort for him to produce even two- or three-word sentences, and he was unable to name most of the common objects he saw every day. Obviously, his ability to practice medicine was affected.

These cases illustrate that our success in life depends largely on the proper operation of both thinking and language skills, and that these skills involve different areas of the brain. When either cognitive or language functions are impaired, we become vulnerable to all sorts of failures and errors. What pitfalls threaten the effectiveness of human cognition? What factors influence our success? How are our thoughts transformed into language? Many of the answers to these questions come from **cognitive psychology,** the study of the mental processes by which the information humans receive from their environment is modified, made meaningful, stored, retrieved, used, and communicated to others (Reed, 2004). Many cognitive psychologists are working with biological psychologists and other neuroscientists to study the brain activity involved in these mental processes. Their collaboration in the field of *cognitive neuroscience* (e.g., D'Esposito, 2003; Fellows et al., 2005) is leading to a better understanding of the relationship between mind and brain.

In this chapter we first consider what thought is and what functions it serves. Then we examine the basic ingredients of thought and the cognitive processes people use as they interact with their environments. These cognitive processes include reasoning, problem solving, and decision making. Next, we discuss language and how it is acquired and used. We cover cognition and language in the same chapter because they often involve the same mental processes. Learning about thought helps us to better understand language, and learning about language helps us to better understand thought.

Basic Functions of Thought

cognitive psychology   The study of the mental processes by which information from the environment is modified, made meaningful, stored, retrieved, used, and communicated to others.

Let's begin our exploration of human cognition by considering the five core functions of thought, which are to *describe, elaborate, decide, plan,* and *guide action.* These functions can be seen as forming a *circle of thought* (see Figure 8.1).

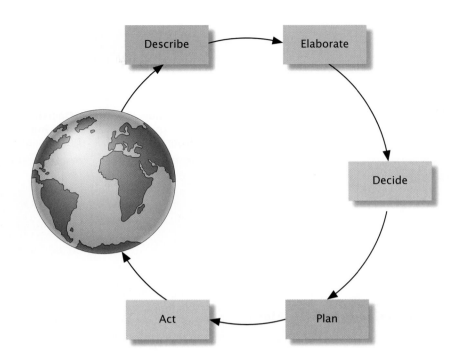

FIGURE 8.1

The Circle of Thought

The circle of thought begins as our sensory systems take in information from the world. Our perceptual system describes and elaborates this information, which is represented in the brain in ways that allow us to make decisions, formulate plans, and guide our actions. As those actions change our world, we receive new information—and the circle of thought begins again.

● The Circle of Thought

Here is an example of what happens when these functions work as they should: Dr. Joyce Wallace, a New York City internist, was trying to figure out what was the matter with a forty-three-year-old patient, "Laura McBride." Laura reported pains in her stomach and abdomen, aching muscles, irritability, dizzy spells, and fatigue (Rouéché, 1986). The doctor's first hypothesis was that Laura had iron-deficiency anemia, a condition in which there is too little oxygen-carrying hemoglobin in the blood. There was some evidence to support that hypothesis. Blood tests showed low hemoglobin and high production of red blood cells, suggesting that Laura's body was attempting to compensate for the loss of hemoglobin. However, other tests revealed normal iron levels. Perhaps she was losing blood through internal bleeding, but an additional test ruled that out. Had Laura been vomiting blood? She said no. Blood in the urine? No. Abnormally heavy menstrual flow? No. During the next week, Laura reported more intense pain, cramps, shortness of breath, and severe loss of energy. Her blood was becoming less and less capable of sustaining her, but if it was not being lost, what was happening to it? When the doctor looked at a smear of Laura's blood under the microscope, she saw that some kind of poison was destroying the red blood cells. What could it be? Laura spent most of her time at home, but her teenage daughters, who lived with her, were healthy. Dr. Wallace asked herself, "What does Laura do that the girls don't?" She repairs and restores paintings. Paint. Lead! She might be suffering from lead poisoning! When a blood test showed a lead level seven times higher than normal, Dr. Wallace knew she had solved this medical mystery at last.

Notice how the circle of thought operated in Dr. Wallace. It began when she received the information about Laura's symptoms that allowed her to *describe* the problem. Next, she *elaborated* on this information by using her knowledge and experience to consider what disorders might cause such symptoms. Then she made a *decision* to investigate a possible cause, such as anemia. To implement this decision, she made a *plan*—to order a blood test—and then *acted* on that plan. But the circle of thought did not stop there. Information from the blood test provided new descriptive information, which Dr. Wallace elaborated further to reach another decision, create a new plan, and guide her next action. Each stage in the circle of thought was also influenced by her *intention*—in this case, to find and cure her patient's problem.

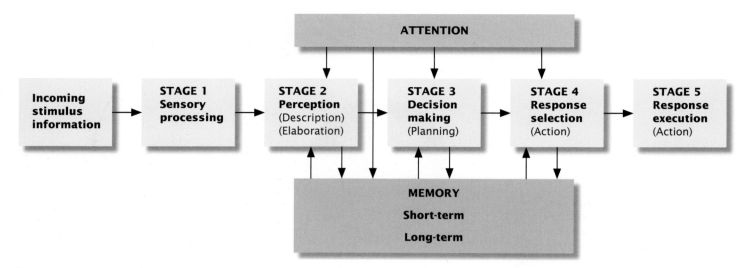

FIGURE 8.2

An Information-Processing Model

According to the information-processing model, each stage in the circle of thought takes a certain amount of time. Some stages depend heavily on both short-term and long-term memory and require some attention—that limited supply of mental energy required for information processing to be carried out efficiently.

Usually, the circle of thought spins so quickly, and its processes are so complex, that it might seem impossible to slow it down enough for scientific analysis. Some psychologists approach this difficult task by studying thought processes as if they were part of a computer-like information-processing system. An **information-processing system** receives information, represents the information with symbols, and then manipulates those representations (Anderson, Bothell, et al., 2004). In this information-processing model, then, **thinking** is defined as the manipulation of mental representations. Figure 8.2 shows how an information-processing model might view the sequence of events that form one spin around the circle of thought. Notice that according to this model, information from the world is transformed somewhat as it passes through each stage of processing.

In the first stage, information about the world reaches the brain by way of the sensory receptors described in the chapter on sensation. This stage does not require attention. In the second stage, the information must be perceived and recognized, using the attentional and perceptual processes described in the chapter on perception. It is also during this stage that the information is consciously elaborated, using short-term and working-memory processes that allow us to think about it in relation to knowledge stored in long-term memory. Once the information has been elaborated in this way, we must decide what to do with it. This third stage—decision making—also demands attention. The decision may be simply to store the information in memory. If, however, a decision is made to take some action, a response must be planned in the third stage and then carried out through a coordinated pattern of responses—the action itself—in the fourth and fifth stages. As suggested in Figure 8.1, this action usually affects the environment, providing new information that is "fed back" to the system for processing in the ongoing circle of thought.

● Measuring Information Processing

The brain damage that Elliot suffered appeared to have mainly affected the decision-making and response-selection stages of information processing. Analyzing the effects of brain damage is just one of several methods that scientists use to study the details of how the entire information-processing sequence normally works and what can interfere with it.

---

information-processing system Mechanisms for receiving information, representing it with symbols, and manipulating it.

thinking The manipulation of mental representations.

"Automatic" Thinking The sensory, perceptual, decision-making, and response-planning components that make up the circle of thought can occur so rapidly that—as when playing a fast-paced video game—we may be unaware of anything other than incoming information and our quick response to it. In such cases, our thinking processes become so well practiced that they are virtually automatic.

On Your Mark . . . The runner who reacts quickest to the starting gun will have an advantage over other competitors, but too much eagerness can cause an athlete to literally jump the gun and lose the race before it starts. Yet trying too hard to avoid a false start can slow reaction time and cost precious time in getting off the mark. This is the speed-accuracy tradeoff in action.

● **Mental Chronometry** Drivers and video-game players know that there is always a slight delay between seeing a red light or a "bad guy" and hitting the brakes or firing the laser gun. The delay occurs because each of the processes described in Figure 8.2 takes some time. Psychologists began the laboratory study of thinking by exploring *mental chronometry*, the timing of mental events (Posner, 1978). Specifically, they examined **reaction time,** the time elapsing between the presentation of a stimulus and the appearance of an overt response to it. Reaction time, they reasoned, should give us an idea of how long it takes for all the processes shown in Figure 8.2 to occur. In a typical reaction-time experiment, a person is asked to say a word or to push a button as rapidly as possible after a stimulus appears. Even in such simple situations, several factors influence reaction times (Wickens, Gordon-Becker, & Liu, 2004).

One important factor in reaction time is the *complexity* of the decision. The more options we have in responding to a set of stimuli, the longer the reaction time. The tennis player who knows that her opponent usually serves to a particular spot on the court will have a simple decision to make when the serve is completed and will react rapidly. But if she faces an opponent whose serve is less predictable, her reaction will be slower, because a more complex decision about which way to move is now required.

Expectancy, too, affects reaction time. People respond faster to stimuli that they are expecting and more slowly to stimuli that surprise them. So your reaction time will be shorter when braking for a traffic light that you knew might turn red than when dodging a ball thrown at you unexpectedly.

Reaction time is also influenced by *stimulus-response compatibility*. If the relationship between a set of stimuli and possible responses is a natural or compatible one, reaction time will be fast. If not, reaction time will be slower. Figure 8.3 illustrates compatible and incompatible relationships. Incompatible stimulus-response relationships are major culprits in causing errors in the use of all kinds of equipment, especially if it is unfamiliar or if the operator is under stress (Segal & Suri, 1999).

Finally, in any reaction-time task, there is a *speed-accuracy tradeoff*. If you try to respond quickly, errors increase. If you try for an error-free performance, reaction time increases (Wickens & Carswell, 2006). At a swimming meet, for example, contestants who try too hard to anticipate the starting gun may have especially quick starts but may also have especially frequent false starts that disqualify them.

● **reaction time** The time between the presentation of a stimulus and an overt response to it.

FIGURE 8.3

Stimulus-Response Compatibility

Imagine standing in front of an unfamiliar stove when a pot starts to boil over. Your reaction time in turning down the heat will depend in part on the stove's design. The response you make will be quicker on the stove shown in the top photo, because each knob is next to the burner it controls. There is compatibility between the source of the stimulus and the location of the response. The stove in the bottom photo shows far less compatibility. Here, which knob you should turn is not as obvious, so your reaction time will be slower.

● **Evoked Brain Potentials** Research on reaction time has helped establish the time required for information processing to occur. It has also revealed how the entire sequence can be made faster or slower. But reaction times alone cannot provide a detailed picture of what goes on between the presentation of a stimulus and the execution of a response. They do not tell us, for example, how long the perception stage lasts. Nor do they tell us whether we respond more quickly to an expected stimulus because we perceive it faster or because we make a decision about it faster. Reaction-time measures have been used in many ingenious efforts to make inferences about such things; but to analyze mental events more directly, psychologists have turned to other methods, such as the analysis of evoked brain potentials.

The **evoked brain potential** is a small, temporary change in voltage on an *electroencephalogram* (EEG) that occurs in response to specific events (Rugg & Coles, 1995). Figure 8.4 shows an example. Each peak on the EEG reflects the firing of large groups of neurons, within different regions of the brain, at different times during the information-processing sequence. The pattern of the peaks provides information that is more precise than overall reaction time. For example, a large positive peak, called the P300, occurs 300 to 500 milliseconds (thousandths of a second) after a stimulus is presented. The exact delay before a P300 occurs is a sensitive measure of how long it takes to complete the first two stages of information processing shown in Figure 8.2. Further, the size of the P300 reflects the operation of attention in the second of those stages. For example, P300s are normally larger in response to unusual or surprising stimuli than to unchanging or predictable ones. If this is not the case, there may be a problem, as was revealed in a study of college students who had suffered concussions. Although these students showed no obvious symptoms of brain damage, their P300s to surprising stimuli were abnormally small, which suggested some lingering disruption in their brains' information-processing capacity (Lavoie et al., 2004).

● **Neuroimaging** Using positron emission tomography (PET), functional magnetic resonance imaging (fMRI), and other neuroimaging techniques described in the chapter on biological aspects of psychology, cognitive neuroscientists can now watch what happens in the brain during information processing (e.g., Amaro & Barker, 2006; Badre & Wagner, 2006). In one study, for example, participants performed a task that required complex problem-solving skills. As shown by the red-shaded areas in Figure 8.5, the frontal lobe of the brain was especially active when this task was still relatively new and difficult. As the participants learned the skills, however, this frontal lobe involvement decreased. When the task was well learned, the hippocampus became especially active (see the green-shaded areas in the bottom panel of Figure 8.5). Activation in the hippocampus suggests that the participants were no longer struggling with a problem-solving task but instead were performing it from memory.

A number of other studies of brain activity during the performance of cognitive tasks have also found that the frontal lobes are especially important for making decisions and solving problems (Wallis, Anderson, & Miller, 2001; Yarkoni et al., 2005; this chapter's Focus on Research Methods shows another example). These tasks involve coordinated activity in many other brain areas, too (Andrés, 2003), but it is certainly no wonder that damage to Elliot's frontal area disrupted his decision-making abilities.

Mental Representations: The Ingredients of Thought

evoked brain potential A small, temporary change in EEG voltage that is evoked by some stimulus.

Just as measuring, stirring, and baking are only part of the story of cookie making, describing the processes involved in thinking tells only part of the story behind the circle of thought. To understand thinking more fully, we also need to know what it is that these processes manipulate. Most psychologists describe the ingredients of

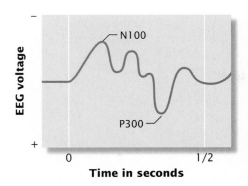

FIGURE 8.4

Evoked Potentials

Here is the average EEG, or brain wave, tracing produced from several trials on which a research participant's name was presented. Evoked potentials are averaged in this way so as to eliminate random variations in the tracings. The result is the appearance of a *negative* peak (N100) followed by a large *positive* peak (P300). Traditionally, positive peaks are shown as decreases on such tracings, whereas negative ones are shown as increases.

FIGURE 8.5

Watching People Think

Cognitive psychologists and other cognitive neuroscientists have found ways to watch brain activity as information processing takes place. These fMRI pictures show activity in two "slices" of the brain of a research participant who was practicing a complex problem-solving task. The areas shown in red were activated early in the learning process. As skill developed, the areas shown in green became activated.

Source: Anderson (2000).

● **concept** A category of objects, events, or ideas that have common properties.

● **formal concept** A concept that can be clearly defined by a set of rules or properties.

thought as *information*. But this is like saying that you make cookies with "stuff." What specific forms does information take in our minds? In other words, how do we mentally represent information? Researchers in cognitive psychology have found that information can be mentally represented in many ways, including as *concepts*, *propositions*, *schemas*, *scripts*, *mental models*, *images*, and *cognitive maps*. Let's consider each of these ingredients of thought and how we manipulate them as we think.

● Concepts

When you think about anything—dogs, happiness, sex, movies, pizza—you are manipulating a basic ingredient of thought called *concepts*. **Concepts** are categories of objects, events, or ideas with common properties (Jahnke & Nowaczyk, 1998). To "have a concept" is to recognize the properties, or *features*, that tend to be shared by the members of the category. For example, the concept "bird" includes such properties as having feathers, laying eggs, and being able to fly. The concept "scissors" includes such properties as having two blades, a connecting hinge, and a pair of finger holes. Concepts allow you to relate each object, event, or idea you encounter to a category you already know. Using concepts, you can say, "No, that's not a dog," or "Yes, that's a car." Concepts also make it possible to think logically. If you have the concepts "whale" and "bird," you can decide whether a whale is bigger than a bird without having either creature in the room with you.

● **Types of Concepts**   Some concepts—called **formal concepts**—can be clearly defined by a set of rules or properties such that members of the concept have all of the defining properties and nonmembers don't. For example, the concept "square" can be defined as "a shape with four equal sides and four right-angle corners." Any object that does not have all of these features simply is not a square, and any object with all these features is a square. To study concept learning in the laboratory, psychologists often use formal concepts, because the members of the concept can be neatly defined (Trabasso & Bower, 1968).

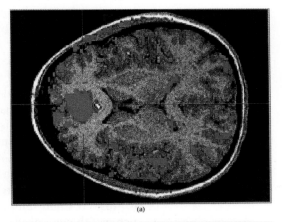

(a)

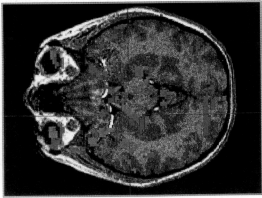

A Natural Concept A space shuttle and a hot-air balloon are two examples of the natural concept "aircraft," but most people think of the space shuttle, with its wings, as the better example. A prototype of the concept is probably an airplane. Members of natural concepts share a kind of "family resemblance" that helps us to recognize items that belong in the same category, even if they are not identical.

TRY THIS There are many other concepts, though, that can't be defined by a fixed set of necessary features. For example, try listing a small set of features that precisely defines the concept of "game." True, most games are competitive, but some—such as pitch-and-catch or ring-around-the-rosey—are not. And although most games require more than one player, pinball, solitaire, and many computer games don't. Similarly, "home" can be defined as the place where you were born, the house in which you grew up, where you live now, your country of origin, the place where you are most comfortable, and so on. These are just two examples of **natural concepts,** concepts that have no fixed set of defining features but instead have a set of typical, or characteristic, features. So just as members of the same family might resemble each other in some ways, but not in every way, members of a natural concept need not have all of its characteristic features. One characteristic feature of the natural concept "bird," for example, is the ability to fly; but an ostrich is a bird even though it cannot fly. It's a bird because it possesses enough other characteristic features of "bird" (feathers, wings, and the like). Having just one bird property is not enough. A snake lays eggs and a bat flies, but neither one is a bird. It is usually a combination of properties that defines a concept. Outside the laboratory, most of the concepts that people use in thinking are natural rather than formal concepts. Natural concepts include relatively concrete object categories, such as "bird" or "house"; abstract idea categories, such as "honesty" or "justice"; and temporary goal-related categories that help people make plans, such as "things I need to pack for my trip" (Barsalou, 1993).

The boundaries of a natural concept are fuzzy, and some members of it are better examples of the concept than others because they share more of its characteristic features (Rosch, 1975). A robin, a chicken, an ostrich, and a penguin are all birds. But a robin is the best example, because a robin can fly and is closer to the size and shape of what most people have learned to think of as a typical bird. A member of a natural concept that possesses all or most of its characteristic features is called a **prototype,** or is said to be *prototypical* (Smith, 1998). A robin, then, is a prototypical bird. The more prototypical a member of a concept is, the more quickly people can decide if it is an example of the concept. As a result, it takes slightly less time for people to answer when asked "Is a robin a bird?" than when asked "Is a penguin a bird?"

● **natural concept** A concept that has no fixed set of defining features but has a set of characteristic features.

● **prototype** A member of a natural concept that possesses all or most of its characteristic features

You Can't Judge a Book by Its Cover
Does this person look like a millionaire to you? Our schemas tell us what to expect about objects, events, and people, but those expectations can sometimes be wrong. This was dramatically illustrated when Gordon Elwood, a Medford, Oregon, man who dressed in rags and collected cans, died and left over $9 million to charity (McMahon, 2000).

● Propositions

We often combine concepts in units known as **propositions.** A proposition is a mental representation that expresses a relationship between concepts. Propositions can be true or false. Suppose you hear that your friend Heather broke up with her boyfriend, Jason. Your mental representation of this event will include a proposition that links your concepts of "Heather" and "Jason" in a particular way. This proposition could be diagrammed (using unscientific terms) as follows: Heather→dumped→Jason.

The diagram looks like a sentence, but it isn't one. Propositions can be expressed as sentences, but they are actually general ideas that can be conveyed in any number of specific ways. In this case, "Jason was dumped by Heather" and "Heather is not dating Jason anymore" would all express the same proposition. If you later discover that it was Jason who caused the breakup, your proposition about the event would change to reflect this new information, shown here as reversed arrows: Heather←dumped←Jason. Propositions are part of the network of associations that many psychologists see as the basis for our knowledge of the world (see Figures 7.9 and 7.10 in the chapter on memory). So hearing the name *Heather*, for example, will activate lots of associated information about her, including the proposition about her relationship to Jason.

● Schemas, Scripts, and Mental Models

Sets of propositions are often so closely associated that they form more complex mental representations called **schemas.** As described in the chapters on perception, memory, and human development, schemas are generalizations that we develop about categories of objects, places, events, and people. Our schemas help us to understand the world. If you borrow a friend's car, your "car" schema will give you a good idea of where to put the ignition key, where the accelerator and brake are, and how to raise and lower the windows. Schemas also create expectations about objects, places, events, and people—telling us that stereo systems have speakers, that picnics occur in the summer, that rock concerts are loud, and so on.

● **Scripts** One particularly useful type of schema is called a script (Anderson, 2000). **Scripts** are schemas about familiar activities, such as going to a restaurant,

● **proposition** A mental representation of the relationship between concepts.

● **schemas** Generalizations about categories of objects, places, events, and people.

● **script** A mental representation of familiar sequences of activity.

FIGURE 8.6

Eating at a Restaurant

Schemas about what happens in restaurants and how to behave in them take the form of a *script*, represented here in four "scenes." Scripts guide our actions in all sorts of familiar situations and also help us to understand descriptions of events occurring in those situations (e.g., "Our service was really slow").

Source: Whitney (2001).

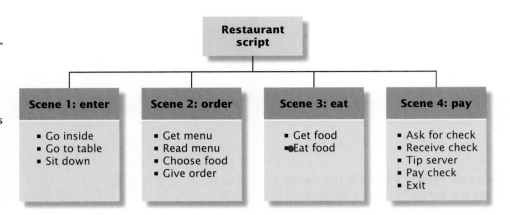

Restaurant script			
Scene 1: enter	**Scene 2: order**	**Scene 3: eat**	**Scene 4: pay**
▪ Go inside ▪ Go to table ▪ Sit down	▪ Get menu ▪ Read menu ▪ Choose food ▪ Give order	▪ Get food ▪ Eat food	▪ Ask for check ▪ Receive check ▪ Tip server ▪ Pay check ▪ Exit

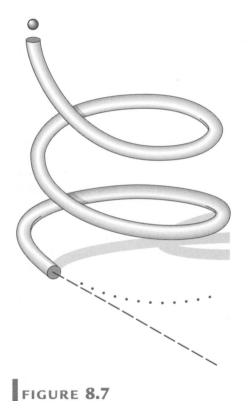

FIGURE 8.7

Applying a Mental Model

TRY THIS Try to imagine the path that the marble will follow when it leaves the curved tube. In one study, most people drew the incorrect (curved) path indicated by the dotted line, rather than the correct (straight) path indicated by the dashed line (McCloskey, 1983). Their errors were based on a faulty mental model of the behavior of physical objects.

mental model A representation of particular situations or arrangements of objects that guides our interaction with them.

visiting a doctor's office, or attending a lecture. Your "restaurant" script, for example, represents the sequence of events you can expect when you go out to eat (see Figure 8.6). That script tells you what to do when you are in a restaurant and helps you to understand stories involving restaurants (Whitney, 2001). Scripts also shape your interpretation of events. For example, on your first day of college, you no doubt assumed that the person standing at the front of the class was a teacher, not a security guard or a janitor.

If our scripts are violated, however, it is easy to misinterpret events. One heart attack victim in London lay for nine hours in the hallway of an apartment building after an ambulance crew smelled alcohol on his breath and assumed he was "sleeping it off." The crew's script for what happens in the poorer sections of big cities told them that someone slumped in a hallway is drunk, not sick. Because script-violating events are unexpected, our reactions to them tend to be slower and less effective than are our reactions to expected events. Your "grocery shopping" script, for example, probably includes pushing a cart, putting items in it, going to the checkout stand, and paying for your purchases. But suppose you are at the back of the store when a robber near the entrance fires a gun and shouts at the manager to open the safe. People sometimes ignore these script-violating events, interpreting gunshots as a car backfiring and shouted orders as "someone fooling around." Others simply "freeze," unsure of what to do, and failing to realize that they could call the police on their cell phones.

● **Mental Models** Related concepts can be organized not only as schemas and scripts but also as **mental models,** which are representations of particular situations or arrangements of objects (Johnson-Laird, 1983). For example, suppose someone tells you, "My living room has blue walls, a white ceiling, and an oval window across from the door." You will mentally represent this information as propositions about how the concepts "wall," "blue," "ceiling," "white," "door," "oval," and "window" are related. However, you will also combine these propositions to create in your mind a three-dimensional model of the room. As more information about the world becomes available, either from existing memories or from new information we receive, our mental models become more complete.

Accurate mental models are excellent guides for thinking about, and interacting with, many of the things we encounter (Ashcraft, 2006). If a mental model is incorrect or incomplete, however, we are likely to make mistakes (see Figure 8.7). For example, if men hold an incorrect mental model of how quickly early-stage prostate cancer spreads, they may choose a more immediate, and more radical, treatment option than may actually be necessary (Denberg, Melhado, & Steiner, 2006).

● Images and Cognitive Maps

Some mental models stem from sets of propositions that describe a situation, but these models are more often based on images in the "mind's eye." For example, take a moment and think about how your best friend would look in a clown   TRY THIS

FIGURE 8.8

Manipulating Images

TRY THIS Are these pairs of objects the same or different? To decide, you will have to rotate one member of each pair. Because manipulating mental images, like manipulating actual objects, takes some time, the speed of your decision will depend on how far you have to mentally rotate one object to line it up with the other for comparison. (The top pair matches, the bottom pair does not.)

Source: Shepard & Metzler (1971).

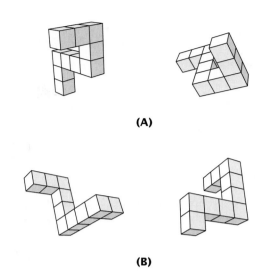

(A)

(B)

suit. The "mental picture" you just got illustrates that thinking often involves the manipulation of **images**—which are mental representations of visual information. Cognitive psychologists refer to mental images as *analogical representations*, because we manipulate these images in a way that is similar, or *analogous,* to manipulating the objects themselves (Reed, 2004). This similarity was demonstrated in a classic study by Roger Shepard and Jacqueline Metzler (1971). They measured how long it took people to decide whether pairs of objects such as those in Figure 8.8 were the same or different. They found that the amount of decision time depended on how far one object had to be "mentally rotated" to compare it with the other. The more rotation was required, the longer the decision took. In other words, rotating the mental image of an object was like rotating the real object. More recent studies using neuroimaging have confirmed that manipulating mental images activates some of the same areas of the brain that are active during comparable tasks with real objects (Farah, 2000).

Our ability to think using images extends beyond the manipulation of stimuli such as those in Figure 8.8. We also create images that serve as mental models of written or spoken descriptions of scenes. In fact, brain areas involved in vision are activated as we construct mental images of those scenes (Mazoyer et al., 2002). You probably created a mental image a minute ago when you read about that blue-walled room, and you would do the same thing when someone gives you directions to that new pizza place in town. In the latter case, you would scan your **cognitive map**—a mental model of familiar parts of your world—to find the location. In doing so, you would use a mental process similar to the visual process of scanning a paper map (Anderson, 2000; Taylor & Tversky, 1992). Manipulating images on a different cognitive map would help you if a power failure left your home pitch dark. Even though you couldn't see a thing, you could still find a flashlight or candle, because your cognitive map would show the floor plan, furniture placement, door locations, and other physical features of your home. You would not have this mental map in an unfamiliar house. There, you would have to walk slowly, arms outstretched, to avoid wrong turns and painful collisions. In the chapter on learning we describe how experience shapes the cognitive maps that help animals navigate mazes and people navigate shopping malls.

Thinking Strategies

- **image** A mental representation of visual information.
- **cognitive map** A mental model of familiar parts of the environment.

We have seen that our thinking capacity is based largely on our ability to manipulate mental representations—the ingredients of thought—much as a baker manipulates the ingredients of cookies (see "In Review: Ingredients of Thought" for a summary of these representations). But whereas the baker's food-processing system combines and transforms flour, sugar, milk, eggs, and chocolate into a

in review Ingredients of Thought

Ingredient	Description	Examples
Concepts	Categories of objects, events, or ideas with common properties; basic building blocks of thought	"Square" (a formal concept); "game" (a natural concept).
Propositions	Mental representations that express relationships between concepts; can be true or false	Assertions such as "The cow jumped over the moon."
Schemas	Sets of propositions that create generalizations and expectations about categories of objects, places, events, and people	A schema might suggest that all grandmothers are elderly, gray haired, and bake a lot of cookies.
Scripts	Schemas about familiar activities and situations; guide behavior in those situations	You pay before eating in fast-food restaurants and after eating in fancier restaurants.
Mental models	Sets of propositions about how things relate to each other in the real world; can be correct or incorrect	Assuming that airflow around an open car will send thrown objects upward, a driver tosses a lighted cigarette butt overhead, causing it to land in the back seat.
Images	Mental representations of visual information	Hearing a description of your blind date creates a mental picture of him or her.
Cognitive maps	Mental representations of familiar parts of the world	You can get to class by an alternate route even if your usual route is blocked by construction.

delicious treat, our information-processing system combines, transforms, and elaborates mental representations in ways that allow us to engage in reasoning, problem solving, and decision making. Let's begin our discussion of these thinking strategies by considering **reasoning,** the process through which we generate and evaluate arguments, as well as reach conclusions about them.

● Formal Reasoning

Astronomers tell us that the temperature at the core of the sun is about 27 million degrees Fahrenheit. They can't put a temperature probe inside the sun, so how can they be so confident about this assertion? Their estimate is based on *inferences* from other things that they know about the sun and about physical objects in general. Telescopic observations of the sun's volume and mass allowed astronomers to calculate its density, using the formula Density = Mass ÷ Volume. These observations also enabled them to measure the energy coming from one small region of the sun and—using what geometry told them about the surface area of spheres—to estimate the energy output from the sun as a whole. Further calculations told them how hot a body would have to be to generate that much energy.

In other words, the astronomers' estimate of the sun's core temperature was based on **formal reasoning** (also called *deductive reasoning*), the process of following a set of rigorous procedures to reach valid, or correct, conclusions. Some of these procedures included the application of specific mathematical formulas to existing data in order to generate new data. Such formulas are examples of **algorithms,** systematic methods that always produce a correct solution to a problem, if a solution exists (Jahnke & Nowaczyk, 1998). The astronomers also followed the **rules of logic,** which are sets of statements that provide a formula for drawing valid conclusions about the world. For example, each step in the

● **reasoning** The process by which people generate and evaluate arguments and reach conclusions about them.

● **formal reasoning** The process of following a set of rigorous procedures for reaching valid conclusions.

● **algorithm** A systematic procedure that cannot fail to produce a correct solution to a problem, if a solution exists.

● **rules of logic** Sets of statements that provide a formula for drawing valid conclusions.

Pitfalls in Formal Reasoning "Elderly people cannot be astronauts; this is an elderly man; therefore, he cannot be an astronaut." The logic of this syllogism is correct, but the first premise is wrong. In 1962, John Glenn became the first American astronaut to orbit the earth. Here he is in 1998, at the age of seventy-seven, just before he returned to space as a crew member on the space shuttle *Discovery*. Most of us try to use formal reasoning to reach correct conclusions, but even perfect logic can lead to incorrect conclusions if we start with false assumptions.

astronomers' thinking took the form of "if-then" statements: If we know how much energy comes from one part of the sun's surface, and if we know how big the whole surface is, then we can calculate the total energy output. You use the same formal reasoning processes when you conclude, for example, that if your friend José is two years older than you are, then his twin brother, Juan, will be two years older, too. Formal reasoning is called *deductive* reasoning because it takes a general rule (e.g., twins are the same age) and applies it to deduce conclusions about specific cases (e.g., José and Juan).

The rules of logic, which are traceable to the Greek philosopher Aristotle, have evolved into a system for drawing correct conclusions from a set of statements known as *premises*. Consider, for example, what conclusion can be drawn from the following premises:

Premise 1: People who study hard do well in this course.

Premise 2: You have studied hard.

According to the rules of logic, it would be valid to conclude that you will do well in this course. Logical arguments that contain two or more premises and a conclusion are known as **syllogisms** (pronounced "SILL-o-jisms"). Notice that the conclusion in a syllogism goes beyond what the premises actually say. The conclusion is an inference based on the premises and on the rules of logic. In this case, the logical rule was this: If something is true of all members of a category, and if A is in that category, then that something will also be true of A.

Your ability to make everyday decisions and solve everyday problems depends heavily on your ability to draw correct inferences about facts. For example, if a course you want to take is open only to seniors and you are a sophomore, you'll infer that it would be a waste of time to try to get in. Here, the syllogism would be:

Premise 1: This class is open only to seniors.

Premise 2: I am not a senior.

Conclusion: I can't take this class.

Logical reasoning skills can be so well learned that they seem to come naturally, but there are some tendencies toward errors in reasoning that seem to come naturally, too. These common pitfalls can lead us astray in our problem solving and decision making. Two of the most important of these pitfalls are *belief bias* and *limits on memory*:

1. *Belief bias.* Sometimes what we already know and believe biases our reasoning processes (e.g., Roberts & Sykes, 2003). For example, consider this syllogism:

Premise 1: Some professors wear ties.

Premise 2: Some men wear ties.

Conclusion: Some professors are men.

The conclusion happens to be true, but it doesn't actually follow logically from these premises. Conclusions such as this one *look* logical and valid, but only because they conform to what our experience has taught us to believe about the world. To see how belief bias affected your view of this syllogism, substitute the word *scarecrows* for *men* in Premise 2. The syllogism now reads: *Some professors wear ties. Some scarecrows wear ties. Therefore, some professors are scarecrows.* No matter what you think of your professors, you would probably not accept this new conclusion as valid.

Belief bias is related to a more general problem in human reasoning, called **confirmation bias**—a tendency to seek evidence and reach conclusions that are consistent with our existing beliefs. Confirmation bias can affect thinking in many situations. When people first fall in love, they often focus only on their

syllogism An argument made up of two propositions, called premises, and a conclusion based on those premises.

confirmation bias The tendency to pay more attention to evidence in support of one's hypothesis than to evidence that refutes that hypothesis.

Anchoring to a Price   The anchoring heuristic operates in many bargaining situations. The asking price of this house, for example, has probably anchored the sellers' perception of its value. As a result, they may be reluctant to accept a lower price, even if information from their sales agent suggests they should. The buyers' judgment of the house's value will also be anchored to some extent by the seller's asking price. Even if they discover the house needs some repairs, they are more likely to offer 90 percent of the price rather than 50 percent.

detail finds its appropriate place. His writing is rather dull and mechanical, occasionally enlivened by somewhat corny puns and flashes of imagination of the sci-fi type. He has a strong drive for competence. He seems to have little feel and little sympathy for other people and does not enjoy interacting with others. Self-centered, he nonetheless has a deep moral sense.

Now if you had been told that there were twenty-five red and five blue jelly beans in a jar, you would probably use that information to guess that the one you drew at random would be red. So knowing that there are five times as many humanities sketches as computer science sketches should guide your guess about Tom's major. Research shows, however, that most people ignore the odds in that situation. They guess that Tom is a computer science major, simply because he seems more representative of that category than of the other one (Tversky & Kahneman, 1974). The odds are against them though, so they will probably be wrong.

The impact of the representativeness heuristic can be seen in many real-life judgments and decisions. One study found, for example, that jurors' decisions to convict or acquit a defendant may depend partly on the degree to which the defendant's actions were representative of a crime category. Someone who abducts a child and asks for ransom (actions that clearly fit the category of "kidnapping") is more likely to be convicted than someone who abducts an adult and demands no ransom—even though both crimes constitute kidnapping and the evidence is equally strong in each case (Smith, 1991).

● **The Availability Heuristic**   Even when people are careful to use probability information to help them judge group membership or to assess a hypothesis, a third heuristic can bias their thinking. The **availability heuristic** involves judging the likelihood of an event or the correctness of a hypothesis based on how easily the hypothesis or examples of that event come to mind (Tversky & Kahneman, 1974). In other words, people tend to choose the hypothesis or predict the event that is most mentally "available" to them, much as they might select the box of cereal that is at the front of the supermarket shelf.

Like other heuristics, this shortcut often works well. After all, frequent events or likely hypotheses are easy to remember. However, the availability heuristic can lead to biased judgments, especially when mental availability does not reflect actual frequency (Morewedge, Gilbert, & Wilson, 2005). For example, news reports about shark attacks and urban shootings lead many people to overestimate how often these memorable, but relatively rare, events actually occur. As a result, these people may suffer undue anxiety over swimming in the ocean or being in certain cities (Bellaby, 2003). Similarly, many students stick with their first responses to multiple choice test questions because it is especially easy to recall those galling occasions on which they changed a right answer to a wrong one. Research shows, though, that changing an answer in light of further reflection is more likely to be correct than incorrect (Kruger, Wirtz, & Miller, 2005).

The heuristics we have discussed represent only three of the many mental shortcuts that people use more or less automatically in making judgments, and they describe only some of the biases and limitations that affect human reasoning. Indeed, research on human thinking has confirmed the ancient idea that we sometimes depend on careful deliberation and sometimes on intuition. Psychologists have formalized this idea in *dual process theories* (Kahneman & Shane, 2005; Reyna & Farley, 2006; Stanovich & West, 2002), which suggest that the quicker, easier intuitive system tends to take over in complex situations or when background knowledge suggests what the right conclusion should be. Intuition has its limits, though, especially when it is based on potentially biasing heuristics that can lead us astray (Myers, 2004). We'll encounter other biases and limitations as we consider two important goals of thinking: problem solving and decision making.

● **availability heuristic**   A mental shortcut through which judgments are based on information that is most easily brought to mind.

A Memorable Outcome The availability heuristic can have a strong impact on people's judgments about the chances of winning a lottery. Splashy media coverage makes it far easier to recall the few people who have won big prizes than the millions whose tickets turned out to be worthless.

Problem Solving

If where you are is not where you want to be, and when the path to getting there is not obvious, you have a *problem*. As suggested by the circle of thought, the most efficient approach to problem solving would be first to diagnose the problem in the elaboration stage, then to come up with a plan for solving it, then to execute the plan, and finally to evaluate the results to determine whether the problem remains (Bransford & Stein, 1993). But people's problem-solving efforts are not always so systematic, which is one reason that medical tests are sometimes given unnecessarily, diseases are sometimes misdiagnosed, and auto parts are sometimes replaced when there is nothing wrong with them.

Strategies for Problem Solving

When you are trying to get from a starting point to some goal, the best path may not necessarily be a straight line. In fact, obstacles may force you to go in the opposite direction temporarily. So it is with problem solving. Sometimes, the best strategy is not to take mental steps aimed straight at your goal. For example, when a problem is especially difficult, it can sometimes be helpful to allow it to "incubate" by setting it aside for a while. A solution that once seemed out of reach may suddenly appear after you think about other things for a while. The benefits of incubation probably arise from forgetting incorrect ideas that may have been blocking the path to a correct solution (Anderson, 2000). Incubation alone may not be enough to solve life's problems, though, so people often use other more direct problem-solving strategies, such as means-ends analysis, working backward, and finding analogies.

● **Means-End Analysis** To use *means-end analysis*, you continuously ask yourself where you are in relation to your final goal, and then decide on the means by which you can get one step closer to it (Newell & Simon, 1972). In other words, rather than trying to solve the problem all at once, you identify a subgoal that will take you toward a solution (this process is referred to as *decomposition*). After reaching that subgoal, you identify another one that will get you even closer to the

Working Backward to Forge Ahead
Whether you are organizing a family vacation or, as Ellen MacArthur did, sailing alone in an around-the-world race, working backward from the final goal through all the steps necessary to reach that goal is a helpful approach to solving complex problems.

solution, and you continue this step-by-step process until the problem is solved. Some students apply this approach to the problem of writing a major term paper. The task might seem overwhelming at first, but their first subgoal is simply to write an outline of what they think the paper should cover. When the outline is complete, they decide whether a paper based on it will satisfy the assignment. If so, the next subgoal might be to search the library and the Internet for information about each section. If they decide that this information is adequate, the next subgoal would be to write a rough draft of the introduction, and so on.

● **Working Backward** The *working-backward* strategy is based on the notion that many problems are like a tree. The trunk is the information you are given. The solution is a twig on one of the limbs. If you work forward by taking the "givens" of the problem and trying to find the solution, it will be easy to branch off in the wrong direction. A more efficient approach may be to start at the twig end and work backward toward your goal (Galotti, 1999). Consider, for example, the problem of planning a climb to the summit of Mount Everest. The best strategy is to figure out, first, what equipment and supplies are needed at the highest camp on the night before the summit attempt. Next, you have to establish how many people are needed to stock that camp the day before, how many people are needed to supply those who must stock the camp, and so on until a plan for the entire expedition is complete. It is easy to overlook the working-backward strategy, however, because it runs counter to the way most of us have learned to think. It is hard to imagine that the first step in solving a problem could be to assume that you have already solved it. Unfortunately, six climbers died on Mount Everest in 1996 in part because of failure to apply this strategy (Krakauer, 1997).

● **Using Analogies** A third problem-solving strategy is trying to find *analogies*, or similarities between today's problem and others you have encountered before. An office manager may find, for example, that a seemingly hopeless conflict between employees can be resolved using the same compromise that worked during a recent family squabble. To take advantage of analogies, we must first recognize the similarities between current and previous problems and then recall the solution that worked before. Most people are surprisingly poor at recognizing such similarities (Anderson, 2000). They tend to concentrate on the surface features that make problems appear different.

**FOCUS ON
RESEARCH METHODS** **Locating Analogical Thinking**

Simply knowing about problem-solving strategies, such as means-end analysis, is not enough. As described in the chapter on motivation and emotion, people must see that the benefits of solving the problem are worth the effort required.

The value of using analogies in problem solving was beautifully illustrated after the Hubble Space Telescope was placed in orbit around the earth in 1990. It

Calvin and Hobbes   by Bill Watterson

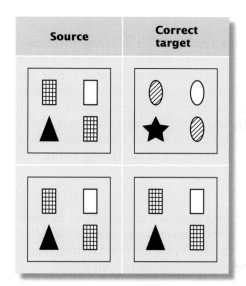

FIGURE 8.10

Comparing Stimulus Patterns

The top row shows an example of the stimulus patterns that were compared in an analogy task. Participants had to say whether the pattern on the right is similar, or *analogous*, to the one on the left. (In this case it is, because even though the specific shapes used in one pattern differ from those in the other pattern, their shading and physical arrangement are similar.) The bottom row shows an example of the patterns that were compared in a "same-different" task. Here, participants were asked only to decide whether the two patterns are *exactly the same* (Wharton et al., 2000).

was designed to take detailed photographs of distant galaxies, but because its main mirror was not focusing light properly, the pictures were blurry. Then NASA engineer James Crocker happened to notice the way a hotel room showerhead pivoted, and it gave him the idea for a system of movable mirrors to correct for the flaw in the Hubble's mirror. When shuttle astronauts installed these mirrors in 1993, the problem was solved (Stein, 1993).

■ What was the researchers' question?

Charles Wharton and his colleagues wanted to know what goes on in the brain when people do this kind of analogical mapping—recognizing similarities between things that appear to be different and even unrelated (Wharton et al., 2000).

■ How did the researchers answer the question?

The researchers knew that PET scan technology could show brain activity while participants performed an analogy task, but how could the activity associated with analogical mapping be separated from everything else going on in the brain at the same time? The answer was to use a *subtraction technique*. They asked people to perform two tasks—one after the other—that involved making comparisons between pairs of stimulus patterns. Both tasks placed similar demands on the brain, but only one of them required the participants to *make analogies* between the patterns (see Figure 8.10). The researchers then compared the resulting PET scans, looking for areas of the brain that were active in the analogy task but not in the other one. What their computers did, in essence, was to take all the brain activity that occurred during the analogy task and "subtract" from it all the activity that occurred during the other task. The activity remaining was presumed to reflect analogical mapping.

■ What did the researchers find?

As you can see in Figure 8.11, the brain areas activated only during the analogy task were in the left hemisphere, particularly in the frontal and parietal areas. Other neuroimaging studies have shown activation of similar areas during abstract problem solving, reasoning, and making simple ethical judgments (e.g., Heekeren et al., 2003; Osherson et al., 1998).

FIGURE 8.11

Brain Activity During Analogical Mapping

Comparing PET scans of brain activity during an analogy task and a task not requiring analogical thinking revealed that making analogies appears to involve areas of the left frontal and parietal lobes, as seen here from below and highlighted in red.

Source: Wharton et al. (2000).

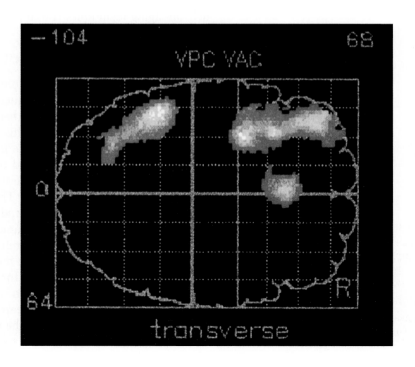

■ What do the results mean?

These results show that it is possible to locate specific brain activities associated with a specific kind of cognitive activity. They also fit well into what we already know about where certain brain functions are localized. As mentioned earlier, the frontal areas of the brain are involved in complex processing tasks, including those requiring coordination of information in working memory with information coming from the senses. There is also evidence that parietal areas are involved in our ability to perceive the arrangements of objects and relationships among them. Both of these regions were activated during the analogy task in this experiment, suggesting that this task required both kinds of abilities.

■ What do we still need to know?

There is no doubt that Wharton and his colleagues devised a clever way to examine the analogical mapping process as it occurs in the human brain, but are the brain areas identified the only ones involved in analogies? Would the same results appear if the analogy task had been verbal instead of visual, requiring participants to make analogies such as "Dark is to light as cold is to _____"? A more recent study suggests that they do (Bunge et al., 2005), though more research will be needed to confirm this.

Consider also that even though the analogy task used in Wharton's study involved processing visual-spatial information (shape, shading, and location) rather than verbal information (words), the PET scans showed activation only on the left side of the brain. This is surprising, because as mentioned in the chapter on biological aspects of psychology, visual-spatial processing is usually handled mainly in the brain's right hemisphere. These results remind us that, as also mentioned in that chapter, the left hemisphere may predominate in verbal tasks and the right in spatial tasks, but both hemispheres are involved to some extent in virtually all complex cognitive activity.

Remember, too, that we have to be careful when interpreting the brain activity detected in neuroimaging studies. Increased activity in a particular brain region doesn't always mean that the region is performing the processing we are trying to locate. The activity observed might also result if the area were being suppressed so as not to interfere with processing going on elsewhere. As discussed in the Thinking Critically section of the biological aspects of behavior chapter, the study of brain activity during higher-level thinking is still quite new, so it will take some time, and a lot more research, to learn how to correctly interpret the data coming from neuroimaging techniques (Buxton et al., 2004; Gonsalves et al., 2005). ■

● Obstacles to Problem Solving

Failing to use analogies is just one example of the obstacles that face problem solvers every day. Difficulties frequently occur at the beginning, during the diagnosis stage, when a person forms and then tests hypotheses about a problem.

As a case in point, consider this true story: In September 1998, John Gatiss was in the kitchen of his rented house in Cheltenham, England, when he heard a faint meowing sound. He couldn't find the source of the sound, but he assumed that a kitten had become trapped in the walls or under the flooring, so he called for the fire brigade to rescue the animal. The sound seemed to be coming from the electric oven, so the rescuers dismantled it, disconnecting the power cord in the process. The sound stopped, but everyone assumed that wherever the kitten was, it had become too frightened to meow. The search was reluctantly abandoned, and the oven was reconnected. Four days later, the meowing began again. This time, Gatiss and his landlord called the Royal Society for the Prevention of Cruelty to Animals (RSPCA), whose inspectors heard the kitten in distress and asked the fire brigade to return. They spent the next three days searching for the cat. First, they tore down parts of the kitchen walls and ripped up the floorboards. Next, they called in plumbing and drainage specialists, who used cables tipped with fiber-optic cameras to search remote cavities where a kitten might hide. Rescuers then brought in members of a disaster search team, who tried to find the kitten using acoustic and ultrasonic equipment designed to locate victims trapped in the debris of earthquakes and explosions. Not a sound could be heard. Increasingly concerned about how much longer the kitten could survive, the fire brigade tried to coax it from hiding with the finest-quality fish, but to no avail. Suddenly, there was a burst of "purring," which to everyone's surprise (and the landlord's dismay), the ultrasonic equipment traced to the clock in the electric oven! Later, the landlord commented that everyone had assumed that Gatiss's hypothesis was correct—that the meowing sound came from a cat trapped somewhere in the kitchen. "I just let them carry on. If there is an animal in there, you have to do what it takes. The funniest thing was that it seemed to reply when we called out to it" (*London Daily Telegraph*, 1998).

How could fifteen fire-rescue workers, three RSPCA inspectors, four drainage workers, and two acoustics experts waste eight days and cause nearly $2,000 in damage to a house in pursuit of a nonexistent kitten? The answer lies in the fact that they, like the rest of us, are prone to four main obstacles to efficient problem solving, described in the following sections.

● **Multiple Hypotheses**   Often, people begin to solve a problem with only a vague notion of which hypotheses to test. Suppose you heard a strange sound in your kitchen. It could be caused by several things, but which hypotheses should you test, and in what order?

People have a difficult time considering more than two or three hypotheses at a time. The limited capacity of short-term memory may be part of the reason (Halford et al., 2005). As discussed in the chapter on memory, we can hold only about seven chunks of information in short-term memory. A single hypothesis, let alone two or three, might include many more than seven chunks, so it might be difficult or impossible to keep them all in mind at once. Further, the availability and representativeness heuristics may lead people to choose the hypothesis that comes most easily to mind and seems most likely to fit the circumstances (Tversky & Kahneman, 1974). That hypothesis may be wrong, though, meaning that the correct hypothesis might never be considered. Mr. Gatiss diagnosed what he heard as distressed meowing because it sounded more like a kitten than a clock and because it was easier to imagine an animal trapped behind the stove than a suddenly faulty clock inside it.

● **Mental Sets**   Sometimes people are so blinded by one hypothesis or strategy that they continue to apply it even when better alternatives should be obvious (a clear case of the anchoring heuristic at work). Once Gatiss reported hearing a "trapped kitten," his description created an assumption that everyone else accepted and no one challenged.

A laboratory example of this phenomenon devised by Abraham Luchins (1942) is shown in Figure 8.12. In each problem shown in the figure, the task is to use three jars of varying sizes to end up with a certain amount of water. For example, in the first problem you are to obtain 21 quarts by using 3 jars that can hold 8, 35, and 3 quarts, respectively. The solution is to fill Jar B to its capacity, 35 quarts, and then use its contents to fill Jar A to its capacity of 8 quarts, leaving 27 quarts in Jar B. Then pour liquid from Jar B to fill Jar C to its capacity twice, leaving 21 quarts in Jar B [27 − (2 × 3) = 21]. In other words, the general solution formula is B − A − 2C. To confirm this, solve the rest of the problems before reading further.

TRY THIS

As you worked, did you notice anything unusual about Problem 7? By the time you reached that one, you had probably developed a **mental set,** a tendency for old patterns of problem solving to persist (Sweller & Gee, 1978). That mental set may have caused you to use the standard solution formula (B − A − 2C) for Problem 7 even though a simpler one (A + C) would have worked just as well. Figures 8.13 and 8.15 show that a mental set can also restrict your perception of the problem itself.

mental set   The tendency for old patterns of problem solving to persist, even when they might not be the best ones available.

FIGURE **8.12**

The Luchins Jar Problem

TRY THIS ⚙ In this problem-solving task, you are trying to end up with the number of quarts of water listed in the first column by filling jars with the capacities shown in the next three columns. Each line represents a different problem, and you have an unlimited supply of water. In dealing with such problems, people often fall prey to mental sets that prevent them from using the most efficient solution. After solving all the problems shown here, read on to see if your performance, too, was affected by a mental set.

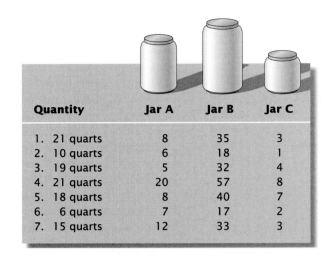

Quantity	Jar A	Jar B	Jar C
1. 21 quarts	8	35	3
2. 10 quarts	6	18	1
3. 19 quarts	5	32	4
4. 21 quarts	20	57	8
5. 18 quarts	8	40	7
6. 6 quarts	7	17	2
7. 15 quarts	12	33	3

A related restriction on problem solving may come from our experience with objects. Once people are accustomed to using an object for one purpose, they may be blinded to its other possible functions. Long experience may produce **functional fixedness,** a tendency to use familiar objects in familiar rather than creative ways (German & Barrett, 2005). Figure 8.14 illustrates an example. An incubation strategy often helps to break mental sets.

● **Ignoring Negative Evidence** On September 26, 1983, Lt. Col. Stanislav Petrov was in command of a secret facility that analyzed information from Russian early-warning satellites. Suddenly, alarms went off as computers found evidence of five U.S. missiles being launched toward Russia. Tension between the two countries was high at the time, so, based on the availability heuristic, Petrov hypothesized that a nuclear attack was under way. He was about to alert his superiors to launch a counterattack on the United States when it occurred to him that if this were a real nuclear attack, it would involve many more than five missiles. Fortunately for everyone, he realized that the "attack" was a false alarm (Hoffman, 1999). As this near-disaster shows, signs, symptoms, or events that do *not* appear can provide important evidence for or against a hypothesis. Compared with evidence that is present, however, the absence of evidence is less likely to be noticed (Hunt & Rouse, 1981). As a result, people have a hard time using missing evidence to help eliminate hypotheses from consideration (Hyman, 2002). In the "trapped kitten" case, when the "meowing" stopped for several days after the stove was reconnected, rescuers assumed that the animal was frightened into silence. They ignored the possibility that their hypothesis was incorrect in the first place.

● **Confirmation Bias** Anyone who has had a series of medical tests knows that diagnosis is not a one-shot decision. Instead, physicians choose their first hypothesis on the basis of observed symptoms and then order tests or evaluate additional symptoms to confirm or reject that hypothesis (Trillin, 2001). This process can be distorted by the *confirmation bias* mentioned earlier: Humans have a strong bias to confirm rather than to reject the hypothesis they have chosen, even in the face of strong evidence against it (Aronson, Wilson, & Akert, 2005; Groopman, 2007). Confirmation bias can be seen as a form of the anchoring heuristic, in that it involves "anchoring" to an initial hypothesis and being unwilling to abandon it. The would-be rescuers of the "trapped kitten" were so intent on their efforts to locate it that they never stopped to question its existence. Similarly, as described in the chapter on social cognition, when evaluating other people's behavior or abilities

FIGURE **8.13**

The Nine-Dot Problem

TRY THIS ⚙ The problem is to draw no more than four straight lines that run through all nine dots on the page without lifting your pen from the paper. Figure 8.15 shows two ways of going beyond mental sets to solve this problem.

FIGURE **8.14**

An Example of Functional Fixedness

TRY THIS Before reading the next sentence, look at this drawing and see if you can figure out how to tie together two strings that are hanging from the ceiling but are out of reach of each other. Several tools are available, yet most people do not think of attaching, say, the pliers to one string and swinging it like a pendulum until it can be reached while holding the other string. This solution is not obvious because we tend to fixate on the function of pliers as a tool rather than as a weight. People are more likely to solve this problem if the tools are scattered around the room. When the pliers are in a tool box, their function as a tool is emphasized, and functional fixedness becomes nearly impossible to break.

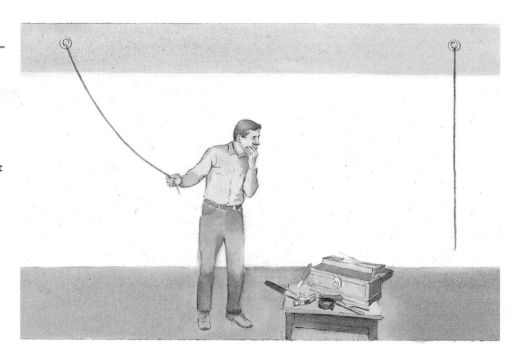

we tend to look for, and pay extra attention to, information that is consistent with any prior beliefs we have about them. This tendency can create positive or negative bias in, say, a teacher's impressions of children's mental abilities or an interviewer's impressions of job candidate's skills (Jussim & Eccles, 1992; Reich, 2004).

● Building Problem-Solving Skills

Some psychologists suggest that it should be possible to train people to avoid the biases that impair problem solving, and their efforts to do so have produced some modest benefits. In one study, cautioning people against their tendency to anchor on a hypothesis reduced the magnitude of confirmation bias and increased participants' openness to alternative evidence (Lopes, 1982).

How do experts avoid some of the obstacles that normally limit problem solving? What do they bring to a situation that a beginner does not? Knowledge based on experience is particularly important (Mayer, 1992). Experts frequently proceed by looking for analogies between current and past problems. Compared with beginners, they are better able to relate new information and new experiences to past experiences and existing knowledge (Anderson, 1995). Accordingly, experts can use existing knowledge to organize new information into chunks, a process described in the chapter on memory. By chunking many elements of a problem into a smaller number of units, experts are better than beginners at visualizing problems clearly and efficiently (Reingold et al., 2001).

Experts can use their experience as a guide because they tend to perceive the similarity between new and old problems more deeply than beginners do. Specifically, experts see the similarity of underlying principles, whereas beginners perceive similarity only in surface features. As a result, experts can more quickly and easily apply these principles to solve the new problem. Although experts are often better problem solvers than beginners, expertise also carries a danger: Their extensive experience may create mental sets. Top-down, knowledge-driven processes can bias experts toward seeing what they expect or want to see and prevent them from seeing a problem in new ways (Groopman, 2007). As in the case of the "trapped kitten," confirmation bias sometimes prevents experts from appreciating that a proposed solution is incorrect. Several studies have shown that although experts

● **functional fixedness** A tendency to think about familiar objects in familiar ways that may prevent using them in other ways.

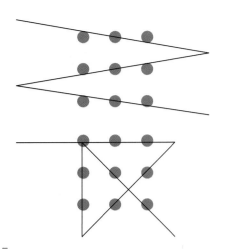

FIGURE 8.15

Two Creative Solutions to the Nine-Dot Problem

Many people find puzzles such as this difficult because their mental sets create artificial limits on the range of possible solutions. In this case, the mental sets involve the tendency to draw within the frame of the dots and to draw through the middle of each dot. As shown here, however, there are other possibilities.

may be more confident in their solutions (Payne, Bettman, & Johnson, 1992), they are not always more accurate than others in such areas as medical diagnosis, accounting, pilot judgment, and predicting political events (Tetlock, 2006; Wickens et al., 1992).

In other words, there is a fine line between using past experience and being trapped by it. Experience alone does not ensure excellence at problem solving, and practice may not make perfect (see Table 8.1). (For a summary of our discussion of human problem solving, see "In Review: Solving Problems.")

■ ● Problem Solving by Computer

Medical and scientific researchers have created artificial limbs, retinas, cochleas, and even hearts to help disabled people move, see, hear, and live more normally. They are developing artificial brains, too, in the form of computer systems that not only see, hear, and manipulate objects but also reason and solve problems. These systems are the product of research in **artificial intelligence (AI)**, a field that seeks to develop computers that imitate the processes of human perception and thought (O'Reilly, 2006). For problems such as those involved in making complex business decisions and medical diagnoses, for example, computerized *expert systems* can already perform as well as humans, and sometimes better (e.g., Khan et al., 2001; Workman, 2005).

● **Symbolic Reasoning and Computer Logic**   Early efforts at developing artificial intelligence focused on computers' enormous capabilities for formal reasoning and symbol manipulation and on their abilities to follow general problem-solving strategies, such as working backward (Newell & Simon, 1972). Valuable as it is, this logic-based approach to AI has important limitations. For one thing, expert systems are successful only in narrowly defined fields. And even within a specific domain, computers show limited ability. There are no ways of putting into computer

TABLE **8.1** Some Expert Opinions	
Experts typically have a large store of knowledge about their area of expertise, but even confidently stated opinions based on this knowledge can turn out to be wrong. In 1768, one expert critic called William Shakespeare's now-revered play Hamlet "the work of a drunken savage" (Henderson & Bernard, 1998). Here are some equally incorrect expert pronouncements from *The Experts Speak* (Cerf & Navasky, 1998).	**On the possibility of painless surgery through anesthesia:** "'Knife' and 'pain' are two words in surgery that must forever be associated. . . . To this compulsory combination we shall have to adjust ourselves." (Dr. Alfred Velpeau, professor of surgery, Paris Faculty of Medicine, 1839) **On the hazards of cigarette smoking:** "If excessive smoking actually plays a role in the production of lung cancer, it seems to be a minor one." (Dr. W. C. Heuper, National Cancer Institute, 1954) **On the stock market (one week before the disastrous 1929 crash that wiped out over $50 billion in investments):** "Stocks have reached what looks like a permanently high plateau." (Irving Fisher, professor of economics, Yale University, 1929) **On the prospects of war with Japan (three years before the December 1941 Japanese attack on Pearl Harbor):** "A Japanese attack on Pearl Harbor is a strategic impossibility." (Maj. George F. Eliot, military science writer, 1938) **On the value of personal computers:** "There is no reason for any individual to have a computer in their home." (Ken Olson, president, Digital Equipment Corporation, 1977) **On the concept of the airplane:** "Heavier-than-air flying machines are impossible." (Lord Kelvin, mathematician, physicist, and president of the British Royal Society, 1895)

in review Solving Problems

Steps	Pitfalls	Remedies
Define the problem	Inexperience: the tendency to see each problem as unique.	Gain experience and practice in seeing the similarity between present problems and previous problems.
Form hypotheses about solutions	Availability heuristic: the tendency to recall the hypothesis or solution that is most available to memory.	Force yourself to entertain different hypotheses.
	Anchoring heuristic or mental set: the tendency to anchor on the first solution or hypothesis and not adjust your beliefs in light of new evidence or failures of the current approach.	Break the mental set, stop, and try a fresh approach.
Test hypotheses	The tendency to ignore negative evidence.	In evaluating a hypothesis, consider the things you should be seeing (but are not) if the hypothesis is true.
	Confirmation bias: the tendency to seek only evidence that confirms your hypothesis.	Look for disconfirming evidence that, if found, would show your hypothesis to be false.

code all aspects of the reasoning of human experts. Sometimes, the experts can only say, "I know it when I see it, but I can't put it into words." Second, the vital ability to draw analogies and make other connections among remote knowledge domains is still beyond the grasp of expert systems, partly because the builders of the systems seldom know ahead of time which other areas of knowledge might lead to insight. They can't always tell computers where to look for new ideas or how to use them. Finally, logic-based AI systems depend on "if-then" rules, and it is often difficult to tell a computer how to recognize the "if" condition in the real world (Dreyfus & Dreyfus, 1988). Consider just one example: *If it's a clock, then set it.* Humans can recognize all kinds of clocks because they have the natural concept of "clock," but computers perform this task very poorly. As discussed earlier, forming natural concepts requires putting into the same category many examples that may have very different physical features—from a bedside digital alarm clock to London's Big Ben.

● **Neural Network Models** Recognizing the problems posed by the need to teach computers to form natural concepts, many researchers in AI have shifted to the *connectionist*, or *neural network*, approach discussed in other chapters. This approach simulates the information processing taking place at many different, but interconnected, locations in the brain. It is very effective for modeling many aspects of perceptual recognition. It has contributed to the development of computers that are able to recognize voices, understand speech, read print, guide missiles, and perform many other complex tasks (Ashcraft, 2006). Some of these computer simulations are being used to improve speech recognition software and to test theories of how infants learn to recognize speech (e.g., Roy & Pentland, 2002; Sroka & Braida, 2005). Google and other "intelligent" Internet search engines are based on neural network models, and connectionist programs have also been used to improve on human decision making in areas ranging from judging meat quality and running credit checks, to detecting credit card fraud and predicting the reappearance of cancer (McNelis, 2004; Rabunal & Dorado, 2006).

The capacities of current neural-network-based computer systems still fall well short of those of the human perceptual system, however. For example, computers are slow to learn how to classify visual patterns, which has led to disappointment in efforts to develop computerized face recognition systems capable of identifying terrorists and other criminals in public places (Feder, 2004). Computers may also fail to show sudden insight when a key common feature is identified. But even

artificial intelligence (AI) The field that studies how to program computers to imitate the products of human perception, understanding, and thought.

Artificial Intelligence Chess master Garry Kasparov had his hands full when he was challenged by "Deep Blue," a chess-playing computer that was programmed so well that it has won games against the world's best competitors, including Kasparov. Still, even the most sophisticated computers cannot perceive and think about the world in general anywhere near as well as humans can. Some observers believe that this situation will eventually change as progress in computer technology—and a deepening understanding of human cognitive processes—leads to dramatic breakthroughs in artificial intelligence.

though neural networks are far from perfect "thinking machines," they are sure to play an important role in psychologists' efforts to build ever more intelligent systems and to better understand the principles of human problem solving.

● **Computer-Assisted Problem Solving** One approach to minimizing the limitations of both computers and humans is to have them work together in ways that create a better outcome than either could achieve alone (e.g., Khan et al., 2001; Workman, 2005). In medical diagnosis, for example, the human's role is to establish the presence and nature of a patient's symptoms. The computer then combines this information in a completely unbiased way to identify the most likely diagnosis (Swets, Dawes, & Monahan, 2000). Similarly, laboratory technologists who examine blood samples for the causes of disease are assisted by computer programs that serve to reduce errors and memory lapses by (1) keeping track of the findings from previous tests, (2) listing possible tests that remain to be tried, and (3) indicating either that certain tests have been left undone or that a new sequence of tests should be done (Guerlain, 1995). This kind of human-machine teamwork can also help in the assessment of psychological problems (Bernstein, Kramer, & Phares, 2008).

Decision Making

Dr. Wallace's patient, Laura McBride, faced a simple decision: risk death by doing nothing or protect herself from lead poisoning. Most decisions are not so easy. Patients must decide whether to undergo a dangerous operation; a college graduate must choose a career; a corporate executive must decide whether to shut down a factory. Unlike the high-speed decisions discussed earlier, these decisions require considerable time, planning, and mental effort.

Even carefully considered decisions sometimes lead to undesirable outcomes, however, because the world is an uncertain place. Decisions made when the outcome is uncertain are called *risky decisions* or *decisions under uncertainty*. Let's consider what psychologists have discovered about why human decisions may lead to unsatisfactory outcomes.

● Evaluating Options

Suppose that you have to choose between (1) an academic major you love but that is unlikely to lead to a good job and (2) a boring major that virtually guarantees a high-paying job. The fact that each option has positive and negative features, or

Analyzing your choices and the possible outcomes of each takes some time and effort, but the results are usually worth it. Like Dilbert's boss, many people prefer to make decisions more impulsively, and although their decisions sometimes turn out well, they often don't (Gladwell, 2005; Myers, 2004).

© Scott Adams/Dist. by United Feature Syndicate, Inc.

attributes, greatly complicates decision making. Deciding which car to buy, which college to attend, or even how to spend the evening are all examples of *multi-attribute decision making* (Edwards, 1977). Often these decisions are further complicated by difficulties in comparing the attributes and in estimating the probabilities of various outcomes.

● **Comparing Attributes**   Part of the difficulty in making multi-attribute decisions lies in the limited capacity of short-term memory. Sometimes, we simply can't keep in mind all of the attributes of all of our options long enough to compare them. Instead, we tend to focus on the one attribute that is most important to us (Tversky, 1972). If, for instance, finishing a degree quickly is most important to you, then you might choose courses based mainly on graduation requirements, without giving much consideration to professors' reputations. (Listing the pros and cons of each option offers a helpful way of keeping them all in mind as you think about decisions.)

Furthermore, in most important decisions, it may be impossible to compare the attributes of our options in terms of money or other objective criteria. In other words, we are often forced to compare "apples and oranges." Psychologists use the term **utility** to describe the subjective value that each attribute holds for each of us. In deciding on a major, for example, you have to think about the positive and negative utilities of each attribute—such as the job prospects and interest level—of each major. Then you must somehow weigh and combine these utilities. Will the positive utility of enjoying your courses be higher than the negative utility of risking unemployment?

● **Estimating Probabilities**   Uncertainty adds other difficulties to the decision-making process: To make a good decision, you should take into account not only the attributes of each option but also the probabilities and risks of their possible outcomes. For example, the economy could change by the time you graduate, closing many of today's job opportunities in one of the majors you are considering and perhaps opening opportunities in another.

In studying risky decision making, psychologists begin by assuming that the best decision is the one that maximizes **expected value**, or the average benefit you could expect if the decision were repeated on several occasions. Suppose someone asks you to buy a charity raffle ticket. You know that it costs $2 to enter and that the probability of winning the $100 prize is one in ten (.10). Assuming you are more interested in the prize money than in donating to the charity, should you enter the contest? The expected value of entering is determined by multiplying the probability of gain (.10) by the size of the gain ($100). The result is the average benefit you would receive if you entered the raffle many times. Next, from this product you subtract the probability of loss, which is 1.0 (the entry fee is a certain loss), multiplied by the amount of the loss ($2). That is, $(.10 \times \$100) - (1.0 \times \$2) = \$8$. Because this $8 expected value is greater than the expected value of not entering (which is zero), you should enter. However, if the odds of winning the raffle were one in a hundred (.01), then the expected value of entering would be $(.01 \times \$100) - (1.0 \times \$2) = -\$1$. In this case, the expected value is negative, so you should not enter the raffle.

● **utility**   A subjective measure of value.

● **expected value**   The total benefit to be expected if a decision were to be repeated several times.

◼ ● Biases and Flaws in Decision Making

Most people think of themselves as logical and rational, but in making decisions about everything from giving up smoking to investing in the stock market, they do not always act in ways that maximize expected value (Farmer, Patelli, & Zovko, 2005; Shiller, 2001). Why not?

● **Gains, Losses, and Probabilities**   For one thing, positive utilities are not mirror images of negative utilities. People usually feel worse—or at least expect to feel worse—about losing a certain amount than they feel good about gaining the same amount (Kermer et al., 2006). This phenomenon is known as *loss aversion* (Dawes, 1998; Tversky & Kahneman, 1991). They may be willing to exert more effort to try to collect a $100 debt, for example, than to try to win a $100 prize.

It also appears that the utility of a specific gain depends not on how large the gain actually is but on what the starting point was. Suppose you can do something to receive a coupon for a free dinner worth $10. Does this gain have the same utility as having an extra $10 added to your paycheck? The amount of gain is the same, but people tend to behave as if the difference in utility between $0 and $10 is much greater than the difference between, say, $300 and $310. So the person who turns down the chance to do an after-work errand across town for an extra $10 on payday might gladly make the same trip to pick up a $10 coupon. This tendency conforms to Weber's law of psychophysics, discussed in the chapter on perception. The subjective value of a gain depends on how much you already have (Dawes, 1998); the more you have, the less it means.

People are also biased in how they perceive probability, and this bias may lead to less-than-optimal decisions. One kind of probability bias comes into play when making decisions about extremely likely or extremely unlikely events. In such cases, we tend to overestimate the probability of the unlikely events and to underestimate the probability of the likely ones (Kahneman & Tversky, 1984). This bias helps explain why people gamble and enter lotteries, even though the odds are against them and the decision to do so has a negative expected value. According to the formula for expected value, buying a $1 lottery ticket when the probability of winning $4 million is 1 in 10 million yields an expected value of minus 60 cents. But because people overestimate the probability of winning, they believe there is a positive expected value. In one study, not even a course that highlighted gambling's mathematical disadvantages could change university students' gambling behavior (Williams & Connolly, 2006). The tendency to overestimate the likelihood of unlikely events is amplified by the availability heuristic: Vivid memories of rare gambling successes and the publicity given to lottery winners help people recall gains rather than losses when deciding about future gambles.

Another bias relating to probability is called the *gambler's fallacy*: People believe that future events in a random process will be changed by past events. This belief is false. For example, if you flip a coin and it comes up heads ten times in a row, the chance that it will come up heads on the eleventh try is still 50 percent. Some gamblers, however, will continue feeding a slot machine that hasn't paid off much for hours, assuming it is "due." This assumption may be partly responsible for the persistence of gambling and other behaviors that are only rewarded now and then. We discuss this phenomenon, called the partial reinforcement extinction effect, in the chapter on learning.

Yet another factor underlying flaws in human decision making is the tendency for people to be unrealistically confident in the accuracy of their predictions. Baruch Fischoff and Donald MacGregor (1982) found a clever way to study this bias. They asked research participants to make a prediction about an event—for example, whether a certain sports team would win—and to say how confident they were about the prediction. After the events took place, the accuracy of the forecasts was compared with the confidence people had expressed in those forecasts. Sure enough,

Bias in Perceiving Risk   After the September 11, 2001, terrorist attacks on the United States, the risks of flying seemed so high that many more people than usual traveled by car instead. But automobile travel is more dangerous overall than flying, so the decision to drive actually increased these people's risk of death. With more cars on the road, traffic fatalities in the last three months of 2001 were about 350 higher than usual (Gigerenzer, 2004). Similar bias in risk perception leads many people to buy big, heavy sport utility vehicles that make them feel safer, even though the risk of serious injury is actually greater in an SUV than it is in a minivan or family sedan (Gladwell, 2004). Their heightened sense of safety may even lead some SUV owners to drive less carefully (Thomas & Walton, 2007), which further increases the injury risk.

the participants' confidence in their predictions was consistently greater than their accuracy. The moral of the story is to be wary when people express confidence that a forecast or decision is correct. They will be wrong more often than they think.

● **How Biased Are We?**   Almost everyone makes decisions they later regret, but these outcomes may not be due entirely to biased thinking about gains, losses, and probabilities. Some decisions are not intended to maximize expected value but rather to satisfy other criteria, such as minimizing expected loss, producing a quick and easy resolution, or preserving a moral principle (Galotti, 2007; McCaffery & Baron, 2006). For example, decisions may depend not just on how likely we are to gain or lose a certain amount of something but also on what that something is. So a decision that could cost or save a human life might be made differently than one that could cost or gain a few dollars, even though the probabilities of each outcome are exactly the same in both cases.

Even the "goodness" or "badness" of decisions can be difficult to measure. Many of them depend on personal values (utilities), which can vary from person to person and from culture to culture. People in individualist cultures, for example, may tend to assign high utilities to attributes that promote personal goals, whereas people in collectivist cultures might place greater value on attributes that bring group harmony and the approval of family and friends (Markus, Kitayama, & Heiman, 1996).

LINKAGES **Group Processes in Problem Solving and Decision Making**

 LINKAGES (a link to Social Influence, p. 757)

Problem solving and decision making often take place in groups. The processes that influence an individual's problem solving and decision making continue to operate when the individual is in a group, but group interactions also shape the outcome.

When groups are trying to make a decision, for example, they usually begin by considering the preferences or opinions stated by various members. Not all of these views have equal influence, though. Views that are shared by the greatest number of

Groups Working at a Distance
Research on group problem solving and decision making now includes "electronic groups," whose members use teleconferencing to work together from a distance. Groups that meet via teleconferencing perform about as well as those meeting face-to-face, but other kinds of electronic communication, such as chat rooms, can impair group performance (Graetz et al., 1998).

group members will have the greatest impact on the group's final decision (Tindale & Kameda, 2000). This means that extreme proposals or opinions will usually have less effect on group decisions than those that are more representative of the majority's views.

Nevertheless, group discussions sometimes result in decisions that are more extreme than the group members would make individually. This tendency toward extreme decisions by groups is called *group polarization* (Rodrigo & Ato, 2002), and it appears to result from two mechanisms. First, most arguments presented during the discussion favor the majority view. Most criticisms are directed at the minority view, and (influenced by confirmation bias) group members tend to seek additional information that supports the majority position (Schulz-Hardt et al., 2000). In this atmosphere, it seems rational to those favoring the majority view to adopt an even stronger version of it (Stasser, 1991). Second, once some group members begin to agree that a particular decision is desirable, other members may try to associate themselves with that decision, perhaps by suggesting an even more extreme version (Kaplan & Miller, 1987).

Are people better at problem solving and decision making when they work in groups than when on their own? This is one of the questions about human thought studied by social psychologists. In a typical experiment, a group of people is asked to solve a problem such as the one in Figure 8.13 or to make a decision about the guilt or innocence of a defendant in a fictional court case. Each person is asked to work alone and then to join with the others to try to agree on a decision. These studies have found that when problems have solutions that can be demonstrated easily to all members, groups will usually outperform individuals at solving them (Laughlin, 1999). When problems have less obvious solutions, groups may be somewhat better at solving them than their average member, but usually no better than their most talented member (Hackman, 1998). And because of the phenomena of *social loafing* and *groupthink* (discussed in the chapter on social influence), people working in a group are often less productive than people working alone (Williams & Sommer, 1997).

Other research (e.g., Stasser, Stewart, & Wittenbaum, 1995) suggests that a critical element in successful group problem solving is the sharing of individual members' unique information and expertise. For example, when asked to diagnose an illness, groups of physicians were much more accurate when they pooled their knowledge (Larson et al., 1998). However, *brainstorming*, a popular strategy that supposedly encourages group members to generate innovative solutions to a

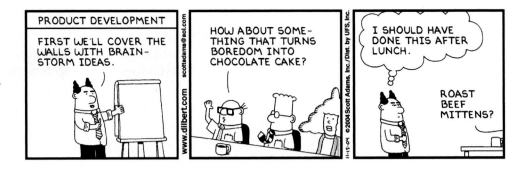

One disadvantage of brainstorming sessions is that running comments and bizarre ideas from some group members can interfere with the creative process in others (Nijstad, Stroebe, & Lodewijkx, 2003).

© Scott Adams/Dist. by United Feature Syndicate, Inc.

problem, may actually produce fewer ideas than are generated by individuals working alone (Kerr & Tindale, 2004). This result may occur because the lively and freewheeling discussion associated with brainstorming can disrupt each member's ability to think clearly and productively (Nijstad, Stroebe, & Lodewijkx, 2003). Further, some participants in a brainstorming session may be reluctant to offer an idea, even a good one, for fear it will be rejected or ridiculed by the group (Kerr & Tindale, 2004). To prevent these problems, some brainstorming groups today meet electronically, using a form of e-mail to present and comment on ideas. Participants in these meetings can offer their suggestions anonymously and without being interrupted, yet still have access to the ideas of all the other members. Because this arrangement allows people to think more clearly and express even "oddball" ideas without fear, electronic brainstorming groups may actually outperform groups that meet face-to-face (Nijstad et al., 2003).

As they work to solve a problem, the members of a group manipulate their own concepts, propositions, images, and other mental representations. How does each person share these private events to help the group perform its task? The answer lies in the use of language, which not only aids group decision making (Kline, 2005), but is a fundamental part of many other human activities. Let's consider what language is and how it develops. ■

Language

Many pet owners swear that their animals "talk" to them. Maybe Harry barks in a particular way when he wants to go outside, or Cleo meows to be fed. But are Harry's barks and Cleo's meows really language? Probably not. These pets are communicating something to their owners, but the noises they make lack many of the components of human language (Slocombe & Zuberbühler, 2005). So although Harry may let out three high-pitched yelps when he wants to go outside, he may bark in exactly the same way when asked whether he agrees with the local leash laws. For this reason, we wouldn't call his barking "language." Humans, however, can use language to express everything from simple requests to abstract principles. They can create stories that pass on cultural information and traditions from one generation to the next. Our language abilities are usually well integrated with our memory, thinking, and other cognitive abilities. As a result, we can speak about our thoughts and memories and think about what people tell us. It is only in cases like that of D. J., when strokes or other forms of damage interfere with the brain's language areas, that we are reminded that language is a very special kind of cognitive ability (Kohnert, 2004).

language Symbols and a set of rules for combining them that provides a vehicle for communication.

grammar A set of rules for combining the words used in a given language.

● The Elements of Language

A **language** has two basic elements: (1) symbols, such as words, and (2) a set of rules, called **grammar,** for combining those symbols. With their knowledge of

Making sure that the surface structures we create accurately convey the deep structures we intend is one of the greatest challenges people face when communicating through language.

approximately 50,000 to 100,000 words (Miller, 1991), humans can create and understand an infinite number of sentences. All of the sentences ever spoken are built from just a few dozen categories of sounds. The power of language comes from the way these rather unimpressive raw materials are organized according to certain rules. This organization occurs at several levels.

● **From Sounds to Sentences** Organization occurs first at the level of sounds. A **phoneme** is the smallest unit of sound that affects the meaning of speech. Changing a phoneme changes the meaning of a spoken word, much as changing a letter in a printed word changes its meaning. *Tea* has a meaning different from *sea*, and *sight* is different from *sigh*.

The number of phonemes in the world's languages varies from a low of thirteen (Hawaiian) to a high of over sixty (Hindi). Most languages have between thirty and fifty phonemes; English uses about forty. With forty basic sounds and an alphabet of only twenty-six letters, you can see that the same letters must sometimes signal different sounds. For example, the letter *a* stands for different phonemes in the words *cat* and *cake*.

Although changing a phoneme affects the meaning of speech, phonemes themselves are not meaningful. We combine them to form a higher level of organization: morphemes. A **morpheme** is the smallest unit of language that has meaning. For example, because they have meaning, *dog* and *run* are morphemes; but so are prefixes such as *un-* and suffixes such as *-ed*, because they, too, have meaning, even though they cannot stand alone.

Words are made up of one or more morphemes. Words, in turn, are combined to form phrases and sentences according to a set of grammatical rules called **syntax**. According to English syntax, a subject and a verb must be combined in a sentence, adjectives typically appear before the nouns that they modify, and so on. Compare the following sentences:

Fatal accidents deter careful drivers.

Snows sudden floods melting cause.

- **phoneme** The smallest unit of sound that affects the meaning of speech.
- **morpheme** The smallest unit of language that has meaning.
- **word** Unit of language composed of one or more morphemes.
- **syntax** The set of rules that govern the formation of phrases and sentences in a language.

The first sentence makes sense, but the second sentence violates English syntax. If the words were reordered, however, they would produce the perfectly acceptable sentence "Melting snows cause sudden floods."

Even if you use English phonemes combined in proper ways to form morphemes strung together according to the laws of English syntax, you may still not end up with an acceptable sentence. Consider the sentence "Rapid bouquets deter sudden neighbors." It somehow sounds right, but it is nonsense. Why? It has syntax, but it ignores the set of rules, called **semantics,** that govern the meaning of words and sentences. For example, because of its meaning, the noun *bouquets* cannot be modified by the word *rapid.*

● **Surface Structure and Deep Structure** So far, we have discussed elements of language that are apparent in the sentences people produce. These elements were the focus of study by linguists for many decades. Then, in 1965, Noam Chomsky started a revolution in the study of language. He argued that if linguists looked only at the language that people produce, they would never uncover the principles that account for all aspects of language. They could not explain, for example, how the sentence "This is my old friend" has more than one meaning. Nor could they account for the close relationship between the meanings of such sentences as "Don't give up just because things look bad" and "It ain't over 'til it's over."

To take these aspects of language into account, Chomsky proposed a more abstract level of analysis. He said that behind the strings of words people produce, called **surface structures,** there is a **deep structure,** an abstract representation of the relationships expressed in a sentence. For example, as shown in Figure 8.16, the surface structure "The shooting of the psychologist was terrible" can represent either

FIGURE 8.16

Surface Structure and Deep Structure

The listener on the right has clearly heard the surface structure of the speaker's message, but has misunderstood its deep structure. Such misunderstandings are common because identical surface structures can correspond to quite different deep structures.

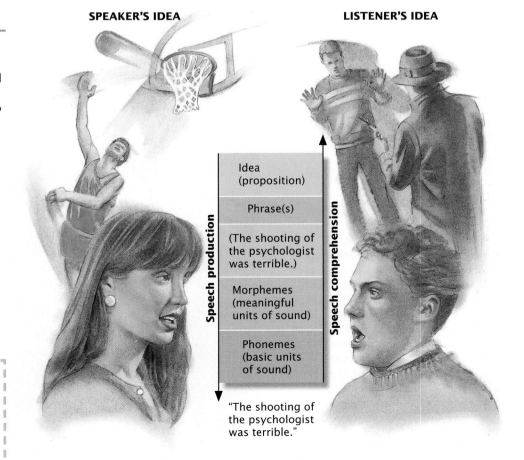

SPEAKER'S IDEA   LISTENER'S IDEA

Speech production →

Idea
(proposition)

Phrase(s)

(The shooting of
the psychologist
was terrible.)

Morphemes
(meaningful
units of sound)

Phonemes
(basic units
of sound)

Speech comprehension ↑

"The shooting of
the psychologist
was terrible."

semantics Rules governing the meaning of words and sentences.

surface structure The order in which words are arranged in sentences.

deep structure An abstract representation of the underlying meanings of a given sentence.

of two deep structures: (1) that the psychologist had terrible aim or (2) that it was terrible that someone shot the psychologist. Chomsky's analysis of deep and surface structures was important because it encouraged psychologists to analyze not just verbal behavior and grammatical rules but also mental representations.

● Understanding Speech

When someone speaks to you in your own language, your sensory, perceptual, and other cognitive systems reconstruct the sounds of speech in a way that allows you to detect, recognize, and understand what the person is saying. The process may seem effortless, but it involves amazingly complex feats of information processing. Scientists trying to develop neural-network-based speech-recognition software systems have discovered just how complex the process is. What makes understanding speech so complicated?

One factor is that the physical features of a particular speech sound are not always the same. This phenomenon is illustrated in Figure 8.17, which shows how the sounds of particular letters differ depending on the sounds that follow them. A second factor complicating our understanding of speech is that each of us creates slightly different speech sounds, even when saying the same words. Third, as people speak, their words are not usually separated by silence. So if the speech spectrograms in Figure 8.17 showed whole sentences, you would not be able to tell where one word ended and the next began.

● Perceiving Words and Sentences
Despite these challenges, humans can instantly recognize and understand the words and sentences produced by almost anyone speaking a familiar language. In contrast, even the best voice-recognition software must learn to recognize words spoken by a new voice, and even then it may make many mistakes. (A man we know recently requested the toll-free number for the Maglite Corporation, and the voice-recognition software in a directory assistance computer gave him the number for Metlife insurance.)

Scientists have yet to discover all the details about how people overcome the challenges of understanding speech, but some general answers are emerging. Just as we recognize objects by analyzing their visual features (see the chapter on perception), it appears that humans identify and recognize the specific—and changing—features of the sounds created when someone speaks. And as in visual perception,

Understanding Spoken Language
The top-down perceptual processes described in the perception chapter help explain why people speaking an unfamiliar language seem to produce a continuous stream of abnormally rapid speech. The problem is that you don't know where each word starts and stops. Without any perceived gaps, the sounds of speech run together, creating the impression of rapid-fire "chatter." People unfamiliar with your language think you are speaking extremely fast, too!

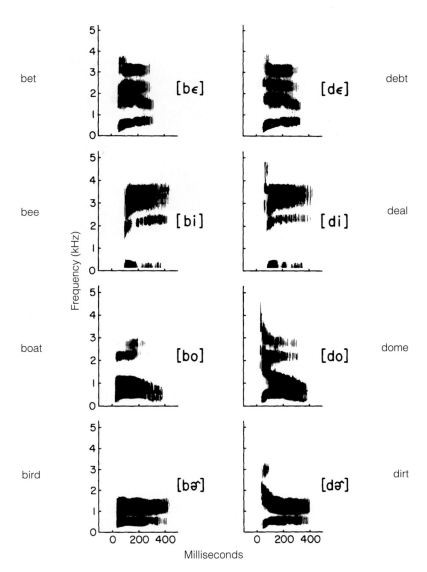

FIGURE 8.17

Speech Spectrograms

These speech spectrograms show what the sound frequencies of speech look like as people say various words. Notice that, even when words begin with the same consonant (such as *b* or *d*), the first part of the speech signal differs depending on what sounds are used in the rest of the word (Jusczyk, Smith, & Murphy, 1981).

Source: Jusczyk, Smith, & Murphy (1981).

this *bottom-up processing* of stimulus features combines with *top-down processing* guided by knowledge-based factors, such as context and expectation, to aid understanding (Samuel, 2001). For example, knowing the general topic of conversation helps you to recognize individual words that might otherwise be hard to understand (Cole & Jakimik, 1978). This ability to use context is especially useful to people with hearing impairments or when trying to understand what someone is saying at a loud party or in other noisy environments (Davis et al., 2005).

Understanding speech can also be guided by nonverbal cues. The frown, the enthusiastic nod, or the bored yawn that accompanies a person's words all carry information that helps you to get the full meaning of the message. So if someone says "Wow, are you smart!" but really means "I think you're a jerk," you will detect the truth based on the context, facial expression, and tone of voice. Without these extra cues, we can easily miss some elements of people's intended deep structure, which is why misunderstandings are more likely when people converse on the telephone or on e-mail rather than face-to-face (Massaro & Stork, 1998).

● The Development of Language

Children the world over develop language with impressive speed. The average six-year-old already has a vocabulary of about 13,000 words (Pinker, 1994). But

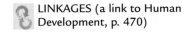

LINKAGES (a link to Human Development, p. 470)

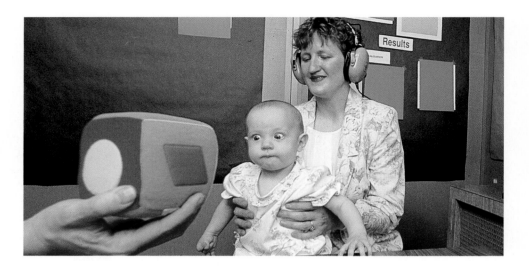

Getting Ready to Talk Long before they utter their first words, babies are getting ready to talk. Experiments in Patricia Kuhl's laboratory show that even six-month-olds tend to look longer at faces whose lip movements match the sounds of spoken words. This tendency reflects babies' abilities to focus on, recognize, and discriminate the sounds of speech, especially in their native language. These abilities are crucial to the development of language (Mayberry, Lock, & Kazmi, 2002).

acquiring a language involves more than just learning vocabulary. We also have to learn how words are combined and how to produce and understand sentences. Psychologists who study the development of language have found that the process begins in the earliest days of a child's life and follows some predictable steps (Saffran, Senghas, & Trueswell, 2001).

● **The First Year** Within the first few months of life, babies can tell the difference between the sounds of their native language and those of other languages (Gerken, 1994), and by ten months of age they pay closer attention to speech in their native language (Werker et al., 1996). In the first year, then, infants become more and more attuned to the sounds that will be important in acquiring their native language. In fact, this early experience with language appears to be vital. Without it, language acquisition can be impaired (Mayberry & Lock, 2003).

The first year is also the time when babies begin to produce **babblings**, which are patterns of meaningless sounds that resemble speech. Infants of all nationalities begin with the same set of babbling sounds. At about nine months, however, babies who hear only English start to lose their German gutturals and French nasals. At this time, babbling becomes more complex and begins to sound like "sentences" in the babies' native language (Goldstein, King, & West, 2003). Starting around this time, too, babies who hear English begin to shorten some of their vocalizations to "da," "duh," and "ma." These sounds seem very much like language, and babies use them in specific contexts and with obvious purpose (Blake & de Boysson-Bardies, 1992). Accompanied by appropriate gestures, they may be used to express joy ("oohwow") or anger ("uh-uh-uh"), to get something that is out of reach ("engh-engh"), or to point out something interesting ("dah!").

By ten to twelve months of age, babies can understand several words—certainly more words than they can say (Fenson et al., 1994). Proper names and object labels are among the earliest words they understand. Often the first word they understand is a pet's name. Proper names and object words—such as *mama, daddy, cookie, doggy,* and *car*—are also among the first words children are likely to say when, at around twelve months of age, they begin to talk (some do this a little earlier and some a little later). Nouns for simple object categories (*dog, flower*) are acquired before more general nouns (*animal, plant*) or more specific names (*collie, rose*; Rosch et al., 1976).

Of course, these early words do not sound exactly like adult language. English-speaking babies usually reduce them to a shorter, easier form, such as "duh" for *duck* or "mih" for *milk*. Children make themselves understood, however, by using gestures, tone of voice, facial expressions, and endless repetitions. If they have a word for an object, they may "overextend" it to cover more ground. So they might use *dog* for cats, bears, and horses. They might use *fly* for all insects and perhaps

babblings The first sounds infants make that resemble speech.

for other small things like raisins and M&Ms (Clark, 1993). Children make these "errors" because their vocabularies are limited, not because they fail to notice the difference between dogs and cats or because they want to eat a fly (Fremgen & Fay, 1980; Rescorla, 1981).

Until they can say the correct words for objects, children overextend the words they have, use all-purpose sounds (such as "dat" or "dis"), and coin new words (such as *pepping* for "shaking the pepper shaker"; Becker, 1994). Being around people who don't understand these overextensions encourages children to learn and use more precise words (Markman, 1994). During this period, children build up their vocabularies one word at a time. They also use their limited vocabulary one word at a time; they cannot yet put words together into sentences.

● **The Second Year**   The one-word stage of speech lasts for about six months. Then, sometime around eighteen months of age, children's vocabularies expand dramatically (Gleitman & Landau, 1994). They may learn several new words each day, and by the age of two, most youngsters can use fifty to well over one hundred words. They also start using two-word combinations to form efficient little sentences. These two-word sentences are called *telegraphic* because, like telegrams or text messages, they are brief and to the point, leaving out anything that is not absolutely essential. So if she wants her mother to give her a book, a twenty-month-old might first say, "Give book," then "Mommy give," and if that does not work, "Mommy book." The child also uses rising tones to indicate a question ("Go out?") and puts stress on certain words to indicate location ("Play *park*") or new information ("*Big* car").

Three-word sentences come next in the development of language. They are still telegraphic, but more nearly complete: "Mommy give book." The child can now speak in sentences that have the usual subject-verb-object form of adult sentences. Other words and word endings begin appearing, too, such as the suffix *-ing*, the prepositions *in* and *on*, the plural *-s*, and irregular past tenses ("It broke," "I ate"; Brown, 1973). Children learn to use the suffix *-ed* for the past tense ("I walked"), but then they often overapply this rule to irregular verbs that they previously used correctly. They'll say, for example, "It breaked," "It broked," or "I eated" (Marcus, 1996).

Children also expand their sentences with adjectives, although at first they make some mistakes. For instance, they are likely to use both *less* and *more* to mean "more" or both *tall* and *short* to mean "tall" (Smith & Sera, 1992).

● **The Third Year and Beyond**   By age three or so, children begin to use auxiliary verbs ("Adam is going") and to ask questions using *wh-* words, such as *what, where, who,* and *why.* They begin to put together clauses to form complex sentences ("Here's the ball I was looking for"). By age five, children have acquired most of the grammatical rules of their native language.

● How Is Language Acquired?

Despite all that has been discovered about the steps children follow in acquiring language, mystery and debate still surround the question of just how they do it. Obviously, children pick up the specific content of language from the speech they hear around them: English children learn English, and Italian children learn Italian. As parents and children share meals, playtime, and conversations, children learn that words refer to objects and actions and what the labels for them are. But how do children learn syntax, the rules of grammar?

● **Conditioning, Imitation, and Rules**   Our discussion of conditioning in the chapter on learning would suggest that children learn syntax because their parents reward them for using it. This sounds reasonable, but observational studies

one-word stage A stage of language development during which children tend to use one word at a time.

show that positive reinforcement is not the main part of the language acquisition story. Parents are usually more concerned about what is said than about its grammatical form (Hirsch-Pasek, Treiman, & Schneiderman, 1984). So when the little boy with chocolate crumbs on his face says, "I not eat cookie," his mother is more likely to say, "Yes, you did" than to ask the child to say, "I did not eat the cookie" and then praise him for grammatical correctness.

Learning through modeling, or imitation, appears to be more influential. Children learn grammar most rapidly when adults demonstrate the correct syntax in the course of a conversation, as in the following example:

CHILD: Mommy fix.

MOTHER: Okay, Mommy will fix the truck.

CHILD: It breaked.

MOTHER: Yes, it broke.

CHILD: Truck broke.

MOTHER: Let's see if we can fix it.

But if children learn syntax by imitation, why would they overgeneralize rules, such as the rule for making the past tense? Why, for example, do children who at one time said "I went" later say "I goed"? Adults never use this form of speech. Its sudden appearance indicates that the child either has mastered the rule of adding *-ed* or has generalized from similar-sounding words (such as *mowed* or *rowed*). In short, neither conditioning nor imitation seems entirely adequate to explain how children learn language. Children must still analyze for themselves the underlying patterns in the language examples they hear around them (Bloom, 1995).

● **Biological Bases for Language Acquisition** The ease with which children everywhere discover these underlying patterns and learn language has led some to argue that language acquisition is at least partly innate. For example, Chomsky believes that we have a built-in *universal grammar*, a mechanism that allows us to identify the basic dimensions of language (Baker, 2002; Chomsky, 1986; Nowak, Komarova, & Niyogi, 2001). One of these dimensions is how important word order is in the syntax of a particular language. In English, for example, word order tells us who is doing what to whom (the sentences "Heather dumped Jason" and "Jason dumped Heather" contain the same words, but they have different meanings). In languages such as Russian, however, word order is less important than the modifiers attached to the word, also called *inflections*. According to Chomsky, a child's universal grammar might initially be "set" to assume that word order is important to syntax, but it would change if the child hears language in which word order is not so important. In Chomsky's system, then, we don't entirely learn language—we develop it as genetic predispositions interact with experience (Senghas & Coppola, 2001).

Evidence that supports claims of a genetic predisposition for language comes from studies of *specific language impairment (SLI)*. Children displaying SLI have trouble acquiring language despite having otherwise normal mental abilities, normal hearing, and adequate early exposure to language sounds (Gopnik & Crago, 1991). Because SLI runs in families, several investigators have proposed that it reflects a defect in the genes that normally provide us with our universal grammar (e.g., Pinker, 1994; Van der Lely, 1994; White, 2006). This is a controversial idea, though, partly because of evidence that people with SLI have specific deficiencies in auditory processing that might account for their difficulty in acquiring grammar (e.g., Stevens, Sanders, & Neville, 2006).

Indeed, the development of language probably reflects the development of more general sensory, motor, and cognitive skills, not just innate, language-specific mechanisms (Bates, 1993). In other words, we probably don't inherit a single, specific "grammar gene" (White, 2006). Still, the existence of SLI and

Learning a Second Language   The notion of a critical period for language acquisition is supported by the fact that, after the age of thirteen or fourteen, people learn a second language more slowly (Johnson & Newport, 1989) and virtually never learn to speak it without an accent (Lenneberg, 1967).

other gene-linked speech and language disorders (Barry, Yasin, & Bishop, 2007) remind us that, as is true for all other aspects of human behavior and mental processes, our language abilities are based partly on biological factors. For example, the unique speech-generating properties of the human mouth and throat, the language-related brain regions such as Broca's area and Wernicke's area (see Figure 3.16), and recent genetic research all suggest that humans are innately "prewired," or biologically programmed, for language (Buxhoeveden et al., 2001; Lai et al., 2001). In addition, there appears to be a *critical period* in childhood during which we can learn language more easily than at any other time (Ridley, 2000). Evidence for the existence of this critical period comes from research on the difficulties adults have in learning a second language (e.g., Lenneberg, 1967) and also by cases in which unfortunate children spent their early years in isolation from human contact and the sound of adult language. Even after years of therapy and language training, these individuals are not able to combine ideas into sentences (Rymer, 1993). These cases suggest that, as mentioned earlier, acquiring the complex features of language depends on being exposed to speech before a certain age.

● **Bilingualism**   Does trying to learn two languages at once, even before the critical period is over, impair the learning of either? Research suggests just the opposite. Although their earliest language utterances may be confused or delayed, children who are raised in a bilingual environment before the end of the critical period seem to show enhanced performance in each language (De Houwer, 1995). There is also some evidence that *balanced bilinguals*—people who developed roughly equal mastery of two languages as children—are superior to others in cognitive flexibility, concept formation, and creativity. It is as if each language offers a slightly different perspective on thinking, and this dual perspective makes the brain more flexible (Hong et al., 2000).

THINKING CRITICALLY   **Can Nonhumans Use Language?**

W̶e have said that it is our ability to acquire and use language that helps set humans apart from all other creatures. Yet those creatures, too, use symbols to communicate. Bees perform a dance that tells other bees where they found sources of nectar; killer whales signal one another as they hunt in groups; and the grunts and gestures of chimpanzees signify varying desires and emotions. These forms of communication do not necessarily have the grammatical characteristics of language, however (Fitch & Hauser, 2004; Povinelli & Bering, 2002; Rendall et al., 2000; Zuberbühler, 2005). Are any animals other than humans capable of learning language?

■ What am I being asked to believe or accept?

Over the past forty years, several researchers have claimed that nonhumans can master language. Chimpanzees and gorillas have been the most popular targets of study, because at maturity they are estimated to have the intelligence of two- or three-year-old children, who are usually well on their way to learning language. Dolphins, too, have been studied because they have a complex communication system and exceptionally large brains relative to their body size (Janik, 2000; Reiss & Marino, 2001). It would seem that if these animals were unable to learn language, their general intelligence could not be blamed. Instead, failure would be attributed to the absence of a genetic makeup that permits language learning.

■ What evidence is available to support the assertion?

The question of whether nonhuman mammals can learn to use language is not a simple one, for at least two reasons. First, language is more than just communication, but defining just when animals are exhibiting that "something more" is a source of debate. What seems to set human language apart from the gestures, grunts, chirps, whistles, or cries of other animals is grammar—a formal set of rules for combining words. Also, because of their anatomical structures, nonhuman mammals will never be able to "speak" in the same way that humans do (Lieberman, 1991; Nishimura et al., 2003). To test these animals' ability to learn language, investigators therefore must devise novel ways for them to communicate.

David and Ann Premack taught their chimp, Sarah, to communicate by placing differently shaped chips, each symbolizing a word, on a magnetic board (Premack, 1971). Lana, a chimpanzee studied by Duane Rumbaugh (1977), learned to communicate by pressing keys on a specially designed computer. A simplified version of American Sign Language (ASL) has been used by Beatrice and Allen Gardner with the chimp Washoe, by Herbert Terrace with Nim Chimsky, a chimp named after Noam Chomsky, and by Penny Patterson with a gorilla named Koko. Finally, Kanzi, a bonobo, or pygmy chimpanzee, studied by Sue Savage-Rumbaugh (1990; Savage-Rumbaugh et al., 1993), learned to recognize spoken words and to communicate by both gesturing and pressing word-symbol keys on a computer that would "speak" them. Kanzi was a special case: He learned to communicate by listening and watching as his mother, Matata, was being taught and then used what he had learned to interact with her trainers.

Studies of these animals suggested that they could use combinations of words to refer to things that were not present. Washoe, Lana, Sarah, Nim, and Kanzi all mastered between 130 and 500 words. Their vocabulary included names for concrete objects, such as *apple* or *me*; verbs, such as *tickle* and *eat*; adjectives, such as *happy* and *big*; and adverbs, such as *again*. The animals combined the words to express wishes such as "You tickle me" or "If Sarah good, then apple." Sometimes their expressions referred to things in the past. When an investigator called attention to a wound that Kanzi had received, the animal responded with "Matata hurt," referring to a disciplinary bite his mother had recently given him (Savage-Rumbaugh, 1990). Finally, all these animals seemed to enjoy their communication tools and used them spontaneously to interact with their caretakers and with other animals.

Most of the investigators mentioned here have argued that their animals mastered a crude grammar (Premack & Premack, 1983; Savage-Rumbaugh, Shanker, & Taylor, 2001). For example, if Washoe wanted to be tickled, she would gesture, "You tickle Washoe." But if she wanted to do the tickling, she would gesture,

Animal Language? Here is Nim Chimsky, learning the sign for "drink" by imitating one of his teachers. Nim died in 2000 at the age of 26, but Koko, the gorilla trained by Penny Patterson, is still with us. In 1998, Patterson made Koko available for an Internet chat session. She relayed on-line questions to Koko in ASL, and a typist sent back Koko's signed responses. This procedure left some questioners wondering whether they were talking to Koko or to her trainer. (You can decide for yourself by reading the transcript of the session at http://www.koko.org/world/talk_aol.html.)

"Washoe tickle you." The correct placement of object and subject in these sentences suggested that Washoe was following a set of rules for word combination—in other words, a grammar (Gardner & Gardner, 1978). Louis Herman and his colleagues documented similar grammatical sensitivity in dolphins, who rarely confused subject-verb order in following instructions given by human hand signals (Herman, Richards, & Wolz, 1984). Furthermore, Savage-Rumbaugh observed several hundred instances in which Kanzi understood sentences he had never heard before. Once, for example, while his back was turned to the speaker, Kanzi heard the sentence "Jeanie hid the pine needles in her shirt." He turned around, approached Jeanie, and searched her shirt to find the pine needles. His actions would seem to indicate that he understood this new sentence the first time he heard it.

■ Are there alternative ways of interpreting the evidence?

Many of the early conclusions about primate language learning were challenged by Herbert Terrace and his colleagues in their investigation of Nim (Terrace et al., 1979) and by other critics' responses to other cases. For example, Terrace noticed many characteristics of Nim's communications that seemed quite different from a child's use of language.

First, he said, Nim's sentences were always very short. For example, Nim could combine two or three gestures but never used strings that conveyed more sophisticated messages. The ape was never able to say anything equivalent to a three-year-old child's "I want to go to Wendy's for a hamburger, OK?" Others have noted that even the most intelligent of primates are unable to master the full grammatical possibilities of either ASL or specially developed artificial languages (Fitch & Hauder, 2004). Second, Terrace questioned whether the animals' use of language demonstrated the spontaneity, creativity, and expanding complexity characteristic of children's language. Many of the animals' sentences were requests for food, tickling, baths, pets, and other pleasurable objects and experiences. Is such behavior really any different from the kind of behavior shown by the family dog who learns to sit up and beg for table scraps? Other researchers also pointed out that chimps are not naturally predisposed to associate seen objects with heard words, as human infants are (Savage-Rumbaugh et al., 1983). Finally, Terrace questioned whether experimenter bias influenced the reports of the chimps' communications. Consciously or

aimed at goals other than maximizing expected value. These goals may be determined by personal and cultural factors.

Language

People's ability to communicate their thoughts depends on their ability to learn and use language.

The Elements of Language *Language* consists of symbols such as words and rules for their combination—a *grammar*. Spoken *words* are made up of *phonemes*, which are combined to make *morphemes*. Combinations of words must have both *syntax* (grammar) and *semantics* (meaning). Behind the word strings, or *surface structures*, is an underlying representation, or *deep structure*, that expresses the relationship among the ideas in a sentence. Ambiguous sentences occur when one surface structure reflects two or more deep structures.

Understanding Speech When people listen to speech in a familiar language, their perceptual system allows them to perceive gaps between words, even when those gaps are not physically present. To understand language generally, and conversations in particular, people use their knowledge of the context and of the world. In addition, understanding is guided by nonverbal cues.

The Development of Language Children develop grammar according to an orderly pattern. *Babblings* and the *one-word stage* of speech come first, then telegraphic two-word sentences. Next come three-word sentences and certain grammatical forms that appear in a somewhat predictable order. Once children learn certain regular verb forms and plural endings, they may overgeneralize rules. Children acquire most of the syntax of their native language by the time they are five years old.

How Is Language Acquired? Conditioning and imitation both play a role in a child's acquisition of language, but neither can provide a complete explanation of how children acquire syntax. Humans may be biologically programmed to learn language. In any event, it appears that language must be learned during a certain critical period if normal language is to occur. The critical-period notion is supported by research on second-language acquisition.

Culture, Language, and Thought Research across cultures, and within North American culture, suggests that although language does not determine what we can think, it does influence how we think.

Consciousness

9

In this chapter, we delve into the topic of consciousness and describe research on altered states of consciousness. We'll examine sleep and dreams, hypnosis, and meditation and how they differ from normal waking consciousness. We'll also look at how consciousness is affected by psychoactive drugs. We have organized the chapter as follows:

There is an old *Sesame Street* episode in which Ernie is trying to find out whether Bert is asleep or awake. Ernie observes that Bert's eyes are closed, and he comments that Bert usually closes his eyes when he is asleep. Ernie also notes that when Bert is asleep, he does not respond to pokes, so naturally, he delivers a few pokes. At first, Bert does not respond. After being poked a few times, though, he awakes, very annoyed, and yells at Ernie for waking him. Ernie then informs Bert that he just wanted to let him know it was time for his nap.

Doctors face a similar situation in dealing with the more than 30 million people each year who receive general anesthesia during surgery. These patients certainly appear to go to sleep, but there is no completely reliable way of knowing whether they are actually unconscious. It turns out that about 0.2 percent of them retain some degree of consciousness during the surgical procedure (Ekman et al., 2004; Sigalovsky, 2003). In rare cases, patients have conscious awareness of surgical pain and remember it later. Although their surgical incisions heal, these people may be psychologically scarred by the experience and may even show symptoms of post-traumatic stress disorder (Schwender et al., 1995). To reduce the possibility of performing surgery on someone who appears unconscious but may not be, some physicans suggest that patients' brain activity should be monitored during every operation (Jameson & Sloan, 2006).

The fact that people can be conscious while "asleep" under the influence of powerful anesthetic drugs illustrates that defining consciousness is quite difficult (Edelman, 2003; Seth et al., 2006). In fact, after decades of discussion and research by philosophers, psychologists, and even physicists, some believe that consciousness is still not yet understood well enough to be precisely defined (Crick & Koch, 1998; King & Pribram, 1995). Given the ethical and legal concerns raised by the need to ensure that patients are not subjected to pain during surgery, medical doctors tend to define *consciousness* as awareness that is demonstrated by either explicit or implicit recall (Schwender et al., 1995). In psychology, the usual definition is somewhat broader: **Consciousness** is generally defined as awareness of your thoughts, actions, feelings, sensations, perceptions, and other mental processes (Metzinger, 2000; Zeman, 2001).

This definition suggests that consciousness is an aspect of many mental processes rather than being a unique mental process on its own. For example, memories can be conscious, but consciousness is not just memory. Perceptions can be conscious, but consciousness is not just perception. The definition also allows for the possibility that humans are not the only creatures that experience consciousness. It appears that some animals whose brains are similar to ours have some capacity for self-awareness, even though they do not have the language abilities to tell us about it. One way to assess this awareness is to determine if a creature recognizes itself in a mirror. Children can do so at about two years of age. Monkeys never display this ability, but chimpanzees do, and so do dolphins (Reiss & Marino, 2001). Although consciousness may not be a uniquely human capacity, it is central to our experience of life (Cotterill, 2001).

In this chapter we consider the nature of consciousness and the ways in which it affects our mental activity and behavior. Then we examine what happens when consciousness is altered by sleep, hypnosis, and meditation. Finally, we explore the changes in consciousness that occur when people use certain drugs.

Keeping an Eye Out Humans are not the only creatures capable of processing information while apparently unconscious. While ducks sleep, one hemisphere of their brains can process visual information from an eye that remains open. Birds positioned where they are most vulnerable to predators, such as at the end of a row, may spend twice as much time in this "alert" sleep than do birds in more protected positions (Rattenborg, Lima, & Amlaner, 1999).

consciousness Awareness of external stimuli and one's own mental activity.

Analyzing Consciousness

Psychologists have been fascinated by the study of consciousness for more than a century, but only in the past thirty-five years or so has consciousness reemerged as an active and vital research area in psychology. As described in the chapter on introducing psychology, behaviorism dominated psychological research in the United States from the 1920s through the 1960s. During that period, the emphasis was on overt behavior, so relatively little research was conducted on mental processes, including the structure and functions of consciousness. But as computerized tomography (CT) scans, PET scans, MRI, and other advanced brain imaging techniques began to appear in the late 1970s, psychologists found it possible to explore the relationship between conscious experience and brain activity with ever greater precision. They can even study differences between mental activity that is conscious and activity that occurs outside of awareness (Faulkner & Foster, 2002). Some scientists who study consciousness today describe their work as *cognitive science* or *cognitive neuroscience*, because their research is closely tied to the subfields of biological psychology, sensation, perception, memory, and human cognition (Koch, 2003). In fact, most cognitive psychologists who study memory, reasoning, problem solving, and decision making can be described as studying various aspects of consciousness.

Other psychologists study consciousness more directly by addressing three central questions about it. First, like the philosophers who preceded them, psychologists have grappled with the *mind-body problem*: What is the relationship between the conscious mind and the physical brain? One approach, known as *dualism*, sees the mind and brain as different. This idea was championed in the 1600s by French philosopher René Descartes. Descartes claimed that a person's soul, or consciousness, is separate from the brain but can "view" and interact with brain events through the pineal gland, a brain structure about the size of a grape. Once a popular point of view, dualism has virtually disappeared from psychology.

Another perspective, known as *materialism*, suggests that mind and brain are one and the same. Materialists argue that complex interactions among the brain's nerve cells create consciousness, much as hardware and software interact to create the image that appears on a computer screen. A good deal of support for the materialist view comes from case studies in which damage to the brain causes disruptions in consciousness.

A second question about consciousness focuses on whether it is a unified phenomenon or several different ones. Does consciousness occur as a single "point" in mental processing or as several parallel mental operations that occur independently? According to the *theater* view, consciousness is a single phenomenon, a kind of "stage" on which all the various aspects of awareness converge to "perform" before the "audience" of your mind. Those adopting the theater view see support for it in the fact that, as described in the perception chapter, the same psychophysical laws govern our subjective experience of the intensity of light, sound, weight, and other stimuli. It is as if each sensory system passes its information to a single "monitor" that coordinates the experience of stimulus magnitude (Teghtsoonian, 1992).

In contrast, the *parallel distributed processing (PDP) models* discussed in the perception chapter describe the mind as processing many parallel streams of information, which interact somehow to create the unitary experience we know as consciousness (John, 2004; Lou et al., 2004). PDP models became influential when research on sensation, perception, memory, cognition, and language suggested that components of these processes are analyzed in separate brain regions. For example, our perception of a visual scene involves activity in a number of separate brain regions that analyze "what" each object is, "where" it is, and whether the object is actually there or merely imagined (Aymoz & Viviani, 2004; Ishai, Ungerleider, &

Haxby, 2000). Scientists still do not know whether these parallel streams of information ever unite in a common brain region.

A third question about consciousness addresses the relationship between conscious and unconscious mental activities. More than a century ago, Sigmund Freud theorized that some mental processes occur without our awareness and that these processes can affect us in many ways. Most aspects of Freud's theory are not supported by modern research, but studies have shown that many important mental activities do occur outside of awareness. Let's examine some of these activities and consider the functions they serve.

Some Functions of Consciousness

Francis Crick and Christof Koch have suggested that one function of consciousness is to produce the best current interpretation of sensory information in light of past experience and to make this interpretation available to the parts of the brain that can act on it (Crick & Koch, 2003). They say that having a *single* conscious representation, rather than multiple ones, allows us to be more decisive in taking action. From this perspective, the conscious brain experiences a representation of the world that is the result of many complex computations. It has access to the results of these computational processes but not to the processes themselves. Some of those processes occur so quickly that our conscious experience can't keep up with them. For example, people playing tennis or a computer game can respond to a fast serve or a threatening alien even before they consciously "see" these stimuli. Although conscious processing is not always the fastest processing available, when dealing with life's most complex problems, consciousness allows the most adaptive and efficient blending of sensory input, motor responses, and knowledge resources in the brain (Baars, 2002).

As described in the chapter on memory, the contents of consciousness at any given moment are limited by the capacity of short-term memory, but the overall process of consciousness allows access to a vast store of memories and other information. In one study, for example, participants paid brief conscious attention to ten thousand different pictures over several days. A week later they were able to recognize more than 90 percent of the photographs. Evidently, mere consciousness of an event helps to store a recognizable memory that can later be brought into consciousness (Kosslyn, 1994).

Over a century ago, psychologist William James compared consciousness to a stream, describing it as ever changing, multilayered, and varying in both quantity and quality. Variations in quantity—in the degree to which one is aware of mental events—result in different *levels of consciousness*. Variations in quality—in the nature of the mental processing available to awareness—are referred to as different *states of consciousness* (Tassi & Muzet, 2001). Appreciating the difference between levels of consciousness and states of consciousness takes a little thought. When you are alert and aware of your mental activity and of incoming sensations, you are fully conscious. At the same time, however, other mental activity is taking place within your brain at varying "distances" from your conscious awareness. These activities are occurring at differing *levels* of consciousness (Morin, 2006). It is when your experience of yourself varies in focus and clarity—as when you sleep or are under the influence of a mind-altering drug—that there are variations in your *state* of consciousness. Let's first consider various levels of consciousness.

Levels of Consciousness

At any moment, the mental events that you are aware of are said to exist at the **conscious level.** For example, look at the Necker cube in Figure 9.1. If you are like most people, you can hold the cube in one orientation for only a few seconds before the other orientation "pops out" at you. The orientation that you experience at any moment is at your conscious level of awareness for that moment.

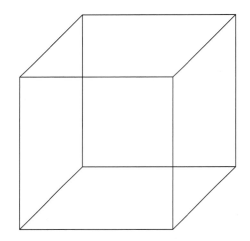

FIGURE 9.1

The Necker Cube

TRY THIS Each of the two squares in the Necker cube can be perceived as either the front or rear surface the cube. Try to make the cube switch of back and forth between these two orientations. Now try to hold only one orientation. You probably cannot maintain the whole cube in consciousness for longer than about three seconds before it "flips" from one orientation to the other.

● **conscious level** The level at which mental activities that people are normally aware of occur.

Some mental events, however, cannot be experienced consciously. For example, you are not directly aware of the fact that your brain is regulating your blood pressure. That kind of mental processing occurs at the **nonconscious level,** totally removed from conscious awareness. Some people can learn to alter a nonconscious process through *biofeedback training.* In this training, you receive information about your biological processes and try to change them. Usually, special equipment is required, but you can approximate a biofeedback session by having a friend take your pulse at one-minute intervals while you sit quietly. First, establish a baseline pulse; then imagine a peaceful scene, or think about lowering your pulse rate. Then ask your friend to softly say whether your pulse is higher or lower compared with the baseline. After four or five minutes of having this information "fed back" to you, you will probably be able to keep your pulse below the original baseline. Yet the pulse-regulating processes themselves remain out of consciousness.

Other mental events are not conscious, but they can either become conscious or influence conscious experience. These mental events make up the *cognitive unconscious* (Reber, 1992), which is further divided into preconscious and unconscious (or subconscious) levels. Mental events at the **preconscious level** are outside of awareness but can easily be brought into awareness. For example, what did you have for dinner last night? The information you needed to answer this question was probably not at a conscious level, but it was at a preconscious level and ready to be brought into awareness. Varying amounts of effort may be required to bring preconscious information into consciousness. When playing a trivia game, for example, it is sometimes easy and sometimes difficult to draw on your storehouse of preconscious memories to come up with obscure facts.

There are still other mental activities that can alter thoughts, feelings, and actions but that are more difficult to bring into awareness (Ratner, 1994). As described in the chapter on personality, Freud suggested that mental events at the **unconscious level**—especially those involving unacceptable sexual and aggressive urges—are actively kept out of consciousness. Many psychologists do not accept this view but still use the term *unconscious* (or *subconscious*) to describe the level of mental activity that influences consciousness but that is not conscious (Dijksterhuis & Nordgren, 2006).

● Mental Processing Without Awareness

A fascinating demonstration of mental processing without awareness was provided by an experiment with patients who had surgery under general anesthesia. While they were still unconscious in the recovery room, an audiotape of fifteen word pairs was played over and over. After regaining consciousness, these patients could not say what words had been played—or even whether a tape had been played at all. Yet when given one word from each of the word pairs on the tape and asked to say the first word that came to mind, the patients were able to produce the other member of the word pair (Cork, Kihlstrom, & Hameroff, 1992).

Even when people are conscious and alert, information can sometimes be processed and used without their awareness (Gaillard et al., 2006). In one study of this phenomenon, participants watched a computer screen as an X flashed in one of four locations. The participants' task was to indicate where the X appeared by rapidly pushing one of four buttons. The X's location seemed to vary randomly, but the movement sequence actually followed a set of complex rules, such as "If the X moves horizontally twice in a row, then it will move vertically next." The participants' responses became progressively faster and more accurate, but their performance instantly deteriorated when the rules were dropped and the Xs began appearing in truly random locations. Without being aware of doing so, these participants had apparently learned a complex rule-bound strategy to improve their performance. However, even when offered $100 to state the rules that had guided the movement sequence, they could not do so, nor were they sure that any such rules existed (Lewicki, 1992).

TRY
THIS

LINKAGES (a link to Perception, p. 157)

nonconscious level A level of mental activity that is inaccessible to conscious awareness.

preconscious level A level of mental activity that is not currently conscious but of which we can easily become conscious.

unconscious level A level of mental activity that influences consciousness but is not conscious.

Evidence for the operation of subconscious mental processing includes research showing that surgery patients may be able to hear and later comply with instructions or suggestions given while they are under anesthesia and of which they have no memory (Bennett, Giannini, & Davis, 1985). Another study found that people have physiological responses to emotionally charged words even when they are not paying attention to them (Von Wright, Anderson, & Stenman, 1975). These and other similar studies provide evidence for the operation of subconscious mental processing (Deeprose & Andrade, 2006).

Reprinted by permission of International Creative Management, Inc. Copyright © 2002 Berkeley Breathed.

BLOOM COUNTY   **by Berke Breathed**

Visual processing without awareness may also occur in cases of blindness caused by damage that is limited to the primary visual cortex. In such cases, fibers from the eyes are still connected to other brain areas that process visual information. Some of these surviving pathways may permit visual processing without visual awareness—a condition known as *blindsight* (Ro et al., 2004; Sahraie et al., 2006). Even though such patients say they see nothing, if forced to guess, they can still locate visual targets, identify the direction and orientation of moving images, reach for objects, name the color of lights, and even discriminate happy from fearful faces that they cannot consciously see (Morris et al., 2001). The same blindsight phenomenon has recently been created in visually normal volunteers using magnetic brain stimulation to temporarily disable the primary visual cortex (Boyer, Harrison, & Ro, 2005; Jolij & Lamme, 2005).

Research on *priming* also demonstrates mental processing without awareness. In a typical priming study, people tend to respond faster or more accurately to previously seen stimuli, even when they cannot consciously recall having seen those stimuli (Abrams & Greenwald, 2000; Kouider & Dupoux, 2005). In one study, people were asked to look at a set of drawings such as those in Figure 9.2 and decide which of the objects could actually exist in three-dimensional space and which could not. The participants were better at classifying pictures that they had seen before, even when they could not remember having seen them (Cooper et al., 1992; Schacter et al., 1991). Some priming effects are short-lived, but others can last for years (Mitchell, 2006).

1   2   3   4   5   6

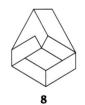

7   8   9   10   11   12

FIGURE 9.2

Possible or Impossible?

TRY THIS   Look at these figures and decide, as quickly as you can, whether each can actually exist. Priming studies show that this task would be easier for figures you have seen in the past, even if you don't recall seeing them. How did you do? (The correct answers appear in the footnote on page 333.)

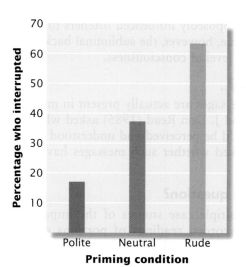

FIGURE 9.3

Priming Behavior Without Awareness

Participants in this study were primed with rude, polite, or neutral words before being confronted with the problem of interrupting a conversation. Though not consciously aware of the priming process, participants who had been exposed to rude words were most likely to interrupt, whereas those previously exposed to polite words were least likely to do so.

Source: Bargh, Chen, & Burrows (1996, Figure 1).

Priming can alter certain behaviors even when participants are not consciously aware of being influenced (Ruiz-Padial & Vila, 2007). For example, experimenters asked participants to unscramble scrambled sentences (e.g., "Finds he it instantly"). For one group of participants, the scrambled sentences all contained words associated with rudeness (e.g., *rude, bother,* and *annoying*). A second group read sentences whose scrambled words were associated with politeness (e.g., *respect, honor,* and *polite*). The scrambled words read by a third group were neutral (e.g., *normally, sends,* and *rapidly*). After completing the unscrambling task, each participant was asked to go to another room to get further instructions from the experimenter. But by design, the experimenter was always found talking to a research assistant. The dependent variable in this experiment was whether participants in the three conditions would interrupt the experimenter. As shown in Figure 9.3, the participants in the "rude priming" condition were most likely to interrupt, whereas those in the "polite priming" condition were least likely to do so. Those in the "neutral" condition fell in between the other two groups (Bargh, Chen, & Burrows, 1996).

The results of priming studies challenge some of the traditional Freudian views about the unconscious. According to Freud, unconscious processes function mainly to protect us from painful or frightening thoughts, feelings, and memories by keeping them out of consciousness (Pervin, 2003). However, many psychologists studying unconscious processes now believe that one of the primary functions of these processes is actually to help us more effectively carry out mundane, day-to-day mental activities (Dijksterhuis et al., 2006; Myers, 2004). For example, your "lucky" choice of the fastest-moving supermarket checkout line might seem to have been based on nothing more than a "hunch," a "gut feeling," or intuition, but previous visits to that store might have given you useful information about the various clerks that you didn't know you had (Adolphs et al., 2005). In a laboratory study that supports this notion, people watched videotaped television commercials while the changing stock prices of fictional companies "crawled" across the bottom of the screen. Later, these people were asked to choose which of these companies they liked best. They couldn't recall anything they had seen about the companies' stock, so they had to make their choice on the basis of their "gut reaction" to the company names. Nevertheless, their choices were not random; they more often chose companies whose stock prices had been rising rather than those whose stock had been falling (Betch et al., 2003).

Many questions about the relationship between conscious and unconscious processes remain to be answered. One of the most significant of these questions is whether conscious and unconscious thoughts occur independently of each other. Priming studies seem to suggest that they are independent, but other research suggests that they may not be. For example, one study found a correlation between unconscious indicators of age prejudice—as seen in implicit memory for negative stereotypes about the elderly—and consciously held attitudes toward the elderly (Hense, Penner, & Nelson, 1995). Another study found similarity between unconscious and conscious forms of ethnic prejudice (Lepore & Brown, 1997). Overall, however, if there is a relationship between explicit and implicit cognitions, it appears to be weak and not yet clearly understood (Dovidio, Kawakami, & Beach, 2001). We consider this issue further in the chapter on social cognition.

FOCUS ON RESEARCH METHODS

Subliminal Messages in Rock Music

According to various Internet web sites, Satanic or drug-related messages have been embedded in the recorded music of rock bands such as Marilyn Manson, Nine Inch Nails, Judas Priest, Led Zeppelin, and the Rolling Stones. The story goes that because these alleged messages were recorded backward, they are *subliminal*

The Cost of Jet Lag Twice a year, thousands of exhibitors freshly arrived from around the world groggily set up dazzling displays at Asia's largest jewelry show. Then they try to wait on customers while keeping track of their treasures. Taking advantage of these jet-lagged travelers' inattentiveness, thieves steal millions of dollars of merchandise at every show (Fowler, 2004).

without external time cues maintain daily rhythms in sleeping and waking, hormone release, eating, urination, and other physiological functions. Under such conditions, these cycles repeat about every twenty-four hours (Czeisler et al., 1999).

Disrupting the sleep-wake cycle can create problems. For example, air travel across several time zones often causes **jet lag,** a pattern of fatigue, irritability, inattention, and sleeping problems that can last several days (Akerstedt, 2007). The traveler's body feels ready to sleep at the wrong time for the new locale. Because it tends to be easier to stay awake longer than usual than to go to sleep earlier than usual, sleep-wake rhythms readjust to altered light-dark cycles more easily when sleep is shifted to a later, rather than an earlier, time (Lemmer et al., 2002). As a result, people usually experience more intense symptoms of jet lag after eastward travel (when time is lost) than after westward travel (when time is gained). Symptoms similar to those of jet lag also appear in workers who repeatedly change between day and night shifts and in people who try to go to sleep early on a Sunday night after a weekend of later-than-usual bedtimes (Czeisler et al., 2005; Di Milia, 2006). For these people, Monday morning "blues" may actually be symptoms of a disrupted sleep-wake cycle. There are also people who suffer because their circadian rhythms are never quite in synch with the local light-dark cycle (Ando, Kripke, & Ancoli-Israel, 2002).

The length of circadian rhythms varies from person to person. Some individuals have a natural tendency to stay up later at night ("owls") or to wake up earlier in the morning ("larks"). But because our circadian-like rhythms continue without external cues about light and dark, there must be a "biological clock" in the brain that keeps track of time. This clock is in the *suprachiasmatic nuclei (SCN)* of the hypothalamus (see Figure 9.8; Kalsbeek et al., 2006). The SCN receives light information from a special set of ganglion cells in the retina that act as photoreceptors and it sends that information to areas in the hindbrain that promote sleep or wakefulness (Albus et al., 2005; Lee et al., 2003; Saper, Scammell, & Lu, 2005). SCN neurons show a rhythm of activity that repeats itself every twenty-four to twenty-five hours, even if the neurons are removed from the brain and put in a laboratory dish (Yamaguchi et al., 2003). When animals with SCN damage receive transplanted SCN cells from another animal, their new circadian rhythms are similar to those of the donor animal (Menaker & Vogelbaum, 1993). SCN neurons also regulate the release of the hormone melatonin from the pineal gland. Melatonin, in turn, appears to be important in maintaining

● **jet lag** A syndrome of fatigue, irritability, inattention, and sleeping problems caused by air travel across several time zones.

FIGURE 9.8

Sleep, Dreaming, and the Brain

Here are some of the brain structures thought to be involved in sleep, dreaming, and other altered states of consciousness discussed later in the chapter. Scientists have discovered two specialized areas in the hypothalamus that appear to coordinate sleep and wakefulness. The preoptic nucleus appears to promote sleep. People with damage in this hypothalamic region find it difficult to ever go to sleep. The posterior lateral hypothalamus appears to promote wakefulness. Damage here causes continuous sleeping from which the person can be awakened only briefly (Salin-Pascual et al., 2001; Saper, Chou, & Scammell, 2001).

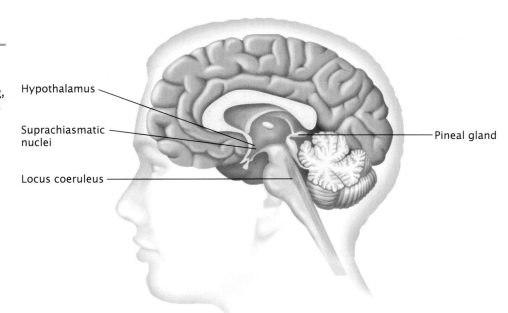

Hypothalamus

Suprachiasmatic nuclei

Locus coeruleus

Pineal gland

circadian rhythms (Beaumont et al., 2004; Cardinali et al., 2002). In fact, many of the symptoms associated with jet lag and other disruptions in sleep-wake cycles can be prevented or treated by taking melatonin (Revell & Eastman, 2005).

● **The Functions of Sleep**   Examining the effects of sleep deprivation may help explain why people sleep at all. People who go without sleep for as long as a week usually do not suffer serious long-term effects, but prolonged sleeplessness does lead to fatigue, irritability, and inattention (Drummond et al., 2000). The effects of short-term sleep deprivation—which is a common condition among busy adolescents and adults—can also take their toll (Arnedt et al., 2005; Steptoe, Peacey, & Wardle, 2006). For example, accidents and serious mistakes in patient care are more likely when medical interns work sleep-disrupting extended hospital shifts than when they work more normal hours (Ayas et al., 2006; Landrigan et al., 2004). Most fatal auto accidents in the

The Effects of Sleep Deprivation
Here, scientists at Loughborough University, England, test the effects of sleep deprivation on motor coordination. Driving while sleep-deprived can be so dangerous that at least one U.S. state (New Jersey) has expanded the definition of reckless driving to include "driving while fatigued." This condition is presumed to be present when someone has had no sleep in the previous twenty-four hours, but research is under way to identify more reliable biological indicators of when a person is dangerously fatigued (Seugnet et al., 2006).

United States occur during the "fatigue hazard" hours of midnight to 6 A.M. (Coleman, 1992), and sleepiness resulting from long work shifts or other causes is a major factor in up to 25 percent of all auto accidents (Barger et al., 2005; Garbarino et al., 2001; Philip et al., 2001). Fatigue also plays a role in many injuries suffered by sleepy young children at play or in day care (Valent, Brusaferro, & Barbone, 2001). Recent research suggests that learning, too, is more difficult after sleep deprivation (Yoo et al., 2007).

Scientists are looking for drugs that can combat the effects of sleep deprivation (Porrino et al., 2005), but there appears to be no substitute for sleep itself. Some researchers suggest that sleep helps restore the body and the brain for future activity and helps to consolidate memories of newly learned facts (Walker & Stickgold, 2006). Restorative functions are especially associated with non-REM sleep, which would help explain why most people get their non-REM sleep in the first part of the night (see Figure 9.6). There is also an apparent need for REM sleep. Sleep-deprived people do not make up lost sleep hour for hour. Instead, they sleep about 50 percent more than usual, then awake feeling rested. But if people are deprived only of REM sleep, they later compensate more directly. In a classic study, participants were awakened whenever their EEG tracings showed REM sleep. When allowed to sleep uninterrupted the next night, the participants "rebounded," nearly doubling the percentage of time spent in REM sleep (Dement, 1960). Even after *total* sleep deprivation, the next night of uninterrupted sleep includes an unusually high percentage of REM sleep (Feinberg & Campbell, 1993). This research suggests that REM has its own special functions. What these special functions might be is still unclear, but there are several possibilities.

First, REM sleep may improve the functioning of neurons that use norepinephrine (Siegel & Rogawski, 1988). Norepinephrine is a neurotransmitter released by cells in the *locus coeruleus* (pronounced "lo-kus seh-ROO-lee-us"; see Figure 9.8). During waking hours, norepinephrine affects alertness and mood. But the brain's neurons lose sensitivity to norepinephrine if it is released continuously for too long. Because the locus coeruleus is almost completely inactive during REM sleep, researchers suggest that REM helps restore sensitivity to norepinephrine and thus its ability to keep us alert (Steriade & McCarley, 1990). Animals deprived of REM sleep show unusually high norepinephrine levels and decreased daytime alertness (Brock et al., 1994).

REM sleep may also be a time for creating and solidifying connections between nerve cells in the brain (Graves, Pack, & Abel, 2001; Maquet, 2001; Peigneux et al., 2001). If so, it would explain why children and infants, whose brains are still developing, spend so much time in REM sleep (see Figure 9.7). Evidence favoring this possibility comes from research showing that REM sleep enhances the creation of neural connections in response to altered visual experience during the development of the visual cortex (Frank et al., 2001). REM sleep may also help solidify and absorb the day's experiences, including newly learned skills (Fenn, Nusbaum, & Margoliash, 2003; Ishikawa et al., 2006). In one study, people who were REM deprived showed poorer retention of a skill learned the day before than people who were either deprived of non-REM sleep or allowed to sleep normally (Karni et al., 1994). Other studies have found that information, including emotional information, is remembered better and longer when followed immediately by sleep, and especially REM sleep (Gais, Lucas, & Born, 2006; Gomez, Bootzin, & Nadel, 2006; Hu, Stylos-Allan, & Walker, 2006). Accordingly, some researchers have suggested that sleep deprivation in the aftermath of a traumatic event might reduce or even prevent the appearance of posttraumatic stress disorder (Wagner et al., 2006).

● Dreams and Dreaming

We have seen that the brain is active in all sleep stages (for a summary of our discussion, see "In Review: Sleep and Sleep Disorders"). Some of this activity is experienced as the storylike sensations and perceptions known as dreams. **Dreams** can last from seconds to minutes and may be organized or chaotic, realistic or fantastic, peaceful or exciting (Hobson & Stickgold, 1994). Sometimes, dreams lead to

● **dream** Story-like sequence of images, sensations, and perceptions occurring mainly during REM sleep.

in review   Sleep and Sleep Disorders

Types of Sleep	Characteristics	Possible Functions
Slow wave (stages 3 and 4)	The deepest stages of sleep, characterized by slowed heart rate and breathing, reduced blood pressure, and low-frequency, high-amplitude brain waves	Refreshing of body and brain; memory consolidation
Rapid eye movement (REM) sleep	Characterized by eye movements, waking levels of heart rate, breathing, blood pressure, and brain waves, but near paralysis in muscles; most dreaming occurs during REM	Restoring sensitivity to norepinephrine, thus improving waking alertness; creating and solidifying nerve cell connections; consolidating memories and new skills

Sleep Disorders	Characteristics	Possible Causes
Insomnia	Difficulty (lasting at least a month) in falling asleep or staying asleep	Worry, anxiety
Narcolepsy	Sudden switching from a waking state to REM sleep	Absence or deficiency in *orexin* (*hypocretin*)
Sleep apnea	Frequent episodes of interrupted breathing while asleep	Genetic predisposition, obesity, faulty breathing-related brain mechanisms, windpipe compression
Sudden infant death syndrome (SIDS)	Interruption of an infant's breathing, resulting in death	Genetic predisposition, faulty breathing-related brain mechanisms
Nightmares	Frightening dreams during REM sleep	Stressful or traumatic events or experiences
Night terrors	Frightening dream images during non-REM sleep	Stressful or traumatic events or experiences
REM behavior disorder	Lack of paralysis during REM sleep allows dreams to be enacted, sometimes with harmful consequences	Malfunction of brain mechanism normally creating REM paralysis

creative insights. For example, after trying for days to write a story about good and evil in the same person, author Robert Louis Stevenson dreamed about a man who drank a potion that turned him into a monster (Hill, 1968). This dream inspired *The Strange Case of Dr. Jekyll and Mr. Hyde.* However, there is no scientific evidence that dreams lead to insights that are any more creative than those coming from waking thoughts.

Some dreaming occurs during non-REM sleep, but most dreams—and the most bizarre and vivid dreams—occur during REM sleep (Dement & Kleitman, 1957; Eiser, 2005) Even when they seem to make no sense, dreams may contain a certain amount of logic. In one study, for example, when segments from some dream reports were scrambled, readers could correctly say which reports had been rearranged and which were intact (Stickgold, Rittenhouse, & Hobson, 1994). And although dreams often involve one person becoming another person or one object turning into another object, it is rare that objects become people or vice versa (Stickgold et al., 1994).

Daytime activities and experiences may influence the content of dreams to some degree (Valli et al., 2006; Wegner, Wenzlaff, & Kozak, 2004). When people were asked to wear red-tinted goggles for a few minutes before going to sleep, they reported more red images in their dreams than people who had not worn the goggles (Roffwarg, Hermann, & Bowe-Anders, 1978). It is also sometimes possible to intentionally direct dream content, especially during **lucid dreaming,** in which the sleeper is aware of dreaming while a dream is happening (Stickgold et al., 2000).

Research leaves little doubt that everyone dreams during every night of normal sleep. Even blind people dream, although their perceptual experiences are usually

● **lucid dreaming** Awareness that a dream is a dream while it is happening.

not visual. Whether you remember a dream depends on how you sleep and wake up. You'll remember more if you awaken abruptly and lie quietly while writing or tape-recording your recollections.

There are many theories about why we dream (Antrobus, 2001; Domhoff, 2001; Eiser, 2005; Revonsuo, 2001). Some researchers see dreaming as a fundamental process by which all mammals analyze and consolidate information that has personal significance or survival value (Porte & Hobson, 1996). This view is supported by the fact that dreaming appears to occur in most mammals, as indicated by the appearance of REM sleep. For example, after researchers disabled the neurons that cause REM sleep paralysis, sleeping cats ran around and attacked, or seemed alarmed by, unseen objects, presumably the images from dreams (Winson, 1990).

According to Freud (1900), dreams are a disguised form of *wish fulfillment*, a way to satisfy unconscious urges or resolve unconscious conflicts that are too upsetting to deal with consciously. So sexual desires might appear in a dream as the rhythmic motions of a horseback ride. Conflicting feelings about a parent might appear as a dream about a fight. Seeing patients' dreams as a "royal road to a knowledge of the unconscious," Freud interpreted their meaning as part of his psychoanalytic therapy (see the chapter on treatment of psychological disorders).

In contrast, the *activation-synthesis theory* describes dreams as the meaningless byproducts of REM sleep (Eiser, 2005; Hobson, 1997). According to this theory, hindbrain arousal during REM sleep creates random messages that *activate* the brain, especially the cerebral cortex. Dreams result as the cortex combines, or *synthesizes*, these random messages as best it can, using stored memories and current feelings to impose a coherent perceptual organization on confusingly random inputs. From this perspective, dreams arise as the brain attempts to make sense of meaningless stimulation during sleep, much as it does during waking hours when trying to find meaningful shapes in cloud formations (Bernstein & Roberts, 1995).

Even if dreams stem from random physiological activity, their content can still have psychological significance. Some psychologists believe that dreams give people a chance to review and address some of the problems they face during waking hours (Cartwright, 1993). This view is supported by evidence that people's current concerns can affect both the content of their dreams and the ways in which dreams are organized and recalled (Domhoff, 1996; Stevens, 1996). However, research using brain imaging techniques shows that while we are asleep, brain areas involved in emotion tend to be overactive, whereas areas controlling logical thought tend to be suppressed (Braun, Balkin, & Wesensten, 1998; Hobson et al., 1998). In fact, as we reach deeper sleep stages, and then enter REM, thinking subsides and hallucinations increase (Fosse, Stickgold, & Hobson, 2001). This is probably why dreams rarely provide realistic, logical solutions to our problems (Blagrove, 1996).

Hypnosis

hypnosis A phenomenon brought on by special induction techniques and characterized by varying degrees of responsiveness to suggestions for changes in experience and behavior.

state theory A theory that hypnosis is an altered state of consciousness.

The word *hypnosis* comes from the Greek word *hypnos*, meaning "sleep," but hypnotized people are not sleeping. People who have been hypnotized say that their bodies felt "asleep," but their minds were active and alert. **Hypnosis** has traditionally been defined as an altered state of consciousness brought on by special techniques and producing responsiveness to suggestions for changes in experience and behavior (Kirsch, 1994b). Most hypnotized people do not feel forced to follow the hypnotist's instructions; they simply see no reason to refuse (Hilgard, 1965). In fact, a desire to cooperate with the hypnotist and active participation in the process greatly increases the likelihood that a person will experience hypnosis (Lynn et al., 2002).

Experiencing Hypnosis

Usually, hypnosis begins with suggestions that the participant feels relaxed and sleepy. The hypnotist then gradually focuses the participant's attention on a particular, often

Inducing Hypnosis In the late 1700s, an Austrian physician named Franz Anton Mesmer became famous for his treatment of physical disorders using *mesmerism*, a forerunner of hypnosis. His procedures included elaborate trance-induction rituals, but despite what you might see in movies and on TV (Barrett, 2006), hypnosis can be induced far more easily, often simply by asking a person to stare at an object, as this man did.

Steve

Steven

Sue

Sue

FIGURE 9.9

Hypnotic Age Regression

TRY THIS Here are the signatures of two adults before hypnotically induced age regression (top of each pair) and while age regressed (bottom of each pair). The lower signatures in each pair look less mature, but was the change due to hypnosis? To find out, ask a friend to write his or her name on a blank sheet of paper, first as usual, and then as if he or she were five years old. If the two signatures look significantly different, what does this say about the cause of certain age-regression effects?

Source: Hilgard (1965).

monotonous set of stimuli while suggesting that the participant should ignore everything else and imagine certain feelings.

There are special tests to measure *hypnotic susceptibility*, the degree to which people respond to hypnotic suggestions (Gfeller, 1994). These tests reveal that about 10 percent of adults are difficult or impossible to hypnotize (Hilgard, 1982). At the other extreme are highly susceptible individuals who report vivid hypnotic experiences. In one study, for example, such individuals were unable to tell the difference between images that a hypnotist told them to imagine and images that were actually projected on a screen (Bryant & Mallard, 2003). Hypnotically susceptible people typically differ from others in several ways, including differences in certain brain structures (Horton et al., 2004), a greater ability to focus attention and ignore distraction (Iani et al., 2006), a more active imagination (Spanos, Burnley, & Cross, 1993), a tendency to fantasize (Lynn & Rhue, 1986), a capacity for processing information quickly and easily (Dixon, Brunet, & Laurence, 1990), a tendency to be suggestible (Kirsch & Braffman, 2001), and more positive attitudes and expectations about hypnosis (Benham et al., 2006; Spanos et al., 1993). As suggested earlier, the willingness to be hypnotized is the most important factor of all. People cannot be hypnotized against their will.

The results of hypnosis can be fascinating. People told that their eyes cannot open may struggle unsuccessfully to open them. They may appear deaf or blind or insensitive to pain. They may be unable to say their own names. Some appear to remember forgotten things. Others show *age regression*, apparently recalling or reenacting their childhoods (see Figure 9.9). Hypnotic effects can last for hours or days through *posthypnotic suggestions*—instructions about behavior that is to take place after hypnosis has ended (such as smiling whenever someone says "England"). Some people show *posthypnotic amnesia*, an inability to recall what happened while they were hypnotized, even after being told what happened.

Ernest Hilgard (1965, 1992) described the main changes that people display during hypnosis. First, hypnotized people show *reduced planfulness*. They tend not to begin actions on their own, waiting instead for the hypnotist's instructions. One participant said, "I was trying to decide if my legs were crossed, but I couldn't tell, and didn't quite have the initiative to move to find out" (Hilgard, 1965, p. 6). Second, they tend to ignore all but the hypnotist's voice and whatever it points out; their *attention is redistributed*. Third, hypnosis enhances the *ability to fantasize*, so participants more vividly imagine a scene or relive a memory. Fourth, hypnotized people display *increased role taking*; they more easily act like a person of a different age or a member of the opposite sex, for example. Fifth, hypnotic participants show *reduced reality testing*, tending not to question if statements are true and more willingly accepting apparent distortions of reality. A hypnotized person might shiver in a warm room if a hypnotist says it is snowing.

Explaining Hypnosis

Hypnotized people and nonhypnotized people act differently and may look different, too (Hilgard, 1965). Do these differences reflect an altered state of consciousness?

Advocates of the **state theory** of hypnosis say that they do. They point to the notable changes in brain activity that occur during hypnosis (Egner, Jamieson, & Gruzelier, 2005; Mohr, Binkofski, et al., 2005; Raij et al., 2005) and to the dramatic effects that hypnosis can produce, including insensitivity to pain and the disappearance of warts (Noll, 1994). They also note that there are slight differences in the way hypnotized and nonhypnotized people carry out suggestions. In one study, hypnotized people and those who had been asked to simulate hypnosis were told to run their hands through their hair whenever they heard the word *experiment* (Orne, Sheehan, & Evans, 1968). Simulators did so only when the hypnotist said the cue word. Hypnotized participants complied no matter who said it. Another study found that hypnotized people complied more often than simulators with a posthypnotic suggestion to mail postcards to the experimenter (Barnier & McConkey, 1998).

FIGURE 9.10

Can Hypnosis Produce Blindness?

The top row looks like gibberish, but if you closed one eye while wearing special glasses, you could detect within it the numbers and letters shown in the lower row. Yet when hypnotized people wore such glasses and were told that they were blind in one eye, they were unable to read the display. This result indicated that, despite the hypnotic suggestion, both their eyes were working normally (Pattie, 1935).

Source: Pattie (1935).

Surgery Under Hypnosis Bernadine Coady, of Wimblington, England, has a condition that makes it dangerous for her to have general anesthesia. In April 1999, when a hypnotherapist failed to show up to help her through a painful foot operation, she used self-hypnosis as her only anesthetic. She imagined the pain as "waves lashing against a sea wall . . . [and] going away, like the tide." Coady's report that the operation was painless is believable because, in December 2000, she underwent the same operation on her other foot, again using only self-hypnosis for pain control (Morris, 2000).

Proponents of the **role theory** of hypnosis argue that hypnosis is *not* a special state of consciousness. They point out, for example, that some of the changes in brain activity associated with hypnosis can also be created without hypnosis (Mohr, Binkofski, et al., 2005). They suggest that hypnotized people are merely complying with social demands and acting in accordance with a special social role (Kirsch, 1994a). From this perspective, then, hypnosis simply provides a socially acceptable reason to follow certain suggestions, much as your annual physical exam provides you with a socially acceptable reason to follow a request to take off your clothes.

Support for role theory comes from several sources. First, nonhypnotized people sometimes display behaviors that are usually associated with hypnosis. For example, contestants on television game shows and reality shows do lots of odd, silly, disgusting, or even dangerous things without first being hypnotized. Second, laboratory experiments show that motivated, but nonhypnotized, volunteers can duplicate many, if not all, aspects of hypnotic behavior, from arm rigidity to age regression (Dasgupta et al., 1995; Orne & Evans, 1965). Other studies using special tests have found that people rendered blind or deaf by hypnosis can still see or hear, even though their actions and beliefs suggest that they cannot (Bryant & McConkey, 1989; Pattie, 1935; see Figure 9.10).

Hilgard's (1992) **dissociation theory** of hypnosis blends role and state theories. He suggested that hypnosis is not a specific state but a general condition that temporarily reorganizes or breaks down our normal control over thoughts and actions. Hypnosis, he said, activates a process called *dissociation*, meaning a split in consciousness (Hilgard, 1979). As a result, body movements normally under voluntary control can occur on their own, and normally involuntary processes (such as reactions to pain) can be controlled voluntarily. Hilgard argued that this relaxation of central control occurs as part of a *social agreement* to share control with the hypnotist. In other words, people usually decide for themselves how to act or what to attend to, perceive, or remember, but during hypnosis, the hypnotist is allowed to control some of these experiences and actions. So Hilgard saw hypnosis as a socially agreed-upon display of dissociated mental functions. Compliance with a social role may account for part of the story, he said, but hypnosis also leads to significant changes in mental processes.

Support for Hilgard's theory comes from brain imaging studies showing that the ability to dissociate certain mental processes is greater in people who are more hypnotically susceptible (Egner et al., 2005). Dissociation was also demonstrated behaviorally by asking hypnotized participants to immerse one hand in ice water (Hilgard, Morgan, & MacDonald, 1975). They were told they would feel no pain, but they were asked to press a button with their other hand if "any part of them" felt pain. These participants said they felt almost no pain, but their button pressing told a different story. Hilgard concluded that a "hidden observer" was reporting on pain that was reaching the person but had been separated, or dissociated, from conscious awareness (Hilgard, 1977).

Much remains to be learned about the nature of hypnosis. Contemporary research continues to test the validity of various explanatory theories of hypnosis, but traditional distinctions between state and role theories have become less important as researchers focus on larger questions, such as why people are susceptible to hypnosis and what roles biological, social, and cognitive factors may play in it (e.g., Lynn & Kirsch, 2006; Raz, Fan, & Posner, 2005).

◗ Applications of Hypnosis

Whatever hypnosis is, it has proven useful, especially in relation to pain (Patterson & Jensen, 2003). Hypnosis seems to be the only anesthetic some people need to block the pain of dental work, childbirth, burns, and surgery (Morris, 2000; Van Sickel, 1992). For others, hypnosis relieves chronic pain from arthritis, nerve damage, migraine headaches, and cancer (Stewart, 2005). Hypnotic suggestion can also help eliminate diarrhea (Tan, Hammond, & Joseph, 2005), reduce nausea and vomiting due to chemotherapy (Redd, 1984), limit surgical bleeding (Gerschman, Reade, & Burrows, 1980), and speed postoperative recovery (Astin, 2004).

Other applications of hypnosis are more controversial, especially the use of hypnosis to aid memory. For example, hypnotic age regression is sometimes attempted in an effort to help people recover lost memories. However, the memories of past events reported by age-regressed individuals are not as accurate as those of non-hypnotized individuals (Lynn, Myers, & Malinoski, 1997). It is doubtful, then, that hypnosis can improve the ability of witnesses to recall details of a crime. In fact, their positive expectations about the value of hypnosis may lead them to unintentionally distort or reconstruct memories of what they saw and heard (Garry & Loftus, 1994; Wells & Olson, 2003). So although hypnosis may not enhance people's memory for information, it may make them more confident about their reports, even if they are inaccurate. As discussed in the memory chapter, confident witnesses tend to be especially impressive to juries.

LINKAGES **Meditation, Health, and Stress**

LINKAGES (a link to Health, Stress, and Coping, p. 547)

Meditation is intended to create an altered state of consciousness characterized by inner peace and tranquility (Walsh & Shapiro, 2006). Some claim that meditation increases people's awareness and understanding of themselves and their environment, improves health, and aids performance in everything from work to tennis (Davidson et al., 2003; Paul-Labrador et al., 2006; Oman, Hedberg, & Thoreson, 2006; Mahesh Yogi, 1994). Meditators also report significant reductions in stress-related problems such as general anxiety, high blood pressure, headache, back pain, and insomnia (Astin et al., 2003; Beauchamp-Turner & Levinson, 1992). Meditators' scores on personality tests indicate increases in overall mental health, self-esteem, and social openness (Janowiak & Hackman, 1994; Sakairi, 1992).

The techniques used to achieve a meditative state differ, depending on belief and philosophy (for example, Eastern meditation, Sufism, yoga, or prayer). However, in the most common meditation methods, attention is focused on just one thing—a word, sound, or object—until the meditator stops thinking about anything and experiences nothing but "pure awareness" (Benson, 1975). In this way, the individual becomes more fully aware of the present moment rather than being caught up in the past or the future.

What a meditator focuses on is far less important than doing so with a passive attitude. To organize attention, meditators might inwardly name every sound or thought that reaches consciousness, focus on the sound of their own breathing, or slowly repeat a *mantra*, which is a soothing word or phrase. During a typical meditation session, breathing, heart rate, muscle tension, blood pressure, and oxygen consumption decrease (Wallace & Benson, 1972), while in the brain blood flow to the thalamus and frontal lobes increases (Cahn & Polich, 2006; Newberg et al., 2001). Meditation also increases the brain's level of dopamine, a neurotransmitter thought to be involved in the experience of reward or pleasure (Kjaer et al., 2002). Most forms of meditation induce alpha-wave EEG activity, the brain wave pattern commonly found in a relaxed, eyes-closed, waking state (see Figure 9.5).

role theory A theory that hypnotized people act in accordance with a special social role that provides a socially acceptable reason to follow the hypnotist's suggestions.

dissociation theory A theory defining hypnosis as a socially agreed-upon opportunity to display one's ability to let mental functions become dissociated.

"Are you not thinking what I'm not thinking?"

Exactly how meditation works is unclear, though its effects on dopamine activity may be one part of the story. Meditation may also create lasting changes in the brain. For example, the prefrontal cortex appears to be thicker in those who practice long-term meditation (Lazar et al, 2005). These changes in neurotransmitter activity and brain structure may affect the brain's responses to the environment, even when meditation is not occurring. In one functional MRI study, people who meditated regularly and those who had never meditated were subjected to a painful stimulus. The meditators reported less pain than the nonmeditators did, and their brains showed less activation in areas that normally process pain signals. When the nonmeditators were retested after having learned and practiced meditation, they, too, experienced less pain and reduced activity in pain-processing areas of their brains (Orme-Johnson et al., 2006).

The changes meditation creates, though, are probably not unique to meditation. Further, the benefits associated with meditation have also been associated with techniques such as biofeedback, hypnosis, tai chi, and just relaxing (Bernstein et al., 2000; Wang, Collet, & Lau, 2004). ■

Psychoactive Drugs

- **psychoactive drug** Substance that acts on the brain to create some psychological effect.

- **psychopharmacology** The study of psychoactive drugs and their effects.

Every day, most people in the world use drugs that alter brain activity and consciousness (Levinthal, 2001). For example, 80 to 90 percent of people in North America use caffeine, the stimulant found in coffee (Gilbert, 1984). A drug is a chemical that is not usually needed for physiological activity and that can affect the body upon entering it. (Some people use the word *drug* to mean therapeutic medicines but refer to nonmedicinal drugs as *substances,* as in *substance abuse.*) Drugs that affect the brain, changing consciousness and other psychological processes, are called **psychoactive drugs.** The study of psychoactive drugs is called **psychopharmacology.**

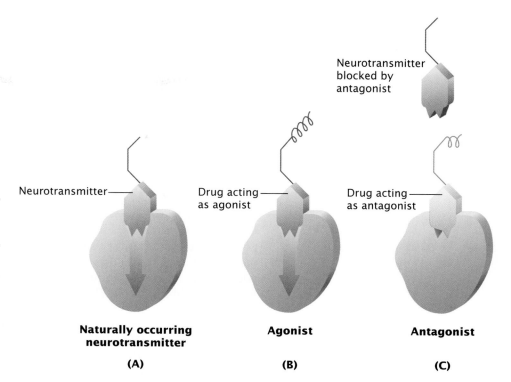

FIGURE 9.11

Agonists and Antagonists

In part (A), a molecule of neurotransmitter interacts with a receptor on a neuron's dendrites by fitting into and stimulating it. Part (B) shows a drug molecule acting as an *agonist*, affecting the receptor in the same way a neurotransmitter would. Part (C) depicts an *antagonist* drug molecule blocking a natural neurotransmitter from reaching and acting upon the receptor.

Neurotransmitter blocked by antagonist

Neurotransmitter —   Drug acting — as agonist   Drug acting — as antagonist

Naturally occurring neurotransmitter   **Agonist**   **Antagonist**

(A)   **(B)**   **(C)**

● Psychopharmacology

Most psychoactive drugs affect the brain by altering the interactions between neurotransmitters and receptors, as described in the chapter on biological aspects of psychology. To create their effects, these drugs must cross the **blood-brain barrier,** a feature of blood vessels in the brain that prevents some substances from entering brain tissue (Neuwelt, 2004). Once past this barrier, a psychoactive drug's effects depend on several factors: With which neurotransmitter systems does the drug interact? How does the drug affect these neurotransmitters or their receptors? What psychological functions are normally performed by the brain systems that use these neurotransmitters?

Drugs can affect neurotransmitters or their receptors through several mechanisms. As shown in Figure 9.11, neurotransmitters fit into their own receptors. However, some drugs are similar enough to a particular neurotransmitter to fool its receptors. These drugs, called **agonists,** bind to the receptor and mimic the effects of the normal neurotransmitter. Other drugs are similar enough to a neurotransmitter to occupy its receptors but cannot mimic its effects. So they bind to a receptor and prevent the normal neurotransmitter from binding. These drugs are called **antagonists.** Still other drugs work by increasing or decreasing the release of a specific neurotransmitter. Finally, some drugs work by speeding or slowing the *removal* of a neurotransmitter from synapses.

Predicting a drug's behavioral effects is complicated by the fact that most psychoactive drugs interact with many neurotransmitter systems. Also, the nervous system may compensate for a drug's effects. For example, repeated exposure to a drug that blocks receptors for a certain neurotransmitter often leads to an increase in the number of receptors available to accept that neurotransmitter.

● The Varying Effects of Drugs

Unfortunately, the chemical properties that give drugs their medically desirable *main effects*, such as pain relief, often create undesirable *side effects* as well.

● **blood-brain barrier** A feature of blood vessels supplying the brain that allows only certain substances to leave the blood and interact with brain tissue.

● **agonist** Drug that mimics the effects of the neurotransmitter that normally binds to a neural receptor.

● **antagonist** Drug that binds to a receptor and prevents the normal neurotransmitter from binding.

● **Substance Abuse** One side effect may be the potential for abuse. **Substance abuse** is a pattern of use that causes serious social, legal, or interpersonal problems for the user (American Psychiatric Association, 2000). Substance abuse may lead to psychological or physical dependence. **Psychological dependence** is a condition in which a person continues to use the drug despite its adverse effects, needs the drug for a sense of well-being, and becomes preoccupied with obtaining the drug. However, the person can still function without the drug. Psychological dependence can occur with or without **physical dependence,** or **addiction,** which is a physiological state in which continued drug use becomes necessary in order to prevent an unpleasant **withdrawal syndrome.** Withdrawal symptoms vary depending on the drug, but they often include an intense craving for the drug and physical effects generally opposite to those of the drug itself. Eventually, drug tolerance may appear. **Tolerance** is a condition in which increasingly larger drug doses are needed to produce the same effect (Sokolowska, Siegel, & Kim, 2002). With the development of tolerance, many addicts need the drug just to prevent the negative effects of not taking it. However, most researchers believe that a craving for the positive effects of drugs is what keeps addicts coming back to drug use (Ciccocioppo, Martin-Fardon, & Weiss, 2004; Everitt & Robbins, 2005). This view is supported by functional MRI studies of addicts who are asked to imagine cocaine or alcohol use. The resulting craving activated regions of the brain related to the rewards, positive emotions, and other pleasures they had learned to associate with using the drug (George et al., 2001; Kilts et al., 2001). Further, stimulating these regions in the brains of rats that had once been physically dependent on cocaine causes them to seek out the drug again (Vorel et al., 2001).

It is tempting to think of "addicts" as being different from the rest of us, but we should never underestimate the ease with which drug dependence can develop in anyone, including ourselves. Physical dependence can develop gradually, without a person's awareness. In fact, scientists believe that the changes in the brain that underlie addiction may be similar to those that occur during learning (Nestler, 2001). All addictive drugs stimulate the brain's "pleasure centers," regions that are sensitive to the neurotransmitter dopamine. Neuronal activity in these areas produces intensely pleasurable feelings; it also helps generate the pleasant feelings of a good meal, a "runner's high," or sex (Grunberg, 1994; Harris & Aston-Jones, 1995). Neuroscientists long believed that these feelings stem directly from the action of dopamine itself, but activity in dopamine systems may actually be more involved in responding to the novelty associated with pleasurable events than in actually creating the experience of pleasure (Bevins, 2001; Garris et al., 1999). In any case, by affecting the regulation of dopamine and other neurotransmitters in the brain's "pleasure centers," addictive drugs have the capacity to create tremendously rewarding effects in most people (Boyd, 2006; Cannon, 2005; Maldonado, Valverde, & Berrendero, 2006). The changes created in the brain by drug addiction can remain long after drug use ends (Diana, Spiqa, & Acquas, 2006), which is one reason that people who succeed in giving up addictive drugs may still be in danger of relapse months or even years later.

● **Expectations and Drug Effects** Drug effects are not determined by biochemistry alone (Crombag & Robinson, 2004). *Learned expectations* also play a role (Bartholow & Heinz, 2006; Siegel, 2005). Several experiments have shown that people who consume alcohol-free drinks that they *think* contain alcohol are likely to behave in line with their expectations about alcohol's effects. So they tend to feel drunk and to become more aggressive, more interested in violent and sexual material, and more easily sexually aroused (Darkes & Goldman, 1993; George & Marlatt, 1986; Lang et al., 1975). And because they know that alcohol impairs memory, these people are more vulnerable to developing false memories about a crime they witnessed on videotape (Assefi & Garry, 2003).

Expectations about drug effects develop, in part, as people watch other people react to drugs (Sher et al., 1996). Because what they see can be different from one

---

● **substance abuse** The self-administration of psychoactive drugs in ways that deviate from a culture's social norms.

● **psychological dependence** A condition in which a person uses a drug despite adverse effects, needs the drug for a sense of well-being, and becomes preoccupied with obtaining it.

● **physical dependence (addiction)** Development of a physical need for a psychoactive drug.

● **withdrawal syndrome** Symptoms associated with discontinuing the use of a habit-forming substance.

● **tolerance** A condition in which increasingly larger drug doses are needed to produce a given effect.

individual and culture to the next, drug effects vary considerably throughout the world (MacAndrew & Edgerton, 1969). In the United States, for example, loss of inhibition, increased anger and violence, and sexual promiscuity are commonly associated with drinking alcohol. These effects are not seen in all cultures, however. In Bolivia's Camba culture, people engage in extended bouts of drinking a brew that is 89 percent alcohol (178 proof). During their binges, the Camba repeatedly pass out, wake up, and start drinking again—all the while maintaining peaceful social relations. The learned nature of responses to alcohol is also demonstrated by cases in which people are exposed to new ideas about the drug's effects. When Europeans brought alcohol to Tahiti in the 1700s, the Tahitians who drank it just became relaxed and disoriented, much as when consuming *kava*, their traditional nonalcoholic tranquilizing drink. But after years of watching European sailors' drunken violence, Tahitian alcohol drinkers became violent themselves. Fortunately, subsequent learning experiences have moderated their response to alcohol (MacAndrew & Edgerton, 1969). Other studies have shown that learned expectations also contribute to the effects of heroin, cocaine, and marijuana (Robbins & Everitt, 1999; Schafer & Brown, 1991; Smith et al., 1992).

As these examples show, the effects of psychoactive drugs are complex and variable. In the chapter on treatment of psychological disorders, we discuss some of the psychoactive drugs being used to help troubled people. Here, we consider several categories of psychoactive drugs that are used primarily for the alterations they produce in consciousness. They include depressants, stimulants, opiates, and hallucinogens.

● Depressants

Depressants, such as alcohol and barbiturates, reduce the activity of the central nervous system. They do so partly by affecting the neurotransmitter GABA. As described in the chapter on biological aspects of psychology, GABA reduces, or inhibits, neuron activity. Depressants increase the availability of GABA, which, in turn, reduces the activity of many neural circuits. So the results of using depressants include relaxation, drowsiness, and sometimes depression (Hanson & Venturelli, 1995).

● **Alcohol**   In the United States, over 100 million people drink *alcohol*. It is equally popular worldwide (Leigh & Stacy, 2004). Alcohol affects several neurotransmitters, including dopamine, endorphins, endocannabinoids, glutamate, serotonin, and most notably, GABA (Daglish & Nutt, 2003; Enoch, 2003; Vinod et al., 2006). For this reason, drugs that interact with GABA receptors can block some of alcohol's effects, as shown in Figure 9.12 (Suzdak et al., 1986). Alcohol also enhances the effect of endorphins (the body's natural painkillers, described in the chapter on sensation). This action may underlie the "high" that people feel when drinking alcohol and may explain why *naltrexone* and *naloxone*, which block endorphins, are better than placebos at reducing alcohol craving and relapse rates in recovering alcoholics (Garbutt et al., 2005). Alcohol also interacts with dopamine systems, a component of the brain's pleasure and reward mechanisms (Thanos et al., 2001). Prolonged alcohol use can have lasting effects on the brain's ability to regulate dopamine levels (Tiihonen et al., 1995). Dopamine agonists reduce alcohol craving and withdrawal effects (Lawford et al., 1995).

Alcohol affects specific brain regions. For example, it reduces activity in the locus coeruleus, an area that helps activate the cerebral cortex (Koob & Bloom, 1988). This reduced activity, in turn, tends to cause cognitive changes and a release of culturally prescribed inhibitions (Casbon et al., 2003). Some drinkers begin talking loudly, acting silly, or telling others what they think of them. Emotional reactions range from giddy happiness to deep despair. Normally shy people may become impulsive or violent. Alcohol's suppression of the hippocampus causes memory problems, making it difficult to form new memories (Givens, 1995). The effects on the hippocampus may

● **depressant**   Psychoactive drug that inhibits the functioning of the central nervous system.

FIGURE **9.12**

GABA Receptors and Alcohol

These rats each received the same amount of alcohol, enough to incapacitate them with drunkenness. The rat on the right then received a drug that reverses alcohol's intoxicating effects by blocking the ability of alcohol to stimulate GABA receptors. Within two minutes, the animal was acting utterly sober. There is a serious problem with the drug, though: It did not reverse the effects of alcohol on the brain's breathing centers. So a person who took the drug could consume a fatal overdose of alcohol without ever feeling drunk. Needless to say, the drug's manufacturer has discontinued its development.

be permanent; brain imaging studies have shown that the hippocampus is smaller in heavy drinkers than in nondrinkers (Beresford et al., 2006). Alcohol's suppression of the cerebellum causes poor motor coordination, and its ability to depress hindbrain mechanisms that control breathing and heartbeat can make overdoses fatal.

As mentioned earlier, some effects of alcohol—such as anger and aggressiveness—depend on both biochemical factors and learned expectations (Goldman, Darkes, & Del Boca, 1999; Kushner et al., 2000). But other effects—especially disruptions in motor coordination, speech, and thought—result from biochemical factors alone. These biological effects depend on the amount of alcohol the blood carries to the brain. It takes the liver about an hour to break down one ounce of alcohol (the amount in one average drink), so alcohol has milder effects if consumed slowly. Effects increase with faster drinking, or with drinking on an empty stomach,

Drinking and Driving Don't Mix
Although practice makes it seem easy, driving a car is a complex information-processing task. As described in the chapter on cognition and language, such tasks require constant vigilance, quick decisions, and skillful execution of responses. Alcohol can impair all these processes, as well as the ability to judge the degree of impairment—thus making drinking and driving a deadly combination that results in 275,000 injuries and almost 17,000 deaths each year in the United States alone (National Highway Traffic Safety Administration, 2005).

thereby speeding the absorption of alcohol into the blood. Even after allowing for differences in average male and female body weight, researchers have found metabolic differences that allow males to tolerate somewhat higher amounts of alcohol. As a result, equal doses of alcohol may create greater effects in women compared with men (York & Welte, 1994). Overindulgence by either sex results in unpleasant physical hangover effects that cannot be prevented or relieved by aspirin, bananas, vitamins, coffee, eggs, exercise, fresh air, honey, pizza, herbal remedies, more alcohol, or any of the dozens of other "surefire" hangover cures you may have heard about (Pittler, Verster, & Ernst, 2005).

Genetics also seems to play a role in determining the biochemical effects of alcohol (Scholz, Franz, & Heberlein, 2005). Some people appear to have a genetic predisposition toward alcohol dependence (Agarwal, 1997; Enoch, 2003), although the specific genes involved have not yet been identified. Others, such as the Japanese, may have inherited metabolic characteristics that increase the adverse effects of alcohol, thus possibly inhibiting the development of alcohol abuse (Iwahashi et al., 1995).

● **Barbiturates** Sometimes called "downers" or "sleeping pills," *barbiturates* are extremely addictive. Small doses cause relaxation, feelings of well-being, loss of muscle coordination, and reduced attention. Higher doses cause deep sleep, but continued use actually distorts sleep patterns (Kales & Kales, 1973). So long-term use of barbiturates as sleeping pills is unwise. Overdoses can be fatal. Withdrawal symptoms are among the most severe for any drug and can include intense agitation, violent outbursts, convulsions, hallucinations, and even sudden death.

● **GHB** *Gamma hydroxybutyrate*, or *GHB*, is a naturally occurring substance similar to the neurotransmitter GABA (Drasbek, Christensen, & Jensen, 2006). Introduced many years ago as a nutritional supplement, a laboratory-manufactured version of GHB (also known as "G") has become a popular recreational drug that is often used at nightclubs. This "club drug" is known for inducing relaxation, elation, loss of inhibition, suggestability, and increased sex drive. Unfortunately, it can also cause nausea and vomiting, headaches, dizziness, loss of muscle control or paralysis, breathing problems, and even death—especially when combined with alcohol or other drugs (Miotto et al., 2001; Stillwell, 2002). Nearly half of those who use GHB report occasions on which it caused loss of memory, and two-thirds report having lost consciousness (Miotto et al., 2001). Because these effects can facilitate sexual assault, GHB is one of several compounds known as "date rape" drugs. As with other depressants, long-term use of GHB can lead to dependence, and suddenly stopping the drug can cause a withdrawal syndrome that can include seizures, hallucinations, agitation, coma, or death (Tarabar & Nelson, 2004).

● Stimulants

Whereas depressants slow down central nervous system activity, **stimulants** speed it up. Amphetamines, cocaine, caffeine, and nicotine are all examples of stimulants.

● **Amphetamines** Also called "uppers" or "speed," *amphetamines* (such as Benzedrine) increase the release and decrease the removal of norepinephrine and dopamine at synapses, causing increased activity at these neurotransmitters' receptors (Bonci et al., 2003). This increased activity results in alertness, arousal, and appetite suppression. These effects are further enhanced by the fact that amphetamines also reduce activity of the inhibitory neurotransmitter GABA (Centonze et al., 2002). The rewarding properties of these drugs are probably due in part to their activation of dopamine systems, because taking dopamine antagonists reduces amphetamine use (Holman, 1994).

stimulant Psychoactive drug that has the ability to increase behavioral and mental activity.

Deadly Drug Use John Entwistle, bass player for The Who, died of a cocaine-related heart attack in 2002. He joined a long list of celebrities (including Chris Farley and Righteous Brother Bobby Hatfield) and an even longer list of ordinary people whose lives have been destroyed by the abuse of cocaine or other drugs.

Amphetamines stimulate both the brain and the sympathetic branch of the autonomic nervous system, raising heart rate and blood pressure, constricting blood vessels, shrinking mucous membranes (relieving stuffy noses), and reducing appetite. Amphetamines also increase response speed, especially in tasks requiring prolonged attention (Koelega, 1993), and they may improve memory for verbal material (Soetens et al., 1995).

Abuse of amphetamines usually begins as an effort to lose weight, stay awake, or experience a "high." Continued use leads to anxiety, insomnia, heart problems, brain damage, movement disorders, confusion, paranoia, nonstop talking, and psychological and physical dependence (Thompson et al., 2004; Volkow et al., 2001). In some cases, the symptoms of amphetamine abuse are virtually identical to those of paranoid schizophrenia, a serious mental disorder associated with malfunctioning dopamine systems.

● **Cocaine** Like amphetamines, *cocaine* increases norepinephrine and dopamine activity and decreases GABA activity, so it produces many amphetamine-like effects (Kolb et al., 2003). Cocaine's particularly quick and powerful effect on dopamine activity may account for its remarkably addictive nature (Bonci et al., 2003; Ciccocioppo et al., 2004; Ungless et al., 2001). Drugs with rapid onset and short duration are generally more addictive than others (Kato, Wakasa, & Yamagita, 1987), which may explain why *crack*—a purified, fast-acting, highly potent, smokable form of cocaine—is especially addictive.

Cocaine stimulates self-confidence, a sense of well-being, and optimism. But continued use brings nausea, overactivity, insomnia, paranoia, a sudden depressive "crash," hallucinations, sexual dysfunction, and seizures (Lacayo, 1995). Overdoses, especially of crack, can be deadly, and even small doses can cause a fatal heart attack or stroke (Klausner & Lewandowski, 2002; Marzuk et al., 1995). Using cocaine during pregnancy harms the fetus (Hurt et al., 1995; Konkol et al., 1994; Snodgrass, 1994), but many of the severe, long-term behavioral problems seen in "cocaine babies" may have at least as much to do with poverty and neglect after birth as with the mother's cocaine use beforehand. Early intervention can reduce the effects of both cocaine and the hostile environment that confronts most cocaine babies (Mayes et al., 2003; Singer et al., 2004).

Ending a cocaine addiction is difficult. One reasonably successful treatment involves a combination of counseling and *buprenorphine*, an opiate antagonist that suppresses cocaine self-administration in addicted monkeys (Fiellin et al., 2006; Montoya et al., 2004). Other drugs that affect selective types of dopamine receptors have been found effective in preventing relapse when mice previously addicted to cocaine were exposed to drug-related cues, but these drugs have not yet been shown to be effective in humans. Still another approach is to use *baclofen*, a drug that reduces the stimulating effects of cocaine by enhancing the inhibitory neurotransmitter GABA (Dobrovitsky et al., 2002). Baclofen has been shown to help reduce cocaine use in addicted people (Shoptaw et al., 2003). The results of other methods have been mixed; fewer than 25 percent of human cocaine addicts who have undergone even long-term pharmacological and psychological treatments are drug-free five years later (*Harvard Mental Health Letter,* 2001).

● **Caffeine** *Caffeine* is the world's most popular drug. It is found in chocolate, many soft drinks, tea, and coffee. A typical cup of coffee has 58–259 mg of caffeine, and even "decaffeinated" coffee may still contain up to 15.8 mg (McCusker, Goldberger, & Cone, 2006; McCusker et al., 2006). Caffeine reduces drowsiness and can enhance cognitive performance and vigilance (Beaumont et al., 2001; Lorist & Tops, 2003). For example, it improves problem solving, increases the capacity for physical work, and raises urine production (Warburton, 1995). At high doses it creates tremors and anxiety. Long-term caffeine use can result in tolerance, as well as physical dependence (Strain et al., 1994). Withdrawal symptoms—including headaches, fatigue, anxiety, shakiness, and craving—appear on the first day of abstinence and last about a week (Silverman et al., 1992). Caffeine may make it harder for women to become pregnant and may increase the risk of miscarriage or stillbirth (Balat et al., 2003; Bech et al., 2005; Rasch, 2003; Wisborg et al., 2003). Moderate daily caffeine use may also cause slight increases in blood pressure (James, 2004), but otherwise it appears to have few, if any, negative effects (Kleemola et al., 2000; Winkelmayer et al., 2005).

● **Nicotine**   A powerful stimulant of the autonomic nervous system (ANS), nicotine is a potent psychoactive ingredient in tobacco. Nicotine's best-known effect is to enhance the action of acetylcholine, but it also increases the release of glutamate, the brain's primary excitatory neurotransmitter (McGehee et al., 1995), and activates the brain's dopamine-related pleasure system (Balfour, 2002). Nicotine has many psychoactive effects, including ANS arousal, elevated mood, and improved memory and attention (Domino, 2003; Ernst et al., 2001; Pomerleau & Pomerleau, 1992). Like heroin and cocaine, nicotine can be physically addictive (White, 1998).

It does not create the "rush" characteristic of many drugs of abuse, but stopping nicotine use often creates a withdrawal syndrome that includes craving, irritability, anxiety, reduced heart rate, and reduced activity in the brain's reward pathways (Epping-Jordan et al., 1998; Hughes, Higgins, & Bickel, 1994). The tendency to become physically dependent on nicotine appears to be at least partly inherited (Li, 2006), so some smokers appear to develop only a psychological dependence (Robinson & Pritchard, 1995). But whatever the blend of physical and psychological dependence, there is no doubt that smoking is a difficult habit for most smokers to break (Breteler et al., 2004; Shiffman et al., 1997). As discussed in the chapter on health, stress, and coping, it is also clearly recognized as a major risk factor for cancer, heart disease, and respiratory disorders (U.S. Department of Health and Human Services, 2001b).

● **MDMA**   "Ecstasy," or *MDMA* (short for 3,4-methylenedioxymethamphetamine), is a popular drug on college campuses in the United States. MDMA increases the activity of dopamine-releasing neurons, so it leads to some of the same effects as those produced by cocaine and amphetamines (Steele, McCann, & Ricaurte, 1994). These include a sense of well-being, increased sex drive, and a feeling of greater closeness to others. But MDMA may also cause dry mouth, hyperactivity, jaw muscle spasms that may result in "lockjaw," elevated blood pressure, fever, dangerously abnormal heart rhythms, and visual hallucinations (Smith, Larive, & Romananelli, 2002). The hallucinations may appear because MDMA is a serotonin agonist and also increases serotonin release (Green, Cross, & Goodwin, 1995). On the day after using MDMA—also known as "XTC," "clarity," "essence," "E," and "Adam"—people often report muscle aches, fatigue, depression, and poor concentration (Peroutka, Newman, & Harris, 1988). With continued use, MDMA's positive effects decrease, but its negative effects persist.

Although it does not appear to be physically addictive, MDMA can be a dangerous, potentially deadly drug, especially when taken by women (Liechti, Gamma, & Vollenweider, 2001; National Institute on Drug Abuse, 2000). In animal studies, high doses permanently damage the brain, particularly serotonin axons (Green et al., 1995). It is not yet clear whether the brain damage seen in these high-dose animal studies also results from the lower doses typically taken by humans (Lyvers, 2006), but both animal studies and human studies indicate that MDMA impairs memory, judgment, and other psychological functions, even after its use is discontinued (Kalechstein et al., 2007; Smith, Tivarus, et al., 2006).

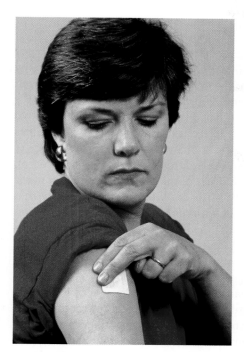

Giving Up Smoking   The chemical effects of nicotine, combined with strongly learned associations between smoking and relaxation, stimulation, mealtimes, alcohol, and a wide variety of pleasant social interactions, make it extremely difficult for most smokers to give up their dangerous habit. The more promising treatment programs available today offer some combination of nicotine replacement (via a patch such as the one this woman is wearing), antismoking drugs such as Chantix or Zyban, and behavioral training in how to resist cravings and cope with the stress of not smoking, especially in smoking-related situations.

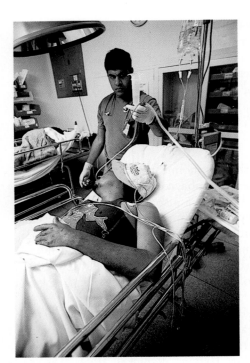

Another Drug Danger Oxycodone, a morphine-like drug prescribed by doctors under the label *OxyContin*, has become popular among recreational substance abusers. Deaths from OxyContin abuse are already on the rise in the United States. (U.S. Drug Enforcement Administration, 2002).

● Opiates

The **opiates** (opium, morphine, heroin, and codeine) are unique in their capacity for inducing sleep and relieving pain (Julien, 2005). *Opium*, derived from the poppy plant, relieves pain and causes feelings of well-being and dreamy relaxation (Cowan et al., 2001). One of its most active ingredients, *morphine*, was first isolated in the early 1800s and is used worldwide for pain relief. Percodan and Demerol are two common morphine-like drugs. *Heroin* is derived from morphine but is three times more powerful, causing intensely pleasurable reactions when first taken.

Opiates have complex effects on consciousness. Drowsy, cloudy feelings occur, perhaps because opiates depress activity in wide areas of the cerebral cortex. But many people also experience euphoria or elation (Bozarth & Wise, 1984). One way that opiates may exert their effects is by acting as agonists for endorphins. When opiates activate endorphin receptors, they are "tricking" the brain into an exaggerated activation of its painkilling and mood-altering systems (Julien, 2005). Like marijuana, which we discuss later, opiates also appear to stimulate the endocannabinoid system, perhaps explaining their euphoric effects (Vigano, Rubino, & Parolaro, 2006).

Opiates are highly addictive, partly because they stimulate a type of glutamate receptor on brain neurons that can physically change the neurons' structure. This change may alter neurons so that they come to require the drug to function properly (Bajo et al., 2006; Martin et al., 2004). Supporting this idea are data showing that glutamate antagonists appear to prevent morphine dependence yet leave the drug's painkilling effects intact (Trujillo & Akil, 1991).

● Hallucinogens

Hallucinogens, also called *psychedelics*, create a loss of contact with reality and alter other aspects of emotion, perception, and thought. They can cause distortions in body image (the user may feel gigantic or tiny), loss of identity (confusion about who one actually is), dream-like fantasies, and hallucinations. Because these effects resemble many severe forms of mental disorder, hallucinogens are also called *psychotomimetics* (mimicking psychosis).

● **LSD**   One of the most powerful hallucinogens is *lysergic acid diethylamide*, or *LSD*, first synthesized from a rye fungus by Swiss chemist Albert Hofmann. In 1938, after Hofmann accidentally ingested a tiny amount of the substance, he discovered the drug's strange effects in the world's first LSD "trip" (Julien, 2005). LSD hallucinations can be quite bizarre. Time may seem distorted, sounds may cause visual sensations, and users may feel as if they have left their bodies. LSD's hallucinatory effects have been attributed partly to its ability to stimulate a specific type of serotonin receptors in the forebrain (Carlson, 1998). Supporting this assertion is evidence that serotonin antagonists greatly reduce LSD's hallucinatory effects (Leonard, 1992). LSD also stimulates a subtype of dopamine receptors whose activation leads to hallucinations and delusions (Minuzzi et al., 2005).

The precise effects of LSD on a particular individual are unpredictable. Unpleasant hallucinations and delusions can occur during a person's first—or two hundredth—LSD experience. Although LSD is not addictive, tolerance to its effects does develop. Some users suffer lasting adverse effects, including severe short-term memory loss, paranoia, violent outbursts, nightmares, and panic attacks (Gold, 1994). Distortions in visual sensations can remain for years after heavy use has ended (Dyck, 2005). Sometimes flashbacks occur, in which a person suddenly returns to an LSD-like state of consciousness weeks or even years after using the drug.

● **Ketamine**   *Ketamine* is an anesthetic widely used by veterinarians to ease pain in animals, and by physicians for sedating critically ill patients or suppressing dangerous seizure activity (Hirota, 2006; Robakis & Hirsch, 2006). But because it also has hallucinogenic effects, ketamine is being stolen and sold as a recreational drug known as

● **opiate**   Psychoactive drug, such as opium, morphine, or heroin, that produces sleep-inducing and pain-relieving effects.

● **hallucinogen**   Psychoactive drug that alters consciousness by producing a temporary loss of contact with reality and changes in emotion, perception, and thought.

"Special K." Its effects include dissociative feelings that create what some users describe as an "out-of-body" or "near death" experience. Unfortunately, ketamine can also cause enduring amnesia and other memory problems (Curran & Monaghan, 2001; Smith et al., 2002). These adverse effects appear to result from damage to memory-related brain structures such as the hippocampus (Jevtovic-Todorovic et al., 2001).

● **Marijuana**   A mixture of crushed leaves, flowers, and stems from the hemp plant (*Cannabis sativa*) makes up *marijuana*. The active ingredient is *tetrahydro-cannabinol*, or THC (Wachtel et al., 2002). When inhaled, THC is absorbed in minutes by many organs, including the brain. It alters blood flow to many brain regions (O'Leary et al., 2002) and continues to affect consciousness for several hours. Low doses of marijuana may initially create restlessness and hilarity, followed by a dreamy, carefree relaxation, an expanded sense of space and time, more vivid sensations, food cravings, and subtle changes in thinking (Kelly et al., 1990).

THC tends to collect in fatty deposits of the brain and reproductive organs, where it can be detected for weeks. The brain contains several receptors for THC. The first to be discovered was named *ananda* (from a Sanskrit word meaning "bliss") and is normally activated by a naturally occurring brain substance called anandamide (Fride & Mechoulam, 1993). Research has now established that the body produces a number of its own "endogenous cannaboids" whose receptors in the brain also respond to THC (Onaivi et al., 2002). Recent research suggests that this *endocannabinoid* system interacts with the pleasure-producing actions of the endorphin and dopamine systems, and it is involved in generating the psychoactive effects of several of the other drugs discussed earlier in this chapter (Maldonado et al., 2006). Scientists hope that it may someday be possible to safely stimulate the endocannabinoid system without producing harmful side effects (Pacher, Batkai, & Kunos, 2006), and to block the system so as to help drug-addicted people discontinue drug use (Huestis et al., 2001).

For a summary of the effects of marijuana and other psychoactive drugs, see "In Review: Major Classes of Psychoactive Drugs."

in review   Major Classes of Psychoactive Drugs

Drug	Trade/Street Name	Main Effects	Potential for Physical/ Psychological Dependence
Depressants			
Alcohol	"booze"	Relaxation, anxiety	High/high
Barbiturates	Seconal, Tuinal, Nembutal ("downers")	reduction, sleep	High/high
GHB	"G," "Jib," "Scoop," "GH Buddy"	Relaxation, euphoria	High/high
Stimulants			
Amphetamines	Benzedrine, Dexedrine, Methadrine ("speed," "uppers," "ice")	Alertness, euphoria	Moderate/high
Cocaine	"coke," "crack"		Moderate to high/high
Caffeine		Alertness	Moderate/moderate
Nicotine	"smokes," "coffin nails"	Alertness	High (?)/high
MDMA	ecstasy, clarity	Hallucinations	Low/(?)
Opiates			
Opium		Euphoria	High/high
Morphine	Percodan, Demerol	Euphoria, pain control	High/high
Heroin	"junk," "smack"	Euphoria, pain control	High/high
Hallucinogens			
LSD/Ketamine	"acid"/"Special K"	Altered perceptions, hallucinations	Low/low
Marijuana (cannabis)	"pot," "dope," "reefer"	Euphoria, relaxation	Low/moderate

THINKING CRITICALLY **Is Marijuana Dangerous?**

Surveys in the United States suggest that about 14.6 million people over the age of twelve use marijuana at least once a month, and that about 3.1 million do so on a daily or almost daily basis (National Institute on Drug Abuse, 2004). U.S. government officials have condemned marijuana use as "dangerous, illegal, and wrong," and concern about the drug has also been voiced in many other countries. At the same time, the medical community has been engaged in serious discussion about whether marijuana should be used for medicinal purposes, and in the United States and around the world many individuals and organizations continue to argue for the decriminalization of marijuana use.

Those who support legalization of marijuana cite its medical benefits. Some doctors claim to have successfully used marijuana in the treatment of problems such as asthma, glaucoma, epilepsy, chronic pain, and nausea from cancer chemotherapy (Abrams et al., 2007; Gorter et al., 2005; Rog et al., 2005; Tramer et al., 2001). There is also evidence that marijuana can affect the immune system in ways that help fight some types of cancer (Parolaro et al., 2002). But some argue that medical legalization of marijuana is premature, because its medicinal value has not been clearly established. They point out, too, that—even though patients may prefer marijuana-based drugs—other medications may be equally effective and less dangerous (e.g., Campbell et al., 2001; Fox et al., 2004; Hall & Degenhardt, 2003).

■ What am I being asked to believe or accept?

Those who see marijuana as dangerous usually assert four beliefs: (1) that marijuana is addictive; (2) that it leads to the use of other drugs, such as heroin; (3) that marijuana intoxication endangers the user and other individuals; and (4) that long-term marijuana use leads to undesirable behavioral changes, disruption of brain functions, and other adverse effects on health.

■ What evidence is available to support the assertion?

Without a doubt, some people do use marijuana to such an extent that it disrupts their lives. According to the criteria normally used to define alcohol abuse, these people are dependent on marijuana—at least psychologically (Stephens, Roffman, & Simpson, 1994). The question of physical dependence (addiction) is less clear, inasmuch as withdrawal from chronic marijuana use has long been thought not to produce any severe physical symptoms. However, some evidence of a mild withdrawal syndrome has been

The Cannabis Controversy Marijuana is illegal in North America and in many other places, too, but the question of whether it should remain so is a matter of hot debate between those who see the drug as a dangerous gateway to more addictive substances and those who view it as a harmless source of pleasure that may also have important medical benefits.

reported in rats. In humans, withdrawal from marijuana may be accompanied by increases in anxiety, depression, and aggressiveness (Budney et al., 2001, 2003; Haney et al., 1999; Smith, 2002). Other research has found that marijuana interacts with the same dopamine and opiate receptors as does heroin, implying that marijuana could be a "gateway drug" to the use of more addictive drugs (Lynskey et al., 2003; Spano et al., 2007).

Regardless of whether marijuana is addictive or leads to other kinds of drug use, it can create a number of problems. It disrupts memory formation, making it difficult to carry out complex tasks (Pope et al., 2001). And despite the fact that people may feel more creative while using marijuana, the drug appears to actually reduce creativity (Bourassa & Vaugeois, 2001). Because marijuana affects muscle coordination, driving while under its influence is quite hazardous. Compounding the danger is the fact that motor impairment continues long after the obvious effects of the drug have worn off. In one study, for example, pilots had difficulty landing a simulated aircraft even a full day after smoking one marijuana cigarette (Yesavage et al., 1985). As for marijuana's effects on intellectual and cognitive performance, long-term use can lead to lasting impairments in reasoning and memory (Bolla et al., 2002; Solowij et al., 2002). One study found that adults who frequently used marijuana scored lower on a twelfth-grade academic achievement test than did nonusers with the same IQs (Block & Ghoneim, 1993). Among long-term users, impairments in memory and attention can persist for years after their drug use has stopped (Solowij et al., 2002). Heavy use of marijuana in teenagers has also been associated with the later appearance of anxiety, depression, and other mental disorders as severe as schizophrenia (Arsenault et al., 2004; Patton et al., 2002; Zammit et al., 2002).

■ Are there alternative ways of interpreting the evidence?

Those who see marijuana as a harmless or even beneficial substance criticize studies such as those just mentioned as providing an inaccurate or incomplete picture of marijuana's effects (Grinspoon, 1999). They argue, for example, that the same dopamine receptors activated by marijuana and heroin are also activated by sex and chocolate—and that few people would call for the criminalization of those pleasures (Grinspoon et al., 1997). Moreover, the correlation between early marijuana use and later use of other drugs could be due more to the people with whom marijuana users become involved than to any property of the drug itself (Fergusson & Horwood, 1997).

The question of marijuana's long-term effects on memory and reasoning is also difficult to resolve, partly because studies of academic achievement scores and marijuana use tend to be correlational in nature. As noted in the chapter on research in psychology, cause and effect cannot easily be determined in such studies. Does marijuana use lead to poor academic performance, or does poor academic performance lead to increased marijuana use? Both possibilities are credible. The same can be said of the correlation between marijuana and mental disorder. Heavy use of marijuana could be a reaction to, or an early symptom of, mental disorder, not necessarily its cause.

■ What additional evidence would help to evaluate the alternatives?

We obviously need more definitive evidence about marijuana's short- and long-term effects, and it should be based on well-controlled experiments with large and representative samples of participants. Still, evaluating the meaning of even the best possible evidence will be difficult. The issues in the marijuana debate involve questions of degree and relative risk. For example, is the risk of marijuana dependence greater than that of alcohol dependence? And what about individual differences? Some people are at much greater risk than others for negative consequences from marijuana use. So far, however, we have not determined what personal characteristics account for these differences. Nor do we know why some people use marijuana only occasionally, whereas others use it so often and in such quantities that it seriously disrupts their ability to function. The physical and psychological factors underlying these differences have yet to be identified.

■ What conclusions are most reasonable?

Those who would decriminalize the use of marijuana argue that when marijuana was declared illegal in the United States in the 1930s, there was no evidence that it was any more harmful than alcohol or tobacco. Scientific evidence supports that claim, but more by illuminating the dangers of alcohol and tobacco than by declaring marijuana safe. In fact, although marijuana is less dangerous than, say, cocaine or heroin, it is by no means harmless. Marijuana easily reaches a developing fetus and should not be used by pregnant women (Fried, Watkinson, & Gray, 1992; Spano et al., 2007); it suppresses some immune functions in humans (Cabral & Dove Pettit, 1998); and marijuana smoke is as irritating to lungs as tobacco smoke (Roth et al., 1998). Further, because possession of marijuana is still a crime almost everywhere in the United States, as well as in many other countries throughout the world, it would be foolish to flaunt existing laws without regard for the legal consequences.

Nevertheless, in Canada, it is legal to grow and use marijuana for medicinal purposes, and the same is true in twelve U.S. states, despite federal laws to the contrary and the threat of federal intervention to enforce those laws (Okie, 2005). Although the American Medical Association has rejected the idea of medical uses for marijuana, scientists are intent on objectively studying its potential value in the treatment of certain diseases, as well as its possible dangers. Their work is being encouraged by bodies such as the National Institute of Medicine (Joy, Watson, & Benson, 1999), and drug companies are working to develop new cannabis-based medicines (Altman, 2000; Tuller, 2004). The United Nations, too, has recommended that governments worldwide sponsor additional work on the medical uses of marijuana (Wren, 1999). Ultimately, the most reasonable conclusions about marijuana use must await the outcome of this research.   ■

LINKAGES

As noted in the chapter on introducing psychology, all of psychology's subfields are related to one another. Our discussion of meditation, health, and stress illustrates just one way in which the topic of this chapter, consciousness, is linked to the subfield of health psychology (which is a focus of the chapter on health, stress, and coping). The Linkages diagram shows ties to two other subfields as well, and there are many more ties throughout the book. Looking for linkages among subfields will help you see how they all fit together and help you better appreciate the big picture that is psychology.

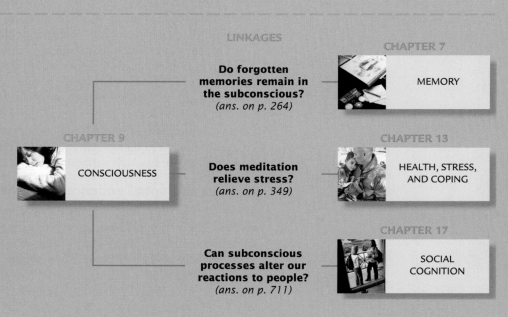

LINKAGES

CHAPTER 9

CONSCIOUSNESS

Do forgotten memories remain in the subconscious?
(ans. on p. 264)

CHAPTER 7

MEMORY

Does meditation relieve stress?
(ans. on p. 349)

CHAPTER 13

HEALTH, STRESS, AND COPING

Can subconscious processes alter our reactions to people?
(ans. on p. 711)

CHAPTER 17

SOCIAL COGNITION

SUMMARY

Consciousness can be defined as awareness of the outside world and of one's own thoughts, feelings, perceptions, and other mental processes.

Analyzing Consciousness

Current research on consciousness focuses on three main questions. First, what is the relationship between the mind and the brain? Second, does consciousness occur as a single "point" in mental processing or as several parallel and independent mental operations? Third, what mental processes are outside awareness, and how do they affect conscious processes?

Some Functions of Consciousness Consciousness produces the best current interpretation of sensory information in light of past experience and makes this interpretation available to the parts of the brain that plan voluntary actions and speech.

Levels of Consciousness Variations in how much awareness you have for a mental function are described by different levels of consciousness. The *preconscious level* includes mental activities that are outside of awareness but can easily be brought to the *conscious level*. At the *unconscious level* are thoughts, memories, and processes that are more difficult to bring to awareness. Mental processes that cannot be brought into awareness are said to occur at the *nonconscious level*.

Mental Processing Without Awareness Awareness is not always required for mental operations. Priming studies show that our responses to some stimuli can be speeded, improved, or modified, even when we are not consciously aware of the priming stimuli.

The Neuropsychology of Consciousness The thalamus and the cerebral cortex are among the brain structures involved in the experience of consciousness. Brain injuries can impair consciousness and reveal ways in which mental processing can occur without conscious awareness.

States of Consciousness A person's *state of consciousness* is constantly changing. When the changes are particularly noticeable, they are called *altered states of consciousness*. Examples include sleep, hypnosis, meditation, and some drug-induced conditions. Cultures vary considerably in the value they place on different states of consciousness.

Sleeping and Dreaming

Sleep is an active and complex state.

Stages of Sleep Different stages of sleep are defined on the basis of changes in brain activity (as recorded by an electroencephalograph, or EEG) and physiological arousal. Sleep normally begins with stage 1 sleep and progresses gradually to stage 4 sleep. Sleep stages 3 and 4 constitute *slow-wave sleep*, which is part of

non-REM sleep. After passing back to stage 2, people enter *rapid eye movement (REM)* sleep, or paradoxical sleep. The sleeper passes through these stages several times each night, gradually spending more time in stage 2 and REM sleep later in the night.

Sleep Disorders Sleep disorders can disrupt the natural rhythm of sleep. Among the most common is *insomnia*, in which one feels tired because of trouble falling asleep or staying asleep. *Narcolepsy* produces sudden daytime sleeping episodes. In *sleep apnea,* people briefly, but repeatedly, stop breathing during sleep. *Sudden infant death syndrome (SIDS)* may be due to brain abnormalities or accidental suffocation. *Nightmares* and *night terrors* are different kinds of frightening dreams. *Sleepwalking* occurs most frequently during childhood. *REM behavior disorder* is potentially dangerous because it allows people to act out REM dreams.

Why Do People Sleep? The cycle of waking and sleeping is a natural *circadian rhythm*, controlled by the suprachiasmatic nuclei in the brain. *Jet lag* can be one result of disrupting the normal sleep-wake cycle. The purpose of sleep is still being debated. Non-REM sleep may aid bodily rest and repair. REM sleep may help maintain activity in brain areas that provide daytime alertness, or it may allow the brain to solidify and absorb the day's experiences.

Dreams and Dreaming *Dreams* are story-like sequences of images, sensations, and perceptions that occur during sleep, most commonly during REM sleep. Evidence from research on *lucid dreaming* suggests that people may sometimes be able to control the content of their dreams. According to activation-synthesis theory, dreams are the meaningless byproducts of brain activity, but they may still have psychological significance.

Hypnosis

Hypnosis is a well-known but still poorly understood phenomenon.

Experiencing Hypnosis Tests of hypnotic susceptibility suggest that some people cannot be hypnotized. Hypnotized people tend to focus attention on the hypnotist and passively follow instructions. Their ability to fantasize and take roles shows improvement, and they may exhibit apparent age regression, experience posthypnotic amnesia, and obey posthypnotic suggestions.

Explaining Hypnosis According to *state theory*, hypnosis is a special state of consciousness. *Role theory* suggests that hypnosis creates a special social role that gives people permission to act in unusual ways. *Dissociation theory* combines aspects of role and state theories, suggesting that hypnotic participants enter into a social contract with the hypnotist to allow normally integrated mental processes to become dissociated and to share control over these processes.

Applications of Hypnosis Hypnosis is useful in the control of pain and the reduction of nausea associated with cancer chemotherapy. Its use as a memory aid is open to serious question.

Psychoactive Drugs

Psychoactive drugs affect the brain, changing consciousness and other psychological processes. *Psychopharmacology* is the field that studies drug effects and their mechanisms.

Psychopharmacology Psychoactive drugs exert their effects primarily by influencing specific neurotransmitter systems and, hence, certain brain activities. To reach brain tissue, drugs must cross the *blood-brain barrier*. Drugs that mimic the receptor effects of a neurotransmitter are called *agonists*, and drugs that block the receptor effects of a neurotransmitter are called *antagonists*. Some drugs alter the release or removal of specific neurotransmitters, thus affecting the amount of neurotransmitter available for receptor effects.

The Varying Effects of Drugs Adverse effects such as *substance abuse* often accompany the use of psychoactive drugs. *Psychological dependence, physical dependence (addiction), tolerance,* and a *withdrawal syndrome* may result. Drugs that produce dependence share the property of directly stimulating certain areas of the brain known as pleasure centers. The consequences of using a psychoactive drug depend both on how the drug affects neurotransmitters and on the user's expectations.

Depressants Alcohol and barbiturates are examples of *depressants*. They reduce activity in the central nervous system, often by enhancing the action of inhibitory neurotransmitters. They have considerable potential for producing both psychological and physical dependence.

Stimulants *Stimulants* such as amphetamines and cocaine increase behavioral and mental activity mainly by increasing the action of dopamine and norepinephrine and decreasing GABA activity. These drugs can produce both psychological and physical dependence. Caffeine, one of the world's most popular stimulants, may also create dependency. Nicotine is a potent stimulant. MDMA is one of several psychoactive drugs that may permanently damage brain tissue.

Opiates *Opiates* such as opium, morphine, and heroin are highly addictive drugs that induce sleep and relieve pain.

Hallucinogens LSD, ketamine, and marijuana are examples of *hallucinogens*, or psychedelics. Hallucinogens alter consciousness by producing a temporary loss of contact with reality and changes in emotion, perception, and thought.

Cognitive Abilities

10

Intelligence tests are used to guide decisions about which children need special education, which job applicants should be hired, which students to admit to college, which individuals should be classified as gifted or retarded, and whether mental functioning has been impaired by head injury or disease. Intelligence tests have even been used to determine who is eligible for the death penalty. With so many important decisions being based on the results of intelligence tests, it is no wonder that there is controversy about them. In theory, these tests measure intelligence, but what does that mean? What, exactly, is "intelligence," where does it come from, and how good are the tests that are designed to measure it? These are some of the questions that we explore in this chapter on cognitive abilities. We have organized the material as follows:

Consider the following sketches of four college seniors and their varying abilities and interests. Do any of these descriptions remind you of anyone you know? Do any of them sound like you?

Jack's big-city "street smarts" were not reflected in his high school grades. After testing revealed a learning disability, Jack worked to compensate for it, graduating with a grade-point average (GPA) of 3.78; but when he took the SAT, his score was only 860 out of a then-possible 1600. He attended a local college, where he was given extra time to complete exams because of his learning disability. He held a half-time job throughout all four years, and his GPA was 2.95. When he completes his undergraduate degree, Jack will apply to master's degree programs in special education.

Deneace earned straight A's in public grade school. She attended a private high school, where she placed in the top fifth of her class and played the violin. Her SAT score was 1340, but because her school did not give letter grades, she had no grade-point average to include in college applications. Instead, she submitted teachers' evaluations and a portfolio containing papers and class projects. Deneace was accepted at several prestigious small colleges, but not at major research universities. She is enrolled in a premed program, and with a GPA of 3.60, Deneace is hoping to be accepted by a medical school.

Ruthie has a wide range of interests and many friends, loves physical activities, and can talk to anybody about almost anything. Her high school grades, however, were only fair, averaging 2.60; but she played four sports, was captain of the state champion volleyball team, and was vice president of her senior class. She scored rather poorly on the SAT but received an athletic scholarship at a large university. She majored in sociology and minored in sport psychology. Focusing on just one sport helped her achieve a 3.25 GPA. She has applied to graduate schools but has also looked into a job as a city recreation director.

George showed an early interest in computers. In high school, he earned straight A's in math, art, and shop, but his overall GPA was only 2.55, and he didn't get along with other students. Everyone was surprised when he scored 1320 on the SAT and went on to major in math and computer science at a large public university. His grades suffered at first as he began to spend time with people who shared his interests, but his GPA is now 3.33. He writes computer animation software and has applied to graduate programs in fields relating to artificial intelligence and human factors engineering.

TRY THIS ▶ Before reading further, rank these four people on **cognitive ability**—the capacity to reason, remember, understand, solve problems, and make decisions. Who came out on top? Now ask a friend to do the same, and see if your rankings match. They may not, because each of the four students is outstanding in different ways.

Deneace might score highest on general intelligence tests, which emphasize remembering, reasoning, and verbal and mathematical abilities. But would these tests measure Ruthie's social skills, Jack's street smarts, or George's computer skills and artistic abilities? If you were hiring an employee or evaluating a student, what characteristics would you want a test to measure? Can test scores be compared without considering the social and academic background of the people who took the tests? The answers to these questions are important because, as our

cognitive ability The capacity to reason, remember, understand, solve problems, and make decisions.

examples illustrate, measures of cognitive abilities often determine the educational and employment opportunities people have or don't have.

There are many kinds of cognitive abilities, but in this chapter we will focus mainly on the abilities that have come to be known as *intelligence*. We can't use x-rays or brain scans to see intelligence itself, so we have to draw conclusions about people's intelligence from what can be observed and measured (Borkenau et al., 2004). This usually means looking at scores on tests designed to measure intelligence.

Testing for Intelligence

There is no universally agreed-upon definition of *intelligence*, but Robert Sternberg (1997b) has offered one that is accepted by many psychologists. Sternberg says that **intelligence** includes three main characteristics: (1) being able to learn, remember, reason, and perform other *information-processing skills*, (2) using those skills to *solve problems*, and (3) being able to *alter or adapt to* new or changing environments. Standard tests of intelligence measure some of these characteristics, but they don't address all of them. Accordingly, some psychologists argue that these tools are not able to capture all that should be tested if we want to get a complete picture of someone's intelligence in its broadest sense. To better understand the controversy, let's take a look at how standard intelligence tests were created, what they are designed to measure, and how well they do their job. Later, we will consider some alternative intelligence tests that have been proposed by those who find fault with traditional ones.

● A Brief History of Intelligence Tests

The story of modern intelligence tests begins in France in 1904, when the French government appointed psychologist Alfred Binet (pronounced "bih-NAY") to a committee whose job was to identify, study, and provide special educational programs for children who were not doing well in school. As part of his work, Binet developed a set of test items that provided the model for today's intelligence tests. Binet assumed that reasoning, thinking, and problem solving all depend on intelligence, so he looked for tasks that would highlight differences in children's ability to do these things (Binet & Simon, 1905). His test included tasks such as unwrapping a piece of candy, repeating numbers or sentences from memory, and identifying familiar objects (Rogers, 1995).

Binet also assumed that children's abilities increase with age. With this in mind, he tried out his test items on children of various ages, and in later versions of his test, categorized each item according to the age at which the typical child could respond correctly. For example, a "six-year-old item" was one that half of six-year-olds could answer. In other words, Binet's test contained a set of *age-graded* items. It measured a child's "mental level"—later called *mental age*—by determining the age level of the most-advanced items a child could consistently answer correctly. Children whose mental age equaled their actual age, or *chronological age*, were considered to be of "regular" intelligence (Schultz & Schultz, 2004).

In 1910, Henry Goddard brought Binet's test to the United States, translated it into English, and began using it at the Vineland (New Jersey) Training School to identify children who were mentally retarded (Zenderland, 1998). Another English-language version of Binet's test was published by Lewis Terman at Stanford University. It became known as the **Stanford-Binet** (Terman, 1916). Table 10.1 gives examples of the kinds of items included on the Stanford-Binet test. Terman added items to measure the intelligence of adults and, following a formula devised by

intelligence Those attributes that center around skill at information processing, problem solving, and adapting to new or changing environments.

Stanford-Binet A test for determining a person's intelligence quotient, or IQ.

TABLE **10.1**   The Stanford-Binet

Here are samples of the types of items included on Lewis Terman's original Stanford-Binet test. As in Alfred Binet's test, an age level was assigned to each item.

Age	Task
2	Place geometric shapes into corresponding openings; identify body parts; stack blocks; identify common objects.
4	Name objects from memory; complete analogies (e.g., fire is hot; ice is _____); identify objects of similar shape; answer simple questions (e.g., "Why do we have schools?").
6	Define simple words; explain differences (e.g., between a fish and a horse); identify missing parts of a picture; count out objects.
8	Answer questions about a simple story; identify absurdities (e.g., in statements like "John had to walk on crutches because he hurt his arm"); explain similarities and differences among objects; tell how to handle certain situations (e.g., finding a stray puppy).
10	Define more difficult words; give explanations (e.g., about why people should be quiet in a library); list as many words as possible; repeat 6-digit numbers.
12	Identify more difficult verbal and pictured absurdities; repeat 5-digit numbers in reverse order; define abstract words (e.g., sorrow); fill in a missing word in a sentence.
14	Solve reasoning problems; identify relationships among points of the compass; find similarities in apparently opposite concepts (e.g., "high" and "low"); predict the number of holes that will appear when folded paper is cut and then opened.
Adult	Supply several missing words for incomplete sentences; repeat 6-digit numbers in reverse order; create a sentence using several unrelated words (e.g., *forest, business-like,* and *dismayed*); describe similarities between concepts (e.g., "teaching" and "business").

Source: Nietzel & Bernstein (1987).

William Stern (1912), revised the scoring procedure. Mental age was divided by chronological age, and the result, multiplied by 100, was called the *intelligence quotient,* or IQ. So a child whose mental age and chronological age were equal would have an IQ of 100, which is considered "average" intelligence. A ten-year-old who scored at the mental age of twelve would have an IQ of 12/10 × 100 = 120. From this method of scoring came the term **IQ test,** a name that is widely used for any test designed to measure intelligence on an objective, standardized scale.

This scoring method allowed testers to rank people on IQ, which was seen as an important advantage by Terman and others who promoted the test in the United States. Unlike Binet—who believed that intelligence improved with education and training—they saw intelligence as a fixed and inherited entity, and they believed that IQ tests could pinpoint who did and who did not have a suitable amount of intelligence. These beliefs were controversial because they were not supported by empirical evidence, and in some instances served to reinforce prejudices against certain people. In other words, enthusiasm for testing outpaced understanding of what was being tested.

Actually, controversy over intelligence testing arose even before the Stanford-Binet was published. In 1918, when the United States entered World War I, the government asked a team of psychologists to develop the first group-administered intelligence tests to assess the cognitive abilities of military recruits. One of these

IQ test   A test designed to measure intelligence on an objective, standardized scale.

Coming to America Early in the twentieth century, immigrants to the United States, including these new arrivals at Ellis Island in New York harbor, were tested for both physical and mental frailties. Especially for those who could not read, speak, or understand English, the intelligence tests they took tended to greatly underestimate their intellectual capacity. Today, psychologists recognize that cognitive abilities are developed partly through education and experience (Cronbach, 1975; Martinez, 2000) and they take much greater care in administering and interpreting intelligence tests.

tests, called the Army Alpha, presented arithmetic problems, verbal analogies (e.g., hot is to cold as high is to _____), and general knowledge questions to those recruits who could read English. The Army Beta test was developed for recruits who could not read or did not speak English; it presented nonverbal tasks, such as visualizing three-dimensional objects and solving mazes. When 47 percent of the recruits scored at a mental age of thirteen years or lower (Yerkes, 1921), one psychologist, C. C. Brigham (1923), drew the incorrect conclusions that (1) from 1890 to 1915 the mental age of immigrants to America had declined and (2) that the main source of this decline was the increase in immigration from southern and eastern Europe. These hasty conclusions were not supported by the testing data, or by other psychologists of the day, and Brigham (1930) later retracted his statements.

In the late 1930s, David Wechsler (1939, 1949) developed new tests designed to improve on the earlier ones in three key ways. First, the new tests included both verbal and nonverbal subtests. Second, the tests were constructed so that success depended less on having formal schooling. Third, each subtest was scored separately, producing a profile that described an individual's performance on all the subtests. Special versions of these tests were developed for adults (the Wechsler Adult Intelligence Scale, or WAIS) and for children (the Wechsler Intelligence Scale for Children, or WISC).

● Intelligence Tests Today

Today's editions of the Wechsler tests and the Stanford-Binet are the most widely used individually administered intelligence tests. The Wechsler Adult Intelligence Scale (WAIS-III) includes fourteen subtests. Seven of them require verbal skills and make up the **verbal scale** of the test. These subtests include such items as remembering a series of digits, solving arithmetic problems, defining vocabulary words, and understanding and answering general-knowledge questions. The other seven subtests have little or no verbal content and make up the **performance scale.** They include tasks that require understanding the relationships between objects and manipulation

● **verbal scale** Subtests in Wechsler tests that measure verbal skills as part of a measure of overall intelligence.

● **performance scale** Subtests in Wechsler tests that measure spatial ability and the ability to manipulate materials as part of a measure of overall intelligence.

FIGURE **10.1**

Performance Items Similar to Those on the Wechsler Intelligence Scale for Children (WISC-IV).

The WISC-IV includes ten standard and five supplemental subtests, grouped into four clusters. The *perceptual reasoning* cluster includes tasks, such as those shown here, that involve assembling blocks, solving mazes, and reasoning about pictures. Tests in the *verbal comprehension* cluster require defining words, explaining the meaning of sentences, and identifying similarities between words. Tests in the *working memory* cluster ask children to recall a series of numbers, put a random sequence of numbers into logical order, and the like. The *processing speed* cluster tests children's ability to search for symbols on a page and to decode simple coded messages.

Source: Simulated items similar to those used in the Wechsler Intelligence Scale for Adults and Children, Copyright © 1949, 1955, 1974, 1981, 1991, and 1997 by Harcourt Assessment, Inc. Reproduced with permission. All rights reserved.

"Wechsler" is a trademark of Harcourt Assessment, Inc. registered in the United States of America and/or other jurisdiction.

Picture completion
What part is missing from this picture?

Block design

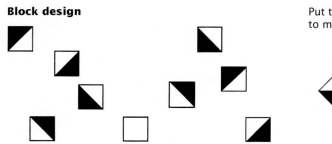

Put the blocks together to make this picture.

of various materials—tasks such as assembling blocks, solving mazes, arranging pictures to form a story, and completing unfinished pictures. Testers using the WAIS-III can compute a verbal IQ, a performance IQ, and an overall IQ, as well as scores that reflect a person's mental processing speed, memory ability, perceptual skills, and understanding of verbal information. The latest edition of the Wechsler Intelligence Scale for Children (WISC-IV; Wechsler, 2003) yields four similar index scores, along with an overall IQ score (see Figure 10.1).

Like the WISC-IV, the new fifth edition of the Stanford-Binet (SB5; Roid, 2003) also consists of ten main subtests. However, the SB5 subtests are designed to measure five different abilities: *fluid reasoning* (e.g., completing verbal analogies), *knowledge* (e.g., defining words, detecting absurdities in pictures),

Taking a New Intelligence Test
New intelligence tests are always being developed to measure newly identified aspects of cognitive abilities (Carroll, 1993). This child is taking the Woodcock-Johnson Tests of Cognitive Abilities, developed in 1997 and currently in its third edition (WJ-III; Woodcock, McGrew, & Mather, 2001). The WJ-III measures eight abilities that are somewhat more specific than those assessed by the Stanford-Binet and Wechsler tests. These eight abilities include fluid reasoning, verbal comprehension and knowledge, quantitative ability, visual-spatial thinking, short-term memory, retrieval from long-term memory, processing of auditory information, and mental processing speed. Testing results in an overall ability score, as well as a profile of scores on these eight abilities.

FIGURE 10.2

The Normal Distribution of IQ Scores in a Population

When the IQ scores in the overall population are plotted on a graph, a bell-shaped curve appears. The average IQ score of any given age group is 100. Half of the scores are higher than 100, and half are lower than 100. Approximately 68 percent of the IQ scores of any age group fall between 84 and 116; about 16 percent fall below 84, and about 16 percent fall above 116.

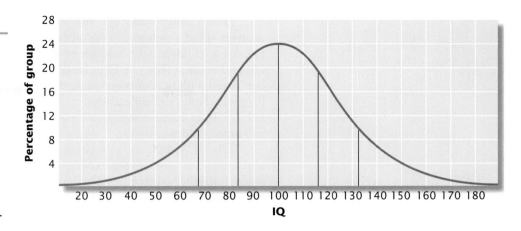

quantitative reasoning (e.g., solving math problems), *visual-spatial processing* (e.g., assembling a puzzle), and *working memory* (e.g., repeating a sentence). Each of these five abilities is measured by one verbal and one nonverbal subtest, so it is possible to calculate a score for each of the five abilities, a total score on all the verbal tests, a total score on all the nonverbal tests, and an overall score for all ten tests combined.

IQ scores are no longer calculated by dividing mental age by chronological age. If you take an IQ test today, the points you earn for each correct answer are added up. That total score is then compared with the scores earned by other people. The average score obtained by people at each age level is assigned the IQ value of 100. Other scores are given IQ values that reflect how far each score deviates from that average. If you do better on the test than the average person in your age group, you will receive an IQ score above 100; how far above depends on how much better than average you do. Similarly, a person scoring below the age-group average will have an IQ below 100. This procedure is based on a well-documented assumption about many characteristics: Most people's scores fall in the middle of the range of possible scores, creating a bell-shaped curve that approximates the normal distribution shown in Figure 10.2. (The statistics appendix provides a fuller explanation of the normal distribution and how IQ tests are scored.) As a result of this scoring method, your **intelligence quotient,** or **IQ score,** reflects your *relative* standing within a population of your age.

● Aptitude and Achievement Tests

Closely related to intelligence tests are aptitude and achievement tests. **Aptitude tests** are designed to measure a person's readiness to learn certain things or perform certain tasks (Corno et al., 2002). Although such tests may contain questions about what you already know, their ultimate goal is to assess your *potential* to learn or to perform well in some future situation. Performing well in college or graduate school, for example, requires well-developed reading and mathematics skills, among other things. The SAT (originally called the *Scholastic Aptitude Test*), the *American College Testing Assessment (ACT),* and the verbal and quantitative components of the *Graduate Record Examination (GRE)* are the aptitude tests most commonly used by colleges and universities in the United States to help guide decisions about which applicants to admit (e.g., Kuncel, Hezlett, & Ones, 2001; Powers, 2004). Corporations also use aptitude tests as part of their employee selection processes. These tests usually involve brief assessments of cognitive abilities; examples include the Otis-Lennon Mental Abilities Test and the Wonderlic Personnel Test (Aiken, 1994). Corporations may also use the General Aptitude Test Battery (GATB) to assess both general and specific skills ranging from learning ability and verbal aptitude to motor coordination and finger dexterity at computer or clerical tasks.

● **intelligence quotient** An index of intelligence that reflects the degree to which a person's score on an intelligence test deviates from the average score of others in the same age group.

● **aptitude test** A test designed to measure a person's capacity to learn certain things or perform certain tasks.

Schools and employers also commonly administer **achievement tests,** which measure what a person has accomplished or learned in a particular area. For example, schoolchildren are tested on what they have learned about language, mathematics, and reading (Linn & Gronlund, 2000). Their performance on these tests is then compared with that of other students in the same grade to evaluate their educational progress. Similarly, college students' scores on the Graduate Record Examination's Subject Tests assess how much they have learned about the field in which they wish to pursue graduate work.

Tests of intelligence, aptitude, and achievement measure related cognitive abilities, so as you might expect, their results are likely to be related, too. One study found a positive correlation between SAT scores and scores on various IQ tests that was almost as high as the correlation among the IQ tests themselves (Frey & Detterman, 2004). In another study, scores on IQ tests were shown to be excellent predictors of British students' scores on national achievement tests (Deary et al., 2007).

Measuring the Quality of Tests

LINKAGES (a link to Personality, p. 581)

What does your IQ or SAT score say about you? Can it predict your performance in school or on the job? Is it a fair summary of your mental abilities? To scientifically answer questions like these, we have to measure the quality of the tests that yield these scores, using the same criteria that apply to tests of personality, language skills, driving, or anything else. Let's review these criteria and then see how they are used to evaluate IQ tests.

A **test** is a systematic procedure for observing behavior in a standard situation and describing it with the help of a numerical scale or a system of categories (Cronbach, 1990). Tests have two major advantages over interviews and other means of evaluating people. First, they are *standardized*; that is, conditions surrounding a test are as similar as possible for everyone who takes it. Standardization helps ensure, for example, that test results will not be significantly affected by who gives and scores the test. Because the biases of those giving or scoring the test do not influence the results, a standardized test is said to be *objective*. Second, tests summarize the test taker's performance with a specific number, known as a *score*. Scores, in turn, allow the calculation of **norms,** which describe the frequency of particular scores. Norms tell us, for example, what percentage of high school students obtained each possible score on a college entrance exam. They also allow us to say whether a person's overall test performance was above or below average and whether that person is particularly strong or weak in certain skill areas, such as verbal reasoning or mathematics.

Any test, including IQ tests, should fairly and accurately measure a person's performance. The two most important things to know about when determining the value of a test are its reliability and validity.

● Reliability

If you stepped on a scale, checked your weight, stepped off, stepped back on, and found that your weight had increased by twenty pounds, you would know it was time to buy a new scale. A good scale, like a good test, must have **reliability;** in other words, the results must be repeatable or stable. Suppose you received a very high score on a reasoning test the first time you took it but a very low score when the test was repeated the next day. Your reasoning ability probably didn't change much overnight, so the test is probably unreliable. The higher the reliability of a test, the less likely it is that its scores will be affected by temperature, hunger, or other irrelevant changes in the environment or the test taker.

● **achievement test** A measure of what a person has accomplished or learned in a particular area.

● **test** A systematic procedure for observing behavior in a standard situation and describing it with the help of a numerical scale or a category system.

● **norm** A description of the frequency at which particular scores occur, allowing scores to be compared statistically.

● **reliability** The degree to which a test can be repeated with the same results.

To estimate the reliability of a test, researchers usually get two sets of scores on the same test from the same people and then compute a *correlation coefficient* between the two (see the chapter on research in psychology and the statistics appendix). If the correlation is high and positive (usually above +.80 or so), the test is considered reliable. The two sets of scores can be obtained in several ways. In the *test-retest* method, a group of people take the same test twice. This method is based on the assumption that whatever is being measured will not change much between the two testing sessions. If you practiced on your keyboard before taking a second test of typing skill, your second score would be higher than the first, but not because the test was unreliable. Using an *alternate form* of the test at the second testing can reduce this practice effect, but great care must be taken to ensure that the tasks on the second test are similar to those on the first. The most common method of assessing reliability is the *split-half* method, in which a correlation coefficient is calculated between each person's scores on two comparable halves of the test (Thorndike & Dinnel, 2001). To be on the safe side, some researchers employ more than one of these methods to check the reliability of their tests.

● Validity

Most scales reliably measure your weight, giving you about the same reading day after day. But what if you use these readings as a measure of your height? This far-fetched example illustrates that a reliable scale reading can be incorrect, or *invalid*, if it is misinterpreted. The same is true of tests. Even the most reliable test might not provide a correct, or valid, measure of intelligence, of anxiety, of typing skill, or of anything else if those are not the things the test really measures. In other words, we can't say that a test itself is "valid" or "invalid." Instead, **validity** refers to the degree to which test scores are interpreted appropriately and used properly (American Educational Research Association, American Psychological Association, and National Council on Measurement in Education, 1999; Messick, 1989). As in our scale example, a test can be valid for one purpose but invalid for another.

To further illustrate this point, suppose you are teaching English to native Spanish speakers who are studying for their U.S. citizenship test. On the first day of class, you give your students a test of their ability to understand a magazine article written in English and find that their scores are quite low. Was the test valid? The answer depends on how you interpret its results. The scores are probably a valid measure of your students' ability to understand written English, but probably not a valid measure of their verbal intelligence. If you had given the test using an article written in Spanish, the resulting scores would have been a valid indicator of verbal intelligence, but not a valid measure of English comprehension.

Evidence about the validity of test scores can be gathered in several ways. For example, we can look at *content validity*, the degree to which the content of a test is a fair and representative sample of what the test is supposed to measure. If an instructor spends only five minutes out of forty lectures discussing the mating behavior of the tree frog and then devotes half of the final exam to this topic, that exam would be low on content validity. It would not allow us to draw accurate conclusions about what students learned in the course as a whole. Similarly, a test that measures only math skills would not have acceptable content validity as an intelligence test. A content-valid test includes items relating to the entire area of interest, not just a narrow slice of it (Linn & Gronlund, 2000).

Another way to evaluate validity is to determine how well test scores correlate with an independent measure of whatever the test is supposed to assess. This independent measure is called a *criterion*. For example, a test of eye-hand coordination would have high *criterion validity* for hiring diamond cutters if scores on the test correlated highly with a test of actual skill at diamond cutting. Why give a test if there is an independent criterion we can measure? The reasons often relate to convenience and cost. It would be silly to hire all applicants for airport security

validity The degree to which test scores are interpreted correctly and used appropriately.

jobs and then fire those who are unskilled if a twenty-minute performance test could identify the best candidates. Criterion validity is called *predictive validity* when test scores are correlated with a criterion that cannot be measured until some time in the future—such as success in a pilot training program or grade-point average at graduation.

We can also look at *construct validity* (pronounced "CON-struct"), the extent to which scores suggest that a test is actually measuring the theoretical construct, such as anxiety, that it claims to measure (Messick, 1989). Suppose you are developing a test of anxiety, and you know that various theories predict that anxiety occurs when people are uncertain about the future. With these theories in mind, you would expect that people waiting for the results of an important medical test should score higher on your anxiety test than those who know they are healthy. If this is not the case, then scores on your test would have low construct validity, at least with regard to most theories of anxiety.

Evaluating Intelligence Tests

Criteria for assessing the reliability and validity of tests have been incorporated into the testing standards established by the American Psychological Association and other organizations (American Educational Research Association et al., 1999). These standards are designed to maintain quality in educational and psychological testing by providing guidelines for the administration, interpretation, and application of tests in such areas as therapy, education, employment, certification or licensing, and program evaluation (Turner et al., 2001). The standards tell us that in evaluating intelligence tests, we must take into account not only the reliability and validity of test scores but also a number of sociocultural factors that might influence those scores.

● The Reliability and Validity of Intelligence Tests

Intelligence tests are generally evaluated on the basis of the stability, or consistency, of IQ scores (reliability) and on their accuracy in guiding statements and predictions about people's cognitive abilities (validity).

● **How Reliable Are Intelligence Tests?**   IQ scores obtained before the age of seven typically correlate only moderately (+.30 to +.60) with scores on intelligence tests given later (Fagan & Detterman, 1992; Fagan, Holland, & Wheeler, 2007; Rose & Feldman; 1995). There are two key reasons that this should be so. First, test items used with very young children are different from those used with older children. Second, in the early years, cognitive abilities change rapidly and at different rates for different children (see the chapter on human development). During the school years, however, IQ scores tend to remain more stable (Mayer & Sutton, 1996). For teenagers and adults, the stability of IQ scores is high, generally between +.85 and +.95. In one study (Deary et al., 2000), the same people took the same intelligence test at age eleven and again at age seventy-seven; the correlation between the two sets of scores was +.73.

Of course, a person's score may vary from one time to another if testing conditions, motivation or anxiety, health status, or other factors change. Scores will also vary across different intelligence tests because each presents a somewhat different collection of items. So a child's scores on the WISC-IV and the SB5 would probably differ somewhat. Accordingly, testers do not usually make decisions about a person's abilities on the basis of a single IQ score. Overall, though, modern intelligence tests usually provide exceptionally consistent results—especially compared with most other kinds of mental tests.

If only measuring intelligence were this easy!

IQ and Job Performance IQ scores are reasonably good at predicting the ability to learn job-relevant information and to deal with unpredictable, changing aspects of the work environment—characteristics that are needed for success in complex jobs such as the ones these navy navigator trainees will undertake.

● **How Valid Are Intelligence Tests?** Intelligence test scores appear to be most valid for assessing aspects of intelligence that are related to schoolwork, such as abstract reasoning and verbal comprehension. The validity of individually administered tests—as measured by correlating IQ scores with high school grades—is reasonably good, about +.50 (Brody & Ehrlichman, 1998). Scores on the Cognitive Abilities Test (Lohman & Hagen, 2001a) and other group-administered tests that focus more specifically on reasoning skills show even higher correlations with school performance (Kuncel, Hezlett, & Ones, 2004). And correlations between intelligence test scores and the level of education that people achieve range from +.60 to +.80 (e.g., Colom & Flores-Mendoza, 2007; Lynn & Mikk, 2007).

There is also evidence that employees who score high on tests of verbal and mathematical reasoning tend to perform better on the job (and are paid more) than those who earned lower scores (Borman, Hanson, & Hedge, 1997; Johnson & Neal, 1998). Later, we describe a study that kept track of people for sixty years and found that children with high IQ scores tended to be well above average in terms of academic and financial success in adulthood (Cronbach, 1996; Oden, 1968; Terman & Oden, 1947). IQ scores also appear to be highly correlated with performance on "real-life" tasks such as reading medicine labels and using the telephone book (Gottfredson, 1997, 2004). So, by the standard measures for judging psychological tests, scores on intelligence tests have good reliability and reasonably good validity for predicting success in school and in many occupations (Schmidt & Hunter, 2004). Indeed, few psychological tests of any kind show better reliability or validity.

● **How Fair Are IQ Tests?** As noted earlier, though, an IQ score is not a perfect measure of how "smart" a person is. Because intelligence tests do not measure the full array of cognitive abilities, a particular test score tells only part of the story, and even that part may be distorted. Those who administer intelligence tests must remember that many factors other than cognitive ability—including one's response to the tester—can influence test performance on a particular day. Children might not do as well if they are suspicious of strangers, for example (Jones & Appelbaum, 1989). And if older adults worry about making mistakes in unfamiliar situations, they may fail to even try to answer some questions, thus artificially lowering their IQ scores.

Test scores can also be affected by anxiety, physical disabilities, and language differences and other cultural barriers (Fagan, 2000; Steele, 1997). As already mentioned, early efforts at intelligence testing in the United States probably underestimated the abilities of people who were unfamiliar with English or with the vocabulary and experiences associated mainly with middle-class culture at the time. For example, consider the question "Which is most similar to a xylophone? (violin, tuba, drum, marimba, piano)." No matter how intelligent children are, if they have never had a chance to see an orchestra or to learn about these instruments, they may miss this question. Accordingly, test designers have developed sophisticated procedures to detect and eliminate obviously biased questions (American Educational Research Association et al., 1999; Serpell, 2000). Furthermore, because intelligence tests now include more than one scale, areas that are most influenced by culture, such as vocabulary, can be assessed separately from areas that are less influenced by cultural factors.

The solutions to many of the technical problems in intelligence tests, however, have not resolved the controversy over the fairness of intelligence *testing*. The debate continues partly because results of intelligence tests can have important consequences. Some students who score well above average on these tests may receive advanced educational opportunities that set them on the road to further high achievement. Those whose relatively low test scores identify them as having special educational needs may find themselves in separate classes that isolate them from other students and carry negative social labels. Obviously, the social consequences of testing can be evaluated separately from the quality of the tests themselves; but those consequences cannot be ignored, especially if they tend to affect some groups more than others.

LINKAGES Emotionality and the Measurement of Cognitive Abilities

LINKAGES (a link to Motivation and Emotion, p. 409)

Emotional arousal is one of the most important noncognitive factors that can potentially influence scores on cognitive ability tests. As described in the chapter on motivation and emotion, people tend to perform best when their arousal level is moderate. Too much arousal, or even too little, tends to result in decreased performance. People whose overarousal impairs their ability to do well in testing situations are said to suffer from *test anxiety*.

These people fear that they will do poorly on the test and that others will think they are "stupid." In a testing situation, they may experience physical symptoms such as heart palpitations and sweating, as well as negative thoughts such as "I am going to blow this exam" (Chapell et al., 2005). In the most severe cases of test anxiety, individuals may be so distressed that they are unable to successfully complete the test.

Test anxiety may affect up to 40 percent of elementary school students and about the same percentage of college students. It afflicts boys and girls equally (Turner et al., 1993). High test anxiety is correlated with lower IQ scores, and even among people with high IQ scores, those who experience severe test anxiety tend to do poorly on tests such as the SAT. Test-anxious elementary school students are likely to receive low grades and to perform poorly on evaluated tasks and on those that require new learning (Campbell, 1986). Some children with test anxiety refuse to attend school, or they "play sick" on test days, creating a vicious circle that further harms their performance on standardized achievement tests.

Anxiety, frustration, and other emotions may also be at work in a testing phenomenon that Claude Steele and his colleagues have identified as *stereotype threat* (Steele & Aronson, 2000). In one study, bright African American students read test

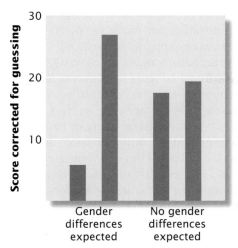

FIGURE 10.3

The Stereotype Threat Effect

In this experiment, male and female college students took a difficult math test. Beforehand, some of the students were told that men usually outscore women on such tests. Women who heard this gender-stereotype information scored lower than those who did not hear it; they also scored lower than the men, even though their mathematical ability was equal to that of the men. Men's scores were not significantly affected by gender-stereotype information (Spencer, Steele, & Quinn, 1997). The stereotype threat effect has been found to be especially strong when women are told that gender differences in math ability are based on genetic causes (Dar-Nimrod & Heine, 2006).

instructions that made them more sensitive to negative stereotypes about the intelligence of their ethnic group. These students performed less well on a standardized test than equally bright African American students whose sensitivity to the stereotypes had not been increased (Steele & Aronson, 2000). In another study, women with good math skills were randomly assigned to one of two groups. The first group was given information that created concern over the stereotype that women aren't as good as men at math. In fact, they were told that men usually do better than women on the difficult math test they were about to take. The second group was not given this information. As shown in Figure 10.3, the women in the second group performed much better on the test than did those in the first. In fact, their performance was equal to that of men who took the same test (Spencer, Steele, & Quinn, 1997). According to Steele, concern over negative stereotypes about the cognitive abilities of the group to which they belong can impair the performance of some women—and some members of ethnic minorities—such that the test scores they earn underestimate their cognitive abilities (Blascovich et al., 2001; Cadinu et al., 2005; Inzlicht & Ben-Zeev, 2000). The extent to which stereotype threat affects performance on the SAT and other abilities tests is uncertain, however (Cullen, Hardison, & Sackett, 2004; Sackett, Hardison, & Cullen, 2004).

The good news for people who suffer from test anxiety is that the counseling centers at most colleges and universities have effective programs for dealing with it. Test anxiety can be remedied through some of the same procedures used to treat other anxiety disorders (see the chapter on treatment of psychological disorders). There is also reason to be cautiously optimistic about reducing the impact of the stereotype threat phenomenon on the academic performance of African Americans and other minority groups. A program at the University of Michigan that directly addresses this phenomenon has produced substantial improvements in the grades of first-year minority students (Cohen & Steele, 2002; Steele, 1997).

These and other research findings indicate that the relationship between anxiety and test performance is a complex one, but one generalization seems to hold true: People who are severely test anxious do not perform to the best of their ability on intelligence tests. ■

● IQ Scores as a Measure of Innate Ability

Concern over the fairness of intelligence tests is based partly on the assumption that a good intelligence test should be able to see through the surface ripples created by an individual's cultural background, experience, and motivation to discover the innate cognitive abilities that lie beneath. Many researchers who study human intelligence argue that this is an impossible task for any test (Cronbach, 1990; Lohman, 1989). Years of research have led them to conclude that intelligence is *developed ability*, influenced partly by genetics but also by educational, cultural, and other life experiences that shape the very knowledge, reasoning, and other skills that intelligence tests measure (Atran, Medin, & Ross, 2005; Garlick, 2003; Plomin & Spinath, 2004). For example, by asking lots of questions, bright children help generate an enriching environment for themselves; thus innate abilities allow people to take better advantage of their environment (Scarr, 1997; Scarr & Carter-Saltzman, 1982). In addition, if their own biologically influenced intelligence allows bright parents to give their children an environment that helps the development of intelligence, their children are favored by both heredity and environment.

Psychologists have explored the influence of genetics on individual differences in intelligence by comparing the correlation between the IQ scores of people who have differing degrees of similarity in their genetic makeup and environment. For example, they have examined the IQ scores of identical twins—pairs with exactly the same genes—who were separated when very young and raised in different environments. They have also examined the scores of identical twins raised together.

(You may want to review the Linkages section of the chapter on research in psychology, as well as the behavioral genetics appendix, for more on the research designs typically used to analyze hereditary and environmental influences.)

These studies find, first, that hereditary factors are strongly related to IQ scores. When identical twins who were separated at birth and adopted by different families are tested many years later, the correlation between their scores is usually high and positive, at least +.60 (e.g., Bouchard & Pedersen, 1999). If one twin receives a high IQ score, the other probably will, too; if one is low, the other is likely to be low as well. However, studies of IQ correlations also highlight the importance of the environment (Scarr, 1998). Consider any two people—twins, siblings, or unrelated children—brought up together in a foster home. No matter what the degree of genetic similarity in these pairs, the correlation between their IQ scores is higher if they share the same home than if they are raised in different environments, as Figure 10.4 shows (Scarr & Carter-Saltzman, 1982).

The role of environmental influences is also seen in the results of studies that compare children's IQ scores before and after environmental changes such as adoption (van IJzendoom & Juffer, 2005). Generally, when children from relatively impoverished backgrounds were adopted into homes offering a more enriching intellectual environment—including interesting materials and experiences, as well as a supportive, responsive adult—they showed modest increases in IQ scores (Weinberg, Scarr, & Waldman, 1992).

A study of French children who were adopted soon after birth demonstrates the importance of both genetic and environmental influences. These children were tested after years of living in their adopted homes. Children whose biological parents were from upper socioeconomic groups (in which higher IQ scores are more common) had higher IQ scores than children whose biological parents came from lower socioeconomic groups, regardless of the socioeconomic status of the adoptive homes (Capron & Duyme, 1989, 1996). These findings were supported by data from the Colorado Adoption Project (Cardon & Fulker, 1993; Cardon et al., 1992), and they suggest that a genetic component of children's cognitive abilities continues to exert an influence even in their adoptive environment. At the same time, when children from low socioeconomic backgrounds were adopted by parents who provided academically enriched environments, their IQ scores rose by twelve to fifteen points (Capron & Duyme, 1989). As described later, exposure to early intervention programs that improve school readiness and academic ability also tends to improve children's scores on tests of intelligence (Neisser et al., 1996; Ripple et al., 1999). Negative effects on cognitive abilities have been associated

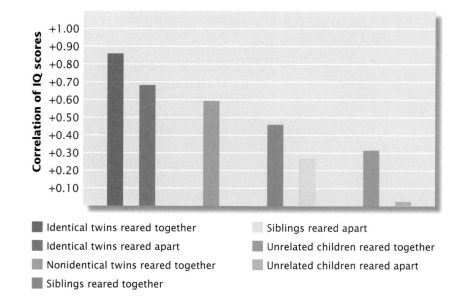

FIGURE 10.4

Correlations of IQ Scores

The correlation in IQ between pairs increases with increasing similarity in heredity or environment.

Source: Reprinted with permission from "Familial Studies of Intelligence: A Review," T. Bouchard et al., *Science,* Vol. 212, #4498, pp. 1055–9, 29 May 1981. Copyright © 1981 American Association for the Advancement of Science.

Research on genetic and environmental influences can help us understand the differences we see *among* people in terms of cognitive abilities and other characteristics, but it cannot tell us how strong each influence is in any *particular* person, including in this person.

with factors such as poverty, poor nutrition, exposure to lead or alcohol, low birth weight, and complications during birth (Matte et al., 2001; Strathearn et al., 2001). Indeed, it has been suggested that living in an impoverished environment does more to impair the development of cognitive skills than living in an enriched environment does to enhance that development (Turkheimer et al., 2003).

Some researchers have concluded that the influence of heredity and environment on differences in cognitive abilities appears to be about equal. Others see a somewhat larger role for heredity (Herrnstein & Murray, 1994; Loehlin, 1989; Petrill et al., 1998; Plomin, 1994), and they are working to identify specific groups of genes that might be associated with variations in cognitive abilities (Posthuma & de Geus, 2006). It is important to understand, though, that estimates of the relative contributions of heredity and environment apply only to groups, not to individuals. It would be inaccurate to say that 50 percent of your IQ score is inherited and 50 percent learned. It is far more accurate to say that about half of the *variability* in the IQ scores of a group of people can be attributed to hereditary influences and about half can be attributed to environmental influences.

Intelligence provides yet another example of nature and nurture working together to shape human behavior and mental processes. It also illustrates how the relative contributions of genetic and environmental influences can change over time. Environmental influences, for example, seem to be greater at younger ages (Plomin, 1994; Plomin & Spinath, 2004) and tend to diminish over the years. So IQ differences in a group of children will probably be affected more by parental help with preschool reading than by, say, the courses they take in junior high school ten years later.

▣ ● Group Differences in IQ Scores

Much of the controversy over the roles played by genes and the environment in intelligence has been sparked by efforts to explain differences in the average IQ scores earned by particular groups of people. For example, the average scores of Asian Americans are typically the highest among various ethnic groups in the United States, followed, in order, by European Americans, Hispanic Americans, and African Americans (e.g., Fagan, 2000; Herrnstein & Murray, 1994; Lynn, 2006; Taylor & Richards, 1991). Similar patterns appear on a number of other tests of cognitive ability and achievement (e.g., Bobko, Roth, & Potosky, 1999; Jencks & Phillips, 1998; Koretz, Lynch, & Lynch, 2000; Sackett et al., 2001). Further, the average IQ scores of people from high-income areas in the United States and elsewhere are consistently higher than those of people from low-income communities with the same ethnic makeup (Jordan, Huttenlocher, & Levine, 1992; McLoyd, 1998; Rowe, Jacobson, & Van den Oord, 1999).

To understand these differences and where they come from, we must remember two things. First, group scores are just that; they do not describe individuals. Although the mean IQ score of Asian Americans is higher than the mean score of European Americans, there will still be large numbers of European Americans who score well above the Asian American mean and large numbers of Asian Americans who score below the European American mean (see Figure 10.5).

Second, increases in average IQ scores in recent decades, and other similar findings, suggest that inherited characteristics are not necessarily fixed. A favorable environment can improve a child's performance somewhat, even if the inherited influences on that child's IQ are negative (Humphreys, 1984). There is also evidence that living in an impoverished environment can impair the development of cognitive skills (Turkheimer et al., 2003).

● **Socioeconomic Differences** Why is there a relationship between IQ scores and socioeconomic status? Four factors seem to be involved. First, parents' jobs and status depend on characteristics related to their own intelligence. This intelligence is

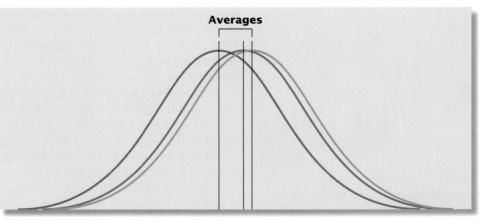

FIGURE **10.5**

A Representation of Ethnic Group Differences in IQ Scores

The average IQ score of Asian Americans is about four to six points higher than the average score of European Americans, who average twelve to fifteen points higher than African Americans and Hispanic Americans. Notice, though, that there is much more variation *within* these groups than there is *among* their average scores.

partly determined by a genetic component that, in turn, contributes to their children's IQ scores. Second, parents' income affects their children's environment in ways that can increase or decrease IQ scores (Bacharach & Baumeister, 1998; Suzuki & Valencia, 1997). Third, motivational differences may play a role. Parents in upper- and middle-income families tend to provide more financial and psychological support for their children's motivation to succeed and excel in academic endeavors (Atkinson & Raynor, 1974; Erikson et al., 2005; Nelson-LeGall & Resnick, 1998). As a result, children from middle- and upper-income families may exert more effort in testing situations and therefore obtain higher scores (Bradley-Johnson, Graham, & Johnson, 1986; Robbins et al., 2004; Zigler & Seitz, 1982). Fourth, because colleges, universities, and businesses usually select people who score high on various cognitive ability tests, those with higher IQs—who tend to do better on such tests—may have greater opportunities to earn more money (Sackett et al., 2001).

● **Ethnic Differences** Some have argued that the average differences in IQ scores among ethnic groups in the United States are due at least partly to heredity (Rowe, 2005; Rushton & Jensen, 2005). Remember, though, that the existence of hereditary differences among individuals *within* groups does not indicate whether differences *between* groups result from similar genetic causes (Lewontin, 1976). As shown in Figure 10.5, variation within ethnic groups is much greater than variation among the mean scores of those groups (Zuckerman, 1990).

We must also take into account the significantly different environments in which average children in various ethnic groups grow up. To take only the most blatant evidence, U.S. Census Bureau figures show 24.9 percent of African American families and 21.8 percent of Hispanic American families living below the poverty level, compared with 10.9 percent of Asian American families and 7.8 percent of European American families. Among children under age eighteen, the figures show about 14.4 percent of European Americans, 33.5 percent of African Americans, 10.3 percent of Asian Americans, and about 28.3 percent of Hispanic Americans living below the poverty line (U.S. Census Bureau, 2006). Compared with European Americans, African Americans are more likely to have parents with poor educational backgrounds, as well as inferior nutrition, health care, and schools (Evans, 2004; Wilson, 1997). All of these conditions are likely to pull down scores on IQ tests (Brooks-Gunn, Klebanov, & Duncan, 1996).

Evidence for the influence of environmental factors on the average black-white difference in IQ scores is supported by data from adoption studies. One such study involved African American children from disadvantaged homes who were adopted by middle- to upper-class European American families in the first years of their lives (Scarr & Weinberg, 1976). When measured a few years later, the mean IQ score of these children was 110. A comparison of this mean score with that of nonadopted children from similar backgrounds suggests that the new environment raised the children's IQ scores at least ten points. A ten-year follow-up study of these youngsters showed that their average IQ scores were still higher than the average scores of African American children raised in disadvantaged homes (Weinberg et al., 1992).

As discussed in the chapter on human development, cultural factors may also contribute to differences among the mean scores of various ethnic groups. For example, those means may partly reflect differences in the value that is placed on academic achievement. In one study of 15,000 African American, Asian American, Hispanic American, and European American high school students, parental and peer influences related to achievement tended to vary by ethnic group (Steinberg, Dornbusch, & Brown, 1992). The Asian American students received strong support for academic pursuits from both their parents and their peers. European American students whose parents expected high academic achievement tended to associate with peers who also encouraged achievement, and they tended to do better academically than African American and Hispanic American students. The parents of the African American students in the study supported academic achievement, but because these students' peers often did not, the students may have been less motivated, and their performance may have suffered. The performance of the Hispanic American students may have suffered because, in this study at least, they were more likely than the others to have authoritarian parents, whose emphasis on obedience (see the chapter on human development) may have created conflicts with the schools' emphasis on independent learning.

In short, it appears that some important nongenetic factors decrease the mean scores of African American and Hispanic American children. Whatever heredity might contribute to children's performance, it may be possible for them to improve greatly, given the right conditions.

Helping with Homework   There are differences in the average IQ scores of European Americans and African Americans, but these differences appear due in large measure to a number of environmental, social, and other nongenetic factors.

● Conditions That Can Raise IQ Scores

A number of environmental conditions can help or deter cognitive development (see the chapter on human development). For example, lack of caring attention or of normal intellectual stimulation can inhibit a child's mental growth. Low test scores have been linked to poverty, chaos, and noise in the home; poor schools; and inadequate nutrition and health care (Alaimo, Olson, & Frongillo, 2001; Kwate, 2001; Weinberg, 1989). Can the effects of bad environments be reversed? Not always, but efforts to intervene in the lives of children and enrich their environments have had some limited success. Conditions for improving children's performance include rewards for progress, encouragement of effort, and creation of expectations for success.

In the United States, the best-known attempt to enrich children's environments is Project Head Start, a set of programs established by the federal government in the 1960s to help preschoolers from lower-income backgrounds. In some of these programs, teachers visit the home and work with the child and parents on cognitive skills. In others, the children attend classes in nursery schools. Some programs emphasize health and nutrition and family mental health and social skills as well. Head Start has brought measurable benefits to children's health, as well as improvements in their academic and intellectual skills (Barnett, 1998; Lee, Brooks-Gunn, & Schnur, 1988; Ramey, 1999).

Do the gains achieved by preschool enrichment programs last? Although program developers sometimes claim long-term benefits (Schweinhart & Weikart, 1991), these claims are disputed (Spitz, 1991). Various findings from more than a thousand such programs are often contradictory, but the effect on IQ scores typically diminishes after a year or two (Woodhead, 1988). A study evaluating two of the better preschool programs concluded that their effects are at best only temporary (Locurto, 1991). These fading effects reflect the fact that IQ scores describe a person's performance compared with others of the same age. To keep the same IQ score, a child must keep improving at the same rate as other children in the same age group (Kanaya, Scullin, & Ceci, 2003). So IQ scores will drop from year to year in children whose rate of cognitive growth falls behind that of their age-mates. This slowing in the cognitive growth rate is often seen when children leave special preschool programs and enter the substandard schools that often serve the poor (Finn-Stevenson & Zigler, 1999; Zigler & Muenchow, 1992; Zigler & Seitz, 1982).

Fading effects have also been seen in programs such as the Abecedarian Project (Ramey, 1992). Children at risk for mental retardation were identified while they were still in the womb. They then received five years of intense interventions to improve their chances of success once they entered school. When they started school, children in this enrichment program had IQ scores that were seven points higher than the scores of at-risk children who were not in the program. At age twelve, they still scored higher on IQ tests, but the size of the difference at that time was just five points. This difference was still evident nearly a decade later, when the participants were assessed at the age of twenty-one (Campbell et al., 2001).

Martin Woodhead (1988) concluded that the primary benefit of early-enrichment programs probably lies in improving children's attitudes toward school. This can be an important benefit because, especially in borderline cases, children with favorable attitudes toward school may be less likely to be held back or placed in special-education classes. Avoiding these experiences may, in turn, help children to retain positive attitudes about school and enter a cycle in which gains due to early enrichment are maintained and amplified on a long-term basis.

● IQ Scores in the Classroom

IQ scores do not provide a crystal ball that can predict a person's destiny, nor are they a measure of some fixed amount of cognitive ability. But might they affect how

Project Head Start This teacher is working in Project Head Start, a U.S. government program designed to enrich the academic environments of preschoolers from lower-income backgrounds and improve their chances of succeeding in grade school.

people are treated and how they behave? Decades ago, Robert Rosenthal and Lenore Jacobson (1968) argued that labels placed on students create teacher expectancies that can become self-fulfilling prophecies. They made this claim on the basis of a study in which they gave grade school teachers the names of students who were about to enter a "blooming" period of rapid academic growth. These students had supposedly scored high on a special test, but the researchers had actually selected the "bloomers" at random. Nevertheless, the IQ scores of two-thirds of the bloomers dramatically increased during the following year. Only one-quarter of the other children showed the same increase. Apparently, the teachers' expectancies about certain children influenced those children in ways that showed up on IQ tests.

Several attempts to replicate these findings have failed, and researchers who reanalyzed the data concluded that they did not support Rosenthal and Jacobson's claims (Elashoff, 1979; Fielder, Cohen, & Feeney, 1971; Thorndike, 1968). Others have found that the effect of teacher expectancies may be statistically significant but that it is relatively small (Jussim, 1989; Snow, 1995). Still, there is little doubt that IQ-based teacher expectancies can have an effect on teachers' interactions with students (Rosenthal, 1994). To find out how, Alan Chaiken and his colleagues (Chaiken, Sigler, & Derlega, 1974) videotaped teacher-child interactions in a classroom in which teachers had been informed (falsely) that certain pupils were particularly bright. They found that the teachers tended to favor the supposedly brighter students—smiling at them more often than at other students, making more eye contact, and reacting more positively to their comments. Children receiving this extra social reinforcement not only get more intense teaching but are also more likely to enjoy school, to have their mistakes corrected, and to continue trying to improve. Later research found that teachers provide a wider range of classroom activities for students for whom they have higher expectations, suggesting another way in which expectancies might influence students' academic achievement and, indirectly, their IQ scores (Blatchford et al., 1989).

These results suggest that the "rich get richer." Those perceived to be blessed with better cognitive abilities are given better opportunities to improve those abilities. There may also be a "poor get poorer" effect. Some studies have found that

in review · Influences on IQ Scores

Source of Effect	Description	Examples of Evidence for Effect
Genetics	Genes appear to play a significant role in differences among people on intelligence test performance.	The IQ scores of siblings who share no common environment are positively correlated. There is a greater correlation between scores of identical twins than between those of nonidentical twins.
Environment	Environmental conditions interact with genetic inheritance. Nutrition, medical care, sensory and intellectual stimulation, interpersonal relations, and influences on motivation are all significant features of the environment.	IQ scores have risen among children who are adopted into homes that offer a stimulating, enriching environment. Correlations between IQs of identical twins reared together are higher than for those reared apart.

teachers tend to be less patient, less encouraging, and less likely to try teaching as much material to students whom they do not consider bright (Cooper, 1979; Trujillo, 1986). Other studies indicate that teachers simply favor students who are most like themselves. Teachers who themselves had difficulty in math, for example, may favor students who have similar difficulties. Further, differential expectations among teachers—and even parents—about the academic potential of boys versus girls may contribute to gender differences in performance in certain areas, such as science (e.g., Crowley et al., 2001). In summary, the operation of teacher expectancies is probably far more complex than Rosenthal and Jacobson originally thought (Snow, 1995).

IQ tests have been criticized for being biased and for labeling people on the basis of scores or profiles. ("In Review: Influences on IQ Scores" lists the factors that can shape IQ scores.) "Summarizing" a person through an IQ score does indeed run the risk of oversimplifying reality and making errors, but intelligence tests can also *prevent* errors by reducing the number of important educational and employment decisions that are made on the basis of inaccurate stereotypes, false preconceptions, and faulty generalizations. For example, boredom or lack of motivation at school might make a child appear mentally slow, or even retarded. But a test of cognitive abilities conducted under the right conditions is likely to reveal the child's potential. The test can prevent the mistake of moving a child of average intelligence to a class for the mentally handicapped. And as Alfred Binet had hoped, intelligence tests have been enormously helpful in identifying children who need special educational attention. So despite their limitations and potential for bias, IQ tests can minimize the likelihood of assigning children to remedial work they do not need or to advanced work they cannot yet handle.

THINKING CRITICALLY **Are Intelligence Tests Unfairly Biased Against Certain Groups?**

We have seen that intelligence tests can undoubtedly have great value, but there is also great concern over the fact that IQ scores can be negatively affected by poverty, inferior educational opportunities, and other environmental factors. This concern focuses on the fact that members of ethnic minorities and other disadvantaged groups have not had an equal chance to develop the knowledge and skills that are required to achieve high IQ scores.

■ What am I being asked to believe or accept?

Some critics claim that standard intelligence tests are not fair. They argue that a disproportionately large number of people in some ethnic minority groups receive low scores on intelligence tests for reasons that are unrelated to cognitive ability, job potential, or other criteria that the tests are supposed to predict (Helms, 1992, 1997; Kwate, 2001; Neisser et al., 1996). They say that using ability and aptitude tests to make decisions about people —such as assigning them to particular jobs or special classes—may unfairly deprive members of some ethnic minority groups of equal employment or educational opportunities.

■ What evidence is available to support the assertion?

Research reveals several possible sources of bias in tests of cognitive abilities. First, as noted earlier, noncognitive factors such as anxiety, lack of motivation, or distrust can impair test performance and may put certain individuals at a disadvantage. For example, children from some minority groups may be less motivated to perform well on standardized tests and less likely to trust the adult tester (Steele, 1997). Consequently, differences in test scores may partly reflect motivational differences among various groups during the testing process.

Second, many test items inevitably reflect the vocabulary and experiences of the dominant middle-class culture in the United States. Those who are less familiar with the knowledge and skills valued by that culture will not score as well as those who are more familiar with them. Not all cultures value the same things, however (Sternberg & Grigorenko, 2004b). A study of Cree Indians in northern Canada revealed that words and phrases associated with *competence* included *good sense of direction*; at the *incompetent* end of the scale was the phrase *lives like a white person* (Berry & Bennett, 1992). A European American might not perform well on a Cree intelligence test based on these criteria. In fact, as illustrated in Table 10.2, poor performance on a culture-specific test is probably due more to unfamiliarity with culture-based concepts than to lack of cognitive ability. Compared with more traditional measures, "culture-fair" tests—such as the Universal Nonverbal Intelligence Test—that reduce dependence on oral skills do produce smaller differences between native English speakers and English-language learners (Bracken & McCallum, 1998).

Third, some tests may reward those who interpret questions as expected by the test designer. Conventional intelligence tests have clearly defined "right" and "wrong" answers. Yet a person may interpret test questions in a manner that is "intelligent" or "correct," but that produces a "wrong" answer. For example, when one child was asked, "In what way are an apple and a banana alike?" he replied, "Both give me diarrhea." The fact that you don't give the answer that the test designer was looking for does not mean that you *can't* (which is why well-trained test administrators would ask for another answer before moving on).

■ Are there alternative ways of interpreting the evidence?

This same evidence might be interpreted as showing that although intelligence tests do not provide a pure measure of innate cognitive ability, they do provide a fair picture of whether a person has developed the skills necessary to succeed in school or in certain jobs. When some people have had more opportunity than others to

---

TABLE 10.2 An Intelligence Test?

TRY THIS How did you do on this "intelligence test"? If, like most people, you are unfamiliar with the material being tested by these rather obscure questions, your score was probably low. Would it be fair to say, then, that you are not very intelligent?	Take a minute to answer each of these questions, and check your answers against the key at the bottom of page 386. 1. What fictional detective was created by Leslie Charteris? 2. What planet travels around the sun every 248 years? 3. What vegetable yields the most pounds of produce per acre? 4. What was the infamous pseudonym of broadcaster Iva Toguri d'Aquino? 5. What kind of animal is Dr. Dolittle's pushmi-pullyu?

develop their abilities, the difference will be reflected in IQ scores. From this point of view, intelligence tests are fair measures of the cognitive abilities developed by people living in a society that, unfortunately, contains some unfair elements. In other words, the tests may be accurately detecting knowledge and skills that are not represented equally in all groups, but this doesn't mean that the tests discriminate *unfairly* among those groups.

To some observers, concern over cultural bias in intelligence tests stems from a tendency to think of IQ scores as measures of innate ability rather than of ability that is developed and expressed in a cultural context—much as athletes develop the physical skills needed to play certain sports (Lohman, 2004). Attempting to eliminate language and other cultural elements from intelligence tests, they say, would eliminate a vital part of what is meant by the term *intelligence* in any culture (Sternberg, 2004). This may be why "culture-fair" tests do not predict academic achievement as well as conventional intelligence tests do (Aiken, 1994; Lohman, 2005). Perhaps familiarity with the culture reflected in intelligence tests is just as important for success at school or work in that culture as it is for success on the tests themselves. After all, the ranking among groups on measures of academic achievement is similar to the ranking for average IQ scores (Sue & Okazaki, 1990).

■ What additional evidence would help to evaluate the alternatives?

If the problem of test bias is really a reflection of differences between various groups' opportunities to develop their cognitive skills, it will be important to conduct research on interventions that can reduce those differences. Making "unfair" cultures fairer by enhancing the skill development opportunities of traditionally disadvantaged groups should lead to smaller differences between groups on tests of cognitive ability (Martinez, 2000). It will also be important to find better ways to encourage members of disadvantaged groups to take advantage of those opportunities (Sowell, 2005).

At the same time, alternative tests of cognitive ability must also be explored, particularly those that include assessment of problem-solving skills and other abilities not measured by most intelligence tests (e.g., Sternberg & Kaufman, 1998). If new tests show smaller between-group differences than traditional tests but have equal or better predictive validity, many of the issues discussed in this section will have been resolved. So far, efforts in this direction have not been successful.

■ What conclusions are most reasonable?

The effort to reduce unfair cultural biases in tests is well founded, but "culture-fair" tests will be of little benefit if they fail to predict success as well as conventional tests do (Anastasi & Urbina, 1997; Sternberg, 1985). Whether one considers this circumstance good or bad, fair or unfair, it is important for people to have information and skills that are valued by the culture in which they live and work. As long as this is the case, tests designed to predict success in such areas are reasonable insofar as they measure a person's skills and access to the information valued by that culture.

In other words, there is probably no value-free, or experience-free, or culture-free way to measure the construct known as intelligence when that construct is defined by the behaviors that a culture values and that are developed through experience in that culture (Laboratory of Comparative Human Cognition, 1982; Sternberg, 1985, 2004). This conclusion has led some researchers to worry less about how cultural influences might "contaminate" tests of innate cognitive abilities and to focus instead on how to help people develop the abilities that are required for success in school and society. As mentioned earlier, if more attention were focused on combating poverty, poor schools, inadequate nutrition, lack of health care, and other conditions that result in lower average IQ scores and reduced economic opportunities for certain groups of people, many of the reasons for concern about test bias might be eliminated. ■

Answer key to Table 10.2: (1) Simon Templar (2) Pluto (3) Cabbage (4) Tokyo Rose (5) A two-headed llama

Understanding Intelligence

We have seen that people who are skilled at using and understanding language, at learning and remembering, and at thinking, problem-solving, and other information-processing tasks are likely to score well on standard intelligence tests such as the Stanford-Binet and the Wechsler. But these standard tests do not measure all the abilities highlighted by other approaches to the concept of "intelligence" (Berry & Bennett, 1992; Carroll, 1993; Eysenck, 1986; Gardner, 1999; Hunt, 1983; Kanazawa, 2004; Meyer & Salovey, 1997; Sternberg, 1996; Sternberg, Lautrey, & Lubart, 2003). Let's consider these approaches and a few of the nontraditional intelligence tests that have emerged from some of them.

● The Psychometric Approach

Standard intelligence tests are associated with the **psychometric approach,** which is a way of studying intelligence that emphasizes the *products* of intelligence, including IQ scores. Researchers taking this approach ask whether intelligence is one general trait or a bundle of more specific abilities. The answer matters, because if intelligence is a single trait, then an employer might assume that someone with a low IQ could not do any tasks well. But if intelligence is composed of many abilities that are somewhat independent of one another, then a poor showing in one area—say, spatial abilities—would not rule out good performance in others, such as understanding information or solving word problems.

Early in the twentieth century, statistician Charles Spearman made a suggestion that began the modern debate about the nature of intelligence. Spearman noticed that scores on almost all tests of cognitive abilities were positively correlated (Spearman, 1904, 1927). That is, people who did well on one test also tended to do well on all of the others. Spearman concluded that these correlations were created by general cognitive ability, which he called **g,** for *general intelligence,* and a group of special intelligences, which he collectively referred to as **s.** The s factors, he said, are the specific information and skills needed for particular tasks.

Spearman argued that people's scores on a particular test depend on both g and s. Further examination of test scores, however, revealed correlations that could not be explained by either g or s; these were called *group factors.* Although Spearman modified his theory to accommodate these group factors, he continued to claim that g represented a measure of mental force, or intellectual power.

In 1938, L. L. Thurstone published a paper criticizing Spearman's mathematical methods. Using the statistical technique of *factor analysis,* Thurstone analyzed the correlations among intelligence tests to identify the underlying factors, or abilities, being measured by those tests. His analyses did not reveal a single, dominating g factor. Instead, he found seven relatively independent *primary mental abilities:* numerical ability, reasoning, verbal fluency, spatial visualization, perceptual ability, memory, and verbal comprehension. Thurstone did not deny that g exists, but he argued that it was not as important as these primary mental abilities in describing a particular person. Similarly, Spearman did not deny the existence of special abilities, but he maintained that g tells us most of what we need to know about a person's cognitive ability.

Raymond B. Cattell (1963) agreed with Spearman, but his own factor analyses suggested that there are two kinds of g, which he labeled *fluid* and *crystallized.* **Fluid intelligence,** he said, is the basic power of reasoning and problem solving. **Crystallized intelligence,** in contrast, involves specific knowledge gained as a result of applying fluid intelligence. It produces, for example, a good vocabulary and familiarity with the multiplication tables.

Who is right? After decades of research and debate, most psychologists today agree that there is a positive correlation among various tests of cognitive ability, a correlation that is due to a factor known as g (e.g., Frey & Detterman, 2004). Further,

● **psychometric approach** A way of studying intelligence that emphasizes analysis of the products of intelligence, especially scores on intelligence tests.

● **g** A general intelligence factor that Charles Spearman postulated as accounting for positive correlations between people's scores on all sorts of cognitive ability tests.

● **s** A group of special abilities that Charles Spearman saw as accompanying general intelligence *(g).*

● **fluid intelligence** The basic power of reasoning and problem solving.

● **crystallized intelligence** The specific knowledge gained as a result of applying fluid intelligence.

it appears that the *g* factor can be measured by many different groups of cognitive tests, even if the tests in each group are entirely different (Johnson et al., 2004).

However, the brain probably does not contain some unified "thing" corresponding to what people call intelligence. Instead, cognitive abilities appear to be organized in "layers," beginning with as many as fifty or sixty narrow and specific skills that can be grouped into seven or eight more general ability factors, all of which combine into *g*, the broadest and most general of all (Carroll, 1993; Gustafsson & Undheim, 1996; Lubinski, 2004). Understanding *g* and how it arises is a major goal of research in cognitive psychology (Colom, Jung, & Haier, 2006; Detterman, 1982, 1987, 1994; Garlick, 2002; van der Maas et al., 2006).

● The Information-Processing Approach

The **information-processing approach** tries to identify the mental *processes* involved in intelligent behavior, not the traits (such as verbal ability) that result in test scores and other *products* of intelligence (Das, 2002; Jensen, 2006; Lohman, 2000; Sternberg, 2000). Researchers taking this approach ask, What mental operations are necessary to perform intellectual tasks? What aspects depend on past learning, and what aspects depend on attention, working memory, and processing speed? In other words, the information-processing approach relates the basic mental processes discussed in the chapters on perception, learning, memory, and cognition to the concept of intelligence. Are there individual differences in these processes that correlate with measures of intelligence? More specifically, are measures of intelligence related to differences in the amount of attention people have available for basic mental processes or in the speed of those processes?

The notion that intelligence may be related to attention builds on the results of research by Earl Hunt and others (Ackerman, 1994; Ackerman, Beier, & Boyle, 2002; Eysenck, 1987; Hunt, 1980). As discussed in the chapter on perception, attention represents a pool of resources or mental energy. When people perform difficult tasks or perform more than one task at a time, they must call on greater amounts of these resources. Does intelligent behavior depend on the amount of attention that can be mobilized? Early research by Hunt (1980) suggests that it does—that people with greater intellectual ability have more attentional resources available. There is also evidence of a positive correlation between IQ scores and performance on tasks requiring attention, such as silently counting the number of words in the "animal" category while reading a list of varied terms aloud (Stankov, 1989).

Another possible link between differences in information processing and differences in intelligence relates to processing speed. Perhaps intelligent people have "faster brains" than other people—perhaps they carry out basic mental processes more quickly. When a task is complex, having a "fast brain" might reduce the chance that information will disappear from memory before it can be used (Jensen, 1993; Larson & Saccuzzo, 1989). A fast brain might also allow people to do a better job of mastering material in everyday life and therefore to build up a good knowledge base (Miller & Vernon, 1992). Hans Eysenck (1986) even proposed that intelligence can be defined as the error-free transmission of information through the brain. Following his lead, some researchers have attempted to measure various aspects of intelligence by looking at activity in particular parts of the brain (Colom et al., 2006; Deary & Caryl, 1993; Eysenck, 1994; Garlick, 2002; Haier, White, & Alkire, 2003). Others have emphasized the importance of working-memory resources in intelligent thinking (e.g., Gray, Chabris, & Braver, 2003; Kyllonen & Christal, 1990; Süss et al., 2002). In fact, some of these researchers conclude that *g* is nothing more than working memory (Jensen, 1998), whereas others believe that *g* is more than memory alone (Ackerman et al., 2002; Mackintosh & Bennett, 2003).

Hypotheses about the role of information-processing skills in intelligence certainly sound reasonable. Research suggests, however, that only a portion of the variation seen in people's performance on general cognitive abilities tests can be

● **information-processing approach** An approach to the study of intelligence that focuses on mental operations, such as attention and memory, that underlie intelligent behavior.

Brainpower and Intelligence The information-processing approach to intelligence suggests that people with the most rapid information processors—the "fastest" brains—should do best on cognitive ability tests, including intelligence tests and college entrance exams. Research suggests that there is more to intelligent behavior than sheer processing speed, though.

accounted for by differences in their speed of access to long-term memory, the capacity of short-term and working memory, or other information-processing abilities (Baker, Vernon, & Ho, 1991; Friedman et al., 2006; Miller & Vernon, 1992).

● The Triarchic Theory of Intelligence

According to Robert Sternberg (1988b, 1999), a complete theory of intelligence must deal with three different types of intelligence: analytic, creative, and practical. *Analytic intelligence*, the kind that is measured by traditional intelligence tests, would help you solve a physics problem; *creative intelligence* is what you would use to compose music; and you would draw on *practical intelligence* to figure out what to do if you were stranded on a lonely road during a blizzard. Sternberg's **triarchic theory of intelligence** deals with all three types of intelligence.

Sternberg recognizes that analytic intelligence is important for success at school and in other areas, but he argues that universities and employers should not select people solely on the basis of tests of this kind of intelligence (Sternberg, 1996; Sternberg & Williams, 1997). Why? Because the tasks posed by tests of analytic intelligence are often of little interest to the people taking them and typically have little relationship to their daily experience. For one thing, each task is usually clearly defined and comes with all the information needed to find the one right answer (Neisser et al., 1996), a situation that seldom occurs in the real world. The practical problems people face every day are generally of personal interest and are related to more common life experiences. That is, they are ill-defined and do not contain all the information necessary to solve them; they typically have more than one correct solution; and there may be several ways of solving them (Sternberg et al., 1995).

It is no wonder, then, that some children who do poorly in school may nevertheless show high degrees of practical intelligence, including—as in the case of Brazilian street children—the ability to live by their wits in hostile environments (Carraher, Carraher, & Schliemann, 1985). And some racetrack bettors whose IQ scores are as low as 82 are experts at predicting race odds at post time by combining many different kinds of complex information about horses, jockeys, and track conditions (Ceci & Liker, 1986). In other words, these people's practical intelligence is unrelated to measures of their IQ.

Sternberg's theory is important because it extends the concept of intelligence into areas that most psychologists traditionally have not examined and because it emphasizes what intelligence means in everyday life. The theory is so broad, however, that many parts of it are difficult to test. For example, methods for measuring

triarchic theory of intelligence Robert Sternberg's theory that describes intelligence as having analytic, creative, and practical dimensions.

PRACTICAL

1. Think of a problem that you are currently experiencing in real life. Briefly describe the problem, including how long it has been present and who else is involved (if anyone). Then describe three different practical things you could do to try to solve the problem. *(Students are given up to 15 minutes and up to 2 pages.)*

2. Choose the answer that provides the **best** solution, given the specific situation and desired outcome.

John's family moved to Iowa from Arizona during his junior year in high school. He enrolled as a new student in the local high school two months ago but still has not made friends and feels bored and lonely. One of his favorite activities is writing stories. What is likely to be the most effective solution to this problem?

A. Volunteer to work on the school newspaper staff.

B. Spend more time at home writing columns for the school newsletter.

C. Try to convince his parents to move back to Arizona.

D. Invite a friend from Arizona to visit during Christmas break.

3. Each question asks you to use information about everyday things. Read each question carefully and choose the best answer.

Mike wants to buy two seats together and is told there are pairs of seats available only in Rows 8, 12, 49, and 95–100. Which of the following is not one of his choices for the total price of the two tickets?

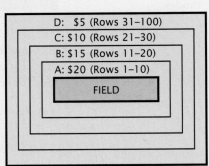

D: $5 (Rows 31–100)
C: $10 (Rows 21–30)
B: $15 (Rows 11–20)
A: $20 (Rows 1–10)
FIELD

A. $10.   **B.** $20.   **C.** $30.   **D.** $40.

CREATIVE

1. Suppose you are the student representative to a committee that has the power and the money to reform your school system. Describe your ideal school system, including buildings, teachers, curriculum, and any other aspects you feel are important. *(Students are given up to 15 minutes and up to 2 pages.)*

2. Each question has a "Pretend" statement. You must suppose that this statement is true. Decide which word goes with the third underlined word in the same way that the first two underlined words go together.

Colors are audible.

flavor is to tongue as shade is to

A. ear.   **B.** light.   **C.** sound.   **D.** hue.

3. First, read how the operation is defined. Then, decide what is the correct answer to the question.

*There is a new mathematical operation called **flix**.*
It is defined as follows:

$$A \text{ flix } B = A + B, \text{ if } A > B$$
but $A \text{ flix } B = A \times B, \text{ if } A < B$
and $A \text{ flix } B = A / B, \text{ if } A = B$

How much is 4 flix 7?

A. 28.   **B.** 11.   **C.** 3.   **D.** –11.

FIGURE 10.6

Testing for Practical and Creative Intelligence

TRY THIS Robert Sternberg argues that traditional tests measure mainly analytic intelligence. Here are sample items from tests he developed to test both practical and creative intelligence. Try answering them before you check the answers at the bottom of the figure. How did you do?

Source: Sternberg (1996).

ANSWERS. Practical: (2) A, (3) B. Creative: (2) A, (3) A.

A Musical Prodigy? According to Gardner's theory of multiple intelligences, skilled artists, athletes, and musicians—such as the young flutist shown here—display forms of intelligence not assessed by standard intelligence tests.

practical "street smarts" have been proposed (Sternberg, 2001; Sternberg et al., 1995), but they remain controversial (Brody, 2003; Gottfredson, 2003). Sternberg and his colleagues have also developed new intelligence tests designed to assess analytic, practical, and creative intelligence, and there is some evidence that scores on these tests can predict success in college and at some jobs at least as well as standard IQ and aptitude tests (Leonhardt, 2000; Sternberg & Kaufman, 1998; Sternberg et al., 1995; Sternberg and The Rainbow Project Coordinators, 2006). Figure 10.6 provides examples of several items from Sternberg's test that are designed to measure practical and creative aspects of intelligence.

● Multiple Intelligences

Some people whose IQ scores are only average, or even below average, may have exceptional ability in certain specific areas (Miller, 1999). One child whose IQ score was just 50 could correctly state the day of the week for any date between 1880 and 1950 (Scheerer, Rothmann, & Goldstein, 1945). He could also play melodies on the piano by ear and sing Italian operatic pieces he had heard. In addition, he could spell—forward or backward—any word spoken to him and could memorize long speeches, although he had no understanding of what he was doing.

Cases such as this are part of the evidence cited by Howard Gardner in support of his theory of **multiple intelligences** (Gardner, 1993, 2002). To study intelligence, Gardner focused on how people learn and use symbol systems such as language, mathematics, and music. He asked, Do these systems all require the same abilities and processes, the same "intelligence"? According to Gardner, the answer is no. All people, he says, possess a number of intellectual potentials, or intelligences, each of which involves a somewhat different set of skills. Biology provides raw capacities; cultures provide symbolic systems—such as language—to use those raw capacities. Although the intelligences normally interact, they can function with some independence, and individuals may develop certain intelligences further than others. ("In Review: Analyzing Cognitive Abilities" summarizes Gardner's theory, along with the other views of intelligence we have discussed.)

● **multiple intelligences** Eight semi-independent kinds of intelligence postulated by Howard Gardner.

in review Analyzing Cognitive Abilities

Approach	Method	Key Findings or Propositions
Psychometric	Define the structure of intelligence by examining factor analyses of the correlations between scores on tests of mental abilities.	Performance on many tests of cognitive abilities is highly correlated, but this correlation, represented by g, reflects a bundle of abilities, not just one trait.
Information processing	Understand intelligence by examining the mental operations involved in intelligent behavior.	The speed of basic processes and the amount of attentional resources available make significant contributions to performance on IQ tests.
Sternberg's triarchic theory	Understand intelligence by examining the information processing involved in thinking, changes with experience, and effects in different environments.	There are three distinct kinds of intelligence: analytic, creative, and practical. IQ tests measure only analytic intelligence, but creative intelligence (which involves dealing with new problems) and practical intelligence (which involves adapting to one's environment) may also be important to success in school and at work.
Gardner's theory of multiple intelligences	Understand intelligence by examining test scores, information processing, biological and developmental research, the skills valued by different cultures, and exceptional people.	Biology provides the capacity for eight distinct "intelligences": linguistic, logical-mathematical, spatial, musical, body-kinesthetic, intrapersonal, interpersonal, and naturalistic.

The specific intelligences that Gardner (1998) proposes are (1) *linguistic* intelligence (reflected in good vocabulary and reading comprehension), (2) *logical-mathematical* intelligence (as indicated by skill at arithmetic and certain kinds of reasoning), (3) *spatial* intelligence (seen in understanding relationships between objects), (4) *musical* intelligence (as in abilities involving rhythm, tempo, and sound identification), (5) *body-kinesthetic* intelligence (reflected in skill at dancing, athletics, and eye-hand coordination), (6) *intrapersonal* intelligence (displayed by self-understanding), (7) *interpersonal* intelligence (seen in the ability to understand and interact with others), and (8) *naturalistic* intelligence (the ability to see patterns in nature). Other researchers have suggested that people also possess *emotional* intelligence, which involves the capacity to perceive emotions and to link them to one's thinking (Meyer & Salovey, 1997; Salovey & Grewal, 2005). Gardner says that traditional intelligence tests sample only the first three of these intelligences, mainly because these are the forms of intelligence most valued in school. To measure intelligences not tapped by standard tests, Gardner suggests collecting samples of children's writing, assessing their ability to appreciate or produce music, and obtaining teacher reports of their strengths and weaknesses in athletic and social skills (Gardner, 1991).

Gardner's view of intelligence is appealing, partly because it allows virtually everyone to be highly intelligent in at least one way. However, critics argue that including athletic or musical skill dilutes the validity and usefulness of the intelligence concept, especially as it is applied in school and in many kinds of jobs. They point out, too, that intrapersonal, interpersonal, body-kinesthetic, or naturalistic abilities are best described as collections of specific skills. Therefore it makes more sense to speak of, say, "interpersonal skills" rather than "interpersonal intelligence." Research on Gardner's theory has been hampered by a lack of dependable measures of the various intelligences he proposes (Lubinski & Benbow, 1995; Visser, Ashton, & Vernon, 2006). Until and unless such measures are developed, say Gardner's critics, his theory will be of little scientific value and serves mainly to draw attention to abilities that are easily ignored by focusing on general intelligence alone.

FOCUS ON
RESEARCH METHODS

Tracking Cognitive Abilities over the Life Span

As described in the chapter on human development, significant changes in cognitive abilities occur from infancy through adolescence, but development does not stop there. One major study has focused specifically on the changes in cognitive abilities that occur during adulthood.

■ What was the researchers' question?

The researchers began by asking what appears to be a relatively simple question: How do adults' cognitive abilities change over time?

■ How did the researchers answer the question?

Answering this question is extremely difficult because findings about age-related changes in cognitive abilities depend to some extent on the methods that are used to observe those changes. None of the methods includes true experiments, because psychologists cannot randomly assign people to be a certain age and then give them mental tests. So changes in cognitive abilities must be explored through a number of other research designs.

One of these, the *cross-sectional study,* compares data collected at the same point in time from people of different ages. However, cross-sectional studies contain a major confounding variable: Because people are born at different times, they may have had very different educational, cultural, nutritional, and medical experiences. This confounding variable is referred to as a *cohort effect.* Suppose two cohorts, or age groups, are tested on their ability to imagine the rotation of an object in space. The cohort born around 1940 might not do as well as the one born around 1980, but does the difference reflect declining spatial ability in the older people? It might, but it might also be due in part to the younger group's greater experience with video games and other spatial tasks. In other words, differences in experience, and not just age, could account for differences in ability between older and younger people in a cross-sectional study.

Changes associated with age can also be examined through *longitudinal studies,* in which a group of people is repeatedly tested as they grow older. But longitudinal designs, too, have some built-in problems. For one thing, fewer and fewer members of an age cohort can be tested over time as death, physical disability, relocation, and lack of interest reduce the sample size. Researchers call this problem the *mortality effect.* Further, the remaining members are likely to be the healthiest in the group and may also have retained better mental powers than the dropouts (Botwinick, 1977). As a result, longitudinal studies may underestimate the degree to which abilities decline with age. Another confounding factor can come from the *history effect.* Here, some event—such as a reduction in health care benefits for senior citizens—might have an effect on cognitive ability scores that is mistakenly attributed to age. Finally, longitudinal studies may be confounded by *testing effects,* meaning that participants may improve over time because of what they learn during repeated testing procedures. People who become "test wise" in this way might even remember answers from one testing session to the next.

As part of the Seattle Longitudinal Study of cognitive aging, K. Warner Schaie (1993) developed a research design that measures the impact of the confounding variables we have discussed and allows corrections to be made for them. In 1956, Schaie identified a random sample of five thousand members of a health maintenance organization (HMO) and invited some of them to volunteer for his study. The volunteers, who ranged in age from twenty to eighty, were given a set of intelligence tests designed to measure Thurstone's primary mental abilities (PMA). The cross-sectional comparisons allowed by this first step were, of course, confounded

LINKAGES (a link to Research in Psychology, p. 41)

by cohort effects. To control for those effects, the researchers retested the same participants seven years later, in 1963. By doing so, the study combined cross-sectional with longitudinal methods in what is called a *cross-sequential with resampling design*. This design allowed the researchers to compare the size of the *difference* in PMA scores between, say, the twenty-year-olds and twenty-seven-year-olds tested in 1956 with the size of the *change* in PMA scores for these same people as they aged from twenty to twenty-seven and from twenty-seven to thirty-four. Schaie reasoned that if the size of the longitudinal change was about the same as the size of the cross-sectional difference, the cross-sectional difference could probably be attributed to aging, not to the era in which the participants were born.

What about the effect of confounding variables on the longitudinal changes themselves? To measure the impact of testing effects, the researchers randomly drew a new set of participants from their original pool of five thousand. These people were of the same age range as the first sample, but they had not yet been tested. If people from the first sample did better on their second PMA testing than the people of the same age who now took the PMA for the first time, a testing effect would be suggested. (In this case, the size of the difference would indicate the size of the testing effect.) To control for history effects, the researchers examined the scores of people who were the same age in different years. For example, they compared people who were thirty in 1956 with those who were thirty in 1963, people who were forty in 1956 with those who were forty in 1963, and so on. If PMA scores were the same for people of the same age no matter what year they were tested, it is unlikely that events that happened in any particular year would have influenced test results. The researchers tested participants six times between 1956 and 1991. On each occasion they retested some previous participants and tested others for the first time.

■ What did the researchers find?

The results of the Seattle Longitudinal Study and other, more limited longitudinal studies suggest a reasonably consistent conclusion: Unless people are impaired by Alzheimer's disease or other brain disorders, their cognitive abilities usually decline very slightly between early adulthood and old age. Some aspects of *crystallized intelligence*, which depends on retrieving information and facts about the world from long-term memory, may remain robust well into old age. Other components of intelligence, however, may have failed quite noticeably by the time people reach sixty-five or seventy. *Fluid intelligence*, which involves rapid and flexible manipulations of ideas and symbols, is the most likely to decline (Bugg et al., 2006; Gilmore, Spinks, & Thomas, 2006; Schaie, 1996; see Figure 12.8 in the chapter on human development). The decline shows up in the following areas:

1. *Working memory.* The ability to hold and organize material in working memory declines beyond age fifty or sixty, particularly when attention must be redirected (Parkin & Walter, 1991).

2. *Processing speed.* There is a general slowing of all mental processes (Salthouse, 1996, 2000). Research has not yet isolated whether this slowing is due to reduced storage capacity, impaired processing efficiency, problems in coordinating simultaneous activities, or some combination of these factors (Babcock & Salthouse, 1990; Li et al., 2004; Salthouse, 1990). For many tasks, this slowing does not create obstacles. But if a problem requires manipulating material in working memory, quick processing of information is critical (Rabbitt, 1977). To multiply two 2-digit numbers mentally, for example, you must combine the subsums before you forget them. In some cases, internal distractions may interfere with older people's processing efficiency (Li et al., 2004).

The Voice of Experience Even in old age, people's crystallized intelligence may remain intact. Their extensive storehouse of knowledge, experience, and wisdom makes older people a valuable resource for the young.

3. *Organization.* Older people seem to be less likely to solve problems by adopting specific strategies, or mental shortcuts (Charness, 2000; Young, 1971). For example, to locate a wiring problem, you might perform a test that narrows down the regions where the problem might be. The tests carried out by older people tend to be more random and haphazard (Young, 1971). This result may occur partly because many older people are out of practice at solving such problems.

4. *Flexibility.* Older people tend to be less flexible in problem solving than their younger counterparts. They are less likely to consider alternative solutions (Salthouse & Prill, 1987), and they require more information before making a tentative decision (Ackerman et al., 2002; Rabbitt, 1977). Laboratory studies suggest that older people are also more likely than younger ones to choose conservative, risk-free options (Botwinick, 1966).

5. *Control of attention.* The ability to direct or control attention declines with age (Kramer et al., 1999). When required to switch their attention from one task to another, older participants typically perform less well than younger ones. Older adults also tend to be overwhelmed by distracting information, which may help account for many of the cognitive problems accompanying aging (Gazzaley et al., 2005).

■ What do the results mean?

This study indicates that different kinds of cognitive abilities change in different ways throughout our lifetimes. In general, there is a gradual, continual accumulation of knowledge about the world, some systematic changes in the limits of cognitive processes, and changes in the way those processes are carried out. This finding suggests that a general decline in cognitive abilities during adulthood is neither inevitable nor universal (Richards et al., 2004).

■ What do we still need to know?

There is an important question that the Schaie (1993) study doesn't answer: Why do age-related changes in cognitive abilities occur? Some researchers suggest that these changes are largely due to a decline in the speed and accuracy with which older people process information (Li et al., 2004; Salthouse, 2000). If this interpretation is correct, it would explain why some older people are less successful than younger ones at tasks that require rapidly integrating several pieces of information in working memory prior to making a choice or a decision.

It is also vital to learn why some people do *not* show declines in cognitive abilities—even when they reach their eighties. By understanding the biological and psychological factors responsible for these exceptions to the general rule, we might be able to reverse or delay some of the intellectual consequences of growing old. ■

Diversity in Cognitive Abilities

Although psychologists still don't agree on the details of what intelligence is, the study of intelligence tests and intelligent behavior has yielded many insights into human cognitive abilities. It also has highlighted the diversity of those abilities. In this section we briefly examine some of that diversity.

● Creativity

If you watch *The Simpsons* on television, you have probably noticed that Bart writes a different "punishment" sentence on the blackboard at the beginning of every episode. To maintain this tradition, the show's writers have had to create a unique—and funny—sentence for each of the hundreds of shows that have aired since 1989.

In every area of human endeavor, there are people who demonstrate **creativity**, the ability to produce new, high-quality ideas or products (Simonton, 1999; Sternberg & Grigorenko, 2004a). Whether a corporate executive or a homemaker, a scientist or an artist, everyone is creative to some degree (Klahr & Simon, 1999). Yet like the concept of intelligence, the concept of creativity is difficult to define (Amabile, Goldfarb, & Brackfield, 1990). Does creativity include innovation based on previous ideas, or must it be utterly new? And must it be new to the world, as in Pablo Picasso's paintings, or only new to the creator, as when a child "makes up" the word *waterbird* without having heard it before? As with intelligence, psychologists have not defined *creativity* as a "thing" that people have or don't have. They have defined it instead as a process or cognitive activity that can be inferred from performance on creativity tests, as well as from the books and computer programs and artwork and other products that result from the creative process (Sternberg & Dess, 2001).

To measure creativity, some psychologists have devised tests of **divergent thinking**, the ability to think along many paths to generate many solutions to a problem (Diakidoy & Spanoudis, 2002). The Consequences Test is an example. It contains items such as "Imagine all of the things that might possibly happen if all national and local laws were suddenly abolished" (Guilford, 1959). Divergent-thinking tests are scored by counting the number of reasonable responses that a person can list for each item and how many of those responses differ from other people's responses. Unfortunately, these tests may underestimate creativity, because even creative people may find it difficult to create on demand in the same way they could, say, spell words or do multiplication problems when asked. Further, there is no guarantee that having the ability to come up with different answers or different ways of looking at a situation will lead to creative products. Creative behavior requires divergent thinking that is appropriate for a given situation or problem. To be productive rather than just weird, a creative person must be firmly anchored to reality, understand society's needs, and learn from the experience and knowledge of others (Sternberg & Lubart, 1992). Teresa Amabile has identified three kinds of cognitive and personality characteristics necessary for creativity (Amabile, 1996; Amabile, Hennessey, & Grossman, 1986):

1. *Expertise* in the field of endeavor, which is directly tied to what a person has learned. For example, a painter or composer must know the paints, techniques, or instruments available.

2. A set of *creative skills*, including willingness to work hard, persistence at problem solving, capacity for divergent thinking, ability to break out of old problem-solving habits, and willingness to take risks. Amabile believes that training can influence many of these skills (some of which are closely linked to the strategies for problem solving discussed in the chapter on cognition and language).

3. The *motivation* to pursue creative production for internal reasons, such as satisfaction, rather than for external reasons, such as prize money. In fact, Amabile and her colleagues found that external rewards can deter creativity (e.g., Amabile et al., 1986). In one study, they asked groups of children or adults to create artistic products such as paintings or stories. Some were simply asked to work on the project. Others were told that their project would be judged for its creativity and excellence and that rewards would be given or winners announced. Experts—who did not know which products were created by which group—judged the work of the "reward" group to be significantly less creative. Similar effects have been found in other studies (Deci, Koestner, & Ryan, 1999, 2001), though research by Robert Eisenberger suggests that there may also be circumstances in which rewarding people's creativity can strengthen it—in much the same way that positive reinforcement strengthens any other behavior (Eisenberger & Rhoades, 2001; Eisenberger & Shanock, 2003).

● **creativity** The capacity to produce new, high-quality ideas or products.

● **divergent thinking** The ability to think along many alternative paths to generate many different solutions to a problem.

Is creativity inherited? To some extent, perhaps it is; but there is evidence that a person's environment—including the social, economic, and political forces within it—can influence creative behavior at least as much as it influences intelligence (Amabile, 2001; Nakamura & Csikszentmihalyi, 2001). For example, the correlation between the creativity scores of identical twins reared apart is lower than that between their IQ scores (Nichols, 1978). Environmental factors, such as growing up around musicians or scientists, may focus one's creativity in a particular area, such as writing music or doing research. There are some notable exceptions, but most people who are creative in one domain are not especially creative in others.

Do you have to be smart to be creative? Creativity does appear to require a certain degree of intelligence (Sternberg, 2001), but not necessarily an extremely high IQ score (Simonton, 1984). Correlations between scores on intelligence tests and on tests of creativity are only modest, between +.10 and +.30 (Barron & Harrington, 1981; Rushton, 1990; Simonton, 1999). This result is not surprising, because creativity as psychologists measure it requires broad, divergent thinking, whereas traditional intelligence tests measure **convergent thinking**—the ability to apply logic and knowledge in order to narrow down the number of possible solutions to a problem. The pace of research on creativity, and its relationship to intelligence, has picked up in recent years (Sternberg & Dess, 2001). One result of that research has been to define the combination of intelligence and creativity in the same person as *wisdom* (Sternberg, 2001; Sternberg & O'Hara, 1999).

● Unusual Cognitive Ability

Our understanding of cognitive abilities has been advanced by research on people whose cognitive abilities are unusual—people who are gifted, mentally retarded, or have learning disabilities (Robinson, Zigler, & Gallagher, 2000).

● **Giftedness**   People who show remarkably high levels of accomplishment in particular domains, or who show promise for such accomplishment, are often referred to as *gifted*. Giftedness is typically measured by school achievement and other evidence of unusually high achievement, such as outstanding science projects, written products, and the like. The potential for this kind of accomplishment is usually measured with intelligence or scholastic aptitude tests. Researchers caution, though, against predicting academic potential from a single measure, such as an IQ score (Hagen, 1980; Lohman & Hagen, 2001b; Thorndike & Hagen, 1996).

In fact, people with unusually high IQs do not necessarily become famous and successful in their chosen fields. One of the best-known studies of the intellectually gifted was conducted by Louis Terman and his colleagues (Oden, 1968; Sears, 1977; Terman & Oden, 1947, 1959). This study began in 1921 with the identification of more than 1,500 children whose IQ scores were very high—most higher than 135 by age ten. Interviews and tests conducted over the next sixty years revealed that few, if any, became truly creative geniuses—such as world-famous inventors, authors, artists, or composers—but that only eleven failed to graduate from high school and that more than two-thirds graduated from college. Ninety-seven earned Ph.D.s; ninety-two, law degrees; and fifty-seven, medical degrees. In 1955 their median family income was well above the national average (Terman & Oden, 1959). In general, they were physically and mentally healthier than the nongifted people and appear to have led happier, or at least more fortunate, lives. These results are consistent with more recent studies showing that people with higher IQ scores tend to live longer (Deary et al., 2004; Gottfredson, 2004; Hart et al., 2003), perhaps because they have the reasoning and problem-solving skills that lead them to take better care of themselves and to avoid danger (Breslau, Lucia, & Alvarado,

convergent thinking   The ability to apply logic and knowledge to narrow down the number of possible solutions to a problem or perform some other complex cognitive task.

The Eagle Has Landed In February 2000, Richard Keebler, twenty-seven, became an Eagle Scout, the highest rank in the Boy Scouts of America. His achievement is notable not only because only 4 percent of all Scouts reach this pinnacle but also because Keebler has Down syndrome. As we come to better understand the potential, not just the limitations, of mentally retarded people, their opportunities and their role in society will continue to expand.

2006; Deary & Der, 2005; Gottfredson & Deary, 2004; see the Focus on Research Methods section of the chapter on health, stress, and coping).

In short, although high IQ scores tend to predict longer, more successful lives (Lubinski et al., 2006; Wai, Lubinski, & Benbow, 2005; Whalley & Deary, 2001), an extremely high IQ does not guarantee special distinction. Some research suggests that gifted children are not fundamentally different from other children; they just have "more" of the same basic cognitive abilities seen in all children (Dark & Benbow, 1993; Singh & O'Boyle, 2004). Other work suggests that there may be other differences as well, such as an unusually intense motivation to master certain tasks or areas of intellectual endeavor (Lubinski et al., 2001; Winner, 2000).

● **Mental Retardation** People whose IQ scores are less than about 70 *and* who fail to display the skill at daily living, communication, and other tasks expected of those their age have traditionally been described as *mentally retarded* (American Psychiatric Association, 1994). They now are often referred to as *developmentally disabled* or *mentally challenged*. People within this very broad category differ greatly in their cognitive abilities, as well as in their ability to function independently in daily life. Table 10.3 shows a classification that divides the range of low IQ scores into categories that reflect these differences.

Some cases of mental retardation have a clearly identifiable cause. The best known example is *Down syndrome*, which occurs when an abnormality during conception results in an extra twenty-first chromosome (Hattori et al., 2000). Children with Down syndrome typically have IQ scores in the range of 40 to 55, though some may score higher than that. There are also several inherited causes of mental retardation. The most common of these is *fragile X syndrome*, caused by a defect on chromosome 23 (known as the *X chromosome*). More rarely, retardation is caused by inheriting *Williams syndrome* (a defect on chromosome 7) or by inheriting a gene for *phenylketonuria*, or PKU (which causes the body to create toxins out of milk and other foods). Retardation can also result from environmental causes, such as exposure to German measles (rubella) or alcohol or other toxins before birth; oxygen deprivation during birth; and head injuries, brain tumors, and infectious diseases (such as meningitis or encephalitis) in childhood (U.S. Surgeon General, 1999).

Familial retardation refers to the 30 to 40 percent of (usually mild) cases in which there is no obvious genetic or environmental cause (American Psychiatric Association,

TABLE **10.3**	**Categories of Mental Retardation**	

These categories are approximate. Especially at the upper end of the scale, many retarded persons can be taught to handle tasks well beyond what their IQ scores might suggest. Furthermore, IQ is not the only diagnostic criterion for retardation. Many people with IQs lower than 70 can function adequately in their communities and so would not be classified as mentally retarded.

Level of Retardation	IQ Scores	Characteristics
Mild	50–70	A majority of all the mentally retarded. Usually show no physical symptoms of abnormality. Individuals with higher IQs can marry, maintain a family, and work in unskilled jobs. Abstract reasoning is difficult for those with the lower IQs of this category. Capable of some academic learning to a sixth-grade level.
Moderate	35–49	Often lack physical coordination. Can be trained to take care of themselves and to acquire some reading and writing skills. Abilities of a 4- to 7-year-old. Capable of living outside an institution with their families.
Severe	20–34	Only a few can benefit from any schooling. Can communicate vocally after extensive training. Most require constant supervision.
Profound	Below 20	Mental age less than 3. Very limited communication. Require constant supervision. Can learn to walk, utter a few simple phrases, and feed themselves.

LINKAGES (a link to Memory, p. 252)

An Inventive Genius Thomas Edison invented the electric light bulb and the phonograph, among many other things, but as a child, he did so poorly in school that his teacher sent him home to be educated by his mother. When students' academic performance falls short of what intelligence tests say they are capable of, a learning disability may be present. However, poor study skills, lack of motivation, and even the need for eyeglasses are among the many factors other than learning disabilities that can create a discrepancy between IQ scores and academic achievement. Accordingly, accurately diagnosing learning disabilities is not an easy task.

1994). In these cases, retardation appears to result from a complex, and as yet unknown, interaction between heredity and environment that researchers are continuing to explore (Croen, Grether, & Selvin, 2001; Spinath, Harlaar, et al., 2004).

People who are mildly mentally retarded differ from other people in three important ways, all of which appear to reflect limitations in working memory and mental processing speed (Campione, Brown, & Ferrara, 1982):

1. They perform certain mental operations more slowly, such as retrieving information from long-term memory. When asked to repeat something they have learned, they are not as quick as a person of normal intelligence.

2. They simply know fewer facts about the world. It is likely that this deficiency is caused by the third problem.

3. They are not very good at remembering to use mental strategies that may be important in learning and problem solving. For example, they do not remember to rehearse material that must be held in short-term memory, even though they know how to do so.

Despite such difficulties, the intellectual abilities of mentally retarded people can be improved to some extent. One program emphasizing positive parent-child communications began when the children were as young as thirty months old. It ultimately helped children with Down syndrome to master reading skills at a second-grade level, providing the foundation for further achievement (Rynders & Horrobin, 1980; Turkington, 1987). However, designing effective programs for retarded children is complicated because the way people learn depends not just on cognitive skills but also on social and emotional factors, including *where* they learn. Currently, there is debate about *mainstreaming*, the policy of teaching children with disabilities, including those who are retarded, in regular classrooms with children who do not have disabilities. Is mainstreaming good for retarded children? A number of studies of the cognitive and social skills of students who have been mainstreamed and those who were separated show few significant differences overall, although it appears that students at higher ability levels may gain more from being mainstreamed than their less mentally able peers (Cole et al., 1991).

● **Learning Disabilities** People who show a significant discrepancy between their measured intelligence and their academic performance may have a *learning disability* (National Information Center for Children and Youth with Disabilities, 2000). Learning disabilities are often seen in people with average or above-average IQs. For example, the problems with reading, writing, and math that Leonardo da Vinci and Thomas Edison had as children may have been due to such a disability; the problems certainly did not reflect a lack of cognitive ability!

There are several kinds of learning disabilities (Myers & Hammill, 1990; Wadsworth et al., 2000). People with *dyslexia* find it difficult to understand the meaning of what they read; they may also have difficulty in sounding out and identifying written words. *Dysphasia* is difficulty with understanding spoken words or with recalling the words needed for effective speech. *Dysgraphia*—problems with writing— appears as an inability to form letters or as the omission or reordering of words and parts of words in one's writing. The least common learning disability, *dyscalculia*, is a difficulty with arithmetic that reflects not poor mathematical ability but rather an impairment in the understanding of quantity and/or in the comprehension of basic arithmetic principles and operations, such as addition and subtraction.

The National Joint Committee on Learning Disabilities (1994) suggests that these disorders are caused by dysfunctions in the brain. However, although evidence from brain imaging and other studies are helping to locate areas of dysfunction (e.g., Pugh et al., 2000; Richards et al., 2000; Wright & Zecker, 2004), specific neurological causes have not yet been found. Accordingly, most researchers describe learning disabilities in terms of dysfunctional information processing (Kujala et al., 2001; Shaw et al., 1995). Diagnosis of a learning disability includes several steps. First, it is important to look for significant weaknesses in a person's listening, speaking, reading, writing, reasoning, or arithmetic skills (Brinckerhoff, Shaw, & McGuire, 1993). The person's actual ability is compared with that predicted by the person's IQ score. Tests for brain damage are also given. To help rule out alternative explanations of poor academic performance, the person's hearing, vision, and other sensory systems are tested, and factors such as poverty, family conflicts, and inadequate instruction are reviewed. Finally, alternative diagnoses such as attention deficit disorder (see the chapter on psychological disorders) must be eliminated.

LINKAGES

As noted in the chapter on introducing psychology, all of psychology's many subfields are related to one another. Our discussion of test anxiety illustrates just one way in which the topic of this chapter, cognitive abilities, is linked to the subfield of motivation and emotion (which is the focus of the chapter by that name). The Linkages diagram shows ties to two other subfields as well, and there are many more ties throughout the book. Looking for linkages among subfields will help you see how they all fit together and better appreciate the big picture that is psychology.

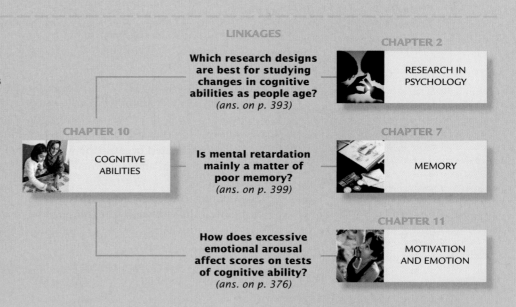

SUMMARY

Cognitive ability refers to the capacity to perform higher mental processes, such as reasoning, remembering, understanding, problem solving, and decision making.

Testing for Intelligence

Psychologists have not reached a consensus on how best to define intelligence. A working definition describes *intelligence* in terms of reasoning, problem solving, and dealing with changing environments.

A Brief History of Intelligence Tests Alfred Binet's pioneering test of intelligence included questions that required reasoning and problem solving of varying levels of difficulty, graded by age. Lewis Terman developed a revision of Binet's test that became known as the *Stanford-Binet*; it included items designed to assess the intelligence of adults as well as children and became the model for *IQ tests*. David Wechsler's tests remedied some of the deficiencies of the earlier IQ tests. Made up of subtests, some of which have little verbal content, these tests

allowed testers to generate scores for different aspects of cognitive ability.

Intelligence Tests Today The Stanford-Binet and Wechsler tests are the most popular individually administered intelligence tests. Both include subtests and provide scores for parts of the test, as well as an overall score. For example, in addition to a full-scale IQ score, the Wechsler tests yield scores for verbal comprehension, perceptual reasoning, working memory, and processing speed. Currently, a person's *intelligence quotient*, or *IQ score*, reflects how far that person's performance on the test deviates from the average performance by people in the same age group. An average performance is assigned an IQ score of 100.

Aptitude and Achievement Tests *Aptitude tests* are intended to measure a person's potential to learn new skills; *achievement tests* are intended to measure what a person has already learned. Both kinds of tests are used by schools for the placement or admission of students and by companies for the selection of new employees.

Measuring the Quality of Tests

Tests have two key advantages over other techniques of evaluation. First, they are standardized, which means that the conditions surrounding a test are as similar as possible for everyone who takes it. Second, they produce scores that can be compared with *norms,* thus allowing people's strengths or weaknesses in various areas to be compared with those of other people.

Reliability A good test must be *reliable,* which means that the results for each person are consistent, or stable. Reliability can be measured by various methods, including the test-retest, alternate-form, and split-half methods.

Validity *Validity* refers to the degree to which test scores are interpreted appropriately and used properly. We cannot say whether a test itself is valid or invalid, but the validity of test scores for a particular purpose can be evaluated in several ways. These include measurement of content validity (the degree to which test items include a fair sample of what the test is supposed to measure), criterion and predictive validity (the correlation between test scores and some present or future criterion), and construct validity (the extent to which the test measures the theoretical construct it was designed to measure).

Evaluating Intelligence Tests

In evaluating intelligence tests, we must consider the reliability and validity of test scores as well as sociocultural factors that might influence those scores.

The Reliability and Validity of Intelligence Tests Intelligence tests are reasonably reliable, and they do a good job of predicting academic success. However, these tests assess only some of the abilities that might be considered aspects of intelligence, and they may favor people most familiar with middle-class culture. Nonetheless, this familiarity is important for academic and occupational success.

IQ Scores as a Measure of Innate Ability Both heredity and the environment influence IQ scores, and their effects interact. The influence of heredity is shown by the high correlation between IQ scores of identical twins raised in separate households and by the similarity in the IQ scores of children adopted at birth and their biological parents. The influence of the environment is revealed by the higher correlation of IQ scores among siblings who share the same environment than among siblings who do not, as well as by the effects of environmental changes such as adoption.

Group Differences in IQ Scores Average IQ scores differ across socioeconomic and ethnic groups. These differences appear to be due to numerous factors, including differences in educational opportunity, motivation to achieve, family support for cognitive development, and other environmental conditions.

Conditions That Can Raise IQ Scores An enriched environment sometimes raises preschool children's IQ scores. Initial gains in cognitive performance that result from interventions such as Project Head Start may decline over time, but the programs may improve children's attitudes toward school.

IQ Scores in the Classroom Like any label, an IQ score can generate expectations that affect both how other people respond to a person and how that person behaves. Children labeled with low IQ scores may be offered fewer or lower-quality educational opportunities. However, IQ scores help educators to identify a student's strengths and weaknesses and to offer the curriculum that will best serve that student.

Understanding Intelligence

Researchers have taken several approaches to understanding the concept of intelligence.

The Psychometric Approach The *psychometric approach* attempts to analyze the structure of intelligence by examining correlations between tests of cognitive ability. Because scores on almost all tests of cognitive ability are positively correlated, Charles Spearman concluded that such tests measure a general factor of mental ability, called *g,* as well as more specific factors, called *s.* As a result of factor analysis, other researchers have concluded that intelligence is not a single general ability but a collection of abilities and subskills needed to succeed on any test of intelligence. Raymond B. Cattell distinguished between *fluid intelligence,* the basic power of reasoning and problem solving, and *crystallized intelligence,* the specific knowledge gained as a result of applying fluid intelligence. Modern theories of intelligence describe it as a hierarchy that is based on a host of specific abilities that fit into about eight groups that themselves combine into a single, general category of cognitive ability.

The Information-Processing Approach The *information-processing approach* to intelligence focuses on the process of intelligent behavior. Varying degrees of correlation have been found between IQ scores and measures of the flexibility and capacity of attention and between IQ scores and measures of the speed of information processing. This approach has helped deepen our understanding of the processes that create individual differences in intelligence.

The Triarchic Theory of Intelligence According to Robert Sternberg's *triarchic theory of intelligence,* there are three different types of intelligence: analytic, creative, and practical. Intelligence tests typically focus on analytic intelligence, but recent research has suggested ways to assess practical and creative intelligence, too.

Multiple Intelligences Howard Gardner's approach to intelligence suggests that biology equips us with the capacities for *multiple intelligences* that can function with some independence—specifically, linguistic, logical-mathematical, spatial, musical, body-kinesthetic, intrapersonal, interpersonal, and naturalistic intelligences.

Diversity in Cognitive Abilities

Research on human cognitive abilities has served to highlight the diversity of those abilities.

Creativity Tests of *divergent thinking* are used to measure differences in *creativity*. In contrast, intelligence tests typically require *convergent thinking*. Although creativity and IQ scores are not highly correlated, creative behavior requires a certain amount of intelligence, along with expertise in a creative field, skills at problem solving and divergent thinking, and motivation to pursue a creative endeavor for its own sake.

Unusual Cognitive Ability Knowledge about cognitive abilities has been expanded by research on giftedness, mental retardation, and learning disabilities. People with very high IQ scores tend to be successful in life, but they are not necessarily geniuses. People are considered mentally retarded if their IQ score is below about 70 and if their communication and daily living skills are less than expected of people their age. Some cases of retardation have a known cause; in familial retardation the mix of genetic and environmental causes is unknown. Compared with people of normal intelligence, retarded people process information more slowly, know fewer facts, and are deficient at knowing and using mental strategies. Despite such difficulties, the intellectual abilities of some mentally retarded people can be improved to some extent. People who show a significant discrepancy between their measured intelligence and their academic performance may have a learning disability. Learning disabilities can take several forms and must be carefully diagnosed.

11

Motivation and Emotion

When your clock goes off in the morning, do you jump out of bed, eager to face the day, or do you bury your head in the blankets? Once you're at your job or on campus, do you always do your best, or do you work just hard enough to get by? Are you generally happy? Do you sometimes worry, or feel sad? In this chapter, we explore the physical, mental, and social factors that motivate behavior in areas ranging from eating to sexuality to achievement. We also examine what emotions are and how they are expressed. Here's how we have organized this material:

One January day, despite temperatures of 30 degrees below zero, Brian Carr caught 155 fish, beating out thirty-six other competitors to win the annual ice-fishing contest at upstate New York's Lake Como Fish and Game Club. He also netted the grand prize of $8 (Shepherd, 1994). Why would thirty-seven people endure such harsh conditions in pursuit of such a small reward?

This is a question about **motivation,** the factors that influence the initiation, direction, intensity, and persistence of behavior (Reeve, 1996). Like the study of *how* people and other animals behave and think, the puzzle of *why* they do so has intrigued psychologists for many decades. Why do we help others or ignore them, eat what we want or stick to a diet, haunt art museums or sleazy bars, attend college or drop out of high school? Why, for that matter, do any of us do whatever it is that we do? In studying motivation, psychologists have noticed that behavior is based partly on the desire to feel certain emotions, such as the joy that comes with winning a contest or climbing a mountain or becoming a parent. They've found, too, that motivation affects emotion, as when hunger makes you irritable. In short, motivation and emotion are closely intertwined.

Let's consider what psychologists have learned so far about motivation. We'll begin with some general theories of motivation and then discuss three specific motives—hunger, sexual desire, and the need for achievement. Next, we examine the nature of emotion, as well as some theories of how and why certain emotions are experienced. We conclude with a discussion of how people communicate their emotions to one another.

Concepts and Theories of Motivation

The concept of motivation helps psychologists accomplish what Albert Einstein once called the whole purpose of science: to discover unity in diversity. Suppose that a man works two jobs, refuses party invitations, wears old clothes, drives a beat-up car, eats food others leave behind at lunch, never gives to charity, and keeps his house at 60 degrees in the dead of winter. In trying to explain why he does what he does, you could propose a separate reason for each behavior: Perhaps he likes to work hard, is afraid of people, hates shopping, is sentimental about his car, doesn't want food to go to waste, thinks the poor should take care of themselves, and feels better when it's cold. Or you could suggest a **motive,** a reason or purpose that provides a single explanation for this man's diverse and apparently unrelated behaviors. That unifying motive might be his desire to save as much money as possible.

This example illustrates the fact that motivation cannot be observed directly. We have to infer, or presume, that motivation is present from what we *can* observe. So psychologists think of motivation, whether it be hunger or thirst or love or greed, as an *intervening variable*—something that is used to explain the relationships between environmental stimuli and behavioral responses. The three different responses shown in Figure 11.1, for example, can be understood as guided by a single unifying motive: thirst. In order for an intervening variable to be considered a motive, it must have the power to change behavior in some way. For example, suppose we arrange for some party guests to eat only salted peanuts and other guests to eat only unsalted peanuts. We will probably find that the people who ate salted peanuts drink more than do those who ate the unsalted nuts. In this situation, we

motivation The influences that account for the initiation, direction, intensity, and persistence of behavior.

motive A reason or purpose for behavior.

can explain the observed differences in drinking in terms of differences in the motive known as thirst.

Figure 11.1 shows that motives can help explain why different stimuli can lead to the same response and why the same stimulus can cause different responses. Motivation also helps explain why behavior varies over time. For example, many people cannot bring themselves to lose weight, quit smoking, or exercise until they have a heart attack or symptoms of other serious health problems. At that point, these people may suddenly start eating a healthier diet, give up tobacco, and exercise regularly (West & Sohal, 2006). In other words, because of changes in motivation, particular stimuli—such as ice cream, cigarettes, and health clubs—trigger different responses at different times.

● Sources of Motivation

The number of possible motives for human behavior seems endless, but psychologists have found it useful to organize them into four somewhat overlapping categories. First, human behavior is motivated by basic *biological factors*, such as the need for food and water (Tinbergen, 1989). *Emotional factors* are a second source of motivation (Izard, 1993). Panic, fear, anger, love, and hatred can influence behavior ranging from selfless giving to brutal murder. Third, *cognitive factors* can motivate behavior (Weiner, 1993). People behave in certain ways—becoming arrogant or timid, for example—partly because of these cognitive factors, which include their perceptions of the world, their beliefs about what they can or cannot do, and their expectations about how others will respond to them. For example, even the least musical contestants who try out for *American Idol* and other talent shows seem utterly confident in their ability to sing. Fourth, motivation may stem from *social factors*, including the influence of parents, teachers, siblings, friends, television, and other sociocultural forces. Have you ever bought a jacket or tried a particular hairstyle not because you liked it but because it was in fashion? This is just one example of how social factors can affect almost all human behavior (Baumeister & Leary, 1995).

Various combinations of all four of these motivational sources appear in four prominent theories of human motivation. None of these theories can fully explain all aspects of how and why we behave as we do, but each of them—instinct theory, drive reduction theory, optimal arousal theory, and incentive theory—helps tell part of the story.

Motivation and Emotion The link between motivation and emotion is obvious in many everyday situations. For example, being motivated to win the U.S. National Spelling Bee creates strong emotions in this contestant as he struggles with a tough word. Sometimes, it is emotion that creates motivation, as when anger leads a parent to become aggressive toward a child or when love leads the parent to provide for that child.

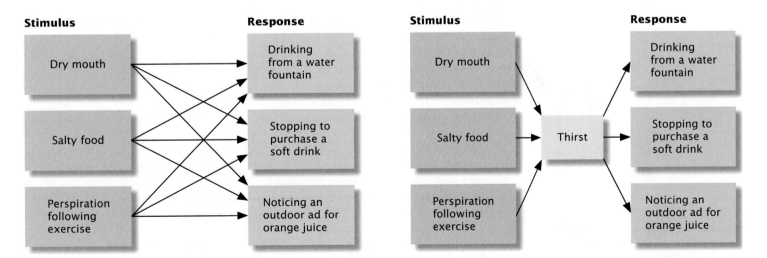

FIGURE 11.1

Motives as Intervening Variables

Motives can explain the links between stimuli and responses that, in some cases, might seem unrelated. In this example, inferring the motive of thirst provides an organizing explanation for why each stimulus triggers the responses shown.

Fixed-Action Patterns   The male three-spined stickleback fish attacks aggressively when it sees the red underbelly of another male. This automatic response is called a *fixed-action pattern* because it can be triggered by almost any red stimulus. These fish have been known to fly into an aggressive frenzy in response to a wooden fish model sporting a red spot, or even to a red truck driving past a window near their tank.

Instinct Theory and Its Descendants

In the early 1900s, many psychologists favored **instinct theory** as an explanation for the motivation of humans and other animals. **Instincts** are automatic, involuntary behavior patterns that are consistently triggered, or "released," by particular stimuli (Tinbergen, 1989). Such behaviors, originally called *fixed-action patterns,* are unlearned, species-typical responses to specific "releaser" stimuli. For example, releaser stimuli cause birds to engage in complex mating dances or to build nests, often doing a good job the first time they try.

In 1908, William McDougall listed eighteen human instincts, including self-assertion, reproduction, pugnacity (aggressiveness), and gregariousness (sociability). Within a few years, McDougall and others had named more than 10,000 more, prompting one critic to suggest that his colleagues had "an instinct to produce instincts" (Bernard, 1924). The problem was that instincts had become labels that do little more than describe behavior. Saying that someone gambles because of a gambling instinct or golfs because of a golfing instinct explains nothing about why these behaviors appear in some people and not others and how they develop.

Today, psychologists have adopted more sophisticated views of the role of inborn tendencies in human motivation. For example, they recognize that a number of human behaviors are present at birth. Among these are sucking and other reflexes, as well as certain facial expressions, such as smiling and grimacing at bitter tastes (Steiner et al., 2001). But they also recognize that inborn tendencies are more flexible than early instinct theories suggested. It turns out that so-called "*fixed*-action patterns—even the simple ones shown by baby chicks as they peck at seeds—actually vary quite a bit among individuals and can be modified by experience (Deich, Tankoos, & Balsam, 1995). Accordingly, these tendencies are now often referred to as *modal action patterns.* Similarly—as discussed in the chapters on learning and psychological disorders—people are not innately afraid of snakes and other potentially dangerous stimuli but rather are biologically *prepared* to learn to fear them. In this contemporary view, then, the behavior of humans and other animals may indeed be motivated by inborn tendencies, but it is not necessarily or entirely "genetically determined." It can be shaped, amplified, or even suppressed, by experience and other factors operating in particular individuals.

Psychologists who take the evolutionary approach suggest that the behavioral predispositions we see in humans and other animals today have evolved in part because they were adaptive for promoting individual survival. In other words, the individuals who possessed these behavioral predispositions and expressed them at

● **instinct theory**   A view that explains human behavior as motivated by automatic, involuntary, and unlearned responses.

● **instinct**   An innate, automatic disposition toward responding in a particular way when confronted with a specific stimulus.

the right times and places were the ones who were more likely than others to survive and reproduce. We are the descendants of ancestral human survivors, so to the extent that our ancestors' behavioral predispositions were transmitted genetically, we should show similar predispositions. Even many aspects of human social behavior, such as helping and aggression, are seen by evolutionary psychologists as motivated by inborn factors—especially by the desire to maximize our genetic contribution to the next generation (Buss, 2004a). We may not be aware of this specific desire, they say, but we nevertheless behave in ways that promote it (Geary, 2000). So you are more likely to hear someone say, "I can't wait to have children" than to say, "I want to pass on my genes."

The evolutionary approach suggests, for example, that people's choice of a marriage partner is influenced by the consequences of the choices made by their ancestors over countless generations. For instance, research in many different cultures shows that both men and women express a strong preference for marrying someone who is kind, understanding, and intelligent—all characteristics associated with creating a good environment for having and raising children (Buss et al., 1990). Evolutionary psychologists also point to sex differences in mating preferences and strategies. They argue that because women can produce relatively few children in their lifetimes, they are more psychologically invested than men are in the survival and development of those children (Townsend, Kline, & Wasserman, 1995). This greater investment is said to motivate women to be choosier than men are when selecting mates. So although women tend to prefer athletic men with symmetrical ("handsome") faces and deep voices, this preference is strongest at the point in the menstrual cycle when fertility peaks and mating with these "genetically fit" men would most likely result in pregnancy (Barber, 1995; Gangestad et al., 2007; Puts, 2005). The rest of the time, say evolutionary psychologists, women are drawn to men whose intelligence, maturity, ambition, and earning power demonstrate the ability to amass resources and mark them as "good providers" who will help raise children and ensure their survival.

It takes some time to assess these resource-related characteristics (he drives a nice car, but can he afford it?), which is why, according to the evolutionary view, women are more likely than men to prefer a period of courtship prior to mating. Men tend to want to begin a sexual relationship sooner than women (Buss & Schmitt, 1993) because, compared with their female partners, they have little to lose from doing so. On the contrary, their eagerness to engage in sex early in a relationship is seen as reflecting their evolutionary ancestors' tendency toward casual sex as a means of maximizing their genetic contribution to the next generation. In fact, evolutionary psychologists suggest that the desire to produce as many children as possible motivates males' attraction to women whose reproductive capacity and genetic fitness are signified by youth, physical beauty, and good health (Symons, 1995).

These ideas have received some support. For instance, in a survey of more than 10,000 men and women in thirty-three countries on six continents and five isolated islands, males generally preferred youth and good health in prospective female mates, and females generally preferred males who were mature and wealthy (Kenrick, 1994). One example of this sex difference is illustrated in Figure 11.2, which shows the age preferences of men and women who advertised for dates in the personal sections of newspapers in the United States. In general, men were interested in women younger than themselves, but women were interested in older men (Kenrick et al., 1995).

Critics argue that such preferences stem from cultural traditions, not genetic predispositions. Among the Zulu of South Africa, where women are expected to build houses, carry water, and perform other physically demanding tasks, men tend to value maturity and ambition in a mate more than women do (Buss, 1989). The

Evolution at Work? The marriage of Rod Stewart and Penny Lancaster, a former model who is twenty-six years his junior, illustrates the worldwide tendency for older men to prefer younger women, and vice versa. This tendency has been interpreted as evidence supporting an evolutionary explanation of mate selection, but skeptics see social and economic forces at work in establishing these preference patterns.

FIGURE **11.2**

Age Preferences in Personal Advertisements

An analysis of 486 personal ads placed in newspapers around the United States showed a sex difference in age preferences. As men got older, their preferences for younger women increased, whereas women, regardless of age, preferred men who were about their own age or older.

Source: Kenrick et al. (1995, Figure 1).

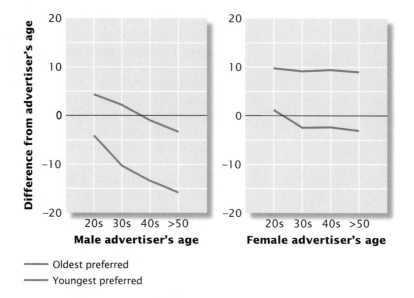

Male advertiser's age   Female advertiser's age

—— Oldest preferred
—— Youngest preferred

fact that women have been systematically denied economic and political power in many cultures may account for their tendency to rely on the security and economic power provided by men (Eagly, Wood, & Johannesen-Schmidt, 2004; Silverstein, 1996). Indeed, an analysis of data from thirty-seven cultures showed that women valued potential mates' access to resources far more in cultures that sharply limited women's reproductive freedoms and educational opportunities (Kasser & Sharma, 1999). Evolutionary theorists acknowledge the role of cultural forces and traditions in shaping behavior, but they ask whether evolutionary factors might contribute to the appearance of these forces and traditions and the relative ease with which gender roles seem to develop in all cultures (Hrdy, 1997, 2003).

By emphasizing the evolutionary roots of human behavior, contemporary versions of instinct theory focus on the ultimate, long-term reasons behind what we do and the circumstances in which evolved predispositions are, or are not, expressed. The theories of motivation discussed next highlight influences that serve as more immediate causes of behavior (Alcock, 2001).

● Drive Reduction Theory

Like instinct theory, drive reduction theory emphasizes internal factors, but it is based on the concept of homeostasis. **Homeostasis** (pronounced "ho-me-oh-STAY-sis") is the tendency to keep physiological systems at a steady level, or *equilibrium*, by constantly making adjustments in response to change. We describe a version of this concept in the chapter on biological aspects of psychology, in relation to feedback loops that keep hormones at desirable levels. According to **drive reduction theory,** an imbalance in homeostasis creates a **need**—a biological requirement for well-being. The brain responds to such needs by creating a psychological state called a **drive**—a feeling of arousal that prompts an organism to take action, restore the balance, and as a result, reduce the drive (Hull, 1943). For example, if you have had no water for some time, the chemical balance of your body fluids is disturbed, creating a biological need for water. One consequence of this need is a drive—thirst—that motivates you to find and drink water. After you drink, the need for water is met, so the drive to drink is reduced. In other words, drives push people to satisfy needs, thereby reducing the drives and the arousal they create (see Figure 11.3).

● **homeostasis** The tendency for organisms to keep their physiological systems at a stable, steady level by constantly adjusting themselves in response to change.

● **drive reduction theory** A theory of motivation stating that motivation arises from imbalances in homeostasis.

● **need** A biological requirement for well-being that is created by an imbalance in homeostasis.

● **drive** A psychological state of arousal created by an imbalance in homeostasis that prompts an organism to take action to restore the balance and reduce the drive.

FIGURE **11.3**

Drive Reduction Theory and Homeostasis

The mechanisms of homeostasis, such as the regulation of body temperature or food and water intake, are often compared to thermostats. If the temperature in a house drops below the thermostat setting, the furnace comes on and brings the temperature up to that preset level, achieving homeostasis. When the temperature reaches the preset point, the furnace shuts off.

Need (biological disturbance)

Unbalanced equilibrium

Drive (psychological state that provides motivation to satisfy need)

Equilibrium restored

Behavior that satisfies need and reduces drive

Optimal Arousal and Personality
According to optimal arousal theory, boldness, shyness, and other personality traits and behavioral tendencies reflect individual differences in the level of arousal that people find ideal for them. As described in the personality chapter, these differences in optimal arousal arise largely from inherited differences in the nervous system (Eysenck, 1990a).

arousal A general level of activation that is reflected in several physiological systems.

optimal arousal theory A theory of motivation stating that people are motivated to behave in ways that maintain what is, for them, an optimal level of arousal.

● Optimal Arousal Theory

Drive reduction theory can account for a wide range of motivated behaviors. But humans and other animals often go to great lengths to do things that don't appear to reduce drives. Consider curiosity. People, rats, monkeys, dogs, and many other creatures explore and manipulate their surroundings, even though these activities do not lead to drive reduction. They will also exert considerable effort simply to enter a new environment, especially if it is complex and full of new or unusual objects (Loewenstein, 1994). We go to the new mall, watch builders work, surf the Internet, and travel the world just to see what there is to see. Some of us also go out of our way to ride roller coasters, skydive, drive race-cars, and do countless other things that, like curiosity-motivated behaviors, do not reduce any known drive (Zuckerman, 1996). In fact, these behaviors cause an *increase* in **arousal,** a general level of activation that is reflected in the state of several physiological systems, including the brain, heart, lungs, and muscles (Plutchik & Conte, 1997).

The realization that we sometimes act in ways that increase arousal and sometimes act in ways that decrease it has led some psychologists to argue that people are motivated to *regulate arousal* so that it stays at roughly the same level most of the time. Specifically, according to **optimal arousal theory,** we are motivated to behave in ways that maintain or restore an ideal, or *optimal* level of arousal (Hebb, 1955). In other words, we try to increase arousal when it is too low and decrease it when it is too high. So after a day of dull chores, you may want to see an exciting movie, but if your day was spent playing baseball, debating a political issue, and helping a friend move, an evening of quiet relaxation may seem ideal.

Where is the optimal level of arousal? In general, people perform best, and may feel best, when arousal is moderate (Teigen, 1994; see Figure 11.4). Too much arousal can hurt performance, as when test anxiety interferes with some students' ability to recall what they have studied or when some athletes "choke" so badly that they miss an easy catch or a simple shot (Smith et al., 2000; Wright et al., 1995). Underarousal, too, can cause problems, as you probably know if you have ever tried to work, drive, or study when you are sleepy. So the optimal level of arousal lies somewhere between these extremes, but exactly where that level is can vary from

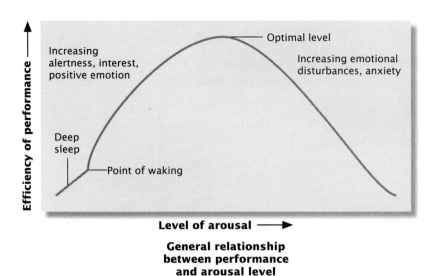

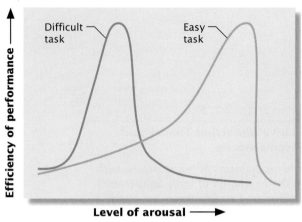

FIGURE 11.4

The Arousal-Performance Relationship

Notice in part (A) that performance is poorest when arousal is very low or very high and best when arousal is at a moderate level. When you are either sleepy or overly excited, for example, it may be difficult to think clearly or to be physically coordinated. In general, optimal performance comes at a lower level of arousal on difficult or complex tasks and at a higher level of arousal on easy tasks, as shown in part (B). Even a relatively small amount of overarousal can cause students to perform far below their potential on difficult tests (Sarason, 1984). Because animal research early in this century by Robert Yerkes and his colleagues provided supportive evidence, this arousal-performance relationship is sometimes referred to as the *Yerkes-Dodson law*, even though Yerkes never actually discussed performance as a function of arousal (Teigen, 1994).

person to person (Zuckerman, 1984). People whose optimal arousal is relatively high try to keep it there, so they are more likely than other people to smoke, drink alcohol, engage in frequent sexual activity, listen to loud music, eat spicy foods, and do things that are novel and risky (Farley, 1986; Zuckerman, 1979). Those with relatively low optimal arousal try to keep it low; so they tend to take fewer risks and behave in ways that are not overly stimulating. Most of these differences in optimal arousal have a strong biological basis and, as discussed in the personality chapter, may help shape other characteristics, such as whether we tend to be introverted or extraverted (Eysenck, 1990a).

●   Incentive Theory

Instinct, drive reduction, and optimal arousal theories of motivation all focus on internal processes that prompt people to behave in certain ways. By contrast, **incentive theory** emphasizes the role of external stimuli that can motivate behavior by pulling us toward them or pushing us away from them. More specifically, people are said to behave in order to get positive incentives and avoid negative incentives. According to incentive theory, then, differences in behavior from one person to another, or in the same person from one situation to another, can be traced to the incentives available and the value a person places on them at the time. If you expect a behavior (such as buying a lottery ticket) to lead to a valued outcome (winning lots of money), you will want to engage in that behavior. The value of an incentive is influenced by physiological, cognitive, and social factors. For example, food is a more motivating incentive when you are hungry than when you are full (Balleine & Dickinson, 1994). As for cognitive and social influences, notice that the value of

● **incentive theory**   A theory of motivation stating that behavior is directed toward attaining desirable stimuli and avoiding unwanted stimuli.

in review	Theories of Motivation
Theory	**Main Points**
Instinct	Innate biological instincts guide behavior.
Drive reduction	Behavior is guided by biological needs and learned ways of reducing drives arising from those needs.
Optimal arousal	People seek to maintain an optimal level of physiological arousal, which differs from person to person. Maximum performance occurs at optimal arousal levels.
Incentive	Behavior is guided by the lure of positive incentives and the avoidance of negative incentives. Cognitive factors influence expectations of the value of various rewards and the likelihood of attaining them.

some things we eat—such as communion wafers or diet shakes—isn't determined by hunger or flavor but by what our culture has taught us about spirituality, health, or attractiveness.

It may seem obvious that people are motivated to approach things they like and to avoid things they don't like, but the story of incentive theory is not quite that simple. Psychologists have found that people sometimes work hard for some incentives only to find that they don't enjoy having them nearly as much as they thought they would (Gilbert, 2006; Wilson & Gilbert, 2005). Indeed, motivation theorists distinguish between wanting and liking. *Wanting* is the process of being attracted to incentives, whereas *liking* is the immediate evaluation of how pleasurable a stimulus is (Berridge, 1999). Studies with laboratory animals have shown that these two systems involve activity in separate parts of the brain, and they involve different neurotransmitters (Peciña et al., 2003). For example, dopamine, a neurotransmitter associated with the pleasure experienced through sex, drugs, and gambling, appears important in activating the wanting system. Some evidence for this idea comes from a study that found an unusual increase in compulsive gambling among people who had begun taking dopamine-enhancing drugs for Parkinson's disease (Dodd et al., 2005). It appears, too, that the wanting system can compel behavior to a far greater extent than does the liking system. For instance, the drug-seeking efforts made by addicted people are often far more intense than the actual pleasure that they get from using the drugs (Robinson & Berridge, 2003). Further, the operation of the wanting system varies according to whether an individual has been deprived (Nader, Bechara, & Van der Kooy, 1997). So although you might like apple pie, your motivation to eat some would be affected by different brain regions, depending on whether the pie is served as an appetizer (when you are hungry) or as a dessert (when you are full).

The theories of motivation we have outlined (see "In Review: Theories of Motivation") complement one another. Each emphasizes different sources of motivation, and each has helped to guide research into motivated behaviors, including eating, sex, and achievement-related activities, which are the topics of the next three sections.

Hunger and Eating

Hunger is deceptively simple; you get hungry when you don't eat. Much as a car needs gas, you need fuel from food. Is there a bodily mechanism that, like a car's gas gauge, signals the need for fuel? What causes hunger? What determines which foods hunger—and the eating of particular types of food—is related to the effects of various neurotransmitters on certain neurons in the brain. One of these neurotransmitters, called *neuropeptide Y*, stimulates increased eating of carbohydrates (Kishi & Elmquist, 2005; Schwartz et al., 2000), whereas another one, *serotonin*, suppresses carbohydrate intake. *Galanin* motivates the eating of high-fat food (Krykouli et al., 1990), whereas *enteristatin* reduces it (Lin et al., 1998). *Endocannabinoids* stimulate eating in general. They affect the same hypothalamic receptors as does the active ingredient in marijuana, which may account for "the munchies," a sudden hunger that marijuana use often creates (Cota et al., 2003; Di Marzo et al., 2001). *Peptide YY3-36* causes a feeling of fullness and reduced food intake (Batterham et al., 2002, 2003).

In other words, several brain regions and many chemicals help to regulate hunger and food selection. These regulatory processes are not set in stone, however. They are shaped, and sometimes overridden, by social, cultural, and other factors.

● Flavor, Cultural Learning, and Food Selection

One factor that can override a set point is the *flavor* of food—the combination of its taste and smell (Carlson, 2001). In one experiment, some animals were offered just a single type of food, whereas others were offered foods of several different flavors. The group getting the varied menu ate nearly four times more than the one-food group. As each new food appeared, the animals began to eat voraciously, regardless of how much they had already eaten (Peck, 1978). Humans behave in similar ways. All things being equal, people eat more food during a multicourse meal than when only one food is served (Raynor & Epstein, 2001). Apparently, the flavor of any particular food becomes less enjoyable as more of it is eaten (Swithers & Hall, 1994). In one study, for example, people rated how much they liked four kinds of food. Then they ate one of the foods and rated all four again. The food they had just eaten now got a lower rating, whereas liking increased for all the rest (Johnson & Vickers, 1993).

Another factor that can override blood-borne signals about satiety is *appetite*, the motivation to seek food's pleasures. For example, the appearance and aroma of certain foods create conditioned physiological responses—such as secretion of saliva, gastric juices, and insulin—in anticipation of eating those foods. (The process is based on the principles of classical conditioning described in the chapter on learning.) These responses then increase appetite. So merely seeing a pizza on television may prompt you to order one—even if you hadn't been feeling hungry—and if you see a delicious-looking cookie, you do not have to be hungry to start eating it. In fact, as described in the chapter on introducing psychology, brain-damaged patients who can't remember anything for more than a minute will eat a full meal ten to thirty minutes after finishing one just like it. They may even start a third meal ten to thirty minutes later, simply because the food looks good (Rozin et al., 1998). In other words, people eat not only to satisfy nutritional needs but also to experience enjoyment.

Eating can also be influenced by *specific hungers*, or desires for particular foods at particular times. These hungers appear to reflect the biological need for the nutrients contained in certain foods. In one study, for example, rats were given three bowls of tasty, protein-free food and one bowl of food that tasted bad but was rich in protein. The rats learned to eat enough of the bad-tasting food to get a proper supply of dietary protein (Galef & Wright, 1995).

These results are remarkable in part because protein and many other nutrients such as fats and vitamins have no taste or odor. So how can they guide food choices? As with appetite, learning is probably involved. The taste and odor of food appears to become associated with the food's nutritional value. Evidence for this kind of learning comes from experiments in which rats received infusions of liquid directly into their stomachs. Some of these infusions consisted of plain water; others

included nutritious cornstarch. Each kind of infusion was paired with a different taste—either sour or bitter—in the animals' normal supply of drinking water. Later, both sour water and bitter water were made available. When the animals got hungry, they showed a strong preference for the water whose taste had been associated with the cornstarch infusions (Drucker, Ackroff, & Sclafani, 1994). Related research shows that children come to prefer flavors that have been associated with high-fat ingredients (Johnson, McPhee, & Birch, 1991). The food industry has applied this research to increase demand for its products. For example, the flavorings that fast-food chains routinely add to French fries and hamburger buns have little or no nutritional value, but after becoming associated with those items, they can help trigger cravings for them (Schlosser, 2001).

The role of learning is also seen when we start to eat in response to sights, sounds, and places that have been associated with eating in the past. If you usually eat when reading or watching television, for example, you may find yourself wanting a snack as soon as you sit down with a book or your favorite show. The same phenomenon has been demonstrated in a laboratory study in which, for several days in a row, hungry rats heard a buzzer just before they were fed. The buzzer eventually became so strongly associated with eating that the rats would start eating when it sounded, even if they had just eaten their fill (Weingarten, 1983). Similarly, even after finishing a big meal, children have been found to resume eating if they enter a room where they have previously had snacks (Birch et al., 1989).

People also learn social rules and cultural traditions that influence eating. Munching popcorn at movies and hot dogs at baseball games are examples from North American culture of how certain social situations can stimulate appetite for particular food items. Similarly, how much you eat may depend on what others do. Courtesy or custom might lead you to eat foods you might otherwise have avoided. The mere presence of other people, even strangers, tends to increase our food consumption (Redd & de Castro, 1992). Most people consume 60 to 75 percent more food when they are with others than when eating alone (Clendenen, Herman, & Polivy, 1995); the same effect has been observed in other species, from monkeys to chickens (Galloway et al., 2005; Keeling & Hurink, 1996). And if others stop eating, we may do the same even if we are still hungry—especially if we want to impress them with our self-control (Herman, Roth, & Polivy, 2003).

Eating and food selection are central to the way people function within their cultures. Celebrations, holidays, vacations, and even daily family interactions often revolve around food and what has been called a *food culture* (Rozin, 1996). As any world traveler knows, there are wide cultural variations in foods and food selection. For example, chewing coca leaves is popular in the Bolivian highlands but illegal in the United States (Burchard, 1992). In China, people in urban areas eat a high-cholesterol diet rich in animal meat, whereas those in rural areas eat so little meat as to be cholesterol deficient (Tian et al., 1995). And the insects known as *palm weevils*, a popular food for people in Papua New Guinea (Paoletti, 1995), are regarded by many Westerners as disgusting (Springer & Belk, 1994). Even within the same general culture, different groups may have sharply contrasting food traditions. Squirrel brains won't be found on most dinner tables in the United States, but some people in the rural South consider them to be a tasty treat. Culture also plays a role in the amount of food we eat. For example, portion sizes in restaurants, grocery stores, and even cookbook recipes tend to be smaller in France, Britain, and other European countries than in the United States (Rozin et al., 2003). Europeans also tend to eat more slowly, which allows satiety signals to reach their brains before they have overindulged. Some of these differences between "slow-food" and "fast-food" cultures might account for why residents of some countries eat less than those in other countries but feel equally satisfied (Geier, Rozin, & Doros, 2006; Slow Food Movement, 2001).

To summarize, eating serves functions that go well beyond nutrition—functions that help to remind us of who we are and with whom we identify.

TRY THIS **Bon Appétit!** The definition of "delicacy" differs from culture to culture. At this elegant restaurant in Mexico, diners pay to feast on baby alligators, insects, and other dishes that some people from other cultures would not eat even if the restaurant paid *them*. To appreciate your own food culture, make a list of foods that are traditionally valued by your family or cultural group but that people from other groups do not, or might even be unwilling, to eat.

● Eating Disorders

Problems in the processes regulating hunger and eating may cause an *eating disorder*. The most common and dangerous examples are obesity, anorexia nervosa, and bulimia nervosa.

●**Obesity** The World Health Organization (WHO) defines **obesity** as a condition in which a person's body-mass index, or BMI, is greater than 30. (BMI is determined by dividing a person's weight in kilograms by the square of the person's height in meters. So someone who is 5 feet 2 inches tall and weighs 164 pounds would be classified as obese, as would someone 5 feet 10 inches tall who weighs 207 pounds. BMI calculators appear on web sites such as www.consumer.gov/weightloss/bmi.htm. People whose BMI is 25 to 29.9 are considered to be overweight. (Keep in mind, though, that a given volume of muscle weighs more than the same volume of fat, so very muscular individuals may have an elevated BMI without being overweight.)

Obesity appears to be on the rise among adults and children in regions as diverse as Europe, Asia, South America, Africa, and especially in the United States (e.g., Vasan et al., 2005; Wang & Lobstein, 2006; Wang et al., 2007). Using the BMI criterion, about 32 percent of adults in the United States are obese (Hedley et al., 2004; Ogden et al., 2006). The problem has become so common that commercial jets have to burn excess fuel to carry heavier loads, parents of obese young children have trouble finding car safety seats to fit them, and the funeral industry has to offer larger than normal coffins and order wider hearses (Dannenberg, Burton, & Jackson, 2004; St. John, 2003; Trifiletti et al., 2006). Obesity is associated with disability and with health problems such as diabetes, high blood pressure, an increased risk of heart attack, and possibly Alzheimer's disease (Gustafson et al., 2003; Lakdawalla, Bhattacharya, & Goldman, 2004; Nanchahal et al., 2005). Particularly alarming is the increase in obesity-associated diabetes among children and adolescents; cases have been confirmed in children as young as four (American Diabetes Association, 2000). In the United States alone, obesity is blamed for about 30,000 deaths each year and for a predicted shortening of life expectancy in the twenty-first century (Adams et al., 2006; Flegal et al., 2005; Olshansky et al., 2005).

The precise reasons for this obesity epidemic are unknown, but possible causes include big portion sizes at fast-food outlets, greater prevalence of high-fat foods, and less physical activity associated with both work and recreation (e.g., Adachi-Mejia et al., 2007; Slentz et al., 2004). These are important factors, because the body maintains a given weight through a combination of food intake and energy output (Keesey & Powley, 1986). Obese people get more energy from food than their body *metabolizes*, or "burns up"; the excess energy, measured in *calories*, is stored as fat. Metabolism declines during sleep and rises with physical activity. Because women tend to have a lower metabolic rate than men, even when equally active, they tend to gain weight more easily than do men with similar diets (Ferraro et al., 1992). Most obese people have normal resting metabolic rates, but they tend to eat above-average amounts of high-calorie, tasty foods and below-average amounts of less tasty foods (Kauffman, Herman, & Polivy, 1995). Further, some obese people are less active than lean people, a pattern that often begins in childhood (Jago et al., 2005; Marshall et al., 2004; Strauss & Pollack, 2001). Spending long hours watching television or playing computer games may contribute to the inactivity seen in overweight children (Hancox & Poulton, 2006).

In short, inadequate physical activity, combined with overeating—especially of the high-fat foods so prevalent in most Western cultures—has a lot to do with obesity. But not everyone who is inactive and eats a high-fat diet becomes obese, and some obese people are as active as lean people, so other factors must also be involved (Blundell & Cooling, 2000; Parsons, Power, & Manor, 2005). Some people probably have a genetic predisposition toward obesity (Bouchard et al., 2007; Farooqi & O'Rahilly, 2004). For example, although most obese people have the

● **obesity** A condition in which a person is severely overweight, as measured by a body-mass index greater than 30.

genes to make leptin, they may not be sensitive to its weight-suppressing effects—perhaps because of genetic codes in leptin receptors in the hypothalamus. Recent brain imaging studies also suggest that obese people's brains may be slower to "read" satiety signals coming from their blood, thus causing them to continue eating when leaner people would have stopped (Liu et al., 2000; Morton et al., 2006). These factors, along with the presence of one or more recently discovered viruses in the body (Dhurandhar et al., 2000), may help explain obese people's tendency to eat more, to accumulate fat, and to feel more hunger than lean people.

Psychological explanations for obesity focus on factors such as learning from examples set by parents who overeat, too little parental control over what and how much children eat, and maladaptive reactions to stress (Birch et al., 2001; Hood et al., 2000). Many people do tend to eat more when under stress, a reaction that may be especially extreme among those who become obese (Dallman et al., 2003).

For most people, and especially for people who are obese, it is a lot easier to gain weight than to lose it and keep it off (Jain, 2005; McTigue et al., 2003). The problem arises partly because our evolutionary ancestors—like nonhuman animals in the wild today—could not always be sure that food would be available. Those who survived lean times were the ones whose genes created tendencies to build and maintain fat reserves (e.g., Hara et al., 2000). These "thrifty genes" are adaptive in famine-plagued environments, but they can be harmful and even deadly in affluent societies in which overeating is unnecessary and in which donut shops and fast-food restaurants are on every corner. Further, if people starve themselves to lose weight, their bodies may burn calories more slowly. This drop in metabolism saves energy and fat reserves and slows weight loss (Leibel, Rosenbaum, & Hirsch, 1995). No wonder health and nutrition experts warn that obese people (and others) should not try to lose a great deal of weight quickly by dramatically cutting food intake (Brownell & Rodin, 1994).

Given the complexity of factors leading to obesity and the seriousness of its health consequences, it is not surprising that many treatment approaches have been developed. Perhaps the most radical approach is *bariatric surgery* (Hamad, 2004). There are several versions of the procedure, all of which involve restructuring the stomach and intestines so that less food energy is absorbed and stored. Despite its costs and risks—postoperative mortality rates are between 0.1 and 2 percent—bariatric surgery is being performed on about 103,000 people a year (Santry, Gillen, & Lauderdale, 2005). The popularity of these procedures has been fueled partly by the examples of NBC TV personality Al Roker and other celebrities whose surgery resulted in dramatic weight loss.

Surgery is recommended mainly for extreme and life-threatening cases of obesity; millions of other people are taking anti-obesity medications (Stafford & Radley, 2003). Among the drugs developed so far is one that prevents fat in foods from being digested (e.g., Finer et al., 2000; Hauptman et al., 2000). Another one appears to dissolve fat (Kolonin et al., 2004), and still another drug has been found to interfere with an enzyme that forms fat. This "fatty acid synthase inhibitor" not only caused rapid weight loss in mice but also reduced their hunger (Loftus et al., 2000). Some of these drugs have not yet been tested for safety and effectiveness in humans, but researchers hope that there may someday be medications that can alter fat deposits or the brain mechanisms involved in overeating and fat storage (Arterburn, Crane, & Veenstra, 2004; Chanoine et al., 2005; Wynne et al., 2005).

Even the best drug treatments are unlikely to solve the problem on their own. In fact, no single anti-obesity treatment is likely to be a safe, effective solution that works for everyone. To achieve the kind of gradual weight loss that is most likely to last, obese people are advised to increase exercise, because it burns calories without slowing metabolism (Tremblay & Bueman, 1995). In fact, a regular regimen of aerobic exercise and weight training *raises* the metabolic rate (Curioni & Lourenço, 2005; Wadden et al., 2005). The most effective weight-loss programs include components designed to reduce food intake, change eating habits and attitudes toward

Thin Is In In Western cultures today, thinness is a much-sought-after ideal, especially among young women who are dissatisfied with their appearance. That ideal is seen in fashion models, as well as in Miss America pageant winners, whose body-mass index has decreased from the "normal" range of 20 to 25 in the 1920s to an "undernourished" 18.5 more recently (Rubinstein & Caballero, 2000; Voracek & Fisher, 2002). In the United States, 35 percent of normal-weight girls—and 12 percent of underweight girls!—begin dieting when they are as young as nine or ten. Correlational studies suggest that many of these children's efforts to lose weight may have come in response to criticism from family members (Barr Taylor et al., 2006a); for some, the result is anorexia.

● **anorexia nervosa** An eating disorder characterized by self-starvation and dramatic weight loss.

● **bulimia nervosa** An eating disorder that involves eating massive amounts of food and then eliminating the food by self-induced vomiting or the use of strong laxatives.

food, and increase energy expenditure through exercise (Bray & Tartaglia, 2000; National Task Force on the Prevention and Treatment of Obesity, 2000; Stice & Shaw, 2004; Wadden et al., 2001).

● **Anorexia Nervosa** At the opposite extreme from obesity is **anorexia nervosa**, an eating disorder characterized by some combination of self-starvation, self-induced vomiting, and laxative use that results in weight loss to below 85 percent of normal (Kaye et al., 2000). About 95 percent of people who suffer from anorexia are young females. Individuals with anorexia often feel hungry, and many are obsessed with food and its preparation, yet they refuse to eat. Anorexic self-starvation causes serious, often irreversible physical damage, including reduction in bone density that enhances the risk of fractures (Grinspoon et al., 2000). The health dangers may be especially high in dancers, gymnasts, and other female athletes with anorexia because the combination of self-starvation and excessive exercise increases their risk for stress fractures and heart problems (Davis & Kapstein, 2006; Sherman & Thompson, 2004). Between 4 and 30 percent of people with anorexia die of starvation, biochemical imbalances, or suicide. Their risk of death is twelve times higher than that of other young women (Millar et al., 2005; National Association of Anorexia Nervosa and Associated Disorders, 2002). Anorexia tends to appear in adolescence, when concern over appearance becomes intense. The incidence of anorexia appears to be on the increase; it now affects about 1 percent of young women in the United States and is a growing problem in many other industrialized nations as well (American Psychiatric Association Work Group on Eating Disorders, 2000; Bulik et al., 2006; Rome et al., 2003).

The causes of anorexia are not yet clear, but they probably involve a combination of factors, including genetic predispositions, biochemical imbalances, social influences, and psychological characteristics (Bulik et al., 2000, 2006; Jacobi et al., 2004; Klump & Culbert, 2007; Ribases et al., 2005). Psychological factors that may contribute to the problem include a self-punishing, perfectionistic personality and a culturally reinforced obsession with thinness and attractiveness (APA Task Force on the Sexualization of Girls, 2007; Dittmar, Halliwell, & Ive, 2006; Dohnt & Tiggermann, 2006; Francis & Birch, 2005; Moradi, Dirks, & Matteson, 2005). Individuals with anorexia appear to develop a fear of being fat, which they take to dangerous extremes. Many of them continue to view themselves as fat or misshapen even as they are wasting away (Feingold & Mazzella, 1998).

Drugs, hospitalization, and psychotherapy are all used to treat anorexia. In many cases, treatment brings recovery and maintenance of normal weight (National Institutes of Health, 2001; Pike et al., 2003), but more effective treatment methods and early intervention methods are still needed (Agras et al., 2004). Prevention programs now being tested with college women at high risk for developing anorexia are showing promising results (e.g., Barr Taylor et al., 2006b; Franko et al., 2005).

● **Bulimia Nervosa** Like anorexia, bulimia nervosa involves intense fear of being fat, but the person may be thin, normal in weight, or even overweight. **Bulimia nervosa** involves eating huge amounts of food (say, several boxes of cookies, a half-gallon of ice cream, and a bucket of fried chicken) and then getting rid of the food through self-induced vomiting or strong laxatives. These "binge-purge" episodes may occur as often as twice a day (Weltzin et al., 1995).

Like people with anorexia, those with bulimia are usually female, and like anorexia, bulimia usually begins with a desire to be slender. However, bulimia and anorexia are separate disorders (Pryor, 1995). For one thing, most people with bulimia see their eating habits as problematic, whereas most individuals with anorexia do not. In addition, bulimia nervosa is usually not life-threatening (Thompson, 1996). There are health consequences, however, including dehydration, nutritional problems, and intestinal damage. Many people with bulimia develop dental problems from the acids associated with vomiting. Frequent vomiting and the

in review · Major Factors Controlling Hunger and Eating

	Stimulate Eating	Inhibit Eating
Biological factors	Levels of glucose and insulin in the blood provide signals that stimulate eating; neurotransmitters that affect neurons in different regions of the hypothalamus also stimulate food intake and influence hungers for specific kinds of foods, such as fats and carbohydrates. Stomach contractions are associated with subjective feelings of hunger, but they do not play a substantial role in the stimulation of eating.	Hormones released into the bloodstream produce signals that inhibit eating; hormones such as leptin, CCK, and insulin act as neurotransmitters or neuromodulators and affect neurons in the hypothalamus and inhibit eating. The ventromedial nucleus of the hypothalamus may be a "satiety center" that monitors these hormones.
Nonbiological factors	Sights and smells of particular foods elicit eating because of prior associations; family customs and social occasions often include norms for eating in particular ways; stress is often associated with eating more.	Values in contemporary U.S. society encourage thinness and thus can inhibit eating.

insertion of objects to trigger it can also cause damage to the throat. More generally, a preoccupation with eating and avoiding weight gain prevents many individuals with bulimia from working productively (Herzog, 1982).

Estimates of the frequency of bulimia range from 1 to 3 percent of adolescent and college-age women (National Institutes of Health, 2001; U.S. Surgeon General, 1999). It appears to be caused by a combination of factors, including perfectionism, low self-esteem, stress, culturally encouraged preoccupation with being thin, depression and other emotional problems, and as-yet-undetermined biological problems that might include defective satiety mechanisms (Crowther et al., 2001; Smith et al., 2007; Stice & Fairburn, 2003; Zalta & Keel, 2006). Treatment for bulimia typically includes individual or group therapy and, sometimes, antidepressant drugs. These treatments help the vast majority of people with bulimia to eat more normally (Herzog et al., 1999).

The health effects of obesity, anorexia, bulimia, and other eating disorders—including recently identified patterns known as binge-eating disorder (Manwaring et al., 2006) and night-eating syndrome (Stunkard, Allison, & O'Reardon, 2005)—remind us that normal patterns of eating are central to our well-being, and explain why psychologists find eating to be such an interesting aspect of human behavior and mental processes. (For a summary of the processes involved in hunger and eating, see "In Review: Major Factors Controlling Hunger and Eating.")

Sexual Behavior

Unlike food, sex is not necessary for an individual's survival. A strong desire for reproduction does help ensure the survival of a species, however. The various factors shaping sexual motivation and behavior differ in strength across species, but they often include a combination of the individual's physiology, learned behavior, and the physical and social environment. For example, one species of desert bird requires adequate sex hormones, a suitable mate, and a particular environment before it begins sexual behavior. During the dry season, it shows no interest in sex, but within ten minutes of the first rain shower the birds vigorously copulate.

Rainfall is obviously much less influential as a sexual trigger for humans. People show a staggering diversity of *sexual scripts*, or patterns of behavior that lead to sex. One survey of college-age men and women identified 122 specific acts and 34 different tactics used for promoting sexual encounters (Greer & Buss, 1994). What happens next? The matter is difficult to address scientifically, because most people are reluctant to respond to specific questions about their sexual practices, let alone to allow researchers to observe their sexual behavior. Yet having valid information about the nature of human sexual behavior is a vital first step for psychologists and other scientists who study such topics as individual differences in sexuality, gender differences in sexual motivation and behavior, sources of sexual orientation, types of sexual dysfunctions, and the pathways through which sexually transmitted diseases (STDs) reach new victims.

FOCUS ON RESEARCH METHODS **A Survey of Human Sexual Behavior**

The first extensive studies of sexual behavior in the United States were done by Alfred Kinsey during the late 1940s and early 1950s (Kinsey, Pomeroy, & Martin, 1948; Kinsey et al., 1953). These were followed in the 1960s by the work of William Masters and Virginia Johnson (1966). Kinsey conducted surveys of people's sex lives; Masters and Johnson actually measured sexual arousal and behavior in volunteers who received natural or artificial stimulation in a laboratory. Together, these studies broke new ground in the exploration of human sexuality, but the people who volunteered for them were probably not a representative sample of the adult population. Accordingly, the results—and any conclusions drawn from them—may not apply to people in general. The results of more recent surveys, such as reader polls in *Cosmopolitan* and other magazines, are also flawed by the use of unrepresentative samples (Davis & Smith, 1990).

■ What was the researchers' question?

Is there a way to gather data on sexual behavior that is more representative and therefore more revealing about people in general? A team of researchers at the University of Chicago believe there is, so they undertook the National Health and Social Life Survey, the first extensive survey of sexual behavior in the United States since the Kinsey studies (Laumann et al., 1994).

■ How did the researchers answer the question?

This survey included important design features that had been neglected in most other surveys of sexual behavior. First, the study did not depend on self-selected volunteers. The researchers sought out a carefully constructed sample of 3,432 people, ranging in age from eighteen to fifty-nine. Second, the sample reflected the sociocultural diversity of the U.S. population in terms of gender, ethnicity, socioeconomic status, geographical location, and the like. Third, unlike previous mail-in surveys, the Chicago study was based on face-to-face interviews. This approach made it easier to ensure that the participants understood each question and could explain their responses. To encourage honesty, the researchers allowed participants to answer some questions anonymously by placing written responses in a sealed envelope.

■ What did the researchers find?

The researchers found that people in the United States have sex less often and with fewer people than many had assumed. For most, sex occurs about once a week, and only with a partner with whom they share a stable relationship. About a third of the participants reported having sex only a few times, or not at all, in the past year. And in contrast to certain celebrities' splashy tales of dozens, even hundreds, of sexual partners per year, the average male survey participant had only six sexual partners in his entire life. The average female respondent reported a lifetime total of two. Further, the survey data suggested that people in committed, one-partner relationships had the most frequent and the most satisfying sex. And although a wide variety of specific sexual practices were reported, the over-whelming majority of heterosexual couples said they tend to engage mainly in penis-vagina intercourse.

■ What do the results mean?

The Chicago survey challenges some of the cultural and media images of sexuality in the United States. In particular, it suggests that people in the United States may be more sexually conservative than one might think on the basis of magazine reader polls and the testimony of guests on daytime talk shows.

■ What do we still need to know?

Many questions remain. The Chicago survey did not ask about some of the more controversial aspects of human sexuality, such as the effects of pornography, the prevalence of pedophilia (sexual attraction to children), and the role in sexual activity of sexual fetishes such as shoes or other clothing. Had the researchers asked about such topics, their results might have painted a less conservative picture. Further, because the original Chicago survey focused on people in the United States, it told us little or nothing about the sexual practices, traditions, and values of people in the rest of the world.

The Chicago team has continued to conduct interviews, and the results are beginning to fill in the picture about sexual behavior in the United States and around the world (Youm & Laumann, 2002). They have found, for example, that nearly one-quarter of U.S. women prefer to achieve sexual satisfaction without partners of either sex. And although people in the United States tend to engage in a wider variety of sexual behaviors than those in Britain, there is less tolerance in the United States of disapproved sexual practices (Laumann & Michael, 2000; Michael et al., 1998). Other researchers have found a number of consistent gender differences in sexuality. For example, men tend to have a stronger interest in and desire for sex than women, whereas women are more likely than men to associate sexual activity with a committed relationship (Baumeister, Catanese, & Vohs, 2001; Peplau, 2003; Regan & Berscheid, 1999).

The results of even the best survey methods—like the results of all research methods—usually raise as many questions as they answer. When do people become interested in sex, and why? How do they choose to express these desires, and why? What determines their sexual likes and dislikes? How do learning and sociocultural factors modify the biological forces that seem to provide the raw material of human sexual motivation? These are some of the questions about human sexual behavior that a survey cannot easily or accurately explore (Benson, 2003b). ■

● The Biology of Sex

Observations in Masters and Johnson's laboratory led to important findings about the **sexual response cycle,** the pattern of physiological arousal during and after sexual activity (see Figure 11.5).

People's motivation to engage in sexual activity has biological roots in **sex hormones.** These hormones include **estrogens, progestins** (the main progestins are *estradiol* and *progesterone*), and **androgens** (the main one is *testosterone*). Each sex hormone flows in the blood of both sexes, but the average man has relatively more androgens, and the average woman has relatively more estrogens and progestins. Sex hormones have both organizational and activational effects on the brain. The *organizational* effects are permanent changes that alter the brain's response to hormones. The *activational* effects are temporary behavioral changes that last only as long as a hormone level remains elevated, such as during puberty or in the ovulation phase of the monthly menstrual cycle.

---

sexual response cycle The pattern of physiological arousal during and after sexual activity.

sex hormones Chemicals in the blood of males and females that have both organizational and activational effects on sexual behavior.

estrogen A sex hormone that circulates in the bloodstream of both men and women; relatively more estrogens circulate in women.

progestin A sex hormone that circulates in the bloodstream of both men and women; relatively more progestins circulate in women.

androgen A sex hormone that circulates in the bloodstream in both sexes; relatively more androgens circulate in men than in women.

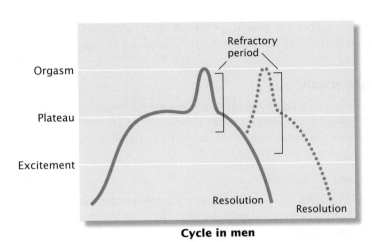

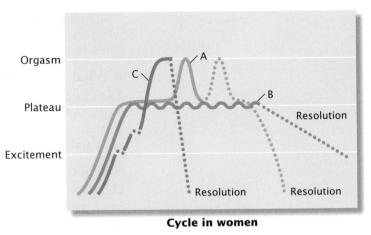

FIGURE 11.5

The Sexual Response Cycle

As shown at left, Masters and Johnson (1966) found that men display one main pattern of sexual response. Women display at least three different patterns from time to time; these are labeled A, B, and C in the right-hand graph. For both men and women, the *excitement* phase begins with sexual stimulation from the environment or one's own thoughts. Continued stimulation leads to intensified excitement in the *plateau* phase, and if stimulation continues, to the intensely pleasurable release of tension in the *orgasmic* stage. During the *resolution* phase, both men and women experience a state of relaxation. Following resolution, men enter a *refractory* phase, during which they are unresponsive to sexual stimulation. Women are capable of immediately repeating the cycle.

Source: Adapted from Masters & Johnson (1966).

In mammals, including humans, the organizational effects of hormones occur around the time of birth, when certain brain areas are sculpted into a "male-like" or "female-like" pattern. These areas are described as *sexually dimorphic*. In rodents, for example, a sexually dimorphic area of the hypothalamus appears to underlie specific sexual behaviors. When these areas are destroyed in male gerbils, the animals can no longer copulate; yet damage to other nearby brain regions does not affect sexual behavior (Yahr & Jacobsen, 1994). Sexually dimorphic areas also exist in the human hypothalamus and elsewhere in the brain (Breedlove, 1994; Kimura, 1999). For example, an area of the hypothalamus called the *bed nucleus of the stria terminalis* (*BnST*) is generally smaller in women than in men. Its possible role in some aspects of human sexuality was suggested by a study of transsexual men—genetic males who feel like women and who may request surgery and hormone treatments in order to appear more female. The BnST in these men was smaller than in other men; in fact, it was about the size usually seen in women (Zhou et al., 1995).

Rising levels of sex hormones during puberty have activational effects, resulting in increased sexual desire and interest in sexual behavior. Generally, estrogens and androgens stimulate females' sexual interest (Burleson, Gregory, & Trevarthen, 1995; Sherwin & Gelfand, 1987). Androgens raise males' sexual interest (Davidson, Camargo, & Smith, 1979). The activational effects of hormones are also seen in reduced sexual motivation and behavior among people whose hormone-secreting ovaries or testes have been removed for medical reasons. Injections of hormones help restore these people's sexual interest and activity.

Because different neurochemicals affect different aspects of sexuality in mammals, the hormones that affect sexual *desire* do not affect the physical ability to have sex (Wallen & Lovejoy, 1993). This fact may explain why castration does not prevent sex crimes in male offenders. Men with low testosterone levels due to medical problems or castration show less sexual desire, but they still show physiological responses to erotic stimuli (Kwan et al., 1983). So a sex offender treated with androgen antagonists or castration would be less likely to seek out sex, but he would still respond as before to his favorite sexual stimuli (Wickham, 2001).

● Social and Cultural Factors in Sexuality

In humans, sexuality is shaped by a lifetime of learning and thinking that modifies the biological "raw materials" provided by hormones. For example, children learn some of their sexual attitudes and behaviors as part of the development of *gender roles*, which we discuss in the chapter on human development. The specific attitudes and behaviors learned depend partly on the nature of those gender roles in a particular culture (Baumeister, 2000; Hyde & Durik, 2000; Peplau, 2003). One survey of the sexual experiences of more than 1,500 college students in the United States, Japan, and Russia found numerous cross-cultural differences in the ways that men and women behave in sexual situations (Sprecher et al., 1994). For example, more women than men in the United States had consented to sex when they did not really want it. In Russia and Japan, men and women were about equally likely to have had this experience.

There are gender differences, too, in what people find sexually appealing. For example, in many cultures, men are far more interested in, and responsive to, pornographic films and other erotic stimuli than women are (Herz & Cahill, 1997; Symons, 1979). The difference in responsiveness was demonstrated in an MRI study that scanned the brain activity of males and females while they looked at erotic photographs (Hamann et al., 2004). As expected, the males showed greater activity in the amygdala and hypothalamus than the females. This result seems to reflect a sex difference in the way male and female brains are "wired." However, it is also important to note that the male and female participants rated the photos to be equally attractive and sexually arousing. In another study, when men reported sexual arousal in response to erotic films, they also showed signs of physiological arousal. For women, self-reports of arousal were not strongly correlated with signs of physiological arousal (Chivers et al., 2004).

These are just a few examples of the fact that sexuality is a product of a complex mixture of factors. Each person's learning history, cultural background, and perceptions of the world interact so deeply with such a wide range of physiological processes that—as in many other aspects of human behavior and mental processes—it is impossible to separate their influence on sexuality. Nowhere is this point clearer than in the case of sexual orientation.

Social Influences on Sexual Behavior
Sexual behavior is shaped by many sociocultural forces. For example, concern over transmission of the AIDS virus during sex has prompted school-based educational programs in the United States to encourage premarital sexual abstinence or "safe sex" using condoms. These efforts have helped to change young people's sexual attitudes and practices (American Academy of Pediatrics, 2001; Everett et al., 2000).

● Sexual Orientation

Sexual orientation refers to the nature of a person's enduring emotional, romantic, or sexual attraction to others (American Psychological Association, 2002a). The most common sexual orientation is **heterosexual,** in which the attraction is to members of the other sex. When attraction focuses on members of one's own sex, the orientation is called **homosexual,** and more specifically, *gay* (for men) and *lesbian* (for women). People who are attracted to members of both sexes are said to have a **bisexual** orientation. Sexual orientation involves feelings that may or may not be translated into corresponding patterns of sexual behavior (Pathela et al., 2006). For example, some people whose orientation is homosexual or bisexual may have sex only with opposite-sex partners. Similarly, people whose orientation is heterosexual may have had one or more same-sex encounters.

In many cultures, heterosexuality has long been regarded as a moral norm, and homosexuality has been seen as a disease, a mental disorder, or even a crime (Hooker, 1993). Attempts to alter the sexual orientation of homosexuals—using psychotherapy, brain surgery, or electric shock—were usually ineffective (American Psychiatric Association, 1999; Haldeman, 1994). In 1973 the American Psychiatric Association dropped homosexuality from the *Diagnostic and Statistical Manual of Mental Disorders,* thus ending its official status as a form of psychopathology. The same change was made by the World Health Organization in its *International Classification of Diseases* in 1993, by Japan's psychiatric organization in 1995, and by the Chinese Psychiatric Association in 2001.

Nevertheless, some people still disapprove of homosexuality. Because gays, lesbians, and bisexuals are often the victims of discrimination and even hate crimes, many are reluctant to let their sexual orientation be known (Bernat et al., 2001; Meyer, 2003). It is difficult, therefore, to paint an accurate picture of the mix of heterosexual, homosexual, and bisexual orientations in the general population. In the Chicago sex survey mentioned earlier, 1.4 percent of women and 2.8 percent of men identified themselves as exclusively homosexual (Laumann et al., 1994), figures much lower than the 10 percent found in Kinsey's studies. However, that survey did not allow respondents to give anonymous answers to questions about sexual orientation. Some researchers suggest that if anonymous responses to those questions had been permitted, the prevalence figures for gay, lesbian, and bisexual orientations would have been higher (Bullough, 1995). In fact, studies that have allowed anonymous responding estimate that gay, lesbian, and bisexual people make up between 2 and 21 percent of the population in the United States, Canada, and Western Europe (Aaron et al., 2003; Bagley & Tremblay, 1998; Binson et al., 1995; Savin-Williams, 2006; Sell, Wells, & Wypij, 1995).

THINKING CRITICALLY **What Shapes Sexual Orientation?**

The question of where sexual orientation comes from is a topic of intense debate in scientific circles, on talk shows, in Internet chat rooms, and in everyday conversations.

■ What am I being asked to believe or accept?

One point of view suggests that genes dictate sexual orientation. According to this view, we do not learn a sexual orientation but rather are born with it.

■ What evidence is available to support the assertion?

In 1995, a report by a respected research group suggested that one kind of sexual orientation—namely, homosexuality in males—was associated with a particular gene on the X chromosome (Hu et al., 1995). This finding was not supported by

- **heterosexual** Referring to sexual motivation that is focused on members of the other sex.
- **homosexual** Referring to sexual motivation that is focused on members of one's own sex.
- **bisexual** Referring to sexual motivation that is focused on members of both sexes.

later studies (Rice et al., 1999), but a growing body of evidence from research in behavioral genetics suggests that genes might indeed influence sexual orientation (Kendler et al., 2000; Pillard & Bailey, 1998). One study examined pairs of monozygotic male twins (whose genes are identical), nonidentical twin pairs (whose genes are no more alike than those of any brothers), and pairs of adopted brothers (who are genetically unrelated). To participate in this study, at least one brother in each pair had to be homosexual. As it turned out, the other brother was also homosexual or bisexual in 52 percent of the identical-twin pairs. This was the case in only 22 percent of the nonidentical twin pairs and in just 11 percent of the pairs of adopted brothers (Bailey & Pillard, 1991). Similar findings have been reported for male identical twins raised apart, whose shared sexual orientation cannot be attributed to the effects of a shared environment (Whitam, Diamond, & Martin, 1993). The few available studies of female sexual orientation have yielded similar results (Bailey & Benishay, 1993; Bailey, Dunne, & Martin, 2000).

Evidence for the role of other biological factors in sexual orientation comes from research on the impact of sex hormones. In adults, differences in the levels of these hormones are not generally associated with differences in sexual orientation. However, hormonal differences during prenatal development might be involved in the shaping of sexual orientation (Lalumière, Blanchard, & Zucker, 2000; Lippa, 2003; Williams et al., 2000). Support for this view is provided by research on a disorder that causes the adrenal glands to secrete extremely high levels of androgens prior to birth (Carlson, 1998). Women exposed to high androgen levels because of this disorder were much more likely to become lesbians than their sisters who had not been exposed (Meyer et al., 1995). Such hormonal influences can alter the structure of the hypothalamus, a brain region known to underlie some aspects of sexual functioning (Swaab & Hofman, 1995). It has been suggested that prenatal exposure to hormones and other chemicals may be responsible for anatomical differences in the hypothalamus that are seen not only in males versus females but also in homosexual versus heterosexual men (Bogaert, 2003, 2006; LeVay, 1991; Savic, Berglund, & Lindström, 2005; Swaab et al., 2001).

A Committed Relationship, with Children Like heterosexual relationships, gay and lesbian relationships can be brief and stormy, or stable and permanent (Kurdek, 2005). These lesbian women's commitment to each other for the long haul can be seen in their decision to adopt a child together. The strong role of biological factors in sexual orientation is supported by research showing that their child's orientation will not be influenced much, if at all, by that of his adopted parents (e.g., Anderssen, Amlie, & Ytteroy, 2002; Stacey & Biblarz, 2001).

Further support for the influence of hormones on sexual orientation comes from a study of *otoacoustic emissions*, which are faint sounds that come from the human ear (McFadden & Pasanen, 1998). These sounds, which are affected by hormones during prenatal development, are louder in heterosexual women than in heterosexual men. In lesbians, however, the sounds are more similar to men's than to heterosexual women's, suggesting a biological process of sexual differentiation. This study did not find a difference between homosexual and heterosexual men, however. A similar pattern of results has emerged from research on *prepulse inhibition*, which is a reduction in the strength of a person's startle reaction to, say, a loud noise when the noise is preceded by a softer sound that serves as a warning (Rahman, Kumari, & Wilson, 2003).

Finally, a biological basis for sexual orientation is suggested by the fact that it is relatively unaffected by environmental factors. Several studies have shown, for example, that the sexual orientation of children's caregivers has little or no effect on those children's own sexual orientation (Anderssen, Amlie, & Ytteroy, 2002; Bailey et al., 1995; Stacey & Biblarz, 2001; Tasker & Golombok, 1995).

■ Are there alternative ways of interpreting the evidence?

Correlations between genetics and sexual orientation, like all correlations, are open to alternative interpretations. As discussed in the chapter on research in psychology, a correlation describes the strength and direction of a relationship between variables, but it does not guarantee that one variable is actually influencing the other. Consider again the data showing that brothers who shared the most genes were also most likely to share a gay sexual orientation. It is possible that what the brothers shared was not a gene for homosexuality but rather a set of genes that influenced their activity levels, emotionality, aggressiveness, or the like. One example is "gender nonconformity" in childhood, the tendency for some boys to display "feminine" behaviors and for some girls to behave in "masculine" ways (Bailey et al., 2000; Knafo, Iervolino, & Plomin, 2005). These general aspects of temperament or personality—and other people's reactions to them—could influence the likelihood of a particular sexual orientation (Bem, 1996). In other words, sexual orientation could arise as a reaction to the way people respond to a genetically determined, but nonsexual, aspect of personality. Prenatal hormone levels, too, could influence sexual orientation by shaping aggressiveness or other nonsexual aspects of behavior.

It is also important to look at behavioral genetics evidence for what it can tell us about the role of *environmental factors* in sexual orientation. When we read that both members of identical twin pairs have a homosexual or bisexual orientation 52 percent of the time, it is easy to ignore the fact that the orientation of the twin pair members was *different* in nearly half the cases. Viewed in this way, the results suggest that genes do not tell the entire story of sexual orientation.

Indeed, evidence that sexual orientation has its roots in biology does not mean that it is determined by genetic and hormonal forces alone. As described in the chapter on biological aspects of psychology, the brains and bodies we inherit are quite responsive to environmental input. The behaviors we engage in and the environmental experiences we have result in physical changes in the brain and elsewhere (Wang et al., 1995). Every time we form a new memory, for example, changes occur in the brain's synapses. So differences in the brains of people with differing sexual orientations could be the effect, not the cause, of their behavior or experiences.

■ What additional evidence would help to evaluate the alternatives?

Much more evidence is needed about the role of genes in shaping sexual orientation. We also have much to learn about the extent to which genes and hormones shape physical and psychological characteristics that lead to the personal and social construction of various sexual orientations. In studying this issue, researchers will want to know more not only about the genetic characteristics of people with different sexual orientations but also about their mental and behavioral styles. Are there personality characteristics associated with different sexual orientations? If so, do those characteristics have a strong genetic component? To what extent are gay men, lesbians, bisexuals and heterosexuals similar—and to what extent are they different—in terms of cognitive styles, biases, coping skills, developmental histories, and the like? And are there any differences in how sexual orientation is shaped in males versus females (Bailey et al., 2000)?

The more we learn about sexual orientation in general, the easier it will be to interpret data relating to its origins. But even defining sexual orientation is not simple because people do not always fall into discrete categories (American Psychological Association, 2002a; Savin-Williams, 2006). Should a man who identifies himself as gay be considered bisexual because he occasionally has heterosexual daydreams? What sexual orientation label would be appropriate for a forty-year-old woman who experienced a few lesbian encounters in her teens but has engaged in exclusively heterosexual sex since then? Progress in understanding the origins of sexual orientation would be enhanced by a generally accepted system for describing and defining exactly what is meant by *sexual orientation* (Stein, 1999).

■ What conclusions are most reasonable?

The evidence available so far suggests that genetic factors, probably operating through prenatal hormones, create differences in the brains of people with different sexual orientations. However, the manner in which a person expresses a genetically influenced sexual orientation will be profoundly shaped by what that person learns through social and cultural experiences (Bancroft, 1994). In short, sexual orientation most likely results from the complex interplay of both genetic and nongenetic mechanisms—both nature and nurture. ■

● Sexual Dysfunctions

The biological, social, and psychological factors that shape human sexual behavior can also result in **sexual dysfunctions,** which are problems in a person's desire for or ability to have satisfying sexual activity (Goldstein & Rosen, 2002). For men, a common problem is *erectile disorder* (once called *impotence),* a persistent inability to have or maintain an erection adequate for sex. Physical causes—such as fatigue, diabetes, hypertension, aging, alcohol or other drugs, and perhaps even genetics—account for some cases, but psychological causes such as anxiety are also common (Everaerd & Laan, 1994; Fischer et al., 2004; Heiman, 2002). *Premature ejaculation*, another common dysfunction, involves a recurring tendency to ejaculate during sex sooner than the man or his partner desires.

For women, the most common sexual dysfunction is *arousal disorder* (once called *frigidity*), which is characterized by a recurring inability to become physiologically aroused during sexual activity (Phillips, 2000; Wilson et al., 1996). Arousal disorder can stem from inadequate genital stimulation, hormonal imbalances, insufficient vaginal lubrication, or inadequate blood flow to the clitoris (Anastasiadis et al., 2002; Wilson et al., 1996). However, it is also often tied to psychological factors such as guilt or self-consciousness, which can affect men as well as women (Davidson & Moore, 1994; Laan et al., 1993).

Many people experience episodes of at least one of these problems at some point in their lives, but such episodes are considered dysfunctions only if they become a persistent and distressing obstacle to sexual functioning (American Psychiatric Association, 1994; Mercer et al., 2003). These dysfunctions affect 30 to 50 percent of adults in the United States and Britain (Heiman, 2002; Laumann, Paik, & Rosen, 1999; Mercer et al., 2003). Fortunately, most of them can be overcome through psychotherapy, medication, or both (Braunstein et al., 2005; de Silva, 1994). For example, Viagra and other drugs that affect blood flow in the penis are effective in treating many cases of erectile disorder (Lue, 2000).

● **sexual dysfunction** A problem with sex that involves sexual motivation, arousal, or orgasmic response.

Achievement Motivation

This sentence was written at 6 A.M. on a beautiful Sunday in June. Why would someone get up that early to work on a weekend? Why do people take their work seriously and try to do the best that they can? People work hard partly due to *extrinsic motivation*, a desire for external rewards such as money. But work and other human behaviors also reflect *intrinsic motivation*, a desire to attain internal satisfaction, including the kind that has been described by some psychologists as *flow* (Csikszentmihalyi, 1990). If you have ever lost track of time while utterly absorbed in some intensely engaging work or recreation or athletics or creative activity, you have experienced flow.

The next time you visit someone's home or office, look at the mementos displayed there. You may see framed diplomas and awards, trophies and ribbons, and photos of children and grandchildren. These badges of achievement affirm that a person has accomplished tasks that merit approval or establish worth. Much of our behavior is motivated by a desire for approval, admiration, and achievement—in short, for *esteem*—from others and from ourselves. In this section, we examine two of the most common avenues to esteem: achievement in general and a job in particular.

● Need for Achievement

Many athletes who already hold world records still train intensely; many people who have built multimillion-dollar businesses still work fourteen-hour days. What motivates these people?

Some psychologists suggest that the answer is a desire for *mastery* or *effectance* (Kusyszyn, 1990; Surtees et al., 2006; White, 1959), the motivation to behave competently. These terms are similar to an earlier concept described by Henry Murray as **need achievement** (Murray, 1938). People with a high need for achievement seek to master tasks—be they sports, business ventures, intellectual puzzles, or artistic creations—and feel intense satisfaction from doing so. They strive for excellence, enjoy themselves in the process, and take great pride in achieving at a high level (McClelland, 1985).

● **Individual Differences** How do people with strong achievement motivation differ from others? To find out, researchers gave children a test to measure their need for achievement (Figure 11.6 shows a test for adults) and then asked them to play a ring-toss game. Children scoring low on the need-achievement test usually stood either so close to the ring-toss target that they couldn't fail or so far away that they couldn't succeed. In contrast, children scoring high on the need-achievement test stood at a moderate distance from the target, making the game challenging but not impossible (McClelland, 1958). These and other experiments suggest that people with high achievement needs tend to set challenging—but realistic—goals. They are interested in their work, actively seek success, take risks when necessary, and are intensely satisfied when they succeed (Eisenberger et al., 2005). But if they feel they have tried their best, people with high achievement motivation are not too upset by failure. Those with low achievement motivation also like to succeed, but instead of joy, success tends to bring them relief at having avoided failure (Winter, 1996).

Differences in achievement motivation also appear in people's goals in achievement-related situations (Molden & Dweck, 2000). Some people tend to adopt *learning goals*. When they play golf, take piano lessons, work at puzzles and problems, go to school, and get involved in other achievement-oriented activities, they do so mainly to get better at those activities. Realizing that they may not yet have the skills necessary to achieve at a high level, they tend to learn by watching others and to struggle with problems on their own rather than asking for help (Mayer & Sutton,

FIGURE 11.6

Assessing Need Achievement

This picture is similar to those included in the Thematic Apperception Test, or TAT (Morgan & Murray, 1935). The strength of people's achievement motivation is inferred from the stories they tell about TAT pictures. A response such as "The young woman is hoping to make her grandmother proud of her" would be seen as reflecting high achievement motivation.

Reprinted by permission of the publishers from Henry A. Murray, THEMATIC APPERCEPTION TEST, Card 12F, Cambridge, Mass.: Harvard University Press, Copyright © 1943 by the President and Fellows of Harvard College, Copyright ©1971 by Henry A. Murray.

need achievement A motive influenced by the degree to which a person establishes specific goals, cares about meeting those goals, and experiences feelings of satisfaction by doing so.

Helping Them Do Their Best
Learning-oriented goals are especially appropriate in classrooms, where students typically have little knowledge of the subject matter. This is why most teachers tolerate errors and reward gradual improvement. They do not usually encourage performance goals, which emphasize doing better than others and demonstrating immediate competence (Reeve, 1996). Still, to help students do their best in the long run, teachers sometimes promote performance goals, too. The proper combination of both kinds of goals may be more motivating than either kind alone (Barron & Harackiewicz, 2001).

1996). When they do seek help, people with learning goals are likely to ask for explanations, hints, and other forms of task-related information, not for quick, easy answers that remove the challenge from the situation. In contrast, people who adopt *performance goals* are usually more concerned with demonstrating the skill they believe they already have. They tend to seek information about how well they have performed compared with others rather than about how to improve their performance (Butler, 1998). When they seek help, it is usually to ask for the right answer rather than for tips on how to find that answer themselves. Because their primary goal is to demonstrate their competence, people with performance goals tend to avoid new challenges if they are not confident that they will be successful, and they tend to quit in response to failure (Grant & Dweck, 2003). Those with learning goals tend to be more persistent and less upset when they don't immediately perform well (Niiya, Crocker, & Bartmess, 2004); having learning goals also predicts better cross-cultural adjustment among international students (Gong & Fan, 2006).

● **Development of Achievement Motivation**   Achievement motivation tends to be learned in early childhood, especially from parents. For example, in one study young boys were given a difficult task at which they were sure to fail. Fathers whose sons scored low on achievement motivation tests often became annoyed as they watched their boys struggle. They discouraged them from continuing, interfered, or even completed the task themselves (Rosen & D'Andrade, 1959). A different pattern of behavior appeared among parents of children who scored high on tests of achievement motivation. Those parents tended to (1) encourage the child to try difficult tasks, especially new ones; (2) give praise and other rewards for success; (3) encourage the child to find ways to succeed rather than merely complaining about failure; and (4) prompt the child to go on to the next, more difficult challenge (McClelland, 1985). Other research with adults shows that even the slightest cues that bring a parent to mind can boost people's efforts to achieve a goal (Shah, 2003).

More general cultural influences also affect the development of achievement motivation. For example, subtle messages about a culture's view of how achievement occurs often appear in the books children read and the stories they hear. Does the story's main character work hard and overcome obstacles, thus creating expectations of a payoff for persistence? Is the character a loafer who drifts aimlessly and then wins the lottery, suggesting that rewards come randomly, regardless of effort?

Children raised in environments that support the development of strong achievement motivation tend not to give up on difficult tasks—even if all the king's horses and all the king's men do!

"Maybe they didn't try hard enough."

If the main character succeeds, is it the result of personal initiative, as is typical of stories in individualist cultures? Or is success based on ties to a cooperative and supportive group, as is typical of stories in collectivist cultures? These themes appear to act as blueprints for reaching culturally approved goals. It should not be surprising, then, that ideas about how people achieve differ from culture to culture. In one study, for example, individuals from Saudi Arabia and from the United States were asked to comment on short stories describing people who succeeded at various tasks. Saudis tended to see the people in the stories as having succeeded because of the help they got from others, whereas Americans tended to attribute success to the personal traits of each story's main character (Zahrani & Kaplowitz, 1993). Achievement motivation is also influenced by how much a particular culture values and rewards achievement. For example, the motivation to excel is likely to be especially strong in cultures in which demanding standards lead students to fear rejection if they fail to attain high grades (Eaton & Dembo, 1997; Hess, Chih-Mei, & McDevitt, 1987).

In short, achievement motivation is strongly influenced by social and cultural learning experiences, as well as by the beliefs about oneself that these experiences help to create. People who come to believe in their ability to achieve are more likely to do so than those who expect to fail (Dweck, 1998; Tuckman, 2003; Wigfield & Eccles, 2000).

● Goal Setting and Achievement Motivation

Why are you reading this chapter instead of watching television or hanging out with your friends? Your motivation to study is probably based on your goal of doing well in a psychology course, which relates to broader goals, such as earning a degree, having a career, and the like. Psychologists have found that we set goals when we recognize a discrepancy between our current situation and how we want that situation to be (Oettingen, Pak, & Schnetter, 2001). Establishing a goal motivates us to engage in behaviors designed to reduce the discrepancy we have identified. The kinds of goals we set can influence the amount of effort, persistence, attention, and planning we devote to a task.

In general, the more difficult the goal, the harder people will try to reach it. This rule assumes, of course, that the goal is seen as realistic. Goals that are impossibly difficult may not motivate maximum effort. It also assumes that the person values the goal. If a difficult goal is set by someone else—as when a parent assigns a teenager to keep a large lawn and garden trimmed and weeded—people may not accept it as their own and may not work very hard to attain it. Setting goals that are clear and specific tends to increase people's motivation to persist at a task (Locke & Latham, 2002). For example, you are more likely to keep reading this chapter if your goal is to "read the motivation section of the motivation and emotion chapter today" than if it is to "do some studying." Clarifying your goal makes it easier to know when you have reached it, and when it is time to stop. Without clear goals, a person can be more easily distracted by fatigue, boredom, or frustration and more likely to give up before completing a task. Clear goals also tend to focus people's attention on creating plans for pursuing them, on the activities they believe will lead to goal attainment, and on evaluating their progress. In short, the process of goal setting is more than just wishful thinking. It is an important first step in motivating all kinds of behavior.

● Achievement and Success in the Workplace

In the workplace, there is usually less concern with employees' general level of achievement motivation than with their motivation to work hard during business hours. In fact, employers tend to set up jobs in accordance with their ideas about how intrinsic and extrinsic motivation combine to shape their employees' performance (Riggio, 1989). Employers who see workers as lazy, dishonest, and lacking in ambition tend to offer highly structured, heavily supervised jobs that give employees little say in deciding what to do or how to do it. These employers assume that workers are motivated mainly by extrinsic rewards—money, in particular. So they tend to be surprised when, in spite of good pay and benefits, employees sometimes express dissatisfaction with their jobs and show little motivation to work hard (Diener & Seligman, 2004; Igalens & Roussel, 1999).

If good pay and benefits alone do not bring job satisfaction and the desire to excel on the job, what does? In Western cultures, low worker motivation comes largely from the feeling of having little or no control over the work environment (Rosen, 1991). Compared with those in rigidly structured jobs, workers tend to be

Teamwork Pays Off Many U.S. companies have followed Japanese examples by redesigning jobs to increase workers' responsibility and flexibility. The goal is to increase productivity and job satisfaction by creating teams in which employees are responsible for solving production problems and making decisions about how best to do their jobs. Team members are publicly recognized for outstanding work, and part of their pay depends on the quality (not just the number) of their products and on the profitability of the company as a whole.

more satisfied and productive if they are (1) encouraged to participate in decisions about how work should be done; (2) given problems to solve, without being told how to solve them; (3) taught more than one skill; (4) given individual responsibility; and (5) given public recognition, not just money, for good performance (Fisher, 2000).

Allowing people to set and achieve clear goals is one way to increase both job performance and job satisfaction (Abramis, 1994). As suggested by our earlier discussion, some goals are especially effective at maintaining work motivation (Katzell & Thompson, 1990). First, effective goals are personally meaningful. When a form letter from a remote administrator tells employees that they should increase production, the employees tend to feel used and not particularly motivated to meet the goal. Before assigning difficult goals, good managers try to ensure that employees accept those goals (Klein et al., 1999). They include employees in the goal-setting process, make sure that the employees have the skills and resources to reach the goal, and emphasize the benefits to be gained from success—perhaps including financial incentives (Locke & Latham, 1990). Second, effective goals are specific and concrete (Locke & Latham, 2002). The goal of "doing better" is usually not a strong motivator, because it provides no direction about how to proceed and it fails to specify when the goal has been met. A specific target, such as increasing sales by 10 percent, is a far more motivating goal. It can be measured objectively, allowing feedback on progress, and it tells workers whether the goal has been reached. Finally, goals are most effective if management supports the workers' own goal setting, offers special rewards for reaching goals, and gives encouragement for renewed efforts after failure (Kluger & DeNisi, 1998).

In summary, motivating jobs offer personal challenges, independence, and both intrinsic and extrinsic rewards. They provide enough satisfaction for people to feel excitement and pleasure in working hard. For employers, the rewards are more productivity, less absenteeism, and greater employee loyalty (Ilgen & Pulakos, 1999).

■● Achievement and Subjective Well-Being

Some people believe that the more they achieve at work and elsewhere, and the more money and other material goods they amass as a result, the happier they will be. Will they? Researchers have been studying what it actually takes to achieve happiness, or more formally, subjective well-being (Seligman et al., 2005; Sheldon & King, 2001). **Subjective well-being** is a combination of a cognitive judgment of satisfaction with life, the frequent experiencing of positive moods and emotions, and the relatively infrequent experiencing of unpleasant moods and emotions (Diener & Biswas-Diener, 2002; Fredrickson & Losada, 2005; Urry et al., 2004).

Research on subjective well-being indicates that, as you might expect, people living in extreme poverty or in war-torn or politically chaotic countries are not as happy as people in better circumstances. And people everywhere react to good or bad events with corresponding changes in mood. As described in the chapter on health, stress, and coping, for example, severe or long-lasting stressors—such as the death of a loved one—can lead to psychological and physical problems. But although events do have an impact, the saddening or elevating effects of major changes, such as being promoted or fired, or even being imprisoned or seriously injured, tend not to last as long as we might think they would (Gilbert et al., 2004). In other words, how happy you are may have less to do with what happens to you than you might expect (Bonanno, 2004; Gilbert & Wilson, 1998; Kahneman et al., 2006; Lyubomirsky, 2001).

Most event-related changes in mood subside within days or weeks, and most people then return to their previous level of happiness (Suh, Diener, & Fujita, 1996). Even when events create permanent changes in circumstances, most people adapt by changing their expectancies and goals, not by radically and permanently changing their baseline level of happiness. For example, people may be thrilled after getting a

● **subjective well-being** A combination of a cognitive judgment of satisfaction with life, the frequent experiencing of positive moods and emotions, and the relatively infrequent experiencing of unpleasant moods and emotions.

big salary increase, but as they get used to having it, the thrill fades, and they may eventually feel just as underpaid as before. In fact, although there are exceptions (Fujita & Diener, 2005; Lucas, 2007), most people's level of subjective well-being tends to be remarkably stable throughout their lives. This baseline level may be related to temperament, or personality, and it has been likened to a set point for body weight (Lykken, 1999). Like many other aspects of temperament, our baseline level of happiness may be influenced by genetics. Twin studies have shown, for example, that individual differences in happiness are more strongly associated with inherited personality characteristics than with environmental factors such as money, popularity, or physical attractiveness (Lykken, 1999; Tellegen et al., 1988).

Beyond inherited tendencies, the things that appear to matter most in generating happiness are close social ties (including friends and a satisfying marriage or partnership), religious faith, and having the resources necessary to allow progress toward one's goals (Diener, 2000; Myers, 2000). So you don't have to be a rich, physically attractive high achiever to be happy, and it turns out that most people in Western cultures are relatively happy (Diener & Diener, 1995; Gow et al., 2005).

These results are consistent with the views expressed over many centuries by philosophers, psychologists, and wise people in all cultures. For example, decades ago, Abraham Maslow (1970) noted that when people in Western cultures experience unhappiness and psychological problems, those problems can often be traced to a *deficiency orientation*. He said that these people seek happiness by trying to acquire the goods and reach the status they don't currently have—but think they need—rather than by appreciating life itself and the material and nonmaterial riches they already have. Others have amplified this point, suggesting that efforts to get more of the things we think will bring happiness may actually contribute to unhappiness if what we get is never "enough" (Diener & Seligman, 2004; Luthar & Latendresse, 2005; Nickerson et al., 2003).

Relations and Conflicts Among Motives

Maslow's ideas about deficiency motivation were part of his more general view of human behavior as reflecting a hierarchy of needs, or motives (see Figure 11.7). Needs at the lowest level of the hierarchy, he said, must be at least partially satisfied before people can be motivated by higher-level goals. From the bottom to the top of Maslow's hierarchy, these five motives are as follows:

1. *Biological,* such as the need for food, water, oxygen, and sleep.

2. *Safety,* such as the need to be cared for as a child and have a secure income as an adult.

3. *Belongingness and love,* such as the need to be part of groups and to participate in affectionate sexual and nonsexual relationships.

4. *Esteem,* such as the need to be respected as a useful, honorable individual.

5. *Self-actualization,* which means reaching one's fullest potential. People motivated by this need explore and enhance relationships with others; follow interests for intrinsic pleasure rather than for money, status, or esteem; and are concerned with issues affecting all people, not just themselves.

Maslow's hierarchy has been very influential over the years, partly because the needs associated with basic survival and security do generally take precedence over those related to self-enhancement or personal growth (Baumeister &

FIGURE 11.7

Maslow's Hierarchy of Motives

TRY THIS ⚙ Abraham Maslow (1970) saw human motives as organized in a hierarchy in which those at lower levels take precedence over those at higher levels. According to this view, self-actualization is the essence of mental health. Take a moment to consider which level of Maslow's hierarchy you are focused on at this point in your life. Which level do you ultimately hope to reach?

Source: Adapted from Maslow (1943).

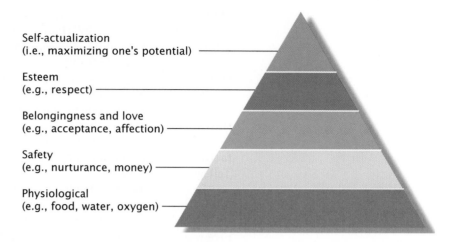

Self-actualization (i.e., maximizing one's potential)

Esteem (e.g., respect)

Belongingness and love (e.g., acceptance, affection)

Safety (e.g., nurturance, money)

Physiological (e.g., food, water, oxygen)

Leary, 1995). But critics see the hierarchy as far too simplistic (Hall, Lindzey, & Campbell, 1998; Neher, 1991). It does not predict or explain, for example, the motivation of people who starve themselves to death to draw attention to political or moral causes. Further, people may not have to satisfy one kind of need before addressing others; we can seek several needs at once. Finally, the ordering of needs within the survival/security and enhancement/growth categories differs from culture to culture, suggesting that there may not be a single, universal hierarchy of needs.

To address some of the problems in Maslow's theory, Clayton Alderfer (1969) proposed *existence, relatedness, growth (ERG) theory,* which places human needs into just three categories: *existence needs* (such as for food and water), *relatedness needs* (e.g., for social interactions and attachments), and *growth needs* (such as for developing one's capabilities). Unlike Maslow, Alderfer doesn't assume that these needs must be satisfied in a particular order. Instead, he sees needs in each category as rising and falling from time to time and from situation to situation. When a need in one area is fulfilled, or even if it is frustrated, a person will be motivated to pursue some other needs. For example, if a breakup frustrates relatedness needs, a person might focus on existence or growth needs by eating more or volunteering to work late.

Choices based on Maslow's proposed hierarchy of needs are not usually this clear, nor are they always dictated strictly by that hierarchy.

LINKAGES | Conflicting Motives and Stress

LINKAGES (a link to Health, Stress, and Coping, p. 520)

As in the case of hunger strikes, in which the desire to promote a cause is pitted against the desire to eat, human motives can sometimes conflict. The usual result is some degree of discomfort. For example, imagine that you are alone and bored on a Saturday night, and you think about going to the store to buy some snacks. What are your motives? Hunger might prompt you to go out, as might the prospect of increased arousal that a change of scene will provide. Even sexual motivation might be involved, as you fantasize about meeting someone exciting in the snack-food aisle. But safety-related motives may also kick in—is your neighborhood safe enough for you to go out alone at night? An esteem motive might come into play, too, making you hesitate to be seen on your own on a weekend night.

These are just a few motives that may shape a trivial decision. When the decision is more important, the number and strength of motivational pushes and pulls are often greater, creating far more internal conflict. Four basic types of motivational conflict have been identified (Miller, 1959):

1. *Approach-approach conflicts*. When a person must choose only one of two desirable activities—say, going with friends to a movie or to a party—an *approach-approach conflict* exists.

2. *Avoidance-avoidance conflicts*. An *avoidance-avoidance conflict* arises when a person must pick one of two undesirable alternatives. Someone forced either to sell the house or to declare bankruptcy faces an avoidance-avoidance conflict.

3. *Approach-avoidance conflicts*. If someone you couldn't stand had tickets to your favorite group's sold-out concert and invited you to come along, what would you do? When a single event or activity has both attractive and unattractive features, an *approach-avoidance conflict* is created.

4. *Multiple approach-avoidance conflicts*. Suppose you must choose between two jobs. One offers a good salary with a well-known company, but it requires long hours and relocation to a miserable climate. The other boasts advancement opportunities, fringe benefits, and a better climate, but also lower pay and an unpredictable work schedule. This is an example of a *multiple approach-avoidance conflict*, in which two or more alternatives each have both positive and negative features. Such conflicts are difficult to resolve partly because it may be hard to compare the features of each option. For example, how much more money per year does it take to compensate you for living in a bad climate?

In fact, all of these conflicts can be difficult to resolve and can create significant emotional arousal and other signs of stress, a topic described in the chapter on health, stress, and coping. Most people in the midst of motivational conflicts are tense, irritable, and more vulnerable than usual to physical and psychological problems. These reactions are especially likely when no choice is obviously "right," when conflicting motives have approximately equal strength, and when the choice can have serious consequences (as in decisions to marry, to split up, or to place an elderly parent in a nursing home). People may take a long time to resolve these conflicts, or they may act impulsively and thoughtlessly, if only to end the discomfort of uncertainty. And even after a conflict is resolved, stress responses may continue in the form of anxiety about the wisdom of the decision or self-blame over bad choices. These and other consequences of conflicting motives can even lead to depression or other serious disorders. ■

TRY THIS **A Stressful Conflict** Think back to the time when you were deciding which college to attend. Was the decision easy and obvious, or did it create a motivational conflict? If there was a conflict, was it an approach-approach, approach-avoidance, or multiple approach-avoidance conflict? What factors were most important in deciding how to resolve the conflict, and what emotions and signs of stress did you experience during and after the decision-making process?

Opponent Processes, Motivation, and Emotion

Resolving approach-avoidance conflicts is often complicated by the fact that some behaviors have more than one emotional effect, and those effects may be opposite to one another. People who ride roller coasters or skydive, for example, often say that the experience is scary, but also thrilling. How do they decide whether or not to repeat these behaviors? One answer lies in the changing value of incentives and the regulation of arousal described in Richard Solomon's *opponent-process theory*, which is discussed in the chapter on learning. Opponent-process theory is based on two assumptions. The first is that any reaction to a stimulus is followed by an opposite reaction, called the *opponent process*. For example, being startled by a sudden sound is typically followed by relaxation and relief. Second, after repeated exposure to the same stimulus, the initial reaction weakens, and the opponent process becomes quicker and stronger.

Research on opponent-process theory has revealed a predictable pattern of emotional changes that helps explain some people's motivation to repeatedly engage in arousing but fearsome activities, such as skydiving. Before each of their first several jumps, people usually experience stark terror, followed by intense relief when they reach the ground. With more experience, however, the terror becomes mild anxiety, and what had been relief grows to a sense of elation that may start to appear *during* the activity (Solomon, 1980). As a result, said Solomon, some people's motivation to pursue skydiving and other "extreme sports" can become a virtual addiction.

The emotions associated with motivational conflicts and with the operation of opponent processes provide just two examples of the close ties between motivation and emotion. Motivation can intensify emotion, as when a normally calm, but extremely hungry person makes an angry phone call about a late pizza delivery. But emotions can also create motivation. For example, most people want to feel happiness, to savor pleasant experiences (e.g., Bryant & Veroff, 2006), and to have other positive emotions, so they engage in whatever behaviors—studying, creating art, investing, beachcombing—they think will lead to those emotions. Similarly, as an emotion that most people want to avoid, anxiety prompts many behaviors, from leaving the scene of an accident to avoiding poisonous snakes. Let's take a closer look at emotions.

The Nature of Emotion

Everyone seems to agree that joy, sorrow, anger, fear, love, and hate are emotions, but it is hard to identify exactly what it is that makes these experiences emotions rather than, say, thoughts or impulses. In fact, some cultures see emotion and thought as the same thing. The Chewong of Malaysia, for example, consider the liver the seat of both what we call thoughts and feelings (Russell, 1991).

Defining Characteristics

Most psychologists in Western cultures see emotions as organized psychological and physiological reactions to changes in our relationship to the world. These reactions are partly private, or *subjective*, experiences and partly objectively measurable patterns of behavior and physiological arousal. The subjective experience of emotion has several characteristics:

1. Emotion is usually *temporary;* it tends to have a relatively clear beginning and end, as well as a relatively short duration. Moods, by contrast, tend to last longer.

2. Emotional experience can be *positive*, as in joy, or *negative*, as in sadness. It can also be a mixture of both, as in the bittersweet feelings of watching one's child leave for the first day of kindergarten.

3. Emotional experience *alters thought processes*, often by directing attention toward some things and away from others. Negative emotions, such as fear, tend to narrow attention. So anxiety about terrorism, for example, might lead you to focus your attention on potential threats in airports and other public places (Yovel & Mineka, 2005). Positive emotions tend to widen our attention, which makes it easier take in a broader range of visual information and perhaps to think more broadly, too (Fredrickson & Branigan, 2005).

4. Emotional experience triggers an *action tendency*, the motivation to behave in certain ways. Positive emotions, such as joy, contentment, and pride, often lead to playfulness, creativity, and exploration of the environment (Cacioppo, Gardner, & Berntson, 1999; Fredrickson, 2001). These behaviors, in turn, can generate further positive emotions by creating stronger social ties, greater skill at problem solving, and the like. The result may be an "upward spiral" of positivity (Fredrickson & Joiner, 2002). Negative emotions, such as sadness and fear, often promote withdrawal from threatening situations, whereas anger might lead to actions aimed at revenge or constructive change. Grieving parents' anger, for example, might motivate them to harm their child's killer. But for John Walsh, whose son was kidnapped and murdered, grief led to helping to prevent such crimes by creating *America's Most Wanted,* a TV show dedicated to bringing criminals to justice.

5. Emotional experiences are *passions* that you feel, usually whether you want to or not. You can exert at least some control over emotions in the sense that they depend partly on how you interpret situations (Gross, 2001). For example, your emotional reaction might be less extreme after a car accident if you remind yourself that no one was hurt and that you are insured. Still, such control is limited. You cannot *decide* to experience joy or sorrow; instead, you "fall in love" or "explode in anger" or are "overcome by grief."

Winners and Losers   Emotional experiences depend in part on our interpretation of situations and how those situations relate to our goals. A single stimulus—the announcement of the results of a cheerleading contest—triggered drastically different emotional reactions in these women, depending on whether they perceived it as making them winners or losers. Similarly, an exam score of 75 percent may thrill you if your best previous score had been 50 percent, but it may upset you if you had never before scored below 90 percent.

FIGURE **11.8**

Brain Regions Involved in Emotion

Incoming sensory information alerts the brain to an emotion-evoking situation. Most of the information goes through the thalamus. The cingulate cortex and hippocampus are involved in the interpretation of this sensory input. Output from these areas goes to the amygdala and hypothalamus, which control the autonomic nervous system via brainstem connections. There are also connections from the thalamus directly to the amygdala. The locus coeruleus is an area of the brainstem that causes both widespread arousal of cortical areas and changes in autonomic activity.

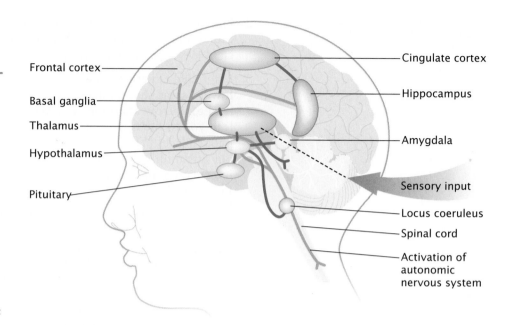

Frontal cortex

Basal ganglia

Thalamus

Hypothalamus

Pituitary

Cingulate cortex

Hippocampus

Amygdala

Sensory input

Locus coeruleus

Spinal cord

Activation of autonomic nervous system

In other words, the subjective aspects of emotions are both *triggered* by the thinking self and felt as *happening* to the self. They reveal each of us as both agent and object, both I and me, both the controller of thoughts and the recipient of passions. The extent to which we are "victims" of our passions versus rational designers of our emotions is a central dilemma of human existence, as much a subject of philosophy and literature as of psychology.

The *objective* aspects of emotion include learned and innate *expressive displays* and *physiological responses*. Expressive displays—such as a smile or a frown—communicate feelings to others. Physiological responses—such as changes in heart rate—are the biological adjustments needed to perform the action tendencies generated by emotional experience. If you throw a temper tantrum or jump for joy, your heart must deliver additional oxygen and fuel to your muscles.

In summary, an **emotion** is a temporary experience with either positive, negative, or mixed qualities. People experience emotion with varying intensity, as happening to them, as generated in part by a mental assessment of situations, and accompanied by both learned and innate physical responses. Through emotion, whether they mean to or not, people communicate their internal states and intentions to others. Emotion often disrupts thinking and behavior, but it also triggers and guides thinking and organizes, motivates, and sustains behavior and social relations.

● The Biology of Emotion

The role of biology in emotion can be seen in mechanisms of the central nervous system and the autonomic nervous system. In the *central nervous system*, several brain areas are involved in the generation of emotions, as well as in our experience of those emotions (Barrett & Wager, 2006). The *autonomic nervous system* gives rise to many of the physiological changes associated with emotional arousal.

● **Brain Mechanisms** Although many questions remain, researchers have described three main aspects of how emotion is processed in the brain. First, it appears that activity in the *limbic system*, especially in the amygdala, is central to emotion (Kensinger & Corkin, 2004; Phelps & LeDoux, 2005; see Figure 11.8). Normal functioning in the amygdala appears critical to the ability to learn emotional associations, recognize emotional expressions, and perceive emotionally

● **emotion** A transitory positive or negative experience that is felt as happening to the self, is generated in part by cognitive appraisal of a situation, and is accompanied by both learned and innate physical responses.

charged words (e.g., Anderson & Phelps, 2001; Suslow et al., 2006). In one brain imaging study, when researchers paired an uncomfortably loud noise with pictures of faces, the participants' brains showed activation of the amygdala while the noise-picture association was being learned (LaBar et al., 1998). In another study, victims of a disease that destroys only the amygdala were found to be unable to judge other people's emotional states by looking at their faces (Adolphs et al., 1994). Faces that normal people rated as expressing strong negative emotions were rated by the amygdala-damaged individuals as approachable and trustworthy (Adolphs, Tranel, & Damasio, 1998).

A second aspect of the brain's involvement in emotion is seen in its control over emotional and nonemotional facial expressions (Rinn, 1984). Take a moment to look in a mirror and put on your best fake smile. The voluntary facial movements you just made, like all voluntary movements, are controlled by the *pyramidal motor system*, a brain system that includes the motor cortex (see Figures 3.16 and 3.17 in the chapter on biological aspects of psychology). However, a smile that expresses genuine happiness is involuntary. That kind of smile, like the other facial movements associated with emotions, is governed by the *extrapyramidal motor system*, which depends on areas beneath the cortex. Brain damage can disrupt either system (see Figure 11.9). People with pyramidal motor system damage show normal facial expressions during genuine emotion, but they cannot fake a smile. In contrast, people with damage to the extrapyramidal system can pose facial expressions at will, but they remain expressionless even when feeling joy or sadness (Hopf, Muller, & Hopf, 1992).

A third aspect of the brain's role in emotion is revealed by research on the cerebral cortex. Its two hemispheres appear to make somewhat different contributions to the perception, experience, and expression of emotion (Davidson, 2000; Davidson, Shackman, & Maxwell, 2004). For example, after suffering damage to the right, but not the left, hemisphere, people no longer laugh at jokes—even though they can still understand the jokes' words, their logic (or illogic), and their punch lines (Critchley, 1991). Further, when people are asked to name the emotions shown in slides of facial expressions, blood flow increases in the right hemisphere more than in the left hemisphere (Gur, Skolnic, & Gur, 1994). People are also faster and more accurate at this emotion-naming task when the facial expressions are presented to the brain's right hemisphere than when they are presented to the left (Hahdahl, Iversen, & Jonsen, 1993).

Precisely how hemispheric differences relate to emotion is not yet entirely clear (Root, Wong, & Kinsbourne, 2006; Vingerhoets, Berckmoes, & Stroobant, 2003). Generally, however, the experiencing of negative emotion, the perception of any emotion exhibited in faces or other stimuli, and the facial expression of any emotion, depend on the right hemisphere more than on the left (Heller, Nitschke, & Miller, 1998; Kawasaki et al., 2001).

If the right hemisphere is relatively dominant in emotion, which side of the face would you expect to be somewhat more involved in expressing emotion? If you said the left side, you are correct, because movements of each side of the body are controlled by the opposite side of the brain (see the chapter on biological aspects of psychology).

● Mechanisms of the Autonomic Nervous System

The autonomic nervous system (ANS) is involved in many of the physiological changes that accompany emotions (see Figure 11.10). If your hands get cold and clammy when you are nervous, it is because the ANS has increased perspiration and decreased the blood flow in your hands.

As described in the chapter on biological aspects of psychology, the ANS carries information between the brain and most organs of the body—the heart and blood vessels, the digestive system, and so on. Each of these organs has its own ongoing activity, but ANS input increases or decreases this activity. By doing so, the ANS

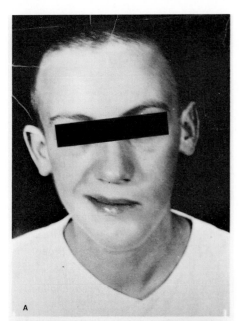

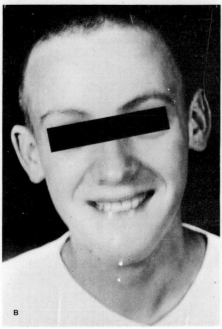

FIGURE 11.9

Control of Voluntary and Emotional Facial Movements

This man has a tumor in his motor cortex that prevents him from voluntarily moving the muscles on the left side of his face. In the photograph at the top he is trying to smile in response to instructions from the examiner. He cannot smile on command, but as shown in the photo at the bottom, he can smile with happiness, because involuntary movements associated with genuine emotion are controlled by the extrapyramidal motor system.

Parasympathetic functions   **Sympathetic functions**

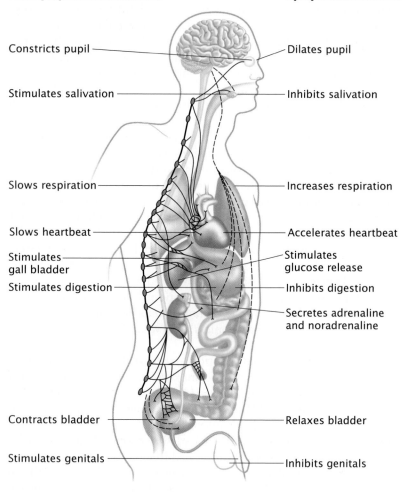

Constricts pupil — Dilates pupil

Stimulates salivation — Inhibits salivation

Slows respiration — Increases respiration

Slows heartbeat — Accelerates heartbeat

Stimulates gall bladder — Stimulates glucose release

Stimulates digestion — Inhibits digestion

Secretes adrenaline and noradrenaline

Contracts bladder — Relaxes bladder

Stimulates genitals — Inhibits genitals

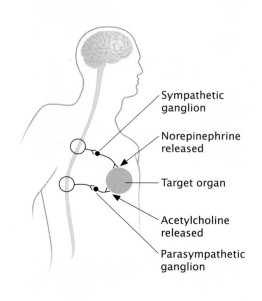

Sympathetic ganglion

Norepinephrine released

Target organ

Acetylcholine released

Parasympathetic ganglion

FIGURE 11.10

The Autonomic Nervous System

 TRY THIS Emotional responses involve activation of the autonomic nervous system, which includes sympathetic and parasympathetic subsystems. Which of the bodily responses depicted here do you associate with emotional experiences?

coordinates the functioning of these organs to meet the body's general needs and to prepare it for change. If you are aroused to take action—to run to catch a bus, say—you need more glucose to fuel your muscles. The ANS frees needed energy by stimulating secretion of glucose-generating hormones and promoting blood flow to the muscles.

As shown in Figure 11.10, the autonomic nervous system is organized into two divisions: the **sympathetic nervous system** and the **parasympathetic nervous system**. Emotions can activate either of these divisions, both of which send axon fibers to each organ in the body. Generally, the sympathetic and parasympathetic fibers have opposite effects on these *target organs*. Axons from the parasympathetic system release *acetylcholine* onto target organs, leading to activity related to the protection, nourishment, and growth of the body. For example, parasympathetic activity increases digestion by stimulating movement of the intestinal system so that more nutrients are taken from food. Axons from the sympathetic system release a different neurotransmitter, *norepinephrine*, onto target organs, helping to prepare the body for vigorous activity. When one part of the sympathetic system is stimulated, other parts are activated "in sympathy" with it. For example, input

● **sympathetic nervous system** The subsystem of the autonomic nervous system that usually prepares the organism for vigorous activity.

● **parasympathetic nervous system** The subsystem of the autonomic nervous system that typically influences activity related to the protection, nourishment, and growth of the body.

from sympathetic neurons to the adrenal medulla causes that gland to release nor-epinephrine and epinephrine into the bloodstream, thereby activating all sympathetic target organs (see Figure 13.3 in the health, stress, and coping chapter). The result is the **fight-or-flight syndrome**, a pattern of increased heart rate and blood pressure, rapid or irregular breathing, dilated pupils, perspiration, dry mouth, increased blood sugar, piloerection ("goose bumps"), and other changes that help prepare the body to combat or run from a threat.

The ANS is not directly connected to brain areas involved in consciousness, so sensations about organ activity reach the brain at a nonconscious level. You may hear your stomach grumble, but you can't actually feel it secrete acids. Similarly, you can't consciously experience the brain mechanisms that alter the activity of your autonomic nervous system. This is why most people don't have direct, conscious control over blood pressure or other aspects of ANS activity. However, there are things you can do to indirectly affect the ANS. For example, to create autonomic stimulation of your sex organs, you might imagine an erotic situation. To raise your blood pressure, you might hold your breath or strain your muscles; to lower it, you can lie down, relax, and think calming thoughts.

Theories of Emotion

How does all this activity in the brain and the autonomic nervous system relate to the emotions we experience? Are autonomic responses to events enough to *create* the experience of emotion, or are those responses the *result* of emotional experiences that begin in the brain? And how are emotional reactions affected by the way we think about events? For over a century now, psychologists have worked at finding the answers to these questions. In the process, they have developed a number of theories that explain emotion mainly in terms of biological or cognitive factors. The main biological theories are those of William James and Walter Cannon. The most prominent cognitive theories are those of Stanley Schachter and Richard Lazarus. In this section we review these theories, along with some research designed to evaluate them.

● James's Peripheral Theory

Suppose you are camping in the woods when a huge bear approaches your tent. You would probably be afraid, and run away. But would you run because you are afraid, or would you be afraid because you ran? The example and the question come from William James, who, in the late 1800s, offered one of the first formal accounts of how physiological responses relate to emotional experience. James argued that you are afraid because you run. Your running and the physiological responses associated with it, he said, follow directly from your perception of the bear. Without these physiological responses, you would feel no fear, because, said James, recognition of physiological responses *is* fear. Because James saw activity in the peripheral nervous system as the cause of emotional experience, his theory is known as a *peripheral theory* of emotion.

At first, James's theory might seem ridiculous; it doesn't make sense to run from something unless you already fear it. James concluded otherwise after examining his own mental processes. He decided that once you strip away all physiological responses, nothing remains of the experience of an emotion (James, 1890). Emotion, he reasoned, must therefore be the result of experiencing a particular set of physiological responses. A similar argument was offered by Carle Lange, a Danish physician, so James's view is sometimes called the *James-Lange theory* of emotion.

fight-or-flight syndrome The physical reactions initiated by the sympathetic nervous system that prepare the body to fight or to run from a threatening situation.

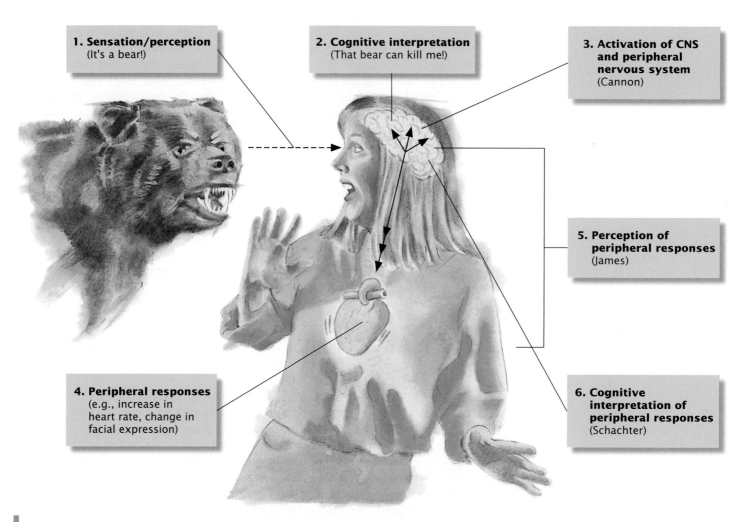

1. Sensation/perception
(It's a bear!)

2. Cognitive interpretation
(That bear can kill me!)

3. Activation of CNS and peripheral nervous system
(Cannon)

5. Perception of peripheral responses
(James)

4. Peripheral responses
(e.g., increase in heart rate, change in facial expression)

6. Cognitive interpretation of peripheral responses
(Schachter)

FIGURE 11.11

Components of Emotion

Emotion is associated with activity in the central nervous system (the brain and spinal cord), with responses elsewhere in the body (called *peripheral* responses), and with cognitive interpretations of events. Emotion theorists have differed about which of these components is essential for emotion. William James focused on the perception of peripheral responses, such as changes in heart rate. Walter Cannon said that emotion could occur entirely within the brain. Stanley Schachter emphasized cognitive factors, including how we interpret events and how we label our peripheral responses to them.

●**Observing Peripheral Responses**   Figure 11.11 outlines the components of emotional experience, including those emphasized by James. First, a perception affects the cerebral cortex, said James; "then quick as a flash, reflex currents pass down through their pre-ordained channels, alter the condition of muscle, skin, and viscus; and these alterations, perceived, like the original object, in as many portions of the cortex, combine with it in consciousness and transform it from an object-simply-apprehended into an object-emotionally-felt" (James, 1890, p. 759). In other words, the brain interprets a situation and automatically directs a particular set of peripheral physiological changes—a racing heart, sinking stomach, facial grimace, perspiration, and certain patterns of blood flow. We are not conscious of the process, said James, until we become aware of these bodily changes; at that point, we experience an emotion. One implication of this view is that each particular emotion is created by a particular pattern of physiological responses. For example, fear would follow from one pattern of bodily responses, and anger would follow from a different pattern.

Notice, too, that according to James's view, emotional experience is not generated by activity in the brain alone. There is no special "emotion center" in the brain where the firing of neurons creates a direct experience of emotion. If this theory is accurate, it might account for the difficulty we sometimes have in knowing our true feelings: We must figure out what emotions we feel by perceiving subtle differences in specific physiological response patterns (Katkin, Wiens, & Öhman, 2001).

●**Evaluating James's Theory**   The English language includes more than 500 labels for emotions (Averill, 1980). Does a different pattern of physiological activity precede each of these specific emotions? Probably not, but research shows that certain emotional states are indeed associated with certain patterns of autonomic activity (Christie & Friedman, 2004; Craig, 2002; Damasio et al., 2000). For example, blood flow to the hands and feet increases in association with anger and declines in association with fear (Levenson, Ekman, & Friesen, 1990). So fear involves "cold feet"; anger does not. A pattern of activity associated with disgust includes increased muscle activity but no change in heart rate. Even when people mentally relive different kinds of emotional experiences, they show different patterns of autonomic activity (Ekman, Levenson, & Friesen, 1983). These emotion-specific patterns of physiological activity have been found in widely different cultures (Levenson et al., 1992). Further, people who are keenly aware of physiological changes in their bodies are likely to experience emotions more intensely than those who are less aware of such changes (Wiens, Mezzacappa, & Katkin, 2000). It has even been suggested that the "gut feelings" that cause us to approach or avoid certain situations might be the result of physiological changes that are perceived without conscious awareness (Bechara et al., 1997; Damasio, 1994; Katkin et al., 2001; Winkielman & Berridge, 2004).

Furthermore, different patterns of autonomic activity are closely tied to specific emotional facial expressions, and vice versa (Ekman, 1993). In one study, when participants were told to make certain facial movements, autonomic changes occurred that resembled those normally accompanying emotion (Ekman et al., 1983; see Figure 11.12). Almost all these participants also reported *feeling the emotion*—such as fear, anger, disgust, sadness, or happiness—associated with the expression they had created, even though they could not see their own expressions and did not realize that they had portrayed a specific emotion. Other studies have confirmed that people feel emotions such as anger or sadness when simply making an "angry" or "sad" face (Schnall & Laird, 2003), and that they can ease these feel-

TRY THIS ings just by relaxing their faces (Duclos & Laird, 2001). To get an idea of how facial expressions can alter, as well as express, emotion, look at a photograph of someone whose face is expressing a strong emotion and try your best to imitate it. Did this create in you the same feelings that the other person appears to be experiencing? The emotional effects of this kind of "face making" appear strongest in people who are the most sensitive to internal bodily cues. When such people pose facial expressions, the emotions created can be significant enough to affect their social judgments. Research participants who were asked to smile, for example, tended to form more positive impressions of other people than did those who received no special instructions (Ohira & Kurono, 1993).

James's theory implies that the experience of emotion would be blocked if a person were unable to detect physiological changes occurring in the body's periphery. So spinal cord injuries that reduce feedback from peripheral responses should reduce the intensity of emotional experiences. Indeed, some people with such injuries have reported reductions in the intensity of their emotions, especially if the injuries are at higher points in the spinal cord, which cuts off feedback from more areas of the body (Hohmann, 1966). Brain imaging studies, too, show differences in the processing of emotional stimuli by people with spinal cord injuries (Nicotra et al., 2006). However, most studies show that when people with spinal injuries continue to pursue their life goals, they experience a full range of emotions, including as much happiness as noninjured people (e.g., Bermond et al., 1991; Cobos et al., 2004). These people report that their emotional experiences are just as intense as before their injuries, even though they notice less intense physiological changes associated with their emotions.

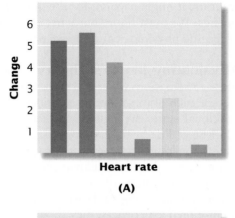

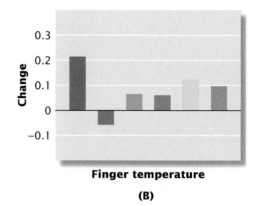

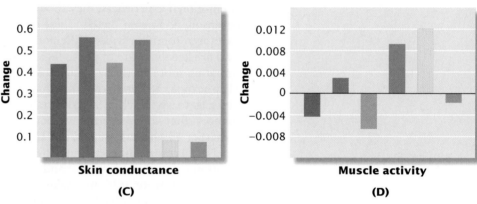

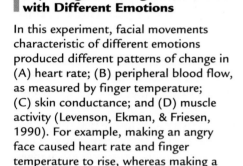

FIGURE 11.12

Physiological Changes Associated with Different Emotions

In this experiment, facial movements characteristic of different emotions produced different patterns of change in (A) heart rate; (B) peripheral blood flow, as measured by finger temperature; (C) skin conductance; and (D) muscle activity (Levenson, Ekman, & Friesen, 1990). For example, making an angry face caused heart rate and finger temperature to rise, whereas making a fearful face raised heart rate but lowered finger temperature.

Source: Levenson, Ekman, & Friesen (1990).

Such reports seem to contradict James's theory. But spinal cord injuries do not usually affect facial expressions, which James included among the bodily responses that are experienced as emotions. A variant of James's theory, the *facial feedback hypothesis*, suggests that involuntary facial movements provide enough peripheral information to create emotional experience (Ekman & Davidson, 1993). This hypothesis helps to explain why posed facial expressions generate the emotions normally associated with them. So the next time you want to cheer yourself up, it might help to smile—even though you don't feel like it (Fleeson, Malanos, & Achille, 2002)!

●**Lie Detection**   James's view that different patterns of physiological activity are associated with different emotions forms the basis for the lie detection industry. If people experience anxiety or guilt when they lie, specific patterns of physiological activity accompanying these emotions should be detectable on instruments, called *polygraphs*, that record heart rate, breathing, perspiration, and other autonomic responses (Granhag & Stromwall, 2004; Iacono & Patrick, 2006).

To examine a criminal suspect using the *control question test*, a polygraph operator would ask questions specific to the crime, such as "Did you stab anyone on April 6, 2007?" Responses to such *relevant questions* are then compared with responses to *control questions*, such as "Have you ever lied to get out of trouble?" Innocent people might have lied at some time in the past and might feel guilty when asked about it, but they should have no reason to feel guilty about what they did on April 6, 2007. So an innocent person should have a stronger emotional response to control questions than to relevant questions (Rosenfeld, 1995). Another approach, called the *directed lie test*, compares a person's physiological reactions when asked to lie about something and when telling what is known to be the truth. Finally, the

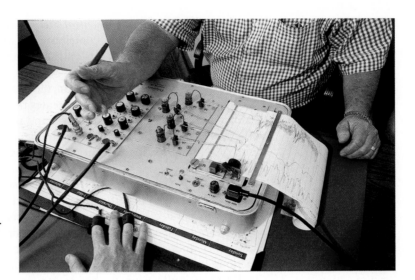

Searching for the Truth Polygraph tests are not foolproof, but they may intimidate people who believe that they are. In a small town where the police could not afford a polygraph, one guilty suspect confessed his crime when a "lie detector" consisting of a kitchen colander was placed on his head and attached by wires to a copy machine (Shepherd, Kohut, & Sweet, 1989).

guilty knowledge test seeks to determine if a person reacts in a notable way to information about a crime that only the criminal would know (Ben-Shakhar, Bar-Hillel, & Kremnitzer, 2002).

Most people do have emotional responses when they lie, but statistics about the accuracy of polygraphs are difficult to obtain. Estimates vary widely, from those suggesting that polygraphs detect 90 percent of guilty, lying individuals (Gamer et al., 2006; Honts & Quick, 1995; Kircher, Horowitz, & Raskin, 1988; Raskin, 1986) to those suggesting that polygraphs mislabel as many as 40 percent of truthful, innocent persons as guilty liars (Ben-Shakhar & Furedy, 1990; Saxe & Ben-Shakhar, 1999). Obviously, the results of a polygraph test are not determined entirely by whether a person is telling the truth. What people think about the act of lying and about the value of the test can also influence the accuracy of its results. For example, people who consider lying to be acceptable—and who do not believe in the power of polygraphs—are unlikely to display emotion-related physiological responses while lying during the test. However, an innocent person who believes in such tests and who thinks that "everything always goes wrong" might show a large fear response when asked about a crime, thus wrongly suggesting guilt (Lykken, 1998).

Polygraphs can catch some liars, but most researchers agree that a guilty person can "fool" a polygraph lie detector and that some innocent people can be mislabeled as guilty (Ruscio, 2005). After reviewing the relevant research literature, a panel of distinguished psychologists and other scientists in the United States expressed serious reservations about the value of polygraph tests in detecting deception and argued against their use as evidence in court or in employee screening and selection (Committee to Review the Scientific Evidence on the Polygraph, 2003). Other lie-detecting techniques now being investigated focus on brain activity and other measures that do not depend on a link between deception and autonomic nervous system responses (Ekman, 2001; Gronau, Ben-Shakhar, & Cohen, 2005; Kozel, Padgett, & George, 2004; Langleben et al., 2005).

● Cannon's Central Theory

James said the experience of emotion depends on feedback from physiological responses occurring outside the brain, but Walter Cannon disagreed (Cannon, 1927/1987). According to Cannon, you feel fear at the sight of a wild bear even before you start to run. He said that emotional experience starts in the central nervous system—specifically, in the thalamus, the brain structure that relays information from most sense organs to the cortex.

According to Cannon's *central theory* (also known as the *Cannon-Bard theory*, in recognition of Philip Bard's contribution), when the thalamus receives sensory information about emotional events and situations, it sends signals to the autonomic nervous system and—at the same time—to the cerebral cortex, where the emotion becomes conscious. So when you see a bear, the brain receives sensory information about it, perceives it as a bear, and *directly* creates the experience of fear while at the same time sending messages to the heart, lungs, and muscles to do what it takes to run away. In other words, Cannon said that the experience of emotion appears directly in the brain, with or without feedback from peripheral responses (see Figure 11.11).

● **Updating Cannon's Theory**   Research conducted since Cannon proposed his theory indicates that the thalamus is actually not the "seat" of emotion but that, through its connections to the amygdala (see Figure 11.8), the thalamus does participate in some aspects of emotional processing (Lang, 1995). For example, studies in laboratory animals and humans show that the emotion of fear is generated by connections from the thalamus to the amygdala (Anderson & Phelps, 2000; LeDoux, 1995). The implication is that strong emotions can sometimes bypass the cortex without requiring conscious thought to activate them. One study showed, for example, that people presented with stimuli such as angry faces display physiological signs of arousal even if they are not conscious of seeing those stimuli (Morris et al., 1998). The same processes might explain why people find it so difficult to overcome an intense fear, or phobia, even though they may consciously know the fear is irrational.

An updated version of Cannon's theory suggests that activity in specific brain areas produces the feelings of pleasure or pain associated with various emotions. This idea arose from studies showing that electrical stimulation of certain brain areas is rewarding. Researchers found that rats kept returning to the place in their cage where they received this kind of stimulation. When the animals were allowed to control delivery of the stimulation by pressing a bar, they pressed it until they were exhausted, ignoring even food and water (Olds & Milner, 1954). Stimulation of other brain regions is so unpleasant that animals work hard to avoid it. The areas of the brain in which stimulation is experienced as especially pleasurable include the dopamine systems, which are activated by drugs such as cocaine. When animals are given drugs that block the action of dopamine, this kind of brain stimulation is no longer experienced as pleasurable (Wise & Rompre, 1989).

The areas of the brain activated by the kind of events that elicit emotion in humans have widespread connections throughout the brain (Fossati et al., 2003). Therefore, the experience of emotion in the central nervous system is probably widely distributed, not narrowly localized in any one "emotion center" (Derryberry & Tucker, 1992). Still, there is evidence to support the main thrust of Cannon's theory: that emotion occurs through the activation of specific circuits in the central nervous system. What Cannon did not foresee is that different parts of the central nervous system may be activated for different emotions and for different aspects of the total emotional experience.

● Cognitive Theories

Suppose you are about to be interviewed for your first job or go out on a blind date or take your first ride in a hot-air balloon. In situations such as these, it is not always easy to know exactly what you are feeling. Is it fear, excitement, anticipation, worry, happiness, dread, or what? Stanley Schachter suggested that the emotions we experience every day are shaped partly by how we interpret the arousal we feel. His cognitive theory of emotion, known as the *Schachter-Singer theory* in recognition of the contributions of Jerome Singer, took shape in the early 1960s, when many psychologists were raising questions about the validity of James's theory of emotion. Schachter argued that the theory was essentially correct—but required a few modifications (Cornelius, 1996). In Schachter's view, feedback about

Labeling Arousal Schachter's cognitive theory of emotion predicts that these people will attribute their physiological arousal to the game they are watching and will label their emotion "excitement." Further, as described in the chapter on health, stress, and coping, the emotions they experience will also depend partly on their cognitive interpretation of the outcome (Lazarus & Folkman, 1984). If their team loses, those who see the defeat as a disaster will experience more negative emotions than those who think of it as a challenge to improve.

physiological changes may not vary enough to create the many shades of emotion that people can experience. He argued instead that emotions emerge from a combination of feedback from peripheral responses and the *cognitive interpretation* of the nature and cause of those responses (Schachter & Singer, 1962). Cognitive interpretation first comes into play, said Schachter, when you perceive the stimulus that leads to bodily responses ("It's a bear!"). Interpretation occurs again when you identify feedback from those responses as a particular emotion (see Figure 11.11). The same physiological responses might be given many different labels, depending on how you interpret those responses. So, according to Schachter, when that bear approaches your campsite, the emotion you experience might be fear, excitement, astonishment, or surprise, depending on how you label your bodily reactions.

Schachter also said that the labeling of arousal depends on **attribution,** the process of identifying the cause of an event. Physiological arousal might be attributed to one of several emotions depending on the information available about the situation. If you are watching the final seconds of a close basketball game, you might attribute your racing heart, rapid breathing, and perspiration to excitement. You might attribute the same physiological reactions to anxiety if you are waiting for a big exam to begin. Schachter predicted that our emotional experiences will be less intense if we attribute arousal to a nonemotional cause. So if you notice your heart pounding before an exam but say to yourself, "Sure my heart's racing—I just drank five cups of coffee!" then you should feel "wired" from caffeine rather than afraid or worried. This prediction has received some support (Mezzacappa, Katkin, & Palmer, 1999; Sinclair et al., 1994), but other aspects of Schachter's theory have not.

Few researchers today fully accept the Schachter-Singer theory, but it did stimulate an enormous amount of valuable research, including studies of **excitation transfer,** a phenomenon in which physiological arousal from one experience carries over to affect emotion in an independent situation (Reisenzein, 1983; Zillmann, 1998). For example, people who have been aroused by physical exercise become more angry when provoked, or experience more intense sexual feelings when in the company of an attractive person, than do people who have been less physically active (Allen et al., 1989). Arousal from fear, like arousal from exercise, can also enhance emotions, including sexual feelings. One study of this transfer took place in Canada, near a deep river gorge. The gorge could be crossed either by a shaky swinging bridge or by a more stable wooden one. A female researcher asked men who had just crossed each bridge to fill out a questionnaire that included a measure of sexual

● **attribution** The process of explaining the causes of an event.

● **excitation transfer** The process of carrying over arousal from one experience to an independent situation.

imagery. The men who met the woman after crossing the more dangerous bridge had much higher sexual imagery scores than the men who had crossed the stable bridge. Furthermore, they were more likely to rate the researcher as attractive (Dutton & Aron, 1974). When the person giving out the questionnaire was a male, however, the type of bridge crossed had no effect on sexual imagery. To test the possibility that the men who crossed the dangerous bridge were simply more adventurous in both bridge crossing and heterosexual encounters, the researcher repeated the study, but with one change. This time, the woman approached the men farther down the trail, long after arousal from the bridge crossing had subsided. Now, the apparently adventurous men were no more likely than others to rate the woman as attractive. So it was probably excitation transfer, not just adventurousness, that produced the original result.

Schachter focused on the cognitive interpretation of our bodily responses to events, but other theorists have argued that it is our cognitive interpretation of *events themselves* that are most important in shaping emotional experiences. For example, as we mentioned earlier, a person's emotional reaction to receiving exam results can depend partly whether the score is seen as a sign of improvement or a grade worthy of shame. According to Richard Lazarus's (1966, 1991) *cognitive appraisal theory* of emotion, these differing reactions can be best explained by how we think exam scores, job interviews, blind dates, bear sightings, and other events will affect our personal well-being. According to Lazarus, the process of cognitive appraisal, or evaluation, begins when we decide whether or not an event is relevant to our well-being. That is, do we even care about it? If we don't, as might be the case if an exam doesn't count toward our grade, we are unlikely to have an emotional experience when we get the results. If the event is relevant to our well-being, we will experience an emotional reaction to it. That reaction will be positive or negative, said Lazarus, depending on whether we see the event as advancing our personal goals or obstructing them. The specific emotion we experience depends on our individual goals, needs, standards, expectations, and past experiences. As a result, a particular exam score can create contentment in one person, elation in another, mild disappointment in someone else, and despair in yet another. Individual differences in goals and standards are at work, too, when a second-place finisher in a marathon race experiences bitter disappointment at having "lost," while someone at the back of the pack may be thrilled just to have completed the race alive (Larsen et al., 2004).

"In Review: Theories of Emotion" summarizes key elements of the theories we have discussed. Research on these theories suggests that both peripheral autonomic responses (including facial responses) and the cognitive interpretation of those responses add to emotional experience. So does cognitive appraisal of events themselves. In addition, the brain can apparently generate emotional experience on its own, independent of physiological arousal. In short, emotion is probably both in the heart

in review Theories of Emotion

Theory	Source of Emotions	Example
James-Lange	Emotions are created by awareness of specific patterns of peripheral (autonomic) responses.	Anger is associated with increased blood flow in the hands and feet; fear is associated with decreased blood flow in these areas.
Cannon-Bard	The brain generates direct experiences of emotion.	Stimulation of certain brain areas can create pleasant or unpleasant emotions.
Cognitive (Schachter-Singer and Lazarus)	Cognitive interpretation of events, and of physiological reactions to them, shapes emotional experiences.	Autonomic arousal can be experienced as anxiety or excitement, depending on how it is labeled. A single event can lead to different emotions, depending on whether it is perceived as threatening or challenging.

and in the head (including the face). The most basic emotions probably occur directly within the brain, whereas the many shades of discernible emotions probably arise from attributions and other cognitive interpretations of physiological responses and environmental events. No theory has completely resolved the issue of which, if any, component of emotion is primary. However, the theories we have discussed have helped psychologists better understand how these components interact to produce emotional experience. Cognitive appraisal theories, in particular, have been especially useful in studying and treating stress-related emotional problems (see the chapters on health, stress, and coping; psychological disorders; and treatment of psychological disorders).

Communicating Emotion

So far, we have described emotion from the inside, as people experience their own emotions. Let's now consider how people communicate emotions to one another. One way they do this is through words. Some people describe their feelings relatively simply, and mainly in terms of pleasantness or unpleasantness. Others include information about the intensity of their emotions (Barrett, 1995; Barrett et al., 2001). In general, women are more likely than men to talk about their emotions and the complexity of their feelings (Barrett et al., 2000; Kring & Gordon, 1998). But humans also communicate emotion through the movement and posture of their bodies (de Gelder et al., 2004; Hadjikhani & de Gelder, 2003), through their tone of voice, and especially through their facial movements and expressions.

Imagine a woman watching television. You can see her face, but not what she sees on the screen. She might be engaged in complex thought, perhaps comparing her investments with those of the experts on CNBC. Or she might be thinking of nothing at all as she loses herself in a rerun of *The Simpsons*. In other words, you won't be able to tell much about what the woman is thinking. But if the TV program creates an emotional experience, you will be able to make a reasonably accurate guess about what she is feeling simply by looking at the expression on her face. The human face can create thousands of different expressions (Zajonc, 1998), and people are good at detecting them. Observers can notice even tiny facial movements—a twitch of the mouth or eyebrow can carry a lot of information (Ambadar, Schooler, & Cohn, 2005). Females consistently outperform males in identifying and interpreting the nonverbal emotion cues conveyed by facial expressions (Hall, 1984). This gender difference appears in infancy (McClure, 2000), suggesting that it may have biological origins that are amplified later through gender-specific socialization. Are emotional facial expressions innate as well, or are they learned? And how are they used in communicating emotion?

● Innate Expressions of Emotion

Charles Darwin observed that some facial expressions seem to be universal (Darwin, 1872/1965). He proposed that these expressions are genetically determined, passed on biologically from one generation to the next. The facial expressions seen today, said Darwin, are those that have been most effective at telling others something about how a person is feeling. If someone is scowling with teeth clenched, for example, you will probably assume that he or she is angry, and you will be unlikely to choose that particular moment to ask for a loan.

Infants provide one source of evidence that some facial expressions are innate. Newborns do not need to be taught to grimace in pain or to smile in pleasure or to blink when startled (Balaban, 1995). Even blind infants, who cannot imitate adults' expressions, show the same emotional expressions as do sighted infants (Goodenough, 1932).

A second line of evidence for innate facial expressions comes from studies showing that for the most basic emotions, people in all cultures show similar facial

TRY THIS ⚙ **What Are They Feeling?** People's emotions are usually "written on their faces." Jot down the emotions you think these people are feeling, and then look at the footnote on page 452 to see how well you "read" their emotions.

responses to similar emotional stimuli (Hejmadi, Davidson, & Rozin, 2000; Matsumoto & Willingham, 2006; Zajonc, 1998). Participants in these studies look at photographs of people's faces and then try to name the emotion each person is feeling. Though there may be some subtle differences from culture to culture (Marsh, Elfenbein, & Ambady, 2003), the overall pattern of facial movements we call a smile, for example, is universally related to positive emotions. Sadness is almost always accompanied by slackened muscle tone and a "long" face. Likewise, in almost all cultures, people contort their faces in a similar way when shown something they find disgusting. And a furrowed brow is frequently associated with frustration (Ekman, 1994).

Anger is also linked with a facial expression recognized by almost all cultures. One study examined artwork—including ceremonial masks—of various Western and non-Western cultures (Aronoff, Barclay, & Stevenson, 1988). The angry, threatening masks of all eighteen cultures contained similar elements, such as triangular eyes and diagonal lines on the cheeks. In particular, angular and diagonal elements carry the impression of threat (see Figure 11.13). One study with high school students found that threat is conveyed most strongly by the eyebrows, followed by the mouth and eyes (Lundqvist, Esteves, & Öhman, 1999).

The Universal Smile The idea that some emotional expressions are innate is supported by the fact that the facial movement pattern we call a smile is related to happiness, pleasure, and other positive emotions in cultures throughout the world.

FIGURE 11.13

Threat Elements of Ceremonial Masks

TRY THIS ⚙ Certain geometric patterns are common to threatening masks in many cultures. "Scary" Halloween pumpkins tend to include these patterns, too. When people in various cultures were asked which member of each of these pairs was more threatening, they consistently chose those, shown here on the left side of each pair, containing triangular and diagonal elements. Cover this caption, then ask a few friends to try the same task. How many of them chose the left-hand elements as being more threatening?

▨ ● Social and Cultural Influences on Emotional Expression

Not all emotional expressions are innate or universal, however (Ekman, 1993). Some are learned through contact with a particular culture, and all of them, even innate expressions, are flexible enough to change as necessary in the social situations in which they occur (Fernández-Dols & Ruiz-Belda, 1995). For example, facial expressions become more intense and change more frequently while people are imagining social scenes as opposed to solitary scenes (Fridlund et al., 1990). Similarly, facial expressions in response to odors tend to be more intense when others are watching than when people are alone (Jancke & Kaufmann, 1994).

Further, although a core of emotional responses is recognized by all cultures (Hejmadi et al., 2000), there is a certain degree of cultural variation in recognizing some emotions (Russell, 1995). In one study, for example, Japanese and North American people agreed about which facial expressions signaled happiness, surprise, and sadness, but they frequently disagreed about which faces showed anger, disgust, and fear (Matsumoto & Ekman, 1989). Members of preliterate cultures, such as the Fore of New Guinea, agree even less with people in Western cultures on the labeling of facial expressions (Russell, 1994). In addition, there are variations in how people in different cultures interpret emotions expressed by tone of voice (Mesquita & Frijda, 1992). For instance, Taiwanese participants were best at recognizing a sad tone of voice, whereas Dutch participants were best at recognizing happy tones (Van Bezooijen, Otto, & Heenan, 1983).

People learn how to express certain emotions in particular ways, as specified by cultural rules. Suppose you say, "I just bought a new car," and all your friends stick their tongues out at you. In North America, this would mean that they are envious or resentful. But in some regions of China, such a display expresses surprise.

Even smiles can vary as people learn to use them to communicate certain feelings. Paul Ekman and his colleagues categorized seventeen types of smiles, including "false smiles," which fake enjoyment, and "masking smiles," which hide unhappiness. They called the smile that occurs with real happiness the Duchenne (pronounced "do-SHEN") smile, after the French researcher who first noticed a difference between spontaneous, happy smiles and posed smiles. A genuine, Duchenne smile includes contractions of the muscles around the eyes (creating a distinctive wrinkling of the skin in these areas), as well as of the muscles that raise the lips and cheeks. Most people are not able to contract the muscles around the eyes during a posed smile, so this feature can be used to distinguish "lying smiles" from genuine ones (Frank, Ekman, & Friesen, 1993).

●**Learning About Emotions** The effects of learning are seen in a child's growing range of emotional expressions. Although infants begin with an innate set of emotional responses, they soon learn to imitate facial expressions and use them for more and more emotions. In time, these expressions become more precise and personalized, so that a particular expression conveys a clear emotional message to anyone who knows that person well.

If facial expressions become *too* personalized, however, no one will know what the expressions mean. Operant shaping (described in the chapter on learning) probably helps keep emotional expressions within certain limits. If you could not see other people's facial expressions or observe their responses to yours, you might show fewer, or less intense, facial signs of emotion. And in fact, as congenitally blind people grow older, their facial expressions tend to become less animated (Izard, 1977).

As children grow, they learn an *emotion culture*—rules that govern what emotions are appropriate in what circumstances and what emotional expressions are allowed. These rules can vary between genders and from culture to culture (LaFrance, Hecht, & Paluck, 2003; Tsai, Levenson, & McCoy, 2006). For example, TV news cameras showed that men in the U.S. military leaving for duty in Iraq tended to keep their emotions in check as they said goodbye to wives, girlfriends, and parents. However, in Italy—where mother-son ties are particularly strong—many male soldiers wailed with dismay and wept openly as they left. In a laboratory study, when viewing a distressing movie with a group of peers, Japanese students exhibited much more control over their facial expressions than did North American students. When they watched the film while alone, however, the Japanese students' faces showed the same emotional expressions as those of the North American students (Ekman, Friesen, & Ellsworth, 1972).

Emotion cultures shape how people describe and categorize feelings, resulting in both similarities and differences across cultures (Russell, 1991). At least five of the seven basic emotions listed in an ancient Chinese book called the *Li Chi*—joy, anger, sadness, fear, love, disliking, and liking—are considered primary emotions by most Western theorists. Yet whereas English has more than 500 emotion-related words, some emotion words in other languages have no English equivalent. The Czech word *litost* apparently has no English word equivalent: "It designates a feeling as infinite as an open accordion, a feeling that is the synthesis of many others: grief, sympathy, remorse, and an indefinable longing" (quoted in Russell, 1991). The Japanese word *ijirashii* also has no English equivalent; it describes the feeling of seeing a praiseworthy person overcoming an obstacle (Russell, 1991).

Similarly, other cultures have no equivalent for some English emotion words. Many cultures do not see anger and sadness as different, for example. The Ilongot, a Philippine head-hunting group, have only one word, *liget*, for both anger and grief (Russell, 1991). Tahitians have words for forty-six different types of anger but no word for sadness and, apparently, no concept of it. One Westerner described a Tahitian man as sad over separation from his wife and child, but the man himself felt *pe'a pe'a*—a general term for feeling ill, troubled, or fatigued—and did not attribute it to the separation.

Cultures differ, too, in terms of the emotions that people would ideally like to experience. One study found, for example, that European Americans and Asian Americans placed higher value on having strong positive emotions than did Hong Kong Chinese (Tsai, Knutson, & Fung, 2006). These results suggest that people from differing cultural backgrounds might differ in the degree to which they experience particular emotions to be pleasant, or upsetting. Such differences, in turn, could underlie cultural variations in subjective well-being, and in stress tolerance (e.g., Laumann et al., 2006; Ott, 2005; Peiro, 2006).

● **Social Referencing** Facial expressions, tone of voice, body postures, and gestures can do more than communicate emotion. They can also influence others' behavior, especially the behavior of people who are not sure what to do. An inexperienced chess player, for instance, might reach out to move the queen, catch sight of a spectator's grimace, and infer that another move would be better. The process of letting another person's emotional state guide our own behavior is called *social referencing* (Campos, 1980).

The visual-cliff studies described in the chapter on perception have been used to create an uncertain situation for infants. To reach its mother, an infant in these experiments must cross the visual cliff (see Figure 5.23). If the apparent drop-off is very small or very large, there is no question about what to do: A one-year-old knows to crawl across in the first case and to stay put in the second case. However, if the apparent drop-off is just large enough (say, two feet) to create uncertainty, the infant relies on its mother's facial expression to decide what to do. In one study, mothers were asked to make either a fearful or a happy face. When the mothers made a fearful face, no infant crossed the glass floor. But when they posed a happy face, most infants crossed (Sorce et al., 1981). Here is yet another example of the adaptive value of sending and receiving emotional communications.

The picture on page 450 shows the wife and daughter of a U.S. Marine helicopter pilot waving goodbye as he departs for deployment in a war zone. Their emotions at the moment probably included sadness, anxiety, worry, dread, uncertainty, hope, and perhaps anger.

As noted in the chapter on introducing psychology, all of psychology's many subfields are related to one another. Our discussion of conflicting motives and stress illustrates just one way in which the topic of this chapter, motivation and emotion, is linked to the subfield of health psychology (which is discussed in the chapter on health, stress, and coping). The Linkages diagram shows ties to two other subfields as well, and there are many more ties throughout the book. Looking for linkages among subfields will help you see how they all fit together and better appreciate the big picture that is psychology.

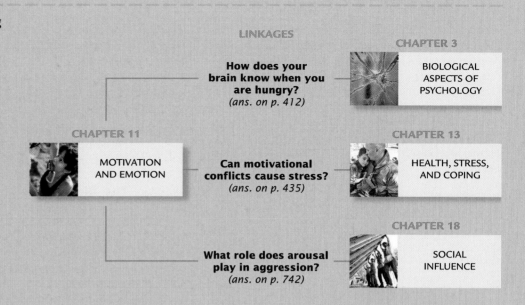

LINKAGES

CHAPTER 11
MOTIVATION AND EMOTION

How does your brain know when you are hungry?
(ans. on p. 412)

CHAPTER 3
BIOLOGICAL ASPECTS OF PSYCHOLOGY

Can motivational conflicts cause stress?
(ans. on p. 435)

CHAPTER 13
HEALTH, STRESS, AND COPING

What role does arousal play in aggression?
(ans. on p. 742)

CHAPTER 18
SOCIAL INFLUENCE

SUMMARY

Motivation refers to factors that influence the initiation, direction, intensity, and persistence of behavior. Emotion and motivation are often linked: Motivation can influence emotion, and people are often motivated to seek certain emotions.

Concepts and Theories of Motivation

Focusing on a *motive* often reveals a single theme within apparently diverse behaviors. Motivation is said to be an intervening variable, a way of linking various stimuli to the behaviors that follow them.

Sources of Motivation   The many sources of motivation fall into four categories: biological factors, emotional factors, cognitive factors, and social factors.

Instinct Theory and Its Descendants   An early argument held that motivation follows from *instincts*, which are automatic, involuntary, and unlearned behavior patterns consistently "released" by particular stimuli. Modern versions of *instinct theory* are seen in evolutionary accounts of helping, aggression, mate selection, and other aspects of social behavior.

Drive Reduction Theory   *Drive reduction theory* is based on *homeostasis*, a tendency to maintain equilibrium in a physical or behavioral process. When disruption of equilibrium creates a *need* of some kind, people are motivated to reduce the resulting *drive* by behaving in some way that satisfies the need and restores balance.

Optimal Arousal Theory   According to *optimal arousal theory*, people are motivated to behave in ways that maintain a level of *arousal* that is optimal for their functioning.

Incentive Theory   *Incentive theory* highlights behaviors that are motivated by attaining desired stimuli (positive incentives) and avoiding undesirable ones (negative incentives).

Hunger and Eating

Eating is controlled by a complex mixture of learning, culture, and biology.

Biological Signals for Hunger and Satiety   The desire to eat *(hunger)* or to stop eating *(satiety)* depends primarily on signals from blood-borne substances such as cholecystokinin (CCK), glucose, insulin, and leptin.

Hunger and the Brain   Activity in the ventromedial nucleus of the hypothalamus results in satiety, whereas activity in the lateral hypothalamus results in hunger. These brain regions might be acting together to maintain a set point of body weight, but control of eating is more complex than that. For example, a variety of neurotransmitters act in various regions of the hypothalamus to create hunger for specific types of foods.

Flavor, Cultural Learning, and Food Selection   Eating may also be influenced by the flavor of food and by appetite for the pleasure of food. Food selection is influenced by biological needs (specific hungers) for certain nutrients, as well as by food cravings, social contexts, and cultural traditions.

Eating Disorders   *Obesity* has been linked to overconsumption of certain kinds of foods, to low energy metabolism, and to genetic factors. People suffering from *anorexia nervosa* starve themselves. Those who suffer from *bulimia nervosa* engage in binge eating, followed by purging through self-induced vomiting or laxatives.

Sexual Behavior

Sexual motivation and behavior result from a rich interplay of biology and culture.

The Biology of Sex   Sexual stimulation generally produces a stereotyped *sexual response cycle*, a pattern of physiological arousal during and after sexual activity. *Sex hormones*, which include *androgens, estrogens,* and *progestins*, occur in different relative amounts in both sexes. They can have organizational effects, such as physical differences in the brain, and activational effects, such as increased desire for sex.

Social and Cultural Factors in Sexuality Gender-role learning and educational experiences are examples of cultural factors that can bring about variations in sexual attitudes and behaviors.

Sexual Orientation Sexual orientation—*heterosexual, homosexual,* or *bisexual*—is increasingly viewed as a sociocultural variable that affects many other aspects of behavior and mental processes. Though undoubtedly shaped by a lifetime of learning, sexual orientation appears to have strong biological roots.

Sexual Dysfunctions Common male *sexual dysfunctions* include erectile disorder and premature ejaculation. Females may experience such problems as arousal disorder.

Achievement Motivation

People gain esteem from achievement in many areas, including the workplace.

Need for Achievement The motive to succeed is called *need achievement*. Individuals with high achievement motivation strive for excellence, persist despite failures, and set challenging but realistic goals.

Goal Setting and Achievement Motivation Goals influence motivation, especially the amount of effort, persistence, attention, and planning we devote to a task.

Achievement and Success in the Workplace Workers are most satisfied when they are working toward their own goals and are getting concrete feedback. Jobs that offer clear and specific goals, a variety of tasks, individual responsibility, and other intrinsic rewards are the most motivating.

Achievement and Subjective Well-Being People tend to have a characteristic level of happiness, or *subjective well-being*, which is not necessarily related to the attainment of money, status, or other material goals.

Relations and Conflicts Among Motives

Human behavior reflects many motives, some of which may be in conflict. Abraham Maslow proposed a hierarchy of five classes of human motives, from meeting basic biological needs to attaining a state of self-actualization. Motives at the lowest levels, according to Maslow, must be at least partially satisfied before people can be motivated by higher-level goals.

Opponent Processes, Motivation, and Emotion Motivated behavior sometimes gives rise to opponent emotional processes, such as the fear and excitement associated with a roller coaster

ride. Opponent-process theory illustrates the close link between motivation and emotion.

The Nature of Emotion

Defining Characteristics An *emotion* is a temporary experience with positive or negative qualities that is felt with some intensity as happening to the self, is generated in part by a cognitive appraisal of a situation, and is accompanied by both learned and innate physical responses.

The Biology of Emotion Several brain mechanisms are involved in emotion. The amygdala, in the limbic system, is deeply involved in various aspects of emotion. The expression of emotion through involuntary facial movement is controlled by the extrapyramidal motor system. Voluntary facial movements are controlled by the pyramidal motor system. The brain's right and left hemispheres play somewhat different roles in emotion. In addition to specific brain mechanisms, both branches of the autonomic nervous system, the *sympathetic nervous system* and the *parasympathetic nervous system*, are involved in physiological changes that accompany emotional activation. The *fight-or-flight syndrome*, for example, follows from activation of the sympathetic system.

Theories of Emotion

James's Peripheral Theory William James's theory of emotion holds that peripheral physiological responses are the primary source of emotion and that awareness of these responses constitutes emotional experience. James's theory is supported by evidence that, at least for several basic emotions, physiological responses are distinguishable enough for emotions to be generated in this way. Distinct facial expressions are linked to particular patterns of physiological change.

Cannon's Central Theory Walter Cannon's theory of emotion proposes that emotional experience occurs independent of peripheral physiological responses and that there is a direct experience of emotion based on activity of the central nervous system. Updated versions of this theory suggest that various parts of the central nervous system may be involved in different emotions and different aspects of emotional experience. Some pathways in the brain, such as that from the thalamus to the amygdala, allow strong emotions to occur before conscious thought can take place. And specific parts of the brain appear to be responsible for the feelings of pleasure or pain in emotion.

Cognitive Theories Stanley Schachter's modification of James's theory proposes that physiological responses are primary sources of emotion but that the cognitive labeling of those responses—a process that depends partly on *attribution*—strongly influences the emotions we experience. Schachter's theory stimulated research on *excitation transfer*. Other cognitive theories, such as that of Richard Lazarus, emphasize that emotional experience depends heavily on how we think about the situations and events we encounter.

Communicating Emotion

Humans communicate emotions mainly through facial movement and expressions, but also through voice tones and bodily movements.

Innate Expressions of Emotion Charles Darwin suggested that certain facial expressions of emotion are innate and universal and that these expressions evolved because they effectively communicate one creature's emotional condition to other creatures. Some facial expressions of basic emotions, such as happiness, do appear to be innate.

Social and Cultural Influences on Emotional Expression Many emotional expressions are learned, and even innate expressions are modified by learning and social contexts. As children grow, they learn an emotion culture, the rules of emotional expression appropriate to their culture. Accordingly, the same emotion may be communicated by different facial expressions in different cultures. Especially in ambiguous situations, other people's emotional expressions may serve as a guide about what to do or what not to do, a phenomenon called *social referencing*.

Human Development

12

Infancy, childhood, adolescence, adulthood, and old age. These words can be read in seconds, but the stages they represent take a lifetime to play out. The story of development is different for each of us, but there are some common threads, too, and developmental psychologists are exploring them. In this chapter, we describe what they have discovered so far about how people change and grow over the course of the life span. Here's how we have organized the material:

Jeff Weise, Lee Boyd Malvo, Dylan Klebold, Eric Harris, Kip Kinkel, and Seung-Hui Cho are just a few of the teenage boys and young men whose deadly shooting sprees in recent years have shocked people in North America and around the world. As thwarted mass murder plots by disgruntled students continue to make news, everyone wants to know what's behind it all. Had these young people watched too much violence on television or played too many violent video games? Were their actions the fault of a "gun culture" that allows children access to firearms? Had they been victims of abuse and neglect? Were their parents too strict—or not strict enough? Did they come from "broken homes," or had they witnessed violence within their own families? Did they behave violently because they were going through a difficult "stage," because they had not been taught right from wrong, because they wanted to impress their peers, because males are more aggressive in general, or because their brains were "defective"? Were they just "bad kids"?

These are the kinds of questions developmental psychologists try to answer. They investigate when certain behaviors first appear and how they change with age. They explore how development in one area, such as moral reasoning, relates to development in other areas, such as aggressive behavior. They look at whether most people develop at the same rate and, if not, whether slow starters ever catch up to early bloomers. They ask why some children become well-adjusted and caring individuals, whereas others become murderers; why some adolescents go on to win honors in college while others drop out of high school. They seek to explain how development throughout the life span is affected by both genetics and the environment, analyzing the extent to which development is a product of what we arrive with at birth (our inherited, biological *nature*) and the extent to which it is a product of what the world provides (the *nurture* of the environment). In short, **developmental psychology** is concerned with the course and causes of the developmental changes that take place over a person's entire lifetime.

In this chapter we examine many such changes. We begin by describing the physical and biological changes that occur from the moment of conception to the moment of birth. Then we discuss cognitive, social, and emotional development during infancy and childhood. Next, we examine the changes and challenges that occur during adolescence. We conclude by considering the significant physical, intellectual, and social changes that take place as people move through early, middle, and late adulthood.

Exploring Human Development

The question of whether development is the result of nature or nurture was the subject of philosophical debate centuries before psychologists began studying it scientifically. In essays published in the 1690s, British philosopher John Locke argued for nurture. He believed that experiences provided by the environment during childhood have a profound and permanent effect. As mentioned in the chapter on introducing psychology, Locke thought of the newborn as a blank slate, or *tabula rasa*. Adults write on that slate, he said, as they teach children about the world and how to behave in it. Some seventy years later, French philosopher Jean-Jacques Rousseau (pronounced "roo-SOH") made the opposite argument. He claimed that children are capable of discovering how the world operates and how they should behave without instruction from adults. According to Rousseau, children should be allowed to grow as their natures dictate, with little guidance or pressure from parents.

developmental psychology The psychological specialty that documents the course of social, emotional, moral, and intellectual development over the life span.

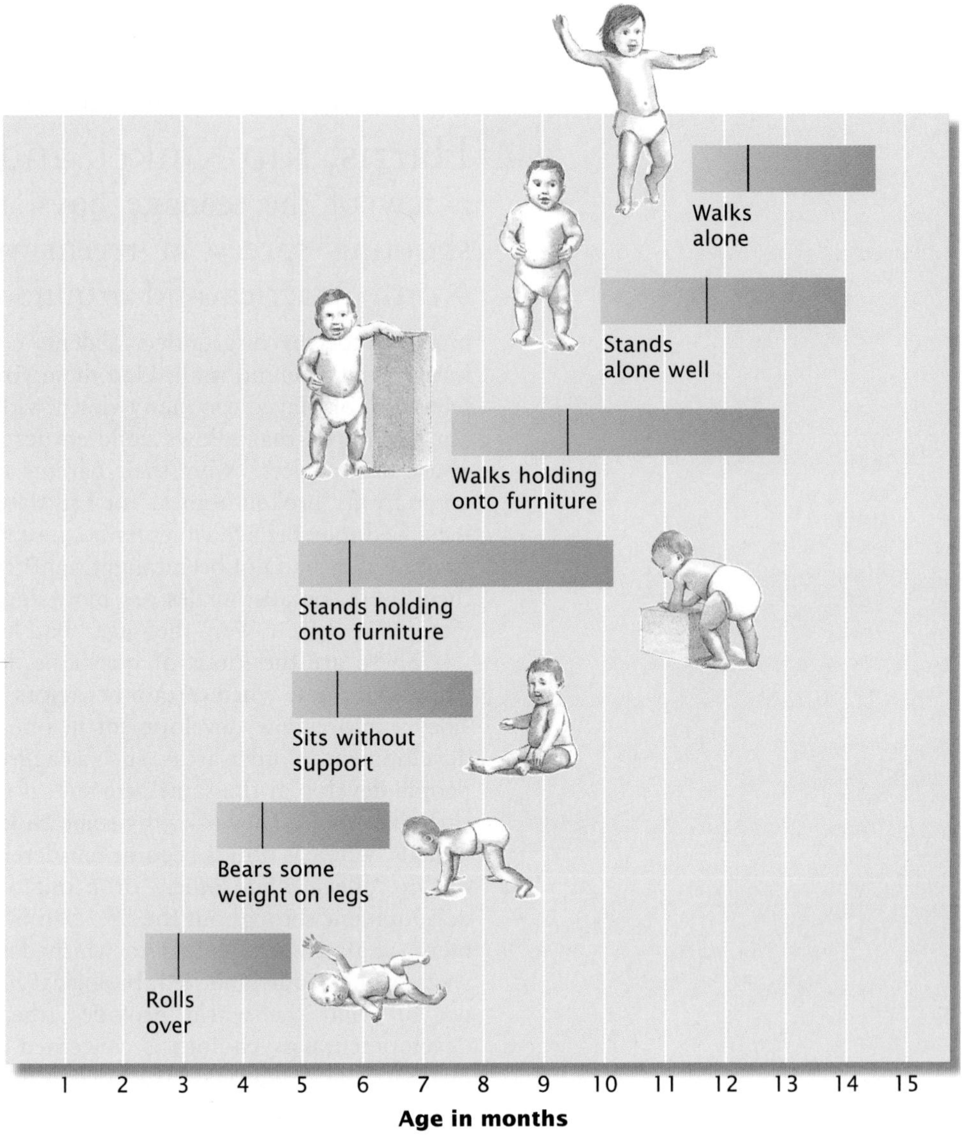

FIGURE 12.1

Motor Development

When did you start walking? The left end of each bar indicates the age at which 25 percent of the infants tested were able to perform a particular behavior; 50 percent of the babies were performing the behavior at the age indicated by the vertical line in the bars. The right end of each bar indicates the age at which 90 percent could do so (Frankenberg & Dodds, 1967). Although different infants, especially in different cultures, achieve milestones of motor development at slightly different ages, all infants—regardless of their ethnicity, social class, or temperament—achieve them in the same order.

Figure bar labels: Walks alone; Stands alone well; Walks holding onto furniture; Stands holding onto furniture; Sits without support; Bears some weight on legs; Rolls over.

Age in months — 1 2 3 4 5 6 7 8 9 10 11 12 13 14 15

The first psychologist to systematically investigate the role of nature in behavior was Arnold Gesell. In the early 1900s, Gesell (pronounced "geh-ZELL") observed many children of all ages. He found that their motor skills, such as standing and walking, picking up a cube, and throwing a ball, developed in a fixed sequence of stages, as Figure 12.1 illustrates. The order of the stages and the age at which they develop, he suggested, are determined by nature and relatively unaffected by nurture. Only under extreme conditions, such as famine, war, or poverty, he claimed, are children thrown off their biologically programmed timetable. Gesell used the term **maturation** to refer to this type of natural growth or change, which unfolds in a fixed sequence relatively independent of the environment. The broader term *development* encompasses not only maturation but also changes that are due to learning.

John B. Watson, founder of the behaviorist approach to psychology, disagreed with Gesell. He claimed that the environment, not nature, molds and shapes development. His research with children left him convinced that we learn everything, from skills to fears. In his words, "there is no such thing as an inheritance of capacity, talent, temperament, mental constitution and characteristics. These things . . . depend on training that goes on mainly in the cradle" (Watson, 1925, pp. 74–75).

maturation   Natural growth or change that unfolds in a fixed sequence relatively independent of the environment.

A Pioneer in the Study of Cognitive Development   Using a variety of research procedures, including his remarkable observational skills, Jean Piaget (1896–1980) investigated the development of cognitive processes in children, including his own son and daughters. He wove his observations and inferences into the most comprehensive and influential theory that had yet been formulated about how thought and knowledge develop from infancy to adolescence.

A Tiger in Training   The development of human behavior is shaped by both heredity and environment—by nature and nurture. The combined and inseparable influence of these two factors in development is perfectly illustrated in the case of professional golfer Tiger Woods. Here he is as a youngster with his father, who not only provided some of Tiger's genes but also served as his golf teacher.

It was the Swiss psychologist Jean Piaget (pronounced "p-ah-ZHAY") who first suggested that nature and nurture work together and that their influences are inseparable and interactive. Piaget had a lifelong interest in human intellectual and cognitive development. His ideas, presented in numerous books and articles published from the 1920s until his death in 1980, influenced the field of developmental psychology more than those of any other person before or since.

Most developmental psychologists now accept the idea that nature and nurture contribute jointly to development—in two ways. First, they operate together to make all people similar in some respects. For example, we all achieve milestones of physical development in the same order and at roughly the same rate. This pattern is a result of the nature of biological maturation supported by the nurture of basic care, nutrition, and exercise. Second, nature and nurture also both operate to make each person unique. The nature of inherited genes and the nurture of widely different family and cultural environments produce differences among individuals in such dimensions as athletic abilities, intelligence, language ability, and personality (Plomin et al., 2002; Spinath, Price, et al., 2004). Heredity creates *predispositions* that interact with environmental influences, including family and teachers, books and computers, friends and random events (Caspi et al., 2002). It is this interaction that produces the developmental outcomes we see in individuals. So Michael Jordan, Michael Jackson, Michael Douglas, and Michael Moore are different from one another and from other men because of both their genes and their experiences.

Just how much nature and nurture contribute varies from one characteristic to another. Nature shapes some characteristics, such as physical size and appearance, so strongly that only extreme environmental conditions can affect them. Variation in height, for example, has been estimated to be 80 to 95 percent genetic. This means that 80 to 95 percent of the differences in height that we see among people are due to their genes. Less than 20 percent of the differences are due to prenatal or postnatal diet or to early illness or other growth-stunting environmental factors. Nature's influence on other characteristics, such as intelligence or personality, is not as strong. Complex traits such as these are influenced by genes, but by many environmental factors as well.

It is impossible for researchers to identify the separate influences that nature and nurture exert on such complex traits, partly because heredity and environment are *correlated*. For instance, highly intelligent biological parents give their children genes related to intelligence and they typically provide a stimulating environment, too.

Heredity and environment also influence each other. Just as the environment promotes or hampers an individual's abilities, those inherited abilities to some extent determine the individual's environment. For example, a stimulating environment full of toys, books, and lessons encourages children's mental development and increases the chances that their full inherited intelligence will emerge. At the same time, more intelligent children seek out environments that are more stimulating, ask more questions, draw more attention from adults, and ultimately learn more from these experiences.

Beginnings

Nowhere are the intertwined effects of nature and nurture clearer than in the womb, as a single fertilized egg becomes a functioning infant.

● Prenatal Development

The process of development begins when sperm from the father-to-be penetrates, or fertilizes, the ovum of the mother-to-be, and a brand-new cell, called a **zygote**, is formed. This new cell carries a genetic heritage from both mother and father (see the behavioral genetics appendix).

● Stages of Prenatal Development
In the first stage of prenatal development, called the *germinal stage*, the zygote divides into many more cells, which by the end of the second week have formed an **embryo** (pronounced "EM-bree-oh"). What follows is the *embryonic stage* of development, during which the embryo quickly develops a heart, nervous system, stomach, esophagus, and ovaries or testes. By two months after conception, when the embryonic stage ends, the inch-long embryo has developed eyes, ears, a nose, a jaw, a mouth, and lips. The tiny arms have elbows, hands, and stubby fingers; the legs have knees, ankles, and toes.

During the remaining seven-month period until birth, called the *fetal stage* of prenatal development, the organs grow and start to function. By the end of the third month, the **fetus** can kick, make a fist, turn its head, open its mouth, swallow, and frown. In the sixth month, the eyelids, which have been sealed, open. The fetus now has taste buds and a well-developed grasp and, if born prematurely, can breathe regularly for as long as twenty-four hours at a time. By the end of the seventh month, the organ systems, though immature, are all functional. In the eighth and ninth months, fetuses respond to light and touch, and they can hear what is going on outside. When they hear an unpleasant sound, they may even respond with movements that look just like a crying newborn (Gingras, Mitchell, & Grattan, 2005). They can also learn. When they hear their mother's familiar voice, their heart beats a little faster, but it slows if they hear a stranger (Kisilevsky et al., 2003).

● Prenatal Risks
Nature determines the timing and stages of prenatal development, but that development is also affected by the nurture provided by the environment of the womb. During prenatal development, a spongy organ called the *placenta*, formed from the outside layer of the zygote, sends nutrients from the mother to the fetus and carries away wastes. It also screens out many potentially harmful substances, including most bacteria. This screening is imperfect, however: Gases and viruses, as well as nicotine, alcohol, and other drugs, can pass through. Severe damage can occur if the baby's mother takes certain drugs, is exposed to toxic substances, or has certain illnesses while organs are forming in the embryonic stage (Koger, Schettler, & Weiss, 2005).

Harmful external substances that invade the womb and result in birth defects are called **teratogens** (pronounced "ta-RAT-a-jens"). Teratogens are especially damaging during the embryonic stage, because it is a **critical period** in prenatal development, a

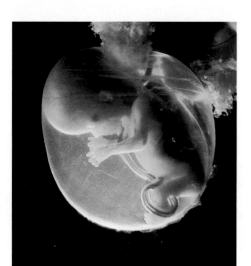

A Fetus at Twelve Weeks At this point in prenatal development, the fetus can kick its legs, curl its toes, make a fist, turn its head, squint, open its mouth, swallow, and take a few "breaths" of amniotic fluid.

zygote A new cell, formed from a father's sperm and a mother's ovum.

embryo The developing individual from the fourteenth day after fertilization until the end of the second month after conception.

fetus The developing individual from the third month after conception until birth.

teratogens Harmful substances that can cause birth defects.

critical period An interval during which certain kinds of growth must occur if development is to proceed normally.

time when certain kinds of growth must occur if the infant's development is to proceed normally. If the heart, eyes, ears, hands, and feet do not appear during this period, they cannot form later on. If they form incorrectly, the defects are permanent. So even before a mother knows she is pregnant, she may accidentally damage her infant by exposing it to teratogens. For example, a baby whose mother has rubella (German measles) during the third or fourth week after conception has a 50 percent chance of being blind, deaf, or mentally retarded or of having a malformed heart. If the mother has rubella later in the pregnancy, after the infant's eyes, ears, brain, and heart have formed, the likelihood that the baby will have one of these defects is much lower. Later, during the fetal stage, teratogens affect the baby's size, behavior, intelligence, and health, rather than the formation of organs and limbs.

Of special concern today are the effects of drugs on infants' development (e.g., Gendle et al., 2004; Jones, 2006). Pregnant women who use substances such as cocaine create a substantial risk for their fetuses, which do not yet have the enzymes necessary to break down the drugs. "Cocaine babies" or "crack babies" may be born premature, underweight, tense, fussy and less likely than other infants to interact smoothly with their mothers (Tronick et al., 2005). They may also suffer delayed physical growth and motor development (Tarr & Pyfer, 1996). Although cocaine babies are more likely to have behavioral and learning problems (Bada et al., 2007; Singer et al., 2002; Tan-Laxa et al., 2004), their cognitive abilities are not necessarily different from those of any baby born into an impoverished environment (Frank et al., 2001; Jones, 2006). How well these children ultimately do in school depends on how supportive that environment turns out to be (Messinger et al., 2004; Singer et al., 2004).

Alcohol is another dangerous teratogen, because it interferes with infants' brain development. Almost half the children born to expectant mothers who abuse alcohol will develop **fetal alcohol syndrome,** a pattern of defects that includes mental retardation and malformations of the face (Jenkins & Culbertson, 1996). Pregnant women who drink as little as a glass or two of wine a day can harm their infants' intellectual functioning (Willford, Leech, & Day, 2006). Those who engage in bouts of heavy drinking triple the odds that their child will develop alcohol-related problems by the age of twenty-one (Baer, Sampson, et al., 2003).

Smoking, too, can affect the developing fetus. Smokers' babies often suffer from respiratory problems, irritability, social and attention problems, and they are at greater risk for nicotine addiction in adolescence and adulthood (Buka, Shenassa, & Niaura, 2003; Law et al., 2003; Linnet et al., 2005; Wakschlag et al., 2006). Worse, they may be born prematurely, and they are usually underweight. Babies who are premature and/or underweight—for whatever reason—are likely to have cognitive and behavioral problems that continue throughout their lives (Bhutta et al., 2002; Jefferis, Power, & Hertzman, 2002).

Defects due to teratogens are most likely to appear when the negative effects of nature and nurture combine. The worst-case scenario is one in which a genetically susceptible infant receives a strong dose of a damaging substance during a critical period of prenatal development. The risk of behavioral and psychological difficulties in later life is also increased for children whose mothers were under significant stress during the first six months of pregnancy (Huizink, Mulder, & Buitelaar, 2004; O'Connor et al., 2005; Van den Bergh & Marcoen, 2004), were depressed (Diego, Field, & Hernandez-Reif, 2005), or got the flu during that period (Brown et al., 2005). However, milder degrees of maternal anxiety or depression during pregnancy may actually advance maturation of the fetus (DiPietro et al., 2006). Fortunately, mental or physical problems resulting from all harmful prenatal factors affect fewer than 10 percent of the babies born in Western nations. Mechanisms built into the human organism maintain normal development under all but the most adverse conditions. The vast majority of fetuses arrive at the end of their nine-month gestation averaging a healthy seven pounds and ready to continue a normal course of development in the world.

fetal alcohol syndrome   A pattern of physical and mental defects found in babies born to women who abused alcohol during pregnancy.

● The Newborn

Determining what newborns are able to see, hear, and do is one of the most fascinating—and frustrating—research challenges in developmental psychology. Young infants are very difficult to study. About 70 percent of the time, they are asleep. When they aren't sleeping, they may be drowsy, crying, or restlessly moving about. It is only when they are in a state of quiet alertness, which occurs infrequently and only for a few minutes at a time, that researchers can assess infants' abilities.

During these brief periods, psychologists present sounds or show objects or pictures, and watch where infants look and for how long. They film the infants' eye movements and record changes in their heart rates, sucking rates, brain waves, body movements, and skin conductance (a measure of perspiration associated with emotion) to learn what infants can see and hear (Kellman & Arterberry, 2006).

● Vision and Other Senses

Infants can see at birth, but their vision is blurry. Researchers estimate that newborns have 20/300 eyesight. In other words, an object 20 feet away looks as clear as it would if viewed from 300 feet by an adult with normal vision. The reason infants' vision is so limited is that their eyes and brains still need time to grow and develop. Newborns' eyes are smaller than those of adults, and the cells in their foveas—the area of each retina on which images are focused—are fewer and far less sensitive. Their eye movements are slow and jerky. Pathways connecting the eyes to the brain are still inefficient, as is the processing of visual information within the brain.

Although infants cannot see small objects on the other side of the room, they are able to see large objects close up. They stare longest at objects that have large visible elements, movement, clear contours, and a lot of contrast—all qualities that exist in the human face (Farroni et al., 2005). In fact, from the time they are born, infants will shift their gaze to track a moving drawing of a face, and they stare at a human face longer than at other figures (Johnson, Dziurawiec, et al., 1991; Valenza et al., 1996). They are particularly interested in eyes, as shown in their preference for faces that are looking directly at them (Farroni et al., 2002). They also experience a certain degree of *size constancy*. This means that objects will appear as the same size despite changes in the size of their image on the eye's retina (see the perception chapter). So a baby perceives the mother's face as remaining about the same size, whether she is looking over the edge of the crib or is close enough to kiss the baby's cheek. By the time they are four months old infants can categorize objects according to their shape (Farran & Brown, 2006), but they do not experience *depth perception* until some time later. It takes about seven months before they begin to use the pictorial depth cues described in the chapter on perception.

The course of development for hearing is similar to that of vision. Infants at birth are not deaf, but they hear poorly. At two or three days of age, they can hear soft voices and notice the difference between tones about one note apart on the musical scale; they also turn their heads toward sounds (Clifton, 1992). But their

A Baby's-Eye View of the World
The photograph on the left simulates what the mother on the right looks like to her newborn infant. Although their vision is blurry, infants particularly seem to enjoy looking at faces. As mentioned in the perception chapter, their eyes will follow a moving face-like drawing, and they will stare at a human face longer than at other figures.

hearing is not as sharp as that of adults until well into childhood. Infants' hearing is particularly attuned to the sounds of speech. When they hear voices, babies open their eyes wider and look for the speaker. By four months of age, they can discriminate differences among almost all of the more than fifty phonetic contrasts in adult languages (Hespos & Spelke, 2004). Infants also prefer certain kinds of speech. They like rising tones spoken by women or children, and they like speech that is high pitched, exaggerated, and expressive. In other words, they like to hear the "baby talk" used by most adults when they talk to babies. They even seem to learn language faster when they hear baby talk (Thiessen, Hill, & Saffran, 2005).

Newborns' sense of smell is similar to that of adults, but again, less well developed. Certain smells and tastes appeal to them more than others. For instance, they like the smell of flowers and the taste of sweet drinks (Ganchrow, Steiner, & Daher, 1983) but dislike the smell of ammonia (in wet diapers). Within a few days after birth, breastfed babies prefer the odor of their own mothers to those of other mothers (Porter et al., 1992). They also develop preferences for the food flavors consumed by their mothers (Mennella & Beauchamp, 1996).

Although limited, an infant's inborn sensory abilities are important for survival and development because they focus the infant's attention on the caregiver. The attraction of newborns to the sweet smell and taste of mother's milk helps them locate appropriate food and identify their caregiver. Their sensitivity to speech allows them to focus on language and encourages the caregiver to talk to them. Because their vision is limited to the distance at which most interaction with a caregiver takes place and is tuned to the special qualities of faces, the caregiver's face is especially noticeable to them. Accordingly, infants are exposed to emotional expressions and come to recognize the caregiver by sight, further encouraging the caregiver to interact. As infants physically mature and learn from their environment, their sensory capacities become more complex and adult-like.

● Reflexes and Motor Skills

In the first few weeks and months after birth, babies demonstrate involuntary, unlearned motor behaviors called *reflexes*. These are swift, automatic movements that occur in response to external stimuli. Figure 12.2 illustrates the *grasping reflex*, one of more than twenty reflexes that have been observed in newborn infants. Another is the *rooting reflex*, which causes the infant to turn its mouth toward a nipple (or anything else) that touches its cheek. And the *sucking reflex* causes the newborn to suck on anything that touches its lips. Many of these reflexes evolved because, like seeing and hearing, they were important for infants' survival. But infants' behavior doesn't remain under the control of these reflexes for long. Most reflexes disappear after the first three or four months, when infants' brain development allows them to control their muscles voluntarily. At that point, infants can develop motor skills, so they are soon able to roll over, sit up, crawl, stand, and by the end of the year, walk (see Figure 12.1).

Until a few years ago, most developmental psychologists accepted Gesell's view that, barring extreme environmental conditions, these motor abilities occur spontaneously as the central nervous system and muscles mature. It turns out, though, that maturation does not tell the whole story, even in normal environments (Thelen, 1995). Consider the fact that many babies today aren't learning to crawl on time—or at all. Why? One reason has to do with the "Back to Sleep" campaign that was launched in the mid-1990s in an effort to prevent sudden infant death syndrome (see the chapter on consciousness). This public health campaign urges parents to put babies to sleep on their backs rather than face-down. The campaign has been successful, but researchers have discovered that many babies who were never placed on their tummies went directly from sitting to toddling, skipping the crawling stage but reaching all other motor milestones on schedule (Kolata & Markel, 2001).

Observation of infants who do learn to crawl has shown that it does not happen suddenly. It takes the development of enough muscle strength to support the abdomen—and some active experimentation—to get the job done. Six infants in one

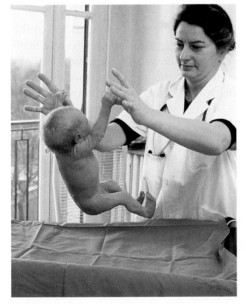

FIGURE 12.2

Reflexes in the Newborn

When a finger is pressed into a newborn's palm, the *grasping reflex* causes the infant to hold on tightly enough to suspend its entire weight. And when a newborn is held upright over a flat surface, the *stepping reflex* leads to walking movements.

study tried various crawling techniques—moving backward, moving one limb at a time, using the arms only, and so on (Freedland & Bertenthal, 1994). It was only after a week or two of trial and error that all six arrived at the same method: moving diagonal limbs (right arm and left leg, left arm and right leg) together. This pattern turned out to be the most efficient way of getting around quickly without tipping over. Such observations suggest that as maturation increases infants' strength, they try out motor patterns and select the ones that work best (Nelson, 1999).

In short, motor development results from a combination of maturation and experience. It is not the result of an entirely automatic sequence genetically etched in the brain. Yet again, we see that nature and nurture influence each other.

Infancy and Childhood: Cognitive Development

In just ten years or so, the tiny infant becomes a competent child who can read a book, write a poem, and argue for access to the family's new computer. Researchers who study *cognitive development* explore the dramatic shifts in thinking, knowing, and remembering that occur between early infancy and later childhood.

● Changes in the Brain

One factor that underlies the cognitive leaps of infancy and childhood is the continued growth and development of the brain. When infants are born, they already have a full quota of brain cells, but the neural networks connecting the cells are immature. With time, the connections grow increasingly complex and then, with pruning, more efficient. Studies reveal how, as different regions of the brain develop more complex and efficient neural networks, new cognitive abilities appear (Nelson, Thomas, & de Haan, 2006).

In the first few months of infancy, the cerebellum is the most mature area of the brain. Its early maturation allows infants to display simple associative abilities, such as sucking more when they see their mother's face or hear her voice. Between six and twelve months of age, neurological development in the medial temporal lobe of the cerebral cortex makes it possible for infants to remember and imitate an action they have seen earlier or to recognize a picture of an object they have never seen but have held in their hands. Neurological development in the frontal cortex, which occurs later in childhood, allows for the development of higher cognitive functions such as reasoning. In other words, brain structures provide the "hardware" for cognitive development. How does the "software" of thinking develop, and how does it modify the "wiring" of the brain's "hardware"? These questions have been pursued by many developmental psychologists, beginning with Piaget.

● The Development of Knowledge: Piaget's Theory

Piaget dedicated his life to a search for the origins of intelligence in infancy and the factors that lead to changes in knowledge over the life span. He was the first to chart the fascinating journey from the simple reflexes of the newborn to the complex understandings of the adolescent. Piaget's theory was not correct in every respect—later we discuss some of its weaknesses—but his ideas about cognitive development still influence research in the field.

Piaget proposed that cognitive development proceeds through a series of distinct *periods* or *stages* (see Table 12.1). He believed that all children's thinking goes through the same stages, in the same order, without skipping—building on previous stages, then moving to higher ones. According to Piaget, the thinking of infants is different from the thinking of children, and the thinking of children is different from that of adolescents. He concluded that children are not just miniature adults and

TABLE 12.1   Piaget's Periods of Cognitive Development

According to Piaget, a predictable set of features characterizes each period of children's cognitive development. The ages associated with the stages are approximate; Piaget realized that some children move through the stages slightly faster or slower than others.

Period	Activities and Achievements
Sensorimotor Birth–2 years	Infants discover aspects of the world through their sensory impressions, motor activities, and coordination of the two. They learn to differentiate themselves from the external world. They learn that objects exist even when they are not visible and that objects are independent of the infant's own actions. They gain some appreciation of cause and effect.
Preoperational 2–4 years	Children cannot yet manipulate and transform information in logical ways, but they now can think in images and symbols.
4–7 years	They become able to represent something with something else, acquire language, and play games that involve pretending. Intelligence at this stage is said to be intuitive, because children cannot make general, logical statements.
Concrete operational 7–11 years	Children can understand logical principles that apply to concrete external objects. They can appreciate that certain properties of an object remain the same despite changes in appearance, and they can sort objects into categories. They can appreciate the perspective of another viewer. They can think about two concepts, such as longer and wider, at the same time.
Formal operational Over 11 years	Only adolescents and adults can think logically about abstractions, can speculate, and can consider what might be or what ought to be. They can work in probabilities and possibilities. They can imagine other worlds, especially ideal ones. They can reason about purely verbal or logical statements. They can relate any element or statement to any other, manipulate variables in a scientific experiment, and deal with proportions and analogies. They reflect on their own activity of thinking.

that they are not dumber than adults. They just think in different ways. Entering each stage involves a *qualitative* change from the previous stage, much as a caterpillar is transformed into a butterfly. What drives children to higher stages is their constant struggle to make sense of their experiences. They are active thinkers who are always trying to construct more advanced understandings of the world.

● **Building Blocks of Development**   To explain how infants and children move to ever-higher stages of understanding and knowledge, Piaget used the concept of **schemas**. As noted in the chapters on perception, memory, and cognition, schemas are the generalizations that form as people experience the world. Schemas organize past experiences and provide a framework for understanding future experiences. Piaget saw schemas as organized patterns of action or thought that children construct as they adapt to the environment; they are the basic units of knowledge, the building blocks of intellectual development. Schemas, he said, can involve behaviors (such as tying a shoelace or sucking), mental symbols (such as words or images), or mental activities (e.g., doing arithmetic "in our head" or imagining actions).

At first, infants form simple schemas. For example, a sucking schema consolidates their experiences of sucking into images of what objects can be sucked on (bottles, fingers, pacifiers) and what kinds of sucking can be done (soft and slow, speedy and vigorous). Later, children form more complex schemas, such as a schema for tying a knot or making a bed. Still later, adolescents form schemas about what it is to be in love.

● **schemas**   Generalizations based on experience that form the basic units of knowledge.

FIGURE 12.3

Accommodation

Because the bars of the playpen are in the way, this child discovers that her schema for grasping and pulling objects toward her will not work. She then adjusts, or accommodates, her schema in order to achieve her goal.

assimilation The process of trying out existing schemas on objects that fit those schemas.

accommodation The process of modifying schemas when familiar schemas do not work.

sensorimotor period The first of Piaget's stages of cognitive development, when the infant's mental activity is confined to sensory perception and motor skills.

Two related processes guide the development of schemas: assimilation and accommodation. In the process of **assimilation,** infants and children take in information about new objects by using existing schemas that will fit the new objects. So when an infant is given a new squeaker toy, he will suck on it, assimilating it into the sucking schema he has developed with his bottle and pacifier. In the same way, a toddler who sees a butterfly for the first time, may assimilate it into her "birdie" schema, because, like a bird, it's colorful and it flies. Now suppose an older child encounters a large dog. How she assimilates this new experience depends on her existing schema of dogs. If she has had positive experiences with a friendly family pet, she will expect the dog to behave the same, and she will greet it happily. If she has been frightened by dogs in the past, she may have a negative schema and react with fear to this new dog. In other words, past experiences affect what and how children think about new ones.

Sometimes, like Cinderella's stepsisters trying to squeeze their oversized feet into the glass slipper, children distort information about a new object to make it fit their existing schema. When squeezing won't work, though, they are forced to change, or accommodate, their schema to the new object. In **accommodation,** children find that a familiar schema cannot be made to fit a new object and so they change the schema (see Figure 12.3). So when the infant discovers that the squeaker toy is more fun when it makes a noise, he accommodates his sucking schema and starts munching on the squeaker instead. When the toddler realizes that butterflies are not birds because they don't have beaks and feathers, she accommodates her "birdie" schema to include two kinds of "flying animals"— birds and butterflies. And if the child with the positive "doggie" schema meets a snarling stray, she discovers that her original schema does not extend to all dogs, and she refines it to distinguish between friendly dogs and aggressive ones. Through assimilation and accommodation, said Piaget, we build our knowledge of the world, block by block.

● **Sensorimotor Development** Piaget (1952) called the first stage of cognitive development the **sensorimotor period** because, he claimed, the infant's mental activity and schemas are confined to sensory functions, such as seeing and hearing, and motor skills, such as grasping and sucking. According to Piaget, during this stage, infants can form schemas only of objects and actions that are present—things they can see or hear or touch. They cannot think about absent objects because they cannot act on them. For infants, then, thinking is doing. They do not lie in the crib thinking about their mother or their teddy bear, because they are not yet able to form schemas that are *mental representations* of objects and actions.

The sensorimotor period ends when infants *can* form mental representations. Now they can think about objects and actions even while the objects are not visible or the actions are not occurring. This is a remarkable milestone, according to Piaget; it frees the child from the here-and-now of the sensory environment and allows for the development of thought. One sign that children have reached this milestone is their ability to find a hidden object. This behavior was of particular interest to Piaget because, for him, it reflected infants' knowledge that they don't have to look at, touch, or suck an object to know that it exists. They know it exists even when it's out of sight. Piaget called this knowledge **object permanence**.

Before they acquire knowledge of object permanence, infants do not search for objects that are placed out of their sight. They act as if out of sight is literally out of mind. The first evidence of developing object permanence appears when infants are four to eight months old. At this age, for the first time, they recognize a familiar object even if part of it is hidden. They know it's their bottle even if they can see only the nipple peeking out from under the blanket. In Piaget's view, infants now have some primitive mental representation of objects. If an object is completely hidden, however, they will not search for it.

Several months later, infants will search briefly for a hidden object, but their search is random and ineffective. Not until they are eighteen to twenty-four months old, Piaget found, did infants look for an object in places other than where they saw it last, sometimes in a completely new place. According to Piaget, infants' concept of the object as permanent is now fully developed. They have a mental representation of the object that is completely separate from their immediate perception of it and they are able to picture and follow events in their minds.

● **New Views of Infants' Cognitive Development** Since Piaget's time psychologists have found new ways to measure what is going on in infants' minds. They use infrared photography to record infants' eye movements, time-lapse photography to detect slight hand movements, special equipment to measure infants' sucking rates, and computer technology to track and analyze it all. Their research shows that infants know a lot more, and know it sooner, than Piaget ever thought they did.

For example, it turns out that infants are not just sensing and moving during the sensorimotor period; they are already thinking as well (Saxe, Tzelnic, & Carey, 2007; Sobel & Kirkham, 2006). For example, they are not just experiencing isolated sights and sounds but combining these experiences. This ability has been demonstrated by studies in which infants were shown two different videos at the same time, but heard the soundtrack for only one of them coming from a speaker placed between the two video screens. The infants tended to look at the video that went with the soundtrack—at a toy bouncing in time with a tapping sound, at Dad's face when his voice was on the audio, or at an angry face when an angry voice was heard (Soken & Pick, 1992; Walker-Andrews et al., 1991). Infants can remember, too. When they are as young as two to three months of age, they can recall a particular mobile that was hung over their cribs a few days before (Rovee-Collier, 1999; see Figure 12.4). Infants can also solve simple problems, such as how to use a little "bridge" to leave a raised platform. In this laboratory situation, infants thought ahead and worked out a plan of attack. When the bridge was wide, they strode across. When it was narrow, they lingered on the platform, explored the bridge with their hands or feet, clung to the handrail with both hands, and took lots of tiny steps or sidled along (Berger & Adolph, 2003).

Young babies even seem to have a sense of object permanence. Piaget had required infants to demonstrate object permanence by making effortful movements, such as

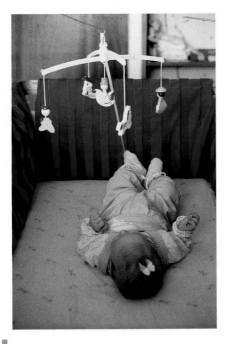

FIGURE 12.4

Infant Memory

This three-month-old infant learned to move a mobile by kicking her left foot, which is tied to the mobile with a ribbon. Even a month later, the baby will show recognition of this particular mobile by kicking more vigorously when she sees it than when she sees another one.

● **object permanence** The knowledge that objects exist even when they are not in view.

removing a cover that had been placed over a hidden object. Researchers now recognize that finding a hidden object under a cover requires several abilities: mentally representing the hidden object, figuring out where it might be, and pulling off the cover. Piaget's tests did not allow for the possibility that infants know a hidden object still exists but do not have adequate strategies for finding it or memory skills for remembering it while they search. When researchers have created situations in which infants merely have to stare to indicate that they know where an object is hidden, even infants under the age of one have demonstrated this cognitive ability, especially when the object is a familiar one (Hespos & Baillargeon, 2001; Keen & Berthier, 2004; Shinskey & Munakata, 2005). And when experimenters simply turn off the lights, infants as young as five months of age will reach for now-unseen objects in the dark (Clifton et al., 1991).

Developmental psychologists generally agree that infants develop some mental representations earlier than Piaget suggested. However, they disagree about whether this knowledge is "programmed" in infants (Spelke et al., 1992), whether it develops quickly through interactions with the world (Baillargeon, 1995), or whether it is constructed by combining old schemas into new ones (Fischer & Bidell, 1991).

FOCUS ON RESEARCH METHODS **Experiments on Developing Minds**

To explore how infants develop mental representations, Renee Baillargeon (pronounced "by-ar-ZHAN") investigated infants' early understanding of the principles of physics. Whether you realize it or not, you know a lot about physics. You know about gravity and balance, for example. But when did you first understand that "what goes up must come down" and that an unbalanced tray will tip over? Are these things you have always known, or did you figure them out through trial and error?

■ What was the researcher's question?

Baillargeon wanted to know when and how babies first develop knowledge about balance and gravity—specifically, about the tendency of unsupported objects to fall.

■ How did the researcher answer the question?

Baillargeon (1994, 2002) devised a creative experimental method to probe infants' knowledge. She showed infants pairs of events, one of which was physically possible and the other, physically impossible. She then determined the infants' interest in each kind of event by measuring the amount of time they spent looking at it. Their tendency to look longer at unexpected events provided an indication of which events violated what the babies knew about the world. Using this method, Baillargeon studied infants' knowledge of balance and gravity.

The independent variable in her studies was the amount of physical support objects had. The dependent variable was the length of time infants spent looking at these objects. Specifically, the infants viewed a red-gloved hand pushing a box from left to right along the top of a platform. On some trials, they saw physically possible events. For example, the hand pushed the box until its edge reached the end of the platform (see event A in Figure 12.5). On other trials, they saw impossible events, as when the hand pushed the box until only the end of its bottom surface rested on the platform or the box was beyond the platform altogether (see events B and C in the figure). On still other trials, the gloved hand held on to the box while pushing it beyond the edge of the platform (as shown in event D). Trials continued until the infants had seen at least four pairs of possible and impossible events in alternating order.

(A)　　　　　　　　　(B)

(C)　　　　　　　　　(D)

FIGURE 12.5

Visual Events Testing Infants' Knowledge of Physics

Infants look longer at things that interest them—that is, at new things rather than things they have seen before and find boring. In her research on the development of knowledge, Renee Baillargeon (1995) has found that physically impossible events (B) and (C)—made possible by an experimenter reaching through a hidden door to support a moving box—attract the most attention from infants. These results suggest that humans understand some basic laws of physics quite early in life.

Source: Baillargeon (1992).

■ What did the researcher find?

Baillargeon found that three-month-old infants looked longest at impossible event C, in which the box was entirely off the platform, whereas they were not particularly interested in either event D (box held by the gloved hand) or event A (box still on the platform). At six and a half months, infants stared intently at both event C (box off the platform) and event B (in which only the end of the box was resting on the platform).

■ What do the results mean?

According to Baillargeon (2002), these results suggest that three-month-old babies know something about physical support. They expect the box to fall if it is entirely off the platform and act surprised when it doesn't. But they do not yet know that a box should fall if its center of gravity is unsupported, as in event B. By the time they are six and a half months old, however, infants apparently know about centers of gravity—that most of the box must be on the platform or it will fall.

Other researchers have questioned whether infants' tendency to stare longer at a particular display necessarily indicates "surprise" (Bogartz, Shinskey, & Speaker, 1997). Perhaps they simply recognize that the image is different from what they remember it to be or find the impossible image more noticeable.

■ What do we still need to know?

The question remains as to which of these interpretations is correct. Do infants possess fundamental knowledge about the world that includes an understanding of complex physical principles, or are they just staring at something because it is novel or vivid? The answer to this question will require further research using varied visual stimuli that allows researchers to determine whether infants stare longer at physically possible events that are just as novel and vivid as physically impossible events (Berger, Tzur, & Posner, 2006).

Researchers also want to discover *how* babies know about physics (Johnson, Amso, & Slemmer, 2003). Does their increasing understanding of physical principles result from their experience with objects, or is the knowledge innate? In an attempt to answer this question, Baillargeon conducted another experiment in which she manipulated infants' experience with objects (the independent variable). After identifying infants ranging in age from three months to six and a half months, she randomly assigned them to receive either normal or extra experience with objects. She then observed the effect of this experience on the infants' understanding of gravity (the dependent variable). After only a few demonstrations in which unsupported objects fell off platforms, infants in the extra-experience group stared longer at a display of an unsupported object that did not fall. Other studies found similar results (Needham & Baillargeon, 1999).

It is still too early to say for sure whether Baillargeon's hypothesis about the importance of experience in developing knowledge is correct, but her results seem to support it (Wang & Baillargeon, 2005). ■

● **Preoperational Development** According to Piaget, the sensorimotor stage of development is followed by the **preoperational period.** During the first half of this period, children begin to understand, create, and use *symbols* (words, images, and objects) to represent things that are not present.

Using and understanding symbols opens up a new world for two- to four-year-olds. As described in the chapter on cognition and language, they begin to use words to stand for objects: *Mommy, cup, me.* At two, for the first time, children are able to play "pretend." They make their fingers "walk" or "shoot" and use a spoon to make a bridge. By the age of three or four, children can symbolize complex roles and events as they play "house," "doctor," or "superhero." They also can use drawing in a symbolic way: Pointing to their scribble, they might say, "This is Mommy and Daddy and me going for a walk."

During the second half of the preoperational stage, according to Piaget, four- to seven-year-olds begin to make intuitive guesses about the world as they try to figure out how things work. However, Piaget observed that they cannot tell the difference

During the second half of the preoperational period, according to Piaget, children believe that inanimate objects are alive and have feelings, intentions, and consciousness.

© Bil Keane, Inc. Reprinted with special permission of King Features Syndicate.

THE FAMILY CIRCUS® By Bil Keane

©1993 Bil Keane, Inc.
Dist. by Cowles Synd., Inc.

"I think the moon likes us. It keeps on followin' us."

TRY
THIS **Testing for Conservation** If you know a child who is between the ages of four and seven, get parental permission to test the child for what Piaget called *conservation*. Show the child two identical lumps of clay and ask which lump is bigger. The child will probably say they are the same. Now roll one lump into a long "rope" and again ask which lump is bigger. If the child says that they are still the same, this is evidence of conservation. If the longer one is seen as bigger, conservation has not yet developed—at least not for this task. The older the child, the more likely it is that conservation will appear, but some children display conservation much earlier than Piaget thought was possible.

between imagination and reality. For example, they might claim that dreams are real and take place outside of themselves as "pictures on the window" or "a circus in my room." They believe that inanimate objects are alive and have intentions, feelings, and consciousness, a belief called *animism*: "Clouds go slowly because they have no legs" and "Empty cars feel lonely." They are also highly *egocentric*, meaning that they appear to believe that the way things look to them is also how they look to everyone else. (This helps to explain why they may stand between you and the TV screen and assume you can still see it, or ask "What's this?" as they look at a picture book in the back seat of the car you're driving.)

Children's thinking is so dominated by what they can see and touch for themselves, Piaget said, that they do not realize that something is the same if its appearance changes. In one study, for example, preoperational children thought that a cat wearing a dog mask was actually a dog—because that's what it looked like (DeVries, 1969). These children do not yet have what Piaget called **conservation**, the ability to recognize that important properties of a substance or object—including its volume, weight, and species—remain constant despite changes in its shape.

In a test of conservation, Piaget first showed children equal amounts of water in two identical containers. He then poured water from one of the containers into a tall, thin glass and the other into a short, wide glass and asked whether one glass contained more water than the other. Children at the preoperational stage of development said that one glass (usually the taller one) contained more. Their conclusion was dominated by the evidence of their eyes. If the glass looked bigger, they thought it contained more. In other words, they did not understand the logical concepts of *reversibility* (you just poured the water from one container to another, so you can pour it back, and it will still be the same amount) or *complementarity* (one glass is taller but also narrower; the other is shorter but also wider). Piaget named this stage "*pre*operational" because children at this stage do not yet understand logical mental operations such as these.

● **Concrete and Formal Operational Thought** Sometime around the age of six or seven, Piaget observed, children develop the ability to conserve number and amount. When this happens, they enter what Piaget called the stage of **concrete operations**. Now, he said, they can count, measure, add, and subtract. Their thinking is no longer dominated by the appearance of things. They can use simple

● **preoperational period** According to Piaget, the second stage of cognitive development, during which children begin to use symbols to represent things that are not present.

● **conservation** The ability to recognize that the important properties of a substance remain constant despite changes in shape, length, or position.

● **concrete operations** According to Piaget, the third stage of cognitive development, during which children's thinking is no longer dominated by visual appearances.

logic and perform simple mental manipulations and mental operations on things. They can also sort objects into classes (such as tools, fruit, and vehicles) or series (such as largest to smallest). Still, concrete operational children can perform their logical operations only on real, concrete objects—sticks and glasses, tools and fruit—not on abstract concepts such as justice and freedom. They can reason about what *is*, but not yet about what is *possible*. The ability to think logically about abstract ideas, according to Piaget, comes in the next stage of cognitive development as children enter adolescence.

This new stage is called the **formal operational period,** and it is marked by the ability to engage in hypothetical thinking, including the imagining of logical consequences. For example, adolescents who have reached this level can consider various strategies for finding a part-time job and recognize that some methods are more likely to succeed than others. They can form general concepts and understand the impact of the past on the present and the present on the future. They can question social institutions; think about the world as it might be and ought to be; and consider the consequences and complexities of love, work, politics, and religion. They can think logically and systematically about symbols and propositions.

Piaget explored adolescents' formal operational abilities by asking them to perform science experiments that involved forming and investigating hypotheses. Research indicates that only about half the people in Western cultures ever reach the formal operational level necessary to succeed in Piaget's experiments (Kuhn & Franklin, 2006). People who have not studied science and math at a high school level are less likely to do well in those experiments (Keating, 1990). In adulthood, people are more likely to use formal operations for problems based on their own occupations; this is one reason that people who think logically at work may still become victims of a home-repair or investment scam (Cialdini, 2001).

■ ● Modifying Piaget's Theory

Piaget was right in pointing out that there are significant shifts with age in children's thinking and that thinking becomes more systematic, consistent, and integrated as children get older. His idea that children are active explorers and constructors of knowledge has been absorbed into contemporary ways of thinking about childhood, and his work has inspired many other psychologists to test his findings and theory with experiments of their own. The results of these experiments suggest that Piaget's theory needs some modification.

What needs to be modified most is Piaget's notion of developmental stages. Researchers have shown that changes from one stage to the next are less consistent and global than Piaget thought. For example, three-year-olds can sometimes make the distinction between physical and mental phenomena; they know the characteristics of real dogs versus pretend dogs (Woolley, 1997). Moreover, they are not always egocentric. In one study, children of this age knew that a white card, which looked pink to them because they were wearing rose-colored glasses, still looked white to someone who was not wearing the glasses (Liben, 1978). Preoperational children can even do conservation tasks if they are allowed to count the number of objects or have been trained to focus on relevant dimensions such as number, height, and width (Gelman & Baillargeon, 1983). Children succeed on conservation tasks at younger ages if their culture values a particular conservation ability (Gardiner & Kosmitzki, 2005); for example, children in cultures where pottery-making is important develop conservation of mass at younger ages than children in North American culture.

Taken together, these studies suggest that children's knowledge and mental strategies develop at different ages in different areas and in "pockets" rather than at global levels of understanding (Sternberg, 1989). Knowledge in particular areas is demonstrated sooner in children who are given specific experience in those areas or who are presented with very simple questions and tasks. Children's reasoning depends not only on their general level of development but also on (1) how easy the

● **formal operational period** According to Piaget, the fourth stage in cognitive development, usually beginning around age eleven, when abstract thinking first appears.

task is, (2) how familiar they are with the objects involved, (3) how well they understand the language being used, and (4) what experiences they have had in similar situations (Siegal, 1997). Research has also shown that the level of a child's thinking varies from day to day and may even shift when the child solves the same problem twice in the same day (Siegler, 1994).

In summary, psychologists today tend to think of cognitive development in terms of rising and falling "waves," not fixed stages—in terms of changing frequencies in children's use of different ways of thinking, not sudden, permanent shifts from one way of thinking to another (Siegler, 2006). Psychologists now suggest that children systematically try out many different solutions to problems and gradually come to select the best of them.

● Information Processing During Childhood

An alternative to Piaget's theory of cognitive development is based on the *information-processing approach* discussed in the chapters on memory and on cognition and language. This approach describes cognitive activities in terms of how people take in information, use it, and remember it. Developmental psychologists taking this approach focus on gradual increases in children's mental capacities rather than on dramatic changes in their stages of development.

Their research demonstrates that as children get older, their information-processing skills gradually get better, and they can perform more complex tasks faster and more easily (Munakata, 2006). First, older children have longer attention spans and are better at filtering out irrelevant information. These skills help them overcome distractions and concentrate intently on a variety of tasks, from hobbies to homework. Second, older children take in information faster and can shift their attention from one task to another more quickly. (This is how they manage to do their homework while watching TV.) Third, older children can process the information they take in more rapidly and efficiently. Compared with younger children, they code information into fewer dimensions and divide tasks into steps that can be dealt with one after another. This helps them to organize and complete their homework assignments. Older children are also better at choosing problem-solving strategies that fit the tasks they are facing (Siegler, 2006).

Children's memory also improves with age (Gathercole et al., 2004). Whereas preschoolers can keep only two or three pieces of information in their short-term memory at the same time, older children can hold four or five pieces of information. Older children can also put more information into their long-term memory storage, so they remember things longer than younger children. After about age seven, children can remember information that is more complex and abstract, such as the gist of what several people have said during a conversation. Their memories are more accurate, extensive, and well organized. Because they have accumulated more knowledge during their years of learning about the world, older children can integrate new information into a more complete network of facts. This makes it easier for them to understand and remember new information. (See "In Review: Milestones of Cognitive Development in Infancy and Childhood.")

LINKAGES (a link to Memory, p. 247)

What accounts for these increases in children's attention, information processing, and memory capacities? It should not be surprising that it's nature plus nurture. As mentioned earlier, maturation of the brain contributes to better and faster information processing as children grow older (Luciana et al., 2005). Experience contributes, too. The importance of experience has been demonstrated by researchers who have tested children's cognitive abilities using familiar versus unfamiliar materials. In one study, for example, Mayan children in Mexico lagged behind their agemates in the United States on standard memory tests for pictures and nouns that the Mexican children had not seen before. But the children did much better when researchers gave them a more familiar task, such as recalling the objects they saw in a model of a Mayan village (Rogoff & Waddell, 1982). The children's memory for

in review — Milestones of Cognitive Development in Infancy and Childhood

Age*	Achievement	Description
3–4 months	Maturation of senses	Immaturities that limit the newborn's vision and hearing are overcome.
	Voluntary movement	Reflexes disappear, and infants begin to gain voluntary control over their movements.
12–18 months	Mental representation	Infants can form images of objects and actions in their minds.
	Object permanence	Infants understand that objects exist even when out of sight.
18–24 months	Symbolic thought	Young children use symbols to represent things that are not present in their pretend play, drawing, and talk.
4 years	Intuitive thought	Children reason about events, real and imagined, by guessing rather than by engaging in logical analysis.
6–7 years	Concrete operations Conservation	Children can apply simple logical operations to real objects. For example, they recognize that important properties of a substance, such as number or amount, remain constant despite changes in shape or position.
7–8 years	Information processing	Children can remember more information; they begin to learn strategies for memorization.

*These ages are approximate; they indicate the order in which children first reach these milestones of cognitive development rather than the exact ages.

these familiar objects was better, presumably because they could process information about them more easily and quickly.

Knowing how to memorize things also improves children's memories. To a great extent, children acquire memorization strategies in school. They learn to repeat information over and over to help fix it in memory, to place information into categories, and to use memory aids such as "*i* before *e* except after *c*" to help them remember. They also learn what situations call for deliberate memorization and what factors, such as the length of a list, affect memory.

LINKAGES Development and Memory

The ability to remember facts, figures, pictures, and objects improves as we get older and more expert at processing information. But take a minute right now and try to recall anything that happened to you when you were, say, one

TRY
THIS

year old. Most people can accurately recall a few memories from age five or six but remember virtually nothing from before the age of three or four (Bauer, 2006; Bruce, Dolan, & Phillips-Grant, 2000).

LINKAGES (a link to Memory, p. 237)

Psychologists have not yet found a fully satisfactory explanation for this "infantile amnesia." Some have suggested that young children lack the memory encoding and storage processes described in the chapter on memory. Yet children two or three years old can clearly recall experiences that happened weeks or even months earlier (Bauer, 2006). Others suggest that infantile amnesia occurs because very young children lack a sense of self. They don't recognize themselves in a mirror, so they may not have a framework for organizing memories about what happens to them (Howe, 2003). However, this explanation cannot apply to the entire period up to three years of age, because children do recognize themselves in the mirror by the time they are two. In fact, research suggests that infants even younger than two can recognize their own faces, as well as their voices on tape (Legerstee, Anderson, & Schaffer, 1998).

Another possibility is that early memories, though "present," are implicit rather than explicit. As described in the chapter on memory, *implicit memories* form automatically and can affect our emotions and behavior even when we do not consciously recall them. Toddlers' implicit memories were demonstrated in a study in which two-and-a-half-year-olds apparently remembered a pitch-dark room where they had participated in an experiment two years earlier (Perris, Myers, & Clifton, 1990). Unlike children who had never been in the room, these children were unafraid and reached for noise-making objects in the dark, just as they had learned to do at the previous session. However, children's implicit memories of their early years, like their explicit memories, are quite limited. In one study, researchers showed photographs of young children to a group of ten-year-olds (Newcombe & Fox, 1994). Some of the photos were of preschool classmates whom the children had not seen since they were five years old. They explicitly recalled 21 percent of their former classmates, and their skin conductance (an index of emotion) indicated that they had implicit memories of an additional 5 percent. Yet these children had no memory of 74 percent of their preschool pals, as compared with adults in another study who correctly identified 90 percent of the photographs of high school classmates they had not seen in thirty years (Bahrick, Bahrick, & Wittlinger, 1975).

Other psychologists have proposed that our early memories are lost because in those years we did not yet have the language skills to talk about, and thus solidify, our memories (Simcock & Hayne, 2002). Still others say that early memories were stored, but because the schemas we used in early childhood to mentally represent them changed in later years, we no longer have the retrieval cues necessary to recall them. Another possibility is that early experiences tend to be merged into generalized event representations, such as "going to Grandma's" or "playing at the beach," so it becomes difficult to remember any specific event. Research on hypotheses such as these may someday unravel the mystery of infantile amnesia (Nelson & Fivush, 2004; Newcombe et al., 2000; Wang, 2006). ■

● Culture and Cognitive Development

To explain cognitive development, Piaget focused on the physical world of objects. Russian psychologist Lev Vygotsky (pronounced "vah-GOT-ski") focused on the social world of people. He viewed cognitive abilities as the product of cultural history. The child's mind, said Vygotsky, grows through interaction with other minds. Dramatic support for this idea comes from cases such as the "Wild Boy of Aveyron," a French child who, in the late 1700s, was apparently lost or abandoned by his parents at an early age and had grown up with animals. At about eleven years of age, he was captured by hunters and sent to Paris, where scientists observed him. What the scientists saw was a dirty, frightened creature who trotted like a wild animal and spent most of his time silently rocking. Although the scientists worked with the boy for more than ten years, he was never able to live unguarded among other people, and he never learned to speak.

Consistent with Vygotsky's ideas, this tragic case suggests that without society, children's minds would not develop much beyond those of animals—that children acquire their ideas through interaction with parents, teachers, and other agents of their culture. Vygotsky's followers have studied the effects of the social world on children's cognitive development—how participation in social routines affects children's developing knowledge of the world (Gauvain, 2001). In Western societies, those routines include shopping, eating at McDonald's, going to birthday parties, and attending religious services. In other cultures they might include helping to make pottery, going hunting, and weaving baskets. Quite early, children develop mental representations, called *scripts*, for these activities (see the chapter on cognition and language). By the time they are three, children can accurately describe the scripts for their routine activities (Nelson, 1986). Scripts, in turn, affect children's knowledge and understanding of cognitive tasks. As mentioned earlier, in cultures in which pottery making is important, children display conservation about the mass of objects sooner than children do in other cultures. Similarly, suburban children can understand conservation problems earlier than inner-city children if the problems are presented, as Piaget's were, like miniature science experiments. But the performance of inner-city children is improved when the task is presented through a more familiar script, such as one involving what a "slick trickster" would do to fool someone (White & Glick, 1978).

Children's cognitive abilities are also influenced by the language of their culture. Consider, for instance, the way people think about relations between objects in space. Children who learn a language that has no words for spatial concepts—such as *in, on, in front of, behind, to the left,* and *to the right*—will acquire cognitive categories that are different from those of people in North America. These individuals do, in fact, have difficulty distinguishing between the left and right sides of objects, and they tend not to use the symbolic associations with left and right hands that North Americans do (Bowerman, 1996; Levinson, 1996).

As a cultural tool, language can also affect academic achievement. For example, Korean and Chinese children show exceptional ability at adding and subtracting large numbers (Miller et al., 1995). As third-graders, they can do in their heads three-digit problems (such as 702 minus 125) that would stump most North American

Encouraging Academic Achievement
Asian American children tend to do better in school than European American children partly because Asian American children's families tend to provide especially strong support for academic achievement.

children. The difference seems due in part to the clear way that Asian languages label numbers from eleven to nineteen. In English, the meaning of the words eleven and twelve, for instance, is not as clear as the Asian *ten-one* and *ten-two*. In addition, Asians use the metric system of measurement and a manual computing device called the *abacus*, both of which are structured around the number ten. Korean math textbooks emphasize this tens structure by presenting the ones digits in red, the tens in blue, and the hundreds in green. Above all, in Asian cultures, educational achievement, especially in mathematics, is encouraged at home and strongly encouraged in school (Naito & Miura, 2001). In short, children's cognitive development is affected in ways large and small by the culture in which they live (Cole, 2006).

▮ ● Improving or Endangering Cognitive Development

Even within a single culture, some children are mentally advanced, whereas others lag behind their peers. Cognitive development is seriously delayed if children are raised in environments that deprive them of the everyday sights, sounds, and feelings provided by conversation and loving interaction with family members, pictures and books, toys and television. Children subjected to this kind of severe deprivation show marked impairment in intellectual development by the time they are two or three years old. They may never fully recover, even if they are given special attention later on. These effects are most clearly seen in youngsters who spent their early years in the understaffed and understimulating orphanages of Russia and Romania (Beckett et al., 2006). If these children are not adopted before they are six months old, their intelligence test scores at the end of childhood are likely to lag behind those of other children by an average of fifteen points.

Children's inherited potential for cognitive development can also be impaired by less extreme conditions of deprivation, including the neglect, malnourishment, noise, and chaos that occur in many poor households (Turkheimer et al., 2003). One study found that children raised in poverty scored nine points lower on intelligence tests by the time they were five years old than did children in families whose incomes were twice the poverty level (Duncan, Brooks-Gunn, & Klebanov, 1994). These

Babies at Risk   The cognitive development of infants raised in this understaffed Russian orphanage will be permanently impaired if they are not given far more stimulation in the orphanage or, better yet, adopted into a loving family at a young age.

differences continue as poor children enter school. Children who remain in poverty have lower IQs and poorer school achievement (McLoyd, 1998; Stipek & Ryan, 1997). They are twice as likely to be held back in grade promotion and three and a half times as likely to drop out of high school (Children's Defense Fund, 2004). One study of more than 10,000 children found that the economic status of a child's family is a much better predictor of the child's later cognitive development than are physical risk factors, such as low birth weight (Jefferis et al., 2002). The effects of poverty come from a buildup of problems that often begins with prenatal complications and continues through childhood with lack of cognitive stimulation and, perhaps most important, harsh and inconsistent parenting (NICHD Early Child Care Research Network, 2005b).

In families above the poverty line, too, children's cognitive development is related to their surroundings, their experiences, and their parents' behavior. For example, eighteen- to thirty-month-old children whose mothers gave them lots of hints, suggestions, and other cognitive guidance during a problem-solving task had higher IQ scores when they were five years old than children whose mothers had simply told them what they needed to do to complete the task (Fagot & Gauvain, 1997). A longitudinal study revealed that the parents of gifted children started stimulating their children's cognitive activity very early on (Gottfried, 1997). When the children were infants, the parents read to them. When the children were toddlers, the parents provided them with reference books, computerized teaching aids, and trips to museums. When the children were preschoolers, the parents drew out their natural curiosity about the world and encouraged their tendency to seek out new learning opportunities themselves. Other studies, too, show that reading to children at a very early age is related to enhanced development of language and other cognitive skills (Raikes et al., 2006). Higher cognitive test scores also tend to be seen in preschoolers whose parents have the income to provide a more stimulating learning environment (Yeung, Linver, & Brooks-Gunn, 2002). Some aspects of that environment are more beneficial than others, though. In one study, third-graders whose parents had bought them a TV for their bedrooms, but not a computer, scored ten to twenty points lower on tests of math, reading, and language than children who had a computer but no bedroom TV (Borzekowski & Robinson, 2005).

When Does Stimulation Become Overstimulation? A child's cognitive development is enhanced by a stimulating environment, but can there be too much stimulation? In the face of an avalanche of electronic media aimed specifically at babies and toddlers, some people are beginning to wonder. These stimulating media include computer "lapware," such as this baby is enjoying, videos and DVDs for even the tiniest infants, and, of course, the *Teletubbies*. Many babies in Western countries are immersed in electronic media for hours each day. In the United States, 20–25 percent of children under two have a TV set in their rooms, and one-third of them have videos in the "Baby Einstein" series (Lewin, 2003; Vandewater et al., 2007). We don't yet know how all this well-intentioned electronic stimulation is affecting young children because we don't yet have enough evidence on which to base conclusions.

To improve the cognitive skills of children who do not get the optimum stimulation and guidance at home, developmental psychologists have provided extra lessons, materials, and educational contact with sensitive adults. In a variety of such programs, ranging from weekly home visits to daily preschools, children's cognitive abilities have been enhanced (Love et al., 2005; Ramey, Ramey, & Lanzi, 2006), and some effects can last into adulthood (Campbell et al., 2001). Music lessons also promote children's cognitive development, especially verbal memory (Ho, Cheung, & Chan, 2003; Schellenberg, 2004). Access to the Internet has been related to improved reading scores and school grades among poor children (Jackson et al., 2006), and even electronic games, although no substitute for adult attention, can provide opportunities for school-age children to hone spatial skills that help improve their performance in math and science (Green & Bavelier, 2003; Subrahmanyam & Greenfield, 1994).

Infancy and Childhood: Social and Emotional Development

Life for a child is more than learning about objects, doing math problems, and getting good grades. It is also about social relationships and emotional reactions. From the first months onward, infants are sensitive to those around them (Mumme & Fernald, 2003), and they are both attracted by and attractive to other people—especially parents and other caregivers.

During the first hour or so after birth, mothers gaze into their infants' eyes and give them gentle touches (Klaus & Kennell, 1976). This is the first opportunity for the mother to display her *bond* to her infant—an emotional tie that begins even before the baby is born. Psychologists once believed that this immediate contact was critical—that the mother-infant bond would never be strong if the opportunity for early interaction was missed. Research has revealed, however, that such interaction in the first few hours is not a requirement for a close relationship (Myers, 1987). With or without early contact, mothers and fathers, whether biological or adoptive, come to form close attachments to their infants by interacting with them day after day.

As the mother gazes at her baby, the baby gazes back. By the time infants are two days old, they recognize—and like—their mother's face; they will suck more vigorously to see a videotaped image of her face than to see that of a stranger (Walton, Bower, & Bower, 1992). Soon, they begin to respond to the mother's facial expressions as well. By the time they are a year old, children use their mothers' emotional expressions to guide their own behavior in uncertain situations (Saarni et al., 2006). If the mother looks frightened when a stranger approaches, for example, the child is more likely to avoid the stranger. As mentioned in the chapter on motivation and emotion, this phenomenon is called *social referencing*. Children can pick up emotion cues from many sources, including television. In one study, after seeing a video in which an adult showed fear of an object, infants later avoided that object (Mumme & Fernald, 2003). As described in the learning chapter, observational learning can sometimes lead to fears, and even phobias.

Infants communicate feelings as well as recognize them. They do so by crying and screaming, but also by more subtle behavior. When they want to interact, they look and smile; when they do not want to interact, they turn away and suck their thumbs (Tronick, 1989).

Forming a Bond   Mutual eye contact, exaggerated facial expressions, and shared "baby talk" are an important part of the early social interactions that promote an enduring bond of attachment between parent and child.

Individual Temperament

From the moment they are born, infants differ from one another in the emotions they express most often. Some infants are happy, active, and vigorous; they splash, thrash, and wriggle. Others are usually quiet. Some infants approach new objects with enthusiasm; others turn away or fuss. Some infants whimper; others kick, scream, and wail. Characteristics such as these make up the infant's **temperament**—the infant's individual style and frequency of expressing needs and emotions. Although temperament mainly reflects nature's contribution to the beginning of an individual's personality, it can also be affected by the prenatal environment, including—as noted earlier—the mother's stress level, smoking, and drug use.

In some of the earliest research on infant temperament, Alexander Thomas and Stella Chess found that most babies fall into one of three general temperament patterns (Thomas & Chess, 1977). *Easy babies* are the most common kind. They get hungry and sleepy at predictable times, react to new situations cheerfully, and seldom fuss. In contrast, *difficult babies* are irregular and irritable. *Slow-to-warm-up babies* react warily to new situations but eventually come to enjoy them. Later research has shown that traces of these early temperament patterns weave their way throughout childhood (Rothbart & Bates, 2006). Easy infants usually stay easy (Zhou et al., 2004); difficult infants often remain difficult, sometimes developing attention and aggression problems in childhood (Else-Quest et al., 2006; Guerin, Gottfried, & Thomas, 1997). Timid, or slow-to-warm-up, toddlers tend to be shy as preschoolers, restrained and inhibited as eight-year-olds, and somewhat anxious as teenagers (Roberts, Caspi, & Moffitt, 2001). The differences even seem to extend into adulthood. In one study, the brains of adults who were timid toddlers reacted especially strongly to novel stimuli (Schwartz et al., 2003).

However, these tendencies are not set in stone. In temperament, as in cognitive development, nature interacts with nurture. Many events take place between infancy and adulthood that can shift an individual's development in one direction or another. For instance, if parents are patient enough to allow their difficult baby to respond to changes in daily routines at a more relaxed pace, the child may become less difficult over time. If the characteristics of parent and infant are in synch, chances increase that temperamental qualities will be stable. Consider, for example, the temperament patterns of Chinese American and European American children. At birth, Chinese American infants are calmer, less changeable, less likely to become upset, and more easily consoled than is typical of European American infants (Kagan et al., 1994). The possibility of an inherited predisposition toward self-control among the Chinese is supported by the fact that only about 2 percent of children in China have a genetic pattern associated with impulse control problems, compared with about 48 percent of children in the United States (Chang et al., 1996). This tendency for self-control is powerfully reinforced by the Chinese culture. Compared with European American parents, Chinese parents are less likely to reward and stimulate babbling and smiling and more likely to maintain close control of their young children. The children, in turn, are less vocal, noisy, and active than European American children (Smith & Freedman, 1983) and, as preschoolers, they show far more impulse control, including in the ability to wait their turn (Sabbagh et al., 2006).

These temperamental differences between children in different ethnic groups illustrate the combined contributions of nature and nurture. There are many other illustrations as well. Mayan infants, for example, are relatively inactive from birth. The Zinacantecos, a Mayan group in southern Mexico, reinforce this innate predisposition toward restrained motor activity by swaddling their infants and by nursing at the slightest sign of movement (Greenfield & Childs, 1991). This combination of genetic predisposition and cultural reinforcement is culturally adaptive. Quiet Mayan infants do not kick off their covers at night, which is important in the cold highlands where they live. Inactive infants are able to spend long periods on their mothers' backs as the mothers work. Infants who do not begin to walk until they can understand some language do not wander into the open fire at the center of the house. This adaptive interplay of innate and cultural factors in the development of temperament operates in all cultures.

temperament An individual's basic disposition, which is evident from infancy.

FIGURE 12.6

Wire and Terrycloth "Mothers"

Here are the two types of artificial mothers used in Harlow's research. Although baby monkeys received milk from the wire mother, they spent most of their time with the terrycloth version, and they clung to it when frightened.

● The Infant Grows Attached

During the first year of life, as infants and caregivers watch and respond to one another, the infant begins to form an **attachment**—a deep, affectionate, close, and enduring relationship—to these important figures. John Bowlby, a British psychoanalyst, drew attention to the importance of attachment after he observed children who had been orphaned in World War II. These children's depression and other emotional scars led Bowlby to develop a theory about the importance of developing a strong attachment to one's primary caregivers, a tie that normally keeps infants close to their caregivers and, therefore, safe (Bowlby, 1951, 1973). Soon after Bowlby presented his theory, researchers in the United States began to investigate how such attachments are formed and what happens when they are not formed, or when they are broken by loss or separation. Some of the most dramatic of these studies were conducted by Harry Harlow.

● Motherless Monkeys—and Children

Harlow (1959) explored two hypotheses about what leads infants to develop attachments to their mothers. The first hypothesis was that attachment occurs because mothers feed their babies. Perhaps food, along with the experience of being fed, creates an emotional bond to the mother. Harlow's second hypothesis was that attachment is based on the warm, comforting contact the baby gets from the mother.

To evaluate these hypotheses, Harlow separated newborn monkeys from their mothers and raised them in cages containing two artificial mothers. One "mother" was made of wire, but it had a rubber nipple from which the infant could get milk (see Figure 12.6). In other words, it provided food but no physical comfort. The other artificial mother had no nipple but was made of soft, comfortable terrycloth. Harlow found that the infants preferred the terrycloth mother, spending most of their time with it, especially when frightened. The terrycloth mother provided feelings of softness and cuddling, which were things the infants needed when they sensed danger.

Harlow also investigated what happens when attachments do not form. He isolated some newborn monkeys from all social contact. After a year of this isolation, the monkeys showed dramatic disturbances. When visited by normally active, playful monkeys, they withdrew to a corner, huddling or rocking for hours. As adults, they were unable to have normal sexual relations. When some of the females did have babies through artificial insemination, they tended to ignore them. When their infants became distressed, the mothers physically abused and sometimes even killed them.

Humans who spend their first few years without a consistent caregiver react in a tragically similar manner. At the Romanian and Russian orphanages mentioned earlier, where children were neglected by institutional caregivers, visitors discovered that the children, like Harlow's deprived monkeys, had not developed attachments to their caregivers; they were withdrawn and engaged in constant rocking (Holden, 1996; Zeanah et al., 2005). Emotional problems continued even after the children were adopted. In one study, researchers observed four-year-old children who had been in a Romanian orphanage for at least eight months before being adopted. The behavior of these children was compared with the behavior of children matched for age and gender who had been adopted before the age of four months (Chisholm, 1997). The late-adopted children were found to have many more serious problems. Depressed or withdrawn, they stared blankly, demanded attention, and could not control their tempers (Holden, 1996). Although they interacted poorly with their adoptive mothers, they were friendly with all strangers, trying to cuddle and kiss them. At age six, a third of late-adopted children still showed no preference for their parents or any tendency to look to them when stressed (Rutter, O'Connor, & ERA Study Team, 2004). Neurologists suggest that the dramatic problems observed in isolated monkeys and humans are the result of developmental brain dysfunction or damage brought on by a lack of touch

● **attachment** A deep and enduring relationship with the person with whom a baby has shared many experiences.

and body movement in infancy and by the absence of early play, conversation, and other normal childhood experiences (Prescott, 1996; Rutter et al., 2004; Wismer Fries et al., 2005).

● **Forming an Attachment** Fortunately, most infants do have a consistent caregiver, usually the mother, to whom they can form an attachment. They learn to recognize her and are able to distinguish her from a stranger at an early age. Some infants vocalize more to their mothers than to a stranger when they are only three months old. These babies are the smart ones; years later, they do better on tests, get higher grades, complete more education, and are more likely to be in stable romantic relationships in their twenties (Roe, 2001). By the age of six or seven months, all infants show signs of preferring their mothers to anyone else—watching her closely, crawling after her, clambering up into her lap, protesting when she leaves, and brightening when she returns (Ainsworth, 1973). After an attachment has been formed, separation from the mother for even thirty minutes can be a stressful experience (Larson, Gunnar, & Hertsgaard, 1991). Soon after, infants develop attachments to their fathers as well (Lamb, 1997). However, interactions with fathers are typically less frequent, and of a somewhat different nature, than with mothers (Parke, 2002). Mothers tend to feed, bathe, dress, cuddle, and talk to their infants, whereas fathers are more likely to play with, jiggle, and toss them, especially sons.

● **Variations in Attachment** The amount of closeness and contact infants seek with either the mother or the father depends to some extent on the infant. Those who are ill, tired, or slow to warm up may require more closeness. Closeness also depends to some extent on the parents. An infant whose parent has been absent, aloof, or unresponsive is likely to need more closeness than one whose parent is accessible and responsive.

Researchers have studied the differences in infants' attachments in a special situation that simulates the natural comings and goings of parents—the so-called *Strange Situation* (Ainsworth et al., 1978). This assessment occurs in an unfamiliar playroom where the infant interacts with the mother and an unfamiliar woman in brief episodes: The infant plays with the mother and the stranger, the mother leaves the baby with the stranger for a few minutes, the mother and the stranger leave the baby alone in the room briefly, and the mother returns to the room.

Videotapes of these sessions show that most infants display a *secure attachment* to the mother in the Strange Situation (Thompson, 2006). In the unfamiliar room, they use the mother as a home base, leaving her side to explore and play but returning to her periodically for comfort or contact. When the mother returns after the brief separation, the infant is happy to see her and receptive when she initiates contact. Some infants, however, display an *insecure attachment*. Their relationship with their mother may be (1) *avoidant*—they avoid or ignore their mother when she returns after the brief separation; (2) *ambivalent*—they are upset when the mother leaves, but when she returns they vacillate between clinging to her and angrily rejecting her efforts at contact; or (3) *disorganized*—their behavior is inconsistent, disturbed, and disturbing; they may begin to cry after their mother has returned and comforted them, or they may reach out for their mother while looking away from her (Moss et al., 2004).

Patterns of attachment vary widely in different parts of the world and are related to how parents treat their children. In northern Germany, for example, where parents promote children's independence with strict discipline, the proportion of infants who display avoidant attachments is quite high (Spangler, Fremmer-Bombik, & Grossman, 1996). In Japan, where mothers are completely devoted to their young children and are seldom apart from them, including at night, children develop an attachment relationship that emphasizes harmony and union; these children cannot bear it when their mothers try to leave the room in the Strange Situation (Rothbaum et al., 2000). These attachment patterns differ from the secure one that

Cultural Differences in Parent-Child Relations Variations in the intimacy of family interactions, including whether infants sleep in their parents' bed, may contribute to cross-cultural differences in attachment patterns.

is most common in the United States, where, with their parents' encouragement, children balance closeness and proximity with exploration and autonomy. In North America, the likelihood that children will develop a secure attachment depends on the mother's attentiveness; if the mother is generally sensitive and responsive to the baby's needs and signals, a secure attachment is likely; if she is rejecting or neglecting, the child's attachment is more likely to be insecure.

● **Consequences of Attachment Patterns** A secure attachment to the mother is reflected in the child's relationships with other people, too. For example, children with secure attachments tend to have better relations with their peers in childhood and adolescence (Thompson, 2006), and they are especially likely to have good relationships with close friends. Securely attached children also require less contact, guidance, and discipline from their teachers and are less likely to seek excessive attention, to act impulsively or aggressively, to express frustration, or to display helplessness (see the chapter on learning; NICHD Early Child Care Research Network, 2006; Sroufe, Fox, & Pancake, 1983). Their teachers like them more and expect more of them.

Why should this be? According to Bowlby, securely attached children develop positive relationships with other people because they develop mental representations, or *internal working models*, of the social world that lead them to expect that, like their mothers, everyone else will respond to them in a positive way. But secure attachment at the age of one doesn't guarantee a life of social competence and emotional well-being. If the mother or other primary caregiver later becomes neglectful or rejecting, due to marital strife, divorce, or depression, for example, the secure attachment is likely to disintegrate and the child may begin to have problems (Thompson, 2006). So although a secure attachment alone does not predict long-term sociability and well-being, in concert with continuing supportive care, it sets the stage for positive psychological growth.

THINKING CRITICALLY **Does Day Care Harm the Emotional Development of Infants?**

With about 60 percent of mothers in North America working outside the home, concern has been expressed about how daily separations from their mothers might affect children, especially infants (Clarke-Stewart & Allhusen, 2005). Some have argued that leaving infants with a baby sitter or putting them in a day-care center damages the quality of the mother-infant relationship and increases the babies' risk for psychological problems later on.

■ **What am I being asked to believe or accept?**

The claim to be evaluated is that daily separations brought about by the need for day care undermine the infant's ability to form a secure attachment, as well as inflict emotional harm.

■ **What evidence is available to support the assertion?**

There is clear evidence that separation from the mother is painful for young children. Furthermore, if separation lasts a week or more, young children may become apathetic and mournful and eventually lose interest in the missing mother (Robertson & Robertson, 1971). But day care does not involve such lasting separations, and research has shown that infants in day care do form attachments to their mothers (Lamb & Ahnert, 2006).

Are their attachments as secure as the attachments formed by infants whose mothers do not work outside the home? Researchers first examined this question by comparing infants' behavior in the Strange Situation. A review of the data showed

The Effects of Day Care Parents are understandably concerned that leaving their infants in a day-care center all day might interfere with the mother-infant attachment or with other aspects of the children's development. Research shows that most infants in day care do form healthy bonds with their parents, but that if children spend many hours in day care between infancy and kindergarten, they are more likely to have behavior problems in school, such as talking back to the teacher or getting into fights with other children (Belsky et al., 2007).

that, on average, infants in full-time day care were somewhat more likely to be classified as insecurely attached. Specifically, 36 percent of the infants in full-time care received this classification, compared with 29 percent of the infants not in full-time day care (Clarke-Stewart, 1989). These results appear to support the suggestion that day care hinders the development of infants' attachments to their mothers.

■ Are there alternative ways of interpreting the evidence?

Perhaps factors other than day care could explain this difference between infants in day care and those at home with their mothers. One such factor could be the method used to assess attachment—the Strange Situation. Infants in these studies were judged insecure if they did not run to their mothers after a brief separation. But maybe infants who experience daily separations from their mothers are less disturbed by the separations in the Strange Situation and therefore seek out less closeness with their mothers. A second factor could be differences between the infants' mothers: Perhaps mothers who value independence in themselves and in their children are more likely to be working and to place their children in day care, whereas mothers who emphasize closeness with their children are more likely to stay home.

■ What additional evidence would help to evaluate the alternatives?

Finding insecure attachment to be more common among the infants of working mothers does not, by itself, prove that day care is harmful. To judge the effects of day care, we must use other measures of emotional adjustment. If infants in day care show consistent signs of troubled emotional relations in other situations (at home, say) and with other caregivers (such as the father), this evidence would support the argument that day care harms children's emotional development. Another useful method would be to statistically control for differences in the attitudes and behaviors of parents who do and do not use day care and then examine the differences in their children.

In fact, this research design has already been employed. In 1990 the U.S. government funded a study of infant day care in ten sites around the country. The psychological and physical development of more than 1,300 randomly selected infants was tracked from birth through age three. The results showed that when factors such as parents' education, income, and attitudes were statistically controlled for, infants in day care were no more likely to have emotional problems or to be insecurely attached to their mothers than infants not in day care. However, in cases in which infants were placed in poor-quality day care, in which the caregivers were insensitive and unresponsive, and in which mothers were insensitive to their babies' needs at home, the infants were less likely to develop a secure attachment to their mothers (Belsky et al., 2007; NICHD Early Childhood Research Network, 2005a, 2006).

■ What conclusions are most reasonable?

Based on available evidence, the most reasonable conclusion appears to be that day care by itself does not lead to insecure attachment or cause emotional harm to infants. But if the care is of poor quality, it can worsen a risky situation at home and increase the likelihood that infants will have problems forming a secure attachment to their mothers. ■

● Relationships with Parents

Like Bowlby, Erik Erikson (1968) saw the first year of life as the time at which infants develop a feeling of basic trust (or mistrust) about the world. According to his theory, an infant's first year represents the first of eight stages of lifelong psychosocial development (see Table 12.2). Each stage focuses on an issue or crisis that is especially important at that time of life. If the crisis is not resolved positively, the person will be psychologically troubled and cope less effectively with later crises. After children have formed emotional attachments to their parents, their next psychological

TABLE 12.2 Erikson's Stages of Psychosocial Development

In each of Erikson's stages of development, a different psychological issue presents a new crisis for the person to resolve. The person focuses attention on that issue and, by the end of the period, has worked through the crisis and resolved it either positively, in the direction of healthy development, or negatively, hindering further psychological development.

Age	Central Psychological Issue or Crisis
First year	**Trust versus mistrust** Infants learn to trust that their needs will be met by the world, especially by the mother—or they learn to mistrust the world.
Second year	**Autonomy versus shame and doubt** Children learn to exercise will, to make choices, and to control themselves—or they become uncertain and doubt that they can do things by themselves.
Third to fifth year	**Initiative versus guilt** Children learn to initiate activities and enjoy their accomplishments, acquiring direction and purpose. Or, if they are not allowed initiative, they feel guilty for their attempts at independence.
Sixth year through puberty	**Industry versus inferiority** Children develop a sense of industry and curiosity and are eager to learn—or they feel inferior and lose interest in the tasks before them.
Adolescence	**Identity versus role confusion** Adolescents come to see themselves as unique and integrated persons with an ideology—or they become confused about what they want out of life.
Early adulthood	**Intimacy versus isolation** Young people become able to commit themselves to another person—or they develop a sense of isolation and feel they have no one in the world but themselves.
Middle age	**Generativity versus stagnation** Adults are willing to have and care for children and to devote themselves to their work and the common good—or they become self-centered and inactive.
Old age	**Integrity versus despair** Older people enter a period of reflection, becoming assured that their lives have been meaningful and ready to face death with acceptance and dignity. Or they are in despair for their unaccomplished goals, failures, and ill-spent lives.

task is to begin to develop a more independent, or autonomous, relationship with them. This task is part of Erikson's second stage, when children begin to exercise their wills, develop some independence from their parents, and begin activities on their own. According to Erikson, children who are not allowed to exercise their wills or begin their own activities will feel uncertain about doing things for themselves and guilty about seeking independence. The extent to which parents allow or encourage their children's autonomy depends largely on their parenting style.

● **Parenting Styles**   Most parents try to channel their children's impulses into socially accepted outlets and to teach them the skills and rules needed to function in their society. As they engage in this *socialization* process, parents tend to display one of four distinct styles (Baumrind, 1971; Maccoby & Martin, 1983). **Authoritarian parents** are relatively strict, punitive, and unsympathetic. They value obedience and try to shape their children's behavior to meet a set standard and to

authoritarian parents   Firm, punitive, and unsympathetic parents who value obedience from the child and authority for themselves.

Parent-Training Programs   Research in developmental psychology on the relationship between parents' socialization styles and children's behavior has helped shape parent-training programs based on both the social-cognitive and the humanistic approaches described in the chapter on personality. These programs are designed to teach parents authoritative methods that can avoid scenes like this.

- **permissive parents**   Parents who give their child great freedom and lax discipline.
- **authoritative parents**   Parents who reason with the child, encourage give-and-take, are firm but understanding.
- **uninvolved parents**   Parents who are indifferent to their children.

curb the children's wills. They do not encourage independence. They are detached and seldom praise their youngsters. **Permissive parents** are more affectionate with their children and give them lax discipline and a great deal of freedom. **Authoritative parents** fall between these two extremes. They reason with their children, encouraging give-and-take, setting limits but also encouraging independence. They are firm but understanding; their demands are reasonable and consistent. As their children get older and better at making decisions they give them more responsibility. **Uninvolved parents** are indifferent to their children. They do whatever is necessary to minimize the costs of having children by investing as little time, money, and effort as possible. They focus on their own needs before their children's. Particularly when children are old enough to be out of the house alone, these parents often fail to monitor their activities.

Research shows some clear relationships between parenting styles and children's social and emotional development (Eisenberg, Fabes, & Spinrad, 2006; Parke & Buriel, 2006; Thompson, 2006). The children of authoritarian parents tend to be unfriendly, distrustful, and withdrawn. They are less likely than other children to be empathic and more likely to be aggressive. They are also more likely to cheat, and, after doing something wrong, they are less likely to feel guilty or accept blame. Children of permissive parents are relatively immature, dependent, and unhappy; they often have tantrums or ask for help when they encounter even slight difficulties. Children raised by authoritative parents tend to be friendly, cooperative, self-reliant, and socially responsible. They do better in school and are more popular than children of other kinds of parents. Children of uninvolved parents are less likely than other children to form secure attachments and more likely to have problems with impulsivity, aggression, noncompliance, moodiness, and low self-esteem.

These studies of parenting styles are interesting and important, but they are limited in several ways. First, they are based on correlations, which, as discussed in the chapter on research in psychology, do not prove causation. Finding consistent correlations between parenting styles and children's behavior does not establish that the parents' behavior is *causing* the differences seen in their children. Socialization is a two-way street: parents' behavior is shaped by their children as well as the reverse. Children's temperament, size, and appearance all influence the way parents treat them (Bugental & Grusec, 2006). Some psychologists have even suggested that it is not the parents' behavior itself that influences children but rather how the children perceive the discipline they receive—as stricter or more lenient than what an older sibling received, for example (Reiss et al., 2000). A second limitation of these studies is that the correlations between parenting styles and children's behavior, though statistically significant, are not terribly large and, therefore, do not apply to every child in every family.

● **Parenting Styles and Culture**   Yet another limitation of parenting studies is that most of them were conducted with European American families. Is the impact of various parenting styles different in other ethnic groups and other cultures? Possibly. Parents in Latino cultures in Mexico, Puerto Rico, and Central America, and in Asian cultures in China and India, for example, tend to be influenced by the collectivist tradition, in which family and community interests are emphasized over individual goals. Children in these cultures are expected to respect and obey their elders and to do less of the questioning, negotiating, and arguing that is encouraged—or at least allowed—in many middle-class European and European American families (Greenfield, Suzuki, & Rothstein-Fisch, 2006; Parke and Buriel, 2006). In short, their parents' style tends to be relatively authoritarian. When parents from these cultures immigrate to the United States, they bring their authoritarian parenting style with them. There is evidence, though, that the authoritarian discipline often seen in Asian American, Hispanic American, and African American families does not have the same negative consequences for children's behavior as it does in European American families (Chao & Tseng, 2002; Slade & Wissow, 2004). The difference is likely due to the fact that different disciplinary styles have different meanings in different cultures, and subcultures. Chinese American parents, for example, use authoritarian discipline to "govern" (*guan*) and provide "training" (*chiao shun*) for their children so that they will know what is expected of them (Chao, 2001). By contrast, European American parents are more likely to use authoritarian discipline to keep children in line and break their will. And in countries such as India and Kenya, where physical punishment tends to be an accepted form of discipline, punishment is associated with less aggression and anxiety than in Thailand and China, where it is rarely used (Lansford et al., 2005). These findings remind us that it is important to evaluate parenting styles in their cultural context. There is no single, universally "best" style of parenting (Parke & Buriel, 2006).

● Peer Friendships and Popularity

Social development over the years of childhood occurs in a world that broadens to include brothers, sisters, playmates, and classmates. Relationships with other children start early (Rubin, Bukowski, & Parker, 2006). By two months of age, infants engage in mutual gazing. By six months, they vocalize and smile at each other. By eight months, they prefer to look at another child rather than at an adult (Bigelow et al., 1990). So, even as infants, people are interested in one another, but it's a long journey from interest to intimacy.

Observations of two-year-olds show that the most they can do with their peers is to look at them, imitate them, and exchange—or grab—toys. By age four, they

Children's Friendships Though relationships with peers may not always be this friendly, they are often among the closest and most positive in a child's life. Friends are more interactive than non-friends; they smile and laugh together more, pay closer attention to equality in their conversation, and talk about mutual goals, not just personal ones. Having at least one close friend in childhood predicts good psychological functioning later on (Reis & Gable, 2003).

begin to play "pretend" together, agreeing about roles and themes. This kind of play is important because it provides a new context for communicating desires and feelings and offers an opportunity to form first "friendships" (Dunn & Hughes, 2001; Rubin et al., 2006). In the school years, peer interaction becomes more frequent, complex, and structured. Children play games with rules, join teams, tutor each other, and cooperate—or compete—in achieving goals. Friends become more important and friendships longer lasting as school-age children find that friends are a source of companionship, stimulation, support, and affection (Hartup & Stevens, 1997). In fact, companionship and fun are the most important aspects of friendship for children at this age. Psychological intimacy does not enter the picture until adolescence (Parker et al., 2001).

Friends help children to establish their sense of self-worth (Harter, 2006). Through friendships, children can compare their own strengths and weaknesses with those of others in a supportive and accepting atmosphere. Some children have more friends than others. When children are asked to nominate the classmates they like the best and the least, those who get the most votes—the *popular children*—tend to be the ones who are friendly, assertive, and good at communication; they help set the rules for their group and they engage in positive social behavior, such as helping others. Especially in early adolescence, children who are athletic, arrogant, or aggressive may also be popular, as long as their aggressiveness is not too extreme (Rubin et al., 2006). Unfortunately, about 10 percent of schoolchildren do not have friends. Some, known as *rejected children*, are actively disliked, either because they are too aggressive and lacking in self-control or because they are anxious and socially unskilled. Others, called *neglected children* are seldom even mentioned in peer nominations; they are isolated, quiet, and withdrawn, but not necessarily disliked. Friendless children tend to do poorly in school and usually experience psychological and behavior problems in later life (Asher & Hopmeyer, 2001; Ladd & Troop-Gordon, 2003). It appears that having even one close, stable friend can protect schoolchildren from loneliness and other problems (Parker et al., 2001). It also appears that the single most important factor in determining children's popularity is the *social skills* that they learn over the years of childhood and adolescence (Rubin et al., 2006).

• Social Skills and Understanding

LINKAGES (a link to Social Cognition, p. 713)

One of the most basic of these social skills is the ability to engage in sustained, responsive interactions with peers. These interactions require cooperation, sharing, and taking turns—behaviors that first appear in the preschool years. A second social skill that children learn is the ability to detect and correctly interpret other people's emotional signals. Much as children's school performance depends on processing academic information, their social performance depends on processing information about other people (Slomkowski & Dunn, 1996). A related set of social skills involves the ability to feel what another person is feeling, or something close to it (*empathy*), and to respond with comfort or help if the person is in distress. Children who understand another person's perspective, who appreciate how that person might be feeling, and who behave accordingly tend to be the most popular members of their peer group (Izard et al., 2001; Rubin et al., 2006). Children who do not have these skills are rejected or neglected; they may become bullies or the victims of bullies.

Parents can help their children develop social skills by engaging them in lots of "pretend" play and other prosocial activities and by encouraging them to express their emotions constructively (Eisenberg et al., 2006; Ladd, 2005). Affectionate mothers who discuss emotions openly and who provide clear messages about the consequences of their child's hurtful behavior effectively encourage the child to be empathic (Eisenberg, 1997). Older siblings, too, can help by acting out social roles during play and by talking about their feelings (Ruffman et al., 1998); teachers' ratings suggest that children without siblings tend to have poorer social skills (Downey & Condron, 2004). Children who have been abused by their parents also tend to lack important interaction skills and are thus more likely to be victimized by their peers (Bolger & Patterson, 2001).

Another social skill that develops in childhood is the ability to control one's emotions and behavior—an ability known as **self-regulation** (Campos, Frankel, & Camras, 2004; Rothbart & Bates, 2006). In the first few years of life, children learn to calm or console themselves by sucking their thumbs or cuddling their favorite blanket. Later, they learn more sophisticated strategies of self-regulation, such as counting to ten, planning ahead to avoid a problem (e.g., getting on the first bus if the school bully usually takes the second one), and recruiting social support (e.g., casually joining a group of big kids to walk past the bully on the playground). Children who cannot regulate their emotions tend to experience anxiety and distress and have trouble recovering from stressful events. They become emotionally overaroused when they see someone in distress and are often unsympathetic and unhelpful (Eisenberg et al., 2006). Further, boys whose emotions are easily aroused and have difficulty regulating this arousal become less and less popular with their peers and may develop problems with aggressiveness (Eisenberg et al., 2004; Fabes et al., 1997; Spinrad et al., 2006).

Self-regulation is most effectively learned when children experience harmonious interactions at home (Saarni et al., 2006). In one study, children who were skilled at regulating their emotions had parents who had soothed them in infancy by holding them, talking to them, and providing distractions. As the children grew older, the parents gradually began to introduce them to new and potentially uncomfortable events (such as their first haircut), all the while remaining close by as a safe base (Fox, 1997). The development of self-regulation may be hampered if parents dismiss children's emotions ("There's no reason for you to feel sad") or threaten to punish emotional expression ("Stop acting like a crybaby or I'll give you something to cry about"; Parke et al., 2005). Among North American children, self-regulation and empathy tend to be enhanced when parents talk about their own feelings and encourage their children to express emotions (Eisenberg, 1997). This phenomenon is not universal, however. For example, Japanese children are usually better emotion regulators than North American children, even though Japanese parents tend not to encourage the expression of strong emotion (Zahn-Waxler et al., 1996).

self-regulation The ability to control one's emotions and behavior.

Emphasis on the development of social skills varies across cultures, but it is widely encouraged. In China, Zambia, and Kenya, for example, the concept of intelligence includes the social skills of being understanding, respectful, responsible, and considerate (Benson, 2003a). In the United States, psychologists are encouraging schools to teach children social skills, including self-regulation, understanding, empathy, and cooperation. It is their hope that this "emotional literacy" or "emotional intelligence" will reduce the prevalence of childhood depression and aggression and even help children's academic achievement (Kress & Elias, 2006).

• Gender Roles

 LINKAGES (a link to Learning, p. 218)

An important aspect of understanding other people and being socially skilled is knowing about social roles, including **gender roles**—the general patterns of appearance and behavior associated with being a male or a female. Gender roles appear in every culture, but they are more pronounced in some of them. One analysis revealed, for example, that where there are smaller male-female differences in social status, gender-role differences are smaller, too (Wood & Eagly, 2002). In North America, some roles—such as homemaker and firefighter—have traditionally been tied to gender, although these traditions are weakening. Research by Deborah Best suggests that children show gender-role expectations earliest in Muslim countries (where the differences in roles are perhaps most extreme), but children in all twenty-five countries she studied eventually developed them (Best, 1992; Williams & Best, 1990).

Gender roles persist because they are deeply rooted in both nature and nurture. Small physical and behavioral differences between the sexes are evident early on (Eagly, 1996). Girls tend to speak and write earlier and to be better at grammar and spelling than boys (Halpern, 1997). Boys tend to be more skilled than girls at manipulating objects, constructing three-dimensional forms, and mentally manipulating complex figures and pictures (Choi & Silverman, 2003). Girls are more attracted than boys are to baby faces (Maestripieri, 2004), and by four months of age, the average duration of mutual gazing between girls and women is four times longer than that between boys and women (Leeb & Rejskind, 2004). Girls are able to read emotional signals at younger ages than boys can, and by school age, they are likely to be more kind, considerate, and empathic. They can also control their emotions better than boys can (Else-Quest et al., 2006). Girls engage in more social conversation and

Learning Gender Roles In every culture, socialization by parents and others typically encourages interests, activities, and other characteristics traditionally associated with a child's own gender.

self-disclosure with their friends and they care more about their friendships than boys do (Rose & Rudolph, 2006). Boys are more physically active and aggressive; they play in larger spaces, enjoying noisier, more strenuous physical games (Rose & Rudolph, 2006). From the age of two, boys engage in riskier behaviors and are injured at a rate that is two to four times that of girls (Morrongiello & Hogg, 2004). On the playground, boys are the overtly aggressive ones; they push and they punch each other more than girls do (Baillargeon et al., 2007; Ostrov, 2006). They are concerned with dominance rather than friendship (Rose & Rudolph, 2006). Girls are more likely to use "relational" or "social" aggression than physical aggression; they hurt with gossip and threats to withdraw friendship rather than with sticks and stones (Crick et al., 2004). Given all these differences, it is not surprising to find that girls are more sensitive and boys are more competitive (Fabes, Martin, & Hanish, 2003).

● **Biological Factors in Gender Roles** A biological contribution to these male-female differences is suggested by several lines of evidence. First, studies show sex differences in anatomy, hormones, and brain organization and functioning (Geary, 1999; Ruble, Martin, & Berenbaum, 2006). Second, cross-cultural research reveals consistent gender patterns even in the face of differing socialization practices (Simpson & Kenrick, 1997). Third, research with nonhuman primates finds sex differences that parallel those seen in human children. In one study, young female animals preferred playing with dolls and young males preferred playing with a toy car, for example (Alexander & Hines, 2002). Finally, research in behavior genetics shows that genes exert a moderate influence on the appearance of gender-typed behaviors (Iervolino et al., 2005).

● **Socialization of Gender Roles** There is no doubt, though, that gender roles are also influenced by socialization, partly by exaggerating whatever gender differences may already exist (Hyde, 2005). From the moment they are born, boys and girls are treated differently. Adults usually play more gently and talk more to infants they believe to be girls than to infants they believe to be boys. They often shower their daughters with dolls and doll clothes, their sons with trucks and tools. They tend to encourage boys to achieve, compete, explore, control their feelings, be independent, and assume personal responsibility. They encourage girls to be reflective, dependent, domestic, obedient, and unselfish (Ruble et al., 2006). Mothers speak with more feeling to girls and in more supportive ways (Kitamura & Burnham, 2003; Leaper, Anderson, & Sanders, 1998). When asked to imagine that their child has been injured, it takes a less severe injury to cause concern about daughters than about sons (Morrongiello & Hogg, 2004). And parents are more likely to stop a fight between their children when a daughter is involved (Martin & Ross, 2005). In these and many other ways, parents, teachers, and television role models consciously or inadvertently pass on their ideas about "appropriate" behaviors for boys and girls (Parke & Buriel, 2006; Ruble et al., 2006). They also convey information about gender-appropriate interests. For example, sixth-grade girls and boys express equal interest in science and earn the same grades. Yet parents underestimate their daughters' interest in science, believe that science is difficult for them, and are less likely to give them scientific explanations when working on a physics task (Tenenbaum & Leaper, 2003).

Children also pick up notions of what is gender-appropriate behavior from their peers (Martin & Fabes, 2001; Rose & Rudolph, 2006). For example, one reason boys tend to be better than girls at computer and video games (Greenfield, 1994) is that boys encourage and reward each other for skilled performance at these games more than girls do (Law, Pellegrino, & Hunt, 1993). Children are also more likely to play with other children of the same sex, and to act in gender-typical ways, when they are on the playground than when they are at home or in the classroom (Luria, 1992).

gender roles Patterns of work, appearance, and behavior that a society associates with being male or female.

● **Cognitive Factors in Gender Roles**   Because most children want to be accepted, especially by peers, they become "gender detectives," always searching for clues about who should do what, who can play with whom, and in what ways girls and boys are different (Martin & Ruble, 2004). In the process, they develop **gender schemas**, which are generalizations about what toys and activities are "appropriate" for boys versus girls and what jobs are "meant" for men versus women (Fagot, 1995). For example, by the time they are three years old, children tend to believe that dolls are for girls and trucks are for boys. Once they have developed these gender schemas and know that they themselves are male or female, children tend to choose activities, toys, and behaviors that are "appropriate" for their own gender (Ruble et al., 2006). They become "sexist self-socializers" as they work at developing the masculine or feminine attributes they view as consistent with their self-image as a male or a female. By the age of eight or nine, they may have become more flexible about what's okay for members of each sex to do—but most still say they wouldn't be friends with a boy who wore lipstick or a girl who played football (Levy, Taylor, & Gelman, 1995). Later in elementary school, when most girls outperform boys in language arts, math, science, and social studies, girls think of themselves as good only in language arts, because that's what they are "supposed" to be good at (Pomerantz, Altermatt, & Saxon, 2002).

In summary, social training by both adults and peers, along with the child's own cognitions about the world, tends to bolster and amplify any biological predispositions that distinguish boys and girls. This process, in turn, creates gender roles that are the joint—and inextricably linked—products of nature and nurture. This and other elements of early development are summarized in "In Review: Social and Emotional Development During Infancy and Childhood."

The efforts of some parents to de-emphasize gender roles in their children's upbringing may help to reduce the magnitude of gender differences in areas such as verbal and quantitative skills. However, some observers believe that other gender differences—such as males' greater ability to visualize the rotation of objects in space and females' greater ability to read facial expressions—are unlikely to change much. In particular, those who adopt the evolutionary approach see these differences as deeply rooted in the distant past, when males' major activity was hunting and females' was child rearing (Buss, 2004a). Other psychologists have suggested that prenatal exposure to male or female hormones influences the organization of male and female brains in ways that make boys more receptive to spatial activities and motion and girls more susceptible to social exchanges (Halpern, 1997). Still others see such differences as reflecting social inequality, not just biological destiny (Wood & Eagly, 2002). Whatever the cause of gender differences, it is important to

in review   Social and Emotional Development During Infancy and Childhood

Age	Relationships with Parents	Relationships with Other Children	Social Understanding
Birth–2 years	Infants form an attachment to the primary caregiver.	Play focuses on toys, not on other children.	Infants respond to emotional expressions of others.
2–4 years	Children become more autonomous and no longer need their parents' constant attention.	Toys are a way of eliciting responses from other children.	Young children can recognize emotions of others.
4–10 years	Parents actively socialize their children.	Children begin to cooperate, compete, play games, and form friendships with peers.	Children learn social rules, like politeness, and roles, like being a male or female; they learn to control their emotions.

Beating the Odds   Some children are able to overcome the difficulties and risks associated with poverty, war, family violence, homelessness and other circumstances to make a success of their lives. These children are said to be *resilient*. This fifteen-year-old girl grew up in a war zone but retains her dream of becoming a doctor.

- **gender schemas**   The generalizations children develop about what toys, activities, and occupations are "appropriate" for males versus females.

- **resilience**   A quality allowing children to develop normally in spite of severe environmental risk factors.

remember that most of them are quite small (Hyde, 2005). So though a popular book suggests that men are from Mars and women are from Venus, a more accurate metaphor would be to say that men are from one state and women are from another (Hyde, 2005).

● Risk and Resilience

Family instability, child abuse, homelessness, parental unemployment, poverty, substance abuse, and domestic violence put many children at risk for various difficulties in social and emotional development (Ackerman, Brown, & Izard, 2004). When parents divorce, for example, their children may develop serious problems (Clarke-Stewart & Brentano, 2006). By two or three years after the divorce, the intense psychological stress is over, and most children are functioning competently, but there can be long-lasting effects. Adults whose parents had divorced when they were children may not live as long as those from intact families, and a high proportion of people who were young adolescents when their parents divorced are unable to form committed relationships even years later. Children are also at risk if their parents have violent fights. Nearly half the children exposed to marital violence exhibit various forms of psychological disorder—a rate six times higher than that in the general population (Garber, 1992).

Children vary in how well they ultimately adjust to all these stressors. Even when the odds are against them, some children are left virtually unscathed by even the most dangerous risk factors. These children are said to be resilient. **Resilience** is a characteristic that permits successful development in the face of significant challenge. It has been studied throughout the world in a wide variety of adverse situations, including war, natural disaster, family violence, and poverty. This research has consistently identified certain qualities in children and their environments that are associated with resilience. Specifically, resilient children tend to be intelligent and to have easy dispositions, high self-esteem, talent, and faith (Masten & Coatsworth, 1998). They are cheerful, focused, and persistent in completing a task (Wills et al., 2001). They also typically have significant relationships with a warm and authoritative parent; with someone in their extended family; or with other caring adults outside the family, at school or in clubs or religious organizations (Rutter, 2006).

Adolescence

The years of middle childhood usually pass smoothly, but adolescence changes things drastically. All adolescents undergo significant changes in size, shape, and physical capacities. Many also experience big changes in their social lives, reasoning abilities, and views of themselves.

● Changes in Body, Brain, and Thinking

A sudden spurt in physical growth is the most visible sign that adolescence has begun. This growth spurt peaks at about age twelve for girls and age fourteen for boys (Tanner, 1978; see Figure 12.7). Suddenly, adolescents find themselves in new bodies. At the end of the growth spurt, females begin to menstruate, and males produce live sperm. This state of being able for the first time to reproduce is called **puberty.**

These dramatic changes in teenagers' bodies are accompanied by significant changes in their brains, especially in parts of the frontal lobes known as the prefrontal cortex (Kuhn, 2006; Spear, 2000; see Figure 3.16 in the chapter on biological aspects of psychology). These areas are vital to the ability to think flexibly, to act appropriately in challenging situations, and to juggle multiple pieces of information. They are also involved in skills such as planning and organization, controlling impulses, and allocating attention.

As described in the Linkages section of the chapter on biological aspects of psychology, the brain overproduces neuronal connections during childhood, but during puberty the connections that are not being used much are eliminated, or "pruned." At the same time, many neurons acquire a sheath of myelin, which speeds their communication with one another. So by the end of adolescence, teenagers' brains have fewer neural connections, but those that remain are more selective,

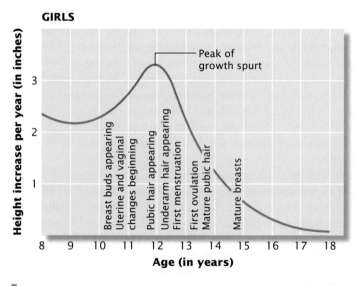

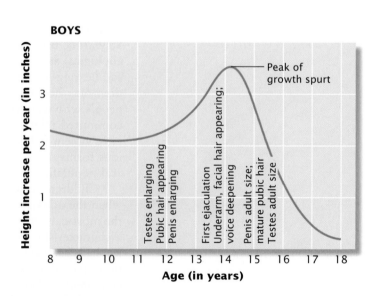

FIGURE 12.7

Physical Changes in Adolescence

At about ten and a half years of age, girls begin their growth spurt, and by age twelve, they are taller than their male peers. Boys begin their growth spurt at about twelve and a half years of age and usually grow faster and for a longer period of time than girls. Adolescents may grow as much as five inches a year. Increases in sex hormones (e.g. estrogen and testosterone) lead to the development of sexual characteristics such as pubic hair. The ages at which these changes occur vary considerably across individuals, but their sequence is the same.

stronger, and more efficient. At the same time, dopamine, a neurotransmitter associated with the experience of pleasure, becomes more prominent.

Changes in the brain are reflected in changes in the ways that adolescents think. As mentioned earlier, Piaget described this new stage of thinking as the *formal operational period*. He said it is marked by the ability to engage in abstract, hypothetical thinking, but researchers now suggest that cognitive changes in adolescence also include a whole range of "executive functions" controlled by the prefrontal cortex (Keil, 2006; Kuhn, 2006). By late adolescence, young people are able to reason better, plan for the future, and foresee consequences. When they investigate an issue they are able to consider and control several factors at once and analyze the impact of what they discover. This ability to engage in strategic, self-organized thinking also allows them to perform more than one mental task at the same time (Luciana et al., 2005). Moreover, they increasingly take charge of their mental life, choosing what to think about, when and where to do so, and how to allocate their mental effort.

● Adolescent Feelings and Behavior

In Western cultures, the changes occurring during *early adolescence*, from ages eleven to fourteen or so, can be disorienting. Adolescents—especially early-maturing girls—may experience bouts of depression, insomnia, and other psychological problems (Ge, Conger, & Elder, 2001; Johnson et al., 2006; Ohring, Graber, & Brooks-Gunn, 2002). This is also the time when eating disorders are likely to first appear (Wilson et al., 1996) and when the incidence of attempted and completed suicides rises (Centers for Disease Control and Prevention, 1999a).

As sex hormones and pleasure-related brain systems become more active, sexual interest stirs, and the prospect of smoking, drinking alcohol, and taking other drugs may become appealing (Patton et al., 2004; Reyna & Farley, 2006). Opportunities to do these things increases, too, because adolescents tend to spend more time with peers than with family, to be more influenced by peers, and to take more risks and seek out more novel sensations than either younger children or adults do (Gardner & Steinberg, 2005; Steinberg, 2007). Of course, a certain amount of adolescent risk-taking and sensation-seeking is normal. In fact, adolescents who engage in moderate risk-taking tend to be more socially competent than those who take no risks, or who take extreme risks (Spear, 2000). Indeed, extreme risk-taking is often maladaptive, leading to excessive use of drugs and alcohol or to reckless and even life-threatening activities. So for some, early adolescence marks the beginning of a downward spiral that ends up in academic failure, delinquency, and substance abuse.

Many of the problems of adolescence are associated with challenges to young people's *self-esteem*, their sense of being worthy, capable, and deserving of respect (Harter, 2006). Adolescents are especially vulnerable if many stressors occur at the same time (Kling et al., 1999). The switch from elementary school to middle school is particularly challenging (Eccles, Lord, & Buchanan, 1996). Their new teachers may have less time to nurture students, and they may exert more control, impose higher standards, and evaluate students' work in a more public way. Under these circumstances, grades may drop, especially for students who were already having trouble in school or who don't have confidence in their own abilities (Rudolph et al., 2001). But grades don't affect self-esteem in all teens. Some base their self-esteem more on athletic success and on their peers' opinions of them than on their academic achievement (Crocker & Wolfe, 2001). In fact, adolescents' academic performance is strongly affected by the peers with whom they spend their time. For example, adolescents whose grades and motivation decline from the end of elementary school to the end of their first year in middle school tend to be those who affiliated themselves with other academic underachievers (Ryan, 2001).

The changes and pressures of adolescence are often played out at home, as adolescents try to have a greater say in a parent-child relationship once ruled mainly by their parents. Serious conflicts may lead to serious problems, including running away, pregnancy, stealing, drug taking, or even suicide—especially among teens who

puberty The condition of being able, for the first time, to reproduce.

do not feel close to their parents (Blum, Beuhring, & Rinehart, 2000). Fortunately, although the bond with parents deteriorates during the transition from early adolescence to midadolescence, most adolescents and young adults maintain a reasonably good relationship with their parents (McGue et al., 2005; van Wel, ter Bogt, & Raaijmakers, 2002). For example, the majority of twelve- to fourteen-year-olds in the National Longitudinal Survey of Youth said that their parents "usually" or "always" helped them to do important things and that they turned first to one of their parents when they had problems (Moore, 2005). Children who report positive relationships with their parents tend not to associate with risk-taking peers in eighth grade or develop problem behaviors in high school (Eisenberg et al., 2005; Goldstein, Davis-Kean, & Eccles, 2005; Soenens et al., 2006).

Teens are most likely to share confidences with parents who keep tabs on their children's activities and expect them to discuss those activities (Smetana et al., 2006; Soenens et al., 2006), but how much involvement and control is enough, and how much is too much? It is not easy for parents to know. In one study, seventh-graders who felt they had a lot of autonomy at home—such as in deciding how late to stay out at night—did more unsupervised socializing with peers in eighth grade and were at greater risk for problem behavior in eleventh grade (Goldstein, Davis-Kean, & Eccles, 2005). At the same time, seventh-graders who thought their parents were too intrusive also ran into problems. They hung out more with deviant peers in eighth grade and, by eleventh grade, showed elevated rates of behavior problems.

● Love and Sex in Adolescence

On top of everything else, adolescence is usually the time when romance first takes center stage (Collins & Steinberg, 2006). Nearly half of fifteen-year-olds and 70 percent of eighteen-year-olds have romantic relationships; 60 percent of these relationships last a year or more (Carver, Joyner, & Udry, 2003). Being in a romantic relationship is linked with feelings of self-worth, competence, and belonging to one's peer group (Collins & Roisman, 2006; Harter, 2006).

Surveys suggest that almost half of teens in the United States have had sexual intercourse by age sixteen (National Center for Chronic Disease Prevention and Health Promotion, 2002). Teens who have sex differ from those who do not in a number of ways. They hold less conventional attitudes and values, and they are more likely to smoke, drink alcohol, and use other drugs (National Center on Addiction and Substance Abuse, 2004). They also have more unsupervised time after school (Cohen et al., 2002), and they are more likely to have a sexually active best friend (Jaccard, Blanton, & Dodge, 2005). Their parents tend to be less educated, to have less control over them, and not to talk openly with them. They are more likely to have spent their childhood without their father (Ellis et al., 2003). The typical pairing of sexually active teens is a "macho" male and a "girly" female (Udry & Chantala, 2003). Adolescents who displayed poorer self-regulatory skills as children are the ones most likely to take greater sexual risks, such as having multiple partners and not using condoms (Raffaelli & Crockett, 2003).

All too often, sexual activity leads to declining school achievement and interest, sexually transmitted diseases, and unplanned and unwanted pregnancies. Teenagers have higher rates of gonorrhea, chlamydia, pelvic inflammatory disease, and other sexually transmitted diseases than any other age group (National Center for Health Statistics, 2000; Ross, 2002). One-fifth of all AIDS cases start in adolescence (Brody, 1998). Although teenage pregnancy rates have been declining lately, nearly 10 percent of all teenage girls in the United States become pregnant before the age of nineteen (National Center for Health Statistics, 2000; Starkman & Rajani, 2002). Girls with low confidence in themselves and their educational future, along with those whose parents have a low level of education, are among the most likely to become pregnant in their teens (Young et al., 2004). More than half of the girls who get pregnant decide to keep their babies and become single mothers.

A teenage pregnancy can create problems for the mother, the baby, and others in the family. For one thing, babies of teenage mothers are less likely than babies

Cyber Love? Many teens develop romantic relationships online, often by exiting a chat room to engage in one-on-one instant messaging after providing "a/s/l" (age, sex, and location) information (Subrahmanyam, Greenfield, & Tynes, 2004). This "pairing off" process allows them to socialize in a relatively anonymous way, but the Internet also carries risks, including exposure to degrading or obscene material and contact with sexual predators (Subrahmanyam, David, & Greenfield, 2006; Wolak, Mitchell, & Finkelhor, 2007).

of older mothers to survive their first year (Phipps, Blume, & DeMonner, 2002). Compared to older parents, teenage parents tend to be less positive and stimulating with their children, and more likely to abuse them (Brooks-Gunn & Chase-Lansdale, 2002). The children of teenage parents, in turn, are more likely to develop behavior problems and to do poorly in school than those whose parents are older (Furstenberg, Brooks-Gunn, & Chase-Lansdale, 1989; Moffitt, 2002). They do better if they have strong attachments to their fathers and if their mothers are prepared for maternal responsibilities and know about children and parenting even before the baby is born (Miller et al., 1996; Whitman et al., 2001). The younger sisters of teenage mothers are also affected by the birth. Often, they must take time away from schoolwork to help care for the child, and they are at increased risk for drug and alcohol use and for becoming pregnant themselves (East & Jacobson, 2001).

● **Violent Adolescents** As described at the beginning of this chapter, some individuals respond to the challenges of adolescence with violence. The roots of teenage violence run deep and lie partly in genetic factors (Brendgen et al., 2005). Aggression is just as stable from childhood to adolescence as intelligence is (Dodge, Coie, & Lynam, 2006). Among the childhood characteristics that increase the risk of violent behavior in adolescence are fearlessness, low intelligence, lack of empathy, lack of emotional self-regulation, and aggressiveness (Eisenberg et al., 2004; Hay et al., 2003; Rutter, 2003). Gender is another important factor: It is no coincidence that teenage killers are almost always boys. In cultures around the world, homicides committed by males outnumber those committed by females by more than thirty to one (Cassel & Bernstein, 2007).

Environmental factors also increase the likelihood of youth violence. These factors include maternal depression and rejection, and involvement in delinquent gangs or with antisocial peers (Rutter, 2003), as well as poverty (Strohschein, 2005), malnutrition (Liu et al., 2004), and exposure to violent television and video games (Comstock & Scharrer, 2006; Nicoll & Kieffer, 2005). Peers are especially influential. In one study, adolescents were more likely to say they would engage in aggressive behaviors if they believed they were in a chat room with popular adolescents who favored aggressive behaviors (Cohen & Prinstein, 2006). Another contributor to violence is the growing use and abuse of anabolic steroids (Grimes, Ricci, & Melloni, 2006). Adolescent violence is also more likely among youngsters who grew up witnessing family violence, clashing with siblings, and/or experiencing abuse (Ehrensaft et al., 2003; Noland et al., 2004). The risk is raised, too, among children who live in neighborhoods plagued by violence and crime (Herrenkohl et al., 2004; Pearce et al., 2003). Young people who are exposed to even a single incident of firearm violence are twice as likely as other children to later engage in violent behavior (Bingenheimer, Brennan, & Earls, 2005).

Fortunately, the effects of all these negative influences can be buffered by protective factors such as religious beliefs, involvement in school activities, and parents' emotional support, supervision, monitoring, and coaching (Brookmeyer, Henrich, & Schwab-Stone, 2005; Herrenkohl et al., 2004; Kliewer et al., 2006; Pearce et al., 2003; Zimmerman, Glew, et al., 2005). In addition, prevention programs involving parent training, social skill training, and classroom intervention show promise for reducing aggression and bullying (Domitrovich, & Greenberg, 2000; Frey et al., 2005). One study found, for example, that showing explicit photos of trauma patients being treated for gunshot wounds helps young people to see violence as less acceptable (Cornwell et al., 2004).

In fact, despite all the dangers and problems of adolescence, most teens in Western cultures do not experience major personal turmoil or family conflicts. Research suggests that in Western cultures, more than half of today's teens find early adolescence relatively trouble-free (Arnett, 1999). Only about 15 percent of the adolescents studied experience serious distress (Steinberg, 1990). The vast majority of adolescents cope well with the changes puberty brings and soon find themselves in the midst of perhaps the biggest challenge of their young lives—preparing themselves for the transition to young adulthood.

● Identity and Development of the Self

In many less developed countries today, as in the United States a century ago, the end of early adolescence, around the age of fifteen, marks the beginning of adulthood: of work, parenting, and grown-up responsibilities. In modern North America, though, the transition from childhood to adulthood often lasts well into the twenties. This lengthened adolescence has created special problems—among them, the matter of finding or forming an identity.

Most adolescents have not previously thought deeply about who they are. When preschool children are asked to describe themselves, they often mention a favorite or habitual activity: "I watch TV" or "I do the dishes" (Keller, Ford, & Meacham, 1978). At age eight or nine, children identify themselves by giving facts such as their sex, age, name, physical appearance, likes, and dislikes. They may still describe themselves in terms of what they do, but they now include how well they do it compared with other children (Secord & Peevers, 1974). Then, at about age eleven, children begin to describe themselves in terms of social relationships, personality traits, and other general, stable psychological characteristics, such as "smart" or "friendly" (Damon & Hart, 1982). By the end of early adolescence, they are ready to develop a personal identity as a unique individual.

Their personal identity may be affected by their **ethnic identity**—the part of a person's identity that reflects the racial, religious, or cultural group to which the person belongs. In melting-pot nations such as the United States, some members of ethnic minorities may identify with their ethnic group—Chinese, Mexican, or Italian, for example—even more than with their national citizenship. Children are aware of ethnic cues such as skin color before they reach the age of three and prefer to play with children from their own group. Minority-group children reach this awareness earlier than other children (Milner, 1983). In high school, most students hang out with members of their own ethnic group. They tend not to know classmates in other ethnic groups well, seeing them more as members of those groups than as individuals

Ethnic Identity Ethnic identity is that part of our personal identity that reflects the racial, religious, or cultural group to which we belong. Ethnic identity often leads people to interact mainly with others who share that same identity.

(Steinberg, Dornbusch, & Brown, 1992). A positive ethnic identity contributes to self-esteem; seeing their own group as superior makes people feel good about themselves and is associated with more positive attitudes about education (Fiske, 1998; Fuligni, Witkow, & Garcia, 2005). However, as described in the chapter on social cognition, the same processes that forge ethnic identity can also sow the seeds of ethnic prejudice. Adolescents who have more extensive contact with members of other ethnic groups in school tend to develop more mature ethnic identities and more favorable attitudes toward people of other ethnicities (Phinney, Ferguson, & Tate, 1997).

● Moral Reasoning

The development of a conscious identity occurs partly because, as mentioned earlier, adolescents have developed a capacity for abstract thinking, self-directed cognitive activity, and other complex "executive functions." Adolescents often find themselves applying these advanced cognitive skills to questions of morality.

● Kohlberg's Stages of Moral Reasoning

To examine how people think about morality, Harvard psychologist Lawrence Kohlberg asked individuals to resolve moral dilemmas. Perhaps the most famous of his dilemmas was the "Heinz dilemma," which requires people to decide whether a man named Heinz should steal a rare and unaffordable drug in order to save his wife from cancer. Kohlberg found that the reasons people give for their moral choices change systematically and consistently with age (Kohlberg & Gilligan, 1971). He proposed that moral reasoning develops in six stages, which are summarized in Table 12.3. These stages are not tightly linked to a person's age. There is a range of ages for reaching each stage, and not everyone reaches the highest level.

Stage 1 and Stage 2 moral judgments are most typical of children under the age of nine and tend to be selfish. Kohlberg called this level **preconventional moral reasoning** because reasoning at this level is not yet based on the conventions or rules that guide social interactions in society. At this level of moral development people are concerned with avoiding punishment or following rules when it is to their own advantage. At the **conventional moral reasoning** level, Stages 3 and 4, people are concerned about other people; they believe that morality consists of following rules and conventions such as duty to their families, to marriage vows, and to their country. Conventional thinkers would never think it was proper to burn their country's flag in protest, for example. The moral reasoning of children and adolescents from ages nine to nineteen is most often at this level. Stages 5 and 6 represent the highest level of moral reasoning, which Kohlberg called **postconventional moral reasoning** because it occurs after conventional reasoning. Moral judgments at this level are based on personal standards or universal principles of justice, equality, and respect for human life rather than on the demands of authority figures or society. People who have reached this level view rules and laws as arbitrary but respect them because they protect human welfare. They believe that individual rights can sometimes justify violating these laws if the laws become destructive. People do not usually reach this level until sometime in young adulthood—if at all. Stage 6 is seen only rarely in extraordinary individuals. Studies of Kohlberg's stages generally support the sequence he proposed (Colby et al., 1983; Turiel, 2006; Walker, 1989).

● Limitations of Kohlberg's Stages

Kohlberg's first four stages appear to be universal. Evidence of them has been found in twenty-seven cultures from Alaska to Zambia. Stages 5 and 6, however, do not always appear (Snarey, 1987). Further, moral judgments made in some cultures do not always fit neatly into Kohlberg's stages. Some people in collectivist cultures—Papua New Guinea, Taiwan, and Israeli kibbutzim, for example—explained their answers to moral dilemmas by pointing to the importance of the community rather than to personal standards. People in India included in their moral reasoning the importance of acting in accordance with one's

ethnic identity The part of a person's identity associated with the racial, religious, or cultural group to which the person belongs.

preconventional moral reasoning Reasoning that is not yet based on the conventions or rules that guide social interactions in society.

conventional moral reasoning Reasoning that reflects the belief that morality consists of following rules and conventions.

postconventional moral reasoning Reasoning that reflects moral judgments based on personal standards or universal principles of justice, equality, and respect for human life.

TABLE 12.3   Kohlberg's Stages of Moral Development

Kohlberg's stages of moral reasoning describe differences in how people think about moral issues. Here are some examples of answers that people at different stages of development might give to the "Heinz dilemma" described in the text. This dilemma is more realistic than you might think. In 1994, a man was arrested for robbing a bank after being turned down for a loan to pay for his wife's cancer treatments; a similar case occurred in 2004.

Stage	What Is Right?	Should Heinz Steal the Drug?
Preconventional		
1	Obeying, and avoiding punishment from, a superior authority	Heinz should not steal the drug because he will be jailed.
2	Making a fair exchange, a good deal	Heinz should steal the drug because his wife will repay him later.
Conventional		
3	Pleasing others and getting their approval	Heinz should steal the drug because he loves his wife and because she and the rest of the family will approve.
4	Doing your duty, following rules and social order	Heinz should steal the drug for his wife because he has a duty to care for her, or he should not steal the drug because stealing is illegal.
Postconventional		
5	Respecting rules and laws, but recognizing that they may have limits	Heinz should steal the drug because life is more important than property.
6	Following universal ethical principles, such as justice, reciprocity, equality, and respect for human life and rights	Heinz should steal the drug because of the principle of preserving and respecting life.

gender and caste and with maintaining personal purity (Shweder et al., 1994). As in other areas of cognitive development, culture plays a significant role in shaping moral judgments.

Gender may also play a role. Carol Gilligan (1982, 1993) has suggested that for females, the moral ideal is not the abstract, impersonal concept of justice that Kohlberg found in males but, rather, the need to protect enduring relationships and fulfill human needs. Gilligan questioned Kohlberg's assumption that the highest level of morality is based on justice. When she asked her research participants about moral conflicts, the majority of men focused on justice, but only half of the women did. The other half focused on caring. Although this difference between men and women has not always been found (Jaffe & Hyde, 2000), there does seem to be an overall tendency for females to focus on caring more than males do and for males to focus on justice more than females do when they are resolving hypothetical moral dilemmas (Turiel, 2006). When resolving real-life moral issues, both men and women focus more on caring than on justice (Walker, 1995).

Taken together, the results of research in many countries and with both genders suggest that moral ideals are not absolute and universal. Moral development is apparently an adaptation to the moral world in which one lives, a world that differs from place to place (Bersoff, 1999). Formal operational reasoning may be necessary for people to reach the highest level of moral reasoning, but formal operational reasoning alone is not sufficient. To some extent, at the highest levels, moral reasoning is a product of culture and history (Turiel, 2006).

● **Moral Reasoning and Moral Action** Moral reasoning is related to moral behavior. In one study, adolescents who committed crimes ranging from burglary to murder tended to see obedience to laws mainly as a way of avoiding jail—a Stage 1 belief. Their nondelinquent peers, who showed Stage 4 reasoning, believed that one should obey laws because they prevent chaos in society (Gregg, Gibbs, & Basinger, 1994). But having high moral reasoning ability is no guarantee that a person will always act morally; other factors, such as the likelihood of being caught in an immoral act also affect behavior (Krebs, 1967). Even a false sense of being watched can make a difference. In one study, people alone in a coffee lounge were nearly three times as likely to pay for their coffee when a poster on the wall portrayed a person's eyes rather than an image of flowers (Bateson, Nettle, & Roberts, 2006).

Children and adolescents can be encouraged to move to higher levels of moral reasoning through exposure to arguments at a higher stage, perhaps as they argue about issues with one another. Hearing about moral reasoning that is one stage higher than their own or encountering a situation that requires more advanced reasoning seems to push people into moral reasoning at a higher level (Enright, Lapsley, & Levy, 1983). The development of moral behavior takes more than abstract knowledge, however. Consider a study of inner-city adolescents who were required to take a high school class that involved community service—working at a soup kitchen for the needy (Youniss & Yates, 1997). As part of the course they also had to write essays on their experience. Over time, the students' essays became more sophisticated, going beyond discussion of, say, homelessness to observations about the distribution of wealth in society and other ideological matters. By the end of the course, the behavior of the students had also changed; they were going to the soup kitchen more often than the course required. In another study, high school students who provided hands-on community service such as feeding the homeless or tutoring underprivileged children became more helpful toward strangers and developed a stronger sense of civic responsibility than did students whose community service did not involve direct helping (Reinders & Youniss, 2006).

In summary, learning to behave in moral ways requires three things: (1) consistent modeling of moral reasoning and behavior by parents and peers, (2) real-life experience with moral issues, and (3) situational factors that support moral actions.

● Emerging Adulthood

For young people in Western cultures, adolescence is typically followed by a period of "emerging adulthood" which lasts from about eighteen to about twenty-five. During this period, they explore life's possibilities through education, dating, and travel before settling into stable adult roles and responsibilities (Arnett, 2000; Roisman et al., 2004). Two tasks are of particular importance for emerging adults: resolving their "identity crisis" and choosing a career direction.

● **Facing the Identity Crisis** According to Erikson (1968), events of late adolescence, such as graduating from high school, going to college, and building new relationships, challenge one's self-concept and precipitate an **identity crisis** (see Table 12.2). In this crisis, the person must develop an integrated self-image as a unique person by pulling together self-knowledge acquired during childhood. If infancy and childhood brought trust, autonomy, and initiative, according to Erikson, individuals will resolve the identity crisis positively, feeling self-confident and competent. If infancy and childhood resulted in feelings of mistrust, shame, guilt, and inferiority, individuals will be confused about their identity and goals.

In Western cultures there is some limited empirical support for Erikson's ideas about the identity crisis. In the period of emerging adulthood, young people do become more open to new experiences (Roberts, Walton, & Viechtbauer, 2006) and consider alternative identities (Waterman, 1982). They "try out" being rebellious,

● **identity crisis** A phase during which an adolescent attempts to develop an integrated self-image.

studious, or detached as they attempt to resolve questions about sexuality, self-worth, industriousness, and independence. Some college students, for example, make a commitment to an identity and then reevaluate that commitment; these students are more likely to repeat their freshman year or change their major (Luyckx, Goossens, & Soenens, 2006). Recreational identities may be especially important; not all college students are successful academically, so they may try out alternative identities associated with extracurricular activities (Eccles & Gootman, 2002). People of college age may also try out identities through online message boards and multiplayer Internet games (Whitlock, Powers, & Eckenrode, 2006).

As young people learn to cope with challenges, handle their emotions, and settle on their identity during emerging adulthood, their psychological well-being tends to improve. The prevalence of serious depression, which tends to be quite high at the end of adolescence, especially for girls, declines (Galambos, Barker, & Krahn, 2006). By the time they are twenty-one, about half of the people studied have resolved the identity crisis in a way that is consistent with their self-image and the historical era in which they are living. They are ready to enter adulthood with self-confidence. Basically the same people who entered adolescence, they now have more mature attitudes and behavior, more consistent goals and values, and a clearer idea of who they are (Savin-Williams & Demo, 1984). Many have become more aware of their obligations to their families (Fuligni & Pedersen, 2002). Those who explore matters of identity more extensively tend to have had opportunities to express and develop their own points of view in a supportive environment at home, at school, and in the community (Grotevant, 1998). For those who fail to resolve identity issues—either because they avoided an identity crisis by accepting whatever identity their parents set for them or because they postponed dealing with the crisis and remain uncommitted and lacking in direction—there are often problems ahead (Hart & Yates, 1997).

● **Choosing a Career, or a Major** Establishing a career direction is much like finding one's identity: There is usually a period of exploration before a vocational choice can be made with any confidence (Blustein, Ellis, & Devenis, 1989). For many emerging adults, the exploration process is quite haphazard, and they find themselves channeled into a career path by chance or circumstances rather than through conscious decisions about what they want to be when they "grow up" (Bright, Pryor, & Harpham, 2005). College students, for example, typically consider only a narrow range of options. In one study, no student considered more than seven academic majors, and most students considered fewer than four (Galotti, 1999).

The final choice tends to be influenced by students' interests and abilities, their gender, their family background, and their previous work experiences (Lent et al., 2002). If students believe they have the skills necessary for success in a particular occupation, they are more likely to develop an interest in that occupation and to seek a career in it (Fouad, Smith, & Zao, 2002). The link between expectations of success and career choice has been demonstrated in the laboratory with college students who were undecided about their choice of a major. Students in the experimental group took and passed (or were told they passed) a brief math test, thus increasing their expectations for success in math. Compared with students who did not take the test, more students in the experimental group enrolled in math or science courses for the following quarter, had selected a math or science major, or expressed interest in a math or science career (Luzzo et al., 1999).

Career choice also depends to some extent on gender. Although girls and boys show equal ability and achievement in high school science courses, college women are less likely than men to major in a basic science, opting instead for a "people-oriented" major such as law, education, or psychology (Miller et al., 2006). Even girls who do choose a basic science major tend to do so because they think it will

So Many Choices Choosing a career is one of the most important decisions you will ever make. As suggested in the chapter on cognition and language, to reach the most informed decision, you should investigate a wide range of occupations, consider the pros and cons of all available majors, take classes in the fields on your "short list," talk to people who work in those fields, and consult with a vocational counselor who can provide career guidance based on interest and aptitude tests.

prepare them for a career helping others rather than because they are interested in that science (Morgan, Isaac, & Sansone, 2001).

The effect of family background on career choice is seen when students seek to follow in their parents' footsteps. In one study, men whose fathers are executives were more likely to major in business than men whose fathers are not executives (Leppel, Williams, & Waldauer, 2001), and other family occupational traditions can lead (or push) other emerging adults toward careers in medicine, law, or science. Prior life experiences have an impact, too. For example, caring for an elderly person might lead to a career in gerontology (Robert & Mosher-Ashley, 2000), and having had psychotherapy may lead to a career in psychiatry (Yakeley, Shoenberg, & Heady, 2004).

Adulthood

As emerging adults enter adulthood itself, the process of development continues. The changes and transitions in adulthood can be divided roughly into three periods: early adulthood (from the midtwenties through the thirties), middle adulthood (ages forty to sixty-five), and late adulthood (older than sixty-five).

● Physical Changes

In *early adulthood*, physical growth continues. Shoulder width, height, and chest size increase. People continue to develop their athletic abilities. For most people, the years of early adulthood are the prime of life.

In *middle adulthood*, one of the most common physical changes is the loss of sensory sharpness. By this time, nearly everyone shows some hearing impairment. People in their early forties become less sensitive to light, and their vision deteriorates somewhat. Increased farsightedness is an inevitable change that usually results in a need for reading glasses. Inside the body, bone mass is dwindling, the risk of heart disease is increasing, and fertility declines. In their late forties or early fifties, women generally experience the shutdown of reproductive capability, a process known as **menopause.** Estrogen and progesterone levels drop, and the menstrual cycle eventually ceases.

In *late adulthood*, men shrink about an inch, and women about two inches, as their posture changes and cartilage disks between the spinal vertebrae become thinner. Hardening of the arteries and a buildup of fat deposits on the artery walls may lead to heart disease. The digestive system slows down and becomes less efficient. In addition, the brain shrinks and the flow of blood to the brain slows. The few reflexes that remained after infancy (such as the knee-jerk reflex) weaken or disappear. Bedtime comes earlier, and naps are more frequent (Park et al., 2002). But as in earlier years, declines in physical functioning can be delayed or diminished by a healthy diet and exercise (Brach et al., 2003; Larson et al., 2006; Seeman & Chen, 2002).

● Cognitive Changes

Adulthood is marked by increases, as well as decreases, in cognitive abilities. Abilities that involve intensive information processing begin to decline in early adulthood, but those that depend on accumulated knowledge and experience increase until beginning to tail off in old age, if at all. In fact, older adults may function as well as, or better than, younger adults in situations that tap their long-term memories and well-learned skills. The experienced teacher may deal with an unruly child more skillfully than the novice, and the senior lawyer may understand the implications of a new law more quickly than the recent graduate. Their years of accumulating and organizing information can make older adults practiced, skillful, and wise.

● **menopause**   The process whereby a woman's reproductive capacity ceases.

● **Cognitive Advances in Early, Middle, and Late Adulthood** In early and middle adulthood, until age sixty at least, important cognitive abilities improve. During this period, adults do better on tests of vocabulary, comprehension, and general knowledge, especially if they use these abilities in their daily lives (Park, 2001). Young and middle-aged adults learn new information and new skills; they remember old information and hone old skills. It is in their forties through their early sixties that people tend to put in the best performance of their lives on complex mental tasks such as reasoning, verbal memory, and vocabulary (Willis & Schaie, 1999).

The nature of thought may also change during adulthood. Adult thought is often more complex and adaptive than adolescent thought (Labouvie-Vief, 1992). Adults can understand, as adolescents cannot, the contradictions inherent in thinking. They see both the possibilities and the problems in every course of action (Riegel, 1975)—in deciding whether to start a new business or to move to a new house, for example. Middle-aged adults are more adept than adolescents or young adults at making rational decisions and at relating logic and abstractions to actions, emotions, social issues, and personal relationships (Tversky & Kahneman, 1981). As they appreciate these relationships, their thought becomes more global, more concerned with broad moral and practical concerns (Labouvie-Vief, 1982). It has been suggested that the achievement of these new kinds of thinking reflects a stage of cognitive development in which people's thinking is *dialectical*. This means they understand that knowledge is relative, not absolute—such that what is seen as wise today may have been thought foolish in times past (Lutz & Sternberg, 1999). They see life's contradictions as an inevitable part of reality, and they tend to weigh various solutions to problems rather than just accepting the first one that springs to mind.

Older people also have the ability to think deeply and wisely about life. Some psychologists have defined *wisdom* as excellence in mind and virtue—knowing about the meaning and conduct of life and ways of achieving a perfect balance between personal interest and the common good (Baltes & Kunzmann, 2004). Old age does not guarantee wisdom, but if it is combined with experiences conducive to the accumulation and refinement of wisdom-related knowledge, growing old can be associated with high levels of wisdom (Baltes et al., 1995). Researchers have found that one component of wisdom—the ability to infer what other people are thinking—remains intact and sometimes even improves over the later adult years. For example, when asked to explain why a burglary suspect in a story surrendered to the police, seventy-year-olds gave better answers than younger adults. Their answers included inferences about the suspect's motives, such as "the burglar surrendered because he thought the policeman knew he had robbed the shop" (Happe, Winner, & Brownell, 1998).

● **Declining Cognitive Abilities in Late Adulthood** It is not until late adulthood—after sixty-five or so—that some intellectual abilities decline noticeably. Generally, the abilities most severely affected are those that require rapid and flexible manipulation of ideas and symbols, active thinking and reasoning, and sheer mental effort (Baltes, 1994; Finkel et al., 2003; Gilmore, Spinks, & Thomas, 2006; see Figure 12.8.). Older adults do just as well as younger ones at tasks they know well, such as naming familiar objects (Radvansky, 1999). It is when they are asked to perform an unfamiliar task or to solve a complex problem they have not seen before that older adults are generally slower and less effective than younger ones (Craik & Rabinowitz, 1984). When facing complex problems, older people apparently suffer from having too much information to sift through (Gazzaley et al., 2005). They have trouble considering, choosing, and executing solutions (Peters et al., 2007). As people age, they grow less efficient at organizing the elements of a problem and at holding and manipulating more than one idea at a time. They have difficulty doing tasks that require them to divide their attention between two activities (Smith et al., 2001) and are slower at shifting their attention back and forth between two

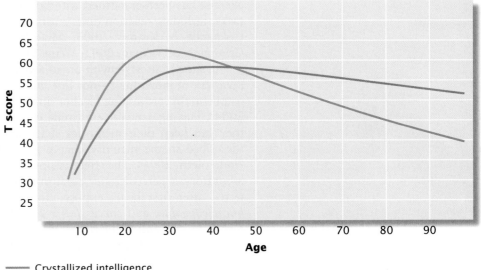

FIGURE **12.8**

Mental Abilities over the Life Span

Mental abilities collectively known as "fluid" intelligence—speed and accuracy of information processing, for example—begin to decline quite early in adult life. Changes in these biologically based aspects of thinking are usually not marked until late adulthood, however. "Crystallized" abilities learned over a lifetime—such as reading, writing, comprehension of language, and professional skills—decline, too, but later, and at a slower pace (Li et al., 2004).

Source: Adapted from Baltes (1994).

activities (Wecker et al., 2005). If older adults have enough time, though, and can separate the two activities, they can perform just as well as younger adults (Hawkins, Kramer, & Capaldi, 1993).

Usually the loss of intellectual abilities in older adults is slow and need not cause major problems (Bashore & Ridderinkhoff, 2002). A study of Swedish adults (Nilsson, 1996) found that memory problems among older adults are largely confined to *episodic memory* (e.g., what they ate for lunch yesterday) rather than to *semantic memory* (general knowledge, such as the name of the capital of Spain). In short, everyday competencies that involve verbal processes are likely to remain intact into advanced old age (Freedman, Aykan, & Martin, 2001; Willis & Schaie, 1999). Unfortunately, however, there is one way in which older adults' declining memories can have negative effects: They may be more likely than younger adults to recall false information as being true (Jacoby & Rhodes, 2006; Park, 2001), making some of them especially prone to victimization by scam artists. For example, the more warnings they hear about a false medical claim—such as that shark cartilage supposedly cures arthritis—the more familiar it becomes, and the more likely they are to believe it. As described in the chapter on memory, younger people are also vulnerable to memory distortions, but they are more likely to remember that false information is false, even when it is familiar.

The decline, and the rate of decline, in cognitive abilities in old age is partly a matter of genetics, but other factors are important, too (Reynolds et al., 2005). For example, long term use of tobacco or alcohol is associated with reductions in the speed and accuracy of thinking among the elderly, and with reductions in IQ scores (Glass et al., 2006). The risk of cognitive decline is much lower for people who are healthy and psychologically flexible; who eat a healthy diet, have a high level of education, income, and occupation; and who live in an intellectually stimulating environment with mentally able spouses or companions (Albert et al., 1995; Morris et al., 2006; Shimamura et al., 1995). Scientists speculate that years of education and/or working at complex jobs multiplies connections among brain regions and creates "cognitive reserves" that can be drawn upon in old age (Milgram et al., 2006; Springer et al., 2005). Continued mental exercise—such as doing puzzles, painting, and talking to intelligent friends—also helps older adults continue to think and remember effectively and creatively (Verghese et al., 2003). Practice at memory and other information-processing tasks may even lead to some improvement in skills impaired by old age and disuse (Erickson et al., 2007; Kramer & Willis, 2002; Rapp, Brenes, & Marsh, 2002). Continued physical exercise helps, too. A lifetime of fitness through dancing or other forms of aerobic exercise has been associated with better maintenance of skills on a variety of mental tasks, including reaction time, reasoning, and divided attention (Abbott et al., 2004; Colcombe & Kramer, 2003; McAuley, Kramer, & Colcombe, 2004; Tabbarah, Crimmins, & Seeman, 2002; Weuve et al., 2004).

In short, a lifestyle with organized activities and the opportunity to interact with a variety of individuals—not just family members—seems to provide the best environment for preventing decline in communication abilities (Keller-Cohen et al., 2004). Having a positive attitude can also be important. People who believe that they can keep their memories sharp are more likely to use mnemonic strategies (described in the memory chapter) that help them to do just that (Lachman & Andreoletti, 2006). The effect of positive expectations has been demonstrated in the laboratory, where memory performance was better among older adults who were tested after first being exposed to positive words (such *as accomplished, alert, knowledgeable,* and *successful*) rather than to negative words, such as *confused, feeble, forgot,* and *senile* (Hess, Hinson, & Statham, 2004).

The greatest threat to cognitive abilities in late adulthood is *Alzheimer's disease,* which strikes 3 percent of the world's population by age seventy-five. As the disease runs its course, its victims become emotionally flat, then disoriented, and then mentally vacant. They usually die prematurely. The average duration of the disease, from onset to death, is seven years. But the age of onset and rate of deterioration depend on a number of factors, such as intelligence (Fritsch et al., 2005; Rentz et al., 2004), gender (Molsa, Marttila, & Rinne, 1995), and education (Mortimer, Snowdon, & Markesbery, 2003). Highly intelligent people show clinical signs of Alzheimer's later than the general population. Women and well-educated people of either gender deteriorate more slowly.

One study of the risk factors for Alzheimer's disease focused on a group of nuns from the School Sisters of Notre Dame. When they took their vows, at ages ranging from eighteen to thirty-two, these women had written autobiographies. Years later, when they were seventy-five to ninety-five years old, they were given cognitive tests, and they gave permission for their brains to be examined after death. The Nun Study found that the women whose autobiographies indicated more limited language abilities did less well on the cognitive tests, were more likely to develop

Staying Alert, Staying Active, Staying Alive Sisters Alcantara, Claverine, and Nicolette of the School Sisters of Notre Dame convent were in their eighties or nineties when this photo was taken. They stayed alert by reading, solving puzzles, playing cards, and participating in vocabulary quizzes. The nuns at this convent are participating in a study of aging and the brain.

Alzheimer's, and died at younger ages than those with richer linguistic abilities (Kemper et al., 2001). Similar findings appeared in a Scottish study of mental ability in childhood and dementia in late adulthood (Whalley et al., 2000). These results suggest that the seeds of Alzheimer's disease may be planted early in life, even though it may not appear for many decades. Genetic influences are certainly involved (Driscoll, McDaniel, & Guynn, 2005).

● Social Changes

In adulthood, people develop new relationships, assume new positions, and take on new roles. These changes do not come in neat, predictable stages but instead follow various paths, depending on each individual's experiences (Lieberman, 1996). Transitions—such as divorcing, getting fired from a job, going back to school, remarrying, losing a spouse to death, being hospitalized, getting arrested, or retiring—are turning points that can redirect a person's life path and lead to changes in personality (Caspi & Shiner, 2006; Roberts, Helson, & Klohnen, 2002).

● Early Adulthood: Work, Marriage, Parenthood
Men and women in industrialized cultures typically enter the adult world in their mid to late twenties. At the beginning of this period, about 20 percent of young adults are still really emerging adults who live with their parents, and just under half are still financially dependent (Cohen et al., 2003). Gradually, they become more conscientious, organized, disciplined, and able to plan, as they decide on an occupation, or at least take a job, and become preoccupied with their careers (Srivastava et al., 2003). They also become more controlled and confident; more socially dominant, conscientious, and emotionally stable; and less angry and alienated (Roberts et al., 2001, 2006).

Young adults become more concerned with matters of romantic love (Whitbourne et al., 1992). Having reached the sixth of Erikson's stages of psychosocial development noted in Table 12.2 (intimacy versus isolation), they begin to focus on forming mature, committed relationships based on sexual intimacy, friendship, or mutual intellectual stimulation. The nature of these relationships is predictable in part from the nature of the person's earlier relations with parents, including the attachment pattern that developed in infancy (Birnbaum et al., 2006; Roisman, 2007; Treboux, Crowell, & Waters, 2004). Young adults whose view of relationships reflects a secure attachment tend to feel valued and worthy of support and affection. They develop closeness easily and have relationships characterized by joy, trust, and commitment. If their view reflects an insecure attachment, however, they tend to be preoccupied with relationships and may feel misunderstood, underappreciated, and worried about being abandoned. Their relationships are often negative, obsessive, and promiscuous. Overall, young adults whose parents have been accepting and supportive tend to develop warm and supportive romantic relationships (Conger et al., 2000). Age also can help people develop loving relationships: During their thirties, most individuals become more agreeable—warm, generous, and helpful (Srivastava et al., 2003). People who are married report the greatest sense of happiness, or well-being, followed by unmarried partners who live together, people in steady relationships, and those in casual relationships. People who have no partners report the lowest levels of happiness, self-esteem, and life satisfaction (Kamp Dush & Amato, 2005) .

For many young adults, the experience of becoming parents represents entry into a major new developmental phase that is accompanied by personal, social, and occupational changes (Palkovitz, Copes, & Woolfolk, 2001). This milestone is usually reached earlier for young adults from lower-income backgrounds, who are more likely to be in full-time employment and less likely to be living at home (Cohen et al., 2003). Often, satisfaction with the marriage or partnership declines once a baby is born (Belsky & Kelly, 1994). Young mothers may experience particular dissatisfaction, especially if parenthood fails to meet their expectations, if they resent the constraints that infants bring, if they see their careers as important, if the infants are temperamentally difficult, if the partnerships are not strong, and if the partners are not supportive (Harwood, McLean, & Durkin, 2007; Shapiro, Gottman, & Carrere, 2000). When the father does not do his share of child care, both mothers and fathers are dissatisfied (Levy-Shiff, 1994). The ability of young parents to provide adequate care for their babies is related to their own attachment histories. New mothers whose attachments to their own mothers were secure tend to be more responsive to their infants, and the infants, in turn, are more likely to develop secure attachments to them (Adam, Gunnar, & Tanaka, 2004; van IJzendoorn, 1995).

The challenges of young adulthood are complicated by the nature of family life today (Halpern, 2005). Forty years ago, about half of North American households consisted of married couples in their twenties and thirties—a breadwinner husband and a homemaker wife—raising at least two children together. This picture now describes only about 10 percent of households (Demo, Allen, & Fine, 2000; Hernandez, 1997). Today, parents are older because young adults are delaying marriage longer and waiting longer to have children. Many are having children without marrying. About 75 percent of African American women become single mothers, and 11 percent of European American college-educated women in their thirties are also choosing single motherhood, a dramatic increase over past decades (Weinraub, Horvath, & Gringlas, 2002). Most of these women become pregnant "the old-fashioned way," but some are taking advantage of technological advances that allow them to conceive through *in vitro fertilization* (Hahn & DiPietro, 2001). Many gay men and lesbians are becoming parents, too. Recent estimates suggest that at least four million families in the United States are headed by openly gay or lesbian adults who became parents by retaining custody of children born in a previous heterosexual marriage, by adopting a child, or by having a child through artificial insemination or surrogacy (Patterson, 2002). Young adult homosexuals face special challenges in making the transition to parenthood. Many of them confront discrimination by health care organizations and employer policies that do not recognize their parental role. They may also experience pervasive hostility, even from members of their own extended families.

Whether they are homosexual or heterosexual, the 60 percent of mothers who hold full-time jobs outside the home often find that the demands of children and career pull them in opposite directions. Devotion to their jobs leaves many of these mothers feeling guilty about spending too little time with their children (Booth et al., 2002), but placing too much emphasis on home life may reduce their productivity at work and threaten their advancement. This stressful balancing act can lead to anxiety, frustration, and conflicts at home and on the job. It affects fathers, too. The husbands of employed women are more involved in child care (Booth et al., 2002), and their contributions to housework have doubled since 1970 (Coltrane, 2001). They can be effective caregivers (Parke, 2002), but mothers still do most of the child care and housework (U.S. Bureau of Labor Statistics, 2004). Research indicates that gay and lesbian parents share duties more equally—and are more satisfied with the division of labor—than is typically the case in heterosexual families (Patterson, 2002).

Nearly half of all marriages in the United States end in divorce (National Center for Health Statistics, 2001), creating yet another set of challenges for adults (Clarke-Stewart & Brentano, 2006). Although it frees people from bad relationships, divorce can leave them feeling anxious, guilty, incompetent, depressed, and lonely. Divorce is also correlated with health problems and, ultimately, with earlier mortality. Often, divorce creates new stressors, including money problems, changes in living circumstances and working hours, and, for custodial parents, a dramatic increase in housework and child-care tasks. One study found that, two years after divorcing, most women were happier than they were during the final year of their marriage but more distressed than were mothers in two-parent families (Hetherington & Stanley-Hagan, 2002). How effectively divorced people deal with these stressors depends on many factors, such as social support, their general

The "Sandwich" Generation During their midlife transition, many people feel "sandwiched" between generations— pressured by the social, emotional, and financial needs of their children on one side and of their aging parents on the other.

psychological stability and coping skills, their ability to form new relationships, and whether or not they remain in conflict with their ex-spouses.

In short, the changes seen in families and family life over the past several decades have made it more challenging than ever to successfully navigate the years of early adulthood.

● Middle Adulthood: Reappraising Priorities

At around age forty, people go through a **midlife transition,** during which they may reappraise and modify their lives and relationships. Many feel invigorated and liberated; some may feel upset and have a "midlife crisis." The contrast between youth and middle age may be especially upsetting for men who matured early in adolescence and were sociable and athletic rather than intellectual (Block, 1971). Women who chose a career over a family now hear the biological clock ticking out their last childbearing years. Women who have had children, however, become more independent and confident and more oriented toward achievement and events outside the family (Helson & Moane, 1987). For both men and women, the emerging sexuality of their teenage children, the emptiness of the nest as children leave home, or the declining health of a parent may precipitate a crisis.

Following the midlife transition, the middle years of adulthood are often a time of satisfaction, happiness, and other positive emotions as people enjoy a wide variety of leisure activities, including just spending time with the family (Mroczek & Spiro, 2005; Taylor, 2001). Many people become concerned with producing something that will outlast them—usually through parenthood or job achievements. Erikson called this concern the crisis of **generativity,** because people begin to focus on producing or generating something. If they do not resolve this crisis, he suggested, people stagnate. Research shows that after the age of forty people are indeed more likely than before to strive for generativity goals (Sheldon & Kasser, 2001; Zucker, Ostrove, & Stewart, 2002). These might include writing a book, helping those in need, developing closer relationships with children and being a good role model for them, and trying to make a lasting contribution to society.

In their fifties, most people become grandparents (Smith & Drew, 2002). This new status often amazes them. For example, a survey of professionals in their fifties found that they could not quite believe they were no longer young (Karp, 1991).

midlife transition A point at around age forty when adults take stock of their lives.

generativity Adult concerns about producing or generating something.

Most described themselves as healthy but acknowledged that their bodies were slowing down. At this age, spending time caring for young grandchildren can be stressful. One study found that grandmothers who spent more time providing care for their grandchildren were at increased risk of coronary heart disease (Lee, Colditz, et al., 2003). Caring for grown children can be stressful, too. Most people in their sixties want their children to be independent and perhaps even ready to support their parents, if necessary. They may have mixed feelings toward adult children who still need financial support (Pillemer & Suitor, 2002). Overall, the degree of happiness and healthiness people experience during middle adulthood depends on how much control they feel they have over their work, finances, marriage, children, and sex life, as well as how many years of education they completed and what kind of job they have (Azar, 1996).

● **Late Adulthood: Retirement and Restriction** Even when they are sixty-five to seventy-five, most people think of themselves as middle-aged, not old (Neugarten, 1977). They are active and influential politically and socially; they often are physically vigorous. Ratings of life satisfaction, well-being, and self-esteem are, on average, as high in old age as during any other period of adulthood (Ben-Zur, 2002; Hamarat et al., 2002; Sheldon & Kasser, 2001). Those who experienced abundant parental support during childhood are particularly likely to have good physical and mental health in late adulthood (Shaw et al., 2004).

This is the time when men and women usually retire from their jobs, but research shows that many people underestimate older people's ability and willingness to work (Clay, 1996). This misperception was once translated into laws that forced workers in the United States to retire at sixty-five regardless of their abilities. Thanks to changes in those laws, most people can now continue working as long as they wish. Being forced to retire can result in psychological and physical problems. In one study of cardiovascular disease, men who retired involuntarily were found to be more depressed, less healthy, and less well-adjusted than those who retired voluntarily (Clay, 1996). Such problems may also occur when husbands retire before their wives do (Rubin, 1998). Men tend to view retirement as a time to wind down, whereas women see it as a time to try new things, to reinvent themselves (Helgesen, 1998). In one study that followed people from childhood through adulthood, researchers found that when previously employed women reached their seventies, they were more active and more concerned about maintaining their independence and continuing their achievements than women who had been homemakers. They were also happier, as well as less depressed and anxious (Holahan, 1994). In general, it seems, retirees are more likely to be satisfied with their lives than people who continue to work through their sixties and seventies (Moen et al., 2000).

More people than ever are reaching old age. In fact, people over seventy-five make up the fastest-growing segment of the population. This group is twenty-five-times larger today than it was a hundred years ago. There are also about 77,000 people in the United States who are older than one hundred, and the Census Bureau predicts that this number will rise to 834,000 by 2050 (Volz, 2000). Old age is not necessarily a time of loneliness and desolation, but it is a time when people generally become more inward looking, cautious, and conforming (Reedy, 1983). It is a time when people develop coping strategies that increasingly take into account the limits of their control—accepting chronic health problems and other things they cannot change (Brandtstadter & Renner, 1990). One such coping strategy is to direct attention to positive thoughts, activities, and memories (Charles, Mather, & Carstensen, 2003; Mather et al., 2004). In fact, when older adults are asked to look at pictures of faces portraying sadness, anger, fear, and happiness, they spend more time looking at the happy faces than the angry ones; college-age students look longer at fearful faces (Isaacowitz et al., 2006).

In old age, people interact with others less frequently, but they enjoy their interactions more (Carstensen, 1997). They find relationships more satisfying, supportive,

Still on a Roll At the age of eighty, actor and race car driver Paul Newman remains a famous example of the many people whose late adulthood is healthy and vigorous. In January 2000, Newman received bruised ribs in a minor accident while preparing to drive his race car in the 24 Hours of Daytona. He was racing again the following month, and he is still racing today.

in review — Milestones of Adolescence and Adulthood

Age	Physical Changes	Cognitive Changes	Social Events and Psychological Changes
Early adolescence (11–15 years)	Puberty brings reproductive capacity and marked bodily changes.	Formal operations and principled moral reasoning become possible for the first time. (This occurs only for some people.)	Social and emotional changes result from growing sexual awareness; adolescents experience mood swings, physical changes, and conflicts with parents.
Late adolescence (16–19 years)	Physical growth continues.	Formal operations and principled moral reasoning become more likely.	An identity crisis accompanies graduation from high school.
Early adulthood (20–39 years)	Physical growth continues.	Increases continue in knowledge, problem-solving ability, and moral reasoning.	People choose a job and often a mate; they may become parents.
Middle adulthood (40–65 years)	Size and muscle mass decrease; fat increases; eyesight declines; reproductive capacity in women ends.	Thought becomes more complex, adaptive, and global.	Midlife transition may lead to change; for most, the middle years are satisfying.
Late adulthood (over 65 years)	Size decreases; organs become less efficient.	Reasoning, mathematical ability, comprehension, novel problem solving, and memory may decline.	Retirement requires adjustments; people look inward; awareness of death precipitates life review.

and fulfilling than they did earlier in life. As they sense that time is running out, they value positive interactions and become selective about their social partners. During the last twenty years of their lives, people gradually restrict their social network to loved ones. As long as there are at least three close friends or relatives in their network, they tend to be content.

The many changes associated with adolescence and adulthood are summarized in "In Review: Milestones of Adolescence and Adulthood."

● Death and Dying

In old age, people become increasingly aware that death is approaching. They watch as their friends disappear. They feel their health deteriorating, their strength waning, and their intellectual capabilities declining. A few years or a few months before death, some people experience a sharp decline in mental functioning known as **terminal drop** (Wilson et al., 2007).

The awareness of impending death brings about the last psychological crisis, according to Erikson's theory, in which people evaluate their lives and accomplishments and affirm them as meaningful (leading to a feeling of integrity) or meaningless (leading to a feeling of despair). People at this stage tend to become more philosophical and reflective. They attempt to put their lives into perspective. They reminisce, resolve past conflicts, and integrate past events. They may also become more interested in the religious and spiritual side of life. This "life review" may trigger anxiety, regret, guilt, and despair, or it may allow people to face their own deaths and the deaths of friends and relatives with a feeling of peace and acceptance (Lieberman & Tobin, 1983).

Even the actual confrontation with death does not have to bring despair and depression. People generally want to be told if they are dying (Hinton, 1967). When

● **terminal drop**   A sharp decline in mental functioning that tends to occur in late adulthood, a few years or months before death.

death finally is imminent, old people strive for a death with dignity, love, affection, physical contact, and no pain (Schulz, 1978). As they think about death, they are comforted by their religious faith, their achievements, and the love of their friends and family (Kastenbaum, Kastenbaum, & Morris, 1989).

● Developmental Trajectories

The life-span development we have described is a bit like the flight of an airplane, beginning with a takeoff, cruising along for a while, and eventually entering its final descent. Like aircraft bound for differing destinations, the flight path, or trajectory, of our lives can be long or short, reach high or low altitudes, and be bumpy or smooth. There may be midcourse corrections during flight, of course, but researchers who have tracked developmental trajectories find a remarkable degree of stability from childhood through adulthood on many dimensions. For example, people who are intelligent and have good memories, who are good with numbers or poor at languages, tend to retain these advantages or disadvantages throughout their lifetimes (e.g., Anstey, Hofer, & Luszcz, 2003; Chodosh et al., 2002). There are also consistencies in personality and social development (Roberts et al., 2001, 2002; Shiner, Masten, & Roberts, 2003). Children who are creative, persistent, enthusiastic about their activities, and motivated to achieve are likely to become adults who take pleasure in their pursuits, enjoy challenges, work hard to succeed, and become effective leaders who handle stress well. Children who take their schoolwork seriously and finish their homework promptly are likely to become adults who are traditional in their views, who plan well, and who are not apt to take risks. Children who exhibit early social competence tend to have good romantic relationships and strong friendships as adults (Shiner et al., 2003). In contrast, highly aggressive children are likely to become antisocial adults (Schaeffer et al., 2003), to develop academic problems in adolescence, and to become more anxious and depressed as young adults, as one kind of problem cascades into the next (Masten et al., 2005). Adolescents who do well in school and have friends and social skills are more successful in work and romance in adulthood (Roisman et al., 2004). In other words, people tend to stay on relatively consistent developmental paths throughout their lives.

● Longevity: The Length of Life

The length of life's trajectory depends on a number of factors. Researchers have discovered, for example, that longevity is greater in women and in people without histories of heavy drinking, smoking, or heart problems. It is also related to personality characteristics such as conscientiousness as a child (Friedman et al., 1995a) and curiosity as an adult (Swan & Carmelli, 1996). People with higher IQ scores and faster reaction times (Deary & Der, 2005) live longer, as do those who experienced more happiness, enthusiasm, contentment, and other forms of *positive affect* during adulthood (Cohen & Pressman, 2006; Pressman & Cohen, 2007).

In fact, adults who had more positive self-perceptions when they were in their fifties and sixties lived seven and a half years longer than those with less positive self-perceptions. This factor was more predictive of longevity than health problems such as high blood pressure, high cholesterol, smoking, lack of exercise, or being overweight (Levy et al., 2002). A network of good friends, even more than close family ties, is also related to longer life (Giles et al., 2005). However, the secret of extreme longevity—one hundred years or more—may lie in a group of genes on chromosome 4 that appears to somehow slow the aging process (Puca et al., 2001).

Older adults can be helped to feel better physically and psychologically if they continue to be socially active and useful. For example, old people who are given parties, plants, or pets are happier and more alert than those who receive less attention, and they do not die as soon (Clark et al., 2001). People who restrict their caloric intake, engage in regular physical and mental exercise, and have a sense of control over important aspects of their lives are also likely to live longer (Krause & Shaw, 2000; Manini et al., 2006; Yaffe et al., 2001). So eat your veggies, stay physically fit, and continue to think actively—not just to live longer later, but to live better now.

LINKAGES

As noted in the chapter on introducing psychology, all of psychology's many subfields are related to one another. Our discussion of infantile amnesia illustrates just one way in which the topic of this chapter, human development, is linked to the subfield of memory (which is the focus of the memory chapter). The Linkages diagram shows ties to two other subfields as well, and there are many more ties throughout the book. Looking for linkages among subfields will help you see how they all fit together and help you better appreciate the big picture that is psychology.

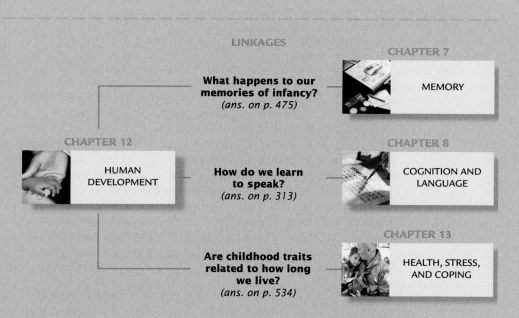

SUMMARY

Developmental psychology is the study of the course and causes of age-related changes in mental abilities, social relationships, emotions, and moral understanding over the life span.

Exploring Human Development

A central question in developmental psychology concerns the relative influences of nature and nurture, a theme that has its origins in the philosophies of John Locke and Jean-Jacques Rousseau. In the twentieth century, Arnold Gesell stressed nature in his theory of development, proposing that development is *maturation*—the natural unfolding of abilities with age. John B. Watson took the opposite view, claiming that development is learning—shaped by the external environment. In his theory of cognitive development, Jean Piaget described how nature and nurture work together. Today we accept the notion that both nature and nurture affect development and ask how and to what extent each contributes.

Beginnings

Prenatal Development Development begins with the union of an ovum and a sperm to form a *zygote*, which becomes an *embryo*. The embryonic stage is a *critical period* for development, a time when certain organs must develop properly or they

never will. Development of organs at this stage is irrevocably affected by harmful *teratogens*, such as drugs and alcohol. After the embryo develops into a *fetus*, adverse conditions during the fetal stage may harm the infant's size, behavior, intelligence, or health. Babies born to women who drink heavily have a strong chance of suffering from *fetal alcohol syndrome*.

The Newborn Newborns have limited but effective senses of vision, hearing, taste, and smell. They exhibit many reflexes, which are swift, automatic responses to external stimuli. Motor development proceeds as the nervous system matures, muscles grow, and the infant experiments with and selects the most efficient movement patterns.

Infancy and Childhood: Cognitive Development

Cognitive development includes the development of thinking, knowing, and remembering.

Changes in the Brain The development of increasingly complex and efficient neural networks in various regions of the brain provides the "hardware" for the increasingly complex cognitive abilities that arise during infancy and childhood.

The Development of Knowledge: Piaget's Theory

According to Piaget, cognitive development occurs in a fixed sequence of stages, as *schemas* are modified through the complementary processes of *assimilation* (fitting new objects or events into existing schemas) and *accommodation* (changing schemas when new objects will not fit existing ones). During the *sensorimotor period*, infants progress from using only simple senses and reflexes to forming mental representations of objects and actions. Thus the child becomes capable of thinking about objects that are not present. The ability to recognize that objects continue to exist even when they are hidden from view is what Piaget called *object permanence*. During the *preoperational period*, children can use symbols, but they do not have the ability to think logically and rationally. Their understanding of the world is intuitive and egocentric. They do not understand the logical operations of reversibility or complementarity. When children develop the ability to think logically about concrete objects, they enter the period of *concrete operations*. At this time they can solve simple problems. They also have an understanding of *conservation*, recognizing that, for example, the amount of a substance is not altered even when its shape changes. The *formal operational period* begins in adolescence and allows a wide range of complex executive functions, including planning, imagining consequences, and thinking logically about abstract ideas.

Modifying Piaget's Theory

Recent research reveals that Piaget underestimated infants' mental abilities. Developmental psychologists now also believe that new levels of cognition are reached not in sharply marked stages of global understanding but more gradually, and in specific areas. Children's reasoning is affected by factors such as task difficulty and degree of familiarity with the objects and language involved.

Information Processing During Childhood

Psychologists who explain cognitive development in terms of information processing have documented age-related improvements in children's attention, their abilities to explore and focus on features of the environment, and their memories.

Culture and Cognitive Development

The specific content of cognitive development, including the development of scripts, depends on the cultural context in which children live.

Improving or Endangering Cognitive Development

How fast children develop cognitive abilities depends to a certain extent on how stimulating and supportive their environments are. Children growing up in poverty are likely to have delayed or impaired cognitive abilities.

Infancy and Childhood: Social and Emotional Development

Infants and their caregivers, from the early months, respond to each other's emotional expressions. When an infant's behavior in an ambiguous situation is affected by the caregiver's emotional expression, social referencing is said to have occurred.

Individual Temperament

Most infants can be classified as having easy, difficult, or slow-to-warm-up *temperaments*. Whether they retain these temperamental styles depends to some extent on their parents' expectations and demands.

The Infant Grows Attached

Over the first year of life, infants form a deep and abiding emotional *attachment* to their mothers or other primary caregivers. This attachment may be secure or insecure.

Relationships with Parents

Parents teach their children the skills and rules needed in their culture using various parenting styles. They can be described as *authoritarian*, *permissive*, *authoritative*, or *uninvolved parents*. Among European and European American parents, those with an authoritative style tend to have more competent and cooperative children. However, parenting styles and their impact depend to some extent upon the culture and conditions in which parents find themselves.

Peer Friendships and Popularity

Over the childhood years, interactions with peers evolve into cooperative and competitive encounters, and friendships become more important.

Social Skills and Understanding

Children become increasingly able to interpret and understand social situations and emotional signals. They begin to express empathy and sympathy and to engage in the *self-regulation* of their emotions and behaviors. They also learn social rules and roles.

Gender Roles

Children develop *gender roles* that are based both on biological differences between the sexes and on implicit and explicit socialization by parents, teachers, peers, and the media. Children are also influenced by *gender schemas*, which affect their choices of activities and toys.

Risk and Resilience

Children who lead successful lives despite such adversities as family instability, child abuse, homelessness, poverty, or war are described as having *resilience*. Factors associated with this characteristic include good intellectual functioning and strong relationships with caring adults.

Adolescence

Adolescents undergo significant changes not only in size, shape, and physical capacity but also, typically, in their social lives, reasoning abilities, and views of themselves.

Changes in Body, Brain, and Thinking

Puberty brings about physical changes that lead to psychological changes. Changes in the brain alter the ways adolescents think. Specifically, they develop the capacity for formal operational thought and the ability to control their own thinking.

Adolescent Feelings and Behavior

Early adolescence is a period of shaky self-esteem. It is also a time when conflict with parents, as well as closeness with and conformity to friends, is likely to rise. A particularly difficult challenge for adolescents is the transition from elementary school to junior high or middle school.

Identity and Development of the Self Late adolescence focuses on finding an answer to the question, Who am I? Adolescents begin to develop an integrated self-image as a unique person, an image that often includes *ethnic identity*.

Moral Reasoning Principled moral judgment—shaped by gender and culture—becomes possible for the first time in adolescence. The development of moral reasoning may progress through *preconventional, conventional,* and *postconventional moral reasoning* stages. A person's moral reasoning may be reflected in moral action.

Emerging Adulthood Going to college challenges the emerging adult's self-concept, precipitating an *identity crisis*. Resolving this identity crisis and choosing a career direction are two major tasks in this stage of life.

Adulthood

Physical, cognitive, and social changes occur throughout adulthood.

Physical Changes Middle adulthood sees changes that include decreased acuity of the senses, increased risk of heart disease, and the end of fertility (*menopause*). Nevertheless, major health problems may not appear until late adulthood.

Cognitive Changes The cognitive changes that occur in early and middle adulthood are generally positive, including improvements in reasoning and problem-solving ability. In late adulthood, some intellectual abilities decline—especially those involved in tasks that are unfamiliar, complex, or difficult. Other abilities, such as recalling facts or making wise decisions, tend not to decline. Individuals with Alzheimer's disease become disoriented and mentally vacant, and they die prematurely.

Social Changes In their twenties, young adults make occupational choices and form intimate commitments. In middle adulthood they become concerned with *generativity*—with producing something that will outlast them. Sometime around age forty, adults experience a *midlife transition*, which may or may not be a crisis. The forties and fifties are often a time of satisfaction. In their sixties, people contend with retirement. They generally become more inward looking, cautious, and conforming. Adults' progress through these ages is influenced by the unique personal events that befall them.

Death and Dying In their seventies and eighties, people confront their own mortality. They may become more philosophical and reflective as they review their lives. A few years or months before death, some individuals experience a sharp decline in mental functioning known as *terminal drop*. They strive for a death with dignity, love, and no pain.

Developmental Trajectories Researchers who have tracked developmental trajectories have found stability from childhood through adulthood in terms of cognitive abilities, personality characteristics, and social skills.

Longevity: The Length of Life Death is inevitable, but certain factors—including healthy diets, exercise, personality traits such as conscientiousness and curiosity, a sense of control over one's life, and genetics—are associated with living longer and happier lives. Older adults feel better and live longer if they receive attention from other people, maintain an open attitude toward new experiences, and keep their minds active.

Health, Stress, and Coping

13

How long will you live? To some extent, the answer lies in your genes, but it is also affected by how you behave, how you think, and what stressors you face. In this chapter, you will learn about several kinds of stressors, how people respond to them, and the relationship between stress reactions and illness. You'll also discover what you can do to protect your own health. We've organized the material as follows:

Twenty-five years ago, acquired immune deficiency syndrome (AIDS) was a rare and puzzling medical condition. Today, it threatens everyone and is one of the major causes of death in the United States (Sepkowitz, 2006). In some African countries, the infection rate among adults from the human immunodeficiency virus (HIV), which causes AIDS, is as high as 20 percent (World Health Organization, 2003). As medical researchers race against time to find a cure for AIDS and a vaccine against HIV, others work to find ways to prolong and improve the lives of people infected with HIV or suffering with AIDS.

In the United States, those infected with HIV can expect to live longer because of new therapies, and indeed, such expectations can be one of many important factors that affect how long AIDS patients live. Geoffrey Reed and his associates asked seventy-four male AIDS patients about the extent to which they had accepted their situation and prepared themselves for the worst (Reed et al., 1994). Some professionals believe that acknowledging the reality of a terminal illness is a psychologically healthy adaptation (e.g., Kübler-Ross, 1975). However, Reed and his associates found that the men who had accepted their situation and prepared themselves for death died an average of nine months earlier than those who had neither accepted nor resigned themselves to their situation. This statistically significant difference is all the more impressive because it cannot be accounted for by differences in the patients' general health status, immune system functioning, or psychological distress. Here is evidence that, compared with those who are "fighters," terminally ill patients who resign themselves to decline and death might actually hasten both, especially if it decreases their motivation to follow the complex medical regimens required to survive (Gifford et al., 2000).

Research such as this has made psychologists and the medical community more aware than ever of psychological factors that can affect health and illness (Ray, 2004). It also reflects the growth of **health psychology**, "a field within psychology devoted to understanding psychological influences on how people stay healthy, why they become ill, and how they respond when they do get ill" (Taylor, 2002, p. 4). Health psychologists use knowledge from many subfields of psychology to enhance understanding of the psychological and behavioral processes associated with health and illness (Smith & Suls, 2004). Their work is part of the broader field of *behavioral medicine*, in which psychologists pursue their health-related goals in cooperation with physicians, nurses, public health workers, and other biomedical specialists. In this chapter we describe some of what has been discovered so far about psychological, social, and behavioral influences on health and how research in health psychology and behavioral medicine is being applied to prevent illness and promote better health. We begin by examining the nature of stressors and people's physical, psychological, and behavioral responses to stress. Then we consider factors that might alter the impact of stressful life events on a person. Next, we consider the psychological factors responsible for specific physical disorders and some behaviors that endanger people's health. We conclude by discussing health psychologists' recommendations for coping with stress and promoting health and some of their programs for doing so.

Health Psychology

health psychology A field in which psychologists conduct and apply research aimed at promoting human health and preventing illness.

Although the field of health psychology is relatively new, the themes underlying it date back to ancient times. For thousands of years, in many cultures around the world, people have believed that their mental state, their behavior, and their health are linked.

Running for Your Life Health psychologists have developed programs to help people increase exercise, stop smoking, eat healthier diets, and make other lifestyle changes that lower their risk of illness and death. They have even helped to ensure community blood supplies by finding ways to make blood donation less stressful (Bonk, France, & Taylor, 2001).

Today, there is scientific evidence to support this belief (Schneiderman, 2004; Antoni & Lutgendorf, 2007). We now know that the stresses of life influence health through their impact on psychological and physiological processes. Researchers have also associated anger, hostility, pessimism, depression, and hopelessness with the appearance of physical illnesses. Traits such as optimism are associated with good health. Similarly, poor health has been linked to behavioral factors such as lack of exercise, inadequate diet, smoking, and abuse of alcohol and other drugs (Freedman et al., 2006; Vollset, Tverdal, & Gjessing, 2006). Good health has been associated with behaviors such as adequate exercise and following medical advice.

Health psychology has become an increasingly important area of research and practice in North America, in part because of changing patterns of illness. Until the middle of the twentieth century, the major causes of illness and death in the United States and Canada were acute infectious diseases, such as influenza, tuberculosis, and pneumonia. With these afflictions now less threatening, chronic illnesses—such as coronary heart disease, cancer, and diabetes—have joined accidents and injuries as the leading causes of disability and death (Guyer et al., 2000). Compared with acute diseases, these modern-day chronic killers tend to develop gradually, and the chances of falling victim to them are substantially affected by psychological, lifestyle, and environmental factors (Taylor, 2002). For example, whether or not a person smokes affects the risk of the five leading causes of death for men and women in the United States (Centers for Disease Control and Prevention, 2001; D'Agostino et al., 2001; see Table 13.1). The psychological and behavioral factors that contribute to these illnesses can be changed by intervention programs such as those that promote nonsmoking, exercise, and healthy eating (e.g., Bazzano et al., 2003; Kraus et al., 2002). In fact, about half the deaths in the United States are due to potentially preventable health-risky behaviors (Greenland et al., 2003; Khot et al., 2003; Mokdad et al., 2004).

Yet as few as 3 percent of people in the United States follow a lifestyle that includes maintaining a healthy weight, getting regular exercise, eating a proper diet, and not smoking (Reeves & Rafferty, 2005). One goal of health psychologists is to help people understand the role they can play in controlling their own health and life expectancy (Nicassio, Meyerowitz, & Kerns, 2004). For example, they have promoted early detection of disease by educating people about the warning signs of cancer, heart disease, and other serious illnesses and encouraging them to seek medical attention while lifesaving treatment is still possible. Health psychologists also study, and help people to understand, the role played by stress in physical health and illness. And clinical health psychologists help individuals cope as effectively as possible with cancer and many other kinds of serious illness.

TABLE 13.1   Lifestyle Behaviors That Affect the Leading Causes of Death in the United States

This table shows five of the leading causes of death in the United States today, along with behavioral factors that contribute to their development (Centers for Disease Control and Prevention, 2001; Jemal et al., 2005).

| Cause of Death | Contributing Behavioral Factor | | | | |
	Alcohol	Smoking	Unhealthy Diet	Inadequate Exercise	Stress
Cancer	X	X	X		?
Heart disease	X	X	X	X	X
Stroke	X	X	X	?	?
Lung disease		X			
Accidents and injury	X	X			X

Source: Data from the Centers for Disease Control and Prevention (2001).

Stress and Stressors

You have probably heard that death and taxes are the only two things you can be sure of in life. If there is a third, it must surely be stress. Stress is basic to life—no matter how wealthy, powerful, attractive, or happy you might be. It comes in many forms—a difficult exam, an automobile accident, waiting in a long line, a day on which everything goes wrong. Mild stress, such as waiting to be with that special person, can be stimulating and motivating, but when circumstances overwhelm our ability to cope with them, the result can be stress that creates physical, psychological, and behavioral problems. In the workplace alone, the impact of stress costs U.S. businesses more than $150 billion each year as a result of employee absenteeism, reduced productivity, and health care costs (Chandola, Brunner, & Marmot, 2006; Schwartz, 2004).

Stress is the negative emotional, cognitive, behavioral, and physiological process that occurs as individuals try to adjust to or deal with stressors. **Stressors,** in turn, are circumstances that disrupt, or threaten to disrupt, individuals' daily functioning and cause people to make adjustments. **Stress reactions** are the physical, psychological, and behavioral responses that occur in the face of stressors (Taylor, 2002). In other words, stress involves a *transaction* between people and their physical and psychological environments. Figure 13.1 lists the main types of stressors and illustrates that when confronted by stressors, people may respond physically (e.g., nausea or fatigue), and psychologically (e.g., anxiety, lack of concentration, or changes in eating habits).

As also shown in Figure 13.1, the transactions between people and their environments can be influenced by *stress mediators*. These mediators include such variables as the extent to which people can predict and control their stressors, how they interpret the threat involved, the amount of social support they perceive as available from family and friends, and their stress-coping skills. (We discuss these mediators in greater detail later.) Mediating factors can either minimize or magnify a stressor's impact. In other words, stress is not a specific event, but an ever-changing *process* in which the nature and intensity of our responses depend not only on what stressors occur, but also on how we think about them, the coping skills we have, and the resources we perceive to be available.

For humans, many stressors have both physical and psychological components. Students, for example, are challenged by psychological demands to do well in their courses, as well as by the physical fatigue that can result from a heavy load of classes, combined perhaps with a job and family responsibilities. Similarly, for victims of arthritis, AIDS, and other chronic illnesses, pain and fatigue are accompanied by worry and other forms of psychological distress. Here, we focus on psychological stressors, which can stimulate some of the same physiological responses as physical stressors (Cacioppo et al., 1995).

● Psychological Stressors

Any event that forces people to accommodate or change can be a psychological stressor. Accordingly, even pleasant events can be stressful. The increased salary and status associated with a promotion may be desirable, but the upgrade usually brings new pressures as well. Similarly, joyful events such as marriage or the birth of a child can be stressful because they require people to adjust to new circumstances and responsibilities. Still, it is typically negative events that have the most adverse psychological and physical effects (Kiecolt-Glaser et al., 2005). These circumstances include catastrophic events, life changes and strains, chronic and acute stressors, and daily hassles.

● **stress** The process of adjusting to circumstances that disrupt, or threaten to disrupt, a person's equilibrium.

● **stressor** An event or situation to which people must adjust.

● **stress reaction** The physical, psychological, and behavioral response that occurs in the face of a stressor.

FIGURE 13.1

The Process of Stress

Stressful events, stress reactions, and stress mediators are all important components of the stress process. Notice that the process involves many two-way relationships. For example, if a person has effective coping skills, stress responses will be less severe. Having milder stress responses can act as a "reward" that strengthens those skills. Further, as coping skills (such as refusing unreasonable demands) improve, certain stressors (such as a boss's unreasonable demands) may become less frequent.

Stressors	**Stress mediators**	**Stress responses**
Life changes and strains	Cognitive appraisal	Physical
Catastrophic events	Predictability	Psychological
Acute stressors	Control	▪ Emotional
Daily hassles	Coping resources and methods	▪ Cognitive
Chronic stressors	Social support	▪ Behavioral

Catastrophic events are sudden, unexpected, potentially life-threatening experiences or traumas, such as physical or sexual assault, military combat, natural disasters, terrorist attacks, and accidents. *Life changes* and *strains* include divorce, illness in the family, difficulties at work, and other circumstances that create demands to which people must adjust (see Table 13.2). *Chronic stressors*—those that continue over a long period of time—include circumstances such as living near a noisy airport or in a high-crime neighborhood, having a serious illness, being unable to earn a decent living, being the victim of discrimination, and even enduring years of academic pressure. *Acute stressors* include painful medical procedures, difficult job interviews, or other disruptive but short-term events. *Daily hassles* are irritations, pressures, and annoyances that might not be significant stressors by themselves but whose cumulative effects can be significant (Almeida, 2005; Evans & Wener, 2006).

● Measuring Stressors

Which stressors are most harmful? To study stress more precisely, psychologists have tried to measure the impact of particular stressors. In 1967, Thomas Holmes and Richard Rahe (pronounced "ray") made a pioneering effort to find a standard way of measuring the stress in a person's life. Working on the assumption that all

Coping with Catastrophe
Catastrophic events such as explosions, hurricanes, plane crashes, school shootings, and other traumas are stressors that can be psychologically devastating for victims, their families, and rescue workers. As was the case in the wake of the 2005 terrorist attacks on the London transit system, health psychologists and other professionals provide on-the-spot counseling and follow-up sessions to help people deal with the consequences of trauma.

TABLE **13.2**   **The Undergraduate Stress Questionnaire**

Here are some items from the Undergraduate Stress Questionnaire, which asks students to indicate whether various stressors have occurred during the previous week (Crandall, Preisler, & Aussprung, 1992).	Has this stressful event happened to you at any time during the last week? If it has, please check the space next to it. If it has not, please leave it blank.

_____ 1. Assignments in all classes due the same day

_____ 2. Having roommate conflicts

_____ 3. Lack of money

_____ 4. Trying to decide on a major

_____ 5. Can't understand your professor

_____ 6. Stayed up late writing a paper

_____ 7. Sat through a boring class

_____ 8. Went into a test unprepared

_____ 9. Parents getting divorced

_____ 10. Incompetence at the registrar's office

change, positive or negative, is stressful, they asked a large number of people to rate—in terms of *life change units* (LCUs)—the amount of change and demand for adjustment associated with events such as divorcing, being fired, retiring, losing a loved one, or becoming pregnant. (Getting married, the event against which raters were told to compare all other stressors, came in as slightly more stressful than losing one's job.) On the basis of these ratings, Holmes and Rahe created the *Social Readjustment Rating Scale*, or *SRRS*. People taking the SRRS receive a stress score equal to the sum of the LCUs for the events they have recently experienced (Holmes & Rahe, 1967).

Numerous studies show that people scoring high on the SRRS and other life-change scales are more likely to suffer physical or mental disorders than those with

A Daily Hassle   Relatively minor daily hassles can combine to create significant physical and psychological stress responses. The frustrations of daily commuting in heavy traffic, for example, can become so intense for some drivers that they may display a pattern of anger and aggression called "road rage." Between 1990 and 1996, more than 10,000 road-rage incidents in the United States alone resulted in 218 deaths and 12,610 injuries (Rathbone & Huckabee, 1999).

lower scores (e.g., Monroe, Thase, & Simons, 1992). Other researchers questioned, though, whether life changes alone can tell the whole story about the effects of stressors because those changes are only one aspect of the total stress process. Some of those researchers developed scales, such as the *Life Experiences Survey*, or *LES* (Sarason, Johnson, & Siegel, 1978), that go beyond the SRRS to measure not just life events, but also people's perceptions, or cognitive appraisal, of how positive or negative the events were, how controllable they were, and how well they were able to cope with the events. This information is particularly important for understanding the impact of life experiences that may have different meanings to different individuals. For example, a woman eager to have a child is likely to see pregnancy as a blessing, but for someone who doesn't want a baby, or can't afford the costs, a positive pregnancy test can be a disaster.

The LES also gives respondents the opportunity to write in and rate any stressors they have experienced that are not on the printed list. This personalized approach is particularly valuable for capturing the differing impact and meaning that experiences may have for men compared with women and for individuals from various cultural or subcultural groups. Divorce, for example, may have very different meanings to people of different religious or cultural backgrounds. Similarly, members of certain ethnic groups are likely to experience stressors—such as prejudice and discrimination—that are not felt by other groups (Lewis et al., 2006; Matthews et al., 2005; Merritt et al., 2006).

Still other researchers have measured stressors and their impact via face-to-face interviews (e.g., Dohrenwend et al., 1993). Different measures yield somewhat differing results (McQuaid et al., 2000; Steffen et al., 2003), but as you might expect, they generally show that events perceived as negative have a stronger negative impact on health than do those that are perceived as positive (De Benedittis, Lornenzetti, & Pieri, 1990).

Stress Responses

Physical and psychological responses to stress often occur together, especially as stressors become more intense. Furthermore, one type of stress response can set off other types. For example, a physical stress response—such as mild chest pain—may lead to the psychological stress response of worrying about having a heart attack. Still, it is useful to consider each category of stress responses one at a time.

● Physical Responses

If you have ever experienced a near accident or some other sudden, frightening event, you know that the acute physical responses to stressors include rapid breathing, increased heartbeat, sweating, and, a little later, shakiness. These reactions are part of a general pattern known as the *fight-or-flight syndrome*. As described in the chapters on biological aspects of psychology and on motivation and emotion, this syndrome prepares the body to face or to flee an immediate threat. When the danger has passed, fight-or-flight responses subside (Gump et al., 2005). However, when stressors are long lasting, these acute responses are only the beginning of a longer sequence of physical and psychological reactions.

●**The General Adaptation Syndrome** Careful observation of humans and other animals led Hans Selye (pronounced "SELL-yay") to suggest that the sequence of physical responses to stress occurs in a consistent pattern and is triggered by the effort to adapt to any stressor. Selye called this sequence the **general adaptation syndrome**, or **GAS** (Selye, 1976). The GAS has three stages, as shown in Figure 13.2.

● **general adaptation syndrome (GAS)** A three-stage pattern of responses triggered by the effort to adapt to any stressor.

FIGURE 13.2

The General Adaptation Syndrome

Hans Selye found that physical reactions to stressors include an initial alarm reaction, followed by resistance and then exhaustion. During the alarm reaction, the body's resistance to stress temporarily drops below normal as it absorbs a stressor's initial impact. Resistance increases and then levels off in the resistance stage, but it ultimately declines if the exhaustion stage is reached.

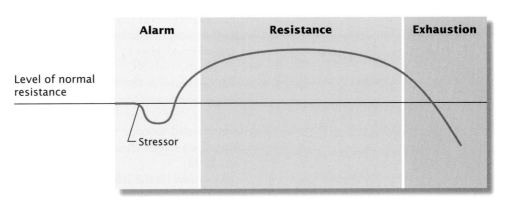

The first stage is the *alarm reaction*, which involves some version of the fight-or-flight syndrome. In the face of a mild stressor such as an overheated room, the reaction may simply involve changes in heart rate, respiration, and perspiration that help the body regulate its temperature. More severe stressors prompt more dramatic alarm reactions, rapidly mobilizing the body's adaptive energy, much as a burglar alarm alerts the police to take action (Kiecolt-Glaser et al., 1998).

Alarm reactions are controlled by the sympathetic branch of the autonomic nervous system (ANS) through organs and glands that make up the *sympatho-adreno-medullary (SAM)* system. As shown on the right side of Figure 13.3, environmental

FIGURE 13.3

Organ Systems Involved in the GAS

Stressors produce a variety of physiological responses that begin in the brain and spread to organs throughout the body. In the sympatho-adreno-medullary system (SAM; blue arrows), for example, the hypothalamus stimulates the release of catecholamines, which mobilize the body for action. Some of these substances may interact with sex hormones to create different physical stress responses and coping methods in men and women (Taylor, Klein, et al., 2000). Through the hypothalamic-pituitary-adrenocortical system (HPA; purple arrows), the hypothalamus causes the pituitary gland to trigger the release of endorphins, the body's natural painkillers. The HPA also stimulates the release of corticosteroids, which help resist stress but also tend to suppress the immune system.

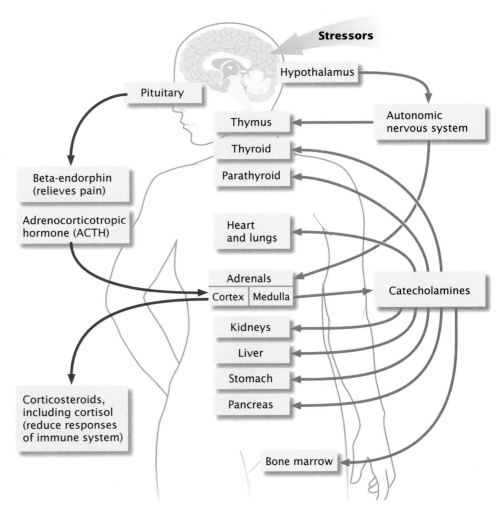

demands (stressors) trigger a process in the brain in which the hypothalamus activates the sympathetic branch of the ANS, which stimulates the medulla (inner part) of the adrenal gland. The adrenal gland, in turn, secretes *catecholamines* (pronounced "kat-uh-KOH-luh-meens")—especially adrenaline and noradrenaline—which circulate in the bloodstream, activating various organs, including the liver, kidneys, heart, and lungs. The results are increased blood pressure, enhanced muscle tension, increased blood sugar, and other physical changes that provide the energy needed to cope with acute stressors. Even brief exposure to a mild stressor can produce major changes in these coordinated physiological mechanisms (Stoney et al., 2002).

As shown on the left side of Figure 13.3, stressors also activate the *hypothalamic-pituitary-adrenocortical (HPA) system*, in which the hypothalamus stimulates the pituitary gland in the brain. The pituitary, in turn, secretes hormones such as adrenocorticotropic hormone (ACTH). Among other things, ACTH stimulates the cortex (outer surface) of the adrenal glands to secrete *corticosteroids*; these hormones release the body's energy supplies and fight inflammation. The pituitary gland also triggers the release of endorphins, the body's natural painkillers.

The overall effect of these stress systems is to generate emergency energy. The more stressors there are and the longer they last, the more resources the body must expend in response.

If stressors persist, the *resistance stage* of the GAS begins. Here, obvious signs of the initial alarm reaction fade as the body settles in to resist the stressor on a long-term basis. The drain on adaptive energy is slower during the resistance stage than it was during the alarm reaction, but the body is still working hard, physiologically, to cope.

This continued campaign of biochemical resistance is costly. It slowly but surely uses up the body's reserves of adaptive energy. The body then enters the third GAS stage, known as *exhaustion*. In extreme cases, such as prolonged exposure to freezing temperatures, the result is death. More commonly, the exhaustion stage brings signs of physical wear and tear, especially in organ systems that were weak in the first place or heavily involved in the resistance process. For example, if adrenaline and cortisol, which help fight stressors during the resistance stage, remain at high levels for an extended time, they can damage the heart and blood vessels. They also suppress the functioning of the body's disease-fighting immune system and promote illnesses ranging from heart disease, high blood pressure, and arthritis to colds and flu (Robles, Glaser, & Kiecolt-Glaser, 2005). Selye referred to illnesses that are caused or worsened by stressors as **diseases of adaptation.**

● Psychological Responses

Selye's model has been very influential, but it has also been criticized for underestimating the role of psychological factors in stress, such as a person's emotional state or the way a person thinks about stressors. These criticisms led to the development of *psychobiological models*, which emphasize the importance of psychological, as well as biological, variables in regulating and producing stress responses (Lazarus & Folkman, 1984; Suls & Rothman, 2004). Psychological responses to stress can appear as changes in emotions, thoughts (cognitions), and behaviors.

● **Emotional Responses** The physical stress responses we have described are usually accompanied by emotional stress responses. If someone pulls a gun and demands your money, you will no doubt experience the GAS alarm reaction, but you will also feel some strong emotion, probably fear and maybe anger. In fact, when people describe stress, they are more likely to say, "I was angry and frustrated!" than "My heart rate increased and my blood pressure went up." In other words, they are likely to mention changes in the emotions they are experiencing.

● **diseases of adaptation** Illnesses that are caused or worsened by stressors.

Another Funeral Even severe emotional stress responses usually ease eventually, but people plagued by numerous stressful events in quick succession—such as those living in strife-torn areas of the Middle East where violent death is all too frequent—may experience increasingly intense feelings of fear, sadness, and helplessness. These reactions can become severe enough to be diagnosed as generalized anxiety disorder, major depressive disorder, or other stress-related problems described in the chapter on psychological disorders.

In most cases, emotional stress responses subside soon after the stressors are gone. However, if stressors continue for a long time or occur in a tight sequence, emotional stress reactions may persist. When people do not have a chance to recover their emotional equilibrium, they commonly report feeling tense, irritable, short-tempered, or anxious more and more of the time.

● **Cognitive Responses** In the busy, noisy intensive care unit of a London hospital, a doctor misplaces a decimal point while calculating the amount of morphine a one-day-old premature baby should receive, and the child dies of a massive overdose (Davies, 1999). Reductions in the ability to concentrate, to think clearly, or to remember accurately are typical cognitive stress responses (Cavenett & Nixon, 2006; Morgan et al., 2006). Sometimes, these problems appear because of *ruminative thinking*, the recurring intrusion of thoughts about stressful events (Lyubomirsky & Nolen-Hoeksema, 1995). Ruminative thoughts about problems in a romantic relationship, for example, can seriously interfere with studying for a test. A related phenomenon is *catastrophizing*, which means dwelling on and overemphasizing the potential consequences of negative events (Sarason et al., 1986). During examinations, test-anxious college students are likely to say to themselves, "I'm falling behind" or "Everyone else is doing better than I am." As catastrophizing or ruminative thinking impairs cognitive functioning, a person

BLOOM COUNTY by **Berke Breathed**

Reprinted by permission of International Creative Management, Inc. Copyright © 2002 Berkeley Breathed.

Stress for $500, Alex The negative effects of stress on memory, thinking, decision making, and other cognitive functions are often displayed by players on quiz shows such as *Jeopardy!* and *Who Wants to Be a Millionaire*. Under the intense pressure of time, competition, and the scrutiny of millions of viewers, contestants may miss questions that seem ridiculously easy to those calmly recalling the correct answers at home.

may experience anxiety and other emotional arousal that adds to the total stress response and futher hampers performance (Beilock et al., 2004).

Overarousal created by stressors can also lead to a narrowing of attention, making it harder to scan the full range of possible solutions to complex problems. In fact, stress-narrowed attention may increase the problem-solving errors described in the chapter on cognition and language. People under stress are more likely to cling to *mental sets*, which are well learned, but not always efficient, approaches to problems. Stress can also intensify *functional fixedness*, the tendency to use objects for only one purpose. Victims of hotel fires, for example, sometimes die trapped in their rooms because, in the stress of the moment, it did not occur to them to use the telephone or a piece of furniture to break a window.

Stressors may also impair judgment and decision making. People who normally consider all aspects of a situation before making a decision may, under stress, act impulsively and sometimes foolishly. High-pressure salespeople try to take advantage of this phenomenon by creating artificially time-limited offers or by telling customers that others are waiting to buy the item they are considering (Cialdini, 2001).

● **Behavioral Responses** Clues about people's physical and emotional stress responses come from changes in how they look, act, or talk. Strained facial expressions, a shaky voice, tremors or spasms, and jumpiness are common behavioral stress responses. Posture can also convey information about stress, a fact well known to skilled interviewers.

Even more obvious behavioral stress responses appear as people attempt to escape or avoid stressors. They may quit their jobs, drop out of school, turn to alcohol, or even attempt suicide. In the month after Hurricane Katrina struck the U.S. gulf coast in 2005, for example, more than double the normal number of calls were placed from the affected area to the National Suicide Prevention Hotline (Breed, 2006). Unfortunately, as discussed in the chapter on learning, escape and avoidance tactics deprive people of the opportunity to learn more adaptive ways of coping with stressful environments, including college. Aggression is another common behavioral response to stressors. All too often, this response is directed at members of one's own family (Polusny & Follette, 1995). So areas devastated by hurricanes and other natural disasters are likely to see not only suicides but also dramatic increases in reports of domestic violence (Curtis, Miller, & Berry, 2000; Rotton, 1990).

LINKAGES Stress and Psychological Disorders

LINKAGES (a link to Psychological Disorders, p. 595)

Physical, psychological, and behavioral stress responses sometimes appear together in patterns known as *burnout* and *posttraumatic stress disorder*. **Burnout** is an increasingly intense pattern of physical and psychological dysfunction in response to a continuous flow of stressors or to chronic stress (Maslach, 2003). As burnout approaches, previously reliable workers or once-attentive spouses may become indifferent, disengaged, impulsive, or accident prone. They may miss work frequently; oversleep; perform their jobs poorly; abuse alcohol or other drugs; and become irritable, suspicious, withdrawn, depressed, and unwilling to talk about stress or anything else (Taylor, 2002). Burnout is particularly common among individuals who do "people work," such as teachers and nurses, and those who perceive themselves as being treated unjustly by employers (Elovainio, Kivimäki, & Vahtera, 2002; Hoobler & Brass, 2006). Recent research suggests a direct and causal relationship between burnout and increased risk for mental and physical health problems (Melamed et al., 2006; Shirom, 2003). Each year, it accounts for a significant percentage of occupational disease claims by U.S. workers (Schwartz, 2004).

A different pattern of severe stress reactions is illustrated by the case of "Mary," a thirty-three-year-old nurse who was raped at knifepoint by an intruder in her apartment (Spitzer et al., 1983). In the weeks following the attack, she became afraid of being alone and was preoccupied with the attack and with the fear that it might happen again. She had additional locks installed on her doors and windows but experienced difficulty concentrating and could not immediately return to work. She was repelled by the thought of sex.

Mary suffered from **posttraumatic stress disorder (PTSD)**, a pattern of adverse reactions following a traumatic and threatening event. Among the characteristic reactions are anxiety, depression, irritability, jumpiness, inability to concentrate or work productively, sexual dysfunction, and difficulty in getting along with others. People suffering from PTSD may also experience sleep disturbances, intense startle responses to noise or other sudden stimuli, and long-term suppression of their immune systems (Goenjian et al., 2001; Guthrie & Bryant, 2005; Johnson, Westermeyer, et al., 2002). The most common feature of PTSD is reexperiencing the trauma through nightmares or vivid memories. In rare cases, *flashbacks* occur in which the person behaves for minutes, hours, or days as if the trauma were occurring again. Posttraumatic stress disorder is most commonly associated with being in military combat, living in a war zone, or experiencing other traumatic events such as terrorist attacks, assault, or rape (e.g., Dohrenwend et al., 2006; Shalev & Freedman, 2005; Shalev et al., 2006). Researchers now believe, though, that some PTSD symptoms can be triggered by any major stressor, including car accidents, being diagnosed with a life-threatening disease, or being stalked (Ironson et al., 1997; Kamphuis & Emmelkamp, 2001; Kangas, Henry, & Bryant, 2005). PTSD symptoms have even been identified in response to community-wide threats such as terrorism or a rash of sniper attacks (Schulden et al., 2006). Research with animals shows that traumatic stressors cause structural and functional changes in the brain (Miller & McEwen, 2006), and brain scanning studies suggest that similar changes in the human brain contribute to the physical and psychological symptoms of PTSD (Kitayama et al., 2005).

Posttraumatic stress disorder may appear immediately following a trauma, or it may not occur until weeks, months, or—rarely—even years later (Gilboa-Schechtman & Foa, 2001; Port, Engdahl, & Frazier, 2001). For some people, though, PTSD never appears, even after severe trauma (Breslau et al., 2005). In fact, some people report enhanced psychological growth after surviving a trauma (Zoellner & Maercker,

● **burnout** A gradually intensifying pattern of physical, psychological, and behavioral dysfunction in response to a continuous flow of stressors.

● **posttraumatic stress disorder (PTSD)** A pattern of adverse and disruptive reactions following a traumatic event.

Life Hanging in the Balance

Symptoms of burnout often plague fire-fighters, police officers, emergency medical personnel, and others who are repeatedly exposed to time pressure, trauma, danger, and other stressors (Fullerton, Ursano, & Wang, 2004). Posttraumatic stress disorder can be another result of these conditions, but it can also appear following a single catastrophic event. Surveys taken in the weeks and months following the terrorist attacks on the World Trade Center revealed that 7.5 percent of adults and 10.6 percent of children who lived near the devastated area experienced symptoms of PTSD (DeLisi et al., 2003; Galea et al., 2002; Hoven et al., 2005; Simeon et al., 2003). Even higher rates of PTSD symptoms were reported by adult survivors of the massive tidal waves that devastated south and southeast Asia in 2004 (van Griensven et al., 2006).

2006). Researchers are working to discover what protective factors are operating in these individuals and whether those factors can be strengthened through PTSD treatment programs (Haskett et al., 2006; Yehuda et al., 2005). Indeed, the majority of people who develop PTSD require professional help, although some seem to recover without it (Bradley et al., 2005; Perkonigg et al., 2005). For most, improvement takes time; for nearly all, the support of family and friends is vital to recovery (Foa et al., 2005).

Stress is also thought to play a role in the development of a number of other psychological disorders, including depression and schizophrenia (see the chapter on psychological disorders). The *diathesis-stress model* suggests that certain people are predisposed to these disorders but that whether or not individuals actually display them depends on the frequency, nature, and intensity of the stressors they encounter. If untreated, stress-related mental health problems can threaten physical health, too. For example, depression or anxiety may leave people unmotivated or forgetful when it comes to taking prescribed medication for high blood pressure or other medical conditions they may have. Similarly, some schizophrenia patients develop delusions that doctors, and the medicines they prescribe, will hurt them and thus begin to avoid both. As a result, all these people are likely to be at increased risk for worsening health. ■

Stress Mediators: Interactions Between People and Stressors

The interaction of particular people with particular stressors can be important in many ways. The stress of combat, for example, is partly responsible for the fact that "friendly fire" deaths and injuries occur in almost every military operation (Adler, 1993). But why does stress disrupt the performance of some people more than others? And why does one individual survive, and even thrive, under the same circumstances that lead another to break down, give up, and burn out? A number of the mediating factors listed in Figure 13.1 help determine how much impact a given stressor will have (Bonanno, 2005; Kemeny, 2003).

▨ ● How Stressors Are Perceived

As discussed in the chapter on perception, our view of the world depends on which stimuli we attend to and how we interpret, or appraise, them. Any potential stressor, whether it is a crowded elevator or a deskful of work, usually has a more negative impact on those who perceive it as a threat than on those who see it as a challenge (Lazarus, 1999; Maddi & Khoshaba, 2005).

Evidence for the effects of cognitive factors on stress responses comes from both laboratory experiments and surveys (e.g., Abelson et al., 2005). Figure 13.4 shows the results of a classic experiment that demonstrated these effects. In this case, the intensity of physiological arousal during a film depended on how the viewers were instructed to think about the film (Lazarus et al., 1965). In a more recent study, students who were first trained to see the threatening aspects of information showed more emotional arousal to a stressful video than those who had been trained to see information as nonthreatening (Wilson et al., 2006). Similarly, physical and psychological symptoms associated with the stress of airport noise, of being diagnosed with a serious illness, of learning about toxins in local soil, or of living with terrorism threats are more common in people who engage in catastrophic thinking about these problems (Bryant & Guthrie, 2005; Lerner et al., 2003; Matthies, Hoeger, & Guski, 2000; Speckhard, 2002). Those who hold a more optimistic outlook tend to show milder stress responses and better health outcomes (de Moor et al., 2006; Taylor et al., 2003).

The influence of cognitive factors weakens somewhat as stressors become more extreme. For example, chronic-pain patients who feel a sense of control over the pain tend to be more physically active, but this effect does not hold for those whose pain is severe (Jensen & Karoly, 1991). Still, even the impact of natural disasters or major stressors such as divorce may be less intense among those who think of them as challenges to be overcome. In other words, many stressful events are not inherently stressful. Their impact depends partly on how people perceive them (Wiedenfeld et al., 1990). An important aspect of this appraisal is the degree to which the stressors are perceived to be predictable or controllable.

▨ ● Predictability and Control

Why is the threat of terrorism so terrorizing? For one thing, knowing that a particular stressor might occur but being uncertain about whether, or when, it will occur tends to increase the stressor's impact (Lerner et al., 2003; Sorrentino & Roney,

FIGURE **13.4**

Cognitive Influences on Stress Responses

Richard Lazarus and his colleagues found that students' physiological stress reactions to a film showing bloody industrial accidents was affected by the way they thought about the film. Those who had been instructed to remain detached from the film (the "intellectualizers") or to think of it as unreal (the "denial" group) were less upset—as measured by sweat-gland activity—than those in an "unprepared" group. These results were among the first to show that people's cognitive appraisal of stressors can affect their responses to those stressors.

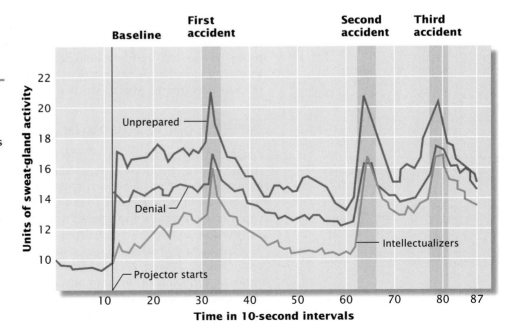

2000). In other words, *predictable* stressors tend to have less impact than those that are unpredictable (Lazarus & Folkman, 1984; Pham, Taylor, & Seeman, 2001), especially when the stressors are intense and relatively brief. Rats given a reliable warning signal every time they are to receive a shock show less severe physiological responses than animals given no warnings (Weinberg & Levine, 1980). Among humans, men and women whose spouses died suddenly tend to display more immediate disbelief, anxiety, and depression than those who had weeks or months to prepare for the loss (Schulz et al., 2001; Swarte et al., 2003). This is not to say that predictability provides total protection against stressors. Laboratory research with animals has shown that predictable stressors, even if relatively mild, can be more damaging than unpredictable ones if they occur over long periods of time (Abbott, Schoen, & Badia, 1984).

The *perception of control* can also mediate the effects of stressors. If people can exert some control over them, stressors usually have less impact on health (e.g., Christensen, Stephens, & Townsend, 1998; Krause & Shaw, 2000). Studies of several thousand employees in the United States, Sweden, and the United Kingdom have found that workers who had little or no control over their work environments were more likely to suffer heart disease and other health problems than workers with a high degree of control over those environments (Bosma et al., 1997; Cheng et al., 2000; Spector, 2002). In another study, researchers randomly selected a group of patients awaiting surgery and gave them a full explanation of the procedures that they could expect to undergo, along with information that would help them manage postsurgical pain (Egbert et al., 1964). After the surgery was over, patients who had been given this information and who felt they had at least some control over the pain they experienced not only were better adjusted than patients in a control group who received no special preparation but also healed faster and could be discharged from the hospital sooner. So impressive are findings such as these that, in many hospitals, it is now standard practice to teach patients how to manage or control the adverse effects of surgery (Broadbent et al., 2003; Gordon et al., 2005).

Simply believing that a stressor is controllable, even if it isn't, can also reduce its impact. This effect was demonstrated in a study in which people with panic disorder (discussed in the chapter on psychological disorders) inhaled a mixture of carbon dioxide and oxygen that typically causes them to experience fear and other symptoms of a panic attack (Sanderson, Rapee, & Barlow, 1989). Half the clients were led to believe (falsely) that they could control the concentration of the mixture. Compared with those who believed they had no control, significantly fewer of the "in control" clients experienced full-blown panic attacks during the session, and their panic symptoms were fewer and less severe.

People who feel they have no control over negative events appear especially prone to physical and psychological problems. They often experience feelings of helplessness and hopelessness that, in turn, may promote depression or other mental disorders (Sarin, Abela, & Auerbach, 2005).

▓▓▓ ● Coping Resources and Coping Methods

People usually suffer fewer ill effects from a stressor if they have adequate coping resources and effective coping methods. *Coping resources* include, for example, the money and time to deal with stressful events. So the physical and psychological responses you experience if your car breaks down are likely to be more negative if you are low on cash and pressed for time than if you have money for repairs and the freedom to take a day off from work.

The impact of stressors can also be reduced by the use of effective *coping methods* (Cote & Pepler, 2002). Most of these methods can be classified as focusing either on problems or on emotions. *Problem-focused* coping involves efforts to alter or eliminate a source of stress, whereas *emotion-focused* techniques are aimed at regulating the negative emotional consequences of the stressor (Folkman et al.,

1986). These two forms of coping sometimes work together. For example, you might deal with the problem of noise from a nearby airport by forming a community action group to push for tougher noise regulations and, at the same time, calm your anger when noise occurs by mentally focusing on the group's efforts to improve the situation (e.g., Hatfield et al., 2002). As mentioned earlier, coping efforts may not always be so adaptive. In the face of a financial crisis or impending exams, for example, some people rely on emotion-focused methods such as using alcohol or other drugs to ease anxiety but take no problem-focused steps to get out of debt or learn difficult material. These emotion-focused strategies may reduce distress in the short run, but the long-term result may be a financial or academic situation that is worse than it was before. Susan Folkman and Richard Lazarus (1988) have devised a widely used questionnaire to assess the specific ways in which people cope with stressors; Table 13.3 shows some examples of responses to their questionnaire.

Particularly when a stressor is difficult to control, it is sometimes helpful to express fully, and think about, the emotions you are experiencing in relation to the stressful event (Langens & Schüler, 2007; Niederhoffer & Pennebaker, 2002). The benefits of this cognitive strategy have been observed among many individuals whose religious beliefs allow them to bring meaning to the death of a loved one, or the devastation of a natural disaster, events that might otherwise seem to be senseless tragedies (Heppner et al., 2006; Powell, Shahabi, & Thoresen, 2003; VandeCreek et al., 2002). And when cancer patients are encouraged to express their feelings about their diagnosis and to search for positive aspects of their illness (such as bringing their family closer together), they experience fewer symptoms, need fewer medical visits, and adjust better to their disease (Antoni et al., 2001; Low, Stanton, & Danoff-Burg, 2006). Humor may also play a role. Some individuals who use humor to help them cope show better adjustment and lower physiological reactivity to stressful events (Martin, 2001; Moran, 2002).

● Social Support

If you have ever benefited from the comforting presence of a good friend during troubled times, you know about another factor that mediates the impact of stressful events—*social support*. Social support consists of resources provided by other

---

TABLE 13.3 Ways of Coping

TRY THIS ⚙ Coping is defined as the cognitive and behavioral efforts to manage specific demands that people perceive as taxing their resources (Folkman et al., 1986). This table illustrates two major approaches to coping measured by the Ways of Coping questionnaire: problem-focused and emotion-focused coping. To get an idea of your own coping style, rank-order the skills listed under each major approach in terms of how often you tend to use each of them. Do you rely on just one or two, or do you adjust your coping strategies to fit different kinds of stressors?

Coping Skills	Example
Problem-focused coping	
Confronting	"I stood my ground and fought for what I wanted."
Seeking social support	"I talked to someone to find out more about the situation."
Planful problem solving	"I made a plan of action, and I followed it."
Emotion-focused coping	
Self-controlling	"I tried to keep my feelings to myself."
Distancing	"I didn't let it get to me; I tried not to think about it too much."
Positive reappraisal	"I changed my mind about myself."
Accepting responsibility	"I realized I brought the problem on myself."
Escape/avoidance (wishful thinking)	"I wished that the situation would go away or somehow be over with."

Source: Adapted from Folkman et al. (1986); Taylor (2002).

You've Got a Friend   Even when social support cannot eliminate stressors, it can help people, such as these breast cancer survivors, to feel less anxious, more optimistic, more capable of control, and more willing to try new ways of dealing with stressors (Trunzo & Pinto, 2003). Those who provide social support may feel better, too (Brown et al., 2003).

people. The friends and social contacts on whom you can depend for support constitute your **social support network** (Burleson, Albrecht, & Sarason, 1994). Social support may take many forms, from eliminating the stressor (as when a friend helps you fix your car) to easing its impact with companionship, ideas for coping, or reassurance that you are cared about and valued and that everything will be all right.

The stress-reducing effects of social support have been documented for a wide range of stressors, including cancer, heart disease, military combat, loss of loved ones, natural disasters, arthritis, AIDS, and even ethnic discrimination (e.g., Antoni & Lutgendorf, 2007; Boden-Albala et al., 2005; Gonzalez et al., 2004; Mookadam & Arthur, 2004; Penner, Dovidio, & Albrecht, 2001). Social support can have health benefits, too. For example, students who get emotional support from friends show better immune system functioning than those with less adequate social support (Cohen & Herbert, 1996). This may be why people in strong social support networks are less vulnerable to colds and flu during exams and other periods of high academic stress (Kop et al., 2005; Pressman et al., 2005; Taylor, Dickerson, & Klein, 2002). Having strong social support is also associated with faster recovery from surgery or illness, possibly because helpful friends and family members encourage patients to follow medical advice (Brummett et al., 2005; Krohne & Slangen, 2005; Taylor, 2002). Stronger social networks are even associated with better mental functioning in old age (Barnes et al., 2004). According to some researchers, having inadequate social support can be as dangerous as smoking, obesity, or lack of exercise in that it nearly doubles a person's risk of dying from disease, suicide, or other causes (House, Landis, & Umberson, 1988; Kiecolt-Glaser & Newton, 2001; Rutledge et al., 2004).

However, the relationship between social support and the impact of stressors is more complex than it might appear. First, just as the quality of social support may influence people's ability to cope with stress, the reverse may also be true: People's ability to cope may determine the quality of social support they receive (McLeod, Kessler, & Landis, 1992). For example, people who complain endlessly about stressors but never try to do anything about them may discourage social support, whereas those with an optimistic, action-oriented approach may attract support.

social support network   The friends and social contacts on whom one can depend for help and support.

Second, *social support* refers not only to relationships with others but also to the recognition that others care and will help (Demaray & Malecki, 2002). Some relationships in a social support network may be stormy and fragile, resulting in interpersonal conflicts that can have an adverse effect on health (Ben-Ari & Gil, 2002; Malarkey et al., 1994).

Finally, having too much support or the wrong kind of support can be as bad as not having enough (Reynolds & Perrin, 2004). For example, people whose friends and family are overprotective may actually put less energy into coping efforts. And in one study of people with physical disabilities, nearly 40 percent of them were found to have experienced emotional distress in response to the well-intentioned help they received from their spouses. This distress, in turn, was a predictor of depression nearly a year later (Newsome & Schulz, 1998). Similarly, people living in crowded conditions might at first perceive the situation as providing lots of social support, but these conditions may eventually become an added source of stress (Lepore, Evans, & Schneider, 1991). Further, the value of social support may depend on the kind of stressor being encountered. So although having a friend present might reduce the impact of some stressors, it might amplify the impact of others. In one study, for example, participants faced with speaking in public experienced it as more threatening—and showed stronger physical and psychological stress responses—when a friend was watching than when they were alone (Stoney & Finney, 2000). In short, the efforts or presence of members of a social support network can sometimes become annoying, disruptive, or interfering, thereby increasing stress and intensifying psychological problems (Newsome, 1999; Ruiz et al., 2006). It has even been suggested that among people under intense stress, the benefits of having a large social support network may be offset by the dangers of catching a cold or the flu from people in that network (Hamrick, Cohen, & Rodriguez, 2002).

● Stress, Personality, and Gender

The impact of stress on health appears to depend not only on how people think about particular stressors but, to some extent, on how they think about and react to the world in general. For instance, stress-related health problems tend to be especially common among people whose "disease-prone" personalities lead them to (1) try to ignore stressors when possible; (2) perceive stressors as long-term, catastrophic threats that they brought on themselves; and (3) be pessimistic about their ability to overcome stressors (e.g., Penninx et al., 2001; Peterson et al., 1988; Segerstrom et al., 1998; Suinn, 2001).

Other cognitive styles, such as those characteristic of "disease-resistant" personalities, help insulate people from the ill effects of stress. These people tend to think of stressors as temporary challenges to be overcome, not catastrophic threats, and they do not constantly blame themselves for bringing them about. Among the most important components of the disease-resistant personality are sociability (e.g., Cohen et al., 2003b) and *dispositional optimism*, the belief or expectation that things will work out positively (Folkman & Moskowitz, 2000; Rosenkranz et al., 2003; Taylor, Kemeny,, et al., 2000). Optimistic people tend to live longer (Giltay et al., 2004, 2006), to experience fewer health consequences following major stressors, and to have more resistance than pessimists to colds and other infectious diseases (Cohen et al., 2003a, 2003b; Kivimaki et al., 2005; Pressman & Cohen, 2005). These data help to explain why optimistic students experience fewer physical symptoms at the end of the academic term (Aspinwall & Taylor, 1992; Ebert, Tucker, & Roth, 2002). Optimistic coronary bypass surgery patients tend to heal faster and stay healthier than pessimists (Scheier et al., 1989) and to experience a higher quality of life following coronary surgery than those with less optimistic outlooks (Fitzgerald et al., 1993). And among HIV-positive men, dispositional optimism has been associated with less psychological distress, fewer worries, and lower perceived risk of developing full-blown AIDS (Johnson & Endler, 2002; Taylor et al., 1992). All these effects appear to be due in part to optimists' tendency to use challenge-oriented, problem-focused coping strategies that attack stressors directly, in contrast to pessimists' tendency to use emotion-focused coping, such as denial and avoidance (Bosompra et al., 2001; Brenes et al., 2002). They also tend to be happier than pessimists, a tendency associated not only with less intense and less dangerous physiological responses to stressors but also with greater success in life (e.g., Lyubomirsky, King, & Diener, 2005; Steptoe, Wardle, & Marmot, 2005).

Indeed, like optimism, happiness and other positive emotions, such as hope and curiosity, have been associated with better health and longer life (Cohen et al., 2003a; Ong et al., 2006; Ostir et al., 2006; Richman et al., 2005). For example, a long-term study of Catholic nuns found that those who wrote with the most positive emotional style when they were young lived longer than those whose writing contained less positive emotions (Danner, Snowden, & Friesen, 2001). Studies like these represent a new line of research in health psychology that focuses on investigating and promoting the positive emotions, behaviors, and cognitive styles associated with better health (Seligman et al., 2005).

Gender may also play a role in responses to stress. In a review of two hundred studies of stress responses and coping methods, Shelley Taylor and her colleagues found that males under stress tended to get angry, avoid stressors, or both, whereas females were more likely to help others and to make use of their social support networks (Taylor, Klein, et al., 2000). Further, in the face of equally intense stressors, men's physiological responses, including changes in heart rate and blood pressure, tend to be more intense than women's (Stoney et al., 1988). This is not true in every case, of course, but why should a significant difference show up at all? The gender-role learning discussed in the chapter on human development surely plays a part (Eagly & Wood, 1999). But Taylor also proposes that women's "tend-and-befriend" style differs from the "fight-or-flight" pattern so often seen in men because of gender differences in how hormones combine under stress. Consider oxytocin (pronounced "ox-see-TOE-sin"), a hormone released in both sexes as part of the general adaptation syndrome (Taylor et al., 2006; Uvnas-Moberg, Arn, & Magnusson, 2005). Oxytocin may interact differently with male and female sex hormones, producing a greater stress reduction effect in women than in men (Grewen et al., 2005). These differences could lead to the more intense emotional and behavioral stress responses often seen among men, responses that may be partly responsible for their greater vulnerability to heart disease and other stress-related illnesses (Kajantie & Phillips, 2006). If that is the case, gender differences in stress responses may help to explain why women in North America live an average of 5.3 years longer than men (Hoyert, Kung, & Smith, 2005). The role of gender-related hormones in stress responding is supported by the fact that there are few, if any, gender differences in children's stress responses. Those differences begin to appear only around adolescence, when sex hormone differences become pronounced (Allen & Matthews, 1997).

FOCUS ON RESEARCH METHODS ▮ **Personality and Health**

 LINKAGES (a link to Personality, p. 561)

The way people think and act in the face of stressors, the ease with which they attract social support, and their tendency to be optimists or pessimists are but a few aspects of their *personalities*.

■ What was the researchers' question?

Are there other personality characteristics that protect or threaten people's health? This was the research question asked by Howard Friedman and his associates (Friedman et al., 1995a, 1995b). In particular, they attempted to identify aspects of personality that increase the likelihood that people will die prematurely from heart disease, high blood pressure, or other chronic diseases.

■ How did the researchers answer the question?

Friedman suspected that an answer might lie in earlier research—specifically, in the Terman Life Cycle Study of Intelligence, named after Louis Terman, author of the Stanford-Binet intelligence test. As described in the chapter on cognitive abilities, the study was originally designed to document the long-term development of 1,528 gifted California children (856 boys and 672 girls)—nicknamed the "Termites" (Terman & Oden, 1947). Friedman and his colleagues found ways of using data from this study to explore the relationship between personality and health.

Starting in 1921, and every five to ten years thereafter, Terman's research team had gathered information about the Termites' personality traits, social relationships, stressors, health habits, and many other variables. The data were collected through questionnaires and interviews with the Termites themselves, as well as with their teachers, parents, and other family members. When, by the early 1990s, about half of the Termites had died, Friedman realized that the Terman Life Cycle Study could serve as a longitudinal study in health psychology. As in most such studies, the independent variable (in this case, personality characteristics) was not actually manipulated (the Termites had obviously not been randomly assigned different personalities by the researchers), but the various personality traits identified in these people could still be related to a dependent variable (namely, longevity—how long they lived). So Friedman and his colleagues gathered the death certificates of the Termites, noted the dates and causes of death, and then looked for associations between personality and longevity.

■ What did the researchers find?

One of the most important predictors of long life turned out to be a personality dimension known as *conscientiousness*, or social dependability (described in the chapter on personality). Termites who, in childhood, had been seen as truthful, prudent, reliable, hard-working, and free from vanity tended to live longer than those whose parents and teachers had identified them as impulsive and lacking in self-control.

Friedman and his colleagues also used the Terman Life Cycle Study to investigate the relationship between social support and health. They compared the life spans of Termites whose parents had divorced or who had been in unstable marriages themselves with those who grew up in stable homes and who had stable marriages. The researchers found that people who had experienced parental divorce during childhood or who themselves had unstable marriages died an average of four years earlier than those whose close social relationships had been less stressful.

■ What do the results mean?

The research of Friedman and his co-workers was based mainly on the analysis of correlations, so it is difficult to draw conclusions about whether differences in personality traits and social support actually caused some Termites to live longer than others. Nevertheless, Friedman and his colleagues searched the Terman data for clues to mechanisms through which personality and other factors might have exerted a causal influence on longevity (Peterson et al., 1998). For example, they evaluated the hypothesis that conscientious, dependable Termites who lived socially stable lives might have followed healthier lifestyles than their impulsive and socially stressed age-mates. People in the latter group did indeed tend to eat less healthy diets and were more likely to smoke, drink to excess, or use drugs. However, these behaviors alone did not fully account for their shorter average life spans. Another possible explanation is that conscientiousness and stability in social relationships create a general attitude of caution that goes beyond eating right and avoiding substance abuse. The researchers found some support for this idea in the Terman data. Termites who were impulsive or low on conscientiousness were somewhat more likely to die from accidents or violence than those who were less impulsive. (A similar finding is reported in the Focus on Research Methods section of the personality chapter.)

■ What do we still need to know?

Although the Terman Life Cycle Study cannot provide definite answers about the relationship between personality and health, it has generated some important clues and a number of intriguing hypotheses to be evaluated in future research with more representative samples of people. Some of that research has already taken place and tends to confirm Friedman's findings about conscientiousness (Hampson et al., 2006). Further, Friedman's decision to reanalyze a set of data on psychosocial development as a way of exploring issues in health psychology stands as a fine example of how a creative researcher can pursue answers to complex questions that are difficult or impossible to study via controlled experiments. ■

Our review of personality and other factors that can alter the impact of stressors should make it obvious that what is stressful for a particular individual is not determined simply by predispositions, coping styles, or situations. (See "In Review: Stress Responses and Stress Mediators.") Even more important are interactions between the person and the situation, the mixture of each individual's coping resources and the specific characteristics of the situations encountered.

in review Stress Responses and Stress Mediators

Category	Examples
Responses	
Physical	Fight-or-flight syndrome (increased heart rate, respiration, and muscle tension; sweating; pupillary dilation); SAM and HPA activation (involving release of catecholamines and corticosteroids); eventual breakdown of organ systems involved in prolonged resistance to stressors.
Psychological	*Emotional:* anger, anxiety, depression, and other emotional states. *Cognitive:* inability to concentrate or think logically, ruminative thinking, catastrophizing. *Behavioral:* aggression and escape/avoidance tactics (including suicide attempts).
Mediators	
Appraisal	Thinking of a difficult new job as a challenge will create less discomfort than focusing on the threat of failure.
Predictability	A tornado that strikes without warning may have a more devastating emotional impact than a long-predicted hurricane.
Control	Repairing a disabled spacecraft may be less stressful for the astronauts doing the work than for their loved ones on Earth, who can do nothing to help.
Coping resources and methods	Having no effective way to relax after a hard day may prolong tension and other stress responses.
Social support	Having no one to talk to about a rape or other trauma may amplify the negative impact of the experience.

psychoneuroimmunology A field of research on the interaction of psychological, social, behavioral, neural, hormonal, and immune system processes that affect the body's defenses against disease.

The Physiology and Psychology of Health and Illness

We have mentioned several studies showing that people under stress are more likely than less stressed people to develop infectious diseases. These studies are part of a much larger body of research in health psychology that sheds light on the relationship between stress and illness. In the following sections we focus on some of the ways in which stress can, directly or indirectly, lead to physical illnesses by affecting the *immune system* and the *cardiovascular system*.

Stress, Illness, and the Immune System

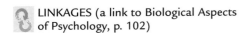

LINKAGES (a link to Biological Aspects of Psychology, p. 102)

As described in the chapter on biological aspects of psychology, components of the immune system act as the body's first line of defense by killing or deactivating foreign or harmful substances in the body, such as viruses and bacteria (Simpson, Hurtley, & Marx, 2000).

The role of physiological stress responses in altering the body's ability to fight disease was demonstrated more than a century ago. On March 19, 1878, at a seminar before the Académie de Médecine de Paris, Louis Pasteur showed his distinguished audience three chickens. One was a healthy bird that had been raised normally. A second bird had been intentionally infected with bacteria but given no other treatment; it was also healthy. The third chicken Pasteur presented was dead. It had been infected with the same bacteria as the second bird, but it had also been stressed by being exposed to cold temperatures. As a result, the bacteria had killed it (Kelley, 1985).

Research conducted since Pasteur's time has greatly expanded knowledge about how stressors affect the body's reaction to disease. **Psychoneuroimmunology** is the field that examines the interaction of psychological, social, behavioral, neural, hormonal, and immune system processes that affect the body's ability to defend itself against disease (Ader, 2001).

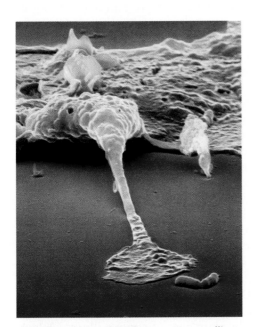

The First Line of Defense A patrolling immune system cell sends out an extension known as a *pseudopod* (pronounced "SUE-doh-pod") to engulf and destroy a bacterial cell before alerting more defenders. Psychological stressors can alter immune system functions through a number of mechanisms. For example, they can activate neural connections between the sympathetic nervous system and organs of the immune system through response systems that have direct suppressant effects on immune function. These suppressant effects are due largely to the release of cortisol and other corticosteroid hormones from the adrenal cortex (see Figure 13.3).

● **The Immune System and Illness** If the immune system is impaired—by stressors, for example—a person is left more vulnerable to colds, mononucleosis, and many other infectious diseases (Potter & Zautra, 1997). It is by disabling the immune system that HIV infection leads to AIDS and leaves the HIV-infected person defenseless against other infections or cancers.

There are many facets to the human immune system. One important component is the action of immune system cells, especially white blood cells, called *leukocytes* (pronounced "LU-koh-sites"), which are formed in the bone marrow and serve as the body's mobile defense units. Leukocytes are called into action when foreign substances are detected. Among the varied types of leukocytes are *B-cells*, which mature in the bone marrow, and *T-cells*, which mature in the thymus. Generally, T-cells kill other cells, and B-cells produce *antibodies*, which are circulating proteins that bind to specific toxins and other foreign cells and begin to deactivate them. *Natural killer cells*, another type of leukocyte, destroy a wide variety of foreign organisms, but they have particularly important antiviral and antitumor functions. Yet another type of immune system cell is the *macrophage* (pronounced "MACK-row-fayj). Macrophages engulf foreign cells and digest them in a process called *phagocytosis*, or "eating cells." These scavengers are able to squeeze out of the bloodstream and enter organs, where they destroy foreign cells.

The activity of immune system cells can be either strengthened or weakened by a number of systems, including the endocrine system and the central and autonomic nervous systems. It is through these connections that stress-related psychological and emotional factors can affect the functioning of the immune system (see Figure 3.24 in the chapter on biological aspects of psychology). The exact mechanisms by which the nervous system affects the immune system are not yet fully understood, but they appear to involve both indirect and direct connections (Rosenkranz et al., 2003). The brain can influence the activity of the immune system indirectly by altering the secretion of hormones (including cortisol secretion by the adrenal gland) that stimulate receptors in circulating T-cells and B-cells. More direct influences occur as nerves affect immune organs, such as the thymus, where T-cells and B-cells are stored (Felten et al., 1991; Maier & Watkins, 2000).

● **The Immune System and Stress** Researchers have found that people under stress are more likely than less stressed people to develop infectious diseases and to experience flare-ups of latent viruses responsible for oral herpes (cold sores) or genital herpes. For example, Sheldon Cohen and his colleagues in the United Kingdom (Cohen et al., 1995) exposed 394 healthy adult volunteers either to one of five respiratory viruses or to a placebo. The participants were then isolated and asked about the number and severity of life stresses they had experienced in the previous year. After controlling for factors such as prior history of colds, exposure to other viruses, and health practices, the researchers found that the more stress the participants had experienced, the greater was the likelihood that their exposure to a virus would result in colds and respiratory infections.

These findings are supported by other research showing that a variety of stressors lead to suppression of the immune system. The effects are especially strong in the elderly (Penedo & Dahn, 2004), but they occur in everyone (Kiecolt-Glaser et al., 2002). For example, one study found that as first-year law students participated in class, took exams, and experienced other stressful aspects of law school, they showed a decline in several measures of immune functioning (Segerstrom et al., 1998). Similarly, reduction in natural killer cell activity has been observed in both men and women following the deaths of their spouses (Irwin et al., 1987), and a variety of immune system impairments have been found in people suffering the effects of separation, divorce, unemployment, lack of social support, and loneliness (Cohen et al., 2007; Kiecolt-Glaser & Glaser, 1992). Providing care for an elderly relative who is mentally or physically incapacitated is a particularly stressful circumstance that has been reliably shown to diminish immune function (Kiecolt-Glaser et al., 2003, 2005; Vitaliano, Zhang, & Scanlan, 2003).

The relationship between stress and the immune system is especially important in persons who are HIV-positive but do not yet have AIDS. Because their immune systems are already seriously compromised, further stress-related impairments could be life-threatening. Research indicates that psychological stressors are associated with the progression of HIV-related illnesses (e.g., Heckman et al., 2004). Unfortunately, people with HIV (and AIDS) face a particularly heavy load of immune-suppressing psychological stressors, including bereavement, unemployment, uncertainty about the future, and daily reminders of serious illness. A lack of perceived control and resulting depression can further amplify their stress responses (Sewell et al., 2000).

● **Moderators of Immune Function** The effects of social support and other stress-moderating factors can be seen in the activity of the immune system. For example, immune system functioning among students who are able to get emotional assistance from friends during stressful periods appears better than among those with less adequate social support (Cohen & Herbert, 1996).

James Pennebaker (2002) suggests that social support may help prevent illness by providing the person under stress with an opportunity to express pent-up thoughts and emotions. Suppressing the emotions associated with stressors, says Pennebaker, is itself a stressor that can lead to further impairment of the immune system (Petrie et al., 1995; Petrie, Booth, & Pennebaker, 1998). For example, the spouses of suicide or accidental-death victims who do not or cannot confide their feelings to others are

Fighting a Deadly Disease The impact of psychological factors on immune system functioning can be seen in the progression of HIV/AIDS. Sustained depression, concealment of gay identity, negative expectancies, and reliance on passive, emotion-focused coping methods such as denial have all been related to faster disease progression. Openly expressing emotions, collaborating closely with doctors, having optimistic expectations, remaining involved in normal activities, finding meaning in the situation, and other active, problem-focused coping strategies have all been associated with slower disease progression (Balbin, Ironson, & Solomon, 1999).

You Can't Fire Me—I Quit! For a time, researchers believed that anyone who displayed the pattern of aggressiveness, competitiveness, and nonstop work known as "Type A" behavior was at elevated risk for heart disease (Friedman & Rosenman, 1974). More recent research shows, however, that the danger lies not in these characteristics alone, but in hostility, a pattern seen in some, but not all, Type A people.

the ones most likely to develop physical illnesses during the year following the death (Pennebaker & O'Heeron, 1984). Disclosing, even anonymously, the stresses and traumas one has experienced is associated with enhanced immune functioning, reduced physical symptoms, and decreased use of health services (Campbell & Pennebaker, 2003; Niederhoffer & Pennebaker, 2002; Rosenberg et al., 2002). This may explain why support groups for problems ranging from bereavement to overeating to alcohol and drug abuse tend to improve participants' quality of life and, to some extent, their physical health status (Taylor, Dickerson, & Klein, 2002). Future research in psychoneuroimmunology promises to reveal more about the complex chain of mental and physical events that determine whether people become ill or stay healthy.

● Stress, Illness, and the Cardiovascular System

Earlier we discussed the role of the sympatho-adreno-medullary (SAM) system in mobilizing the body's defenses during times of threat. Because the SAM system is linked to the cardiovascular system, its repeated activation in response to stressors has been associated with the development of coronary heart disease (CHD), high blood pressure (hypertension), and stroke. The link appears especially strong in people who show intense physiological reactivity to stressors (Ming et al., 2004; Treiber et al., 2001). For example, among healthy young adult research participants, those whose blood pressure rose most dramatically in response to a mild stressor, or a series of stressors, were the ones most likely to develop hypertension later in life (Light et al., 1999; Matthews et al., 2004).

As also mentioned earlier, these physiological reactions to stressors—and the chances of suffering stress-related health problems—depend partly on personality, especially on how people tend to think about stressors and about life in general. For example, the trait of *hostility*—particularly when accompanied by irritability and impatience—has been associated with the appearance of coronary heart disease (Bunde & Suls, 2006; Day & Jreige, 2002; Krantz & McCeney, 2002; Smith, 2003a).

THINKING CRITICALLY **Does Hostility Increase the Risk of Heart Disease?**

Health psychologists see hostility as characterized by suspiciousness, resentment, frequent anger, antagonism, and distrust of others (Krantz & McCeney, 2002; Stoney & Engebretson, 1994; Williams, 2001). The identification of hostility as a risk factor for coronary heart disease and *myocardial infarction*, or *MI* (commonly known as heart attack), could be an important breakthrough in better understanding the chief cause of death in the United States and most other Western nations (Centers for Disease Control and Prevention, 2001; Hu et al., 2000). But is hostility as dangerous as health psychologists suspect?

■ What am I being asked to believe or accept?

Many researchers claim that individuals displaying hostility are at increased risk for coronary heart disease and heart attack (e.g., Bleil et al., 2004; Boyle et al., 2004). This risk, they say, is independent of other risk factors such as heredity, diet, smoking, and drinking.

■ What evidence is available to support the assertion?

The precise mechanism underlying the relationship between hostility and heart disease is not clear, but there are several possibilities. The risk of CHD and MI may be elevated in hostile people because these people tend to have an unusually strong reaction to stressors, especially when challenged. During interpersonal conflicts, for example, people predisposed to hostile behavior display not only overt hostility but also unusually large increases in blood pressure, heart rate, and other aspects of SAM reactivity (Brondolo et al., 2003; Suls & Wan, 1993). In addition, it takes hostile individuals longer than normal to get back to their resting levels of SAM functioning (Gerin et al., 2006). Like a driver who damages a car by flooring the accelerator and applying the brakes at the same time, these "hot reactors" may create excessive wear and tear on the arteries of the heart as their increased heart rate forces blood through tightened vessels. Increased sympathetic nervous system activation not only puts a strain on the coronary arteries but also leads to surges of stress-related hormones from the adrenal glands, including the catecholamines (adrenaline and noradrenaline). High levels of these hormones are associated with increases in cholesterol and other fatty substances that are deposited in arteries and contribute to atherosclerosis (hardening of the arteries) and CHD (Bierhaus et al., 2003; Stoney & Hughes, 1999). And in fact, cholesterol and triglycerides do appear to be elevated in hostile people, even when they are not under stress (Dujovne & Houston, 1991; Engebretson & Stoney, 1995).

Hostility might also affect heart disease risk less directly, through its impact on social support. Some evidence suggests that hostile people take less advantage of their social support networks than other people do (Lepore, 1995). Some may not have much social support available, possibly because they have offended potential supporters. Whatever the case, failure to use the support they do have may intensify the impact of stressful events on hostile people. The result may be increased anger, antagonism, and, ultimately, additional stress on the cardiovascular system.

■ Are there alternative ways of interpreting the evidence?

Studies suggesting that hostility causes CHD or MI are not true experiments. Researchers cannot manipulate the independent variable, hostility, by creating it in some people but not others, nor can they create experimental conditions in which individuals who differ only in terms of hostility are compared on heart disease, the dependent variable. So although the available evidence suggests an association between hostility and heart disease, it cannot confirm that hostility is causing heart disease. Accordingly, we have to consider other possible explanations of the hostility–heart disease relationship.

Some researchers suggest that higher rates of heart problems among hostile people are due not to the impact of hostility on autonomic reactivity and hormone surges but, rather, to a third variable that accounts for the other two. Specifically, genetically determined autonomic reactivity might increase the likelihood of both hostility and heart disease (Krantz et al., 1988). Supporting this alternative interpretation is evidence that people with an inherited predisposition toward strong physiological responses to the stressors of everyday life not only have a higher risk for CHD but also tend to be more hostile (Cacioppo et al., 1998). It is at least plausible, then, that some individuals are biologically predisposed to exaggerated autonomic reactivity and to hostility, each of which is independent of the other.

It has also been suggested that hostility may be only one of many traits linked to heart disease. Depressiveness, hopelessness, pessimism, and anxiety may be involved, too (Frasure-Smith & Lespérance, 2005; Kubzansky, Davidson, & Rozanski, 2005; Nicholson, Fuhrer, & Marmot, 2005; Suls & Bunde, 2005).

■ What additional evidence would help to evaluate the alternatives?

One way of testing whether hostile people's higher rates of heart disease are related to their hostility or to a more general tendency toward intense physiological arousal is to examine how hostile individuals react to stressors under circumstances in which their hostility is deactivated. Researchers have done exactly this by observing the physiological reactions of hostile people as they endure the stress of surgery under general anesthesia. The results indicate that, even while unconscious, hostile people show unusually strong autonomic reactivity (Krantz & Durel, 1983). So it is more likely that oversensitivity to stressors, not hostile thinking, is causing this exaggerated response. This possibility is supported by research showing that, compared with other people, individuals who have strong blood pressure responses to stressors also show different patterns of brain activity during stress (Gianaros et al., 2005).

To more fully illuminate the role of hostility in the development of heart disease, future research will have to take into account a number of important possibilities: (1) Some individuals may be biologically predisposed to react to stress and challenge with hostility and increased cardiovascular activity, which in turn may contribute to heart disease; (2) hostile people may amplify and perpetuate their stress through aggressive thoughts and actions, which in turn may provoke others and elicit additional stressors; and (3) people high in hostility may harm their health to a greater extent than less hostile people by smoking, drinking, overeating, failing to exercise, and engaging in other high-risk behaviors (Houston & Vavac, 1991).

■ What conclusions are most reasonable?

Although there is some inconsistency among various studies, most researchers continue to find that hostile individuals have a higher risk of heart disease and heart attacks than do other people (Krantz & McCeney, 2002; Stansfeld & Marmot, 2002). However, the causal relationship is probably more complex than researchers first thought; it appears that many interacting factors affect the relationship between hostility and CHD.

We must also keep in mind that the relationship between heart problems and hostility may not be universal. The relationship does appear to hold for women, as well as for men, and for individuals in various ethnic groups (e.g., Nakano & Kitamura, 2001; Olson et al., 2005; Stoney & Engebretson, 1994; Yoshimasu et al., 2002). However, final conclusions must await further research that examines the impact of gender, culture, and ethnicity on the link between hostility and heart disease (Finney, Stoney, & Engebretson, 2002). ■

▪● Risking Your Life: Health-Endangering Behaviors

As we have seen, many of today's major health problems are caused or amplified by preventable behaviors such as those listed in Table 13.1.

●**Smoking** Smoking is the single most preventable risk factor for fatal illnesses in the United States (U.S. Surgeon General, 2004). It accounts for 440,000 deaths each year—which is 20 percent of all U.S. deaths and more than those caused by all other drugs, car accidents, suicides, homicides, and fires combined (Centers for Disease Control and Prevention, 2002a; U.S. Department of Health and Human Services, 2001b; Mokdad et al., 2004). Even nonsmokers who inhale second-hand smoke face an elevated risk for respiratory diseases, including lung cancer, and for cardiovascular diseases as well (Menzies et al., 2006; Vineis et al., 2005; Wen et al., 2006), a fact that has fueled a militant nonsmokers' rights movement in North America and in some European countries.

Although smoking is declining in the United States overall—only about 23.5 percent of adults now smoke—the rate is higher (almost 28 percent) for those between the ages of eighteen and twenty-four and much higher (40.8%) among American Indians and Alaskan Natives (American Lung Association, 2002; Centers for Disease Control and Prevention, 2002a). In North America, only about 4 percent of smokers who try to quit on their own remain abstinent, and only 27 to 30 percent of those using nicotine replacement and/or behavior modification programs achieve long-term success (American Lung Association, 2002; Lancaster et al., 2006). Still, persistence can pay off: There are more than 45 million former smokers in the United States alone (Niaura & Abrams, 2002). Improving this success rate and preventing adolescents from taking up smoking remain among health psychology's greatest challenges.

●**Unsafe Sex** About 40 million people worldwide are HIV-positive, and about 21 million have died from AIDS (Sepkowitz, 2006; World Health Organization, 2003). About a million people in the United States have AIDS or HIV (Centers for Disease Control, 2005), though as many as 300,000 HIV victims are unaware of being infected (Glynn & Rhodes, 2005; Sepkowitz, 2006). With growing public awareness that using condoms can prevent HIV infection, and with the availability of better treatment methods, the number of new AIDS cases and AIDS deaths began to fall in the United States during the 1990s. AIDS deaths are continuing to fall somewhat, but the number of new HIV/AIDS cases is again on the rise. Current estimates are that about 40,000 HIV infections occur each year, many of which stem from heterosexual contact with people who don't know they are infected (Centers for Disease Control and Prevention, 2005; Sepkowitz, 2006).

In short, not everyone is getting the HIV/AIDS prevention message. Like smoking and many other health-threatening behaviors, unprotected sex is disproportionately common among low-income individuals, many of whom are members of ethnic minority groups. As a result, African American women's risk of contracting HIV is fifteen times higher than that of European American women. African American men are three times more likely than European American men to contract HIV; in fact, AIDS is the leading cause of death among African American men between the ages of twenty-five and forty-four (Centers for Disease Control and Prevention, 2005).

Promoting Healthy Behavior

Health psychologists are deeply involved in the development of smoking cessation programs, in campaigns to prevent young people from taking up smoking, in obesity-prevention efforts, and in the fight against the spread of HIV infection and AIDS

Doctor's Orders Despite their physicians' instructions, many patients fail to take their blood pressure medication and continue to eat unhealthy diets. Noncompliance with medical advice is especially common when cultural values and beliefs conflict with that advice. Aware of this problem, health psychologists are developing culture-sensitive approaches to health promotion and disease prevention (Kazarian & Evans, 2001).

(e.g., Carey et al., 2004; Durantini et al., 2006; Morisky et al., 2006; Stice, Shaw, & Nathan, 2006). They have also helped promote early detection of disease. Encouraging women to perform breast self-examinations and men to do testicular self-examinations are just two examples of health psychology programs that can save thousands of lives each year (Taylor, 2002). Health psychologists have also explored the reasons behind some people's failure to follow treatment regimens that are vital to the control of diseases such as diabetes, heart disease, HIV/AIDS, and high blood pressure (Bartlett, 2002; Gonzalez et al., 2004). Understanding these reasons and devising procedures that encourage greater adherence to medical advice could speed recovery, prevent unnecessary suffering, decrease costs, and save many lives (Barclay et al., 2007; Simpson et al., 2006).

Health psychologists' efforts to prevent, reduce, or eliminate behaviors that pose health risks and to increase healthy behavior patterns are called **health promotion** (Smith, Orleans, & Jenkins, 2004). For example, they have developed many of the health promotion programs now used in school systems to teach children and adolescents the skills necessary to turn down cigarettes, drugs, and unprotected sex. To meet the more difficult challenge of modifying existing health-threatening behaviors, health psychologists go into workplaces and communities with the goal of altering diet, smoking, and exercise patterns, promoting safe driving habits, helping elderly people to avoid falling, and teaching stress-management techniques (Langenberg et al., 2000; Lisspers et al., 2005; Tuomilehto et al., 2001). These programs may have the added advantage of creating savings in future medical treatment costs (Blumenthal et al., 2002; Schneiderman et al., 2001).

● Health Beliefs and Health Behaviors

Health psychologists are also trying to understand the thought processes that lead people to engage in health-endangering behaviors and that can interfere with efforts to adopt healthier lifestyles. Their research has led to intervention programs that seek to change these patterns of thinking, or at least take them into account. In one study, for example, women who avoid thinking about the risks of breast cancer were more likely to get a mammogram screening after receiving health information that was tailored to their cognitive styles (Williams-Piehota et al., 2005).

This cognitive approach to health psychology is embodied in various *health-belief models*. One of the most influential of these models was developed by Irwin

health promotion The process of altering or eliminating behaviors that pose risks to health, as well as encouraging healthy behavior patterns.

© Steve Kelley/Copley News Service.

Rosenstock (1974). This model is based on the assumption that people's decisions about health-related behaviors (such as smoking) are guided by four main factors:

1. Perceiving a *personal threat* of, or susceptibility to, developing a specific health problem. (Do you believe that *you* will get lung cancer from smoking?)

2. Perceiving the seriousness of the illness and the consequences of having it. (How serious do *you* think lung cancer is, and what will happen if you get it?)

3. The belief that changing a particular behavior will reduce the threat. (Will giving up smoking prevent *you* from getting lung cancer?)

4. A comparison of the *perceived costs* of enacting a health-related behavior change and the *benefits expected* from that change. (Will the reduced chance of getting cancer in the future be worth the discomfort and loss of pleasure associated with not smoking?)

This health-belief model suggests that the people most likely to quit smoking would be those who believe that they are at risk for getting cancer from smoking, that cancer is serious and life-threatening, that quitting will reduce their chances of getting cancer, and that the benefits of preventing cancer clearly outweigh the difficulties associated with quitting.

Other cognitive factors not included in Rosenstock's model may also be important, however. For example, people are unlikely to try to quit smoking unless they believe they can succeed. So *self-efficacy*, the belief that one is able to perform some behavior, is an additional consideration in decisions about health behaviors (Armitage, 2005; Bandura, 1992). A related factor is the person's intention to engage in a behavior designed to improve health or protect against illness (Albarracín et al., 2001; Schwarzer, 2001; Webb & Sheeran, 2006).

Health-belief models have been useful in predicting a variety of health behaviors, including exercise (McAuley, 1992), safe-sex practices (Fisher, Fisher, & Rye, 1995), following doctors' orders (Bond, Aiken, & Somerville, 1992), and having vaccinations and routine mammograms (Brewer et al., 2007; Champion & Huster, 1995). These models have also shaped health promotion efforts. For example, interventions with individuals at high risk for AIDS, particularly adolescents and African American women, include programs to improve knowledge about the disease and skill in demanding safe sex (e.g., DiClemente et al., 2004).

● Changing Health Behaviors: Stages of Readiness

Changing health-related behaviors depends not only on a person's health beliefs but also on that person's readiness to change. According to James Prochaska and his colleagues, the process of successful change occurs in five stages (Prochaska, DiClemente, & Norcross, 1992; Schumann et al., 2005):

1. *Precontemplation.* The person does not perceive a health-related problem and has no intention of changing in the foreseeable future.

2. *Contemplation.* The person is aware of a health-related behavior that should be changed and is seriously thinking about changing it. People often get stuck here. Smokers, for example, have been known to spend years "thinking about" quitting.

3. *Preparation.* The person has a strong intention to change; has specific plans to do so; and may already have taken preliminary steps, such as cutting down on smoking.

4. *Action.* The person at this stage is engaging successfully in behavior change. Because "backsliding," or relapse, is so common when trying to change health-related behaviors, people must remain successful for up to six months before they officially reach the final stage.

5. *Maintenance.* The person uses skills learned along the way to continue the healthy behavior and to prevent relapse.

These stages may actually overlap somewhat; for example, some "precontemplators" might actually be starting to contemplate change (Herzog & Blagg, 2007). In any case, the path from precontemplation through maintenance may not be a smooth one. Usually, people relapse and repeat one or more of the previous stages before finally achieving stability in the healthy behavior they desire (Polivy & Herman, 2002). For example, smokers typically require three to four cycles through the stages and up to seven years before they finally reach the maintenance stage (Piasecki, 2006).

Programs for Coping with Stress and Promoting Health

An important part of health psychologists' health promotion work has been to improve people's stress-coping skills (e.g., Keogh, Bond, & Flaxman, 2006). Let's consider a few specific procedures and programs associated with this effort.

● Planning to Cope
Just as people with money in the bank have a better chance of weathering a financial crisis, those with effective coping skills may escape some of the more harmful effects of intense stress. Like family money, the ability to handle stress appears to come naturally to some people, but coping can also be learned (Lewis Claar & Blumenthal, 2003).

The first step in learning to cope with stress is to make a systematic assessment of the degree to which stress is disrupting your life. This assessment involves (1) identifying the specific events and situations, such as conflicts or life changes, that are operating as stressors, and (2) noting the effects of these stressors, such as headaches, lack of concentration, or excessive drinking. Table 13.4 lists the other steps in a program to cope with stress. Notice that the second step is to select an appropriate goal. Should you try to eliminate stressors or try to change your response to them? Knowing the difference between changeable and unchangeable stressors is important. Stress-related problems are especially common among people who either exhaust themselves trying to change unchangeable stressors or miss opportunities to change stressors that can be changed (Folkman, 1984).

Bear in mind that no single method of coping with stressors is right for everyone, or every stressor. As mentioned earlier, for example, denying the existence of an uncontrollable stressor may be fine in the short run but may eventually lead to problems if no other coping method is used (Suls & Fletcher, 1985). Similarly, people who rely exclusively on an active problem-solving approach may handle controllable stressors well but find themselves nearly helpless in the face of uncontrollable ones (Murray & Terry, 1999). The most successful stress managers may be those who can adjust their coping methods to the demands of changing situations and differing stressors (Taylor, 2002).

Taking Time Out The workplace is the number one source of stress for many people in the United States. On January 1, 2000, Raymond Fowler, who was then chief executive officer of the American Psychological Association, joined the ranks of those whose elevated blood pressure, heart problems, and other physical stress responses necessitated a temporary leave of absence from highly stressful jobs (Fowler, 2000). The National Institute for Occupational Safety and Health (1999) suggests a wide range of other behavioral coping options for stressed employees who cannot afford to take time off.

TABLE 13.4   **Stages in Coping with Stress**

Many successful programs for systematically coping with stress guide people through several stages and are aimed at removing stressors that can be changed and at reducing responses to stressors that cannot be changed (Taylor, 2002).

Stage	Task
1. Assessment	Identify the sources and effects of stress.
2. Goal setting	List the stressors and stress responses to be addressed. Designate which stressors are and are not changeable.
3. Planning	List the specific steps to be taken to cope with stress.
4. Action	Implement coping plans.
5. Evaluation	Determine the changes in stressors and stress responses that have occurred as a result of coping methods.
6. Adjustment	Alter coping methods to improve results, if necessary.

LINKAGES (a link to Treatment of Psychological Disorders, p. 644)

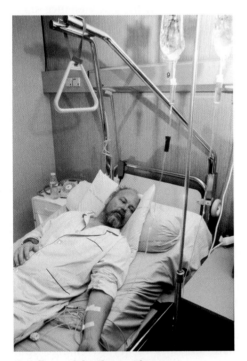

Dealing with Chemotherapy
Progressive relaxation training can be used to ease a variety of health-related problems. For example, one study found that this training resulted in significant reductions in anxiety, physiological arousal, and nausea following cancer chemotherapy (Burish & Jenkins, 1992).

● **progressive muscle relaxation training** A procedure for learning to relax that involves tensing muscles and then releasing the tension in those muscles.

● **Developing Coping Strategies**   Like stress responses, strategies for coping with stress can be cognitive, emotional, behavioral, or physical. *Cognitive coping strategies* involve changing how we think about stressors. For example, students with heavy course loads may experience anxiety, confusion, discouragement, lack of motivation, and the desire to run away from it all. Frightening, catastrophizing thoughts about their tasks (for example, "What if I fail?") magnify these stress responses. Cognitive coping strategies replace catastrophic thinking with thoughts in which stressors are viewed as challenges rather than threats (Ellis & Bernard, 1985). This substitution process is called *cognitive restructuring* (Lazarus, 1971; Meichenbaum, 1977). It can be done by practicing calmer, more rational and constructive thoughts such as "All I can do is the best I can." Cognitive coping does not eliminate stressors, but it can help people perceive them as less threatening and thus make them less disruptive while generating a more hopeful emotional state (Antoni et al., 2001; Chesney et al., 2003).

Seeking and finding social support from others are effective *emotional coping strategies*. The perception that you have such support and that you are cared for and valued by others tends to be an effective buffer against the ill effects of many stressors (Taylor, 2002; Taylor, Klein, et al., 2000). Research suggests that having enhanced social support is associated with improved immune function (Kiecolt-Glaser & Newton, 2001) and more rapid recovery from illness (Taylor, 2002).

Behavioral coping strategies involve changing behavior in ways that minimize the impact of stressors. Time management is one example. If it seems that you are always pressed for time, consider developing a time management plan. The first step is to use a calendar or day planner to record how you spend each hour of each day in a typical week. Next, analyze the information to locate when and how you might be wasting time and how you might use your time more efficiently. Then set out a schedule for the coming week and stick to it. Make adjustments in subsequent weeks as you learn more realistic ways to manage your time. Time management can't create more time, but it can help control catastrophizing thoughts by providing reassurance that there is enough time for everything and a plan for handling everything you have to do. ⚙️→ TRY THIS

Physical coping strategies are aimed at directly altering the undesirable physiological responses that occur before, during, or after the appearance of stressors. The most common physical coping strategy is some form of drug use. Prescription medications are sometimes an appropriate coping aid, especially when stressors are severe and acute, such as the sudden death of one's child. But if people depend on prescriptions or other drugs, including alcohol, to help them face stressors, they often attribute any success to the drug, not to their own skill. Furthermore, the drug effects that blunt stress responses may also interfere with the ability to apply coping strategies. The resulting loss of perceived control over stressors may make those stressors even more threatening and disruptive.

in review	Methods for Coping with Stress	
Type of Coping Method	**Examples**
Cognitive	Thinking of stressors as challenges rather than as threats; avoiding perfectionism.
Emotional	Seeking social support; getting advice.
Behavioral	Implementing a time-management plan; where possible, making life changes to eliminate stressors.
Physical	Progressive relaxation training; exercise; meditation.

Nonchemical methods of reducing physical stress reactions and improving functioning include progressive muscle relaxation training (Bernstein, Borkovec, & Hazlett-Stevens, 2000; Scheufele, 2000), physical exercise (Anshel, 1996), biofeedback (Sarafino & Goehring, 2000), and meditation and tai chi (Li et al., 2001), among others (Taylor, 2002).

Progressive muscle relaxation training is one of the most popular physical methods for coping with stress. Edmund Jacobson developed the technique during the 1930s (Jacobson, 1938). Today, progressive muscle relaxation is learned by tensing a group of muscles (such as the hand and arm) for a few seconds, then releasing the tension and focusing on the resulting feelings of relaxation. This procedure is repeated for each of sixteen muscle groups throughout the body (Bernstein et al., 2000). Once people develop some skill at relaxation, they can use it to calm themselves down anywhere and anytime, often without lying down. ("In Review: Methods for Coping with Stress" summarizes our discussion of stress-coping methods.)

LINKAGES

As noted in the chapter on introducing psychology, all of psychology's many subfields are related to one another. Our discussion of posttraumatic stress disorder illustrates just one way in which the topic of this chapter, health, stress, and coping, is linked to the subfield of psychological disorders (which is the focus of the chapter by that name). The Linkages diagram shows ties to two other subfields as well, and there are many more ties throughout the book. Looking for linkages among subfields will help you see how they all fit together and help you better appreciate the big picture that is psychology.

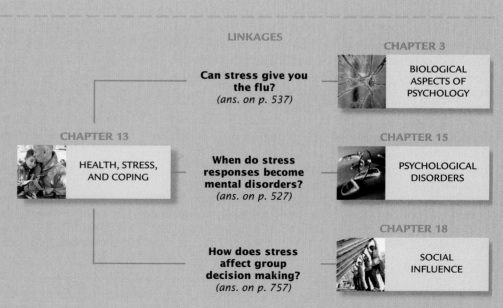

SUMMARY

Health Psychology

The development of *health psychology* was prompted by recognition of the link between stress and illness, as well as the role of behaviors such as smoking, in elevating the risk of illness. Researchers in this field explore how psychological factors are related to physical disease and vice versa. Health psychologists also help people to behave in ways that prevent or minimize disease and promote health.

Stress and Stressors

The term *stress* refers in part to *stressors*, which are events and situations to which people must adjust. More generally, stress is viewed as an ongoing, interactive process that takes place as people adjust to and cope with their environment. Stressors may be physical or psychological.

Psychological Stressors Psychological stressors include life changes and strains, catastrophic events, acute stressors, daily hassles, and chronic stressors.

Measuring Stressors Stressors can be measured by tests such as the Social Readjustment Rating Scale (SRRS) and the Life Experiences Survey (LES), as well as by surveys of daily hassles, but scores on such tests provide only a partial picture of the stress in an individual's life.

Stress Responses

Responses to stressors can be physical or psychological. They can occur alone or in combination, and the appearance of one response can stimulate others.

Physical Responses Physical stress responses include changes in sympatho-adreno-medullary (SAM) activation, such as increases in heart rate, respiration, and many other processes, as well as hypothalamic-pituitary-adrenocortical (HPA) activation, including the release of corticosteroids. These responses are part of a pattern known as the *general adaptation syndrome*, or *GAS*. The GAS has three stages: alarm, resistance, and exhaustion. The GAS helps people resist stress, but if present too long, it can lead to depletion of physiological resources, as well as to physical illnesses, which Hans Selye called *diseases of adaptation*.

Psychological Responses Psychological stress responses can be emotional, cognitive, and behavioral. Cognitive stress reactions include ruminative thinking; catastrophizing; and disruptions in the ability to think clearly, remember accurately, and solve problems efficiently. Behavioral stress responses include irritability, aggression, absenteeism, and even suicide attempts. Extreme or chronic stressors can lead to *burnout* or *posttraumatic stress disorder (PTSD)*.

Stress Mediators: Interactions Between People and Stressors

The fact that different individuals react to the same stressors in different ways can be explained in part by stress mediators, such as the extent to which individuals can predict and control their stressors, how they interpret the threat involved, the social support they get, and their stress-coping skills.

How Stressors Are Perceived Many stressors are not inherently stressful; their impact depends partly on how people perceive them. In particular, stressors appraised as threats are likely to have greater impact than those appraised as challenges.

Predictability and Control Knowing that a particular stressor might occur but being uncertain whether it will occur tends to increase the stressor's impact, as does lack of control over stressors.

Coping Resources and Coping Methods The people most likely to react strongly to a stressor are those whose coping resources and coping methods are inadequate.

Social Support Social support, which consists of resources provided by other persons, can lessen the impact of stressors. The friends and social contacts on whom a person can depend for support constitute that person's *social support network*.

Stress, Personality, and Gender Certain personality characteristics help insulate people from the ill effects of stress. One such characteristic appears to be dispositional optimism, the belief or expectation that things will work out positively. Gender can also play a role in stress responses.

The Physiology and Psychology of Health and Illness

Stress, Illness, and the Immune System *Psychoneuroimmunology* is the field that examines the interaction of psychological and physiological processes that affect the body's ability to defend itself against disease. When a person is under stress, some of the hormones released from the adrenal gland, such as cortisol, reduce the effectiveness of the cells of the immune system (for example, T-cells, B-cells, natural killer cells, and macrophages) in combating foreign invaders such as viruses.

Stress, Illness, and the Cardiovascular System Heart disease is a major cause of death in most Western countries, including the United States. People who are hostile appear to be at greater risk for heart disease than other people, possibly because their heightened reactivity to stressors can damage their cardiovascular system.

Risking Your Life: Health-Endangering Behaviors   Many of the major health problems in Western cultures are related to preventable behaviors such as smoking and having unsafe sex.

Promoting Healthy Behavior

The process of altering or eliminating health-risky behaviors and fostering healthy behavior patterns is called *health promotion.*

Health Beliefs and Health Behaviors   People's health-related behaviors are partly guided by their beliefs about health risks and what they can do about them.

Changing Health Behaviors: Stages of Readiness   The process of changing health-related behaviors may involve several stages, including precontemplation, contemplation, preparation, action, and maintenance. Understanding which stages people are in and helping them move through these stages are important tasks in health psychology.

Programs for Coping with Stress and Promoting Health To cope with stress, people must recognize the stressors affecting them, note their effects, and develop ways of handling them. Important coping skills include cognitive restructuring, as well as using emotional and behavioral means to minimize the intensity and impact of stressors. *Progressive muscle relaxation training* and other physical coping strategies can reduce physical stress reactions. These coping procedures are often part of health psychologists' disease-prevention and health-promotion efforts.

14

Personality

If you've ever been stuck in a traffic jam, you've probably noticed that some people are tolerant and calm. Others become so fearful and cautious that they worsen the congestion. Still others get so impatient and angry that they may trigger a shouting match or cause an accident. How people handle frustration is just one aspect of their personalities. In this chapter, we examine the concept of personality, review some of the tests that psychologists have developed to measure it, and look at how personality theories and research are being applied in everyday life. Here's how we have organized the material:

It has been estimated that U.S. businesses lose more than $60 billion each year as a result of employee theft (Gatewood & Feild, 2001). Millions more are spent on security and surveillance designed to curb these losses, but it would be far better if companies could simply avoid hiring dishonest employees in the first place. Some firms have tried to screen out potential thieves by requiring prospective employees to take "lie detector" polygraph tests. As described in the chapter on motivation and emotion, however, these tests may not be reliable or valid. In fact, the federal government has banned their use in most kinds of employee selection.

Thousands of companies have turned instead to paper-and-pencil "integrity" tests designed to identify job applicants who are likely to steal or behave in other dishonest or irresponsible ways (Wanek, Sackett, & Ones, 2003). Some of these tests simply ask applicants if they have stolen from previous employers and if they might steal in the future. Such questions can screen out people who are honest about their stealing, but most people who steal would probably also lie to conceal previous crimes or criminal intentions. Accordingly, some companies now use tests to assess applicants' general psychological characteristics and compare their scores with those of current or past employees. Applicants whose characteristics are most like the company's honest employees are hired; those who appear similar to dishonest employees are not hired.

Can undesirable employee behaviors be predicted on the basis of such tests? To some extent, they can. For example, scores on the *Reliability Scale*—which includes questions about impulsivity and disruptive behavior during school years—are significantly correlated with a broad range of undesirable activities in the workplace (Hogan, 2005). But psychological tests are far from perfect predictors of those activities (Mumford et al., 2001). Although better than polygraph tests, psychological tests still fail to detect dishonesty in some people, and worse, they may falsely identify some honest people as potential thieves. The best that companies can hope for is to find tests that will help reduce the overall likelihood of hiring dishonest people.

The use of psychological tests to help select honest employees is a more formal version of the process that most of us use when we meet someone new. We observe the person's behavior, form impressions, and draw conclusions—often within just a few seconds (Borkenau et al., 2004)—about how that person will act at other times or under other circumstances. Like the employer, we are looking for clues to *personality*. Although there is no universally accepted definition, psychologists generally view **personality** as the unique pattern of enduring thoughts, feelings, and actions that characterize a person. Personality research, in turn, focuses on understanding the origins or causes of the similarities and differences among people in their patterns of thinking, emotion, and behavior.

With such a large agenda, personality researchers must incorporate information from many other areas of psychology. In fact, personality psychology lies at the crossroads of all psychological research (Funder, 2004). It is the merging, in a particular individual, of all the psychological, behavioral, and biological processes discussed in this book. To gain a full understanding of anyone's personality, for example, you must know something about that person's developmental experiences (including cultural influences), genetic and other biological characteristics, perceptual and other information-processing habits and biases, typical patterns of emotional expression, and social skills. Psychologists also want to know about personality in general, such as how it develops and changes across the life span, why some people are usually optimistic whereas others are usually pessimistic, and how consistent or inconsistent people's behavior tends to be from one situation to the next.

personality The pattern of psychological and behavioral characteristics by which each person can be compared and contrasted with others.

In this chapter we describe four approaches to the study of personality and some of the ways in which personality theory and research are being applied. We begin by presenting the *psychodynamic approach*, which was developed by Sigmund Freud and later modified by a number of people he influenced. Next, we describe the *trait approach*, which focuses on the consistent patterns of thoughts, feelings, and actions that form individual personalities. Then we present the *social-cognitive approach*, which explores the roles of learning and cognition in shaping human behavior. Finally, we consider the *humanistic approach*, with its emphasis on personality as a reflection of personal growth and the search for meaning in life. After reviewing these approaches, we describe how psychologists measure and compare people's personalities. We also give some examples of how psychological tests are being used in personality research and in other ways as well.

The Psychodynamic Approach

Some people think they can understand personality by simply watching people. Someone with an "outgoing personality," for example, shows it by acting friendly and sociable. But is that all there is to personality? Not according to Sigmund Freud. Trained as a medical doctor in the late 1800s, Freud spent most of his life in Vienna, Austria, treating patients who displayed "neurotic" disorders, such as blindness or paralysis, for which there was no physical cause. Freud's experience with these patients, as well as his reading of the works of Charles Darwin and other scientists of his day, led him to believe that our personalities, behavior, and behavior disorders are determined mainly by basic drives and past psychological events (Allen, 2006). He agreed, too, with Sir Francis Galton and other nineteenth-century writers when he proposed that people may not know why they feel, think, or act the way they do, because these activities are partly controlled by the unconscious part of the personality—the part of which we are not normally aware (Funder, 2004). From these ideas Freud created the **psychodynamic approach** to personality, which assumes that our thoughts, feelings, and behavior are determined by the interaction of various unconscious psychological processes (Schultz & Schultz, 2005).

Founder of the Psychodynamic Approach   Here is Sigmund Freud with his daughter, Anna, who became a psychoanalyst herself and eventually developed a revised version of her father's theories.

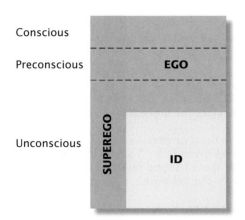

Conscious

Preconscious

Unconscious

EGO

SUPEREGO

ID

FIGURE **14.1**

Freud's Model of Personality

According to Freud, some parts of the personality are conscious, whereas others are unconscious. Between these levels is the *preconscious*, which Freud saw as the location of memories and other material not usually in awareness but that can be brought into consciousness with little or no effort.

- **psychodynamic approach** Freud's view that personality is based on the interplay of unconscious mental processes.

- **id** The unconscious portion of personality that contains basic impulses and urges.

- **libido** The psychic energy contained in the id.

- **pleasure principle** The id's operating principle, which guides people toward whatever feels good.

- **ego** The part of the personality that mediates conflicts between and among the demands of the id, the superego, and the real world.

- **reality principle** The operating principle of the ego that creates compromises between the id's demands and those of the real world.

- **superego** The component of personality that tells people what they should and should not do.

- **defense mechanism** A psychological response that helps protect a person from anxiety and guilt.

- **psychosexual stages** Periods of personality development in which, according to Freud, conflicts focus on particular issues.

▮ ● The Structure and Development of Personality

Freud believed that people have certain basic impulses or urges—related not only to food and water, but also to sex and aggression. In most translations of his writings, the term *instinct* is used to describe these impulses and urges, though Freud did not believe that they are all inborn and unchangeable, as the word *instinct* might imply (Schultz & Schultz, 2005). He did believe, though, that our desires for love, knowledge, security, and the like arise from these more basic impulses. He said that each of us faces the task of figuring out how to satisfy basic urges. Our personality develops, he claimed, as we struggle with that task, and it is reflected in the ways we go about satisfying a range of urges.

● **Id, Ego, and Superego** As shown in Figure 14.1, Freud described the structure of personality as having three major components: the id, the ego, and the superego (Allen, 2006).

He saw the **id** as the unconscious portion of personality, in which two kinds of "instincts" reside. There are life instincts, which he called *Eros*. They promote positive, constructive behavior and reflect a source of energy (sometimes called *psychic energy*) known as **libido**. There are also death instincts, or *Thanatos*, which Freud saw as responsible for aggression and destructiveness (Hergenhahn & Olson, 2007). The id operates on the **pleasure principle**, seeking immediate satisfaction of both kinds of instincts, regardless of society's rules or the rights or feelings of others. The hungry person who pushes to the front of the line at Burger King would be satisfying an id-driven impulse.

Parents, teachers, and others soon begin to place more and more restrictions on children's expression of their id impulses. In the face of these restrictions, a second part of the personality—the **ego**—develops from the id. The ego tries to find ways to get what a person wants in the real world, as opposed to the fantasy world of the id. Operating on the **reality principle**, the ego makes compromises between the id's unreasoning demands for immediate satisfaction and the practical limits imposed by the social world. The ego would lead that hungry person at Burger King to wait in line and think about what to order rather than risk punishment by pushing ahead.

As children learn about the rules and values of society, they tend to adopt them. This process of *internalizing* parental and cultural values produces the third component of personality. It is called the **superego**, and it tells us what we should and should not do. The superego becomes our moral guide, and it is just as relentless and unreasonable as the id in its demand to be obeyed. It would make the hungry person at Burger King feel guilty for even thinking about violating society's rules.

● **Conflicts and Defenses** Freud described the inner clashes among the three personality components as *intrapsychic* or *psychodynamic conflicts*. He believed that each person's personality is shaped by the number, nature, and outcome of these conflicts. Freud said that the ego's primary function is to prevent the anxiety or guilt we would feel if we became aware of our socially unacceptable id impulses or if we thought about violating the superego's rules (Engler, 2003). Sometimes, the ego motivates sensible actions, as when a parent asks for help in dealing with impulses to abuse a child. However, the ego may also use **defense mechanisms**, which are unconscious tactics that protect against anxiety and guilt by either preventing threatening material from surfacing or disguising it when it does (Porcerelli et al., 2004) (see Table 14.1).

● **Stages in Personality Development** Freud proposed that personality develops during childhood in a series of **psychosexual stages**. Failure to resolve the problems and conflicts that appear at a given stage can leave a person *fixated*—that is, unconsciously preoccupied with the area of pleasure associated with that stage. Freud believed that the stage at which a person became fixated in childhood can be seen in adult personality characteristics.

TABLE **14.1**   **Ego Defense Mechanisms**

TRY THIS According to Freud, defense mechanisms deflect anxiety or guilt in the short run, but they sap energy. Further, using them to avoid dealing with the source of problems can make those problems worse in the long run. Try listing some incidents in which you or someone you know might have used each of the defenses described here. What questions would a critical thinker ask to determine whether these behaviors were unconscious defense mechanisms or actions motivated by conscious intentions?

Defense Mechanism	Description
Repression	Unconsciously pushing threatening memories, urges, or ideas from conscious awareness: A person may experience loss of memory for unpleasant events.
Rationalization	Attempting to make actions or mistakes seem reasonable: The reasons or excuses given (e.g., "I spank my children because it is good for them") sound rational, but they are not the real reasons for the behavior.
Projection	Unconsciously attributing one's own unacceptable thoughts or impulses to another person: Instead of recognizing that "I hate him," a person may feel that "He hates me."
Reaction formation	Defending against unacceptable impulses by acting opposite to them: Sexual interest in a married co-worker might appear as strong dislike instead.
Sublimation	Converting unacceptable impulses into socially acceptable actions, and perhaps symbolically expressing them: Sexual or aggressive desires may appear as artistic creativity or devotion to athletic excellence.
Displacement	Deflecting an impulse from its original target to a less threatening one: Anger at one's boss may be expressed through hostility toward a clerk, a family member, or even a pet.
Denial	Simply discounting the existence of threatening impulses: A person may vehemently deny ever having had even the slightest degree of physical attraction to a person of the same sex.
Compensation	Striving to make up for unconscious impulses or fears: A business executive's extreme competitiveness might be aimed at compensating for unconscious feelings of inferiority.

In Freud's theory, a child's first year or so is called the **oral stage,** because the mouth—which infants use to eat and to explore everything from toys to their own hands and feet—is the center of pleasure during this period. Freud said fixation at the oral stage can stem from weaning that is too early or too late and may result in adult characteristics ranging from overeating or childlike dependence (late weaning) to the use of "biting" sarcasm (early weaning).

TRY THIS Which of Freud's ego defense mechanisms is operating here? (Check the answer at the bottom of page 556.)

© Scott Adams/Dist. by United feature Syndicate, Inc.

The Oral Stage   According to Freud, personality develops in a series of psychosexual stages. At each stage, a different part of the body becomes the primary focus of pleasure. This baby would appear to be in the oral stage.

- **oral stage**   The first of Freud's psychosexual stages, in which the mouth is the center of pleasure and conflict.

- **anal stage**   The second of Freud's psychosexual stages, usually occurring during the second year of life, in which the focus of pleasure and conflict shifts from the mouth to the anus.

- **phallic stage**   The third of Freud's psychosexual stages, in which the focus of pleasure and conflict shifts to the genital area.

- **Oedipus complex**   A pattern described by Freud in which a boy has sexual desire for his mother and wants to eliminate his father's competition for her attention.

- **Electra complex**   A pattern described by Freud in which a young girl develops an attachment to her father and competes with her mother for his attention.

- **latency period**   The fourth of Freud's psychosexual stages, in which sexual impulses lie dormant.

- **genital stage**   The last of Freud's psychosexual stages, which begins during adolescence, when sexual impulses appear at the conscious level.

The **anal stage** occurs during the second year, when the child's ego develops to cope with parental demands for socially appropriate behavior. For example, in most Western cultures, toilet training clashes with the child's freedom to have bowel movements at will. Freud said that if toilet training is too harsh or begins too early, it can produce an anal fixation that leads, in adulthood, to stinginess or excessive neatness (symbolically withholding feces). If toilet training is too late or too lax, however, the result could be a kind of anal fixation that is reflected in adults who are disorganized or impulsive (symbolically expelling feces).

According to Freud, between the ages of three and five, the child's focus of pleasure shifts to the genital area. Because he emphasized male psychosexual development, Freud called this period the **phallic stage** (*phallus* is another word for penis). He believed that during this stage, a boy experiences sexual desire for his mother and a desire to eliminate, or even kill, his father, with whom the boy competes for the mother's affection. (Freud named this pattern of impulses the **Oedipus complex** because it reminded him of the plot of *Oedipus Rex*, the classical Greek play in which Oedipus, upon returning to his homeland, unknowingly slays his father and marries his mother.) The boy's fantasies make him fear that his powerful "rival" (his father) will castrate him. To reduce this fear, the boy's ego represses his incestuous desires and leads him to "identify" with his father and try to be like him. It is during this stage that the male's superego begins to develop.

According to Freud, a girl begins the phallic stage with a strong attachment to her mother. When she realizes that boys have penises and girls don't, though, she supposedly develops *penis envy* and transfers her love to her father. This pattern has become known as the **Electra complex** because it parallels the plot of another classical Greek play, but Freud himself never used that label. To avoid her mother's disapproval, the girl identifies with and imitates her, thus forming the basis for her own superego.

Freud believed that unresolved conflicts from the phallic stage can lead to many problems in adulthood, including difficulties in dealing with authority figures and an inability to maintain a stable love relationship.

As the phallic stage draws to a close and its conflicts are dealt with by the ego, a peaceful interval begins. During this **latency period**, which lasts through childhood, sexual impulses stay in the background as the youngster focuses on education, same-sex peer play, and the development of social skills. In adolescence, when sexual impulses reappear at a conscious level, the genitals again become the focus of pleasure. Thus begins what Freud called the **genital stage**, which he saw as lasting for the rest of a person's life.

● Variations on Freud's Personality Theory

Freud's ideas—especially those involving the Oedipus and Electra complexes and the role of infantile sexuality—were, and still are, controversial. Even many of Freud's followers did not entirely agree with him. Some of them have been called *neo-Freudian* theorists, because they maintained many of the basic ideas in Freud's theory but developed their own approaches. Others are known as *ego psychologists*, because their ideas focused more on the ego than on the id (Larsen & Buss, 2005).

● **Jung's Analytic Psychology**   Carl Jung (pronounced "yoong") was the most prominent of Freud's early followers to chart his own theoretical course. Jung (1916) emphasized that libido is not just sexual instinct but rather a more general life force that includes an innate drive for creativity, for growth-oriented resolution of conflicts, and for the productive blending of basic impulses with real-world demands. Jung did not identify specific stages in personality development. He suggested instead that people gradually develop differing degrees of *introversion* (a tendency to reflect on one's own experiences) or *extraversion* (a tendency to focus on the social world), along with differing tendencies to rely on specific psychological functions, such as thinking versus feeling. Combinations of these differing tendencies, said Jung (1933), create personalities that display distinctive and predictable patterns of behavior.

Jung also claimed there is a *collective unconscious*, which contains the memories we have inherited from our human and nonhuman ancestors (Hergenhahn & Olson, 2007). According to Jung, we are not consciously aware of these memories, but they are responsible for our innate tendencies to react in particular ways to certain things. For example, Jung believed that our collective memory of mothers influences how each of us perceives our own mother. Although the notion of a collective unconscious is widely accepted by followers of Jung, there is no empirical evidence that it exists. In fact, Jung himself acknowledged that it would be impossible to objectively demonstrate the existence of a collective unconscious (Feist & Feist, 2002).

● **Other Neo-Freudian Theorists**   Jung was not the first or the only theorist to challenge Freud. Alfred Adler, once a loyal follower of psychoanalysis, came to believe that the power behind the development of personality comes not from id impulses but from an innate desire to overcome infantile feelings of helplessness and to gain some control over the environment. Adler (1927/1963) referred to this process as *striving for superiority*, by which he meant a drive for fulfillment as a person, not just a desire to do better than others. Other prominent neo-Freudians, including Erik Erikson, Erich Fromm, and Harry Stack Sullivan, focused on how people's personalities are shaped by those around them. They argued that once our biological needs are met, the attempt to meet social needs (to feel protected, secure, and accepted, for example) is the primary influence on personality. And according to these theorists, the strategies people use to meet these social needs, such as by dominating others or being dependent on them, become central features of their personalities.

The first feminist personality theorist, Karen Horney (pronounced "HORN-eye"), disputed Freud's view that women's lack of a penis causes them to envy men and feel inferior to them. Horney (1937) argued that, in fact, it is men who envy women: Realizing that they cannot bear children and that they often play only a small role in raising them, males see their lives as having less meaning or substance than women's. Horney called this condition *womb envy*. She argued further that when women feel inferior, it is because of the personal and political restrictions that men have placed upon them, not because of penis envy (Larsen & Buss, 2005). Horney's position on this issue reflected her strong belief that cultural factors, rather than instincts, play a major role in personality development (Hergenhahn & Olson, 2007). This greater emphasis on cultural influences is one of the major theoretical differences between Freud and the neo-Freudians generally.

● Contemporary Psychodynamic Theories

Some of the most influential psychodynamic approaches to personality now focus on *object relations*—that is, on how people's perceptions of themselves and others influence their view of, and reactions to, the world (Pervin, Cervone, & John, 2005). Early object relations theorists such as Melanie Klein (1991), Otto Kernberg (1984), Heinz Kohut (1984), and Margaret Mahler (1968), saw the first relationships between infants and their love objects—usually the mother and other primary caregivers—as vitally important in the development of personality (Klein, 1975; Kohut, 1984; Sohlberg & Jansson, 2002). In their view, these relationships shape a person's thoughts and feelings about social relationships later in life (Pervin et al., 2005).

Today, object relations theory finds its clearest expression in research on the kinds of relationships, or *attachments*, that infants form with their primary caregivers. Ideally, infants form a secure early bond to their mothers or other caregivers,

An Early Feminist   After completing medical school at the University of Berlin in 1913, Karen Horney (1885–1952) trained as a Freudian psychoanalyst. She accepted some aspects of Freud's views, including the idea of unconscious motivation, but she eventually developed her own neo-Freudian theory. She saw the need for security as more important than biological instincts in motivating infants' behavior. She also rejected Freud's notion that the psychological development of females is influenced by penis envy.

The defense mechanism illustrated in the cartoon on page 554 is displacement.

tolerate gradual separation from this "attachment object," and eventually develop the ability to relate to others as independent, secure individuals (Ainsworth, 1989; Bowlby, 1973). As described in the chapter on human development, however, some infants do not develop this *secure attachment*. Instead, they may display various kinds of *insecure attachments*. There is indeed evidence that the nature of early child-parent attachments is associated with differences in self-image, identity, security, and social relationships in adolescence, adulthood, and even old age (Consedine & Magai, 2003; Mattanah, Hancock, & Brand, 2004; Rholes, Simpson, & Friedman, 2006). In one study, people who had insecure attachment showed much stronger physiological stress reactions to interpersonal conflicts than did people whose attachments were secure (Powers et al., 2006). Another study found that people with insecure attachments were much less likely to be helpful when they encountered a person in distress (Mikulincer & Shaver, 2005). A third study found that children who, because of abuse, neglect, or rejection, miss the opportunity to become securely attached to their mothers or other adults may suffer severe disturbances in their later relationships (Aizawa, 2002).

● Evaluating the Psychodynamic Approach

Freud's personality theory is probably the most comprehensive and influential psychological theory ever proposed, and it has influenced modern Western thinking about medicine, literature, religion, sociology, and anthropology. It has also shaped a wide range of psychotherapy techniques and stimulated the development of several personality assessments, including the projective tests described later in this chapter. Some of Freud's ideas have received support from research on cognitive processes. For example, psychologists have found that people do employ several of the defense mechanisms Freud described (Cramer, 2003), although it is unclear whether these always operate at an unconscious level. As mentioned in the chapter on consciousness, there is also evidence that people's thoughts and actions can be influenced by unrecalled events and experiences (Andersen & Miranda, 2000; Andersen & Chen, 2002; Ferguson & Bargh, 2004) and perhaps by emotions that are not consciously felt (Winkielman & Berridge, 2004). Some researchers believe that unconscious processes may affect people's health (Goldenberg et al., 2005).

However, Freud's psychodynamic theories have several weaknesses. For one thing, they are based almost entirely on case studies of a few individuals. As discussed in the chapter on research in psychology, conclusions drawn from case studies may not apply to people in general. Nor was Freud's sample representative of people in general. Most of his patients were upper-class Viennese women who not only had psychological problems but also were raised in a culture in which discussion of sex was considered to be uncivilized. Moreover, Freud's thinking about personality reflected Western European and North American values, which may or may not be helpful in understanding people in other cultures (Schultz & Schultz, 2005). For example, the concepts of ego and self that are so central to Freud's personality theory (and those of his followers) are based on the self-oriented values of individualist cultures. These values may be less central to personality development in the more collectivist cultures of, say, Asia and South America (Matsumoto, 2000).

Freud's conclusions may have been distorted by other biases as well. Freudian scholars suggest for example, that Freud might have modified reports of what happened during therapy to better fit his theory (Esterson, 2001; Schultz & Schultz, 2005). He may also have asked leading questions that influenced patients to "recall" events from their childhood that never really happened (Esterson, 2001). Today, there are similar concerns that some patients who recover allegedly repressed memories about childhood sexual abuse by parents may actually be reporting false memories implanted by their therapists (Loftus, 2004).

Freud's focus on male psychosexual development and his notion that females envy male anatomy have also caused both female and male feminists to reject some or all of his ideas. In the tradition of Horney, some contemporary female neo-Freudians have proposed theories that focus specifically on the psychosexual development of women (Sayers, 1991).

Finally, as judged by today's standards, Freud's theory is not very scientific. His definitions of id, ego, unconscious conflict, and other concepts lack the precision required for scientific measurement and testing (Stanovich, 2004). His belief that human beings are driven mainly by unconscious desires ignores evidence that much human behavior goes beyond impulse gratification. The conscious drive to reach personal, social, and spiritual goals is also an important determinant of behavior, as is learning from others.

Some of the weaknesses in Freudian theory have been addressed by those who have altered some of Freud's concepts and devoted more attention to social influences on personality. Attempts have also been made to increase precision and objectivity in the measurement of psychodynamic concepts (e.g., Barber, Crits-Christoph, & Paul, 1993). Research on concepts from psychodynamic theory is, in fact, becoming more sophisticated and increasingly reflects interest in subjecting psychodynamic principles to experimental tests (e.g., Betan et al., 2005; Wegner, Wenzlaff, & Kozak, 2004; Westen, 2005). Still, the psychodynamic approach is better known for generating hypotheses about personality than for scientifically testing them. Accordingly, this approach to personality is now much less influential in mainstream psychology than it was in the past (Allen, 2006; Carver & Scheier, 2004).

The Trait Approach

If you were to describe the personality of someone you know, it would probably take the form of a small number of descriptive statements. Here is an example:

> She is a truly caring person, a real extravert. She is generous with her time, and very conscientious about everything she does. Yet sometimes she is not very assertive or confident. She always gives in to other people's demands because she wants to be accepted by them.

In other words, most people describe others by referring to the kind of people they are ("extravert," "conscientious"); to the thoughts, feelings, and actions that are most typical of them ("caring," "not very assertive," "generous"); or to their needs ("wants to be accepted"). Together, these statements describe personality *traits*—the inclinations or tendencies that help to direct how a person usually thinks and behaves (Pervin et al., 2005).

The **trait approach** to personality makes three basic assumptions:

1. Personality traits are relatively stable and therefore predictable over time. So a gentle person tends to stay that way day after day, year after year (Costa & McCrae, 2002).

2. Personality traits are relatively stable across situations, and they can explain why people act in predictable ways in many different situations. A person who is competitive at work will probably also be competitive on the tennis court or at a party.

3. People differ in how much of a particular personality trait they possess; no two people are exactly alike on all traits. The result is an endless variety of unique human personalities.

● **Traits Versus Types**   Theories about enduring differences in people's personality characteristics go back at least as far as Hippocrates, a physician of ancient Greece. He suggested that a certain temperament, or basic behavioral tendency, is associated with each of four bodily fluids, or humors: blood, phlegm, black bile, and

● **trait approach**   A perspective in which personality is seen as a combination of characteristics that people display over time and across situations.

Selecting a Jury Some psychologists employ type and trait theories of personality as they advise prosecution or defense attorneys about which potential jurors are most likely to be sympathetic to their side of a court case.

yellow bile. Personality, said Hippocrates, depends on how much of each humor a person has. His terms for the four humor-based personalities—sanguine (optimistic), phlegmatic (slow, lethargic), melancholic (sad, depressive), and choleric (angry, irritable)—still survive today.

Notice that Hippocrates was describing personality *types*, not traits. Traits involve *quantitative* differences among people—such as how much of a certain characteristic they possess. Types involve *qualitative* differences, such as whether someone possesses a certain characteristic at all. When people are "typed," they are said to belong to one class or another—such as male or female. Modern type theories of personality try to do the same by placing people in one category or another (Funder, 2004). For example, Avshalom Caspi and his colleagues claim to have identified three qualitatively different basic personality types (Caspi, 1998; Robins, John, & Caspi, 1998). These include the *well-adjusted person*, who is flexible, resourceful, and successful with other people; the *maladjusted overcontrolling person*, who is too self-controlled to enjoy life and is difficult for others to deal with; and the *maladjusted undercontrolling person*, whose excessive impulsiveness can be dangerous both for the person and for others. (This chapter's Focus on Research Methods section contains more information on these and other types.)

Type theories have recently gained acceptance among some personality researchers, but the majority of researchers doubt that it's possible to compress the dazzling range of human characteristics into a just few discrete types (McRae et al., 2006). Accordingly, the trait approach to personality remains much more influential. Trait theorists are interested in measuring the relative strength of the many personality characteristics that they believe are present in everyone (see Figure 14.2). Most of today's trait theories of personality have their origins in the work of Gordon Allport, Raymond Cattell, and Hans Eysenck.

● Allport's Trait Theory

Gordon Allport spent thirty years searching for the traits that combine to form personality. He found nearly 18,000 dictionary terms that can be used to describe human behavior (Allport & Odbert, 1936), but he noticed that many of these terms referred to the same thing (e.g., *hostile, nasty,* and *mean* all convey a similar meaning). So if you were to jot down the personality traits that describe a close friend or relative, you would probably be able to capture that individual's personality using only about seven

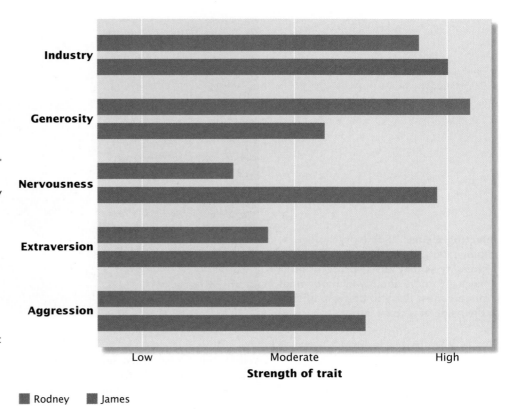

FIGURE 14.2

Two Personality Profiles

TRY
THIS   Trait theory describes personality in terms of the strength of particular dimensions, or traits. Here are trait profiles for Rodney, an inner-city social worker, and James, a sales clerk. Compared with James, Rodney is about equally industrious; more generous; and less nervous, extraverted, and aggressive. Just for fun, mark this figure to indicate how strong you think you are on each of the listed traits. Trait theorists suggest that this should be easy for you to do because, they say, virtually everyone displays a certain amount of almost any personality characteristic.

■ Rodney   ■ James

trait labels. Allport believed that the set of labels chosen to describe a particular person reflects that person's *central traits*—those that are usually obvious to others and that organize and control behavior in many different situations. Central traits are roughly equivalent to the descriptive terms used in letters of recommendation (*reliable* or *distractible*, for example) that are meant to convey what can be expected from a person most of the time (Schultz & Schultz, 2005). Allport also believed that people possess *secondary traits*—those that are more specific to certain situations and control far less behavior. "Dislikes crowds" is an example of a secondary trait.

Allport's research helped to lay the foundation for modern research on personality traits. However, his emphasis on the uniqueness of each individual personality made it difficult to draw conclusions about the structure of human personality in general (McAdams, 1997).

● The Big-Five Model of Personality

In recent years, trait approaches have continued to focus on identifying and describing the core structure of personality. This work owes much to Allport and also to a British psychologist named Raymond Cattell. Cattell asked people to rate themselves and others on many of the trait-descriptive terms that Allport had identified. He then used a mathematical technique called *factor analysis* to study which of these terms were related to one another. Factor analysis can reveal, for example, whether someone who is moody is also likely to be anxious, rigid, and unsociable. Cattell believed that the sets of traits clustering together in this analysis would reflect a set of basic personality *factors* or dimensions. His analyses eventually identified sixteen such factors, including shy versus bold, trusting versus suspicious, and relaxed versus tense. Cattell believed that these factors are found in everyone, and he measured their strength using a test called the *Sixteen Personality Factor Questionnaire*, or 16PF (Cattell, Eber, & Tatsuoka, 1970).

More recent factor analyses by researchers such as Paul Costa and Robert McCrae have led many trait theorists to believe that personality is organized around

TABLE **14.2** The Big-Five Personality Dimensions

Here is a list of the adjectives that define the big-five personality factors. You can more easily remember the names of these factors by noting that their first letters spell the word *ocean*.

Dimension	Defining Descriptors
Openness to experience	Artistic, curious, imaginative, insightful, original, wide interests, unusual thought processes, intellectual interests
Conscientiousness	Efficient, organized, planful, reliable, thorough, dependable, ethical, productive
Extraversion	Active, assertive, energetic, outgoing, talkative, gesturally expressive, gregarious
Agreeableness	Appreciative, forgiving, generous, kind, trusting, noncritical, warm, compassionate, considerate, straightforward
Neuroticism	Anxious, self-pitying, tense, emotionally unstable, impulsive, vulnerable, touchy, worrying

Source: Adapted from McCrae & John (1992).

only five basic factors (McCrae & Costa, 2004). The components of this so-called **big-five model**, or five-factor model, of personality are *openness to experience, conscientiousness, extraversion, agreeableness,* and *neuroticism* (see Table 14.2). The importance of the big-five model is suggested by the fact that different investigators find these factors (or a set very similar to them) when they factor-analyze data from personality inventories, peer ratings of personality characteristics, checklists of descriptive adjectives, and many other sources (Costa & McCrae, 1995; John & Srivastava, 1999). The fact that some version of the big-five factors reliably appears in many countries and cultures—including Canada, China, the Czech Republic, Germany, Greece, Finland, India, Japan, Korea, the Philippines, Poland, and Turkey (Allik & McCrae, 2004; Ashton et al., 2004; Yamagata et al., 2006)—provides further evidence that these few dimensions may represent the most important components of human personality (McCrae & Terracciano, 2005).

Many trait theorists believe that the big-five model represents a major breakthrough in examining the personalities of people who come from different backgrounds, differ in age, and live in different parts of the world (Carver & Scheier, 2004). It has certainly enabled psychologists to provide a comprehensive description of the basic similarities and differences in people's personalities and to explore how these factors are related to everything from attachment styles and personality disorders to subjective well-being and even future weight gain (e.g., Brummett et al., 2006; Diener, 2000; Lynam & Widiger, 2001; Noftle & Shaver, 2006).

■ ● Biological Trait Theories

Some personality theorists are interested not only in what traits form the core of human personality but also in why people differ on these traits. Their research suggests that trait differences reflect the operation of some important biological factors.

● Eysenck's Biological Trait Theory
Like Cattell, British psychologist Hans Eysenck (pronounced "EYE-sink") used factor analysis to study the structure of personality and thus helped lay the groundwork for the big-five model. Eysenck suggested that most people's traits could be described using two main dimensions—*introversion-extraversion* and *emotionality-stability* (Eysenck 1990a, 1990b; see Figure 14.3):

1. *Introversion-extraversion.* Extraverts are sociable and outgoing, enjoy parties and other group activities, take risks, and love excitement and change.

big-five model A view based on factor-analytic studies suggesting the existence of five basic components of human personality: openness, conscientiousness, extraversion, agreeableness, and neuroticism; also called the five-factor model.

Animal Personalities The idea that personality can be described in terms of five main dimensions seems to hold for some animals as well as humans. The five animal dimensions vary from, but are still related to, human traits. For example, hyenas differ from one another in terms of dominance, excitability, agreeableness (toward people), sociability (toward each other), and curiosity. Some of these same traits have been observed in other species, including dogs, horses, orangutans, and chimpanzees (Gosling, 2001; Gosling, Kwan, & John, 2003; King, Weiss, & Farmer, 2005; Weiss, King, & Perkins, 2006; Wolf et al., 2007). Cat lovers often report such traits in their pets, too.

Introverts tend to be quiet, thoughtful, and reserved, enjoying solitary pursuits and avoiding excitement and social involvement.

2. *Emotionality-stability.* At one extreme of the emotionality-stability dimension are people who display such characteristics as moodiness, restlessness, worry, anxiety, and other negative emotions. Those at the opposite extreme are calm, even-tempered, relaxed, and emotionally stable. (This dimension is also often called *neuroticism.*)

FIGURE 14.3

Eysenck's Main Personality Dimensions

TRY THIS According to Eysenck, varying degrees of emotionality-stability and introversion-extraversion combine to produce predictable trait patterns. Notice that an introverted but stable person is likely to be controlled and reliable, whereas an introverted emotional person is likely to be rigid and anxious. (The traits appearing in the quadrants created by crossing these two personality dimensions correspond roughly to Hippocrates' four temperaments.) Which section of the figure do you think best describes your personality traits? How about those of a friend or a relative? Did you find it any easier to place other people's personalities in a particular section than it was to place your own personality? If so, why do you think that might be?

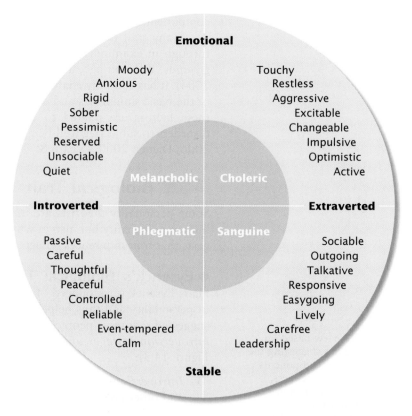

Eysenck argued that the variations in personality characteristics that we see among individuals can be traced to inherited differences in their nervous systems, especially in their brains. These biological differences, he said, create variations in people's typical levels of physiological arousal and in their sensitivity to stress and other environmental stimulation. For example, as mentioned in the motivation and emotion chapter, people who inherit a nervous system that normally operates below their optimum arousal level will always be on the lookout for excitement, change, and social contact in order to increase their arousal. As a result, these people will be *extraverted*. In contrast, people whose nervous system is normally "overaroused" will tend to avoid excitement, change, and social contact in order to reduce arousal to their optimum level. In short, they will be *introverted*. What about the emotionality-stability dimension? Eysenck said that people who score toward the stability side have nervous systems that are relatively insensitive to stress; those who are more emotional have nervous systems that react more strongly to stress.

● **Gray's Approach-Inhibition Theory** Jeffrey Gray, another British psychologist, agrees with Eysenck about the two basic dimensions of personality, but he offers a different explanation of the biological factors underlying them (Gray, 1991; Gray & McNaughton, 2000). According to Gray, differences among people in introversion-extraversion and emotionality-stability stem from two related systems in the brain: the behavioral approach system and the behavioral inhibition system. The *behavioral approach system*, or *BAS*, is made up of brain regions that affect people's sensitivity to rewards and their motivation to seek those rewards (Pickering & Gray, 1999). The BAS has been called a "go" system, because it is responsible for how impulsive or uninhibited a person is. The *behavioral inhibition system*, or *BIS*, involves brain regions that affect sensitivity to potential punishment and the motivation to avoid being punished. The BIS is a "stop" system that is responsible for how fearful or inhibited a person is. People with an active behavioral approach system tend to experience positive emotions; people with an active behavioral inhibition system are more likely to experience negative ones (Zelenski & Larsen, 1999).

In explaining Eysenck's personality dimensions, Gray sees extraverts as having a sensitive reward system (BAS) and an insensitive punishment system (BIS). Introverts are just the opposite—they are relatively insensitive to rewards but highly sensitive to punishment. Similarly, emotionally unstable people are much more sensitive to both rewards and punishments than are those who are emotionally stable.

Gray's theory has its critics (e.g., Corr, 2002), but it is now more widely accepted than Eysenck's theory—primarily because it is being supported by other research (e.g., Johnson, Ruggero, & Carver, 2005; Mitchell & Nelson-Gray, 2006) and because it is more consistent with what neuroscientists know about brain structures, neurotransmitters, and how they operate (Franken, Muris, & Georgieva, 2006; Reuter et al., 2006; Wacker, Chavanon, & Stemmler, 2006).

THINKING CRITICALLY **Are Personality Traits Inherited?**

Gray's approach-inhibition theory is one of several new biologically oriented explanations of the origins of personality traits (e.g., Zuckerman, 2004). A related approach involves investigating the genetics of these traits. Consider the case of identical twins who were separated at five weeks of age and did not meet again for thirty-nine years. Both men drove Chevrolets, chain-smoked the same brand of cigarettes, had divorced women named Linda, were remarried to women named Betty, had sons named James Allan, had dogs named Toy, enjoyed similar hobbies, and had served as sheriff's deputies (Tellegen et al., 1988).

■ What am I being asked to believe or accept?

Case studies like these have helped focus the attention of behavioral geneticists on the possibility that some core aspects of personality might be partly, or even largely, inherited (Bouchard, 2004; Ebstein, 2006; Noblett & Coccaro, 2005; Yamagata et al. 2006).

■ What evidence is available to support the assertion?

The evidence and the arguments regarding this assertion are much like those presented in the chapter on cognitive abilities, in which we discuss the origins of differences in intelligence. Stories about children who seem to "have" their parents' or grandparents' bad temper, generosity, or shyness are often presented in support of the heritability of personality. And in fact, family resemblances in personality do provide an important source of evidence. Several studies have found moderate but significant correlations between children's personality test scores and those of their parents and siblings (Davis, Luce, & Kraus, 1994; Loehlin, 1992).

Even stronger evidence comes from studies conducted around the world comparing identical twins raised together, identical twins raised apart, nonidentical twins raised together, and nonidentical twins raised apart (Grigorenko, 2002). Whether they are raised apart or together, identical twins (who have exactly the same genes) tend to be more alike in personality than nonidentical twins (whose genes are no more similar than those of other siblings). This research also shows that identical twins are more alike than nonidentical twins in general temperament, such as how active, sociable, anxious, and emotional they are, their positive attributes, and where they fall on the big-five dimensions (Borkenau et al., 2002; Yamagata et al., 2006). On the basis of such twin studies, behavioral geneticists have concluded that at least 30 percent, and perhaps as much as 60 percent, of the differences among people in terms of personality traits are due to genetic factors (Caspi, Roberts, & Shiner, 2005).

■ Are there alternative ways of interpreting the evidence?

Family resemblances in personality could reflect genetic or social influence. So an obvious alternative interpretation of this evidence might be that family similarities come not from common genes but from a common environment, especially from the examples set by parents and siblings. Children learn many rules, skills, and behaviors

Family Resemblance Do children inherit personality traits in the same direct way as they may inherit facial features, coloration, and other physical characteristics? Research in behavioral genetics suggests that personality is the joint product of genetically influenced behavioral tendencies and the environmental conditions each child encounters.

by watching those around them; perhaps they learn their personalities as well (Funder, 2004). The fact that siblings who aren't twins are less alike than twins are may well result from what are called *nonshared environments* (Plomin, 2004). A child's place in the family birth order, differences in the way parents treat each of their children, and accidents and illnesses that alter a particular child's life or health are examples of nonshared factors that can have a differential impact on each individual (Loehlin, Neiderhiser, & Reiss, 2003). Nontwins are more likely than twins, especially identical twins, to be affected by nonshared environmental factors.

■ What additional evidence would help to evaluate the alternatives?

One way to evaluate the idea that personality is inherited would be to locate genes that are associated with certain personality characteristics (Ebstein, 2006). Genetic differences have already been tentatively associated with certain behavior disorders, but most behavioral genetics researchers doubt that there are direct links between specific genes and particular personality traits (Caspi et al., 2005; Reif & Lesch, 2003).

Another way to evaluate the role of genes in personality is to study people in infancy, before the environment has had a chance to exert its influence. If the environment were entirely responsible for personality, all newborns should be essentially alike. However, as discussed in the chapter on human development, they show immediate differences in *temperament*—varying markedly in activity, sensitivity to the environment, tendency to cry, and interest in new stimuli (Rothbart & Derryberry, 2002). These differences suggest biological and perhaps genetic influences.

To evaluate the relative contributions of nature and nurture beyond infancy, psychologists have examined the characteristics of adopted children. If adopted children are more like their biological parents than their adoptive parents, this suggests the influence of heredity in personality. If they are more like their adoptive families, a strong role for environmental factors in personality would be suggested. In actuality, adopted children's personalities tend to resemble the personalities of their biological parents and siblings more than those of the families in which they are raised (Plomin et al., 1998).

Further research is needed to determine more clearly what aspects of the environment are most important in shaping personality. So far, the evidence suggests that elements in the shared environment that affect all children in the family to varying degrees (socioeconomic status, for example) are probably not the main reason that identical twins show similar personalities. As mentioned earlier, however, nonshared environmental influences may be very important in personality development (Harris, 2000; Loehlin et al., 2003). In fact, some researchers believe that nonshared influences must be considered even when trying to explain the greater similarities between identical twins reared apart than among nontwin siblings reared together. Additional research on the role of nonshared factors in personality development and the ways in which these factors might differentially affect twin and nontwin siblings' development is obviously vital. It will also be important to investigate the ways in which the personalities of individual children may affect the nature of the environment in which they are raised (Krueger, Markon, & Bouchard, 2003; see also the behavioral genetics appendix).

■ What conclusions are most reasonable?

Even those researchers, such as Robert Plomin, who support genetic theories of personality caution that we should not replace "simple-minded environmentalism" with the equally incorrect view that personality is almost completely biologically determined (Plomin & Crabbe, 2000). As with cognitive abilities, it is pointless to talk about heredity *versus* environment as causes of personality, because nature and nurture always intertwine to exert joint and simultaneous influences. For example, we know that genetic factors affect the environment in which people live (e.g., their families) and how they react to their environment, but it also turns out that environmental factors can influence which of a person's genes are activated and how much those genes affect the person's behavior (Cacioppo et al., 2000; Pickering & Gray, 1999).

With these findings in mind, we would be well advised to draw rather tentative conclusions about the sources of differences in people's personalities. The evidence available so far suggests that genetic influences do appear to contribute significantly to personality differences. However, it is important to understand the implications of this statement. As noted earlier, there is no evidence of a single gene for any specific personality trait (Plomin, 2002). The genetic contribution to personality most likely comes through the influence of sets of genes that shape people's nervous systems and their general predispositions toward certain temperaments (Arbelle et al., 2003; Ebstein, 2006; Grigorenko, 2002). Temperamental factors—such as how active, emotional, and sociable a person is—then combine with environmental factors, such as a person's interactions with other people, to produce specific features of personality (Caspi et al., 2005). For example, children who inherit a tendency toward emotionality might play less with other children, withdraw from social interactions, and thereby fail to learn important social skills (Eisenberg, Fabes, & Murphy, 1995). These experiences and tendencies, in turn, might lead to the self-consciousness and shyness seen in introverted personalities.

Notice, though, that genetic predispositions toward particular personality characteristics may or may not appear in behavior, depending on whether the environment supports or suppresses them. Changes in genetically influenced traits are not only possible but may actually be quite common as children grow (Cacioppo et al., 2000). So even though there is a strong genetic basis for shyness, many children learn to overcome this tendency and become rather outgoing (Rowe, 1997). In summary, it appears that rather than inheriting specific traits, people inherit the raw materials out of which personality is shaped by the world. ■

● Evaluating the Trait Approach

The trait approach, especially the big-five model, has gained such wide acceptance that it tends to dominate contemporary research in personality. Yet there are several problems and weaknesses associated with this approach.

For one thing, trait theories seem better at describing people than at understanding them. It is easy to say, for example, that Marilyn is nasty to others because she has a strong hostility trait; but other factors, such as the way people treat her, could also be responsible. Indeed, trait theories have typically focused more on *how* people behave than on *why* they act as they do (Mischel, 2004a, 2004b). Nor do trait theories say much about how traits are related to the thoughts and feelings that precede, accompany, and follow behavior. Do introverts and extraverts decide to act as they do, can they behave otherwise, and how do they feel about their actions and experiences? Some personality psychologists are now linking their research to that of cognitive psychologists in an effort to better understand how thoughts and emotions influence, and are influenced by, personality traits (e.g., Shoda & LeeTiernan, 2002). And as suggested in the previous section, other psychologists have become interested in the role of genes, brain structures, and neurotransmitters as causes of the individual differences we see among people's personality traits (e.g., DeYoung, Peterson, & Higgins, 2005; Netter, 2006).

Still, the trait approach has been faulted for offering a short list of traits that provides, at best, a fixed and superficial description of personality that fails to capture how traits combine to form a complex and dynamic individual (Block, 2001; Funder, 2004). Also, some people have questioned whether there are exactly five core dimensions of personality. Some research suggests, for example, that there might be a sixth dimension, namely honesty and humility (Lee, Ogunfowora, & Ashton, 2005). Others have questioned whether the factors are exactly the same in all cultures (Cross & Markus, 1999). But even if the big-five model is correct and universal, its factors are not all-powerful, because situations also affect behavior. For example, people high in extraversion are not always sociable. Whether they behave sociably depends, in part, on where they are and who else is present.

In fairness, early trait theorists, such as Allport, did implicitly acknowledge the importance of situations in influencing behavior, but it is only recently that consideration of person-situation interactions has become an explicit part of trait-based approaches to personality. This change is largely the result of research conducted by psychologists who have taken a social-cognitive approach to personality, which we describe next.

The Social-Cognitive Approach

The **social-cognitive approach** to personality differs from the psychodynamic and trait approaches in two important ways. First, social-cognitive theorists look to *conscious* thoughts and emotions for clues to how people differ from one another and what guides their behavior (Mischel, 2004b). Second, the social-cognitive approach did not grow out of clinical cases or other descriptions of people's personalities. It was based instead on the principles of animal and human learning described in the chapter on learning. In fact, the founders of the social-cognitive approach were originally known as *social-learning theorists* because of their view that what we call *personality* consists mainly of the thoughts and actions we learn through observing and interacting with family and others in social situations (Bandura & Walters, 1963; Funder, 2004).

● Roots of the Social-Cognitive Approach

Elements of the social-cognitive approach can be traced back to the behaviorism of John B. Watson. As described in the chapter on introducing psychology, Watson (1925) used research on classical conditioning to support his claim that all human behavior, from mental disorder to scientific skill, is determined by learning. B. F. Skinner broadened the behavioral approach by emphasizing the importance of operant conditioning in learning. Through what he called **functional analysis**, Skinner tried to understand behavior in terms of the function it serves in obtaining rewards or avoiding punishment. For example, if observations show that a schoolboy's aggressive behavior occurs mainly when a certain teacher is present, it may be that aggression is tolerated by that teacher, and might even be rewarded with special attention. Rather than describing personality traits, then, functional analysis summarizes what people find rewarding, what they are capable of doing, and what skills they lack.

The principles of classical and operant conditioning launched social-learning explanations of personality, but because they were focused on observable behavior, they were of limited usefulness to researchers who wanted to explore the role of thoughts in guiding behavior. As the social-learning approach evolved into the social-cognitive approach, it incorporated learning principles but also went beyond them.

Today, proponents of this very popular approach to personality seek to assess and understand how learned patterns of thoughts and feelings contribute to behavior and how behavior and its consequences alter cognitive activity, as well as future actions. In dealing with that aggressive schoolboy, for example, social-cognitive theorists would want to know not only what he has learned to do in certain situations (and how he learned it) but also what he thinks about himself, his teachers, his behavior—and his expectations about each (Shoda & Mischel, 2006).

● Prominent Social-Cognitive Theories

Julian Rotter, Albert Bandura, and Walter Mischel have presented the most influential social-cognitive personality theories.

social-cognitive approach An approach in which personality is seen as the patterns of thinking and behavior that a person learns.

functional analysis Analyzing behavior by studying what responses occur under what conditions of operant reward and punishment.

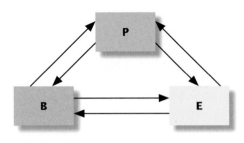

B = Behavior

E = The external environment

P = Personal factors, such as thoughts, feelings, and biological events

FIGURE 14.4

Reciprocal Determinism

Bandura's notion of reciprocal determinism suggests that personal factors (such as cognitions, or thoughts), behavior, and the environment are constantly affecting one another. For example, a person's hostile thoughts may lead to hostile behavior, which creates even more hostile thoughts. At the same time, the hostile behavior offends other people, which creates a threatening environment that causes the person to think and act in even more negative ways. As increasingly negative thoughts alter the person's perceptions of the environment, that environment seems to be more threatening than ever (Bushman et al., 2005).

● **self-efficacy** According to Bandura, learned expectations about the probability of success in given situations.

● **Rotter's Expectancy Theory** Julian Rotter (1982) argued that learning creates cognitions, known as *expectancies*, that guide behavior. Specifically, he said that a person's decision to engage in a behavior is determined by (1) what the person expects to happen following the behavior and (2) the value the person places on the outcome. For example, people spend a lot of money on clothes to be worn at a job interview because (1) past learning leads them to expect that doing so will help get them the job, and (2) they place a high value on having the job. To Rotter, then, behavior is determined not only by the kinds of consequences that Skinner called *positive reinforcers* but also by the expectation that a particular behavior will result in those consequences (Mischel, 2004b).

Rotter himself focused mainly on how expectations shape particular behaviors in particular situations, but several of the researchers he influenced also examined people's more general expectations about what controls life's rewards and punishments. Those researchers noticed that some people (*internals*) are inclined to expect events to be controlled by their own efforts. These individuals assume that what they achieve and the reinforcements they receive are due to efforts they make themselves. Others (*externals*) are more inclined to expect events to be determined by external forces over which they have no control. When externals succeed, they are likely to believe that the success was due to chance or luck.

Research on differences in generalized expectancies does show that they are correlated with differences in behavior. For example, when threatened by a hurricane or other natural disaster, internals—in accordance with their belief that they can control what happens to them—are more likely than externals to buy bottled water and make other preparations (Sattler, Kaiser, & Hittner, 2000). When confronted with a personal problem, internals are more likely than externals to work to solve this problem. Externals are more likely to see it as being unsolvable (Gianakos, 2002). Internals also tend to work harder than externals at staying physically healthy, and as a result may lower their risk of cancer and heart disease (Stürmer, Hasselbach, & Amelang, 2006). They are less likely to drink alcohol, or—if they do drink—less likely to drive while intoxicated (Cavaiola & Desordi, 2000). Internals tend to be more careful with money (Lim, Teo, & Loo, 2003), and internal college students tend to be better informed about the courses they take, including what they need to do to get a high grade. Perhaps as a result, internals tend to get better grades than externals (Dollinger, 2000).

● **Bandura and Reciprocal Determinism** In his social-cognitive theory, Albert Bandura (1999; 2006) sees personality as shaped by the ways in which thoughts, behavior, and the environment interact and influence one another. He points out that whether people learn through direct experience with rewards and punishments or through the observational learning processes described in the chapter on learning, their behavior creates changes in their environment. Observing these changes, in turn, affects how they think, which then affects their behavior, and so on in a constant web of mutual influence that Bandura calls *reciprocal determinism* (see Figure 14.4).

According to Bandura, an especially important cognitive element in this web of influence is perceived **self-efficacy**—the learned expectation of success. Bandura says that what we do, and what we try to do, is largely controlled by our perceptions or beliefs about our chances of success at a particular task or problem. The higher our perceived self-efficacy in relation to a particular situation or task, the greater our actual accomplishments in that situation or task (Zimmerman & Schunk, 2003). So going into a job interview with the belief that you have the skills necessary to be hired may lead to behaviors that help you get the job.

Perceived self-efficacy about a specific behavior can interact with a person's expectancies about the consequences of behavior in general, thus helping to shape the person's psychological well-being (Maddux & Gosselin, 2003; see Figure 14.5). For example, if a person has low perceived self-efficacy and also expects that nothing

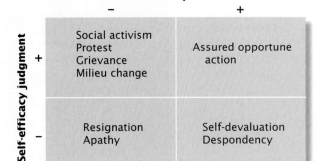

FIGURE **14.5**

Self-Efficacy and Psychological Well-Being

According to Bandura, if people with high self-efficacy perceive the environment as unresponsive to their best efforts, they may become resentful and socially active protesters. If they perceive the environment as responsive to their efforts, they are more likely to be both active and self-assured.

anyone does has much effect on the world, the result may be apathy. But if a person with low perceived self-efficacy also believes that other people are enjoying the benefits of their efforts, the result may be self-criticism and depression.

● **Mischel's Cognitive/Affective Theory**   Social-cognitive theorists argue that learned beliefs, feelings, and expectancies characterize each individual and make that individual different from other people. Walter Mischel calls these characteristics *cognitive person variables*, and he believes that they outline the dimensions along which individuals differ (Mischel, 2004b).

According to Mischel, the most important cognitive person variables are (1) *encodings* (the beliefs the person has about the environment and other people), (2) *expectancies* (what the person expects to follow from various behaviors and what the person believes he or she is capable of doing), (3) *affects* (feelings, emotions, and affective responses), (4) *goals and values* (the things a person believes in and wants to achieve), and (5) *competencies and self-regulatory plans* (the thoughts and actions the person is capable of, as well as the ability to engage in planned, self-controlled, and goal-directed behavior (Shoda & Mischel, 2006).

To predict a person' behavior in a particular situation, says Mischel, we need to know about these cognitive person variables, as well as about the features of the situation the person will face. In short, the person and the situation interact to produce behavior. Mischel's view has been called an "if-then" theory, because he proposes that *if* people encounter a particular situation, *then* they will engage in the characteristic behaviors (called *behavioral signatures*) they have learned to display in that situation (Kammrath, Mendoza-Denton, & Mischel, 2005).

Mischel was once highly critical of trait theories of personality, but now sees his own theory as generally consistent with that approach. In fact, the concept of behavioral signatures is quite similar to the concept of traits. However, Mischel still argues that trait theorists underestimate the power of situations to alter behavior and do not pay enough attention to the cognitive and emotional processes that underlie people's overt actions. Despite their remaining differences, most advocates of the trait and social-cognitive approaches are now focusing on the similarities between their views (Cervone, 2005; Fleeson, 2004). This trend toward reconciliation has helped to clarify the relationship between personal and situational variables and how they affect behavior under various conditions. Many of the conclusions that have emerged are consistent with Bandura's concept of reciprocal determinism:

1. Personal dispositions (which include traits and cognitive person variables) influence behavior only in relevant situations. The trait of anxiousness, for example, may predict anxiety, but only in situations in which an anxious person feels threatened.

2. Personal dispositions can lead to behaviors that alter situations that, in turn, promote other behaviors. For example, a hostile child can trigger aggression in others and thus start a fight.

The Impact of Situations Like the rest of us, Arnold Schwarzenegger behaves differently in different situations, including when acting in his *Terminator* movies and when serving as the governor of California. Mischel's theory of personality emphasizes that person-situation interactions are important in determining behavior.

3. People choose to be in situations that are in tune with their personal dispositions. Introverts, for instance, are likely to choose quiet environments, whereas extraverts tend to seek out livelier, more social circumstances.

4. Personal dispositions are more important in some situations than in others. Under circumstances in which many different behaviors would all be appropriate—a company picnic, for example—what people do may be predicted from their dispositions (extraverts will probably play games and socialize while introverts watch). However, in situations such as a funeral, in which fewer options are socially acceptable, personal dispositions will not differentiate one person from another; everyone is likely to be quiet and somber.

Today, social-cognitive theorists devote much of their research to examining how cognitive person variables develop, how they are related to stress and health, and how they interact with situational variables to affect behavior.

● Evaluating the Social-Cognitive Approach

The original behavioral view of personality appealed to many people. It offered an objective, experimentally oriented approach that operationally defined its concepts, relied on empirical data for its basic principles, and based its applications on the results of empirical research (Pervin et al., 2005). However, its successor, the social-cognitive approach, has gained even wider acceptance because it blends theories from behavioral and cognitive psychology and applies them to such socially important areas as aggression, the effects of mass media on children, and the development of self-regulatory processes that enhance personal control over behavior. The popularity of this approach also stems from the ease with which its principles can be translated into treatment procedures for many types of psychological disorders (O'Donohue, Fisher, & Hayes, 2003; see the chapter on treatment of psychological disorders).

Still, the social-cognitive approach has not escaped criticism. Psychodynamic theorists point out that social-cognitive theories leave no role for unconscious thoughts and feelings in determining behaviors (e.g., Westen, 1998). Some advocates of trait theory complain that social-cognitive theorists have focused more on explaining why traits are unimportant than on why situations are important and that they have failed to identify what it is about specific situations that brings out certain behaviors (Friedman & Schustack, 2003; Funder, 2004). The social-cognitive approach has also been faulted for failing to present a general theory of personality, offering instead a set of more limited theories that share certain common assumptions about the nature of personality (Feist & Feist, 2002). Most generally, the social-cognitive approach is considered incapable of capturing the complexity, richness, and uniqueness that some critics see as inherent in human personality (Carver & Scheier, 2004). According to these critics, a far more attractive alternative is provided by the humanistic approach to personality.

The Humanistic Approach

Unlike theories that emphasize the instincts and learning processes that humans seem to share with other animals, the **humanistic approach** to personality focuses on mental capabilities that set humans apart: self-awareness, creativity, planning, decision making, and responsibility. Those who adopt the humanistic approach see human behavior as motivated mainly by an innate drive toward growth that prompts people to fulfill their unique potential. And like the planted seed whose natural potential is to become a flower, people are seen as naturally inclined toward goodness, creativity, love, and joy. Humanistic psychologists also believe that to explain people's actions in any particular situation, it is more important to understand their view of the world than their instincts, traits, or learning experiences. To humanists, that world view is a bit different for each of us, and it is this unique *phenomenology* (pronounced "feh-naw-men-ALL-oh-gee"), or way of perceiving and interpreting the world, that shapes personality and guides behavior (Kelly, 1980). From this perspective, then, no one can understand another person without somehow perceiving the world through that person's eyes. All behavior, even seemingly weird behavior, is presumed to be meaningful to the person displaying it. Because it emphasizes the importance of looking at people's perceptions, this approach is sometimes called the *phenomenological approach*.

What Is Reality?   Each of these people has a different perception of what happened during the play that started this argument—and each is sure he is right! Disagreement about the "same" event illustrates phenomenology, each person's unique perceptions of the world. The humanistic approach sees these perceptions as shaping personality and guiding behavior. As described in the perception chapter, our perceptions are often influenced by top-down processing. In this case, expectations and motivation stemming from differing loyalties are likely to influence reality—and reactions—for each team's players, coaches, and fans.

humanistic approach   A view in which personality develops through an actualizing tendency that unfolds in accordance with each person's unique perceptions of the world.

The humanistic approach to personality has many roots. The idea that each person perceives a different reality reflects the views of existential philosophers such as Søren Kierkegaard and Jean-Paul Sartre. The idea that people actively shape their own reality stems in part from the Gestalt psychologists, whose work is described in the chapter on perception, and from George Kelly, a psychologist who also influenced social-cognitive theorists. We can also hear echoes of Alfred Adler and other psychodynamic theorists who emphasized the positive aspects of human nature and the importance of the ego in personality development. Humanistic theories of personality have, themselves, helped to fuel research in positive psychology, which focuses on character strengths such as wisdom, courage, and humanity, as well as on happiness, thriving, and other aspects of human experience associated with maximum personal development and functioning (Peterson, 2006; Ryan & Deci, 2000; Seligman, 2002).

● Prominent Humanistic Theories

By far, the most prominent humanistic theories of personality are those of Carl Rogers and Abraham Maslow.

● Rogers's Self Theory
In his extensive writings, Carl Rogers (e.g., 1961, 1970, 1980) emphasized the **actualizing tendency**, which he described as an innate inclination toward growth and fulfillment that motivates all human behavior and is expressed in a unique way by each individual (Raskin & Rogers, 2001). Rogers saw personality as the expression of that actualizing tendency as it unfolds in each individual's uniquely perceived reality (Hergenhahn & Olson, 2007). The centerpiece of Rogers's theory is the *self*, the part of experience that a person identifies as "I" or "me." According to Rogers, those who accurately experience the self—with all its preferences, abilities, fantasies, shortcomings, and desires—are on the road to what Kurt Goldstein (1939) had called *self-actualization*. The progress of people whose experiences of the self become distorted, however, is likely to be slowed or stopped.

Rogers saw personality development beginning early, as children learn to need other people's approval, or as he called it, *positive regard*. Evaluations by parents, teachers, and others soon begin to affect children's self-evaluations. When these

Seeking Self-Actualization According to Rogers, conditions of worth can make it harder for children to become aware of and accept aspects of themselves that conflict with their parents' values. Progress toward self-actualization can be enhanced by associating with those whose positive regard is less conditional on displaying any particular pattern of behavior.

● **actualizing tendency** According to Rogers, an innate inclination toward growth that motivates all people.

P. BYRNES.

"Just remember, son, it doesn't matter whether you win or lose—unless you want Daddy's love."

Parents are not usually this obvious about creating conditions of worth, but according to Rogers, the message gets through in many more subtle ways.

evaluations are in agreement with a child's own self-evaluations, the child reacts in a way that matches, or is *congruent* with, self-experience. The child not only experiences positive regard but also evaluates the self as "good" for having earned approval. This positive self-experience becomes part of the **self-concept**, which is the way one thinks of oneself. But what if a positive self-experience is evaluated negatively by others, as when a little boy is teased by his father for having fun playing with dolls? In this case, the child must either do without a parent's positive regard or, more likely, reevaluate the self-experience—deciding perhaps that "I don't like dolls" or "Feeling good is bad."

In other words, said Rogers, personality is shaped partly by the actualizing tendency and partly by evaluations made by others. In this way, people come to like what they are "supposed" to like and to behave as they are "supposed" to behave. This socialization process is adaptive, because it helps people to function in society, but it often requires that they suppress their self-actualizing tendency and distort their experience. Rogers argued that psychological discomfort, anxiety, or even mental disorder can result when the feelings people experience or express are *incongruent*, or at odds, with their true feelings.

Incongruence is likely, said Rogers, when parents and teachers act in ways that lead children to believe that their worth as people depends on displaying the "right" attitudes, behaviors, and values. These **conditions of worth** are created whenever *people* are evaluated instead of their behavior. For example, parents who find their toddler smearing finger paint on the dog are unlikely to say, "I love you, but I don't approve of this particular behavior." They are more likely to shout, "Bad boy!" or "Bad girl!" This reaction sends a subtle message that the child is lovable and worthwhile only when well behaved. As a result, the child's self-experience is not "I like painting Fang, but Mom and Dad don't approve," but instead, "Playing with paint is bad, and I am bad if I like it, so I don't like it," or "I like it, so I must be bad." The child may eventually display overly neat and tidy behaviors that do not reflect the real self but, rather, are part of the ideal self dictated by the parents.

● **self-concept** The way one thinks of oneself.

● **conditions of worth** According to Rogers, the feelings an individual experiences when the person, instead of the person's behavior, is evaluated.

The Joys of a Growth Orientation
According to Maslow's theory of personality, the key to personal growth and fulfillment lies in focusing on what we have, not on what we don't have or on what we have lost. Rachel Barton could have let the accident that took her leg destroy her career as a concert violinist, and with it, her joy in life—but she didn't. Researchers in the field of positive psychology are studying the development of resilience, as well as other character strengths, as part of an effort to understand and promote all the things that can go right in human life (Peterson, 2006).

As with Freud's concept of superego, conditions of worth are first set up by external pressure but eventually become part of the person's belief system. So Rogers saw rewards and punishments as important in personality development not just because they shape overt behavior but also because they can so easily create distorted self-perceptions and incongruence.

● **Maslow's Growth Theory**   Like Rogers, Abraham Maslow (1954, 1971) considered personality to be the expression of a basic human tendency toward growth and self-actualization. In fact, Maslow believed that self-actualization is not just a human capacity but a human need. As described in the motivation and emotion chapter, he placed self-actualization as the highest in a hierarchy of motives, or needs. Yet, said Maslow, people are often distracted from seeking self-actualization because they focus on needs that are lower on the hierarchy.

Maslow saw most people as controlled by a **deficiency orientation**, the preoccupation with perceived needs for material things, especially things they do not have. Ultimately, he said, deficiency-oriented people come to see life as a meaningless exercise in disappointment and boredom, and they may begin to behave in problematic ways. For example, in an attempt to satisfy the need for love and belongingness, people may focus on what love can give them (security), not on what they can give to another. This deficiency orientation may lead a person to be jealous and to focus on what is missing in relationships. As a result, the person will never truly experience either love or security.

In contrast, people with a **growth orientation** do not focus on what is missing but draw satisfaction from what they have, what they are, and what they can do. This orientation opens the door to what Maslow called *peak experiences*, in which people feel joy, even ecstasy, in the mere fact of being alive, being human, and knowing that they are utilizing their fullest potential.

● Evaluating the Humanistic Approach

The humanistic approach to personality is consistent with the way many people view themselves. It gives a central role to each person's immediate experiences and emphasizes the uniqueness of each individual. The humanistic approach and its phenomenological perspective inspired the person-centered therapy of Rogers and other forms of psychotherapy (see the chapter on treatment of psychological disorders). This approach also underlies various short-term personal growth experiences—such as sensitivity training and encounter groups designed to help people become more

● **deficiency orientation**   According to Maslow, a preoccupation with perceived needs for things a person does not have.

● **growth orientation**   According to Maslow, a tendency to draw satisfaction from what is available in life, rather than to focus on what is missing.

Psychological Disorders

15

Many people pursue what other people consider odd hobbies, such as collecting string, but when does oddness become abnormality? In this chapter, we discuss the ways in which society answers that question. We also describe the main types of psychological disorders, their possible causes, their legal status, and how they have been explained over the centuries. We have organized our presentation as follows:

During his first year at college, Mark began to worry about news stories describing the deadly diseases resulting from HIV, the virus that causes AIDS. He took a blood test for HIV and was relieved when it showed no infection. But then he wondered if he might have contracted HIV after he took the test. Internet research revealed that HIV antibodies may not appear until six months after infection. Mark took another blood test, also negative, but he still worried when he learned that the AIDS virus can live outside of the human body for anywhere from ten minutes to several hours or even days.

Given this uncertainty, Mark concluded that HIV can live indefinitely outside of the body and could therefore be anywhere and everywhere. He decided that the only safe course was not just sexual abstinence but absolute cleanliness. Mark began to scrub himself whenever he touched doorknobs, money, walls, floors—anything. People with HIV, he thought, could have touched these things, or they might have bled on the street and he might have tracked their infected blood into his car and house and bathroom. Eventually he felt the need to scrub everything around him up to forty times in each direction; it took him several exhausting hours just to shower and dress. He washed the shower knobs before touching them and, once in the shower, felt that he had to wash his body in cycles of thirteen strokes. If his feet touched the bare floor, he had to wash them again before putting on his underwear to ensure that his feet would not contaminate the fabric. He was sure that his hands, rubbed raw from constant washing, were especially susceptible to infection, so he wore gloves at all times except in the summer, when he wrapped his fingers in flesh-colored bandages. The process of protecting himself from infection was wearing him out and severely restricting his activities; he could not go anywhere without first considering the risk of infection.

Mark's case provides an example of someone who suffers from a psychological disorder, also called a *mental disorder* or *psychopathology*. **Psychopathology** is generally defined as patterns of thought, emotion, and behavior that result in personal distress or a significant impairment in a person's social or occupational functioning. Surveys reveal that in any given year in the United States alone, about 30 percent of adults—about 60 million people—display some form of mental disorder and that about half of all Americans can expect to experience a disorder by age seventy-five (Kessler, Berglund, et al., 2005; Kessler, Chiu, et al., 2005; National Institute of Mental Health, 2006; World Health Organization Mental Health Survey Consortium, 2004; see Figure 15.1). These overall rates of mental disorder are found, with only minor variations, in all segments of U.S. society, including males and females in all ethnic groups and in the young and old. Many of these disorders appear quite early in life. In any given year, about 20 percent of U.S. children display significant mental disorders (Costello et al., 2003; U.S. Surgeon General, 1999), and about three-quarters of adult disorders first appear by age twenty-four; half begin as early as fourteen (Egan & Asher, 2005; Kessler, Berglund, et al., 2005).

Bear in mind, though, that the prevalence of psychological disorders may be even higher than the percentages just cited. For one thing, major survey studies have examined fewer than half of all known psychological disorders. Further, these studies count each case only once, even though about 45 percent of people who are diagnosed with one disorder actually display *comorbidity,* meaning that they are diagnosed as having two or even three disorders (Kessler, Chiu, et al., 2005; National Institute of Mental Health, 2006). Finally, surveys fail to count people whose symptoms are not quite severe enough to be labeled as a disorder, but who

psychopathology Patterns of thinking, feeling, and behaving that are maladaptive, disruptive, or uncomfortable for those who are affected or for those with whom they come in contact.

FIGURE 15.1

Incidence of Specific Psychological Disorders

Several large-scale surveys of adults in the United States revealed that about 30 percent of them experience some form of mental disorder in any given year and that almost half of them have displayed a disorder at some time in life. Indeed, one recent survey suggested that only about 20 percent of adults in the U.S. are both free of any form of mental disorder and flourishing (Keyes, 2007). The data shown here summarize the lifetime findings by category of disorder. The same general patterns appear among the more than 400 million people worldwide who suffer from some form of psychological disorder (Andrade et al., 2002; Bjil et al., 2003; Liu et al., 2002; World Health Organization Mental Health Survey Consortium, 2004).

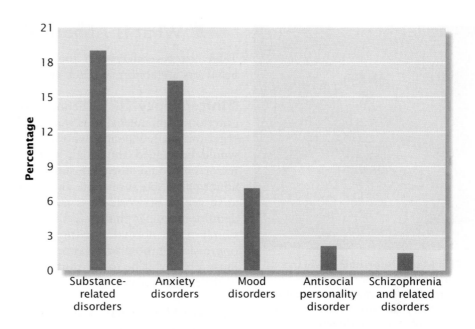

are nevertheless suffering and whose functioning is somewhat impaired (Faravelli et al., 2006).

Psychological disorders are enormously costly in terms of human suffering, wasted potential, and lost resources (e.g., Adler et al., 2006; Kessler, Adler, et al., 2006). They are the leading cause of disability in the United States and Canada for persons aged fifteen to forty-four (National Institute of Mental Health, 2006), and a similar pattern appears around the world. One study found that psychological disorders ranked second (after cardiovascular disease) in producing disability and shortened life expectancy in industrialized economies (World Health Organization Mental Health Survey Consortium, 2004). The impact of these disorders is even greater in less-developed countries where treatment is less available (Druss, Rosenheck, & Sledge, 2000; Gureje et al., 2006; Kawakami et al., 2005; Medina-Mora et al., 2005; Miller, 2006; Stewart et al., 2003).

Beyond causing personal suffering and disability, psychological disorders also impose a huge financial burden on families, communities, and society (Druss et al., 2000; Lyons & McLoughlin, 2001; Marcotte & Wilcox-Goek, 2001; Stewart et al., 2003). Let's consider how these disorders are defined and classified.

Defining Psychological Disorders

A California woman's husband dies, and in her grief she stays in bed all day, weeping, refusing to eat, at times holding "conversations" with him. In India, a Hindu holy man on a pilgrimage rolls along the ground across a thousand miles of deserts and mountains, pelted by monsoon rains, until he reaches the sacred place he seeks. In the Middle East, a young man straps explosives to his body and detonates them in a crowded market, killing himself and dozens of others. In London, a British artist randomly scratches parked cars as part of his "creative process." Eight percent of adults in the United States say they have seen a UFO (CNN/Time, 1997), and hundreds of people around the world claim to have been abducted by space aliens (Clancy, 2005). These examples and countless others raise the question of where to draw the line between normality and abnormality, between eccentricity, criminality, and mental disorder.

Is This Man Abnormal? Whether unusual individuals are labeled "abnormal" and perhaps given treatment for psychological disorder depends on a number of factors, including how *abnormality* is defined by the culture in which they live, who is most directly affected by their behavior, and how much distress they suffer or cause.

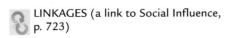

LINKAGES (a link to Social Influence, p. 723)

impaired functioning Difficulty in fulfilling appropriate and expected family, social, and work-related roles.

● What Is Abnormal?

There are several criteria for judging whether people's thinking, emotions, or behaviors are abnormal. Each criterion has value but also some flaws.

●**Infrequency** If we define *normality* as what most people do, an obvious criterion for abnormality is *statistical infrequency*—that which is unusual. By this criterion, the few people who believe that space aliens are stealing their thoughts would be judged abnormal, and the many people who worry about crime or terrorism would not. But statistical infrequency alone is a poor criterion for abnormality, because some characteristics that appear only rarely—such as creative genius or world-class athletic ability—may be highly valued. Further, this definition implies that only those who conform to all aspects of the majority's standards are normal. Equating nonconformity with abnormality can result in the oppression of those who express minority views in a society. Finally, just how rare must a behavior be to warrant the designation of "abnormal"? The dividing line is not easy to locate.

●**Norm Violation** Abnormality can also be defined in terms of whether someone violates social norms—the cultural rules that tell us how we should and should not behave in various situations, especially in relation to others (see the chapter on social influence). According to this *norm violation* criterion, when people behave in ways that are bizarre, unusual, or disturbing enough to violate social norms, they may be described as abnormal. From this perspective, identifying psychopathology and deciding who "has it" depends in part on how a society defines *normal* and *abnormal* (Castillo, 1997).

Like infrequency, though, norm violation alone is an inadequate measure of abnormality. For one thing, some norm violations are better characterized as eccentric or illegal than as abnormal. People who seldom bathe or who stand too close during conversation violate social norms, but are they abnormal or merely annoying? Further, whose norms are we talking about? Social norms vary across cultures, subcultures, and historical eras, so actions that qualify as abnormal in one part of the world might be perfectly acceptable elsewhere.

●**Personal Suffering** Another criterion for abnormality is *personal suffering*. In fact, experiencing distress is the criterion that people often use in deciding that their psychological problems are severe enough to require treatment. But personal suffering alone is an inadequate criterion for abnormality. It does not take into account the fact that people are sometimes distressed about characteristics (such as being gay or lesbian) that are not mental disorders. Further, people can display psychological disorders without experiencing distress if the disorders have impaired their ability to recognize how maladaptive their behavior is. Those who sexually abuse children, for example, create far more distress in victims and their families than they suffer themselves.

● Behavior in Context: A Practical Approach

Because no single criterion is entirely adequate for identifying abnormality, mental health practitioners and researchers tend to adopt a *practical approach* that combines aspects of all the criteria we have discussed. They consider the *content* of behavior (what the person does); the sociocultural *context* in which the person's behavior occurs; and the *consequences* of the behavior for that person, as well as for others. This practical approach pays special attention to whether a person's thoughts, behavior, or emotions cause **impaired functioning**—that is, difficulty in fulfilling appropriate and expected family, social, and work-related roles (U.S. Surgeon General, 1999; Wakefield, 1999).

Situational Factors in Defining Abnormality   When men in Delhi, India, need a restroom, they can take advantage of outdoor urinals like this one. In some countries, it is even acceptable for men to urinate against buildings on city streets. In the United States and many other places, though, males who urinate anywhere other than the relative privacy of a men's room are considered to be deviant and might even be arrested for indecent exposure. In other words, situational factors can determine whether a particular behavior is labeled "normal" or "abnormal." Make a list of the reasons you would give for, or against, calling these men "abnormal." Which criteria for abnormality did you use?

What is "appropriate" and "expected" depends on age, gender, and culture, as well as on the particular situation and historical era in which people find themselves. For example, the same short attention span that is considered normal in a two-year-old would be considered inappropriate and problematic in an adult. There are gender-specific norms as well. In some countries, for example, it is more appropriate for women than for men to display emotion. Kisses, tears of happiness, and long embraces are common when women greet each other after a long absence. Men tend to simply shake hands or, at most, hug briefly. Because of cultural differences, hearing a dead relative's voice calling from the afterlife would be more acceptable in certain North American Indian tribes than among, say, the families of suburban Toronto. Situational factors are important, too. Falling to the floor and speaking an unintelligible language is considered appropriate, even desirable, during the worship services of certain religious groups, but the same behavior would be seen as inappropriate, and a sign of disorder, in a college classroom. Finally, judgments about behavior are shaped by changes in social trends and cultural values. For example, the American Psychiatric Association once listed homosexuality as a mental disorder but dropped this category from its *Diagnostic and Statistical Manual of Mental Disorders* in 1973. In taking this step, it was responding to changing views of homosexuality that were prompted in part by the political and educational efforts of gay and lesbian rights groups.

In summary, it is difficult, and probably impossible, to define a specific set of behaviors that everyone, everywhere, will agree constitutes abnormality. The practical approach defines abnormality as including those patterns of thought, behavior, and emotional reaction that significantly impair people's functioning within their culture (Wakefield, 1992).

Explaining Psychological Disorders

Since the dawn of civilization, people throughout the world have tried to understand the causes of psychological disorder. The earliest explanations of abnormal behavior focused on possession by gods or demons. Disordered people were seen either as innocent victims of spirits or as social or moral deviants suffering supernatural

An Exorcism The exorcism being performed by this Buddhist monk in Thailand is designed to cast out the evil forces seen as causing this child's disorder. Supernatural explanations of mental disorder remain influential among religious groups in many cultures and subcultures around the world (Fountain, 2000). Awareness of this influence in the United States and Europe has increased recently following cases in which people have died during exorcism rituals (e.g., Christopher, 2003; Radford, 2005).

punishment. In Europe during the late Middle Ages, for example, people who displayed threatening or unusual behavior were seen as controlled by the devil or other evil beings. Supernatural explanations of psychological disorders are still invoked today in many cultures around the world—including certain ethnic and religious subcultures in North America (Glazer et al., 2004; Nickell, 2001; Tagliabue, 1999).

● The Biopsychosocial Model

More generally, however, researchers in Western cultures attribute psychopathology to three other causes: biological factors, psychological processes, and sociocultural contexts. For many decades, there was controversy over which of these three causes is most important, but it is now widely agreed that they can all be important. Accordingly, researchers have adopted a **biopsychosocial model** in which mental disorders are seen as caused by the combination and interaction of biological, psychological, and sociocultural factors, each of which contributes in varying degrees to particular problems in particular people (Krueger & Markon, 2006; Nater et al., 2006; U.S. Surgeon General, 1999).

●**Biological Factors** The *biological factors* thought to be involved in causing mental disorders include physical illnesses, disruptions or imbalances in bodily processes, and genetic influences. This *medical model* of psychopathology has a long history. For example, the ancient Greek physician Hippocrates said that psychological disorders resulted from imbalances among four *humors*, or bodily fluids (blood, phlegm, black bile, and yellow bile). According to Hippocrates, depression ("melancholia") resulted from an excess of black bile. In ancient Chinese cultures, psychological disorders were seen as resulting from an imbalance of *yin* and *yang*, the dual forces of the universe flowing in the physical body.

As the medical model gained prominence in Western cultures after the Middle Ages, specialized hospitals for the insane were established throughout Europe. Treatment in these early asylums consisted mainly of physical restraints, laxative purges, bleeding of "excess" blood, and induced vomiting. Cold baths, fasts, spinning chairs, and other physical discomforts were also used in efforts to "shock" patients back to normality.

● **biopsychosocial model** A view of mental disorders as caused by a combination of interacting biological, psychological, and sociocultural factors.

Visiting Bedlam   As shown here in William Hogarth's portrayal of "Bedlam" (slang for London's St. Mary's of Bethleham hospital), most asylums of the 1700s were little more than prisons. Notice the well-dressed visitors; in those days, people could buy tickets to tour the cells and gawk at the patients.

The medical model led to a view of abnormality as *mental illness*, and in fact, most people in Western cultures today still tend to seek medical doctors and hospitals for the diagnosis and treatment of psychological disorders (Wang et al., 2006). The medical model is now more properly called the **neurobiological model**, because it explains psychological disorders in terms of particular disturbances in the anatomy and chemistry of the brain and in other biological processes, including genetic influences (e.g., Kendler, 2005; Plomin & McGuffin, 2003). Neuroscientists and others who adopt a neurobiological approach study the causes and treatment of these disorders as they would study any physical illness, seeing problematic symptoms stemming primarily from an underlying neurological disturbance that can be diagnosed, treated, and cured.

The importance of biological factors in psychopathology has been demonstrated in many psychological disorders. *Dementia*, for example, is characterized by a loss of mental functions, including disturbances in memory, personality, and cognitive abilities. The most frequent causes of dementia are progressive deterioration of the brain as a result of aging or long-term alcohol abuse; acute diseases and disorders such as encephalitis, brain tumors, or head injury; and drug intoxication. Alzheimer's disease is a severe form of dementia seen mostly in the elderly. Research in neuroscience and behavioral genetics has also identified biological factors in a number of other psychological disorders to be described later, including schizophrenia, bipolar disorders, some forms of anxiety disorder, and autism and attention deficit disorder (Kendler, 2001).

●**Psychological Processes**   If biological factors provide the "hardware" of mental disorders, the "software" includes psychological factors, such as our wants, needs, and emotions; our learning experiences; our attachment history; and our way of looking at the world. The roots of this **psychological model** of mental disorders can be seen in ancient Greek literature and drama dealing with the *psyche*, or mind—especially with the mind's struggles to resolve inner conflicts or to overcome the effects of stressful events. These ideas took center stage in the late 1800s, when Sigmund Freud challenged the assumption that psychological disorders had only physical causes. As described in the personality chapter, Freud's explanations of

● **neurobiological model**   A modern name for the medical model, in which psychological disorders are seen as reflecting disturbances in the anatomy and chemistry of the brain and in other biological processes.

● **psychological model**   A view in which mental disorder is seen as arising from psychological processes.

mental disorders were part of his *psychodynamic approach*. He believed that those disorders are the result of unresolved, mostly unconscious conflicts that begin in childhood. These conflicts pit people's inborn impulses against the limits placed on those impulses by society. More recent psychodynamic explanations—such as *object relations* theory—focus less on unconscious urges and more on the role of attachment and other early interpersonal relationships (Bienenfeld, 2005; Schultz & Schultz, 2005).

Other theories discussed in the personality chapter suggest other psychological processes that can contribute to the development of mental disorders. For example, *social-cognitive* theorists, also known as *social learning* theorists, see most psychological disorders as resulting from the interaction of past learning and current situations. Just as people learn to avoid hot grills after being burned, say these theorists, bad experiences in school or a dental office can "teach" people to fear such places. Social-cognitive theorists also emphasize that learned expectations, schemas, and other mental processes discussed in the chapter on cognition and language can influence the development of disorders (e.g., Johnson-Laird, Mancini, & Gangemi, 2006). Depression, for example, is seen as stemming from negative events, such as losing a job, but also from the irrational or maladaptive thoughts that people have learned in relation to these events—thoughts such as "I never do anything right."

Finally, the *humanistic* approach to personality suggests that behavior disorders appear when a person's natural tendency toward healthy growth is blocked, usually by a failure to be aware of, and to express, true feelings. When this happens, the person's perceptions of reality become distorted. The greater the distortion, the more serious the psychological disorder. Humanistic psychologists also focus on the meanings that people attach to events and how those meanings can lead to adaptive or maladaptive reactions.

●Sociocultural Context

Together, neurobiological and psychological factors go a long way toward explaining many forms of mental disorder. Still, these factors relate mainly to causes residing within the individual. The **sociocultural model** of disorder suggests that we cannot fully explain all forms of psychopathology without also looking outside the individual—especially at the social and cultural factors that form the background of abnormal behavior. Looking for causes of disorders in this *sociocultural context* means paying attention to factors such as gender, age, and marital status; the physical, social, and economic situations in which people live; and the cultural values, traditions, and expectations in which they are immersed (Evans et al., 2000; Lim, 2006; Martinez-Taboas, 2005). Sociocultural context influences not only what is and is not labeled "abnormal" but also who displays what kind of disorder and how likely they are to receive treatment for it.

Consider gender, for instance. The greater tolerance in many cultures for the open expression of emotional distress among women, but not men, may contribute to the higher rates of depression seen in women compared with men (Hightower, 2005; Wupperman & Neumann, 2006). Similarly, the view held in many cultures that excessive alcohol consumption is less appropriate for women than for men is a sociocultural factor that may help explain higher rates of alcohol abuse among men in those cultures (Helzer et al., 1990; Timko, Finney, & Moos, 2005).

Sociocultural factors can influence the overall prevalence of disorders, too. For instance, anxiety disorders and depression tend to be less common in Japan than in Western countries, including the United States (Kawakami et al., 2005). And many kinds of psychological disorders increase in frequency among people living in countries ravaged by wars or other stressful conditions (Karam et al., 2006).

Sociocultural factors also influence the form that abnormality takes. For example, depression is a *culture-general* disorder—appearing virtually everywhere in the world—but the symptoms that sufferers report tend to differ depending on cultural background (Falicov, 2003; Hopper & Wanderling, 2000). In Western cultures, emotional and physical components of disorders are generally viewed separately, so

 LINKAGES (a link to Learning, p. 204)

sociocultural model A way of looking at mental disorders in relation to gender, age, ethnicity and other social and cultural factors.

symptoms of depression tend to revolve around despair and other signs of emotional distress. But in China, Japan, and certain other Asian cultures, emotional and physical experiences tend to be viewed as one, so a depressed person is as likely to report stomach or back pain as to complain of sadness (Karasz, 2005; Kleinman, 2004; Nakao & Yano, 2006).

There are also culture-specific forms of disorder. For instance, Puerto Rican, Guatemalan, Mexican, and Dominican Hispanic women sometimes experience *ataques de nervios* ("attack of nerves"), a unique way of reacting to stress that includes heart palpitations, shaking, shouting, nervousness, depression, and, on occasion, fainting or seizure-like episodes (Baer, Weller, et al., 2003; Spiegel, 1994). Another example can be found in Southeast Asia, southern China, Malaysia, and West African nations where a disorder called *koro* is occasionally observed. Victims of this condition, who are usually male, fear that their penis will shrivel, retract into the body, and cause death (in females, the fear relates to shriveling of the breasts). Epidemics of *koro*, often triggered by economic hard times, appear only in cultures that hold the specific supernatural beliefs that explain it (Dzokoto & Adams, 2005; Tseng et al., 1992).

In short, sociocultural factors create differing stressors, social roles, opportunities, experiences, and avenues of expression for different groups of people. They also help shape the disorders and symptoms to which certain categories of people are prone, and they even affect responses to treatment. For example, among people diagnosed with schizophrenia, those living in a developing country such as India are much more likely to improve than those living in a more developed country, such as the United States (Hopper & Wanderling, 2000). We don't yet know for certain what is responsible for this difference, but it may have something to do with the ways in which schizophrenia is understood in different cultures. In the West, schizophrenia is considered a chronic, debilitating, potentially dangerous, long-term illness. As a result, many people diagnosed with schizophrenia find themselves left on the fringes of society. In some non-Western societies, the disorder is seen as less severe and less resistant to treatment. Perhaps this more optimistic view encourages more intense efforts at socialization and, as a result, better outcomes (Mathews, Basily, & Mathews, 2006). Whatever the explanation, these data highlight the fact that any attempt to fully explain psychological disorders must take sociocultural factors into account.

● Diathesis-Stress as an Integrative Explanation

The biopsychosocial model is currently the most comprehensive and influential approach to explaining psychological disorders. It is prominent partly because it encompasses so many important causal factors, including biological imbalances, genetically inherited characteristics, brain damage, enduring psychological traits, socioculturally influenced learning experiences, stressful life events, and many more.

But how do all these factors interact to actually create disorder? Most researchers believe that inherited characteristics, biological processes, and early learning experiences combine to create a predisposition, or *diathesis* (pronounced "dye-A-thuh-sis"), for a psychological disorder. Whether or not a person actually develops symptoms of a disorder depends on the nature and amount of stress the person encounters (Turner & Lloyd, 2004; U.S. Surgeon General, 1999). For example, a person may have inherited a biological tendency toward depression or may have learned depressing patterns of thinking, but these predispositions may not be expressed as a depressive disorder unless the person is faced with a financial crisis or suffers the loss of a loved one. If such major stressors don't occur, or if the person has adequate skills for coping with them, depressive symptoms may never appear or may be relatively mild (Canli et al., 2006).

This way of thinking about the biopsychosocial model is known as the **diathesis-stress approach.** It assumes that biological, psychological, and sociocultural factors can predispose us toward a disorder but that it takes a certain amount of stress to actually trigger that disorder. People with a strong diathesis

diathesis-stress approach Viewing psychological disorders as arising when a predisposition for a disorder combines with sufficient amounts of stress to trigger symptoms.

TABLE 15.1 **The Biopsychosocial Model of Psychopathology**

Here are the factors that would be considered by the biopsychosocial model, and combined in the diathesis-stress approach, to explain the case of José, a fifty-five-year-old electronics technician. A healthy and vigorous father of two adult children, he was recently forced to take medical leave because of a series of sudden, uncontrollable panic attacks in which he experienced dizziness, heart palpitations, sweating, and fear of impending death. The attacks also kept him from his favorite pastime, scuba diving, but he has been able to maintain a part-time computer business out of his home. (Panic disorder is discussed in more detail later in this chapter; the outcome of this case is described in the chapter on treatment of psychological disorders.)

Explanatory Domain	Possible Contributing Factors
Neurobiological/medical	José may have organic disorders (e.g., genetic tendency toward anxiety; brain tumor, endocrine dysfunction; neurotransmitter imbalance).
Psychological: psychodynamic	José has unconscious conflicts and desires. Instinctual impulses are breaking through ego defenses into consciousness, causing panic.
Psychological: social-cognitive	Physical stress symptoms are interpreted as signs of serious illness or impending death. Panic is rewarded by avoidance of work stress and the opportunity to stay home.
Psychological: humanistic	José fails to recognize his genuine feelings about work and his place in life, and he fears expressing himself.
Sociocultural	A culturally based belief that "a man should not show weakness" amplifies the intensity of stress reactions and delays José's decision to seek help.
Diathesis-stress summary	José has a biological (possibly genetic) predisposition to be overly responsive to stressors. The stress of work and extra activity exceeds his capacity to cope and triggers panic as a stress response.

are more vulnerable, so even relatively mild stress might be enough to create a problem. People whose diathesis is weaker might not show signs of a disorder until stress becomes extreme or prolonged. Another way to think about the notion of diathesis-stress is in terms of *risk*: The more risk factors for a disorder a person has—whether in the form of genetic tendencies, personality traits, cultural traditions, or stressful life events—the more likely it is that the person will display a form of psychological disorder associated with those risk factors.

Table 15.1 provides an example of how the diathesis-stress approach and the factors contained in the biopsychosocial model of disorder might explain a particular case of psychopathology. Throughout this chapter, you'll see how these concepts are being applied in an effort to understand the causes of several other psychological disorders (Hankin & Abela, 2005; Hastings & Nuselovici, 2006).

Classifying Psychological Disorders

Although definitions of abnormality differ somewhat within and across cultures, there is a set of culture-general and culture-specific behavior patterns that characterize what most mental health professionals consider to be psychopathology. Most of these behavior patterns qualify as disorders because they result in impaired functioning, a main criterion of the practical approach to defining abnormality. It has long been the goal of those who study abnormal behavior to organize these patterns into a system of diagnostic categories.

The main purpose of diagnosing psychological disorders is to determine the nature of people's problems. Once the characteristics of the problems are understood, the most appropriate method of treatment can be chosen. Diagnoses are also important for research on the causes of mental disorders. If researchers can accurately and reliably classify people into particular disorder categories, they will have a better chance of spotting genetic flaws, biological abnormalities, cognitive processes, and environmental experiences that people in the same category might share. Finding that people in a certain diagnostic category share a set of features that differs from those seen in other categories could provide clues about which features are related to the development of each disorder. In short, proper classification can lead to the discovery of causes.

In 1952 the American Psychiatric Association published the first edition of what has become the official North American diagnostic classification system, the *Diagnostic and Statistical Manual of Mental Disorders (DSM)*. Each new edition of the *DSM* has included more categories of disorders. The latest editions, *DSM-IV* and *DSM-IV-TR* (which contains some text revisions), include more than three hundred specific diagnostic labels (American Psychiatric Association, 1994, 2000). Each of these editions was designed to further improve the quality of the diagnostic system by taking into account the results of the most recent research on psychopathology.

Mental health professionals outside North America diagnose mental disorders using the classification systems that appear in the tenth edition of the World Health Organization's *International Classification of Diseases (ICD-10)* and its companion volume, the second edition of the *International Classification of Impairments, Disabilities and Handicaps (ICIDH-2)*. To facilitate international communication about—and cross-cultural research on—psychopathology, *DSM-IV* was designed to be compatible with these manuals, and efforts are under way to remove inconsistencies existing between the systems (Helzer & Hudziak, 2002; Regier et al., 2005; Widiger et al., 2006).

■■ ● A Classification System: *DSM-IV*

DSM-IV describes the abnormal patterns of thinking, emotion, and behavior that define various mental disorders. For each disorder, *DSM* provides specific criteria outlining the conditions that must be present before a person can be given that diagnostic label. Diagnosticians using *DSM-IV* can evaluate troubled people on as many as five dimensions, or *axes* (the plural of *axis*). In keeping with the biopsychosocial model, evaluations on all relevant dimensions are combined to create a broad outline of the person's biological and psychological problems, as well as of any sociocultural factors that might contribute to them. As shown in Table 15.2, major mental disorders, such as schizophrenia or major depressive disorder, are recorded on Axis I. Personality disorders, mental retardation, and other lifelong conditions that tend not to change much over time are noted on Axis II. Any medical conditions that might be important in understanding the person's cognitive, emotional, or behavioral problems are listed on Axis III. On Axis IV the diagnostician notes any psychosocial and environmental factors that are important for understanding the person's psychological problems. These factors include, for example, the loss of a loved one, physical or sexual abuse, discrimination, unemployment, poverty, homelessness, inadequate health care, or conflict with religious or cultural traditions. Finally, a rating (from 100 down to 1) of the person's current level of psychological, social, and occupational functioning appears on Axis V. Here is a sample *DSM-IV* diagnosis for a person who received labels on all five axes:

Axis I	Major depressive disorder, single episode; alcohol abuse.
Axis II	Dependent personality disorder.
Axis III	Alcoholic cirrhosis of the liver.
Axis IV	Problems with primary support group (death of spouse).
Axis V	Global assessment of functioning: 50

TABLE 15.2 The *Diagnostic and Statistical Manual of Mental Disorders (DSM)* of the American Psychiatric Association

Axis I of the fourth edition *(DSM-IV)* lists the major categories of mental disorders.

Personality disorders and mental retardation are listed on Axis II.

Axis I (Clinical Syndromes)

1. ***Disorders usually first diagnosed in infancy, childhood, or adolescence.*** Problems such as hyperactivity, childhood fears, conduct disorders, frequent bed-wetting or soiling, and other problems in normal social and behavioral development. Autistic disorder (severe impairment in social, behavioral, and language development), as well as learning disorders.

2. ***Delirium, dementia, and amnestic and other cognitive disorders.*** Problems caused by physical deterioration of the brain due to aging, disease, drugs or other chemicals, or other possible unknown causes. These problems can appear as an inability to "think straight" (delirium) or as loss of memory and other intellectual functions (dementia).

3. ***Substance-related disorders.*** Psychological, behavioral, physical, social, or legal problems caused by dependence on, or abuse of, a variety of chemical substances, including alcohol, heroin, cocaine, amphetamines, hallucinogens, marijuana, and tobacco.

4. ***Schizophrenia and other psychotic disorders.*** Severe conditions characterized by abnormalities in thinking, perception, emotion, movement, and motivation that greatly interfere with daily functioning. Problems involving false beliefs (delusions).

5. ***Mood disorders (also called affective disorders).*** Severe disturbances of mood, especially depression, overexcitement (mania), or alternating episodes of each extreme (as in bipolar disorder).

6. ***Anxiety disorders.*** Specific fears (phobias); panic attacks; generalized feelings of dread; rituals of thought and action (obsessive-compulsive disorder) aimed at controlling anxiety; and problems caused by traumatic events, such as rape or military combat (see the chapter on health, stress, and coping for more on posttraumatic stress disorder.

7. ***Somatoform disorders.*** Physical symptoms, such as paralysis and blindness, that have no physical cause. Unusual preoccupation with physical health or with nonexistent physical problems (hypochondriasis, somatization disorder, pain disorder).

8. ***Factitious disorders.*** False mental disorders, which are intentionally produced to satisfy some psychological need.

9. ***Dissociative disorders.*** Psychologically caused problems of consciousness and self-identification—e.g., loss of memory (amnesia) or the development of more than one identity (multiple personality).

10. ***Sexual and gender identity disorders.*** Problems of (a) finding sexual arousal through unusual objects or situations (like shoes or exposing oneself), (b) unsatisfactory sexual activity (sexual dysfunction; see the chapter on motivation and emotion), or (c) identifying with the opposite gender.

11. ***Eating disorders.*** Problems associated with eating too little (anorexia nervosa) or binge eating followed by self-induced vomiting (bulimia nervosa). (See the chapter on motivation and emotion.)

12. ***Sleep disorders.*** Severe problems involving the sleep-wake cycle, especially an inability to sleep well at night or to stay awake during the day. (See the chapter on consciousness.)

13. ***Impulse control disorders.*** Compulsive gambling, stealing, or fire setting.

14. ***Adjustment disorders.*** Failure to adjust to, or deal well with, such stressors as divorce, financial problems, family discord, or other unhappy life events.

Axis II (Personality Disorders and Mental Retardation)

1. ***Personality disorders.*** Diagnostic labels given to individuals who may or may not receive an Axis I diagnosis but who show lifelong behavior patterns that are unsatisfactory to them or that disturb other people. These patterns may involve unusual suspiciousness, unusual ways of thinking, self-centeredness, shyness, overdependency, excessive concern with neatness and detail, or overemotionality, among others.

2. ***Mental retardation.*** As described in the chapter on cognitive abilities, the label of mental retardation is applied to individuals whose measured IQ is less than about 70 *and* who fail to display the skills of daily living, communication, and other tasks expected of people their age.

Notice that the terms *neurosis* and *psychosis* are not included as they once were in *DSM*. They were dropped because they are too vague, but some mental health professionals still sometimes use them as shorthand descriptions. *Neurosis* refers to conditions in which some form of anxiety is the major characteristic. *Psychosis* refers to conditions involving severe thought disorders that leave people "out of touch with reality" or unable to function on a daily basis. The disorders once gathered under these headings now appear in various Axis I categories in *DSM-IV*.

Further changes will undoubtedly appear in *DSM-V*, a new edition of *DSM* that is currently under development. For example, because it is common for certain kinds of disorders, such as anxiety and depression, to appear together, *DSM-V* diagnoses may include some labels that designate "mixed" disorders (Barlow & Campbell, 2000). Or there may be a mood-anxiety category that contains three subcategories: distress disorders (e.g., depression, generalized anxiety disorder, posttraumatic stress disorder), bipolar disorders (e.g., bipolar I and bipolar II disorders), and fear disorders (e.g., panic disorder, phobias) (Watson, 2005). Another proposal is to organize *DSM-V* around symptom clusters or symptom dimensions rather than around specific diagnostic categories (Vollebergh et al., 2001; Widiger & Simonsen, 2005; Widiger & Trull, 2007; Zachar & Kendler, 2007). The idea behind this *dimensional approach* would be to create a set of symptom "building blocks" that could be combined in many different ways so as to better describe the precise contours of each person's problems. Ratings of the severity of symptoms in each dimension would paint an even more detailed and meaningful picture of the problems a person is experiencing, a picture that would be of more use to clinicians (Krueger & Markon, 2006; Samuel & Widiger, 2006). Still other proposals for *DSM-V* include basing diagnoses on the results of brain imaging and analysis of people's genetic characteristics (Beutler & Malik, 2002; Bracha, 2006; Helzer & Hudziak, 2002; Maj et al., 2002).

To broaden the diagnostic process even further, some researchers have suggested that mental health professionals should consider not just people's weaknesses and problems, but also their character strengths, virtues, prosocial values, and other psychological resources upon which they can potentially build during treatment. For example, each problem-oriented *DSM* diagnosis could be supplemented by a list of the strengths (such as resilience, courage, kindness, and tolerance) that contribute to the level of functioning rating that is noted on Axis V. Some researchers have even offered comprehensive lists of human strengths and values from which diagnosticians can choose (Park, Peterson, & Seligman, 2004; Peterson, 2006). From the perspective of *positive psychology*, then, diagnosis via the *DSM* alone is seen as valuable, but incomplete. It not only tends to ignore people's strengths and values, but it also fails to recognize that people who *lack* certain character strengths and prosocial values can experience or cause a significant amount of discomfort and social impairment, even if they don't meet the "official" criteria for mental disorder.

● Evaluating the Diagnostic System

Many possible changes are on the horizon, but how good is the diagnostic system now in use? One way to evaluate *DSM-IV* is to consider *interrater reliability*, the degree to which different mental health professionals give the same person the same diagnostic label. Some studies indicate that interrater agreement is as high as 83 percent for schizophrenia and mood disorders. Agreement on many other Axis I categories, such as anxiety, mood disorders, and schizophrenia is also high (e.g., Brown et al., 2001; Jakobsen et al., 2005; Nathan & Langenbucher, 1999; Simpson et al., 2002). Still other categories, such as somatoform disorders and Axis II personality disorders, remain more difficult to diagnose reliably (Mayou et al., 2005; Shedler & Westen, 2004; Westen, Shedler, & Bradley, 2006; Zanarini et al., 2000). The reliability of a diagnosis depends partly on the extent to which clinicians all use similar assessment methods. For example, interrater agreement appears highest overall when diagnosis is based on structured or semistructured interviews that systematically address various areas of functioning and provide uniform guidelines for interpretation of the answers that people give (Rogers, 2003; Widiger & Sanderson, 1995).

Do diagnostic labels give accurate information that guides correct inferences about people? This *validity* question is difficult to answer because it is hard to find a fully acceptable standard for accuracy. Should a diagnosis be evaluated by comparing it with judgments of experts or with neurological measurements? Should it be evaluated by how well it predicts the diagnosed person's behavior? Despite having no single standard available, there is evidence to support the validity of most *DSM* criteria (e.g.,

Deep-Soboslay et al., 2006; Keenan & Wakschlag, 2004; Langenbucher & Nathan, 2006; Simon & von Korff, 2006). As with reliability, though, validity is stronger for some diagnoses (e.g., schizophrenia, depression) than for others (e.g., ADHD, somatoform disorders). Validity is likely to improve further as diagnostic labels—and the diagnostic system—are refined in *DSM-V* to reflect what researchers are learning about the characteristics, causes, courses, and cultural factors involved in various disorders.

Still, the diagnostic system is far from perfect (Beutler & Malik, 2002; Kendell & Jablensky, 2003; Krueger & Markon, 2006; Nestadt et al., 2005; Widiger & Sankis, 2000). First, as already mentioned, people's problems often do not fit neatly into a single category; mixed (or "comorbid") disorders are common. Second, the same symptom (such as sleeplessness) may appear as part of more than one disorder. Third, *DSM-IV* specifies that, in order to be given a particular diagnosis, a person must display a certain number of symptoms at a certain level of severity for a certain period of time. If these criteria are met, a person is said to "have" a certain disorder. But in setting these criteria, the authors of *DSM-IV* had to identify some rather arbitrary boundaries between "having" a disorder and "not having" it. These sharp boundaries fail to capture the varying levels of distress that different people might be experiencing. Further, diagnostic criteria often specify that there be "clinically significant impairment," but they provide few if any guidelines for what that phrase means. When mental health professionals must decide for themselves whether a particular person's symptoms are severe enough to warrant a particular diagnosis, personal bias can creep into the system (Kim & Ahn, 2002; Widiger & Clark, 2000). All of these factors can lead to misdiagnosis in some cases. Concern over this possibility is especially relevant as the nations of North America and Western Europe become increasingly multicultural. The current *DSM* disorder categories sometimes fail to take into account the ways that different cultures influence the experience and expression of distress. Diagnosticians in these countries are encountering more and more people whose cultural backgrounds they may not fully understand and whose behavior they may misunderstand.

Some people whose behavior differs enough from cultural norms to cause annoyance feel that society should tolerate their "neurodiversity" instead of giving them a diagnostic label (Harmon, 2004). In the same vein, Thomas Szasz (pronounced "zaws") and other critics of the medical model (e.g., Caplan, 1995; Kutchins & Kirk, 1997; Peterson, 2003; Snyder & Lopez, 2006; Szasz, 2003; Wampold, Ahn, & Coleman, 2001) argue that labeling people instead of describing them is dehumanizing because it ignores features that make each person unique. Calling people "schizophrenics" or "alcoholics," Szasz says, may actually encourage the behaviors associated with these labels and undermine the confidence of clients (and therapists) about the chances of improvement.

In summary, the current system for diagnosing psychological disorders has not satisfied everyone, and it is unlikely that any system ever will. No shorthand diagnostic label can fully describe a person's problems or predict exactly how that person will behave. All that can be reasonably expected of a diagnostic system is that it is based on the latest research on psychopathology and that it provides informative, general descriptions of the types of problems displayed by people who have been placed in various categories (First et al., 2004).

THINKING CRITICALLY **Is Psychological Diagnosis Biased?**

Some researchers and clinicians worry that problems with the reliability and validity of the diagnostic system are due partly to bias in its construction and use. They point out, for example, that if the diagnostic criteria for various disorders are based on research that focused on one culture, one gender, one ethnic group, or one age group, those criteria might not apply to other groups. Moreover, because diagnosticians, like other people, hold expectations and make assumptions about males versus females and about individuals from differing cultures or ethnic groups, those cognitive biases could color their judgments. This "prejudging" process could lead to the application of diagnostic criteria in ways that are slightly, but significantly, different from one case to the next (Bjorklund, 2006; Garb, 1997; Hartung & Widiger, 1998; Poland & Caplan, 2004). For example, one recent study found that clinicians reading identical case reports were more likely to label patients as schizophrenic if they thought the patients were male (Hoye et al., 2006).

■ What am I being asked to believe or accept?

Here, we focus on ethnicity as a possible source of bias in diagnosing psychopathology. It is of special interest because there is evidence that, like social class and gender, ethnicity is an important sociocultural factor in the development of mental disorder. So the assertion to be considered is that clinicians in the United States base their diagnoses partly on clients' ethnic background and, more specifically, that there is bias in diagnosing African Americans.

■ What evidence is available to support the assertion?

Several facts suggest the possibility of ethnic bias in psychological diagnosis. For one thing, African Americans receive the diagnosis of schizophrenia more frequently than European Americans do (Barnes, 2004; Kilbourne et al., 2004; Minsky et al., 2003). In fact, one study found that certain kinds of odd symptoms tend to be diagnosed as a mood disorder in European Americans but as schizophrenia in African Americans (Neighbors et al., 2003). Further, relative to their presence in the general population, African Americans are overrepresented in public mental hospitals, where the most serious forms of disorder are seen, and underrepresented in private hospitals and outpatient clinics, where less severe problems are treated (Barnes, 2004; Snowden & Cheung, 1990; U.S. Surgeon General, 1999). African Americans are also more likely than European Americans to be discharged from mental hospitals without a definitive diagnosis, suggesting that clinicians have more difficulty in diagnosing their disorders (Sohler & Bromet, 2003). Other research suggests that emergency room physicians are less likely to recognize psychiatric disorders in African American patients than in patients from other groups (Kunen et al., 2005).

There is also evidence that African Americans and members of other ethnic minority groups are underrepresented in research on mental disorders. One review found that minority participants were included in less than 30 percent of the research published in five leading clinical psychology journals over a seventeen-year period (Iwamasa, Sorocco, & Koonce, 2002). If such underrepresentation leaves clinicians less sensitive to the operation of sociocultural factors in certain groups, the quality of their diagnoses could be affected. For example, a European American diagnostician might interpret an African American patient's suspiciousness as evidence of paranoid thinking, when it might actually reflect the patient's history of unpleasant experiences with white authority figures (Whaley, 2001).

■ Are there alternative ways of interpreting the evidence?

Differences among ethnic groups in diagnosis or treatment do not automatically indicate bias based on ethnicity. Perhaps there are real differences in psychological functioning across different ethnic groups. If, relative to other groups, African Americans are exposed to more risk factors for disorder, such as poverty, violence, or other major stressors, they could be more vulnerable to more serious forms of mental disorder (Plant & Sachs-Ericsson, 2004; Turner & Lloyd, 2004). And poverty, not diagnostic bias, could be responsible for the fact that African Americans more often seek help at less expensive public hospitals than at more expensive private ones. Indeed African Americans are more likely than European Americans to bring mental health problems to hospital emergency rooms rather than to family physicians or other mental health service providers. So perhaps African Americans are less likely to come to the attention of mental health professionals until their disorders have become more severe (Nelson, 2006). Finally, there is no guarantee that diagnostic criteria would be significantly different, or that clinicians would do better at diagnosis, if more African Americans had been included in psychopathology research samples.

■ What additional evidence would help to evaluate the alternatives?

So do African Americans actually display more signs of schizophrenia, or do diagnosticians just perceive them as more disordered? One way of approaching this question is to conduct experiments in which diagnosticians assign labels to clients on the basis of case histories, test scores, and the like. In some studies, the cases are selected so that pairs of clients show about the same degree of disorder, but one member of the pair is identified as European American and the other as African American. In other studies, the same case materials, identified as representing either African American or European American patients, are presented to different diagnosticians. Bias in diagnosis would be suggested if, for example, patients identified as African American were seen as more seriously disordered than others.

The results of such studies are mixed. Most have found little or no ethnic bias (e.g., Angold et al., 2002; Garb, 1997; Kales, 2005a, 2005b; Littlewood, 1992), but because the diagnosticians could have been aware of the purpose of the research, they might have gone out of their way to be unbiased (Abreu, 1999). Some evidence of diagnostic bias against African Americans *has* been found when clinicians were unaware of the purpose of the research (e.g., Baskin, Bluestone, & Nelson, 1981; Jones, 1982).

Bias has also appeared in studies aimed at identifying the factors influencing clinicians' diagnostic judgments following extensive interviews with patients. One study conducted in a hospital setting found that in arriving at their diagnoses, psychiatrists were more likely to attribute hallucinations and paranoid thinking to African American patients than to patients who were not African American. Symptoms of mood disorders were more likely to be attributed to those who were not African American (Trierweiler et al., 2000). As noted earlier, these differences could reflect differences in the rate of disorder in different populations, but when people were interviewed in their own homes as part of large-scale mental health surveys, the diagnosis of schizophrenia was given only slightly more often to African Americans than to European Americans (Robins & Regier, 1991; Snowden & Cheung, 1990). In other words, ethnic bias is suggested, at least for some diagnoses, for patients who are evaluated in mental hospitals (Trierweiler et al., 2000, 2005).

■ What conclusions are most reasonable?

Just as *DSM-IV* is imperfect, so are those who use it. As described in the chapters on cognition and language and on social cognition, biases and stereotypes affect human thinking to some extent in virtually every social situation. It should not be surprising, then, that they operate in diagnosis as well. But diagnostic bias does not necessarily reflect deliberate discrimination. At least one study has shown that, like the processes of prejudice discussed in the chapter on social cognition, diagnostic bias based on ethnicity can operate unconsciously, without the diagnostician's awareness (Abreu, 1999). So no matter how precisely researchers specify the criteria for assigning diagnostic labels, cognitive biases and stereotypes are likely to threaten the objectivity of the diagnostic process (Funtowicz & Widiger, 1999; Poland & Caplan, 2004; Trierweiler et al., 2000).

But a blanket conclusion that the entire diagnostic system is biased against African Americans would be far too general, especially because there is evidence that, given the same symptom information, clinicians are just as likely to assign certain diagnoses, such as depression, to African Americans as to European Americans (Kales et al., 2005a, 2005b). Another study found that African American youngsters were *less* likely than European American adolescents to receive conduct disorder diagnoses (Pottick et al., 2007). It is probably more accurate to say that there may be a small amount of bias in the way diagnosticians interpret the symptoms of schizophrenia in African Americans and European Americans.

To minimize such bias, Hope Landrine (1991) suggests that diagnosticians focus more intently than ever on the fact that their concepts of "normality" and "abnormality" are affected by sociocultural values that they may not share with a given client (see Kales et al., 2006; Trierweiler et al., 2005). And Steven Lopez (1989) argues that diagnosticians must become more aware that the cognitive shortcuts and biases that affect everyone else's thinking and decision making can impair their own clinical judgments. In fact, studies of memory, problem solving, decision making, social attributions, and other aspects of culture and cognition may turn out to hold the key to reducing whatever bias may exist in the diagnosis of psychological disorders. Meanwhile, perhaps the best way to counteract clinicians' cognitive shortcomings is to teach them to base their diagnoses solely on published diagnostic criteria, standardized interview formats, and statistically validated decision rules (aided, perhaps, by specialized computer programs) rather than relying on their potentially biased clinical impressions (Akin & Turner, 2006; Bernstein, Kramer, & Phares, 2008). ■

We don't have the space to cover all the *DSM-IV* categories, so we will sample several of the most prevalent and socially significant ones. As you read, try not to catch "medical student's disease." Just as medical students often think they have the symptoms of every illness they read about, some psychology students worry that their behavior (or that of a relative or friend) signals a mental disorder. Remember that everyone has problems sometimes. Before deciding that you or someone you know needs psychological help, consider whether the content, context, and functional impairment associated with the behavior would qualify it as abnormal according to the criteria of the practical approach.

Anxiety Disorders

If you have ever been tense before an exam, a date, or a job interview, you have some idea of what anxiety feels like. Increased heart rate, sweating, rapid breathing, a dry mouth, and a sense of dread are common features of anxiety. Brief episodes of moderate anxiety are a normal part of life for most people. But when anxiety is so intense and long-lasting that it impairs a person's daily functioning, it is called an **anxiety disorder**.

● Types of Anxiety Disorders

Here we discuss four types of anxiety disorders: *phobia, generalized anxiety disorder, panic disorder,* and *obsessive-compulsive disorder.* Another type, called posttraumatic stress disorder, is described in the chapter on health, stress, and coping. Together, these are the most common psychological disorders in North America; about 29 percent of the U.S. population will have an anxiety disorder at some point in their lives (Kessler, Berglund, et al., 2005).

●Phobia   An intense, irrational fear of an object or situation that is not likely to be dangerous is called a **phobia.** People who experience phobias usually realize that their fears are groundless, but that's not enough to make the anxiety go away. The continuing discomfort and avoidance of the object or event may greatly interfere with daily life. Thousands of phobias have been described; Table 15.3 lists just a few.

DSM-IV classifies phobias into specific, social, and agoraphobia subtypes. **Specific phobias** include fear and avoidance of heights, blood, animals, automobile

● **anxiety disorder**   A condition in which intense feelings of apprehension are long-standing and disruptive.

● **phobia**   An anxiety disorder involving strong, irrational fear of an object or situation that does not objectively justify such a reaction.

● **specific phobia**   An anxiety disorder involving fear and avoidance of heights, animals, and other specific stimuli and situations.

TABLE 15.3	**Some Phobias**		

Name	Feared Stimulus	Name	Feared Stimulus
Acrophobia	Heights	Aerophobia	Flying
Claustrophobia	Enclosed places	Entomophobia	Insects
Hematophobia	Blood	Gamophobia	Marriage
Gephyrophobia	Crossing a bridge	Ophidiphobia	Snakes
Kenophobia	Empty rooms	Xenophobia	Strangers
Cynophobia	Dogs	Melissophobia	Bees

Phobia is the Greek word for "morbid fear," after the Greek god Phobos. Phobias are usually named by attaching the word *phobia* to the Greek word for the feared object or situation.

or air travel, and other specific stimuli and situations. In the United States and other developed nations, they are the most prevalent of the anxiety disorders, affecting approximately 9 percent of adults and children (Kessler, Chiu, et al., 2005; National Institute of Mental Health, 2006; U.S. Surgeon General, 1999). Here is an example:

> Mr. L. was a fifty-year-old office worker who became terrified whenever he had to drive over a bridge. For years, he avoided bridges by taking round-about ways to and from work, and he refused to be a passenger in anyone else's car, just in case they might use a bridge. Even this very inconvenient adjustment failed when Mr. L. was transferred to a position requiring frequent automobile trips, many of which were over bridges. He refused the transfer and lost his job.

Social phobias involve anxiety about being criticized by others or acting in a way that is embarrassing or humiliating. The anxiety is so intense and persistent that it impairs the person's normal functioning. Common social phobias are fear of public speaking or performance ("stage fright"), fear of eating in front of others, and fear of using public restrooms (Kleinknecht, 2000; Noyes & Hoehn-Saric, 2006).

It's a Long Way Down Almost everyone is afraid of something, but about 9 percent of U.S. adults suffer from a specific phobia, in which fear interferes significantly with daily life. For example, people with acrophobia (fear of heights) would not do well in a job that requires being in this high position.

Anxiety and Depression People who experience anxiety disorders—particularly panic disorder, generalized anxiety disorder, or posttraumatic stress disorder—are likely to display some other mental disorder as well, most often depression (Kaufman & Charney, 2000; Roy-Byrne et al., 2000). Accordingly, the next edition of the *DSM* may include a new category, called *mixed anxiety-depression disorder*, to identify people whose symptoms of anxiety and depression combine to impair their daily functioning.

Generalized social phobia is a more severe form in which fear occurs in virtually all social situations (Mineka & Zinbarg, 2006; Williams et al., 2005). Sociocultural factors can alter the nature of social phobias. For example, in Japan, where cultural training emphasizes group-oriented values and goals, a common social phobia is *tai-jin kyofu sho*, the fear of embarrassing those around you (Kleinknecht, 1994).

Agoraphobia is a strong fear of being away from a safe place, such as home; of being away from a familiar person, such as a spouse or close friend; or of being in a place (such as a crowded theater or mall) that might be difficult to leave or where help may be unavailable. These fears can cause serious problems. People who suffer from agoraphobia typically avoid social situations and refuse to shop, drive, or use public transportation. They may be unable to work and can easily become isolated. In severe cases, agoraphobia can make leaving home such a frightening prospect that people become housebound, unwilling to even try going out alone. Most individuals who display agoraphobia have a history of panic attacks, which we describe later. Their intense fear of public places occurs partly because they don't want to risk triggering an attack by going to places in which they had a previous attack or where they feel an attack would be dangerous or embarrassing (Kessler, Chiu, et al., 2006).

Like other phobias in Western cultures, agoraphobia is more often reported by women. However, in other cultures, such as India, where being a housebound woman is considered less unusual than in the United States, those diagnosed as agoraphobic tend to be male (Raguram & Bhide, 1985). Although agoraphobia occurs at only about one tenth the rate of specific phobias (about 0.8 percent for agoraphobia versus 9 percent for specific phobias in any given year), it is the phobia that most often leads people to seek treatment, mainly because it interferes so severely with everyday life (National Institute of Mental Health, 2006; U.S. Surgeon General, 1999).

●**Generalized Anxiety Disorder** Excessive and long-lasting anxiety that is not focused on any particular object or situation marks **generalized anxiety disorder (GAD).** Because the problem occurs in almost all situations and because the person cannot pinpoint its source, this type of anxiety is sometimes called *free-floating anxiety*. For weeks at a time, the person feels anxious and worried, sure that some disaster is about to happen. The person becomes jumpy and irritable; sound sleep is impossible. Fatigue, inability to concentrate, and physiological signs of anxiety are also common. Generalized anxiety disorder affects about 3.1 percent of the U.S. population in any given year and about 5 percent of the population at some point in their lives (Kessler, Berglund, et al., 2005; U.S. Surgeon General, 1999). This disorder tends to appear somewhat later in life than most of the other anxiety disorders (the median age of onset is thirty-one years old for GAD compared with the teens or early twenties for phobias). Generalized anxiety disorder is more common in women, often accompanying other problems such as depression or substance abuse (Wittchen & Hoyer, 2001).

●**Panic Disorder** For some people, anxiety takes the form of **panic disorder.** Like the man described in Table 15.1, people suffering from panic disorder experience recurrent, terrifying *panic attacks* that seem to come without warning or obvious cause. These attacks are marked by intense heart palpitations, pressure or pain in the chest, dizziness or unsteadiness, sweating, and feeling faint. Often, victims believe they are having a heart attack. They may worry constantly about suffering future panic episodes and thus restrict their activities to avoid possible embarrassment. As noted earlier, fear of experiencing panic attacks while alone or away from home can lead to agoraphobia; indeed, it does so in about one-third of people with panic disorder (Carter & Barlow, 1995; National Institute of Mental Health, 2006; Robins & Regier, 1991). Panic disorder can continue for years, with periods of improvement followed by recurrence (Ehlers, 1995). As many as 30 percent of the people in the United States have experienced at least one panic attack within the previous year (Ehlers, 1995), but only about 2 to 3 percent of the adult population

---

● **social phobia** An anxiety disorder involving strong, irrational fears relating to social situations.

● **agoraphobia** An anxiety disorder involving strong fear of being alone or away from the security of home.

● **generalized anxiety disorder (GAD)** A condition that involves relatively mild but long-lasting anxiety that is not focused on any particular object or situation.

● **panic disorder** An anxiety disorder involving sudden panic attacks.

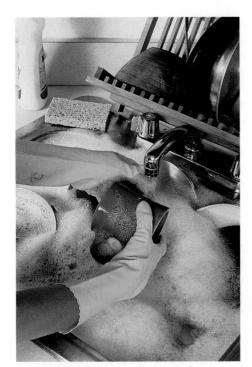

A Cleaning Compulsion Obsessive-compulsive disorder is diagnosed when a culturally expected degree of cleanliness becomes an obsessive preoccupation with germs and a disruptive compulsion to clean things. Though learning and stress appear to play the major role in shaping and triggering this and other anxiety disorders, biological factors, including genetically inherited characteristics and deficiencies in certain neurotransmitters in the brain, may result in an oversensitive nervous system and a predisposition toward anxiety.

develops full-blown panic disorder in any given year (American Psychiatric Association, 2000; Kessler, Berglund, et al., 2005; Kessler, Chiu, et al., 2006). Here is one example:

> Geri, a thirty-two-year-old nurse, had her first panic attack while driving on a freeway. Afterward, she would not drive on freeways. Her next attack occurred while with a patient and a doctor in a small examining room. A sense of impending doom flooded over her, and she burst out of the office and into the parking lot, where she felt immediate relief. From then on, fear of another attack made it impossible for her to tolerate any close quarters, including crowded shopping malls. She eventually quit her job because of terror of the examining rooms.

● **Obsessive-Compulsive Disorder** Anxiety is also at the root of obsessive-compulsive disorder (OCD), which affects about 1 percent of the population in any given year in the United States and elsewhere (Crino, Slade, & Andrews, 2005; Kessler, Chiu, et al., 2005; National Institute of Mental Health, 2006). Like Mark, whose story opened this chapter, people displaying obsessive-compulsive disorder are plagued by persistent, upsetting, and unwanted thoughts—called *obsessions*—that often center on the possibility of infection, contamination, or doing harm to themselves or others. They do not actually carry out harmful acts, but the obsessive thoughts motivate ritualistic, repetitive behaviors—called *compulsions*—that are performed in an effort to avoid some dreaded outcome or to reduce feelings of anxiety associated with the obsessions (Noyes & Hoehn-Saric, 2006). For example, Mark engaged in incessant, ritualized cleaning to protect himself from infection. Other common compulsions include rituals such as checking locks; repeating words, images, or numbers; counting things; or arranging objects "just so." Obsessions and compulsions are much more intense than the familiar experience of having a repetitive thought or tune "in the back of your mind" or rechecking that a door is locked. In obsessive-compulsive disorder, the obsessions and compulsions are intense, disturbing, and often strange intrusions that can severely impair daily activities. (*DSM-IV* defines compulsions as occupying more than one hour a day.) Many people who display this disorder recognize that their thoughts and actions are irrational, but they still experience severe agitation and anxiety if they try to interrupt their obsessions or give up their compulsive behaviors.

● Causes of Anxiety Disorders

As with all the forms of psychopathology we will consider, the exact causes of anxiety disorders are a matter of some debate. However, there is good evidence that biological, psychological, and social factors all contribute. Biological predispositions, distortions in thinking, and certain learning experiences appear to be particularly important (U.S. Surgeon General, 1999; Williams et al., 2005). The exact nature and combination of causal factors varies from one anxiety disorder to the next. For example, the brain regions involved in panic disorder are not identical to those involved in obsessive-compulsive disorder, and the learning experiences contributing to specific phobia may differ from those contributing to agoraphobia.

● **Biological Factors** Most anxiety disorders, including panic disorder, obsessive-compulsive disorder, and generalized social phobia, appear to run in families (Bolton et al., 2006; Grabe et al., 2006; Stewart et al., 2007). This tendency may be partly due to environmental factors that affect members of the same family, but it also suggests that people may inherit a predisposition to develop anxiety disorders (e.g., Fyer et al., 2006). Genetic influences on these disorders are suggested by research showing that if one identical twin has an anxiety disorder, the other is more likely also to have an anxiety disorder than is the case in nonidentical twin pairs (Bolton et al., 2006; Kendler, Jacobson, et al., 2002). Data from twin, family, and

● **obsessive-compulsive disorder (OCD)** An anxiety disorder involving repetitive thoughts and urges to perform certain rituals.

other studies suggest, for example, that genetic influences play a relatively strong role in panic disorder and generalized anxiety disorder, particularly when there is early onset of symptoms (Bolton et al., 2006; Hettema, Neale, & Kendler, 2001; Neumeister et al., 2004). Some evidence suggests that genetic factors appear to influence social phobia more strongly in males than in females (Kendler, Jacobson, et al., 2002), but overall the genetic and environmental risk factors for anxiety disorders are similar in men and women (Hettema et al., 2005).

Some inherited predispositions may be rather specific. For instance, one study has found that identical twins were more likely than other siblings to share phobias about small animals and social situations but not about heights or enclosed spaces (Skre et al., 2000). Other research suggests that there may be a link between obsessive-compulsive disorder and a specific gene known as SLC1A1 (Leckman & Kim, 2006). It will take much more research, however, to determine the degree to which various anxiety disorders are influenced by specific genetic factors or more general ones. For example, people who display anxiety disorders may have inherited an autonomic nervous system that is oversensitive to stress and easily conditioned, thus predisposing them to react with intense anxiety to a wide range of situations (Ahmad et al., 2002; Bracha, 2006; Miller et al., 2005; Zinbarg & Barlow, 1996). A predisposition for developing anxiety disorders may also stem from abnormalities in the brain's neurotransmitter activity. Excessive activity of norepinephrine circuits in certain parts of the brain has been linked with panic disorder, and dysregulation of serotonin has been associated with obsessive-compulsive disorder and social phobia (Lanzenberger et al., 2007). Supporting this view is evidence that medications that affect these neurotransmitters are often effective in the treatment of OCD and other anxiety disorders (Bartz & Hollander, 2006).

● **Psychological Factors** Although biological predispositions may set the stage for anxiety disorders, most researchers agree that environmental stressors and psychological factors, including cognitive processes and learning, are crucial to the development of most anxiety disorders (Mineka & Zinbarg, 2006; Moses & Barlow, 2006; Schmidt et al., 2000; Stein, Chavira, & Jang, 2001). To see the effects of environmental stressors, one need only look at the dramatic rise in cases of post-traumatic stress disorder following military combat, natural disasters, or terrorist attacks (Galea et al., 2002; Hoven et al., 2005). The impact of learning can be seen in families in which parents don't socialize much, tend to be suspicious of others, and constantly exaggerate life's everyday dangers. These parents might unwittingly promote social anxiety in their children—especially children born with a tendency toward shyness—by influencing them to interpret social situations as threatening. Abuse or other traumatic childhood experiences also increase the risk of developing an anxiety disorder, particularly panic disorder (Safren et al., 2002).

People suffering from an anxiety disorder often exaggerate the dangers in their environment, thereby creating an unrealistic expectation that bad events are going to happen (Wenzel et al., 2006; Wilson et al., 2006). This expectation leads them to be constantly on the lookout for negative events (Foa et al., 1996; Leahy et al., 2005; Wells & Matthews, 2006). Further, because they tend to underestimate their capacity to control threatening events, they are likely to experience anxiety and desperation if and when feared events do occur. Their lack of perceived control, in turn, can lead these people to avoid, or overreact to, threatening situations (Wells & Matthews, 2006; White et al., 2006). As an example, consider the development of a panic attack. Unexplained symptoms of physical arousal may set the stage for a panic attack, but it is the person's sensitivity to and cognitive interpretation of those symptoms that can determine whether or not the attack actually develops (Lim & Kim, 2005; Schmidt, Lerew, & Jackson, 1999). In fact, panic attacks are less likely in panic-disorder patients who believe they can control the source of their discomfort (Rapee et al., 1992; White et al., 2006). In short, a number of dysfunctional beliefs and cognitive distortions are associated with the development of anxiety disorders.

LINKAGES Anxiety Disorders and Learning

 LINKAGES (a link to Learning, p. 204)

The learning principles discussed in the chapter on learning also play an important role in anxiety disorders. For example, upsetting thoughts—about money or illness, for example—often create anxiety and worry, especially when people are already under stress or feel incapable of dealing with their problems. As the thoughts become more persistent, anxiety increases. If doing something such as, say, cleaning the kitchen temporarily relieves the anxiety, that behavior may be strengthened through the process of negative reinforcement discussed in the chapter on learning. But cleaning can't eliminate the obsessive thoughts, so they return, and the actions become compulsive, endlessly repeated rituals that keep the person trapped in a vicious circle of anxiety. To social-cognitive theorists, then, obsessive-compulsive disorder is a pattern that is sparked by distressing thoughts and maintained by operant conditioning (Abramowitz et al., 2006).

Phobias, too, may be partly based on learning, especially on the principles of classical conditioning and observational learning described in the learning chapter. The feared object becomes an aversive conditioned stimulus after being associated with a traumatic event that acts as an unconditioned stimulus (Öst, 1992). Fear of dogs, for example, may result from a dog attack. But fear can also be learned merely by seeing or hearing about other people's bad experiences. These fears can even be learned by watching TV or movies (Cook & Mineka, 1990). Perhaps you know someone who became reluctant to take a shower after seeing the horrific shower-room murder scene in Alfred Hitchcock's film *Psycho* or one of its many remakes. Once phobias are learned, avoiding the feared object or situation prevents the person from finding out that there is nothing to fear. This cycle of avoidance helps explain why many phobias do not simply extinguish, or disappear, on their own.

Why are phobias about snakes and spiders so common, even though people are seldom harmed by them? And why are there so few cases of electrical-shock phobia, even though lots of people receive accidental electrical shocks? As discussed in the

Learning by Watching Many phobias, including those involving needles, blood, and medical-related situations, are acquired vicariously—by what we see and hear. In fact, fear developed through observational learning can be as strong as fear developed through direct experience. Fearlessness can also be learned vicariously. By simply watching the boy in the dental chair as he learns to relax with his dentist, the other youngster is less likely to be distressed when it is his turn.

chapter on learning, the answer may be that we are *biologically prepared* to learn associations between certain stimuli and certain responses. These stimuli and responses, then, would be especially easy to link through conditioning (Hamm, Vaitl, & Lang, 1989). Specifically, we may be biologically prepared to learn to fear and to avoid stimuli that had the potential to harm our evolutionary ancestors (Skre et al., 2000; Staddon & Ettinger, 1989).

The notion that people are biologically prepared to learn certain phobias is supported by laboratory evidence. For example, a group of Swedish psychologists attempted to condition people to fear certain stimuli by associating those stimuli with electrical shocks (Öhman, Dimberg, & Öst, 1985). The research participants developed approximately equal conditioned anxiety reactions to photos of houses, human faces, and snakes. Later, however, when they were tested without shock, their fear reaction to snakes remained long after their reaction to houses and faces had faded. A series of investigations with animals has also supported preparedness theory (Cook & Mineka, 1990). If a monkey sees another monkey behaving fearfully in the presence of a snake, it quickly develops a strong and persistent fear of snakes. However, if the snake is entwined in flowers, the observer monkeys come to fear only the snake, not the flowers. So the fear conditioning appears to be selective, focusing only on potentially dangerous creatures such as snakes or crocodiles (Zinbarg & Mineka, 1991), not on harmless objects.

Learning is obviously important in the development of fear, but learning principles alone cannot explain why exposure to certain stimuli creates anxiety disorders in some people and not in others (Field, 2006). Why is it, for example, that some survivors of the terrorist attacks of 9/11 developed phobias or posttraumatic stress disorder and others did not? As suggested by the diathesis-stress approach, and as discussed in the chapter on health, stress, and coping, the impact of people's experiences is heightened or dampened by other factors, such as their genetic and biological vulnerability to stress, their previous experiences with frightening events, their expectations and other cognitive habits, and the social support and other conditions that follow the trauma (Armfield, 2006; Mineka & Zinbarg, 2006). In short, learning—including the learning that supports the development of anxiety disorders—occurs more quickly among those who are biologically and psychologically prepared for it. ■

TRY THIS **Biological Preparedness** Being predisposed to learn to fear snakes and other potentially dangerous stimuli makes evolutionary sense. Humans and other animals who rapidly learn a fear response to objects or situations that they see causing fright in their parents or peers are more likely to survive to reproduce, thus passing on their genes to the next generation. Make a list of the things that you might be especially afraid of. How did these fears develop? And how many of them appear to have "survival value"?

Somatoform Disorders

A young athlete began to suffer fainting spells that prevented her from competing in track and field events, but doctors could find nothing physically wrong. After a program of stress management, however, her symptoms disappeared, and she was able to rejoin her team (Lively, 2001). Sometimes people show symptoms of a *somatic,* or bodily, disorder, even though it has no physical cause. Because these conditions reflect psychological problems that take somatic form, they are called **somatoform disorders.** The classic example is **conversion disorder,** a condition in which people appear to be, but are not, blind, deaf, paralyzed, or insensitive to pain in various parts of the body. (An earlier term for this disorder was *hysteria.*) Conversion disorders are rare, accounting for only about 2 percent of diagnoses (American Psychiatric Association, 1994, 2000). Although they can occur at any point in life, they usually appear in adolescence or early adulthood.

Conversion disorders differ from true physical disabilities in several ways (Allin, Streeruwitz, & Curtis, 2005). First, they tend to appear when a person is under severe stress. Second, they often help reduce that stress by allowing the person to avoid unpleasant or threatening situations. Third, the person may show remarkably little concern about what is apparently a rather serious problem. Finally, the symptoms may be neurologically impossible or improbable, as Figure 15.2 illustrates. One university student, for example, experienced visual impairment that began each Sunday evening and became total blindness by Monday morning. Her vision would begin to return on Friday evenings and was fully restored in time for weekend football games and other social activities. She expressed no particular concern over her condition (Holmes, 1991).

Can people who display a conversion disorder actually see and hear and move, even though they act as if they cannot? Observations and experiments suggest that they can. Supposedly paralyzed people have been seen to sleep-walk, and supposedly blind or deaf people make use of sights and sounds to guide their behavior (e.g., Blake, 1998; Grosz & Zimmerman, 1970). But this does not mean that they are *malingering,* or faking. In fact, conversion disorder is diagnosed only when the symptoms are *not* being faked. Rather than destroying sensory or motor ability, the conversion process may prevent the person from being aware of information that the brain is still processing (Ballmaier & Schmidt, 2005; Harvey, Stanton, & David, 2006).

Another somatoform disorder is **hypochondriasis** (pronounced "hye-poh-kon-DRY-a-sis"), a strong, unjustified fear that one has cancer, heart disease, AIDS, or other serious physical problems. The fear prompts frequent visits to physicians and reports of numerous symptoms. Their preoccupation with illness often leads hypochondriacs to become experts on their most feared diseases. In some ways, hypochondriasis is like an anxiety disorder in that it involves health concerns and includes elements of phobia, panic, and obsessive-compulsiveness. However, whereas a person suffering from anxiety disorder might have an irrational fear of getting a serious illness, the person diagnosed with hypochondriasis is excessively concerned about already *having* the illness and is much more likely to seek unnecessary medical treatments (Hiller et al., 2006; Neziroglu, McKay, & Yaryura-Tobias, 2000). A related condition, called **somatization disorder,** is characterized by dramatic, but vague, reports about a multitude of physical problems rather than any specific illness. **Pain disorder** is marked by complaints of severe, often constant pain (typically in the neck, chest, or back) with no physical cause.

Some cases of somatoform disorder may be related to childhood experiences in which a person learns that symptoms of physical illness bring special attention, care, and privileges (Abramowitz & Braddock, 2006; Barsky et al., 1994). Others, including conversion disorder, may be triggered by severe stressors (Ballmaier & Schmidt, 2005; Ovsiew, 2006; Spiegel, 1994). Cognitive factors also come into play. When given information about their health, people with hypochondriasis are

somatoform disorders Psychological problems in which there are symptoms of a physical disorder without a physical cause.

conversion disorder A somatoform disorder in which a person displays blindness, deafness, or other symptoms of sensory or motor failure without a physical cause.

hypochondriasis A somatoform disorder involving strong, unjustified fear of having physical illness.

somatization disorder A somatoform disorder in which there are numerous physical complaints without verifiable physical illness.

pain disorder A somatoform disorder marked by complaints of severe pain with no physical cause.

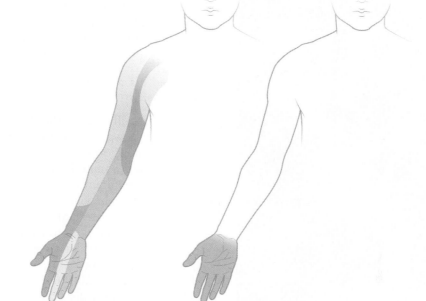

(A)   (B)

FIGURE 15.2

Glove Anesthesia

In "glove anesthesia," a form of conversion disorder, lack of feeling stops abruptly at the wrist, as in Part B. But as shown in Part A, the nerves of the hand and arm blend, so if they were actually impaired, part of the arm would also lose sensitivity. Other neurologically impossible symptoms of conversion disorder include sleepwalking at night on legs that are "paralyzed" during the day.

strongly biased to focus on threat-confirming information but to ignore reassuring information (Smeets, de Jong, & Mayer, 2000).

Based on such findings, many researchers have adopted a diathesis-stress approach to explaining somatoform disorders. The results of their work suggest that certain people may have biological and psychological traits that make them especially vulnerable to somatoform disorders, particularly when combined with a history of physical illness. Among these traits are self-consciousness and oversensitivity to physical sensations. If such people experience a number of long-lasting stressors, intense emotional conflicts, or severe traumas, they are more likely than others to display physical symptoms in association with emotional arousal (Abramowitz & Braddock, 2006; Siti, 2004).

Sociocultural factors may shape the nature of some somatoform disorders. In many Asian, Latin American, and African cultures, it is not unusual for people to experience severe physical symptoms in association with psychological or interpersonal conflicts (Brislin, 1993; recall our earlier examples of *ataque de nervios* and *koro)*. However, the overall *rate* of somatoform disorders appears to be about the same across cultures (Becker, 2004; Kohrt et al., 2005).

Dissociative Disorders

If you have ever spent many hours driving on a boring highway, you may have suddenly realized that you had little or no recollection of what happened during the previous half-hour. This common experience does not signal a mental disorder, but when disruptions in a person's memory, consciousness, or identity are more intense and long-lasting, they are known as **dissociative disorders.** These disruptions can come on gradually, but they usually occur suddenly and last from a few hours to many years.

Consider the case of John, a thirty-year-old computer manufacturing executive:

John was a meek person who was dependent on his wife for companionship and emotional support. It came as a jolt when she announced that she was leaving him to live with his younger brother. John did not go to work the

dissociative disorders Rare conditions that involve sudden and usually temporary disruptions in a person's memory, consciousness, or identity.

A Famous Case of Dissociative Identity Disorder In this scene from the film *Sybil*, Sally Field portrays a woman diagnosed with dissociative identity disorder, previously known as multiple personality disorder. Sybil appeared to have as many as seventeen distinct personalities. The causes of such dramatic cases, and the reasons behind their increasing prevalence in recent years, is a matter of intense debate.

next day. In fact, nothing was heard from him for two weeks until he was arrested for public drunkenness and assault in a city more than three hundred miles from his home. During those two weeks, John lived under another name at a cheap hotel and worked selling tickets at a pornographic movie theater. When he was interviewed, John did not know his real name or his home address, could not explain how he had reached his present location, and could not remember much about the previous two weeks.

John's case illustrates the dissociative disorder known as **dissociative fugue** (pronounced "fewg"), which is characterized by a sudden loss of personal memory and the adoption of a new identity in a new locale. Another dissociative disorder, **dissociative amnesia**, also involves sudden memory loss. As in fugue, all personal identifying information may be forgotten, but the person does not leave home or create a new identity. These rare conditions attract intense publicity because they are so dramatic. As with other forms of disorder, explanations for dissociative disorder symptoms can vary from culture to culture. For instance, some dissociative-disorder patients in China, Malaysia, India, and Africa report being possessed by spirits or one of their religion's gods (Ng, 2000; van Duiji, Cardena, & de Jong, 2005).

The most famous dissociative disorder is **dissociative identity disorder (DID)**, formerly known as—and still commonly called—*multiple personality disorder (MPD)*. A person diagnosed with DID appears to have more than one identity, each of which speaks, acts, and writes in a different way. Each personality seems to have its own memories, wishes, and (often conflicting) impulses. Here is a case example:

Mary, a pleasant and introverted thirty-five-year-old social worker, was referred to a psychiatrist for hypnotic treatment of chronic pain. At an early interview she mentioned the odd fact that though she had no memory of using her car after coming home from work, she often found that it had been driven fifty to one hundred miles overnight. It turned out that she also had no memory of large parts of her childhood. Mary rapidly learned self-hypnosis for pain control, but during one hypnotic session, she suddenly began speaking in a hostile manner. She told the doctor her name was Marian, and that it was "she" who had been taking long evening drives. She also called Mary "pathetic" for "wasting time" trying to please other people. Eventually, six other identities emerged, some of whom told of having experienced parental abuse in childhood. (Spitzer et al., 1994)

For about a decade after 1970, there was a minor "epidemic" of DID as well as an increase in the number of alternate personalities per case (some patients reported over twenty of them). This upsurge in DID may have occurred because clinicians were looking for it more carefully or because the conditions leading to it became more prevalent, but it may have also been influenced by movies such as *Sybil* and by tell-all books written by people who had been diagnosed with DID (Kihlstrom, 2005). These media influences might have increased the status of DID as a socio-culturally approved method of expressing distress (Hacking, 1995; Spanos, 1994). Such concerns were partly responsible for the change in designation from *multiple personality disorder* to *dissociative identity disorder*. The authors of *DSM-IV* wanted to downplay the notion that people harbor multiple personalities that can easily be "contacted" through hypnosis or related techniques. The new name was chosen to suggest, instead, that dissociation, or separation, between one's memories and other aspects of identity can be so dramatic that people experiencing it may come to believe that they have more than one personality (Gleaves, May, & Cardena, 2001; Spiegel, 1994).

How do dissociative disorders develop? Psychodynamic theorists see massive repression of unwanted impulses or memories as the basis for creating a "new person" who acts out otherwise unacceptable impulses or recalls otherwise unbearable memories (Ross, 1997). Social-cognitive theorists focus on the fact that everyone is

dissociative fugue A dissociative disorder involving sudden loss of memory and the assumption of a new identity in a new locale.

dissociative amnesia A dissociative disorder marked by a sudden loss of memory.

dissociative identity disorder (DID) A dissociative disorder in which a person reports having more than one identity.

capable of behaving in different ways, depending on circumstances (e.g., rowdy in a bar, quiet in a museum); but in rare cases, they say, this variation can become so extreme that an individual feels—and is perceived by others as being—a "different person." Further, dissociative symptoms may be strengthened by reward as people find that a sudden memory loss or shift in behavior allows them to escape stressful situations, responsibilities, or punishment for misbehavior (Lilienfeld & Lynn, 2003; Lilienfeld et al., 1999). The difficulty in evaluating these hypotheses had once been attributed to the rarity of dissociative disorders, but the availability of more cases, especially cases of DID, has only added to the causal controversy.

Research available so far on dissociative disorders supports four conclusions. First, memory loss and other forms of dissociations are genuine phenomena and as seen in dissociative fugue, they can sometimes become extreme. Second, many people displaying DID have experienced events they would like to forget or avoid. The majority (some clinicians believe all) have suffered severe, unavoidable, persistent abuse in childhood (Foote et al., 2006; Kihlstrom, 2005; Ross et al., 1991). Third, like Mary, most of these people appear to be skilled at self-hypnosis, through which they can induce a trance-like state. Fourth, most found that they could escape the trauma of abuse, at least temporarily, by creating "new personalities" to deal with stress (Spiegel, 1994). However, not all abused children display DID, and there is evidence that DID can indeed be triggered by media stories or by suggestions made to clients by their therapists (Spanos, 1996).

This evidence has led some skeptics to question the very existence of multiple personalities (Acocella, 1998; Merckelbach, Devilly, & Rassin, 2002). They point to research showing, for example, that people who display DID may be more aware than they think they are of the memories and actions of each apparent identity (Allen, 2002; Allen & Iacono, 2001). Research on the existence and effects of repressed memories (discussed in the memory chapter) is sure to have an impact on our understanding of, and the controversy over, the causes of DID. ("In Review: Anxiety, Somatoform, and Dissociative Disorders" presents a summary of our discussion of these disorders.)

The debate and skepticism about dissociative identity disorder—including whether it is caused partly by therapists' expectations—is not confined to professional journals. This drawing appeared in *The New Yorker* magazine.

"Would it be possible to speak with the personality that pays the bills?"

in review Anxiety, Somatoform, and Dissociative Disorders

Disorder	Subtypes	Major Symptoms
Anxiety disorders	Phobias	Intense, irrational fear of objectively nondangerous situations or things, leading to disruptions of behavior
	Generalized anxiety disorder	Excessive anxiety not focused on a specific situation or object; free-floating anxiety
	Panic disorder	Repeated attacks of intense fear involving physical symptoms such as faintness, dizziness, and nausea
	Obsessive-compulsive disorder	Persistent ideas or worries accompanied by ritualistic behaviors performed to neutralize anxiety-driven thoughts
Somatoform disorders	Conversion disorder	A loss of physical ability (e.g., sight, hearing) that is related to psychological factors
	Hypochondriasis	Preoccupation with, or belief that one has, a serious illness in the absence of any physical evidence
	Somatization disorder	Wide variety of somatic complaints that occur over several years and are not the result of a known physical disorder
	Pain disorder	Preoccupation with pain in the absence of physical reasons for the pain
Dissociative disorders	Dissociative amnesia/fugue	Sudden loss of memory, which may result in relocation and the assumption of a new identity
	Dissociative identity disorder (multiple personality disorder)	Appearance within the same person of two or more distinct identities, each with a unique way of thinking and behaving

Mood Disorders

Everyone's mood, or *affect*, tends to rise and fall from time to time. However, when people experience extremes of mood—wild elation or deep depression—for long periods, when they shift from one extreme to another, and especially when their moods are not consistent with the events around them, they are said to show a **mood disorder** (also known as an *affective disorder*). We will describe two main types: depressive disorders and bipolar disorders.

● Depressive Disorders

Depression can range from occasional, normal "down" periods to episodes severe enough to require hospitalization. A person suffering **major depressive disorder** feels sad and overwhelmed, typically losing interest in activities and relationships and taking pleasure in nothing (Getzfeld, 2006; Sloan, Strauss, & Wisner, 2001). Despite the person's best efforts, everything from conversation to bathing is an unbearable, exhausting effort. Changes in eating habits resulting in weight loss or weight gain often accompany major depressive disorder, as does sleep disturbance or, less often, excessive sleeping. Problems in working, concentrating, making decisions, and thinking clearly are also common. More often than not, there are also symptoms of an accompanying anxiety disorder (Zimmerman, McDermut, & Mattia, 2000). In extreme cases, depressed people may express false beliefs, or **delusions**—worrying, for example, that the government is planning to punish them. Major depressive disorder may come on suddenly or gradually. It may consist of a single episode or, more

● **mood disorder** Conditions in which a person experiences extreme moods, such as depression or mania.

● **major depressive disorder** A mood disorder in which a person feels sad and hopeless for weeks or months.

● **delusions** False beliefs, such as those experienced by people suffering from schizophrenia or extreme depression.

commonly, repeated depressive periods. These episodes can last for weeks or months; the average length of the first one is four to nine months (Durand & Barlow, 2006). Exaggerated feelings of inadequacy, worthlessness, hopelessness, or guilt are common in major depressive disorder. Here is a case example:

> Mr. J. was a fifty-one-year-old industrial engineer. . . . Since the death of his wife five years earlier, he had been suffering from continuing episodes of depression marked by extreme social withdrawal and occasional thoughts of suicide. . . . He drank and, when thoroughly intoxicated, would plead to his deceased wife for forgiveness. He lost all capacity for joy. . . . Once a gourmet, he now had no interest in food and good wine . . . and could barely manage to engage in small talk. As might be expected, his work record deteriorated markedly. Appointments were missed and projects haphazardly started and left unfinished. (Davison & Neale, 1990, p. 221)

Depression is not always so extreme. In a less severe pattern of depression, called **dysthymic disorder,** the person experiences the sad mood, lack of interest, and loss of pleasure associated with major depression, but less intensely and for a longer period. (The duration must be at least two years to qualify as dysthymic disorder.) Mental and behavioral disruption are also less severe; people exhibiting dysthymic disorder rarely require hospitalization.

Major depressive disorder occurs sometime in the lives of about 17 percent of people in North America and Europe (Hasin et al., 2005; Kessler et al., 1994, 2003; U.S. Surgeon General, 1999); in any given year, about 9.5 percent of these populations are experiencing the disorder (Kessler et al., 1994, 2003; U.S. Surgeon General, 1999). Unfortunately, it is becoming more common, both in the United States and elsewhere. The World Health Organization estimates that if current trends continue, depression will become the second-leading cause of disability and premature death in developed economies (World Health Organization Mental Health Survey Consortium, 2004). However, the incidence of the disorder varies considerably across cultures and sub-cultures. For example, depression occurs at much higher rates in urban Ireland than in urban Spain (Judd et al., 2002), though it is not always clear whether such differences reflect real differences in rates of depression or differences in the application of diagnostic criteria (Judd et al., 2002). There are gender differences in some cultures, too. In the United States and other Western countries, females are two to three times more likely than males to experience major depressive disorder; 10 to 25 percent of women and 5 to 12 percent of men will display this disorder during their lifetimes (American Psychiatric Association, 2000; Weissman et al., 1993). This difference is smaller in the less economically developed countries of the Middle East, Africa, and Asia (Ayuso-Mateos et al., 2001; Culbertson, 1997; World Health Organization, 2003). Depression can occur at any age, but two peaks of prevalence appear across the life span. The first occurs in late adolescence or young adulthood, and the second during old age (Cross-National Collaborative Group, 2002; Durand & Barlow, 2006; Fassler & Dumas, 1997; Sowdon, 2001).

Depression is often found in combination with other psychological disorders and medical conditions; it is especially likely to be diagnosed along with posttraumatic stress disorder, obsessive-compulsive disorder, and other anxiety disorders, as well as with substance use disorders, physical disabilities, and recovery from heart attack (Mitra et al., 2005; O'Brien, 2006). As mentioned earlier, some researchers believe that the overlap between anxiety and depression is significant enough to warrant combining them into a single category in the next edition of the *DSM* (Moses & Barlow, 2006).

● **Suicide and Depression**   Suicide is associated with a variety of psychological disorders, but it is most closely tied to depression and other mood disorders (Balázs et al., 2006). Some form of depression has been implicated in 40 to 70 percent of suicides (Angst, Angst, & Stassen, 1999; Oquendo & Mann, 2001). In fact, thinking about suicide is a symptom of depressive disorders. Hopelessness about the future—another

dysthymic disorder   A mood disorder involving a pattern of comparatively mild depression that lasts for at least two years.

depressive symptom—and a desire to seek instant escape from problems are also related to suicide attempts (Beck et al., 1990; Brown et al., 2000).

About 31,000 people in the United States commit suicide each year, or about 86 persons per day, and ten to twenty times that many people attempt it (Centers for Disease Control and Prevention, 2004). This puts the U.S. suicide rate at about 10 per 100,000 individuals, making suicide the eleventh-leading cause of death. Worldwide, the suicide rate is as high as 25 per 100,000 in some northern and eastern European countries and Japan (Lamar, 2000; World Health Organization, 2003) and as low as 6 per 100,000 in countries with stronger religious prohibitions against suicide, such as Greece, Italy, Ireland, and the nations of the Middle East.

Suicide rates also differ considerably depending on sociocultural factors such as age, gender, and ethnicity (Centers for Disease Control and Prevention, 2002b, 2002c; Oquendo et al., 2001). In the United States, suicide is most common among people over sixty-five years old, especially men. The suicide rate for men who are eighty-five or older is 55 per 100,000; for women in this age group, it is only 4 per 100,000 (Centers for Disease Control and Prevention, 2004). However, since 1950 suicide among those aged fifteen to twenty-four has tripled. And though the rate has begun to level off in the last decade (Centers for Disease Control and Prevention, 2006), suicide is still the third-leading cause of death, after accidents and homicides, among people in this age group (Centers for Disease Control and Prevention, 2002b, 2006). Suicide is the second-leading cause of death among college students. About 10,000 try to kill themselves each year, and about 1,000 succeed. These figures are much higher than for eighteen- to twenty-four-year-olds in general, but much lower than for the elderly (U.S. Surgeon General, 1999). Women attempt suicide three times as often as men, but men are four times as likely to actually kill themselves (Centers for Disease Control and Prevention, 2006). The gender difference is even greater among people who have been diagnosed with depression. In this group, the male suicide rate of 65 per 100,000 is ten times higher than the rate for women (Blair-West et al., 1999; Centers for Disease Control and Prevention, 1999b).

Suicide rates also differ across ethnic groups (Centers for Disease Control and Prevention, 2002c; Oquendo et al., 2001; see Figure 15.3). Among males in the United States, for example, the overall rate for American Indians is 19.1 per 100,000, compared with 19.4 for European Americans, 9.7 for Asian Americans, 10.7 for Hispanic Americans, and 10.4 for African Americans. The same pattern of ethnic differences appears among women, though the actual rates are much lower (Centers for Disease Control and Prevention, 2002c).

FIGURE 15.3

Suicide Rates in Various Ethnic Groups

The suicide rates among ethnic groups in the United States vary widely. For example, the rate among American Indians is almost twice that of African Americans. In 2002, more teenagers and young adults died from suicide than from cancer, heart disease, AIDS, birth defects, stroke, pneumonia and influenza, and chronic lung disease *combined* (Centers for Disease Control and Prevention, 2002c, 2004).

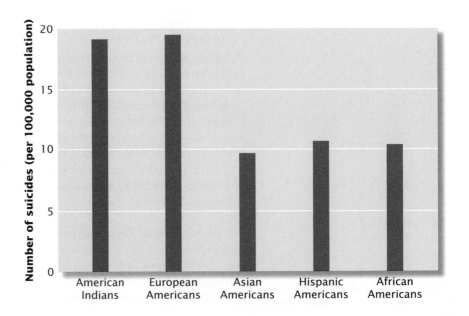

Predicting who will commit suicide is difficult. For one thing, suicidal thoughts are quite common—about 3 percent of all adults and as many as 10 percent of college students report having had such thoughts in the previous year (Brener, Hassan, & Barrios, 1999; Kessler, Berglund, Borges, et al., 2005). Still, the results of hundreds of research studies provide some predictive guidelines, and new instruments are being developed to make prediction even more accurate (Smyth & MacLachian, 2005). In the United States, at least, suicide is most likely among European American males, especially those older than forty-five, single or divorced, and living alone. The risk of suicide is also heightened among people diagnosed with a mood disorder, anxiety disorder, or schizophrenia (Boardman & Healy, 2001; Khan et al., 2002; Rihmer, 2001). Among the elderly, suicide is most common in males who suffer depression over health problems (e.g., Brown, Bongar, & Cleary, 2004). The risk is higher, too, in people who have made a specific plan, given away possessions, and are impulsive (Centers for Disease Control and Prevention, 2004). A previous suicide attempt may not always be a good predictor of eventual suicide, because such attempts may have been help-seeking gestures, not failed efforts to die (McIntosh, 2003; Nock & Kessler, 2006). In fact, although about 10 percent of unsuccessful attempters try again and succeed, most people who commit suicide had made no prior attempts (Clark & Fawcett, 1992).

It is often said that people who talk about suicide will never try it. This is a myth. On the contrary, those who say they are thinking of suicide are much more likely than other people to attempt suicide. In fact, according to Edwin Schneidman (1987), 80 percent of suicides are preceded by some kind of warning, whether direct ("I think I'm going to kill myself") or vague ("Sometimes I wonder if life is worth living"). Although not everyone who threatens suicide follows through, if you suspect that someone you know is thinking about suicide, encourage the person to contact a mental health professional or a crisis hotline. If the danger is immediate, make the contact yourself, and ask for advice about what to do. Many suicide attempts—including those triggered by other suicides in the same town or school—can be prevented by social support and other forms of help for people at high risk (Centers for Disease Control and Prevention, 2004; Mann et al., 2005). For more information, visit suicide-related web sites, such as that of the American Association of Suicidology (www.suicidology.org).

● Bipolar Disorders

The alternating appearance of two emotional extremes, or poles, characterizes *bipolar I disorder*. We have already described one emotional pole: depression. The other is **mania,** which is an extremely agitated, usually elated, emotional state. People in a manic state tend to be utterly optimistic, boundlessly energetic, certain of having extraordinary powers and abilities, and bursting with all sorts of ideas. They become irritated with anyone who tries to reason with them or "slow them down." During manic episodes individuals may make impulsive and unwise decisions, including spending their life savings on foolish schemes.

In **bipolar I disorder,** manic episodes may alternate with periods of deep depression. Sometimes, periods of relatively normal mood separate these extremes (Tohen et al., 2003). This pattern has also been called *manic depression*. Compared with major depressive disorder, bipolar I disorder is rare. It occurs in only about 1 percent of adults, and it affects men and women about equally. Another 1 percent of adults display *bipolar II disorder,* in which major depressive episodes alternate with episodes known as *hypomania,* which are less severe than the manic phases seen in bipolar I disorder (Merikangas et al., 2007). Both versions can severely disrupt a person's ability to work or maintain social relationships (Kessler, Berglund, Demler, et al., 2005; National Institute of Mental Health, 2006).

Somewhat more common is *cyclothymic disorder*, the bipolar equivalent of dysthymia. Cyclothymic disorder involves episodes of depression and mania, but the

● **mania** An elated, very active emotional state.

● **bipolar I disorder** A mood disorder in which a person alternates between deep depression and mania.

in review Mood Disorders

Type	Typical Symptoms	Related Features
Major depressive disorder	Deep sadness, feelings of worthlessness, changes in eating and sleeping habits, loss of interest and pleasure	Lasts weeks or months; may occur in repeating episodes; severe cases may include delusions; danger of suicide
Dysthymic disorder	Similar to major depressive disorder, but less severe and longer lasting	Hospitalization usually not necessary
Bipolar I disorder	Alternating extremes of mood, from deep depression to mania, and back	Manic episodes include impulsivity, unrealistic optimism, high energy, severe agitation
Cyclothymic disorder	Similar to bipolar disorder, but less severe	Hospitalization usually not necessary

intensity of both moods is less severe than in bipolar I disorder. As with depression, bipolar disorders are often accompanied by anxiety disorders (Freeman, Freeman, & McElroy, 2002). ("In Review: Mood Disorders" summarizes the main types of mood disorders.)

■● Causes of Mood Disorders

Research on the causes of mood disorders has focused on biological, psychological, and sociocultural risk factors. The more of these risk factors people have, the more likely they are to experience a mood disorder.

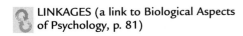

LINKAGES (a link to Biological Aspects of Psychology, p. 81)

●**Biological Factors**   The role of genetics in mood disorders, especially in bipolar disorders, is suggested by twin studies and family studies (Cho et al., 2005; Hayden & Nurnberger, 2006; Kendler et al., 2006). For example, bipolar disorder is much more likely to be seen in both members of genetically identical twin pairs than in fraternal, or nonidentical, twins (Bowman & Nurnberger, 1993; McGuffin et al., 2003). Family studies also show that those who are closely related to people with a bipolar disorder are more likely than others to develop that disorder themselves (Althoff et al., 2005; Blackwood, Visscher, & Muir, 2001). Major depressive disorder is also more likely to be shared among family members, and especially by identical twins (Detera-Wadleigh & McMahon, 2004; Levinson, 2006). This genetic influence is especially strong in female twins (Bierut et al., 1999). Findings such as these suggest that genetic influences tend to be stronger for mood disorders, and especially for bipolar I disorder, than for most other disorders. Researchers are making progress at identifying regions on various chromosomes that appear related to the genetic transmission of vulnerability to bipolar disorder and other affective disorders (e.g., Greenwood et al., 2006; Levinson et al., 2007). These include genes on chromosome 13 that are involved in the operation of the neurotransmitter serotonin (Detera-Wadleigh & McMahon, 2004; Hariri et al., 2005; Jacobs et al., 2006; Wilhelm et al., 2006).

Other biological factors that may contribute to mood disorders include malfunctions in regions of the brain devoted to mood, imbalances in the brain's neurotransmitter systems, malfunctioning of the endocrine system, disruption of biological rhythms, and underdevelopment in the frontal lobes, hippocampus, or other brain areas (Jans et al., 2007; Milak et al., 2005; Shankman et al., 2007;

Staley et al., 2006; Strakowski, DelBello, & Adler, 2005). All of these conditions may themselves be influenced by genetics. The brain regions involved in mood are many, including the prefrontal cortex, the hippocampus, the amygdala, and other components of the limbic system (Blumberg et al., 2003; MacQueen et al., 2003). There are so many of these regions, in fact, and so many different pathways through which their activity can be disrupted, that different mood disorders might reflect problems in different brain regions (Davidson et al., 2002; Elliott et al., 2002). Malfunctions in some of the same regions are also involved in the symptoms of anxiety disorders, which may help account for the fact that mood and anxiety disorders often appear together (Middeldorp et al., 2005).

As for the role of neurotransmitters, norepinephrine, serotonin, and dopamine were implicated in mood disorders decades ago, when scientists discovered that drugs capable of altering these brain chemicals also relieved depression. Early research suggested that depression was triggered by too little of these neurotransmitters, whereas unusually high levels caused mania. However, the neurochemical causes now appear far more complex. For example, mood disorders may result in part from changes in the sensitivity of the neuronal receptors at which these chemicals have their effects in the brain. The precise nature of these neurotransmitter-receptor mechanisms, and just how they affect mood, is not yet fully understood.

Mood disorders have also been related to malfunctions in the endocrine system, especially the hypothalamic-pituitary-adrenocortical system (HPA). As described in the chapter on health, stress, and coping this system is involved in the body's responses to stress. Research shows, for example, that as many as 70 percent of depressed people secrete abnormally high levels of the stress hormone cortisol (Dinan, 2001; Posener et al., 2000).

The cycles of mood swings seen in bipolar disorders and in recurring episodes of major depressive disorder suggest that mood disorders may be related to stressful triggering events (Hammen, 2005; Keller & Nesse, 2006; Miklowitz & Alloy, 1999). They may also be related to disturbances in the body's biological clock, which is described in the chapter on consciousness. This second possibility seems especially likely in the 15 percent of depressed people who consistently experience a calendar-linked pattern of depressive episodes known as *seasonal affective disorder* (SAD). During months of shorter daylight, these people slip into severe depression, accompanied by irritability and excessive sleeping (Durand & Barlow, 2006). Their depression tends to lift as daylight hours lengthen (Faedda et al., 1993). Disruption of biological rhythms is also suggested by the fact that many depressed people tend to have trouble sleeping—perhaps partly because during the day their biological clocks are telling them it is the middle of the night. Resetting the biological clock through methods such as sleep deprivation or light stimulation has relieved depression in many cases (Golden et al., 2005; Lewy et al., 2006).

● **Psychological and Social Factors** Researchers have come to recognize that whatever biological causes are involved in mood disorders, their effects are always combined with those of psychological and social causes. As mentioned earlier, the very nature of depressive symptoms can depend on the culture in which a person lives. Biopsychosocial explanations of mood disorders also emphasize the impact of anxiety, negative thinking, personality traits, family interactions, and the other psychological and emotional responses triggered by trauma, losses, and other stressful events (Kendler, Hettema, et al., 2003; Kendler, Kuhn, & Prescott, 2004; Rice et al., 2006; Steunenberg et al., 2006). For example, the higher incidence of depression among females—and especially among poor, ethnic minority, single mothers—has been attributed to several factors. Women have greater exposure than men to certain adverse experiences during childhood (e.g., sexual abuse) and adulthood (e.g., domestic violence, poverty). When these risk factors combine with depressive ways of thinking and loss of social support, depression becomes more likely (Miranda & Green, 1999; Nolen-Hoeksema, 2006). Environmental stressors

Treating SAD Seasonal affective disorder (SAD) can often be relieved by exposure to full-spectrum light for as little as a couple of hours a day (Terman & Terman, 2005).

affect men, too, which may be one reason why gender differences in depression are smaller in countries in which men and women face equally stressful lives (Bierut et al., 1999; Maier et al., 1999).

A variety of social-cognitive theories suggest that the way people think about their stressors can increase or decrease the likelihood of mood disorders. One of these theories stemmed from the research on *learned helplessness* described in the chapter on learning. Just as animals become inactive and appear depressed when they have no control over negative events (El Yacoubi et al., 2003), humans may experience depression as a result of feeling incapable of controlling their lives, especially the stressors confronting them (Klein & Seligman, 1976; Seligman, 1991). But most of us have limited control, so why aren't we all depressed? The ways in which people learn to think about events in their lives may hold the key. For example, Aaron Beck's (1967, 1976) cognitive theory of depression suggests that depressed people develop mental habits of (1) blaming themselves when things go wrong; (2) focusing on and exaggerating the negative side of events; and (3) jumping to overly generalized, pessimistic conclusions. Such cognitive habits, says Beck, are errors that lead to depressing thoughts and other symptoms of depression (Beck & Beck, 1995; Evans et al., 2005). Depressed people, in fact, do think about significant negative events in ways that are likely to increase or prolong their depression (Gotlib & Hammen, 1992; Gotlib et al., 2004; Strunk, Lopez, & DeRubeis, 2006).

Social-cognitive theories of depression are somewhat consistent with the psychodynamically oriented *object relations* approach discussed in the chapter on personality. Both views suggest that negative patterns of thinking can be acquired through maladaptive experiences in childhood. For example, research indicates that children whose early relationships with parents or other primary caregivers were characterized by deprivation or abuse are especially likely to develop depression in later life (Gotlib & Hammen, 1992). It may be that close, protective, predictable, and responsive early relationships are necessary if children are to form healthy views of themselves, positive expectations about others, and a sense of control over the environment (Bowlby, 1980; Ivanova & Israel, 2005; Main, 1996).

Severe, long-lasting depression is especially common among people who see their lack of control or other problems as caused by a permanent, generalized lack of personal competence rather than by a temporary condition or an external cause (Seligman et al., 1988). This *negative attributional style* is seen by some researchers as a partly inherited trait that leaves people prone to depression because they attribute negative events to their own characteristics and believe they will never be capable of doing better (Alloy, Abramson, & Francis, 1999; Hankin, Fraley, & Abela, 2005; Hunt & Forand, 2005). Are depressed people's unusually negative beliefs about themselves actually helping to cause their depression, or are they merely symptoms of it? A number of studies have assessed the attributional styles of large samples of nondepressed people and then kept in touch with them to see if, in the face of equivalent stressors, individuals with negative self-beliefs are more likely to become depressed. These longitudinal studies suggest that a negative attributional style is, in fact, a risk factor for depression, not just a result of being depressed (Evans et al., 2005; Garber, Keiley, & Martin, 2002; Gibb et al., 2004; Satterfield, Folkman, & Acree, 2002). In one study, for example, adolescents who held strong negative self-beliefs were more likely than other youngsters to develop depression when faced with stress later in life (Lewinsohn, Joiner, & Rohde, 2001).

Social-cognitive theorists also suggest that whether depression continues or worsens depends in part on how people respond once they start to feel depressed. Those who ruminate, or continuously dwell, on negative events, on why they occur, and even on the feelings of depression are likely to feel more and more depressed (Just & Alloy, 1997; Rimes & Watkins, 2005). According to Susan Nolen-Hoeksema (1990, 2001), this *ruminative style* is especially common in women and may help explain gender differences in the frequency of depression. When men start to feel sad, she says, they tend to use a *distracting style*. That is, they engage in activity that distracts them from their concerns and helps bring them out of their depressed mood (Hankin & Abramson, 2001; Just & Alloy, 1997; Nolen-Hoeksema, Morrow, & Fredrickson, 1993).

Notice that social-cognitive explanations of depression are consistent with the diathesis-stress approach to disorder. These explanations suggest that certain cognitive styles constitute a predisposition (or diathesis) that makes a person vulnerable to depression. The actual occurrence of depression is then made more likely by stressors. In fact, most episodes of major depressive disorder are preceded by the onset of major stressors, such as the loss of a loved one. As suggested in the chapter on health, stress, and coping, the depressing effects of these stressors are likely to be magnified in people who lack social support, who have inadequate coping skills, and who must face other stressful conditions such as poverty (e.g., Stice, Ragan, & Randall, 2004).

Given the number and complexity of biological, psychological, social, and situational factors potentially involved in causing mood disorders, the biopsychosocial model and the diathesis-stress approach appear to be especially appropriate guides to future research (Kendler, Gardner, & Prescott, 2006). Studies based on these guides are already bearing fruit. One study looked at the role of genetics and stressful events in shaping mood disorders in a large group of female twin pairs. Both factors were associated with major depression. Specifically, the women at highest genetic risk were also the most likely to become depressed following a significant stressor (Kendler, Thornton, & Gardner, 2000, 2001; Kendler et al., 2005). Another study found that people with a particular version of a single gene were more likely than others to experience depressive symptoms in relation to stressful events (Caspi et al., 2003). On the basis of studies like these, Kenneth Kendler and his colleagues (Kendler, Gardner, & Prescott, 2002) identified specific sets of risk factors for depression in women that appear at five developmental stages, including childhood, early adolescence, late adolescence, adulthood, and in the year preceding the diagnosis of depression. They recently identified a slightly different model of risk factors for men (Kendler, Gardner, & Prescott, 2006).

In the final analysis, it may turn out that each subtype in the spectrum of mood disorders is caused by a unique combination of factors. The challenge for researchers is to identify these subtypes and map out their causal ingredients.

Schizophrenia

Here is part of a letter that arrived in the mail several years ago:

Dear Sirs:

Pertaining to our continuing failure to prosecute violations of minor's rights to sovereign equality which are occurring in gestations being compromised by the ingestation of controlled substances, . . . the skewing of androgyny which continues in female juveniles even after separation from their mother's has occurred, and as a means of promulflagitating my paying Governor Hickel of Alaska for my employees to have personal services endorsements and controlled substance endorsements, . . . the Iraqi oil being released by the United Nations being identified as Kurdistanian oil, and the July, 1991 issue of the Siberian Review spells President Eltsin's name without a letter y.

The disorganization and strange content of this letter suggest that its writer suffers from **schizophrenia** (pronounced "skit-so-FREE-nee-uh"), a pattern of extremely disturbed thinking, emotion, perception, and behavior that seriously impairs the ability to communicate and relate to others and disrupts most other aspects of daily functioning (Freedman, 2003). Schizophrenia is one of the most severe and disabling of all mental disorders. Its core symptoms are seen virtually everywhere in the world, occurring in

● **schizophrenia** A severe and disabling pattern of disturbed thinking, emotion, perception, and behavior.

1 to 2 percent of the population (American Psychiatric Association, 1994, 2000; Ho, Black, & Andreasen, 2003; National Institute of Mental Health, 2006). In the United States, it appears about equally in various ethnic groups, but like most disorders, it tends to be diagnosed more frequently in economically disadvantaged populations. Schizophrenia is seen about equally in men and women, although in women it generally appears later in life, tends to be less severe, and responds better to treatment (Aleman, Kahn, & Selten, 2003; American Psychiatric Association, 2000; Häfner, 2003; U.S. Surgeon General, 1999).

Schizophrenia tends to develop in adolescence or early adulthood. About 75 percent of the time, its onset is gradual, with the earliest signs appearing as much as five years before the first major schizophrenic episode. In other cases, the onset is more rapid. About 40 percent of people with schizophrenia improve with treatment and are able to function reasonably well. The rest show continuous or intermittent symptoms that permanently disrupt their functioning (an der Heiden & Haefner, 2000; Hegarty et al., 1994). Those who also have a drug abuse problem are at increased risk for becoming homeless. It has been estimated that 10 to 13 percent of homeless individuals in the United States suffer from schizophrenia (Fischer & Breakey, 1991; Olfson et al., 1999; Timms, 2005).

One of the best predictors of the course of schizophrenia is *premorbid adjustment*, which is the level of functioning a person had achieved before schizophrenic symptoms first appeared. Improvement is more likely in those who had reached higher levels of education and occupation and who had established supportive relationships with family and friends (Keshavan, et al., 2005; Rabinowitz et al., 2002).

LINKAGES (a link to Cognition and Language, p. 282)

Symptoms of Schizophrenia

People displaying schizophrenia have problems in how they think and what they think. The nineteenth-century psychiatrist Eugen Bleuler (pronounced "bloy-ler") coined the word *schizophrenia*, or "split mind," to refer to the oddities of schizophrenic thinking. However, schizophrenia does not mean "split personality," as in dissociative identity disorder (multiple personality disorder). It refers instead to a splitting of normally integrated mental processes, such as thoughts and feelings. For instance, some schizophrenics may giggle while claiming to feel sad.

Schizophrenic thought and language are often disorganized. *Neologisms* ("new words" that have meaning only to the person speaking them) are common. The appearance of "promulflagitating" in the preceding letter is one example. That letter also illustrates *loose associations*, the tendency for one thought to be logically unconnected, or only slightly related, to the next. Sometimes the associations are based on double meanings or on the way words sound (*clang associations*). For example, "My true family name is Abel or A Bell. We descended from the clan of Abel, who originated the bell of rights, which we now call the bill of rights." In the most severe cases, a jumble of words known as *word salad* reflects utterly chaotic thoughts: "Upon the advisability of held keeping, environment of the seabeach gathering, to the forest stream, reinstatement to be placed, poling the paddleboat, of the swamp morass, to the forest compensation of the dunce" (Lehman, 1967, p. 627).

The *content* of schizophrenic thinking is also disturbed. Often it includes a bewildering assortment of delusions, or false beliefs. These delusions tend to fall into three general categories (Kimhy et al., 2005). *Delusions of influence* focus on the belief that one's body, thinking, or behavior are being controlled by external forces. Patients with these delusions might claim that the CIA has implanted a control device in their brains (delusions of control). They might believe that other people's thoughts are appearing in their mind (thought insertion) or that they can broadcast their thoughts to others (thought broadcasting). *Self-significant delusions* involve exaggerated beliefs about oneself. People with these delusions may believe, for example, that certain TV commercials contain coded messages about their innermost secrets, that they are truly an emperor, the pope, or even God (delusions of

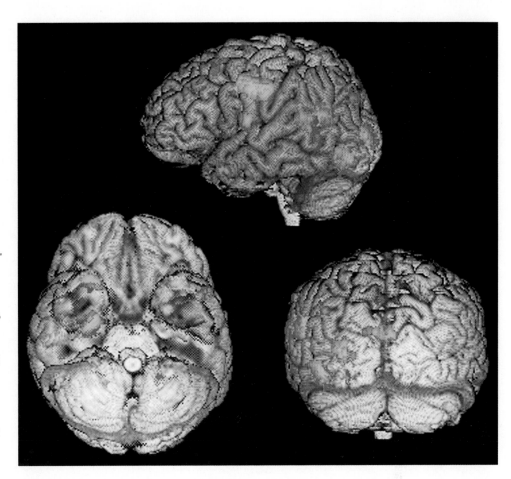

FIGURE 15.4

Brain Activity During Hallucinations

These are brain images of a twenty-three-year-old schizophrenia patient who was hallucinating rolling, disembodied heads that spoke to him. PET scans revealed heightened activity in visual and auditory (language) *association* cortex, rather than in the *primary* cortex regions for these senses. The posterior cingulate cortex (part of the limbic system) was also activated; it is known to be affected by drugs that produce hallucinations (Silbersweig et al., 1995).

grandeur), or that they are guilty of some terrible sin. People displaying *delusions of persecution* believe that others are out to harass or harm them. They may claim, for example, that they are always being followed, that space aliens are trying to steal their internal organs or that they are the targets of an assassin. Such delusions tend to be deeply entrenched and resistant to change, no matter how strong the evidence against them (Woodward et al., 2006).

People with schizophrenia often report that they cannot focus their attention. They may feel overwhelmed as they try to attend to everything at once. Various perceptual disorders may also appear. The person may feel detached from the world and see other people as flat cutouts. The body may feel like a machine, or parts of it may seem to be dead or rotting. **Hallucinations,** or false perceptions, are common, often taking the form of voices. These voices may sound like an overheard conversation, or they may tell the person to do or not to do things. They may also comment on, narrate, or (most often) harshly criticize the person's actions or characteristics. Hallucinations can also create sights, smells, tastes, and touch sensations even when no external stimuli are present. As shown in Figure 15.4, the brain areas activated during hallucinations are related to those that respond to real sights and sounds (Shergill et al., 2000). The emotional expressiveness of people with schizophrenia is often muted, but when they do show emotion, it is frequently exaggerated or inappropriate. They may cry for no apparent reason or fly into a rage in response to a simple question.

Some schizophrenia patients are extremely agitated, constantly moving their limbs, making facial grimaces, or pacing the floor in highly ritualistic sequences. Others become so withdrawn that they move very little. Lack of motivation and poor social skills, deteriorating personal hygiene, and an inability to function in everyday situations are other common characteristics of schizophrenia.

● **hallucinations**   A symptom of disorder in which people perceive voices or other stimuli when there are no stimuli present.

TABLE 15.4 Subtypes of Schizophrenia

Mental health professionals still use these *DSM-IV* subtypes when diagnosing schizophrenia, but many researchers now tend to categorize patients in terms of whether positive or negative symptoms of schizophrenia predominate in a given case (Villalta-Gil et al., 2006).

Type	Frequency	Prominent Features
Paranoid schizophrenia	40 percent of schizophrenics; usually appears after age 25–30	Delusions of grandeur or persecution; anger; anxiety; argumentativeness; extreme jealousy; onset often sudden; signs of impairment may be subtle.
Disorganized schizophrenia	5 percent of all schizophrenics; high prevalence in homeless population	Delusions; hallucinations; incoherent speech; facial grimaces; inappropriate laughter/giggling; neglected personal hygiene; loss of bladder/bowel control.
Catatonic schizophrenia	8 percent of all schizophrenics	Disordered movement, alternating between immobility (stupor) and wild excitement. In stupor, the person does not speak or attend to communication; also, the body is rigid or can be posed in virtually any posture (a condition called *waxy flexibility*).
Undifferentiated schizophrenia	40 percent of all schizophrenics	Patterns of disordered behavior, thought, and emotion that do not fall easily into any other subtype.
Residual schizophrenia	Varies	Applies to people who have had prior episodes of schizophrenia but are not currently displaying symptoms.

● Categorizing Schizophrenia

DSM-IV lists five major subtypes of schizophrenia: paranoid, disorganized, catatonic, undifferentiated, and residual (see Table 15.4). These subtype labels convey a certain amount of useful information, but they don't always provide an accurate picture of patients' behavior, because some symptoms appear in more than one subtype. Further, people originally diagnosed in one subtype might later display characteristics of another subtype. Finally, the *DSM-IV* subtypes may not be linked very closely to the various biological conditions thought to underlie schizophrenia (Barch, 2006; Fenton & McGlashan, 1991; Jablensky, 2006).

Accordingly, many researchers now categorize schizophrenia in ways that focus more precisely on the kinds of symptoms that patients display. One method of categorizing schizophrenia highlights the positive or negative aspects of symptoms. Disorganized thoughts, delusions, and hallucinations are sometimes called **positive symptoms** of schizophrenia, because they appear as undesirable *additions* to a person's mental life (Andreasen et al., 1995; Iancu et al., 2005; Racenstein et al., 2002). In contrast, the absence of pleasure and motivation, lack of emotional reactivity, social withdrawal, reduced speech, and other deficits seen in schizophrenia are sometimes called **negative symptoms,** because they appear to *subtract* elements from normal mental life (Nicholson & Neufeld, 1993). Describing patients in terms of positive and negative symptoms does not require that they be placed in one category or the other. In fact, many patients exhibit both positive and negative symptoms. However, it is important to know whether negative or positive symptoms predominate, because when symptoms are mainly negative, schizophrenia is usually more severe and less responsive to treatment (Milev et al., 2005; Prikryl et al., 2006). In these cases, patients typically experience long-term disability. Such

● **positive symptoms** Schizophrenic symptoms such as disorganized thoughts, hallucinations, and delusions.

● **negative symptoms** Schizophrenic symptoms such as absence of pleasure, lack of speech, and flat affect.

Catatonic Stupor The symptoms of schizophrenia often occur in characteristic patterns. This woman's lack of motivation and other negative symptoms of schizophrenia are severe enough that she appears to be in a catatonic stupor. Such patients may become rigid or, as in this case, show a waxy flexibility that allows them to be "posed" in virtually any position. Diagnosticians using the traditional subtype system would probably label her as displaying catatonic schizophrenia.

disability has also been associated with positive symptoms if they are severe (e.g., Fenton & McGlashan, 1994; Racenstein et al., 2002).

Another way of categorizing schizophrenia symptoms focuses on whether they are *psychotic* (hallucinations, delusions), *disorganized* (incoherent speech, chaotic behavior, inappropriate affect), or *negative* (e.g., lack of speech or motivation). Other researchers have suggested categorizing schizophrenia symptoms as positive, negative, or depressive (Haefner & Maurer, 2000). The fact that, like positive and negative symptoms, these dimensions of schizophrenia are to some extent independent from one another suggests to some researchers that each symptom cluster or dimension may ultimately be traceable to different causes. For this reason, schizophrenia is often referred to as the *schizophrenia spectrum*, implying that each cluster may develop differently and require different treatments (Tsuang, Stone, & Faraone, 2000).

● Causes of Schizophrenia

The search for the causes of schizophrenia has been more intense than for any other psychological disorder. The findings so far confirm one thing: As with other disorders, there are biological, psychological, and social factors at work in causing or worsening all forms of schizophrenia (Sullivan, Kendler, & Neale, 2003).

●**Biological Factors** Research in behavioral genetics shows that schizophrenia runs in families (Asarnow et al., 2001; Dubertret et al., 2004). One family study found, for instance, that 16 percent of the children of schizophrenic mothers—compared with 2 percent of those of nonschizophrenic mothers—developed schizophrenia themselves over a twenty-five-year period (Parnas et al., 1993). Even if they are adopted by nonschizophrenic families, the children of schizophrenic parents are ten times more likely to develop schizophrenia than adopted children whose biological parents are not schizophrenic (Kety et al., 1994; Tienari et al., 2003). Still, it is unlikely that a single gene transmits schizophrenia (Chumakov et al., 2002; Plomin & McGuffin, 2003). For example, among identical-twin pairs in which one member displays schizophrenia, 40 percent of the other members will, too; but 60 percent will not (McGue, 1992).

It is more likely that some people inherit a predisposition, or diathesis, for schizophrenia that involves several genes, and researchers are currently focusing on some likely candidates, including genes known as *5-HT-sub(5A) receptor gene, DTNBP1, RGS4,* and *a-7 neuronal nicotinic receptor subunit (CHRNA7).* These genetic factors appear to combine with other genetic and nongenetic factors to cause the disorder (DeRosse et al., 2006; Fan et al., 2006; Law, Cotton, & Berger, 2006; Levitt et al., 2006; Vazza et al., 2007).

The search for biological causes of schizophrenia also focuses on a number of abnormalities in the structure, functioning, and chemistry of the brain that tend to appear in people with schizophrenia (e.g., Andrews et al., 2006; Neves-Pereira et al., 2005; Tamminga & Holcomb, 2005). Numerous brain imaging studies have shown that, compared with other mental patients, many schizophrenia patients have less tissue in thalamic regions, prefrontal cortex, and some subcortical areas (Behrendt, 2006; Conklin & Iacono, 2002; Csernansky et al., 2004; Ettinger et al., 2007; Highley et al., 2003; Selemon et al., 2003). As shown in Figure 15.5, shrinkage of tissue in these regions leads to corresponding enlargement of the brain's fluid-filled spaces, called *ventricles.* The brain areas in which anatomical abnormalities have been found are active in emotional expression, thinking, and information processing—functions that are disordered in schizophrenia (Conklin & Iacono, 2002; Csernansky et al., 2004; Highley et al., 2003; Pol et al., 2002; Selemon et al., 2003; Velakoulis et al., 2006). Enlarged ventricles and reduced prefrontal cortex are more often found in patients whose schizophrenic symptoms are predominantly negative (Sigmundsson et al., 2001). Continued tissue loss has

FIGURE 15.5

Brain Abnormalities in Schizophrenia

Here is a magnetic resonance imaging (MRI) comparison of the brains of identical twins. The schizophrenic twin, on the right, has greatly enlarged ventricles (see arrows) and correspondingly less brain tissue, including in the hippocampal area, a region involved in memory and emotion. The same results appeared in fourteen other identical-twin pairs. By contrast, no significant differences appeared between members of a seven-pair control group of normal identical twins (Suddath et al., 1990). These results support the idea that brain abnormalities are associated with schizophrenia and, because identical twins have the same genes, that such abnormalities may stem from nongenetic factors (Baare et al., 2001).

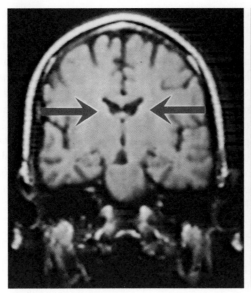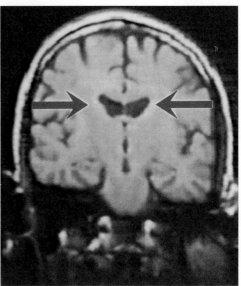

been associated with worsening of negative symptoms (Ho et al., 2003; Mathalon et al., 2001). Patients with mainly positive symptoms tend to have essentially normal-looking brains (Andreasen, 1997).

Hundreds of studies of brain functioning in people diagnosed with schizophrenia provide general support for the idea that their impairments in information processing and other cognitive abilities are related to structural abnormalities (Gur et al., 2000; Jeon & Polich, 2003; Lee, Williams, et al., 2003; Niznikiewicz et al., 1997). For example, patients with predominantly negative symptoms are especially likely to display cognitive deficits associated with prefrontal-cortex problems (Wible et al., 2001). This research is providing important clues (Barch, 2006), but it will take even more research to determine the extent to which, or exactly how, specific structural abnormalities are related to the cognitive problems seen in various forms of schizophrenia.

Researchers are also investigating the possibility that abnormalities in brain chemistry—especially in neurotransmitter systems that use dopamine—play a role in causing or intensifying schizophrenic symptoms (Seeman et al., 2005). Because drugs that block the brain's dopamine receptors often reduce hallucinations, delusions, disordered thinking, and other positive symptoms of schizophrenia, some investigators speculate that schizophrenia results from excess dopamine. However, the relationship between dopamine and schizophrenia is quite complex (Carlsson & Lecrubier, 2004). For example, it may be that changes in the ratio of dopamine to other neurochemicals, particularly in the region of the thalamus, are involved in the difficulties experienced by people with schizophrenia in distinguishing genuine sights and sounds from those produced by neural "noise" within the brain (Buchsbaum et al., 2006; Winterer, 2006).

Some researchers are seeking to integrate genetic, neurological, and environmental explanations of schizophrenia by looking for *neurodevelopmental abnormalities* (Meyer et al., 2005; Rapoport et al., 2005). Perhaps, they say, some forms of schizophrenia arise from disruptions in brain development during the period from before birth through childhood, when the brain is growing and its various functions are maturing. Studies have shown, for instance, that prenatal exposure to physical traumas, influenza, or other viral infections is associated with increased risk for developing schizophrenia (AbdelMalik et al., 2003; Brown et al., 2005; Subotnik et al., 2006). Similarly, low birthweight children are more likely to have the brain abnormalities described earlier. These abnormalities are especially likely in children of schizophrenic parents (Cannon et al., 1993; Lawrie et al., 2001). Even parental age may make a difference. Children whose fathers were older than forty-five at the time the children were conceived appear to be at elevated risk for developing schizophrenia, possibly because of a sperm cell mutation (Dalman & Allebeck, 2002). These neurodevelopmental factors may help explain why children of schizophrenic parents tend to show the kinds of subtle cognitive and intellectual problems associated with brain abnormalities (Ashe, Berry, & Boulton, 2001; Cannon et al., 1994; McGlashan & Hoffman, 2000; Neumann et al., 1995).

The expression of a genetically transmitted predisposition for brain abnormality may be enhanced by environmental factors such as maternal drug use during pregnancy, oxygen deprivation or other complications during birth, childhood malnutrition, and the like (Sørensen et al., 2003). For example, as mentioned earlier, smaller-than-normal prefrontal lobes and other brain structures appear to constitute an inherited predisposition for schizophrenia. However, reduced brain growth alone is not sufficient to cause the disorder. When only one member of an identical twin pair has schizophrenia, both tend to have unusually small brains, but the schizophrenic twin's brain in each pair is the smaller of the two (Baare et al., 2001). This finding suggests that some environmental influence caused degeneration in an already underdeveloped brain, making it even more prone to function abnormally.

●**Psychological and Sociocultural Factors** Psychological processes and sociocultural influences can contribute to the appearance of schizophrenia and influence its course (Jenkins & Barrett, 2003; Kealy, 2005; Pitschel-Walz et al., 2001). These factors include maladaptive learning experiences, dysfunctional cognitive habits, and stressful family communication patterns (Cantor-Graae & Selten, 2005; Wicks et al., 2005). For example, criticism by family members—sometimes called *expressed emotion*—is associated with more severe symptoms (Nomura et al., 2005). And schizophrenia patients living with relatives who are critical, unsupportive, or emotionally overinvolved are especially likely to relapse following improvement (Hooley, 2004). Family members' negative attitudes may be a source of stress that increases the chances that disruptive or odd behaviors will persist or worsen. Keep in mind, though, that the strange and often disturbing behavior of a family member with schizophrenia can place tremendous strain on the rest of the family, making it harder for them to remain helpful and supportive (Kymalainen et al.,

in **review** Schizophrenia	
Aspect	**Key Features**
Common Symptoms	
Disorders of thought	Disturbed content, including delusions; disorganization, including loose associations, neologisms, and word salad
Disorders of perception	Hallucinations, or false perceptions; poorly focused attention
Disorders of emotion	Flat affect; inappropriate tears, laughter, or anger
Possible Causes	
Biological	Genetics; abnormalities in brain structure; abnormalities in dopamine systems; neurodevelopmental problems
Psychological	Learned maladaptive behavior; disturbed patterns of family communication

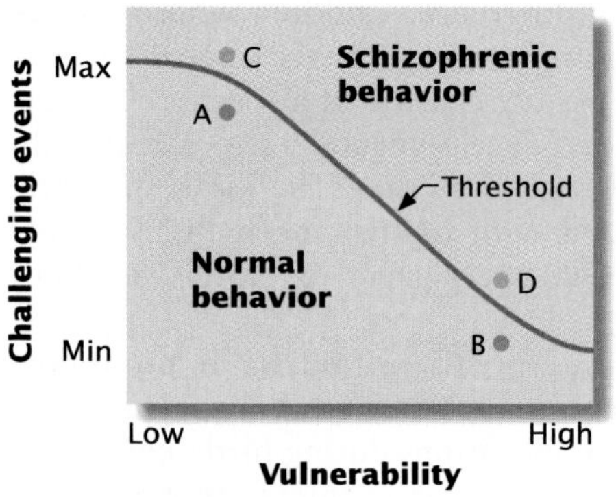

FIGURE 15.6

The Vulnerability Theory of Schizophrenia

According to this theory, a person can cross the threshold into schizophrenia as a result of many combinations of predisposition and stress. A strong predisposition for schizophrenia and little environmental stress (point D), a weak predisposition and a lot of stress (point C), or any other sufficiently potent combination can lead to the disorder. Points A and B represent combinations of vulnerability and stress that would not lead to schizophrenia.

2006; Rosenfarb, Bellack, & Aziz, 2006). In any case, patients who are helped to cope with potentially damaging family influences tend to have better long-term outcomes (Bustillo et al., 2001; Velligan et al., 2000).

Vulnerability Theory All the causal theories of schizophrenia we have discussed are consistent with the diathesis-stress approach, which assumes that various forms of stress can activate a person's predisposition for disorder. ("In Review: Schizophrenia" summarizes these theories, as well as the symptoms of schizophrenia.) The diathesis-stress approach is embodied in the *vulnerability theory* of schizophrenia (Cornblatt & Erlenmeyer-Kimling, 1985). This theory suggests that (1) vulnerability to schizophrenia is mainly biological; (2) different people have differing degrees of vulnerability; (3) vulnerability is influenced partly by genetic influences on development and partly by neurodevelopmental abnormalities associated with environmental risk and (4) psychological components—such as exposure to poor parenting or high-stress families, having inadequate coping skills, and the like—may help determine whether schizophrenia actually appears and may also influence the course of the disorder (Walker & Diforio, 1998; Wearden et al., 2000).

Many different blends of vulnerability and stress can lead to schizophrenia, as Figure 15.6 illustrates. People whose genetic characteristics or developmental influences leave them vulnerable to develop schizophrenia may be especially likely to do so if they are later exposed to learning experiences, family conflicts, and other stressors that trigger and maintain schizophrenic patterns of thought and action. Those same experiences and stressors would not be expected to lead to schizophrenia in people who are less vulnerable to developing the disorder. In other words, schizophrenia is a highly complex disorder—probably a spectrum of related disorders (Kirkpatrick et al., 2001; Lenzenweger, McLachlan, & Rubin, 2007)—whose origins lie in many biological, psychological, and social domains, some of which are yet to be discovered.

Personality Disorders

Personality disorders are long-standing, inflexible ways of behaving that are not so much severe mental disorders as dysfunctional styles of living (Clarkin, 2006). These disorders affect all areas of functioning and, beginning in childhood or adolescence, create problems for those who display them and for others (Millon & Davis, 1996). Some psychologists view personality disorders as interpersonal strategies (Kiesler, 1996) or as the extreme, rigid, and maladaptive expressions of personality traits (Widiger, 1997). The ten personality disorders listed on Axis II of *DSM-IV* are grouped into three clusters that share certain features (see Table 15.5).

The *odd-eccentric* cluster—referred to as *cluster A*—includes paranoid, schizoid, and schizotypal personality disorders. People diagnosed as having schizotypal personality disorder, for example, display some of the peculiarities seen in schizophrenia but are not disturbed enough to be labeled as schizophrenic. Rather than hallucinating, these people may report "illusions" of sights or sounds. They may also exhibit "magical thinking," including odd superstitions or beliefs (such as that they have extrasensory perception or that salt under the mattress will prevent insomnia).

The *dramatic-erratic* cluster—called *cluster B*—includes the histrionic, narcissistic, borderline, and antisocial personality disorders. The main characteristics of narcissistic personality disorder, for example, are an exaggerated sense of self-importance, extreme sensitivity to criticism, a constant need for attention, and a tendency to arrogantly overestimate personal abilities and achievements. People displaying this disorder feel entitled to special treatment by others but are markedly lacking in empathy *for* others.

personality disorders Long-standing, inflexible ways of behaving that create a variety of problems.

TABLE 15.5 Personality Disorders

Here are brief descriptions of the ten personality disorders listed on Axis II of *DSM-IV*.

Type	Typical Features
Paranoid	Suspiciousness and distrust of others, all of whom are assumed to be hostile.
Schizoid	Detachment from social relationships; restricted range of emotion.
Schizotypal	Detachment from, and great discomfort in, social relationships; odd perceptions, thoughts, beliefs, and behaviors.
Dependent	Helplessness; excessive need to be taken care of; submissive and clinging behavior; difficulty in making decisions.
Obsessive-compulsive	Preoccupation with orderliness, perfection, and control.
Avoidant	Inhibition in social situations; feelings of inadequacy; oversensitivity to criticism.
Histrionic	Excessive emotionality and preoccupation with being the center of attention; emotional shallowness; overly dramatic behavior.
Narcissistic	Exaggerated ideas of self-importance and achievements; preoccupation with fantasies of success; arrogance.
Borderline	Lack of stability in interpersonal relationships, self-image, and emotion; impulsivity; angry outbursts; intense fear of abandonment; recurring suicidal gestures.
Antisocial	Shameless disregard for, and violation of, other people's rights.

The *anxious-fearful* cluster—*cluster C*—includes dependent, obsessive-compulsive, and avoidant personality disorders. Avoidant personality disorder, for example, is similar to social phobia in the sense that persons labeled with this disorder tend to be "loners" with a long-standing pattern of avoiding social situations and of being particularly sensitive to criticism or rejection. They want to be with others but are too inhibited.

Personality disorder diagnoses are among the most controversial. The controversy arises partly because persons with these diagnoses sometimes produce more distress in others than in themselves, so the role of social and moral judgment in deciding who is disordered comes into play (Clark, 2006). In addition, the overlap among symptoms of some of the personality disorders makes diagnosis difficult. Studies that use symptom checklists or other behavioral measures, as well as those that use molecular genetic data, generally identify either three or four clusters, not always what would be expected according to *DSM-IV* (Fossati et al., 2006; Livesley, 2005). Some critics have suggested that there is gender bias in the application of diagnoses—pointing to the fact that women are labeled as borderline much more often than men, while men are labeled as antisocial more often than women (Bjorklund, 2006; Boggs et al., 2005). Even the stability of personality disorders over the lifetime has been questioned (Durbin & Klein, 2006). Some aspects of personality disorders diagnoses may be revised in *DSM-V*, but as yet there is no strong consensus about what changes should be made.

From the perspective of public welfare and safety, the most serious, costly, and intensively studied personality disorder is **antisocial personality disorder** (e.g., Scott et al., 2001). It is marked by a long-term pattern of irresponsible, impulsive, unscrupulous, even criminal behavior beginning in childhood or early adolescence. In

● **antisocial personality disorder**
A personality disorder involving impulsive, selfish, unscrupulous, even criminal behavior.

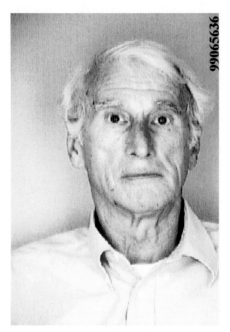

A Classic Case of Antisocial Personality Disorder Alfred Jack Oakley meets women through personal ads, claiming to be a millionaire movie producer, pilot, and novelist. In reality, he is a penniless con artist who uses smooth talk and charm to gain the women's trust so he can steal from them. In January 2000, after being convicted of stealing a Florida woman's Mercedes, Oakley complimented the prosecutor's skills and the jury's wisdom and claimed to feel remorseful. The judge appeared to see through this ploy ("I don't believe there is a sincere word that ever comes out of your mouth"), but it was still effective enough to get him probation instead of jail time!

the 1800s, this pattern was called *moral insanity*, because the people displaying it appear to have no morals or common decency. The terms *sociopath* or *psychopath* are sometimes still used. All these labels share a common foundation of referring to social norm violation and deception (Warren & South, 2006), but the current "antisocial personality" label more accurately portrays people displaying the disorder as troublesome and sometimes dangerous, but not "insane" by the legal standards we will discuss shortly. About 3 percent of men and about 1 percent of women in the United States fall into this diagnostic category (American Psychiatric Association, 1994, 2000).

At their least troublesome, people exhibiting antisocial personality disorder are a nuisance. They are charming, intelligent "fast talkers" who borrow money and fail to return it. They are arrogant and self-centered manipulators who con people into doing things for them, usually by lying and taking advantage of people's decency and trust. A hallmark of people with antisocial personality disorder is a lack of anxiety, remorse, or guilt, whether they have wrecked a borrowed car or killed an innocent person (Gray et al., 2003; Hare, 1993). Fortunately, these individuals tend to become less active and dangerous after the age of forty or so (Stoff, Breiling, & Maser, 1997).

Perhaps you are wondering whether terrorists and suicide bombers should be classified as antisocial personalities—after all, they exhibit violent and disruptive behavior in the extreme. Some terrorists do exhibit the characteristics of antisocial personality disorder, but many do not (Martens, 2004). Acts of terrorism might better be explained from the perspective of social and political psychology—terrorists are persons spurred to take extreme destructive measures by political and religious ideologies during intense group conflict. In short, the psychology of group conflict and war might better explain the terrorism of today, just as it might have explained the terrifying behavior of Japanese kamikaze pilots during World War II.

As for the causes of antisocial personality disorder, theories abound. Some studies suggest a genetic predisposition (Slutske et al., 2001). Genes appear implicated in nearly all disorders; however, the available evidence suggests that the genetic contribution to antisocial behaviors that begin in adolescence or adulthood is modest at best. In contrast, forms of antisocial activity that appear in early childhood appear to have a stronger genetic component (Arseneault et al., 2003). Genes may influence brain development; reduced brain size and reductions in the hippocampal regions are associated with antisocial personality (Barkataki et al., 2006; van Goozen et al., 2007). Genes may also contribute to chronic underarousal of both the autonomic and central nervous systems (Dolan & Park, 2002; Lindberg et al., 2005). This underarousal may render people less sensitive to punishment and more likely to seek exciting stimulation than is normally the case (Herpertz et al., 2001; Stoff et al. 1997).

Other evidence suggests more specific information-processing defects. For example, people diagnosed with antisocial personality disorder perform less well than others do on neuropsychological tests of the ability to make plans (Dolan & Park, 2002). There seem to be specific problems, too, in the processing of fear-related information among people whose symptoms of antisocial personality disorder include extreme emotional detachment (Levenston et al., 2000; Patrick, Bradley, & Lang, 1993). In one study, film clips of delinquent acts were shown to young men with antisocial personality and to non-APD males. The APD males reported lower levels of guilt and fear and higher levels of excitement and happiness while watching (Cimbora & McIntosh, 2003). This diminished responsiveness may be partly explained by a finding that, compared to those without APD, antisocial adolescents have more difficulty simply remembering emotional material (Dolan & Fullam, 2006). Deficits in the ability to encode, recall, and respond to emotional material might help explain the apparent "fearlessness" (and foolishness) of some of their behavior.

Broken homes, rejection by parents, poor discipline, lack of good parental models, lack of attachment to early caregivers, impulsivity, conflict-filled childhoods, and poverty have all been suggested as psychological and social factors contributing to the development of antisocial personality disorder (Lahey et al., 1995; Lyman & Gudonis, 2005; Tremblay et al., 1994). The biopsychosocial model suggests that antisocial personality disorder results when these psychosocial and environmental conditions interact with genetic predispositions to low arousal and the sensation seeking and impulsivity associated with it (Gray et al., 2003; Rutter, 1997). Environmental and/or genetic factors can suppress the development of antisocial personality disorder, too. In one study, for example, boys whose environments heightened their risk of antisocial behavior were less likely to display such behavior if they had inherited a particular gene (Caspi et al., 2002). Research suggests that identification of antisocial personalities prior to the development of their more treatment-resistant traits may offer the best hope for dealing with this disorder (Crawford, Cohen, & Brooks, 2001; Lynam, 1996; Stoff et al., 1997).

FOCUS ON RESEARCH METHODS — **Exploring Links Between Child Abuse and Antisocial Personality Disorder**

One of the most prominent environmental factors associated with the more violent forms of antisocial personality disorder is the experience of abuse in childhood (MacMillan et al., 2001). However, most of the studies that have found a relationship between childhood abuse and antisocial personality disorder were based on potentially biased reports (Monane, Leichter, & Lewis, 1984; Rosenbaum & Bennett, 1986). People with antisocial personalities—especially those with criminal records—are likely to make up stories of abuse in order to shift blame for their behavior onto others. Even if these people's reports were accurate, however, most of the studies lacked a control group of people from similar backgrounds who were not antisocial. Because of this research design flaw, it is virtually impossible to separate the effects of reported child abuse from the effects of poverty or other factors that might also have contributed to the development of antisocial personality disorder.

■ What was the researcher's question?

Can childhood abuse cause antisocial personality disorder? To help answer this question and to correct some of the flaws in earlier studies, Cathy Widom (1989) used a prospective research design, first finding cases of childhood abuse and then looking for the effects of that abuse on adult behavior.

■ How did the researcher answer the question?

Widom began by identifying 416 adults whose backgrounds included official records of having been physically or sexually abused before the age of eleven. She then explored the stories of these people's lives, as told in police and school records, as well as in two-hour diagnostic interviews. To reduce experimenter bias and distorted reporting, Widom ensured that the interviewers were unaware of the purpose of the study and that the respondents were told only that the researchers wanted to learn about people who had grown up in a midwestern U.S. metropolitan area in the late 1960s and early 1970s. Widom also selected a comparison group of 283 people who had no history of abuse but who were similar to the abused sample in terms of age, gender, ethnicity, hospital of birth, schools attended, and area of residence. Her goal was to obtain a nonabused control group that had been exposed to approximately the same environmental risk factors and socioeconomic conditions as the abused children.

■ What did the researcher find?

First, Widom (1989) tested the hypothesis that exposure to abuse in childhood is associated with criminality and/or violence in later life. She found that 26 percent of the abused youngsters went on to commit juvenile crimes, 29 percent were arrested as adults, and 11 percent committed violent crimes. These percentages were significantly higher than the figures for the nonabused group. The association between criminality and abuse was stronger for males than for females and stronger for African Americans than for European Americans. And overall, victims of physical abuse were more likely to commit violent crimes as adults than were victims of sexual abuse.

Next, Widom tested the hypothesis that childhood abuse is associated with the development of antisocial personality disorder (Luntz & Widom, 1994). She found that the abused group exhibited a significantly higher rate of antisocial personality disorder (13.5 percent) than did the comparison group (7.1 percent). The apparent role of abuse in antisocial personality disorder was particularly pronounced in men, and it remained strong even when other factors—such as age, ethnicity, and socio-economic status—were accounted for in the statistical analyses. It is interesting to note that one other factor—failure to graduate from high school—was also strongly associated with the appearance of antisocial personality disorder, whether or not childhood abuse had occurred.

■ What do the results mean?

Widom's research supported earlier studies in finding an association between child-hood abuse and criminality, violence, and antisocial personality disorder. Further, although her study did not permit a firm conclusion that abuse alone causes antisocial personality disorder, the data from its prospective design added strength to the argument that abuse may be an important causal factor (Widom, 2000). This interpreta-tion is supported by the results of research by other investigators (Jaffee et al., 2004). Finally, Widom's work offers yet another reason—as if more reasons were needed—why it is so important to prevent the physical and sexual abuse of children. The long-term consequences of such abuse can be tragic not only for its immediate victims but also for those victimized by the violence, criminal actions, and antisocial behavior per-petrated by some abused children as they grow up (Weiler & Widom, 1996).

■ What do we still need to know?

Widom's results suggest that one or more of the factors leading teenagers to drop out (or be thrown out) of high school might help create antisocial personality disorder even in children who were not abused. Some of her more recent work suggests, too, that exposure to poverty and other stressors can be as important as abuse in promot-ing antisocial personality disorder (Horwitz et al., 2001). Further research is needed to discover whether antisocial personality disorder stems from abuse itself, from one of the factors accompanying it, or from some other specific combination of known and still-unknown risk factors. The importance of combined and interacting risk fac-tors is suggested by the fact that abuse is often part of a larger pool of experiences, such as exposure to deviant models, social rejection, poor supervision, and the like.

In fact, another of Widom's more recent studies (Horwitz et al., 2001) supported the conclusion that childhood abuse increases the likelihood of encountering later stressful life events and that it is some of these events that lead to an increase risk of antisocial personality disorder. In other words, childhood abuse might create general vulnerability for a variety of psychological disorders and life stressors, but the chain of events that promote the development of any particular disorder, such as antisocial personality disorder, are not yet fully understood.

We need to know more, too, about why such a small percentage of the abused children in Widom's sample displayed violence, criminal behavior, and antisocial personality disorder. What genetic characteristics or environmental experiences serve to protect children from at least some of the devastating effects of abuse (Rind & Tromovitch, 1997; Rind, Tromovitch, & Bauserman, 1998)? As described in the chapter on human development, some clues have already been found (Caspi et al., 2002; Wills et al., 2001), but a better understanding of these protective elements is needed if there are to be effective programs for the prevention of antisocial personality disorder. ■

A Sampling of Other Psychological Disorders

The disorders described so far represent some of the most prevalent and socially disruptive psychological problems encountered in cultures around the world. Several others are mentioned in other chapters. For example, mental retardation is covered in the chapter on cognitive abilities; sexual dysfunctions are mentioned in the chapter on motivation and emotion; posttraumatic stress disorder is described in the chapter on health, stress, and coping; and sleep disorders are discussed in the chapter on consciousness. Here, we consider two other significant psychological problems: disorders of childhood and substance-related disorders.

Psychological Disorders of Childhood

The physical, cognitive, emotional, and social changes seen in childhood—and the stress associated with them—can create or worsen psychological disorders in children. Stress can do the same in adults, but childhood disorders are not just miniature versions of adult psychopathology. Because children's development is still incomplete and because their capacity to cope with stress is limited, children are often vulnerable to special types of disorders. Two broad categories encompass the majority of childhood behavior problems: externalizing disorders and internalizing disorders (Lahey et al., 2004; Nigg, 2000).

The *externalizing*, or *undercontrolled*, category includes behaviors that are particularly disturbing to people in the child's environment. Lack of control shows up as *conduct disorders* in about 9.5 percent of children and adolescents, mostly boys, and appears most frequently at around 11 or 12 years of age (Nock et al., 2006). Conduct disorders are characterized by a relatively stable pattern of aggression, disobedience, destructiveness, and other problematic behaviors (Kalb & Loeber, 2003). Often these behaviors involve criminal activity, and they may signal the development of antisocial personality disorder (Loeber & Stouthamer-Loeber, 1998; Lyman & Gudonis, 2005).

There may be a genetic predisposition toward externalizing disorders, including conduct disorders (Gelhorn et al., 2005; Hicks et al., 2004). For example, many children who display conduct disorder have parents who display antisocial personality disorder. Further, externalizing disorders are especially likely to appear in children with temperamentally high activity levels (Mesman & Koot, 2000). There is no doubt, however, that environmental and parenting factors also help to shape these children's behavior, and that these factors interact with genetic factors (Hanish et al., 2005; Laird et al., 2001; Leve, Kim, & Pears, 2005; Scourfield et al., 2004).

Another kind of externalizing problem, *attention deficit hyperactivity disorder (ADHD)*, is seen in 3 to 7 percent of children, mostly boys. A diagnosis of ADHD is given to children who are impulsive and unable to concentrate on an activity as well as other children their age can (Nigg, 2001). *DSM-IV* lists three subtypes of this disorder: primarily inattentive, primarily impulsive, and combined inattention and impulsivity. As the name implies, many of these children are *hyperactive*. That is, they have great difficulty sitting still or otherwise controlling their physical activity. Their impulsiveness and lack of self-control contribute to significant impairments in learning and to an astonishing ability to annoy and exhaust those around them (Henker & Whalen, 1989). The day-to-day behavior problems of children diagnosed with ADHD are reflected in poor performance on certain clinical tests of attention, memory, decision making, and other information-processing tasks. As a result, ADHD is being increasingly viewed as a neurological condition rather than just "bad" behavior (Ollendick & Prinz, 2002; Sergeant, Geurts, & Oosterlaan, 2002).

TRY THIS **Active or Hyperactive?** Normal behavior for children in one culture might be considered hyperactive in other cultures. Do people in the *same* culture disagree on what is hyperactive? To find out, ask two or three friends to join you in observing a group of children at a playground, a schoolyard, a park, or some other public place. Ask your friends to privately identify which children they would label as "hyperactive," and then count how many of their choices agree with yours and with each other's.

Inheritance of a genetic risk factor has been proposed as a likely cause of ADHD, with many studies focusing on genes that regulate dopamine, a neurotransmitter important in the functioning of the attention system (Levy, Hay, & Bennett, 2006; Waldman & Gizer, 2006). But other factors, including brain damage, poisoning from lead or other household substances, and low birth weight, may play a causal role, too (Daly et al., 1999; Linnet et al., 2003; Mick et al., 2002; Spencer, 2002). In some cases, problems in parenting may increase the risk for this disorder (Clarke et al., 2002). Exactly how all these factors might combine is still not clear. Also uncertain is exactly what constitutes hyperactivity. Cultural standards about acceptable activity levels in children vary, so a "hyperactive" child in one culture might be considered merely "active" in another. In fact, when mental health professionals from four cultures used the same rating scales to judge the presence and severity of hyperactivity in a videotaped sample of children's behavior, the Chinese and Indonesians rated the children as significantly more hyperactive than did their American and Japanese colleagues (Mann et al., 1992; see also Jacobson, 2002). Such findings remind us again that sociocultural factors can be important determinants of what is acceptable, and thus what is abnormal, in various parts of the world.

A second group of child behavior problems falls into the *internalizing*, or *over-controlled*, category. Children in this category experience distress, especially depression and anxiety, and may be socially withdrawn. Those displaying *separation anxiety disorder*, for example, constantly worry that they will be lost, kidnapped, or injured or that some harm may come to a parent (usually the mother). The child clings desperately to the parent and becomes upset or sick at the prospect of any separation. Refusal to go to school (sometimes called "school phobia") is often the result. Children whose temperaments are shy or withdrawn are at a higher risk for internalizing disorders, but they are also associated with environmental factors, including being rejected by peers and (especially for girls) being raised by a single parent (Mesman & Koot, 2000; Prinstein & La Greca, 2002).

A few childhood disorders, such as *pervasive developmental disorders*, do not fall into either the externalizing or internalizing category. Children diagnosed with these disorders show severe problems in communication and impaired social relationships. They also often display repetitive, stereotyped behaviors and unusual preoccupations and interests (American Psychiatric Association, 2000; Filipek et al., 1999). The disorders in this group, also known as *autistic spectrum disorders*, share many of these core symptoms, although the severity of those symptoms may vary (Çeponien et al., 2003; Constantino & Todd, 2003). Estimates of the prevalence of autistic spectrum disorders range from 10 to 20 children per 10,000 births (Bryson & Smith, 1998; Filipek et al., 1999) to as high as 62 per 10,000 (Chakrabarti & Fombonne, 2001). About half of these children suffer *autistic disorder*, which can be the most severe of the group. The earliest signs of autistic disorder usually appear within the first thirty months after birth, as these babies show little or no evidence of forming an attachment to their caregivers. Language development is seriously disrupted in most of these children; half of them never learn to speak at all. They have great difficulty engaging in tasks that require shared attention, and they often focus on nonsocial aspects of human interaction such as clothing rather than on social aspects such as eye contact, facial expression, and tone of voice (Klin et al., 2002). Those who display high-functioning autism or a less severe autistic spectrum disorder called *Asperger's disorder* have impaired relationships, engage in repetitive behaviors, and may memorize arcane facts or activities (such as sports scores or ZIP codes), but they show few severe cognitive deficits and are able to function adaptively and, in some cases, independently as adults (e.g., Grandin, 1996).

Possible biological roots of autistic disorder include genetic factors (Freitag, 2007; Gupta & State, 2007; Veenstra-VanderWeele & Cook, 2004) or neurodevelopmental abnormalities affecting language and communication (Akshoomoff, 2005; Belmonte et al., 2004; Courchesne et al., 2001). Researchers have recently focused on specific kinds of neurons that serve to relate observed actions of others (e.g., smiling) with regions in one's own brain where that same action would be initiated. These "mirror neurons" apparently allow us to have an idea of what is going on in other peoples' minds. The functioning of such neurons appears disturbed in persons with autism, partly explaining why these individuals seem to operate with little appreciation for what others might be thinking or feeling (Williams et al., 2006). Researchers today have rejected the once-popular hypothesis that autistic disorder is caused by cold and unresponsive parents.

Disorders of childhood differ from adult disorders not only because the patterns of behavior are distinct but also because their early onset disrupts development. To take one example, children whose separation anxiety causes spotty school attendance may not only fall behind academically but also fail to form the relationships with other children that promote normal social development. Some children never make up for this deficit. They may drop out of school and risk a life of poverty, crime, and violence. Moreover, children are dependent on others to obtain help for their psychological problems, and all too often those problems may go unrecognized or untreated. For some, the long-term result may be adult forms of mental disorder.

● Substance-Related Disorders

Childhood disorders, especially externalizing disorders, often lead to *substance-related disorders* in adolescence and adulthood. *DSM-IV* defines substance-related disorders as the use of psychoactive drugs for months or years in ways that harm the user or others. These disorders create major political, economic, social, and health problems worldwide. The substances involved most often are alcohol and other depressants (such as barbiturates), opiates (such as heroin), stimulants (such as cocaine or amphetamines), and hallucinogens (such as LSD).

As mentioned in the chapter on consciousness, one effect of using some substances (including alcohol, heroin, and amphetamines) is **addiction,** a physical need for the substance. *DSM-IV* calls addiction *physiological dependence.* Usually, addiction is evident when the person begins to need more and more of a substance to achieve the desired state. This condition is called building a *tolerance.* When addicted people stop using the substance, they experience painful, often terrifying, and potentially dangerous *withdrawal symptoms* as the body tries to readjust to a substance-free state. People can also display *psychological dependence,* sometimes called *behavioral dependence.* In such cases, a drug has become their primary source of reward, and their lives essentially revolve around getting and using it. People who are psychologically dependent on a drug often display problems that are at least as serious as, and sometimes more difficult to treat than, those of people who are physiologically addicted.

Even when use of a drug does not create psychological or physiological dependence, some people may use it in a way that is harmful to themselves or others. For example, they may rely on the drug to bolster self-confidence or to avoid depression, anger, fear, or other unpleasant feelings. However, the drug effects these people seek may also impair their ability to hold a job, care for their children, or drive safely. This pattern of behavior, defined in *DSM-IV* as *substance abuse,* creates significant social, legal, and interpersonal problems.

In short, substance-related disorders can be extremely serious, even when they do not involve addiction. The chapter on consciousness includes a discussion of how consciousness can be affected by a wide range of psychoactive drugs. Here we focus more specifically on problems associated with the use of alcohol, heroin, and cocaine.

● **Alcohol Use Disorders**   According to a large national survey, in 2001–2002 the twelve-month prevalence of alcohol abuse, as defined in *DSM-IV,* was 4.65 percent of adults (Grant et al., 2004). *Alcohol abuse* is characterized by a pattern of continuous or intermittent drinking that may lead to *alcohol dependence,*

addiction   Development of a physical need for a psychoactive drug.

an addiction that almost always causes severe social, physical, and other problems (U.S. Department of Health and Human Services Office of Applied Studies, 2003). Males outnumber females in this category by about three to one, although the problem is on the rise among women and among teenagers of both genders. Abuse is greater among European Americans and American Indians than among African Americans and Hispanics; it is lowest among Asians (Chassin, Pitts, & Prost, 2002; Grant et al., 2004). Binge drinking, which peaks in late adolescence and early adulthood, can have serious consequences, including impaired academic performance and injury or death from driving while intoxicated. Prolonged overuse of alcohol can result in life-threatening liver damage, reduced cognitive abilities, vitamin deficiencies that can lead to an irreversible brain disorder called *Korsakoff's psychosis* (severe memory loss), and a host of other physical ailments. Many of these adverse effects appear to be due to the fact that excessive alcohol consumption causes deterioration in several brain areas (Hommer et al., 2001; Pfefferbaum et al., 2001).

Alcohol dependence or abuse, commonly referred to as **alcoholism**, has been implicated in half of all the traffic fatalities, homicides, and suicides that occur each year (National Institute on Alcohol Abuse and Alcoholism [NIAAA], 2001). Alcoholism also has a stronger association to rape, child abuse, and many other forms of violence than other drugs do (Martin, Maxwell, et al., 2004). It contributes to elevated rates of hospitalization and absenteeism from work, resulting in total costs to society of over $180 billion each year in the United States alone (NIAAA, 2001). It is estimated that about half of U.S. adults have a close relative who is an active or recovering alcoholic and that about 25 percent of children are exposed to adults who display alcohol abuse or dependence (NIAAA, 2001). Children growing up in families in which one or both parents abuse alcohol are at increased risk for developing a host of mental disorders, including substance-abuse disorders (Hoffmann & Cerbone, 2002). And, as described in the chapter on human development, children of mothers who abused alcohol during pregnancy may be born with fetal alcohol syndrome.

The biopsychosocial model suggests that alcohol use disorders stem from a combination of genetic characteristics (including inherited aspects of temperament such as impulsivity and emotionality) and what people learn in their social and cultural environment (Kendler, Jacobson, et al., 2003; Petry, 2001; Wall et al., 2001). For example, the children of alcoholics are more likely than others to become alcoholics themselves; and if the children are identical twins, both are at increased risk for alcoholism, even when raised apart (Kendler et al., 1992; McGue, 1999; Slutske et al., 1998). These findings could be explained by genetics, by learning (modeling), or by both. Now that the human genome has been decoded, researchers are focusing on specific chromosomes and gene complexes as likely candidates for alcohol vulnerability. However, the genetics of addiction is complex, and there are likely multiple pathways to alcoholism (Crabbe, 2002; Higuchi, Matsushita, & Kashima, 2006). As with other disorders, alcoholism probably arises as many genes interact with one another and with environmental events, including parental influences (Duncan et al., 2006; Kaufman et al., 2007). For example, one study of the sons of identical twins found that they were at elevated risk for alcoholism if their own father was an alcoholic, but not if the father's identical twin was alcoholic (Jacob et al., 2003). Something in these boys' nonalcoholic family environment had apparently moderated whatever genetic tendency toward alcoholism they might have inherited.

Expectations, such as that alcohol will create good feelings and helps to cope with stressors, play an important role in the development of alcohol use disorders. Shaped by experience and by exposure to others who drink, the network of memories to which alcohol is associated influence the amount one drinks (Reich & Goldman, 2005). If drinking becomes a person's main stress-coping strategy, alcohol use can become abuse and often addiction (NIAAA, 2001; see Table 15.6). The stress-reduction theory of alcoholism has been supported by studies showing that alcohol can reduce animals' learned fear of a particular location and that animals in a stressful conflict situation will choose to drink alcohol if it is available. The stress-

● **alcoholism** A pattern of drinking that may lead to addiction and almost always causes severe social, physical, and other problems.

TABLE 15.6   **Social Drinking Versus Alcoholism**

Social drinking differs markedly from alcoholism, but it is all too easy for people to drift from social to alcoholic drinking patterns. Alcoholism can include heavy drinking on a daily basis, on weekends only, or in isolated binges lasting weeks or months (NIAAA, 2000).	**Social Drinkers**	**Alcoholics**
	Sip drinks.	Gulp drinks.
	Usually drink in moderation and can control the amount consumed.	Drink increasing quantities (develop tolerance); sometimes drink until blacking out; may not recall events that occur while drinking.
	Usually drink to enhance the pleasure of social situations.	Drink for the chemical effect, often to relieve tension or face problems; often drink alone, including in the morning to reduce hangover or to face the day.
	Do not usually think about or talk about drinking in nondrinking situations	Become preoccupied with getting their next drink, often sneaking drinks during working hours or at home.
	Do not experience physical, social, or occupational problems caused by drinking.	Suffer physical disorders, damaged social relationships, and impaired capacity to work because of drinking.

reducing effects of alcohol have also been shown in humans, though not consistently (Armeli et al., 2003; Cooper et al., 1992). The emotion-regulating effects of alcohol may be more significant in young women who engage in occasional binge drinking than in boys who started drinking early in life and continue to drink heavily (Chassin et al., 2002; Timko et al., 2005).

The importance of social and cultural learning is further suggested by evidence that alcoholism is more common among ethnic and cultural groups (such as the Irish and English) in which frequent drinking tends to be socially reinforced than among groups (such as Jews, Italians, and Chinese) in which all but moderate drinking tends to be discouraged (see Gray & Nye, 2001; Wilson et al., 1996). Moreover, variations in social support for drinking can result in differing consumption patterns within a cultural group. For example, one study found significantly more drinking among Japanese men living in Japan (where social norms for males' drinking are quite permissive) compared with those living in Hawaii or California, where excessive drinking is less strongly supported (Kitano et al., 1992). Learning would also help explain why rates of alcoholism are higher than average among bartenders, cocktail servers, and others who work where alcohol is available and drinking is socially reinforced or even expected (Fillmore & Caetano, 1980). (Of course, it is also possible that attraction to alcohol led some of these people into such jobs in the first place.)

●**Heroin and Cocaine Dependence**   Like alcoholics, heroin and cocaine addicts suffer many serious physical problems, both as a result of the drugs themselves and of the poor eating and other unhealthy habits associated with drug use. The risk of death from an overdose, contaminated drugs, or AIDS (contracted through blood in shared needles), as well as from suicide, is also always present. Dependence on these drugs tends to be more prevalent among males, especially young males (Compton et al., 2007; Warner et al., 1995).

Continued use or overdoses of cocaine can cause problems ranging from nausea and hyperactivity to paranoid thinking, sudden depressive "crashes," and even death. Cocaine use has been on the decline since 1985, but it is still a serious problem. Surveys indicate that 7.7 percent of high school seniors in the United States have used cocaine at some time in their lives, and millions more teens and adults still use it on occasion (Johnston et al., 2004). The widespread availability of crack, a powerful and relatively cheap form of cocaine, has made it one of the most dangerous and addicting of all drugs. Pregnant women who use cocaine are much more likely than nonusers to lose their babies through spontaneous abortion, placental detachment, early fetal death, or stillbirth.

Addiction to substances such as heroin and cocaine is largely a biological process brought about by the physiological effects of the drugs (Phillips et al., 2003). Explaining why people start using them is more complicated. Beyond the obvious and immediate pleasure that these drugs provide, the causes of initial drug abuse are less well established than the reasons for alcohol abuse. One line of theorizing suggests that a complex genetic predisposition toward behavioral dysregulation or compulsion leads some people to abuse many kinds of drugs (Crabbe, 2002; Kreek et al., 2005; NIAAA, 2001). A study supporting this possibility found a link between alcoholism in biological parents and drug abuse in adopted-away sons (Cadoret et al., 1995). The same study also found a link between antisocial personality traits in biological parents and antisocial acts—including drug abuse—in the sons they had put up for adoption.

A number of psychological and environmental factors have been proposed as promoting initial drug use (Alessi et al., 2002; Brems & Namyniuk, 2002; Hoffmann & Cerbone, 2002). These include peer pressure, thrill seeking, seeing parents using drugs, being abused in childhood, efforts to cope with stressors or to ease anxiety or depression, and associating drug use with pleasant experiences (Baker et al., 2004; Dube et al., 2003; Putnam, 2003). Research has not yet established why continued drug use occurs in some people and not in others, but again, it is likely that a biological predisposition sets the stage on which specific psychological processes and stressors play out their roles in specific social and cultural contexts (Kendler, Jacobson, et al., 2003).

Mental Illness and the Law

Cheryl was barely twenty when she married Glen, a graduate student in biology. They moved into a large apartment complex near the university and within three years had two sons. Cheryl's friends had always been impressed by the attention and affection she showered on her boys; she seemed to be the ideal mother. She and Glen had serious marital problems, however, and she felt trapped and unhappy. One day Glen came home to find that Cheryl had stabbed both children to death. At her murder trial, she was found not guilty by reason of insanity and was placed in a mental institution.

This verdict reflects U.S. laws and rules that protect people with severe psychological disorders when they are accused of crimes (Cassel & Bernstein, 2007). Similar laws and rules are in effect in many other countries as well. The protection takes two forms.

First, under certain conditions, people designated as mentally ill may be protected from prosecution. If, at the time of their trial, individuals accused of a crime are unable to understand the proceedings and charges against them or to assist in their own defense, they are declared to be *mentally incompetent to stand trial*. In such cases, defendants are sent to a mental institution until they are judged to have become mentally competent. If still not competent after a court-specified period—two years, in most cases—a defendant may be ruled permanently ineligible for trial and either committed in civil court to a mental institution or released. Release is rare, however, because competency to stand trial requires only minimal mental abilities. If drugs can produce even temporary mental competence, the defendant will usually go to trial (Nietzel, 1999).

Second, mentally ill defendants may be protected from punishment. In most U.S. states, they may be judged *not guilty by reason of insanity* if, at the time of the crime, mental illness prevented them from (1) understanding what they were doing, (2) knowing that what they were doing was wrong, or (3) resisting the impulse to

Assessment of Mental Competence
Andrea Yates admitted to drowning her five children in the bathtub of her Houston, Texas, home in 2001. She had twice tried to kill herself in previous years, and she was reportedly depressed at the time of the murders. Accordingly, she pleaded not guilty by reason of insanity. The court's first step in deciding her fate was to confine her in a mental institution for assessment of her mental competency to stand trial. Following testimony of psychologists who examined her, she was found competent, tried, and sentenced to life in prison. Her conviction was overturned on appeal, though, and at a second trial in 2006, she was found not guilty by reason of insanity and committed to a mental hospital.

do wrong. The first two of these criteria—understanding the nature or wrongfulness of an act—are "cognitive" criteria known as the M'Naughton rule. This rule stems from an 1843 case in England in which a man named Daniel M'Naughton, upon hearing "instructions from God," tried to kill British prime minister Robert Peel. He was found not guilty by reason of insanity and put into a mental institution for life. The third criterion, which is based on a defendant's emotional state during a crime, is known as the irresistible-impulse test. All three criteria were combined in a rule proposed by the American Law Institute (ALI) in 1962 and now followed by about one-third of the U.S. states: "A person is not responsible for criminal conduct if at the time of such conduct as a result of mental disease or defect he lacks substantial capacity either to appreciate the criminality (wrongfulness) of his conduct or to conform his conduct to the requirements of law" (ALI, 1962, p. 66).

In 1984, after John Hinckley, Jr., was found not guilty by reason of insanity under the ALI rule for his attempted assassination of President Ronald Reagan, the U.S. Congress passed the Insanity Defense Reform Act, which eliminated the irresistible-impulse criterion from the definition of insanity in federal cases. About 75 percent of the U.S. states have passed similar or related reform laws (Giorgi-Guarnieri et al., 2002). As a result, about half the states employ some version of the narrower M'Naughton rule (American Psychiatric Association, 2003). These laws highlight the fact that *insanity* is a legal term, not a psychiatric diagnosis; it does not appear in *DSM-IV* (Cassel & Bernstein, 2007). When defendants plead insanity, judges and juries must decide whether or not these people understood what they were doing or had control over their actions. Defendants who are judged not guilty by reason of insanity and who still display a psychological disorder are usually required to receive treatment, typically through commitment to a hospital, until judged to be cured or no longer dangerous.

Insanity rules have been faulted on several grounds. Some critics argue that everyone, even those who meet legal criteria for insanity, should be held responsible for their actions and punished for their crimes. Others point out significant problems in the implementation of insanity rules. For one thing, different experts often give conflicting, highly technical testimony about a defendant's sanity at the time of a crime. (In the case mentioned at the beginning of this section, one expert said Cheryl was sane; another concluded she was insane.) Jurors are then left in the difficult position of deciding which expert to believe and what to make of the experts' diagnostic judgments. Their task is complicated by the fact that people suffering from mental disorders—even those as severe as schizophrenia—are still capable of some rational decision making and of controlling some aspects of their behavior (Grisso & Appelbaum, 1995; Matthews, 2004). Concern over such problems has led four U.S. states—Montana, Idaho, Utah, and Kansas—to abolish the insanity defense. Other states have tried less extreme reforms. In thirteen states, it is now possible for juries to find defendants *guilty but mentally ill*. These defendants still serve a sentence, and although they are supposed to receive treatment while confined, they seldom do (Cassel & Bernstein, 2007). A second reform already noted is that federal courts no longer use the irresistible-impulse criterion in defining insanity. Third, federal courts and some state courts now require defendants to prove that they were insane at the time of their crime, rather than requiring the prosecution to prove that the defendants were sane.

Does the insanity defense allow lots of criminals to "get away with murder"? No. Although certain high-profile cases might suggest otherwise, the insanity plea is used in fewer than 1 of every 200 felony cases in the United States—usually when the defendant displays severe psychological disorder—and this plea is successful in only 2 of every 1,000 attempts (American Psychiatric Association, 2003; Silver, Cirincione, & Steadman, 1994). Further, the few defendants found not guilty by reason of insanity are usually hospitalized for two to nine times as long as they would have spent in prison had they been convicted (Silver, 1995; Steadman, 1993). For example, John Hinckley, Jr., has been in St. Elizabeth's Hospital in Washington, D.C., since 1982, and despite his annual efforts to be released and court approval for some visits with his parents outside the hospital, he is unlikely to be freed anytime soon.

In summary, legislators, victims' rights groups, civil liberties advocates, and ordinary citizens are constantly seeking the proper balance between protecting the rights of defendants and protecting society from dangerous criminals. In doing so, the sociocultural values that shape views about what is abnormal also influence judgments about the extent to which abnormality should relieve people of responsibility for criminal behavior.

LINKAGES

As noted in the chapter on introducing psychology, all of psychology's many subfields are related to one another. Our discussion of the role of learning principles in the development of phobias illustrates just one way in which the topic of this chapter, psychological disorders, is linked to the subfield of learning (which is the focus of the chapter by that name). The Linkages diagram shows ties to two other subfields as well, and there are many more ties throughout the book. Looking for linkages among subfields will help you see how they all fit together and better appreciate the big picture that is psychology.

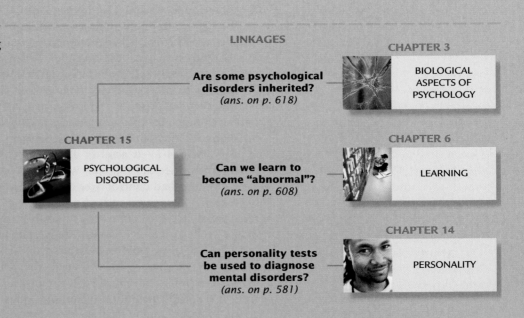

LINKAGES

CHAPTER 15
PSYCHOLOGICAL DISORDERS

Are some psychological disorders inherited?
(ans. on p. 618)

CHAPTER 3
BIOLOGICAL ASPECTS OF PSYCHOLOGY

Can we learn to become "abnormal"?
(ans. on p. 608)

CHAPTER 6
LEARNING

Can personality tests be used to diagnose mental disorders?
(ans. on p. 581)

CHAPTER 14
PERSONALITY

SUMMARY

Psychopathology involves patterns of thinking, feeling, and behaving that cause personal distress or that significantly impair a person's social or occupational functioning.

Defining Psychological Disorders

Some disorders show similarity across cultures, but the definition of abnormality is largely determined by social and cultural factors.

What Is Abnormal? The criteria for judging abnormality include statistical infrequency (a comparison with what most people do), norm violation, and personal suffering. Each of these criteria is flawed to some extent.

Behavior in Context: A Practical Approach The practical approach to defining abnormality, which considers the content, context, and consequences of behavior, emphasizes the question of whether individuals show *impaired functioning* in fulfilling the roles appropriate for particular people in particular settings, cultures, and historical eras.

Explaining Psychological Disorders

Abnormal behavior has been attributed, at one time or another, to many different factors, including the action of supernatural forces.

The Biopsychosocial Model In today's *biopsychosocial model*, mental disorders are attributed to the combination and interaction of biological, psychological, and sociocultural factors. Biological factors are emphasized by the medical, or *neurobiological model*, which sees psychological disorders as reflecting disturbances in the anatomy and chemistry of the brain and in other biological processes. The causal factors emphasized by the *psychological model* of mental disorders include unconscious conflicts, disruptions in attachment, learning, or maladaptive cognitive schemas. The *sociocultural model* focuses on factors that help define abnormality and influence the form that disorders take in different parts of the world.

Diathesis-Stress as an Integrative Explanation No single aspect of the biopsychosocial model can adequately explain all psychological disorders. The *diathesis-stress approach* takes into account all the causal factors in that model by suggesting that biological, psychological, and sociocultural characteristics create predispositions for disorder and that the symptoms of a disorder appear only in the face of sufficient amounts of stress.

Classifying Psychological Disorders

There seems to be a set of behavior patterns that roughly defines abnormality in most cultures. Classifying these patterns helps to identify the features, causes, and most effective methods of treating various psychological disorders.

A Classification System: *DSM-IV* The dominant system for classifying abnormal behavior in North America is the American Psychiatric Association's *Diagnostic and Statistical Manual of Mental Disorders (DSM-IV)* and its most recent text revision (*DSM-IV-TR*). It includes more than three hundred specific categories of mental disorders. As with medical illnesses, categories for psychological disorders are periodically revised as research accumulates.

Evaluating the Diagnostic System Research on the reliability and validity of *DSM-IV* shows that it is a useful, but imperfect, classification system.

Anxiety Disorders

Long-standing and disruptive patterns of anxiety characterize *anxiety disorders*.

Types of Anxiety Disorders The most prevalent type of anxiety disorder is *phobia*, which includes *specific phobias*, *social phobias*, and *agoraphobia*. Other anxiety disorders are *generalized anxiety disorder*, which involves nonspecific anxiety; *panic disorder*, which brings unpredictable attacks of intense anxiety; and *obsessive-compulsive disorder (OCD)*, in which uncontrollable repetitive thoughts and ritualistic actions occur.

Causes of Anxiety Disorders The most influential explanations of anxiety disorders suggest that they may develop through the combination of a biological predisposition for strong anxiety reactions and the impact of fear-enhancing thought patterns and learned anxiety responses.

Somatoform Disorders

Somatoform disorders, including *conversion disorder*, involve physical problems that have no apparent physical cause. Other examples are *hypochondriasis*, an unjustified concern about being ill; *somatization disorder*, in which the person complains of numerous, unconfirmed physical complaints; and *pain disorder*, in which pain is felt in the absence of a known physical cause.

Dissociative Disorders

Dissociative disorders involve rare conditions such as *dissociative fugue*, *dissociative amnesia*, and *dissociative identity disorder*, *or DID* (multiple personality disorder), in which a person suffers memory loss or develops two or more identities.

Mood Disorders

Mood disorders, also known as affective disorders, involve extreme moods of long duration that may be inconsistent with events.

Depressive Disorders *Major depressive disorder* is marked by feelings of inadequacy, worthlessness, and guilt; in extreme cases, delusions may also occur. *Dysthymic disorder* includes similar but less severe symptoms persisting for a long period. Suicide is often related to these disorders.

Bipolar Disorders Alternating periods of depression and *mania* characterize bipolar I disorder, which is also known as *manic depression. Cyclothymic disorder*, an alternating pattern of less extreme mood swings, is more common.

Causes of Mood Disorders Mood disorders have been attributed to biological causes such as genetics—which underlie disruptions in neurotransmitter and endocrine systems—and irregularities in biological rhythms. Both loss of significant sources of reward and maladaptive patterns of thinking are among the psychological causes proposed. A predisposition toward some of these disorders appears to be inherited, although their appearance may be determined by a diathesis-stress process.

Schizophrenia

Schizophrenia is perhaps the most severe and puzzling disorder of all.

Symptoms of Schizophrenia Among the symptoms of schizophrenia are problems in thinking, perception (often including *hallucinations*), attention, emotion, movement, motivation, and daily functioning.

Categorizing Schizophrenia Although *DSM-IV* lists five major subtypes of schizophrenia (paranoid, disorganized, catatonic, undifferentiated, and residual), many researchers today favor viewing it as a spectrum disorder involving displays of *positive symptoms* (such as hallucinations and disorganized thoughts) and *negative symptoms* (such as lack of speech and restricted emotional expression). Each category of symptoms may be traceable to different causes. Predominantly negative symptoms tend to be associated with more severe disorder and less successful treatment outcomes.

Causes of Schizophrenia Genetic factors, neurotransmitter problems, abnormalities in brain structure and functioning, and neurodevelopmental abnormalities are biological factors implicated in schizophrenia. Psychological explanations have focused on maladaptive learning experiences and disturbed family interactions. The diathesis-stress approach, often described in terms

of the vulnerability model, remains a promising framework for research into the multiple causes of schizophrenia.

Personality Disorders

Personality disorders are long-term patterns of maladaptive behavior that may be disturbing to the person displaying them and/or to others. Examples include schizotypal, avoidant, narcissistic, and *antisocial personality disorders*.

A Sampling of Other Psychological Disorders

Psychological Disorders of Childhood Childhood disorders can be categorized as externalizing disorders (such as conduct disorders or attention deficit hyperactivity disorder) and internalizing disorders (in which children show overcontrol and experience distress, as in separation anxiety disorder). Pervasive developmental disorders do not fall into either category and include the autistic spectrum disorders. In autistic disorder, which can be the most severe of these, children show no interest in, or attachment to, others.

Substance-Related Disorders *Substance-related disorders* involving alcohol and other drugs affect millions of people. *Addiction* to, psychological dependence on, or abuse of these substances contributes to disastrous personal and social problems, including physical illnesses, accidents, and crime. Genetic factors may create a predisposition for *alcoholism,* but learning, cultural traditions, and other psychosocial processes are also important. In the case of dependence on heroin and cocaine, stress reduction, imitation, thrill seeking, and parental modeling have been proposed as important causal factors, along with genetics. The exact causes of initial use of these drugs, however, are not fully understood.

Mental Illness and the Law

Current rules protect people accused of crimes from prosecution or punishment if they are mentally incompetent at the time of their trials or if they were legally insane at the time of their crimes. Difficulty in establishing the mental state of defendants and other knotty problems have created dissatisfaction with those rules and prompted a number of reforms, including the "guilty but mentally ill" verdict.

Treatment of Psychological Disorders 16

Many movies and television dramas include scenes in a psychotherapist's office, but even the best of them tell only part of the story of how psychological disorders can be treated. In this chapter we describe a wide range of treatment options, from "talking therapy" to drugs. We also summarize the results of research on the effectiveness of treatment and on efforts to prevent psychological disorders. Here's how we have organized the material:

In the chapter on psychological disorders, we described José, an electronics technician who was forced to take medical leave from his job because of repeated panic attacks (see Table 15.1). After four months of diagnostic testing turned up no physical problems, José's physician suggested that he see a psychologist. José resisted at first, insisting that his condition was not "just in his head," but he eventually began psychological treatment. Within a few months, his panic attacks had stopped, and José had returned to all his old activities. After the psychologist helped him reconsider his workload, José decided to retire from his job in order to pursue more satisfying work at his home-based computer business.

José's case is by no means unique. During any given year in the United States alone, about 15 percent of adults and about 21 percent of children are receiving some form of treatment for a psychological disorder (Kancelbaum, Singer, & Wong, 2004; Kessler, Demler, et al., 2005; Wang, Lane, et al., 2005). The cost of treating these disorders is just one part of their economic impact—which amounts to a staggering $150 billion per year, including disability payments and lost productivity. Fortunately, the cost of treatment is more than made up for by the savings it creates. Compared with untreated patients, those who receive treatment for psychological disorders typically need fewer mental and physical health services later on (American Psychological Association, 2002c; Chiles, Lambert, & Hatch, 1999; Schoenbaum, Sherbourne, & Wells, 2005).

The most common targets of treatment are problems involving anxiety, mood, impulse control, substance abuse, or some combination of these (Kessler, Demler, et al., 2005). Many people also seek treatment for problems that are not officially diagnosed as disorders, such as relationship conflicts or difficulties associated with grief, divorce, retirement, or other life transitions.

In this chapter, we describe a variety of treatment methods, most of which are based on the theories of stress and coping, personality, and psychological disorders reviewed in the chapters on those topics. First we examine the basic features common to all forms of treatment. Then we discuss approaches that rely on **psychotherapy**, the treatment of psychological disorders through psychological methods, such as talking about problems and exploring new ways of thinking and acting. These methods are based on psychodynamic, humanistic, or social-cognitive (behavioral) theories of disorder and treatment. We then consider biological approaches to treatment, which consist of prescription drugs and other physical therapies.

Although we discuss different psychotherapy methods in separate sections, keep in mind that the majority of mental health professionals see themselves as *eclectic* or *integrative* therapists. In other words, they might lean toward one set of methods, but when working with particular clients or particular problems, they employ other methods as well (Hayes & Harris, 2000; Magnavita, 2006; Slife & Reber, 2001).

Basic Features of Treatment

All treatments for psychological disorders share certain basic features. These common features include a *client* or patient, a *therapist* who is accepted as being capable of helping the client, and the establishment of a *special relationship* between the client and therapist. In addition, all forms of treatment are based on some *theory* about the causes of the client's problems. That theory may presume causes ranging

Medieval Treatment Methods
Methods used to treat psychological disorders have always been related to the presumed causes of those disorders. In medieval times, when demonic possession was widely blamed for abnormal behavior, physician-priests tried to make the victim's body an uncomfortable place for evil spirits. Here, we see a depiction of demons fleeing as an afflicted person's head is placed in an oven.

from magic spells to infections and everything in between (Frank & Frank, 1991). The theory, in turn, leads to procedures for dealing with the client's problems. So traditional healers combat supernatural forces with ceremonies and prayers, medical doctors treat chemical imbalances with drugs, and psychologists focus on altering psychological processes through psychotherapy.

People receiving treatment for psychological disorders can be inpatients or outpatients. *Inpatients* are treated in a hospital or other residential institution. They are voluntarily or involuntarily committed to these institutions because their problems are severe enough to create a threat to their own well-being or the safety of others. Depending on their level of functioning, inpatients may stay in the hospital for a few days or weeks or—in rare cases—several years. Their treatment almost always includes psychoactive drugs. *Outpatients* receive psychotherapy and/or drugs while living in the community. Compared with inpatients, outpatients tend to have fewer and less severe symptoms of disorder and to function better in social and occupational situations (Mendlowicz et al., 1998; Sanguineti et al., 1996; White & Litovitz, 1998).

Those who provide psychological treatment are a diverse group (Robiner, 2006). **Psychiatrists** are medical doctors who have completed specialty training in the treatment of psychological disorders. Like other physicians, they are authorized to prescribe drugs for the relief of psychological problems. **Psychologists** who offer psychotherapy have usually completed a doctoral degree in clinical or counseling psychology, often followed by additional specialized training. Except in New Mexico and Louisiana, psychologists are not authorized to prescribe drugs, though this privilege may eventually be granted to specially trained psychologists elsewhere (Heiby, DeLeon, & Anderson, 2004). Other treatment providers include *clinical social workers, marriage and family therapists,* and *licensed professional counselors,* all of whom typically hold a master's degree in their respective professions and provide therapy in a variety of settings, such as hospitals, clinics, and private practice. *Psychiatric nurses, substance abuse counselors,* members of the clergy working as *pastoral counselors,* and a host of paraprofessionals also provide therapy services, often as part of a hospital or outpatient treatment team (Bernstein, Kramer, & Phares, 2008).

The general goal of treatment is to help troubled people change their thinking, feelings, and behavior in ways that relieve discomfort, promote happiness, and improve their overall functioning as parents, students, workers, and the like. To

psychotherapy The treatment of psychological disorders through talking and other psychological methods.

psychiatrists Medical doctors who have completed special training in the treatment of psychological disorders.

psychologists Among therapists, those whose education includes completion of a master's or (usually) a doctoral degree in clinical or counseling psychology, often followed by additional specialty training.

Group Therapy for War Veterans
Some psychotherapy occurs in one-to-one office sessions, but some treatment is conducted with couples, families, and groups in hospitals, community health centers, and facilities for former mental hospital residents. Therapy is also offered in prisons, at military bases, in drug and alcoholism treatment centers, and in many other places.

reach this goal, some therapists try to help clients gain insight into the hidden causes of problems. Others seek to promote growth through more genuine self-expression, and still others help clients learn and practice new ways of thinking and acting. The particular methods used in each case—whether some form of psychotherapy, a drug treatment, or both—depend on the problems, preferences, and financial circumstances of the client; the time available for treatment; and the therapist's theoretical leanings, methodological preferences, and professional qualifications. Later, we will discuss drugs and other biological treatments; here, we consider several forms of psychotherapy, each of which is based on a different theoretical explanation of mental disorder.

Psychodynamic Psychotherapy

The field of formal psychotherapy began in the late 1800s when, as described in the chapter on personality, Sigmund Freud established the psychodynamic approach to understanding psychological disorders. Central to his approach, and to modern revisions of it, is the assumption that personality and behavior reflect the efforts of the ego to referee conflicts, usually unconscious, among various components of the personality.

Freud's method of treatment, **psychoanalysis,** was aimed at understanding these unconscious conflicts and how they affect the client, but most other forms of psychotherapy also incorporate some of his ideas. These include (1) a one-to-one treatment approach; (2) searching for relationships between an individual's life history and current problems; (3) emphasizing the role of thoughts, emotions, and motivations; and (4) focusing on the client-therapist relationship. We will describe Freud's original methods first and then consider some more recent treatments that are rooted in his psychodynamic approach.

● Classical Psychoanalysis

psychoanalysis A method of psychotherapy that seeks to help clients gain insight by recognizing and understanding unconscious thoughts and emotions.

Classical psychoanalysis developed mainly out of Freud's medical practice. He was puzzled by patients who suffered from "hysterical" ailments—blindness, paralysis, or other symptoms that had no apparent physical cause (see our discussion of *conversion*

Freud's Consulting Room During psychoanalytic sessions, Freud's patients lay on this couch, free-associating or describing dreams and everyday events, while he sat in the chair behind them (this famous couch is now at The Freud Museum in London, which you can visit online at http://www.freud.org.uk/). According to Freud, even apparently trivial behavior may carry messages from the unconscious. Forgetting a dream or missing a therapy appointment might reflect a client's unconscious resistance to treatment. Even accidents may be meaningful. The waiter who spills hot soup on an elderly male customer might be seen as acting out unconscious aggressive impulses against a father figure.

disorders in the chapter on psychological disorders). Inspired by his colleague Josef Breuer's dramatic success in using hypnosis to treat hysterical symptoms in a patient known as "Anna O." (Breuer & Freud, 1895/1974), Freud tried similar methods with other hysteria patients but found them to be only partially and temporarily successful. Eventually, Freud merely asked patients to lie on a couch and report whatever thoughts, memories, or images came to mind, a process Freud called *free association.*

The results of this "talking cure" were surprising. Freud was struck by how many of his patients reported childhood memories of sexual abuse, usually by a parent or other close relative (Esterson, 2001). Freud wondered whether child abuse was rampant in Vienna, whether he was seeing a biased sample of patients, or whether his patients' memories were being distorted in some way. He eventually concluded that his patients' memories of abuse probably reflected unconscious childhood wishes and fantasies, not reality. He also believed that hysterical symptoms stem from unconscious conflicts over those wishes and fantasies.

As a result, Freud's psychoanalysis came to focus on exploring the unconscious and the conflicts raging within it. Classical psychoanalytic treatment aims first to help troubled people gain *insight* into their problems by recognizing unconscious thoughts and emotions. Then they are encouraged to discover, or *work through*, the many ways in which those unconscious elements continue to motivate maladaptive thinking and behavior in everyday life. The treatment may require as many as three to five sessions per week, usually over several years. Generally, the psychoanalyst is compassionate but emotionally neutral as the patient slowly develops an understanding of how past conflicts determine current problems (Gabbard, 2004).

To gain glimpses of the unconscious—and of the sexual and aggressive impulses he believed reside there—Freud looked for meaning in his patients' free associations, their dreams, their everyday behaviors, and their relationship with him. He believed that hidden beneath the obvious or *manifest content* of dreams is *latent content* that reflects the wishes, impulses, and fantasies that the dreamer's defense mechanisms keep out of consciousness during waking hours. He focused also on what have become known as "Freudian slips" of the tongue and other seemingly insignificant, but potentially meaningful, behaviors. So if a patient mistakenly used the name of a former girlfriend while talking about his wife, Freud might wonder if the patient unconsciously regrets his marriage. Similarly, when patients expressed dependency, hostility, or even love toward him, Freud saw it as an unconscious process in which childhood feelings and conflicts about parents and other significant people were being transferred to the therapist. Analysis of this *transference*, this "new edition" of the patient's childhood conflicts and current

Analysis of the transference in this therapy relationship would be quite a challenge! This parody of psychoanalysis illustrates the point that therapists focus not only on their client's feelings toward them but also on their feelings toward clients—called *countertransference*. For example, if transference leads a client to treat the therapist as a mother, the therapist might, because of countertransference, unintentionally begin treating the client as her child.

"What do you think I think about what you think I think you've been thinking about?"

problems, became another important psychoanalytic method (Gabbard, 2004). Freud believed that focusing on the transference allows patients to see how old conflicts haunt their lives and helps them to resolve these conflicts (Arlow, 1995).

● Contemporary Variations on Psychoanalysis

Classical psychoanalysis is still practiced, but not as much as it was several decades ago (Gabbard, 2004; Horgan, 1996). The decline is due to many factors, including disenchantment with Freud's personality theory; the expense of classical psychoanalysis; its limited usefulness with children; and the availability of many alternative forms of treatment, including variations on classical psychoanalysis (e.g., Roseborough, 2006; Russ, 2006; Stricker, 2006).

Some of these variations were developed by the neo-Freudian theorists discussed in the chapter on personality. As noted there, those theorists tended to place less emphasis than Freud did on the past and on unconscious impulses stemming from the id. They also tended to stress the role of social relationships in clients' problems and how the power of the ego can be harnessed to solve those problems (Gray, 2005). *Ego analysis* (Hartmann, 1958; Klein, 1960) and *individual analysis* (Adler, 1927/1963) were among the first treatments to be based on neo-Freudian theories. Some were designed for treating children (Freud, 1946; Klein, 1960). More recent variations on psychoanalysis alter the format of treatment so that it is less intense, less expensive, and more appropriate for a broader range of clients (Hoyt, 1995; Messer & Kaplan, 2004). Some of these variants have come to be known as *short-term psychodynamic therapy* because they aim to provide benefits in far less time than is required in classical psychoanalysis (Levenson, 2003; Rawson, 2006). However, virtually all modern psychodynamic therapies still focus attention on

Play Therapy   Modern versions of psychoanalytic treatment include fantasy play and other techniques that make the approach more useful with children. A child's behavior and comments while playing with puppets representing family members, for example, are seen as a form of free association that the therapist hopes will reveal important unconscious material, such as fear of abandonment (Carlson, Watts, & Maniacci, 2006).

unconscious as well as conscious aspects of mental life, on the impact of internal conflicts, and on transference analysis as a key element in treatment (Levy et al., 2006; Luborsky & Luborsky, 2006; Vanheule et al., 2006).

In a particularly popular short-term psychodynamic approach known as *object relations therapy*, the powerful need for human contact and support takes center stage. Object relations therapists believe that most of the problems that bring clients to treatment ultimately stem from their relationships with others, especially their mothers or other early caregivers. (The term *object* usually refers to a person who has emotional significance for the client.) Psychotherapists who adopt an object relations perspective take a much more active role in therapy sessions than classical analysts do—particularly by directing the client's attention to evidence of certain conflicts, rather than waiting for free association or other more subtle methods to reveal these conflicts. Object relations therapists work to develop a nurturing relationship with their clients, providing a "second chance" for them to receive the support that might have been lacking in infancy and to counteract some of the consequences of maladaptive early attachment patterns (Kahn & Rachman, 2000; Wallerstein, 2002). For example, object relations therapists take pains to show that they will not abandon their clients, as might have happened to these people in the past. *Interpersonal therapy*, too, is rooted partly in neo-Freudian theory (Sullivan, 1954), but it focuses on helping clients explore and overcome the problematic effects of interpersonal events that occur *after* early childhood—events such as the loss of a loved one, conflicts with a parent or a spouse, job loss, or social isolation (Mufson, Polack, & Moreau, 2004; Stuart & Robertson, 2003).

In another version of psychodynamic treatment, the therapist looks for a "core conflict" that appears repeatedly across a variety of relationships, including in the therapy relationship (Luborsky & Luborsky, 2006). In one case, for example, "Katie" reported recurring dreams about breaking glass and accidentally cutting her therapist (Vaughan, 1998). She also recalled two childhood incidents in which she broke glassware after wandering away from her mother; in one incident, her mother cut herself while cleaning up the glass. Katie's therapist suggested that these dreams and memories indicated a core conflict about wanting to be independent of her mother, yet also close to her. Addressing this conflict during therapy helped Katie to realize that professional success did not require her to reject or hurt the people she cared about.

With their focus on interpersonal relationships rather than instincts, their emphasis on clients' potential for self-directed problem solving, and the reassurance and emotional support they provide, contemporary variants on classical psychoanalysis have helped the psychodynamic approach retain its influence among mental health professionals (Stiles et al., 2006; Westen & Gabbard, 1999).

Humanistic Psychotherapy

Whereas some therapists revised Freud's ideas, others developed radical new therapies based on the humanistic approach to personality, which we describe in the personality chapter. *Humanistic psychologists*, sometimes called *phenomenologists*, see people as capable of consciously controlling their own actions and taking responsibility for their own decisions. Most humanistic therapists believe that human behavior is motivated not by sexual or aggressive impulses but rather by an innate drive toward personal growth and improvement that is guided from moment to moment by the way people perceive their world. Disordered behavior, they say, reflects a blockage of natural growth brought on by distorted perceptions or lack of awareness of feelings. Accordingly, humanistic therapy operates on the following assumptions:

1. Treatment is an encounter between equals, not a cure provided by an expert. It is a way to help clients restart their natural growth and to feel and behave more in line with that growth.

2. Clients will improve on their own, given the right conditions. These ideal conditions promote clients' awareness, acceptance, and emotional expression. So, like psychodynamic therapy, humanistic therapy promotes insight, but it is insight into current feelings and perceptions, not into unconscious childhood conflicts.

3. Ideal conditions in therapy can best be established through a relationship in which clients feel fully accepted and supported as human beings, no matter how problematic or undesirable their behavior may be. It is the client's experience of this relationship that brings beneficial changes. (As noted earlier, this assumption is also important in object relations therapy.)

4. Clients must remain responsible for choosing how they will think and behave.

Of the many humanistically oriented treatments in use today, the most influential are client-centered therapy, developed by Carl Rogers (1951), and Gestalt therapy, developed by Frederick and Laura Perls.

● Client-Centered Therapy

Carl Rogers was trained in psychodynamic therapy methods during the 1930s, but he soon began to question their value. He especially disliked being a detached expert observer whose task was to "figure out" the client. Convinced that a less formal approach would be more effective for the client and more comfortable for the therapist, Rogers allowed his clients to decide what to talk about and when, without direction, judgment, or interpretation by the therapist (Raskin & Rogers, 2001). This approach, now called **client-centered therapy** or **person-centered therapy**, relies on the creation of a relationship that reflects three intertwined attitudes of the therapist: unconditional positive regard, empathy, and congruence.

● Unconditional Positive Regard
The attitude Rogers called **unconditional positive regard**, also known as **acceptance**, is expressed by treating the client as a valued person, no matter what. Rogers believed that experiencing unconditional

client-centered therapy (person-centered therapy) A therapy that allows the client to decide what to talk about, without direction, judgment, or interpretation from the therapist.

unconditional positive regard (acceptance) A therapist attitude that conveys a caring for, and acceptance of, the client as a valued person.

empathy The therapist's attempt to appreciate and understand how the world looks from the client's point of view.

reflection An active listening method in which a therapist conveys empathy by paraphrasing clients' statements and noting accompanying feelings.

acceptance by the therapist helps clients to overcome the sense that their value as a person depends on being successful, intelligent, attractive, or meeting the other *conditions of worth* described in the personality chapter. Acceptance is communicated through the therapist's willingness to listen to the client without interrupting and without making judgments or expressing opinions. The therapist doesn't have to approve of everything the client says but must accept each statement as reflecting the client's view of the world. Client-centered therapists also avoid giving advice, because acceptance includes trusting clients to solve their own problems. They don't want their advice to convey the unspoken suggestion that clients are incompetent and dependent on the therapist's help.

● **Empathy**   Client-centered therapists also try to appreciate the client's point of view. This goes far beyond saying "I know what you mean." It involves an effort to see the world as each client sees it, and not to look at clients from the outside. In other words, client-centered therapists work at developing **empathy**, an emotional understanding of what the client might be thinking and feeling. They convey empathy by showing that they are *actively listening* to the client. Like other skillful interviewers, they make eye contact with the client, nod in recognition as the client speaks, and give other signs of careful attention. They also use **reflection**, a paraphrased summary of the client's words that emphasizes the feelings and meanings that appear to accompany them. Reflection confirms the communication, shows that the therapist is interested, and helps the client to perceive and focus on the thoughts and feelings being expressed. Here is an example:

> CLIENT: This has been such a bad day. I've felt ready to cry any minute, and I'm not even sure what's wrong!

> THERAPIST: You really do feel so bad. The tears just seem to well up inside, and I wonder if it's a little scary to not even know why you feel this way.

Notice that in rephrasing the client's statements, the therapist reflected back not only the obvious feelings of sadness but also the fear in the client's voice. Most clients respond to empathic reflection by elaborating on their feelings. In this example, the client went on to say, "It *is* scary, because I don't like to feel in the dark about myself. I have always prided myself on being in control." Clients do this, said Rogers, simply because the therapist expresses the desire to listen and understand

A Client-Centered Therapy Group
Carl Rogers (shown here in shirtsleeves) believed that, as successful treatment progresses, clients become more self-confident, more aware of their feelings, more accepting of themselves, more comfortable and genuine with other people, more reliant on self-evaluation than on the judgments of others, and more effective and relaxed.

Existential Therapy Rogers's and Perls's methods of treatment represent two prominent examples of humanisitic therapies, but there are others, too. For example, Rollo May (1969; May, Angel, & Ellenberger,1958), Viktor Frankl (1963), and Irwin Yalom (1980) developed therapies based on existential philosophy, which highlights such uniquely human concerns as our freedom to choose our actions, being responsible for those actions, feeling alone in the world, trying to find meaning and purpose in our lives, and confronting the prospect of death (Yalom, 2002). *Existential therapy* is designed to help people accept and deal with these concerns head-on rather than to continue ignoring or avoiding them. Because people can feel lost, alone, and unsure of life's meaning without displaying serious behavior problems, existential therapists see their approach as applicable to anyone, whether or not they are officially diagnosed with some form of mental disorder.

without asking disruptive questions. Empathic listening tends to be so effective in promoting self-understanding and awareness that it is used across a wide range of therapies (Corsini & Wedding, 2001; Miller & Rollnick, 2002). Even outside the realm of therapy, people who are thought of as easy to talk to are usually "good listeners" who reflect back the important messages they hear from others.

● **Congruence** Rogerian therapists also try to convey **congruence** (sometimes called *genuineness*) by acting in ways that are consistent with their feelings during therapy. For example, if they are confused by what a client has said, they would say so rather than trying to pretend that they always understand everything. When the therapist's acceptance and empathy are genuine, the client is able to see that relationships can be built on openness and honesty. Ideally, this experience will help the client become more congruent in other relationships.

Here is an excerpt that illustrates the three therapist attitudes we have described.

CLIENT: . . . I cannot be the kind of person I want to be. I guess maybe I haven't the guts or the strength to kill myself, and if someone else would relieve me of the responsibility or I would be in an accident I, I . . . just don't want to live.

THERAPIST: At the present time things look so bad that you can't see much point in living. [Note the empathic reflection and the attitude of acceptance.]

CLIENT: Yes. I wish I'd never started this therapy. I was happy when I was living in my dream world. There I could be the kind of person I wanted to be. But now there is such a wide, wide gap between my ideal and what I am. . . . [Notice that the client responds to reflection by giving more information.]

THERAPIST: It's really a tough struggle digging into this like you are, and at times the shelter of your dream world looks more attractive and comfortable. [Note the use of empathic reflection.]

CLIENT: My dream world or suicide. . . . So I don't see why I should waste your time—coming in twice a week—I'm not worth it—what do you think?

THERAPIST: It's up to you. . . . It isn't wasting my time. I'd be glad to see you whenever you come but it's how you feel about it. . . . [Note the congruence in stating an honest desire to see the client and the acceptance in trusting her capacity and responsibility for choice.]

CLIENT: You're not going to suggest that I come in oftener? You're not alarmed and think I ought to come in every day until I get out of this?

THERAPIST: I believe you are able to make your own decision. I'll see you whenever you want to come. [Note again the attitude of acceptance.]

CLIENT: (With a note of awe in her voice) I don't believe you are alarmed about—I see—I may be afraid of myself but you aren't afraid for me. [Here the client experiences the therapist's confidence in her; in the end, the client chose not to commit suicide.] (adapted from Rogers, 1951, p. 49)

Gestalt Therapy

Another form of humanistic treatment was developed by Frederick S. (Fritz) Perls, along with his wife, Laura. A European psychoanalyst, Perls was greatly influenced by research in *Gestalt psychology*. (As described in the chapter on perception, Gestalt psychologists emphasized the idea that people actively organize their perceptions of the world.) He believed that (1) people create their own versions of reality and

● **congruence** A consistency between the way therapists feel and the way they act toward clients.

(2) people's natural psychological growth continues only as long as they perceive, remain aware of, and act on their true feelings. Growth stops and symptoms appear, said Perls, when people are not aware of all aspects of themselves (Perls, 1969; Perls, Hefferline, & Goodman, 1951).

Fritz and Laura Perls based Gestalt therapy on these beliefs. Like client-centered therapy, **Gestalt therapy** seeks to create conditions in which clients can become more unified, self-aware, and self-accepting—and thus ready to grow again. However, Gestalt therapists use more direct and dramatic methods than do Rogerians. Often working in group settings, Gestalt therapists prod clients to become aware of feelings and impulses that they have disowned and to discard feelings, ideas, and values that are not really their own. For example, the therapist or other group members might point out inconsistencies between what clients say and how they behave. Gestalt therapists pay particular attention to clients' gestures and other kinds of "body language" that appear to conflict with what the clients are saying (Kepner, 2001). They may also ask clients to engage in imaginary dialogues, or "conversations," with other people, with parts of their own personalities, and even with objects (Elliott, Watson, & Goldman, 2004a, 2004b). Like a shy person who can be socially outgoing only while masked at a costume party, clients often find that these dialogues help to get them in touch with, and express, their feelings (Paivio & Greenberg, 1995; Woldt & Toman, 2005).

In recent years, client-centered and other forms of humanistic therapy have declined in popularity (Norcross, Hedges, & Castle, 2002), but Carl Rogers's contributions to psychotherapy remain significant. In particular, his emphasis on the importance of the therapeutic relationship in bringing about change has been adopted by many other treatment approaches (Kirschenbaum & Jourdan, 2005).

Behavior Therapy

Psychodynamic and humanistic approaches to therapy assume that if clients gain insight or self-awareness about underlying problems, the symptoms created by those problems will disappear. Behavior therapists emphasize a different kind of client insight, namely that most psychological problems are *learned behaviors* that can be changed by taking action to learn new ones, not by searching for underlying causes (Martin & Pear, 2002; Miltenberger, 2003).

For example, consider again José, the electronics technician whose panic attacks are described in the chapter on psychological disorders. Some of these attacks had occurred while he was scuba diving, so he began making excuses when friends invited him to go on diving trips. Avoiding diving situations eased his anxiety temporarily but it did nothing to solve the problem. Could José reduce his fear without first discovering its "underlying meaning"? *Behavior therapy* would offer just such an alternative by first identifying the signals, rewards and punishments, and other learning-based factors that maintain José's fear and then helping him to develop new responses in feared situations.

These goals are based on both the *behavioral approach* to psychology and the *social-cognitive approach* to personality and disorder. As described in the chapters on introducing psychology, on personality, and on psychological disorders, these approaches emphasize the role of learning in the development of personality, as well as in most psychological disorders. Accordingly, behaviorists tend to see those disorders as examples of the maladaptive thoughts and actions that a client has learned. For instance, behavior therapists believe that fear of leaving home (*agoraphobia*) develops through classically conditioned associations between being away from home and having panic attacks. The problem is maintained in part through operant conditioning: Staying home and making excuses for doing so are rewarded by reduced anxiety. Therapists adopting a behavioral approach argue that if learning experiences can create problems, they can also help to alleviate problems.

● **Gestalt therapy** An active treatment designed to help clients get in touch with genuine feelings and disown foreign ones.

So even if the experiences that led to today's problems began in the client's childhood, behavior therapy seeks to solve those problems by creating beneficial new experiences using the principles discussed in the chapter on learning.

Inspired by John B. Watson, Ivan P. Pavlov, B. F. Skinner, and others who studied learning during the 1920s and 1930s, researchers in the late 1950s and early 1960s began to systematically apply the principles of classical conditioning, operant conditioning, and observational learning to alter disordered human behavior (Ullmann & Krasner, 1965). By 1970, behavioral treatment had become a popular alternative to psychodynamic and humanistic methods (Craighead, Craighead, & Ilardi, 1995).

The most notable features of behavioral treatment include the following:

1. Development of a productive therapist-client relationship. As in other therapies, this relationship enhances clients' confidence that change is possible and makes it easier for them to speak openly and to cooperate in treatment (Creed & Kendall, 2005; Lejuez et al., 2005).

2. A careful listing of the behaviors and thoughts to be changed (Umbreit et al., 2006). This assessment—and the establishment of specific treatment goals—often replaces the formal diagnosis used in some other therapy approaches. So instead of treating "depression" or "obsessive-compulsive disorder," behavior therapists work to change the specific thoughts, behaviors, and emotional reactions that cause people to receive these diagnostic labels.

3. A therapist who acts as a kind of teacher/assistant by providing learning-based treatments, giving "homework" assignments, and helping the client make specific plans for dealing with problems, rather than just talking about them (Shelton & Levy, 1981).

4. Continuous monitoring and evaluation of treatment, along with constant adjustments to any procedures that are not effective (Farmer & Nelson-Gary, 2005). Because ineffective procedures are soon altered or abandoned, behavioral treatment tends to be one of the briefer forms of therapy.

Behavioral treatment can take many forms. By tradition, those that rely mainly on classical conditioning principles are usually referred to as **behavior therapy**. Those that focus on operant conditioning methods are usually called **behavior modification**. And behavioral treatment that focuses on changing thoughts as well as overt behaviors is called **cognitive-behavior therapy**. These methods, especially cognitive-behavior therapy, are among the most important and influential approaches to psychological treatment available today (Durlak, 2006).

Techniques for Modifying Behavior

Among the most important behavior therapy methods are systematic desensitization, exposure techniques, modeling, positive reinforcement, extinction, punishment, and aversion conditioning.

●**Systematic Desensitization** Joseph Wolpe (1958) developed one of the first behavioral methods for helping clients overcome phobias and other forms of anxiety. Called **systematic desensitization**, it is a method in which the client visualizes a series of anxiety-provoking stimuli while remaining relaxed. Wolpe believed that this process gradually weakens the learned association between anxiety and the feared object, until the fear disappears.

Wolpe first helped his clients learn to relax, often using the *progressive relaxation training* procedures described in the chapter on health, stress, and coping. Then, while relaxed, the clients would be asked to imagine an item from a *desensitization hierarchy*, a sequence of increasingly fear-provoking situations (see Table 16.1). The clients would imagine one hierarchy item at a time, moving to a more difficult scene only after tolerating the previous one without distress. Wolpe found that once clients

behavior therapy Treatments that use classical conditioning principles to change behavior.

behavior modification Treatments that use operant conditioning methods to change behavior.

cognitive-behavior therapy Learning-based treatment methods that help clients change the way they think, as well as the way they behave.

systematic desensitization A behavioral treatment for anxiety in which clients visualize a graduated series of anxiety-provoking stimuli while remaining relaxed.

flooding An exposure technique for reducing anxiety that involves keeping a person in a feared, but harmless, situation.

exposure techniques Behavior therapy methods in which clients remain in the presence of strong anxiety-provoking stimuli until the intensity of their emotional reactions decrease.

TABLE **16.1**   A Desensitization Hierarchy

Desensitization hierarchies are lists of increasingly fear-provoking situations that clients visualize while using relaxation methods to remain calm. Here are a few items from the beginning and the end of a hierarchy that was used to help a client overcome fear of flying.	1. You are reading a newspaper and notice an ad for an airline. 2. You are watching a television program that shows a group of people boarding a plane. 3. Your boss tells you that you need to take a business trip by air. 4. You are in your bedroom packing your suitcase for your trip. ． ． ． 12. Your plane begins to move as you hear the flight attendant say, "Be sure your seat belt is securely fastened." 13. You look at the runway as the plane is readied for takeoff. 14. You look out the window as the plane rolls down the runway. 15. You look out the window as the plane leaves the ground.

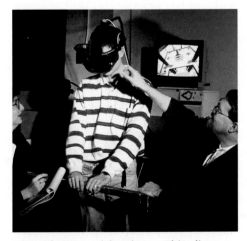

Virtual Desensitization   This client fears heights. He is wearing a virtual reality display that creates the visual experience of being in a glass elevator which, under the therapist's careful control, seems to gradually rise higher and higher. After learning to tolerate these realistic images without anxiety, clients are better able to fearlessly face the situations they once avoided.

could calmly imagine being in feared situations, they were better able to deal with them in reality later on.

Wolpe's original treatment package is not used as much as it once was (McGlynn, Smitherman, & Gothard, 2004), partly because of research indicating that desensitization is especially effective if it slowly and carefully presents clients with real (rather than imagined) hierarchy items (Bouton, 2000, 2002; Choy, Fyer, & Lipsitz, 2007; Marks, 2002; Tryon, 2005). This *in vivo*, or "real life," desensitization was once difficult to arrange or control, especially in cases involving fear of flying, heights, or highway driving, for example. However, *virtual reality graded exposure* now makes it possible for clients to "experience" extremely vivid and precisely graduated versions of feared situations without actually being exposed to them. In one study, clients who feared heights wore a head-mounted virtual reality helmet that gave them the impression of standing on bridges of gradually increasing heights, on outdoor balconies at higher and higher floors, and in a glass elevator as it slowly rose forty-nine stories (Rothbaum et al., 1995). The same technology has been used successfully in the treatment of many other anxiety disorders, ranging from fear of spiders or air travel to social phobia and posttraumatic stress disorder (Anderson, Rothbaum, & Hodges, 2003; Glantz, Rizzo, & Graap, 2003; Maltby, Kirsch, & Mayers, 2002; Rothbaum, 2006; Wiederhold & Wiederhold, 2005).

Exactly why systematic desensitization works is not clear. Traditionally, clinicians believed that change occurs because of basic learning processes—either through classical conditioning of a new, calmer response to the fear-provoking stimulus or through extinction, as the object or situation that had been a conditioned fear stimulus repeatedly occurs without being paired with pain or any other aversive unconditioned stimulus (Hermans et al., 2006; McNeil & Zvolensky, 2000). More recent explanations emphasize that desensitization also modifies clients' cognitive processes, including their expectation that they can deal calmly and successfully with previously feared situations (McNeil & Zvolensky, 2000).

●**Exposure Techniques**   Extinction is also the basis of **flooding**, an anxiety-reduction treatment that keeps people in a feared but harmless situation and prevents them from engaging in their normally rewarding pattern of escape (O'Donohue, Hayes, & Fisher, 2003). Because they continuously expose clients to feared stimuli, flooding and other similar methods are called **exposure techniques**. The clients are flooded with fear at first, but after an extended period of exposure to the feared

Treating Fear Through Flooding
Flooding is designed to extinguish anxiety by allowing it to occur without the harmful consequences the person dreads. This man's fear of flying is obvious here, on takeoff, but it is likely to diminish during and after an uneventful flight. Like other behavioral treatments, flooding is based on the idea that phobias and other psychological disorders are learned and can thus be "unlearned." Some therapists prefer more gradual exposure methods similar to those of *in vivo* desensitization, which start with situations that are lower on the client's fear hierarchy.

stimulus (a frog, say) without experiencing pain, injury, or any other dreaded result, the association between the feared stimulus and the fear response gradually weakens, and the conditioned fear response is extinguished (Basoglu, Livanou, & Salcioglu, 2003; McNally, 2007). In one study, twenty clients who feared needles were exposed for two hours to the sight and feel of needles, including mild finger pricks, harmless injections, and blood samplings (Öst, Hellström, & Kåver, 1992). Afterward, all but one of these clients were able to have a blood sample drawn without experiencing significant anxiety.

Although often highly effective, flooding is equivalent to immediately exposing a fearful client to the most distressing item on a desensitization hierarchy. Therefore, some therapists and clients prefer more gradual exposure methods, especially when a client's fear is not focused on a specific stimulus (Hecker & Thorpe, 1992). In dealing with agoraphobia, for instance, the therapist might provide gradual exposure by escorting the client away from home for increasing periods and eventually venturing into shopping malls and other previously avoided places (Barlow, Raffa, & Cohen, 2002; Craske et al., 2003). Clients can also practice gradual exposure methods on their own. They might be instructed, for example, to spend a little more time each day looking at photos of some feared animal or to spend some time alone in a dental chair or waiting room. In one study, clients suffering from various phobias made as much progress after six hours of instruction in gradual self-exposure methods and daily "homework" exercises as did those who received an additional nine hours of therapist-aided gradual exposure (Al-Kubaisy et al., 1992). Effective self-treatment using gradual exposure has also been reported in cases of panic disorder (Hecker et al., 1996) and obsessive-compulsive disorder (Fritzler, Hecker, & Losee, 1997).

● **Modeling**   Behavior therapists sometimes help clients to develop more desirable behaviors by demonstrating those behaviors. In **modeling** treatments, the client watches the therapist or other people perform desired behaviors, thus learning skills vicariously, or second-hand, without going through a lengthy shaping process (Bidwell & Rehfeldt, 2004). In fear treatment, for example, modeling can teach the client how to respond fearlessly while vicariously extinguishing conditioned fear responses. One therapist showed a twenty-four-year-old student with a severe spider phobia how to kill spiders with a fly swatter and had her practice this skill at home with rubber spiders (MacDonald & Bernstein, 1974). The combination of live modeling with gradual practice is called *participant modeling,* and it is one of the most powerful treatments for fear (Bandura, Blanchard, & Ritter, 1969; Faust, Olson, & Rodriguez, 1991; see Figure 16.1).

Modeling is also a major part of *social skills training* and *assertiveness training,* which teach clients how to interact with people more comfortably and effectively. The goals of **social skills training** range from helping socially phobic singles make conversation on dates to rebuilding the abilities of mental patients so they can interact more normally with people outside the hospital (Al-Kubaisy & Jassim, 2003; McQuaid et al., 2000; Spence, Donovan, & Brechman-Toussaint, 2000; Trower, 1995). In **assertiveness training,** the therapist helps clients learn to be more direct and expressive in social situations. So instead of sheepishly agreeing to be seated at a badly located restaurant table, clients learn to be comfortable making "I-statements," such as "I would rather sit over there, by the window." Notice that *assertiveness* does not mean aggressiveness; instead it involves clearly and directly expressing both positive and negative feelings and standing up for one's own rights while respecting the rights of others (Alberti & Emmons, 1986; Paterson, 2000). Assertiveness training is often conducted in groups and involves both modeling and role playing of specific situations (Spence, 2003). For example, group assertiveness training has helped wheelchair-bound adults more comfortably handle the socially awkward situations in which they sometimes find themselves (Gleuckauf & Quittner, 1992; Weston & Went, 1999).

● **modeling**   Demonstrating desirable behaviors as a way of teaching them to clients.

● **assertiveness training and social skills training**   Methods for teaching clients how to interact with others more comfortably and effectively.

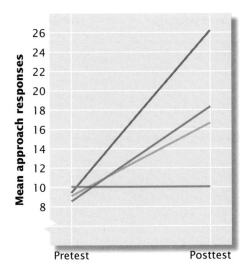

Mean approach responses (y-axis: 8, 10, 12, 14, 16, 18, 20, 22, 24, 26)
Pretest — Posttest

——— Live modeling with participation
——— Symbolic modeling
——— Systematic desensitization
——— Control

FIGURE 16.1

Participant Modeling

In this study, participant modeling was compared with systematic desensitization, symbolic modeling (watching filmed models), and no treatment (control). Notice that, compared with no treatment, all three methods helped snake-phobic clients approach live snakes, but participant modeling was clearly the best. Ninety-two percent of the participants in that group were virtually free of any fear. The value of participant modeling has been repeatedly confirmed (e.g., Öst, Salkovskis, & Hellström, 1991).

- **positive reinforcement** A therapy method that uses rewards to strengthen desirable behaviors.

- **token economy** A system for improving the behavior of institutionalized clients in which desirable behaviors are rewarded with tokens that can be exchanged for desired items or activities.

- **extinction** The gradual disappearance of a conditioned response or operant behavior through nonreinforcement.

- **punishment** A therapy method that weakens undesirable behavior by following it with an unpleasant stimulus.

- **aversion conditioning** A method that uses classical conditioning to create a negative response to a particular stimulus.

● **Positive Reinforcement** Behavior therapists also use systematic **positive reinforcement** to change problematic behaviors and to teach new skills in cases ranging from childhood tantrums and juvenile delinquency to schizophrenia and substance abuse (e.g., Lussier et al., 2006). Using operant conditioning principles, they set up *contingencies*, or rules, that specify the behaviors to be strengthened through reinforcement. In one study, language-impaired autistic children were given grapes, popcorn, or other items they liked in return for saying "please," "thank you," and "you're welcome" while exchanging crayons and blocks with a therapist. The therapist first modeled the behavior by saying the appropriate words. The children almost immediately began to utter the phrases themselves and were reinforced for doing so. The effects of positive reinforcement generalized to situations involving other toys, and, as indicated in Figure 16.2, the new skills were still evident at a follow-up session six months later (Matson et al., 1990).

When working with severely retarded or disturbed clients in institutions, behavior therapists sometimes establish a **token economy,** a system in which desirable behaviors are positively reinforced with coin-like tokens or points that can be exchanged later for snacks, access to television, or other rewards (Ayllon, 1999; LePage et al., 2003; Paul & Lentz, 1977; Seegert, 2003). The goal is to shape behavior patterns that will persist outside the institution.

● **Extinction, Punishment, and Aversion Conditioning** Just as reinforcement can make desirable behaviors more likely, other behavioral techniques can make undesirable behaviors less likely. One operant conditioning method, for example, promotes the **extinction** of undesirable behaviors by removing the reinforcers that normally follow those behaviors. So a person who gets satisfying attention by disrupting a classroom, damaging property, or violating hospital rules might be placed in a quiet, boring "time out" room for a few minutes in order to interrupt reinforcement for this misbehavior (e.g., Kee, Hill, & Weist, 1999; Reitman & Drabman, 1999). When such behavior no longer "pays off," people usually stop performing it, though the process of change can be slow. Still, extinction-based programs are often chosen when dealing with children and retarded or seriously disturbed adults because they provide a gentle way to eliminate undesirable behaviors (Ducharme & Van Houten, 1994).

Sometimes, though, the only way to eliminate a dangerous or disruptive behavior is through **punishment,** an operant conditioning technique in which undesirable behavior is followed by an unpleasant but harmless stimulus, such as a shouted "No!" or a mild electrical shock. However, before behavior therapists use punishment with the institutionalized clients, other impaired adults, or children for whom it might be appropriate and beneficial, they must consider certain ethical and legal questions: Would the client's life be in danger without treatment? Have all other methods failed? Has an ethics committee reviewed and approved the procedures? And has the client or a close relative formally agreed to the treatment? (Kazdin, 1994a). When the answer to these questions is yes, punishment can be an effective, sometimes lifesaving, treatment—as in the case illustrated in Figure 6.11 in the chapter on learning. And even then, punishment is best used only long enough to eliminate undesirable behavior and in combination with other behavioral methods designed to reinforce more appropriate behavior (Hanley et al., 2005).

When unwanted behaviors—such as using addictive drugs, gambling, or engaging in certain sexual offenses—have become deeply habitual and immediately rewarding, not even punishment may be effective in eliminating them. In such cases, behavior therapists may try to make these behaviors less attractive, thus making it easier for clients to give them up. Methods for reducing the appeal of certain stimuli are known as *aversion therapy*. The name reflects the fact that these methods rely on a classical conditioning principle called **aversion conditioning** to associate nausea, painful electrical shock, or some other unpleasant stimulus with the actions, thoughts, or situations the client wants to stop or avoid (e.g., Bordnick et al., 2004).

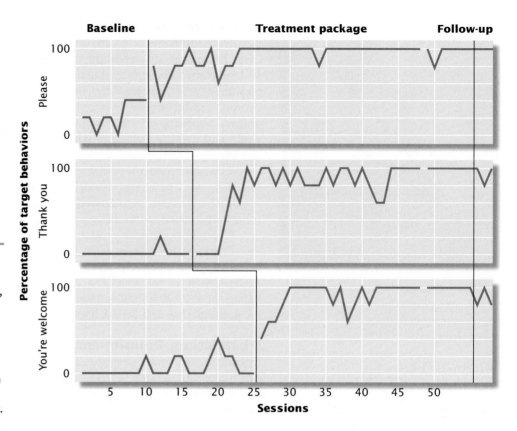

Positive Reinforcement for an Autistic Child

During each pretreatment baseline period, an autistic child rarely said "please," "thank you," or "you're welcome," but these statements began to occur once they were modeled, then reinforced. Did modeling and reinforcement actually cause the change? Probably, because each type of response did not start to increase until the therapist began demonstrating it.

Because aversion therapy is unpleasant and uncomfortable, because it may not work with all clients (Flor et al., 2002), and because its effects are often temporary, behavior therapists use this method relatively rarely, only when it is the best treatment choice, and only long enough to allow the client to learn a more desirable alternative behavior.

● Cognitive-Behavior Therapy

Like psychodynamic and humanistic therapists, behavior therapists recognize that depression, anxiety, and many other behavior disorders can stem from how clients think about themselves and the world. And like other therapists, behavior therapists also try to change their clients' troublesome ways of thinking. However, the methods used by behavior therapists—known collectively as *cognitive-behavior therapy*—rely on learning principles to help clients change the way they think (e.g., Dobson, 2003; O'Donohue et al., 2003). Suppose, for example, that a client suffers intense anxiety in social situations, despite having excellent social skills. In a case such as this, social skills training would be unnecessary. Instead, the behavior therapist would use cognitive-behavioral methods designed to help the client identify the recurring thoughts (such as "I shouldn't draw attention to myself") that get in the way of self-expression and create discomfort. Once these cognitive obstacles are brought to light, the therapist models—and encourages the client to develop and practice—new and more adaptive ways of thinking. As these new cognitive skills are learned, it becomes easier and more rewarding for clients to let these new thoughts guide their behavior (Meichenbaum, 1995).

● **Rational-Emotive Behavior Therapy** One prominent form of cognitive-behavior therapy is **rational-emotive behavior therapy (REBT)**. Developed by Albert Ellis (1962, 1993, 1995, 2004a, 2004b), REBT is based on the notion that anxiety, guilt, depression, and other psychological problems are caused by how people think

rational-emotive behavior therapy (REBT) A treatment designed to identify and change self-defeating thoughts that lead to anxiety and other symptoms of disorder.

Albert Ellis   Rational-emotive behavior therapy (REBT) focuses on altering the self-defeating thoughts that Ellis believed underlie people's behavior disorders. Ellis argued, for example, that students do not get upset because they fail a test but because they have learned to believe that failure is a disaster that indicates they are worthless. Many of Ellis's ideas have been incorporated into various forms of cognitive-behavior therapy, and they helped Ellis himself to deal rationally with the health problems he encountered near the end of his life (Ellis, 1997).

about events, not by the events themselves. Ellis's therapy aims first at identifying self-defeating beliefs, usually in the form of *shoulds* or *musts*, such as "I should be loved or approved by everyone" or "I must be perfect in order to be worthwhile." After the client learns to recognize thoughts like these and to see how they can cause problems, the therapist uses modeling, encouragement, and logic to help the client replace them with thoughts that are more realistic. The client is then given "homework" assignments to try out these new ways of thinking in everyday situations. Here is part of an REBT session with a woman who suffered from panic attacks. She has just said that it would be "terrible" if she had an attack in a restaurant and that people "should be able to handle themselves!"

> THERAPIST: . . . The reality is that . . . "shoulds" and "musts" are the rules that other people hand down to us, and we grow up accepting them as if they are the absolute truth, which they most assuredly aren't.
>
> CLIENT: You mean it is perfectly okay to, you know, pass out in a restaurant?
>
> THERAPIST: Sure!
>
> CLIENT: But . . . I know I wouldn't like it to happen.
>
> THERAPIST: I can certainly understand that. It would be unpleasant, awkward, inconvenient. But it is illogical to think that it would be terrible, or . . . that it somehow bears on your worth as a person.
>
> CLIENT: What do you mean?
>
> THERAPIST: Well, suppose one of your friends calls you up and invites you back to that restaurant. If you start telling yourself, "I might panic and pass out and people might make fun of me and that would be terrible," . . . you might find you are dreading going to the restaurant, and you probably won't enjoy the meal very much.
>
> CLIENT: Well, that is what usually happens.
>
> THERAPIST: But it doesn't have to be that way. . . . The way you feel, your reaction . . . depends on what you choose to believe or think, or say to yourself. (Masters et al., 1987)

Cognitive-behavior therapists use many techniques related to REBT to help clients learn to think and act in more adaptive ways. Behavioral techniques aimed at replacing upsetting thoughts with alternative thinking patterns are called *cognitive restructuring* (Lazarus, 1971). Using these techniques, clients develop calming thoughts that they can use as part of *self-instruction* during exams, tense discussions, and other anxiety-provoking situations. The calming thoughts might be something like "OK, you can handle this if you just focus on the task and don't worry about being perfect" (Meichenbaum, 1977). Sometimes, the methods are expanded into *stress inoculation training*, in which clients imagine being in a stressful situation, then practice newly learned cognitive skills to remain calm (Meichenbaum, 1995). In one study of stress inoculation training, first-year law students tried out calming new thoughts during role-playing exercises that exposed them to stressful classroom-style questioning, hostile feedback, and a competitive learning atmosphere. Following training, these students showed reductions in troublesome responses to stressors as well as improved academic performance (Sheehy & Horan, 2004).

● **Beck's Cognitive Therapy**   Behavior therapists seek a different kind of cognitive restructuring by using Aaron Beck's **cognitive therapy** (Beck, 1976, 1995, 2005). Beck's treatment approach is based on the idea that certain psychological disorders—especially those involving depression and anxiety—can be traced to errors in logic, or what he calls *cognitive distortions*. Common cognitive distortions include *catastrophizing* (e.g., "If I fail my driver's test the first time, I'll never pass it and that'll be the end of my social life"), *all-or-none thinking* (e.g., "Everyone ignores me"),

● **cognitive therapy**   A treatment in which the therapist helps clients to notice and change negative thoughts associated with anxiety and depression.

TABLE 16.2 Some Examples of Negative Thinking

TRY THIS Here are just a few examples of the kinds of thoughts that cognitive-behavior therapists see as underlying anxiety, depression, and other behavior problems. After reading this list, try writing an alternative thought that clients could use to replace each of these ingrained cognitive habits. Then jot down a "homework assignment" that you would recommend to help clients challenge each maladaptive statement, and thus develop new ways of thinking about themselves.

"I shouldn't draw attention to myself."

"I will never be any good at this."

"It will be so awful if I don't know the answer."

"Everyone is smarter than I am."

"Nobody likes me."

"I should be able to do this job perfectly."

"What if I panic?"

"I'll never be happy."

"I should have accomplished more by this point in my life."

and *personalization* (e.g., "I know those people are laughing at *me*"). Beck points out that these learned cognitive distortions occur so quickly and automatically that the client never stops to consider that they might not be true.

Cognitive therapy is an active, structured, problem-solving approach in which the therapist first helps clients to identify the distorted thoughts and beliefs that precede anxiety, depression, eating disorders, and other psychological problems (Beck & Rector, 2005; Drinkwater & Stewart, 2002; Hendricks & Thompson, 2005; Pardini & Lochman, 2003; see Table 16.2). Then, much as in the five-step critical thinking system illustrated throughout this book, those thoughts and beliefs are treated as hypotheses to be scientifically tested rather than as assertions to be uncritically accepted (Hatcher, Brown, & Gariglietti, 2001). Accordingly, therapist and client take the role of "investigators" who develop ways to test beliefs such as "I'm no good around the house." They might decide on tasks that the client will attempt as "homework"—such as cleaning out the basement, cooking a meal, paying bills, or cutting the grass. Success at accomplishing even one of these tasks provides concrete evidence to challenge a false belief that has supported depression, thus helping to reduce it. As therapy progresses, clients become more skilled at recognizing, and then correcting, the cognitive distortions related to their problems.

As mentioned in the chapter on psychological disorders, however, the cognitive roots of depression, anxiety, and some other disorders may involve more than specific thoughts and beliefs about certain situations (Beck, 2002). They may be associated with a more general cognitive style that leads people to expect the worst and to consider any negative events to be confirmation that they are completely and permanently incompetent or unlovable (Peterson, 1995; Peterson & Seligman, 1984). Accordingly, cognitive-behavior therapists help depressed clients, for example, to develop more optimistic ways of thinking and to reduce their tendency to blame themselves for negative outcomes (Persons, Davidson, & Tompkins, 2001). In some cases, cognitive restructuring is combined with practice at using logical thinking, anxiety management techniques, and skill training—all designed to help clients experience success and develop confidence in situations in which they had previously expected to fail (Beck & Beck, 1995). Some cognitive therapists have also encouraged clients to use traditional Eastern practices such as meditation (see the chapter on consciousness) to help monitor problematic thoughts. This combined approach is called *mindfulness-based cognitive therapy* (Ma & Teasdale, 2004; Segal, Williams, & Teasdale, 2001). Research in the field of positive psychology suggests, too, that the effects of cognitive behavior therapy may be enhanced through exercises deigned to promote positive emotions—such as identifying and using personal strengths, and making a list of three things that have gone well each day (Seligman, Berkowitz, et al., 2005; Seligman, Rashid, & Parks, 2006).

group therapy Psychotherapy involving several unrelated clients.

Group, Family, and Couples Therapy

The psychodynamic, humanistic, and behavioral treatments we have described are often conducted with individuals, but they can also be adapted for use with groups of clients or with family units (Petrocelli, 2002; Thorngren & Kleist, 2002).

Group Therapy

Group therapy refers to the treatment of several unrelated clients under the guidance of a therapist who encourages helpful interactions among group members. Many groups are organized around a particular problem (such as alcoholism) or a particular type of client (such as adolescents). In most cases, six to twelve clients meet with their therapist at least once a week for about two hours. All group members agree to hold confidential everything that occurs during these sessions.

Group therapy offers several features not found in individual treatment (Marmarosh, Holtz, & Schottenbauer, 2005; Yalom, 1995). First, group therapy allows the therapist to see clients interacting with one another, which can be helpful in identifying problems in clients' interpersonal styles. Second, clients discover that they are not alone as they listen to others and realize that many people struggle with difficulties similar to theirs. This realization tends to lift each client's expectations for improvement, a factor important in all forms of treatment. Third, group members can boost one another's self-confidence and self-acceptance as they come to trust and value one another. Fourth, clients learn from one another by sharing ideas for solving problems and giving one another honest feedback about how each member "comes across" to others. Fifth, perhaps through mutual modeling, the group experience makes clients more willing to share their feelings and more sensitive to other people's needs and messages. Finally, group therapy allows clients to try out new skills—such as assertiveness—in a safe and supportive environment.

Some of the advantages of group therapy are also put to use in *self-help organizations*. Self-help groups, such as Alcoholics Anonymous (AA), are made up of people who share some problematic experience and meet to help one another. There are

A Circle of Friends This meeting of Overeaters Anonymous is but one example of the self-help movement in North America, a growing network of inexpensive mental health and anti-addiction services offered by volunteer helpers, including friends and relatives of troubled people. A recent edition of one small-town Florida newspaper listed 104 local self-help groups focused on problems ranging from alcohol abuse to weight control. The services provided by these nonprofessional groups make up about 20 percent of the total mental health and anti-addiction services offered in the United States (Borkman, 1997; Regier et al., 1993; Swindle et al., 2000).

self-help groups for a wide range of problems, including alcohol and drug addiction, childhood sexual abuse, cancer, overeating, overspending, bereavement, compulsive gambling, and schizophrenia, among many others (e.g., Humphreys, 2004; Kurtz, 2004). The worldwide self-help movement has grown dramatically in recent decades, partly because many troubled people prefer to seek help from friends, teachers, or other "unofficial" helpers before turning to mental health practitioners (Swindle et al., 2000). Dozens of self-help organizations operate through hundreds of thousands of local chapters, enrolling 10 million to 15 million participants in the United States and about half a million in Canada (Barlow et al., 2000; Norcross et al., 2000; Swindle et al., 2000).

Lack of reliable data makes it difficult to assess the value of many self-help groups, but available information suggests that active members may experience moderate improvement in their lives (Kelly, 2003; Mains & Scogin, 2003; Masudomi et al., 2004; Moos et al., 2001). Some professional therapists view these groups with suspicion; others encourage clients to participate in them as part of their treatment or as a first step toward more formal treatment (Haaga, 2000; Salzer, Rappaport, & Segre, 1999), especially in cases of eating disorders, alcoholism, and other substance-related problems (Dunne & Fitzpatrick, 1999; Guimon, 2004; Scheidinger, 2004).

● Family and Couples Therapy

As its name implies, **family therapy** involves treatment of two or more individuals from the same family system, one of whom—often a troubled child or adolescent—is the initially identified client. The term *family system* highlights the idea that the problems displayed by one family member usually reflect problems in the functioning of the entire family (Cox & Paley, 2003; Pilling et al., 2002; Williams, 2005).

Whether family therapy is based on psychodynamic, humanistic, or cognitive-behavioral approaches, the family itself becomes the client, and treatment involves as many members as possible (Novick & Novick, 2005). In fact, the goal of family therapy is not just to ease the identified client's problems but also to create greater harmony and balance within the family by helping each member understand the family's interaction patterns (Blow & Timm, 2002). As with group therapy, the family format gives the therapist a chance to see how the initially identified client interacts with others, thus providing a basis for discussion of topics that are important in the operation of the family system.

Family therapists who emphasize psychodynamic theory point out that if the parents in a family have not worked out conflicts with their own parents, these conflicts will surface in relation to their spouses and children (Scharff & Scharff, 2003). Accordingly, these family therapy sessions might focus on the parents' problems with their own parents and, when possible, include members of the older generation. A related approach, called *structural family therapy*, concentrates on family communication patterns. It focuses on changing the rigid patterns and rituals that create *alliances* (such as mother and child against father), because these alliances maintain conflicts and prevent healthy communication within the family. Structural family therapists argue that when dysfunctional communication patterns are eliminated, problematic interactions will decrease because family members no longer need them in order to survive in the family system (McLendon, McLendon, & Petr, 2005).

Behavior therapists often use family therapy sessions as meetings at which family members can discuss and agree on behavioral "contracts" (e.g., Hayes et al., 2000). Based on operant conditioning principles, these contracts establish rules and reinforcement contingencies that help parents encourage their children's desirable behaviors (while discouraging undesirable ones) and help spouses become more supportive of each other (O'Farrell, 1995; Sanders & Dadds, 1993).

Therapists of many theoretical persuasions also offer **couples therapy,** in which communication between partners is the main focus of treatment (Christensen et al., 2004; Gurman & Jacobson, 2002). Discussion in couples therapy sessions is usually

● **family therapy**   Treatment of two or more individuals from the same family.

● **couples therapy**   A form of therapy focusing on improving communication between partners.

TABLE 16.3 **Some "Rules for Talking" in Couples Therapy**

TRY THIS Many forms of couples therapy help partners improve communication by establishing rules such as these. Think about your own experience in relationships or your observations of couples as they interact, and then write down some rules you would add to this list. Why do you think it would be important for couples to follow the rules on your list?

1. Always begin with something positive when stating a problem.

2. Use specific behaviors rather than derogatory labels or overgeneralizations to describe what is bothersome about the other person.

3. Make connections between those specific behaviors and feelings that arise in response to them (e.g., "It makes me sad when you . . .").

4. Admit your own role in the development of the problem.

5. Be brief; don't lecture or harangue.

6. Maintain a focus on the present or the future; don't review all previous examples of the problem or ask "why" questions, such as "Why do you always . . . ?"

7. Talk about observable events; don't make inferences about them (e.g., say, "I get angry when you interrupt me" rather than "Stop trying to make me feel stupid").

8. Paraphrase what your partner has said, and check out your own perceptions of what was said before responding. (Note that this suggestion is based on the same principle as Rogers's empathic listening.)

aimed at identifying and improving the problematic interactions that are interfering with a couple's happiness and intimacy. In behavioral marital therapy, for example, couples learn to abide by certain "rules for talking," such as those listed in Table 16.3 (Shadish & Baldwin, 2005). Another version of couples therapy focuses on strengthening the bond between partners by teaching them how to deal with their unsolvable problems and recover from their fights by expressing at least five times as many positive statements as negative ones (Gottman, Driver, & Tabares, 2002).

Some therapists even offer programs designed to *prevent* marital problems in couples whose interactions suggest that they are at high risk for developing discord (Gottman, Gottman, & Declaire, 2006; Jacobson et al., 2000; Laurenceau et al., 2004). "In Review: Approaches to Psychological Treatment" summarizes key features of the main approaches to treatment that we have discussed so far.

Fortunately, most couples are not this far out of touch, but couples therapy aims to identify the communication problems that do exist in the relationship and to help the partners speak to each other more directly and listen to each other more carefully.

"I'm sorry, dear. I wasn't listening. Could you repeat what you've said since we've been married?"

in review Approaches to Psychological Treatment

Dimension	Classical Psychoanalytic	Contemporary Psychodynamic	Humanistic	Behavioral/ Cognitive-Behavioral
Nature of the human being	Driven by sexual and aggressive urges	Driven by the need for human relationships	Has free will, choice, and capacity for self-actualization	Is a product of social learning and conditioning; behaves on the basis of past experience
Therapist's role	Neutral; helps client explore meaning of free associations and other material from the unconscious	Active; develops relationship with client as a model for other relationships	Facilitates client's growth; some therapists are active, some are nondirective	Teacher/trainer who helps client replace undesirable thoughts and behaviors; active, action oriented
Focus	Emphasizes unresolved unconscious conflicts from the distant past	Understanding the past, but focusing on current relationships	Here and now; focus on immediate experience	Current behavior and thoughts; may not need to know original causes to create change
Goals	Psychosexual maturity through insight; strengthening of ego functions	Correction of effects of failures of early attachment; development of satisfying intimate relationships	Expanded awareness; fulfillment of potential; self-acceptance	Changes in thinking and behaving in particular classes of situations; better self-management
Typical methods	Free association; dream analysis; analysis of transference	Analysis of interpersonal relationships, including the client-therapist relationship	Reflection-oriented interviews designed to convey unconditional positive regard, empathy, and congruence; exercises to promote self-awareness	Systematic desensitization, social skills training, positive reinforcement, extinction, aversion conditioning, punishment, and cognitive restructuring

Evaluating Psychotherapy

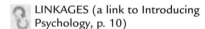 LINKAGES (a link to Introducing Psychology, p. 10)

Most psychotherapists and their clients believe in psychotherapy's effectiveness (*Consumer Reports*, 1995), but confirming this belief with experimental research has proved to be challenging and controversial (Beutler, 2002; Dawes, 1994; Laurenceau, Hayes, & Feldman, 2007; Norcross, Beutler, & Levant, 2005; Seligman, 1996; Weisz, Weersing, & Henggeler, 2005; Westen, Novotny, & Thompson-Brenner, 2004).

The value of psychotherapy was first widely questioned in 1952, when British psychologist Hans Eysenck reviewed studies in which thousands of clients had received either traditional psychodynamic therapy, various other therapies, or no treatment. To the surprise and dismay of many therapists, Eysenck (1952) concluded that the percentage of clients who improved following any kind of psychotherapy was actually lower than that of people who received no treatment.

Critics argued that in drawing his conclusions, Eysenck had ignored studies that supported the value of psychotherapy and that he had misinterpreted his data (Bergin, 1971; de Charms, Levy, & Wertheimer, 1954; Luborsky, 1972). They pointed out, for example, that untreated clients might have been less disturbed than those in treatment. Further, they said, untreated clients might have received informal treatment from their medical doctors. Finally, the physicians who judged untreated clients' progress might have used less demanding criteria than the psychotherapists who rated their own clients. In fact, when some of these critics conducted their own counts of successes and failures, they concluded that psychotherapy tends to be more helpful than no treatment (Bergin, 1971).

Debate over Eysenck's findings—and the contradictory reports that followed them—highlighted several factors that make it so hard to answer the apparently simple question: Does psychotherapy work? For one thing, there is the problem of how to measure improvement in psychotherapy. Should it be measured with psychological tests, behavioral observations, interviews, or a combination of all three? And what kinds of tests should be used? Where should clients be observed (and by whom)? Should equal weight be given to interviews with clients, friends, relatives, therapists, and teachers? The fact that these various measures don't always tell the same story about improvement makes it that much more difficult for researchers to compare or combine the results of different studies and draw conclusions about the overall effectiveness of treatment (De Los Reyes & Kazdin, 2006; Krause, 2005; Sass, Twohig, & Davies, 2004).

The question of effectiveness is further complicated by the broad range of clients, therapists, and treatments involved in psychotherapy. Clients differ not only in terms of their problems but also in terms of their motivation to solve them and in the amount of stress and social support present in their environments. Therapists differ, too, not only in skill, experience, and personality but also in which of the hundreds of available treatment procedures they might select (Feltham, 2000; Wampold, 2005), and how long treatment lasts (Barkham et al., 2006). Further, differences in the nature and quality of the client-therapist relationship from one case to another can significantly alter the course of treatment, the clients' faith in the procedures, and their willingness to cooperate (Lambert & Barley, 2001; Zuroff & Blatt, 2006). Because clients' responses to psychotherapy can be influenced by all these factors, results from any particular treatment evaluation study might not tell us much about how well different therapists, using different methods, would do with other kinds of clients and problems (Kazdin, 1994b; Roth & Fonagy, 2005). Consider the example of a study in which "kindly college professors" were found to be as effective as experienced psychotherapists in helping people solve their problems (Strupp & Hadley, 1979). This result would appear relevant to the question of psychotherapy's effectiveness, but a careful reading of the study shows that the clients were college students with minor problems, not severe psychological disorders. Further, the fact that these students already had a relationship with their professors might have given the professors an edge over unfamiliar therapists (Chambless & Hollon, 1998). So the outcome of this study probably does not apply to the outcome of professional psychotherapy in general.

THINKING CRITICALLY | Are All Forms of Therapy Equally Effective?

LINKAGES (a link to Personality, p. 584)

In short, the general question of whether psychotherapy "works" is difficult or impossible to answer scientifically in a way that applies to all therapies for all disorders (Roth & Fonagy, 2005). However, the findings of several research reviews (Anderson & Lambert, 1995; Galatzer-Levy et al., 2000; Leichsenring, Rabung, & Leibing, 2004; Shadish et al., 2000; Smith, Glass, & Miller, 1980; Weisz & Jensen, 1999) have reinforced therapists' beliefs that psychotherapy does work (see Figure 16.3). In fact, most therapists believe that the theoretical approach and treatment methods they use are superior to those of other therapists (e.g., Giles, 1990; Mandelid, 2003). They can't all be right, of course, so what is going on?

FIGURE **16.3**

An Analysis of Psychotherapy Effects

These curves show the results of one large-scale analysis of the effects of psychotherapy. Notice that on average, people who received therapy for their problems were better off than 80 percent of troubled people who did not. The overall effectiveness of psychotherapy has also been confirmed in a more recent analysis of ninety treatment outcome studies (Shadish et al., 2000).

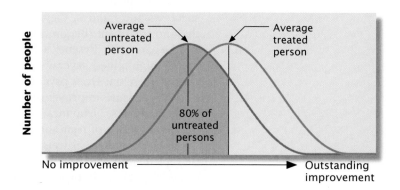

■ What am I being asked to believe or accept?

Some researchers argue that the success of psychotherapy doesn't have much to do with theories about the causes of psychopathology, or even with the specific treatment methods that are used in treatment. All approaches, they say, are equally effective. This has been called the "Dodo Bird Verdict," after the *Alice in Wonderland* character who, when called upon to judge a race, answered, "Everybody has won and all must have prizes" (Duncan, 2002; Luborsky, Singer, & Luborsky, 1975).

■ What evidence is available to support the assertion?

Some evidence does suggest that there are no significant differences in the overall effectiveness of psychodynamic, humanistic, and behavioral therapies. Statistical methods, called *meta-analysis*, that combine the results of a large number of therapy studies have shown that the three treatment approaches are associated with about the same degree of success overall (Lambert & Bergin, 1994; Luborsky et al., 2002; Luborsky, Rosenthal, & Diguer, 2003; Shadish et al., 2000; Smith et al., 1980; Wampold et al., 1997; Weisz, McCarty, & Valeri, 2006).

■ Are there alternative ways of interpreting the evidence?

It is possible, however, that evidence for the Dodo Bird Verdict is based on statistical methods that tend to make all treatments look equally effective, even if they are not. For example, a meta-analysis that averages the results of many studies might miss important differences in the impact of particular treatments for particular problems. To understand how this might happen, suppose that Therapy A works better than Therapy B in treating anxiety but that Therapy B works better than Therapy A in cases of depression. If you combined the results of treatment studies with both kinds of clients, the average effects of each therapy would be about the same, making it appear that the two treatments are about equally effective.

Differences in the effects of specific treatment procedures might also be overshadowed by the beneficial *common factors* shared by almost all forms of therapy—such as the support of the therapist, the hope and expectancy for improvement that therapy creates, and the trust that develops between client and therapist (Greenberg, Constantino, & Bruce, 2006; Kazantzis, Lampropoulos, & Deane, 2005; Vocisano et al., 2004). Therapists whose personal characteristics can motivate clients to change might promote that change no matter what specific therapeutic methods they use (Elkin, 1999; Hubble, Duncan, & Miller, 1999).

■ What additional evidence would help to evaluate the alternatives?

Debate is likely to continue over the question of whether, on average, all forms of psychotherapy are equally effective. But many researchers believe that this is the wrong question to ask. In their view, it is pointless to compare the effects of psychodynamic, humanistic, and behavioral methods in general. It is more important, they say, to address what Gordon Paul called the "ultimate question" about psychotherapy: "What treatment, by whom, is most effective for this individual with that specific problem, under what set of circumstances?" (Paul, 1969, p. 44).

■ What conclusions are most reasonable?

Statistical analyses show that various treatment approaches appear to be about equally effective overall. But this does not mean that every specific psychotherapy method works in the same way or that every psychotherapy experience will be equally beneficial. Clients entering therapy must realize that the success of their treatment can still be affected by how severe their problems are, the quality of the relationship they form with a therapist, and the appropriateness of the therapy methods chosen for their problems. ■

Like those seeking treatment, many clinical psychologists, too, are eager for more specific scientific evidence about the effectiveness of particular therapies for particular kinds of clients and disorders. These empirically oriented clinicians are concerned that all too often, a therapist's choice of therapy methods depends more heavily on personal preferences or current trends than on scientific evidence of effectiveness (Lynn, Lilienfeld, & Lohr, 2003; Nathan, Stuart, & Dolan, 2000; Norcross et al., 2005; Tavris, 2003). They believe that advocates of any treatment—whether it is object relations therapy or systematic desensitization—must demonstrate that its benefits are the result of the treatment itself and not just of the passage of time, the effects of repeatedly measuring progress, the client's motivation and personal characteristics, or other confounding factors. A movement toward this same kind of *evidence-based practice* has also appeared in the medical and dental professions (Borry, Schotsmans, & Dierickx, 2006; Niederman & Richards, 2005).

Empirically oriented psychologists also want to see evidence that the benefits of treatment are *clinically significant*. To be clinically significant, therapeutic changes must be not only measurable but also substantial enough to make treated clients' feelings and actions similar to those of people who have not experienced these clients' disorders (Kendall & Sheldrick, 2000). For example, a reduction in treated clients' scores on an anxiety test might be *statistically significant*, but if those clients do not now feel and act more like people without an anxiety disorder, the change is probably not clinically significant (see Figure 16.4). The need to demonstrate the clinical significance of treatment effects has become clearer than ever as increasingly cost-conscious clients—and their health insurance companies—decide whether, and how much, to pay for various psychotherapy services (Levant, 2005; Makeover, 2004; Nelson & Steele, 2006).

FIGURE 16.4

Clinical Significance

Evaluations of psychological treatments must consider the clinical, as well as statistical, significance of observed changes. Here, the shaded area shows the range of deviant behaviors per minute displayed at home by normal boys. The solid line shows the average rate of deviant behaviors for boys in an operant conditioning treatment for severe behavior problems. The improvement following reinforcement of appropriate behavior was not only statistically significant (compared with the pretreatment baseline) but also clinically significant, inasmuch as the once-deviant behavior came to resemble that of normal boys.

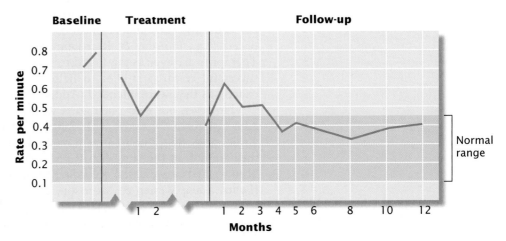

By scientific tradition, the ideal way to evaluate treatment effects is through experiments in which clients are randomly assigned to various treatments or control conditions and their progress is objectively measured over time.

FOCUS ON
RESEARCH METHODS

Which Therapies Work Best for Which Problems?

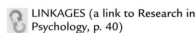
LINKAGES (a link to Research in Psychology, p. 40)

To help clinicians select treatment methods on the basis of that kind of empirical evidence, the American Psychological Association's Division of Clinical Psychology created a task force on effective psychotherapies (Task Force on Promotion and Dissemination of Psychological Procedures, 1995), now called the Committee on Science and Practice (Sanderson, 2003).

■ What was the researchers' question?

The question addressed by this task force was: Which therapies have proven themselves most effective in treating various kinds of psychological disorders?

■ How did the researchers answer the question?

Working with other empirically oriented clinical psychologists, members of this task force examined the outcomes of thousands of experiments that evaluated psychotherapy methods used to treat mental disorder, marital distress, and health-related behavior problems in adults, children, and adolescents (Baucom et al., 1998; Chambless & Ollendick, 2001; Compas et al., 1998; DeRubeis & Crits-Christoph, 1998; Foley, 2004; Kazdin & Weisz, 1998; Kendall & Chambless, 1998; Norcross, 2002).

■ What did the researchers find?

The task force found that a number of treatments—known as **empirically supported therapies**, or ESTs—have been validated by controlled experimental research (Chambless & Ollendick, 2001; DeRubeis & Crits-Christoph, 1998; Kendall & Chambless, 1998; Norcross, 2001, 2002). Table 16.4 contains some examples of these therapies. Notice that the treatments identified as effective for particular problems in adult clients are mainly behavioral, cognitive, and cognitive-behavioral methods but that certain psychodynamic therapies (e.g., interpersonal therapy and brief dynamic therapy) also made the list (Chambless & Ollendick, 2001; Svartberg, Stiles, & Seltzer, 2004).

■ What do the results mean?

The authors of the report on ESTs, as well as those who support their efforts, claim that by relying on analysis of experimental research, they have accomplished a scientific evaluation of various treatments and generated a list of methods from which clinicians and consumers can choose with confidence when dealing with specific disorders (e.g., Hunsley & Rumstein-McKean, 1999; Kendall & Chambless, 1998). Therapists are even being urged to follow the *treatment manuals* that were used in successful research studies to help them deliver empirically supported therapies exactly as they were intended (Addis, 1997; Wade, Treat, & Stuart, 1998).

However, not everyone agrees with the conclusions or recommendations of the APA task force (Norcross et al., 2005; Westen & Bradley, 2005; Westen et al., 2004). Critics note, first, that treatment methods are not necessarily discredited just because they are not on the latest list of ESTs. Some of these treatments might not yet have been studied or validated according to the efficacy criteria selected by the task force (Lantz, 2004; Westen & Morrison, 2001). These critics also have doubts about the value of some of those criteria. They point to research showing that had the task force used different outcome criteria, it might have reached different—and perhaps less

● **empirically supported therapies (ESTs)** Treatments whose effects have been validated by controlled experimental research.

TABLE **16.4**   **Some Empirically Supported Therapies**

Treatments listed as "efficacious and specific" (pronounced "effeh-KAY-shus") were shown to be superior to no treatment or to some alternative treatment in at least two experiments in which clients were randomly assigned to various treatment conditions. These experiments are called randomized clinical trials, or RCTs. Also included in this category are treatments supported by scientific outcome measures from a large number of carefully conducted case studies. Treatments listed as "probably efficacious" are supported by at least one RCT or by a smaller number of rigorously evaluated case studies. Those listed as "possibly efficacious" are supported by a mixture of data, generally from single-case studies or other nonexperimental studies (Chambless & Ollendick, 2001). More information about these ESTs is available at http://www.apa.org/divisions/div12/rev_est/. Other reviews of empirical research are aimed at identifying potentially harmful therapies (Lilienfeld, 2007).

Problem	Efficacious and Specific	Probably Efficacious	Possibly Efficacious
Major depressive disorder	Behavior therapy Cognitive-behavior therapy Interpersonal therapy	Brief dynamic therapy Social problem solving Self-control therapy	
Specific phobia	Exposure therapy	Systematic desensitization	
Agoraphobia/panic disorder	Cognitive-behavior therapy	Couples training + exposure therapy	
Generalized anxiety disorder	Cognitive-behavior therapy	Applied relaxation therapy	
Obsessive-compulsive disorder	Exposure therapy + response prevention	Cognitive therapy Family-assisted exposure therapy + response prevention + relaxation	Rational emotive behavior therapy + exposure therapy
Posttraumatic stress disorder		Exposure Stress inoculation Cognitive therapy + stress inoculation + exposure	Structured psychodynamic treatment
Schizophrenia	Behavioral family therapy	Family systems therapy Social skills training Supportive group therapy	Cognitive therapy (for delusions)
Alcohol abuse and dependence	Community reinforcement	Cue exposure therapy Behavioral marital therapy + anti-alcohol drug, disulfiram Social skills training (with inpatients)	
Opiate abuse and dependence		Behavior therapy Brief dynamic therapy Cognitive therapy	
Marital discord	Behavioral marital therapy	Insight-oriented marital therapy	

Source: Chambless & Ollendick (2001).

optimistic—conclusions about the value of some empirically supported treatments (Bradley, Heim, & Westen, 2005; Thompson-Brenner, Glass, & Westen, 2003). There is concern, too, about the wisdom of categorizing treatments as either "supported" or "unsupported." These simple either-or judgments seem reassuring, but may fail to give a complete picture of the impact of various treatments on various clients with various problems (Krause & Lutz, 2006; Westen & Bradley, 2005). Critics argue further that the list of ESTs is based on research that may not be relevant to clinicians working in the real world of clinical practice. They note that experimental studies of psychotherapy have focused mainly on relatively brief treatments for highly specific disorders, even though most clients' problems tend to be far more complex (Westen & Bradley, 2005). These studies focus, too, on the therapeutic procedures used rather than on the characteristics and interactions of therapists and clients (Cornelius-White, 2002; Garfield, 1998; Hilliard, Henry, & Strupp, 2000; Westen et al., 2004). This emphasis on procedure is a problem, critics say, because the outcome of therapy in these experiments might have been strongly affected by client-therapist factors, such as whether the random pairing of clients and therapists resulted in a match or a mismatch on certain personal characteristics. In real clinical situations, clients and therapists are not paired up at random (Goldfried & Davila, 2005; Hill, 2005; Hohman & Shear, 2002). Finally, because therapists participating in experimental research were required to follow standard treatment manuals, they were not free to adapt treatment methods, as they normally would, to the needs of particular clients (Garfield, 1998). Perhaps, say critics, when there is less experimental control over the treatment situation, all therapies really are about equally effective, as suggested by the statistical analyses of outcome research we mentioned earlier (Shadish et al., 2000; Smith et al., 1980).

In short, critics reject the EST list as a useful guide. In fact, some see it as an incomplete and ultimately misleading document (Westen & Bradley, 2005). They also worry that widespread use of treatment manuals would make psychotherapy mechanical and less effective and would discourage therapists' from developing new treatment methods (Addis & Krasnow, 2000; Beutler, 2000; Garfield, 1998).

■ What do we still need to know?

The efforts of the APA task force represent an important step in responding to Paul's (1969) "ultimate question" about psychotherapy: "What treatment, by whom, is most effective for this individual with that specific problem, under what set of circumstances?" We still have a long way to go, but empirically oriented clinical psychologists are determined to find scientific answers to this question. As suggested by critics of the EST list, the challenge now is to combine research on EST methods with research on the common factors they share and to create a picture of psychotherapy effectiveness that is based on both sets of data (Messer, 2004; Westen & Bradley, 2005). So researchers are focusing not only on the long-term efficacy of psychotherapy—in naturalistic as well as laboratory settings—but also on the role of the therapeutic relationship in promoting that efficacy (Morrison, Bradley, & Westen, 2003; Nathan, Stuart, & Dolan, 2000; Wampold, Lichtenberg, & Waehler, 2002; Westen & Morrison, 2001). Ideally, their work will speed the development of evidence-based practice in psychology (Levant, 2005; Messer, 2004), in which therapists are guided by research that is clinically relevant as well as empirically supported (Arkowitz & Lilienfeld, 2006). ■

Choosing a Therapist

We have seen that the Dodo Bird Verdict is probably incorrect, and it is certainly incomplete. Although different treatments can be equally effective in addressing some disorders, empirical research shows that for other disorders certain therapies tend to be more effective than others. For example, when differences show up in comparative studies of adult psychotherapy, they reveal a small to moderate advantage for behavioral and cognitive-behavioral methods, especially in the treatment of phobias and certain other anxiety disorders (Barrowclough et al., 2001; Butler et al., 2006; DeRubeis & Crits-Christoph, 1998; Eddy et al., 2004; Hollon, Stewart, & Strunk, 2006; Schnurr et al., 2007; Lambert & Bergin, 1994; Weisz et al., 1995), as well as bulimia nervosa, an eating disorder (Hendricks & Thompson, 2005; Wilson, 1997). The same tends to be true for child and adolescent clients (Epstein et al., 1994; Weiss & Weisz, 1995; Weisz et al., 1995).

This research provides valuable guidelines for matching treatments to disorders, but it doesn't guarantee success. The outcome of any given case will also be affected by client characteristics, therapist characteristics, and the quality of the relationship that develops between them (e.g., Hill, 2005; Sherer & Schreibman, 2005). Indeed, the client-therapist relationship plays a consistent role in the success of all forms of treatment (Constantino et al., 2005; Horvath, 2005; Karver et al., 2006; Uwe, 2005; Zuroff & Blatt, 2006). Certain people seem to be particularly effective in forming productive human relationships. Even without formal training, these people can sometimes be as helpful as professional therapists because of personal qualities that are inspiring, healing, and soothing to others (Stein & Lambert, 1995). Their presence in self-help groups may well underlie some of the success of those groups and, among professionals, may help account for the success of many kinds of formal therapy.

Before choosing a therapist and treatment approach, then, clients should keep Paul's "ultimate question" in mind. They should carefully consider (1) what treatment approach, methods, and goals they find most comfortable and appealing; (2) information about the therapist's "track record" of clinically significant success with a particular method for treating problems similar to those they face; and (3) the likelihood of forming a productive relationship with the therapist. This last consideration assumes special importance when client and therapist do not share similar cultural backgrounds.

● Cultural Factors in Psychotherapy

Imagine that after moving to an unfamiliar country to pursue your education or career, you become severely depressed. A friend there refers you to a therapist who specializes in depression. At your first session the therapist stares at you intently, touches your head for a moment, and says, "You have taken in a spirit from the river, and it is trying to get out. I will help." The therapist then begins chanting softly and appears to go into a trance. What would you think? Would you return for a second visit? If you are like most people raised in a Western culture, you probably wouldn't continue treatment, because this therapist may not share your beliefs and expectations about what is wrong with you and what should be done about it.

Similar sociocultural clashes can also occur within a particular country if clients bring to therapy a cultural or subcultural world view that is not shared by their therapist (Seeley, 2006). Suppose, for example, that a therapist suggests that a client's panic attacks are a reaction to stress, but the client is sure that they come as punishment for having offended a dead ancestor. That client may not easily accept a treatment based on the principles of stress management. Similarly, a therapist who believes that people should confront and overcome life's problems might run into trouble when treating clients whose cultural or religious training encourages calmly accepting these problems (Sundberg & Sue, 1989). In such cases, the result may be much like two people singing a duet using the same music but different lyrics (Martinez et al., 2005).

In the United States, cultural clashes may be partly to blame for the underuse of, or withdrawal from, mental health services by recent immigrants, as well as by African Americans, Asian Americans, Hispanic Americans, American Indians, and members of other minority populations (Duran et al., 2005; Gone, 2004; Neighbors et al., 2007; Sanders-Thompson et al., 2004; Wang, Lane, et al., 2005). In other words, cultural differences, including religious differences and differences in sexual orientation, can create enough miscommunication or mistrust to threaten the quality of the client-therapist relationship (Jones, Botsko, & Gorman, 2003; Wintersteen, Mensinger, & Diamond, 2005). Accordingly, major efforts are under way to ensure that cultural differences between clients and therapists do not interfere with the delivery of treatment to anyone who wants or needs it. Virtually every mental health training program in North America is seeking to recruit more students from traditionally underserved minority groups to eventually make it easier to match clients with therapists from similar cultural backgrounds (e.g., Kersting, 2004; Rogers & Molina, 2006).

In the meantime, many minority clients are likely to encounter a therapist from a differing background, so researchers have also examined the value of matching therapeutic techniques with clients' culturally based expectations and preferences (Jones et al., 2003; Li & Kim, 2004; Muñoz & Mendelson, 2005). For example, many clients from collectivist cultures—in which the emphasis is on meeting the expectations of family and friends rather than satisfying personal desires—might expect to receive instructions from a therapist about how to overcome problems. How would such clients respond to a therapist whose client-centered treatment emphasizes more individualist goals, such as being independent and taking responsibility for the direction of change? David Sue and his students have investigated the hypothesis that the collectivist values of Asian cultures would lead Asians and Asian Americans to prefer a directive, problem-solving approach over nondirective, client-centered methods. Sue (1992) found that a preference for directive treatment was highest among foreign-born Asians compared with American-born Asians and European Americans. There are still individual differences, however, so two people from the same culture may react quite differently to a treatment that group research suggests should be ideal for both of them. In Sue's (1992) study, for example, more than a third of the foreign-born Asians preferred the nondirective approach, and 28 percent of the European Americans preferred the directive approach.

Today, psychotherapists are more sensitive than ever to the cultural values of particular groups and to the difficulties that can impair intercultural communication (Ali, Liu, & Humedian, 2004; Hays & Iwamasa, 2006; Hwang, 2006; Martinez et al., 2005). Some U.S. states now require clinical and counseling psychologists to complete courses or gain supervised experience focused on the role of cultural factors in therapy before being licensed. This training helps clinicians appreciate, for example, that it is considered impolite in some cultures to make eye contact with a stranger. Having that information makes it easier for them to recognize that clients from those cultures are not necessarily depressed, lacking in self-esteem, or inappropriately submissive just

Preparing for Therapy Special pretreatment orientation programs may be offered to clients who, because of sociocultural factors, are unfamiliar with the rules and procedures of psychotherapy. These programs provide a preview of what psychotherapy is, how it can help, and what the client is expected to do to make it more effective (Reis & Brown, 2006).

because they look at the floor during an interview. Graduate students are receiving similar training and practical experience as part of their course work in clinical or counseling psychology (Kersting, 2004; Smith, Constantine, et al., 2006).

There is no guarantee that cultural sensitivity training will improve treatment results (Ramirez et al., 1996; Shin et al., 2005), but there is some evidence that it can help (e.g., Constantine, 2002; Razali, Aminah, & Umeed, 2002). Although it is unrealistic to expect all therapists to be equally effective with clients of every ethnic or religious background, cultural sensitivity training offers a way to improve their *cultural competence*, an extension of Carl Rogers's concept of empathy. When therapists appreciate the client's view of the world, it is easier for them to set goals that are in harmony with that view (Dyche & Zayas, 2001; Pedersen & Draguns, 2002; Stuart, 2004). Minimizing the chances of cultural misunderstanding and miscommunication is one of the many ethical obligations that therapists assume whenever they work with a client. Let's consider some others.

● Rules and Rights in the Therapeutic Relationship

Treatment can be an intensely emotional experience, and the relationship established with a therapist can profoundly affect a client's life. Professional ethics and common sense require the therapist to ensure that this relationship does not harm the client. For example, the American Psychological Association's *Ethical Principles of Psychologists and Code of Conduct* forbids a sexual relationship between therapist and client—during treatment and for at least two years afterward—because of the severe harm it can cause the client (American Psychological Association, 2002b; Behnke, 2004).

These same ethical standards require therapists, with a few exceptions, to keep strictly confidential everything a client says in therapy. Confidentiality is one of the most important features of a successful therapeutic relationship, because it allows the client to discuss unpleasant or embarrassing feelings, behaviors, or events without fear that the therapist might disclose this information to others. Professionals sometimes consult with one another about their clients, but they do not identify clients by name, and they do not reveal information to outsiders (even to members of the client's family) without the client's consent. The APA's code of ethics also includes standards for protecting confidentiality for the growing number of clients who seek psychological services via *telehealth* or *e-health* channels, which include telephone, videophone, e-mail, or other Internet links (APA, 2002b; Barnett & Scheetz, 2003; Christensen, Griffiths, & Jorm, 2004; Mohr, Hart, et al., 2005; Ruskin et al., 2004). One of these standards, for example, requires therapists to inform clients that others might be able to gain access to their e-mail messages and that no formal client-therapist relationship exists in e-mail exchanges.

Professional rules about confidentiality are backed up in most U.S. states by laws recognizing that information revealed in therapy—like information given to a priest, a lawyer, or a physician—is privileged communication. In 1996, a U.S. Supreme Court ruling also established psychotherapist-client privilege in the federal courts (DeBell & Jones, 1997; Knapp & VandeCreek, 1997). This means that by asserting *privilege*, a therapist can refuse, even in court, to answer questions about a client or to provide personal notes or tape recordings from therapy sessions (Kaplan, 2005). The law may require a therapist to violate confidentiality only under special circumstances, including those in which: (1) a client is so severely disturbed or suicidal that hospitalization is needed, (2) a client uses his or her mental condition and history of therapy as part of his or her defense in a civil or criminal trial, (3) the therapist must defend against a client's charge of malpractice, (4) a client reveals information about sexual or physical abuse of a child, and (5) the therapist believes a client may commit a violent act against a specific person.

This last condition poses a dilemma: Suppose a client says, "Someday I'm going to kill that brother of mine!" Should the therapist consider this a serious threat and

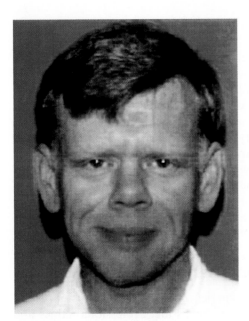

Rights of the Mentally Ill In 1996, after years of odd behavior—including vague threats against government officials and claims that the government was spying on him through TV satellite dishes—Russell Eugene Weston, Jr., was diagnosed with paranoid schizophrenia. He was hospitalized for seven weeks but had to be released when doctors determined that he was not a threat to himself or others as long as he took his prescribed medication. He failed to do so, however, and in July of 1998, Weston killed two police officers during an armed rampage at the U.S. Capitol Building. Cases such as his are frustrating to mental health professionals whose decisions about hospitalization must balance the rights of mental patients against those of the public.

warn the brother? In most cases, there is no real danger, but there have been tragic exceptions. For example, Prosenjit Poddar, a graduate student receiving therapy at the University of California at Berkeley in 1969, revealed his intention to kill Tatiana Tarasoff, a young woman whom he had dated the previous year but who later rejected him. The therapist took the threat seriously, consulted his supervisor, and asked the campus police to take Mr. Poddar to a hospital. They did not do so, however, and neither Ms. Tarasoff nor her parents were warned about the possible danger (Ewing & McCann, 2006). After dropping out of therapy, the client killed Tarasoff, whose parents later sued the university, the campus police, and the therapist. They won their case, thus setting an important precedent (Yufik, 2005). Several U.S. states now have laws that make a therapist liable for failing to take steps to protect those who are threatened with violence by the therapist's clients (Bersoff, 1999). Other states allow therapists more discretion in warning or protecting potential victims (Stromberg, Schneider, & Joondeph, 1993).

In the United States, people are protected from being casually committed to mental hospitals (Johnson, 2004). Federal court decisions have given clients threatened with commitment the right to have written notice; an opportunity to prepare a defense with the help of an attorney; a court hearing, with a jury if desired; and the right to take the Fifth Amendment to avoid self-incrimination. Furthermore, before people can be forcibly committed, the state must provide "clear and convincing" evidence that they are not only mentally ill but also gravely disabled or an "imminent danger" to themselves or others. Most states now require a periodic review of every committed person's records to determine whether release is appropriate.

While hospitalized, patients have the right to receive treatment, but they also have the right to refuse certain forms of treatment (Stromberg et al., 1988). These rules are designed to protect hospitalized mental patients from abuse, neglect, or exploitation, but they can also create difficulties and dangers. Consider Russell Eugene Weston, Jr., a former mental patient who was hospitalized after being charged with the murders of two police officers in 1998. Facing a possible death penalty but judged mentally incompetent to stand trial, he asserted his right to refuse drug treatment that would make him competent. After a long legal battle, Weston was forced to take medication. Prosecutors successfully argued that the right to refuse treatment does not extend to hospitalized patients who pose a danger to themselves or others (Manahan, 2004).

Hospitalized patients who do not pose these dangers—including those whose dangerous impulses are being suppressed by drug treatment—have the right to be subjected to minimal restriction of their freedom (Bell, 2005). Accordingly, they are released from mental hospitals, usually with a supply of medication that they are to take on their own. Unfortunately, not all these patients follow doctors' orders. Like Weston, Andrew Goldstein was not considered dangerous as long as he took his antipsychotic medication, but after being released from a New York City mental hospital in December 1998, he stopped doing so. About two weeks later, Goldstein pushed Kendra Webdale to her death under the wheels of a subway train (Perlin, 2003). Cases such as these put the staff at mental health facilities in a bind—they worry about being sued if they keep patients unnecessarily confined *or* if someone is harmed by a patient they have released too soon. In an effort to strike a balance between the rights of mental patients and those of the public, several states now have laws requiring outpatient treatment for people who are dangerous when not medicated. The New York Statute is known as Kendra's Law (Appelbaum, 2005).

Biological Treatments

Drugs that can ease the symptoms of psychological disorders are the latest and most effective in a long line of biological treatments based on the idea that psychological problems have physical causes. Hippocrates, a physician of ancient Greece, was

Hospital Restraints Here are examples of the chains, straitjackets, belts, and covered bathtubs that were used to restrain disruptive patients in North American and European mental hospitals in the 1800s and well into the 1900s. These devices were gentle compared with some of the methods endorsed in the late 1700s by Benjamin Rush. Known as the "father of American psychiatry," Rush advocated curing patients by frightening or disorienting them—for example, by placing them in a coffinlike box, which was then briefly immersed in water.

among the first to propose this idea, and the treatments he prescribed included rest, special diets, laxatives, and abstinence from alcohol or sex. In the mental hospitals of Europe and North America during the sixteenth through eighteenth centuries, treatment of psychological disorders was based in part on Hippocrates' methods and consisted mainly of physical restraints, laxative purges, draining of "excess" blood, and induced vomiting. Cold baths, hunger, and other physical discomforts were also used in efforts to shock patients back to normality (Jones, 1923). Even as recently as the mid-1900s, physicians treated most forms of psychological disorder by means of brain surgery or electric shock.

● Psychosurgery

Psychosurgery involves the destruction of brain tissue for the purpose of treating mental disorder. Among the first to try these procedures was a Portuguese neurosurgeon named António Egas Moniz. In 1935 he developed a technique, called *prefrontal lobotomy,* in which small holes are drilled in the forward portion of the skull and a sharp instrument is inserted and moved from side to side to cut connections between the prefrontal cortex and the rest of the brain (Freeman & Watts, 1942; Moniz, 1948). The theory was that emotional reactions in disturbed people become exaggerated due to neural processes in the frontal lobes and that the lobotomy disrupts these processes. During the 1940s and 1950s, psychosurgery became almost routine in the treatment of schizophrenia, depression, anxiety, aggressiveness, and obsessive-compulsive disorder (Valenstein, 1980). Unfortunately, brain surgery is risky, and sometimes fatal; its benefits are uncertain; and its side effects and complications, including epilepsy, are irreversible (Balon, 2004; Martin et al., 2001; Rueck, Andreewitch, & Flyckt, 2003). Today, psychosurgery is performed only in rare cases in which all else has failed, and—guided by brain imaging techniques—it focuses on much smaller brain areas than those involved in lobotomies (Anderson & Booker, 2006; Dougherty et al., 2002; Feldman & Goodrich, 2001).

● Electroconvulsive Therapy

In the 1930s, a Hungarian physician named Ladislaus Von Meduna used a drug to induce convulsions in schizophrenics. He believed—incorrectly—that because schizophrenia and epilepsy rarely occur in the same person, epileptic-like seizures might

psychosurgery Surgical procedures that destroy tissue in small regions of the brain in an effort to treat psychological disorders.

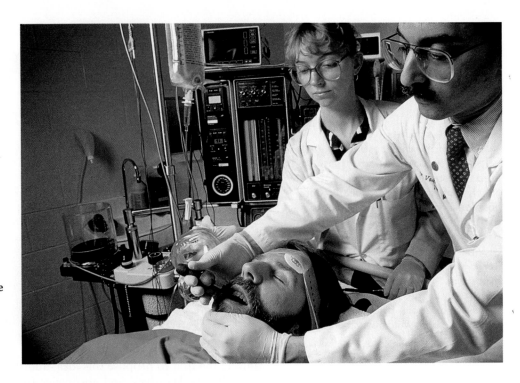

Electroconvulsive Therapy Estimates of the number of people receiving ECT each year in the United States range from 30,000 to over 100,000 (Hermann et al., 1995; Mathew, Amiel, & Sackeim, 2005). A survey in the United Kingdom suggests that about 12,000 patients a year are receiving ECT (U.K. Statistical Bulletin, 1999). Because of its dramatic and potentially dangerous nature, the use of ECT remains controversial (Breggin, 1997). Critics want it outlawed, but proponents say the benefits of ECT for certain patients outweigh its potential costs.

combat schizophrenia. In 1938, Italian physicians Ugo Cerletti and Lucio Bini created seizures by passing an electric current through schizophrenics' brains. During the next twenty years or so, this procedure, called **electroconvulsive therapy (ECT)**, became a routine treatment for schizophrenia, depression, and sometimes mania. Although many patients improved, they often relapsed. The benefits of ECT also had to be weighed against side effects such as memory loss, confusion, speech disorders, and in some cases, death due to cardiac arrest (Lickey & Gordon, 1991; Shiwach, Reid, & Carmody, 2001). To make ECT safer, patients are now given an anesthetic so that they are unconscious before the shock is delivered, along with a muscle relaxant to prevent bone fractures during convulsions. Also, the shock now lasts only about half a second and is usually delivered to only one side of the brain (Sackeim et al., 2000). Finally, in contrast to the dozens of treatments administered decades ago, patients now receive only about six to twelve shocks, one approximately every two days (Fink, 1999).

The use of ECT has declined since the 1950s, but it is still performed more frequently in the United States than coronary bypass operations, appendectomies, and tonsillectomies (Mathew, Amiel, & Sackeim, 2005). It is administered mainly to patients suffering severe depression (and occasionally to manic patients) who do not respond to drug treatments (Daly et al., 2001; de Macedo-Soares et al., 2005; Rasmussen, 2003). ECT can be effective in some of these cases—especially when followed up with medication—and it does not appear to cause brain damage, even when administered repeatedly (e.g., Anghelescu et al., 2001; Dwork et al., 2004; Kellner et al., 2005, 2006; Sackeim et al., 2001). No one knows for sure how and why ECT works (Greenberg & Kellner, 2005; Rudorfer, Henry, & Sackeim, 1997), but the fact that it helps some patients has led ECT researchers to seek even safer methods of inducing seizures. Among the techniques being investigated are *magnetic seizure therapy (MST)*, which creates seizures with timed pulses of magnetic energy (Lisanby, 2004), and a related, but less intense procedure called *repetitive transcranial magnetic stimulation (rTMS)* (Couturier, 2005; Schutter, 2005). *Deep brain stimulation (DBS)* does not cause seizures, but requires the placement of electrodes in the brain to provide continuous pulses of electricity to particular target area. Some researchers suggest that DBS may be of value in severe cases of depression and obsessive-compulsive disorder that are unresponsive to any other treatments (Hardesty & Sackeim, 2007).

■● Psychoactive Drugs

The use of psychosurgery and ECT declined after the 1950s, not only because of their complications and general distastefulness but also because *psychoactive drugs* had begun to emerge as more convenient and effective treatment alternatives. These drugs are now the most common biological treatment for all forms of psychological disorder. In the chapters on biological aspects of psychology and on consciousness, we discuss how psychoactive drugs affect neurotransmitter systems and consciousness. Here, we describe how drugs are used to combat schizophrenia, depression, mania, and anxiety.

●**Neuroleptics**   One group of drugs, called **neuroleptics** or *antipsychotics*, dramatically reduces the intensity of psychotic symptoms such as hallucinations, delusions, paranoid suspiciousness, disordered thinking, and confused speech in many mental patients, especially those with schizophrenia. The most widely used antipsychotic drugs are the *phenothiazines* (pronounced "fee-noh-THIGH-uh-zeens"), of which the first, *chlorpromazine* (marketed as *Thorazine* in the United States and as *Largactil* in Canada and the United Kingdom), has been especially popular. Another neuroleptic, *haloperidol* (*Haldol*), is about as effective as the phenothiazines, but it creates less sedation (Julien, 2005). Patients who do not respond to one type of neuroleptic may respond to the other (Davis, Chen, & Glick, 2003). Between 60 and 70 percent of patients receiving these drugs show improvement, though fewer than 30 percent respond well enough to live successfully on their own (Freedman, 2003).

Neuroleptics also have side effects ranging from dry mouth and dizziness to symptoms similar to those of Parkinson's disease, including muscle rigidity, restlessness, tremors, and slowed movement. Some of these side effects can be treated with medication, but at least 25 percent of patients who take chlorpromazine or haloperidol for several years develop an irreversible movement disorder called *tardive dyskinesia (TD)*, which causes uncontrollable, repetitive actions, often including twitching of the face and flailing of the arms and legs, and thrusting of the tongue (Miller, McEvoy, et al., 2005).

Among a newer generation of antipsychotic drugs (also called *atypical neuroleptics*) is *clozapine* (*Clozaril*), which has effects like those of the phenothiazines but is less likely to cause movement disorders (Louzá & Bassit, 2005; Rochon et al., 2005). Although no more effective overall than the phenothiazines, clozapine has helped many patients who did not respond to the phenothiazines or haloperidol (Green & Patel, 1996; Rabinowitz et al., 2001). Unfortunately, taking clozapine carries a slight risk of developing a fatal blood disease called *agranulocytosis* (Ginsberg, 2006). Weekly blood tests to detect early signs of this disease greatly increase the cost of using this drug.

Several other atypical neuroleptics have been introduced lately, including *risperidone* (*Risperdal*), *olanzapine* (*Zyprexa*), *quetiapine* (*Seroquel*), *ziprasidone* (*Geodon*), and most recently, *aripiprazole* (*Abilify*). These medications are expensive, but they have fewer side effects than clozapine, and they do not cause agranulocytosis (Correll, Leucht, & Kane, 2004). Like clozapine, they also appear to reduce the "negative" symptoms of schizophrenia, such as lack of emotion, social withdrawal, and reduced speech (e.g., Fleischhacker & Widschwendter, 2006; Kapur, Sridhar & Remington, 2004; Potkin et al., 2003). There is some doubt, though, as to whether these newest atypical neuroleptics are significantly more effective than older drugs (Matza, Baker, & Revicki, 2005), partly because 60 to 80 percent of patients may stop taking them due to weight gain, nervous tics, and other bothersome side effects (Lieberman et al., 2005; Swartz et al., 2007).

●**Antidepressants**   Soon after antipsychotic drugs appeared, they were joined by **antidepressants**, a class of drugs that is now the most widely prescribed treatment for depression (National Institute for Clinical Excellence, 2004; Olfson et al., 2002).

● **electroconvulsive therapy (ECT)**
Brief electrical shock administered to the brain, usually to reduce depression that does not respond to drug treatments.

● **neuroleptics**   Drugs that alleviate the symptoms of severe disorders such as schizophrenia.

● **antidepressants**   Drugs that relieve depression.

Although these drugs have almost immediate effects on neurotransmitters (usually increasing the availability of serotonin or norepinephrine in the brain), their effects on depressive symptoms do not appear for a week or two and maximum effects may take even longer (Quitkin et al., 2003; Taylor et al., 2006). The fact that these drugs affect specific neurotransmitters is consistent with some theories about the biology of depression discussed in the chapter on psychological disorders, although the time lag suggests that the effects occur through a long-term compensatory process in the nervous system.

There are several classes of antidepressant drugs. The *monoamine oxidase inhibitors (MAOIs)* are used to treat many cases of depression, especially clients who also experience anxiety and panic (Julien, 2005). The *tricyclic antidepressants (TCAs)* are another popular class of antidepressants. The TCAs have been prescribed more frequently than MAOI drugs because they seem to work somewhat better and have fewer side effects. However, overdoses of TCAs can be fatal, as can taking TCAs and drinking alcohol at the same time (Nutt, 2005a). Still, if side effects are controlled, tricyclics can be effective in treating depression and can also reduce the severity of panic attacks in some cases of panic disorder.

Today, the most popular medications for depression are those that affect the neurotransmitter *serotonin*. The most prominent drug in this group is *fluoxetine (Prozac)*, which after its introduction in 1986, quickly became the most widely used antidepressant in the United States (Brambilla et al., 2005). Its popularity is due to the fact that it is as effective as older antidepressants and, in most cases, has milder side effects—mainly weight gain, sexual dysfunction, and gastrointestinal problems (Nutt, 2005a; Patten et al., 2005). An improved version of Prozac, containing a purer active ingredient called *R-fluoxetine*, has now been developed (Norman & Olver, 2004). Other, even newer antidepressants, including *venlafaxine (Effexor), nefazodone (Serzone), bupropion (Wellbutrin), escitalopram (Lexapro)*, and *duloxetine (Cymbalta)*, are also now on the market (Brambilla et al., 2005; Hirschfeld & Vornik, 2004; Zimmerman, Posternak, et al., 2005).

About 50 to 60 percent of patients who take antidepressant drugs experience improved mood, greater physical activity, increased appetite, and better sleep (Hollon, Thase, & Markowitz, 2002). This degree of improvement is seen in only 10 to 20 percent of the most severe cases of psychotic depression, however (Agency for Healthcare Research and Quality, 1999; U.S. Surgeon General, 1999). It has long been assumed that these results were due to the drugs' active ingredients, but there is now some doubt about this assumption. An analysis of clinical trial data submitted to the U.S. Food and Drug Administration by the makers of six widely prescribed antidepressant drugs showed that in 57 percent of the trials, antidepressant drugs did only a little better than placebo medication ("sugar pills") at relieving depression (Kirsch et al., 2002). Defenders of antidepressant medications argue that even relatively small effects are better than none (e.g., Thase, 2002), whereas critics contend that those effects are too small to matter (e.g., Moncrieff & Kirsch, 2005; Wampold et al., 2005).

● **Lithium and Anticonvulsants** In 1949, J. F. Cade discovered that a mineral salt of the element *lithium*, when taken regularly, could prevent the mania associated with bipolar disorders in some patients (Schou, 2001). In fact, for 30 to 50 percent of patients with bipolar disorder, lithium is effective in preventing both manic and depressive episodes, thereby earning its label as a *mood stabilizer* (Baldessarini & Tondo, 2000; Geddes et al., 2004; Manji, Bowden, & Belmaker, 2000). Without lithium, the typical bipolar patient has a manic episode about every fourteen months and a depressive episode about every seventeen months (Lickey & Gordon, 1991). With lithium, attacks of mania occur as rarely as every nine years (Bowden, 2000; Geddes et al., 2004). The lithium dosage must be exact and carefully controlled, however, because taking too much can cause nausea, vomiting, tremor, fatigue, slurred speech, and, if the overdose is severe, coma or death

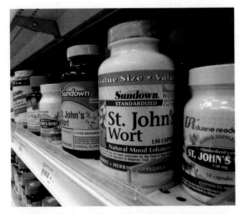

A Natural Cure? An herbal remedy from the plant called *Saint John's wort* has become a popular nonprescription treatment for depression. One of its active ingredients, *hypericin*, is thought to affect serotonin much as Prozac does. Double-blind, placebo-controlled studies have shown Saint John's wort to be as effective as Prozac for depression (e.g., Hammerness, Basch, & Ulbricht, 2003; Hypericum Depression Trial Study Group, 2002; Szegedi et al., 2005). The design of some of these studies has been questioned, however (e.g., Spira, 2001), so final conclusions about the safety and effectiveness of Saint John's wort must await the results of further research.

(Johnson, 2002). Further, lithium is not useful for treating a manic episode in progress because, as in the case of antidepressants, it takes a week or two of regular use before its effects are seen. So, as with the antidepressants, lithium's effects probably occur through some form of long-term adaptation as the nervous system adjusts to the presence of the drug. Combining lithium with other mood-stabilizing drugs, such as carbamazepine, has shown enhanced benefits but also more adverse side effects (Baethge et al., 2005).

In recent years, anticonvulsant drugs such as *divalproex* and *lamotrigine* (*Epival/Depakote*; *Lamictal*) have been used as an alternative to lithium in treating mania (e.g., Daban et al., 2006; Delbello et al., 2006). Compared with lithium, these drugs cause fewer side effects, are less dangerous at higher doses, and are easier to regulate (Bowden, 2000, 2003; Hirschfeld et al., 1999). However, their long-term benefits in reducing mania and the risk of suicide are not as well established, so lithium is still considered the treatment of choice against which other drugs are measured (Calabrese et al., 2005; Capriani et al., 2005; McAllister-Williams, 2006).

●**Anxiolytics** During the 1950s, a new class of drugs called *tranquilizers* was shown to reduce mental and physical tension and other symptoms of anxiety. The first of these drugs, called *meprobamate* (*Miltown* or *Equanil*), acts somewhat like barbiturates, meaning that overdoses can be fatal (Allen, Greenblatt, & Noel, 1977). Newer tranquilizers, known as *benzodiazepines*—such as *chlordiazepoxide* (*Librium*) and *diazepam (Valium)*—do not pose this danger and have become the worldwide drug treatment of choice for anxiety (Stevens & Pollack, 2005). Today, these and other anti-anxiety drugs, now called **anxiolytics** (pronounced "ang-zee-oh-LIT-iks"), continue to be the most widely prescribed of all legal drugs (Stevens & Pollack, 2005).

Anxiolytics have an immediate calming effect and are quite useful in reducing anxiety, including in cases of generalized anxiety disorder and posttraumatic stress disorder. One of the newest of the benzodiazepines, *alprazolam (Xanax)*, has also become especially popular for the treatment of panic disorder and agoraphobia (Verster & Volkerts, 2004). Another benzodiazepine, *clonazepam (Klonopin)*, is also being used, alone or in combination with other anxiolytics, in the treatment of anxiety ranging from phobias to panic disorder. But benzodiazepines can have bothersome side effects such as sleepiness, lightheadedness, and impaired psychomotor and mental functioning. Combining these drugs with alcohol can have fatal consequences, and continued use can lead to tolerance and physical dependence (Chouinard, 2004). Furthermore, after heavy or long-term use, attempts to stop taking benzodiazepines, particularly if the change is sudden, can result in severe withdrawal symptoms, including seizures and a return of anxiety more intense than the patient had originally experienced (Lemoine et al., 2006; Rickels et al., 1993).

An anxiolytic called *buspirone (BuSpar)* provides an alternative anxiety treatment that eliminates some of these problems, but it acts more slowly. As with the antidepressants, buspirone's effects do not occur for days or weeks after treatment begins. As a result, many patients stop taking it because they think it has no effect other than dizziness, headache, and nervousness (Stahl, 2002; Wagner et al., 2003). Yet buspirone can ultimately equal benzodiazepines in reducing generalized anxiety (Gorman, 2003; Rickels & Rynn, 2002). Further, it does not seem to promote dependence, has fewer side effects than the benzodiazepines, and does not interact dangerously with alcohol.

Because depression often accompanies anxiety, antidepressant drugs such as fluoxetine (Prozac), paroxetine (Paxil), clomipramine (Anafranil), fluvoxamine (Luvox), and sertraline (Zoloft) are also used in treating anxiety-related problems such as panic disorder, social phobia, obsessive-compulsive disorder, and posttraumatic stress disorder (e.g., Gorman, 2003; Julien, 2005; Nutt, 2005b; Rickels et al., 2003). Table 16.5 lists the effects and side effects of the psychoactive drugs we have described.

anxiolytics Drugs that reduce feelings of anxiety.

TABLE 16.5   A Sampling of Psychoactive Drugs Used for Treating Psychological Disorders

Psychoactive drugs have been successful in dramatically reducing the symptoms of many psychological disorders. Critics point out that drugs can have troublesome side effects, however, and they may create dependence, especially after years of use (e.g., Breggin, 1997). They note, too, that drugs do not "cure" mental disorders (National Institute of Mental Health, 1995), that their effects are not always strong (Kirsch et al., 2002), and that temporary symptom relief may make some patients less likely to seek a permanent solution to their psychological problems.

For Schizophrenia: Neuroleptics (Antipsychotics)

Chemical Name	Trade Name	Effects and Side Effects
Chlorpromazine	Thorazine	Reduce hallucinations, delusions, incoherence, jumbled thought processes; cause movement-disorder side effects, including tardive dyskinesia
Haloperidol	Haldol	
Clozapine	Clozaril	Reduces psychotic symptoms; causes no movement disorders, but raises risk of serious blood disease
Risperidone	Risperdal	Reduces positive and negative psychotic symptoms without risk of blood disease
Ziprasidone	Geodon	Reduces positive and negative psychotic symptoms without causing weight gain
Aripiprazole	Abilify	Reduces positive and negative psychotic symptoms without weight gain and with few side effects

For Mood Disorders: Antidepressants and Mood Elevators

Tricyclics

Imipramine	Tofranil	Act as antidepressants, but also have antipanic action; cause sleepiness and other moderate side effects; potentially dangerous if taken with alcohol
Amitriptyline	Elavil, Amitid	

Other Antidepressants

Fluoxetine	Prozac	Have antidepressant, antipanic, and anti-obsessive action
Clomipramine	Anafranil	
Fluvoxamine	Luvox	
Sertraline	Zoloft	
Escitalopram	Lexapro	

Other Drugs

Lithium carbonate	Carbolith, Lithizine	Calms mania; reduces mood swings of bipolar disorder; overdose harmful, potentially deadly
Divalproex	Depakote	Is effective against mania, with fewer side effects
Lamotrigine	Lamictal	Is effective in delaying relapse in bipolar disorder; most benefits associated with depression

For Anxiety Disorders: Anxiolytics

Benzodiazepines

Chlordiazepoxide	Librium	Act as potent anxiolytics for generalized anxiety, panic, stress; extended use may cause physical dependence and withdrawal syndrome if abruptly discontinued
Diazepam	Valium	
Alprazolam	Xanax	Also has antidepressant effects; often used in agoraphobia (has high dependence potential)
Clonazepam	Klonopin	Often used in combination with other anxiolytics for panic disorder

Other Anti-anxiety Agents

Buspirone	BuSpar	Has slow-acting anti-anxiety action; no known dependence problems

in review Biological Treatments for Psychological Disorders

Method	Typical Disorders Treated	Possible Side Effects	Mechanism of Action
Electroconvulsive therapy (ECT)	Severe depression	Temporary confusion, memory loss	Uncertain
Psychosurgery	Schizophrenia, severe depression, obsessive-compulsive disorder	Listlessness, overemotionality, epilepsy	Uncertain
Psychoactive drugs	Anxiety disorders, depression, obsessive-compulsive disorder, mania, schizophrenia	Variable, depending on drug used: movement disorders, physical dependence	Alteration of neurotransmitter systems in the brain

● **Human Diversity and Drug Treatment** Drug treatments are designed to benefit everyone in the same way ("In Review: Biological Treatments for Psychological Disorders" summarizes our discussion of drugs and other biological treatments), but it turns out that the same psychoactive drug dose can have significantly different effects in people from various ethnic groups and in men versus women (e.g., Esel et al., 2005; Seeman, 2004). For example, compared with Asians, Caucasians must take significantly higher doses of the benzodiazepines, haloperidol, clozapine, lithium, and possibly the tricyclic antidepressants in order to obtain equally beneficial effects (Lin & Poland, 1995; Matsuda et al., 1996). In addition, African Americans may show a faster response to tricyclic antidepressants than European Americans and may respond to lower doses of lithium (Strickland et al., 1991). There is also some evidence that compared with European Americans or African Americans, Hispanic Americans require lower doses of antipsychotic drugs to get the same benefits (Ruiz et al., 1999). Some of these ethnic differences are thought to be related to genetically regulated differences in drug metabolism, whereas others may be due to dietary practices.

Males and females may respond in about the same way to tricyclic antidepressants (Wohlfarth et al., 2004), but women may maintain higher blood levels of these and other therapeutic psychoactive drugs and may show better response to neuroleptics (Hildebrandt et al., 2003; Salokangas, 2004). They also may be more vulnerable to adverse effects such as tardive dyskinesia (Yonkers et al., 1992). These gender differences in drug response appear less related to estrogen than to other hormonal or body-composition differences between men and women, such as the ratio of body fat to muscle (Salokangas, 2004). Continued research on these and other dimensions of human diversity will undoubtedly lead to more effective and safer drug treatments (Thompson & Pollack, 2001).

▇▇ ● Evaluating Psychoactive Drug Treatments

Despite the widespread success of psychoactive drugs in the treatment of psychological disorders, critics point out several problems with them. First, even if a disorder has physical components, drugs may mask the problem without curing it. This masking effect is desirable in treating otherwise incurable physical conditions such as diabetes, but it may divert attention from potentially effective nondrug approaches to psychological problems. So although anti-anxiety drugs may be an aid to psychotherapy, these drugs alone cannot teach people to cope with the source of their anxiety. Critics are concerned that psychiatrists, and especially general practitioners, rely too heavily on anxiolytics and other drugs to solve patients' psychological problems (Glenmullen, 2000). The antidepressant Prozac, for instance, is being widely prescribed—overprescribed, critics say—for problems ranging from hypersensitivity

There is widespread concern that psychiatrists, and especially general practitioners, rely too heavily on drugs to deal with psychological problems, including those of adolescents and children (Olfson et al., 2006; Zuvekas, Vitiello, & Nordquist, 2006). This trend appears due in part to drug ads that fuel consumer demand, but drugs are not always the answer. In one case, medication failed to stop a paranoid schizophrenia patient from repeatedly running away from a mental hospital, but allowing him to use a telephone at a nearby shopping mall eliminated the problem. A psychologist discovered that the man had been afraid to use "bugged" hospital phones and kept escaping to call his mother (Rabasca, 1999).

"I medicate first and ask questions later."

to criticism and fear of rejection to low self-esteem and premenstrual problems. Second, abuse of some drugs (such as the anti-anxiety benzodiazepines) can result in physical or psychological dependence. Third, drug side effects can range from minor problems, such as the thirst and dry mouth caused by some antidepressants, to movement disorders such as tardive dyskinesia caused by certain neuroleptics. The most serious of these side effects are relatively rare, but some are irreversible, and it is impossible to predict in advance who will develop them. Although a clear causal link has not been confirmed (Gibbons et al., 2005; Simon et al., 2006), recent research has led the U.S. National Institute of Mental Health (NIMH) and regulatory agencies in Canada and Britain to issue warnings about the danger of suicidal behavior in children and adolescents who are given Prozac and similar antidepressant drugs (Bridge et al., 2007; Gualtieri & Johnson, 2006; Hammad, Laughren, & Racoosin, 2006; Martinez et al., 2005; NIMH, 2004; Olfson, Marcus, & Shaffer, 2006; Whittington, Kendall, & Pilling, 2005). Warnings have also been issued about the elevated risk of death in elderly patients who are taking antipsychotic medications (U.S. Food and Drug Administration, 2005; Wang, Schneeweiss, et al., 2005). There is concern, too, about whether psychoactive drugs are as effective as they appear to be, especially in research sponsored by the drug companies that make them (Chan et al., 2004; Heres et al., 2006; Melander et al., 2003; Moncrieff & Kirsch, 2005).

● Drugs and Psychotherapy

With these issues in mind, many clinicians and clients wonder which is better, drugs or psychotherapy. Can they be effectively combined? A considerable amount of research is being conducted to address these questions.

Although occasionally a study does show that one approach or the other is more effective, there is no clear consensus. Overall, neither form of therapy is clearly superior for treating problems such as anxiety disorders and major depressive disorder (Smits, O'Cleirigh, & Otto, 2006; Thase et al., 2007). For example, large-scale studies of treatment for severe depression found that behavior therapy, cognitive-behavior therapy, and interpersonal psychotherapy can be as effective as an antidepressant drug (Butler et al., 2006; DeRubeis et al., 2005; Dimidjian et al., 2006; Hollon et al.,

2002; March et al., 2004; Nemeroff et al., 2003; Spanier et al., 1996). Cognitive-behavior therapy has also equaled drug effects in the treatment of phobias (Clark et al., 2003; Davidson et al., 2004; Otto et al., 2000; Thom, Sartory, & Jöhren, 2000), panic disorder (Klosko et al., 1990; Mitte, 2005a), generalized anxiety disorder (Gould et al., 1997; Mitte, 2005b), and obsessive-compulsive disorder (Abramowitz, 1997; Kozak, Liebowitz, & Foa, 2000). Further, the dropout rate from psychotherapy may be lower than from drug therapies (Casacalenda, Perry, & Looper, 2002; Hollon et al., 2005; Mitte, 2005b), and the benefits of many kinds of psychotherapy may last longer than those of drug therapies (e.g., Bockting et al., 2005; Hollon et al., 2002, 2006; Segal, Gemar, & Williams, 2000; Thom et al., 2000), thus making psychotherapy more cost-effective than medication in the long run (Barrett, Byford, & Knapp, 2005).

What about combining drugs and psychotherapy? Recent research suggests that doing so can sometimes be helpful (Hofmann et al., 2006; Miklowitz et al., 2007; Winston, Been, & Serby, 2005). Combined treatment is recommended in cases of bipolar disorder (Otto, Smits, & Reese, 2005) and produces slightly better results than either psychotherapy or drugs alone in people suffering from severe, long-term depression (Friedman et al., 2004; Hegerl, Plattner, & Moller, 2004). The combination of drugs and psychotherapy also has been shown to be more effective than either method alone in treating attention deficit hyperactivity disorder, obsessive-compulsive disorder, alcoholism, stammering, compulsive sexual behavior, and panic disorder (Barlow et al., 2000; Engeland, 1993; Keller et al., 2000; March et al., 2004; Roy-Byrne et al., 2005). The combined approach may be especially useful for clients who are initially too distressed to cooperate in psychotherapy. A related approach, already shown successful with clients who had been taking drugs for panic disorder and depression, is to use psychotherapy to prevent relapse and make further progress as drug treatment is discontinued (e.g., Lam et al., 2003). Preliminary evidence also suggests that a drug called D-cycloserine might be helpful in preventing the reappearance of fears being extinguished through exposure techniques or other forms of behavior therapy (Choy et al., 2007; Davis et al., 2005, 2006; Hofmann et al., 2006; Ressler et al., 2004).

However, many other studies have found little advantage in combining drugs and psychotherapy (e.g., Davidson et al., 2004; Elkin, 1994; Nemeroff et al., 2003; Spiegel & Bruce, 1997). One research team compared the effects of gradual in vivo exposure and an anti-anxiety drug (Xanax) in the treatment of agoraphobia. Clients receiving gradual exposure alone showed better short- and long-term benefits than those getting either the drug alone or a combination of the drug and gradual exposure (Echeburua et al., 1993).

Perhaps the most conservative strategy for treating most cases of anxiety and depression is to begin with cognitive or interpersonal psychotherapy (which have no major negative side effects) and then to add or switch to drug treatment if psychotherapy alone is ineffective (Jacobs et al., 2004; Schatzberg et al., 2005). Often, clients who do not respond to one method will be helped by the other (e.g., Heldt et al., 2006). Someday, research may offer better guidelines as to which clients should be treated with psychotherapy alone, medication alone, a combination of the two (Hollon et al., 2005).

LINKAGES

Biological Aspects of Psychology and the Treatment of Psychological Disorders

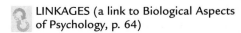

LINKAGES (a link to Biological Aspects of Psychology, p. 64)

As described in the chapter on biological aspects of psychology, human feelings, thoughts, and actions—whether normal or abnormal—are ultimately the result of biological processes, especially those involving neurotransmitters and their receptors in the brain. Because different neurotransmitters are especially prominent in particular brain regions or circuits, altering the functioning of particular neurotransmitter systems has relatively specific psychological and behavioral effects.

Let's consider some of the ways in which therapeutic psychoactive drugs affect neurotransmitters and their receptors. Some therapeutic drugs cause neurons to fire, whereas others reduce or inhibit such firing. For example, benzodiazepines (e.g., Valium and Xanax) exert their anti-anxiety effects by helping the inhibitory neurotransmitter GABA bind to receptors and thus suppress neuron firing. This increased inhibitory effect acts as a sort of braking system that slows the activity of GABA-sensitive neurons involved in the experience of anxiety. However, benzodiazepines also slow the action of all neural systems that use GABA, including those associated with motor activity and mental processing, which are spread throughout the brain. The result is the decreased motor coordination and clouded thinking that appear as benzodiazepines' side effects. Research suggests that it might soon be possible to develop drugs that will bind only to certain kinds of GABA receptors and thus greatly reduce these side effects (Gorman, 2005).

Other therapeutic drugs are receptor *antagonists* (see Figure 9.11 in the chapter on consciousness), acting to block the receptor site normally used by a particular neurotransmitter. The phenothiazines, for example, exert their antipsychotic effects by blocking receptors for dopamine, a neurotransmitter that is important for movement, as described in the chapter on biological aspects of psychology. Blocking dopamine seems to normalize the jumbled thinking of many schizophrenia patients, but it can also create severe disorders—including tardive dyskinesia—in the movement systems that are also controlled by dopamine.

Finally, some psychoactive drugs exert their therapeutic influence by increasing the amount of a neurotransmitter available to act on receptors. This effect usually occurs because the drug slows a process called *reuptake,* by which the neurotransmitter would normally return to the brain cell from which it was released. The tricyclic antidepressants, for example, operate by slowing the reuptake of norepinephrine. Prozac, Anafranil, and some other antidepressants are called *selective serotonin reuptake inhibitors (SSRIs)* because they slow the reuptake of serotonin. Others, such as Effexor, slow the reuptake of both serotonin and norepinephrine. These effects are consistent with biological theories suggesting that some cases of depression are traceable to faulty norepinephrine or serotonin systems. ■

LINKAGES (a link to Consciousness, p. 351)

Community Psychology: From Treatment to Prevention

It has long been argued that even if psychologists knew exactly how to treat every psychological problem, there would never be enough mental health professionals to help everyone who needs it (Albee, 1968). This view fostered the rise of **community psychology**, an approach whose goals are to treat people in their local communities and to work for social changes (such as lower unemployment) that may help prevent psychological disorders (Nelson & Prilleltensky, 2004).

One aspect of community psychology, the *community mental health movement*, arose during the 1960s amid growing concern that patients were not improving after years of confinement in mental hospitals. The plan was that these patients would be released from their hospitals and would receive newly available antipsychotic drugs and other mental health services in newly funded community mental health centers. This *deinstitutionalization* process did spare patients the boredom and isolation of the hospital environment, but the mental health services available in the community never matched the need for them (Leff, 2006). Some former

● **community psychology** A movement to minimize or prevent psychological disorders through changes in social systems and through community mental health programs.

Community Mental Health Efforts
Professional and nonprofessional staff members of community mental health centers provide traditional therapy and mental health education, along with walk-in facilities and hotlines for people who are suicidal or in crises because of rape or domestic violence. They also offer day treatment to former mental patients, many of whom are homeless.

hospital patients and many people whose disorders might once have sent them to mental hospitals are now living in halfway houses and other community-based facilities where they receive *psychosocial rehabilitation*. These community support services are not deigned to "cure" severe disorders, but to help troubled people to cope with their problems and develop the social and occupational skills necessary for semi-independent living (Coldwell & Bender, 2007; Cook et al., 2005). All too many others with severe psychological disorders do not receive or fail to respond to rehabilitation, and are to be found enduring the dangers of urban homelessness or of confinement in jails and prisons (Teplin et al., 2005; U.S. Department of Health and Human Services, 2001b; World Health Organization World Mental Health Survey Consortium, 2004).

Community psychology also attempts to prevent psychological disorders by addressing poverty, substandard housing, and other stressful social problems that may underlie some disorders (Tucker & Herman, 2002; Weissberg, Kumpfer, & Seligman, 2003; Xue et al., 2005). Researchers in the field of positive psychology applaud this approach, suggesting that the development of many disorders could be further minimized by teaching skills that promote mental well-being and by offering programs designed to help young people build the character strengths they need to be resilient in the face of stress (Keyes, 2007; Seligman et al., 2005; Wallace & Shapiro, 2006). Another dimension of community psychology involves detecting psychological problems in their earliest stages and keeping them from becoming worse. Examples include programs for the prevention of depression and suicide (Gillham et al., 2007; Horowitz & Garber, 2006; Lynch et al., 2005; Spence, Sheffield, & Donovan, 2005); programs such as Project Head Start that help preschoolers whose backgrounds put them at risk for school failure and delinquency (Foster et al., 2006; Reid, Webster-Stratton, & Baydar, 2004; Shaw, Dishion, et al., 2006); and efforts to identify children who are at risk for disorders due to aggressiveness, parental divorce, or being rejected or victimized at school (e.g., Frey et al., 2005; Lochman & Wells, 2004; Martinez & Forgatch, 2001). Still other interventions aim to head off anxiety disorders or schizophrenia in children and adults (McGorry et al., 2002; Rapee et al., 2005), to prevent child abuse and other domestic violence (Duggan et al., 2004; Whitaker et al., 2006), and to promote health consciousness in ethnic minority communities (Borg, 2002).

LINKAGES

As noted in the chapter on introducing psychology, all of psychology's many subfields are related to one another. Our discussion of treating psychological disorders through the use of psychoactive drugs illustrates just one way in which the topic of this chapter, the treatment of psychological disorders, is linked to the subfield of biological psychology (see the chapter on biological aspects of psychology). The Linkages diagram shows ties to two other subfields as well, and there are many more ties throughout the book. Looking for linkages among subfields will help you see how they all fit together and better appreciate the big picture that is psychology.

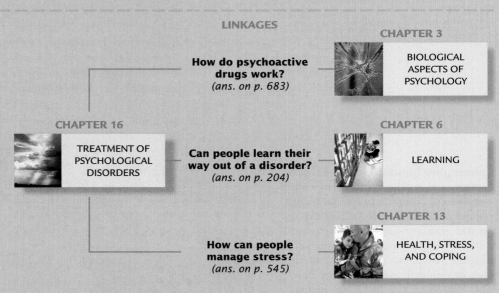

LINKAGES

How do psychoactive drugs work?
(ans. on p. 683)

CHAPTER 3
BIOLOGICAL ASPECTS OF PSYCHOLOGY

CHAPTER 16
TREATMENT OF PSYCHOLOGICAL DISORDERS

Can people learn their way out of a disorder?
(ans. on p. 204)

CHAPTER 6
LEARNING

How can people manage stress?
(ans. on p. 545)

CHAPTER 13
HEALTH, STRESS, AND COPING

SUMMARY

Psychotherapy for psychological disorders is usually based on psychodynamic, humanistic, or social-cognitive (behavioral) theories of personality and behavior disorder. Most therapists combine features of these theories in an eclectic approach. The biological approach is reflected in the use of drugs and other physical treatment methods.

Basic Features of Treatment

All forms of treatment for psychological disorders include a client; a therapist; an underlying theory of behavior disorder; a set of treatment procedures suggested by the underlying theory; and the development of a special relationship between the client and therapist, which may make it easier for improvement to occur. Therapy may be offered to inpatients and outpatients in many different settings by *psychologists, psychiatrists*, and other mental health professionals. The goal of treatment is to help people change their thinking, feelings, and behavior so that they will be happier and function better. This goal may be pursued by promoting insight into hidden causes of behavior problems, by fostering personal growth through genuine self-expression, or by helping clients learn new ways of thinking and acting.

Psychodynamic Psychotherapy

Psychodynamic psychotherapy, which began with Sigmund Freud's methods of *psychoanalysis*, seeks to help clients gain insight into unconscious conflicts and impulses and then to explore how those factors have created disorders.

Classical Psychoanalysis Exploration of the unconscious is aided by the use of free association, dream interpretation, and analysis of transference.

Contemporary Variations on Psychoanalysis Some variations on psychoanalysis focus less on the id, the unconscious,

and the past and more on helping clients harness the ego to solve problems in the present. Other forms of psychodynamic treatment retain most of Freud's principles but use a more flexible format. Object relations therapy, for example, examines the effects of early relationships with caregivers and how those relationships affect current ones.

Humanistic Psychotherapy

Humanistic (or phenomenological) psychotherapy helps clients to become more aware of discrepancies between their feelings and their behavior. According to the humanistic approach, these discrepancies are at the root of behavior disorders and can be resolved by the client once they are brought to light in the context of a genuine, trusting relationship with the therapist.

Client-Centered Therapy Therapists using Carl Rogers's *client-centered therapy*, also known as *person-centered therapy*, help mainly by adopting attitudes toward the client that express *unconditional positive regard (acceptance)*, *empathy*, and *congruence*. These attitudes create a nonjudgmental atmosphere that facilitates the client's honesty with the therapist, with himself or herself, and with others. One way of creating this atmosphere is through *reflection*.

Gestalt Therapy Therapists employing the *Gestalt therapy* of Fritz and Laura Perls use more active techniques than do Rogerian therapists, often confronting and challenging clients.

Behavior Therapy

Behavior therapy, behavior modification, and *cognitive-behavior therapy* use learning principles to reduce clients' undesirable patterns of thought and behavior and to strengthen more desirable alternatives.

Techniques for Modifying Behavior Common behavioral treatments include *systematic desensitization, flooding* and other *exposure techniques, modeling, social skills training,* and *assertiveness training.* Behavior therapists also use *positive reinforcement* (sometimes in a *token economy*), *extinction, punishment,* and *aversion conditioning* to make desirable behaviors more likely or problematic behaviors less likely.

Cognitive-Behavior Therapy Many behavior therapists employ cognitive-behavior therapy to help clients change the way they think, as well as the way they behave. Among the specific cognitive-behavior therapy methods are *rational-emotive behavior therapy (REBT)*, cognitive restructuring, stress inoculation training, and *cognitive therapy.*

Group, Family, and Couples Therapy

Therapists of all theoretical persuasions may offer therapy to several clients at once. Clients' interactions with one another can enhance the effects of treatment.

Group Therapy *Group therapy* may involve a variety of people and problems, or it may focus on particular types of clients and problems. The group format is also adopted in many self-help organizations, such as Alcoholics Anonymous.

Family and Couples Therapy *Family therapy* involves treatment of two or more individuals from the same family system. In *couples therapy*, the clients are spouses or other intimate partners. In both formats, treatment usually focuses on improving communication and other interactions among the people involved.

Evaluating Psychotherapy

There is some disagreement about exactly how to measure improvement following psychotherapy and how best to ensure that observed improvement was actually due to the treatment itself and not to some other factor. Meta-analyses have found that clients who receive psychotherapy are better off than most people who receive no treatment but that no single approach is uniformly better than all others for all clients and problems. Still, some methods appear effective enough in the treatment of particular disorders to have been listed by an American Psychological Association task force as *empirically supported therapies (ESTs)*.

Choosing a Therapist

Research is needed to discover which combinations of therapists, clients, and treatments are ideally suited to alleviating particular psychological problems. Several factors, including personal preferences, must be considered when choosing a treatment approach and a therapist.

Cultural Factors in Psychotherapy The effects of cultural differences in values and goals between therapist and client have attracted increasing attention. Efforts are under way to minimize the problems that these differences can create.

Rules and Rights in the Therapeutic Relationship Whatever the specific form of treatment, the client's rights include the right to confidentiality; the right to receive or, sometimes, to refuse treatment; and the right to protection from unnecessary confinement.

Biological Treatments

Biological treatment methods seek to relieve psychological disorders by physical rather than psychological means.

Psychosurgery *Psychosurgery* procedures once involved mainly prefrontal lobotomy; when used today, usually as a last resort, they focus on more limited areas of the brain.

Electroconvulsive Therapy In *electroconvulsive therapy (ECT)*, an electric current is passed through the patient's brain, usually in an effort to relieve severe depression.

Psychoactive Drugs Today the most prominent form of biological treatment is the prescription of psychoactive drugs, including drugs that are used to treat schizophrenia (the *neuroleptics*, or antipsychotics), mood disorders (*antidepressants, lithium*, and *anticonvulsants*), and anxiety disorders (*anxiolytics*). There appear to be significant differences among members of various ethnic groups and between men and women in the dosages of psychoactive drugs necessary to produce clinical effects.

Evaluating Psychoactive Drug Treatments Psychoactive drugs have proven impressively effective in many cases, but critics point out a number of undesirable side effects associated with these drugs, the risks of abuse, and the dangers of over-reliance on chemical approaches to human problems that might have other solutions.

Drugs and Psychotherapy So far, neither psychotherapy nor drug treatment has been found clearly superior overall for treating problems such as anxiety or depression. Combining drugs and psychotherapy may help in some cases, but their joint effect may not be any greater than the effect of either one alone.

Community Psychology: From Treatment to Prevention

The realization that there will never be enough therapists to treat everyone who needs help prompted the development of *community psychology*. Community mental health programs and efforts to prevent mental disorders are the two main elements of community psychology.

Social Cognition

17

Your view of yourself, and what you think about others, play major roles in shaping your behavior every day. In this chapter, we explore the ways in which perception, learning, emotion, and other factors affect how people think about themselves and others. We'll consider topics such as how we form first impressions, how we develop attitudes—including prejudiced attitudes—and why we may like (or love) one person and dislike another. We have organized the material as follows:

The death toll in the September 11, 2001, terrorist attacks on the United States exceeded 3,000, the largest number of people to die violently on American soil in a single day since 1862, during the U.S. Civil War. Almost all of the questions that can be asked about these attacks, and about terrorism in general, relate to human behavior. For example, what could lead people to kill themselves, along with thousands of innocent people, in the name of political or religious beliefs? Why did hundreds of New York City firefighters, police officers, emergency medical workers, and others enter the World Trade Center's burning towers to save the lives of others while risking, and some ultimately losing, their own? Why did some of the people who were fleeing the damaged buildings return to their offices after hearing an announcement telling them to do so? Is there any reason to hope that someday the hatred and distrust that brought about this disaster can be reduced or eliminated?

We may never have final answers to such questions, but some partial answers may come from **social psychology,** the scientific study of how people's thoughts and feelings influence their behavior toward others and how the behavior of others influences people's own thoughts, feelings, and behavior. In this chapter we focus on **social cognition,** the mental processes associated with the ways in which people perceive and react to other individuals and groups (Wyer, 2004). Specifically, we will examine how people think about themselves and others, how they form and change attitudes, why and how they use stereotypes to judge other people (sometimes in unfair and biased ways), and why they like and dislike other people. In the companion chapter on *social influence*, we describe how social factors affect individuals, helping to shape behaviors that range from despicable acts of aggression to inspiring acts of heroism and self-sacrifice.

Social Influences on the Self

In the chapters on human development and personality, we describe how each individual develops within a cultural context and the ways in which collectivist and individualist cultures emphasize different core values and encourage contrasting definitions of the self. In this section we highlight the processes through which people in each culture help to shape two important components of the self. The first is our **self-concept,** the beliefs we hold about who we are and what characteristics we have. The second is our **self-esteem,** the evaluations we make about how worthy we are as human beings (Crocker & Park, 2004).

Social Comparison

People spend a lot of time thinking about themselves, trying to evaluate their own perceptions, opinions, values, abilities, and the like (Mussweiler, 2003). Decades ago, Leon Festinger (1954) pointed out that self-evaluation involves two types of questions: those that can be answered by taking objective measurements and those that cannot. So you can determine your height or weight by measuring it, but how do you answer questions about your cognitive ability, social skills, athletic talent, or the quality of your relationships? Here, there are no yardsticks to act as objective measurement criteria. In these cases, we make one of two types of comparisons. If we use a **temporal comparison,** we consider the way we are now in relation to how

social psychology The study of how people's thoughts, feelings, and behavior influence, and are influenced by, the behavior of others.

social cognition Mental processes associated with people's perceptions of, and reactions to, other people.

self-concept The way one thinks of oneself.

self-esteem The evaluations people make about how worthy they are as human beings.

temporal comparison Using one's previous performance or characteristics as a basis for judging oneself in the present.

The Muhammad Ali Effect When former world heavyweight boxing champion Muhammad Ali was once asked why he did so poorly on an intelligence test, he replied, "I only said I was the greatest, not the smartest." Research in the United States and in Holland suggests that most people, like Ali, consider it more important to be moral and honest than to be smart. They also believe that they are more honest than other people. This helps to maintain self-esteem (Van Lange & Sedikides, 1998).

we were in the past (Zagefka & Brown, 2005). Using a **social comparison,** we evaluate ourselves in relation to others. So if you use others as a basis for evaluating how intelligent, athletic, interesting, or attractive you are, you are using social comparison (Buunk et al., 2005).

Who serves as your basis of comparison? Festinger said that people usually look to others who are similar to themselves. If you are curious about how good a swimmer you are, you are likely to compare yourself with the people you normally compete against, not with Olympic champions. In other words, you tend to choose swimmers at your own level of experience and ability. The categories of people to which you see yourself belonging and to which you usually compare yourself are called **reference groups.**

The performance of people in a reference group can influence your self-esteem (Seta, Seta, & McElroy, 2006). For example, if being a good swimmer is very important to you, knowing that someone in your reference group swims much faster than you do can lower your self-esteem. People use a wide variety of strategies to protect or maintain their self-esteem (Leary, 2004; Pyszczynski et al., 2004). Sometimes they choose to compare themselves with those who are not as good as they are, a strategy called *downward social comparison*. They may also engage in *upward social comparison*, comparing themselves with people who do much better (Buunk et al., 2005). Both kinds of social comparisons can make people feel better about themselves. Downward social comparisons remind them that although their performance or their lives may not be ideal, things could be far worse. The comfort provided by such reminders helps explain the popularity of television talk shows whose guests are stuck in unpleasant, dysfunctional, and even bizarre family situations. But people may also feel better after comparing themselves with those who are doing much better than they are (Buunk & Oldersma, 2001). This result occurs partly because seeing people who are better off than we are can create optimism about improving our own situation (Buunk & Oldersma, 2001). We may tell ourselves "If they can do it, so can I!"

Some people use a related tactic to maintain their self-esteem through upward social comparison. Specifically, they tell themselves that a superior performer is not similar enough to be in their reference group. They may even exaggerate the ability of the other person so that their own performance doesn't look so bad when viewed in light of such an able competitor (Mussweiler, 2003). If you can convince yourself that you lost every hole during a golf game because your opponent is almost as good as Tiger Woods, Michele Wie, or some other world-class golfer, then it is easier to believe that your performance wasn't so terrible and that you would do just fine against someone with normal athletic skills.

An unfavorable comparison of your own status with that of others can produce **relative deprivation**—the belief that no matter how much you are getting in terms of recognition, status, money, and so forth, it is less than you deserve (Brehm, Kassin, & Fein, 2005). The concept of relative deprivation explains why an actor who receives $5 million to star in a film feels abused if a costar is receiving $10 million. It also explains the far more common situation in which employees become dissatisfied when they see themselves as underpaid or underappreciated in comparison to their co-workers (Tougas et al., 2005). When large groups of people experience relative deprivation, political unrest may follow. Social and political turmoil usually begins after the members of a deprived group experience some improvement in their lives and begin to compare their circumstances with those in other groups (Worchel et al., 2000). With this improvement comes higher expectations about what they deserve. When these expectations are not met, violence may follow. A feeling among citizens of poor countries that the United States enjoys and exploits its great prosperity may have played a role in creating the hatred that led to the attack on the World Trade Center, a symbol of U.S. financial strength (Plous & Zimbardo, 2004).

● **social comparison** Using other people as a basis of comparison for evaluating oneself.

● **reference groups** Categories of people to which people compare themselves.

● **relative deprivation** The belief that, in comparison to a reference group, one is getting less than is deserved.

**FOCUS ON
RESEARCH METHODS** **Self-Esteem and the Ultimate Terror**

Why is self-esteem so important to so many people? An intriguing answer to this question comes from the *terror management theory* proposed by Jeff Greenberg, Tom Pyszczynski, and Sheldon Solomon. This theory is based on the notion that humans are the only creatures capable of thinking about the future. One result of this ability is the realization that we will all eventually die, and the sense of terror it may bring. We can't change this reality, but terror management theory suggests that humans cope with anxiety about death by developing a variety of self-protective psychological strategies, including efforts to establish and maintain high self-esteem (Pyszczynski et al., 2004; Solomon, Greenberg, & Pyszczynski, 2004).

■ What was the researchers' question?

In one series of experiments, Greenberg and his colleagues (1992) asked whether high self-esteem would, in fact, serve as a buffer against anxiety—specifically, the anxiety brought on by thoughts about death and pain.

■ How did the researchers answer the question?

About 150 students at several North American universities participated in these studies, each of which followed a similar format. The first step in each experiment was to manipulate the independent variable, in this case the participants' self-esteem. To do this, the researchers gave the students feedback on a test they had taken earlier in the semester. Half the participants received esteem-building feedback, such as that their scores indicated high intelligence or a stable personality. The other half received feedback that was neutral (i.e., neither flattering nor unflattering). Next, the students' self-esteem was measured, and these measures showed that the positive feedback actually did produce higher self-esteem than the neutral feedback. In the third phase of each experiment, the researchers manipulated a second independent variable by causing some anxiety in half of the participants in each of the two feedback groups. In one study, for example, anxiety was created by showing some students a film containing pictures of dead people and discussions of death. The others saw a film that did not arouse emotion. In two other experiments, anxiety was created by leading some of the participants to believe (falsely) that they would be receiving a mild electrical shock. Afterward, the participants' anxiety was measured by their self-reports or by monitoring galvanic skin resistance (GSR), an anxiety-related measure of perspiration.

■ What did the researchers find?

Self-reports or GSR measures revealed that participants in all three experiments were significantly less upset by an anxiety-provoking experience (the death film or the threat of shock) if they had first received esteem-building feedback about their previous test performance.

■ What do the results mean?

The researchers concluded that these results offer support for terror management theory, and specifically for the notion that self-esteem is important as a buffer against anxiety and other negative feelings. The results may help explain why the maintenance of self-esteem is such a powerful human motive (Tesser, 2001). People do not like to feel anxious, and increased self-esteem reduces most people's anxiety.

■ What do we still need to know?

Additional research by Greenberg and his associates, as well as by others, has provided additional support for terror management theory. For instance, the theory

FIGURE **17.1**

A Schema-Plus-Correction

People who see an object like this tend to use a preexisting mental representation (their schema of a square) and then correct or modify it in some way (here, with a notch).

(Cloutier, Mason, & Macrae, 2005). Consider Figure 17.1. Consistent with Gestalt principles, most people would describe it as "a square with a notch in one side," not as eight straight lines. The reason is that they interpret new information using the mental representations, or *schemas*, they already have about squares. In short, they interpret this diagram as a square with a slight modification.

Schemas about people, too, can have a significant influence on our perception of them. First of all, schemas influence what we pay attention to and what we ignore. Characteristics or events that are consistent with our schema about another person usually get more attention than those that are inconsistent with that schema. As a result, we tend to process information about the other person more quickly if it confirms our beliefs about, say, that person's gender or ethnic group than if it violates those beliefs (Smith & Queller, 2001). Second, schemas influence what we remember about others. One study demonstrated that if people thought a woman they saw in a video was a waitress, they later recalled that she had a beer with dinner and owned a TV set. If they thought she was a librarian, they remembered that she was wearing glasses and liked classical music (Cohen, 1981). Finally, schemas affect our judgment about other people's behavior. As an example, Thomas Hill and his colleagues (1989) found that participants' ratings of male and female friends' sadness were influenced not only by the friends' actual behavior but also by the participants' general schemas about whether men or women experience more sadness.

In other words, through "top-down" processing, schemas can influence—and sometimes bias—person perception in the same way in which schemas about objects can affect object perception. And just as schemas help us read sentences in which words have missing letters, they also allow us to efficiently "fill in the blanks" about people. So we don't usually ask our doctors or bus drivers to show us their credentials. Our schemas about these people lead us to perceive them as competent, confident, skilled, and experienced. And usually these perceptions are correct. It is only when our expectations are violated that we realize that schemas can create errors in our judgment about other people.

● First Impressions

The schemas we have about people act as lenses that shape our first impressions of them. Those impressions, in turn, influence both our perceptions of their behaviors

May I Help You? Schemas help us to quickly categorize people and respond appropriately to them, but they can also create narrow-mindedness and even prejudice. If this woman does not fulfill your schema—your mental representation—of how carpenters are supposed to look, you might be less likely to ask her advice on your home improvement project. One expert carpenter who manages the hardware department of a large home improvement store told us that most customers walk right past her in order to ask the advice of one of her less experienced male clerks.

Noticeable features or actions help shape our impressions of others. Those impressions may or may not be correct.

© Scott Adams/Dist. by United Feature Syndicate, Inc.

and our reactions to those behaviors. First impressions are formed quickly, usually change slowly, and typically have a long-lasting influence. No wonder first impressions are so important in the development of social relations. How do people form impressions of other people? And why are they so resistant to change?

TRY THIS ● **Forming Impressions** Think about your first impression of a close friend. It probably formed rapidly, because as mentioned earlier, existing schemas create a tendency to automatically infer a great deal about a person on the basis of limited information. One study found that people could make judgments about how trustworthy and competent a person was after seeing that person's face for only a tenth of a second (Willis & Todorov, 2006). Other attributes, such as an ethnic name, might have caused you to draw inferences about your friend's religion, food preferences, or temperament. Clothing or hairstyle might have led you to make assumptions about your friend's political views or taste in music. These inferences and assumptions may or may not have been accurate. How many turned out to be true in your friend's case?

One schema has a particularly strong influence on our first impressions: We tend to assume that people we meet will have attitudes and values similar to our own (Hoyle, 1993). So all else being equal, we are inclined to like other people. However, it doesn't take much negative information to change our minds. The main reason for this is that most of us don't expect other people to act negatively toward us. When unexpectedly negative behaviors do occur, they capture our attention and lead us to believe that these behaviors reflect something negative about the other person (Taylor, Peplau, & Sears, 2006). For example, we know that there are many reasons why people might be nice to us—because they are kind, because they like our best friends, or because they want to sell us a car. But if they do something negative—such as insult us or steal our lecture notes—the most likely explanation is that they are unfriendly or have other undesirable personality traits. In other words, negative behavior carries more weight than positive behavior in shaping first impressions (Smith & Mackie, 2000).

● **Lasting Impressions** Does your friend seem the same today as when you first met? First impressions can change, but the process is usually slow. One reason is that negative first impressions may cause us to avoid certain people, thus reducing our exposure to new information that might change our view of them (Denrell, 2005). Further, most people want to keep their social environment simple and easy to understand (Kenrick, Neuberg, & Cialdini, 2005). We cling to our beliefs about the world, often using our schemas to preserve a reality that fits our expectations. Holding on to existing impressions appears to be part of this effort. If your friend has recently said or done something that violates your expectations, your view of her probably did not change much, if at all. In fact, you may have acted to preserve your impression by thinking something like, "She's just not herself today." In other words, impressions are slow to change because the meaning we give to new information about people is shaped by what we already know or believe about them (Kenrick et al., 2005).

Self-Fulfilling Prophecies in the Classroom If teachers inadvertently spend less time helping children who impressed them as "dull," those children may not learn as much, thus fulfilling the teachers' expectations. If the girl in the back row has not impressed this teacher as being bright, how likely do you think it is that she will be called on?

● **Self-Fulfilling Prophecies** Another reason first impressions tend to be stable is that we often do things that cause others to confirm our impressions (Madon et al., 2004). If teachers expect particular students to do poorly in mathematics, those students may sense this expectation, exert less effort, and perform below their ability level. Similarly, if mothers expect their young children to eventually abuse alcohol, they are more likely to do so than the children of mothers who didn't convey that expectation (Madon et al., 2006). When, without our awareness, schemas cause us to subtly lead people to behave in line with our expectations, a **self-fulfilling prophecy** is at work.

In one experiment on self-fulfilling prophecies, men and women participated in "get-acquainted" conversations over an intercom system. They could not see each other, but before the conversations took place, the men were shown photographs and told that they were pictures of their partners. Some saw a photograph of an obese woman, whereas others saw a picture of a woman of normal weight. In fact, the photographs bore no relationship to the women's actual appearance. Judges who had not seen any of the participants listened to tapes of the conversations and rated the women's behavior and personalities. The women who had been portrayed as normal in weight were rated as more articulate, lively, interesting, exciting, and fun to be with. Apparently, when the men thought their partners were of normal weight, they were more friendly and engaging, and this behavior drew more positive reactions from the women. In contrast, men who thought their partners were overweight behaved in ways that drew comparatively dull responses (Snyder & Haugen, 1995).

Self-fulfilling prophecies also help maintain judgments about groups. If you assume that members of a certain ethnic group are unfriendly, for example, you might be defensive or even hostile when you meet a member of that group. If the person reacts to your behavior with hostility, your prophesy would be fulfilled and you would have an even stronger impression that "all those people" are unfriendly (Ross & Jackson, 1991).

● **self-fulfilling prophecy** A process through which an initial impression of someone leads that person to behave in accordance with that impression.

■ ● Explaining Behavior: Attribution

So far, we have considered how people form impressions about the characteristics of other people. But our perceptions of others include another key element: explanations of their behavior. People tend to form *implicit theories* about why people (including themselves) behave as they do and about what behavior to expect in the future. Psychologists use the term **attribution** to describe the process people go through to explain the causes of behavior (including their own).

As an example, suppose a classmate fails to return some borrowed notes on time. You could attribute this behavior to many causes, from an unavoidable emergency to simple selfishness. Which of these alternatives you choose is important because it will help you to *understand* your classmate's behavior, *predict* what will happen if this person asks to borrow something in the future, and decide how to *control* the situation should it arise again. Similarly, your decision to stick with a troubled relationship or end it may be influenced by whether you attribute your partner's recent indifference to stressful circumstances or to a loss of love.

People tend to attribute behavior in a particular situation to either internal causes (characteristics of the person) or external causes (characteristics of the situation). If you thought your classmate's failure to return your notes was due to lack of consideration or laziness, you would be making an *internal attribution*. If you thought that the oversight was caused by time pressure or a family crisis, you would be making an *external attribution*. And if you failed an exam, you could explain it by concluding either that you're not very smart (internal attribution) or that your job responsibilities didn't leave you enough time to study (external attribution). The attribution that you make, in turn, might determine how much you study for the next exam or even whether you decide to stay in school.

● **Sources of Attributions**   Harold Kelley (1973) proposed an influential theory of how people (whom Kelley called *observers*) make attributions about the actions of other people (whom Kelley called *actors*). To illustrate this theory, suppose you are at your parents' home for the weekend. You want to invite your friend Ralph to stay for dinner, but your father says no. According to Kelley, understanding the reasons for your father's behavior requires information about three key variables: consensus, consistency, and distinctiveness (Kelley, 1973):

1. *Consensus* is the degree to which other people's behavior is similar to the actor's—in this case, your father. If everyone you know avoids Ralph, your father's behavior has a high degree of consensus, and you would attribute his reaction to an external cause (probably something about Ralph). However, if everyone except your father likes Ralph, your father's negative response would have low consensus. In that case you would probably attribute the response to something about your father, such as rudeness or having a personal dislike for Ralph.

2. *Consistency* is the degree to which the behavior is the same across time and/or situations. If your father has invited Ralph to dinner several times in the past but rejects him this time, the consistency of his behavior is low. Low consistency suggests that your father's behavior is attributable to external causes, such as conflicts at work that have left your father feeling unsociable. If your father's behavior toward Ralph is always hostile, it has high consistency. But is your father's consistent behavior attributable to an internal cause (his consistent rudeness) or to an external cause (consistent conflicts at work)? This question is difficult to answer without information about distinctiveness.

3. *Distinctiveness* concerns the extent to which the actor's response to one situation stands out from responses to similar situations. If your father is nasty to all your friends, his behavior toward Ralph has low distinctiveness. Behavior

attribution   The process of explaining the causes of people's behavior, including our own.

that is low in distinctiveness is usually attributable to internal causes, such as personality traits. However, if your dad gets along with everyone except Ralph, his behavior has high distinctiveness, and your attribution about the cause of his behavior is likely to shift toward a cause other than your father's personality, such as how Ralph acts.

In summary, Kelley's theory suggests that people are most likely to make internal attributions about an actor's behavior when there is low consensus, high consistency, and low distinctiveness. If you observe your boss insulting customers (a situation of low consensus, inasmuch as most people in business are polite to customers) every day (high consistency) no matter who the customers are (low distinctiveness), you would probably attribute this behavior to the boss's personality rather than to the customers' unreasonable demands or some other external cause. But if you saw the boss on just one day (low consistency) being rude (low consensus) to one particular customer (high distinctiveness), you would probably attribute the incident to the customer's behavior, an external factor.

● **Culture and Attribution** Most theories of causal attribution were developed by North American psychologists who implicitly assumed that people all over the world use the same kinds of information to make similar kinds of attributions. However, there is substantial evidence to suggest that this may not be true (Lehman, Chiu, & Schaller, 2004). For example, Joan Miller and David Bersoff (1994) found that students from the United States and students from India made very different attributions about the reasons why people would do a favor for someone who had just helped them. The Americans attributed the behavior to an external cause (feeling an obligation to repay a favor), but the Indians attributed it to an internal cause (liking to help people). Miller (1994) suggested that the differences in the two groups' responses reflected differences in their cultural experiences. The results of Miller and Bersoff's experiment highlight once again the danger of assuming that phenomena seen in European American cultures generalize to all cultures. Cross-cultural differences in attribution and other aspects of social cognition may help to explain why people in different cultures sometimes have so much difficulty in understanding one another.

Why Are They Helping? Helping occurs all around the world, but research shows that people's attributions, or explanations, about why it happens can differ from culture to culture.

Attributional Bias Men whose thinking is colored by the ultimate attribution error might assume that women who succeed at tasks associated with traditional male gender roles are just lucky, but that men succeed at those tasks because of their skill (Deaux & LaFrance, 1998). When this attributional bias is in operation, people who are perceived as belonging to an out-group, whether on the basis of their gender, age, sexual orientation, religion, ethnicity, or other characteristics, may be denied fair evaluations and equal opportunities.

● Biases in Attribution

Whatever their background, most people are usually logical in their attempts to explain behavior (Trope, Cohen, & Alfieri, 1991). However, they are also sometimes prone to *attributional biases* that can distort their views of behavior (Gilbert, 1998).

● **The Fundamental Attribution Error** North American psychologists have paid special attention to the **fundamental attribution error**, a tendency to over-attribute the behavior of others to internal factors, such as personality traits (Moskowitz, 2005). Imagine that you hear a student give an incorrect answer in class. You will probably attribute this behavior to an internal cause and assume that the person is not very smart. In doing so, however, you might be failing to consider the possible influence of various external causes, such as lack of study time.

A related form of cognitive bias is called the *ultimate attribution error*. Through this error, when members of a social or ethnic *out-group* (people we see as "different") do something positive, we attribute their behavior to luck or some other external cause. But we attribute their negative behavior to an internal cause, such as dishonesty (Pettigrew, 1979). At the same time, when members of an *in-group* (people we see as being like ourselves) do good deeds, we attribute the behavior to integrity or other internal factors. If they do something bad, we attribute it to some external cause. Because of the ultimate attribution error, members of the out-group receive little credit for their positive actions, and members of the in-group get little blame for their negative actions. Biases such as the ultimate attribution error help maintain people's negative views of out-groups and positive views of their own in-group (Fiske, 1998).

Like other aspects of social cognition, the fundamental attribution error may not be universal (Miyamoto & Kitayama, 2002). Researchers have found, for example, that people in collectivist cultures such as India, China, Japan, and Korea are less likely than those in the individualist cultures of North America and Europe to attribute people's behavior to internal causes. Instead, these people tend to see behavior as due to an interaction between individual characteristics and the situations or contexts in which the person is immersed (Lehman et al., 2004).

Researchers have also pointed out that attributing behavior to internal causes may not always be an "error." Sometimes an internal attribution may simply be the most reasonable attribution to make, given the information available (Sabini, Siepmann, & Stein, 2001). Further, David Funder (2004) has argued that, in many situations, personality characteristics and other internal factors are indeed the true causes of behavior. In other words, according to Funder, social perception is much more accurate than many psychologists have previously recognized.

● **Other Attributional Biases** The inclination toward internal attributions is much less pronounced when people explain their own behavior. Here, in fact, another bias tends to come into play: the **actor-observer bias**. Whereas people often attribute other people's behavior to internal causes, they tend to attribute their own behavior to external factors, especially when the behavior is inappropriate or inadequate. For example, when Australian students were asked why they sometimes drive too fast, they focused on circumstances such as being late, but saw other people's dangerous driving as a sign of aggressiveness or immaturity (Harré, Brandt, & Houkamau, 2004). Similarly, when you drive slowly, it's because you are looking for an address, or for some other good reason, not because you're a dimwitted loser like that jerk who crawled along in front of you yesterday.

The actor-observer bias occurs mainly because people have different kinds of information about their own behavior and about others' behavior. When *you* are acting in a situation—giving a speech, perhaps—the information that is most available to you is likely to be external and situational, such as the temperature of the room and the size of the audience. You also have a lot of information about other external factors, such as the amount of time you had to prepare your talk or the

● **fundamental attribution error** A bias toward overattributing the behavior of others to internal causes.

● **actor-observer bias** The tendency to attribute other people's behavior to internal causes while attributing our own behavior (especially errors and failures) to external causes.

upsetting argument that occurred this morning. If your speech is disorganized and boring, you can easily attribute it to one or all of these external causes. But when you observe someone else, the most noticeable stimulus in the situation is *that person*. You do not know what happened to the person last night or this morning, so you are likely to attribute whatever he or she does to enduring internal characteristics (Moskowitz, 2005).

Of course, people do not always attribute their own behavior to external forces. In fact, the degree to which they do so depends on whether the outcome of their behavior is positive or negative. In one study, when people were asked what they saw as the cause of their good and bad experiences when shopping online, they tended to take personal credit for positive outcomes but to blame the computer for the negative ones (Moon, 2003). In other words, these people showed a **self-serving bias,** the tendency to take personal credit for success but to blame external causes for failure. This tendency has been found in almost all cultures, but as with the fundamental attribution error, it is usually more pronounced among people from individualistic Western cultures than among those from collectivist Eastern cultures (Mezulis et al., 2004).

■ ● The Self-Protective Functions of Social Cognition

The self-serving bias occurs partly because, as noted earlier, people are motivated to maintain their self-esteem—and ignoring negative information is one way to do so. If you just failed an exam, it is painful to admit that your grade was fair, so you might blame your performance on an unreasonably demanding instructor. Other forms of social cognition also help people think about their failures and shortcomings in ways that protect their self-esteem (Gilbert et al., 2004).

One example is *unrealistic optimism,* the tendency to believe that positive events (such as financial success or having a gifted child) are more likely to happen to yourself than to others and that negative events (such as being in an accident or having cancer) are more likely to happen to others than to yourself (Lin & Raghubir, 2005; see "In Review: Some Biases in Social Perception").

in review Some Biases in Social Perception

Bias	Description
Importance of first impression	Ambiguous information is interpreted in line with a first impression, and the initial schema is recalled better and more vividly than any later correction to it. Actions based on this impression may elicit behavior that confirms it.
Fundamental attribution error	The tendency to attribute the behavior of others to internal factors.
Actor-observer bias	The tendency for actors to attribute their own behavior to external causes and for observers to attribute the behavior of others to internal factors
Self-serving bias	The tendency to attribute one's successes to internal factors and one's failures to external factors.
Unrealistic optimism	The tendency to assume that positive events are more likely, and negative events are less likely, to occur to oneself than to others.

Unrealistic optimism is fueled, in part, by another self-protective form of social cognition called *unique invulnerability*. For example, when motorcyclists in England were asked to estimate the chances that they would be in a serious traffic accident during the next twelve months, virtually all of them said that this was far less likely to happen to them than to other motorcycle riders (Rutter, Quine, & Albery, 1998).

Remember that *unrealistic* optimism is not the same as the optimistic (but realistic) perspective on life that, as mentioned in the chapter on health, stress, and coping, is associated with good physical and mental health (Radcliffe & Klein, 2002). In fact, unrealistic optimism can have the opposite effects because it tends to persist even in the face of contradictory evidence and it can lead to potentially harmful behaviors. In one study, unrealistically optimistic smokers not only underestimated their chances of getting lung cancer but also were less likely than others to believe that smoking causes lung cancer or that quitting can lower their risk (Dillard, McCaul, & Klein, 2006). Similarly, one reason that people engage in risky sexual behaviors (e.g., unprotected sex with multiple partners) is that they estimate the risks of unsafe sex to be much lower for themselves than for other people (Taylor et al., 1992).

Like the defense mechanisms described in the personality chapter, self-protective cognitive biases can help us temporarily escape from unpleasant thoughts and feelings. But these biases also set the stage for a somewhat distorted view of reality and can create problems in the long run. For example, although unrealistic optimism may reduce anxiety and blunt the impact of stress for a while, it may also keep people from taking the rational steps necessary for long-term protection of their health, well-being, and safety (Ayanian & Cleary, 1999).

Attitudes

People's views about health or safety reflect their *attitudes*, an aspect of social cognition that social psychologists have studied longer and more intensely than any other. An **attitude** is the tendency to think, feel, or act positively or negatively toward objects in our environment (Albarracín, Johnson, & Zanna, 2005). Attitudes play an important role in guiding how we act toward other people, what political causes we support, which products we buy, and countless other daily decisions.

The Structure of Attitudes

Social psychologists have long viewed attitudes as having three components (Fabrigar, MacDonald, & Wegener, 2005; see Figure 17.2). The *cognitive* component is a set of beliefs about the attitude object. The emotional, or *affective*, component includes feelings about the object. The *behavioral* component is the way people act toward the object. If these components were always in harmony, we would be able to predict people's behavior toward the homeless, for example, on the basis of the thoughts or feelings they express and vice versa. This is often not the case, however (Bohner & Schwarz, 2001). Many people's positive thoughts and supportive emotions regarding homeless people are never translated into actions aimed at helping them.

What determines whether people's behavior will be consistent with the cognitive and affective components of their attitudes? Several factors are important. For one thing, behavior is more likely to be consistent with attitude when people see the attitude as important and relevant to their lives (Kenrick et al., 2005). Second, consistency is more likely when the behavioral component of the attitude is in line with a *subjective norm*, our view of how important people in our lives want us to act. Conflict between attitudes and subjective norms may cause us to behave in

- **self-serving bias** The tendency to attribute our successes to internal characteristics while blaming our failures on external causes.

- **attitude** A predisposition toward a particular cognitive, emotional, or behavioral reaction to objects.

FIGURE 17.2

Three Components of an Attitude

Various attitude components may or may not be consistent with one another. For example, people may think that drunken driving is wrong (cognitive component) and be upset by its tragic consequences (affective component), yet they may still get behind the wheel after drinking too much (behavioral component).

Attitude toward drunk driving		Assessment methods
Cognitive component (belief)	Believes driving after drinking is dangerous	Paper-and-pencil tests (questionnaires)
Affective component (feeling)	Is upset by widespread drunk driving	Physiological indices (heart rate, GSR)
Behavioral component (action)	Participates in demonstrations against drunk driving	Directly observed behaviors

TRY THIS **A Reminder about Poverty** Photographs such as this one are used by fund-raising organizations to remind us of the kind thoughts and charitable feelings we have toward needy people and other social causes. As a result, we may be more likely to behave in accordance with the cognitive and affective components of our attitudes and make a donation to these causes. Browse through several newspapers and popular magazines and calculate the percentage of such photos you find in ads for charitable organizations.

ways that are inconsistent with our attitudes (Ajzen & Fishbein, 2005). For example, someone who believes that the rights of gay men and lesbians should be protected might not campaign for this cause because doing so would upset family members or friends who are against it. Third, attitude-consistent behavior is more likely when people have *perceived control,* the belief that they can actually perform such behavior (Ajzen & Fishbein, 2005). The cognitive and affective components of your attitude about the homeless may be positive, but if you don't believe you can do anything about it, you are not likely to even try. Fourth, *direct experience* with the attitude object increases the likelihood of attitude-consistent behavior (Glasman & Albarracín, 2006). This is because attitudes based on direct experiences are more stable and memorable and thus more likely to come into play when the attitude object is present. Accordingly, you might be more likely to actively support, and perhaps even participate in, efforts to help the homeless if you have come to know a homeless person on your campus than if you have only read about their plight.

The importance of direct experience in creating consistency among attitude components reflects the cognitive network theories described in the chapters on learning and memory. According to these theories, attitudes are stored in long-term memory as networks of cognitions—interconnected evaluations and beliefs about attitude objects (Tourangeau, Rips, & Rasinski, 2000; see also Figure 7.10 in the memory chapter). When you encounter an attitude object, the cognitions associated with it in your cognitive network are activated. If your thoughts and feelings are well defined and come easily to mind, then your behavior is likely to be consistent with them. If not, there may be less consistency (Glasman & Albarracín, 2006).

● Forming Attitudes

People are not born with specific attitudes toward specific objects, but their attitudes about new objects begin to appear in early childhood and continue to emerge throughout life. How do attitudes form? Some of the variation we see in people's attitudes may reflect genetic influences inherited from their parents (Abrahamson, Baker, & Caspi, 2002), but what they *learn* from their parents and others appears to play the major role in attitude formation. In childhood, modeling and other forms of social learning are especially important. Children learn not only the names of objects but also what they should believe and feel about them and how they should act toward them. For example, a parent may teach a child not only that snakes are reptiles but also that they should be feared and avoided. So as children learn concepts such as "reptile" or "work," they learn attitudes about those concepts, too.

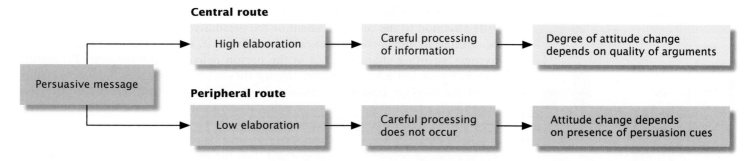

Central route

| Persuasive message | → | High elaboration | → | Careful processing of information | → | Degree of attitude change depends on quality of arguments |

Peripheral route

| | → | Low elaboration | → | Careful processing does not occur | → | Attitude change depends on presence of persuasion cues |

FIGURE 17.3

The Elaboration Likelihood Model of Attitude Change

The central route to attitude change involves carefully processing and evaluating the content of a message (high elaboration). The peripheral route involves low elaboration, or processing, of the message and relying on persuasion cues such as the attractiveness of the person making the argument (Cacioppo, Petty, & Crites, 1993).

Attitudes can also be influenced by classical and operant conditioning. In one study demonstrating this process, certain cartoon characters were associated with positive words (e.g., *excellent*) and images (e.g., an ice cream sundae), whereas others were associated with negative words and images (Olson & Fazio, 2001). Afterward, participants in this study liked the characters associated with the positive stimuli much more than those associated with the negative ones. No wonder so many advertisers present enjoyable music or attractive images in association with the products they are trying to sell (Aronson, Wilson, & Akert, 2005; Pratkanis & Aronson, 2001)! As for operant conditioning, parents, teachers, and peers actively shape children's attitudes by rewarding them for stating particular views. The *mere-exposure effect* is influential as well: All else being equal, attitudes toward an object will become more positive the more frequently people are exposed to it (Winkielman & Cacioppo, 2004). One study found that even newborns showed a preference for stories that their mother had repeatedly read aloud while they were still in the womb (Cacioppo, Berntson, & Petty, 1997). The mere-exposure effect helps explain why we sometimes come to like a song only after hearing it several times—and why we may come to like products and candidates only after being repeatedly exposed to commercials and political ads.

● Changing Attitudes

Although mere exposure can help to form new attitudes, it is not very effective at changing existing ones (Crano & Prislin, 2006). If you are already strongly against requiring motorcyclists to wear helmets, for example, that attitude is unlikely to change much no matter how often you see riders wearing their helmets. Changing attitudes usually requires more active efforts, mainly in the form of persuasive messages. The nearly $100 billion a year spent on advertising in the United States alone provides just one example of how people are constantly trying to change our attitudes. Stop for a moment and make a list of other examples, perhaps starting with the messages of groups concerned with abortion or recycling—and don't forget your friends who want you to think the way they do.

TRY THIS

● **Two Routes to Attitude Change** Whether a persuasive message succeeds in changing attitudes depends primarily on three factors: (1) the person communicating the message, (2) the content of the message, and (3) the audience who receives it (Johnson, Maio, & Smith-McLallen, 2005). The **elaboration likelihood model** of attitude change provides a framework for understanding when and how these factors affect attitude change. As shown in Figure 17.3, the model is based on the notion that persuasive messages can change people's attitudes through one of two main routes.

elaboration likelihood model A model suggesting that attitude change can be driven by evaluation of the content of a persuasive message (central route) or by irrelevant persuasion cues (peripheral route).

LOW INVOLVEMENT

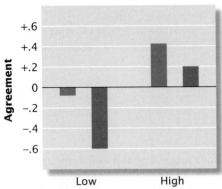

HIGH INVOLVEMENT

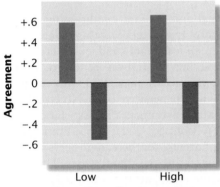

■ Strong arguments   ■ Weak arguments

FIGURE 17.4

Personal Involvement and Routes to Attitude Change

In the study represented here, students' reactions to messages supporting exit exams for seniors depended on whether they thought the policy would begin immediately (high involvement) or only after they had graduated (low involvement). In the low-involvement condition, students followed a peripheral route to attitude change, agreeing with messages from expert communicators regardless of how logical they were. More involved students followed a central route, changing their minds only if the message contained a strong, logical argument.

Source: Data from Petty, Cacioppo, & Goldman (1981); Petty, Cacioppo, & Schumann (1983).

● **cognitive dissonance theory**   A theory asserting that attitude change is driven by efforts to reduce tension caused by inconsistencies between attitudes and behaviors.

The first is called the *peripheral route* because, when it is activated, we devote little attention to the central content of the persuasive message. Instead, we tend to be affected by the *persuasion cues* that surround it, such as the confidence, attractiveness, or other characteristics of the person delivering the message. Persuasion cues influence attitude change even though they say nothing about the logic or validity of the message content. Commercials in which movie stars or other attractive nonexperts praise pain relievers or political candidates are designed to operate via the peripheral route to attitude change.

By contrast, when the *central route* to attitude change is activated, the content of the message becomes more important than the characteristics of the communicator in determining attitude change. A person following the central route uses logical steps—such as those outlined in the Thinking Critically sections of this book—to rationally analyze the content of the persuasive message. This analysis considers the validity of the message's claims, determines whether the message leaves out important information, assesses alternative interpretations of evidence, and so on.

What determines which route people will follow? Personal involvement with the content of the message is one important factor. The elaboration likelihood model proposes that the more personally involving a topic is, the more likely it is that the central route will be activated (Fabrigar et al., 2005). Suppose, for example, that you heard someone arguing for the elimination of student loans in Chile. This message might persuade you via the peripheral route if it came from someone who looked attractive and sounded intelligent. However, you would be more likely to follow the central route if the message proposed doing away with student loans at your own school. You might be persuaded, but only if the logic of the message was undeniable (see Figure 17.4). This is why celebrity endorsements tend to be most effective when the products being advertised are relatively unimportant to the audience.

"Cognitive busyness" is another factor affecting which attitude-change route is activated. If you are busy thinking about other things while a message is being delivered, you will be unable to pay much attention to its content. In this case, activation of the peripheral route becomes more likely. Personality characteristics are also related to attitude-change processes. For example, people with a strong *need for cognition* like to engage in thoughtful mental activities and are therefore more likely to use the central route to attitude change (Suedfeld & Tetlock, 2001). In contrast, people whose discomfort with uncertainty creates a *need for closure* are more likely to use the peripheral route (Cacioppo et al., 1996).

Persuasive messages are not the only means of changing attitudes. Another approach is to get people to act in ways that are inconsistent with their current attitudes in the hope that they will adjust those attitudes to match their behavior. Often, such adjustments do occur. Cognitive dissonance theory and self-perception theory each attempt to explain why.

● **Cognitive Dissonance Theory**   Leon Festinger's (1957) classic **cognitive dissonance theory** holds that people want their thoughts, beliefs, and attitudes to be consistent with one another and with their behavior. When people experience inconsistency, or *dissonance*, among these elements, they become anxious and are motivated to make them more consistent (Elliot & Devine, 1994; Olson & Stone, 2005). For example, someone who believes that "smoking is unhealthy" but must also acknowledge that "I smoke" would be motivated to reduce the resulting dissonance. Because it is often difficult to change behavior, people usually reduce cognitive dissonance by changing inconsistent attitudes. So rather than quit smoking, the smoker might decide that smoking is not so dangerous.

In one of the first studies of cognitive dissonance, Festinger and his colleague Merrill Carlsmith asked people to turn pegs in a board, a very dull task (Festinger & Carlsmith, 1959). Later, some of these people were asked to persuade a person waiting to participate in the study that the task was "exciting and fun." Some were told

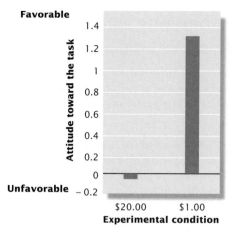

FIGURE 17.5

Cognitive Dissonance and Attitude Change

According to cognitive dissonance theory, people who were paid $20 to say a boring task was enjoyable had clear justification for lying, so they should experience little dissonance between what they said and what they thought about the task. In fact, their attitudes toward the task did not change much. However, participants who received just $1 had little justification to lie and reduced their dissonance mainly by displaying a more positive attitude toward the task.

that they would be paid $1 to tell this lie; others were promised $20. After they had talked to the waiting person, their attitudes toward the dull task were measured.

Figure 17.5 shows the surprising results. The people who were paid just $1 to lie liked the dull task more than those who were paid $20. Why? Festinger and Carlsmith (1959) argued that telling another person that a boring task is enjoyable will produce dissonance (between the thoughts "I think the task is boring" and "I am saying it is fun"). To reduce this dissonance, the people who were paid just $1 adopted a favorable attitude toward the task, making their cognitions consistent: "I think the task is fun" and "I am saying it is fun." But if a person has adequate justification for the behavior, any dissonance that exists will be reduced simply by thinking about the justification. The participants who were paid $20 thought they had adequate justification for lying and so did not need to change their attitudes toward the task.

Hundreds of other experiments have also found that when people publicly engage in behaviors that are inconsistent with their privately held attitudes, they are likely to change their attitudes to be consistent with their behavior (Cooper, Mirabile, & Scher, 2005). These experiments have also found that behavior-attitude inconsistency will produce attitude change when (1) the inconsistency causes some distress or discomfort and (2) changing attitudes will reduce this distress or discomfort. But what causes the discomfort in the first place? There is considerable debate among attitude researchers about this question (Crano & Prislin, 2006).

Currently, the most popular of several possible answers is that discomfort results when people's positive self-concept is threatened by the recognition that they have done something inconsistent with that self-concept. For example, if they have encouraged another person to do something that they themselves didn't believe in or that they themselves wouldn't do, this inconsistency makes most people feel uncomfortable, so they change their attitudes to reduce or eliminate such feelings (Stone, 2003; Stone & Cooper, 2001). If people can persuade themselves that they really believed in what they did, the perceived inconsistency disappears, and their positive self-concepts are restored. Changing one's private attitude to match one's public actions is one way to accomplish this self-persuasion. Claude Steele's work on *self-affirmation* supports this explanation of why dissonance causes discomfort (e.g., Steele, Spencer, & Lynch, 1993). He has found that people will not change their attitudes after recognizing their own attitude-behavior inconsistency if they can do something else that makes them look good and feel good about themselves (e.g., showing how smart or competent they are). In other words, when people do not need to change their attitudes to reestablish a positive view of themselves, they don't.

The circumstances that lead to cognitive dissonance may be different in the individualist cultures of Europe and North America than in collectivist cultures such as Japan and China. In individualist cultures, dissonance typically arises from behaving in a manner inconsistent with one's own beliefs, because this behavior causes self-doubt. But in collectivist cultures, dissonance typically arises when such behavior causes the person to worry about one's reputation with others (Kitayama et al., 2004). Cultural values also operate in shaping dissonance-reducing strategies. For example, people from individualistic cultures can reduce the unpleasant feelings that accompany dissonance by affirming their value as unique individuals, whereas people from collectivist cultures can reduce the same kind of feelings by affirming the value of the groups to which they belong (Hoshino-Browne et al., 2005).

● **Self-Perception Theory** Over the years, cognitive dissonance theory has been challenged by other explanations of why attitudes change when they are inconsistent with behavior (Dunning, 2001). The first and strongest of these challenges came from Daryl Bem's (1967) self-perception theory. Unlike dissonance theory, self-perception theory does not assume that people experience discomfort when their attitudes are inconsistent with their behaviors. According to Bem, situations often arise in which people are not quite sure about their attitudes. When this happens, Bem says, people look at their own behavior under particular circumstances and then infer what their

● **self-perception theory** A theory suggesting that attitudes can change as people consider their behavior in certain situations and then infer what their attitude must be.

in review Forming and Changing Attitudes	
Type of Influence	**Description**
Modeling and conditioning	Attitudes are usually formed through observation of how others behave and speak about an attitude object, as well as through classical and operant conditioning.
Elaboration likelihood model	People change attitudes through either a central or peripheral route, depending on factors such as personal involvement, "cognitive busyness," and personality characteristics.
Cognitive dissonance and self-perception	Inconsistencies between attitudes and behaviors can produce attitude change, as can reviewing one's behavior in light of circumstances.

attitude must be. The person says, "If I did that under those circumstances, my attitude must be this." This process makes their attitudes consistent with their behavior, but the process is not driven by tension or discomfort.

Self-perception explanations of attitude change seem reasonable, but two kinds of evidence are inconsistent with it. First, people actually do become physiologically aroused and feel uncomfortable when they experience an inconsistency between their attitudes and behavior, and their discomfort is reduced when they change their attitudes to match their behavior (Elliot & Devine, 1994). This finding suggests that some kind of internal tension is, in fact, created by cognitive dissonance. Second, people adjust their attitudes to match their behavior even when they are unable to reflect on that behavior—a process that is crucial to self-perception theory. In one experiment, for example, researchers studied the effects of attitude-behavior inconsistencies in people suffering from anterograde amnesia, a condition described in the memory chapter that leaves its victims unable to recall what they have said or done minutes earlier. Like the participants in other attitude-change experiments, these people, too, changed their attitudes to be more consistent with their behavior (Lieberman et al., 2001).

Although these results do not support self-perception theory, they do not entirely invalidate it. It may be that self-perception theory applies best either when people have no prior attitude toward some object or when the discrepancy between their attitude and their behavior is slight. For instance, if you know you like Coca-Cola, but you also know that you just drank a Pepsi, this self-perception may drive an attitude change toward Pepsi even though you did not experience any dissonance. However, when attitudes are strong and clearly defined, and the inconsistency between attitudes and behaviors is larger and more important to a person's self-concept, attitude change appears to occur mainly because of cognitive dissonance (Dunning, 2001). ("In Review: Forming and Changing Attitudes" summarizes some of the major processes through which attitudes are formed and changed.)

LINKAGES **Biological and Social Psychology**

Social psychologists' research on thoughts, feelings, and behaviors was once entirely separate from research on the biological processes that underlie those thoughts, feelings, and behaviors (Cacioppo & Berntson, 2005). Social psychologists believed that it was not possible to reduce complex social psychological processes to the firing of neurons or the secretion of hormones. For their part, biological psychologists, more commonly known as *neuroscientists*, viewed the study of social psychology as having little, if any, relevance to the understanding of behavioral genetics or the functioning of the nervous, endocrine, or immune systems. Recently, however, scientists in both subfields have begun to take a closer look at each other's research and how their subfields are related. The result has been the emergence of a new specialty called *social neuroscience* (Cacioppo & Bernston, 2005; Decety & Keenan, 2006). This new specialty focuses on the neurological aspects of social processes and is part of a more general trend toward research on the interaction of biological and social processes.

There are already many reasons to believe that this research approach will be valuable. For example, the chapter on health, stress, and coping contains numerous examples of how social stressors can have health-related biological consequences. Health psychologists have also found that the quality of a person's social relationships can affect biological processes ranging from the functioning of the immune system to the healing of wounds (Kiecolt-Glaser et al., 1998; Robles & Kiecolt-Glaser, 2003; Uchino, Cacioppo, & Kiecolt-Glaser, 1996). The social environment can affect even the way genes express themselves. In one study, for example, monkeys were selectively bred to react strongly to even mild stressors. These animals' oversensitivity appeared to be based on a specific gene, but researchers found it possible to modify the effects of this gene by changing the monkeys' social situation. When the animals were paired with a warm, nurturant foster mother, their oversensitivity diminished significantly, and it remained low even when they were later separated from her (Suomi, 1999).

LINKAGES (a link to Biological Aspects of Psychology, p. 73)

Researchers are also beginning to identify the biological underpinnings of many social processes. One example can be seen in studies of how the amygdala—a brain structure that plays a significant role in emotion—is related to the stereotypes and prejudice described in the next section. Using functional magnetic resonance imaging technology, researchers found that European Americans who were prejudiced against African Americans showed significantly more amygdala activity when looking at pictures of black people than when looking at pictures of white people (Hart et al., 2000; Phelps et al., 2000). More recently, researchers have used fMRI to study people's emotional reactions to other people's distress (Lamm, Batson, & Decety, 2007). They found patterns of brain activity that were quite different depending on whether the individual experienced empathy for a distressed person or simply observed the person's distress. Studies such as this one are helping to shed light on the biological aspects of empathy, and they may eventually lead to a broader understanding of the factors influencing people's motivation to help each other (Tankersley, Stowe, & Huettel, 2007; see the chapter on social influence). Social neuroscientists have also used electroencephalography (EEG) and other techniques to record the brain activity associated with positive and negative attitudes about people and objects (e.g., Amodio et al., 2004). Their research has shown that these evaluative reactions are associated with activity in specific brain regions (Cacioppo, Crites, & Gardner, 1996).

Social neuroscience is still in its infancy; the first journal devoted to social neuroscience research only began publication in 2006 (Decety & Keenan, 2006). However, this new field already shows great promise for improving our understanding of the linkages among social, cognitive, and biological phenomena, as well as of complex social and physiological processes (Cacioppo et al., 2007). ■

Prejudice and Stereotypes

All of the principles that underlie impression formation, attribution, and attitudes come together to create prejudice and stereotypes. **Stereotypes** are the perceptions, beliefs, and expectations a person has about members of some group. They are schemas about entire groups of people (Dion, 2003). Usually, stereotypes involve the false assumption that all members of a group share the same characteristics. The characteristics that make up the stereotype may be positive, but they are usually negative.

stereotypes False assumptions that all members of some group share the same characteristics.

FIGURE **17.6**

The Impact of Stereotypes on Behavior

TRY THIS When these men suddenly appeared on a video screen, participants were supposed to "shoot" them, but only if they appeared to be armed (Correll et al., 2002). Stereotypes about whether white men or black men are more likely to be armed significantly affected the errors made by participants in firing their video game "weapons." Cover these photos with a pair of index cards; then ask a few friends to watch as you show each photo, one at a time, for just an instant, before covering it again. Then ask your friends to say whether either man appeared to be armed. Was one individual more often seen as armed? If so, which one?

● **prejudice** A positive or negative attitude toward an entire group of people.

● **discrimination** Differential treatment of various groups; the behavioral component of prejudice.

The most common and powerful stereotypes focus on observable personal attributes, particularly ethnicity, gender, and age (Operario & Fiske, 2001).

The stereotypes people hold can be so ingrained that their effects on behavior can be automatic and unconscious (Banaji, Lemm, & Carpenter, 2001; Blair, Judd, & Fallman, 2004). In one study, for example, European American and African American participants played a video game in which white or black men suddenly appeared on a screen holding objects that might be weapons (Correll et al., 2002; see Figure 17.6). The participants were instructed to immediately "shoot" an armed man, but not an unarmed one. Under this time pressure, the participants' errors were not random. If they "shot" an unarmed man, he was significantly more likely to be black than white. If they failed to "shoot" an armed man he was more likely to be white than black. These differences occurred among both European American and African American participants but were most pronounced among those who held the strongest cultural stereotypes about blacks.

Stereotyping often leads to **prejudice**, which is a positive or negative attitude toward an individual based simply on membership in some group (Dion, 2003). The literal meaning of the word *prejudice* is "prejudgment." Many theorists believe that prejudice, like other attitudes, has cognitive, affective, and behavioral components. Stereotyped thinking is the cognitive component of prejudicial attitudes. The hatred, admiration, anger, and other feelings people have about stereotyped groups make up the affective component. The behavioral component of prejudice involves **discrimination**, which is differing treatment of individuals who belong to different groups.

● Theories of Prejudice and Stereotyping

Prejudice and stereotyping may occur for several reasons (Duckitt, 1994). Let's consider three explanatory theories, each of which has empirical support and accounts for some, but not all, instances of stereotyping and prejudice.

● **Motivational Theories** For some people, prejudice against certain groups might enhance their sense of security and help them meet certain personal needs. This idea was first proposed by Theodor Adorno and his associates more than fifty years ago (Adorno et al., 1950). It has since been revised and expanded by Bob Altemeyer (2004; Altemeyer & Hunsberger, 2005). Specifically, these researchers suggest that prejudice may be especially likely among people who display a personality trait called *authoritarianism*. According to Altemeyer, authoritarianism is composed of three elements: (1) an acceptance of conventional or traditional values, (2) a willingness to unquestioningly follow the orders of authority figures, and (3) an inclination to act aggressively toward individuals or groups identified by these authority figures as threatening the values held by one's in-group. People with an authoritarian orientation tend to view the world as a threatening place (Winter, 1996), and one way to protect themselves from perceived threats is to identify strongly with their in-group and to dislike, reject, and perhaps even punish anyone who is a member of other groups (Cottrell & Neuberg, 2005). Looking down on, and discriminating against, out-groups—such as gay men and lesbians, African Americans, or Muslims, for example—may help people with authoritarian tendencies to feel safer and feel better about themselves (Haddock & Zanna, 1998).

Another motivational explanation of prejudice employs the concept of social identity discussed earlier. Recall that whether they are authoritarian or not, most people are motivated to identify with their in-group and tend to see it as better than other groups (Brewer & Pierce, 2005). As a result, members of an in-group often see all members of out-groups as less attractive and less socially acceptable than in-group members and may thus treat them badly (Jackson, 2002). In other words, prejudice may result when people's motivation to enhance their own self-esteem causes them to disrespect other people.

● **Cognitive Theories**   Stereotyping and prejudice may also result from the social-cognitive processes people use in dealing with the world. There are so many other people, so many situations in which one meets them, and so many possible behaviors they might perform that we cannot possibly attend to and remember them all. Therefore, we use schemas and other cognitive shortcuts to organize and make sense out of our social world (Moskowitz, 2005). These cognitive processes allow us to draw accurate and useful conclusions about other people, but sometimes they lead to inaccurate stereotypes. For example, one effective way to deal with social complexity is to group people into *social categories*. Rather than remembering every detail about everyone we have ever encountered, we tend to put other people into categories, such as doctor, senior citizen, Republican, student, Italian, and the like (Dovidio, Kawakami, & Gaertner, 2000). To further simplify perception of these categories, we tend to see their members as being quite similar to one another. In fact, members of one ethnic group may find it harder to distinguish among specific faces within other ethnic groups than within their own group (Michel et al., 2006). People also tend to assume that all members of a different group share the same beliefs and values and that those beliefs and values differ from their own (Dion, 2003). Finally, as noted in the chapter on perception, people's attention tends to be drawn to distinctive stimuli. Rude behavior by even a few members of an easily identified ethnic group may lead other people to see an *illusory correlation* between rudeness and ethnicity (Hamilton & Sherman, 1994). As a result, they may incorrectly believe that all members of that group are rude.

● **Learning Theories**   Like other attitudes, prejudice can be learned. Some prejudice is learned on the basis of conflicts between members of different groups, but people also develop negative attitudes toward groups with whom they have had little or no contact. Learning theories suggest that children can pick up prejudices just by watching and listening to parents, peers, and others (Taylor et al., 2006). Movies and television may also portray ethnic or other groups in ways that teach stereotypes and prejudice (Brehm et al., 2005). One study found, for example, that local news coverage often gives the impression that African Americans are responsible for a higher percentage of crimes than is actually the case (Romer, Jamieson, & deCoteau, 1998). No wonder so many young children already know about the supposed negative characteristics of certain groups long before they ever meet members of those groups (Baron & Banaji, 2006; Quintana, 1998).

Schemas and Stereotypes   The use of schemas to assign certain people to certain categories can be helpful when deciding who is a customer and who is a store employee, but it can also lead to inaccurate stereotypes. After the September 11, 2001, terrorist attacks on New York and Washington, D.C., many people began to think of all Muslims as potential terrorists and to discriminate against them. This false assumption and the problems it has created for Muslims in the United States was one of the many awful side effects of the terrorist attacks.

Fighting Ethnic Prejudice Negative attitudes about members of ethnic groups are often based on negative personal experiences or the negative experiences and attitudes people hear from others. Cooperative contact between equals can help promote mutual respect and reduce ethnic prejudice.

● Reducing Prejudice

One clear implication of the cognitive and learning theories of prejudice and stereotyping is that members of one group are often ignorant or misinformed about the characteristics of people in other groups (Dovidio, Gaertner, & Kawakami, 2003). Before 1954, for example, most black and white children in the United States knew very little about one another because they went to separate schools. Then the Supreme Court declared that segregated public schools should be prohibited. By ruling segregation to be unconstitutional, the court created a real-life test of the **contact hypothesis,** which states that stereotypes and prejudice toward a group will diminish as contact with that group increases (Pettigrew & Tropp, 2006).

Did the desegregation of U.S. schools confirm the contact hypothesis? In a few schools, integration was followed by a decrease in prejudice, but in most places either no change occurred or prejudice actually increased (Oskamp & Schultz, 1998). However, these results did not necessarily disprove the contact hypothesis. In-depth studies of schools in which desegregation was successful suggested that contact alone was not enough. Integration reduced prejudice only when certain social conditions were created (Pettigrew & Tropp, 2006). First, members of the two groups had to be of roughly equal social and economic status. Second, school authorities had to promote cooperation and interdependence between the members of different ethnic groups by having them work together on projects that required relying on one another to reach success. Third, the contact between group members had to occur on a one-on-one basis. It was only when people got to know one another as individuals that the errors contained in stereotypes became apparent. Finally, the members of each group had to be seen as typical and not unusual in any significant way. When these four conditions prevailed, the children's attitudes toward one another became more positive. The same effects have appeared in adults, and in other countries, too. In Italy, for example, people who had equal-status contact with black immigrants from North Africa displayed less prejudice against them than did Italians who had no contact with those immigrants (Kirchler & Zani, 1995).

Elliot Aronson (1997) describes a teaching strategy, called the *jigsaw technique,* that helps create the conditions that reduce prejudice. The strategy calls for children from several ethnic groups to work as a team to complete a task, such as writing a

contact hypothesis The idea that stereotypes and prejudice toward a group will diminish as contact with the group increases.

report about a famous person in history. Each child learns, and provides the team with, a separate piece of information about this person, such as place of birth (Aronson, 1990). Studies show that children from various ethnic groups who are exposed to the jigsaw technique and other cooperative learning experiences show substantial reductions in prejudice toward other groups (Aronson, 1997). The success reported in these studies has greatly increased the popularity of cooperative learning exercises in classrooms in the United States. Such exercises may not eliminate all aspects of ethnic prejudice in children, but they seem to be a step in the right direction.

Can friendly, cooperative, interdependent contact reduce the more entrenched forms of prejudice seen in adults? It may. When equal-status adults work jointly toward a common goal, bias and distrust can be reduced, particularly among those in ethnic majority groups (Tropp & Pettigrew, 2005). This is especially true if they come to see themselves as members of the same group rather than as belonging to opposing groups (Dovidio et al., 2000; Fiske, 2000). The challenge to be met in creating such cooperative experiences in the real world is that the participants must be of equal status—a challenge made more difficult in many countries by the sizable status differences that still exist between ethnic groups (Kenworthy et al., 2006).

In the final analysis, contact provides only part of the solution to the problems of stereotyping, prejudice, and discrimination. To reduce ethnic prejudice, we must develop additional educational techniques that address the social cognitions and perceptions that lie at the core of bigotry and hatred toward people who are different from ourselves (Bigler & Liben, 2007; Monteith, Zuwerink, & Devine, 1994).

THINKING CRITICALLY Is Ethnic Prejudice Too Ingrained Ever to Be Eliminated?

 LINKAGES (a link to Consciousness, p. 329)

There is little doubt that overt forms of ethnic prejudice have decreased dramatically in the United States over the past forty to fifty years. For example, in the 1950s fewer than half of European American college students surveyed said they were willing to live in integrated neighborhoods. More recent surveys indicate that about 95 percent say they would be willing to do so. And four decades ago, fewer than 40 percent of European Americans said they would vote for an African American presidential candidate; over 95 percent now say they might do so (Dovidio & Gaertner, 1998). Despite these changes, research in social psychology suggests that more subtle aspects of prejudice and discrimination may remain as entrenched in the United States today as they were fifteen or even twenty years ago (Dovidio & Gaertner, 2000).

■ What am I being asked to believe or accept?

Even people who see themselves as unprejudiced and who disavow ethnic stereotypes and discrimination still hold negative stereotypes about ethnic out-groups and, in certain situations, will display prejudice and discrimination toward them (Dovidio, Kawakami, & Beach, 2001). Some people claim, therefore, that negative attitudes toward ethnic out-groups are so deeply ingrained in all of us that ethnic prejudice can never be eliminated.

■ What evidence is available to support the assertion?

Evidence for this assertion focuses primarily on prejudice against African Americans by European Americans. It comes, first, from studies testing the theory of *aversive racism* (Hodson, Dovidio, & Gaertner, 2004). This theory holds that even though many European Americans consider ethnic prejudice to be unacceptable, or aversive, they will still sometimes display it—especially when they can do so without admitting, even to themselves, that they are prejudiced.

In one test of this theory, a male experimenter telephoned male and female European Americans who were known to believe in ethnic equality. The man claimed to be a stranded motorist who was trying to call a service station from a pay phone. When told he had called the wrong number, the man replied that he was out of coins and asked the person he'd reached to call a service station for him. If people listened long enough to learn of the man's problem, they were just as likely to contact the service station whether the caller "sounded" European American or African American. However, if the caller "sounded" African American, these supposedly unprejudiced people were almost five times as likely to hang up even before the caller could ask for help (Gaertner & Dovidio, 1986). In other studies, female European American college students were asked to help another female student who was doing poorly on some task. When the student's poor performance was described as being due to the difficulty of the task, the students agreed to help, regardless of the other student's ethnicity. But if the problem was said to be due to lack of effort, help was offered much more often to European Americans than to African Americans (Frey & Gaertner, 1986; McPhail & Penner, 1995). These findings suggest that even people who do not display prejudice in most situations may do so in others.

A second line of evidence for the entrenched nature of prejudice comes from research showing that many people hold negative stereotypes about ethnic minorities (and women) but are unaware that they do so. These negative stereotypes can also be *activated* without conscious awareness, even among people who believe they are free of prejudice (Banaji et al., 2001; Wheeler & Petty, 2001). To demonstrate these phenomena, researchers have used the priming procedures described in the chapter on consciousness to activate unconscious thoughts and feelings that can alter people's reactions to stimuli without their awareness. In one study, for example, white participants were exposed to subliminal presentations of pictures of black individuals (Chen & Bargh, 1997). The participants were not consciously aware that they had seen these pictures, but when they interacted with a black man soon afterward, those who had been primed with the pictures acted more negatively toward him and saw him as more hostile than did people who had not been primed. Priming apparently activated these participants' negative ethnic stereotypes. It is also possible to prime unconscious negative stereotypes about other groups, including women and the elderly (Glick & Fiske, 2001; Hense, Penner, & Nelson, 1995). All of these findings suggest that stereotypes are so well learned and so ingrained in people that they may be activated automatically and without conscious awareness (Dovidio et al., 2001).

■ Are there alternative ways of interpreting the evidence?

The evidence presented so far suggests that it may be impossible to eliminate ethnic prejudice, because everyone harbors unconscious negative stereotypes about various groups. But this evidence does not necessarily mean that unconscious stereotypes affect everyone in the same way. Perhaps they have a greater impact on people who are more overtly prejudiced.

■ What additional evidence would help to evaluate the alternatives?

One way to evaluate this possibility is to compare the responses of prejudiced and unprejudiced people in various experimental situations. In one mock-trial study, for example, overtly prejudiced white jurors recommended the death penalty more often for black defendants than for white defendants found guilty of the same crime. Low-prejudice white jurors showed this bias only when they believed that a black member of the jury also favored giving the death penalty (Dovidio et al., 1997). Priming studies, too, show that although negative stereotypes can be primed in both prejudiced and unprejudiced people, it is easier to do in people who openly display their ethnic bias (Dovidio et al., 2000). Furthermore, activation of these stereotypes may be less likely to affect the conscious attitudes and behavior of unprejudiced people. So when unconscious stereotypes are activated in unprejudiced people, the effects tend to appear in subtle ways, such as in facial expressions or other nonverbal behaviors (Kawakami, Dion, & Dovidio, 1998; Lepore & Brown, 1997; Vanman et al., 2004).

LINKAGES (a link to Perception, p. 157)

■ What conclusions are most reasonable?

Taken together, research evidence presents a mixed picture regarding the possibility of eliminating ethnic prejudice. True, people in the United States are not nearly as colorblind as we might hope, and ethnic prejudice may be so ingrained in some people as to be subconscious. However, research suggests that it may still be possible to eliminate even subconscious stereotypes (Kawakami, Dovidio, & van Kamp, 2005; Plant & Peruche, 2005; Wheeler & Fiske, 2005). It also appears that when unprejudiced people are made aware of their negative beliefs about some target group, they will actively work to prevent those beliefs from influencing their behavior toward members of that group (Amodio et al., 2004; Devine, Plant, & Buswell, 2000). In short, prejudice is ingrained, but it can also be reduced, and it makes sense to do everything possible to reduce it. In the United States, as in any multicultural country, survival as a civilized society requires that we all continue to fight against overt and covert forms of stereotyping, prejudice, and discrimination. This goal is more important than ever, as fear of, and the fight against, international terrorism can make it all too easy to misjudge and mistreat innocent people based on their ethnicity. ■

Interpersonal Attraction

TRY THIS **Proximity and Liking**
Research on environmental factors in attraction suggests that, barring bad first impressions, the more often we make contact with someone—as neighbors, classmates, or co-workers, for example—the more we tend to like that person. Does this principle apply in your life? To find out, think about how and where you met each of your closest friends. If you can think of cases in which proximity did not lead to liking, what do you think interfered with the formation of friendship?

Research on prejudice suggests some of the reasons why people, from childhood on, may come to dislike or even hate other people. An equally fascinating aspect of social cognition is why people like or love other people. Folklore tells us that "opposites attract," but also that "birds of a feather flock together." Although valid to some degree, neither of these statements is entirely accurate in all cases. We begin our coverage of interpersonal attraction by discussing the factors that lead to initial attraction. We then examine how liking sometimes develops into more intimate relationships.

● Keys to Attraction

Whether you like someone or not depends partly on situational factors and partly on personal characteristics.

● **The Environment** One of the most important determinants of attraction is simple physical proximity (Berscheid & Reis, 1998). As long as you do not initially dislike a person, your liking for that person will increase with additional contact. For example, Richard Moreland and Scott Beach (1992) varied the number of times that several experimental assistants (posing as students) attended a class. Even though none of the assistants ever spoke to anyone in the class, they were rated by the other students as more likable the more often they attended. A more recent study found that these higher ratings generalized to individuals who resembled the people who had been present (Rhodes, Halberstadt, & Brajkovich, 2001). This proximity phenomenon—another example of the mere-exposure effect mentioned earlier—helps account for the fact that next-door neighbors are usually more likely to become friends than people who live farther from one another. Chances are, most of your friends are people whom you met as neighbors, co-workers, or classmates (Liben-Nowell et al., 2005).

The circumstances under which people first meet also influence attraction. In accordance with the conditioning principles discussed in the chapter on learning, you are much more likely to be attracted to a stranger if you meet in comfortable, rather than uncomfortable, physical conditions. Similarly, if you are rewarded in the presence of a stranger, the chances that you will like that stranger are increased, even if the stranger was not the one who gave the reward. In one study, for example, an experimenter judged people's creativity while another person watched. Compared with those

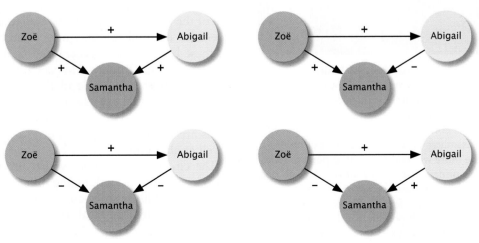

FIGURE 17.7

Attitude Similarity and Attraction

This graph shows the results of a study in which participants learned about another person's attitudes. Their liking for that person was strongly related to the proportion of the other person's attitudes that were similar to the participants' own attitudes.

Source: Adapted from Byrne & Nelson (1965).

who received a negative evaluation, participants who were evaluated positively tended to like the observer more (Griffitt & Guay, 1969). At least among strangers, then, liking can occur through associating someone with something pleasant.

● **Similarity** People also tend to like those they perceive as similar to themselves on variables such as age, religion, smoking or drinking habits, or being a "morning" or "evening" person (Buston & Emlen, 2003; Rushton & Bons, 2005). As shown in Figure 17.7, similarity in attitudes is an especially important influence on attraction. This relationship has been found among children, college students, adult workers, and senior citizens (Taylor et al., 2006).

Similarity in attitudes toward mutual acquaintances is a particularly good predictor of liking, because in general, people prefer relationships that are *balanced*. As illustrated in Figure 17.8, if Zoe likes Abigail, the relationship is balanced as long as they agree on their evaluation of a third person, Samantha, regardless of whether they like or dislike that third person. However, the relationship will be imbalanced if Zoe and Abigail disagree on their evaluation of the third person.

One reason why we like people with similar views of the world is that we expect such people to think highly of us (Condon & Crano, 1988). Like many important relationships, it's hard to say whether attraction is a cause or an effect of similarity. For example, you might like someone because his attitudes are similar to yours, but it is also possible that as a result of liking him, your attitudes will become more similar to his (Davis & Rusbult, 2001). Even if your own attitudes don't change, you may change your *perceptions* of the liked person's attitudes such that those attitudes seem more similar to yours (Brehm, 1992).

● **Physical Attractiveness** Physical characteristics are another important factor in attraction, particularly during the initial stages of a relationship (Berscheid & Reis, 1998). From preschool through adulthood, physical attractiveness is a key to popularity with members of both sexes (e.g., Langlois et al., 2000). Consistent with the **matching hypothesis** of interpersonal attraction, however, people tend to date, marry, or form other committed relationships with those who are similar to themselves in physical attractiveness (Yela & Sangrador, 2001). One possible reason for this outcome is that people tend to be most attracted to those with the greatest physical appeal, but they also want to avoid being rejected by such individuals. So it may be compromise, not preference, that leads people to pair off with those who are roughly equivalent to themselves in physical attractiveness (Carli, Ganley, & Pierce-Otay, 1991).

FIGURE 17.8

Balanced and Imbalanced Relationships

Here are some common examples of balanced and imbalanced patterns of relationships among three people. The plus and minus signs refer to liking and disliking, respectively. Balanced relationships are comfortable and harmonious. Imbalanced ones often bring conflict.

Balanced relationships   **Imbalanced relationships**

FIGURE 17.9

Sex Differences in Date and Mate Preferences

According to evolutionary psychologists, men and women have developed different strategies for selecting sexual partners. These psychologists say that women became more selective than men because they can have relatively few children and want a partner who is able to help care for those children. Here are some data supporting this idea. When asked about the intelligence of people they would choose for one-night stands, dating, and sexual relationships, women preferred much smarter partners than men did. Only when the choices concerned steady dating and marriage did the men's preference for bright partners equal that of the women. Critics of the evolutionary approach explain such sex differences as reflecting learned social norms and expectations of how men and women should behave (Eagly & Wood, 1999; Miller, Putcha-Bhagavatula, & Pedersen, 2002).

Source: Kenrick et al. (1993).

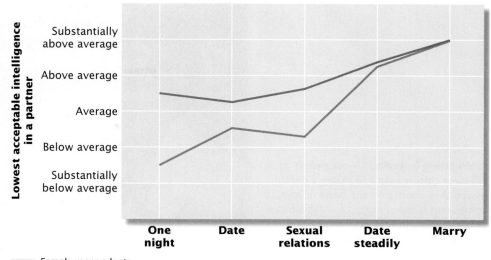

● Female respondents
● Male respondents

● Intimate Relationships and Love

There is much about intimate relationships that psychologists do not—and may never—understand, but they are learning all the time. As mentioned in the chapter on motivation and emotion, evolutionary psychologists suggest that men and women employ different mating strategies and that each gender looks for different attributes in a potential mate (Buss, 2004b; Li & Kenrick, 2006). For example, in short-term relationships, at least, women may be much more selective than men about the intelligence of their partners (Buss, 2004b; see Figure 17.9).

● **Intimate Relationships** Eventually, people who are attracted to each other usually become *interdependent*, which means that the thoughts, emotions, and behaviors of one person affect the thoughts, emotions, and behaviors of the other (Rusbult & Van Lange, 2003). Interdependence is one of the defining characteristics of intimate relationships.

Another key component of successful intimate relationships is *commitment*, which is the extent to which each party is psychologically attached to the relationship and wants to remain in it (Amodio & Showers, 2005). People feel committed to a relationship when they are satisfied with the rewards they receive from it, when they have invested significant tangible and intangible resources in it, and when there are few attractive alternative relationships available to them (Bui, Peplau, & Hill, 1996).

● **Analyzing Love** Although some people think love is simply a strong form of liking, recent research suggests that romantic love and liking are quite separate emotions, at least in the sense that they activate separate areas of the brain (Aron et al., 2005; Emanuele et al., 2006). And although romantic love and sexual desire are often experienced together, they, too, seem to be separate emotions associated with different patterns of physiological arousal (Diamond, 2004). Further, most theorists agree that there are several different types of love (Brehm et al., 2005). One widely accepted view distinguishes between *passionate love* and *companionate love* (Hendrick & Hendrick, 2003). Passionate love is intense, arousing, and marked by both strong physical attraction and deep emotional attachment. Sexual feelings are strong, and thoughts of the loved one intrude on a person's awareness frequently. Companionate love is less arousing but psychologically more intimate. It is marked by mutual concern for the welfare of the other (Kim & Hatfield, 2004).

● **matching hypothesis** The notion that people are most likely to form relationships with those who are similar to themselves in physical attractiveness.

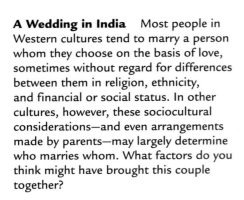

A Wedding in India   Most people in Western cultures tend to marry a person whom they choose on the basis of love, sometimes without regard for differences between them in religion, ethnicity, and financial or social status. In other cultures, however, these sociocultural considerations—and even arrangements made by parents—may largely determine who marries whom. What factors do you think might have brought this couple together?

Robert Sternberg (1997a) has offered a more comprehensive analysis of love. According to his *triangular theory,* the three basic components of love are *passion, intimacy,* and *commitment.* Various combinations of these components result in different types of love, as illustrated in Figure 17.10. For example, Sternberg suggests that *romantic love* involves a high degree of passion and intimacy, yet lacks substantial commitment to the other person. *Companionate love* is marked by a great deal of intimacy and commitment but little passion. *Consummate love* is the most complete and satisfying. It is the most complete because it includes a high level of all three components, and it is the most satisfying because the relationship is likely to fulfill many of the needs of each partner.

Cultural factors have a strong influence on the value that people place on love. In North America and the United Kingdom, for example, the vast majority of people believe that they should love the person they marry. By contrast, in India and Pakistan, about half the people interviewed in a survey said they would marry someone they did not love if that person had other qualities that they desired (Levine et al., 1995). Many such cultural differences in the role of love in marriage are likely to continue, but some of them, such as the differences that had once existed between the United States and China, for example, seem to be disappearing (Hatfield & Rapson, 2006).

● **Strong and Weak Marriages**   Long-term studies of successful and unsuccessful marriages suggest that premarital attitudes and feelings predict marital success. For example, one study found that couples who had a close, intimate relationship and similar attitudes when they were dating were more likely to still be married fifteen years later (Hill & Peplau, 1998; Neff & Karney, 2005). Also, still-married couples were more likely to have had a premarital relationship that was rewarding and balanced.

Among married couples, women—but not men—generally tend to be more satisfied with their marriage when the partners talk a lot about the relationship (Acitelli, 1992). Partners in successful marriages also tend to share each other's view of themselves and the other, even if that view is a negative one (Swann, De La Ronde, & Hixon, 1994). The perception that the relationship is fair and equitable also enhances marital satisfaction (Grote & Clark, 2001). After the birth of a first child, for example, many wives find that they have much more work than they had

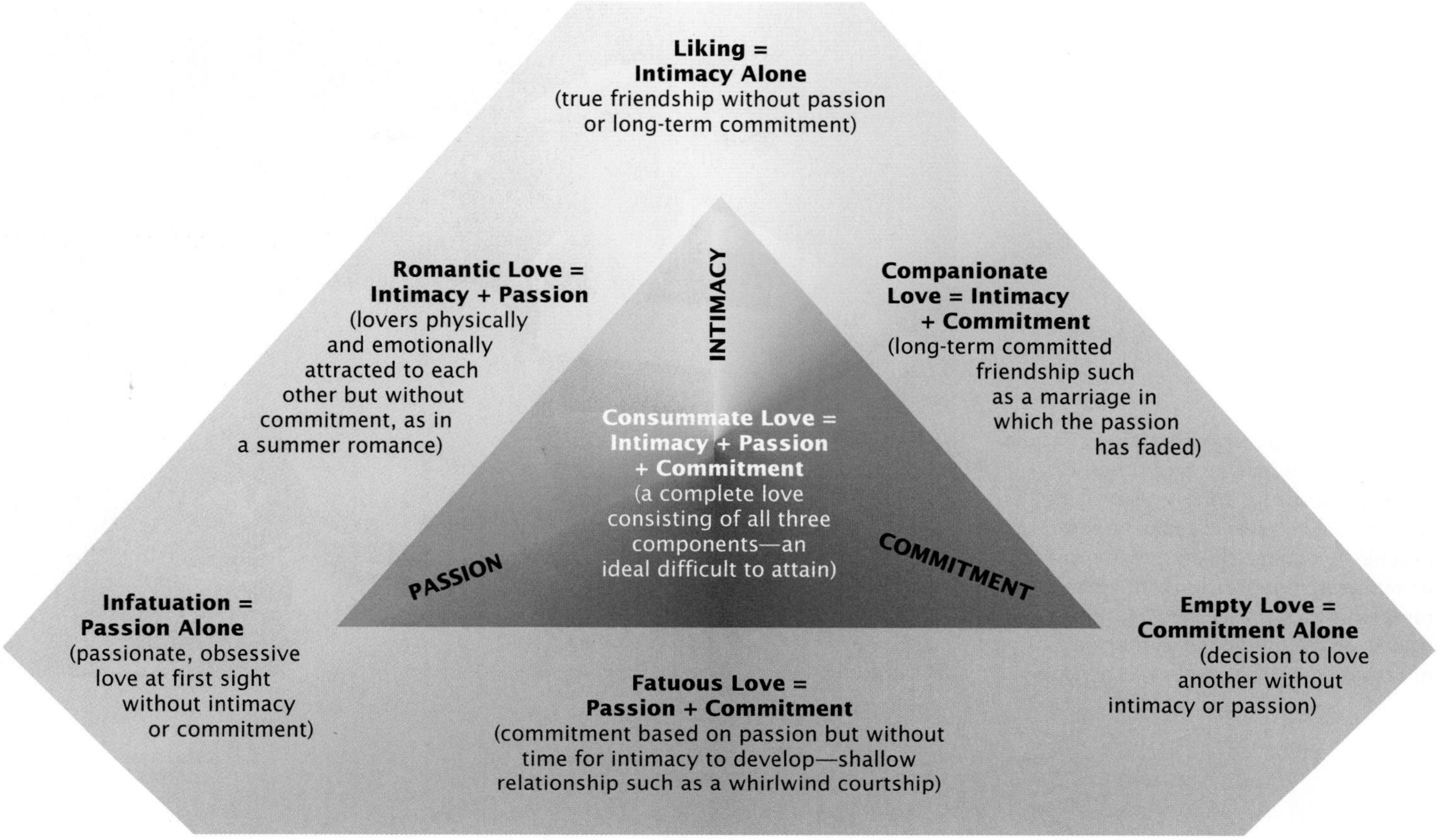

**Liking =
Intimacy Alone**
(true friendship without passion
or long-term commitment)

**Romantic Love =
Intimacy + Passion**
(lovers physically
and emotionally
attracted to each
other but without
commitment, as in
a summer romance)

INTIMACY

**Companionate
Love = Intimacy
+ Commitment**
(long-term committed
friendship such
as a marriage in
which the passion
has faded)

**Consummate Love =
Intimacy + Passion
+ Commitment**
(a complete love
consisting of all three
components—an
ideal difficult to attain)

PASSION

COMMITMENT

**Infatuation =
Passion Alone**
(passionate, obsessive
love at first sight
without intimacy
or commitment)

**Empty Love =
Commitment Alone**
(decision to love
another without
intimacy or passion)

**Fatuous Love =
Passion + Commitment**
(commitment based on passion but without
time for intimacy to develop—shallow
relationship such as a whirlwind courtship)

FIGURE 17.10

A Triangular Theory of Love

According to Sternberg, different types of love result when the three basic components in his triangular theory occur in different combinations. Sternberg has also explored factors associated with falling in love (Sternberg, Hojjat, & Barnes, 2001). Preliminary results suggest that people who share similar views about what a loving relationship should be like are much more likely to fall in love with each other, and remain committed to the relationship, than are people whose views on love are dissimilar.

Source: Sternberg (1988b), pp. 500, 520.

anticipated. If their husbands do not share this work to the degree they expected, wives' marital satisfaction tends to decrease (Hackel & Ruble, 1992; McNulty & Karney, 2004).

One particularly interesting line of research suggests that even brief observations of couples' interactions can predict whether those couples will divorce and when (Driver & Gottman, 2004). Among couples who divorced relatively soon after marriage, the partners tended to express both positive and negative feelings toward one another, but they were unable to control the way they expressed these feelings, especially the negative ones. Communication became increasingly hurtful and eventually broke down (Driver et al., 2003). A different picture emerged, however, in couples who divorced after many years of marriage. These people did not necessarily express negative emotions toward one another. They simply became less and less likely to communicate *any* feelings. The increasing emotional distance between the spouses created a sense of isolation that eventually led to divorce (Gottman & Levenson, 2002). These findings can help us understand why people in a long, and apparently strong, marriage might suddenly announce that they are divorcing—and why they may remain friends afterward. These people may still like each other, but no longer love each other (Gottman & Levenson, 2000; Huston et al., 2001).

TRY THIS **Happy and Healthy** People in marriages and other long-term relationships that are satisfying tend to enjoy better physical and psychological health than those in unsatisfying relationships. In light of research described in the chapter on health, stress, and coping, make a list of reasons why this might be the case.

LINKAGES

As noted in the chapter on introducing psychology, all of psychology's many subfields are related to one another. Our discussion of brain activity and attitudes illustrates just one way in which the topic of this chapter, social cognition, is linked to the subfield of biological psychology (see the chapter on biological aspects of psychology). The Linkages diagram shows ties to two other subfields as well, and there are many more ties throughout the book. Looking for linkages among subfields will help you see how they all fit together and better appreciate the big picture that is psychology.

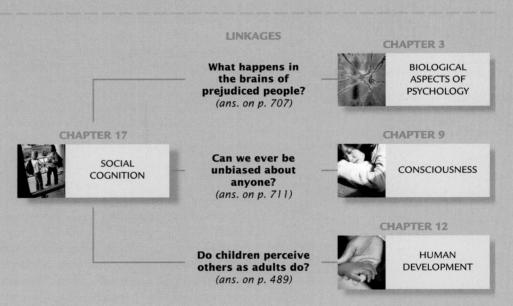

SUMMARY

Social cognition (the mental processes through which people perceive and react to others) is one aspect of *social psychology* (the study of how people influence, and are influenced by, other people).

Social Influences on the Self

People's social and cultural environments affect their thoughts and feelings about themselves, including their *self-esteem* and their *self-concept*.

Social Comparison   When people have no objective criteria by which to judge themselves, they engage in *social comparison* (using others) or *temporal comparison* (using themselves at an earlier time) as their standard. Such comparison can affect self-evaluation, or self-esteem. Categories of people that are habitually used for social comparison are known as *reference groups*. Comparison to reference groups sometimes produces *relative deprivation*, which in turn can cause personal and social turmoil.

Social Identity Theory A person's *social identity* is formed from beliefs about the groups to which the person belongs. Social identity affects the beliefs we hold about ourselves. It permits us to feel part of a larger group, engendering loyalty and sacrifice from group members but also potentially creating bias and discrimination toward people who are not members of the group.

Self-Schemas Through social comparison and the formation of social identity, people develop mental representations of their views and beliefs about themselves. These mental representations, called *self-schemas*, are part of one's self-concept. Self-schemas can affect people's emotional reactions to events.

Social Perception

Social perception concerns the processes by which people interpret information about others, form impressions of them, and draw conclusions about the reasons for their behavior.

The Role of Schemas Schemas, the mental representations about people and social situations that we carry into social interactions, affect what we pay attention to, what we remember, and how we judge people and events.

First Impressions First impressions are formed easily and quickly, in part because people apply existing schemas to their perceptions of others. First impressions change slowly because once we form an impression about another person, we try to maintain it. Schemas, however, can create *self-fulfilling prophecies*, leading people to act in ways that bring out in others behavior that is consistent with expectations.

Explaining Behavior: Attribution *Attribution* is the process of explaining the causes of people's behavior, including our own. Observers tend to attribute behavior to causes that are either internal or external to the actor. In general, they do this by looking at three aspects of the behavior: consensus, consistency, and distinctiveness. People from different cultures may sometimes reach different conclusions about the causes of an actor's behavior.

Biases in Attribution Attributions are affected by biases that systematically distort one's view of behavior. The most common attributional biases are the *fundamental attribution error* (and its cousin, the ultimate attribution error), the *actor-observer bias*, and the *self-serving bias*. Personal and cultural factors can affect the extent to which people exhibit attributional biases.

The Self-Protective Functions of Social Cognition People often protect themselves from admitting something threatening about themselves through unrealistic optimism and a feeling of unique invulnerability.

Attitudes

An *attitude* is the tendency to respond positively or negatively to a particular object. Attitudes affect a wide range of behaviors.

The Structure of Attitudes Many theorists believe that attitudes consist of cognitive (beliefs), affective (feelings), and behavioral (actions) components. However, it is often difficult to predict a specific behavior from a person's beliefs or feelings about an object. Cognitive theories propose that attitudes consist of evaluations of an object that are stored in memory. This approach suggests that the likelihood of attitude-behavior consistency depends on the accessibility of evaluations in memory, on subjective norms, on perceived control over the behavior, and on prior direct experience with the attitude object.

Forming Attitudes Attitudes can be learned through modeling, as well as through classical or operant conditioning. They are also subject to the mere-exposure effect: All else being equal, people develop greater liking for a new object the more often they are exposed to it.

Changing Attitudes The effectiveness of a persuasive message in changing attitudes is influenced by the characteristics of the person who communicates it, by its content, and by the audience receiving it. The *elaboration likelihood model* suggests that attitude change can occur through either a peripheral or a central route, depending on a person's ability and motivation to carefully consider an argument. Another approach to attitude change is to change a person's behavior in the hope that the person's attitude will be adjusted to match the behavior. *Cognitive dissonance theory* holds that if inconsistency between attitudes and behavior creates discomfort related to a person's self-concept or self-image, the person will be motivated to reduce that discomfort. *Self-perception theory* suggests that such attitude changes occur in some cases as people look to their behavior for clues about what their attitudes are.

Prejudice and Stereotypes

Stereotypes often lead to *prejudice* and *discrimination*.

Theories of Prejudice and Stereotyping Motivational theories of prejudice suggest that some people have a need to disrespect and dislike others. This need may stem from the trait of authoritarianism, as well as from a strong social identity. In either case, feeling superior to members of out-groups helps these people to feel better about themselves. As a result, in-group members tend to discriminate against members of out-groups. Cognitive theories suggest that people categorize others into groups in order to reduce social complexity. And learning theories maintain that stereotypes, prejudice, and discriminatory behaviors can be learned from parents, peers, and the media.

Reducing Prejudice The *contact hypothesis* proposes that intergroup contact can reduce prejudice and lead to more favorable attitudes toward a stereotyped group—but only if the contact occurs under specific conditions, such as when there is equal status between group members. Helping diverse people to feel as if they belong to the same group can also reduce intergroup prejudice.

Interpersonal Attraction

Keys to Attraction Interpersonal attraction is a function of many variables. Physical proximity is important because it allows people to meet. The situation in which they meet is important because positive or negative aspects of the situation tend to be associated with the other person. Characteristics of the other person are also important. Attraction tends to be greater when two people share similar attitudes and characteristics. Physical appearance plays a role in attraction. Initially, attraction is strongest to those who are most physically attractive. But for long-term relationships, the *matching hypothesis* applies: People tend to choose others whose physical attractiveness is about the same as theirs.

Intimate Relationships and Love A defining characteristic of intimate relationships is interdependence, and a key component of successful relationships is commitment. Commitment, in turn, is affected by the rewards coming from the relationship, by the resources invested in it, and by the possible alternatives open to each party. Robert Sternberg's triangular theory suggests that love is a function of three components: passion, intimacy, and commitment. Varying combinations of these three components create different types of love. Couples who have long and successful marriages are likely to perceive the relationship as fair to both parties, and they are likely to share warm and loving feelings for each other.

Social Influence

18

If you are like most people, there is probably at least one thing you do in private that you would never do when someone else is around. In this chapter we describe many other ways in which the presence and behavior of other people affect our own behavior, and how we, in turn, affect the behavior of others. Here's how we have organized our presentation:

In the days following the September 11, 2001, attacks on the World Trade Center and the Pentagon—and also after anthrax bacteria were mailed to news organizations and the U.S. Congress—cities throughout the United States experienced a substantial increase in false bomb threats, anthrax hoaxes, and other "copycat" crimes apparently inspired by the terrorists' actions. Unfortunately, this phenomenon is not unusual. After the murderous rampage at Columbine High School in April of 1999, for example, a number of students at other high schools were arrested for threatening similar acts of violence against their classmates. Copycat threats were also made following the horrific massacre at Virginia Tech University in April of 2007. Well-publicized suicides, too, are often copied (Romer, Jamieson, & Jamieson, 2006). After German television reported the case of a young man who killed himself by jumping in front of a train, there was a dramatic increase in railway suicides (Schmidtke & Hafner, 1988). Even telecasts of major professional boxing matches are typically followed by a small increase in murders.

Do these correlations mean that media coverage of violence triggers copycat violence? As described in the chapter on learning, televised violence can play a causal role in aggressive behavior, but there are additional reasons to believe that when suicides and murders become media events, they stimulate people to imitate them. For one thing, many of the people who kill themselves soon after a notable suicide bear a strong similarity to the original victim (Cialdini, 2001). The copycat railway suicides in Germany, for example, were committed almost exclusively by other young German men. Further, murder victims in the days following a professional championship fight are more likely to be young white men if the losing boxer was white, and more likely to be young black men if the loser was black (Miller et al., 1991).

Copycat, or imitative, crimes illustrate the effects of **social influence,** the process whereby a person's behavior is directly or indirectly affected by the words or actions of other people. This chapter begins with a discussion of social influence itself, after which we consider several related aspects of how we are influenced by others, including the processes of conformity, compliance, and obedience. Then we explore the causes and consequences of aggression, helping, and altruism. Finally, we examine circumstances in which people jointly influence one another's behavior, especially circumstances in which people compete with one another for some scarce resource or work together in groups to solve some problem.

Social Influence

Copycat crimes are but one illustration of the fact that people can influence the way other people think, feel, and act, even without specifically trying to do so. There are countless others. For example, simply asking people if they have thought about buying a car in the coming year dramatically increases the chance they will actually purchase a car (Fitzsimons & Shiv, 2001). The most widespread, yet subtle, form of social influence is communicated through social norms.

Norms are learned, socially based rules that prescribe what people should or should not do in various situations (Cialdini & Goldstein, 2004). Norms are

social influence The process whereby one person's behavior is affected by the words or actions of others.

norms Socially based rules that prescribe what people should or should not do in various situations.

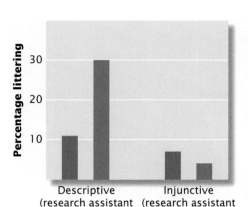

FIGURE 18.1

Descriptive and Injunctive Norms

When both descriptive norms (a littered parking lot) and injunctive norms (a person discarding paper in the parking lot) were consistent with littering, 30 percent of the people crossing the parking lot also littered. But after seeing a person picking up a bag in the parking lot (creating an injunctive norm against littering), very few people engaged in littering, whether or not the lot was littered (Reno, Cialdini, & Kallgren, 1993). Applying these findings to combat alcohol abuse on campus, some student health campaigns now create descriptive norms for responsible drinking by citing statistics showing that most students drink in moderation (Zernike, 2000). Such campaigns might also change injunctive norms by portraying excessive drinking as socially unacceptable (Larimer et al., 2004).

Source: Adapted from Reno, Cialdini, & Kallgren (1993).

• **deindividuation** A psychological state occurring in group members that results in loss of individuality and a tendency to do things not normally done when alone.

transmitted by parents, teachers, clergy, peers, and other agents of culture. Although they often cannot be verbalized, norms are so powerful that people usually follow them automatically. At movie theaters in North America and Britain, for example, norms tell us that we should get in line to buy a ticket rather than crowd around the ticket window; they also lead us to expect that others will do the same. By informing people of what is expected of them and others, norms make social situations less uncertain and more comfortable (Schultz et al., 2007).

Robert Cialdini (2001) has described social norms as either descriptive or injunctive. *Descriptive norms* indicate how most other people actually behave in a given situation. They tell us what actions are common in the situation and thereby implicitly give us permission to act in the same way. The fact that most people do not cross a street until the green light or "walk" sign appears is an example of a descriptive norm. *Injunctive norms* give more specific information about the actions that others find acceptable and those that they find unacceptable. Subtle pressure exists to behave in accordance with these norms. A sign that reads "Do not cross on red" or the person next to you saying the same thing is an example of an injunctive norm.

A study by Raymond Reno and his colleagues (Reno, Cialdini, & Kallgren, 1993) illustrates the differing effects of these two types of norms. The participants were people who walked through a parking lot just after being handed an advertising leaflet. The experimenters arranged for the participants to see another person (who was working with the experimenters) either toss a paper bag on the ground or pick one up from the ground. On half the trials of this experiment, the parking lot was littered with paper; on the other half, the lot was clean. As shown in Figure 18.1, the descriptive norm—seeing another person litter in an already messy environment—appeared to communicate that "many people do this," and a relatively high percentage of people dropped their leaflet in the littered parking lot. By contrast, the injunctive norm—seeing someone pick up litter—appeared to communicate that even though many people litter, it's not the right thing to do. When this norm was evident, fewer than 5 percent of the people dropped their leaflet in the littered parking lot. Later research has shown that norms are most likely to actually reduce littering when a person focuses on and believes in the relevant norm (Kallgren, Reno, & Cialdini, 2000)

One very powerful injunctive norm is *reciprocity*, the tendency to respond to others as they have acted toward you (Cialdini & Goldstein, 2004). Restaurant servers often apply this norm by leaving some candy with the bill. Customers who receive this gift tend to reciprocate by leaving a larger tip than customers who don't get candy (Strohmetz et al., 2002). The reciprocity norm probably exists in every culture, but other norms are not universal (Miller, 2001). For instance, people around the world differ greatly in terms of the physical distance they maintain between themselves and others during conversation. People from South America usually stand much closer to one another than do people from North America. And as suggested in the chapter on psychological disorders, behavior considered normal and friendly in one culture may be seen as abnormal, and even offensive, in another.

The social influence exerted by norms creates orderly social behavior. But social norms can also lead to a breakdown in order. For example, **deindividuation** is a phenomenon in which a person becomes "submerged in a group" and loses the sense of individuality (Cialdini & Goldstein, 2004). When people experience deindividuation, they become emotionally aroused and feel intense closeness with the group. This increased awareness of group membership may create greater adherence to the group's norms, even if those norms promote antisocial behavior. In other words, through deindividuation, people appear to become "part of the herd," and they may perform acts that they would not do otherwise. Fans at rock concerts and athletic events have trampled one another to death in their frenzy to get the best seats.

Clothing and Culture The social norms that guide how people dress and behave in various situations are part of the culturally determined socialization process described in the chapter on human development. The process is the same worldwide. Parents, teachers, peers, religious leaders, and others communicate their culture's social norms to children, but differences in those norms result in quite different behaviors from culture to culture.

Deindividuation Robes, hoods, and group rituals help create deindividuation in these Ku Klux Klansmen by focusing their attention on membership in their organization and on its values. The hoods also hide their identities, which reduces their sense of personal responsibility and accountability and makes it easier for them to engage in hate crimes and other cowardly acts of bigotry. Deindividuation operates in other groups, too, ranging from lynch mobs and terrorist cells to political protesters and urban rioters. In short, people who feel themselves to be anonymous members of a group may engage in antisocial acts that they might not perform on their own.

Normally mild-mannered people may find themselves throwing rocks or fire bombs at police during political protests.

The greater the sense of personal anonymity, the more influence the group appears to have (Lea, Spears, & de Groot, 2001). An analysis of newspaper accounts of lynchings in the United States over a fifty-year period showed that larger lynch mobs were more savage and vicious than smaller ones (Mullen, 1986). Deindividuation provides an example of how, given the right circumstances, quite normal people can engage in destructive, even violent, behavior.

LINKAGES **Motivation and the Presence of Others**

LINKAGES (a link to Motivation and Emotion, p. 429)

In the chapter on motivation and emotion, we noted that social factors such as parental attitudes toward achievement often affect motivation. But a person's current motivational state is also affected by the mere presence of other people. As an illustration, consider what was probably the first experiment in social psychology, conducted by Norman Triplett in 1897.

Triplett noticed that bicycle racers tended to go faster when other racers were nearby than when they were alone. Did seeing one another remind the racers of the need to go faster to win? To test this possibility, Triplett arranged for bicyclists to complete a twenty-five-mile course under three conditions: riding alone in a race against the clock; riding with another cyclist, but not in competition; or

Social Facilitation   Premier athletes like Lindsay Davenport, shown here winning the women's singles championship at Wimbledon in 2005, are able to perform at their best even though large crowds are present. In fact, the crowds probably help them do well, because the presence of others tends to increase arousal, which enhances the performance of familiar and well-learned skills, such as tennis strokes. However, arousal created by an audience tends to interfere with the performance of unfamiliar and poorly developed skills. This is one reason that professional athletes who show flawless grace in front of thousands of fans are likely to freeze up or blow their lines in front of a small production crew when trying for the first time to tape a TV ad or a public service announcement.

competing directly with another rider. The cyclists went much faster when another rider was present than when they were simply racing against time. This was true even when they were not competing against the other person. Something about the presence of the other person, not just competition, produced increased speed.

The term **social facilitation** describes circumstances in which the mere presence of other people can improve performance. This improvement does not always occur, however. The presence of other people sometimes hurts performance, a process known as **social impairment**. For decades these results seemed contradictory. Then Robert Zajonc (pronounced "ZYE-onze") suggested that both effects could be explained by one process: arousal.

The presence of other people, said Zajonc, increases a person's general level of arousal or motivation (Zajonc, 1965). Why? One reason is that being watched by others increases our sense of being evaluated, producing worry that in turn increases emotional arousal (Penner & Craiger, 1992). Arousal increases the tendency to perform those behaviors that are most *dominant*—the ones we know best—and this tendency can either help or hinder performance. If you are performing an easy, familiar task, such as riding a bike, the increased arousal caused by the presence of others should allow you to ride even faster than normal. But if the task is hard or unfamiliar—such as trying new dance steps or playing a piano piece you just learned—the most dominant responses may be incorrect and cause your performance to suffer. In other words, the impact of other people on performance depends on whether the task is easy or difficult.

The presence of others may affect performance in other ways as well. For example, having an audience may distract us from the task at hand or cause us to focus on only one part of it, thus impairing performance (Aiello & Douthitt, 2001).

If a person is not merely in the presence of others but is actually working on a task with them, the impact of their presence changes somewhat. In these situations, people typically exert less effort than they do when performing alone, a phenomenon called **social loafing** (Karau & Williams, 1997). Whether the task is pulling on a rope, clapping as loudly as possible, or trying to solve puzzles, people tend to work harder when performing alone than with others (Baron, Kerr, & Miller, 1992; Geen, 1991). There are at least three reasons behind this social

- **social facilitation**   A phenomenon in which the presence of others improves a person's performance.
- **social impairment**   A reduction in performance due to the presence of other people.
- **social loafing**   Exerting less effort when performing a group task than when performing the same task alone.

loafing phenomenon. First, it is usually much harder to evaluate the performance of individuals when they are working as part of a group. As a result, it is simply easier to succeed at loafing when in a group. Second, rewards may come to a group whether or not every member exerts maximum effort. Third, a group's rewards are usually divided equally among its members rather than according to individual effort (Karau & Williams, 1997).

In North American and other Western countries, social loafing can be seen in all kinds of groups, from volunteer committees to search parties. Because social loafing can reduce productivity in business situations, it is important for managers to develop ways of evaluating the efforts of every individual in a work group, not just the overall output of the team. Social loafing can also be reduced by strategies that cause people to like the group and identify with it (Karau & Williams, 1997), and by the punishment that social loafers tend to receive from other, harder-working group members (Barclay, 2006).

Social loafing is much less common in Eastern cultures, such as those of China and Japan. In fact, in collectivist cultures, working in a group usually produces *social striving*—defined as greater individual effort when working in a group (Matsumoto, 2000). This difference in the effects of group membership on individual efforts probably reflects the value that collectivist cultures place on coordinated and cooperative group activities. This orientation serves to discourage social loafing. ■

Conformity and Compliance

Suppose you are with three of your friends. One says that Franklin Roosevelt was the greatest president in the history of the United States. You think that the greatest president was Abraham Lincoln, but before you can say anything, another friend agrees that it was Roosevelt, and then the other one does as well. What would you do? Disagree with all three? Maintain your opinion but keep quiet? Change your mind?

Mass Conformity   The faithful who gather at Mecca, at the Vatican, and at other holy places around the world exemplify the power of religion and other social forces to produce conformity to group norms.

Standard line

(A)

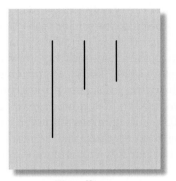

Test lines

(B)

FIGURE 18.2

Stimulus Lines for Conformity Studies

TRY THIS ⚙ Participants in Asch's (1956) experiments saw a new set of lines like these on each trial. The middle line in Part B matches the one in Part A, but when several of Asch's assistants chose an incorrect line, so did many of the participants. Try re-creating this experiment with four friends. Secretly ask three of them to choose the line on the left when you show this drawing, then see if the fourth person conforms to the group norm. If not, do you think it was something about the person, the length of the incorrect line chosen, or both that led to nonconformity? Would conformity be more likely if the first three people were to choose the line on the right? (Read on for more about this possibility.)

Source: Asch (1955).

• **conformity** Changing one's behavior or beliefs to match those of others, generally as a result of real or imagined, though unspoken, group pressure.

• **compliance** Adjusting one's behavior because of an explicit or implicit request.

When people change their behavior or beliefs to match those of other members of a group, they are said to conform. **Conformity** occurs as a result of group pressure, real or imagined (Cialdini & Goldstein, 2004). You probably have experienced such group pressure when everyone around you stood to applaud a performance you thought was not that great. You might have conformed by standing as well, though no one told you to do so. The group's behavior created a silent, but influential, pressure to follow suit. **Compliance,** in contrast, occurs when people adjust their behavior because of a request. The request can be clear and *explicit,* such as when someone says, "Could you do me a favor?," or subtle and *implicit,* as when someone simply looks at you in a way that lets you know the person needs a favor.

● The Role of Norms

Conformity and compliance are usually generated by spoken or unspoken norms. In a classic experiment, Muzafer Sherif (1937) charted the formation of a group norm by taking advantage of a perceptual illusion, called the *autokinetic phenomenon.* In this illusion, a stationary point of light in a pitch dark room appears to move. Estimates of the amount of movement tend to stay the same over time—if an observer is alone. But when Sherif tested several people at once, asking each person to say aloud how far the light moved on repeated trials, their estimates tended to converge. They had established a group norm. Even more important, when the individuals from the group were later tested alone, they continued to be influenced by this norm.

In another classic experiment, Solomon Asch (1956) examined how people would respond when they faced a norm that already existed but was obviously wrong. The participants in this experiment saw a standard line like the one in Figure 18.2(A); then they saw a display like that in Figure 18.2(B). Their task was to pick out the line in the display that was the same length as the one they had first been shown.

Each participant performed this task in a small group of people who posed as fellow participants, but who were actually the experimenter's assistants. There were two conditions. In the control condition, the real participant responded first. In the experimental condition, the participant did not respond until after the assistants did. The assistants chose the correct response on six trials, but on the other twelve trials they all gave the same obviously incorrect response. So on twelve trials, each participant was confronted with a "social reality" created by a group norm that conflicted with the physical reality created by what the person could clearly see. Only 5 percent of the participants in the control condition ever made a mistake on this easy task. However, among participants who heard the assistants' responses before giving their own, about 70 percent made at least one error by conforming to the group norm. An analysis of 133 studies conducted in seventeen countries reveals that conformity in Asch-type situations has declined somewhat in the United States since the 1950s, but it still occurs. It is especially likely in collectivist cultures, in which conformity to group norms is emphasized (Cialdini et al., 2001).

Pressure for conformity can even affect reports about personal experiences. In one study that used a procedure similar to Asch's, participants were shown a number of objects. Later, the same objects were shown again, along with some new ones, and the participants were asked to say whether they had seen each object in the previous display. When tested alone, the participants' memories were quite accurate, but hearing another person's opinion about which objects had or had not been shown before strongly affected their memory of which objects they had seen (Hoffman et al., 2001).

● Why Do People Conform?

Why did so many people in Asch's experiment, and others like it, give incorrect responses when they were capable of near-perfect performance? One possibility is that they displayed public conformity, giving an answer they did not believe simply because it was the socially desirable thing to do. Another possibility is that they experienced *private acceptance*: Perhaps the participants used other people's responses as legitimate evidence about reality, were convinced that their own perceptions were wrong, and actually changed their minds. Morton Deutsch and Harold Gerard (1955) reasoned that if conformity disappeared when people gave their responses without identifying themselves, then Asch's findings must reflect public conformity, not private acceptance. Actually, conformity does decrease when people respond anonymously instead of publicly, but it doesn't disappear (Deutsch & Gerard, 1955). So people sometimes say things in public that they don't believe, but hearing other people's responses also influences their private beliefs (Moscovici, 1985).

Why are group norms so powerful? Research suggests three influential factors (Cialdini & Goldstein, 2004). First, people want to be correct, and norms provide information about what is right and wrong. This factor may help explain why some extremely disturbed or distressed people consider stories about suicide to be "social proof" that self-destruction is a reasonable way out of their problems (Cialdini, 2001). Second, people want others to like them, so they may seek favor by conforming to the norms that those others have established. Third, conforming to group norms may increase a person's sense of self-worth, especially if the group is valued or has high prestige (Cialdini & Goldstein, 2004). The process may occur without our awareness (Lakin & Chartrand, 2003). For example, observations of interviews by Larry King, the television talk-show host, revealed that he tended to imitate the speech patterns of high-status guests but not low-status ones (Gregory & Webster, 1996).

Finally, norms influence the distribution of social rewards and punishments (Cialdini, 1995). From childhood on, people in many cultures learn that going along with group norms is good and earns rewards. (These positive outcomes presumably help compensate for not always being able to say or do exactly what we please.) People also learn that breaking a norm may bring punishments ranging from scoldings for small transgressions to imprisonment for violation of norms that have been translated into laws.

■ When Do People Conform?

People do not always conform to social influence. In the original Asch studies, for example, nearly 30 percent of the participants did not go along with the research assistants' obviously incorrect judgments. Countless experiments have probed the question of what combinations of people and circumstances do and do not lead to conformity.

● **Ambiguity of the Situation** *Ambiguity*, or uncertainty, is very important in determining how much conformity will occur. As the physical reality of a situation becomes less certain, people rely more and more on others' opinions, and conformity to a group norm becomes increasingly likely (Cialdini & Goldstein, 2004).

TRY THIS You can demonstrate this aspect of conformity on any street corner. First, create an ambiguous situation by having several people look at the sky or the top of a building. When passersby ask what is going on, be sure everyone excitedly reports seeing something interesting but fleeting—perhaps a faint light or a tiny, shiny object. If you are especially successful, conforming newcomers will begin persuading other passersby that there is something fascinating to be seen.

● **Unanimity and Size of the Majority** If ambiguity contributes so much to conformity, why did so many of Asch's participants conform to a judgment that was so clearly wrong? The answer has to do with the *unanimity* of the group's judgment and the number of people expressing it. Specifically, people experience great pressure to conform as long as the majority is unanimous. If even one other person in the group disagrees with the majority view, conformity drops greatly. When Asch (1951) arranged for just one assistant to disagree with the others, fewer than 10 percent of the real participants conformed. Once unanimity is broken, it becomes much

easier to disagree with the majority, even
with the person's own view (Turner, 1991

Conformity also depends on the size of
phenomenon by varying the number of a
Conformity to incorrect norms grew as th
But most of the growth in conformity occ
one to about three or four members. Furt
after Asch's research, Bibb Latané (prono
phenomenon with his *social impact theory*
an individual depends not only on group s
group is to the person. And according to
size of a majority depends on how big the
ity from, say, two to three will have muc
sixty to sixty-one. The reason is that the increase from sixty to sixty-one is psychologically much smaller than the change from two to three; it attracts far less notice in
relative terms. Does this explanation sound familiar? The principles underlying it are
similar to those of Weber's law, which, as described in the chapter on perception, gov-
erns our experience of changes in brightness, weight, and other physical stimuli.

● **Minority Influence**   Conformity can also result from *minority influence*, by
which a minority in a group influences the behavior or beliefs of a majority (Crano
& Prislin, 2006). This phenomenon is less common than majority influence, but
minorities can be influential, especially when they are established members of the
group, they agree with one another, and persist in their views (David & Turner,
2001). Perhaps because the views of a numerical minority are examined especially
carefully (Martin & Hewstone, 2003), minority-influenced change often takes a
while to occur and may involve only a moderate adjustment of the majority view
(Alvaro & Crano, 1997; Crano & Chen, 1998).

● **Gender**   Early research on conformity suggested that women conform more
than men, but this gender difference stemmed mainly from the fact that the tasks
used in those experiments were often more familiar to men than to women. This fact
is important because people are especially likely to conform when they are faced
with an unfamiliar situation (Cialdini & Goldstein, 2004). No male-female differences in conformity have been found in research using materials that are equally
familiar to both genders (Maupin & Fisher, 1989).

So why do some people still perceive women as more conforming than men
despite evidence to the contrary? Part of the answer may lie in their perception of the
relative social status of men and women. People who think of women as having lower
social status than men in most social situations are likely to see women as easier to
influence, even though men and women conform equally often (Eagly, 1987).

● Inducing Compliance

In the conformity experiments we have described, the participants experienced psychological pressure to conform to the views or actions of others, even though no one
specifically asked them to do so. In contrast, *compliance* involves changing what
you say or do because of a request.

How is compliance brought about? Many people believe that the direct approach
is always best: If you want something, ask for it. But salespeople, political strategists,
social psychologists, and other experts have learned that often the best way to get
something is to ask for something else. Three examples of this strategy are the foot-
in-the-door technique, the door-in-the-face procedure, and the low-ball approach.

The *foot-in-the-door technique* works by getting a person to agree to a small
request and then gradually presenting larger ones. In the original experiment on
this strategy, homeowners were asked to do one of two things. Some were asked

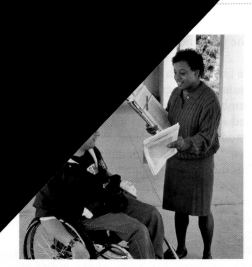

Sign Here, Please Have you ever been asked to sign a petition in favor of a political, social, or economic cause? Supporters of these causes know that people who comply with this small request are the best ones to contact later with requests to do more. Complying with larger requests is made more likely because it is consistent with the signer's initial commitment to the cause. If you were contacted after signing a petition, did you agree to donate money or perhaps become a volunteer?

to allow a large, unattractive "Drive Carefully" sign to be placed on their front lawns. Approximately 17 percent of the people approached in this way complied with the request. In the foot-in-the-door condition, however, homeowners were first asked only to sign a petition supporting legislation aimed at reducing traffic accidents. Several weeks later, when a different person asked these same people to put the "Drive Carefully" sign on their lawns, 55 percent of them complied (Freedman & Fraser, 1966).

Why should the granting of small favors lead to granting larger ones? First, people are usually far more likely to comply with a request that costs little in time, money, effort, or inconvenience. Second, complying with a small request makes people think of themselves as being committed to the cause or issue involved (Burger & Guadango, 2003). This change occurs through the processes of self-perception and cognitive dissonance discussed in the chapter on social cognition. In the study just described, participants who signed the petition might have thought, "I must care enough about traffic safety to do something about it." Compliance with the higher-cost request (displaying the sign) then became more likely because it was consistent with these people's self-perceptions and past actions (Burger & Caldwell, 2003).

The foot-in-the-door technique can be quite effective. Steven Sherman (1980) created a 700 percent increase in the rate at which people volunteered to work for a charity simply by first getting them to say that, in a hypothetical situation, they would volunteer if asked. For some companies, the foot in the door is a request that potential customers merely answer a few questions. The request to buy something comes later. Others offer a small gift, or "door opener," as salespeople call it. Acceptance of the gift not only allows a foot in the door, but may also activate the reciprocity norm: Many people who get something free of charge feel obligated to reciprocate by buying something—especially if the request to do so is delayed for a while (Cialdini, 2001; Guadagno et al., 2001).

The *door-in-the-face procedure* offers a second way of obtaining compliance (Pascual & Guéguen, 2005). This strategy begins with a request for a favor that is likely to be denied. The person making the request then concedes that asking for the initial favor was excessive and substitutes a lesser alternative—which was what the person really wanted in the first place! Because the person appears willing to compromise and because the new request seems modest in comparison with the first

OK, OK, I'll Be Home by One! The door-in-the-face approach is sometimes used successfully by teenagers to influence parents to comply with many kinds of requests. After asking to stay out overnight, a youngster whose curfew is normally 11 P.M. might be allowed to stay out until 1 A.M.—a "compromise" that was actually the original goal.

one, it is more likely to be granted than if it had been made at the outset. Here again, compliance appears to be due partly to activation of the reciprocity norm. The door-in-the-face strategy often lies at the heart of the bargaining that takes place among political groups and between labor and management (Ginges et al., 2007).

A third technique for gaining compliance, called the *low-ball approach*, is commonly used by car dealers and other salespeople. The first step in this strategy is to obtain a person's oral commitment to do something, such as to purchase a car at a certain price. Once this commitment is made, the cost of fulfilling it is increased, often because of an "error" in computing the car's price. Why do buyers end up paying much more than originally planned for "low-balled" items? Apparently, once people say they will do something, they feel obligated to follow through, especially when the commitment was made in public and when the person who obtains the initial commitment also makes the higher-cost request (Burger & Cornelius, 2003). In other words, as described in relation to cognitive dissonance theory in the chapter on social cognition, people like to be consistent in their words and deeds. In this case, it appears that people try to maintain a positive self-image by acting in accordance with their previously stated intention, even though it may cost them a great deal to do so.

Obedience

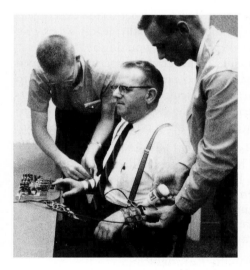

FIGURE 18.3

Studying Obedience in the Laboratory

In this photograph from Milgram's original experiment, a man is being strapped into a chair with electrodes on his arm. Although participants in the experiment didn't know it, the man was actually one of the experimenter's research assistants and received no shock.

Compliance involves a change in behavior in response to a request. In the case of **obedience**, the behavior change comes in response to a *demand* from an authority figure. In the 1960s, Stanley Milgram developed a laboratory procedure at Yale University to study obedience. In his first experiment, he used newspaper ads to recruit forty male volunteers between the ages of twenty and fifty. Among the participants were professionals, white-collar businessmen, and unskilled workers (Milgram, 1963).

Imagine you are one of the people who answered the ad. When you arrive for the experiment, you join a fifty-year-old gentleman who has also volunteered and has been scheduled for the same session. The experimenter explains that the purpose of the experiment is to examine the effects of punishment on learning. One of you—the "teacher"—will help the "learner" remember a list of words by administering an electrical shock whenever he makes a mistake. Then the experimenter turns to you and asks you to draw one of two cards out of a hat. Your card says "TEACHER." You think to yourself that this must be your lucky day.

Now the learner is taken into another room and strapped into a chair, as shown in Figure 18.3. Electrodes are attached to his arms. Meanwhile, you are shown a shock generator featuring thirty switches. The experimenter explains that the switch on the far left administers a mild, 15-volt shock and that each succeeding switch increases the shock by 15 volts. The switch on the far right delivers 450 volts. The far left section of the shock generator is labeled "slight shock." Looking across the panel, you see "moderate shock," "very strong shock," and at the far right, "danger—severe shock." The last two switches are ominously labeled "XXX." The experimenter explains that you, the teacher, will begin by reading a list of word pairs to the learner. Then you will go through the list again, presenting just one word of each pair. It is the learner's task to say which word went with it. After the first mistake, you are to throw the switch to deliver 15 volts of shock. Each time the learner makes another mistake, you are to increase the shock by 15 volts.

You begin, following the experimenter's instructions. But after the learner makes his fifth mistake and you throw the switch to give him 75 volts, you hear a loud moan. At 90 volts, the learner cries out in pain. At 150 volts, he screams and asks to be let out of the experiment. You look to the experimenter, who says, "Proceed with the next word."

No shock was actually delivered in Milgram's experiments. The learner was always an employee of the experimenter, and the moans and other signs of pain came from a prerecorded tape. But you don't know that. What would you do in this

obedience Changing behavior in response to a demand from an authority figure.

FIGURE **18.4**

Results of Milgram's Obedience Experiment

When Milgram asked a group of undergraduates and a group of psychiatrists to predict how participants in his experiment would respond, they estimated that no more than 2 percent would go all the way to 450 volts. In fact, 65 percent of the participants did so. What do you think you would have done in this situation?

Source: Milgram (1963).

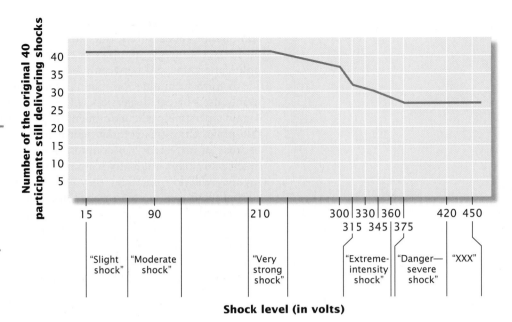

situation? Suppose you continue and eventually deliver 180 volts. The learner screams that he cannot stand the pain any longer and starts banging on the wall. The experimenter says, "You have no other choice; you must go on." Would you continue? Would you keep going even when the learner begged to be let out of the experiment and then fell silent? Would you administer 450 volts of potentially deadly shock to a perfect stranger just because an experimenter demanded that you do so?

Figure 18.4 shows that only 5 participants in Milgram's experiment stopped before 300 volts, and 26 out of 40 participants (or 65 percent) went all the way to the 450-volt level. The decision to continue was difficult and stressful for the participants. Many protested repeatedly; but each time the experimenter told them to continue, they did so. Here is a partial transcript of what a typical participant said:

[After throwing the 180-volt switch:] He can't stand it. I'm not going to kill that man in there. Do you hear him hollering? He's hollering. He can't stand it. What if something happens to him? I'm not going to get that man sick in there. He's hollering in there. Do you know what I mean? I mean, I refuse to take responsibility. He's getting hurt in there. . . . Too many left here. Geez, if he gets them wrong. There are too many of them left. I mean, who is going to take responsibility if anything happens to that gentleman?

[After the experimenter accepts responsibility:] All right. . . .

[After administering 240 volts:] Oh, no, you mean I've got to keep going up the scale? No, sir, I'm not going to kill that man. I'm not going to give him 450 volts.

[After the experimenter says, "The experiment requires that you go on":] I know it does, but that man is hollering in there, sir.

This participant administered shock up to 450 volts. (Milgram, 1974, p. 74)

● Factors Affecting Obedience

Milgram had not expected so many people to deliver such apparently intense shocks. Was there something about his procedure that produced this high level of obedience? To find out, Milgram and other researchers varied the original procedure in a number of ways. The overall level of obedience to an authority figure was usually quite high, but the degree of obedience was affected by several factors.

Proximity and Obedience
Milgram's research suggested that the close physical proximity of an authority figure is one of several factors that can enhance obedience to authority (Rada & Rogers, 1973). This proximity principle is employed in the military, where no one is ever far away from the authority of a higher-ranking person.

● **Experimenter Status and Prestige**   In Milgram's original study, the experimenter's status and prestige as a Yale University professor created two kinds of social power that affected the participants. The first was *expert social power*, which is the ability to influence people because they assume the person in power is a knowledgeable and responsible expert. The second was *legitimate social power*, which is the ability to influence people because they assume the person in power has the right or legitimate authority to tell them what to do (Blass & Schmitt, 2001).

To test the effects of reduced status and prestige, Milgram rented an office in a rundown building in Bridgeport, Connecticut. He then placed a newspaper ad for people to participate in research sponsored by a private firm. There was no mention of Yale. In all other ways, the experimental procedure was identical to the original. Under these less impressive circumstances, the level of obedience dropped, but not as much as you might expect; 48 percent of the participants continued to the maximum level of shock, compared with 65 percent in the original study. Milgram concluded that people still would obey instructions that could cause great harm to another even if the authority figure was not associated with a prestigious institution. Evidently, people's willingness to follow orders from an authority operates somewhat independently of the setting in which the orders are given.

● **The Behavior of Others**   To study how the behavior of fellow participants might affect obedience, Milgram (1965) created a situation in which there were apparently three teachers. Teacher 1 (in reality, a research assistant) read the words to the learner. Teacher 2 (another research assistant) stated whether or not the learner's response was correct. Teacher 3 (the actual participant) was to deliver a shock when mistakes were made. At 150 volts, when the learner began to complain that the shock was too painful, Teacher 1 said he would not participate any longer and left the room. The experimenter asked him to come back, but he refused. The experimenter then instructed Teachers 2 and 3 to continue by themselves. The experiment went on for several more trials. However, at 210 volts, Teacher 2 said that the learner was suffering too much and refused to participate further. The experimenter then told Teacher 3 (the actual participant) to continue the procedure. In this case, only 10 percent of the participants (compared with 65 percent in the original study) continued to deliver shocks all the way up to 450 volts. In other words, as research on conformity would suggest, the presence of others who disobey appears to be the most powerful factor in reducing obedience.

Civil Disobedience Not everyone is blindly obedient to authority. In 1955, Rosa Parks was arrested and fingerprinted in Montgomery, Alabama, after refusing an order to move to the "colored" section in the back of a segregated bus. Her courageous act of disobedience sparked the civil rights movement in the United States.

● **Personality Characteristics** Were the participants in Milgram's original experiment heartless creatures who would have given strong shocks even if there had been no pressure on them to do so? Quite the opposite; most of them were nice people who were influenced by experimental situations to behave in apparently anti-social ways. In a later demonstration of the same phenomenon, college students playing the role of prison guards behaved with aggressive heartlessness toward other students who were playing the role of prisoners (Zimbardo, 1973). A more recent illustration of this phenomenon occurred among some U.S. soldiers who were assigned to guard or interrogate prisoners in Afghanistan and Iraq.

Still, not everyone is equally obedient to authority. For example, people high in *authoritarianism* (a characteristic discussed in the chapter on social cognition) are more likely than others to comply with an experimenter's request to shock the learner (Blass, 1991). Support for this idea comes from data suggesting that German soldiers who obeyed orders to kill Jews during World War II were higher on author-itarianism than other German men of the same age and background (Steiner & Fahrenberg, 2000).

● Evaluating Milgram's Studies

How relevant are Milgram's forty-five year-old studies in today's world? Consider this fact: The U.S. Federal Aviation Administration attributes some commercial air-line accidents to a phenomenon it calls "captainitis." This phenomenon occurs when the captain of an aircraft makes an obvious error, but none of the other crew members is willing to challenge the captain's authority by pointing out the mistake. As a result, planes have crashed and people have died (Kanki & Foushee, 1990). Obedience to authority may also have operated during the World Trade Center attack on September 11, 2001, when some people who had started for the exits returned to their offices after hearing an ill-advised public address announcement telling them to do so. Most of these people died as a result. Such events suggest that Milgram's findings are still relevant and important. Similar kinds of obedience have

May I Take Your Order?   In February of 2004, the managers of four fast-food restaurants in Boston, Massachusetts, received calls from someone claiming to be a police detective on the trail of a robbery suspect. The caller said that the suspect might be one of the restaurant's employees and told the managers to strip-search all of them for evidence of guilt. The calls turned out to be hoaxes, but every manager obeyed this bizarre order, apparently because it appeared to come from a legitimate authority. In a similar case, hospital nurses obeyed medical treatment orders given by a teenager who claimed he was a doctor (Kenrick, Neuberg, & Cialdini, 2005).

been observed in experiments conducted in many countries, from Europe to the Middle East, with female as well as male participants. In short, people appear to be as obedient today as they were when Milgram conducted his research (Blass, 2000; Smith & Bond, 1999).

Nevertheless, many aspects of Milgram's work still provoke debate. (For a summary of Milgram's results, plus those of studies on conformity and compliance, see "In Review: Types of Social Influence.")

in review   Types of Social Influence

Type	Definition	Key Findings
Conformity	A change in behavior or beliefs to match those of others	In cases of ambiguity, people develop a group norm and then adhere to it.
		Conformity occurs because people want to be right, because they want to be liked by others, and because conformity to group norms is usually reinforced.
		Conformity usually increases with the ambiguity of the situation, as well as with the unanimity and psychological size of the majority.
Compliance	A change in what is said or done because of a request	Compliance increases with the foot-in-the-door technique, which begins with a small request and works up to a larger one.
		The door-in-the-face procedure can be used, too. After making a large request that is denied, the person substitutes a less extreme alternative that was desired all along.
		The low-ball approach also elicits compliance. A person first obtains an oral commitment for something, then claims that only a higher-cost version of the original request will suffice.
Obedience	A change in behavior in response to an explicit demand, typically from an authority figure	People may inflict great harm on others when an authority demands that they do so.
		Even though people obey orders to harm another person, they often agonize over the decision.
		People are most likely to disobey orders to harm someone when they see another person disobey such orders.

LINKAGES (a link to Research in Psychology, p. 54)

● **Ethical Questions** Although the "learners" in Milgram's experiment suffered no discomfort, the participants did. Milgram (1963) saw participants "sweat, stutter, tremble, groan, bite their lips, and dig their fingernails into their flesh" (p. 375). Against the potential harm inflicted by Milgram's experiments stand the potential gains. For example, people who learn about Milgram's work often take his findings into account when deciding how to behave in social situations (Sherman, 1980). But even if social value has come from Milgram's studies, the question remains: Was it ethical for Milgram to treat his participants as he did?

In the years before his death in 1984, Milgram defended his experiments (e.g., Milgram, 1977). He argued that his debriefing of the participants after the experiment prevented any lasting harm. For example, to demonstrate that their behavior was not unusual, Milgram told participants that most people went all the way to the 450-volt level. He also explained that the learner did not experience any shock; in fact, the learner came in and chatted with each participant. On a later questionnaire, 84 percent of the participants said that they had learned something important about themselves and that the experience had been worthwhile. Milgram argued, therefore, that the experience was actually a positive one. Still, today's committees charged with protecting human participants in research would be unlikely to approve Milgram's experiments, and less controversial ways to study obedience have now been developed (Blass, 2004).

● **Questions about Meaning** Do Milgram's dramatic results mean that most people are putty in the hands of authority figures and that most of us would blindly follow inhumane orders from our leaders? Some critics have argued that Milgram's results cannot be interpreted in this way because his participants knew they were in an experiment and may simply have been playing a cooperative role. If so, the social influence processes identified in his studies may not explain obedience in the real world today (Berkowitz, 1999).

Most psychologists believe, however, that Milgram not only demonstrated the power of obedience to authority, but also revealed a basic truth about human behavior—namely, that under certain circumstances, human beings are capable of unspeakable acts of brutality toward other humans. Sadly, examples abound. And one of the most horrifying aspects of human inhumanity—whether it is the Nazis' campaign of genocide against Jews sixty years ago or the campaigns of terror under way today—is that the perpetrators are not necessarily demented, sadistic fiends. Most of them are, in many respects, "normal" people who have been influenced by economic and political situations, and the persuasive power of their leaders, to behave in a demented and fiendish manner.

In short, inhumanity can occur even without pressure for obedience. For example, a good deal of people's aggressiveness toward other people appears to come from within. Let's now consider human aggressiveness and some of the circumstances that influence its expression.

Aggression

Aggression is an action intended to harm another person. It is all too common. Nearly 1.4 million violent crimes are committed each year in the United States, including nearly 94,000 rapes and nearly 17,000 murders (Federal Bureau of Investigation, 2006). In fact, homicide is the second-leading cause of death for people in the United States between the ages of fifteen and twenty-four (National Center for Injury Prevention and Control, 2002). One of the most disturbing aspects of these figures is that about 85 percent of all murder victims knew their assailants, and over 70 percent of rapists were romantic partners, friends, relatives, or acquaintances of their victims (U.S. Department of Justice, 2007). Further, about one-third of married

aggression An act that is intended to cause harm to another person.

people in the United States, and a significant proportion of dating couples, display aggression toward each other that ranges from pushing, shoving, and slapping to beatings and the threatened or actual use of weapons (Cornelius & Resseguie, 2007; Durose et al., 2005).

LINKAGES (a link to Introducing Psychology, p. 10)

■● Why Are People Aggressive?

An early theory of human aggression was offered by Sigmund Freud, who suggested it was partly due to *Thanatos*, the death instincts described in the chapter on personality. Freud proposed that aggression is an instinctive biological urge that builds up in everyone and must be released. Sometimes, he said, the release takes the form of physical or verbal abuse against others. At other times, the aggressive impulse is turned inward and leads to suicide or other self-damaging acts.

A somewhat more complicated view is offered by evolutionary psychologists. As discussed in the introductory chapter, these psychologists believe that human social behavior is related to our evolutionary heritage. From this perspective, aggression is seen to have helped prehistoric people compete for mates, thus resulting in the survival of their genes in the next generation. Through the principles of natural selection, then, aggressive tendencies were passed on through successive generations.

Evolutionary theories of the origins of aggression are popular, but even evolutionary theorists realize that "nature" alone cannot fully account for aggression. "Nurture," in the form of environmental factors, also plays a large role in when and why people are aggressive. We know this partly because there are large differences in aggression from culture to culture. The murder rate in the Philippines, for example, is forty-six times higher than in China or Finland; and the U.S. murder rate is almost nine times higher than in those latter two countries (Barclay & Tavares, 2002). These data suggest that even if aggressive *impulses* are universal, the emergence of aggressive *behavior* reflects an interplay of nature and nurture (Malamuth & Addison, 2001). No equation can predict when people will be aggressive, but years of research have revealed a number of important biological, learning, and environmental factors that combine in various ways to produce aggression in various situations.

● Genetic and Biological Mechanisms

There is strong evidence for hereditary influences on aggression, especially in animals (Cairns, Gariepy, & Hood, 1990). In one study, the most aggressive members of a large group of mice were interbred. Then the most aggressive of their offspring were also interbred. After this procedure was followed for twenty-five generations, the resulting animals would immediately attack any mouse put in their cage. Continuous inbreeding of the least aggressive members of the original group produced animals that were so nonaggressive that they would refuse to fight even when attacked (Lagerspetz & Lagerspetz, 1983). Research on human twins reared together or apart suggests that there is a genetic component to aggression in people as well (Vierikko et al., 2006). However, other research suggests that people do not necessarily inherit the tendency to be aggressive; instead, they may inherit certain temperaments, such as impulsiveness or emotional oversensitivity in social situations, that in turn make aggression more likely (Eisenberger et al., 2007; Hennig et al., 2005).

Several parts of the brain influence aggression (Anderson & Bushman, 2002a). One is the limbic system, which includes the amygdala, the hypothalamus, and related areas (see Figure 3.13 in the chapter on biological aspects of psychology). Damage to these structures may produce *defensive aggression*, which includes heightened aggressiveness to stimuli that are not usually threatening or a decrease in the responses that normally inhibit aggression (Coccaro, 1989; Eichelman, 1983). The cerebral cortex may also be involved in aggression (e.g., Pietro et al., 2000; see Figure 3.16). For example, one study found that the prefrontal area of the cortex metabolized glucose significantly more slowly in murderers than in nonmurderers (Raine, Brennan, & Mednick, 1994).

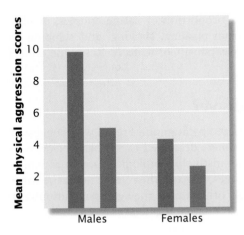

■ Participants exposed to high doses of testosterone during prenatal development

■ Unexposed participants

FIGURE **18.5**

Testosterone and Aggression

In the study illustrated here, the children of women who had taken testosterone during pregnancy to prevent miscarriage became more aggressive than the mothers' other children of the same sex who had not been exposed to testosterone during prenatal development. This outcome held for both males and females.

Source: Data from Reinisch, Ziemba-Davis, & Sanders (1991).

Hormones such as *testosterone*—the masculine hormone that is present in both sexes—may also play an important role in aggression (van Bokhoven et al. 2006). Experiments have shown that aggressive behavior increases or decreases dramatically with the level of testosterone in the human bloodstream (Klinesmith, Kasser, & McAndrew, 2006). Among criminals, those who commit violent crimes have higher levels of testosterone than those whose crimes are nonviolent. And among murderers, those with higher levels of testosterone are more likely than others to have known their victims and to have planned their crimes before committing them (Dabbs, Riad, & Chance, 2001).

Testosterone may have its most significant and durable influence not so much through its day-to-day variations as through its impact on early brain development. One natural test of this hypothesis occurred when pregnant women were given testosterone in an attempt to prevent miscarriages. Accordingly, their children were exposed to high doses of testosterone during prenatal development. Figure 18.5 shows that these children grew up to be more aggressive than their same-sex siblings who were not exposed to testosterone during prenatal development (Reinisch, Ziemba-Davis, & Sanders, 1991). Another study found that girls who had been prenatally exposed to elevated levels of testosterone by virtue of having shared the womb with a male twin were more aggressive than girls who had a female twin (Cohen-Bendahan et al., 2005).

Drugs that alter central nervous system functioning can also affect the likelihood that a person will act aggressively. Alcohol, for example, can substantially increase some people's aggressiveness. Canadian researchers have found that in almost 70 percent of the acts of aggression they studied, the aggressors had been drinking alcohol. And the more alcohol the aggressors consumed, the more aggressive they were (Wells, Graham, & West, 2000). No one knows exactly why alcohol increases aggression, but there is no doubt that many people associate drinking with both aggressive thoughts and aggressive actions (Bartholow & Heinz, 2006; Graham et al., 2006). As described in the consciousness chapter, this association may result in part from observing the drunken aggressiveness that is common in many cultures.

Research on the effects of other drugs on aggression has produced some surprising findings. One might expect, for example, that using stimulants would increase aggressiveness and that taking tranquilizers would reduce it, but the opposite appears to be true. Whereas amphetamine stimulants do not usually make people more aggressive, opiates (e.g., heroin and morphine) and some tranquilizers may do so (Taylor & Hulsizer, 1998). It is not clear why heroin users are more likely than amphetamine users to be aggressive. Some have suggested that heroin addicts' aggression reflects their desperate need to get money, by any means, to buy more drugs. But if this were so, we should also see increased aggression among people who are addicted to amphetamines and cocaine—because these addictions, too, are very expensive. Further, opiates increase people's aggressiveness even in controlled laboratory settings (Taylor & Hulsizer, 1998), suggesting that these drugs have biochemical effects that lead directly to aggression. The nature of these effects is presently unknown.

● **Learning and Cultural Mechanisms** Cross-cultural research makes it clear that although biological factors may increase or decrease the likelihood of aggression, learning also plays a role. Aggressive behavior is much more common in individualist than in collectivist cultures, for example (Oatley, 1993). Cultural differences in the expression of aggression appear to stem in part from differing cultural values. In contrast to many so-called advanced peoples, the Utku, an Inuit culture, view aggression in any form as a sign of social incompetence. In fact, the Utku word for "aggressive" also means "childish" (Oatley, 1993). The effects of culture on aggression can also be seen in the fact that the incidence of aggression in a given culture changes over time as cultural values change (Matsumoto, 2000).

Aggression can even differ from one part of a country to another. Consider the fact that more males in the southern United States commit homicide than do males in the northern states (Cassel & Bernstein, 2007). As discussed later, this regional difference in the homicide rate may be related to the South's higher temperatures, but Richard Nisbett and his colleagues (e.g., Cohen & Nisbett, 1997) have proposed that it is due to a *culture of honor* that is more commonly endorsed by southern males. One key aspect of this cultural orientation is the need to defend one's honor, with violence if necessary, in response to a perceived insult. Studies testing this notion have indeed found that southern-born college students reacted much more angrily to a provocation than did northern-born students (Cassel & Bernstein, 2007; Cohen et al., 1996). The results of other regional U.S. studies, though, raise doubts about whether the culture of honor is any more prevalent in the south than in the north (Chu, Rivera, & Loftin, 2000).

The frequency of aggressive acts can certainly be altered by rewards or punishment. People become more aggressive when rewarded for aggressiveness and less aggressive when punished for aggression (Geen, 1998). People also learn many aggressive responses by watching others (Bingenheimer, Brennan, & Earls, 2005; Bushman & Anderson, 2001). Children, in particular, learn and perform many of the aggressive acts that they see modeled by others (Bandura, 1983). Albert Bandura's "Bobo" doll experiments, which are described in the chapter on learning, provide impressive demonstrations of the power of observational learning. The significance of observational learning is highlighted by studies of the effects of televised violence, also discussed in that chapter. For example, the amount of violent content watched on television when children are between six and ten predicts aggressiveness in these children even fifteen years later (Huesmann et al., 2003). Fortunately, not everyone who sees aggression becomes aggressive; individual differences in temperament, the modeling of nonaggressive behaviors by parents, and other factors can temper the effects of violent television. Nevertheless, observational learning, including the learning that comes through exposure to violent television, does play a significant role in the development and display of aggressive behavior (Anderson & Murphy, 2003; Bushman & Anderson, 2001). Even listening to music whose lyrics describe or endorse violence can increase aggressive thoughts and hostile feelings (Anderson, Carnagey, & Eubanks, 2003).

In short, a person's accumulated experiences—including culturally transmitted teachings—combine with daily rewards and punishments to influence whether, when, and how aggressive acts occur (Baron & Richardson, 1994; Bettencourt et al., 2006).

Following Adult Examples Learning to express aggression is especially easy for children who, like these children, see aggressive acts modeled for them all too often.

THINKING CRITICALLY **Do Violent Video Games Make People More Aggressive?**

A lot of research has been conducted on the impact of violent television on aggressiveness, but what about other forms of violent entertainment, such as video games? When these games first appeared in the late 1970s they contained little or no violence, but by the 1990s violent versions such as *Mortal Kombat* and *Street Fighter* had become extremely popular, and the current flood of graphically violent games remain the favorites of young game-players. For example, one survey of fourth-graders found that 59 percent of girls and 73 percent of boys preferred violent video games over nonviolent ones. In response to complaints from parents groups, the video-game industry devised a rating system designed to keep the most violent games out of the hands of preteens and young teenagers, but many of the games that the system deems appropriate for these groups still contain considerable violent content (Funk et al., 1999). Further, fewer than 1 percent of young teenagers in one survey said that their parents had ever stopped them from buying a video game because of its violence rating (Walsh, 2000). In other words, children in the United States have essentially unrestricted access to violent video games. If they can't buy a violent game in a store, they can always download it from the Internet.

■ What am I being asked to believe or accept?

The parents groups who have objected to this situation are basing their concerns on the claim that playing violent video games can alter behavior in undesirable ways. Specifically, they say that exposure to violent video games increases the frequency of aggressive thoughts, feelings, and actions in people who play them (Anderson, Gentile, & Buckley, 2007).

■ What evidence is available to support the assertion?

Evidence for this claim comes from correlational and laboratory experiments on violent video games. Correlational studies have examined the relationship between the amount of time people spend playing these games and how aggressive they are. When Craig Anderson and Brad Bushman (2001) analyzed the combined results of a large number of these correlational studies, they found a statistically significant positive relationship. That is, the more time people spent playing violent video games, the more aggressive they tended to be.

In laboratory experiments on violent video games, researchers randomly assign participants to groups, then expose them for varying lengths of time to games that contain varying amounts of violence and allow varying degrees of player involvement. After manipulating these independent variables, the researchers measure some aspect of aggression, which is the dependent variable in these experiments. Finally, they compare the amount of aggressiveness displayed by participants in the various groups. In one such experiment, participants played a violent video game in which the researchers manipulated: (1) whether the player could actively participate as one of the characters in the game or could only watch the actions of the game's characters, and (2) whether or not the characters bled when they were wounded (Farrar, Krcmar, & Nowak, 2006). They found that participants expressed more hostility and aggressive intentions when they were able to "be" characters in the game and when their victims bled when wounded. The combined results of several experiments like this one show that playing violent video games increases players' aggressive thoughts, feelings, and actions. There is also some evidence that playing violent video games may make people less likely to help other people (Anderson & Bushman, 2001).

■ Are there alternative ways of interpreting the evidence?

Like research on the effects of television violence, the results of correlational and experimental studies of violent video games have been questioned on several counts.

The correlational studies have been challenged mainly because correlations do not allow us to draw conclusions about cause and effect. True, greater aggressiveness is associated with longer exposure to violent video games, but is this because the games are causing aggressiveness or because aggressive people are more inclined to play violent video games? The laboratory experiments have been criticized mainly because their methods may not reflect, and their results may not apply to, what goes on in the world outside the laboratory (Goldstein, 2001). Do violent video games played in a lab have the same effects as they do when played at home, perhaps with friends? Do artificial laboratory measures of aggressiveness really tell us anything about how a person is likely to behave toward other people in daily life? Although experiments give researchers the control necessary to support cause-effect conclusions, critics argue that those conclusions might be of limited value in understanding the true impact of violent video games on aggressiveness.

At least one reviewer has suggested that studies whose results fail to show a relationship between violent video games and aggression are less likely to be published than those that do show such a relationship (Ferguson, 2007). Other skeptics point out that even if a statistically significant cause-effect relationship between violent video games and aggression does exist, it is not a very strong one (Sherry, 2001), especially when compared with other influences. They suggest, for example, that people's aggressiveness is affected far less intensely by violent video games (and violent television) than by other factors, such as what children learn by seeing their families and friends behaving aggressively.

■ What additional evidence would help to evaluate the alternatives?

Part of the controversy over the impact of violent video games could be resolved if we had data from longitudinal studies that track the behavior of people who choose to engage in varying amounts of violent game-playing over many years. If the relationship between amount of exposure and amount of aggression remains over ten or fifteen years, as it does in the case of violent television (Bushman & Huesmann, 2001), the claim that exposure to violent video games can make people more aggressive becomes that much more plausible.

It would also be valuable to know what happens in the brains of people who play violent video games, and scientists are currently studying this question using a variety of neuroscience techniques. In one recent study, changes in event-related brain activity (see Figure 8.4 in the cognition and language chapter) indicated that playing violent video games made participants less sensitive to, and less upset by, seeing violence (Bartholow, Bushman, & Sestir, 2006). Another study (Weber, Ritterfied & Mathiak, 2006) using functional magnetic resonance imaging (fMRI) found that exposure to violent aspects of video games activates brain areas that are commonly associated with aggression. Such studies cannot confirm that violent video games cause aggression, but their results support the possibility of a causal link and begin to provide some explanations about why that link might exist.

■ What conclusions are most reasonable?

Given the evidence available so far, it appears reasonable to say that violent video games probably have at least some short-term effects on the people who play them. Questions about how strong the causal relationship is, and how long it might last, have not yet been answered. On the basis of the principles described in the chapter on learning, some researchers believe that violent video games might actually have a stronger impact on aggression than violent television because (1) game players can literally practice aggression as they engage in violent electronic acts and (2) they are rewarded for those violent acts by reaching the game's next level (e.g., Bushman & Anderson, 2007). Are these researchers correct? Are the effects of violent video games that strong, and are they likely to be long-lasting influences on aggressiveness? It will take much more research to definitively answer these questions, but it seems reasonable to suspect that the effects of prolonged exposure to violent video games will be quite similar to that of long exposure to violent television.

LINKAGES (a link to Motivation and Emotion, p. 409)

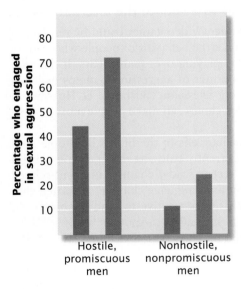

80
70
60
50
40
30
20
10

Percentage who engaged in sexual aggression

Hostile, promiscuous men

Nonhostile, nonpromiscuous men

■ Small amount of pornography watched
■ Large amount of pornography watched

FIGURE 18.6

Pornography and Sexual Aggression

Extensive exposure to pornography does not by itself make most men more likely to engage in sexual aggression. However, among men who are hostile toward women and have a history of sexual promiscuity, those who view a lot of pornography are much more likely to engage in sexual aggression.

Source: Adapted from Malamuth (1998).

When Are People Aggressive?

In general, people are more likely to be aggressive when they are both physiologically aroused and experiencing angry or hostile thoughts and feelings (Anderson & Bushman, 2002a). They tend either to lash out at those who make them angry or to displace their anger onto defenseless targets such as children or pets. However, aggression can also be made more likely by other forms of emotional arousal. One emotion that has long been considered to be a major cause of aggression is *frustration*, which occurs when we are prevented from reaching some goal.

● **Frustration and Aggression** Suppose that a friend interrupts your studying for an exam by coming over to borrow a book. If things have been going well and you are feeling confident about the exam, you are likely to be friendly and helpful. But what if you are feeling frustrated because your friend's visit is the fifth interruption in the last hour? Under these emotional circumstances, you may react aggressively, perhaps snapping at your startled visitor for bothering you.

Your aggressiveness in this situation conforms to the predictions of the **frustration-aggression hypothesis,** originally developed by John Dollard and his colleagues (Dollard et al., 1939). They proposed that frustration always results in aggression and that aggression will not occur unless a person is frustrated. Research on this hypothesis, however, has shown that it is too simple and too general. For one thing, frustration sometimes produces depression and withdrawal, not aggression (Berkowitz, 1998). In addition, not all aggression is preceded by frustration (Berkowitz, 1994).

After many years of research, Leonard Berkowitz (1998) suggested some substantial modifications to the frustration-aggression hypothesis. First, he proposed that it may be stress in general rather than frustration in particular that can produce a readiness to act aggressively. Once this readiness exists, cues in the environment that are associated with aggression will often lead a person to behave aggressively. The cues might be guns or knives, televised scenes of people arguing, violent song lyrics or game images, and the like. Neither stress alone nor the cues alone are sufficient to set off aggression. When combined, however, they often do set it off. Support for this aspect of Berkowitz's theory has been quite strong (Anderson & Bushman, 2002b).

Second, Berkowitz argues that the direct cause of most kinds of aggression is *negative affect,* or unpleasant emotion. He says that the greater the negative affect, whether it is caused by frustrating circumstances or other sources, the stronger the readiness to behave aggressively (Berkowitz, 1998). Negative affect can be aroused by pain, for example. Research suggests that people in pain do tend to become aggressive, no matter what caused their pain. In one study, participants whose hands were placed in painfully cold water became more aggressive toward other people than participants whose hands were in water of room temperature (Berkowitz, 1998).

● **Generalized Arousal** Imagine you have just jogged three miles. You are hot, sweaty, and out of breath, but you are not angry. Still, the physiological arousal caused by jogging may increase the probability that you will become aggressive if, say, a passerby shouts an insult (Zillmann, 1988). Why? The answer lies in a phenomenon described in the chapter on motivation and emotion: Arousal from one experience may carry over to an independent situation, producing what is called *excitation transfer.* So the physiological arousal caused by jogging may intensify your reaction to an insult (Harrison, 2003).

By itself, however, generalized arousal does not lead to aggression. It is most likely to produce aggression when the situation contains some reason, opportunity, or target for aggression (Zillmann, 2003). In one study, for example, people engaged in two minutes of vigorous exercise. Then they had the opportunity to deliver electrical shock to another person. The participants chose high levels of shock only if they were first

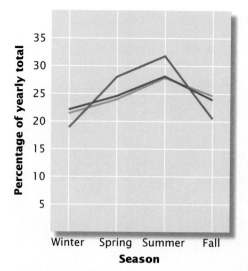

Rape

Murder

Other violent crime

FIGURE 18.7

Effects of Temperature on Aggression

Studies from around the world indicate that aggressive behaviors are most likely to occur during hot summer months. These studies support the idea that environmental factors can affect aggression.

Source: Anderson & Anderson (1998).

insulted (Zillmann, Katcher, & Milavsky, 1972). Apparently, the arousal resulting from the exercise made aggression more likely; the insult "released" it.

Other research suggests that men who are aroused by watching violent pornography might be more likely to commit rape or other forms of aggression against women. In one experiment, for example, male participants were told that a person in another room (actually an employee of the experimenter) would be performing a learning task and that they were to administer an electric shock every time the person made a mistake. The intensity of shock could be varied (as in the Milgram studies, no shock actually reached the employee), but participants were told that changing the intensity would not affect the speed of learning. So the shock intensity (and presumed pain) that they chose to administer was considered to be a measure of aggression. Before the learning trials began, some participants watched a film in which several men had sex with the same woman, against her will. These participants' aggressiveness during the learning experiment was greater than that of men who did not watch the film (Donnerstein, 1984). There was no parallel increase in aggression against other men, indicating that the films don't create a generalized increase in aggression but do create an increase in aggressiveness directed toward women (Aronson, Wilson, & Akert, 2005).

Such effects do not appear in all men, however. One study of about 2,700 men in the United States found that men who are not hostile toward women and who do not tend to have a lot of casual sex showed little if any change in sexual aggressiveness after viewing aggressive pornography. In contrast, among men who are high in promiscuity and hostility, watching aggressive pornography was followed by a dramatic increase in the chances that these men would engage in sexual aggression (Malamuth, Addison, & Koss, 2000). In fact, 72 percent of the men who frequently used pornography and were high in promiscuity and hostility had actually engaged in sexually aggressive acts (see Figure 18.6).

These findings are in keeping with the notion that aggression is not caused solely by a person's characteristics or by the particular situation a person is in. Instead, the occurrence and intensity of aggression are determined by the joint influence of individual characteristics and environmental circumstances (Klinesmith et al., 2006).

● **Environmental Influences on Aggression**   The links between stress, arousal, and aggressive behavior point to the possibility that stressful environmental conditions can make aggressive behavior more likely (Anderson, 2001). This possibility is one of the research topics in **environmental psychology**, the study of the relationship between people's physical environment and their behavior (Bell et al., 2000). One aspect of the environment that clearly affects social behavior is the weather, especially temperature. High temperature is a source of stress and arousal, so it might be expected to correlate with aggressiveness. The results of many studies conducted in several countries show that many kinds of aggressive behavior are indeed more likely to occur during hot summer months than at any other time of the year (Anderson et al., 2000; Bushman, Wang, & Anderson, 2005; see Figure 18.7).

Noise also tends to make people more likely to display aggression, especially if the noise is unpredictable and irregular (Geen & McCown, 1984). Living arrangements, too, can influence aggressiveness. Compared with the tenants of crowded apartment buildings, those in buildings with relatively few residents are less likely to behave aggressively (Bell et al., 2000). This difference appears to be due in part to how people feel when they are crowded. Crowding tends to create physiological arousal and to make people tense, uncomfortable, and more likely to report negative feelings (Oskamp & Schultz, 1998). This arousal and tension can influence people to like one another less and to be more aggressive. One study of juvenile delinquents found that the number of behavior problems they displayed (including aggressiveness) was directly related to how crowded their living conditions had become (Ray et al., 1982).

● **frustration-aggression hypothesis** A proposition that frustration always leads to some form of aggressive behavior.

● **environmental psychology** The study of the relationship between behavior and the physical environment.

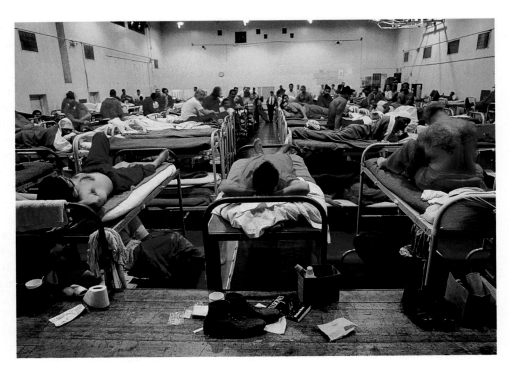

Crowding and Aggression Studies of prisons suggest that as crowding increases, so does aggression (Paulus, 1988). Environmental psychologists are working with architects on the design of prisons that minimize the sense of crowding and that may help prevent some of the violence that endangers staff and prisoners.

Altruism and Helping Behavior

Like all acts of terrorism, the 2001 attacks on the World Trade Center and the Pentagon were examples of human behavior at its worst. But like all tragedies, they drew responses that provide inspiring examples of human behavior at its best. Michael Benfante and John Cerqueira were working in the World Trade Center when one of the hijacked planes struck their building. They headed for a stairwell, but they didn't just save themselves. Although it slowed their own escape, they chose to carry Tina Hansen, a wheelchair-bound co-worker, down sixty-eight flights of stairs to safety. David Theall was in his Pentagon office when another hijacked plane hit the building not far from his desk. He could have escaped the rubble immediately, but he first located a dazed officemate and led him, along with seven other co-workers, to safety. And no one will ever forget the heroism of the hundreds of New York City firefighters, police officers, and emergency workers who risked their lives, and lost their lives, while trying to save others. Acts of selflessness and sacrifice were common that day, and in the days and weeks and months that followed. Police officers, medical personnel, search-and-rescue specialists, and just ordinary people came to New York from all over the United States to help clear wreckage, look for survivors, and recover bodies. More than $1 billion in donations to the Red Cross and other charitable organizations poured in to help victims; one celebrity telethon raised $150 million in two hours. There was also a dramatic increase in many other forms of prosocial behavior, including volunteering to work for all kinds of charities (Penner et al., 2005; see Figure 18.8).

All of these actions are examples of **helping behavior,** which is defined as any act that is intended to benefit another person. Helping can range from picking up dropped packages to donating a kidney. Closely related to helping is **altruism,** an unselfish concern for another's welfare (Penner et al., 2005). Let's consider some of the reasons for helping and altruism, along with some of the conditions under which people are most likely to help others.

helping behavior Any act that is intended to benefit another person.

altruism An unselfish concern for another's welfare.

One of Many Heroes   Along with his colleague Michael Benfante, John Cerqueira (shown here) risked his life on September 11, 2001, to help a handicapped co-worker escape from the sixty-eighth floor of the World Trade Center. Hundreds of other heroic acts of helping took place that day, and less dramatic examples occur every day throughout the world.

Photo courtesy of North Carolina State University, Cerqueira's alma mater.

● Why Do People Help?

The tendency to help others begins early, although at first it is not spontaneous. In most cultures, very young children generally help others only when they are asked to do so or are offered a reward (Grusec, Davidov, & Lundell, 2002). Still, Carolyn Zahn-Waxler and her associates found that almost half of the two-year-olds they observed acted helpfully toward a friend, a family member, or even a stranger (Warneken & Tomasello, 2006; Zahn-Waxler et al., 1992). As they grow older, children use helping behavior to gain social approval, and their efforts at helping become more elaborate. The role of social influence in the development of helping is seen as children follow examples set by people around them. Their helping behaviors are

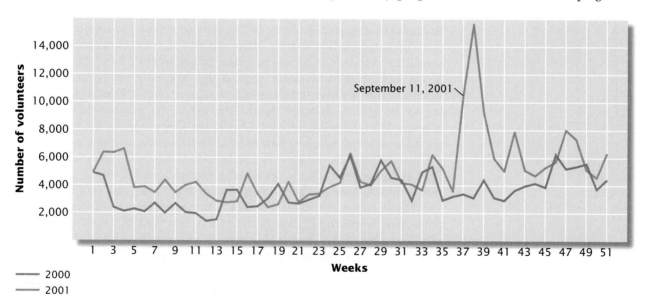

FIGURE **18.8**

The Impact of 9/11 on Volunteering

The 2001 terrorist attacks on New York and Washington, D.C., prompted a flood of volunteers who offered to work for charities and service organizations nationwide. As shown here, volunteerism during the three weeks after the attacks nearly tripled in comparison to the same three weeks in the previous year.

A Young Helper Even before their second birthdays, some children offer help to those who are hurt or crying by snuggling, patting, or offering food or even their own teddy bears.

shaped by the norms established by their families and the broader culture (Grusec & Goodnow, 1994). In addition, children are praised and given other rewards for helpfulness but are scolded for selfishness. Eventually children come to believe that being helpful is good and that they are good when they are helpful. By the late teens, people often help others even when no one is watching and no one will know that they did so (Grusec et al., 2002). There are three major theories about why people help even when they cannot expect any external rewards for doing so.

● **Arousal: Cost-Reward Theory** One approach to explaining why people help is called the **arousal: cost-reward theory** (Piliavin et al., 1981). This theory proposes that people find the sight of a victim distressing and anxiety provoking, and that this experience motivates them to do something to reduce the unpleasant arousal. Several studies have shown that all else being equal, the more physiologically aroused bystanders are, the more likely they are to help someone in an emergency (Dovidio et al., 2006). Before rushing to a victim's aid, however, the bystander will first evaluate two aspects of the situation: the costs associated with helping and the costs (to the bystander and the other person) of not helping. Whether or not the bystander actually helps depends on the outcome of this evaluation (Dovidio et al., 1991). If the costs of helping are low (as when helping someone pick up a dropped grocery bag) and the costs of not helping are high (as when the other person is physically unable to do this alone), the bystander will almost certainly help. However, if the costs of helping are high (as when the task is to load a heavy box into a car) and the costs of not helping are low (as when the person is strong enough to manage the task alone), the bystander is unlikely to offer help. This theory is attractive partly because it is comprehensive enough to provide a framework for explaining research findings on the factors that affect helping.

One of these factors is the *clarity of the need for help*, which has a major impact on whether people provide help (Dovidio et al., 1991). In one study, undergraduate students were waiting alone in a campus building when a staged "accident" took place outside. A window washer screamed as he and his ladder fell to the ground. He then began to clutch his ankle and groan in pain. All of the students looked out a window to see what had happened, but only 29 percent of them did anything to help. Other students experienced the same situation with one important difference: The man *said* he was hurt and needed help. In this case, more than 80 percent of the students came to his aid (Yakimovich & Saltz, 1971). Why so many? Apparently, this one additional cue eliminated any uncertainty about whether the person needed help. This cue also raised the perceived costs to the victim of not offering help. As these costs become higher, helping becomes more likely. If this laboratory study seems unrealistic, consider the case of a sixty-two-year-old woman in Darby, Pennsylvania. She was walking to the grocery store in March 2000 when she was pushed from behind by an attacker. She fended him off and then did her shopping as usual. It was only when she got home and her daughter saw the handle of a knife protruding from her back that she realized that the assailant had stabbed her! No one in the grocery store said anything to her about the knife, let alone offered to help. Why? The most likely explanation is that the woman didn't say or do anything to suggest that help was needed.

The *presence of others* also has a strong influence on the tendency to help. Somewhat surprisingly, though, their presence actually tends to suppress helping behavior. One of the most highly publicized examples of this phenomenon was the Kitty Genovese incident, which occurred on a New York City street in 1964. During a thirty-minute struggle, a man stabbed Genovese repeatedly, but none of the dozens of neighbors who witnessed the attack intervened or even called the police until it was too late to save her life. A similar case occurred on November 27, 2000, in London, when a ten-year-old boy who had been stabbed by members of a street gang lay ignored by passersby as he bled to death. After each case, journalists and social commentators expressed dismay about the cold, uncaring attitudes that seem to exist among people who live in big cities. But psychologists believe that something about the situation surrounding such events deters people from helping.

● **arousal: cost-reward theory** A theory attributing people's helping behavior to their efforts to reduce the unpleasant arousal they feel in the face of someone's need or suffering.

Diffusion of Responsibility   Does the man on the sidewalk need help? The people nearby probably are not sure and might assume that, if he does, someone else will assist him. Research on factors affecting helping and altruism suggests that if you ever need help, especially in a crowd, it is important not only to clearly ask for help but also to tell a specific onlooker to take specific action (for example, "You, in the yellow shirt, please call an ambulance!").

The numerous studies of helping behavior stimulated by the Genovese case revealed a phenomenon that may explain the inaction of Genovese's neighbors and those passersby in London. This phenomenon is known as the **bystander effect:** Usually, as the number of people who witness an emergency increases, the likelihood that one of them will help decreases (Garcia, et al., 2002). One explanation for why the presence of others often reduces helping is that each person thinks someone else will help the victim. That is, seeing other bystanders allows each individual to experience a *diffusion of responsibility* for taking action, which lowers the costs of not helping (Dovidio et al., 2006).

The degree to which the presence of other people inhibits helping may depend on who those other people are. When they are strangers, perhaps poor communication inhibits helping. People often have difficulty speaking to strangers, particularly in an emergency, and without speaking, they have difficulty knowing what the others intend to do. According to this logic, if people are with friends rather than strangers, they should be less uncomfortable, more willing to discuss the problem, and thus more likely to help.

In one experiment designed to test this idea, an experimenter left a research participant in a waiting room, either alone, with a friend, with a stranger, or with a stranger who was an assistant to the experimenter (Latané & Rodin, 1969). The experimenter then stepped behind a curtain into an office. For a few minutes, she could be heard opening and closing the drawers of her desk, shuffling papers, and so on. Then there was a loud crash, and she screamed, "Oh, my god . . . My foot, I . . . I can't move it. Oh, my ankle . . . I can't get this . . . thing off me." Then the participant heard her groan and cry.

Would the participant go behind the curtain to help? Once again, people were most likely to help if they were alone. When one other person was present, participants were more likely to communicate with each other, and to offer help, if they were friends than if they were strangers. When the stranger was the experimenter's assistant (who had been instructed not to help), very few participants offered to help. Other studies have confirmed that bystanders' tendency to help increases when they know one another (Rutkowski, Gruder, & Romer, 1983).

Research suggests that the *personality of the helper* also plays a role in helping. Some people are simply more likely to help than others. Consider, for example, the Christians who risked their lives to save Jews from the Nazi Holocaust. Researchers

● **bystander effect**   A phenomenon in which the chances that someone will help in an emergency decrease as the number of people present increases.

interviewed hundreds of these rescuers many years later and compared their personalities with those of people who had a chance to save Jews but did not do so (Midlarsky, Jones, & Corley, 2005; Oliner & Oliner, 1988). The rescuers were found to have more empathy (the ability to understand or experience another's emotional state), more concern about others, a greater sense of responsibility for their own actions, and a greater sense of self-efficacy (confidence in the success of their efforts). Louis Penner and his associates (Penner, 2002; Penner & Finkelstein, 1998) have found that these kinds of personality traits predict a broad range of helping behaviors, from the speed with which bystanders intervene in an emergency to the amount of time volunteers spend helping AIDS victims. Consistent with the arousal: cost-reward theory, these personality characteristics are also correlated with people's estimates of the costs of helping and not helping. For example, empathic individuals usually estimate the costs of not helping as high, and people with a sense of self-efficacy usually rate the costs of helping as low (Penner et al., 1995). These patterns of cost estimation may partially explain why such people tend to be especially helpful.

Valuable as it is, the arousal: cost-reward theory cannot account for all aspects of helping. For instance, it cannot easily explain why *environmental factors* affect helping. Research conducted in several countries has revealed, for example, that people in urban areas are generally less helpful than those in rural areas (Aronson et al., 2005). Why? The explanation probably has more to do with the stressors found in cities than with city living itself. Evidence for this possibility comes from a study conducted in thirty-six North American cities. Researchers found that people's tendency to help was related more strongly to a city's population *density* (the number of people per square mile) than to the size of the city (Levine et al., 1994). The higher the density, the less likely people were to help others. Similar results have been found in other places such as the United Kingdom, the Middle East, and Africa (Hedge & Yousif, 1992; Yousif & Korte, 1995). Two explanations have been suggested for this association between environmental stress and reduced likelihood of helping. The first is that stressful environments create bad moods—and generally speaking, people in bad moods are less likely to help (Salovey, Mayer, & Rosenhan, 1991). A second possibility is that noise, crowding, and other urban stressors create too much stimulation. To reduce this excessive stimulation, people may pay less attention to their surroundings, which might include individuals who need help.

It is also difficult for the arousal: cost-reward theory to predict what bystanders will do when the cost of helping and the cost of not helping are *both* high. In these cases, helping (or not helping) may depend on several situational factors and, sometimes, on the personality of the potential helper. There may also be circumstances in which cost considerations may not be the major cause of a decision to help or not help. A second approach to helping considers some of these circumstances.

● **Empathy-Altruism Theory** The second approach to explaining helping is embodied in **empathy-altruism theory**, which maintains that people are more likely to engage in *altruistic*, or unselfish, helping—even when the cost of helping is high—if they feel empathy toward the person in need (Batson, 1998). In one experiment illustrating this phenomenon, participants listened to a tape-recorded interview with a female student. The student told the interviewer that her parents had been killed in an automobile accident, that they had had no life insurance, and that she was now faced with the task of finishing college while taking care of a younger brother and sister. She said that these financial burdens might force her to quit school or give up her siblings for adoption. None of this was true, but the participants were told that it was. Further, before listening to the woman's story, half the participants were given additional information about her that was designed to promote strong empathy. Later, all the participants were asked to help the woman raise money for herself and her siblings (Batson et al., 1997). The critical question was whether the participants who heard the additional empathy-promoting information would help more than those who did not have that information. Consistent

empathy-altruism theory A theory suggesting that people help others because of empathy with their needs.

with the empathy-altruism theory, more participants in the empathy condition than in the nonempathy condition offered to help (see Figure 18.9).

Were those who offered help in this experiment being utterly altruistic, or could there be a different reason for their actions? This is a hotly debated question. Some researchers dispute the claim that this study illustrated truly altruistic helping. They suggest that people help in such situations for more selfish reasons, such as relieving the distress they experienced after hearing of the woman's problems (Maner et al., 2002). The final verdict on this question is not yet in.

● **Evolutionary Theory** The evolutionary approach to social psychology offers a third way of explaining helping. This approach views many human social behaviors as echoes of actions that contributed to the survival of our prehistoric ancestors (Buss, 2004a). At first glance, it might not seem reasonable to apply evolutionary theory to helping and altruism, because helping others at the risk of one's own well-being doesn't appear adaptive. If we die while trying to save others, it will be their genes, not ours, that will survive. In fact, according to Charles Darwin's concept of the survival of the fittest, helpers—and their genes—should have disappeared long ago. Contemporary evolutionary theorists suggest, however, that Darwin's thinking about natural selection focused too much on the survival of the fittest *individuals* and not enough on the survival of their genes in others. Accordingly, the concept of survival of the fittest has been replaced by the concept of *inclusive fitness*, the survival of one's genes in future generations (Hamilton, 1964; Kruger, 2003). Because we share genes with our relatives, helping or even dying for a cousin, a sibling, or above all, our own child potentially increases the likelihood that at least some of our genetic characteristics will be passed on to the next generation through the beneficiary's future reproduction (Burnstein & Branigan, 2001). So *kin selection*—helping a relative to survive—may produce genetic benefits even if it provides no personal benefits for the helper (Kruger, 2003).

There is considerable evidence that kin selection occurs among birds, squirrels, and other animals. The more closely the animals are related, the more likely they are to risk their lives for one another. Studies in a wide variety of cultures show the same pattern of helping among humans (Buss, 2004a). People in the United States are three times as likely to donate a kidney to a relative as to a nonrelative (Borgida,

FIGURE 18.9

The Effect of Empathy on Helping

After hearing a staged interview with a woman who supposedly needed to raise money for her family, participants in this experiment were asked to help her. Those who were led to empathize with the woman were much more likely to offer their help than those who did not empathize. These results are consistent with the empathy-altruism theory of helping.

Source: Adapted from Batson et al. (1997).

Family Ties Research indicates that people are more likely to donate organs to family members than to strangers. This pattern may reflect greater attachment or a stronger sense of social obligation to relatives than to others. Psychologists who take an evolutionary approach suggest that such helpful attitudes and actions have evolved because they are adaptive. When, as in the case of these sisters, one family member donates a kidney to save the life of another, the genes they share are more likely to survive.

Conner, & Monteufel, 1992), and identical twins (who have exactly the same genes) are much more willing to help one another than are fraternal twins or siblings, who share only 50 percent of their genes (Segal, 1999).

FOCUS ON RESEARCH METHODS Does Family Matter?

In and of themselves, data on kin selection do not confirm evolutionary explanations of helping and altruism. The greater tendency to donate organs to relatives could also be due to the effects of empathy toward more familiar people, pressure from family members, or other social influence processes. To control for the effects of these confounding variables, some researchers have turned to the laboratory to study the role of evolutionary forces in helping behavior.

■ What was the researchers' question?

Eugene Burnstein, Christian Crandell, and Shinobu Kitayama (1994) wanted to know whether people faced with a choice of whose life to save would behave in line with the concept of kin selection. These investigators reasoned that if kin selection does affect helping, the more genetically related two people are—the more genes they share in common—the more inclined they should be to save each other's life. Further, if this kind of helping evolved because it preserves one's own genes in others, the tendency to save a close relative should be lessened if that relative is unlikely to produce offspring and thereby help preserve the helper's genes.

■ How did the researchers answer this question?

The most direct way to test these predictions would be to put people's lives in danger and then observe which (if any) of their relatives try to save them. Such an experiment would be unthinkable, of course, so Burnstein and his colleagues used a simulation, or *analogue*, methodology. Specifically, they asked people to imagine a series of situations and then to say how they would respond if the situation were real.

The participants in their analogue experiment were 110 men and 48 women enrolled at universities in Japan and the United States. The first independent variable was the kind of help that was needed. On the basis of random assignment, some participants were asked to imagine life-or-death situations in which there was time to save only one of three people who were asleep in separate rooms of a burning house. The remaining participants were asked to imagine everyday situations in which they had time to help only one of three people who each needed a small favor. The other independent variables were the characteristics of the people needing help in each situation—their age, gender, physical health, and genetic relatedness to the potential helper. The dependent variable was the participants' choice of which person they would help.

■ What did the researchers find?

In accordance with evolutionary theory, the participants were more than twice as likely to say they would save the life of a close relative than that of an unrelated friend. Also, the more closely related the endangered people were to the potential helpers, the more likely they were to be saved. Did these results occur simply because people tend to help closer relatives in any situation? Probably not. When the participants imagined situations in which only small favors were involved, they were only slightly more likely to help a close relative than a distant one.

Another major prediction of evolutionary theory was supported as well. Several different findings indicated that even close relatives might not be saved if they were unlikely to produce offspring. For example, the participants were more willing to do a small favor for a seventy-five-year-old relative than for a ten- or eighteen-year-old

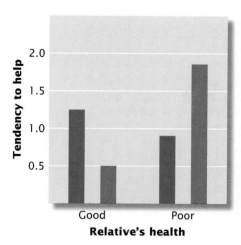

FIGURE 18.10

Kin Selection and Helping

In this analogue experiment, students said they would be more likely to save the life of a healthy relative than a sick one but more likely to do a favor for the sick relative. Results like these have been cited in support of evolutionary theories of helping behavior.

Source: Burnstein, Crandell, & Kitayama (1994).

relative, but they were much more likely to save the lives of the younger relatives. Similarly, they were more likely to do a favor for a sick relative than for a healthy one; but in a life-or-death situation, they chose to save the healthy relative more often than the sick one (see Figure 18.10). Finally, the participants were more likely to save the life of a female relative than that of a male relative, unless the female was past childbearing age. There were no substantial differences between the responses of students in the United States and those in Japan.

■ **What do the results mean?**

The results of this experiment generally support the concept of kin selection, which says that the tendency to help close relatives evolved because, genetically speaking, it helps the helper. Specifically, if we save the life of a relative and that relative is able to produce offspring, more of our genes will be represented in the next generation. Evolutionary psychologists see these results as providing confirmation that kin selection affects the decisions people make about saving the life of another person, and thus that there is an evolutionary basis for helping.

■ **What do we still need to know?**

The findings reported by Burnstein and his colleagues are consistent with the predictions of evolutionary theory, but they must be interpreted with caution and in light of the methods that were used to obtain them. Analogue studies give clues to behavior—and allow experimental control—in situations that approximate, but may not precisely duplicate, situations outside the laboratory. These studies tend to be used when it would be unethical or impractical to expose people to "the real thing." The more closely the analogue approximates the natural situation, the more confident we can be that conclusions drawn about behavior observed in the laboratory will apply, or generalize, to the world beyond the laboratory.

In an analogue experiment such as this one, we might question how closely the natural situation was approximated. For one thing, the participants predicted what their responses would be in hypothetical situations. Those responses might be different if the students were actually in the situations described. So although the analogue methodology in this study allowed the researchers to show that kin selection *could* play a role in human helping behavior, they did not demonstrate that it *did* play a role.

The study also failed to identify the mechanisms whereby biological tendencies are translated into thoughts that lead to helpful actions (Kruger, 2003). It is highly unlikely that the participants were thinking, "I'll help a close relative because it will preserve my genes." So what conscious thoughts or feelings led to their choices? Another analogue study by Josephine Korchmaros and David Kenny (2001) may provide a partial answer to this question. The people who needed help in this simulation were described using the names of the participants' actual family members. The researchers also measured the strength of the emotional ties between the participants and these particular people. The results suggested that genetic closeness was related to emotional closeness. Perhaps, then, emotional closeness provides the mechanism that drives the choice of whom to help. It may be that we are biologically predisposed to feel emotionally closer to closer relatives and thus more likely to help them if their lives are in danger. These feelings, in turn, serve to increase the chances that some of our genes will survive in those close relatives.

This is a reasonable possibility, but remember that even though evolutionary theory may explain some general human tendencies to help, it cannot predict the behavior of specific individuals in specific situations (Penner et al., 2005). Like all other behavior, helping and altruism depend on the interplay of many genetic and environmental factors—including interactions between particular people and particular situations. (See "In Review: Theories of Helping Behaviors" for a summary of the major reasons why people help and the conditions under which they are most likely to do so.) ■

in review Theories of Helping Behaviors

Theory	Basic Premise	Important Variables
Arousal: cost-reward	People help in order to reduce the unpleasant arousal caused by another person's distress. They attempt to minimize the costs of doing this.	Factors that affect the costs of helping and of not helping
Empathy-altruism	People sometimes help for utterly altruistic reasons. They are motivated by a desire to increase another person's well-being.	The amount of empathy that one person feels for another
Evolutionary	People help relatives because it increases the chances that the helper's genes will survive in future generations.	The biological relationship between the helper and the recipient of help

Cooperation, Competition, and Conflict

Helping is one of several ways in which people *cooperate* with one another. **Cooperation** is any type of behavior in which people work together to attain a common goal (Dovidio et al., 2006). For example, several law students might form a study group to help one another pass a difficult exam. But people can also engage in **competition,** trying to attain a goal for themselves while denying that goal to others. So those same students might later compete with one another for a single job opening at a prestigious law firm. Finally, **conflict** results when one person or group believes that another stands in the way of their achieving a goal. When the students become attorneys and represent opposing parties in a legal dispute, they will be in

Cooperation, Competition, Conflict, and Cash Cooperation, competition, and conflict can all be seen on *Survivor,* a television series in which people try to win money by staying the longest in some remote location. Early on, contestants cooperate with members of their own teams, but as more and more people are eliminated, even team members compete with one another. When only two people remain, each stands in the way of the other's goal of winning, so they are in direct conflict.

conflict. One way in which psychologists have learned about all three of these behaviors is by studying social dilemmas (Weber, Kopelman, & Messick, 2004).

● Social Dilemmas

Social dilemmas are situations in which an action that produces rewards for one individual will, if adopted by all others, produce negative consequences for everyone (Dawes & Messick, 2000). For instance, it might be in a factory owner's short-term self-interest to save the costs of pollution control by releasing untreated toxic waste into the environment. But if all factories do the same, the air and water will eventually become poisonous for everyone. Social psychologists have studied situations like this by conducting experiments on the two-person "prisoner's dilemma."

● **The Prisoner's Dilemma**   The **prisoner's dilemma** is based on a scenario in which two people are separated for questioning immediately after being arrested on suspicion of having committed a serious crime (Komorita & Parks, 1996). The prosecutor believes they are guilty but doesn't have enough evidence to convict them. Each prisoner can either confess or not, but they are told that if they both refuse to confess, each will be convicted of a minor offense and will be jailed for one year. If they both confess, the prosecutor will recommend a five-year sentence for each. However, if one prisoner remains silent and the other confesses to what they did, the prosecutor will allow the confessing prisoner to go free, whereas the other will serve the maximum ten-year sentence.

Each prisoner faces a dilemma. Figure 18.11(A) outlines the possible outcomes. Obviously, the strategy that will guarantee the best *mutual* outcome—short sentences for both prisoners—is cooperation. In other words, neither should confess. But the prisoner who remains silent runs the risk of receiving a long sentence if the other prisoner confesses. Further, the prisoner who confesses will benefit if the other prisoner doesn't talk. In other words, each prisoner has an incentive to compete for freedom by confessing. But if they *both* compete and confess, each will end up going to jail for longer than if they had kept quiet.

In the typical prisoner's dilemma experiment, two people sit at separate control panels. Each of them has a red button and a black button, one of which is to be pushed on each of many trials. Pressing the black button is a cooperative response. Pressing the red button is a competitive response. For example, on a given trial, if both participants press their black buttons, each wins $5. If both press their red buttons, they earn only $1. However, if one player presses the red button and the other presses the black button, the one who pressed the red button will win $10, and the other will win nothing.

Figure 18.11(B) shows the possible outcomes for each trial. Over the course of the experiment, the combined winnings of the players are greatest if each presses the black button—that is, if they cooperate. By pressing the black button, however, a player becomes open to exploitation, because on any trial the other might press the red button and take all the winnings. So each player stands to benefit the most individually by pressing the red button occasionally. The prisoner's dilemma is what psychologists call a *mixed-motive conflict*—there are good reasons to cooperate and also good reasons to compete.

What happens when people play this game? Overall, there is a strong tendency to respond competitively. People find it difficult to resist the competitive choice on any given trial (Komorita & Parks, 1996). This choice wins them more money on that trial, but in the long run they gain less than they would have gained through cooperation.

If acting competitively leads to smaller rewards in the long run, why do people persist in competing? There seem to be two reasons (Komorita, 1984). First, winning more than an opponent seems to be rewarding in itself. In the prisoner's dilemma game, many people want to outscore an opponent even if the result is that

● **cooperation**   Any type of behavior in which people work together to attain a goal.

● **competition**   Behavior in which individuals try to attain a goal for themselves while denying that goal to others.

● **conflict**   The result of a person's or group's belief that another person or group stands in the way of their achieving a valued goal.

● **social dilemmas**   Situations in which actions that produce rewards for one individual will produce negative consequences if adopted by everyone.

● **prisoner's dilemma**   A social dilemma in which mutual cooperation guarantees the best mutual outcome.

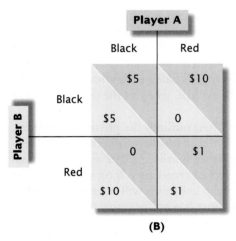

FIGURE 18.11

The Prisoner's Dilemma

In the prisoner's dilemma, mutual cooperation benefits each person and mutual competition is harmful to both. However, one party can take advantage of the other's cooperativeness. These diagrams show the potential payoffs for prisoners—and research participants—in prisoner's dilemma situations.

- **resource dilemma** A situation in which people must share a common resource, creating conflicts between the short-term interests of individuals and the long-term interests of the group.

- **zero-sum game** A social situation in which one person's gains are subtracted from another person's resources, so that the sum of the gains and losses is zero.

they win less money overall. Second, and more important, once several competitive responses are made, the competition seems to feed on itself (Insko et al., 1990). Each person becomes distrustful of the other, and cooperation becomes increasingly difficult. The more competitive one person acts, the more competitive the other becomes (McClintock & Liebrand, 1988).

● **Resource Dilemmas** Psychologists interested in cooperation, competition, and conflict have also concentrated on social dilemmas in which people share a common resource. In this situation, called a **resource dilemma** (Pruitt, 1998), there are built-in conflicts between the interests of the individual and those of the group, and also between people's short-term and long-term interests (Schroeder, 1995). There are two kinds of resource dilemmas. In the *commons dilemma*, people have to decide how much to take from a common resource. In the *public goods dilemma*, people must decide how much to contribute to a common resource. An example of the commons dilemma would be a situation in which farmers all want to draw water for their crops from the same lake. Each individual farmer would benefit greatly from unrestricted use of the water, but if all the farmers did the same, the water would soon be gone. Tax laws provide an example of the public goods dilemma. You would benefit greatly in the short run if you didn't pay any taxes, but if everyone failed to pay, no one would have police and fire protection, highway repairs, national defense, or other vital government services. How can people facing such dilemmas be prompted to cooperate?

● Promoting Cooperation

Communication can reduce people's tendency to act competitively (Pruitt, 1998). Unfortunately, however, not all communication increases cooperation, just as not all contact between ethnic groups reduces prejudice. If the communication takes the form of a threat, people may interpret the threat itself as a competitive response and are likely to respond competitively (Gifford & Hine, 1997). Furthermore, the communication must be relevant. In one social dilemma study, cooperation increased only when people spoke openly about the dilemma and how they would be rewarded for various responses. Praising one another for past cooperation was most beneficial (Orbell, van de Kragt, & Dawes, 1988).

People can also communicate silently through the strategy they use. In the prisoner's dilemma, the most effective strategy for producing long-term cooperation is to use basic learning principles and play *tit-for-tat*. This means rewarding cooperative responses with cooperation and punishing competitiveness by being competitive in return. Cooperating after a cooperative response and competing after a competitive response produces a high degree of cooperation over time (Nowak, May, & Sigmund, 1995). But competing after a cooperative response may harm the relationship and threaten future cooperation (Monterosso et al., 2002). So players usually learn that the only way to come out ahead is to cooperate. There is even evidence from computer simulation studies that societies whose members use cooperative strategies with one another are more likely to survive and prosper than are societies whose members act competitively (Ginges et al., 2007; Nowak et al., 1995).

● Interpersonal Conflict

In social dilemmas and other situations in which people are *interdependent*—that is, when what one person does always affects the other—cooperation usually leads to the best outcomes for everyone. This doesn't mean, however, that cooperation always occurs. People from collectivist cultures, in which cooperation is emphasized, are generally less likely to act selfishly in a social dilemma, but conflict in such situations does appear in all cultures (Smith & Bond, 1999). Conflict is especially likely when people are involved in a **zero-sum game**. This is a situation in which one person's gains are subtracted from the other person's resources. It is called *zero sum*

"There's quite a power struggle going on."

because when you add up the gains and losses, you get zero. Election campaigns, lawsuits over a deceased relative's estate, and competition between children for a toy are all examples of zero-sum games.

There are four major causes of interpersonal conflict (Baron, Byrne, & Branscombe, 2006). The first is traceable to incompatible interests. Suppose, for example, that at a company with twenty offices, only five have windows. Not all employees can have a window, so they will be in conflict as they compete for this scarce resource. Some managers report spending as much as 20 percent of their time dealing with interpersonal conflicts arising from incompatible interests (Thomas & Schmidt, 1976). More subjective factors play a role in the second cause of interpersonal conflict, namely attributing unfriendly or selfish motives to others. For example, conflict is likely to emerge if people who must share some resource, such as printer paper, attribute a shortage of that resource to the other people's selfishness (Samuelson & Messick, 1995). Sometimes these attributions are accurate, but often conflict results from the kinds of attributional errors discussed in the chapter on social cognition. In this case, the paper shortage might have occurred because someone simply forgot to order a new supply.

Attributional errors are related to a third source of interpersonal conflict: faulty communication. A comment intended as a compliment is sometimes interpreted as a snide remark, and constructive criticism is sometimes perceived as a personal attack. Such miscommunication can start a cycle of increasingly provocative actions, in which each person believes the other is being aggressive and unfair (Pruitt & Carnevale, 1993).

A final cause of interpersonal conflict is the tendency to magnify the differences between one's own views and those of others. For example, people may see themselves as fair and objective during discussions of a developer's plans for a wilderness area, but see the developer as utterly biased and concerned only with profit. This tendency often results in the impression that it will be harder to resolve a situation than is actually the case.

● **Managing Conflict**   Interpersonal conflict can damage relationships among people and impair the effectiveness of organizations, but it can also lead to beneficial changes. Industrial/organizational psychologists have found that often it is much better to manage conflict effectively than to try to eliminate it. The most common way of managing organizational conflict is through *bargaining*. Each side—labor and management, for example—produces a series of offers and counteroffers until a solution emerges that is acceptable to both sides. At its best, bargaining can produce a win-win situation in which each side gets what is most important and gives up what is less important (Carnevale & Pruitt, 1992).

If bargaining fails, *third-party interventions* may be useful. Like a therapist working with a couple, an outside mediator can often help the two sides in an organizational conflict focus on important issues, defuse emotions, clarify positions and proposals, and make suggestions that allow each side to compromise without losing face (Pruitt, 1998).

Other techniques for managing conflict, especially conflict over resources, involve the introduction of *superordinate goals* or a *superordinate identity* (Williams, Jackson, & Karau, 1995). For example, if people who are competing for scarce resources can be made to feel that they are all part of the same group and share the same goals, they will act less selfishly and manage the limited resources more efficiently. Focusing on larger common goals was part of what created the unprecedented level of cooperation among people all over the United States following the terrorist attacks of September 11, 2001.

In short, although interpersonal conflict can be harmful if left unchecked, it can also be managed in a way that benefits the group. Much as psychotherapy can help people resolve personal conflict in a way that leads to growth, interpersonal conflict within an organization can be handled in a way that leads to innovations, increased loyalty and motivation, and other valuable changes.

Group Processes

Although Western industrialized cultures tend to emphasize individuals over groups, the fact remains that most important governmental and business decisions in those cultures and elsewhere are made by groups, not individuals (Kerr & Tindale, 2004). Sometimes group processes are effective. Perhaps you recall the extraordinary team-work displayed by engineers, emergency workers, and volunteers that led to the dramatic rescue of nine men trapped in a flooded Pennsylvania coal mine in July 2002. At other times, group processes can have disastrous results, as we will see later. In the chapter on cognition and language, we describe some of the factors that influence the nature and quality of group decisions. Here, we consider some of the social psychological processes that often occur in groups to alter the behavior of their members and the quality of their collective efforts.

● Group Leadership

A good leader can help a group pursue its goals; a poor one can get in the way of a group's functioning. What makes a good leader? Psychologists once thought that the personalities of good and bad leaders were about the same, but we now know that certain personality traits often distinguish effective from ineffective leaders. For example, using tests similar to those that measure the big-five traits described in the chapter on personality, Colin Silverthorne (2001) examined the characteristics of leaders in the United States, Thailand, and China. He found that effective leaders in all three countries tended to score high on agreeableness, emotional stability, extraversion, and conscientiousness. Other researchers have found that in general, effective leaders are intelligent, success oriented, flexible, and confident in their ability to lead (Chemers, Watson, & May, 2000; Foti & Hauenstein, 2007). Having particular personality traits does not guarantee good leadership ability, however. People can be effective leaders in one situation, but ineffective in another (Chemers, 2000). The reason is that effective leadership also depends on the characteristics of the group members, the task at hand, and most important, the interaction between these factors and the leader's style (Yun, Faraj, & Sims, 2005).

For many years, leadership research focused on two main types of leaders, known as *task-oriented and person-oriented*. **Task-oriented leaders** provide close supervision, lead by giving directives, and generally discourage group discussion (Yukl & Van Fleet, 1992). Their style may not endear them to group members. **Person-oriented leaders** provide loose supervision, ask for group members' ideas, and are generally concerned with subordinates' feelings. They are usually well liked by the group, even when they must discipline a group member (Brehm, Kassin, & Fein, 2005).

More recently, some researchers have proposed that there are additional leadership styles. One of these is seen in *transactional leaders*, whose leadership behavior depends on the actions of those they lead. For example, transactional leaders reward those who behave as the leader wishes, and they correct or punish those who behave otherwise. In contrast, there are also *transformational or charismatic leaders* (Bass & Riggio, 2006). Rather than focusing on rewarding or punishing specific behaviors, these people concentrate on creating a vision of the group's goals, inspiring others to pursue that vision, and giving their followers reason to respect and admire them. Transformational leaders, such as Sir Winston Churchill and Dr. Martin Luther King, Jr., have dramatically changed the world for the better, and many less famous leaders of social or business groups have done the same on a smaller scale.

Do men or women make better leaders? Alice Eagly and her colleagues have studied differences between men and women in leadership styles (e.g., Eagly, Karau, & Makhijani, 1995). Their initial research found that, overall, men and women are equally capable leaders. It also looked as though men tend to be more effective when

task-oriented leader A leader who provides close supervision, leads by directives, and generally discourages group discussion.

person-oriented leader A leader who provides loose supervision, asks for group members' ideas, and is concerned with subordinates' feelings.

A Different Kind of Coach Many football coaches are task-oriented leaders whose tough discipline and emotional outbursts are legendary. Only a few, such as Indianapolis Colts coach Tony Dungy, are charismatic leaders. Dungy's leadership style is calm and low-key; rather than shouting at his players, he inspires them to focus on his vision of success and to do their best to achieve it. Their love for him is evident here as they carry Dungy off the field after winning the Super Bowl in 2007.

success requires a task-oriented leader, and that women tend to be more effective when success requires a more person-oriented leader. In other words, it appeared that people of each gender tend to be most effective when they are acting in a manner consistent with gender-role traditions (Eagly & Karau, 1991; Eagly et al., 1995). Perhaps this was because some people did not like female leaders who act in a "masculine" manner or occupy leadership positions traditionally held by men (Eagly, Makhijani, & Klonsky, 1992).

A somewhat different picture of gender differences in leadership has emerged from Eagly's more recent research (Eagly, Johannesen-Schmidt, & van Engen, 2003). She found that, compared with males, female leaders are generally more likely to display a transformational leadership style. Further, women whose leadership style is transactional tend to be more encouraging than transactional male leaders. That is, the transactional female leaders tend to focus more on using rewards rather than punishments to modify group members' behaviors. In addition, and in contrast to earlier findings, Eagly's results suggest that women may be slightly more effective leaders overall than men, even though they may still face challenges in convincing some followers to accept them as legitimate authorities (Eagly, 2005; Eagly et al., 2003).

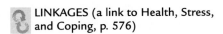

LINKAGES (a link to Health, Stress, and Coping, p. 576)

● Groupthink

The emphasis on group decisions in most large organizations is based on the belief that a group of people working together will make better decisions than will individuals working alone. As noted in the chapter on cognition and language, this belief is generally correct; yet under certain circumstances, groups have been known to make amazingly bad decisions (Kerr & Tindale, 2004). Consider an example from 1986, when officials at the National Aeronautics and Space Administration (NASA) ignored engineers' warnings about the effects of cold weather and decided to launch the space shuttle *Challenger*. The spacecraft exploded seventy-three seconds after liftoff, killing everyone aboard. After analyzing disastrous decisions such as this one, Irving Janis (1989) proposed that they can be attributed to a phenomenon called **groupthink**. Groupthink occurs, he said, when group members are unable to realistically evaluate the options available to them or to fully consider the potential negative consequences of the option they are considering. It is particularly likely when

groupthink A pattern of thinking in which group members fail to evaluate realistically the wisdom of various options and decisions.

members of a group place a higher value on reaching a decision than on being sure they have reached the best decision.

Trying to reach a consensus before a group acts is not necessarily a bad strategy. In fact, it usually produces a good decision and positive feelings about the group (Smith & Mackie, 2000). But according to Janis, the drive toward consensus is likely to produce groupthink and bad decisions when four conditions are present: (1) the consensus is not based on all the facts at hand, (2) group members all share certain biases, (3) members who disagree with the majority view are punished or even ejected from the group, and (4) the group leader puts pressure on the members to reach consensus. This last condition appeared to play a crucial role in the U.S. government's decision to support a disastrously unsuccessful invasion of Cuba by anti-Castro Cubans in 1961. Before the final decision was made, several advisers were told that President John F. Kennedy had made up his mind to support the invasion and that it was time to "close ranks with the president." This situation created enormous pressure for conformity (McCauley, 1989).

Some researchers have questioned the prevalence and dangers of groupthink (e.g., Aldag & Fuller, 1993; Park, 2000). They point out that groupthink is not the only cause of poor group decisions and that the conditions that make for groupthink don't actually create it. These conditions can even lead to good decisions (Kerr & Tindale, 2004). For example, having a strong, directive leader can sometimes improve group performance, and occasionally highly cohesive groups do quite well. But there are instances where groupthink does occur, and some researchers have worked on developing techniques to help groups avoid it (Galinsky & Kray, 2004; Kray & Galinsky, 2003).

One way to avoid groupthink is to designate someone to take the unpopular role of "devil's advocate"—to constantly challenge the group's emerging consensus and offer additional alternatives. This person forces the group to consider all the facts and every possible decision option (Janis, 1985; Risen, 1998). Another technique is to encourage the expression of diverse opinions by allowing them to be presented anonymously. The group members might sit at separate computers and type out messages about all the options that occur to them. Each message is displayed for all to see on an electronic mail system that hides each sender's identity. This procedure allows the group to discuss the options via e-mail without knowing who is saying what. Research on this technique suggests that it is effective in stimulating logical debate and making people less inhibited about disagreeing with the group (O'Brien, 1991).

LINKAGES

As noted in the chapter on introducing psychology, all of psychology's subfields are related to one another. Our discussion of how the presence of other people affects a person's motivation to perform illustrates just one way in which the topic of this chapter, social influence, is linked to the subfield of motivation and emotion (see the chapter on that topic). The Linkages diagram shows ties to two other subfields as well, and there are many more ties throughout the book. Looking for linkages among subfields will help you see how they all fit together and help you better appreciate the big picture that is psychology.

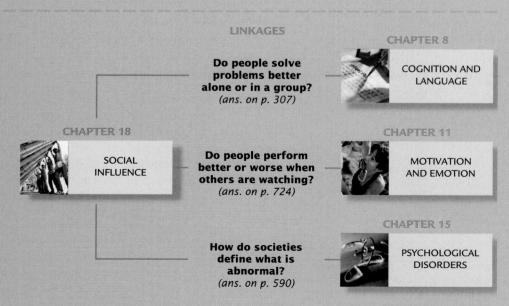

LINKAGES

Do people solve problems better alone or in a group?
(ans. on p. 307)

CHAPTER 8
COGNITION AND LANGUAGE

CHAPTER 18
SOCIAL INFLUENCE

Do people perform better or worse when others are watching?
(ans. on p. 724)

CHAPTER 11
MOTIVATION AND EMOTION

How do societies define what is abnormal?
(ans. on p. 590)

CHAPTER 15
PSYCHOLOGICAL DISORDERS

SUMMARY

Social Influence

Norms establish the rules for what should and should not be done in a particular situation. Descriptive norms indicate what most other people do and create pressure to do the same. Injunctive norms provide specific information about what others approve or disapprove of. *Deindividuation* is a psychological state in which people in a group temporarily lose their individuality, focus on the group's norms, and may engage in antisocial acts that they would not normally perform. *Social facilitation, social impairment,* and *social loafing* provide three other examples of how the presence of other people can affect an individual's behavior.

Conformity and Compliance

When behavior or beliefs change as the result of unspoken or implicit group pressure, *conformity* has occurred; when the change is the result of a request, *compliance* has occurred.

The Role of Norms   People tend to follow the normative responses of others, and groups create norms when none already exist.

Why Do People Conform?   People sometimes exhibit public conformity without private acceptance. At other times, the responses of other people have a genuine impact on private beliefs. People conform because they want to be right, because they want to be liked, and because they tend to be rewarded for doing so.

When Do People Conform?   People are most likely to conform when the situation is ambiguous, as well as when others in the group are in unanimous agreement. Up to a point, conformity usually increases as the number of people holding the majority view grows larger. Persistent and unanimous *minority influence* can also produce some conformity.

Inducing Compliance   Effective strategies for inducing compliance include the foot-in-the-door technique, the door-in-the-face procedure, and the low-ball approach.

Obedience

Obedience involves complying with an explicit demand, typically from an authority figure. Research by Stanley Milgram indicates that levels of obedience are high even when obeying an authority appears to result in pain and suffering for another person.

Factors Affecting Obedience

People obey someone who has certain kinds of social power. Obedience declines when the status of the authority figure declines, as well as when others are observed to disobey. Some people may be more likely to obey orders than others.

Evaluating Milgram's Studies

Because participants in Milgram's studies experienced considerable stress, the experiments have been questioned on ethical grounds. Nevertheless, Milgram's research showed that even apparently "normal" people can be influenced to inflict pain on others.

Aggression

Aggression is an act intended to harm another person.

Why Are People Aggressive?   Sigmund Freud saw aggression as due partly to self-destructive instincts. More recent theories attribute aggressive tendencies to genetic factors, brain dysfunctions, and hormonal influences. Learning is also important. People learn to display aggression by watching others and by being rewarded for aggressive behavior. There are wide cultural differences in the incidence of aggression.

When Are People Aggressive?   A variety of emotional factors play a role in aggression. The *frustration-aggression hypothesis* suggests that frustration can lead to aggression, particularly if cues that invite or promote aggression are present. Recent research indicates that stress and negative feelings play a major role in aggression. Arousal from sources unrelated to aggression, such as exercise, can also make aggressive responses more likely. Research in *environmental psychology* suggests that factors such as high temperature, noise, and crowding increase the likelihood of aggressive behavior.

Altruism and Helping Behavior

Human behavior is also characterized by *helping behavior* and *altruism.*

Why Do People Help?   There are three major theories of why people help others. According to the *arousal: cost-reward theory*, people help in order to reduce the unpleasant arousal they experience when others are in distress. Their specific reaction to a suffering person depends on the costs associated with helping or not helping. Helping behavior is most likely when the costs of helping are low and the costs of not helping are high. Perceptions of cost are affected by the clarity of the need for help, diffusion of responsibility, and personality traits. Environmental factors also affect willingness to help. The *empathy-altruism theory* suggests that helping can be truly unselfish if the helper feels empathy for the person in need. Evolutionary theory suggests that humans have an innate tendency to help others, especially relatives, because doing so increases the likelihood that family genes will survive.

Cooperation, Competition, and Conflict

Cooperation is behavior in which people work together to attain a goal. *Competition* exists when individuals try to attain a goal while denying that goal to others. *Conflict* occurs when a person or group believes that someone stands in the way of something of value.

Social Dilemmas In *social dilemmas*, selfish behavior that benefits individuals in the short run may spell disaster in the long run if adopted by an entire group. Two kinds of social dilemmas are the *prisoner's dilemma* and *resource dilemmas*. When given a choice between cooperation and competition in a social dilemma, people often compete with one another. This is true even though they may receive fewer rewards for competing than for cooperating.

Promoting Cooperation Communication between competing parties can increase cooperation, especially if the communication is not threatening and is relevant to the situation. One of the most effective strategies for producing long-term cooperation in a prisoner's dilemma is rewarding cooperative responses with cooperation and punishing competitive responses with competitiveness.

Interpersonal Conflict In *zero-sum games*, competition is almost inevitable, because there can be only one winner.

Incompatible interests, attribution of another's behavior to unfriendly motives, faulty communication, and magnification of differences are frequent sources of interpersonal conflict. Bargaining, third-party interventions, and reminders about broader goals and shared identity are helpful procedures for managing conflict.

Group Processes

Many of the world's most important decisions are made by groups.

Group Leadership No single personality type or behavioral style always results in good leadership. *Task-oriented leaders* provide close supervision, lead by giving directives, and generally discourage group discussion. *Person-oriented leaders* provide loose supervision, ask for group members' ideas, and are generally concerned with subordinates' feelings. Transformational leaders try to inspire and motivate the group; transactional leaders tend to reward appropriate behaviors and punish inappropriate ones.

Groupthink The pattern of thinking called *groupthink* can occur when the desire to reach a group decision becomes more important than the need to reach the best decision.

Neuropsychology

O ur eyes, in cooperation with our brains, allow most of us to see the world in three-dimensional depth and in full color, but some people suffer conditions that leave them unaware of half of that world. Even though their eyes are working properly, when these people look at a nice round pizza, they see only half a pizza. They are not suffering from a mental illness of the kind we review in the chapter on psychological disorders, but they most definitely have a problem somewhere in their brains. Understanding what the problem is, exactly where it is, and how it affects a person's behavior and mental processes takes us into the realm of *neuropsychology*, which is the focus of this chapter. Here is how we have organized our presentation:

by Joel I. Shenker and Douglas A. Bernstein

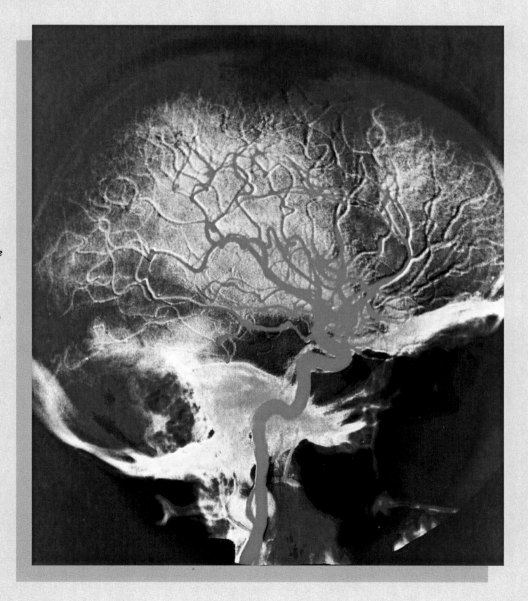

Something was wrong with Max. He put away his car keys, his wallet, and a pair of dress shoes in their usual places, but when he tried looking for them later, he had no idea where they were. "You're just getting forgetful," his wife teased. But at breakfast one day, he used a piece of bacon to stir his coffee. Then, mistaking a candle on the table for a glass of orange juice, he tried to drink it, and he used a pancake as a napkin, wiping his mouth with it before placing it carefully on his lap. He seemed puzzled by these mistakes. His wife took him to a doctor. Suppose you were that doctor. How could you determine what was wrong with Max? There would be many possibilities to consider. Maybe he is choosing to do silly things to annoy his wife for some reason. But if he is not acting oddly on purpose, just where does the problem lie? Perhaps something is amiss in his brain. The problem might reside somewhere in his memory systems, but it might also be in the realm of attention or some other psychological function. Of course, the problem might be something less specific. Perhaps he has just been working too hard or is having a reaction to a medication or some sort of dietary deficiency. He might even be suffering from depression or from an unrecognized infection that is affecting his ability to remember and concentrate. In this chapter, we explore *neuropsychology*, a subfield in which specially trained psychologists study patients such as Max in an effort to pinpoint the nature and cause of a wide variety of puzzling behavioral and psychological problems. We will describe how this subfield developed, what it has revealed about the relationship between brain functions and psychological functions, and how neuropsychologists study patients on a case-by-case basis. We will also describe some of the most interesting examples of what can go wrong in the brain and how these problems can affect people's thoughts, actions, and abilities.

Foundations of Neuropsychology

Neuropsychology is the subfield of psychology whose goal is to explore and understand the relationships among brain processes, human behavior, and psychological functioning. *Neuropsychologists* are interested in how brain processes, and disruptions of those processes, affect a wide range of human abilities, including cognitive functioning (such as language, memory, attention, mathematical, and visual-spatial skills), motor functioning (such as walking or threading a needle), emotional functioning (such as the ability to express emotions and understand other people's emotional expressions), and social functioning (such as daily interactions with others). They are interested, too, in how dysfunctions in the brain relate to changes in personality and to the appearance of psychological disorders such as depression.

The field of neuropsychology rests on two main assumptions. The first is that many complicated mental tasks, such as memory or decision making, involve many subtasks that can be tested and studied separately (Lezak, Loring, & Howieson, 2004). For example, as described in earlier chapters, the ability to form a new memory usually requires a person to be awake, to pay attention, to receive sensations, to perceive those sensations, to form mental representations of that information, to be motivated to remember the information, and to have the language or other verbal skills necessary to express the information when it is retrieved from memory. If any of these subtasks fail, a person's memory could fail in any number of everyday situations. With this assumption about subtasks in mind, neuropsychologists

neuropsychology The subfield of psychology whose goal is to explore and understand the relationship between brain processes, human behavior, and psychological functioning.

must not only figure out what complicated mental tasks a person can and cannot do, but also identify the failure of one or more subtasks that may be at the root of the problem.

The second main assumption of neuropsychology is that different psychological processes are controlled by different brain regions, or by different combinations of brain regions (Fodor, 1983; Heilman & Valenstein, 2003). Neuropsychologists use this assumption to draw conclusions about each patient they examine. After deciding what psychological processes are impaired, they work backward to infer what brain region, or combinations of regions, may not be working properly. This "working backward" approach is valuable, because many kinds of brain damage or disease are too subtle to be identified by physical examination or by various brain-scanning procedures (Nadeau & Crosson, 1995).

Using these two main assumptions, some neuropsychologists conduct research on how the human brain controls and organizes separate parts of complicated mental activities. These scientists, known as **experimental neuropsychologists,** most often study people with brain damage, but they sometimes do research on people with normal brains, too. Their aim is to add to our knowledge of brain functioning among people in general. **Clinical neuropsychologists** use this knowledge to try to understand the problems that appear in particular individuals such as Max. They look for the best way examine each person so as to determine the likelihood of brain damage or dysfunction, to determine what psychological processes are impaired, exactly how they are impaired, and which processes are still operating properly (Heilman & Valenstein, 2003; Lezak et al., 2004). Most clinical neuropsychologists are to be found in hospitals and other health care settings, where they work with physicians to test people with brain damage.

For example, Max's physician decided to have him tested by a clinical neuropsychologist, who showed Max a long series of simple drawings of common objects and asked him to name each one. Experimental neuropsychological research on thousands of people provided *norms* that told the neuropsychologist what kind of performance she could expect on this test from people of Max's age and educational background. She could then compare his performance to these norms. As it turned out, Max's responses were not normal. For example, looking at the drawing of a pencil, he said he saw "a long narrow protrusion of some kind." He called a paperclip "an object curling into itself." For eyeglasses he said "that's two circular devices suspended together." Clearly he was not naming things well—but why? Could his vision be bad? No, because he could correctly read words even when they were in small print. He could also produce reasonably accurate copies of the drawings, even though he could not always name them. This meant that he had sensed and perceived the drawings' shapes and angles and spatial relationships. Did Max have a general problem with memory, as his wife had suggested? To test that idea, the neuropsychologist read him lists of words and later asked him to recall them. He did about as well on this memory test as most of people his age and level of education, so his memory seemed normal. The neuropsychologist next considered whether Max was no longer able to understand the concepts represented in the drawings. But this possibility was ruled out when he correctly defined what is meant by a pencil, a paperclip, eyeglasses, and other objects shown in the drawings. So he knew what these objects are, and in fact, when examples of them were placed into his hands while he was blindfolded, he could instantly name them. So Max could recognize the objects by touching them, but not by looking at them.

Why? The neuropsychologist concluded that Max still had normal function within brain areas that process basic visual sensations, but that something was wrong in the brain regions that normally convert those sensations into recognizable visual perceptions. Her knowledge of research told the neuropsychologist that this problem, called a *visual agnosia*, can occur when parts of the temporal lobes on both sides of the brain are not working properly (Bauer & Demery, 2003). Max's physician used that information to focus his medical care on those brain regions.

experimental neuropsychologist A neuropsychologist who conducts research on how the brain controls and organizes separate parts of complicated mental activities.

clinical neuropsychologist A neuropsychologist who uses tests and other methods to try to understand neuropsychological problems and intact functions in individual patients.

Max's case illustrates several important aspects of what neuropsychologists have learned about how the brain operates. Let's review some of what they have discovered, and how these discoveries occurred.

● A Brief History of Neuropsychology

Max's case shows **localization of function,** the idea that a specific psychological function can be affected by damage to a specific brain area. This concept probably seems obvious to you, especially if you have read about the brain in the chapters on biological aspects of psychology, sensation, and consciousness. But this "commonsense" notion was once a matter of considerable debate (Tyler & Malessa, 2000). In fact, for centuries, philosophers and scientists had been speculating about the role of different brain areas in different psychological functions (Kaitaro, 2001).

Early in the 1800s, for example, the dominant view was that the brain worked more or less as a single organ, such that no particular part was any more important than any other part in the control of mental life. An anatomist named Franz Gall disagreed with this view, suggesting instead that particular brain areas controlled particular aspects of cognitive functioning (Zola-Morgan, 1995). This suggestion actually turned out to be correct, and his legacy would be more widely honored except for the fact that Gall also mistakenly believed that brain areas, like muscles, get bigger as people use them. He believed, too, that each brain area is associated with certain behavior patterns or personality traits, such as honesty or love or aggressiveness. Finally, Gall assumed that as brain areas grew larger, there would be corresponding bumps in the skull just above them. After creating a map showing which brain areas were supposedly controlling which traits, he thought it should be possible to assess a person's psychological makeup by feeling the bumps on the surface of the skull. Gall's approach, which was known as *phrenology*, was a hit with the public because it appeared to offer a simple way to measure personality (Benjamin & Baker, 2004). But assessing personality by feeling people's skulls was a far-fetched and easily refuted notion that led Gall's scientific colleagues to dismiss virtually everything he said about the brain's role in psychology. In fact, the ridicule heaped on phrenology tended to spread to any and all theories about localization of function.

In 1861, though, everything changed. A famous and widely respected French surgeon, Paul Broca, was asked to see a hospitalized patient whose leg had gangrene, a serious deep-tissue infection. In this era before antibiotics, gangrene often required a surgeon to amputate the affected limb, which is why Broca was consulted. It so happened that, many years earlier, this patient had had a stroke, a condition in which one of the blood vessels in the brain is blocked, causing permanent damage. The stroke left him unable to say anything but the word *tan*, which became the staff's nickname for him. Despite his speech difficulties, Tan could apparently understand language because he easily followed verbal commands. Before anything could be done about Tan's gangrene, he died, and Broca ordered an autopsy. It showed a small lesion, or area of damage, in the left frontal lobe of Tan's brain (see Figure 19.1). Broca wondered if this lesion was related to Tan's speech problems, and if so, how such a small lesion could cause such a major and specific problem. Not long afterward, Broca requested an autopsy on another patient who had had language problems similar to Tan's, and discovered a brain lesion in the same place as Tan's.

If lesions in this spot were somehow linked to these patients' speech disorders, it would support the previously dismissed idea of localization of function. Indeed, it would suggest that a particular brain area is involved in controlling a particular function, namely speech (Broca, 1861, 1865). This is precisely what Broca hypothesized when he shared his observations in a lecture to the Anthropological Society of Paris. And because, unlike Gall, Broca held such high status in the scientific community, his

localization of function The idea that a specific psychological function can be affected by damage to a specific brain area.

modules Regions of the brain that perform their own unique kind of analysis of the information they receive.

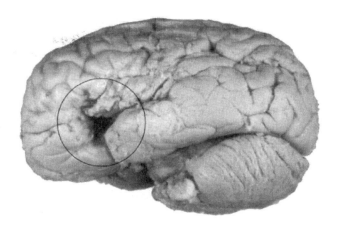

FIGURE 19.1

Tan's Brain

When Tan died, surgeon Paul Broca discovered severe damage in the left frontal lobe of the cerebral cortex, just in front of the primary motor cortex. This area, which now bears Broca's name, is involved in the ability to produce normal speech.

endorsement of localization of function made it respectable again. In fact, it created an upsurge of scholarly interest in localization of brain function that is still seen today. The resulting explosion of brain research that occurred in the last century and a half has not only confirmed localization, but established that localization is more complex than anyone in Broca's time would ever have guessed. ·

● Modules and Networks

More recent theories about localization of function have introduced the idea that the brain is organized into discrete regions called **modules**, each of which performs its own unique kind of analysis of the information it receives (Fodor, 1983; Uttal, 2003). According to this *modularity* view, each module, located in a unique brain area, acts somewhat like a circuit board in a computer. That is, a module does not itself "control" any particular function, but it adds a needed piece to complete a larger puzzle that allows speech or some other function to occur. The analysis performed by a particular module can be used in many kinds of brain functions. And each brain function—whether it is detecting the edges of an object or making a decision about something—is accomplished through the support of a different team, or *network*, of modules (Mesulam, 1990). It is as if the brain were the head of a company with a vast array of employees, each with a specific skill, who can be organized and reorganized from one moment to the next into many different work teams to perform many different tasks.

Speaking and understanding language, for example, involves a network of modules in several different brain areas. This means that damage to any part of the network will affect a person's language ability in some way, but the exact effect will depend on which part of the network is damaged. In Tan's case, for example, the lesion in his left frontal lobe disrupted his ability to speak, but left him with the ability to understand what was said to him.

The brain regions underlying language are a particularly good example of a network that uses several modules. One of the interesting consequences of a system that is organized in this way is the potential for a *disconnection syndrome*. Such syndromes occur when various modules in a network, though themselves intact, are prevented from interacting (Geschwind, 1968). A classic example is *alexia without agraphia*, which literally means inability to read while still being able to write (Imtiaz, Nirodi, & Khaleeli, 2001). The brain damage shown in Figure 19.2 could produce this kind of disconnection syndrome. Here, there is damage to the left occipital lobe, causing loss of vision, but only for what is on the right side of the visual field. Vision of the left side of the world can still occur. However, there is also damage to part of the corpus callosum, a structure that connects the left and right hemispheres of the brain. This particular part normally allows visual information from the left side of the world to cross from the right hemisphere into the left

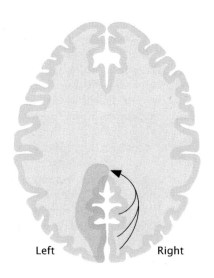

Left   Right

FIGURE 19.2

Alexia Without Agraphia

This is a classic example of a disconnection syndrome. Brain damage (in darker blue) has occurred in the left occipital lobe and part of the corpus callosum. As a result, no visual information can enter the left hemisphere. The left hemisphere brain regions that create writing are intact, so these patients can write. But because feedback from the visual system cannot get back to the language processing systems of the left hemisphere, the patients cannot read what they have written.

hemisphere, but now this pathway is blocked. Because the language-producing regions of the left hemisphere are intact, the person can still talk and write normally, but can only see what lies in their left visual field. That information goes to the right hemisphere, but because it cannot cross from there into the left hemisphere, where most language functions reside, people with this kind of disconnection syndrome have difficulty reading what they have written. In effect, the visual processing of the words is disconnected from the brain regions that are needed to understand the meaning of the words.

● Lesion Analysis

Much as Broca did so long ago, experimental neuropsychologists today still study localization of function by looking at the results of brain damage. This aspect of their work is sometimes called **lesion analysis** (Aharonov et al., 2003). To get an idea of how lesion analysis works, suppose that a man with normal mathematical ability has a stroke that damages his left parietal lobe (see the chapter on biological aspects of psychology for the location of this area). Afterward, like other people with similar brain damage, he no longer can do mathematical calculations. Do these observations confirm that the ability to do math is localized in the left parietal lobe in human brains? Possibly, but not necessarily. Critical thinking by experimental neuropsychologists leads them to consider other possibilities, too.

For example, we have already seen that complex psychological functions often require the cooperation of several different modules in several different parts of the brain. So although mathematical ability may well be impaired by damage to the left parietal lobe, it might also be affected by damage to other regions in the "mathematics" network. Experimental neuropsychologists explore this possibility by studying the changes in math ability seen in large numbers of people with damage to many different regions of the brain. If they find that math ability is affected by left parietal lobe damage, but nowhere else, they would be more confident in asserting that mathematical ability is localized in that area. If they find that damage in other areas also affects math ability, they would realize that this ability is not as localized as it might at first seem.

But lesion analysis must also address the question of just *what* function it is that has been damaged. For example, doing a mathematical calculation might require you to use several kinds of abilities—such as recognizing numbers and symbols, remembering the rules of addition or multiplication, keeping several numbers "in your head" as you do calculations, and being able to read or hear the math problem and report your answer. So if a brain lesion makes it hard for you to talk, you would not be able to answer the question "how much is two and two." But this doesn't mean there is anything wrong with your mathematical ability.

To help figure out exactly what problems a brain-damaged patient actually has, experimental neuropsychologists look at a complex mental task, such as reading or doing math, and try to identify all the abilities that a person's brain must combine to succeed at that task. They then try to determine which of these abilities are actually separate, or *dissociated*, perhaps because they are based in different brain modules in particular brain regions. One way to establish a dissociation between abilities is to study which components of a mental task are affected by which kinds of brain damage. An important example of dissociated abilities is described in the chapter on biological aspects of psychology: Damage to a particular area in the left frontal lobe disrupts a person's ability to speak fluently, but leaves the person able to understand what others say. Damage to a different area in the left temporal lobe does the opposite, leaving the person able to speak easily, but unable to understand what others are saying. We will discuss these conditions again later in this chapter. ("In Review: Foundations of Neuropsychology" summarizes milestones in the history of neuropsychology.)

lesion analysis Research conducted by experimental neuropsychologists in an attempt to understand localization of function by looking at the results of brain damage.

in review Foundations of Neuropsychology

Principle	Main Figure or Era	Key Idea(s)
Phrenology	Franz Gall, early 1800s	Argument that each person's psychological makeup depends on the size of different areas of cerebral cortex, as inferred by feeling bumps on the skull
Localization of function	Paul Broca, mid-1800s	The idea that a specific psychological function could depend on a specific brain area
Modularity	Late 1900s	A revision of localization in which each brain area is seen as performing different, unique computations, which contribute to various psychological functions
Networks	Late 1900s	A perspective suggesting that different complex psychological functions rely on unique combinations of brain modules
Lesion analysis	1800s to the present	An approach to experimental neuropsychology in which psychological functions are linked to particular brain areas by studying patients with damage to those areas and comparing these people with people who have damage elsewhere or no damage

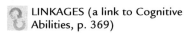 LINKAGES (a link to Cognitive Abilities, p. 369)

●● Neuropsychological Testing

So far we have discussed how the brain is organized, and how neuropsychologists go about studying ways in which its functioning is related to behavior and behavior problems. Let's now consider how they decide when a person has such problems. Consider memory, for example. We all forget things sometimes, even such familiar things as our best friend's phone number, the name of our roommate's brother, or where we left our car keys. But how much forgetfulness is normal and how much does it take to be labeled as excessive or problematic?

To answer this question, neuropsychologists typically give patients a large number of tests designed to assess a wide range of mental functions, such as general intelligence, memory, reading, motor coordination, naming pictures, finding targets in a visual display, and the like. Some neuropsychologists prefer to use an individualized set of assessments uniquely tailored to each patient. In this way they hope to measure the specific problems that a given patient is most likely to have. In other cases, patients are given a standardized test battery, which includes a predetermined set of tests that are designed to complement one another and comprehensively address all aspects of psychological functioning. Many such test batteries have been carefully prepared and validated. Among the best-known examples are the *Halstead-Reitan Battery*, the *Wechsler Adult Intelligence Scale*, and the *Luria-Nebraska Neuropsychology Battery*. Standardized batteries offer the advantage of giving each patient the same tests in the same way, but they don't allow the neuropsychologist to tailor the testing to focus on a patient's particular problems or unique situation. Accordingly, most clinical neuropsychologists start with a standard test battery, then administer additional tests that are particularly relevant to each case.

By giving many different tests, the clinical neuropsychologist can get a glimpse into many different aspects of a person's psychological functioning and also measure each area separately. Analyzing the overall pattern of results may help to pinpoint where the difficulties in the brain may lie. But the results of neuropsychological testing, like the results of personality testing, intelligence testing, or academic testing, must be interpreted with caution. Many factors, such as age, education, and cultural background, for example, can affect a person's performance on neuropsychological tests. With this in mind, each patient's performance on these tests must be compared with established averages, or norms. These norms are based on the test performance of thousands of people of the patient's own age, educational level, and cultural background, but with no known brain damage. Norms also give clinical neuropsychologists an idea of how often normal people's scores vary from the average, and by how much. Having this information helps establish whether a score that looks deviant at first glance is actually as unusual as it seems. Norms might also reveal that even a small deviation from the average is very unusual and indicative of a potential problem.

● Training for Neuropsychology

It is no wonder, then, that a considerable part of a clinical neuropsychologist's training is focused on learning about a large number of different kinds of neuropsychological tests, on exactly how to give them and score them, and on how to combine and interpret their results so as to reach the most accurate conclusions about patients' problems and the likely source of those problems (Boake, Yeates, & Donders, 2002). Neuropsychologists typically train in graduate school, earning a Ph.D. degree in clinical psychology, with a special focus on neuropsychology and the many topics related to it. Before they can get a license to practice on their own, however, they must complete an internship. The internship usually includes a year or more of neuropsychological practice performed under the close supervision and mentoring of a licensed clinical neuropsychologist, typically in a university hospital setting. Once licensed, clinical neuropsychologists tend to be hired by health facilities where there is a need for testing patients for possible brain damage. Indeed, many neuropsychologists are employed directly by a hospital, though some may join a specialty clinic where they work closely with physicians who focus on the diagnosis and treatment of brain disorders. Others may work in highly specialized facilities offering programs focusing only on patients with stroke or brain trauma. Experimental neuropsychologists are usually employed as professors in a university setting, where they teach students, conduct their own research, and participate in testing patients as time permits.

Mechanisms of Brain Dysfunction

We have been talking a lot about brain damage, and perhaps you are wondering how brains get hurt.

● Stroke

As you may have guessed by now, strokes are a common source of brain damage. What is a stroke, exactly? The problem arises because the brain receives all the oxygen, sugar (glucose), and other nutrients it needs from the rich supply of blood flowing through it (see Figure 19.3). But brain cells cannot store much of this energy, so they must have a supply of fresh blood at all times (Acker & Acker, 2004). If a vessel bringing blood into some part of the brain becomes blocked, the brain tissue in that part of the brain will die, and whatever function that part of the brain usually does will be disrupted or destroyed (Caplan, 2004, 2005). When someone's behavior or mental processes are affected by loss of the blood supply in some part of the brain, the person is said to have had a **stroke**. Even very tiny strokes can cause disabling symptoms if they take place in vital brain areas, but strokes in less vital areas might cause no symptoms at all.

Strokes can be quite dangerous. In fact, they are the third-leading cause of death in the United States. They tend to occur as people get older, but young adults and even children have been known to have them. Unlike heart attacks, in which the blood supply to the heart muscle is disrupted, a stroke usually involves little or no pain because there are no pain receptors in brain tissue. So a stroke victim may not

● **stroke** A loss of blood supply to some part of the brain, resulting in disruption of some aspect of behavior or mental processes.

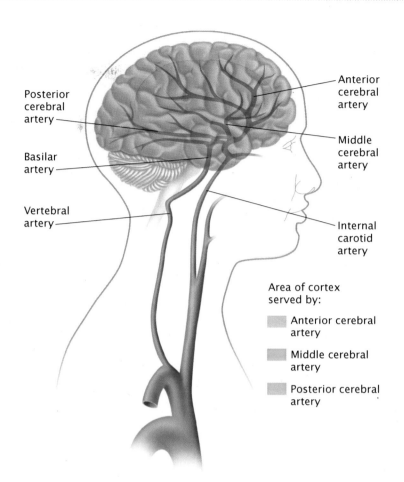

FIGURE 19.3

The Brain's Blood Supply

TRY THIS Blood reaches the brain either through the carotid arteries on either side of the neck or through vertebral arteries entering through the base of the skull. Once in the brain, these arteries branch into the anterior cerebral artery, the middle cerebral artery, and the posterior cerebral artery. Each artery provides blood to specific brain areas. As a result, a blockage in each particular blood vessel damages a specific, predictable part of the brain. Review the chapter on biological aspects of psychology to remind yourself of what functions are associated with each area of the cerebral cortex. Then make a list of the functions that would most likely be affected by blockage in each of the arteries shown in this figure.

immediately realize that anything is wrong. The resulting delay in seeking medical attention can be costly, because treatments that can help reduce the effects of a stroke must be given as soon as possible after the stroke occurs.

Like explosions that break windows a block away, strokes affect not only the area in which brain tissue has died, but also the area surrounding it. Fortunately, if cells in the area around a stroke have not actually died, they may start working again (Baron, 2005). As a result, some people experience some recovery of the functions that were lost when the stroke occurred. The amount of recovery depends on many factors, including the quality and speed of medical treatment, how large the stroke is (and where the stroke is), the health of the remaining blood vessels and brain tissue, and what kinds of rehabilitation programs are undertaken after the stroke (Fink & Caplan, 2003; Frizzell, 2005; Heiss & Teasel, 2006).

● Trauma

Another major cause of brain damage is **trauma**, a sudden impact on the brain caused when a person's head is struck by a baseball bat, a bullet, or some other object, or when the head suddenly moves or stops moving, as when a person is thrown violently against a head restraint during an accident. Traumatic events such as these can cause damage because the brain is not firmly attached to the skull. Instead, it floats within it, suspended in a bath of *cerebrospinal fluid*. So when the skull is struck or the head suddenly and violently accelerates or decelerates, the brain will slide in one direction inside its bony case, and then bounce backward. As the soft globe of brain bounces back and forth and bumps up against bone, nerve fibers in many places may stretch and tear.

The amount of brain damage resulting from trauma depends greatly on the amount of force involved in such situations. Further, unlike in strokes, where only

trauma An impact on the brain caused by a blow or sudden, violent movement of the head.

in **review**	Mechanisms of Brain Dysfunction		
Brain Problem	**Starts**	**Underlying Process**	**Symptoms**
Stroke	Suddenly	Blocked blood flow in some part of the brain	Specific to the area of the brain that is destroyed
Trauma	Suddenly	Brain slides back and forth inside the skull	Often nonspecific, diffuse
Neurodegeneration	Gradually	A subset of neuron cell types becomes diseased and stops working properly	Specific to the types of brain cells affected

the area in and around a disrupted blood supply is likely to be affected, the damage and disruption caused by trauma may be widespread. So whereas stroke patients may show very specific kinds of neuropsychological deficits, sometimes with striking dissociations between functions that are lost and those that are preserved, people with head injuries may display deficits that are far more diffuse, harder to specify, and involve more aspects of functioning (Wade, 2004). Perhaps as a result, we know much more about the neuropsychological symptom patterns that follow strokes than we do about those following brain traumas.

● Neurodegeneration

Unlike the sudden symptoms that result from brain damage caused by stroke and trauma, other brain problems develop bit by bit. These more slowly developing symptoms often result from **neurodegeneration** (Mayeux, 2003), a term that refers to a gradual process of cell damage in the brain. Three of the most prominent examples of neurodegenerative diseases are Alzheimer's disease, Parkinson's disease, and Huntington's disease. Each type of neurodegenerative disease affects a particular kind of brain cell, or cells in a particular part of the brain, causing them to be the first to stop working properly (Cummings, 2003) and leaving the victim without the mental or physical functions those cells had once supported. The pattern of symptoms resulting from each neurodegenerative disease is different enough that neuropsychological testing of a patient can usually lead to a diagnosis of which disease is affecting that patient (Cummings, 2003; Manning, 2004).

Some kinds of neurodegeneration appear to be caused by infections, nutritional deficiencies, or genetic abnormalities, but despite intense research, we still do not know the ultimate causes of most such diseases. ("In Review: Mechanisms of Brain Dysfunction" summarizes the major causes of brain injury and dysfunction.)

Neuropsychological Disorders

Let's now take a closer look at the *syndromes,* or patterns of symptoms, that clinical neuropsychologists typically see in patients who have suffered stroke, trauma, or neurodegenerative disease. These syndromes are referred to as **neuropsychological disorders** and include amnestic disorders, disorders of consciousness, disorders of perceptual function, disorders of language and communication, disorders of higher movement, and disorders involving dementia.

● Amnestic Disorders

LINKAGES (a link to Memory, p. 270)

Amnestic disorders are those that involve memory loss (often referred to as *amnesia*). Quite often, it is a specific concern about memory problems that brings people to

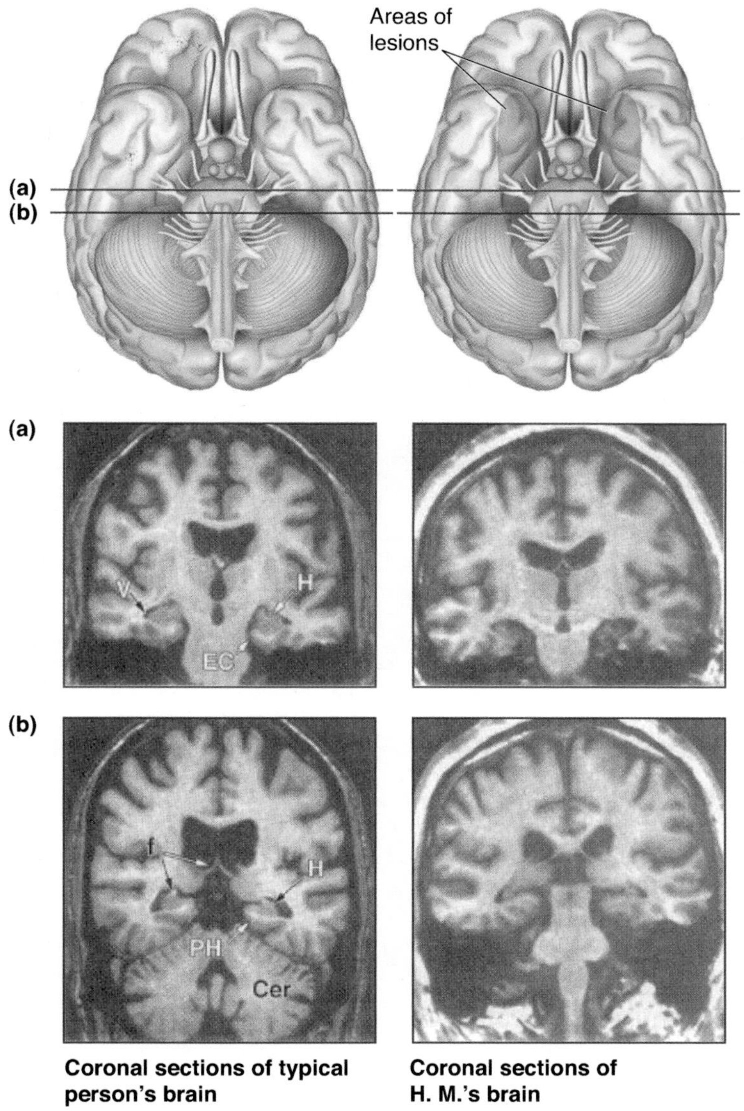

Areas of lesions

(a)
(b)

(a)

(b)

Coronal sections of typical person's brain

Coronal sections of H. M.'s brain

FIGURE **19.4**

H. M.'s Brain Surgery

H. M. underwent surgery that removed the hippocampus, amygdala, and part of the association cortex from both temporal lobes. As shown in these MRI scans comparing an intact brain with H. M.'s brain after surgery, H. M. has some hippocampus (H) but no entorhinal cortex (EC). In this image, (V) refers to the lateral ventricle, (f) refers to the fornix, (PH) refers to the parahippocampal cortex, and (Cer) refers to the cerebellum.

clinical neuropsychologists for evaluation. These people are concerned partly because they rely heavily on memory, and any threat to its integrity can be extremely upsetting. But patients also tend to highlight memory problems because we all have a tendency to interpret almost any psychological deficit as being related to memory (Lezak et al., 2004). As in Max's case, for example, people who begin having trouble naming objects may assume they are "forgetting" words, even though the problem could actually be one of language or visual recognition. Many older individuals, too, seek neuropsychological assessment because of worry that even minor forgetfulness might be early signs of Alzheimer's disease. We discuss Alzheimer's in the section on dementia, but memory loss can occur in other neuropsychological syndromes, too (Lucas, 2005).

For example, the ability to create new long-term memories can be impaired by damage in the brain's medial temporal lobes ("medial" means toward the middle of the brain), and in the hippocampus in particular (Milner, 2005). Consider the famous case of H. M. (Scoville & Milner, 1957). In 1953, at the age of twenty-seven, H. M. had brain surgery to remove parts of both his left and right temporal lobes, including parts of the hippocampus on both sides (see Figure 19.4). The surgery was successful at stopping H. M.'s severe epileptic seizures, but it left him with a dense amnestic syndrome that persists to this day (Mackay, 2006). Although he

neurodegeneration A gradual process of cell damage in the brain, usually caused by disease.

neuropsychological disorders Patterns of symptoms seen in patients who have suffered stroke, trauma, or neurodegenerative disease.

amnestic disorders Neuropsychological disorders, such as anterograde amnesia, that involve memory loss.

FIGURE 19.5

Memory without Awareness

People with amnesia from medial temporal lobe damage may learn from experiences that they cannot recall. This stimulus shows a degraded version of a drawing. Using stimuli similar to these, participants with amnesia first saw a very degraded version, then one less so, then less, and so on until they could name the item. Patients with amnesia were able to name items earlier if they had seen them before, even when they could not recall having seen them.

can recall most details of his life from before the surgery, he has had difficulty ever since in forming new memories. In other words, as discussed in the memory chapter, he has *anterograde amnesia*. When he meets someone new, he is unable to recall the meeting, so the person always seems to be a stranger no matter how many times they meet again. Similarly, the new terms he has heard over the years—such as "computer," "videotape," "cell phone," and "Jacuzzi"—have never made it into his vocabulary. He can't even remember that time is passing, so he has had few clues that he is getting older; to a great extent, he is mentally stuck in the 1950s.

Yet many of H. M.'s other mental capacities have remained largely intact, providing a striking example of the dissociation that can occur between abilities lost and those retained after brain damage. His language function remains good; he is able to recognize objects; he can think and reason; he remains intelligent, pleasant, and sociable; and he can carry on very normal sounding conversations. But even he is quite aware of his memory problem. He put it as follows (Corkin, 2002):

> Right now, I'm wondering, have I done or said something amiss? You see, at this moment everything looks clear to me, but what happened just before? That's what worries me. It's like waking from a dream. I just don't remember.

H. M. has been carefully studied for years, and the lessons learned from him have prompted research on memory loss in other people after medial temporal lobe damage. When other people have amnesia caused by damage to the hippocampus, just like H. M., they also have difficulty remembering the new experiences or events of their lives. But, also like H. M., it turns out that these individuals can still learn new skills and habits as a result of their new experiences. When they do a task over and over, they get better at it, meaning that they do form some kind of a memory. Nonetheless, they have no awareness for this learning and do not recall the experiences that led to it (see Figure 19.5).

Anterograde amnesia and other amnestic syndromes can be caused by events other than surgery in the hippocampus and medial temporal lobe. For example, certain brain infections, such as herpes encephalitis (Stefanacci et al., 2000), tend to damage these same parts of the brain and create an amnestic syndrome similar to that of H. M. Strokes, too, can sometimes damage these regions, though they are usually on just one side of the brain, so the amnestic syndrome may not be as noticeable. Finally, as described later, these regions, and the memory functions they normally perform, can also be impaired by Alzheimer's disease (Van Hoesen, Hyman, & Damasio, 1991).

The hippocampus is not the only structure involved in memory. For example, as described in the chapter on biological aspects of psychology, the thalamus processes information from all the senses except smell and sends it on to the cerebral cortex for further processing. But the medial dorsal (the middle and top) region of the thalamus is also part of the brain's *limbic system*, an interconnected set of structures that includes the hippocampus (see Figure 19.6). The medial dorsal thalamus is seldom damaged by trauma or stroke, but it is often damaged by *Korsakoff's syndrome* (Butters, 1981), a condition in people whose thiamine (vitamin B_1) is depleted by inadequate nutrition or alcoholism. Running low on thiamine is dangerous because this vitamin is needed to process glucose (sugar) for energy. Nerve cells of the medial dorsal thalamus are especially dependent on this function of thiamine (Marti, Singleton, & Hiller-Sturmhofel, 2003), and if thiamine deficiency is severe, nerve cells there are more likely to die than in other brain regions (Visser et al., 1999). The result is an anterograde amnesia with an additional unusual feature. Korsakoff's syndrome patients are prone to *confabulation*—in other words they create false memories (Butters, 1981). These individuals believe that they have had experiences that they have not actually had, and

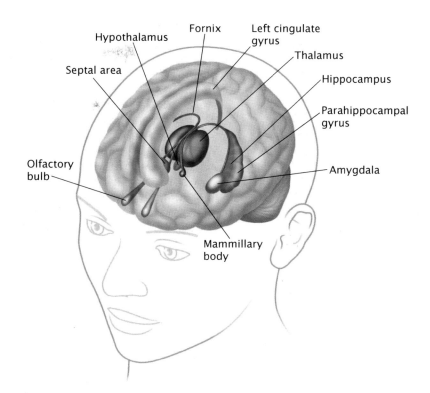

FIGURE 19.6

The Limbic System

A number of closely connected structures form the limbic system, which controls many aspects of motivation and emotion.

they "recall" them as if they were real. Other amnestic syndromes do not usually produce confabulation, so when a clinical neuropsychologist is testing a patient with severe anterograde amnesia and finds confabulation, too, a medial dorsal thalamic amnesia is often suspected.

Disorders of Consciousness

Sometimes, problems in the brain can create **disorders of consciousness,** which impair people's ability to be conscious, or accurately aware, of the world around them (Bleck & Klawans, 1986; Plum & Posner, 2000). One such problem occurs when there is disruption or damage to the *reticular formation,* also known as the *reticular activating system,* or *RAS.* The RAS is a long, tube-like structure that begins in the base of the brain and extends upward, eventually splitting into two halves that reach into both sides of the thalamus. As its name implies, the RAS normally serves to increase and decrease arousal in the rest of the brain, and helps to create our daily cycles of wakefulness and sleep (Izac & Eeg, 2006). If the RAS is severely damaged, the result can be an unconscious state known as a *coma.* People with lesser amounts of RAS damage may enter a *persistent vegetative state (PVS)* (Bekinschtein et al., 2005). Unlike coma patients, people suffering PVS may open their eyes and appear to wake up during the day, and close their eyes and appear to sleep at night. They may also show a wider array of automatic movements than do coma patients. For example, when food is put the mouth of someone in a PVS, chewing movements may occur, and sounds and touches may sometimes trigger facial expressions. But though EEG and high-tech scanning procedures show activity in some areas of these individuals' brains (Brenner, 2005; Laureys, 2004; Schiff et al., 2005), the patients remain unaware of their environment. The chances for recovery are often poor following significant damage to the RAS.

disorders of consciousness
Neuropsychological disorders in which there are impairments in the ability to be conscious, or accurately aware, of the world.

Even if the RAS is working properly to stimulate the rest of the brain, consciousness can be impaired if there are widespread disruptions in the functioning of both sides of the cerebral cortex, where other aspects of awareness are controlled (Stevens & Bhardwaj, 2006). Impairment of both sides of the cortex is most commonly caused by drugs such as alcohol or sleeping pills, but other causes include fever, seizures, chemical imbalances in the blood, hormonal disorders, or infections that have spread to the blood (Plum & Posner, 2000).

Other disorders of consciousness have more complex and changing effects. People with *delirium*, for example, enter alternating periods of abnormally impaired consciousness and abnormally elevated levels of consciousness (Ferro, 2001). The impairments in consciousness appear in many mental functions, usually including poor attention, poor memory, and disorientation. Elevated consciousness may appear as hallucinations (hearing sounds or seeing things that are not really there), or in periods of mental agitation for no apparent reason. Indeed, a key feature of delirium is the waxing and waning, the rising and falling, of consciousness (Plum & Posner, 2000). These patients may appear sleepy and "out of it" one minute, and then far too attentive the next, as shown by reactions to every little sight and sound. Common causes of delirium include fever, poisons, infections that have reached the bloodstream, and the side effects of medication. Delirium can sometimes create a medical emergency, but most of the time its psychological effects are not permanent. Delirium usually goes away when the underlying medical cause is corrected.

Neuropsychological testing of people in delirium is difficult (Milisen et al., 2006). Their attention and awareness can vary, sometimes dramatically, over the course of testing. In general, performance on almost any test is very poor, probably because delirium patients cannot pay attention long enough or well enough to cooperate with the testing process. Indeed, their typical pattern of performance on neuropsychological tests is that there is no pattern—everything may look impaired.

Still other disorders of consciousness don't involve problems in people's level of consciousness, but in the nature, or content, of their consciousness. For example, a person may have a stroke that causes total paralysis of one side of the body, but the person may have no awareness that there is anything wrong. This condition is called *anosognosia* (pronounced "a-nose-ag-NOSE-ya"), which means an absence of knowledge of disease (Babinski, 1914; Heilman, Barrett, & Adair, 1998; McGlynn & Schacter, 1989). In such cases, it appears that brain damage causes not only an impairment in functioning, but an impairment in the ability to know about that impairment. This makes sense, because the brain is the organ that we use to figure out when something is wrong. So if you have pain in your arm, sensory neurons tell the brain about it. But if the brain itself is hurt, it has nowhere to send its message.

Anosognosia can occur in association with a variety of problems, from paralysis to blindness to amputation of a limb (McGlynn & Schacter, 1989), and it is particularly likely after damage to the right side of the brain (Nathanson, Bergman, & Gordon, 1952; Stone, Halligan, & Greenwood, 1993). Anosognosia is relatively common, occurring, for example, in about 25 percent of all stroke victims (Starkstein et al., 1992). An unfortunate result is that these patients may not be motivated to get the prompt medical attention needed to limit the amount of damage that a stroke can cause. Anosognosia may fade over time, or it may persist. When it does persist, it impairs patients' cooperation with rehabilitative treatments. They don't understand that something is wrong, so they don't see the treatment as necessary. There may be ways to improve awareness of neurological deficits, though. In one case, a man was unaware of the sudden and bizarre involuntary movements he had been making for several years. He could not see these movements, even when looking at himself in a mirror, but when doctors arranged for him to see himself on videotape, he instantly saw the problem (Shenker et al., 2004).

THINKING CRITICALLY Can Someone Be Partially Paralyzed and Not Know It?

In anosognosia, a person denies any neurological deficit because there is no understanding that a problem exists. This phenomenon was first described long ago in relation to strokes that caused *hemiparesis*, a weakness or partial paralysis that affects just one side of the body (Babinski, 1914). Skeptics have argued that people with hemiparesis are still fully capable of knowing that they are partially paralyzed, but that this knowledge would be so upsetting that they simply cannot admit it, even to themselves. According to this skeptical argument, anosognosia is not based on true unawareness, but on the operation of an unconscious mental process similar to the ego defense mechanism that Freud called denial (see the chapter on personality).

■ What am I being asked to believe or accept?

Arguing against these skeptics are those who say that anosognosia occurs because the brain damage that causes hemiparesis also damages the parts of the brain that would allow the person to know that something is wrong. As a result, patients who seem unaware of hemiparesis or other problems are, in fact, truly unaware of them (Heilman et al., 1998; McGlynn & Schacter, 1989).

■ What evidence is available to support the assertion?

Those who believe that anosognosia is genuine unawareness point out that if it were the result of an ego defense mechanism, it would operate in a general way to deny any and all potentially upsetting deficits. Yet evidence from neurological examinations shows that some hemiparesis patients, for example, are aware that an arm is weak but not that a leg is weak (Berti, Ladavas, & Corti, 1996; Bisiach et al., 1986). Others are aware that they have a speech disturbance, but not weakness in a limb (Bisiach et al., 1986; Breier et al., 1995).

Another problem with the ego defense mechanism argument is that anosognosia occurs much more often after right hemisphere brain damage, which causes left-side hemiparesis, than it does when left hemisphere brain damage causes right-side hemiparesis. It would seem that weakness on either side should be about equally upsetting and equally likely to cause anosognosia. In fact, because most people are right-handed, weakness on the right side might be even more upsetting and therefore *more* likely to result in psychologically motivated denial.

Additional evidence against the ego defense mechanism hypothesis comes from research showing that anosognosia can occur even when there is no threat of permanent paralysis. In a procedure pioneered by June Wada (Strauss & Wada, 1983), participants being evaluated for possible brain surgery had an anesthetic injected into one side of their brain at a time (Adair et al., 1995; Gilmore et al., 1992). This *Wada technique* temporarily "turns off" either the left hemisphere or the right hemisphere, without causing any permanent brain damage. When the right hemisphere was "turned off" in this way, participants became paralyzed on the left side of their bodies. When they were asked about their experience, they recalled most details correctly but most of them displayed anosognosia—that is, they said that they did not notice any weakness or paralysis. When the left hemisphere was anesthetized, though, patients not only became weak on the right side, but later reported awareness of the paralysis. These data are hard to explain as being due to ego defense mechanisms, because, once participants had recovered from their left-side paralysis, why would they be motivated to deny that it had occurred?

■ Are there alternative ways of interpreting the evidence?

One problem with the Wada technique is that it is difficult to compare what patients are experiencing at the time the left and right hemispheres are anesthetized. The problem is that because speech areas are on the left side, people are usually unable to speak when their left hemisphere is "turned off." This doesn't happen on the right side, so the only way to do a direct comparison of the experience of left versus right hemisphere inactivation is to ask the patient questions after the anesthetic has worn off. If it were possible to talk to people during the left hemisphere inactivation, perhaps they would show anosognosia because, at that particular moment, there could be enough distress to motivate denial.

This interpretation is supported by research conducted decades ago with patients who had suffered a stroke causing hemiparesis (Weinstein & Kahn, 1955). When these patients' families were interviewed, it turned out that those patients who, before their stroke, had tended to cope with stress through denial were the ones most likely to deny their hemiparesis. Patients who did not show anosognosia were described by their families as less likely to have previously used denial as a coping mechanism. These data suggest that denial of hemiparesis is just an exaggeration of a person's established stress-coping tendencies.

■ What additional evidence would help to evaluate the alternatives?

The results of this and other family report studies might be affected by *retrospective bias* (Heilman et al., 1998). That is, once they know that their relative is denying hemiparesis, family members might be more likely to recall similar episodes of denial in the relative's past, and to forget about episodes in which the patient had coped with stress in other ways. Similarly, if a relative isn't denying the symptoms caused by a stroke, perhaps family members will be less likely to recall incidents in which the patient did use denial in stressful situations.

One way around the problem of retrospective bias would be to do a *prospective* study, in which a large group of individuals is identified, their typical stress-coping tendencies are assessed, and then they are contacted on a regular basis for many years. The ego defense mechanism hypothesis would be supported in such a study if the people in the group who were most likely to use denial as a coping mechanism are also the ones most likely to display anosognosia following a stroke.

■ What conclusions are most reasonable?

It is probably true that some individuals who suffer neurological deficits may use denial or other psychological defense mechanisms to avoid facing their distressing problems, but given the neurological evidence we have reviewed, it seems reasonable to conclude that many cases of anosognosia reflect a true lack of awareness of neurological deficit. ■

● Disorders of Perception

As described in the chapter on perception, the information we receive from our eyes, ears, and other senses must be analyzed by the brain in order to organize, recognize, interpret, and understand it if we are to make sense of the world. These vital perceptual functions depend on the normal operation of specific regions of the brain. For example, visual information passes from the eyes to and through the thalamus, and then to particular areas in the occipital lobe of the cerebral cortex where the information is analyzed further. From there, visual information is sent along two separate, but parallel pathways. Along each of these pathways are a series of connected cortical regions that perform specialized analyses that allow us to experience different aspects of visual perception (Ungerleider & Mishkin, 1982; see Figure 19.7). The pathway leading toward the ventrolateral temporal lobe (on the sides of the head— "ventral" means toward the bottom part of the brain, "lateral" means toward the outside of the brain) has been called the "what" system because the cortical regions along this pathway help us to decide what it is that we are seeing—a dog or a car, for example. The pathway leading toward to the parietal lobe (near the top of the head) has been called the "where" system because it processes information about the location of objects and where those objects are in relation to one another.

● **disorders of perception**
Neuropsychological disorders in which there are impairments in the ability to organize, recognize, interpret, and make sense of incoming sensory information.

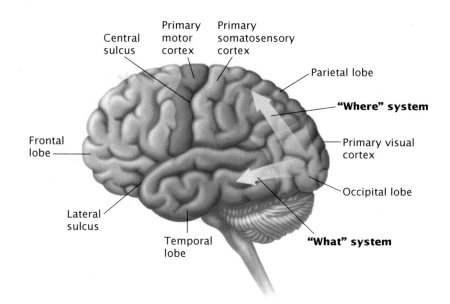

FIGURE 19.7

"What" Versus "Where" Visual Pathways

Research suggests that visual information reaching the primary visual cortex is sent along two separate but parallel systems. The "where" system focuses on an object's location in space and how it is moving. The "what" system determines the identity of the object.

FIGURE 19.8

A "Global-Local" Stimulus

TRY THIS People with simultanagnosia have difficulty seeing an H in this stimulus but see the Ts easily. Try showing this pattern to several friends. Unless any of them are suffering a similar neuropsychological disorder, you should be able to confirm that they will report seeing both the little Ts and the larger letter H.

This system helps us to understand, for example, that the dog is sitting in the car. Damage to our perceptual systems can result in **disorders of perception.**

For example, damage to the "what" pathway causes a condition called *visual agnosia* (Bauer & Demery, 2003). As in the case of Max, individuals with visual agnosia can see objects in the world, they can describe them, and they can even draw them, but they no longer know what the objects are based on their appearance (Rubens & Benson, 1971). So a visual agnosia patient can correctly define the word *apple* and, based on how it feels, correctly state that the neurologist has placed an apple in the person's hand. In other words, these patients still know what apples and other objects are, but they have lost the ability to link visual images of these objects to the part of the brain where that knowledge is stored.

Visual agnosia may leave patients unable to name anything they see, but sometimes the problem occurs only in relation to certain categories of objects (Bauer & Demery, 2003). For example, some people have visual agnosia only for manufactured objects, such as a car or a book or a drinking glass, but can still correctly identify on sight a tree, a dog, or any other living thing. In other cases, it may only be manufactured objects that can be named on sight (Farah, McMullen, & Meyer, 1991; Kurbat, 1997). These case observations suggest that information about natural versus manufactured objects must be processed in different ways by different brain areas. Visual agnosias can be even more specific. For example, there appears to be a special brain system dedicated to visual recognition of faces (Farah, 1996). When this aspect of the "what" system is damaged, the result is *prosopagnosia*, a condition in which a person can no longer recognize faces, even very familiar ones, and even the patient's own face in a photograph or mirror (Barton et al., 2004). The facial recognition system appears to depend on temporal lobe structures; most people who develop prosopagnosia have damage to these areas on both sides of the brain (Ettlin et al., 1992), but sometimes a lesion on the right side alone is enough to produce a facial recognition syndrome (Barton et al., 2002).

What happens when there is damage to the "where" system? As you might expect, this kind of damage creates problems in the visual perception of objects in space and how they are related to one another. A particularly interesting example is called *simultanagnosia* (Wolpert, 1924), a condition in which a person can see parts of a visual scene but has difficulty perceiving the whole scene. In a sense, a person with simultanagnosia can see the "trees" but cannot see the "forest." So if simultanagnosia patients were to look at the pattern shown in Figure 19.8, they could see all the "Ts," but not the larger letter "H" formed by the smaller letters.

One patient described her perceptions as follows (Shenker, 2005):

EXAMINER: What do you see?

PATIENT: I see T. T, T, T, . . . Do I keep going?

EXAMINER: Anything else?

PATIENT: T, T, T, T . . . lots of T's.

EXAMINER: Are there any other letters?

PATIENT: No.

EXAMINER: Is there an H?

PATIENT: No, just T's

EXAMINER: Is there a big letter?

PATIENT: No I don't see one.

EXAMINER: Is there a big letter H?

PATIENT: No.

EXAMINER: Do the little letters together form the shape of a big letter H?

PATIENT: I don't see how.

EXAMINER: (outlines the H with finger) Do you see how this is a big H?

PATIENT: I don't see an H.

Simultanagnosia has been associated with damage or dysfunction on both sides of the brain, in the upper part of the parietal lobes (Coslett & Saffran, 1991). Damage to the "where" system in a different region of the parietal lobes can cause a condition known as *hemineglect* (Heilman, Valenstein, & Watson, 2000). This condition, usually occurring after a stroke, involves difficulty in seeing, responding to, or acting on information coming from either the right, or more often, the left side of the world (Heilman, Watson, & Valenstein, 2003). The side of space that is neglected is usually opposite to the side where the parietal lobe lesion is located. A person with hemineglect will ignore food on one side of a dinner plate, fail to put makeup on one side of the face, and pay no attention to voices coming from one side of the room. As shown in Figure 19.9, when asked to draw a picture of, say, a flower or a clock, only half a drawing will be completed—the half on the side of space to which the person is still paying attention.

One of the most fascinating aspects of hemineglect is that it cannot be explained as being due to a lack of sensation on one side or the other. For patients with left hemineglect, it is as if the concept of "leftness" is lost, and so the left side of things is simply ignored (Bisiach, Capitani, & Tansini, 1979). This ignoring process is easy to demonstrate in some patients. The neuropsychologist simply holds up one hand on each side of the patient's visual field and then asks the patient to say when any fingers are wiggling. In some cases of hemineglect, patients will be able to correctly report when fingers are wiggling on the right, *or* on the left, as long as the wiggling is only on one side. When there is wiggling on both sides, though, these patients may only report seeing it on the side to which they pay attention. These cases demonstrate that some hemineglect patients are capable of seeing both sides of space; they don't have a pure sensory problem. They are simply more likely to pay attention to one side of the world, and to ignore the other.

Other patients with hemineglect also have sensory problems. They may be blind in their left visual field, for example. It may seem surprising, but neuropsychologists can show that even in these patients, the tendency to ignore one side of space cannot be explained by their sensory loss. For example, patients with left hemineglect may not respond to the sound of a voice coming from the left. Is it because of a problem in their left ear? No, because the sound was heard by their right ear, too. Also, left hemineglect patients may ignore the left side of an object, even if the entire object appears in their right visual field.

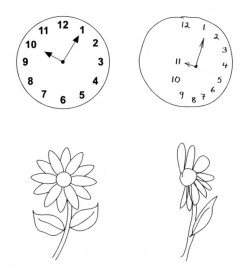

FIGURE 19.9

Examples of Neglect on a Drawing Test

When shown an object and asked to draw it, patients with hemineglect often leave out details from the neglected side of the object.

FOCUS ON
RESEARCH METHODS

Studying Hemineglect

Proving that hemineglect cannot be explained by sensory problems alone can be tricky. After all, in many cases of hemineglect the brain damage that caused it also caused a loss of sensation from the same side. Also, most tests for hemineglect rely on giving a person some kind of sensory information to respond to. How can one show that hemineglect is not due to a sensory problem if you can only test for it by having people respond to the sensations they receive?

■ What was the researcher's question?

Edoardo Bisiach (Bisiach, Luzzatti, & Perani, 1979) reasoned that if hemineglect were truly a problem with understanding that a particular side of space exists, then this problem should persist even for a scene that is not viewed directly, but is instead put together using only one's imagination.

■ How did the researcher answer the question?

Bisiach tested patients who had right hemisphere lesions and left-sided hemineglect. He created randomly shaped stimuli that looked a bit like clouds. The stimuli were passed behind a vertical slit, so that as the image moved across, patients could see only a small "slice" of it at a time (see Figure 19.10). In other words, the only way to "see" the whole stimulus was to imagine all the "slices" assembled in the "mind's eye." Patients were shown two of these passing images at a time, one passing by the top part of the slit, and the other passing by the bottom part of the slit. On some trials, the two stimuli were identical. On other trials, only their left sides were different, and on still others only their right sides were different. The patients' task was to decide if the two stimuli were the same or different.

■ What did the researcher find?

Patients with left-sided hemineglect were able to determine when the stimuli were different if the right sides were different. But these patients could not detect differences between the stimuli if the left sides were different.

■ What do the results mean?

Because of the slit, the patients could not see the left and right sides of the images at the same time. This means that their failure to notice differences on only the left side did not result because they couldn't see the left side of space. Instead, these results appear to suggest that hemineglect occurs when patients ignore stimulation that is on a particular side of space, even when they are assembling that stimulation through memory and imagination.

FIGURE 19.10

Studying Hemineglect

Here are examples of the random cloudlike shapes used by Bisiach, Luzzatti, & Perani (1979) to explore whether hemineglect is a sensory problem. Hemineglect patients could see only vertical "slices" of these shapes as the patterns passed behind a narrow vertical slit. So to "see" these shapes as whole patterns and to decide whether pairs of patterns were the same or different, the patients had to build an image of each pattern in their minds.

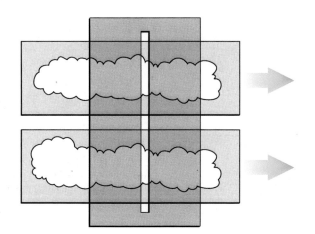

■ What do we still need to know?

Different kinds of hemineglect are produced by damage in different parts of the brain (Watson & Heilman, 1979). So it is not clear if Bisiach's patients, who had damage in their parietal lobes, are representative of all hemineglect patients. Notice, too, that the stimuli in Bisiach's study were all visual. Would the same results appear in research using imagined touches or sounds, for example? These are questions to be answered by further research on the fascinating topic of hemineglect. ■

LINKAGES Language Disorders and the Brain

LINKAGES (a link to Biological Aspects of Psychology, p. 86)

When people suffer disruptions in the functioning of brain regions that normally support their ability to speak, read, write, and understand language, specific aspects of these language skills will fail, resulting in corresponding disorders in the person's language abilities. The precise nature of these **language disorders,** also called *aphasias*, can be identified through careful and detailed neuropsychological testing. In this section we discuss several subtypes of aphasias (Caplan, 2003a), each of which is associated with damage or dysfunction in a particular area of the brain's language centers.

Most aphasias occur as a result of damage to the left side of the brain, often from stroke or trauma, but sometimes from a neurodegenerative disease process called *frontotemporal degeneration (FTD)* (Boxer & Miller, 2005; Neary & Snowden, 1996). As a result of this process, nerve cells start to die in the front section of the brain's temporal or frontal lobes, often on one side more than on the other (Neary, Snowden, & Mann, 1993; see Figure 19.11). The result is similar to a stroke because FTD tends to affect a fairly specific brain area, but unlike the sudden symptoms of a stroke, FTD symptoms develop gradually over a period of years. If FTD is focused on the language-related regions of the brain's left hemisphere, the result is a condition called *primary progressive aphasia* (Grossman & Ash, 2004; Mesulam, 2001). Let's consider where these brain regions are, what they normally do, and what else can happen when their functioning is disrupted.

As described in the chapter on biological aspects of psychology, there are several "language areas" in the brain. These interconnected regions work together as a network, and all of them must work properly in order for us to use and understand language. For example, it appears that *Broca's area* is vital to our ability to translate thoughts into words or writing that will be clear and meaningful to others. People who suffer damage to Broca's area (see Figure 19.12) display **Broca's aphasia,** which is seen mainly in the loss of language fluency. That is, they are no longer able to smoothly and easily express themselves (Kertesz, 1993). Instead, they speak in a halting, sputtering manner, and only with great effort, and often with much frustration. There may be other symptoms as well, including a change in the kinds of words that individuals produce (Benson & Geschwind, 1971). Most of the words that patients with Broca's aphasia can still speak or write are those that refer to concrete objects, such as *book* or *pillow* or *water*, rather than those that refer to abstract ideas such as *justice* or *literature* or *weather*. These patients also tend to use mainly concrete nouns and verbs, leaving out the more abstract articles, adjectives, and adverbs they once spoke or wrote. This change in word usage results in a "telegraphic" speaking style that recalls a bygone era when people sending telegrams had to pay for each word in a message. A Broca's aphasia patient who once would have said "Please give me the spoon" might now say simply "Give spoon." Sometimes, Broca's aphasia patients make mistakes when naming objects. Such naming errors are called *paraphasias*, and in Broca's aphasia they tend to be *phonemic paraphasias*, or errors in the way a word should sound. So a person with Broca's

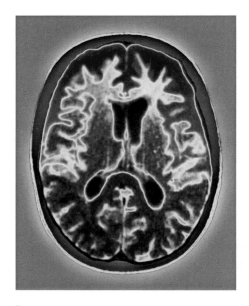

FIGURE 19.11

Frontotemporal Degeneration

In frontotemporal degeneration, a relatively limited part of the brain can become extremely shrunken, as shown here.

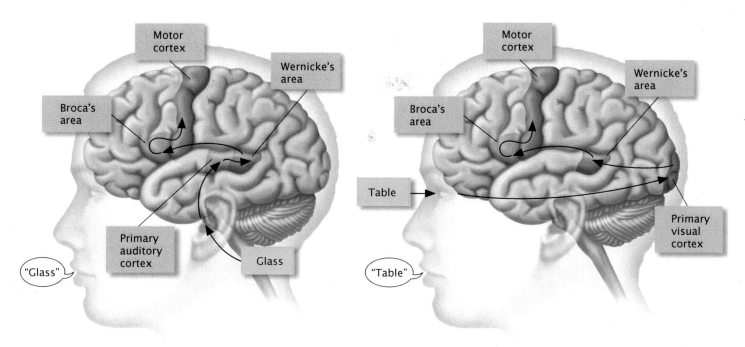

Repeating a Spoken Word

(A)

Reading a Word Out Loud

(B)

FIGURE 19.12

The Wernicke-Geschwind Model of Aphasia

The Wernicke-Geschwind model of aphasia accounts for many, but not all, of the findings associated with the major aphasias. The pathways shown in part A transmit information when a participant is instructed to repeat a spoken word. The image shown in part B traces the flow of information when the person is asked to read a written word out loud.

aphasia might look at a pen and call it *peb*. Finally, people with Broca's aphasia may have some difficulty understanding what they see and hear (Caplan, 2003a, 2003b).

People with damage to *Wernicke's area* (see Figure 19.12) display a different set of problems (Goodglass & Kaplan, 1982), because this area is involved in the ability to understand the meaning of sensory information. These people have difficulty understanding what they read, or what others are saying (Kertesz, 1993). In fact, because everything everyone says sounds like nonsense to a person with **Wernicke's aphasia,** the world must seem like a suddenly strange and even unfriendly place where everyone *else* has a problem. Further, although people with Wernicke's aphasia can still speak fluently and effortlessly, what they say is far from normal. Most notably, they make *semantic paraphasias*, which are naming errors in which they may use words that have the wrong meaning. So when trying to name a pen they may call it a "book." In contrast to Broca's aphasia, people with Wernicke's aphasia tend to use lots of adverbs, adjectives, and articles, but relatively few nouns and verbs. As a result these people's speech sounds rather empty of content. For example, when attempting to describe a picture of a woman and her children in the kitchen, a Wernicke's aphasia patient may say "Over here is the top of the rest for the other rapid sheesh of many red sitters." This kind of output, combined with naming errors, can make the speech of a person with Wernicke's aphasia sound so disorganized that it may be mistaken for the "word salad" associated with some cases of severe schizophrenia (Sambunaris & Hyde, 1994; see the chapter on psychological disorders). Yet, because they do not recognize all the mistakes they are making, or appreciate the oddness of their speech, people with Wernicke's aphasia are often puzzled and upset when others do not seem to understand them or respond to them correctly.

language disorders Neuropsychological disorders in which there are disruptions in the ability to speak, read, write, and understand language.

Broca's aphasia A language disorder in which there is a loss of fluent speech.

Wernicke's aphasia A language disorder in which there is a loss of ability to understand written or spoken language and to produce sensible speech.

The brain's left hemisphere is the focus of most language disorders, but communication problems can also occur when the right hemisphere is damaged. In general, people with right hemisphere damage can still speak words fairly normally and can understand the words that they hear and see fairly well. However, they may lose the ability to use tone of voice to express meaning, or to use other people's tone of voice to help them understand what those people mean. This problem, called *aprosodia*, can take several forms (Ross, 1981). For example, damage to the right frontal lobe can cause an *expressive aprosodia*, in which the person speaks in such a dull monotone that they may be forced to say something like "I am angry" in order to get their emotional meaning across. Yet they may still be able to correctly understand and use cues from other people's tone of voice. By contrast, people with damage to the right temporal and parietal regions may have a *receptive aprosodia,* which means that they can use tone of voice correctly when they speak, but have difficulty understanding the meaning of other people's tone of voice. So if someone were to sarcastically say "Well, that was really smart," meaning just the opposite, a person with receptive aprosodia may miss the sarcasm, pay attention only to the words themselves, and say "Thanks!" ▪

● Disorders of Movement

The brain's motor pathways are "wired" to our muscles in ways that allow us to move our limbs and body, but the knowledge of how to move in ways that effectively accomplish our goals is not built into that system. Using silverware, pedaling a bicycle, sucking on a straw, or swinging a hammer are just a few examples of the thousands of coordinated movements that each of us has had to learn from experience. A network of special brain systems control such learned motor skills by instructing the brain's motor control centers to make the movements needed for each action sequence (see Figure 19.13). These brain areas tell the motor system what combinations of movements to make for a specific kind of task. If a part of

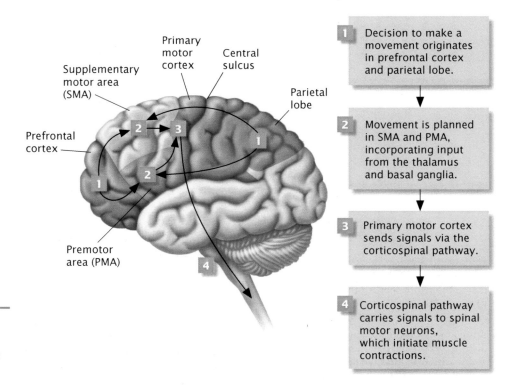

FIGURE 19.13

The Initiation of Voluntary Movement

A network of brain regions is involved in initiating voluntary movements.

1. Decision to make a movement originates in prefrontal cortex and parietal lobe.

2. Movement is planned in SMA and PMA, incorporating input from the thalamus and basal ganglia.

3. Primary motor cortex sends signals via the corticospinal pathway.

4. Corticospinal pathway carries signals to spinal motor neurons, which initiate muscle contractions.

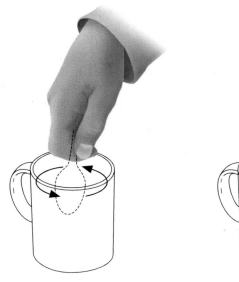  

Correct pantomime   **Apraxic behavior**

FIGURE 19.14

An Example of Apraxic Motor Behavior

When imitating the movements involved in using a common object, an individual with apraxia may mistakenly use an arm or a leg to represent that object. So instead of showing how they would move in order to use a tool, they act as if their limb is the tool itself.

this special network is damaged, the result is some form of *apraxia*, or **disorders of movement,** in which learned motor skills are disrupted (McClain & Foundas, 2004).

There are two main types of apraxia (Heilman & Gonzalez-Rothi, 2003). In *ideational apraxia*, the individual movements needed to perform a task are all correctly executed, but in the wrong order. So, although a person with ideational apraxia can still open a tube of toothpaste, wet her toothbrush, squeeze paste onto the brush, insert the brush in her mouth, and do a good job of brushing, she might begin to brush before putting toothpaste on her brush, or she might squeeze the toothpaste tube first, and then try to unscrew the cap.

A more common problem is *ideomotor apraxia*, which involves difficulties not in the sequence of skilled movements, but in performing the skilled movements. So a person with ideomotor apraxia will try to execute each step in tooth-brushing in its proper order, but may have difficulty in positioning her hand to hold on to the brush, and may be unable to make the proper sequence of arm and hand motions required to actually brush her teeth. In one kind of ideomotor apraxia, the person may use a finger or other body part as if it were a tool, perhaps brushing with the finger, or using it to try to turn a screw. In such cases, the person cannot seem to figure out how to use the brush or screwdriver or other tool they once used with skillful ease (see Figure 19.14).

● Dementia

We have already seen that, in cases of delirium, people show reduced or heightened levels of consciousness, and many psychological abilities may all fail at once. But these multiple deficits are usually reversible, such that when the toxin or other cause of delirium disappears, the deficits do, too. In conditions known as **dementia,** however, there is no waxing and waning of consciousness; wakefulness and alertness remain normal, but many other mental functions are impaired (Knopman & Selnes, 2003; Manning, 2004). To receive a diagnosis of dementia a person must have developed a notable impairment of memory, along with impairment in some other area of psychological function such as perceptual ability, language, or learned motor skills. In addition, the impairments must be significant enough to cause problems in

disorders of movement
Neuropsychological disorders in which there are impairments in the ability to perform or coordinate previously normal motor skills.

dementia Neuropsychological disorders in which there are significant and disruptive impairments in memory, as well as perceptual ability, language, or learned motor skills.

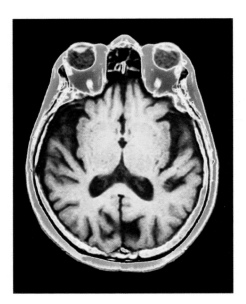

FIGURE 19.15

Brain Atrophy in Alzheimer's Disease

Alzheimer's disease causes some brain cells to stop working and eventually die, whereas other brain cells may be unaffected. Where brain cells die off, the cortex shrinks, leaving gaping wide spaces.

the person's ability to function at work, in social situations, or in everyday tasks such as driving, cooking, or balancing a checkbook. In most cases, but not all, dementia is gradual, progressive, and irreversible.

A condition known as *mild cognitive impairment (MCI)* may precede the appearance of some kinds of dementia (Dubois, 2004; Petersen & Morris, 2005). In *amnestic MCI*, for example, a person displays much below average memory skills on neuropsychological tests, but no other deficits, and may have adapted well enough to the memory loss that it has not caused a significant disruption in daily functioning. People with amnestic MCI often get worse, though, and about 12–15 percent of them each year progress to the point that they receive a diagnosis of dementia (Petersen et al., 1999). Identifying people when they are still in this relatively early stage of memory loss may be important because some studies suggest that medication can stabilize memory and delay the development of full-fledged dementia (Petersen et al., 2005; Tabert et al., 2006).

Dementia is usually caused by a progressive neurodegenerative brain disorder, and the most common of these, accounting for about half of all cases, is *Alzheimer's disease* (Cummings, 2004). About 4.5 million people have Alzheimer's disease in the United States alone, where its economic costs are set at more than $100 billion a year, and where its costs in personal suffering are incalculable (U.S. Department of Health and Human Services, 2001a; Wimo & Winblad, 2001). The percentage of people with Alzheimer's disease doubles after about every five years after the age of sixty. As a result, about 10 percent of people over age sixty-five and 47 percent of people over eighty-five suffer from this disease (Kukull et al., 2002; U.S. Department of Health and Human Services, 2001a). With more people than ever living longer and longer lives, current estimates suggest that by the year 2050 Alzheimer's disease will affect nearly 13.2 million people in the United States (Hebert et al., 2003).

Alzheimer's disease was first described in 1907 by a German neurologist, Alois Alzheimer (Devi & Quitschke, 1999). He told of a fifty-one-year-old woman called Auguste D., who before her death displayed what Alzheimer described as an "early onset senility" (see Figure 19.15). When he examined her brain after she died, he found two types of microscopic abnormalities. The first were degenerated nerve cells that had twisted into misshapen *tangles*. The second were clumps of protein deposits, called *amyloid plaques*, lying around the outside of dead and dying nerve cells. To this day, the ultimate diagnosis of Alzheimer's disease depends on the appearance of these tangles and plaques (Graeber & Mehraein, 1999).

Studying the brains of deceased Alzheimer's patients has shown that the anatomical basis of the disease mainly involves neurons that use the neurotransmitter *acetylcholine* (Perry, 1980). This disease particularly affects neurons in the parietal and medial temporal lobes on both sides of the brain (Cummings, 2004; Knopman & Selnes, 2003). Because the parietal lobes are important for locating objects in space, Alzheimer's disease patients have difficulty drawing certain kinds of shapes, and they may easily get lost as they drive or walk. Many Alzheimer's patients are endangered every day by wandering away from home or from the care facility in which they are living. Because the left parietal lobe contains brain areas important for language, patients with Alzheimer's disease may also develop *anomia*, a condition in which it becomes hard to name objects even if they know what the objects are. The left parietal lobe usually also contains brain areas that are important for learned skills such as using a hammer or a spoon, so these kinds of functions can also become impaired enough to lead to apraxia. And because the medial temporal lobes contain the hippocampus, patients with Alzheimer's disease become unable to form new memories. Old memories, the ones already formed and stored elsewhere, usually remain accessible until the disease has progressed further. So as in the case of

H. M., Alzheimer's' disease patients may remember details from their early adulthood, yet they may not remember a conversation they had yesterday. Finally, because the temporal lobes are also important for the ability to interpret visual sensations, patients with Alzheimer's disease sometimes develop visual agnosia, an inability to recognize the objects they see.

In a final type of dementia, memory loss and other psychological deficits are not caused by Alzheimer's or any other kind of neurodegenerative disease. This condition, called *vascular dementia*, is brought about by restrictions in the supply of blood to the brain. We have already mentioned that when a blood vessel in the brain is blocked, the brain cells die in the tissue that normally receives oxygen and nutrients from that blood vessel (Caplan, 2005). Sometimes this loss of blood supply occurs in very tiny blood vessels, resulting in the death of only a tiny amount of brain tissue. Such injuries may not cause symptoms when they first occur, especially if vital areas are not affected, but if many small injuries occur repeatedly, more and more brain tissue is lost, and the cumulative effect can be an impairment of memory and other psychological functions (Fisher, 1989).

The symptoms of vascular dementia usually differ from those of Alzheimer's disease (Knopman, 2006). These patients show memory loss, including difficulty in remembering recent events, but in contrast to Alzheimer's disease, the hippocampus is usually relatively well preserved. So vascular dementia patients should still be able to form new memories. Why, then, do these people have difficulty remembering new material? The answer often is that they have more of a problem in retrieving recent memories than in forming them. This subtle difference highlights the importance of careful neuropsychological testing. A proper testing protocol can help establish the exact cause of a dementia. This information is vital, because new medications are becoming available that can stop or slow the progression of certain dementias (Cummings, 2004). It is important for physicians to know exactly what form of dementia they are dealing with in each case so that they can prescribe the correct medication. Choosing the right drug at the right time can help patients enjoy a better quality of life for a longer time and can delay for years the need for nursing home care (Geldmacher et al., 2003). ("In Review: Major Neuropsychological Disorders" summarizes the various dysfunctions discussed here.)

in review Major Neuropsychological Disorders

Syndrome	Affected Person Has Difficulty...	Area(s) of Brain Malfunction
Apraxia	Making learned skilled movements even if not weak or confused.	Usually left cerebral hemisphere parietal or frontal lobes
Visual agnosia	Attaching meaning to visual sensations.	Temporal lobes, often bilateral
Anosognosia	Becoming aware of the loss of neurological function.	Usually right cerebral hemisphere
Hemineglect	Paying attention to one side of space.	Usually right parietal lobe
Aphasia	Using language as a communication system.	Usually left cerebral hemisphere
Aprosodia	Using tone of voice as a communication tool.	Usually right cerebral hemisphere
Dementia	With memory, and at least one other psychological ability, that is severe enough to impair functioning.	Variable, depending on the cause of the dementia

LINKAGES

As noted in the introductory chapter, all of psychology's subfields are related to one another. Our discussion of language disorders illustrates just one way in which the topic of this chapter, neuropsychology, is linked to the subfield of biological psychology, which is described in the chapter on biological aspects of psychology. The Linkages diagram shows ties to two other subfields, and there are many more ties throughout the book. Looking for linkages among subfields will help you see how they all fit together and help you better appreciate the big picture that is psychology.

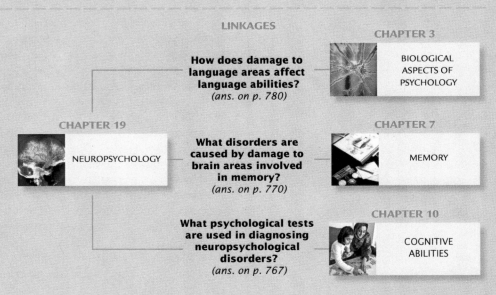

LINKAGES

CHAPTER 19

NEUROPSYCHOLOGY

How does damage to language areas affect language abilities?
(ans. on p. 780)

CHAPTER 3

BIOLOGICAL ASPECTS OF PSYCHOLOGY

What disorders are caused by damage to brain areas involved in memory?
(ans. on p. 770)

CHAPTER 7

MEMORY

What psychological tests are used in diagnosing neuropsychological disorders?
(ans. on p. 767)

CHAPTER 10

COGNITIVE ABILITIES

SUMMARY

Neuropsychology is the subfield of psychology whose goal is to explore and understand the relationship between brain processes, human behavior and psychological functioning.

Foundations of Neuropsychology

There are two main assumptions in neuropsychology. The first is that complicated mental tasks such as memory involve many subtasks that can be studied separately. The second is that different psychological processes are controlled by different brain regions, or different combinations of brain regions. *Experimental neuropsychologists* use these assumptions as they conduct research on how the brain controls and organizes human mental activity. *Clinical neuropsychologists* use the results of neuropsychological research to try to understand the nature and location of brain disorders seen in individual patients.

A Brief History of Neuropsychology Neuropsychology's early history focused on debates over *localization of function*, the idea that specific psychological functions are governed by specific parts of the brain. Early evidence for this notion was dismissed by serious scientists, but by the 1860s localization of function began to be accepted and it now forms the basis for much of what we know about neuropsychological functioning.

Modules and Networks Recent theories of localization center on the idea that the brain is organized into *modules*, each of which performs its own unique analysis of information and each of which works together with varying combinations of other modules throughout the brain to perform all aspects of behavior and mental processes.

Lesion Analysis Experimental neuropsychologists today use *lesion analysis* to try to understand the complexities of localization of function; they look at how damage (lesions) in particular places in the brain relate to the appearance of particular problems.

Neuropsychological Testing Clinical neuropsychologists use a wide variety of neuropsychological tests to help determine the nature of a patient's neuropsychological problems and even to suggest where in the brain the problem may lie. These tests may consist of a standardized group of instruments, such as the Halstead-Reitan Battery, or they may be an individualized combination of tests chosen by the neuropsychologist with a particular patient in mind. In most cases, a standard battery is followed by some additional individualized tests.

Training for Neuropsychology To develop their skills, clinical neuropsychologists typically earn a Ph.D. in clinical psychology, with a focus on neuropsychology, and then complete a postdoctoral internship.

Mechanisms of Brain Dysfunction

Brain dysfunctions can be caused by a number of conditions.

Stroke One of the main causes of brain damage and dysfunction is a *stroke*, which occurs when the blood supply to a part of the brain is blocked, causing the death of cells in that region and the loss of that brain region's ability to perform its normal control over some aspect of behavior or mental processing. Strokes can be disabling, and sometimes, deadly.

Trauma Damage and dysfunction can also result from *trauma*, a sudden impact on the brain caused by a blow to the head, sudden and violent head movements, or other events that literally shake the brain inside the skull. The amount of damage and dysfunction following such events depends mainly on the amount of force involved.

Neurodegeneration Finally, *neurodegeneration*, the gradual process of damage to brain cells, can be caused by diseases such as Alzheimer's, Parkinson's, and Huntington's, or by infections, nutritional deficiencies, or genetic abnormalities.

Neuropsychological Disorders

The syndromes, or patterns of symptoms, associated with stroke, trauma, and neurodegenerative diseases appear as several kinds of *neuropsychological disorders*.

Amnestic Disorders The hallmark of *amnestic disorders* is some significant disruption or loss of memory, as seen in conditions such as anterograde amnesia, in which new memories do not form.

Disorders of Consciousness In *disorders of consciousness*, there is impairment in a person's normal awareness of the world. These conditions can range from loss of consciousness, as in coma or persistent vegetative state, to delirium, in which the patient alternates between reduced and elevated degrees of consciousness. In cases of anosognosia, a person may be paralyzed on one side of the body but have no awareness of the problem.

Disorders of Perception When people suffer disorders of perception, they may become unable to understand what objects, or certain categories of objects, are by looking at them (visual agnosia), may be unable to recognize faces (prosopagnosia), or have difficulty assembling the specific parts of a visual scene into a coherent whole (simultanagnosia). Patients suffering a perceptual disorder called hemineglect ignore one half of the world.

Language Disorders and the Brain *Language disorders* usually result from damage to language areas on the left side of the brain and take the form of aphasias, in which the ability to speak or understand language is disrupted. The many forms of aphasia include *Broca's aphasia*, in which people can no longer speak fluently, and *Wernicke's aphasia*, which makes it difficult for people to understand what they read or hear; and though they can speak fluently, their speech makes little or no sense. Damage in the right side of the brain can result in aprosodia, the loss of ability to use tone of voice to express one's meaning or to understand the meaning of other people's speech.

Disorders of Movement *Disorders of movement*, also known as apraxias, involve the inability to perform various motor skills, or the inability to perform those skills in the correct order.

Dementia Patients with *dementia* suffer gradually more significant and, usually, irreversible, loss of many mental functions, including impairment of memory, perception, language, and motor skills. It is usually caused by progressive neurodegenerative disorders such as Alzheimer's disease, though it may also be caused by restrictions of the brain's blood supply. A condition known as mild cognitive impairment may precede the appearance of some forms of dementia.

Industrial/Organizational Psychology 20

I f you have a full-time or part-time job, you know that workdays blend demands, challenges, difficulties, and rewards—all of which can affect job satisfaction. Understanding the causes and effects of job satisfaction is just one aspect of industrial/organizational (I/O) psychology, the topic of this chapter. We will describe how I/O psychologists conduct their research, and how they apply that research to improve the performance and welfare of workers and of the organizations that employ them. The chapter is organized as follows:

by Paul E. Spector and Douglas A. Bernstein

Suppose that you are the manager at a department store. You want to hire someone to head up the cosmetics department, but you are not sure how to choose the best person for the job. Should you rely on interviews with each of the candidates, or should you also give them some psychological tests? Perhaps you decide to do both, but what questions should you ask during the interviews? What kinds of tests should you use? And how should you interpret the results? Further, what happens after you have made your hiring decision? Do you have procedures available to train, motivate, supervise, and reward employees so that they perform at their best and are happy in their work? For answers to questions like these, many human resources managers and other company executives seek the help of *industrial/organizational (I/O) psychologists*. We briefly mentioned I/O psychology in the chapter on introducing psychology; here we describe it more detail, including a summary of what I/O psychologists do, and some of the ways that their work has benefited organizations and employees.

An Overview of Industrial/Organizational Psychology

We have said that psychology is the science of behavior and mental processes. The subfield of **industrial/organizational (I/O) psychology** is the science of behavior and mental processes in the workplace. Industrial/organizational psychologists conduct scientific research on all sorts of people-oriented workplace topics, such as what personality traits predict good performance under stress, or what social factors cause conflict in work groups. I/O psychologists are also hands-on practitioners who help organizations apply research findings to problems such as matching employees to jobs, or maximizing cooperation in workplace teams. The link between scientific research and professional practice can be especially strong in I/O psychology because the workplace provides both a natural laboratory for studying psychological questions and a setting in which research-based answers can be applied and evaluated.

Industrial/organizational psychologists address two main goals in their research and practice. The first is *promoting effective job performance* by employees, which ultimately leads to enhanced performance by the organization as a whole. The second goal is to contribute to human welfare by *improving the health, safety, and well-being of employees*. This second goal is important in itself but is also related to the first one. Effective organizations are those whose employees not only are capable of performing their jobs well but also are healthy and well adjusted in the workplace.

Industrial/organizational psychology emerged early in the 1900s as psychologists began to apply laboratory-based principles of learning, memory, and motivation to solve practical problems in the workplace. Over the years, research and applications in I/O psychology have continued to be influenced by laboratory research in many of psychology's subfields, including cognitive psychology, personality, motivation and emotion, health psychology, and especially social psychology. The work of I/O psychologists is also shaped by findings in fields beyond psychology, including business management, engineering, and medicine.

Like psychologists in other subfields, I/O psychologists hold graduate degrees in their specialty. The popularity of that specialty has grown rapidly in recent decades, both in North America and throughout the industrialized world (Spector, 2003). According to a survey by the Society for Industrial and Organizational Psychology,

industrial/organizational (I/O) psychology The science of behavior and mental processes in the workplace.

Teaching I/O Psychology Some graduates pursue careers in I/O psychology after completing a master's degree, but salaries and opportunities are better for those with a Ph.D. For example, virtually all I/O psychologists who are hired as college or university professors have completed a doctoral degree. Master's or doctoral training in I/O psychology is available at more than 100 universities in the United States, 9 in Canada, and more than 80 in other countries (Society for Industrial and Organizational Psychology, 2007).

about 34.5 percent of I/O psychologists are employed as professors in college or university departments of psychology, business, or related fields. Another 30 percent own or work in consulting firms that provide services to private and public organizations on a fee-based freelance basis. About 30 percent are hired as technical specialists by private corporations, and about 5.6 percent act as research scientists in the public sector, including in government agencies (Medsker, Katkowski, & Furr, 2003). Let's now consider some of the specific kinds of work that I/O psychologists do in these various settings.

Assessing People, Jobs, and Job Performance

If you apply for a job with a large corporation or government agency, you will probably be asked to take one or more standardized tests of personality or mental ability, and to participate in other assessments whose results will help determine whether you have the "right stuff" for the job you seek. These assessment programs are usually designed by I/O psychologists. In fact, I/O psychologists are asked to develop or conduct some sort of assessment task more often than any other. Accordingly, the development and evaluation of new and better assessment devices is one of the main areas for scientific research in I/O psychology.

Knowledge, Skills, Abilities, and Other Characteristics

Industrial/organizational assessments are often used to describe the human attributes necessary for doing jobs successfully. Those attributes are referred to collectively as *KSAOs*, which stands for knowledge, skill, ability, and other personal characteristics. *Knowledge* refers to what the person already knows. *Skill* refers to how good a person is at doing a particular task. *Ability* is defined as the person's relatively enduring capacities in areas such as thinking, physical coordination, and the like. Skills and abilities are closely related; some researchers consider skills to be the products of innate abilities (Muchinsky, 2003). *Other personal characteristics* can be almost anything else about a person, including attitudes, personality traits, physical characteristics, preferences, values, and the like.

TABLE **20.1** Knowledge, Skill, Ability, and Other Characteristics (KSAOs)					
Here are examples of the kinds of KSAOs required for successful performance by people working in two different jobs.	**Job Title**	**Knowledge**	**Skill**	**Ability**	**Other**
	Secretary	Knowledge of office procedures	Skill in using a word-processing program	Ability to communicate with others	Willingness to follow instructions
	Plumber	Knowledge of county building codes	Skill in using a wrench	Good hand-eye coordination	Willingness to work in dirty environments

● Job Analysis

How do organizations know which KSAOs are important for which jobs? The answer lies in **job analysis,** in which I/O psychologists collect information about particular jobs and job requirements. This job analysis information is then used to guide decisions about whom to hire and what kind of training is needed to succeed at a particular job (Brannick & Levine, 2002). There are two major approaches to job analysis. The *job-oriented approach* describes the tasks involved in doing a job, such as wiring circuit boards, creating a computer database, or driving a truck. The *person-oriented approach* describes the KSAOs needed to do those job tasks (see Table 20.1). Some job analyses take one approach or the other, but many provide information about both tasks and KSAOs. A job analysis report can be a relatively superficial description, a microscopically detailed examination, or anything in between. The approach taken and level of detail included in a job analysis depend mainly on how the report will be used. When the analysis will guide the hiring of employees, it should contain enough detail to make it clear what needs to be done in a particular job and to show, in a court of law if necessary, how the selection process is related to the requirements established by the job analysis. The person-oriented approach is the most useful one for this purpose, because it describes the KSAOs that the employer should be looking for in the new employee.

Job analysis can also help organizations recognize the need to train employees, and it can even outline the kind of training required. Suppose you have five job openings, but when you test candidates for hiring or promotion, too few of them possess the KSAOs that a job analysis says are necessary for success in these positions. Obviously, some training will be needed, and because the job analysis lists specific KSAOs, you can use that analysis to determine exactly what the training should include. Suppose a job analysis reveals that people in a computer sales position must be familiar with the *Linux* operating system. As a result, you would provide *Linux* training for all individuals hired for that position unless they already knew that operating system.

The most common method of job analysis is to ask current employees (known as *job incumbents*) to fill out questionnaires about what they do in the workplace. However, a somewhat more reliable picture may emerge when specially trained job analysts observe people as they do their jobs, or even perform those jobs themselves (Dierdorff & Wilson, 2003). If one goal of the analysis is to compare various jobs, I/O psychologists might use an instrument such as the *Position Analysis Questionnaire*, or *PAQ* (McCormick, Jeanneret, & Mecham, 1972). The 189 items on the PAQ can describe almost any job in terms of a particular set of characteristics, or dimensions, such as the degree to which a job involves communicating with people, lifting heavy objects, doing mental arithmetic, or the like. The results of thousands of job analyses have been collected in the U.S. Department of Labor's *Occupational Information Network, or O*NET* (Peterson et al., 2001). This computer database contains analyses of approximately 1,100 groups of jobs, including the KSAOs and tasks involved in each, and how each job fits into its organizational context. Accessible on line at http://online.onetcenter.org, *O*NET* is an excellent source of information about occupations for anyone who is in the process of choosing a career.

● **job analysis** The process of collecting information about jobs and job requirements that is used to guide hiring and training decisions.

■ ● Measuring Employee Characteristics

I/O psychologists use a wide variety of instruments to measure a person's knowledge, skill, ability, and other characteristics. These instruments range from simple paper-and-pencil tests—perhaps an arithmetic test for a sales clerk—to a multiday program of hands-on activities that simulates the tasks required of a midlevel manager. Some assessments are used to select new employees, others are designed to choose employees for promotion, and still others are meant to determine how well employees are doing their jobs at the moment. The three main methods to measure employee characteristics are psychological tests, selection interviews, and assessment centers.

● Psychological Tests

A *psychological test* is a systematic procedure for observing behavior in a standard situation and describing it on a number scale or a system of categories (Anastasi & Urbina, 1997). Some tests present a standardized series of problems or questions, each of which has one correct answer, much like the multiple choice exams used in some college classrooms. Others are more like essay exams in which the respondent is asked to, say, describe an ideal sales organization. These essay-type exams are not scored by a computer but by experts who use job analysis information and/or their own job experience to judge the correctness or quality of the responses. Still other tests require the respondent to demonstrate skill by performing a task such as typing a letter, debugging a computer program, repairing a car, or giving a sales talk.

The tests I/O psychologists most often use to measure general mental ability and skill are the standard IQ tests described in the cognitive abilities chapter. These tests are relatively inexpensive and easy to administer, and they do a reasonably good job at predicting how well people will do in a wide variety of occupational tasks (Bertau, Anderson, & Salgado, 2005; Jansen & Vinkenburg, 2006; Rooy et al., 2006). Tests of job-relevant knowledge—such as basic accounting principles or stock-trading rules and regulations—may also be used to confirm that an individual has the information necessary to succeed at a particular job. Finally, personality tests are used to assess a wide variety of other employee characteristics. As described in the personality chapter, some of these tests provide information about personality dimensions that may be relevant to hiring decisions. For example, a person's score on *conscientiousness* (i.e., reliability and industriousness) has been linked to job performance across many occupations (Dudley et al., 2006; Thoresen et al., 2003; Witt & Ferris, 2003). Personality-related *integrity tests* are sometimes used to identify people who have tendencies that might lead them to steal or engage in other disruptive acts (Alliger & Dwight, 2000; Ones & Viswesvaran, 2001). These are usually paper-and-pencil tests that ask respondents about their thoughts or temptations regarding theft, their perceptions of norms regarding dishonesty, their own social conformity, and their history of associating with delinquents (Wanek, Sackett, & Ones, 2003).

● Selection Interviews

A *selection interview* is designed to determine an applicant's suitability for a job. Interviews usually take place in person, though some are conducted by telephone, videoconferencing, or even e-mail. As mentioned in the personality chapter, interviews can be structured or unstructured (open-ended). In a *structured interview*, the interviewer has prepared a list of specific topics or even specifically worded questions to be covered in a particular order (Chapman & Zweig, 2005). In *unstructured interviews*, the course of the conversation is more spontaneous and variable. Following some interviews, especially structured interviews, the candidate's responses will be rated on a set of dimensions such as product knowledge, clarity of expression, poise, or the like. After other interviews, the interviewer's subjective impression of the candidate is used to make a yes-or-no judgment about the candidate's suitability for the job.

Research consistently shows that structured interviews are far more effective than unstructured interviews in leading to good hiring decisions (e.g., Huffcutt & Arthur, 1994). The difference is due largely to the fact that structured interviews

A Matter of Degree When hiring employees for some jobs, organizations often rely on credentials rather than knowledge tests. For example, an undergraduate degree in any major may be enough to qualify for some white-collar jobs because it is assumed that college graduates have enough general knowledge and "mental horsepower" to succeed. For jobs in medicine, law, accounting, engineering, and other specialty fields, candidates' knowledge is assumed if they have completed a particular degree program or earned a particular license. These assumptions are usually correct, but credentials alone do not always guarantee competence.

Conducting structured interviews ensures that each prospective employee will be asked about the things that are most important to the employer when filling a job. It is easy to see what kind of workers this boss is seeking.

© Scott Adams/Dist. by United Feature Syndicate, Inc.

focus specifically on job-related knowledge and skills, especially interpersonal skills, whereas unstructured interviews do not (Huffcutt et al., 2001). Further, lack of structure makes it easier for personal bias to enter the hiring picture. Ratings from an unstructured interview might have more to do with the interviewer's personal bias about the candidates than with the candidates' objective qualifications. There is some evidence that job candidates tend to prefer interview-based assessments over test-based assessments. This preference is of interest, especially when competing for top candidates, because those who have positive views of the selection process are more likely to like the organization and to accept a job offer (Hausknecht, Day, & Thomas, 2004).

● **Assessment Centers**   An **assessment center** is an extensive set of exercises designed to determine an individual's suitability for a particular job. Assessment centers are often used to hire or promote managers, but they can be employed in relation to other positions as well. A typical assessment center consists of two to three days of exercises that simulate various aspects of a job and that are rated by a team of judges (e.g., Spychalski et al., 1997). The *in-basket* is a typical assessment center exercise for managers. Candidates are seated at a desk and asked to imagine that they have just taken over a new management job. On the desk is the "previous manager's" overflowing in-basket, containing correspondence, memos, phone messages, and other items. The candidate's task is to go through all this material and write on the back of each item what action should be taken to deal with it, and when. Later, experts read what the candidate has written and assign an appropriateness score to each action. For example, candidates who prioritize tasks well—taking immediate action on critical matters and delaying action on less important ones—would receive higher scores than those who, say, deal with each task in the order in which it is encountered regardless of its importance.

Other assessment center exercises tap interpersonal skills. The job candidate might be asked to play the role of a manager who is working with others to solve a problem, or who must discipline a problem employee. As in the in-basket task, each candidate is given a score by each judge on the knowledge, skills, abilities, and other job-related characteristics displayed during each exercise. Later, the evaluation team meets to arrive at a group evaluation, using total scores from all assessment center exercises to classify individuals in terms of their suitability for a particular position.

Considerable evidence supports the value of assessment centers (Arthur et al., 2003; Jansen & Vinkenburg, 2006). For example, the assessment center scores earned by first-year college students predicted their performance as teachers several years after graduation (Shechtman, 1992). Assessment centers have also successfully predicted the performance of police officers, pilots, and managers, among others (Dayan, Kasten, & Fox, 2002; Lievens et al., 2003; McEvoy & Beatty, 1989).

● **Measuring Job Performance**

Almost all employees of medium to large organizations receive an annual **job performance appraisal,** which, much like a student's report card, provides an evaluation of how well they are doing in various aspects of their work. Organizations

assessment center   An extensive set of exercises designed to determine an individual's suitability for a particular job.

job performance appraisal   The process of evaluating how well employees are doing in various aspects of their work.

use these appraisals to guide decisions about employee salary raises, bonuses, and about whether to keep, promote, or fire particular individuals. The appraisals are also used to give employees feedback on the quality and quantity of their work (Rynes, Gerhart, & Parks, 2005). The feedback function of job performance appraisals is important because it helps employees recognize what they are doing right, and what they need to do differently to reach their own goals, and to promote the goals of the organization.

● **Establishing Performance Criteria**   One of the most important roles for I/O psychologists in designing job performance appraisal systems is to help establish *criteria*, or benchmarks, that define what the organization means by "good" or "poor" performance (see Table 20.2). These criteria can be theoretical, or actual. A *theoretical criterion* is a statement of what we mean by good (or poor) performance, in theory. A theoretical criterion for good teaching, for example, might be "promotes student learning." This criterion certainly sounds reasonable, but notice that it does not specify how we would measure it in order to decide if a particular teacher is actually promoting student learning. So we also need an *actual criterion*, which specifies what we should measure to determine if the theoretical criterion has been met. An actual criterion for good teaching might be defined in terms of students' performance on a standardized test of what their teacher has taught them. If, on average, the students reach or exceed some particular score, the teacher will have satisfied one of the school district's criteria for good teaching.

Keep in mind, though, that the match between theoretical criteria and actual criteria is never perfect. The actual criterion chosen should provide a sensible way to assess the theoretical criterion, but the actual criterion may be flawed. For one thing, actual criteria are usually incomplete. There is probably more to good teaching, for example, than just assuring that students reach a particular score on a particular test. The teacher may have done a great (or poor) job at teaching material that did not happen to be covered on that test. Second, factors other than the employee's performance can affect the actual criterion. Perhaps students' scores on a standardized test were affected partly by the work of a good (or poor) teacher they encountered before their current teacher was hired. I/O psychologists are sensitive to these problems, and they usually recommend that job performance appraisals be based on several actual criteria, not just one.

● Methods of Performance Appraisal

The information used in job performance appraisals can come from objective measures and subjective measures.

TABLE 20.2   **Examples of Theoretical and Actual Criteria**

Here are some theoretical and actual criteria for several kinds of jobs. Notice that theoretical criteria tend to be rather vague, so for purposes of job performance appraisals, they must be backed up by actual criteria. By evaluating employees on how well they have reached actual criteria, organizations can decide whether the theoretical criteria have been met, and they can act accordingly.

Job	Theoretical Criterion	Actual Criterion
Architect	Design buildings	Number of buildings designed
Car salesperson	Sell cars	Number of cars sold per month
Police officer	Fight crime	Number of arrests made per month
Roofer	Install roofs	Square feet of shingles installed per month
Scientist	Make scientific discoveries	Number of articles published in scholarly journals

● **Objective Measures** *Objective measures* of job performance include counting the frequency of particular behaviors or the results of those behaviors. The number of calls made by a telemarketer, the number of computers shipped out by a factory worker, and the total value of items sold per month by a shoe store employee are just three examples of objective measures of job performance. Other objective measures might include records about the number of days employees are absent from work, how often they are late for work, or the number of complaints that have been filed against them (Roth, Huffcutt, & Bobko, 2003). Objective appraisal measures are especially valuable because they provide a close link between theoretical and actual performance criteria. If the theoretical criterion for good performance as a salesperson is to sell a company's products, the most closely linked actual criterion would be an objective count of the number of those products sold per month.

Objective methods of job performance are not appropriate for all jobs, however, because some performance criteria cannot be evaluated by counting things (Rynes et al., 2005). For example, it would make no sense to evaluate a teacher's job performance by counting the number of students taught per year. Teachers usually have no control over their class size and, in any case, an enrollment count tells us nothing about what the students learned. In other words, except for the simplest jobs, objective measures may fail to assess all the aspects of performance that are of interest to an organization. A salesperson might have sold twenty cars last month, but it would also be important to know how this was accomplished. If the person used high-pressure tactics that harmed the organization's reputation, the sales count tells only part of the story of this employee's performance. Similarly, this month's top salesperson might have done well only after inheriting a territory full of loyal customers who buy the company's products no matter what.

● **Subjective Measures** No wonder, then, that I/O psychologists sometimes recommend that objective performance measures be supplemented, or sometimes even replaced, by subjective measures (Rynes et al., 2005). *Subjective measures* of job performance take the form of a supervisor's judgments about various aspects of an employee's work. Typically, the supervisor records these judgments on a graphic rating form or a behavior-focused rating form.

Graphic rating forms list several criterion-related dimensions of job performance and provide a space for the supervisor to rate each employee's performance on each dimension, using a scale ranging from, say, 1 to 10 or from poor to excellent (see Figure 20.1). These graphic ratings can be valuable, but they do reflect the supervisor's

FIGURE 20.1

A Graphic Rating Form Used in Subjective Job Performance Appraisal

Supervisors often use graphic rating forms such as this one in subjective job performance appraisals. The ratings are based on the supervisor's personal experience with the employee and on subjective impressions of that employee's work.

Rate employee on each dimension on the left by checking the appropriate box corresponding to the level of performance for the past year.

Dimension	Poor	Fair	Satisfactory	Above satisfactory	Outstanding
Customer service					
Management of time					
Professional appearance					
Teamwork					
Work quality					
Work quantity					

subjective judgment. And as in unstructured interviews, factors other than the employee's performance can influence the results (Wong & Kwong, 2005). For example, most graphic ratings contain *leniency error*, meaning that supervisors tend to use only the top of the scale. As a result, almost all employees in most organizations receive ratings that are "satisfactory" or better. Many supervisors also show *halo error*, meaning that the same rating tends to be given on each dimension. So if Tasha receives an "outstanding" rating on one dimension, she will probably be rated at or near "outstanding" on all the others. Similarly, if Jack is rated as only "satisfactory" on one scale, he will probably get "satisfactory" ratings on the rest of them.

To some extent, these "errors" reflect reality. After all, most people try to do their jobs well, and they may do about equally well (or equally poorly) in various aspects of their work (Balzer & Sulsky, 1992; Solomonson & Lance, 1997). However, when using graphic rating forms, supervisors may not carefully discriminate those aspects of job performance that are satisfactory from those that need improvement. Further, many tend to "go easy" on their employees, especially if they like them (Ferris et al., 1994) or if other factors such as "political correctness" are operating in the situation (Tziner, Murphy, & Cleveland, 2005). This kind of bias can result in favoritism in which supervisors intentionally inflate ratings beyond what an employee's performance deserves (Fried & Tiegs, 1995; Rynes et al., 2005). Supervisors who are biased against certain employees on ethnic or other grounds may give those employees undeservedly low ratings (Stauffer & Buckley, 2005).

To help minimize the errors and bias associated with graphic rating forms, I/O psychologists developed *behavior-focused rating forms*, which ask supervisors to rate employees on specific behaviors rather than general dimensions of performance (Smith & Kendall, 1963). These forms contain lists of *critical incidents* that illustrate different levels of performance—from extremely effective to extremely ineffective—on important job dimensions (Flanagan, 1954). A critical incident list relating to customer relations, for example, might include "listens patiently," "tries to reach a compromise," "coldly states store policy," and "angrily demands that complaining customers leave." Once these behavior-focused forms are constructed, supervisors choose which incidents are most typical of each employee.

Behavior-based rating forms help supervisors and their employees come to a better understanding of what constitutes good and poor performance. Somewhat surprisingly, however, these forms do not appear to eliminate the impact of supervisor bias and error (Bernardin & Beatty, 1984; Latham et al., 1993). ("In Review: Assessing People, Jobs, and Job Performance" summarizes our discussion of these topics.)

in review Assessing People, Jobs, and Job Performance

Target of Assessment	Typical Purpose	What Is Assessed	Examples
Employees	Employee selection	Knowledge, skill, ability, and other personal characteristics (KSAOs)	Tests of ability, achievement, or personality; structured or unstructured interviews; assessment centers requiring simulated job tasks
Jobs	Matching employees to jobs; identifying training needs	Job tasks and personal attributes needed for the job	Job-oriented analysis (identifies required tasks); person-oriented analysis (identifies KSAOs required for success)
Job performance	Feedback on performance; decisions about retention, salary adjustments, or promotion	Work activities and/or products; supervisors' reports	Evaluating employees' work in relation to theoretical and actual criteria as measured by objective (counting) or subjective (rating) methods

Recruiting and Selecting Employees

LINKAGES (a link to Personality, p. 583)

We have described a number of assessment methods developed by I/O psychologists to help organizations hire, train, and evaluate employees. Let's now consider the role of I/O psychology in finding candidates for employment, and in selecting the right people for each job.

● Recruitment Processes

It is generally agreed that people are an organization's most valuable assets, because it is people who are ultimately responsible for success in achieving an organization's goals. Accordingly, there is often intense competition among organizations to recruit the "best and brightest" employees. It is a disciplined competition, however. There is no point in hiring this year's top ten accounting graduates if your organization only needs two new accountants. So the first step in effective recruiting is to determine what employees are needed and then go after applicants to fill those needs.

Determining employment needs means more than just counting empty chairs, though. Analyses by I/O psychologists help organizations determine how many people in each position are needed at the moment, and how many will be needed in the future. Suppose, for example, that a computer company anticipates a 20 percent growth in business over the next five years. That growth will require a 20 percent increase in the number of customer service representatives, but how many new representatives should be hired each month? An I/O psychologist's analysis would help answer this question. The analysis would take into account the growth projections as well as estimates of how many representatives quit each year, and whether the existing ratio of customer service employees to customers is too high, too low, or about right for efficient operation. In making recommendations about recruitment plans, I/O psychologists must also consider the intensity of demand for employees in various occupations. More active recruitment plans will be necessary to attract the best people in high-demand areas (see Table 20.3).

Once employment needs are established and the competitive landscape has been explored, the next step in recruitment is to persuade people with the right kinds of knowledge, skill, ability, and other characteristics to apply for the jobs to be filled. The six most common methods for identifying and attracting candidates include: (1) newspaper advertising; (2) posting jobs on Hotjobs.com, Monster.com, or other recruitment web sites; (3) interviewing graduating seniors on college campuses; (4) collecting information from current employees about potential candidates; (5) working with employment agencies, recruiting consultants, and private "head hunting" firms; and (6) accepting applications from job seekers who appear on their own ("walk-ins"). The recruitment methods used for any particular job will depend on how easy or difficult it is to attract high-quality applicants, and on the importance of the position in the organization. For relatively low-level positions requiring few skills, it may be possible to rely on walk-in applicants to fill available positions. Much more effort and several different recruitment methods may be required to attract top-notch candidates for higher-level jobs that demand extensive experience and skill.

● Selection Processes

Selecting the right employee for a particular job is generally a matter of using tests, interviews, and assessment centers to find the best fit between each candidate's characteristics and the tasks and characteristics that a job analysis identified as necessary for successful performance. This matching strategy would suggest that a candidate who is better at written communication than at computer skills would do better in, say, the marketing department than at the computer help desk.

TABLE 20.3   Fast-Growing Occupations

The U.S. Department of Labor estimates that these twenty occupations will see the most growth in demand between now and 2012. Industrial/organizational psychologists must take such trends into account when making recommendations about where to make the strongest efforts at recruiting new employees.

Occupation	Percent Growth
Medical assistant	59
Network systems and data communications analyst	57
Physician assistant	49
Social and human service assistant	49
Home health aides	48
Medical records and health information technicians	47
Physical therapist aides	46
Computer software engineer, applications	46
Computer software engineer, systems software	45
Physical therapist assistant	45
Fitness trainer and aerobics instructor	44
Database administrator	44
Veterinary technologist and technician	44
Hazardous materials removal worker	43
Dental hygienist	43
Occupational therapist aide	43
Dental assistant	42
Personal and home care aide	40
Self-enrichment education teacher	40
Computer systems analyst	39

Source: U.S. Department of Labor (2004).

Is this strategy the best way to select employees? Usually it is, but I/O psychologists help assure that the characteristics identified as predicting success at particular jobs are, in fact, associated with success. To do this, they conduct **validation studies,** which are research projects designed to determine how well a particular test, interview, or other assessment method predicts an employee's job performance (Chan, 2005). For example, on the basis of a job analysis conducted years ago, a department store might require applicants for sales clerk positions to pass a test of mental arithmetic. A validation study could determine whether scores on that test are actually related to sales clerks' performance. The easiest way to conduct this study would be to ask a representative sample of the store's current sales clerks to take the arithmetic test. A correlation coefficient would then be computed that describes the relationship between their test scores and some objective or subjective performance criterion, such as monthly sales figures or a supervisor's ratings. If those who score highest on the mental arithmetic test also do best at their jobs, the test can be seen as valid for predicting job performance. If not, it may be that for clerks using today's computerized sales terminals, mental arithmetic is no longer as important to job success as it was in the past.

A large body of results from I/O psychology research is available to tell organizations which types of tests and other assessments are valid in predicting performance in which types of jobs. Having this database available saves organizations a great deal of time and money, because it eliminates the need to conduct their own validation studies for each assessment device they use in selecting employees for every job they want to fill.

validation study   Research project that determines how well a test, interview, or other assessment method predicts job performance.

Ensuring Equal Opportunity
Affirmative action (AA) is an important element of the U.S. government's *Uniform Guidelines on Employee Selection Procedures.* A major goal of AA was to encourage organizations to actively seek job applicants from underrepresented minority groups and, in the process, ensure that qualified minority candidates are not overlooked. Critics claim, though, that AA establishes quota systems in which certain percentages of people from particular groups must be hired or promoted, even if they are not all well qualified. AA has thus become an increasingly controversial aspect of employment law.

● Legal Issues in Recruitment and Selection

The United States and many other industrialized countries have established the principle that hiring, firing, and promotion processes should not discriminate against anyone on the basis of characteristics that have nothing to do with job performance. This principle has been translated into laws designed to protect all employees and job candidates against unfair discrimination. U.S. laws have also identified, and created special safeguards for, several *protected classes*–including women, Asians, Blacks, Hispanics, American Indians, and other groups whose members have been discriminated against in the past. Together, these laws make it illegal for employers in the United States to discriminate in hiring or promotion on the basis of a candidate's age, ethnicity, gender, national origin, disability, or religion. In some states and in some other countries, discrimination on the basis of sexual orientation is also prohibited.

In 1978, I/O psychologists helped the U.S. government create its *Uniform Guidelines on Employee Selection Procedures,* a document that outlines the steps organizations must take to assure fairness in hiring and promotion. The most important element of these guidelines is the requirement that personnel decisions be based solely on job-related criteria. This means that, in choosing new employees, for example, organizations should hire those whose knowledge, skill, ability, and other characteristics match the KSAO requirements previously established by the job analysis process described earlier. The guidelines also state that organizations should use only those test scores and other assessment data that validation studies have established as good predictors of job performance.

Training Employees

Every year, organizations in the industrialized world spend billions on training their employees (Thompson et al., 2002). I/O psychologists are often directly involved in establishing the need for training, in designing training methods and content, and in evaluating the outcome of training efforts. Some I/O psychologists actually conduct training programs, but in most cases these programs are delivered by professional trainers and/or by experts on the topic of the training.

Assessing Training Needs

To help organizations identify which employees need what kind of training, I/O psychologists typically carry out a *training needs assessment* that takes into account the organization's job categories, its workforce, and its goals (Goldstein, 1993). One aspect of this assessment is to look at job analysis reports. As mentioned earlier, the need for training is indicated when job analyses reveal that certain jobs require KSAOs that employees do not have, or that could be strengthened. A second aspect of a training needs assessment is to give employees a chance to describe the training they would like to have. This information often emerges from *personal development plans* that employees and their supervisors create. These plans usually include an evaluation of the person's strengths and weaknesses; the weaknesses suggest where training might be useful. For example, if the supervisor notes that an individual is awkward when making presentations, a course in public speaking might be worthwhile. Finally, the I/O psychologist will look at the goals of the organization. If those goals include reducing workplace accidents, or improving communication with international customers, then training in safety procedures or foreign language skills would be in order.

Designing Training Programs

In designing training programs for use by organizations, I/O psychologists are always mindful of the basic principles that govern the learning and remembering of new information and skills. These principles, which are described in the learning and memory chapters, guide efforts to promote *transfer of training, feedback, training in general principles, overlearning*, and *sequencing*.

● **Transfer of Training**   The most valuable training programs are those that teach knowledge and skills that will generalize, or transfer, to the workplace. If employees don't see how to apply what they have learned so as to improve their job performance, the training effort will have been wasted. Promoting *transfer of training* is not always easy, so I/O psychologists develop written materials and active learning exercises that not only clarify the link between training and application, but also give employees a chance to apply new knowledge and skills in simulated work situations. So trainees might first complete reading assignments, attend lectures, and watch videos illustrating effective approaches to dealing with customer complaints, or defusing an office conflict. Then they might form groups to role-play using these approaches in a variety of typical workplace scenarios.

● **Feedback**   People learn new skills quicker when they receive *feedback* on their performance (Smither, London, & Reilly, 2005). In organizational training, this feedback usually comes from the trainer and/or other trainees. It takes the form of positive reinforcement following progress, constructive suggestions following errors or failure, and constant encouragement to continue the effort to learn. For example, after one trainee has role-played a new way to deal with an angry customer or a disgruntled employee, the trainer might play a videotape of the effort so that everyone can offer comments, compliments, and suggestions for improvement.

● **Training in General Principles**   People tend to learn better, and remember more of what they learn, when they can put new information in a broader context—in other words, when they get some insight into how the information or skill they are learning fits into a bigger picture (Baldwin & Ford, 1988). The Linkages sections in this book are designed specifically to promote this kind of learning. In organizational settings, the "big picture" approach takes the form of *training in general principles*, which teaches not only how to do things in particular ways, but also why it is important to do so. When training new customer service agents at a hotel, a bank, or an airline, for example, trainers often include an orientation to the basic characteristics of

Applying General Principles Training programs for employees who portray cartoon characters at major theme parks emphasize the general principle that the organization's goal is to create a fantasy world for customers. This aspect of training helps the employees understand why it is important to follow the rule about remaining in character at all times. The carefully cultivated fantasy world would be disrupted if children were to see "Mickey Mouse" or "Bugs Bunny" holding his headgear under his arm while smoking a cigarette!

these businesses, including how competitive they are. Understanding their company's need to survive intense competition helps employees recognize the importance of courtesy training in determining whether a customer remains a customer or goes elsewhere.

● **Overlearning**   Practice makes perfect in all kinds of teaching and training, so I/O psychologists emphasize the need for employees to practice using the information and skills learned in a training program until they reach a high level of performance. In fact, many training programs encourage employees to continue practicing until they are not only highly competent, but are able to perform the skill or use the information automatically, without having to think much about it. This *overlearning* is seen in many everyday situations, most notably among experienced drivers, who can easily get from one place to another without paying much attention to the mechanics of steering, braking, and turning. Athletes and musicians, too, practice until their skills seem to unfold on their own. In the workplace, overlearning can save time and improve efficiency. For example, members of an experienced medical team can perform surgery using skills and information that, through overlearning, have become second nature to them. They do not have to stop and think about how critical tasks must be done; they simply do them.

● **Sequencing**   Is it better to cram organizational training into one or two long, intense sessions over a single weekend, or to schedule it in several shorter sessions over a longer period? Obviously, the intense, or *massed training* approach is less expensive and less disruptive to employees' work schedules than *distributed training*. However, I/O psychologists know that, as described in the learning chapter, people do not retain as much after massed training as they do after distributed training (Bjork, 1999; Donovan & Radosevich, 1999). Among other problems, massed training can create boredom, inattention, and fatigue, all of which interfere with the learning and retention of new material. As most students can appreciate, an employee might remain motivated and interested during a one-hour training session but will probably be exhausted and inattentive by the end of an eight-hour training marathon. With this in mind, organizational training programs are often set up on a distributed schedule whenever possible.

● Evaluating Training Programs

Did a training program produce enough benefits to the organization to make it worth the time and money it cost? Should it be repeated? If so, should it be refined in some way? I/O psychologists are prepared to conduct research on these important evaluation questions. As described in the chapter on research in psychology, controlled experiments offer a way to draw reasonably strong cause-effect conclusions about the impact of a training program. A representative sample of employees who need training would be selected, then randomly assigned either to receive training or to spend an equivalent amount of time away from their jobs pursuing some alternative activity. The value of the training program could then be measured in terms of the size of the difference in job performance between the trained (experimental) group and the untrained (control) group. However, organizations rarely request experimental research on their training programs. Most of them merely hope that what seemed to be valuable training did, in fact, deliver information and skill-building that will be retained by employees and that will transfer to improve their job performance. Accordingly, evaluation tends to focus on nonexperimental designs using criteria such as employees' reactions to training, what they remember about it, and the changes in behavior that follow it.

● **Evaluation Criteria**   The first kind of evaluation criteria, called *training-level criteria*, includes data collected immediately after a training session. Trainees are typically asked to fill out questionnaires about how much they liked the training and how valuable they feel it was. Training sessions that receive low ratings on enjoyment, value, and effectiveness are not likely to be repeated in the same format, especially if the sessions are also low on other criteria.

A second class of criteria, called *trainee learning criteria*, includes information about what trainees actually learned from the training program. These criteria are usually measured by a test, similar to a college final exam, that is designed to determine each trainee's knowledge and skill in the areas covered by the training material. In some cases, alternative forms of this test are given to the trainees both before and after training to assess how much improvement has taken place.

Finally, *performance-level criteria* measure the degree to which the knowledge and skills learned in training transferred to the employee's workplace behavior. If employees now know how to do a better job on the assembly line or at the hotel's front desk but do not apply this knowledge to improve their performance, the training program has not been successful. So organizations often evaluate training on the basis of criteria such as number or quality of products produced, frequency of customer complaints, and the like. Significant improvements following training might be a result of that training, but because so few organizations conduct controlled experimental evaluations of training, drawing this conclusion is usually risky. The improvement might have had less to do with the training than with some uncontrolled factor, such as a downturn in the economy that motivated employees to work harder in an effort to keep their jobs.

I/O psychologists recommend evaluating training programs on as many criteria as possible, because the apparent value of training can depend on which criterion you consider. A program that looks great on one criterion might be dismal on another. In particular, many programs that get high employee ratings on enjoyment, value, and other training-level criteria fail to show effectiveness in terms of increased productivity, efficiency, or other performance-level criteria (Alvarez, Salas, & Garofano, 2004; May & Kahnweiler, 2000). One training program that was designed to improve employees' interviewing skills received high ratings from the trainees, who showed improved interviewing during training. Unfortunately, these skills did not transfer to real interview situations (Campion & Campion, 1987). ("In Review: Recruiting, Selecting, and Training Employees" summarizes our discussion of these topics.)

in review Recruiting, Selecting, and Training Employees

Process	Methods
Recruitment	Perform hiring needs assessment; place ads in newspapers and on web sites; contact employment agencies; conduct campus interviews; solicit nominations from current employees; accept walk-in applications.
Selection	Measure candidates' knowledge, skill, ability, and other personal characteristics using interviews, tests, and assessment centers; conduct validation studies to ensure that these KSAO criteria predict job success.
Training	Conduct training needs assessment; design training to promote transfer of training, feedback, understanding of general principles, overlearning, and distributed practice sequencing; evaluate training in terms of employee ratings of the experience and improvement in employee performance.

Employee Motivation

In the chapter on motivation and emotion, we define *motivation* as the reason why people behave as they do. It includes biological, emotional, cognitive, and social factors that influence the direction, intensity, and persistence of behavior (Reeve, 1996; Spector, 2003). These factors are as important in the workplace as they are anywhere else. We can see motivation affecting the *direction* of work-related behavior in people's decisions about whether to work, and what kind of job to seek. The effect of motivation on the *intensity* of work can be seen in how often an employee misses work, shows up late, works overtime, or goes beyond the call of duty. Motivation is also reflected in a worker's *persistence* at a task. Some employees give up as soon as difficulties arise, perhaps not bothering to pursue information if it is hard to find. Others keep trying, using every strategy possible until their efforts are successful.

Let's consider three theories that have been used by I/O psychologists to help understand employee motivation. One theory focuses on general factors that can affect behavior in the workplace and all other areas of life, too. The others highlight factors that are more specifically associated with motivation in the workplace.

ERG Theory

In the chapter on motivation and emotion, we describe Abraham Maslow's (1943, 1970) theory in which human behavior is seen as based on a hierarchy of motives. These motives range from such basic physiological needs as food and water to higher needs, such as for esteem and self-actualization (see Figure 11.7). Maslow believed that people have to at least partially satisfy needs at the lower levels of the hierarchy before they will be motivated by higher-level goals. As discussed in the motivation and emotion chapter, though, this is not always true. Hunger strikers, for example, ignore their need for food in order to pursue a protest that brings them closer to self-actualization.

To address some of the problems in Maslow's theory, Clayton Alderfer (1969) proposed **existence, relatedness, growth (ERG) theory,** which places human needs into three rather than five categories: *Existence needs* are things, such as food and water, that are necessary for survival. *Relatedness needs* include the need for social contact, especially having satisfying interactions with, and attachments to, others. *Growth needs* are those involving the development and use of a person's capabilities. These three categories of needs form a continuum from the most concrete (existence) to the most abstract (growth), but ERG theory does not suggest that they must be satisfied in a particular order. Instead, the strength of people's needs in each category is seen as rising and falling from time to time and from one situation to the next. If a need in one area is fulfilled or frustrated, a person may be motivated to pursue some other needs. For example, after a relationship breakup frustrates relatedness needs, a person might focus on existence or growth needs by eating more or volunteering to work late. Similarly, losing a job frustrates growth needs, so a laid-off employee might focus on relatedness needs by seeking the social support of friends. Finally, a person obsessed with work-related growth needs might ignore friends until after a big project is completed and it is time to party.

I/O psychologists apply ERG theory in the workplace by helping organizations recognize that employees may not be as motivated to pursue job-related growth needs if other need categories are frustrated or unfulfilled. We will see later, for example, that many organizations now allow flexible working hours in the hope that employees will be more motivated on the job once they can more easily satisfy family-oriented relatedness needs.

existence, relatedness, growth (ERG) theory A theory of motivation that focuses on employees' needs at the level of existence, relatedness, and growth.

expectancy theory A theory of workplace motivation in which employees act in accordance with expected results and how much they value those results.

goal setting theory A theory of workplace motivation focused on the idea that employees' behavior is shaped by their intention to achieve specific goals.

job satisfaction The degree to which people like or dislike their jobs.

Expectancy Theory

A second approach to employee motivation is similar in many ways to Julian Rotter's (1954, 1982) expectancy theory (which we discuss in the personality chapter). It seeks to explain how cognitive processes affect the impact of salary, bonuses, and other rewards on employees' behavior (Vroom, 1964). The main assumption of **expectancy theory** in the workplace is that employees behave in accordance with (1) what results they expect their actions to bring, and (2) how much they value those results. For example, workers' motivation to put out extra effort will increase if they (1) expect a bonus for doing so, and (2) if they value a bonus and think that it is large enough to be worth the effort. Both expectancy and value are a matter of individual perception, though, so it is difficult to use expectancy theory to predict employee motivation from considering outcomes alone. If some workers don't believe that a supervisor will actually provide a bonus for extra work, or if certain individuals are not strongly focused on money, the prospect of a bonus may not be equally motivating for all employees.

Workplace tests of expectancy theory provide strong support for it. One review of seventy-seven studies (Van Eerde & Thierry, 1996) showed that how hard employees work and the quality of their work are strongly related to their expectancies about rewards and to the value they place on those rewards. In short, people tend to work hard when they believe it will be worth it to do so. Part of the task faced by I/O psychologists is to help organizations make high performance worthwhile to their employees.

Goal Setting Theory

A third approach to employee motivation, called **goal setting theory,** focuses on the idea that behavior at work is affected not only by general needs and expectations, but also by workers' intention to achieve specific goals. These goals can be short term, such as finishing a report by the end of the week, or long term, such as earning a promotion within the next two years. A basic prediction of goal setting theory is that employees will be motivated to choose, engage in, and persist at behaviors that take them closer to their goals.

Goal setting theory has proven quite useful in motivating employees. There is evidence that arranging for employees to spend some time setting specific goals can lead to better job performance (Locke & Latham, 1990). Many organizations today encourage their employees to engage in goal setting activities, but I/O psychologists remind managers that some goals are more useful than others. As described in the motivation and emotion chapter, the most motivating goals are those that are (1) chosen, or at least accepted, by the employees; (2) difficult enough to be challenging, but not so difficult as to be impossible; and (3) specific enough (e.g., "increasing sales by 10 percent") to allow employees to keep track of their progress and know when they have succeeded (Latham, 2004; Locke, 2000). These same characteristics can apply to group as well as individual goals (Wegge & Haslam, 2005).

Job Satisfaction

Success in achieving workplace goals is one of many factors that can affect **job satisfaction,** the degree to which people like or dislike their jobs. Like other attitudes described in the chapter on social cognition, job satisfaction is made up of cognitive, emotional, and behavioral components (Schleicher, Watt, & Greguras, 2004). The cognitive component of job satisfaction includes *beliefs* about the job, such as "this job is too demanding" or "this job always presents new challenges."

TABLE 20.4	Facets of Job Satisfaction	
Here are the results of a 1999 Gallup poll in which workers in the United States reported on their attitudes toward eight facets of their jobs. Notice that workers tend to have differing attitudes about differing facets. For example, workers can be satisfied with their co-workers and supervisors, but not satisfied with their salaries.	**Facet**	**Percent Satisfaction**
	Relationships with co-workers	94
	Physical safety conditions of work	91
	Supervisor	82
	Job security	81
	Health insurance	73
	Salary	70
	Promotion opportunities	64
	Retirement plan	61

Source: Gallup (1999).

The emotional component includes positive or negative *feelings* about the job, such as boredom, excitement, anxiety, or pride. Finally, the behavioral component of job satisfaction is seen in how people *act* in relation to their work, perhaps showing up early and staying late or maybe taking every opportunity to avoid work by calling in "sick."

● Measuring Job Satisfaction

In an effort to accurately measure employees' level of job satisfaction, I/O psychologists explore all three of these attitude components. They also assess employees' attitudes about their jobs in general (a *global approach*) and about various aspects of it (a *facet approach*; see Table 20.4).

In most cases, job satisfaction is measured using questionnaires. Some questionnaires, such as the *Job in General Scale* (Ironson et al., 1989) take a global approach. Others, such as the *Job Satisfaction Survey* (Spector, 1985) are made up of subscales designed to assess attitudes about several job facets, including pay, promotion, benefits, co-workers, and supervision (see Figure 20.2).

FIGURE 20.2

Pay Satisfaction Subscale from the Job Satisfaction Survey

Here are just four items from the pay satisfaction subscale of the Job Satisfaction Survey (Spector, 1985). As its name implies, this subscale focuses on employees' attitudes about the pay they receive in their jobs. Other subscales assess attitudes toward other job facets, such as promotion opportunities, benefits, co-workers, and supervisors.

Please circle the one number for each question that comes closest to reflecting your opinion about it.	Disagree very much	Disagree moderately	Disagree slightly	Agree slightly	Agree moderately	Agree very much
1. I feel I am being paid a fair amount for the work I do.	1	2	3	4	5	6
2. Raises are too few and far between.	1	2	3	4	5	6
3. I feel unappreciated by the organization when I think about what they pay me.	1	2	3	4	5	6
4. I feel satisfied with my chances for salary increases.	1	2	3	4	5	6

Surveys of job satisfaction usually find that some employees are more satisfied than others, and these differences can affect how various employees do their jobs.

CLOSE TO HOME ©2004 John McPherson. Reprinted with permission of Universal Press Syndicate. All rights reserved.

● Factors Affecting Job Satisfaction

Satisfaction with a job in general, or with its various facets, can vary widely from one person to the next, even when people do the same job in the same organization (Bond & Bunce, 2003; Schleicher et al., 2004; Staw & Cohen-Charash, 2005). In other words, some employees like jobs, or facets of jobs, that others hate. I/O psychologists have studied several environmental and personal factors that can influence people's job satisfaction. Among the environmental factors are the requirements of the job, how much it pays, and how it affects workers' lives outside of the workplace. Among the personal factors are workers' gender, age, and ethnicity.

● **Job Requirements**   Some jobs, such as those of assembly-line workers, involve performing the same relatively simple tasks again and again throughout the workday. Other jobs, such as those in management, are more complex, requiring workers to perform a different set of tasks each day, often in response to unpredictable requests or demands. Is the complexity of a job related to workers' job satisfaction? In general, yes; people tend to be more satisfied with jobs that are more complex (Fried & Ferris, 1987; Melamed, Fried, & Froom, 2001). As described in the chapter on motivation and emotion, this higher satisfaction may relate to the fact that more complex jobs tend to be more interesting, more challenging, and more likely to create a sense of responsibility and control in setting and achieving goals (Maynard, Joseph & Maynard, 2006). However, not everyone responds to complex jobs in the same way (Jex et al., 2002). A complex job may create dissatisfaction among people who do not have the KSAOs to do it successfully (Hackman & Oldham, 1980). Even individuals who have the necessary knowledge and skills may be dissatisfied with a complex job if their personality characteristics lead them to prefer simpler, less intellectually demanding work (Loher et al., 1985).

● **Salary**   Many workers feel underpaid, but as discussed in the motivation and emotion chapter, higher salaries alone do not necessarily lead to higher levels of job satisfaction (Igalens & Roussel, 1999). One study of recent college graduates found a correlation of only +.17 between starting salary and overall job satisfaction (Brasher & Chen, 1999). A main reason for such a low correlation is that a good salary may not compensate for unsatisfactory aspects of a job, such as poor working conditions, lack of respect from supervisors, or the like. In fact, knowing that salary and pay raise decisions are made in a fair way can be more important to job satisfaction than the amount of money employees receive (Currall et al., 2005; Liao & Rupp, 2005; Simons & Roberson, 2003). As a result, students working at low-paying jobs may be more satisfied than executives who earn six-figure salaries. The student's satisfaction may come from knowing that everyone doing the same job is getting the same pay, whereas the executives may experience *relative deprivation*, the perception that others are unfairly receiving more benefits for the same or lesser effort (see the social cognition chapter).

● **Work-Family Conflict**   The number of two-career couples and single-parent families is on the increase in the industrialized world (e.g., Demo, Allen, & Fine, 2000; Weinraub, Horvath, & Gringlas, 2002). With this increase comes increasing conflict between the demands of a job and the demands of family life (Eby et al., 2005; O'Driscoll, Brough, & Kalliath, 2006). One common example of such conflict is when the need to care for a sick child or attend a school play interferes with a parent's work responsibilities. The amount of conflict between the demands of job and family are strongly and consistently related to job satisfaction (Ford, Heinen, & Langkamer, 2007). Both men and women report lower job satisfaction when work-family conflict is high, though the effects may last longer for women (Baltes & Heydens-Gahir, 2003; Grandey, Cordeiro, & Crouter, 2005; Lapierre & Allen, 2006). Working with I/O psychologists, many organizations deal with this source of job dissatisfaction by establishing *family-friendly work policies* that help employees

Minimizing Work-Family Conflict
To help working couples deal with both job demands and family obligations, many organizations have adopted family-friendly programs and policies, including workplace day-care services and the availability of flexible work schedules (flextime). These programs and policies have been associated with higher levels of job satisfaction and less absenteeism among employees with children (Baltes et al., 1999; Scandura & Lankau, 1997).

balance work and family responsibilities. One of these policies, called *flextime*, allows parents to work an eight-hour day, but frees them from the standard nine-to-five schedule. One parent can come to work at, say, 9:30 A.M. after taking the children to school, and then stay on the job beyond 5 P.M. to complete an eight-hour day. The other parent can start work at, say, 7:30 A.M., then leave early to pick up the children from school.

● **Gender, Age, and Ethnicity** The many studies that have compared job satisfaction in men and women have found few, if any, differences—even when the men and women compared were doing quite different jobs (e.g., Greenhaus, Parasuraman, & Wormley, 1990; Moncrief et al., 2000). Job satisfaction is related to age, though, with older workers tending to be more satisfied than younger ones (Brush, Moch, & Pooyan, 1987). However, some studies suggest that the picture is a bit more complicated than that (Clark, Oswald, & Warr, 1996; Hedge, Borman, & Lammlein, 2006). For example, among people who enter the world of work immediately after high school or junior college, job satisfaction may at first be quite high, but may soon begin to decline, especially among males. Satisfaction ratings then tend to increase slowly, but steadily, from about age thirty to retirement. This pattern may occur because young workers with relatively little education may find themselves in jobs that are not only poorly paid, but that also offer few of the features associated with job satisfaction, such as complexity, control over time, opportunity to set goals and tasks, and the like (White & Spector, 1987).

Some studies of workers in the United States have found slightly higher job satisfaction among Whites than among people of color (e.g., Jones & Schaubroeck, 2004; Tuch & Martin, 1991), but others have found no differences (e.g., Brush et al., 1987). In fact, when comparisons are made across groups doing the same jobs, ethnicity does not appear to be a major factor in job satisfaction.

THINKING CRITICALLY **Is Job Satisfaction Genetic?**

In the chapter on motivation and emotion, we described evidence that people's overall level of happiness, or *subjective well-being*, may be determined partly by genetic influences. Could those same influences operate in the workplace in relation to job satisfaction?

■ What am I being asked to believe or accept?

Richard Arvey and his colleagues (1989) have suggested that differences in job satisfaction reflect genetic predispositions toward liking or not liking a job.

■ What evidence is available to support the assertion?

As mentioned in the chapters on human development and personality, people's temperament and personality are influenced by genetics. Research in I/O psychology shows that these genetically influenced personality characteristics are related to people's job satisfaction. In one study, for example, hostility and other personality traits that were measured in adolescence were found to be significantly related to job satisfaction up to fifty years later (Staw, Bell, & Clausen, 1986). These data suggest that job satisfaction is at least indirectly shaped by inherited predispositions.

However, Arvey and his colleagues (1989) conducted what may be the only study to directly investigate the role of genetics in job satisfaction. They selected a sample of thirty-four pairs of genetically identical twins who had been separated and raised in different environments. They then arranged for these people to complete job satisfaction questionnaires. The questionnaire responses showed a strong positive correlation between the twins' job satisfaction; if one twin was satisfied, the other one tended to be satisfied, too. If one was dissatisfied, the other twin tended to be dissatisfied, as well. The researchers suggested that because the members of each twin pair had been raised in different environments, genetic factors were at least partly responsible for creating the observed similarity in job satisfaction ratings.

■ Are there alternative ways of interpreting the evidence?

These results suggest a strong genetic influence, but they could have been affected by factors other than a genetic predisposition to be satisfied or dissatisfied with a job. For example, although the twins grew up in different home environments, their work environments might have been quite similar. If so, it may have been these similar work environments that produced similar satisfaction ratings. Why would separated twins have similar kinds of working environments? For one thing, the innate abilities, interests, behavioral tendencies, or appearance that identical twins might share could have led them into similar kinds of jobs. Some pairs might have selected jobs that tend to be satisfying, whereas other pairs entered jobs that tend to be less satisfying. A pair of bright, athletic, or musically talented twins might have found it possible to have complex, interesting, and challenging jobs and to enjoy a high level of satisfaction. A less fortunate set of twins, having been unable to qualify for the kind of job they might want, may have settled for more routine work that leaves them feeling unsatisfied. In other words, it may be that genes don't shape job satisfaction itself, but do help to shape characteristics that influence people's access to satisfying work.

■ What additional evidence would help to evaluate the alternatives?

One way to assess the impact of job characteristics on the high correlation in twins' job satisfaction ratings is to look at the nature of the twins' jobs. When Arvey and his colleagues did this, they found that the twins did tend to hold jobs that were similar in several ways, including in overall job complexity and some of the skills required. A more complete assessment of the jobs and job environments would be required, however, to determine the strength of these nongenetic factors in creating positively correlated job satisfaction ratings.

■ What conclusions are most reasonable?

Research in I/O psychology suggests that individual differences in job satisfaction are probably related to workers' characteristics, some of which are influenced by genetics. However, the precise mechanisms through which genetics might affect job satisfaction are not yet clear (Ilies & Judge, 2003). It is most likely that job satisfaction, like so many other aspects of behavior and mental processes, is shaped by both genetic and environmental influences. There is no single reason why people differ in terms of job satisfaction. How satisfied we are with our work can be predicted to some extent by job characteristics and to some extent by personal characteristics (Gerhart, 2005), but the outcome in a given case is ultimately a matter of who does what job in what organization. ■

● Consequences of Job Satisfaction

Organizations spend a lot of time, money, and effort to try to maintain a reasonable level of job satisfaction among their employees. They do so, if for no other reason, because job satisfaction is linked to a variety of positive consequences for individuals, their co-workers, and their organizations. Dissatisfaction with a job can lead to numerous negative consequences.

● **Job Performance**   Research shows that people who are satisfied with their jobs tend to be more motivated, to work harder, and to perform better than employees who are dissatisfied (e.g., Fisher, 2003; Judge et al., 2001). In one study, for example, public school teachers' job satisfaction was positively correlated with the academic achievements of their students (Currall et al., 2005). Positive correlations between job satisfaction and performance make sense, and though a correlation cannot itself confirm that satisfaction is causing good performance, it is certainly consistent with that conclusion. In fact, a recent meta-analysis supports the view that job satisfaction and commitment to the organization shape performance rather than the other way around (Harrison, Newman, & Roth, 2006).

● **Organizational Citizenship Behavior**   Job satisfaction is also associated with **organizational citizenship behavior (OCB)**, a willingness to go beyond formal job requirements in order to help co-workers and/or the organization (Borman, et al., 2001; Ilies, Scott, & Judge, 2006). OCB tends to occur in return for fair treatment employees have received from others or in an effort to support a group to which employees feel connected (Kamdar, McAllister, & Turban, 2006; Moorman & Byrne, 2005). As in the case of job performance, it is difficult to determine whether job satisfaction causes increased OCB, or whether engaging in OCB causes increased job satisfaction. Further, organizational citizenship behavior can be caused by factors other than job satisfaction. Some cases of OCB might occur as part of a strategy designed to get a pay raise, promotion, or other personal goal. In one study, for example, employees who believed it would help their promotion chances engaged in high levels of OCB before being promoted, then reduced their OCB afterward (Hui, Lam, & Law, 2000). Another study found that teachers on temporary contracts felt less secure about their jobs and also engaged in more organizational citizenship behaviors than did teachers who held permanent positions (Feather & Rauter, 2004).

● **Turnover**   Every organization must deal with a certain amount of *turnover*, or loss of employees. Some turnover is involuntary, as in cases of disability or dismissal, but much of it is voluntary (Harman et al., 2007). Some employees simply quit, and they tend to be employees whose job satisfaction is low (e.g., Griffeth, Hom, & Gaertner, 2000). However, in order to avoid unemployment, few dissatisfied workers actually quit until and unless they have found another job (Kammeyer-Mueller et al., 2005). So job dissatisfaction is related more strongly to turnover when people are able to find other jobs (Trevor, 2001). When alternative employment is unavailable, even dissatisfied workers tend to stay on the job. Efforts to reduce turnover include establishing supportive relationships between new employees, called *protégés*, and more experienced employees, known as *mentors*. Such

organizational citizenship behavior (OCB)   A willingness to go beyond formal job requirements in order to help co-workers and/or the organization.

mentoring programs can be effective, especially when they involve structured rather than informal meetings, and when care is taken to match protégés with mentors who are most likely to help them (Allen, Eby, & Lentz, 2006; Ortiz-Walters & Gilson, 2005; Payne & Huffman, 2005).

● **Absenteeism** You might expect that absenteeism, like voluntary turnover, would be strongly related to job satisfaction. However, the correlation between job satisfaction and attendance is surprisingly weak (Farrell & Stamm, 1988). True, there is a tendency for dissatisfied employees to be absent more frequently than those who are satisfied. But other factors, including personal or family illness, work-family conflicts, and the financial consequences of missing work are far more important in determining who shows up and who doesn't (Dalton & Mesch, 1991; Erickson, Nichols, & Ritter, 2000).

● **Aggression and Counterproductive Work Behavior** Job dissatisfaction is one cause of workplace aggression, as well as of theft and other forms of *counterproductive work behavior (CWB)*. Assaults or murders involving co-workers or supervisors are rare (LeBlanc, Dupre, & Barling, 2006), but theft, computer hacking, and other forms of CWB by employees and former employees are commonplace. Employee theft in the United States alone costs organizations billions of dollars each year (Gatewood & Feild, 2001). In fact, employees steal more from their employers than do shoplifters (Hollinger et al., 1996). The direct and indirect costs of other forms of CWB, such as sabotage, working slowly, or doing jobs incorrectly, are staggering. But CWB can be hard to detect, so much of it goes unnoticed (Bennett & Robinson, 2000).

As illustrated in Figure 20.3, it is often stress in the workplace that leads to job dissatisfaction and negative emotions, such as anger and anxiety (Spector, Fox, & Domalgaski, 2006). These emotions, in turn, can result in CWB, especially among employees who feel they have little or no control over stressors (Fox, Spector, & Miles, 2001) or who feel they have been treated unfairly (Aquino, Tripp, & Bies, 2006; Greenberg, 2002; Penney & Spector, 2005). Why does lack of control matter? As described in the chapter on health, stress, and coping, when people feel they have control over the work situation, they are more likely to perceive stressors as challenges to be overcome, and to try constructive means of doing so. Suppose, for example, that a supervisor suddenly assigns a difficult task to an employee who must complete it by the next day or face serious consequences. If the employee feels sufficiently in control of the situation to complete the task on time, this stressful assignment is likely to be perceived as a challenge to be mastered. If the employee doesn't have that sense of control and believes it is impossible to meet the deadline, this assignment will probably create dissatisfaction and negative emotions such as angry resentment. This person is at elevated risk for engaging in CWB directed at the supervisor, the organization, or other employees.

LINKAGES (a link to Health, Stress, and Coping, p. 527)

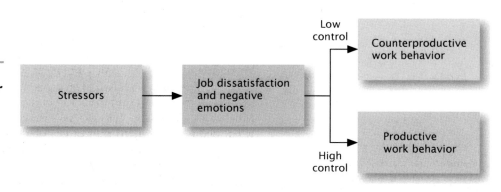

FIGURE 20.3

Job Satisfaction and Counterproductive Work Behavior

Workplace stressors can lead to job dissatisfaction, which leads to negative emotions and counterproductive work behavior, especially among employees who feel mistreated and unable to control stressors.

LINKAGES　　**Aggression in the Workplace**

LINKAGES (a link to Social Influence, p. 737)

In the chapter on social influence, we describe a number of biological, psychological, and environmental factors that appear responsible for creating and/or triggering human aggression and violence. These factors operate in the workplace, too, though incidents of aggression between or against workers differ in some ways from violence outside of the workplace (Hershcovis et al., 2007).

For example, whereas most murder victims in the United States knew their assailants (Cassel & Bernstein, 2007), about 85 percent of workplace homicides are committed against employees by strangers (LeBlanc & Barling, 2004). In other words, despite well-publicized cases of disgruntled employees killing co-workers or supervisors, employees actually perpetrate only about 15 percent of workplace homicides and less than 10 percent of workplace assaults (LeBlanc & Barling, 2004). Convenience store clerks, taxi drivers, and other employees who deal directly with the public, handle money, and work alone at night are at particular risk to be victims of workplace aggression (Le Blanc et al., 2006). Most aggression against these people is *instrumental aggression*, meaning that the aggressor's intent is not necessarily to injure, but to achieve a goal such as getting money or other valuables (Merchant & Lundell, 2001). Though the perpetrator often uses a weapon to intimidate the employee, these aggressive incidents do not usually result in physical injury.

Most cases of injury in the workplace occur in the course of aggressive assaults on doctors, nurses, and other health workers, sales clerks, and food servers by patients or customers (Büssing & Höge, 2004; LeBlanc & Barling, 2004). Often, these injuries occur under stressful circumstances—such as during emergency room treatment—in which pain, anger, fatigue, and frustration lead to an impulsive, emotional, aggressive outburst. In contrast to instrumental aggression, the perpetrator's intent in these cases is to injure the employee victim.

When aggression does occur between or among employees, the assault is usually verbal, not physical, and the result is usually resentment and bruised feelings, not bruised bodies (Grubb et al., 2005). Like road rage incidents, employee-to-employee aggression is often the byproduct of an impulsive, emotional outburst under time pressure or other stressful conditions, including workplace injustices or abusive supervision (Inness, Barling, & Turner, 2005). Sometimes, though, this form of aggression may reflect an attempt by one employee to control others through bullying or intimidation (Bies, Tripp, & Kramer, 1997; Grubb et al., 2005). ■

Occupational Health Psychology

In the chapter on health, stress, and coping, we defined *health psychology* as a field devoted to understanding psychological factors in how people stay healthy, why they become ill, and how they respond when they do get ill (Taylor, 2002). **Occupational health psychology** is concerned with psychological factors that affect the health, safety, and well-being of employees in the workplace. I/O psychologists help to promote the goals of occupational health psychology by consulting with organizations about ways to reduce threats to employees posed by undue stress, accidents, and hazards. Their success in this enterprise is reflected in the fact that today, most workplaces are safer and healthier than employees' own homes (National Safety Council, 2004).

occupational health psychology
A field concerned with psychological factors that affect the health, safety, and well-being of employees.

● Physical Conditions Affecting Health

Many physical conditions in the workplace have the potential to cause illness and injury (Lund et al., 2006). Accordingly, in the United States, the government's

Occupational Safety and Health Administration (OSHA) establishes regulations designed to minimize employees' exposure to hazards arising from infectious agents, toxic chemicals, dangerous machinery, and the like. For example, to guard against the spread of AIDS, U.S. doctors, dentists, nurses, and other health care workers have been asked to follow a set of safety procedures called *universal precautions.* These precautions include wearing disposable gloves when drawing blood, giving injections, or performing dental procedures, and also discarding needles and other sharp objects into special sealed containers.

Procedures like these can be effective in reducing the spread of disease, but because of heavy workloads and lack of encouragement from supervisors, health care workers do not always follow them (McDiarmid & Condon, 2005). I/O psychologists can play a role in this aspect of occupational health psychology by helping to promote organizational support for following proper safety procedures and by designing safety training that employees will actually use in the workplace (Smith-Crowe, Burke, & Landis, 2003). They also help protect employees' health by creating reminders to use caution on the job, and by consulting with organizations to minimize stressors that can lead to illness or injury.

One of these stressors comes in the form of jobs that require performing certain movements in the same way over long periods of time, such as turning a screwdriver or making cut after cut in pieces of plastic. Eventually, these movements can create *repetitive strain injuries* in which joints become inflamed, sometimes producing permanent damage. The most familiar of these injuries is *carpal tunnel syndrome*, a condition of the wrist that produces pain, numbness, and weakness in the fingers. Although typically associated with using a computer keyboard or mouse, carpal tunnel syndrome can be caused by many other activities involving the fingers and wrists. Psychologists have been involved in two approaches to prevent repetitive strain injuries. First, as described in the introductory chapter, *engineering psychologists* (also called *human factors psychologists*) consult with industrial designers to create tools and equipment that are less physically stressful to use. As a result, people who perform typing tasks for many hours each day now usually place a pad in front of their keyboard that provides support and also helps keep their wrists from twisting. Second, I/O psychologists are working with organizations to assure that employees whose jobs require repetitive actions be allowed to take breaks that are long enough and frequent enough to rest the body parts at risk for strain injuries. These psychologists are also working with employees themselves to assure that they follow the recommended break schedule.

● Work Schedules, Health, and Safety

The flextime arrangements mentioned earlier that allow some employees to adjust their working hours is but one part of a more general trend away from the traditional nine-to-five workday. As many organizations expand their hours of service,

Doing It Over and Over Performing the same movements on the job hour after hour and day after day can lead to *repetitive strain injuries*. This employee's keyboard movements resulted in a painful and potentially disabling condition called *carpal tunnel syndrome*. Wearing a wrist brace can reduce the pain somewhat, but I/O and engineering psychologists know that improved wrist support for keyboard users can help prevent the problem in the first place.

including to twenty-four hours a day, seven days a week, more and more employees are on the job during what once would have been considered "odd hours." They may work at night or on weekends, and they follow shift patterns once associated mainly with hospital, law enforcement, and factory employees. Others are working more than eight hours a day, but less than five days a week, and in the face of staffing cutbacks, still others may be working more than forty hours a week. Whether undertaken by choice or by assignment, these nontraditional work schedules can create stress and fatigue that can adversely affect employees' health.

● **Rotating Shift Work**   These negative effects can be especially great among employees who change work shifts from week to week—rotating from evenings to days to nights, for example (Demerouti et al., 2004). As described in the chapter on consciousness, these shift changes disrupt employees' *circadian rhythms* of eating, sleeping, and wakefulness, resulting in a number of unpleasant mental and physical symptoms. A major problem with working night shifts, for example, is fatigue, irritability, and reduced cognitive sharpness resulting from difficulty in getting to sleep, or staying asleep, during the day (Daus, Sanders, & Campbell, 1998; Rouch et al., 2005). Some shift workers also experience upset stomachs and other symptoms of digestive distress. Such problems are especially common after long periods of rotating shift work, but they may be far less troubling for workers who are assigned to night shifts long enough to get used to their "backward" schedule (Barton & Folkard, 1991).

● **Long Shifts and Long Weeks**   Many organizations today are establishing longer-than-normal work shifts. For example, some have set up ten-hour shifts that allow employees to work forty hours in four days, thus creating an extra day off. Others have replaced three eight-hour work shifts with a more efficient system of two twelve-hour shifts that allows workers even more time off. There is evidence that many employees tend to like such arrangements, and that longer shifts can lead to greater job satisfaction and better job performance (Baltes et al., 1999).

However, extended workdays may create health and performance problems for some workers in some jobs (Lamberg, 2004). This possibility is suggested by research on drivers of intercity buses. Those who drove longer routes that required being on the road for up to fourteen hours a day with few rest breaks tended to use stimulants to stay alert; to drink alcohol to counteract the stimulants after arrival; and to experience sleep disturbances, various physical symptoms, anxiety, and fatigue. They were also more likely than shorter-shift drivers to be involved in accidents (Raggatt, 1991).

There are also dangers in requiring employees to work more than forty-eight hours per week, especially when they would prefer not to do so. These involuntary workweek extensions have been associated with a number of employee health problems, particularly heart disease (Sparks et al., 1997). Accordingly, nations of the European Union have adopted regulations setting workweeks at a maximum of forty-eight hours. So far, there are no such government regulations in the United States.

● Stress, Accidents, and Safety

Though most accidents occur outside the workplace, workplace safety is still a major focus of organizations, and of I/O psychologists. In the United States alone, 5,734 workers were killed and 4.2 million others were injured on the job in just one recent year (U.S. Bureau of Labor Statistics, 2007). Motor vehicle accidents account for nearly half of workplace fatalities. Falls and equipment accidents account for about another one-third of these deaths.

Longer than normal work shifts and extended workweeks are just one source of the occupational stress that contributes to the fatigue, inattention, cognitive impairment, sleepiness, and other problems that elevate the risk of workplace accidents.

Staying Sharp I/O psychologists' research on the negative impact of extended work shifts has led to organizational and U.S. government rules requiring rest breaks at fixed intervals for commercial airline pilots, long-haul bus and truck drivers, and others whose jobs require constant attention to complex tasks and systems. These rules also limit the total number of hours these employees can work in any twenty-four-hour period.

I/O psychologists have identified many other individual and organizational factors that contribute to accidents, including, for example, inadequate job training or guidance, overwork, job insecurity, sexual harassment, ethnic prejudice, and bullying (Berdahl & Moore, 2006; Hoel, Faragher, & Cooper, 2004; Sparks, Faragher, & Cooper, 2001). Perhaps most important of all is a poor *climate of safety*, which includes a lack of safety training, too little supervisor emphasis on following safety rules, and workers' tendency to ignore those rules (Griffin & Neal, 2000). Accidents are least common in organizations that provide adequate safety training for employees, conduct thorough and frequent safety inspections, and assure that supervisors consistently communicate the need for safety (Wallace, Popp, & Mondore, 2006).

Work Groups and Work Teams

A great deal of workplace activity is accomplished by groups of individuals working together. Industrial/organizational psychologists have been at the forefront of efforts to help organizations maximize the effectiveness and efficiency of work groups and work teams. A **work group** is defined as at least two people who interact as they perform the same or different tasks. The four servers waiting on customers during the dinner shift at a restaurant would be an example of a work group. A **work team** is a special kind of work group in which (1) the members' activities are coordinated with and depend on one another; (2) each member has a specialized role; and (3) members are working to accomplish a common goal (West, Borrill, & Unsworth, 1998). The entire staff on duty during the restaurant's dinner shift would be considered a work team. All members of the team are working on the same task with the same goal in mind, namely to serve that evening's customers as quickly and efficiently as possible. Further, each team member has a specialized role: Greeters seat customers, servers take orders and deliver the food prepared by the cooks, and managers monitor progress, direct employees, and fill in at various tasks as needed. Whether it involves food service, brain surgery, automobile repair, or other workplace activities, an effective work team performs like the proverbial well-oiled machine.

work group At least two people who interact with one another as they perform the same or different workplace tasks.

work team A work group in which the members' specialized activities are coordinated and interdependent as they work toward a common goal.

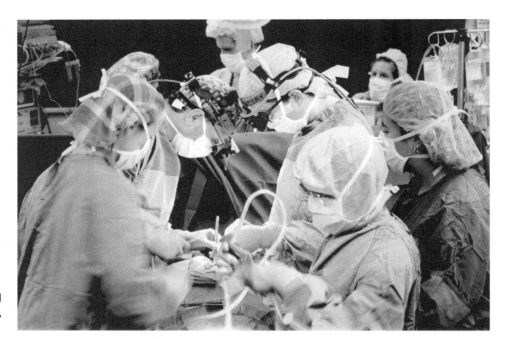

Medical Teamwork The doctors, nurses, and technicians who join forces to perform surgery are a perfect example of a work team. Everyone on the surgical team is devoted to the same goal of completing a successful operation, but each performs a somewhat different task in a coordinated manner under the direction of the surgeon, who acts as the team leader.

Promoting this kind of efficiency, especially in work groups and work teams whose members come from diverse cultural and ethnic backgrounds, is one of the most important challenges faced by I/O psychologists today (Kozlowski & Ilgen, 2006; Silverthorne, 2005). In addressing this challenge, they have distinguished between the "surface diversity" seen in ethnic and gender differences and the "deep diversity" of work group members' differing attitudes and values (Harrison et al., 2002). So they seek to improve the performance of diverse work groups partly by helping them to overcome any problems relating to surface diversity, but also by encouraging them to capitalize on deep diversity through the identification and exploitation of members' differing, perhaps even unique, perspectives, expertise, and knowledge (Phillips et al., 2004; Van Knippenberg, DeDreu, & Homan, 2004).

● Autonomous Work Teams

In most organizations, work groups and work teams operate in a traditional way, meaning that all team members report to a manager who directs and supervises their activities. However, a growing number of organizations today are establishing **autonomous work teams (AWTs)** that manage themselves and do not report to anyone for routine daily supervision. Instead, once AWTs are given a work assignment, it is up to them to determine how best to accomplish their goal, and then to work together to achieve it. The classic example of AWTs is seen in the manufacturing sector. Automobiles and other consumer products were once built on long assembly lines by large numbers of workers who each performed only one small part of the process before passing the product on to another worker who performed the next step. In autonomous work teams, however, each member rotates among jobs, such that everyone does every aspect of assembly from time to time. The team members also design and order their own tools, conduct their own product inspections to assure quality and performance, and even participate in hiring and firing decisions. Saturn and Volvo automobiles and other large pieces of equipment are assembled in AWT factories that feature a series of workstations where perhaps a half-dozen employees assemble the entire product, or a substantial portion of it.

Autonomous work teams have benefits for employees and for organizations. In one comparison study, employees in AWT factories reported higher levels of job satisfaction than did employees of traditional factories (Cordery, Mueller, & Smith,

autonomous work teams (AWTs) Self-managed employee groups that do not report to anyone for routine daily supervision.

1991). Further, the productivity of AWTs has been shown to be at least as good, and sometimes better than, traditional arrangements (Hoegl & Parboteeah, 2006; Stewart, 2006) despite the fact that AWTs cost less in the long run because organizations don't need as many supervisors (Banker et al., 1996; Glassop, 2002). AWTs may be particularly effective when they are created in organizations that had previously suffered from an inefficient and unsatisfying work climate (Morgeson et al., 2006).

● Group Leadership

Even in autonomous work teams, leaders usually emerge (Taggar, Hackett, & Saha, 1999). And AWTs are themselves embedded in organizations that operate through a leadership hierarchy. At each level, designated leaders direct or supervise the activities of others, set group- and organization-wide objectives, decide how individual employees can best contribute to those objectives, and make sure employees perform the tasks assigned to them. Let's consider some of the characteristics of good leaders, how good leaders behave, and how they relate to various members of their work groups and work teams.

● What Makes a Good Leader?

One way to study leadership is to look at lots of leaders to see if particular kinds of knowledge, skill, ability, or other personal characteristics are associated with those who are effective and those who are ineffective. Much of what social and I/O psychologists have learned about the KSAOs of effective leaders comes from their research on managers (e.g., Peterson et al., 2003; Zaccarco, 2007). That research suggests that some characteristics are seen by almost everyone as necessary for good leadership. One study conducted in sixty-two countries found that intelligence and trustworthiness, for example, were universally rated as important traits of good leaders (House et al., 1999). These results are supported by other studies showing that intelligence is consistently important for competent managerial performance (Hogan, Curphy, & Hogan, 1994; Judge, Colbert, & Ilies, 2004). In other words, smarter leaders tend to be better leaders. The value of other leadership traits can depend on social, cultural, and situational factors (Felfe & Goihl, 2002). For instance, a willingness to take risks tends to be seen as a positive leadership trait in some countries and as a negative trait in other countries (House et al., 1999).

● How Do Good Leaders Behave?

Another way to study leadership is to look at what effective and ineffective leaders do. The foundation for this research was provided by the Ohio State leadership studies, which began in 1945. The first step in this extensive program was to collect 1,800 critical incidents of effective and ineffective leader behavior. An incident of "effective" leadership might be to suggest that a troubled employee transfer to a less demanding job. An incident of "ineffective" leadership might be to shout at an employee who questioned the leader's decision. These and other studies have revealed that specific kinds of leader behaviors can have profound effects on group members and organizations. For example, one study found that army platoons led by active and involved leaders were especially effective under combat conditions (Bass et al., 2003).

The Ohio State researchers identified two dimensions on which leaders typically vary. The first, called *consideration*, is the degree to which a leader shows concern for the welfare of employees, including friendly and supportive behavior that makes the workplace more pleasant. The second dimension, called *initiating structure*, is the degree to which a leader coordinates employee efforts by assigning tasks and clarifying expectations so that group members know what is required of them to perform well.

As described in the social influence chapter, person-oriented leaders tend to be high on the consideration dimension, and task-oriented leaders tend to be high on the initiating structure dimension. The place where managers fall on each of these dimensions of leadership style can have important effects on employees (Judge, Piccolo, & Ilies, 2004; Keller, 2006; Zaccaro, 2007). In one study, workers in a truck manufacturing plant were asked to rate their immediate supervisors on the consideration and initiating structure dimensions (Fleishman & Harris, 1962). These ratings were then related to the number of formal complaints these employees filed against their supervisors, and the rate at which they quit their jobs (voluntary turnover). There were more grievances and much higher turnover among employees whose supervisors had been rated low on consideration than among those whose supervisors had been rated high on consideration. More grievances were also filed by employees whose supervisors were higher on initiating structure, but there is more to that part of the story. The highest rates of grievance and turnover occurred among employees whose supervisors who were not only high on initiating structure, but also low on consideration. As long as supervisors were high on consideration, they could be high on initiating structure without creating a lot of grievances and turnover. In other words, it is possible for a leader to be firm but fair, thus promoting maximum performance with a minimum of complaints and employee losses.

● **Leader-Member Interactions** Are leadership styles like the relatively stable traits described in the personality chapter? Do they create consistent leadership behaviors toward all group members in all situations? Some leaders might fit this description, but **leader-member exchange (LMX) theory** suggests that most leaders tend to adopt different styles with two different kinds of subordinates (Dansereau, Graen, & Haga, 1975). Leaders tend to offer the most consideration and best treatment to subordinates who make up the employee *in-group*. These individuals tend to be the best performers and are seen by the leader as competent, trustworthy, loyal, and dependable (Bauer & Green, 1996). As such, in-group members' opinions and requests tend to carry more weight with the leader than do those of *out-group* employees, who are seen by the leader as less competent, less reliable, and potentially expendable. Leaders give out-group employees less opportunity to influence decisions and tend to supervise them by giving high structure and low consideration (Dansereau et al., 1975). Almost eighty studies of leader-member interaction patterns support the existence of employee in-groups and out-groups, and the tendency for in-group members to experience more job satisfaction and less occupational stress (Gerstner & Day, 1997; Schyns, 2006).

FOCUS ON RESEARCH METHODS

Can People Learn to Be Charismatic Leaders?

Some people's leadership abilities are so effective that they are described as charismatic (pronounced "kare-iz-MATIC"). A *charismatic leader* is one who inspires followers to embrace a vision of success and to make extraordinary efforts to achieve things they would not have done on their own. Charismatic leaders like Martin Luther King, Jr., and Winston Churchill captured the imaginations of their followers. Dr. King led the fight for civil rights in the 1960s, inspiring countless thousands of followers to overcome entrenched opposition and personal danger to achieve the long-sought goal of equality under the law for African Americans. Prime Minister Churchill rallied the British people to resist and overcome the effects of Nazi air attacks during the darkest days of 1940 and throughout World War II. It has long been assumed that charismatic leadership is a byproduct of a charismatic personality, not something that one can learn.

■ What was the researcher's question?

I/O psychologists wonder, though, whether that assumption is correct. Might it be possible to train leaders to be charismatic, and if so, how would such training affect

leader-member exchange (LMX) theory A theory suggesting that leaders tend to supervise in-group and out-group employees in different ways.

A Charismatic Leader Former British prime minister Margaret Thatcher is considered by many to exemplify the kind of leader whose charisma inspires followers to accomplish what they might not otherwise have done.

the job satisfaction and performance of those leaders' employees? Julian Barling, Tom Weber, and E. Kevin Kelloway (1996) addressed these questions by designing and evaluating a charisma-building training program for corporate managers.

How did the researchers answer this question?

Their study was conducted in twenty branches of a large Canadian banking corporation. The managers of these branches were randomly assigned to a charisma training group or a no-training control group. Two weeks before training began, and five months after it was completed, the people working for each manager filled out a questionnaire on which they rated their manager's charisma on three dimensions. They also reported on their own level of job satisfaction. The financial performance of each branch office was measured before and after training, too.

Charisma training was delivered in five sessions over a three-month period. At the first session, managers met as a group to spend an entire day learning what makes charismatic leaders charismatic, and practicing these behaviors in order to increase their own charisma. In the next four sessions, managers worked individually with one of the researchers, receiving additional training, getting feedback on performance, and setting goals for further progress.

What did the researchers find?

All the results indicated that this training program had a positive impact on managers' charisma. First, branch employees' ratings showed increased charisma for managers in the training group. There was a small decline in charisma for those in the control group. Second, those who worked for the charisma-trained managers reported higher levels of job satisfaction after training was over than did those of the untrained managers. Finally, the financial performance of the trained managers' branches increased, whereas that of the untrained group decreased somewhat.

What do the results mean?

This charisma training program may not have produced a Martin Luther King, Jr., or a Winston Churchill, but its impact supports the notion that charisma can be taught, at least to some extent (Frese, Beimel, & Schoenborn, 2003). The trained managers became more charismatic and more effective than their untrained colleagues, suggesting that charisma involves behavior that can be learned by people with many different personality characteristics.

What do we still need to know?

The findings of this study are encouraging, but we should be cautious in interpreting them. For one thing, the changes seen in the trained managers might have been due to factors other than the training itself. As described in the chapter on research in psychology, improvements following some treatment may be due partly or largely to placebo effects or other factors that create positive expectations among research participants. If the managers expected to be better at their jobs as a result of training, and if their subordinates expected them to be better managers, it could have been these expectations, not the training, that caused the behavior changes and/or the increased charisma ratings (Groves, 2005). Even the improved financial performance could have been the result of expectation-driven efforts to do better, efforts that had nothing to do with training itself. Interpreting the results of this experiment would have been easier if members of the untrained group had participated in some sort of placebo control program that, like the charisma training, would have raised their expectations, and those of their employees.

If the training program was, in fact, responsible for the improvements seen, it would be important to know if its effects will last beyond the five-month follow-up period. If it does have long-term effects, it would then be important to evaluate the charisma training with leaders in other kinds of organizations, and at other levels of leadership. It will take time and a lot of research to explore these matters, but if charisma can indeed be taught, we may someday see candidates for political office lining up to take charisma training courses. ■

LINKAGES

As noted in the introductory chapter, all of psychology's many subfields are related to one another. Our discussion of aggression in the workplace illustrates just one way in which the topic of this chapter, industrial/organizational psychology, is linked to the subfield of social psychology, which is covered in the chapters on social cognition and social influence. The Linkages diagram shows ties to two other subfields as well, and there are many more ties throughout the book. Looking for linkages among subfields will help you see how they all fit together and better appreciate the big picture that is psychology.

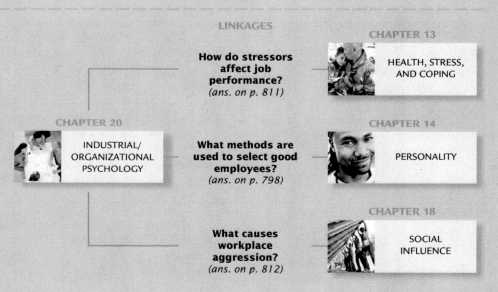

SUMMARY

An Overview of Industrial/Organizational Psychology

Industrial/organizational (I/O) psychology is the science of behavior and mental processes in the workplace. I/O psychologists not only study the psychology of the workplace but also apply psychological research to enhance the performance of employees and organizations, and to improve the health, safety, and well-being of employees. I/O psychology grew out of experimental psychology early in the twentieth century as psychologists began to apply laboratory research to workplace problems.

Assessing People, Jobs, and Job Performance

The development and evaluation of methods for assessing employees, jobs, and job performance is one of the main areas for scientific research in I/O psychology.

Knowledge, Skills, Abilities, and Other Characteristics The human attributes necessary for doing jobs successfully are referred to collectively as *KSAOs*, which stands for knowledge, skill, ability, and other personal characteristics.

Job Analysis A *job analysis* is the assessment of jobs and job requirements. It may either be job oriented (describing job tasks), person oriented (describing the KSAOs necessary to perform job tasks), or both. Organizations use job analysis information for many purposes, including to guide employee hiring and training.

Measuring Employee Characteristics The three main methods used to measure employee characteristics are psychological tests, interviews, and assessment centers. Tests can focus on employees' knowledge, abilities, skills, and other characteristics, such as personality traits. A selection interview is designed to determine an applicant's suitability for a job. It can be structured or unstructured, but structured interviews are far more effective in selecting successful employees than unstructured interviews, in which no preplanned questions are asked. An *assessment center* is an extensive set of exercises used to determine if a person is suited for a particular job.

Measuring Job Performance Most organizations give an annual *job performance appraisal* to all employees. Much like a school report card, these appraisals describe how well a person is doing in several different job domains. Performance is measured in relation to general (theoretical) criteria as well as in relation to more specific (actual) criteria.

Methods of Performance Appraisal *Objective measures* of performance appraisal rely on counting behaviors or the results of behaviors. These measures are valuable, but they are not appropriate for evaluating performance in jobs that have little or no objectively measurable output. *Subjective measures* can be used in any job situation, but because they rely on supervisor ratings of performance, these measures may be distorted by judgment bias or error.

Recruiting and Selecting Employees

Assessment tools are used frequently by I/O psychologists to help hire people who will be best able to succeed in particular jobs.

Recruitment Processes The first step in effective recruiting is to determine what employees are needed and then attract applicants to fill those needs, using employment agencies, newspaper and Internet advertising, and campus visits; encouraging nominations from current employees; and accepting walk-in applications.

Selection Processes The I/O psychology approach to hiring is to use scientific principles to match the needs of the job to the KSAOs of applicants. Establishing the KSAO requirements of a job helps determine which employee assessment tools will be most appropriate, and *validation studies* may be used to confirm that particular scores on the chosen assessments actually predict success on the job.

Legal Issues in Recruitment and Selection Many industrialized countries have established laws and regulations barring discrimination in hiring, firing, or promotion based on ethnicity, age, gender, or any other characteristics that have nothing to do with job performance.

Training Employees

I/O psychologists help organizations to establish the need for training, to design training methods and content, and to evaluate the outcome of training.

Assessing Training Needs Using a training needs assessment, organizations determine what training employees need to perform their jobs safely and well. Training needs assessments can focus on what KSAOs are required for specific jobs, on what training employees say they need, and on the objectives of the organization, such as to improve production and decrease accidents.

Designing Training Programs The design of training programs is guided by research on the processes through which people acquire new information and skills. These principles, such as generalization, reinforcement, insight, and practice, are translated into employee training that emphasizes transfer of training (applying newly learned skills in the workplace), feedback (providing reinforcement for progress and guidance and encouragement following errors), training in general principles (providing "big picture" information to show the relevance of training), overlearning (practicing new skills to the point of automaticity), and sequencing (distributing training over time to improve learning and retention).

Evaluating Training Programs A training program can be evaluated in terms of how trainees felt about the training (training-level criteria), what trainees actually learned during training (trainee learning criteria), and/or the degree to which trainees used what was learned during training in doing their jobs (performance-level criteria).

Employee Motivation

Motivation in the workplace refers to factors that influence the direction, intensity, and persistence of employees' behavior. Three motivational theories have special workplace applications.

ERG Theory *ERG theory* divides human needs into existence needs (such as food and water), relatedness needs (e.g., social contact), and growth needs (the development and use of one's capabilities). It suggests that the strength of each type of need affects workers' motivation to do their jobs well.

Expectancy Theory According to *expectancy theory*, employees work hard if they expect a valued reward to result from their efforts. These expectations, and the value placed on particular rewards, differ from person to person.

Goal Setting Theory *Goal setting theory* suggests that workers' motivation stems mainly from their desire to achieve short- and long-term goals. Organizations are advised to help employees set clear, specific goals that are challenging but not impossible.

Job Satisfaction

Job satisfaction is a cluster of attitudes that reflect the degree to which people like their jobs.

Measuring Job Satisfaction Job satisfaction is usually assessed using questionnaires that ask employees to say how they feel about their job in general (global approach) or about pay, supervision, or other specific job components (facet approach).

Factors Affecting Job Satisfaction I/O psychologists have studied several environmental and personal factors that can influence people's job satisfaction. Among the environmental factors are the requirements of the job, how much it pays, and how it affects workers' lives outside of the workplace. Among the personal factors are workers' gender, age, and ethnicity. For the most part, complex jobs tend to be more satisfying than simple jobs. Salary itself may be a less important factor in job satisfaction than the fairness of the salary system. Excessive work-family conflict can reduce job satisfaction. Because of temperament and experience, some individuals may have a tendency to be more satisfied with their jobs than others.

Consequences of Job Satisfaction Job satisfaction has been associated with better job performance and with *organizational citizenship behavior*, but it isn't clear if satisfaction is a cause or an effect of these attributes. Job dissatisfaction is clearly at work in causing people to quit their jobs (turnover), but has a smaller effect on absenteeism. Job dissatisfaction can also lead to aggression and counterproductive work behavior (CWB) such as theft or sabotage. CWB is especially likely among dissatisfied employees who work under conditions of high stress and low perceived control.

Occupational Health Psychology

Occupational health psychology is concerned with psychological factors that affect the health, safety, and well-being of employees.

Physical Conditions Affecting Health A number of physical conditions in the workplace can affect health, including infectious agents, toxic chemicals, dangerous machinery, and stressors such as the need to perform repetitive actions.

Work Schedules, Health, and Safety Work schedules have implications for health and well-being. Rotating shift work, extended shifts, and longer-than-normal workweeks have been associated with a variety of problems ranging from fatigue and sleeping problems to substance abuse and increased risk of heart disease.

Stress, Accidents, and Safety Most accidents in the United States occur outside of work, but workplace safety is still a major concern. Reducing workplace accidents can be accomplished not only by reducing occupational stressors, but also by promoting a climate of safety. Workplace accidents are least frequent in organizations that provide rigorous safety training, conduct frequent safety inspections, and encourage adherence to safety procedures.

Work Groups and Work Teams

A *work group* is a collection of people who interact on the job, whereas a *work team* is a group in which members depend on one another as they work at specialized, yet coordinated tasks aimed at accomplishing a common goal.

Autonomous Work Teams Unlike traditional, closely supervised work teams, *autonomous work teams* are assigned tasks, then allowed to manage themselves, solve their problems, and even influence hiring and firing decisions, all of which tends to result in greater job satisfaction among autonomous work team members than among members of traditional teams.

Group Leadership Leaders direct or supervise the activities of others, set group and organizational objectives, and assure that employees perform their assigned tasks. Certain characteristics, such as intelligence, tend to be universally seen as a desirable leadership attribute; others, such as a willingness to take risks, may not be seen as ideal in all cultures. Two dimensions of leadership style have been found to exert strong effects on employees' performance and job satisfaction. Consideration, which means showing concern for the welfare of employees, is associated with person-oriented leaders, while initiating structure (coordinating employee efforts by assigning tasks) is associated with task-oriented leaders. Leaders who are low on consideration tend to have less satisfied employees and higher turnover rates than those who are high on consideration. Leaders high on initiating structure may also create such problems, unless they are also high on consideration. *Leader-member exchange theory* suggests that leaders adopt different kinds of styles toward in-group and out-group employees. Charismatic leaders have the ability to influence and inspire employees to accomplish things they would not have done on their own. Charisma tends to promote job satisfaction in employees, and there is some evidence that training programs might help managers enhance organizational effectiveness by becoming more charismatic.

References

Aaron, D. J., Chang, Y.-F., Markovic, N., & LaPorte, R. E. (2003). Estimating the lesbian population: A capture-recapture approach. *Journal of Epidemiology and Community Health, 57,* 207–209.

Abbott, B. B., Schoen, L. S., & Badia, P. (1984). Predictable and unpredictable shock: Behavioral measures of aversion and physiological measures of stress. *Psychological Bulletin, 96,* 45–71.

Abbott, R. D., White, L. R., Ross, G. W., Masaki, K. H., Curb, J. D., & Petrovitch, H. (2004). Walking and dementia in physically capable elderly men. *Journal of the American Medical Association, 292,* 1447–1453.

AbdelMalik, P., Husted, J., Chow, E. W., & Bassett, A. S. (2003). Childhood head injury and expression of schizophrenia in multiply affected families. *Archives of General Psychiatry, 60,* 231–236.

Abelson, J. L., Liberzon, I., Young, E. A., & Khan, S. (2005). Cognitive modulation of the endocrine stress response to a pharmacological challenge in normal and panic disorder subjects. *Archives of General Psychiatry, 62,* 668–675.

Abi-Hashem, N. (2000). Psychology, time, and culture. *American Psychologist, 55,* 342–343.

Abraham, W. C. (2006). Memory maintenance: The changing nature of neural mechanisms. *Current Directions in Psychological Science, 15,* 5–8.

Abrahamson, A. C., Baker, L. A., & Caspi, A. (2002). Rebellious teens? Genetic and environmental influences on the social attitudes of adolescents. *Journal of Personality and Social Psychology, 83,* 1392–1408.

Abramis, D. J. (1994). Work role ambiguity, job satisfaction, and job performance: Meta-analyses and review. *Psychological Reports, 75,* 1411–1433.

Abramowitz, J. S. (1997). Effectiveness of psychological and pharmacological treatments for obsessive-compulsive disorder: A quantitative review. *Journal of Consulting and Clinical Psychology, 65,* 44–52.

Abramowitz, J. S., & Braddock, A. E. (2006). Hypochondriasis: Conceptualization, treatment, and relationship to obsessive-compulsive disorder. *Psychiatric Clinics of North America, 29,* 503–519.

Abramowitz, J. S., Khandker, M., Nelson, C. A., Deacon, B. J., & Rygwall, R. (2006). The role of cognitive factors in the pathogenesis of obsessive-compulsive symptoms: A prospective study. *Behaviour Research and Therapy, 44,* 1361–1374.

Abrams, D. I., Jay, C. A., Shade, S. B., Vizoso, H., Reda, H., Press, S., Kelly, M.E., Rowbotham, M.C., & Petersen, K. L. (2007). Cannabis in painful HIV-associated sensory neuropathy. *Neurology, 68,* 515–521.

Abrams, R. L., & Greenwald, A. G. (2000). Parts outweigh the whole (word) in unconscious analysis of meaning. *Psychological Science, 11,* 118–124.

Abreu, J. M. (1999). Conscious and unconscious African American stereotypes: Impact on first impression and diagnostic ratings by therapists. *Journal of Consulting and Clinical Psychology, 67,* 387–393.

Acitelli, L. K. (1992). Gender differences in relationship awareness and marital satisfaction among young married couples. *Personality and Social Psychology Bulletin, 18,* 102–110.

Acker, T., & Acker, H. (2004). Cellular oxygen sensing need in CNS function: Physiological and pathological implications. *Journal of Experimental Biology, 207*(Pt. 18), 3171–3188.

Ackerman, B. P., Brown, E. D., & Izard, C. E. (2004). The relations between contextual risk, earned income, and the school adjustment of children from economically disadvantaged families. *Developmental Psychology, 40,* 204–216.

Ackerman, D. (1995). *Mystery of the senses.* Boston: WGBH-TV/Washington, DC: WETA-TV.

Ackerman, P. L. (1994). Intelligence, attention, and learning: Maximal and typical performance. In D. K. Detterman (Ed.), *Current topics in human intelligence* (Vol. 4, pp. 1–27). Norwood, NJ: Ablex.

Ackerman, P. L., Beier, M. E., & Boyle, M. O. (2002). Individual differences in working memory within a nomological network of cognitive and perceptual speed abilities. *Journal of Experimental Psychology: General, 131,* 567–589.

Acocella, J. (1998, April 6). The politics of hysteria. *New Yorker,* pp. 64–79.

Adachi-Mejia, A. M., Longacre, M. R., Gibson, J. J., Beach, M. L., Titus-Ernstoff, & Dalton, M. A. (2007). Children with a TV in their bedroom at higher risk for overweight. *International Journal of Obesity, 31,* 644–651.

Adair, J. C., Gilmore, R. L., Fennell, E. B., Gold, M., & Heilman, K. M. (1995). Anosognosia during intracarotid barbiturate anesthesia: Unawareness or amnesia for weakness. *Neurology, 45*(2), 241–243.

Adam, E. K., Gunnar, M. R., & Tanaka, A. (2004). Adult attachment, parent emotion, and observed parenting behavior: Mediator and moderator models. *Child Development, 75,* 110–122.

Adams, K. F., Schatzkin, A., Harris, T. B., Kipnis, V., Mouw, T., Ballard-Barbash, R., et al. (2006). Overweight, obesity, and mortality in a large prospective cohort of persons 50 to 71 years old. *New England Journal of Medicine, 355,* 763–778.

Adams, R. J., Courage, M. L., & Mercer, M. E. (1991). Deficiencies in human neonates' color vision: Photoreceptoral and neural explanations. *Behavioral Brain Research, 43,* 109–114.

Adams, W. J., Graf, E. W., & Ernst, M. O. (2004). Experience can change the "light from above" prior. *Nature Neuroscience, 7,* 1057–1058.

Addis, M. E. (1997). Evaluating the treatment manual as a means of disseminating empirically validated psychotherapies. *Clinical Psychology: Science and Practice, 4,* 1–11.

Addis, M. E., & Krasnow, A. D. (2000). A national survey of practicing psychologists' attitudes toward psychotherapy treatment manuals. *Journal of Consulting and Clinical Psychology, 68,* 331–339.

Ader, R. (2001). Psychoneuroimmunology. *Current Directions in Psychological Science, 10,* 94–98.

Ader, R., Felten, D., & Cohen, N. (1990). Interactions between the brain and the immune system. *Review of Pharmacology and Toxicology, 30,* 561–602.

Adler, A. (1963). *The practice and theory of individual psychology.* Paterson, NJ: Littlefield Adams. (Original work published 1927)

Adler, D. A., McLaughlin, T. J., Rogers, W. H., Chang, H., Lapitsky, L., & Lerner, D. (2006). Job performance deficits dues to depression. *American Journal of Psychiatry, 163,* 1569–1576.

Adler, T. (1993, March). Bad mix: Combat stress, decisions. *APA Monitor,* p. 1.

Adolphs, R., Tranel, D., & Damasio, A. R. (1998). The human amygdala in social judgment. *Nature, 393*(6684), 470–474.

Adolphs, R., Tranel, D., & Damasio, H., & Damasio, A. (1994). Impaired recognition of emotion in facial expressions following bilateral damage to the human amygdala. *Nature, 372*(6507), 669–672.

Adolphs, R., Tranel, D., Koenigs, M., & Damasio, A. R. (2005). Preferring one taste over another without recognizing either. *Nature Neuroscience, 8,* 860–861.

Adorno, T. W., Frenkel-Brunswik, E., Levinson, D. J., & Sanford, R. N. (1950). *The authoritarian personality.* New York: Harper & Row.

Agarwal, D. P. (1997). Molecular genetic aspects of alcohol metabolism and alcoholism. *Pharmacopsychiatry, 30*(3), 79–84.

Agency for Healthcare Research and Quality (AHRQ). (1999). *Treatment of depression–newer pharmacotherapies* (Evidence Report/Technology Assessment, Number 7, Pub. No. 99–E014). Rockville, MD: Author.

Agras, W. S., Brandt, H. A., Bulik, C. M., Dolan-Sewell, R., Fairburn, C. G., Halmi, K. A., et al. (2004). Report of the National Institutes of Health workshop on overcoming barriers to treatment research in anorexia nervosa. *International Journal of Eating Disorders, 35,* 509–521.

Aharonov, R., Segev, L., Meilijson, I., & Ruppin, E. (2003). Localization of function via lesion analysis. *Neural Computation, 15,* 885–913.

Ahmad, R. H., Venkata, S. M., Alessandro, T., Bhaskar, K., Francesco, F., Goldman, D., et al. (2002). Serotonin transporter genetic variation and the response of the human amygdala. *Science, 297,* 400–403.

Aiello, J. R., & Douthitt, E. A. (2001). Social facilitation from Triplett to electronic performance monitoring. *Group Dynamics, 5,* 163–180.

Aiken, L. R. (1994). *Psychological testing and assessment* (8th ed.). Boston: Allyn & Bacon.

Ainsworth, M. D. S. (1973). The development of infant-mother attachment. In B. M. Caldwell & H. N. Ricciuti (Eds.), *Review of child development research* (Vol. 3, pp. 1–94). Chicago: University of Chicago Press.

Ainsworth, M. D. S. (1989). Attachments beyond infancy. *American Psychologist, 44,* 709–716.

Ainsworth, M. D. S., Blehar, M. D., Waters, E., & Wall, S. (1978). *Patterns of attachment: A psychological study of the Strange Situation.* Hillsdale, NJ: Erlbaum.

Aizawa, N. (2002). Grandiose traits and hypersensitive traits of the narcissistic personality. *Japanese Journal of Educational Psychology, 50,* 215–224.

Ajzen, I., & Fishbein, M. (2005). The influence of attitudes on behavior. In D. Albarracín, B. T. Johnson, & M. P. Zanna (Eds.), *Handbook of attitudes* (pp. 173–221). Mahwah, NJ: Erlbaum.

Akerstedt, T. (2007). Altered sleep/wake patterns and mental performance. *Physiology and Behavior, 90,* 209–218.

Akin, W. M., & Turner, S. M. (2006). Toward understanding ethnic and cultural factors in the interviewing process. *Psychotherapy: Theory, Research, Practice, Training, 43,* 50–64.

Akshoomoff, N. (2005). The neuropsychology of autistic spectrum disorders. *Developmental Neuropsychology, 27*, 307–310.

Alaimo, K., Olson, C. M., & Frongillo, E. A., Jr. (2001). Food insufficiency and American school-aged children's cognitive, academic, and psychosocial development. *Pediatrics, 108*, 44–53.

Albarracín, D., Johnson, B. T., Fishbein, M., & Muellerleile, P. A. (2001). Theories of reasoned action and planned behavior as models of condom use: A meta-analysis. *Psychological Bulletin, 127*, 142–161.

Albarracín, D., Johnson, B. T., & Zanna, M. P. (Eds.). (2005). *Handbook of attitudes.* Mahwah, NJ: Erlbaum.

Albee, G. W. (1968). Conceptual models and manpower requirements in psychology. *American Psychologist, 23*, 317–320.

Albers, M. W., Tabert, M. H., & Devanand, D. P. (2006). Olfactory dysfunction as a predictor of neurodegenerative disease. *Current Neurology and Neuroscience Reports, 6*, 379–386.

Albert, M. S., Savage, C. R., Blazer, D., Jones, K., Berkman, L., & Seeman, T. (1995). Predictors of cognitive change in older persons: MacArthur studies of successful aging. *Psychology and Aging, 10*, 578–589.

Alberti, R. E., & Emmons, M. L. (1986). *Your perfect right: A guide to assertive living* (5th ed.). San Luis Obispo, CA: Impact.

Alberto, P. A., Troutman, A. C., & Feagin, J. R. (2002). *Applied behavior analysis for teachers* (6th ed.). Englewood Cliffs, NJ: Prentice Hall.

Albus, H., Vansteensel, M. J., Michel, S., Block, G. D., & Meijer, J. H. (2005). A GABAergic mechanism is necessary for coupling dissociable ventral and dorsal regional oscillators within the circadian clock. *Current Biology, 15*, 886–893.

Alcock, J. (2001). *Animal behavior: An evolutionary approach* (7th ed.). Sunderland, MA: Sinauer.

Aldag, R. J., & Fuller, S. R. (1993). Beyond fiasco: A reappraisal of the groupthink phenomenon and a new model of group decision processes. *Psychological Bulletin, 113*, 533–552.

Alderfer, C. P. (1969). An empirical test of a new theory of human needs. *Organizational Behavior and Human Performance, 4*, 142–175.

Aldridge, J. W. (2005). Interpreting correlation as causation? *Science, 308*(5724), 954.

Aleman, A., Kahn, R. S., & Selten, J.-P. (2003). Sex differences in the risk of schizophrenia: Evidence from meta-analysis. *Archives of General Psychiatry, 60*, 565–571.

Aleman, A., Rutten, G. J., Sitskoorn, M. M., Dautzenberg, G., & Ramsey, N. F. (2001). Activation of striate cortex in the absence of visual stimulation: An fMRI study of synesthesia. *NeuroReport, 12*, 2827–2830.

Alessi, S. M., Roll, J. M., Reilly, M. P., & Johanson, C.-E. (2002). Establishment of a diazepam preference in human volunteers following a differential-conditioning history of placebo versus diazepam choice. *Experimental & Clinical Psychopharmacology, 10*, 77–83.

Alexander, G. M., & Hines, M. (2002). Sex differences in response to children's toys in nonhuman primates (*Cercopithecus aethiops sabaeus*). *Evolution and Human Behavior, 23*, 467–479.

Alexander, K. W., Quas, J. A., Goodman, G. S., Ghetti, S., Edelstein, R. S., Redlich, A. D., et al. (2005). Traumatic impact predicts long-term memory for documented child sexual abuse. *Psychological Science, 16*, 33–40.

Ali, R., Liu, W. M., & Humedian, M. (2004). Islam 101: Understanding the religion and therapy implications. *Professional Psychology: Research and Practice, 35*, 635–642.

Alison, L., Kebbell, M., & Lewis, P. (2006). Considerations for experts in assessing the credibility of recovered memories of child sexual abuse: The importance of maintaining a case-specific focus. *Psychology, Public Policy, and the Law, 12*, 419–441.

Al-Kubaisy, T. F., & Jassim, A. L. (2003). The efficacy of assertive training in the acquisition of social skills in Iraqi social phobics. *Arab Journal of Psychiatry, 14*, 68–72.

Al-Kubaisy, T., Marks, I. M., Logsdail, S., Marks, M. P., Lovell, K., Sungur, M., & Araya, R. (1992). Role of exposure homework in phobia reduction: A controlled study. *Behavior Therapy, 23*, 599–621.

Allen, B. P. (2006). *Personality theories: Development, growth, and diversity* (5th ed.). Boston, MA: Pearson.

Allen, J. B., Kenrick, D. T., Linder, D. E., & McCall, M. A. (1989). Arousal and attraction: A response-facilitation alternative to misattribution and negative-reinforcement models. *Journal of Personality and Social Psychology, 57*, 261–270.

Allen, J. J. B. (2002). The role of psychophysiology in clinical assessment: ERPs in the evaluation of memory. *Psychophysiology, 39*, 261–280.

Allen, J. J. B., & Iacono, W. G. (2001). Assessing the validity of amnesia in dissociative identity disorder: A dilemma for the DSM and the courts. *Psychology, Public Policy and Law, 7*, 311–344.

Allen, L. S., Hines, M., Shryne, J. E., & Gorski, R. A. (1989). Two sexually dimorphic cell groups in the human brain. *Journal of Neuroscience, 9*, 497–506.

Allen, M. D., Greenblatt, D. J., & Noel, B. J. (1977). Meprobamate overdosage: A continuing problem. *Clinical Toxicology, 11*, 501–515.

Allen, M. T., & Matthews, K. A. (1997). Hemodynamic responses to laboratory stressors in children and adolescents: The influences of age, race and gender. *Psychophysiology, 34*, 329–339.

Allen, T. D., Eby, L. T., & Lentz, E. (2006). The relationship between formal mentoring program characteristics and perceived program effectiveness. *Personnel Psychology, 59*, 125–153.

Alliger, G. M., & Dwight, S. A. (2000). A meta-analytic investigation of the susceptibility of integrity tests to faking and coaching. *Educational and Psychological Measurement, 60*, 59–72.

Allik, J., & McCrae, R. R. (2004). Toward a geography of personality traits: Patterns of profiles across 36 cultures. *Journal of Cross-Cultural Psychology, 35*, 13–28.

Allin, M., Streeruwitz, A., & Curtis, V. (2005). Progress in understanding conversion disorder. *Neuropsychiatric Disease and Treatment, 1*, 205–209.

Alloy, L. B., Abramson, L. Y., & Francis, E. L. (1999). Do negative cognitive styles confer vulnerability to depression? *Current Directions in Psychological Science, 8*, 128–132.

Allport, G. W., & Odbert, H. S. (1936). Trait names: A psycholexical study. *Psychological Monographs, 47*(1, Whole No. 211).

Almeida, D. M. (2005). Resilience and vulnerability to daily stressors assessed via diary methods. *Current Directions in Psychological Science, 14*, 64–68.

Alston, J. H. (1920). Spatial condition of the fusion of warmth and cold in heat. *American Journal of Psychology, 31*, 303–312.

Altemeyer, B. (2004). Highly dominating, highly authoritarian personalities. *Journal of Social Psychology, 144*, 421–447.

Altemeyer, B., & Hunsberger, B. (2005). Fundamentalism and authoritarianism. In R. Paloutzian & C. Park (Eds.), *Handbook of the psychology of religion and spirituality* (pp. 378–393). New York: Guilford Press.

Althoff, R. R., Faraone, S. V., Rettew, D. C., Morley, C. P., & Hudziak, J. J. (2005). Family, twin, adoption, and molecular genetic studies of juvenile bipolar disorder. *Bipolar Disorders, 7*, 598–609.

Altman, J., & Das, G. D. (1965). Autoradiographic and histological evidence of postnatal hippocampal neurogenesis in rats. *Journal of Comparative Neurology, 124*, 319–335.

Altman, L. K. (2000, April 10). Company developing marijuana for medical uses. *New York Times.* Retrieved December 13, 2004, from http://www.mapinc.org/drugnews/v00/n474/a01.html

Aluja-Fabregat, A., & Torrubia-Beltri, R. (1998). Viewing of mass media violence, perception of violence, personality and academic achievement. *Personality and Individual Differences, 25*, 973–989.

Alvarez, K., Salas, E., & Garofano, C. M. (2004). An integrated model of training evaluation and effectiveness. *Human Resource Development and Review, 3*, 385–416.

Alvaro, E. M., & Crano, W. D. (1997). Indirect minority influence: Evidence for leniency in source evaluation and counterargumentation. *Journal of Personality and Social Psychology, 72*, 949–964.

Amabile, T. M. (1996). *Creativity in context: Update to "The Social Psychology of Creativity."* Boulder, CO: Westview.

Amabile, T. M. (2001). Beyond talent: John Irving and the passionate craft of creativity. *American Psychologist, 56*, 333–336.

Amabile, T. M., Goldfarb, P., & Brackfield, S. C. (1990). Social influences on creativity: Evaluation, coaction, and surveillance. *Creativity Research Journal, 3*, 6–21.

Amabile, T. M., Hennessey, B. A., & Grossman, B. S. (1986). Social influences on creativity: The effects of contracted-for reward. *Journal of Personality and Social Psychology, 50*, 14–23.

Amaro, E., Jr., & Barker, G. J. (2006). Study design in fMRI: Basic principles. *Brain and Cognition, 60*, 220–232.

Ambadar, Z., Schooler, J. W., & Cohn, J. F. (2005). Deciphering the enigmatic face. *Psychological Science, 16*, 403–410.

American Academy of Pediatrics. (2001). Condom use by adolescents. *Pediatrics, 107*, 1463–1469.

American Diabetes Association. (2000). Type 2 diabetes in children and adolescents. *Diabetes Care, 23*, 381–389.

American Educational Research Association, American Psychological Association, & National Council on Measurement in Education. (1999). *Standards for educational and psychological testing.* Washington, DC: American Educational Research Association.

American Law Institute. (1962). *Model penal code: Proposed offical draft.* Philadelphia: Author.

American Lung Association. (2002). *Trends in tobacco use.* Retrieved July 23, 2003, from http//www/lungusa.org/data/smoke/SMK1.pdf

American Psychiatric Association. (1994). *Diagnostic and statistical manual of mental disorders* (4th ed.). Washington, DC: Author.

American Psychiatric Association. (1999). Position statement on psychiatric treatment and sexual orientation. *American Journal of Psychiatry, 156*, 1131.

American Psychiatric Association. (2000). *Diagnostic and statistical manual of mental disorders* (4th ed., rev.). Washington DC: Author.

American Psychiatric Association. (2003). *The insanity defense.* Retrieved May 26, 2004, from http://www.psych.org/public_info/insanity.cfm.

American Psychiatric Association Work Group on Eating Disorders. (2000). Practice guidelines for the treatment of patients with eating disorders (revision). *American Journal of Psychiatry, 157,* 1–39.

American Psychological Association. (1993). *Violence and youth: Psychology's response.* Washington: DC: Author.

American Psychological Association. (2002a). *Answers to your questions about sexual orientation and homosexuality.* Retrieved December 13, 2004, from http://www.apa.org/pubinfo/answers.html#whatis

American Psychological Association. (2002b). Ethical standards of psychologists and code of conduct. *American Psychologist, 57,* 1060–1073.

American Psychological Association. (2002c). *Medical cost offset.* Retrieved December 13, 2004, from http://www.apa.org/practice/offset3.html.

American Psychological Association. (2006). *2003 doctorate employment survey.* Washington, DC: APA Research Office.

American Psychological Association Committee on Animal Research and Ethics. (2006). *Research with animals in psychology.* Retrieved January 11, 2007, from http://www.apa.org/science/animal2.html.

American Psychological Association, Task Force on the Sexualization of Girls. (2007). *Report of the APA Task Force on the Sexualization of Girls.* Washington, DC: American Psychological Association.

American Society for Microbiology. (2000, September 18). *America's dirty little secret—our hands.* Washington, DC: Author.

Amodio, D. M., Harmon-Jones, E., Devine, P. G., Curtin, J. J., Hartley, S. L., & Covert, A. E. (2004). Neural signals for the detection of unintentional race bias. *Psychological Science, 15,* 88–93.

Amodio, D. M., & Showers, C. J. (2005). "Similarity breeds liking" revisited: The moderating role of commitment. *Journal of Social and Personal Relationships, 22,* 817–836.

an der Heiden, W., & Haefner, H. (2000). The epidemiology of onset and course of schizophrenia. *European Archives of Psychiatry and Clinical Neuroscience, 250,* 292–303.

Anastasi, A., & Urbina, S. (1997). *Psychological testing* (7th ed.). Upper Saddle River, NJ: Prentice-Hall.

Anastasiadis, A. G., Davis, A. R., Salomon, L., Burchardt, M., & Shabsigh, R. (2002). Hormonal factors in female sexual dysfunction. *Current Opinion in Urology, 12,* 503–507.

Andersen, S. M., & Chen, S. (2002). The relational self: An interpersonal social-cognitive theory. *Psychological Review, 109,* 619–645.

Andersen, S. M., & Miranda, R. (2000). Transference: How past relationships emerge in the present. *Psychologist, 13,* 608–609.

Anderson, A. K., & Phelps, E. A. (2000). Expression without recognition: Contributions of the human amygdala to emotional communication. *Psychological Science, 11,* 106–111.

Anderson, A. K., & Phelps, E. A. (2001). Lesions of the human amygdala impair enhanced perception of emotionally salient events. *Nature, 411,* 305–309.

Anderson, B. L. (2004). The role of occlusion in the perception of depth, lightness, and opacity. *Psychological Review, 110,* 785–801.

Anderson, C. A. (2001). Heat and violence. *Current Directions in Psychological Science, 10,* 33–38.

Anderson, C. A. (2004). An update on the effects of playing violent video games. *Journal of Adolescence, 27,* 113–122.

Anderson, C. A., & Anderson, K. B. (1998). Temperature and aggression: Paradox, controversy, and a (fairly) clear picture. In R. G. Geen & E. Donnerstein (Eds.), *Human aggression* (pp. 248–298). San Diego: Academic Press.

Anderson, C. A., Anderson, K. B., Dorr, N., DeNeve, K. M., & Flanagan, M. (2000). Temperature and aggression. In M. Zanna (Ed.), *Advances in experimental social psychology* (Vol. 32, pp. 63–133). New York: Academic Press.

Anderson, C. A., Berkowitz, L., Donnerstein, E., Huesmann, L. R., Johnson, J. D., Linz, D., et al. (2003). The influence of media violence on youth. *Psychological Science in the Public Interest, 4,* 81–110.

Anderson, C. A., & Bushman, B. J. (2001). Effects of violent video games on aggressive behavior, aggressive cognition, aggressive affect, physiological arousal, and prosocial behavior: A meta-analytic review of the scientific literature. *Psychological Science, 12,* 353–359.

Anderson, C. A., & Bushman, B. J. (2002a). Human aggression. *Annual Review of Psychology, 53,* 27–51.

Anderson, C. A., & Bushman, B. J. (2002b). Media violence and the American public revisited. *American Psychologist, 57,* 448–450.

Anderson, C. A., Carnagey, N. L., & Eubanks, J. (2003). Exposure to violent media: The effects of songs with violent lyrics on aggressive thoughts and feelings. *Journal of Personality and Social Psychology, 84,* 960–971.

Anderson, C. A., & Dill, K. E. (2000). Video games and aggressive thoughts, feelings, and behavior in the laboratory and in life. *Journal of Personality and Social Psychology, 78,* 772–790.

Anderson, C. A., Gentile, D. A., & Buckley, K. E. (2007). *Violent video game effects on children and adolescents: Theory, research, and public policy.* Oxford, Oxford University Press.

Anderson, C. A., & Murphy, C. R. (2003). Violent video games and aggressive behavior in young women. *Aggressive Behavior, 29,* 423–429.

Anderson, C., John, O. P., Keltner, D., & Kring, A. M. (2001). Who attains social status? Effects of personality and physical attractiveness in social groups. *Journal of Personality and Social Psychology, 81,* 116–132.

Anderson, E. M., & Lambert, M. J. (1995). Short-term dynamically oriented psychotherapy: A review and meta-analysis. *Clinical Psychology Review, 9(6),* 503–514.

Anderson, J. R. (1995). *Learning and memory: An integrated approach.* New York: Wiley.

Anderson, J. R. (2000). *Cognitive psychology and its implications* (5th ed). New York: Worth.

Anderson, J. R., Bothell, D., Byrne, M.D., Douglass, S., Lebiere, C., & Qin, Y. (2004). An integrated theory of the mind. *Psychological Review, 111,* 1036–1060.

Anderson, M. C., & Green, C. (2001). Suppressing unwanted memories by executive control. *Nature, 410,* 366–369.

Anderson, M. C., Ochsner, K. N., Kuhl, B., Cooper, J., Robertson, E., Gabrieli, S. W., et al. (2004). Neural systems underlying the suppression of unwanted memories. *Science, 303,* 232–235.

Anderson, M. E., Johnson, D. C., & Batal, H. A. (2005). Sudden infant death syndrome and prenatal maternal smoking: Rising attributed risk in the *Back to Sleep* era. *BMC Medicine, 3,* 4.

Anderson, P., Rothbaum, B. O., & Hodges, L. F. (2003). Virtual reality exposure in the treatment of social anxiety. *Cognitive and Behavioral Practice, 10(3),* 240–247.

Anderson, S. W., & Booker, M. B. (2006). Cognitive behavioral therapy versus psychosurgery for refractory obsessive-compulsive disorder. *Journal of Neuropsychiatry & Clinical Neurosciences, 18,* 129.

Anderssen, N., Amlie, C., & Ytteroy, E. A. (2002). Outcomes for children with lesbian or gay parents: A review of studies from 1978 to 2000. *Scandinavian Journal of Psychology, 43,* 335–351.

Ando, K., Kripke, D. F., & Ancoli-Israel, S. (2002). Delayed and advanced sleep phase symptoms. *Israel Journal of Psychiatry and Related Sciences, 39,* 11–18.

Andrade, L., Walters, E. E., Gentil, V., & Laurenti, R. (2002). Prevalence of ICD-10 mental disorders in a catchment area in the city of São Paolo, Brazil. *Social Psychiatry and Psychiatric Epidemiology, 37,* 316–325.

Andreasen, N. C. (1997). Linking mind and brain in the study of mental illnesses: A project for a scientific psychopathology. *Science, 275,* 1586–1593.

Andreasen, N. C., Arndt, S., Alliger, R., Miller, D., & Flaum, M. (1995). Symptoms of schizophrenia. *Archives of General Psychiatry, 52,* 341–351.

Andrés, P. (2003). Frontal cortex as the central executive of working memory: Time to revise our view. *Cortex, 39,* 871–895.

Andrew, D., & Craig, A. D. (2001). Spinothalamic lamina I neurons selectively sensitive to histamine: A central neural pathway for itch. *Nature Neuroscience, 4,* 72–77.

Andrews, B., Brewin, C., Ochera, J., Morton, J., Bekerian, D. A., Davies, G. M., & Mollon, P. (2000). The timing, triggers, and quality of recovered memories in therapy. *British Journal of Clinical Psychology, 39,* 11–26.

Andrews, J., Wang, L., Csernansky, J. G., Gado, M. H., & Barch, D. M. (2006). Abnormalities of thalamic activation and cognition in schizophrenia. *American Journal of Psychiatry, 163,* 463–469.

Anghelescu, I., Klawe, C. J., Bartenstein, P., & Szegedi, A. (2001). Normal PET after long-term ETC. *American Journal of Psychiatry, 158,* 1527.

Angold, A., Erkanli, A., Farmer, E. M. Z., Fairbank, J. A., Burns, B. J., Keeler, G., & Costello, E. J. (2002). Psychiatric disorder, impairment, and service use in rural African American and white youth. *Archives of General Psychiatry, 59,* 893–901.

Angst, J., Angst, F., & Stassen, H. H. (1999). Suicide risks inpatients with major depressive disorder. *Journal of Clinical Psychiatry, 60(Suppl. 2),* 57–62.

Annenberg Public Policy Center. (1999). *The 1999 state of children's television report: Programming for children over broadcast and cable television.* Washington, DC: Author.

Annenberg Public Policy Center. (2000). *Media in the home: The fifth annual survey of parents and children 2000.* Washington, DC: Author.

Anshel, M. (1996). Coping styles among adolescent competitive athletes. *Journal of Social Psychology, 136,* 311–323.

Anstey, K. J., Hofer, S. M., & Luszcz, M. A. (2003). Cross-sectional and longitudinal patterns of dedifferentiation in late-life cognitive and sensory function: The effects of age, ability, attrition, and occasion of measurement. *Journal of Experimental Psychology: General, 132,* 470–487.

Antoni, M. H. & Lutgendorf, S. (2007). Psychosocial factors and disease progression in cancer. *Current Directions in Psychological Science, 16,* 42–46.

Antoni, M. H., Lehman, J., Kilbourn, K., Boyers, A., Yount, S., Culver, J., et al. (2001). Cognitive-behavioral stress management intervention enhances optimism and the sense of positive contributions among women under treatment for early-stage breast cancer. *Health Psychology, 20,* 20–32.

Antrobus, J. (2001). Rethinking the fundamental process of dream and sleep mentation production: Defining new questions that avoid the distraction of REM versus NREM comparisons. *Sleep and Hypnosis, 3,* 1–8.

APA Office of Ethnic Minority Affairs. (2000). *Guidelines for research in ethnic minority communities.* Washington, DC: American Psychological Association.

Appelbaum, P. S. (2005). Assessing Kendra's Law: Five years of outpatient commitment in New York. *Psychiatric Services, 56,* 791–792.

Aquino, K., Tripp, T. M., & Bies, R. J. (2006). Getting even or moving on? Power, procedural justice, and types of offense as predictors of revenge, forgiveness, reconciliation, and avoidance in organizations. *Journal of Applied Psychology, 91,* 653–668.

Arbelle, S., Benjamin, J., Golin, M., Kremer, I., Belmaker, R. H., & Ebstein, R. P. (2003). Relation of shyness in grade school children to the genotype for the long form of the serotonin transporter promoter region polymorphism. *American Journal of Psychiatry, 160,* 671–676.

Arkowitz, H., & Lilienfeld, S. O. (2006). Psychotherapy on trial. *Scientific American Mind, April/May,* 42–49.

Arlow, J. (1995). Psychoanalysis. In R. J. Corsini & D. Wedding (Eds.), *Current psychotherapies* (5th ed., pp. 15–50). Itasca, IL: Peacock.

Armeli, S., Tennen, H., Todd, M., Carney, M. A., Mohr, C., Affleck, G., & Hromi, A. (2003). A daily process examination of the stress-response dampening effects of alcohol consumption. *Psychology of Addictive Behaviors, 17,* 266–276.

Armfield, J. M. (2006). Cognitive vulnerability: A model of the etiology of fear. *Clinical Psychology Review, 26,* 746–768.

Armitage, C. J. (2005). Can the theory of planned behavior predict the maintenance of physical activity? *Health Psychology, 24,* 235–245.

Arnedt, J. T., Owens, J., Crouch, M., Stahl, J., & Carskadon, M. A. (2005). Neurobehavioral performance of residents after heavy night call vs after alcohol ingestion. *Journal of the American Medical Association, 294,* 1025–1033.

Arnett, J. J. (1999). Adolescent storm and stress, reconsidered. *American Psychologist, 54,* 317–326.

Arnett, J. J. (2000). Emerging adulthood: A theory of development from the late teens through the twenties. *American Psychologist, 55,* 469–480.

Aron, A., Fisher, H. E., Mashek, D. J. Strong, G., Li, H-F. & Brown, L. L. (2005). Reward, motivation and emotion systems associated with early-stage intense romantic love. *Journal of Neurophysiology, 94,* 327–337.

Aronoff, J., Barclay, A. M., & Stevenson, L. A. (1988). The recognition of threatening stimuli. *Journal of Personality and Social Psychology, 54,* 647–655.

Aronson, E. (1990). Applying social psychology to desegregation and energy conservation. *Personality and Social Psychology Bulletin, 16,* 118–132.

Aronson, E. (1997). *The jigsaw classroom.* New York: Longman.

Aronson, E. (1999). *The social animal* (8th ed.). New York: Worth/Freeman.

Aronson, E. (2004). Reducing hostility and building compassion: Lessons from the jigsaw classroom. In A. G. Miller (Ed.), *The social psychology of good and evil* (pp. 469–488). New York: Guilford Press.

Aronson, E., Wilson, T. D., & Akert, R. M. (2005). *Social psychology* (5th ed.). Upper Saddle River, NJ: Prentice Hall.

Arseneault, L., Cannon, M., Witton, J., & Murray, R. M. (2004). Causal association between cannabis and psychosis: Examination of the evidence. *British Journal of Psychiatry, 184,* 110–117.

Arseneault, L., Moffitt, T. E., Caspi, A., Taylor, A., Rijsdijk, F. V., et al. (2003). Strong genetic effects on cross-situational antisocial behavior among 5-year-old children according to mothers, teachers, examiner-observers, and twins' self-reports. *Journal of Child Psychology and Psychiatry, 44,* 832–848.

Arterberry, M. E., Yonas, A., & Bensen, A. S. (1989). Self-produced locomotion and development of responsiveness to textural gradients. *Developmental Psychology, 25,* 976–982.

Arterburn, D. E., Crane, P. K., & Veenstra, D. L. (2004). The efficacy and safety of sibutramine for weight loss: A systematic review. *Archives of Internal Medicine,164,* 994–1003.

Arthur, W. Jr., Day, E. A., McNelly, T. L., & Edens, P. S. (2003). A meta-analysis of the criterion-related validity of assessment center dimensions. *Personnel Psychology, 56,* 125–154.

Arvey, R. D., Bouchard, T. J., Segal, N. L., & Abraham, L. M. (1989). Job satisfaction: Environmental and genetic components. *Journal of Applied Psychology, 74,* 187–192.

Asarnow, R. F., Nuechterlein, K. H., Fogelson, D., Subotnik, K. L., Payne, D. A., Russell, A. T., et al. (2001). Schizophrenia and schizophrenia-spectrum personality disorders in the first-degree relatives of children with schizophrenia: The UCLA family study. *Archives of General Psychiatry, 58,* 581–588.

Asch, S. E. (1951). Effects of group pressure upon the modification and distortion of judgments. In H. Guetzkow (Ed.), *Groups, leadership, and men* (pp. 177–190). Pittsburgh, PA: Carnegie Press.

Asch, S. E. (1955). Opinions and social pressure. *Scientific American, 193,* 31–35.

Asch, S. E. (1956). Studies of independence and conformity: A minority of one against a unanimous majority. *Psychological Monographs, 70,* 1–70.

Ascherio, A., Chen, H., Weisskopf, M. G., O'Reilly, E., McCullough, M. L., Calle, E. E., et al. (2006). Pesticide exposure and risk for Parkinson's disease. *Annals of Neurology, 60,* 197–203.

Ashcraft, M. H. (2006). *Cognition* (4th ed.). Upper Saddle River, NJ: Prentice Hall.

Ashe, P. C., Berry, M. D., & Boulton, A. A (2001). Schizophrenia, a neurodegenerative disorder with neurodevelopmental antecedents. *Progress in Neuro-Psychopharmacology and Biological Psychiatry, 25,* 691–707.

Asher, S. R., & Hopmeyer, A. (2001). Loneliness in childhood. In G. Bear, K. Minke, & A. Thomas (Eds.), *Children's needs II: Psychological perspectives.* Silver Spring, MD: National Association of School Psychologists.

Ashmore, R. D., Deaux, K., McLaughlin-Volpe, T. (2004). An organizing framework for collective identity: Articulation and significance of multidimensionality. *Psychological Bulletin, 130,* 80–114.

Ashton, M. C., Lee, K., Perugini, M., Szarota, P., de Vries, R. E., Di Blas, L., et al. (2004). A six-factor structure of personality-descriptive adjectives: Solutions from psycholexical studies in seven languages. *Journal of Personality and Social Psychology, 86,* 356–366.

Aspinwall, L. G., & Taylor, S. E. (1992). Modeling cognition adaptation: A longitudinal investigation of the impact of individual differences and coping on college adjustment and performance. *Journal of Personality and Social Psychology, 63,* 989–1003.

Assefi, N. P., Sherman, K. J., Jacobsen, C., Goldberg, J., Smith, W. R., & Buchwald, D. (2005). A randomized clinical trial of acupuncture compared with sham acupuncture in fibromyalgia. *Annals of Internal Medicine, 143,* 10–19.

Assefi, S. L., & Garry, M. (2003). Absolut® memory distortions: Alcohol placebos influence misinformation effect. *Psychological Science, 14,* 77–80.

Associated Press. (2002, March 9). Odds and ends. *Naples Daily News.* Retrieved August 27, 2003, from http://www.nctimes.net/news/2002/20020313/wwww.html

Associated Press. (2003, January 10). Man to get $900,000 for 20 years spent in prison for rape he did not commit. *Naples Daily News.*

Associated Press. (2004, November 1). *Genetic disorder deprives kindergartner of natural alarms.* Retrieved September 26, 2006, from http://www.msnbc.msn.com/id-/6379795/.

Associated Press. (2006, April 23). *Six middle schoolers arrested after planning massacre.* Retrieved September 26, 2006, from http://www.foxnews.com/story/0,2933,192726,00.html.

Astin, J. A. (2004). Mind-body therapies for the management of pain. *Clinical Journal of Pain, 20,* 27–32.

Astin, J. A., Shapiro, S. L., Eisenberg, D. M., & Forys, K. L. (2003). Mind-body medicine: State of the science, implications for practice. *Journal of the American Board of Family Practice, 16,* 131–147.

Aston-Jones, G. (2005). Brain structures and receptors involved in alertness. *Sleep Medicine, 6*(Suppl. 1), S3–7.

Atkinson, J. W., & Raynor, J. O. (1974). *Personality, motivation, and achievement.* Washington, DC: Hemisphere.

Atkinson, R. C., & Shiffrin, R. M. (1968). Human memory: A proposed system and its control processes. In K. Spence (Ed.), *The psychology of learning and motivation* (Vol. 2, pp. 89–195). New York: Academic Press.

Atran, S., Medin, D. L., & Ross, N. O. (2005). The cultural mind: Environmental decision making and cultural modeling within and across populations. *Psychological Review, 112,* 744–776.

Auld, D. S., & Robitaille, R. (2003). Glial cells and neurotransmission: An inclusive view of synaptic function. *Neuron, 40,* 389–400.

Averill, J. S. (1980). On the paucity of positive emotions. In K. R. Blankstein, P. Pliner, & J. Polivey (Eds.), *Advances in the study of communication and affect: Vol. 6. Assessment and modification of emotional behavior.* New York: Plenum.

Ayache, D., Corre, A., Can Prooyen, S., & Elbaz, P. (2003). Surgical treatment of otosclerosis in elderly patients. *Otolaryngological Head and Neck Surgery, 129,* 674–677.

Ayanian, J., & Cleary, P. (1999). Perceived risks of heart disease and cancer among cigarette smokers. *Journal of the American Medical Association, 281,* 1019–1021.

Ayas, N. T., Barger, L. K., Cade, B. E., Hashimoto, D. M., Rosner, B., Cronin, J. W., et al. (2006). Extended work duration and the risk of self-reported percutaneous injuries in interns. *Journal of the American Medical Association, 296,* 1055–1062.

Ayllon, T. (1999). *How to use token economy and point systems* (2nd ed.). Austin, TX: Pro-Ed.

Aymoz, C., & Viviani, P. (2004). Perceptual asynchronies for biological and non-biological visual events. *Vision Research, 44,* 1547–1563.

Ayuso-Mateos, J. L., Vazquez-Barquero, J. L., Dowrick, C., Lehtinen, V., Dalgard, O. S., Casey, P., et al. (2001). Depressive disorders in Europe: Prevalence figures fromt he ODIN study. *British Journal of Psychiatry, 179,* 308–316.

Azar, B. (1996, November). Project explores landscape of midlife. *APA Monitor,* p. 26.

Baare, W. F. C., van Oel, C. J., Hushoff, H. E., Schnack, H. G., Durston, S., Sitskoorn, M. M., & Kahn, R. S. (2001). Volumes of brain structures in twins discordant for schizophrenia. *Archives of General Psychiatry, 58,* 33–40.

Baars, B. J. (2002). The conscious access hypothesis: Origins and recent evidence. *Trends in Cognitive Science, 6,* 47–52.

Babcock, R., & Salthouse, T. (1990). Effects of increased processing demands on age differences in working memory. *Psychology and Aging, 5,* 421–428.

Babinski, J. (1914). Contribution a l'etude dies troubles mentaux dans l'hemiplegie organique cerebrale (anosognosia). *Reveu Neurologie (Paris), 27,* 845–847.

Bacharach, V. R., & Baumeister, A. A. (1998). Direct and indirect effects of maternal intelligence, maternal age, income, and home environment on intelligence of preterm, low-birth-weight children. *Journal of Applied Developmental Psychology, 19,* 361–375.

Backman, L., & Nilsson, L. (1991). Effects of divided attention on free and cued recall of verbal events and action events. *Bulletin of the Psychonomic Society, 29,* 51–54.

Bach-Mizrachi, H., Underwood, M. D., Kassir, S. A., Bakalian, M. J., Sibille, E., Tamir, H., et al. (2006). Neuronal tryptophan hydroxylase mRNA expression in the human dorsal and median raphe nuclei: Major depression and suicide. *Neuropsychopharmacology: Official Publication of the American College of Neuropsychopharmacology, 31,* 814–824.

Bada, H. S., Das, A., Bauer, C. R., Shankaran, S., Lester, B., LaGasse, L., et al. (2007). Impact of prenatal cocaine exposure on child behavior problems through school age. *Pediatrics, 119,* 348–359.

Baddeley, A. (1982). *Your memory: A user's guide.* New York: Macmillan.

Baddeley, A. (1992). Working memory. *Science, 255,* 556–559.

Badre, D., & Wagner, A. D. (2006). Computational and neurobiological mechanisms underlying cognitive flexibility. *Proceedings of the National Academy of Sciences, 103,* 7186–7191.

Baer, J. S., Sampson, P. D., Barr, H. M., Connor, P. D., & Streissguth, A. P. (2003). A 21-year longitudinal analysis of the effects of prenatal alcohol exposure on young adult drinking. *Archives of General Psychiatry, 60,* 377–385.

Baer, R. D., Weller, S. C., De Alba Garcia, J. G., Glazer, M., et al. (2003). A cross-cultural approach to the study of the folk illness nervios. *Culture, Medicine, and Psychiatry, 27,* 315–337.

Baethge, C., Baldessarini, R. J., Mathiske-Schmidt, K., Hennen, J., Berghofer, A., et al., (2005). Long-term combination therapy versus monotherapy with lithium and carbamazepine in 46 bipolar I patients. *Journal of Clinical Psychiatry, 66,* 174–182.

Bagley, C., & Tremblay, P. (1998). On the prevalence of homosexuality and bisexuality, in a random survey of 750 men aged 18–27. *Journal of Homosexuality, 36,* 1–18.

Bahrick, H. P., Bahrick, P. O., & Wittlinger, R. P. (1975). Fifty years of memory for names and faces: A cross-cultural approach. *Journal of Experimental Psychology: General, 104,* 54–75.

Bahrick, H. P., & Hall, L. K. (1991). Lifetime maintenance of high school mathematics content. *Journal of Experimental Psychology: General, 120,* 20–33.

Bahrick, H. P., Hall, L. K., & Berger, S. A. (1996). Accuracy and distortion in memory for high school grades. *Psychological Science, 7,* 265–271.

Bahrick, H. P., Hall, L. K., Noggin, J. P., & Bahrick, L. E. (1994). Fifty years of language maintenance and language dominance in bilingual Hispanic immigrants. *Journal of Experimental Psychology: General, 123,* 264–283.

Bailey, J. M., & Benishay, D. S. (1993). Familial aggregation of female sexual orientation. *American Journal of Psychiatry, 150,* 272–277.

Bailey, J. M., Bobrow, D., Wolfe, M., & Mikach, S. (1995). Sexual orientation of adult sons of gay fathers. *Developmental Psychology, 31*(1), 124–129.

Bailey, J. M., Dunne, M. P., & Martin, N. G. (2000). Genetic and environmental influences on sexual orientation and its correlates in an Australian twin sample. *Journal of Personality and Social Psychology, 78,* 524–536.

Bailey, J. M., & Pillard, R. C. (1991). A genetic study of male sexual orientation. *Archives of General Psychiatry, 48,* 1086–1096.

Baillargeon, R. (1992). A model of physical reasoning in infancy. In C. Rovee-Collier & L. P. Lipsett (Eds.), *Advances in infancy research.* Norwood, NJ: Ablex.

Baillargeon, R. (1994). How do infants learn about the physical world? *Current Directions in Psychological Science, 3,* 133–139.

Baillargeon, R. (1995). Physical reasoning in infancy. In M. S. Gazzaniga (Ed.), *The cognitive neurosciences* (pp. 181–204). Cambridge, MA: MIT Press.

Baillargeon, R. (2002). The acquisition of physical knowledge in infancy: A summary in eight lessons. In U. Goswami (Ed.), *Blackwell handbook of childhood cognitive development* (pp. 47–83). Malden, MA: Blackwell.

Baillargeon, R. H., Zoccolillo, M., Keenan, K., Côté, S., Pérusse, D., Wu., H.-X., et al. (2007). Gender differences in physical aggression: A prospective population-based survey of children before and after 2 years of age. *Developmental Psychology, 43,* 13–26.

Bajo, M., Crawford, E. F., Roberto, M., Madamba, S. G., & Siggins, G. R. (2006). Chronic morphine treatment alters expression of N-methyl-D-aspartate receptor subunits in the extended amygdala. *Journal of Neuroscience Research, 83,* 532–537.

Baker, L. T., Vernon, P. A., & Ho, H. (1991). The genetic correlation between intelligence and speed of information processing. *Behavior Genetics, 21,* 351–367.

Baker, M. C. (2002). *The atoms of language: The mind's hidden rules of grammar.* New York: Basic Books.

Baker, T. B., Piper, M. E., McCarthy, D. E., & Majeskie, M. R. (2004). Addiction motivation reformulated: An affective processing model of negative reinforcement. *Psychological Review, 111,* 33–51.

Bakker, J., Honda, S., Harada, N., & Balthazart, J. (2003). The aromatase knockout (ArKO) mouse provides new evidence that estrogens are required for the development of the female brain. *Annals of the New York Academy of Science, 1007,* 251–262.

Balaban, M. T. (1995). Affective influences on startle in five-month-old infants: Reactions to facial expressions of emotion. *Child Development, 66*(1), 28–36.

Balat, O., Balat, A., Ugur, M. G., & Pence, S. (2003). The effect of smoking and caffeine on the fetus and placenta in pregnancy. *Clinical and Experimental Obstetrics and Gynecology, 30,* 57–59.

Balázs, J., Benazzi, F., Rihmer, Z, Annamaria, A., Akiskal, K. K., et al. (2006). The close link between suicide attempts and mixed (bipolar) depression: Implications for suicide prevention. *Journal of Affective Disorders, 91,* 133–138.

Balbin, E. G., Ironson, G. H., & Solomon, G. F. (1999). Stress and coping: The psychoneuroimmunology of HIV/AIDS. *Baillieres Best Practice and Research. Clinical Endocrinology and Metabolism, 13,* 615–633.

Balcetis, E., & Dunning, D. (2006). See what you want to see: Motivational influences on visual perception. *Journal of Personality and Social Psychology, 91,* 612–625.

Baldessarini, R. J., & Tondo, L. (2000). Does lithium treatment still work? Evidence of stable responses over three decades. *Archives of General Psychiatry, 57,* 187–190.

Baldwin, T. T., & Ford, J. K. (1988). Transfer of training: A review and directions for future research. *Personnel Psychology, 41,* 63–105.

Balfour, D. J. (2002). The neurobiology of tobacco dependence: A commentary. *Respiration, 69,* 7–11.

Ball, K., & Sekuler, R. (1992). Cues reduce direction uncertainty and enhance motion detection. *Perception and Psychophysics, 30,* 119–128.

Balleine, B., & Dickinson, A. (1994). Role of cholecystokinin in the motivational control of instrumental action in rats. *Behavioral Neuroscience, 108*(3), 590–605.

Ballmaier, M., & Schmidt, R. (2005). Conversion disorder revisited. *Functional Neurology, 20,* 105–113.

Balon, R. (2004). Developments in treatment of anxiety disorders: Psychotherapy, pharmacotherapy, and psychosurgery. *Depression and Anxiety, 19*(2), 63–76.

Baltes, B. B., Briggs, T. E., Huff, J. W., Wright, J. A., & Neumann, G. A. (1999). Flexible and compressed workweek schedules: A meta-analysis of their effects on work-related criteria. *Journal of Applied Psychology, 84,* 496–513.

Baltes, B. B., & Heydens-Gahir, H. A. (2003). Reduction of work–family conflict through the use of selection, optimization, and compensation behaviors. *Journal of Applied Psychology, 88,* 1005–1018.

Baltes, P. B. (1994, August). *Life-span developmental psychology: On the overall landscape of human development.* Invited address presented at the annual meeting of the American Psychological Association, Los Angeles.

Baltes, P. B., & Kunzmann, U. (2004). The two faces of wisdom: Wisdom as a general theory of knowledge and judgment about excellence in mind and virtue vs. wisdom as everyday realization in people and produces. *Human Development, 47,* 290–299.

Baltes, P. B., Staudinger, U. M., Maercker, A., & Smith, J. (1995). People nominated as wise: A comparative study of wisdom-related knowledge. *Psychology and Aging, 10,* 155–166.

Balzer, W. K., & Sulsky, L. M. (1992). Halo and performance appraisal research: A critical examination. *Journal of Applied Psychology, 77,* 975–985.

Banaji, M., Lemm, K. M., & Carpenter, S. J. (2001). The social unconscious. In A. Tesser & N. Schwarz (Eds.), *Blackwell handbook of social psychology: Intraindividual processes* (pp. 134–158). Oxford, UK: Blackwell.

Bancroft, J. (1994). Homosexual orientation: The search for a biological basis. *British Journal of Psychiatry, 164,* 437–440.

Bandura, A. (1965). Influence of a model's reinforcement contingencies on the acquisition of imitative responses. *Journal of Personality and Social Psychology, 1,* 589–595.

Bandura, A. (1983). Psychological mechanisms of aggression. In R. G. Geen & C. I. Donnerstein (Eds.), *Aggression: Theoretical and empirical reviews* (Vol. 1, pp. 1–40). New York: Academic Press.

Bandura, A. (1992). Self-efficacy mechanism in psychobiologic functioning. In R. Schwarzer (Ed.), *Self-efficacy: Thought control of action* (pp. 355–394). Washington, DC: Hemisphere.

Bandura, A. (1999). Social cognitive theory of personality. In L. Pervin & O. John (Eds.), *Handbook of personality: theory and research* (2nd ed., pp. 154–198). New York: Guilford.

Bandura, A. (2006). Toward a psychology of human agency. *Perspectives on Psychological Science, 1,* 164–180.

Bandura, A., Blanchard, E. B., & Ritter, B. (1969). The relative efficacy of desensitization and modeling approaches for inducing behavioral, affective, and attitudinal changes. *Journal of Personality and Social Psychology, 13,* 173–199.

Bandura, A., Ross, D., & Ross, S. A. (1963). Imitation of film-mediated aggressive models. *Journal of Abnormal and Social Psychology, 66,* 3–11.

Bandura, A., & Walters, R. H. (1963). *Social learning and personality development.* New York: Holt, Rinehart & Winston.

Banich, M. T. (2004). *Cognitive neuroscience and neuropsychology.* Boston: Houghton Mifflin.

Banich, M. T., & Heller, W. (1998). Evolving perspectives on lateralization of function. *Current Directions in Psychological Science, 7,* 1–2.

Banker, R. D., Field, J. M., Schroeder, R. G., & Sinha, K. K. (1996). Impact of work teams on manufacturing performance: A longitudinal field study. *Academy of Management Journal, 39,* 867–890.

Bantick, S. J., Wise, R. G., Ploghaus, A., Clare, S., Smith, S. M., & Tracey, I. (2002). Imaging how attention modulates pain in humans using functional MRI. *Brain, 125,* 310–319.

Bara, B. G., Bucciarelli, M., & Johnson-Laird, P. N. (1995). Development of syllogistic reasoning. *American Journal of Psychology, 108,* 157–193.

Barber, J. P., Crits-Christoph, P., & Paul, C. C. (1993). Advances in measures of psychodynamic formulations. *Journal of Consulting and Clinical Psychology, 61,* 574–585.

Barber, N. (1995). The evolutionary psychology of physical attractiveness: Sexual selection and human morphology. *Ethology and Sociobiology, 16,* 395–424.

Barch, D. M. (2006). The cognitive neuroscience of schizophrenia. *Annual Review of Clinical Psychology, 1,* 321–353.

Barclay, G., & Tavares, C. (2002). *International comparisons of crime statistics.* London: Home Office.

Barclay, J. R., Bransford, J. D., Franks, J. J., McCarrell, N. S., & Nitsch, K. (1974). Comprehension and semantic flexibility. *Journal of Verbal Learning and Verbal Behavior, 13,* 471–481.

Barclay, P. (2006). Reputational benefits for altruistic punishment. *Evolution and Human Behavior, 27,* 325–344.

Barclay, T. R., Hinkin, C. H., Castellon, S. A., Mason, K. I., Reinhard, M. J., Marion, S. D., et al. (2007). Age-associated predictors of medication adherence in HIV-positive adults: health beliefs, self-efficacy, and neurocognitive status. *Health Psychology, 26,* 40–49.

Bareyre, F. M., Kerschensteiner, M., Raineteau, O., Mettenleiter, T. C., & Schwab, M. E. (2004). The injured spinal cord spontaneously forms a new intraspinal circuit in adult rats. *Nature Neuroscience, 7,* 269–277.

Barger, L. K., Cade, B. E., Ayas, N. T., Cronin, J. W., Rosner, B., Speizer, F. E., et al. (2005). *New England Journal of Medicine, 352,* 125–134.

Bargh, J. A., Chen, M., & Burrows, L. (1996). Automaticity of social behavior: Direct effects of trait construct and stereotype activation on action. *Journal of Personality and Social Psychology, 71,* 245–262.

Barkataki, I., Kumari, V., Das, M., Taylor, P., & Sharma, T. (2006). Volumetric structural brain abnormalities in men with schizophrenia or antisocial personality disorder. *Behavioral Brain Research, 169,* 239–247.

Barker, L. M. (1997). *Learning and behavior: Biological, psychological, and sociocultural perspectives* (2nd ed.). Upper Saddle River, NJ: Prentice-Hall.

Barkham, M., Connell, J., Stiles, W. B., Miles, J. N. V., Margison, F., Evans, C., et al. (2006). Dose-effect relations and responsive regulation of treatment duration: The good enough level. *Journal of Consulting and Clinical Psychology, 74,* 160–167.

Barlow, D. H., & Campbell, L. A. (2000). Mixed anxiety-depression and its implications for models of mood and anxiety disorders. *Comprehensive Psychiatry, 41,* 55–60.

Barlow, D. H., Gorman, J. M., Shear, M. K., & Woods, S. W. (2000). Cognitive-behavioral therapy, imipramine, or their combination for panic disorder: A randomized controlled trial. *Journal of the American Medical Association, 283,* 2529–2536.

Barlow, D. H., Raffa, S. D., & Cohen, E. M. (2002). Psychosocial treatments for panic disorders, phobias, and generalized anxiety disorder. In P. E. Nathan & J. M. Gorman (Eds.), *A guide to treatments that work* (2nd ed., pp. 301–335). London: Oxford University Press.

Barnes, A. (2004). Race schizophrenia, and admission to state psychiatric hospitals. *Administration and Policy in Mental Health, 31,* 241–252.

Barnes, L. L., Mendes de Leon, C. F., Wilson, R. S., Bienias, J. L., & Evans, D. A. (2004). Social resources and cognitive decline in a population of older African Americans and whites. *Neurology, 63,* 2322–2326.

Barnett, J. E., & Scheetz, K. (2003). Technological advances and telehealth: Ethics, law, and the practice of psychotherapy. *Psychotherapy: Theory, Research, Practice, and Training, 40,* 86–93.

Barnett, W. S. (1998). Long-term cognitive and academic effects of early childhood education of children in poverty. *Preventive Medicine: An International Devoted Practice & Theory, 27,* 204–207.

Barnier, A. J., & McConkey, K. M. (1998). Posthypnotic responding away from the hypnotic setting. *Psychological Science, 9,* 256–262.

Baron, A. S., & Banaji, M. R. (2006). The development of implicit attitudes. *Psychological Science 17,* 53–58.

Baron, J. C. (2005). How healthy is the acutely reperfused ischemic penumbra? *Cerebrovascular Disease, 20*(Suppl. 2), 25–31.

Baron, R. A., & Byrne, D. (2004). *Social psychology* (10th ed.) Boston: Allyn & Bacon.

Baron, R. A., Byrne, D., & Branscombe, N. R. (2006). *Social psychology* (11th ed.). Boston: Allyn & Bacon.

Baron, R. A., & Richardson, D. C. (1994). *Human aggression* (2nd ed.). New York: Plenum.

Baron, R. S., Kerr, N. L., & Miller, N. (1992). *Group process, group decision, group action.* Pacific Grove, CA: Brooks/Cole.

Barr Taylor, C., Bryson, S., Celio Doyle, A. A., Luce, K. H., Cunning, D., Abascal, L. B., et al. (2006a). The adverse effect of negative comments about weight and shape from family and siblings on women at high risk for eating disorders. *Pediatrics, 118,* 731–738.

Barr Taylor, C., Bryson, S., Luce, K. H., Cunning, D., Celio Doyle, A. A., Abascal, L. B., et al. (2006b). Prevention of eating disorders in at-risk college-age women. *Archives of General Psychiatry, 63,* 881–888.

Barrett, B., Byford, S., & Knapp, M. (2005). Evidence of cost-effective treatments for depression: A systematic review. *Journal of Affective Disorders, 84,* 1–13.

Barrett, D. (2006). Hypnosis in film and television. *American Journal of Clinical Hypnosis, 49*(1), 13–30.

Barrett, L. F. (1995). Valence focus and arousal focus: Individual differences in the structure of affective experience. *Journal of Personality and Social Psychology, 69,* 153–166.

Barrett, L. F., Gross, J., Christensen, T. C., & Benvenuto, M. (2001). Knowing what you're feeling and knowing what to do about it: Mapping the relation between emotion differentiation and emotion regulation. *Cognition and Emotion, 15,* 713–724.

Barrett, L. F., Lane, R. D., Sechrest, L., & Schwartz, G. E. (2000). Sex differences in emotional awareness. *Personality and Social Psychology Bulletin, 26,* 1027–1035.

Barrett, L. F., & Wager, T. D. (2006). The structure of emotion. *Current Directions in Psychological Science, 15,* 79–83.

Barron, F., & Harrington, D. M. (1981). Creativity, intelligence, and personality. *Annual Review of Psychology, 52,* 439–476.

Barron, K. E., & Harackiewicz, J. M. (2001). Achievement goals and optimal motivation: Testing multiple goal models. *Journal of Personality and Social Psychology, 80,* 706–722.

Barrowclough, C., King, P., Colville, J., Russell, E., Burns, A., & Tarrier, N. (2001). A randomized trial of the effectiveness of cognitive-behavioral therapy and supportive counseling for anxiety symptoms in older adults. *Journal of Consulting and Clinical Psychology, 69,* 756–762.

Barry, J. G., Yasin, I., & Bishop, D. V. M. (2007). Heritable risk factors associated with language impairments. *Genes, Brain & Behavior, 6,* 66–76.

Barsalou, L. W. (1993). Flexibility, structure, and linguistic vagary in concepts: Manifestations of a compositional system of perceptual symbols. In A. F. Collins, S. E. Gathercole, M. A. Conway, & P. E. Morris (Eds.), *Theories of memory* (pp. 29–102). Hillsdale, NJ: Erlbaum.

Barsky, A. J., Wool, C., Barnett, M. C., & Cleary, P. D. (1994). Histories of childhood trauma in adult hypochondriacal patients. *American Journal of Psychiatry, 151,* 397–401.

Bartels, A., & Zeki, S. (2000). The neural basis of romantic love. *Neuroreport, 11,* 3829–3834.

Bartholow, B. D., Bushman, B. J., & Sestir, M. A. (2006). Chronic violent video game exposure and desensitization to violence: Behavioral and event-related brain potential data. *Journal of Experimental Social Psychology, 42,* 532–539.

Bartholow, B. D., & Heinz, A. (2006). Alcohol and aggression without consumption: Alcohol cues, aggressive thoughts, and hostile perception bias. *Psychological Science, 17,* 30–37.

Bartlett, J. A. (2002). Addressing the challenges of adherence. *Journal of Acquired Immune Deficiency Syndrome, 29*(Suppl. 1), S2–S10.

Barton, J., & Folkard, S. (1991). The response of day and night nurses to their work schedules. *Journal of Occupational Psychology, 64,* 207–218.

Barton, J. J., Cherkasova, M., & O'Connor, M. (2001). Covert recognition in acquired and developmental prosopagnosia. *Neurology, 57,* 1161–1168.

Barton, J. J., Cherkasova, M. V., Press, D. Z., Intriligator, J. M., & O'Connor, M. (2004). Perceptual functions in prosopagnosia. *Perception, 33*(8), 939–956.

Barton, J. J., Press, D. Z., Keenan, J. P., & O'Connor, M. (2002). Lesions of the fusiform face area impair perception of facial configuration in prosopagnosia. *Neurology, 58*(1), 71–78.

Bartoshuk, L. M. (1991). Taste, smell, and pleasure. In R. C. Bollef (Ed.), *The hedonics of taste* (pp. 15–28). Hillsdale, NJ: Erlbaum.

Bartoshuk, L. M. (2000). Comparing sensory experiences across individuals: Recent psychophysical advances illuminate genetic variation in taste perception. *Chemical Senses, 25,* 447–460.

Bartz, J. A., & Hollander, E. (2006). Is obsessive-compulsive disorder an anxiety disorder? *Progress in Neuro-Psychopharmacology & Biological Psychiatry, 30,* 338–352.

Bashore, T. R., & Ridderinkhof, K. R. (2002). Older age, traumatic brain injury, and cognitive slowing: Some convergent and divergent findings. *Psychological Bulletin, 128,* 151–198.

Baskin, D., Bluestone, H., & Nelson, M. (1981). Ethnicity and psychiatric diagnosis. *Journal of Clinical Psychology, 37,* 529–537.

Basoglu, M., Livanou, M., & Salcioglu, E. (2003). A single session with an earthquake simulator for traumatic stress in earthquake survivors. *American Journal of Psychiatry, 160,* 788–790.

Bass, B. M., Avolio, B. J., Jung, D. I., & Berson, Y. (2003). Predicting unit performance by assessing transformational and transactional leadership. *Journal of Applied Psychology, 88,* 207–218.

Bass, B. M., & Riggio, R. E. (2006). *Transformational leadership* (2nd ed.). Mahwah, NJ: Erlbaum.

Bass, E., & Davis, L. (1994). *The courage to heal* (3rd ed.). New York: Harper Perennial Library.

Bates, E. (1993, March). *Nature, nurture, and language development.* Paper presented at the biennial meeting of the Society for Research in Child Development, New Orleans.

Bateson, M., Nettle, D., & Roberts, G. (2006). Cues of being watched enhance cooperation in a real-world setting. *Biology Letters, 2,* 412–414.

Batson, C. D. (1998). Altruism and prosocial behavior. In D. Gilbert, S. T. Fiske, & G. Lindzey (Eds.), *Handbook of social psychology* (Vol. 2, 4th ed., pp. 282–316). Boston: McGraw-Hill.

Batson, C. D., Sager, K., Garst, E., & Kang, M. (1997). Is empathy-induced helping due to self-other merging? *Journal of Personality and Social Psychology, 73,* 495–509.

Batterham, R. L., Cohen, M. A., Ellis, S. M., Le Roux, C. W., Withers, D. J., Frost, G. S., et al. (2003). Inhibition of food intake in obese subjects by peptide YY3-36. The *New England Journal of Medicine, 349,* 941–948.

Batterham, R. L., Cowley, M. A., Small, C. J., Herzog, H., Cohen, M. A., Dakin, C. L., et al. (2002). Gut hormone PYY3-36 physiologically inhibits food intake. *Nature, 418,* 650–654.

Baucom, D. H., Shoham, V., Mueser, K. T., Daiuto, A. D., & Stickle, T. R. (1998). Empirically supported couple and family interventions for marital distress and adult mental health problems. *Journal of Consulting and Clinical Psychology, 66,* 53–88.

Bauer, P. J. (2006). Event memory. In W. Damon & R. M. Lerner (Series Eds.) & D. Kuhn & R. Siegler (Vol. Eds.), *Handbook of child psychology: Vol. 2. Cognition, perception, and language* (6th ed., pp. 373–425). New York: Wiley.

Bauer, R. M., & Demery, J. A. (2003). Agnosia. In K. M. Heilman & E. Valenstein (Eds.), *Clinical neuropsychology* (4th ed.). New York: Oxford.

Bauer, T. N., & Green, S. G. (1996). Development of leader-member exchange: A longitudinal test. *Academy of Management Journal, 39,* 1538–1567.

Baumeister, R. F. (2000). Gender differences in erotic plasticity: The female sex drive as socially flexible and responsive. *Psychological Bulletin, 126,* 347–374.

Baumeister, R. F., Campbell, J. D., Krueger, J. I., & Vohs, K. D. (2003). Does high self-esteem cause better performance, interpersonal success, happiness, or healthier lifestyles? *Psychological Science in the Public Interest, 4,* 1–44.

Baumeister, R. F., Catanese, K. R., & Vohs, K. D. (2001). Is there a gender difference in strength of sex drive? *Personality and Social Psychology Review, 5,* 242–273.

Baumeister, R. F., & Leary, M. R. (1995). The need to belong: Desire for interpersonal attachments as a fundamental human motivation. *Psychological Bulletin, 117*(3), 497–529.

Baumrind, D. (1971). Current patterns of parental authority. *Developmental Psychology Monographs, 4*(1, part 2).

Baumrind, D., Larzelere, R. E., & Cowan, P. A. (2002). Ordinary physical punishment: Is it harmful? Comment on Gershoff. *Psychological Bulletin, 128,* 580–589.

Bayley, P. J., Hopkins, R. O., & Squire, L. R. (2003). Successful recollection of remote autobiographical memories by amnesic patients with medial temporal lobe lesions. *Neuron, 38,* 135–144.

Bazzano, L. A., He, J., Ogden, L. G., Loria, C. M., & Whelton, P. K. (2003). Dietary fiber intake and reduced risk of coronary heart disease in US men and women. *Archives of Internal Medicine, 163,* 1897–1904.

Beatty, J. (1995). *Principles of behavioral neuroscience.* Dubuque: Brown and Benchmark.

Beauchamp, G. K., Katahira, K., Yamazaki, K., Mennella, J. A., Bard, J., & Boyse, E. A. (1995). Evidence suggesting that the odortypes of pregnant women are a compound of maternal and fetal odortypes. *Proceedings of the National Academy of Sciences of the United States of America, 92,* 2617–2621.

Beauchamp-Turner, D. L., & Levinson, D. M. (1992). Effects of meditation on stress, health, and affect. *Medical Psychotherapy: An International Journal, 5,* 123–131.

Beaumont, M., Batejat, D., Pierard, C., Coste, O., Doireau, P., Van Beers, P., et al. (2001). Slow release caffeine and prolonged (64-h) continuous wakefulness: effects on vigilance and cognitive performance. *Journal of Sleep Research, 10*(4), 265.

Beaumont, M., Batejat, D., Pierard, C., Van Beers, P., Denis, J. B., Coste, O., et al. (2004). Caffeine or melatonin effects on sleep and sleepiness after rapid eastward transmeridian travel. *Journal of Applied Physiology, 96,* 50–58.

Bech, B. H., Nohr, E. A., Vaeth, M., Henriksen, T. B., & Olsen, J. (2005). Coffee and fetal death: A cohort study with prospective data. *American Journal of Epidemiology, 162,* 983–990.

Bechara, A., Damasio, H., Tranel, D., & Damasio, A. R. (1997). Deciding advantageously before knowing the advantageous strategy. *Science, 275,* 1293–1295.

Beck, A. T. (1967). *Depression: Clinical, experimental and theoretical aspects.* New York: Harper & Row.

Beck, A. T. (1976). *Cognitive therapy and the emotional disorders.* New York: International Universities Press.

Beck, A. T. (1995). Cognitive therapy: A 30-year retrospective. In S. O. Lilienfeld (Ed.), *Seeing both sides: Classic controversies in abnormal psychology* (pp. 303–311). Pacific Grove, CA: Brooks/Cole. (Original work published 1991)

Beck, A. T. (2002). Cognitive models of depression. In R. L. Leahy & E. T. Dowd (Eds.), *Clinical advances in cognitive psychotherapy: Theory and Application* (pp. 29–61). New York: Springer.

Beck, A. T. (2005). The current state of cognitive therapy: A 40-year retrospective. *Archives of General Psychiatry, 62,* 953–959.

Beck, A. T., Brown, G., Berchick, R. J., Stewart, B. L., & Steer, R. A. (1990). Relationship between hopelessness and ultimate suicide: A replication with psychiatric outpatients. *American Journal of Psychiatry, 147,* 190–195.

Beck, A. T., & Rector, N. A. (2005). Cognitive approaches to schizophrenia: Theory and therapy. *Annual Review of Clinical Psychology, 1,* 577–606. Behnke, S. (2004, December). Sexual involvements with former clients: A delicate balance of core values. *Monitor on Psychology,* 76–77.

Beck, J. S., & Beck, A. T. (1995). *Cognitive therapy: Basics and beyond.* New York: Guilford.

Becker, J. A. (1994). "Sneak-shoes," "sworders" and "nose-beards": A case study of lexical innovation. *First Language, 14,* 195–211.

Becker, S. M. (2004). Detection of somatization and depression in primary care in Saudi Arabia. *Social Psychiatry and Psychiatric Epidemiology, 39,* 962–969.

Beckett, C., Maughan, B., Rutter, M., Castle, J., Colvert, E., Groothues, C., et al. (2006). Do the effects of early severe deprivation on cognition persist into early adolescence? Findings from the English and Romanian adoptees study. *Child Development, 77,* 696–711.

Beede, K. E., & Kass, S. J. (2006). Engrossed in conversation: The impact of cell phones on simulated driving performance. *Accident Analysis and Prevention, 38,* 415–421.

Behnke, S. (2003). *Hierarchical neural network for image interpretation.* New York: Springer.

Behnke, S. (2004). Sexual involvements with former clients: A delicate balance of core values. *Monitor on Psychology, December,* 76–77.

Behrendt, R. (2006). Dysregulation of thalamic sensory "transmission" in schizophrenia: Neurochemical vulnerability to hallucinations. *Journal of Psychopharmacology, 20,* 356–372.

Beilock, S. L., Kulp, C. A., Holt, L. E., & Carr, T. H. (2004). More on the fragility of performance: Choking under pressure in mathematical problem solving. *Journal of Experimental Psychology: General, 133,* 584–600

Beirne, R. O., Zlatkova, M. B., & Anderson, R. S. (2005). Changes in human short-wavelength-sensitive and achromatic resolution acuity with retinal eccentricity and meridian. *Visual Neuroscience, 22,* 79–86.

Bekinschtein, T., Tiberti, C., Niklison, J., Tamashiro, M., Ron, M., Carpintiero, S., et al. (2005). Assessing level of consciousness and cognitive changes from vegetative state to full recovery. *Neuropsychological Rehabilitation, 15*(3–4), 307–322.

Belin, P., Zatorre, R. J., & Ahad, P. (2002). Human temporal-lobe response to vocal sounds. *Brain Research and Cognitive Brain Research, 13,* 17–26.

Bell, B. E., & Loftus, E. F. (1989). Trivial persuasion in the courtroom: The power of (a few) minor details. *Journal of Personality and Social Psychology, 56,* 669–679.

Bell, P. A., Greene, T. C., Fisher, J. D., & Baum, A. (2000). *Environmental psychology* (5th ed.). Belmont, CA : Wadsworth.

Bell, S. (2005). What does the "right to health" have to offer mental health patients? *International Journal of Law and Psychiatry, 28,* 141–153.

Bella, S. D., & Peretz, I. (2003). Congenital amusia interferes with the ability to synchronize with music. *Annals of the New York Academy of Science, 999,* 166–169.

Bellaby, P. (2003). Communication and miscommunication of risk: Understanding UK parents' attitudes to combined MMR vaccination. *British Medical Journal, 327,* 725–728.

Belli, R. F., & Loftus, E. F. (1996). The pliability of autobiographical memory: Misinformation and the false memory problem. In D. C. Rubin (Ed.), *Remembering our past: Studies in autobiographical memory* (pp. 157–179). New York: Cambridge University Press.

Belmonte, M. K., Cook, E. H., Jr, Anderson, G. M., Rubenstein, J. L., Greenough, W. T., Beckel-Mitchener, A., et al. (2004). Autism as a disorder of neural information processing: Directions for research and targets for therapy [Electronic version]. *Molecular Psychiatry, 9,* 646–663.

Belsky, J., & Kelly, J. (1994). *The transition to parenthood.* New York: Dell.

Belsky, J., Vandell, D. L., Burchinal, M., Clarke-Stewart, K. A., McCartney, K., Owen, M.T., & The NICHD Early Child Care Research Network. (2007). Are there long-term effects of early child care? *Child Development 78,* 681–701.

Bem, D. J. (1967). Self-perception: An alternative interpretation of cognitive dissonance phenomenon. *Psychological Review, 74,* 183–200.

Bem, D. J. (1996). Exotic becomes erotic: A developmental theory of sexual orientation. *Psychological Review, 103,* 320–335.

Ben-Ari, A., & Gil, S. (2002). Traditional support systems: Are they sufficient in a culturally diverse academic environment? *British Journal of Social Work, 32,* 629–638.

Benecke, M. (1999). Spontaneous human combustion: Thoughts of a forensic biologist. *Skeptical Inquirer, 22,* 47–51.

Benedetti, F., & Amanzio, M. (1997). The neurobiology of placebo analgesia: From endogenous opioids to cholecystokinin. *Progress in Neurobiology, 52,* 109–125.

Benedetti, F., Arduino, C., & Amanzio, M. (1999). Somatotopic activation of opioid systems by target-directed expectations of analgesia. *Journal of Neuroscience, 19,* 3639–3648.

Benham, G., Woody, E. Z., Wilson, K. S., & Nash, M. R. (2006). Expect the unexpected: Ability, attitude, and responsiveness to hypnosis. *Journal of Personality and Social Psychology, 91,* 342–350.

Benjamin, K., Wilson, S. G., & Mogil, J. S. (1999). *Journal of Pharmacology & Experimental Therapeutics, 289,* 1370–1375.

Benjamin, L. T., Jr. (2000). The psychology laboratory at the turn of the 20th century. *American Psychologist, 55,* 318–321.

Benjamin, L. T., Jr., & Baker, D. B. (2004). *From séance to science: A history of the profession of psychology in America.* Belmont, CA: Thomson Wadsworth.

Bennett, H. L., Giannini, J. A., & Davis, H. S. (1985). Nonverbal response to intraoperational conversation. *British Journal of Anaesthesia, 57,* 174–179.

Bennett, K. K., & Elliott, M. (2002). Explanatory style and health: Mechanisms linking pessimism to illness. *Journal of Applied Social Psychology, 32,* 1508–1526.

Bennett, R. J., & Robinson, S. L. (2000). Development of a measure of workplace deviance. *Journal of Applied Psychology, 85,* 349–360.

Ben-Shakhar, G., Bar-Hillel, M., & Kremnitzer, M. (2002). Trial by polygraph: Reconsidering the use of the guilty knowledge technique in court. *Law & Human Behavior, 26,* 527–541.

Ben-Shakhar, G., & Furedy, J. J. (1990). *Theories and applications in the detection of deception: A psychophysiological and international perspective.* New York: Springer-Verlag.

Benson, D. F., & Geschwind, N. (1971). Aphasia and related cortical disturbances. In A. B. Baker & L. H. Baker (Eds.). *Clinical neurology.* New York: Harper & Row.

Benson, E. (2003a). Intelligence across cultures. *Monitor on Psychology, 34*(2), 56–58.

Benson, E. (2003b). Sex: The science of sexual arousal. *Monitor on Psychology, 34,* 50.

Benson, H. (1975). *The relaxation response.* New York: Morrow.

Ben-Zur, H. (2002). Coping, affect and aging: The roles of mastery and self-esteem. *Personality & Individual Differences, 32*(2), 357–372.

Berdahl, J. L., & Moore, C. (2006). Workplace harassment: Double jeopardy for minority women. *Journal of Applied Psychology, 91,* 426–436.

Berenbaum, S. A., & Resnick, S. M. (1997). Early androgen effects on aggression in children and adults with congenital adrenal hyperplasia. *Psychoneuroendocrinology, 22,* 505–515.

Beresford, J., & Blades, M. (2006). Children's identification of faces from lineups: The effects of lineup presentation and instructions on accuracy. *Journal of Applied Psychology, 91,* 1102–1113.

Beresford, T. P., Arciniegas, D. B., Alfers, J., Clapp, L., Martin, B., Du, Y., Liu, D., Shen, D., & Davatzikos, C. (2006). Hippocampus volume loss due to chronic heavy drinking. *Alcoholism, Clinical and Experimental Research, 30,* 1866–1870.

Berger, A., Henderson, M., Nadoolman, W., Duffy, V., Cooper, D., Saberski, L., & Bartoshuk, L. (1995). Oral capsaicin provides temporary relief for oral mucositis pain secondary to chemotherapy/radiation therapy. *Journal of Pain and Symptom Management, 10,* 243–248.

Berger, A., Tzur, G., & Posner, M. I. (2006). Infant brains detect arithmetic errors. *Proceedings of the National Academy of Sciences, 103,* 12649–12653.

Berger, S. E., & Adolph, K. E. (2003). Infants use handrails as tools in a locomotor task. *Developmental Psychology, 39,* 594–605.

Bergin, A. E. (1971). The evaluation of therapeutic outcomes. In A. E. Bergin & S. L. Garfield (Eds.), *Handbook of psychotherapy and behavior change: An empirical analysis* (pp. 217–270). New York: Wiley.

Berglund, H., Lindström, P., & Savic, I. (2006). Brain response to putative pheromones in lesbian women. *Proceedings of the National Academy of Sciences of the USA, 103,* 8269–8274.

Beriault, M., & Larivee, S. (2005). French review of EMDR efficacy: Evidences and controversies. *Revue de Psychoeducation, 34,* 355–396.

Berkowitz, L. (1994). Is something missing? Some observations prompted by the Cognitive-neoassociationist view of anger and emotional aggression. In L. R. Huesmann (Ed.), *Human aggression: Current perspectives* (pp. 35–60). New York: Plenum.

Berkowitz, L. (1998). Affective aggression: The role of stress, pain, and negative affect. In R. G. Geen & E. Donnerstein (Eds.), *Human aggression* (pp. 49–72). San Diego: Academic Press.

Berkowitz, L. (1999). Evil is more than banal: Situationism and the concept of evil. *Personality and Social Psychology Review, 3,* 246–253.

Berliner, D. L., Monti-Bloch, L., Jennings-White, C., & Diaz-Sanchez, V. (1996). The functionality of the human vomeronasal organ (VNO): Evidence for steriod receptors. *Journal of Steriod Biochemical Molecular Biology, 58,* 259–265.

Berman, W. H., & Bradt, G. (2006). Executive consulting: "Different strokes for different folks." *Professional Psychology: Research and Practice, 37,* 244–253.

Bermond, B., Fasotti, L., Nieuwenhuyse, B., & Schuerman, J. (1991). Spinal cord lesions, peripheral feedback and intensities of emotional feelings. *Cognition and Emotions, 5,* 201–220.

Bernard, L. L. (1924). *Instinct.* New York: Holt, Rinehart & Winston.

Bernardin, H. J., & Beatty, R. W. (1984). *Performance appraisal: Assessing human behavior at work.* Boston: Kent.

Bernat, J. A., Calhoun, K. S., Adams, H. E., & Zeichner, A. (2001). Homophobia and physical aggression toward homosexual and heterosexual individuals. *Journal of Abnormal Psychology, 110,* 179–187.

Berns, G. S., McClure, S. M., Pagnoni, G., & Montague, P. R. (2001). Predictability modulates human brain response to reward. *Journal of Neuroscience, 21,* 2793–2798.

Bernstein, D. A. (1970). The modification of smoking behavior: A search for effective variables. *Behaviour Research and Therapy, 8,* 133–146.

Bernstein, D. A., Borkovec, T. D., & Hazlett-Stevens, H. (2000). *Progressive relaxation training: A manual for the helping professions* (2nd ed.). New York: Praeger.

Bernstein, D. A., Kramer, G. P., & Phares, V. (2008). *Introduction to clinical psychology* (7th ed.). Upper Saddle River, NJ: Prentice Hall.

Bernstein, D. M., Laney, C., Morris, E. K., & Loftus, E. F. (2005). False beliefs about fattening foods can have healthy consequences. *Proceedings of the National Academy of Sciences of the USA, 102,* 13724–13731.

Bernstein, D. M., & Roberts, B. (1995). Assessing dreams through self-report questionnaires: Relation with past research and personality. *Dreaming: Journal of the Association for the Study of Dreams, 5,* 13–27.

Bernstein, I. L. (1978). Learned taste aversions in children receiving chemotherapy. *Science, 200,* 1302–1303.

Berridge, K. C. (1999). Pleasure, pain, desire and dread: Biopsychological components and relations. In D. Kahneman, E. Diener, & N. Schwarz (Eds.), *Understanding the quality of life: Scientific perspectives on enjoyment and suffering.* New York: Russell Sage Foundation.

Berry, J. W., & Bennett, J. A. (1992). Cree conceptions of cognitive competence. *International Journal of Psychology, 27,* 73–88.

Berscheid, E., & Reis, H. T. (1998). Attraction and close relationships. In D. Gilbert, S. T. Fiske, & G. Lindzey (Eds.), *Handbook of social psychology* (Vol. 2, 4th ed., pp. 193–281). Boston: McGraw-Hill.

Bersoff, D. M. (1999). Why good people sometimes do bad things: Motivated reasoning and unethical behavior. *Personality and Social Psychology Bulletin, 25,* 28–39.

Bersoff, D. N. (1999). *Ethical conflicts in psychology* (2nd ed.). Washington, DC: American Psychological Association.

Bertau, C., Anderson, N., & Salgado, J. F. (2005). The predictive validity of cognitive ability tests: A UK meta-analysis. *Journal of Occupational and Organizational Psychology, 78,* 387–409.

Berti, A., Ladavas, E., & Corti, M. D. (1996). Anosognosia for hemiplegia, neglect dyslexia, and drawing neglect: Clinical findings and theoretical implications. *Journal of the International Neuropsychological Association, 2,* 426–440.

Besli, R., Saylam, C., Veral, A., Karl, B., & Ozek. C. (2004). The existence of the vomeronasal organ in human beings. *Journal of Craniofacial Surgery, 15,* 730–735.

Best, D. (1992, June). *Cross-cultural themes in developmental psychology.* Paper presented at workshop on cross-cultural aspects of psychology. Western Washington University, Bellingham.

Best, J. B. (1999). *Cognitive psychology* (5th ed.). Belmont, CA: Brooks/Cole.

Betan, E., Heim, A. K., Conklin, C. Z., & Westen, D. (2005). Countertransference phenomena and personality pathology in clinical practice: An empirical investigation. *American Journal of Psychiatry, 162,* 890–898.

Betch, T., Hoffman, K., Hoffrage, U., & Plessner, H. (2003). Intuition beyond recognition: When less familiar events are liked more. *Experimental Psychology, 50,* 49–54.

Bettencourt, B. A., Talley, A., Benjamin, A. J., & Valentine, J. (2006). Personality and aggressive behavior under provoking and neutral conditions: A meta-analytic review. *Psychological Bulletin. 132,* 751–777.

Beutler, L. E. (2000). David and Goliath: When empirical and clinical standards of practice meet. *American Psychologist, 55,* 997–1007.

Beutler, L. E. (2002). The dodo bird is extinct. *Clinical Psychology: Science and Practice, 9,* 30–34.

Beutler, L. E., & Malik, M. L. (Eds.). (2002). *Rethinking DSM: A psychological perspective.* Washington DC: American Psychological Association.

Bevan, S., & Geppetti, P. (1994). Protons: small stimulants of capsaicin-sensitive sensory nerves. *Trends in Neuroscience, 17,* 509–512.

Bevins, R. A. (2001). Novelty seeking and reward: Implications for the study of high-risk behaviors. *Current Directions in Psychological Science, 10,* 189–193.

Bhagat, R. S., Kedia, B. L., Harveston, P. D., & Triandis, H. C. (2002). Cultural variations in the cross-border transfer of organizational knowledge: An integrative framework. *Academy of Management Review, 27,* 204–221.

Bhatt, R. S., & Bertin, E. (2001). Pictorial cues and three-dimensional information processing in early infancy. *Journal of Experimental Child Psychology, 80,* 315–332.

Bhopal, R., Vettini, A., Hunt, S., Wiebe, S., Hanna, L., & Amos, A. (2004). Review of prevalence data in, and evaluation of methods for cross cultural adaptation of, UK surveys on tobacco and alcohol in ethnic minority groups. *British Medical Journal, 328,* 76.

Bhutta, A. T., Cleves, M. A., Casey, P. H., Cradock, M. M., & Anand, K. J. S. (2002). Cognitive and behavioral outcomes of school-aged children who were born preterm. *JAMA, 288,* 728–737.

Bickis, M., Kelly, I. W., & Byrnes, G. (1995). Crisis calls and temporal and lunar variables: A comprehensive study. *Journal of Psychology, 129,* 701–711.

Bidwell, M. A., & Rehfeldt, R. A. (2004). Using video modeling to teach a domestic skill with an embedded social skill to adults with severe mental retardation. *Behavioral Interventions, 19,* 263–274.

Bienenfeld, D. (2005). *Psychodynamic theory for clinicians.* New York: Lippincott Williams & Wilkins.

Bierhaus, A., Wolf, J., Andrassy, M., Rohleder, N., Humpert, P. M., Petrov, D., et al. (2003). A mechanism converting psychosocial stress into mononuclear cell activation. *Proceedings of the National Academy of Sciences, 100,* 1920–1925.

Bierut, L. J., Heath, A. C., Bucholz, K. K., Dinwiddie, S. H., Madden, P. A., Statham, D. J., et al. (1999). Major depressive disorder in a community-based twin sample: Are there different genetic and environmental contributions for men and women? *Archives of General Psychiatry, 56,* 557–563.

Bies, R. J., Tripp, T. M., & Kramer, R. M. (1997). At the breaking point: Cognitive and social dynamics of revenge in organizations. In R. A. Giacalone & J. Greenberg (Eds.), *Antisocial behavior in organizations* (pp. 18–36). Thousand Oaks, CA: Sage.

Bigelow, A., MacLean, J., Wood, C., & Smith, J. (1990). Infants' responses to child and adult strangers: An investigation of height and facial configuration variables. *Infant Behavior and Development, 13,* 21–32.

Bigler, R. S., & Liben, L. S. (2007). Developmental intergroup theory: Explaining and reducing children's social stereotyping and prejudice. *Current Directions in Psychological Science, 16,* 162–166.

Biklen, D. (1990). Communication unbound: Autism and praxis. *Harvard Educational Review, 60,* 290–314.

Billing, J., & Sherman, P. W. (1998). Antimicrobial functions of spices: Why some like it hot. *Quarterly Review of Biology, 73,* 3–49.

Binet, A., & Simon, T. (1905). Methodes nouvelles pour le diagnostic du niveau intellectuel des anormaux. *L'Annee Psychologique, 11,* 191–244.

Bingenheimer, J. B., Brennan, R. T., & Earls, F. J. (2005). Firearm violence exposure and serious violent behavior. *Science, 308,* 1323–1326.

Binson, D., Michaels, S., Stall, R., Coates, T. J., Gagnon, J. H., & Catania, J. A. (1995). Prevalence and social distribution of men who have sex with men: United States and its urban centers. *Journal of Sex Research, 32*(3), 245–254.

Birch, H. G. (1945). The relation of previous experience to insightful problem solving. *Journal of Comparative Psychology, 38,* 367–383.

Birch, L. L., Fisher, J. O., Grimm-Thomas, K., Markey, C. N., Sawyer, R., & Johnson, S. L. (2001). Confirmatory factor analysis of the Child Feeding Questionnaire: A measure of parental attitudes, beliefs and practices about child feeding and obesity proneness. *Appetite, 36,* 201–210.

Birch, L. L., McPhee, L., Sullivan, S., & Johnson, S. (1989). Conditioned meal initiation in young children. *Appetite, 13,* 105–113.

Birnbaum, G. E., Reis, H. T., Mikulincer, M., Gillath, O., & Orpaz, A. (2006). When sex is more than just sex: Attachment orientations, sexual experience, and relationship quality. *Journal of Personality & Social Psychology, 91,* 929–943.

Bisiach, E., Capitani, E., & Tansini, E. (1979). Detection from left and right hemifields on single and double simultaneous stimulation. *Perceptual and Motor Skills, 48*(3, Pt. 1), 960.

Bisiach, E., Luzzatti, C., & Perani, D. (1979). Unilateral neglect, representational schema and consciousness. *Brain, 102*(3), 609–618.

Bisiach, E., Vallar, G., Perani, D., Papagano, C., & Berti, A. (1986). Unawareness of disease following lesions of the right hemisphere: Anosognosia for hemiplegia and anosognosia for hemianopia. *Neuropsychologia, 24,* 471–482.

Bjil, R. V., de Graaf, R., Hiripi, E., Kessler, R. C., Kohn, R., Offord, D. R., et al. (2003). The prevalence of treated and untreated mental disorders in five countries. *Health Affairs, 22,* 122–133.

Bjork, R. A. (1999). Assessing our own competence: Heuristics and illusions. In D. Gopher & A. Koriat (Eds.), *Attention and performance XVII. Cognitive regulation of performance: Interaction of theory and application* (pp. 435–459). Cambridge: MIT Press.

Bjork, R. A. (2001, March). How to succeed in college: Learn how to learn. *American Psychological Society Observer, 14,* 9.

Bjork, R. A., & Linn, M. C. (2006). The science of learning and the learning of science. *APS Observer, 19,* 29, 39.

Bjorklund, D. F., & Green, B. L. (1992). The adaptive nature of cognitive immaturity. *American Psychologist, 47,* 46–54.

Bjorklund, P. (2006). No man's land: Gender bias and social constructivism in the diagnosis of borderline personality disorder. *Issues in Mental Health Nursing, 27,* 3–23.

Black, J. E., & Greenough, W. T. (1991). Developmental approaches to the memory process. In J. L. Martinez & R. P. Kesner (Eds.), *Learning and memory: A biological view* (2nd ed.). San Diego: Academic Press.

Blackwood, D. H. R., Visscher, P. M., & Muir, W. J. (2001). Genetic studies of bipolar affective disorder in large families. *British Journal of Psychiatry, 178*(Suppl. 14), 134–136.

Blagrove, M. (1996). Problems with the cognitive psychological modeling of dreaming. *Journal of Mind and Behavior, 17,* 99–134.

Blair, I. V., Judd, C. M., & Fallman, J. L. (2004). The automaticity of race and Afrocentric facial features in social judgments. *Journal of Personality and Social Psychology, 87,* 763–778.

Blair, P. S., Sidebotham, P., Berry, P. J., Evans, M., & Fleming P. J. (2006). Major epidemiological changes in sudden infant death syndrome: A 20-year population-based study in the UK. *Lancet, 367,* 314–319.

Blair-West, G. W., Cantor, C. H., Mellsop, G. W., & Eyeson-Annan, M. L. (1999). Lifetime suicide risk in major depression: Sex and age determinants. *Journal of Affective Disorders, 53,* 171–178.

Blaisdell, A. P., Sawa, K., & Leising, K. J. (2006). Causal reasoning in rats. *Science, 311,* 1020–1022.

Blake, J., & de Boysson-Bardies, B. (1992). Patterns in babbling: A cross-linguistic study. *Journal of Child Language, 19,* 51–74.

Blake, R. (1998). What can be "perceived" in the absence of visual awareness? *Current Directions in Psychological Science, 6,* 157–162.

Blakemore, S. J., Wolpert, D., & Frith, C. (2000). Why can't you tickle yourself? *Neuroreport, 11,* R-11–R-16.

Blakeslee, S. (2001, August 28). Therapies push injured brains and spinal cords into new paths. *New York Times.* Retrieved July 28, 2003, from http://www.nytimes.com/2001./08/28/health/anatomy/28REHA.html

Blakeslee, S. (2002, September 22). Exercising toward repair of the spinal cord. *The New York Times,* p. 36.

Blascovich, J., Spencer, S. J., Quinn, D., & Steele, C. (2001). African Americans and high blood pressure: The role of stereotype threat. *Psychological Science, 12,* 225–229.

Blass, T. (1991). Understanding behavior in the Milgram obedience experiment: The role of personality, situations, and their interactions. *Journal of Personality and Social Psychology, 60,* 398–413.

Blass, T. (2000). The Milgram paradigm 35 years later: Some things we know about obedience to authority. In T. Blass (Ed.), *Current perspectives on the Milgram paradigm* (pp. 35–59). Mahwah, NJ: Erlbaum.

Blass, T. (2004). *The man who shocked the world: The life and legacy of Stanley Milgram.* New York: Basic Books.

Blass, T., & Schmitt, C. (2001). The nature of perceived authority in the Milgram paradigm: Two replications. *Current Psychology: Developmental, Learning, Personality, Social, 20,* 115–121.

Blatchford, P., Burke, J., Farquhar, C., & Plewis, I. (1989). Teacher expectations in infant school: Associations with attainment and progress, curriculum coverage and classroom interaction. *British Journal of Educational Psychology, 59,* 19–30.

Bleck, T. P., & Klawans, H. L. (1986). Neurologic emergencies. *Medical Clinics of North America, 70*(5), 1167–1184.

Bleil, M. E., McCaffery, J. M., Muldoon, M. F., Sutton-Tyrrell, K., & Manuck, S. B. (2004). Anger-related personality traits and carotid artery atherosclerosis in untreated hypertensive men. *Psychosomatic Medicine, 66,* 633–639.

Block, J. (2001). Millennial contrarianism: The Five-Factor approach to personality description 5 years later. *Journal of Research in Personality, 35,* 98–107.

Block, J. A. (1971). *Lives through time.* Berkeley: Bancroft Books.

Block, R. I., & Ghoneim, M. M. (1993). Effects of chronic marijuana use on human cognition. *Psychopharmacology, 110*(1–2), 219–228.

Blood, A. J., & Zatorre, R. J. (2001). Intensely pleasurable responses to music correlate with activity in brain regions implicated in reward and emotion. *Proceedings of the National Academy of Science, 98,* 11818–11823.

Bloom, L. (1995). *The transition from infancy to language: Acquiring the power of expression.* New York: Cambridge University Press.

Blow, A. J., & Timm, T. M. (2002). Promoting community through family therapy: Helping clients develop a network of significant social relationships. *Journal of Systematic Therapies, 21,* 67–89.

Blum, R. W., Beuhring, T., & Rinehart, P. M. (2000). *Protecting teens: Beyond race, income and family structure.* Minneapolis, MN: Center for Adolescent Health, University of Minnesota.

Blumberg, H. P., Leung, H.-C., Skudlarski, P., Lacadie, C. M., Fredericks, C. A., Harris, B. C., et al. (2003). A functional magnetic resonance imaging study of bipolar disorder: State- and trait-related dysfunction in ventral prefrontal cortices. *Archives of General Psychiatry, 60,* 601–609.

Blumberg, M. S., & Lucas, D. E. (1994). Dual mechanisms of twitching during sleep in neonatal rats. *Behavioral Neuroscience, 108*(6), 1196–1202.

Blume, E. S. (1998). *Secret survivors: Uncovering incest and its aftereffects in women.* New York: Ballantine.

Blumenthal, J. A., Babyak, M., Wei., J., O'Conner, C., Waugh, R., Eisenstein, E., et al. (2002). Usefulness of psychosocial treatment of mental stress-induced myocardial ischemia in men. *American Journal of Cardiology, 89,* 164–168.

Blundell, J. E., & Cooling, J. (2000). Routes to obesity: Phenotypes, food choices, and activity. *British Journal of Nutrition, 83,* S33–S38.

Blustein, D. L., Ellis, M. E., & Devenis, L. D. (1989). The development and validation of a two-dimensional model of the commitment to career choices process. *Journal of Vocational Behavior, 35,* 342–378.

Boake, C., Yeates, K. O., & Donders, J. (2002). Association of postdoctoral programs in clinical neuropsychology: Update and new directions. *Clinical Neuropsychology, 16*(1), 1–6.

Boardman, A. P., & Healy, D. (2001). Modeling suicide risk in affective disorders. *European Psychiatry, 16,* 400–405.

Bobko, P., Roth, P. L., & Potosky, D. (1999). Derivation and implications of a meta-analytic matrix incorporating cognitive ability, alternative predictors, and job performance. *Personnel Psychology, 52,* 561–590.

Bockting, C. L. H., Schene, A. H., Spinhoven, P., Koeter, M. W. J., Wouters, L. F., Huyser, J., et al. (2005). Preventing relapse/recurrence in recurrent depression with cognitive therapy: A randomized controlled trial. *Journal of Consulting and Clinical Psychology, 73,* 647–657.

Boden, M. A. (2006). *Computer models of mind.* Cambridge, UK: Cambridge University Press.

Boden-Albala, B., Litwak, E., Elkind, M. S., Rundek, T., & Sacco, R. L. (2005). Social isolation and outcomes post stroke. *Neurology, 64,* 1888–1892.

Boehning, D., & Snyder, S. H. (2003). Novel neural modulators. *Annual Review of Neuroscience, 26,* 105–131.

Bogaert, A. F. (2003). Number of older brothers and social orientation: New tests and the attraction/behavior distinction in two national probability samples. *Journal of Personality and Social Psychology, 84,* 644–652.

Bogaert, A. F. (2006). Biological versus nonbiological older brothers and men's sexual orientation. *Proceedings of the National Academy of Sciences, 103,* 10771–10774.

Bogartz, R. S., Shinskey, J. L., & Speaker, C. J. (1997). Interpreting infant looking: The event set x event set design. *Developmental Psychology, 33,* 408–422.

Bogen, J. E. (1995). On the neurophysiology of consciousness: I. An overview. *Consciousness and Cognition, 4,* 52–62.

Boggs, C. C., Morey, L. C., Skodol, A. E., Shea, M. T., & Sanislow, C. A. (2005). Differential impairment as an indicator of sex bias in DSM-IV criteria for four personality disorders. *Psychological Assessment, 17,* 492–496.

Bohner, G., & Schwarz, N. (2001). Attitudes persuasion and behavior. In A. Tesser & N. Schwarz (Eds.), *Blackwell handbook of social psychology: Intraindividual processes* (pp. 413–435). Oxford, UK: Blackwell.

Boles, D. B. (2005). A large-sample study of sex differences in functional cerebral lateralization. *Journal of Clinical and Experimental Neuropsychology: Official Journal of the International Neuropsychological Society, 27,* 759–768.

Bolger, K. E., & Patterson, C. J. (2001). Developmental pathways from child maltreatment to peer rejection. *Child Development, 72,* 549–568.

Bolla, K. I., Brown, K., Eldreth, D., Tate, K. & Cadet, J. L. (2002). Dose-related neurocognitive effects of marijuana use. *Neurology, 59,* 1337–1343.

Bolton, D., Eley, T. C., O'Connor, T. G., Perrin, S., Rabe-Hesketh, S., & et al. (2006). Prevalence and genetic and environmental influences on anxiety disorders in 6-year-old twins. *Psychological Medicine, 36,* 335–344.

Bonanno, G. A. (2004). Loss, trauma, and human resilience: Have we underestimated the human capacity to thrive after extremely aversive events? *American Psychologist, 59,* 20–28.

Bonanno, G. A. (2005). Resilience in the face of potential trauma. *Current Directions in Psychological Science, 14,* 135–138.

Bonci, A., Bernardi, G., Grillner, P., & Mercuri, N. B. (2003). The dopamine-containing neuron: Maestro or simple musician in the orchestra of addiction? *Trends in Pharmacological Science, 24,* 172–177.

Bond, F. W., & Bunce, D. (2003). The role of acceptance and job control in mental health, job satisfaction, and work performance. *Journal of Applied Psychology, 88,* 1057–1067.

Bond, G., Aiken, L., & Somerville, S. (1992). The Health Beliefs Model and adolescents with insulin-dependent diabetes mellitus. *Health Psychology, 11,* 190–198.

Boniecki, K. A. & Moore, S. (2003). Breaking the silence: Using a token economy to reinforce classroom participation. *Teaching of Psychology, 30,* 224–227.

Bonk, V. A., France, C. R., & Taylor, B. K. (2001). Distraction reduces self-reported physiological reactions to blood donation in novice donors with a blunting coping style. *Journal of Psychosomatic Medicine, 63,* 447–452.

Bonner, R. (2001, August 24). Death row inmate is freed after DNA test clears him. *The New York Times.*

Bonwell, C. C., & Eison, J. A. (1991). *Active learning: Creating excitement in the classroom.* Washington, DC: George Washington University.

Booth, C. B., Clarke-Stewart, K. A., Vandell, D. L., McCartney, K., & Owen, M. T. (2002). Child-care usage and mother-infant "quality time." *Journal of Marriage and the Family, 64,* 16–26.

Bordnick, P. S., Elkins, R. L., Orr, T. E., Walters, P., & Thyer, B. A. (2004). Evaluating the relative effectiveness of three aversion therapies designed to reduce craving among cocaine abusers. *Behavioral Interventions, 19,* 1–24.

Borg, M. B., Jr. (2002). The Avalon Garden men's association: A community health psychology case study. *Journal of Health Psychology, 7,* 345–357.

Borgida, E., Conner, C., & Monteufel, L. (1992). Understanding living kidney donors: A behavioral decision-making perspective. In S. Spacapan & S. Oskamp (Eds.), *Helping and being helped* (pp. 183–212). Newbury Park, CA: Sage.

Borkenau, P., Mauer, N., Riemann, R., Spinath, F. M., & Angleitner, A. (2004). Thin slices of behavior as cues of personality and intelligence. *Journal of Personality and Social Psychology, 86,* 599–614.

Borkenau, P., Riemann, R., Angleitner, A., & Spinath, F. M. (2002). Similarity of childhood experiences and personality resemblance in monozygotic and dizygotic twins: A test of the equal environments assumption. *Personality & Individual Differences, 33,* 261–269.

Borkman, T. J. (1997). A selected look at self-help groups in the U.S. *Health and Social Care in the Community, 5,* 357–364.

Borman, W. C., Hanson, M. A., & Hedge, J. W. (1997). Personnel selection. *Annual Review of Psychology, 48,* 299–337.

Borman, W. C., Penner, L. A., Allen T. D. & Motowidlo, S. (2001). Personality predictors of citizenship performance. *International Journal of Selection and Assessment, 9,* 52–69.

Borry, P., Schotsmans, P., & Dierickx, K. (2006). Evidence-based medicine and its role in ethical decision-making. *Journal of Evaluation in Clinical Practice, 12,* 306–311.

Borzekowski, D. L., & Robinson, T. N. (2005). The remote, the mouse, and the no. 2 pencil: The household media environment and academic achievement among third grade students. *Archives of Pediatrics & Adolescent Medicine, 159,* 607–613.

Bosma, H., Marmot, M. G., Hemingway, H., Nicholson, A. C., Brunner, E., & Stansfeld, S. A. (1997). Low job control and risk of coronary heart disease in Whitehall II (prospective cohort) study. *British Medical Journal, 314,* 558–565.

Bosompra, K., Ashikaga, T., Worden, J. K., & Flynn, B. S. (2001). Is more optimism associated with better health? Findings from a population-based survey. *International Quarterly of Community Health Education, 20,* 29–58.

Botwinick, J. (1961). Husband and father-in-law: A reversible figure. *American Journal of Psychology, 74,* 312–313.

Botwinick, J. (1966). Cautiousness in advanced age. *Journal of Gerontology, 21,* 347–353.

Botwinick, J. (1977). Intellectual abilities. In J. E. Birren & K. W. Schaie (Eds.), *Handbook of the psychology of aging.* New York: Van Nostrand Reinhold.

Bouchard, L., Tremblay, A., Bouchard, C., & Perusse, L. (2007). Contribution of several candidate gene polymorphisms in the determination of adiposity changes: Results from the Quebec family study. *International Journal of Obesity, 31,* 891–899.

Bouchard, T. J., Jr. (2004). Genetic influence on human psychological traits: A survey. *Current Directions in Psychological Science, 13,* 148–151.

Bouchard, T. J., Jr., & Pedersen, N. (1999). Twins reared apart: Nature's double experiment. In M. C. LaBuda & E. L. Grigorenko (Eds.), *On the way to individuality: Current methodological issues in behavioral genetics* (pp. 71–93). Hauppauge, NY: Nova Science.

Bourassa, M., & Vaugeois, P. (2001). Effects of marijuana use on divergent thinking. *Creativity Research Journal, 13,* 411–416.

Bouret, S. G., Draper, S. J., & Simerly, R. B. (2004). Trophic action of leptin on hypothalamic neurons that regulate feeding. *Science, 304,* 108–110.

Bouton, M. E. (2000). A learning theory perspective on lapse, relapse, and the maintenance of behavior change. *Health Psychology, 19,* 57–63.

Bouton, M. E. (2002). Context, ambiguity, and unlearning: Sources of relapse after behavioral extinction. *Biological Psychiatry, 52,* 976–986.

Bouton, M., Mineka, S., & Barlow, D. (2001). A modern learning theory perspective on the etiology of panic disorder. *Psychological Review, 107,* 4–32.

Bowden, C. L. (2000). Efficacy of lithium in mania and maintenance therapy of bipolar disorder. *Journal of Clinical Psychiatry, 61,* 35–40.

Bowden, C. L., Calabrese, J. R., Sachs, G., Yatham, L. N., Asghar, S. A., Hompland, M., et al. (2003). A placebo-controlled 18-month trial of lamotrigine and lithium maintenance treatment in recently manic or hypomanic patients with bipolar I disorder. *Archives of General Psychiatry, 60,* 392–400.

Bower, G. H. (1975). Cognitive psychology: An introduction. In W. K. Estes (Ed.), *Handbook of learning and cognitive processes* (Vol. 1, pp. 25–80). Hillsdale, NJ: Erlbaum.

Bowerman, M. (1996). The origins of children's spatial semantic categories: Cognitive versus linguistic determinants. In J. J. Gumperz & S. C. Levinson (Eds.), *Rethinking linguistic relativity: Studies in the social and cultural foundations of language* (No. 17, pp. 145–176). Cambridge: Cambridge University Press.

Bowlby, J. (1951). *Maternal care and mental health.* Geneva: World Health Organization.

Bowlby, J. (1973). *Attachment and loss: Vol. 2. Separation.* New York: Basic Books.

Bowlby, J. (1980). *Loss: Sadness and depression.* New York: Basic Books.

Bowman, E. S., & Nurnberger, J. I. (1993). Genetics of psychiatry diagnosis and treatment. In D. L. Dummer (Ed.), *Current psychiatric therapy* (pp. 46–56). Philadelphia: Saunders.

Boxer, A. L., & Miller, B. L. (2005). Clinical features of frontotemporal dementia. *Alzheimer Disease and Associated Disorders, 19* (Suppl. 1), S3–S6.

Boyd, S. T. (2006). The endocannabinoid system. *Pharmacotherapy, 26*(12 Pt. 2), 218S–221S.

Boyer, J. L., Harrison, S., & Ro, T. (2005). Unconscious processing of orientation and color without primary visual cortex. *Proceedings of the National Academy of Sciences of the USA, 102,* 16875–16879.

Boyle, S. H., Williams, R. B., Mark, D. B., Brummett, B. H., Siegler, I. C., Helms, M. J., & Barefoot, J. C. (2004). Hostility as a predictor of survival in patients with coronary artery disease. *Psychosomatic Medicine, 66,* 629–632.

Bozarth, M. A., & Wise, R. A. (1984). Anatomically distinct opiate receptor fields mediate reward and physical dependence. *Science, 224,* 516–518.

Brach, J. S., FitzGerald, S., Newman, A. B., Kelsey, S., Kuller, L., VanSwearingen, J. M., & Kriska, A. M. (2003). Physical activity and functional status in community-dwelling older women. *Archives of Internal Medicine, 163,* 2565–2571.

Bracha, H. S. (2006). Human brain evolution and the "neuroevolutionary time-depth principle": Implication for the reclassification of fear-circuitry-related tratins in DSM-V and for studying resilience to war zone-related posttraumatic stress disorder. *Progress in Neuro-Psychopharmacology & Biological Psychiatry, 30,* 827–853.

Bracken, B. A., & McCallum, R. S. (1998). *Universal Nonverbal Intelligence Test (UNIT).* Boston: Riverside.

Bradley, R., Greene, J., Russ, E., Dutra, L., & Westen, D. (2005). A multidimensional meta-analysis of psychotherapy for PTSD. *American Journal of Psychiatry, 162,* 214–227.

Bradley, R., Heim, A. K., & Westen, D. (2005). Transference patterns in the psychotherapy of personality disorders: Empirical investigation. *British Journal of Psychiatry, 186,* 342–349.

Bradley-Johnson, S., Graham, D. P., & Johnson, C. M. (1986). Token reinforcement on WISC-R performance for white, low-socioeconomic, upper and lower elementary-school-age students. *Journal of School Psychology, 24,* 73–79.

Brainerd, C. J., & Reyna, V. F. (2005). *The science of false memory.* New York: Oxford University Press.

Brainerd, C. J., Reyna, V. F., Wright, R., & Mojardin, A. H. (2003). Recollection rejection: False memory editing in children and adults. *Psychological Review, 110,* 762–784.

Brambilla, P., Cipriani, A., Hotopf, M., & Barbul, C. (2005). Side-effect profile of fluoxetine in comparison with other SSRIs, tricyclic, and newer antidepressants: A meta-analysis of clinical trial data. *Pharmacopsychiatry, 38,* 69–77.

Brandimonte, M. A., Hitch, G. J., & Bishop, D. V. M. (1992). Influence of short-term memory codes on visual image processing: Evidence from image transformation tasks. *Journal of Experimental Psychology: Learning, Memory, and Cognition, 18,* 157–165.

Brandtstadter, J., & Renner, G. (1990). Tenacious goal pursuit and flexible goal adjustment: Explication and age-related analysis of assimilative and accommodative strategies of coping. *Psychology and Aging, 5,* 58–67.

Brannick, M., & Levine, E. (2002). *Job analysis.* Thousand Oaks: CA: Sage.

Bransford, J. D., & Johnson, M. K. (1972). Contextual prerequisites for understanding: Some investigations of comprehension and recall. *Journal of Verbal Learning and Verbal Behavior, 11,* 717–726.

Bransford, J. D., & Stein, B. S. (1993). *The ideal problem solver* (2nd ed.). New York: Freeman.

Brasher, E. E., & Chen, P. Y. (1999). Evaluation of success criteria in job search: A process perspective. *Journal of Occupational and Organizational Psychology, 72,* 57–70.

Braun, A. E., Balkin, T. J., & Wesensten, N. J. (1998). Dissociated pattern of activity in visual cortices and their projections during human rapid eye movement sleep. *Science, 279,* 91–95.

Braunstein, G. D., Sundwall, D. A., Katz, M., Shifren, J. L., Buster, J. E., Simon, J. A., et al. (2005). Safety and efficacy of a testosterone patch for the treatment of hypoactive sexual desire disorder in surgically menopausal women: A randomized, placebo-controlled trial. *Archives of Internal Medicine, 165,* 1582–1589.

Bray, G. A., & Tartaglia, L. A. (2000). Medicinal strategies in the treatment of obesity. *Nature, 404,* 672–677.

Bredt, D. S., & Nicoll, R. A. (2003). AMPA receptor trafficking at excitatory synapses. *Neuron, 40,* 361–379.

Breed, A. G. (2006, January 28). Stress from Katrina is called "recipe for suicide." *Naples Daily News,* p. 4A.

Breedlove, S. M. (1994). Sexual differentiation of the human nervous system. *Annual Review of Psychology, 45,* 389–418.

Breggin, P. R. (1997). *Brain-disabling treatments in psychiatry : Drugs, electroshock, and the role of the FDA.* New York: Springer.

Brehm, S. (1992). *Intimate relationships.* New York: McGraw-Hill.

Brehm, S., Kassin, S., & Fein, S. (2005). *Social psychology* (6th ed.). Boston: Houghton Mifflin.

Breier, J. I., Adair, J. C., Gold, M., Fennell, E. B., Gilmore, R. L., & Heilman, K. M. (1995). Dissociation of anosognosia for hemiplegia and aphasia during left-hemisphere anesthesia. *Neurology, 45,* 65–67.

Brelsford, J. W. (1993). Physics education in a virtual environment. In *Proceedings of the 37th Annual Meeting of the Human Factors and Ergonomics Society.* Santa Monica, CA: Human Factors.

Bremner, J. D., Shobe, K. K., & Kihlstrom, J. F. (2000). False memories in women with self-reported childhood sexual abuse. *Psychological Science, 11,* 333–337.

Bremner, J. D., Vythilingam, M., Vermetten, E., Southwick, S. M., McGlashan, T., Nazeer, A., et al. (2003). MRI and PET study of deficits in hippocampal structure and function in women with childhood sexual abuse and posttraumatic stress disorder. *American Journal of Psychiatry, 160,* 924–932.

Bremner, J. D., Vythilingam, M., Vermetten, E., Vaccarino, V., & Charney, D. S. (2004). Deficits in hippocampal and anterior cingulate functioning during verbal declarative memory encoding in midlife major depression. *American Journal of Psychiatry, 161,* 637–645.

Brems, C., & Namyniuk, L. (2002). The relationship of childhood abuse history and substance use in an Alaska Sample. *Substance Use and Misuse, 37,* 473–494.

Brendgen, M., Dionne, G., Girard, A., Boivin, M., Vitaro, F., & Pérusse, D. (2005). Examining genetic and environmental effects on social aggression: A study of 6-year-old twins. *Child Development, 76,* 930–946.

Brener, N. D., Hassan, S. S., & Barrios, L. C. (1999). Suicidal ideation among college students in the United States. *Journal of Consulting and Clinical Psychology, 67,* 1004–1008.

Brenes, G. A., Rapp, S. R., Rejeski, W. J., & Miller, M. E. (2002). Do optimism and pessimism predict physical functioning? *Journal of Behavioral Medicine, 25,* 219–231.

Brennan, F. X. & Charnetski, C. J. (2000). Explanatory style and Immunoglobulin A (IgA). *Integrative Physiological & Behavioral Science, 35,* 251–255.

Brennen, T., Baguley, T., Bright, J., & Bruce, V. (1990). Resolving semantically induced tip-of-the-tongue states for proper nouns. *Memory & Cognition, 18,* 339–347.

Brenner, L., & Ritter, R. C. (1995). Peptide cholecystokinin receptor antagonist increases food intake in rats. *Appetite, 24,* 1–9.

Brenner, R. P. (2005). The interpretation of the EEG in stupor and coma. *Neurologist, 11*(5), 271–284.

Breslau, N., Lucia, V. C., & Alvarado, G. F. (2006). Intelligence and other predisposing factors in exposure to trauma and posttraumatic stress disorder: A follow-up study at age 17 years. *Archives of General Psychiatry, 63,* 1238–1245.

Breslau, N., Reboussin, B. A., Anthony, J. C., & Storr, C. L. (2005). The structure of posttraumatic stress disorder: Latent class analysis in 2 community samples. *Archives of General Psychiatry, 62,* 1343–1351.

Breslin, P. A., & Beauchamp, G. K. (1997). Salt enhances flavour by suppressing bitterness. *Nature, 387,* 563.

Breteler, M. H., Hilberink, S. R., Zeeman, G., & Lammers, S. M. (2004). Compulsive smoking: The development of a Rasch homogeneous scale of nicotine dependence. *Addiction and Behavior, 29,* 199–205.

Breuer, J., & Freud, S. (1974). Studies on hysteria. In J. A. Strachey (Ed. & Trans.), *The Pelican Freud library* (Vol. 3). Harmondsworth, England: Penguin. (Original work published 1895)

Brewer, J. B., Zhao, Z., Desmond, J. E., Glover, G. H., & Gabriel, J. D. E. (1998). Making memories: Brain activity that predicts how well visual experience will be remembered. *Science, 281,* 1185–1187.

Brewer, M. B., & Hewstone, M. (2004). *Self and social identity.* Malden, MA: Blackwell Publishing.

Brewer, M. B., & Pierce, K. P. (2005). Social identity complexity and outgroup tolerance. *Personality and Social Psychology Bulletin, 31,* 428–437.

Brewer, N. T., Chapman, G. B., Gibbons, F. X., Gerrard, M., McCaul, K. D., & Weinstein, N. D. (2007). *Health Psychology, 26,* 136–145.

Brewer, W. F. (1977). Memory for the pragmatic implications of sentences. *Memory & Cognition, 5,* 673–678.

Brewer, W. F., & Treyens, J. C. (1981). Role of schemata in memory for places. *Cognitive Psychology, 13,* 207–230.

Bridge, J. A., Iyengar, S., Salary, C. B., Barbe, R. P., Birmaher, B., Pincus, H. A., et al. (2007). Clinical response and risk for reported suicidal ideation and suicide attempts in pediatric antidepressant treatment: A meta-analysis of randomized controlled trials. *Journal of the American Medical Association, 297,* 1683–1696.

Brigham, C. C. (1923). *A study of American intelligence.* Princeton, NJ: Princeton University Press.

Brigham, C. C. (1930). Intelligence tests of immigrant groups. *Psychological Review, 37,* 158–165.

Bright, J. E. H., Pryor, R. G. L., & Harpham, L. (2005). The role of chance events in career decision making. *Journal of Vocational Behavior, 66,* 561–576.

Brinckerhoff, L. C., Shaw, S. F., & McGuire, J. M. (1993). *Promoting postsecondary education for students with learning disabilities.* Austin, TX: Pro-Ed.

Brinkhaus, B., Witt, C. M., Jena, S., Linde, K., Streng, A., Wagenpfeil, S., et al. (2006). Acupuncture in patients with chronic low back pain: A randomized controlled trial. *Archives of Internal Medicine, 166,* 450–457.

Brislin, R. (1993). *Understanding culture's influence on behavior.* Fort Worth: Harcourt, Brace, Jovanovich.

British Medical Association. (2000). *Acupuncture: Efficacy, safety, and practice.* London: Harwood Academic.

Broadbent, E., Petrie, K. J., Alley, P. G., & Booth, R. J. (2003). Psychological stress impairs early wound repair following surgery. *Psychosomatic Medicine, 65,* 865–869.

Broca, P. (1861). Remargues sur le siege de la faculte de la porle articulee, suives d'une observation d'aphemie (perte de parole). *Bulletin Societie Anatomie, 36,* 330–357.

Broca, P. (1865). Sur la faculté du langage articulé. *Bulletin Societe Anthropologie Paris, 6,* 337–393.

Brock, J. W., Farooqui, S. M., Ross, K. D., & Payne, S. (1994). Stress-related behavior and central norepinephrine concentrations in the REM sleep-deprived rat. *Physiology and Behavior, 55*(6), 997–1003.

Brody, A. L., Mandelkern, M. A., London, E. D., Olmstead, R. E., Farahi, J., Scheibal, D., et al. (2006). Cigarette smoking saturates brain alpha 4 beta 2 nicotinic acetylcholine receptors. *Archives of General Psychiatry, 63,* 907–915.

Brody, G. H. (2004). Siblings' direct and indirect contributions to child development. *Current Directions in Psychological Science, 13,* 124–126.

Brody, J. E. (1998, September 15). Personal health: Teenagers and sex—Younger and more at risk. *New York Times* (Web Archive).

Brody, N. (2003). Construct validation of the Sternberg Triarchic Abilities Test: Comment and reanalysis. *Intelligence, 31,* 319–330.

Brody, N., & Ehrlichman, H. (1998). *Personality psychology: The science of individuality.* Upper Saddle River, NJ: Prentice-Hall.

Brondolo, E., Rieppi, R., Erickson, S. A., Bagiella, E., Shapiro, P. A., McKinley, P., & Sloan, R. P. (2003). Hostility, interpersonal interactions, and ambulatory blood pressure. *Psychosomatic Medicine, 65,* 1003–1011.

Brookmeyer, K. A., Henrich, C. C., & Schwab-Stone, M. (2005). Adolescents who witness community violence: Can parent support and prosocial cognitions protect them from committing violence? *Child Development, 76,* 917–929.

Brooks-Gunn, J., & Chase-Lansdale, P. L. (2002). Adolescent parenthood. In M. H. Bornstein (Ed.), *Handbook of parenting* (2nd ed). Mahwah, NJ: Erlbaum.

Brooks-Gunn, J., Klebanov, P. K., & Duncan, G. J. (1996). Ethnic differences in children's intelligence test scores: Role of economic deprivation, home environment, and maternal characteristics. *Child Development, 67,* 396–408.

Brown, A. L., Campione, J. C., Webber, L. S., & McGilly, K. (1992). Interactive learning environments: A new look at assessment and instruction. In B. Gifford & M. C. O'Connor (Eds.), *Changing assessments: Alternative views of aptitude, achievement, and instruction* (pp. 121–212). Boston: Kluever.

Brown, A. S. (2004). *The déjà vu experience.* New York: Psychology Press.

Brown, A. S., Begg, M. D., Gravenstein, S., Schaefer, C. A., Wyatt, R. J., Bresnahan, M., et al. (2005). Serologic evidence of prenatal influenza in the etiology of schizophrenia. *Obstetrical and Gynecological Survey, 60,* 77–78.

Brown, A. S., & Nix, L. A. (1996). Age-related changes in the tip-of-the-tongue experience. *American Journal of Psychology, 109,* 79–91.

Brown, C. (2003, January 31). The man who mistook his wife for a deer. *The New York Times Magazine.* Retrieved December 13, 2004, from http://query.nytimes.com/gst/abstract.html?res=F10614FB395D0C718CDDAB0894DB404482

Brown, G. K., Beck, A. T., Steer, R. A., & Grisham, J. R. (2000). Risk factors for suicide in psychiatric outpatients: A 20-year prospective study. *Journal of Consulting and Clinical Psychology, 68,* 371–377.

Brown, J. (1958). Some tests of the decay theory of immediate memory. *Quarterly Journal of Experimental Psychology, 10,* 12–21.

Brown, L. M., Bongar, B., & Cleary, K. M. (2004). A profile of psychologists' views of critical risk factors for completed suicide in older adults. *Professional Psychology: Research and Practice, 35,* 90–96.

Brown, R., & Kulik, J. (1977). Flashbulb memories. *Cognition, 5,* 73–99.

Brown, R., & McNeill, D. (1966). The "tip-of-the-tongue" phenomenon. *Journal of Verbal Learning and Verbal Behavior, 5,* 325–337.

Brown, R. A. (1973). *First language.* Cambridge: Harvard University Press.

Brown, S. L., Nesse, R. M., Vinokur, A. D., & Smith, D. M. (2003). Providing social support may be more beneficial than receiving it: Results from a prospective study of mortality. *Psychological Science, 14,* 320–327.

Brown, T., DiNardo, P. A., Lehman, C, & Campbell, L. A. (2001). Reliability of DSM-IV anxiety and mood disorders: Implications for classification of emotional disorders. *Journal of Abnormal Psychology, 110,* 49–58.

Browne, K. D., & Hamilton-Giachritsis, C. (2005). The influence of violent media on children and adolescents: A public health approach. *Lancet, 365,* 702–710.

Brownell, K. D., & Rodin, J. (1994). The dieting maelstrom: Is it possible and advisable to lose weight? *American Psychologist, 49*(9), 781–791.

Broytman, O., & Malter, J. S. (2004). Anti-Abeta: The good, the bad, and the unforeseen. *Journal of Neuroscience Research, 75,* 301–306.

Bruce, D., Dolan, A., & Phillips-Grant, K. (2000). On the transition from childhood amnesia to the recall of personal memories. *Psychological Science, 11,* 360–364.

Bruce, H. M. (1969). Pheromones and behavior in mice. *Acta Neurologica Belgica, 69,* 529–538.

Bruck, M., Cavanagh, P., & Ceci, S. J. (1991). Fortysomething: Recognizing faces at one's 25th reunion. *Memory and Cognition, 19,* 221–228.

Brummett, B. H., Babyak, M. A., Williams, R. B., Barefoot, J. C., Costa, P.T., & Siegler, I. C. (2006). NEO personality domains and gender predict levels and trends in body mass index over 14 years during midlife *Journal of Research in Personality, 40,* 222–236.

Brummett, B. H., Mark, D. B., Siegler, I. C., Williams, R. B., Babyak, M. A., Clapp-Channing, N. E., & Barefoot, J. C. (2005). Perceived social support as a predictor of mortality in coronary patients: Effects of smoking, sedentary behavior, and depressive symptoms. *Psychosomatic Medicine, 67,* 40–45.

Brüning, J. C., Gautam, D., Burks, D. J., Gillette, J., Schubert, M., Orban, P. C., et al. (2000). Role of brain insulin receptor in control of body weight and reproduction. *Science, 289,* 2122–2125.

Brunvald, J. H. (1989). *Curses! Broiled again! The hottest urban legends going.* New York: Norton.

Brush, D. H., Moch, M. K., & Pooyan, A. (1987). Individual demographic differences and job satisfaction. *Journal of Occupational Behaviour, 8,* 139–155.

Bruyer, R. (1991). Covert face recognition in prosopagnosia. *Brain and Cognition, 15,* 223–235.

Bryant, F. B., & Veroff, J. (2006). *The process of savoring: A new model of positive experience.* Mahwah, NJ: Erlbaum.

Bryant, R. A., & Guthrie, R. M. (2005). Maladaptive appraisals as a risk factor for posttraumatic stress. *Psychological Science, 16,* 749–752.

Bryant, R. A., & Mallard, D. (2003). Seeing is believing: The reality of hypnotic hallucinations. *Consciousness and Cognition, 12,* 219–230.

Bryant, R. A., & McConkey, K. M. (1989). Hypnotic blindness: A behavioral and experiential analysis. *Journal of Abnormal Psychology, 98,* 71–77.

Bryson, S. E., & Smith, I. M. (1998). Autism. *Mental Retardation and Developmental Disabilities Research Reviews, 4,* 97–103.

Buccino, G., Vogt, S., Ritzl, A., Fink, G. R., Zilles, K., Freund, H. J., et al. (2004). Neural circuits underlying imitation learning of hand actions: An event-related fMRI study. *Neuron, 42,* 323–334.

Buchsbaum, M. S., Christian, B. T., Lehrer, D. S., Narayanan, T. K., Shi, B., et al. (2006). D2/D3 dopamine receptor binding with (F-18) fallypride in thalamus and cortex of patients with schizophrenia. *Schizophrenia Research, 85,* 232–244.

Buckner, R. L., & Wheeler, M. E. (2001). The cognitive neuroscience of remembering. *Nature Reviews Neuroscience, 2,* 1–12.

Budney, A. J., Hughes, J. R., Moore, B. A., & Novy, P. L. (2001). Marijuana abstinence effects in marijuana smokers maintained in their home environment. *Archives of General Psychiatry, 58,* 917–924.

Budney, A. J., Moore, B. A., Vandrey, R. G., & Hughes, J. R. (2003). The time course and significance of cannabis withdrawal. *Journal of Abnormal Psychology, 112,* 393–402.

Bugental, D. B., & Grusec, J. E. (2006). Socialization processes. In W. Damon & R. M. Lerner (Series Eds.) & N. Eisenberg (Vol. Ed.), *Handbook of child psychology: Vol. 3. Social, emotional, and personality development* (6th ed., pp. 366–428). New York: Wiley.

Bugg, J. M., Zook, N. A., DeLosh, E. E., Davalos, D. B., & Davis, H. P. (2006). Age differences in fluid intelligence: Contributions of general slowing and frontal decline. *Brain and Cognition, 62,* 9–16.

Bui, K.-V. T., Peplau, L. A., & Hill, C. T. (1996). Testing the Rusbult model of relationship commitment and stability in a 15-year study of heterosexual couples. *Personality and Social Psychology Bulletin, 22,* 1244–1257.

Buka, S. L., Shenassa, E. D., & Niaura, R. (2003). Elevated risk of tobacco dependence among offspring of mothers who smoked during pregnancy: A 30-year prospective study. *American Journal of Psychiatry, 160,* 1978–1984.

Bulevich, J. B., Roediger, H. L., Balota, D. A., & Butler, A. C. (2006). Failures to find suppression of episodic memories in the think/no-think paradigm. *Memory and Cognition.*

Bulik, C. M., Sullivan, P. F., Tozzi, F., Furberg, H., Lichtenstein, P., & Pedersen, N. L. (2006). Prevalence, heritability, and prospective risk factors for anorexia nervosa. *Archives of General Psychiatry, 63,* 305–312.

Bulik, C. M., Sullivan, P. F., Wade, T. D., & Kendler, K. S. (2000). Twin studies of eating disorders: A review. *International Journal of Eating Disorders, 27,* 1–20.

Buller, D. J. (2005). *Adapting minds: Evolutionary psychology and the persistent quest for human nature.* Cambridge, MA: MIT Press.

Bullock, T. H., Bennett, M. V., Johnston, D., Josephson, R., Marder, E., & Fields, R. D. (2005). Neuroscience: The neuron doctrine, redux. *Science, 310,* 791–793.

Bullough, V. L. (1995, August). Sex matters. *Scientific American,* pp. 105–106.

Bunde, J., & Suls, J. (2006). A quantitative analysis of the relationship between the Cook-Medley hostility scale and traditional coronary artery disease risk factors. *Health Psychology, 25,* 493–500.

Bunge, S. A., Wendelken, C., Badre, D., & Wagner, A. D. (2005). Analogical reasoning and prefrontal cortex: Evidence for separable retrieval and integration mechanisms. *Cerebral Cortex, 15,* 239–249.

Burchard, R. E. (1992). Coca chewing and diet. *Current Anthropology, 33*(1), 1–24.

Burger, J. M., & Caldwell, D. F. (2003). The effects of monetary incentives and labeling on the foot-in-the-door effect: Evidence for a self-perception process. *Basic and Applied Social Psychology, 25,* 235–241.

Burger, J. M., & Cornelius, T. (2003). Raising the price of agreement: Public commitment and the lowball compliance procedure. *Journal of Applied Social Psychology, 33,* 923–934.

Burger, J. M., & Guadagno, R. E. (2003). Self-concept clarity and the foot-in-the-door procedure. *Basic and Applied Social Psychology, 25,* 79–86.

Burish, T., & Jenkins, R. (1992). Effectiveness of biofeedback and relaxation training in reducing the side effects of cancer chemotherapy. *Health Psychology, 11,* 17–23.

Burleson, B. R., Albrecht, T. L., & Sarason, I. G. (Eds.). (1994). *Communication of social support: Messages, interactions, relationships, and community.* Thousand Oaks, CA: Sage.

Burleson, M. H., Gregory, W. L., & Trevarthen, W. R. (1995). Heterosexual activity: Relationship with ovarian function. *Psychoneuroendocrinology, 20*(4), 405–421.

Burnstein, E., & Branigan, C. (2001). Evolutionary analyses in social-psychology. In A. Tesser & N. Schwarz (Eds.), *Blackwell handbook of social psychology: Intraindividual processes* (pp. 3–21). Oxford, UK: Blackwell.

Burnstein, E., Crandell, C., & Kitayama, S. (1994). Some Neo-Darwinian decision rules for altruism: Weighing cues for inclusive fitness as a function of the biological importance of the decision. *Journal of Personality and Social Psychology, 67,* 773–789.

Burr, D. C., Morrone, C., & Fiorentini, A. (1996). Spatial and temporal properties of infant colour vision. In F. Vital-Durand, J. Atkinson, & O. J. Braddick (Eds.), *Infant vision* (pp. 63–77). Oxford: Oxford University Press.

Burton, A. M., Wilson, S., Cowan, M., & Bruce, V. (1999). Face recognition in poor-quality video: Evidence from security surveillance. *Psychological Science, 10,* 243–248.

Burton, K. D., Lydon, J. E., D'Alessandro, D. U., & Koestner, R. (2006). The differential effects of intrinsic and identified motivation on well-being and performance: Prospective, experimental, and implicit approaches to self-determination theory. *Journal of Personality and Social Psychology, 91,* 750–762.

Bushman, B. J. (1998). Priming effects of media violence on the accessibility of aggressive constructs in memory. *Personality and Social Psychology Bulletin, 24,* 537–545.

Bushman, B. J., & Anderson, C. A. (2001). Media violence and the American public: Scientific facts versus media misinformation. *American Psychologist, 56,* 477–489.

Bushman, B. J., & Anderson, C. A. (2007). Measuring the strength of the effect of violent media on aggression. *American Psychologist, 62,* 253–254.

Bushman, B. J., Bonacci, A. M., Pedersen, W. C., Vasquez, E. A., & Miller, N. (2005). Chewing on it can chew you up: Effects of rumination on triggered displaced aggression. *Journal of Personality and Social Psychology, 88,* 969–983.

Bushman, B. J., & Huesmann, L. R. (2000). Effects of televised violence on aggression. In D. Singer & J. Singer (Eds.), *Handbook of children and the media* (pp. 223–254). Thousand Oaks, CA: Sage.

Bushman, B. J., & Huesmann, L. R. (2001). Effects of televised violence on aggression. In D. G. Singer & J. L. Singer (Eds.), *Handbook of children and the media* (pp. 223–254). Thousand Oaks, CA: Sage.

Bushman, B. J., Wang, M. C., & Anderson, C. A. (2005). Is the curve relating temperature to aggression linear or curvilinear? Assaults and temperature in Minneapolis reexamined. *Journal of Personality and Social Psychology, 89,* 62–66.

Buss, A. H. (1989). Personality as traits. *American Psychologist, 44,* 1378–1388.

Buss, D. M. (2004a). *Evolutionary psychology: The new science of the mind* (2nd ed.). Boston: Allyn & Bacon.

Buss, D. M. (2004b). *The evolution of desire: Strategies of human mating.* New York: Basic Books.

Buss, D. M., & Schmitt, D. P. (1993). Sexual strategies theory: An evolutionary perspective on human mating. *Psychological Review, 100,* 204–232.

Buss, D. M., Abbott, M., Angleitner, A., Biaggio, A., Bianco-Villasenor, A., Bruchon Schweitzer, M., et al. (1990). International preferences in selecting mates. *Journal of Cross-Cultural Psychology, 21,* 5–47.

Büssing, A., & Höge, A. (2004). Aggression and violence against home care workers. *Journal of Occupational Health Psychology, 9,* 206–219.

Bustillo, J. R., Lauriello, J., Horan, W. P., & Keith, S. J. (2001). The psychosocial treatment of schizophrenia: An update. *American Journal of Psychiatry, 158,* 163–175.

Buston, P. M., & Emlen, S. T. (2003). Cognitive processes underlying human mate choice: The relationship between self-perception and mate preference in Western society. Proceedings of the National Academy of Sciences, 100, 8805–8810.

Butcher, J. N. (2004). Personality assessment without borders: Adaptation of the MMPI-2 across cultures. *Journal of Personality Assessment, 83,* 90–104.

Butcher, J. N., & Rouse, S. V. (1996). Personality: Individual differences and clinical assessment. *Annual Review of Psychology, 47,* 87–111.

Butler, A. C., Chapman, J. E., Forman, E. M., & Beck, A. T. (2006). The empirical status of cognitive-behavioral therapy: A review of meta-analyses. *Clinical Psychology Review, 26,* 17–31.

Butler, R. (1998). Information seeking and achievement motivation in middle childhood and adolescence: The role of conceptions of ability. *Developmental Psychology, 35,* 146–163.

Butters, N. (1981). The Wernicke-Korsakoff syndrome: A review of psychological, neuropathological and etiological factors. *Currents in Alcohol, 8,* 205–232.

Buunk, B. P., & Oldersma, F. L. (2001). Social comparisons and close relationships. In G. Fletcher & M. Clark (Eds.), *Blackwell handbook of social psychology: Interpersonal processes* (pp. 388–408). Oxford, UK: Blackwell.

Buunk, B. P., Zurriaga, R., Peiró, J. M., Nauta, A., & Gonsalvez, I. (2005). Social comparisons at work as related to a cooperative social climate and to individual differences in social comparison orientation. *Applied Psychology: An International Review, 54,* 61–80.

Buxhoeveden, D. P., Switala, A. E., Roy, E., Litaker, M., & Casanova, M. F. (2001). Morphological differences between minicolumns in human and nonhuman primate cortex. *American Journal of Physical Anthropology, 115,* 361–371.

Buxton, R. B., Uludag, K., Dubowitz, D. J., & Liu, T. T. (2004). Modeling the hemodynamic response to brain activation. *Neuroimage, 23*(Suppl. 1), S220–233.

Byrne, D., & Nelson, D. (1965). Attraction as a linear function of proportion of positive reinforcements. *Journal of Personality and Social Psychology, 1,* 659–663.

Cabanac, M., & Morrissette, J. (1992). Acute, but not chronic, exercise lowers the body weight set-point in male rats. *Physiology and Behavior, 52,* 1173–1177.

Cabeza, R., & Nyberg, L. (2000). Imaging cognition II: An empirical review of 275 PET and MRI studies. *Journal of Cognitive Neuroscience, 12,* 1–47.

Cabeza, R., Rao, S. M., Wagner, A. D., Mayer, A. R., & Schacter, D. L. (2001). Can medial temporal lobe regions distinguish true from false? An event-related functional MRI study of veridical and illusory recognition memory. *Proceedings of the National Academy of Science, 98,* 4805–4810.

Cabot, P. J. (2001). Immune-derived opioids and peripheral antinociception. *Clinical and Experimental Pharmacology and Physiology, 28,* 230–232.

Cabral, G. A., & Dove Pettit, D. A. (1998). Drugs and immunity: Cannabinoids and their role in decreased resistance to infectious disease. *Journal of Neuroimmunology, 83,* 116–123.

Cacioppo, J. T., Amaral, D. G., Blanchard, J. J., Cameron, J. L., Carter, C. S., Crews, D., et al. (2007) Social neuroscience: Progress and implications for mental health. *Perspectives on Psychological Science, 2,* 99–123.

Cacioppo, J. T. & Berntson, G. G. (Eds.) (2005). *Social neuroscience: Key readings.* New York: Psychology Press.

Cacioppo, J. T., Berntson, G. G., & Petty, R. E. (1997). Persuasion. *Encyclopedia of human biology* (Vol. 6, pp. 679–690). San Diego: Academic Press.

Cacioppo, J. T., Berntson, G. G., Sheridan, J. F., & McClintock, M. K. (2000). Multilevel integrative analyses of human behavior: Social neuroscience and the complementing nature of social and biological approaches. *Psychological Bulletin, 126,* 829–843.

Cacioppo, J. T., Crites, S. L., & Gardner, W. L. (1996). Attitudes to the right: Evaluative processing is associated with lateralized late positive event-related brain potentials. *Personality and Social Psychology Bulletin, 22,* 1205–1219.

Cacioppo, J. T., Gardner, W. L., Berntson, G. G. (1999). The affect system has parallel and integrative processing components: Form follows function. *Journal of Personality and Social Psychology, 76,* 839–855.

Cacioppo, J. T., Malarkey, W. B., Kiecolt-Glaser, J. K., Uchino, B. N., Sgoutas-Emch, S. A., Sheridan, J. F., et al. (1995). Heterogeneity in neuroendocrine and immune responses to brief psychological stressors as a function of autonomic cardiac activation. *Psychosomatic Medicine, 57,* 154–164.

Cacioppo, J. T., Petty, R. E., & Crites, S. L. (1993). Attitude change. In V. S. Ramachandran (Ed.), *Encyclopedia of human behavior* (pp. 261–270). San Diego: Academic Press.

Cacioppo, J. T., Petty, R. E., Feinstein, J. A, Jarvis, W., & Blair, G. (1996). Dispositional differences in cognitive motivation: The life and times of individuals varying in need for cognition. *Psychological Bulletin, 119,* 197–253.

Cacioppo, J. T., Poehlmann, K. M., Kiecolt-Glaser, J. K., Malarkey, W. B., Burleson, M. H., Berntson, G. G., & Glaser, R. (1998). Cellular immune responses to acute stress in female caregivers of dementia patients and matched controls. *Health Psychology, 17,* 182–189.

Cadinu, M., Maass, A., Rosabianca, A., & Kiesner, J. (2005). Why do women underperform under stereotype threat? *Psychological Science, 16,* 572–578.

Cadoret, R. J., Yates, W. R., Troughton, E., Woodworth, G., & Stewart, M. A. (1995). Adoption study demonstrating two genetic pathways to drug abuse. *Archives of General Psychiatry, 52,* 42–52.

Cahill, L., & McGaugh, J. L. (1998). Mechanisms of emotional arousal and lasting declarative memory. *Trends in Neuroscience, 21,* 294–299.

Cahn, B. R., & Polich, J. (2006). Meditation states and traits, EEG, ERP, and neuroimaging studies. *Psychological Bulletin, 132,* 180–211.

Cain, D. J., & Seeman, J. (Eds.). (2002). *Humanistic psychotherapies: Handbook of research and practice.* Washington, DC: APA Books.

Cairns, R. B., Gariepy, J., & Hood, K. E. (1990). Development, microevolution, and social behavior. *Psychological Review, 97,* 49–65.

Calabrese, J. R., Shelton, M. D., Rapport, D. J., Youngstrom, E. A., Jackson, K., Bilali, S., et al. (2005). A 20-month, double-blind, maintenance trial of lithium versus divalproex in rapid-cycling bipolar disorder. *American Journal of Psychiatry, 162,* 2152–2161.

Callen, D. J. A., Black, S. E., Gao, F., Caldwell, C. B., & Szalai, J. P. (2001). Beyond the hippocampus: MRI volumetry confirms widespread limbic atrophy in AD. *Neurology, 57,* 1669–1674.

Cameron, H. A., Tanapat, P., & Gould, E. (1998). Adrenal steroids and N-methyl-D-aspartate receptor activation regulate neurogenesis in the dentate gyrus of adult rats through a common pathway. *Neuroscience, 82,* 349–354.

Campbell, F. A., Pungello, E. P., Miller-Johnson, S., Burchinal, M., & Ramey, C. T. (2001). The development of cognitive and academic abilities: Growth curves from an early childhood educational experiment. *Developmental Psychology, 37,* 231–242.

Campbell, F. A., Tramer, M. R., Carroll, D., Reynolds, D. J., Moore, R. A., & McQuay, H. J. (2001). Are cannabinoids an effective and safe treatment option in the management of pain? A qualitative systematic review. *British Medical Journal, 323,* 13–16.

Campbell, R. S., & Pennebaker, J. W. (2003). The secret life of pronouns: Flexibility in writing style and physical health. *Psychological Science, 14,* 60–65.

Campbell, S. B. (1986). Developmental issues. In R. Gittelman (Ed.), *Anxiety disorders of childhood* (pp. 24–57). New York: Guilford.

Campion, M. A., & Campion, J. E. (1987). Evaluation of an interviewee skills training program in a natural field experiment. *Personnel Psychology, 40,* 676–691.

Campione, J. C., Brown, A. L., & Ferrara, R. A. (1982). Mental retardation and intelligence. In R. J. Sternberg (Ed.), *Handbook of human intelligence* (pp. 392–490). Cambridge: Cambridge University Press.

Campos, J. J. (1980). Human emotions: Their new importance and their role in social referencing. *Research and Clinical Center for Child Development, 1980–81 Annual Report,* 1–7.

Campos, J. J., Frankel, C. B., & Camras, L. (2004). On the nature of emotion regulation. *Child Development, 75,* 377–394.

Campos, L., & Alonso-Quecuty, M. L. (2006). Remembering a criminal conversation: Beyond eyewitness testimony. *Memory, 14,* 27–36.

Candia, V., Rosset-Llobet, J., Elbert, T., & Pascual-Leone, A. (2005). Changing the brain through therapy for musicians' hand dystonia. *Annals of the New York Academy of Sciences, 1060,* 335–342.

Canli, T., Qui, M., Omura, K., Congdon, E., Haas, B. W., Amin, Z., et al. (2006). Neural correlates of epigenesist. *Proceedings of the National Academy of Sciences, 103,* 16033–16038.

Cann, A., & Ross, D. A. (1989). Olfactory stimuli as context cues in human memory. *American Journal of Psychology, 102,* 91–102.

Cannon, C. P. (2005). The endocannabinoid system: A new approach to control cardiovascular disease. *Clinical Cornerstone, 7(2–3),* 17–26.

Cannon, T. D., Mednick, S. A., Parnas, J., Schulsinger, F., Praestholm, J., & Vestergaard, A. (1993). Developmental brain abnormalities in the offspring of schizophrenic mothers. *Archives of General Psychiatry, 50,* 551–564.

Cannon, T. D., Zorrilla, L. E., Shtasel, D., Gur, R. E., Gur, R. C., Marco, E. J., Moberg, P., & Price, A. (1994). Neuropsychological functioning in siblings discordant for schizophrenia and healthy volunteers. *Archives of General Psychiatry, 51,* 651–661.

Cannon, W. B. (1987). The James-Lange theory of emotions: A critical examination and an alternative theory. Special issue: 100 years of the American Journal of Psychology. *American Journal of Psychology, 100(3–4),* 567–586. (Original work published 1927)

Cannon, W. B., & Washburn, A. L. (1912). An explanation of hunger. *American Journal of Physiology, 29,* 444–454.

Cantor-Graae, E., & Selten, J.-P. (2005). Schizophrenia and migration: A meta-analysis and review. *American Journal of Psychiatry, 162,* 2–24.

Caplan, D. (2003a). Aphasic syndromes. In K. M. Heilman & E. Valenstein (Eds.), *Clinical neuropsychology* (4th ed.). New York: Oxford.

Caplan, D. (2003b). Syntactic aspects of language disorders. In K. M. Heilman & E. Valenstein (Eds.), *Clinical neuropsychology* (4th ed.). New York: Oxford University Press.

Caplan, L. R. (2004). Clinical diagnosis of patients with cerebrovascular disease. *Primary Care, 31(1),* 95–109.

Caplan, L. R. (2005). Stroke. *Review of Neurological Disorders, 2,* 223–225.

Caplan, P. J. (1995). *They say you're crazy. How the world's most powerful psychiatrists decide who's normal.* Reading, MA: Addison-Wesley.

Capriani, A., Pretty, H., Hawton, K., & Geddes, J. R. (2005). Lithium in the prevention of suicidal behavior and all-cause mortality in patients with mood disorders: A systematic review of randomized trials. *American Journal of Psychiatry, 162,* 1805–1819.

Capron, C., & Duyme, M. (1989). Assessment of effects of socio-economic status on IQ in a full cross-fostering study. *Nature, 340,* 552–553.

Capron, C., & Duyme, M. (1996). Effect of socioeconomic status of biological and adoptive parents on WISC-R subtest scores of their French adopted children. *Intelligence, 22,* 259–276.

Caramazza, A., & Hillis, A. E. (1991). Lexical organization of nouns and verbs in the brain. *Nature, 349,* 788–790.

Cardemil, E. V., Reivich, K. J., & Seligman, M. E. P. (2002). The prevention of depressive symptoms in low-income minority middle school students [Electronic version]. *Prevention and Treatment, 5.*

Cardinali, D. P., Bortman, G. P., Liotta, G., Perez Lloret, S., Albornoz, L.E., Cutrera, R.A., et al. (2002). A multifactorial approach employing melatonin to accelerate resynchronization of sleep-wake cycle after a 12 time-zone westerly transmeridian flight in elite soccer athletes. *Journal of Pineal Research, 32,* 41–46.

Cardon, L. R., & Fulker, D. W. (1993). Genetics of specific cognitive abilities. In R. Plomin, & G. McClearn (Eds.), *Nature, nurture, and psychology* (pp. 99–120). Washington, DC: American Psychological Association.

Cardon, L. R., Fulker, D. W., DeFries, J. C., & Plomin, R. (1992). Multivariate genetic analysis of specific cognitive abilities in the Colorado Adoption Project at age 7. *Intelligence, 16,* 383–400.

Cardon, L. R., Smith, S. D., Fulker, D. W., Kimberling, W. J., Pennington, B. F., & DeFries, J. C. (1994). Quantitative trait locus for reading disability on chromosome 6. *Science, 266,* 276–279.

Carey, M. P., Carey, K. B., Maisto, S. A., Gordon, C. M., Schroeder, K. E. E., & Vanable, P. A. (2004). Reducing HIV-risk behavior among adults receiving outpatient psychiatric treatment: Results from a randomized controlled trial. *Journal of Consulting and Clinical Psychology, 72,* 252–268.

Carli, L. L. (1999). Cognitive reconstruction, hindsight, and reactions to victims and perpetrators. *Personality and Social Psychology Bulletin, 25,* 966–979.

Carli, L. L., Ganley, R., & Pierce-Otay, A. (1991). Similarity and satisfaction in romantic relationships. *Personality and Social Psychology Bulletin, 17,* 419–426.

Carlson, J., Watts, R. E., & Maniacci, M. (2006). Play therapy. In J. Carlson, R. E. Watts, & M. Maniacci (Eds.), *Adlerian therapy: Theory and practice* (pp. 227–248). Washington, DC: American Psychological Association.

Carlson, N. R. (1998). *Physiology of behavior.* Boston: Allyn & Bacon.

Carlson, N. R. (2001). *Physiology of behavior* (7th ed.). Boston: Allyn & Bacon.

Carlsson, A., & Lecrubier, Y. (Eds.). (2004). *Progress in dopamine research schizophrenia.* New York: Taylor & Francis.

Carlsson, K., Petrovic, P., Skare, S., Petersson, K. M., & Ingvar, M. (2000). Tickling expectations: Neural processing in anticipation of a sensory stimulus. *Journal of Cognitive Neuroscience, 12,* 691–703.

Carmichael, L. L., Hogan, H. P., & Walter, A. A. (1932). An experimental study of the effect of language on the reproduction of visually perceived form. *Journal of Experimental Psychology, 15,* 73–86.

Carmignoto, G., & Fellin, T. (2006). Glutamate release from astrocytes as a non-synaptic mechanism for neuronal synchronization in the hippocampus. *Journal of Physiology, Paris, 99,* 98–102.

Carnevale, P. J., & Pruitt, D. G. (1992). Negotiation and mediation. *Annual Review of Psychology, 43,* 531–582.

Carpenter, J. T. (2004). EMDR as an integrative psychotherapy approach: Experts explore the paradigm prism. *Psychotherapy Research, 14,* 135–136.

Carr, G. D., Moretti, M. M., & Cue, B. J. H. (2005). Evaluating parenting capacity: Validity problems with the MMPI-2, PAI, CAPI, and ratings of child adjustment. *Professional Psychology: Research and Practice, 36,* 188–196.

Carraher, T. N., Carraher, D., & Schliemann, A. D. (1985). Mathematics in the streets and in the schools. *British Journal of Developmental Psychology, 3,* 21–29.

Carrasco, M., & McElree, B. (2001). Covert attention accelerates the rate of visual information processing. *Proceedings of the National Academy of Science, 98,* 5363–5367.

Carrigan, M. H., & Levis, D. J. (1999). The contributions of eye movements to the efficacy of brief exposure treatment for reducing fear of public speaking. *Journal of Anxiety Disorders, 13,* 101–118.

Carroll, J. B. (1993). *Human cognitive abilities: A survey of factor-analytic studies.* New York: Cambridge University Press.

Carroll, J. B., Neitz, M., Hofer, H., Neitz, J., & Williams, D. R. (2004). Functional photoreceptor loss revealed with adaptive optics: An alternate cause of color blindness. *Proceedings of the National Academy of Sciences, 101,* 8461–8466

Carstensen, L. (1997, August). *Psychology and the aging revolution: Changes in social needs and social goals across the lifespan.* Paper presented at the annual convention of the American Psychological Association.

Carter, M. M., & Barlow, D. H. (1995). Learned alarms: The origins of panic. In W. T. O'Donohue & L. Krasner (Eds.), *Theories of behavior therapy: Exploring behavior change* (pp. 209–228). Washington, DC: American Psychological Association.

Cartwright, R. D. (1978). *A primer on sleep and dreaming.* Reading, MA: Addison-Wesley.

Cartwright, R. D. (1993). Who needs their dreams? The usefulness of dreams in psychotherapy. *Journal of the American Academy of Psychoanalysis, 21(4),* 539–547.

Carver, C. S., & Scheier, M. F. (2002). The hopeful optimist. *Psychological Inquiry, 13,* 288–290.

Carver, C. S., & Scheier, M. (2004). *Perspectives on personality* (5th ed.). Boston, MA: Pearson.

Carver, K., Joyner, K., & Udry, J. R. (2003). National estimates of adolescent romantic relationships. In P. Florsheim (Ed.), *Adolescent romantic relations and sexual behavior: Theory, research, and practical implications* (pp. 23–56). Mahwah, NJ: Erlbaum.

Casacalenda, N., Perry, J. C., & Looper, K. (2002). Remission in major depressive disorder: A comparison of pharmacotherapy, psychotherapy, and control conditions. *American Journal of Psychiatry, 159*, 1354–1360.

Casbon, T. S., Curtin, J. J., Lang, A. R., & Patrick, C. J. (2003). Deleterious effects of alcohol intoxication: Diminished cognitive control and its behavioral consequences. *Journal of Abnormal Psychology, 112*, 476–487.

Case, L., & Smith, T. B. (2000). Ethnic representation in a sample of the literature of applied psychology. *Journal of Consulting and Clinical Psychology, 68*, 1107–1110.

Casey, B. J., Galvan, A., & Hare, T. A. (2005). Changes in cerebral functional organization during cognitive development. *Current Opinion in Neurobiology, 15*, 239–244.

Caspi, A. (1998). Personality development across the life course. In W. Damon & N. Eisenberg (Eds.), *Handbook of child psychology: Vol. 3. Social, emotional, and personality development* (5th ed., pp. 311–388). New York: Wiley.

Caspi, A. (2000). The child is the father of man: Personality continuities from childhood to adulthood. *Journal of Personality and Social Psychology, 78*, 158–172.

Caspi, A., Begg, D., Dickson, N., Harrington, H., Langley, J., Moffitt, T. E., & Silva, P. A. (1997). Personality differences predict health-risk behaviors in young adulthood: Evidence from a longitudinal study. *Journal of Personality and Social Psychology, 73*, 1052–1063.

Caspi, A., Harrington, H., Milne, B., Amell, J. W., Theodore, R. F., & Moffitt, T. E. (2003). Children's behavioral styles at age 3 are linked to their adult personality traits at age 26. *Journal of Personality, 71*, 495–513.

Caspi, A., Henry, B., McGee, R. O., Moffitt, T. E., & Silva, P. A. (1995). Temperamental origins of child and adolescent behavior problems: From age 3 to Age 15. *Child Development, 66*, 55–68.

Caspi, A., McClay, J., Moffitt, T. E., Mill, J., Martin, J., Craig, I. W., et al. (2002). Role of genotype in the cycle of violence in maltreated children. *Science, 297*, 851–854.

Caspi, A., Roberts, B. W., & Shiner, R. L. (2005). Personality development: Stability and change. *Annual Review of Psychology, 56*, 453–484.

Caspi, A., & Shiner, R. L. (2006). Personality development. In W. Damon & R. M. Lerner (Series Eds.) & N. Eisenberg (Vol. Ed.), *Handbook of child psychology: Vol. 3, Social, emotional, and personality development* (6th ed., pp. 300–365). New York: Wiley.

Caspi, A., & Silva, P. A. (1995). Temperamental qualities at age 3 predict personality traits in young adulthood: Longitudinal evidence from a birth cohort. *Child Development, 66*, 468–498.

Caspi, A., Sugden, K., Moffitt, T. E., Taylor, A., Craig, I.W., Harrington, H., et al. (2003). Influence of life stress on depression: Moderation by a polymorphism in the 5-HTT gene. *Science, 301*, 386–389.

Cassel, E., & Bernstein, D. A. (2007). *Criminal behavior* (2nd ed.). Mahwah, NJ: Erlbaum.

Castillo, R. (Ed.). (1997). *Meanings of madness*. Stamford, CT: Wadsworth.

Castro, L., & Toro, M. A. (2004). The evolution of culture: From primate social learning to human culture. *Proceedings of the National Academy of Sciences, 101*, 10235–10240.

Caterina, M. J., Schumacher, M. A., Tominaga, M., Rosen, T. A., Levine, J. D., & Julius, D. (1997). The capsaicin receptor: A heat-activated ion channel in the pain pathway. *Nature, 389*, 816–824.

Cattell, R. B. (1963). Theory of fluid and crystallized intelligence: A critical experiment. *Journal of Educational Psychology, 54*, 1–22.

Cattell, R. B., Eber, H. W., & Tatsuoka, M. (1970). *Handbook for the sixteen personality factor questionnaire (16PF)*. Champaign, IL: Institute for Personality Testing.

Cavaiola, A. A., & Desordi, E. G. (2000). Locus of control in drinking driving offenders and nonoffenders. *Alcoholism Treatment Quarterly, 18*, 63–73.

Cavenett, T., & Nixon, D. V. (2006). The effect of arousal on memory for emotionally-relevant information: A study of skydivers. *Behaviour Research and Therapy, 44*, 1461–1469.

Ceci, S. J., Huffman, M. L. C., Smith, E., & Loftus, E. F. (1994). Repeatedly thinking about a non-event: Source misattributions among preschoolers. *Consciousness and Cognition, 3*, 388–407.

Ceci, S. J., & Liker, J. K. (1986). A day at the races: A study of IQ, expertise and cognitive complexity. *Journal of Experimental Psychology: General, 115*, 255–266.

Centers for Disease Control and Prevention. (1999a). *Chronic diseases and their risk factors*. Washington, DC: U.S. Government Printing Office.

Centers for Disease Control and Prevention. (1999b). *Suicide deaths and rates per 100,000*. Retrieved December 7, 2004, from http://www.cdc.gov/ncipc/data/us9794/suic.htm

Centers for Disease Control and Prevention. (2001). Deaths: Preliminary data for 2000. *National Vital Statistics Reports, 49*, 1–40.

Centers for Disease Control and Prevention. (2002a). Cigarette smoking among adults—United States, 2000. *Morbidity and Mortality Weekly Report*, July 26.

Centers for Disease Control and Prevention. (2002b). *National Center for Health Statistics faststats, A to Z: Suicide.*

Centers for Disease Control and Prevention. (2002c). *Table 47: Death rates for suicide, according to sex, race, Hispanic origin, and age: United States, selected years 1950–1999*. Retrieved September 25, 2002 from http://www/cdc.gov/nchs/faststats/pdf/nvsr49_11tb1/pds.

Centers for Disease Control and Prevention. (2004). Web-based injury statistics query and reporting system (WISQARS). Retrieved December 7, 2004, from http://www.cdc.gov/ncipc/wisquars.

Centers for Disease Control and Prevention. (2005). *HIV/AIDS Surveillance Report, 2004* (Vol. 16). Atlanta: US Department of Health and Human Services, Centers for Disease Control and Prevention.

Centers for Disease Control and Prevention. (2006). WISQARS website and "Fatal Injury Reports." Retrieved February 8, 2006, from http://www.cdc.gov/ncipc/wisqars/.

Centerwall, L. (1990). Controlled TV viewing and suicide in countries: Young adult suicide and exposure to television. *Social Psychiatry and Social Epidemiology, 25*, 149–153.

Centonze, D., Picconi, B., Baunez, C., Borrelli, E., Pisani, A., Bernardi, G., & Calabresi, P. (2002). Cocaine and amphetamine depress striatal GABAergic synaptic transmission through D2 dopamine receptors. *Neuropsychopharmacology, 26*, 164–175.

Cepeda, N. J., Pashler, H., Vul, E., Wixted, J., & Rohrer, D. (2006). Distributed practice in verbal recall tasks: A review and quantitative synthesis. *Psychological Bulletin, 132*, 354–380.

Çeponien, R., Lepisto, T., Shesakova, A., Vanhala, R., Alku, P., Naatanen, R., & Yaguchi, K. (2003). Speech-sound-selective auditory impairment in children with autism: They can perceive but do not attend. *Proceedings of the National Academy of Sciences, 100*, 5567–5572.

Cerf, C., & Navasky, V. (1998). *The experts speak: The definitive compendium of authoritative misinformation*. New York: Villard.

Cervone, D. (2005). Personality architecture: Within-person structures and processes. *Annual Review of Psychology, 56*, 423–452.

Chaiken, A. L., Sigler, E., & Derlega, V. J. (1974). Nonverbal mediators of teacher expectancy effects. *Journal of Personality and Social Psychology, 30*, 144–149.

Chakrabarti, S., & Fombonne, E. (2001). Pervasive developmental disorders in preschool children. *Journal of the American Medical Association, 285*, 3093–3099.

Chambless, D. L., & Hollon, S. D. (1998). Defining empirically supported therapies. *Journal of Consulting and Clinical Psychology, 66*, 7–18.

Chambless, D. L., & Ollendick, T. H. (2001). Empirically supported psychological treatments. *Annual Review of Psychology, 52*, 685–716.

Champion, V., & Huster, G. (1995). Effect of interventions on stage of mammography adoption. *Journal of Behavioral Medicine, 18*, 159–188.

Chan, A., Asbjørn, H., Haahr, M. T., Gøtzsche, P. C., & Altman, D. G. (2004). Empirical evidence for selective reporting of outcomes in randomized trials. *Journal of the American Medical Association, 291*, 2457–2465.

Chan, D. (2005). Current directions in personnel selection research. *Current Directions in Psychological Science, 14*, 220–223.

Chandola, T., Brunner, E., & Marmot, M. (2006). Chronic stress at work and the metabolic syndrome: Prospective study. *British Medical Journal, 332*, 521–525.

Chang, E. F., & Merzenich, M. M. (2003). Environmental noise retards auditory cortical development. *Science, 300*, 498–502.

Chang, F.-M., Kidd, J.R., Kivak, K.J., Pakstis, A.J., & Kidd, K.K. (1996). The worldwide distribution of allele frequencies at the human dopamine D4 receptor locus. *Human Genetics, 98*, 91–101.

Chanoine, J. P., Hampl, S., Jensen, C., Boldrin, M., & Hauptman, J. (2005). Effect of orlistat on weight and body composition in obese adolescents: A randomized controlled trial. *Journal of the American Medical Association, 293*, 2873–2883.

Chao, R. K. (2001). Extending research on the consequences of parenting style for Chinese Americans and European Americans. *Child Development, 72*, 1832–1843.

Chao, R., & Tseng, V. (2002). Parenting of Asians. In M. H. Bornstein (Ed.), *Handbook of parenting: Vol. 4. Social conditions and applied parenting* (2nd ed., pp. 59–93). Mahwah, NJ: Erlbaum.

Chapell, M. S., Blanding, Z. B., Silverstein, M. E., Takahashi, M., Newman, B., Gubi, A., & McCann, N. (2005). Test anxiety and academic performance in undergraduate and graduate students. *Journal of Educational Psychology, 97*, 268–274.

Chapman, D. Z., & Zweig, D. I. (2005). Developing a nomological network for interview structure: Antecedents and consequences of the structured selection interview. *Personnel Psychology, 58*, 673–702.

Chapman, S., & Morrell, S. (2000). Barking mad? Another lunatic hypothesis bites the dust. *British Medical Journal, 321*, 1561–1563.

Charles, S. T., Mather, M., & Carstensen, L. L. (2003). Aging and emotional memory: The forgettable nature of negative images for older adults. *Journal of Experimental Psychology: General, 132*, 310–324.

Charleton, T., Gunter, B., & Coles, D. (1998). Broadcast television as a cause of aggression? Recent findings from a naturalistic study. *Emotional and Behavioral Difficulties, 3*, 5–13.

Charness, N. (2000). Can acquired knowledge compensate for age-related declines in cognitive efficiency? In S. H. Qualls & N. Abeles, (Eds.), *Psychology and the aging revolution: How we adapt to longer life* (pp. 99–117). Washington, DC: American Psychological Association.

Chase, T. N. (1998). The significance of continuous dopaminergic stimulation in the treatment of Parkinson's disease. *Drugs, 55*(Suppl. 1), 1–9.

Chassin, L., Pitts, S. C., & Prost, J. (2002). Binge drinking trajectories from adolescence to emerging adulthood in a high-risk sample: Predictors and substance abuse outcomes. *Journal of Consulting and Clinical Psychology, 70,* 67–78.

Chastain, G., & Thurber, S. (1989). The SQ3R study technique enhances comprehension of an introductory psychology textbook. *Reading Improvement, 26,* 94–96.

Chemers, M. M. (2000). Leadership research and theory: A functional integration. *Group Dynamics, 4,* 27–43.

Chemers, M. M., Watson, C. B., & May, S. T. (2000). Dispositional affect and leadership effectiveness: A comparison of self-esteem, optimism, and efficacy. *Personality and Social Psychology Bulletin, 26,* 267–277.

Chen, J., Magavi, S. S. P., & Macklis, J. D. (2004). Neurogenesis of corticospinal motor neurons extending spinal projections in adult mice. *Proceedings of the National Academy of Sciences of the USA, 101,* 16357–16362.

Chen, M., & Bargh, J. A. (1997). Nonconscious behavioral confirmation processes: The self-fulfilling consequences of automatic stereotype activation. *Journal of Experimental Social Psychology, 33,* 541–560.

Chen, R., Cohen, L. G., & Hallett, M. (2002). Nervous system reorganization following injury. *Neuroscience, 111,* 761–773.

Chen, R., Tilley, M. R., Wei, H., Zhou, F., Zhou, F. M., Ching, S., et al. (2006). Abolished cocaine reward in mice with a cocaine-insensitive dopamine transporter. *Proceedings of the National Academy of Sciences of the United States of America, 103,* 9333–9338.

Cheng, L.-C., Tavazoie, M., & Doetsch, F. (2005). Stem cells: From epigenetics to microRNAs. *Neuron, 46,* 363–367.

Cheng, Y., Kawachi, I., Coakley, E. H., Schwartz, J., & Colditz, G. (2000). Association between psychosocial work characteristics and health functioning in American women: Prospective study. *British Medical Journal, 320,* 1432–1436.

Chesney, M. A., Chambers, D. B., Taylor, J. M., Johnson, L. M., & Folkman, S. (2003). Coping effectiveness training for men living with HIV: Results from a randomized clinical trial testing a group-based intervention. *Psychosomatic Medicine, 65,* 1038–1046.

Children's Defense Fund. (2004). *The state of America's children 2004.* Washington DC: Children's Defense Fund.

Chiles, J. A., Lambert, M. J., & Hatch, A. L. (1999). The impact of psychological interventions on medical cost offset: A meta-analytic review. *Clinical Psychology: Science and Practice, 6,* 204–220.

Chisholm, K. (1997, June). Trauma at an early age inhibits ability to bond. *APA Monitor,* p. 11.

Chivers, M. L., Rieger, G., Latty, E., & Bailey, J. M. (2004). A sex difference in the specificity of sexual arousal. *Psychological Science, 15,* 736–744.

Cho, H. J., Meira-Lima, I., Cordeiro, Q., Michelon, L., Sham, P., Vallada, H., et al. (2005). Population-based and family-based studies on the serotonin transporter gene polymorphisms and bipolar disorder: A systematic review and meta-analysis. *Molecular Psychiatry, 10,* 771–781.

Cho, Z. H., Chung, S. C., Jones, J. P., Park, J. B., Park, H. J., Lee, H. J., et al. (1998). New findings of the correlation between acupoints and corresponding brain cortices using functional MRI. *Proceedings of the National Academy of Sciences, 95,* 2670–2673.

Chodosh, J., Reuben, D. B., Albert, M. S., & Seeman, T. E. (2002). Predicting cognitive impairment in high-functioning community-dwelling older persons: MacArthur studies of successful aging. *Journal of the American Geriatrics Society, 50*(6), 1051–1060.

Choi, J., & Silverman, I. (2003). Processes underlying sex differences in route-learning strategies in children and adolescents. *Personality and Individual Differences, 34,* 1153–1166.

Chomsky, N. (1986). *Knowledge of language: Its nature, origin, and use.* New York: Praeger.

Chouinard, G. (2004). Issues in the clinical use of benzodiazepines: Potency, withdrawal, and rebound. *Journal of Clinical Psychiatry, 65*(Suppl. 5), 7–21.

Choy, Y., Fyer, A. J., & Lipsitz, J.D. (2007). Treatment of specific phobia in adults. *Clinical Psychology Review, 27,* 266–286.

Christensen, A., Atkins, D. C., Berns, S., Wheeler, J., Baucom, D. H., & Simpson, L. E. (2004). Traditional versus integrative behavioral couple therapy for significantly and chronically distressed married couples. *Journal of Consulting and Clinical Psychology, 72,* 176–191.

Christensen, H. C., Schüz, J., Kosteljanetz, M., Poulsen, H. S., Boice, J. D., Jr., McLaughlin, J. K., & Johansen, C. (2005). Cellular telephones and risk for brain tumors: A population-based, incident case-control study. *Neurology, 64,* 1189–1195.

Christensen, H., Griffiths, K. M., & Jorm, A. F. (2004). Delivering interventions for depression by using the Internet: Randomized controlled trial. *British Medical Journal, 328,* 265.

Christensen, K. A., Stephens, M. A. P., & Townsend, A. L. (1998). Mastery in women's multiple roles and well-being: Adult daughters providing care to impaired parents. *Health Psychology, 17,* 163–171.

Christie, I. C., & Friedman, B. H. (2004). Autonomic specificity of discrete emotion and dimensions of affective space: A multivariate approach. *International Journal of Psychophysiology, 51,* 143–153.

Christopher, K. (2003). Autistic boy killed during exorcism. *Skeptical Inquirer, 27,* 11.

Chu, R., Rivera, C., & Loftin, C. (2000). Herding and homicide: An examination of the Nisbett-Reaves hypothesis. *Social Forces, 78,* 971–987.

Chua, H. F., Boland, J. E., & Nisbett, R. E. (2005). Cultural variation in eye movements during scene perception. *Proceedings of the National Academy of Sciences of the USA, 102,* 12629–12633.

Chugani, H. T., & Phelps, M. E. (1986). Maturational changes in cerebral function in infants determined by 18FDG positron emission tomography. *Science, 231,* 840–843.

Chumakov, I., Blumenfeld, M., Guerassimenko, O., Cavarec, L., Palicio, M., Abderrahim, H., et al. (2002). Genetic and physiological data implicating the new human gene G72 and the gene for D-amino acid oxidase in schizophrenia. *Proceedings of the National Academies of Science, 99,* 13675–13680.

Cialdini, R. B. (1995). Principles and techniques of social influence. In A. Tesser (Ed.), *Advanced social psychology* (pp. 257–282). New York: McGraw-Hill.

Cialdini, R. B. (2001). *Influence: Science and practice* (4th ed.). Boston: Allyn & Bacon.

Cialdini, R. B., & Goldstein, N. J. (2004). Social influence: Compliance and conformity. *Annual Review of Psychology, 55,* 591–621.

Cialdini, R. B., Wosinska, W. B., Barrett, D. W., Butner, J., & Gornik-Durose, M. (2001). The differential impact of two social influence principles on individualists and collectivists in Poland and the United States. In W. Wosinska, R. B. Cialdini, D.W. Barrett, & J. Reykowski (Eds.), *The practice of social influence in multiple cultures: Applied social research* (pp. 33–50). Mahwah, NJ: Erlbaum.

Ciccocioppo, R., Martin-Fardon, R., & Weiss, F. (2004). Stimuli associated with a single cocaine experience elicit long-lasting cocaine-seeking. *Nature Neuroscience, 7,* 495–496.

Ciccocioppo, R., Sanna, P. P., & Weiss, F. (2001). Cocaine-predictive stimulus induces drug-seeking behavior and neural activation in limbic brain regions after multiple months of abstinence: Reversal by D1 antagonists. *Proceedings of the National Academy of Sciences, 98,* 1976–1981.

Cimbora, D. M., & McIntosh, D. N. (2003). Emotional responses to antisocial acts in adolescent males with conduct disorder: A link to affective morality. *Journal of Clinical Child and Adolescent Psychology, 32,* 296–301.

Clancy, S. A. (2005). *Abducted: How people come to believe they were kidnaped by aliens.* Cambridge, MA: Harvard University Press.

Clancy, S. A., McNally, R. J., Schacter, D. L., Lenzenweger, M. F., & Pitman, R. K. (2002). Memory distortion in people reporting abduction by aliens. *Journal of Abnormal Psychology, 111,* 455–461.

Clancy, S. A., Schacter, D. L., McNally, R. J., & Pittman, R. K. (2000). False recognition in women reporting recovered memories of sexual abuse. *Psychological Science, 11,* 26–31.

Clark, A., Oswald, A., & Warr, P. (1996). Is job satisfaction U-shaped in age? *Journal of Occupational and Organizational Psychology, 69,* 57–81.

Clark, D. C., & Fawcett, J. (1992). Review of empirical risk factors for evaluation of the suicidal patient. In B. Bongar (Ed.), *Suicide: Guidelines for assessment, management, and treatment* (pp. 16–48). New York: Oxford University Press.

Clark, D. M., Ehlers, A., McManus, F., Hackmann, A., Fennell, M., Campbell, H., et al. (2003). Cognitive therapy versus fluoxetine in generalized social phobia: A randomized placebo-controlled trial. *Journal of Consulting and Clinical Psychology, 71,* 1058–1067.

Clark, E. V. (1993). *The lexicon in acquisition.* Cambridge: Cambridge University Press.

Clark, F., Azen, S. P., Carlson, M., Mandel, D., LaBree, L., Hay, J., Zemke, R., Jackson, J., & Lipson, L. (2001). Embedding health-promoting changes into the daily lives of independent-living older adults: Long-term follow-up of occupational therapy intervention. *Journal of Gerontology: Psychological Sciences, 56B,* 60.

Clark, L. A. (2006). The role of moral judgment in personality disorder diagnosis. Journal of Personality Disorders, 20, 184–185.

Clarke, L., Ungerer, J., Chahoud, K., Johnson, S., Stiefel, I. (2002). Attention deficit hyperactivity disorder is associated with attachment insecurity. *Clinical Child Psychology and Psychiatry, 7,* 179–198.

Clarke-Stewart, A., & Allhusen, V. (2005). *What we know about childcare.* Cambridge, MA: Harvard University Press.

Clarke-Stewart, A., & Brentano, C. (2006). *Divorce: Causes and consequences.* New Haven, CT: Yale University Press.

Clarke-Stewart, K. A. (1989). Infant day care: Maligned or malignant? *American Psychologist, 44,* 266–273.

Clarkin, J. F. (2006). Conceptualization and treatment of personality disorders. Psychotherapy Research, 16, 1–11.

Clausen, J., Sersen, E., & Lidsky, A. (1974). Variability of sleep measures in normal subjects. *Psychophysiology, 11,* 509–516.

Clay, R. (1996, December). Some elders thrive on working into later life. *APA Monitor,* p. 35.

Clay, R. A. (2000). Often, the bells and whistles backfire. *Monitor on Psychology, 31,* 64–65.

Clendenen, V. I., Herman, C. P., & Polivy, J. (1995). Social facilitation of eating among friends and strangers. *Appetite, 23,* 1–13.

Cleveland, M. J., Gibbons, F. X., Gerrard, M., Pomery, E. A., & Brody, G. H. (2005). The impact of parenting on risk cognitions and risk behavior: A study of mediation and moderation in a panel of African American adolescents. *Child Development, 76,* 900–916.

Clifton, R. K. (1992). The development of spatial hearing in human infants. In L. A. Werner & E. W. Rubel (Eds.), *Developmental psychoacoustics* (pp. 135–157). Washington, DC: American Psychological Association.

Clifton, R. K., Rochat, P., Litovsky, R., & Perris, E. (1991). Object representation guides infants' reaching in the dark. *Journal of Experimental Psychology: Human Perception and Performance, 17,* 323–329.

Cloutier, J., Mason, M. F., & Macrae, C. N. (2005). The perceptual determinants of person construal: Reopening the social-cognitive toolbox. *Journal of Personality and Social Psychology, 88,* 885–894.

CNN/Time. (1997). Poll: U.S. hiding knowledge of aliens. *CNN/Time.* Retrieved December 13, 2004, from http://www-cgi.cnn.com/US/9706/15/ufo.poll/index.html

Cobos, P., Sánchez, M., Pérez, N., & Vila, J. (2004). Effects of spinal cord injuries on the subjective component of emotions. *Cognition and Emotion, 18,* 281–287.

Coccaro, E. F. (1989). Central serotonin and impulsive aggression. *British Journal of Psychiatry, 155,* 52–62.

Cohen, C. E. (1981). Person categories and social perception: Testing some boundaries of the processing effects of prior knowledge. *Journal of Personality and Social Psychology, 40,* 441–452.

Cohen, D., & Nisbett, R. (1997). Field experiments examining the culture of honor: The role of institutions in perpetuating norms about violence. *Personality and Social Psychology Bulletin, 23,* 1188–1199.

Cohen, D., Nisbett, R. E., Bowdle, B. F., & Schwarz, N. (1996). Insult, aggression, and the southern culture of honor: An "experimental ethnography." *Journal of Personality and Social Psychology, 70,* 945–960.

Cohen, D. A., Farley, T. A., Taylor, S. N., Martin, D. H., & Schuster, M. A. (2002). When and where do youths have sex? The potential role of adult supervision. *Pediatrics, 110,* e66.

Cohen, E., Bieschke, J., Percivalle, R. M., Kelly, J. W., & Dillin, A. (2006). Opposing activities protect against age onset proteotoxicity. *Science, 313,* 1604–1610.

Cohen, F., Kemeny, M. E., Zegans, L. S., Johnson, P., Kearney, K. A., & Strites, D. P. (2007). Immune function declines with unemployment and recovers after stressor termination. *Psychosomatic Medicine, 69,* 225–234.

Cohen, G. L., & Prinstein, M. J. (2006). Peer contagion of aggression and health risk behavior among adolescent males: An experimental investigation of effects on public conduct and private attitudes. *Child Development, 77,* 967–983.

Cohen, G. L., & Steele, C. M. (2002). A barrier of mistrust: How negative stereotypes affect cross-race mentoring. In J. Aronson (Ed.), *Improving academic achievement: Impact of psychological factors on education* (pp. 303–327). San Diego, CA: Academic Press.

Cohen, N. J., & Corkin, S. (1981). The amnesic patient H. M.: Learning and retention of a cognitive skill. *Neuroscience Abstracts, 7,* 235.

Cohen, N. J., & Squire, L. R. (1980). Preserved learning and retention of pattern analyzing skills in amnesia: Dissociation of knowing how and knowing that. *Science, 210,* 207–210.

Cohen, P., Kasen, S., Chen, H., Hartmark, C., & Gordon, K. (2003). Variations in patterns of developmental transitions in the emerging adulthood period. *Developmental Psychology, 39,* 657–669.

Cohen, S., Doyle, W. J., Skoner, D. P., Gwaltney, J. M., Jr., & Newsom, J. T. (1995). State and trait negative affect as predictors of objective and subjective symptoms of respiratory viral infections. *Journal of Personality and Social Psychology, 68,* 159–169.

Cohen, S., Doyle, W. J., Turner, R. B., Alper, C. M., & Skoner, D. P. (2003a). Emotional style and susceptibility to the common cold. *Psychosomatic Medicine, 65,* 652–657.

Cohen, S., Doyle, W. J., Turner, R. B., Alper, C. M., & Skoner, D. P. (2003b). Sociability and susceptibility to the common cold. *Psychological Science, 14,* 389–395.

Cohen, S., & Herbert, T. B. (1996). Health psychology: Psychological factors and physical disease from the perspective of human psychoneuroimmunology. *Annual Review of Psychology, 47,* 113–142.

Cohen, S., & Pressman, S. D. (2006). Positive affect and health. *Current Directions in Psychological Science, 15,* 122–125.

Cohen-Bendahan, C. C. C., Buitelaar, J. K., van Goozen, S. H. M., Orlebeke, J. F., & Cohen-Kettenis, P. T. (2005). Is there an effect of prenatal testosterone on aggression and other behavioral traits? A study comparing same-sex and opposite-sex twin girls. *Hormones and Behavior, 47,* 230–237.

Colak, A., Soy, O., Uzun, H., Aslan, O., Barut, S., Belce, A., et al. (2003). Neuroprotective effects of GYKI 52466 on experimental spinal cord injury in rats. *Journal of Neurosurgery, 98,* 275–281.

Colby, A., Kohlberg, L., Gibbs, J., & Lieberman, M. (1983). A longitudinal study of moral judgment. *Monographs of the Society for Research in Child Development, 48*(1, Serial No. 200).

Colcombe, S., & Kramer, A. F. (2003). Fitness effects on the cognitive function of older adults: A meta-analytic study. *Psychological Science, 14,* 125–130.

Coldwell, C. M., & Bender, W. S. (2007). The effectiveness of assertive community treatment for homeless populations with severe mental illness: A meta-analysis. *American Journal of Psychiatry, 164,* 393–399.

Cole, K. N., Mills, P. E., Dale, P. S., & Jenkins, J. R. (1991). Effects of preschool integration for children with disabilities. *Exceptional Children, 58,* 36–45.

Cole, M. (2006). Culture and cognitive development in phylogenetic, historical, and ontogenetic perspective. In W. Damon & R. M. Lerner (Series Eds.) & D. Kuhn & R. Siegler (Vol. Eds.), *Handbook of child psychology: Vol. 2, Cognition, perception, and language* (6th ed., pp. 636–686). New York: Wiley.

Cole, R. A., & Jakimik, J. (1978). Understanding speech: How words are heard. In G. Underwood (Ed.), *Strategies of information processing* (pp. 67–116). London: Academic Press.

Coleman, D. (1992). Why do I feel so tired? Too little, too late. *American Health, 11*(4), 43–46.

Collacott, E. A., Zimmerman, J. T., White, D. W., & Rindone, J. P. (2000). Bipolar permanent magnets for the treatment of chronic low back pain: A pilot study. *Journal of the American Medical Association, 283,* 1322–1325.

Collins, A. M., & Loftus, E. F. (1975). A spreading activation theory of semantic processing. *Psychological Review, 82,* 407–428.

Collins, R. L., Elliott, M. N., Berry, S. H., Kanouse, D. E., Kunkel, D., Hunter, S. B., et al. (2004). Watching sex on television predicts adolescent initiation of sexual behavior. *Pediatrics, 114,* e280–e289.

Collins, W. A., & Roisman, G. I. (2006). The influence of family and peer relationships in the development of competence during adolescence. In A. Clarke-Stewart & J. Dunn (Eds.), *Families count: Effects on child and adolescent development.* New York: Cambridge University Press.

Collins, W. A., & Steinberg, L. (2006). Adolescent development in interpersonal context. In W. Damon & R. M. Lerner (Series Eds.) & N. Eisenberg (Vol. Ed.), *Handbook of child psychology: Vol. 3, Social, emotional, and personality development* (pp. 1003–1068). New York: Wiley.

Colloca, L., & Benedetti, F. (2005). Placebos and painkillers: Is mind as real as matter? *Nature Reviews Neuroscience, 6,* 545–552.

Colom, R., & Flores-Mendoza, C. E. (2007). Intelligence predicts scholastic achievement irrespective of SES factors: Evidence from Brazil. *Intelligence, 35,* 243–251.

Colom, R., Jung, R. E., & Haier, R. J. (2006). Distributed brain sites for the g-factor of intelligence. *Neuroimage, 31,* 1359–1365.

Colombo, M., D'Amato, M. R., Rodman, H. R., & Gross, C. G. (1990). Auditory association cortex lesions impair auditory short-term memory in monkeys. *Science, 247,* 336–338.

Coltheart, M. (2006). What has functional neuroimaging told us about the mind (so far)? *Cortex: A Journal Devoted to the Study of the Nervous System and Behavior, 42,* 323–331.

Coltrane, S. (2001). Research on household labor: Modeling and measuring the social embeddedness of routine family work. In R. M. Milardo (Ed), *Understanding families into the new millennium: A decade in review.* Minneapolis, MN: National Council on Family Relations.

Committee to Review the Scientific Evidence on the Polygraph. (2003). *The polygraph and lie detection.* Washington, DC: National Academies Press.

Compagnone, N. A., & Mellon, S. H. (2000). Neurosteroids: Biosynthesis and function of these novel neuromodulators. *Frontiers of Neuroendocrinology, 21,* 1–56.

Compas, B. E., Haaga, D. A. F., Keefe, F. J., Leitenberg, H., & Williams, D. A. (1998). Sampling of empirically supported psychological treatments from health psychology: Smoking, chronic pain, cancer, and bulimia nervosa. *Journal of Consulting and Clinical Psychology, 66,* 89–112.

Compton, W. M., Thomas, Y. F., Stinson, F. S., & Grant, B. F. (2007). Prevalence, correlates, disability, and comorbidity of DSM-IV drug abuse and dependence in the United States. *Archives of General Psychiatry, 64,* 566–576.

Comstock, G., & Scharrer, E. (2006). Media and popular culture. In W. Damon & R. M. Lerner (Series Eds.) & K. A. Renninger & I. E. Sigel (Vol. Eds.), *Handbook of child psychology: Vol. 4, Child psychology in practice* (6th ed., pp. 817–863). New York: Wiley.

Condon, J. W., & Crano, W. D. (1988). Inferred evaluation and the relationship between attitude similarity and interpersonal attraction. *Journal of Personality and Social Psychology, 54,* 789–797.

Cone, E. J., Fant, R. V., Rohay, J. M., Caplan, Y. H., Ballina, M., Reder, R. F., et al. (2004). Oxycodone involvement in drug abuse deaths: II. Evidence for toxic multiple drug-drug interactions. *Journal of Analytical Toxicology, 28,* 616–624.

Conger, R. D., Cui, M., Bryant, C. M., & Elder, G. H. (2000). Competence in early adult romantic relationships: A developmental perspective on family influences. *Journal of Personality and Social Psychology, 79*(2), 224–237.

Conklin, H. M., & Iacono, W. G. (2002). Schizophrenia: A neurodevelopmental perspective. *Current Directions in Psychological Science, 11,* 33–37.

Conrad, R. (1964). Acoustic confusions in immediate memory. *British Journal of Psychology, 55,* 75–84.

Consedine, N. S., & Magai, C. (2003). Attachment and emotion experience in later life: The view from emotions theory. *Attachment and Human Development, 5,* 165–187.Constantino, J. N., & Todd, R. D. (2003). Autistic traits in the general population: A twin study. *Archives General Psychiatry, 60,* 524–530.

Constantine, M. G. (2002). Predictors of satisfaction with counseling: Racial and ethnic minority clients' attitudes toward counseling and ratings of their counselors' general and multicultural competence. *Journal of Counseling Psychology, 49,* 255–263.

Constantino, J. N., & Todd, R. D. (2003). Autistic traits in the general population: A twin study. *Archives General Psychiatry, 60,* 524–530.

Constantino, M. J., Arnow, B. A., Blasey, C., & Agras, W. S. (2005). The association between patient characteristics and the therapeutic alliance in cognitive-behavioral and interpersonal therapy for bulimia nervosa. *Journal of Consulting and Clinical Psychology, 73,* 203–211.

Constantino, M. J., Arnow, B. A., Blasey, C., & Agras, W. S. (2005). The association between patient characteristics and the therapeutic alliance in cognitive-behavioral and interpersonal therapy for bulimia nervosa. *Journal of Consulting and Clinical Psychology, 73,* 203–211.

Consumer Reports. (1995, November). Mental health: Does therapy help? *Consumer Reports,* pp. 734–739.

Conte, J. M., & Gintoft, J. N. (2005). Polychronicity, big five personality dimensions, and sales performance. *Human Performance, 18,* 427–444.

Conway, M. A., Cohen, G., & Stanhope, N. (1991). On the very long-term retention of knowledge acquired through formal education: Twelve years of cognitive psychology. *Journal of Experimental Psychology: General, 120,* 395–409.

Cook, J. A., Lehman, A. F., Drake, R., McFarlane, W. R., Gold, P. B., Leff, H. S., et al. (2005). Integration of psychiatric and vocational services: A multisite randomized, controlled trial of supported employment. *American Journal of Psychiatry, 162,* 1948–1956.

Cook, M., & Mineka, S. (1990). Selective associations in the observational conditioning of fear in rhesus monkeys. Journal of Experimental Psychology: Animal Behavior Processes, 16, 372–389.

Cooper, A. (2004). *The inmates are running the asylum: Why high tech products drive us crazy and how to restore the sanity* (2nd ed.). New York: Pearson.

Cooper, H. (1979). Pygmalion grows up: A model for teacher expectation communication and performance influence. *Review of Educational Research, 49,* 389–410.

Cooper, J., Mirabile, R., & Scher, S. J. (2005). Actions and attitudes: The theory of cognitive dissonance. In T. Brock & M. Green (Eds.), *Persuasion: Psychological insights and perspectives* (2nd ed., pp. 63–79). Thousand Oaks, CA: Sage Publications, Inc.

Cooper, M. L., Russell, M., Skinner, J. B., Frone, M. R., & Mudar, P. (1992). Stress and alcohol use: The moderating effects of gender, coping, and alcohol expectancies. *Journal of Abnormal Psychology, 101,* 139–152.

Corbetta, M., Miezin, F. M., Dobmeyer, S., Shulman, G. L., & Petersen, S. E. (1991). Selective and divided attention during visual discriminations of shape, color, and speed: Functional anatomy by positron emission tomography. *Journal of Neuroscience, 11,* 2383–2402.

Corden, B., Critchley, H. D., Skuse, D., & Dolan, R. J. (2006). Fear recognition ability predicts differences in social cognitive and neural functioning in men. *Journal of Cognitive Neuroscience, 18,* 889–897.

Cordery, J. L., Mueller, W. S., & Smith, L. M. (1991). Attitudinal and behavioral effects of autonomous group working: A longitudinal field study. *Academy of Management Journal, 34,* 464–476.

Coren, S. (1999). Psychology applied to animal training. In A. Stec & D. Bernstein (Eds.), *Psychology: Fields of application.* Boston: Houghton Mifflin.

Cork, R. C., Kihlstrom, J. F., & Hameroff, S. R. (1992). Explicit and implicit memory dissociated by anesthetic technique. *Society for Neuroscience Abstracts, 22,* 523.

Corkin, S. (2002). What's new with the amnesic patient H. M.? *Nature Reviews Neuroscience, 3,* 153–160.

Cornblatt, B., & Erlenmeyer-Kimling, L. E. (1985). Global attentional deviance in children at risk for schizophrenia: Specificity and predictive validity. *Journal of Abnormal Psychology, 94,* 470–486.

Cornelius, R. R. (1996). *The science of emotion.* Upper Saddle River, NJ: Prentice-Hall.

Cornelius, T. L., & Resseguie, N. (2007). Primary and secondary prevention programs for dating violence: A review of the literature. *Aggression and Violent Behavior, 12,* 364–375.

Cornelius-White, J. H. D. (2002). The phoenix of empirically supported therapy relationships: The overlooked person-centered bias. *Psychotherapy: Theory, Research, Practice, Training, 39,* 219–222.

Corno, L., Cronbach, L. J., Kupermintz, H., Lohman, D. F., Mandinach, E. B., Porteus, A. W., & Talbert, J. E. (2002). *Remaking the concept of aptitude: Extending the legacy of Richard E. Snow.* Hillsdale, NJ: Erlbaum.

Cornoldi, C., DeBeni, R., & Baldi, A. P. (1989). Generation and retrieval of general, specific, and autobiographic images representing concrete nouns. *Acta Psychologica, 72,* 25–39.

Cornwell, E. E., Yonas, M., Allen, F., & Antkowiak, B. (2004). *Reducing youth violence.* Paper presented at the annual meeting of the Society of Black Academic Surgeons, Washington, DC.

Corr, P. J. (2002). J. A. Gray's reinforcement sensitivity theory: Tests of the joint subsystems hypothesis of anxiety and impulsivity. *Personality and Individual Differences, 33,* 511–532.

Correll, C. U., Leucht, S., & Kane, J. M. (2004). Lower risk for tardive dyskinesia associated with second-generation antipsychotics: A systematic review of 1-year studies. *American Journal of Psychiatry, 161,* 414–425.

Correll, J., Park, B., Judd, C. M., & Wittenbrink, B. (2002). The police officer's dilemma: Using ethnicity to disambiguate potentially threatening individuals. *Journal of Personality and Social Psychology, 83,* 1314–1329.

Corsini, R. J., & Wedding, D. (2001). *Current psychotherapies* (6th ed.). Itasca, IL: Peacock.

Corwin, M. J., Lesko, S. M., Heeren, T., Vezina, R. M., Hunt, C. E., Mandell, F., et al. (2003). Secular changes in sleep position during infancy: 1995–1998. *Pediatrics, 111,* 52–60.

Coslett, H. B., & Saffran, E. (1991). Simultanagnosia. To see but not two see. *Brain, 114* (Pt. 4), 1523–1545.

Cosmides, L., & Tooby, J. (2004). *What is evolutionary psychology? Explaining the new science of the mind.* New Haven, CT: Yale University Press.

Costa, P. (2001, June). *New insights on personality and leadership provided by the five-factor model.* Paper presented at Annual Convention of American Psychological Society, Toronto, Canada.

Costa, P. T., & McCrae, R. R. (2002). Looking backwards: Changes in mean levels of personality traits from 80 to 12. In D. Cervone, & W. Mischel (Eds.), *Advances in personality science* (pp. 196–217). New York: Guilford Press.

Costa, P. T., Jr., & McCrae, R. R. (1992). *Revised NEO Personality Inventory: NEO PI and NEO Five-Factor Inventory (NEO FFI: Professional Manual).* Odessa, FL: Psychological Assessment Resources.

Costa, P. T., Jr., & McCrae, R. R. (1995). Primary traits of Eysenck's P-E-N system: Three- and five-factor solutions. *Journal of Personality and Social Psychology, 69,* 308–317.

Costello, E. J., Mustillo, S., Erkanli, A., Keeler, G., & Angold, A. (2003). Prevalence and development of psychiatric disorders in childhood and adolescence. *Archives of General Psychiatry, 60,* 837–844.

Costermans, J., Lories, G., & Ansay, C. (1992). Confidence level and feeling of knowing in question answering: The weight of inferential processes. *Journal of Experimental Psychology: Learning, Memory, and Cognition, 18,* 142–150.

Cota, D., Marsicano, G., Lutz, B., Vicennati, V., Stalla, G.K., Pasquali, R., & Pagotto, U. (2003). Endogenous cannabinoid system as a modulator of food intake. *International Journal of Obesity, 27,* 289–301.

Cota, D., Proulx, K., Smith, K. A. B., Kozma, S. C., Thomas, G., Woods, S. C., et al. (2006). Hypothalamic mTOR signaling regulates food intake. *Science, 312,* 927–930.

Cote, J. K., & Pepler, C. (2002). A randomized trial of a cognitive coping intervention for acutely ill HIV-positive men. *Nursing Research, 51,* 237–244.

Cotterill, R. M. (2001). Cooperation of the basal ganglia, cerebellum, sensory cerebrum and hippocampus: Possible implications for cognition, consciousness, intelligence and creativity. *Progress in Neurobiology, 64,* 1–33.

Cottrell, C. A., & Neuberg, S. L. (2005). Different emotional reactions to different groups: A sociofunctional threat-based approach to prejudice. *Journal of Personality and Social Psychology, 88,* 770–789.

Courchesne, E., Karns, C. M., Davis, H. R., Ziccardi, R., Carper, R. A., Tigue, Z. D., et al. (2001). Unusual brain growth patterns in early life in patients with autistic disorder: An MRI study. *Neurology, 57,* 245–254.

Couturier, J. L. (2005). Efficacy of rapid-rate repetitive transcranial magnetic stimulation in the treatment of depression: A systematic review and meta-analysis. *Journal of Psychiatry and Neuroscience, 30,* 83–90.

Cowan, C. A., Atienza, J., Melton, D. A., & Eggan, K. (2005). Nuclear reprogramming of somatic cells after fusion with human embryonic stem cells. *Science, 309,* 1369–1373.

Cowan, D. T., Allan, L. G., Libretto, S. E., & Griffiths, P. (2001). Opiod drugs: A comparative survey of therapeutic and "street" use. *Pain, 2,* 193–203.

Cowan, N. (1988). Evolving concepts of memory storage, selective attention, and their mutual constraints within the human information-processing system. *Psychological Bulletin, 104,* 163–191.

Cox, M. J., & Paley, B. (2003). Understanding families as systems. *Current Directions in Psychological Science, 12,* 193–196.

Crabbe, J. C. (2002). Alcohol and genetics: new models. *American Journal of Medical Genetics, 114,* 969–974.

Crabbe, J. C., Phillips, T. J., Buck, K. J., Cunningham, C. L., & Belknap, J. K. (1999). Identifying genes for alcohol and drug sensitivity: Recent progress and future directions. *Trends in Neuroscience, 22,* 173–179.

Craig, A. D. (2002). How do you feel? Interoception: the sense of the physiological condition of the body. *Nature Reviews: Neuroscience, 3,* 655–666.

Craig, A. D., & Bushnell, M. C. (1994). The thermal grill illusion: Unmasking the burn of cold pain. *Science, 265,* 252–254.

Craighead, W. E., Craighead, L. W., & Ilardi, S. S. (1995). Behavior therapies in historical perspective. In B. M. Bongar & L. E. Beutler (Eds.), *Comprehensive textbook of psychotherapy: Theory and practice.* New York: Oxford University Press.

Craik, F. I. M., & Lockhart, R. S. (1972). Levels of processing: A framework for memory research. *Journal of Verbal Learning and Verbal Behavior, 11,* 671–684.

Craik, F. I. M., Moroz, T. M., Moscovitch, M., Stuss, D. T., Winocur, G., Tulving, E., & Kapur, S. (1999). In search of the self: A positron emission topography study. *Psychological Science, 10,* 26–34.

Craik, F. I. M., & Rabinowitz, J. C. (1984). Age differences in the acquisition and use of verbal information. In H. Bouma & D. G. Bouwhuis (Eds.), *Attention and performance* (Vol. 10, pp. 471–499). Hillsdale, NJ: Erlbaum.

Cramer, P. (2003). Personality change in later adulthood is predicted by defense mechanism use in early adulthood. *Journal of Research in Personality, 37,* 76–104.

Crandall, C. S., Preisler, J. J., & Aussprung, J. (1992). Measuring life event stress in the lives of college students: The Undergraduate Stress Questionnaire (USQ). *Journal of Behavioral Medicine, 15,* 627–662.

Crano, W. D., & Chen, X. (1998). The leniency contract and persistence of majority and minority influence. *Journal of Personality and Social Psychology, 74,* 1437–1450.

Crano, W. D., & Prislin, R. (2006). Attitudes and persuasion. *Annual Review of Psychology, 57,* 345–374.

Craske, M. G., DeCola, J. P., Sachs, A. D., & Pontillo, D. C. (2003). Panic control treatment for agoraphobia. *Journal of Anxiety Disorders, 17,* 321–333.

Crawford, T. N., Cohen, P., & Brooks, J. S. (2001). Dramatic-erratic personality disorder symptoms: II. Developmental pathways from early adolescence to adulthood. *Journal of Personality Disorders, 15,* 336–350.

Crawley, J. N., & Corwin, R. L. (1994). Biological actions of cholecystokinin. *Peptides, 15*(4), 731–755.

Creed, T. A., & Kendall, P. C. (2005). Therapist alliance-building behavior within a cognitive-behavioral treatment for anxiety in youth. *Journal of Counseling and Clinical Psychology, 73,* 498–505.

Creem, S. H., & Proffitt, D. R. (2001). Defining the cortical visual systems: "What," "where," and "how." *Acta Psychologia, 107,* 43–68.

Creery, D., & Mikrogianakis, A. (2004). Sudden infant death syndrome. *Clinical Evidence, 12,* 545–555.

Crick, F., & Koch, C. (1998). Consciousness and neuroscience. *Cerebral Cortex, 8,* 97–107.

Crick, F., & Koch, C. (2003). A framework for consciousness. *Nature Neuroscience, 6,* 119–126.

Crick, N. R., Ostrov, J. M., Appleyard, K., Jansen, E. A., & Casas, J. F. (2004). Relational aggression in early childhood: "You can't come to my birthday party unless. . . ." In M. Putallaz & K. L. Bierman (Eds.), *Aggression, antisocial behavior, and violence among girls: A developmental perspective.* (pp. 71–89). New York: Guilford Press.

Crino, R., Slade, T., & Andrews, G. (2005). The changing prevalence and severity of obsessive-compulsive disorder criteria from DSM-III to DSM-IV. American Journal of Psychiatry, 162, 876–882.

Critchley, E. M. (1991). Speech and the right hemisphere. *Behavioural Neurology, 4*(3), 143–151.

Crocker, J., & Park, L. E. (2004). The costly pursuit of self-esteem. *Psychological Bulletin, 130,* 392–414.

Crocker, J., & Wolfe, T. (2001). Contingencies of self-worth. *Psychological Review, 108,* 593–623.

Croen, L. A., Grether, J. K., & Selvin, S. (2001). The epidemiology of mental retardation of unknown cause. *Pediatrics, 107,* 86.

Crombag, H. S., & Robinson, T. E. (2004). Drugs, environment, brain, and behavior. *Current Directions in Psychological Science, 13,* 107–111.

Cronbach, L. J. (1975). Five decades of public controversy over mental testing. *American Psychologist, 30,* 1–14.

Cronbach, L. J. (1990). *Essentials of psychological testing* (5th ed.). New York: Harper & Row.

Cronbach, L. J. (1996). Acceleration among the Terman males: Correlates in midlife and after. In C. P. Benbow & D. J. Lubinski (Eds.), *Intellectual talent: Psychometric and social issues* (pp. 179–191). Baltimore: Johns-Hopkins University Press.

Cross, I. (2003). Music as a biocultural phenomenon. *Annals of the New York Academy of Sciences, 999,* 106–111.

Cross, S. E., & Madson, L. (1997). Models of the self: Self-construals and gender. *Psychological Bulletin, 122,* 5–37.

Cross, S. E., & Markus, H. R. (1999). The cultural constitution of personality. In L. Pervin & O. John (Eds.), *Handbook of personality research* (2nd ed., pp. 378–398). New York: Guilford.

Cross-National Collaborative Group. (2002). The changing rate of major depression: Cross-national comparisons. *Journal of the American Medical Association, 268,* 3098–3105.

Crowley, K., Callahan, M. A., Tenenbaum, H. R., & Allen, E. (2001). Parents explain more often to boys than to girls during shared scientific thinking. *Psychological Science, 12,* 258–261.

Crowther, J. H., Sanftner, J., Bonifazi, D. Z., & Shepherd, K. L. (2001). The role of daily hassles in binge eating. *International Journal of Eating Disorders, 29,* 449–454.

Cruz, A., & Green, B. G. (2000). Thermal stimulation of taste. *Nature, 403,* 889–892.

Csernansky, J. G., Schindler, M. K., Splinter, N. R., Wang, L., Gado, M., Selemon, L. D., et al. (2004). Abnormalities of thalamic volume and shape in schizophrenia. *American Journal of Psychiatry, 161,* 896–902.

Csikszentmihalyi, M. (1990). *Flow: The psychology of optimal experience.* New York: Harper & Row.

Culbertson, F. M. (1997). Depression and gender. An international review. *American Psychologist, 52,* 25–31.

Cullen, M. J., Hardison, C. M., & Sackett, P. R. (2004). Using SAT–grade and ability–job performance relationships to test predictions derived from stereotype threat theory. *Journal of Applied Psychology, 89,* 220–230.

Cummings, J. L. (2003). Toward a molecular neuropsychiatry of neurodegenerative diseases. *Annals of Neurology, 54*(2), 147–154.

Cummings, J. L. (2004). Alzheimer's disease. *New England Journal of Medicine, 351,* 56–67.

Curioni, C. C., & Lourenço, P. M. (2005). Long-term weight loss after diet and exercise: A systematic review. *International Journal of Obesity, 29,* 1168–1174.

Currall, S. C., Towler, A. J., Judge, T. A., & Kohn, L. (2005). Pay satisfaction and organizational outcomes. *Personnel Psychology, 58,* 613–640.

Curran, H. V., & Monaghan, L. (2001). In and out of the K-hole: A comparison of the acute and residual effects of ketamine in frequent and infrequent ketamine users. *Addiction, 96,* 749–760.

Curry, D. T., Eisenstein, R. D., & Walsh, J. K. (2006). Pharmacologic management of insomnia: Past, present, and future. *Psychiatric Clinics of North America, 29,* 871–893.

Curtis, T., Miller, B. C., & Berry, E. H. (2000). Changes in reports and incidence of child abuse following natural disasters. *Child Abuse & Neglect, 24,* 1151–1162.

Cusack, K., & Spates, C. R. (1999). The cognitive dismantling of eye movement desensitization and reprocessing (EMDR) treatment of posttraumatic stress disorder (PTSD). *Journal of Anxiety Disorders, 13,* 87–99.

Czeisler, C. A., Duffy, J. F., Shanahan, T. L., Brown, E. N., Mitchell, J. F., Rimmer, D. W., et al. (1999). Stability, precision, and near 24-hour period of the human circadian pacemaker. *Science, 284,* 2177–2181.

Czeisler, C. A., Walsh, J. K., Roth, T., Hughes, R. J., Wright, K. P., Kingsbury, L., et al. (2005). Modafinil for excessive sleepiness associated with shift-work sleep disorder. *New England Journal of Medicine, 353,* 476–486.

Daban, C., Martínez-Arán, A., Torrent, C., Sánchez-Moreno, J., Goikolea, J. M., Benabarre, A., et al. (2006). Cognitive functioning in bipolar patients receiving lamotrigine: Preliminary results. *Journal of Clinical Psychopharmacology, 26,* 178–181.

Dabbs, J. M., Jr., Riad, J. K., & Chance, S. E. (2001). Testosterone and ruthless homicide. *Personality and Individual Differences, 31,* 599–603.

Daglish, M. R., & Nutt, D. J. (2003). Brain imaging studies in human addicts. *European Neuropsychopharmacology, 13,* 453–458.

D'Agostino, R. B., Sr., Grundy, S., Sullivan, L. M., & Wilson, P. (2001). Validation of the Framingham coronary heart disease prediction scores: Results of a multiple ethnic groups investigation. *Journal of the American Medical Association, 286,* 180–187.

Daley, K. C. (2004). Update on sudden infant death syndrome. *Current Opinion in Pediatrics, 16,* 227–232.

Dallman, M. F., Pecoraro, N., Akana, S. F., La Fleur, S. E., Gomez, F., Houshyar, H., et al. (2003). Chronic stress and obesity: A new view of "comfort food." *Proceedings of the National Academies of Science, 100,* 11696–11701.

Dalman, C., & Allebeck, P. (2002). Parental age and schizophrenia: Further support for an association. *American Journal of Psychiatry, 159,* 1591–1592.

Dalton, D. R., & Mesch, D. J. (1991). On the extent and reduction of avoidable absenteeism: An assessment of absence policy provisions. *Journal of Applied Psychology, 76,* 810–817.

Daly, G., Hawi, Z., Fitzgerald, M., & Gill, M. (1999). Mapping susceptibility loci in attention deficit hyperactivity disorder: Preferential transmission of parental alleles at DAT1, DBH and DRD5 to affected children. *Molecular Biology, 4,* 192–196.

Daly, J. J., Prudic, J., Devanand, D. P., Nobler, M. S., Mitchell, S., Lisanby, S. H., et al. (2001). ECT in bipolar and unipolar depression: Differences in speed of response. *Bipolar Disorders, 3,* 95–104.

Damasio, A. R. (1994). *Descartes' error.* New York: Putnam.

Damasio, A. R., Grabowski, T. J., Bechara, A., Damasio, H., Ponto, L. L. B., Parvizi, J., & Hichwa, R. D. (2000). Subcortical and cortical brain activity during the feeling of self-generated emotions. *Nature Neuroscience, 3,* 1049–1056.

Damon, W., & Hart, D. (1982). The development of self-understanding from infancy through adolescence. *Child Development, 53,* 841–864.

Dannenberg, A. L., Burton, D. C., & Jackson, R. J. (2004). Economic and environmental costs of obesity: The impact on airlines. *American Journal of Preventive Medicine, 27,* 264–264.

Danner, D. D., Snowden, D. A., & Friesen, W. V. (2001). Positive emotions in early life and longevity findings from the nun study. *Journal of Personality and Social Psychology, 80,* 804–813.

Dansereau, F., Jr., Graen, G., & Haga, W. J. (1975). A vertical dyad linkage approach to leadership with formal organizations. *Organizational Behavior and Human Performance, 13,* 46–78.

Dapretto, M., Davies, M. S., Pfeifer, J. H., Scott, A. A., Sigman, M., Bookheimer, S. Y., et al. (2006). Understanding emotions in others: Mirror neuron dysfunction in children with autism spectrum disorders. *Nature Neuroscience, 9,* 28–30.

Darchia, N., Campbell, I. G., & Feinberg, I. (2003). Rapid eye movement density is reduced in the normal elderly. *Sleep, 26,* 973–977.

Dark, V. J., & Benbow, C. P. (1993). Cognitive differences among the gifted: A review and new data. In D. K. Detterman (Ed.), *Current topics in human intelligence* (Vol. 3, pp. 85–120). Norwood, NJ: Ablex.

Darkes, J., & Goldman, M. S. (1993). Expectancy challenge and drinking reduction. *Journal of Clinical and Consulting Psychology, 61,* 344–353.

Dar-Nimrod, I., & Heine, S. J. (2006). Exposure to scientific theories affects women's math performance. *Science, 314,* 435.

Darwin, C. E. (1965). *The expression of emotions in man and animals.* Chicago: University of Chicago Press. (Original work published 1872)

Das, J. P. (2002). A better look at intelligence. *Current Directions in Psychological Science, 11,* 28–33.

Dasgupta, A. M., Juza, D. M., White, G. M., & Maloney, J. F. (1995). Memory and hypnosis: A comparative analysis of guided memory, cognitive interview, and hypnotic hypermnesia. *Imagination, Cognition, and Personality, 14*(2), 117–130.

Dass, B., Olanow, C. W., & Kordower, J. H. (2006). Gene transfer of trophic factors and stem cell grafting as treatments for Parkinson's disease. *Neurology, 66,* S89–103.

Daus, C. S., Sanders, D. N., & Campbell, D. P. (1998). Consequences of alternative work schedules. In C. L. Cooper & I. T. Robertson (Eds.), *International review of industrial and organizational psychology 1998* (pp. 185–223). Chichester, UK: Wiley.

Davachi, L., Mitchell, J. P., & Wagner, A. D. (2003). Multiple routes to memory: Distinct medial temporal lobe processes build item and source memories. *Proceedings of the National Academy of Sciences, 100,* 2157–2162.

David, B., & Turner, J. C. (2001). Majority and minority influence: A single process self-categorization analysis. In C. K. De Dreu & N. K. De Vries (Eds.), *Group consensus and minority influence: Implications for innovation* (pp. 91–121). Malden, MA: Blackwell.

Davidson, J. K., & Moore, N. B. (1994). Guilt and lack of orgasm during sexual intercourse: Myth versus reality in college women. *Journal of Sex Education and Therapy, 20*(3), 153–174.

Davidson, J. M., Camargo, C. A., & Smith, E. R. (1979). Effects of androgen on sexual behavior in hypogonadal men. *Journal of Clinical Endocrinological Metabolism, 48,* 955–958.

Davidson, J. R., Foa, E. B., Huppert, J. D., Keefe, F. J., Franklin, M. E., Compton, J. S., et al. (2004). Fluoxetine, comprehensive cognitive behavioral therapy, and placebo in generalized social phobia. *Archives of General Psychiatry, 61,* 1005–1013.

Davidson, R. J. (2000). Affective style, psychopathology, and resilience: Brain mechanisms and plasticity. *American Psychologist, 55,* 1196–1214.

Davidson, R. J., Ekman, P., Saron, C., Senulis, J., & Friesen, W. V. (1990). Approach-withdrawal and cerebral asymmetry: Emotional expression and brain physiology: I. *Journal of Personality and Social Psychology, 58,* 330–341.

Davidson, R. J., Kabat-Zinn, J., Schumacher, J., Rosenkranz, M., Muller, D., Santorelli, S. F., et al. (2003). Alterations in brain and immune function produced by mindfulness meditation. *Psychosomatic Medicine, 65,* 564–570.

Davidson, R. J., Pizzagalli, D., Nitschke, J. B., & Putnam, K. (2002). Depression: Perspectives from affective neuroscience. *Annual Review of Psychology, 53,* 545–574.

Davidson, R. J., Shackman, A. J., & Maxwell, J. S. (2004). Asymmetries in face and brain related to emotion. *Trends in Cognitive Science, 8,* 389–391.

Davies, C. (1999, April 21). Junior doctor is cleared in baby overdose death. *London Daily Telegraph,* p. 2.

Davis, C., & Kapstein, S. (2006). Anorexia nervosa with excessive exercise: A phenotype with close links to obsessive-compulsive disorder. *Psychiatry Research, 142,* 209–217.

Davis, C., & Strachan, S. (2001). Elite female athletes with eating disorders: A study of psychopathological characteristics. *Journal of Sport & Exercise Psychology, 23,* 245–253.

Davis, J. A., & Smith, T. W. (1990). *General social surveys, 1972–1990: Cumulative codebook.* Chicago: National Opinion Research Center.

Davis, J. D., Gallagher, R. J., Ladove, R. F., & Turansky, A. J. (1969). Inhibition of food intake by a humoral factor. *Journal of Comparative and Physiological Psychology, 67,* 407–414.

Davis, J. L., & Rusbult, C. (2001). Attitude alignment in close relationships. *Journal of Personality and Social Psychology, 81,* 65–84.

Davis, J. M., Chen, N., & Glick, I. D. (2003). A meta-analysis of the efficacy of second-generation antipsychotics. *Archives of General Psychiatry, 60,* 553–564.

Davis, M., Myers, K. M., Ressler, K. J., & Rothbaum, B. O. (2005). Facilitation of extinction of conditioned fear by D-cycloserine. *Current Directions in Psychological Science, 14,* 214–219.

Davis, M., Ressler, K., Rothbaum, B. O., & Richardson, R. (2006). Effects of D-cycloserine on extinction: Translation from preclinical to clinical work. *Biological Psychiatry, 60,* 369–375.Davis, M. H., Johnsrude, I. S., Hervais-Adelman, A., Taylor, K., & McGettigan, C. (2005). Lexical information drives perceptual learning of distorted speech: Evidence from the comprehension of noise-vocoded sentences. *Journal of Experimental Psychology: General, 134,* 222–241.

Davis, M. H., Luce, C., & Kraus, S. J. (1994). The heritability of characteristics associated with dispositional empathy. *Journal of Personality, 60,* 369–391.

Davis, R. A., & Moore, C. C. (1935). Methods of measuring retention. *Journal of General Psychology, 12,* 144–155.

Davison, G. C., & Neale, J. M. (1990). *Abnormal psychology* (5th ed.). New York: Wiley.

Davison, P. R., & Parker, K. C. H. (2001). Eye movement desensitization and reprocessing (EMDR): A meta-analysis. *Journal of Consulting and Clinical Psychology, 69,* 305–316.

Dawe, L. A., Platt, J. R., & Welsh, E. (1998). Spectral-motion aftereffects and the tri-tone paradox among Canadian subjects. *Perception and Psychophysics, 60,* 209–220.

Dawes, R. M. (1994). *House of cards: Psychology and psychotherapy built on myth.* New York: Free Press.

Dawes, R. M. (1998). Behavioral decision making and judgment. In D. Gilbert, S. T. Fiske, & G. Lindzey (Eds.), *Handbook of social psychology* (Vol. 1, 4th ed., pp. 497–549). Boston: McGraw-Hill.

Dawes, R. M., & Messick, D. M. (2000). Social dilemmas. *International Journal of Psychology, 35,* 111–116.

Dawson-Basoa, M., & Gintzler, A. R. (1997). Involvement of spinal cord delta opiate receptors in the antinociception of gestation and its hormonal simulation. *Brain Research, 757,* 37–42.

Day, A. L., & Jreige, S. (2002). Examining Type A behavior pattern to explain the relationship between job stressors and psychosocial outcomes. *Journal of Occupational Health Psychology, 7,* 109–120.

Dayan, K., Kasten, R., & Fox, S. (2002). Entry-level police candidate assessment center: An efficient tool or a hammer to kill a fly? *Personnel Psychology, 55,* 827–849.

de Araujo, I. E., Rolls, E. T., Velazco, M. I., Margot, C., & Cayeux, I. (2005). Cognitive modulation of olfactory processing. *Neuron, 46,* 671–679.

Deary, I. J., Strand, S., Smith, P., & Fernandes, C. (2007). Intelligence and educational achievement. *Intelligence, 35,* 13–21.

Deary, I. J., & Caryl, P. G. (1993). Intelligence, EEG and evoked potentials. In P. A. Vernon (Ed.), *Biological approaches to the study of human intelligence* (pp. 259–315). Norwood, NJ: Ablex.

Deary, I. J., & Der, G. (2005). Reaction time explains IQ's association with death. *Psychological Science, 16*(1), 64–69.

Deary, I. J., Whalley, L. J., Lemmon, H., Crawford, J. R., & Starr, J. M. (2000). The stability of individual differences in ability from childhood to old age: Follow up of the 1932 Scottish mental survey. *Intelligence, 28,* 49–55.

Deary, I. J., Whiteman, M. C., Starr, J. M., Whalley, L. J., & Fox., H. C. (2004). The impact of childhood intelligence on later life: Following up the Scottish mental surveys of 1932 and 1947. *Journal of Personality and Social Psychology, 86,* 130–147.

Death Penalty Information Center. (2007). *Innocence and the death penalty.* Washington, DC: Death Penalty Information Center. Retrieved September 26, 2006, from http://www.deathpenaltyinfo.org/article.php?did=412&scid=6.

Deaux, K., & LaFrance, M. (1998). Gender. In D. Gilbert, S. T. Fiske, & G. Lindzey (Eds.), *Handbook of social psychology* (Vol. 1, 4th ed., pp. 778–828). Boston: McGraw-Hill.

DeBell, C., & Jones, R. D. (1997). As good as it seems? A review of EMDR experimental research. *Professional Psychology: Research and Practice, 28,* 153–163.

De Benedittis, G., Lornenzetti, A., & Pieri, A. (1990). The role of stressful life events in the onset of chronic primary headache. *Pain, 40,* 65–75.

Decety, J., & Keenan, J. (2006). Editorial. *Social Neuroscience, 1,* 1–2.

de Charms, R., Levy, J., & Wertheimer, M. (1954). A note on attempted evaluations of psychotherapy. *Journal of Clinical Psychology, 10,* 233–235.

Deci, E. L, Koestner, R., & Ryan, R. M. (1999). The undermining effect is a reality after all—Extrinsic rewards, task interest, and self-determination: Reply to Eisenberger, Pierce, and Cameron (1999) and Lepper, Henderlong, and Gingras (1999). *Psychological Bulletin, 125,* 692–700.

Deci, E. L., Koestner, R., & Ryan, R. M. (2001). A meta-analytic review of experiments examining the effects of extrinsic rewards on intrinsic motivation. *Psychological Bulletin, 125,* 627–668.

Deci, E. L., & Ryan, R. M. (2000). The "what" and "why" of goal pursuits: Human needs and the self-determination of behavior. *Psychological Inquiry, 11,* 227–268.

Deeb, S. S. (2005). The molecular basis of variation in human color vision. *Clinical Genetics, 67,* 369–377.

Deeb, S. S., & Kohl, S. (2003). Genetics of color vision deficiencies. *Developmental Ophthalmology, 37*, 170–187.

Deeprose, C., & Andrade, J. (2006). Is priming during anesthesia unconscious? *Consciousness and Cognition, 15*, 1–23.

Deep-Soboslay, A., Akil, M., Martin, C. E., Bigelow, L. B., Herman, M. M., et al. (2006). Reliability of psychiatric diagnosis in postmortem research. Biological Psychiatry, 57, 96–101.

de Gelder, B., Frissen, I., Barton, J., & Hadjikhani, N. (2003). A modulatory role for facial expressions in prosopagnosia. *Proceedings of the National Academies of Science, 100*, 13105–13110.

de Gelder, B., Snyder, J., Greve, D., Gerard, G., & Hadjikhani, N. (2004). Fear fosters flight: A mechanism for fear contagion when perceiving emotion expressed by a whole body. *Proceedings of the National Academy of Sciences of the USA, 101*, 16701–16706.

De Houwer, A. (1995). Bilingual language acquisition. In P. Fletcher & B. MacWhinney (Eds.), *The handbook of child language* (pp. 219–250). Cambridge, MA: Blackwell.

Deich, J. D., Tankoos, J., & Balsam, P. D. (1995). Systematic changes in gaping during the ontogeny of pecking in ring doves (*Streptopelia risoria*). *Developmental Psychobiology, 28*, 147–163.

de Lacoste-Utamsing, C., & Holloway, R. L. (1982). Sexual dimorphism in the human corpus callosum. *Science, 216*, 1431–1432.

Delamater, A. R. (2004). Experimental extinction in Pavlovian conditioning: Behavioural and neuroscience perspectives. *Quarterly Journal of Experimental Psychology, 57B*, 97–132.

Delbello, M. P., Kowatch, R. A., Adler, C. M., Stanford, K. E., Welge, J. A., Barzman, D. H., et al. (2006). A double-blind randomized pilot study comparing quetiapine and divalproex for adolescent mania. *Journal of the American Academy of Child & Adolescent Psychiatry, 45*, 305–313.

DeLisi, L. E., Maurizio, A., Yost, M., Papparozzi, C. F., Fulchino, C., Katz, C. L., et al. (2003). A survey of New Yorkers after the Sept. 11, 2001, terrorist attacks. *American Journal of Psychiatry, 160*, 780–783.

Delmolino, L. M., & Romanczyk, R. G. (1995). Facilitated communication: A critical review. *The Behavior Therapist 18*, 27–30.

De Los Reyes, A., & Kazdin, A. E. (2006). Conceptualizing changes in behavior in intervention research: The range of possible changes model. *Psychological Review, 113*, 554–583.

De Macedo-Soares, M. B., Moreno, R. A., Rigonatti, S. P., & Lafer, B. (2005). Efficacy of electroconvulsive therapy in treatment-resistant bipolar disorder: A case series. *Journal of ECT, 21*, 31–34.

Demaray, M. K., & Malecki, C. K. (2002). Critical levels of perceived social support associated with student adjustment. *School Psychology Quarterly, 17*, 213–241.

Dement, W. (1960). The effect of dream deprivation. *Science, 131*, 1705–1707.

Dement, W., & Kleitman, N. (1957). Cyclic variations in EEG during sleep and their relation to eye movements, body motility and dreaming. *Electroencephalography and Clinical Neurophysiology, 9*, 673–690.

Demerouti, E., Geurts, S. A. E., Bakker, A. B., & Euwema, M. (2004). The impact of shiftwork on work-home conflict, job attitudes, and health. *Ergonomics, 47*, 987–1002.

Demo, D. H., Allen, K. R., & Fine, M. A. (Eds.). (2000). *Handbook of family diversity.* New York: Oxford University Press.

de Moor, J. S., de Moor, C. A., Basen-Engquist, K., Kudelka, A., Bevers, M. W., & Cohen, L. (2006). Optimism, distress, health-related quality of life, and change in cancer antigen 125 among patients with ovarian cancer undergoing chemotherapy. *Psychosomatic Medicine, 68*, 555–562.

Denberg, T. D., Melhado, T. V., & Steiner, J. F. (2006). Patient treatment preferences in localized prostate carcinoma: The influence of emotion, misconception, and anecdote. *Cancer, 107*, 620–630.

Denrell, J. (2005). Why most people disapprove of me: Experience sampling in impression formation. *Psychological Review, 112*, 951–978.

Denton, G. (1980). The influence of visual pattern on perceived speed. *Perception, 9*, 393–402.

DePrince, A. P., & Freyd, J. J. (2004). Forgetting trauma stimuli. *Psychological Science, 15*, 488–492.

de Rios, M. D. (1992). Power and hallucinogenic states of consciousness among the Moche: An ancient Peruvian society. In C. A. Ward (Ed.), *Altered states of consciousness and mental health: A cross-cultural perspective.* Newbury Park, CA: Sage.

Derogowski, J. B. (1989). Real space and represented space: Cross-cultural perspectives. *Behavior and Brain Sciences, 12*, 51–73.

DeRosse, P., Funke, B., Burdick, K. E., Lencz, T., & Ekholm, J. M. (2006). Dysbindin genotype and negative symptoms of schizophrenia. American Journal of Psychiatry, 163, 532–534.

Derrington, A. M., & Webb, B. S. (2004). Visual system: How is the retina wired up to the cortex? *Current Biology, 14*, R14–15.

Derry, C. J., Derry, S., McQuay, H. J., & Moore, R. A. (2006). Systematic review of systematic reviews of acupuncture published 1996–2005. *Clinical Medicine, 6*, 381–386.

Derryberry, D., & Tucker, D. M. (1992). Neural mechanisms of emotion. *Journal of Consulting and Clinical Psychology, 60*, 329–338.

DeRubeis, R. J., Hollon, S. D., Amsterdam, J. D., Shelton, R. C., Young, P. R., Salomon, R. M., et al. (2005). Cognitive therapy vs medications in the treatment of moderate to severe depression. *Archives of General Psychiatry, 62*, 409–416.

DeSchepper, B., & Treisman, A. (1996). Visual memory for novel shapes: Implicit coding without attention. *Journal of Experimental Psychology: Learning, Memory and Cognition 22*, 27–47.

Deshpande, D. M., Kim, Y. S., Martinez, T., Carmen, J., Dike, S., Shats, I., et al. (2006). Recovery from paralysis in adult rats using embryonic stem cells. *Annals of Neurology, 60*, 32–44.

de Silva, P. (1994). Psychological treatment of sexual problems. *International Review of Psychiatry, 6*(2–3), 163–173.

D'Esposito, M. (Ed.). (2003). *Neurological foundations of cognitive neuroscience.* Cambridge, MA: MIT Press.

D'Esposito, M., Detre, J. A., Alsop, D. C., & Shin, R. K. (1995). The neural basis of the central executive system of working memory. *Nature, 378*, 279–281.

Destexhe, A., & Marder, E. (2004). Plasticity in single neuron and circuit computations. *Nature, 431*, 789–795.

Detera-Wadleigh, S. D., & McMahon, F. J. (2004). Genetic association studies in mood disorders: Issues and promise. International Review of Psychiatry, 16, 301–310.

Detterman, D. K. (1982). Does "g" exist? *Intelligence, 6*, 99–108.

Detterman, D. K. (1987). Theoretical notions of intelligence and mental retardation. *American Journal of Mental Deficiency, 92*, 2–11.

Detterman, D. K. (1994). A system theory of intelligence. In D. K. Detterman (Ed.), *Current topics in human intelligence: Vol. 4. Theories of Intelligence* (pp. 85–115). Norwood, NJ: Ablex.

Deutsch, M., & Gerard, H. B. (1955). A study of normative and informative social influences on individual judgments. *Journal of Abnormal and Social Psychology, 51*, 629–636.

Devanand, D. P., Pradhaban, G., Liu, X., Khandji, A., De Santi, S. Segal, S., et al. (2007). Hippocampal and entorhinal atrophy in mild cognitive impairment: Prediction of Alzheimer's disease. *Neurology, 68*, 828–836.

Devi, G., & Quitschke, W. (1999). Alois Alzheimer, neuroscientist (1864–1915). *Alzheimer Disease and Associated Disorders, 13*(3), 132–137.

Devilly, G. J., Varker, T., Hansen, K., & Gist, R. (2007). An analogue study of the effects of psychological debriefing on eyewitness testimony. *Behaviour Research and Therapy, 45*, 1245–1254.

Devine, P. G. (1989). Stereotypes and prejudice: Their automatic and controlled components. *Journal of Personality and Social Psychology, 56*, 5–18.

Devine, P., Plant, E. A., & Buswell, B. N. (2000). Breaking the prejudice habit: Progress and obstacles. In S. Oskamp (Ed.), *Reducing prejudice and discrimination* (pp. 175–190). Hillsdale, NJ: Erlbaum.

DeVries, R. (1969). Constancy of generic identity in the years three to six. *Monographs of the Society for Research in Child Development, 34* (3, Serial No. 127).

Devulder, J., Crombez, E., & Mortier, E. (2002). Central pain: An overview. *Acta Neurologica Belgia, 102*, 97–103.

DeYoung, C. G., Peterson, J. B., & Higgins, D. M. (2005). Sources of openness/intellect: Cognitive and neuropsychological correlates of the fifth factor of personality. *Journal of Personality, 73*, 825–858.

Dhurandhar, N. V., Israel, B. A., Kolesar, J. M., Mayhew, G. F., Cook, M. E., & Atkinson, R. L. (2000). Increased adiposity in animals due to a human virus. *International Journal of Obesity, 24*, 989–996.

Diakidoy, I. N., & Spanoudis, G. (2002). Domain specificity in creativity testing: A comparison of performance on a general divergent-thinking test and a parallel, content-specific test. *Journal of Creative Behavior, 36*, 41–61.

Diamond, L. M. (2004). Emerging perspectives on distinctions between romantic love and sexual desire. *Current Directions in Psychological Science, 13*, 116–119.

Diana, M., Spiga, S., & Acquas, E. (2006). Persistent and reversible morphine withdrawal–induced morphological changes in the nucleus accumbens. *Annals of the New York Academy of Sciences, 1074*, 446–457.

Dickerson, F. B., Tenhula, W. N., & Green-Paden, L. D. (2005). The token economy for schizophrenia: Review of the literature and recommendations for future research. *Schizophrenia Research, 75*, 405–416.

Dickinson, A. (2001). Causal learning: Association versus computation. *Current Directions in Psychological Science, 10*, 127–132.

DiClemente, R. J., Wingood, G. M., Harrington, K. F., Lang, D. L., Davies, S. L., Hook, E. W., III, et al. (2004). Efficacy of an HIV prevention intervention for African American adolescent girls: A randomized controlled trial. *Journal of the American Medical Association, 292*, 171–179.

Diego, M. A., Field, T., & Hernandez-Reif, M. (2005). Prepartum, postpartum, and chronic depression effects on neonatal behavior. *Infant Behavior & Development, 28*, 155–164.

Diego, M. A., Field, T., & Hernandez-Reif, M. (2005). Vagal activity, gastric motility, and weight gain in massaged preterm neonates. *Journal of Pediatrics, 147,* 50–55.

Diener, E. (2000). Subjective well-being: The science of happiness and a proposal for a national index. *American Psychologist, 55,* 34–43.

Diener, E. (2003). What is positive about positive psychology: The curmudgeon and Pollyanna. *Psychological Inquiry, 14,* 115–120.

Diener, E., & Biswas-Diener, R. (2002). Will money increase subjective well-being? *Social Indicators Research, 57,* 119–169.

Diener, E., & Diener, C. (1995). Most people are happy. *Psychological Science, 7,* 181–185.

Diener, E., & Seligman, M. E. P. (2004). Beyond money: Towards an economy of well-being. *Psychological Science in the Public Interest, 5,* 1–31.

Dierdorff, E. C., & Wilson, M. A. (2003). A meta-analysis of job analysis reliability. *Journal of Applied Psychology, 88,* 635–646.

Dijksterhuis, A., Bos, M. W., Nordgren, L. F., & van Baaren, R. B. (2006). On making the right choice: The deliberation-without-attention effect. *Science, 311,* 1005–1007.

Dijksterhuis, A., & Nordgren, L. F. (2006). A theory of unconscious thought. *Perspectives on Psychological Science, 1,* 95–109.

Dillard, A. J., McCaul, K. D., & Klein, W. M. P. (2006). Unrealistic optimism in smokers: Implications for smoking myth endorsement and self-protective motivation. *Journal of Health Communication, 11,* 93–102.

Di Marzo, V., Goparaju, S. K., Wang, L., Liu, J., Batkai, S., Jarai, Z., et al. (2001). Leptin-regulated endocannabinoids are involved in maintaining food intake. *Nature, 410,* 822–825.

Dimidjian, S., Hollon, S. D., Dobson, K. S., Schmaling, K. B., Kohlenberg, R. J., Addis, M. E., et al. (2006). Randomized trial of behavioral activation, cognitive therapy, and antidepressant medication in the acute treatment of adults with major depression. *Journal of Consulting and Clinical Psychology, 74,* 658–670.

Di Milia, L. (2006). Shift work, sleepiness, and long distance driving. *Transportation Research, 9,* 278–285.

Dinan, T. G. (2001). Novel approaches to the treatment of depression by modulating the hypothalamic-pituitary-adrenal axis. *Human Psychopharmacology: Clinical and Experimental, 16,* 89–93.

Dingus, T. A., Klauer, S. G., Neale, V. L., Petersen, A., Lee, S. E., Sudweeks, J., et al. (2006). *The 100-car naturalistic driving study, Phase II: Results of the 100-car field experiment* (Contract No. DTNH22–00–C–07007). Washington, DC: National Highway Traffic Safety Administration.

Dion, K. (2003). Prejudice, racism and discrimination. In T. Millon & M. Lerner (Eds.), *Handbook of psychology: Volume 5: Personality and social psychology* (pp. 507–536). Hoboken, NJ: Wiley.

DiPietro, J. A., Novak, M. F., Costigan, K. A., Atella, L. D., & Reusing, S. P. (2006). Maternal psychological distress during pregnancy in relation to child development at age two. *Child Development, 77,* 573–587.

Dittmar, H., Halliwell, E., & Ive, S. (2006). Does Barbie make girls want to be thin?: The effect of experimental exposure to images of dolls on the body image of 5- to 8-year-old girls. *Developmental Psychology, 42,* 283–292.

Dixon, M., Brunet, A., & Laurence, J.-R. (1990). Hypnotizability and automaticity: Toward a parallel distributed processing model of hypnotic responding. *Journal of Abnormal Psychology, 99,* 336–343.

Dobrovitsky, V., Pimentel, P., Duarte, A., Froestl, W., Stellar, J. R., & Trzcinska, M. (2002). CGP 44532, a GABAB receptor agonist, is hedonically neutral and reduces cocaine-induced enhancement of reward. *Neuropharmacology, 42,* 626–632.

Dobson, K. S. (Ed.). (2003). *Handbook of cognitive-behavioral therapies* (2nd ed.). New York: Guilford.

Dodd, M. L., Klos, K. J., Bower, J. H., Geda, Y. E., Josephs, K. A., & Ahlskog, J. E. (2005). Pathological gambling caused by drugs used to treat Parkinson disease. *Archives of Neurology, 62,* 1377–1381.

Dodge, K. A., Coie, J. D., & Lynam, D. (2006). Aggression and antisocial behavior in youth. In W. Damon & R. M. Lerner (Series Eds.) & N. Eisenberg (Vol. Ed.), *Handbook of child psychology:Vol. 3, Social, emotional, and personality development* (6th ed., pp. 719–788). New York: Wiley.

Dodson, C., & Reisberg, D. (1991). Indirect testing of eyewitness memory: The (non)effect of misinformation. *Bulletin of the Psychonomic Society, 29,* 333–336.

Dohnt, H., & Tiggermann, M. (2006). The contribution of peer and media influences to the development of body satisfaction and self-esteem in young girls: A prospective study. *Developmental Psychology, 42,* 929–936.

Dohrenwend, B. P., Raphael, K. G., Schwartz, S., Stueve, A., & Skodol, A. (1993). The structured event probe and narrative rating method for measuring stressful life events. In L. Goldenberger & S. Breznitz (Eds.), *Handbook of stress: Theoretical and clinical aspects* (2nd ed.). New York: The Free Press.

Dohrenwend, B. P., Turner, J. B., Turse, N. A., Adams, B. G., Koenen, K. C., & Marshall, R. (2006). The psychological risks of Vietnam for U.S. veterans: A revisit with new data and methods. *Science, 313,* 979–982.

Dolan, M., & Fullam, R. (2006). Memory for emotional events in violent offenders with antisocial personality disorder. Personality and Individual Differences, 38, 1657–1667.

Dolan, M., & Park, I. (2002). The neuropsychology of antisocial personaity disorder. *Psychological Medicine, 32,* 417–427.

Dollard, J., Doob, L., Miller, N., Mowrer, O. H., & Sears, R. R. (1939). *Frustration and aggression.* New Haven, CT: Yale University Press.

Dollinger, S. J. (2000). Locus of control and incidental learning: An application to college students. *College Student Journal, 34,* 537–540.

Domhoff, G. W. (1996). *Finding meaning in dreams: A quantitative approach.* New York: Plenum.

Domhoff, G. W. (2001). A new neurocognitive theory of dreams. *Dreaming: Journal of the Association for the Study of Dreams, 11,* 13–33.

Domino, E. F. (2003). Effects of tobacco smoking on electroencephalographic, auditory evoked and event related potentials. *Brain and Cognition, 53,* 66–74.

Domitrovich, C. E., & Greenberg, M. T. (2000). The study of implementation: Current findings from effective programs that prevent mental disorders in school-aged children. *Journal of Educational and Psychological Consultation, 11,* 193–221.

Domjan, M. (2005). Pavlovian conditioning: A functional perspective. *Annual Review of Psychology, 56,* 179–206.

Donegan, N. H., & Thompson, R. F. (1991). The search for the engram. In J. L. Martinez & R. P. Kesner (Eds.), *Learning and memory: A biological view* (2nd ed.). San Diego: Academic Press.

Donnerstein, E. (1984). Pornography: Its effects on violence against women. In N. M. Malamuth & E. Donnerstein (Eds.), *Pornography and sexual aggression.* New York: Academic Press.

Donnerstein, E., Slaby, R. G., & Eron, L. D. (1995). The mass media and youth aggression. In L. Eron, J. Gentry, & P. Schlegel (Eds.), *Reason to hope: A psychosocial perspective on violence and youth* (pp. 219–250). Washington, DC: American Psychological Association.

Donovan, J. J., & Radosevich, D. J. (1999). A meta-analytic review of the distribution of practice effect: Now you see it, now you don't. *Journal of Applied Psychology, 84,* 795–805.

Dougherty, D. D., Baer, L., Cosgrove, G. R., Cassem, E. H., Price, B. H., Nierenberg, A. A., et al. (2002). Prospective long-term follow-up of 44 patients who received cingulotomy for treatment-refractory obsessive-compulsive disorder. *American Journal of Psychiatry, 159,* 269–275.

Dovidio, J. F., & Gaertner, S. L. (2000). Aversive racism and selection decisions: 1989 and 1999. *Psychological Science, 11,* 319–323.

Dovidio, J. F., Gaertner, S. L., & Kawakami, K. (2003). Intergroup contact: The past, present, and the future. *Group Processes and Intergroup Relations, 6,* 5–20.

Dovidio, J. F., Kawakami, K., & Beach, K. R. (2001). Implicit and explicit attitudes: Examination of the relationship between measures of intergroup bias. In R. Brown & S. Gaertner (Eds.), *Blackwell handbook of social psychology: Vol. 4. Intergroup relations* (pp. 175–197). Oxford, England: Blackwell.

Dovidio, J. F., Kawakami, K., & Gaertner, S. L. (2000). Reducing contemporary prejudice: Combating explicit and implicit bias ai the individual and intergroup level. In S. Oskamp (Ed.), *Reducing prejudice and discrimination* (pp. 137–163). Hillsdale, NJ: Erlbaum.

Dovidio, J. F., Piliavin, J. A., Gaertner, S. L., Schroeder, D. A., & Clark, R. D., III. (1991). The arousal: cost-reward model and the process of intervention: A review of the evidence. In M. Clark (Ed.), *Review of personality and social psychology: Vol. 12. Prosocial behavior* (pp. 86–118). Newbury Park, CA: Sage.

Dovidio, J. F., Piliavin, J. A., Schroeder, D. A., & Penner, L. (2006). *The social psychology of prosocial behavior.* Mahwah, NJ: Lawrence Erlbaum Associates Publishers.

Dovidio, J. F., Smith, J. K., Donnella, A. G., & Gaertner, S. L. (1997). Racial attitudes and the death penalty. *Journal of Applied Social Psychology, 27,* 1468–1487.

Downey, D. B., & Condron, D. J. (2004). Playing well with others in kindergarten: The benefit of siblings at home. *Journal of Marriage and Family, 66,* 333–350.

Downey-Lamb, M. M., & Woodruff-Pak, D. S. (1999). Early detection of cognitive deficits using eyeblink classical conditioning. *Alzheimer's Reports, 2,* 37–44.

Dowson, D. I., Lewith, G. T., & Machin, D. (1985). The effects of acupuncture versus placebo in the treatment of headache. *Pain, 21,* 35–42.

Doyle, J. (2005). *True witness: Cops, courts, science, and the battle against misidentification.* New York: Palgrave Macmillan.

Draganski, B., Gaser, C., Busch, V., Schuierer, G., Bogdahn, U., & May, A. (2004). Neuroplasticity: Changes in grey matter induced by training. *Nature, 427,* 311–312.

Drasbek, K. R., Christensen, J., & Jensen, K. (2006). Gamma-hydroxybutyrate—a drug of abuse. *Acta Neurologica Scandinavica, 114,* 145–156.

Drayna, D., Manichaikul, A., de Lange, M., Snieder, H., & Spector, T. (2001). Genetic correlates of musical pitch recognition in humans. *Science, 291,* 1969–1972.

Dreyfus, H. L., & Dreyfus, S. E. (1988). Making a mind versus modeling the brain: Intelligence back at a branchpoint. In S. R. Graubard (Ed.), *The artificial intelligence debate.* Cambridge: MIT Press.

Drinkwater, J., & Stewart, A. (2002). Cognitive behavior therapy for young people. *Current Opinion in Psychiatry, 15,* 377–381.

Driscoll, I., McDaniel, M. A., & Guynn, M. J. (2005). Apolipoprotein E and prospective memory in normally aging adults. *Neuropsychology, 19,* 28–34.

Driver, J., Tabares, A., Shapiro, A., Nahm, E. Y., & Gottman, J. M. (2003). Interactional patterns in marital success and failure: Gottman laboratory studies. In F. Walsh (Ed.), *Normal family processes: Growing diversity and complexity* (3rd ed., pp. 493–513). New York: Guilford.

Driver, J. L., & Gottman, J. M. (2004). Daily marital interactions and positive affect during marital conflict among newlywed couples. *Family Process, 43,* 301–314.

Drucker, D. B., Ackroff, K., & Sclafani, A. (1994). Nutrient-conditioned flavor preference and acceptance in rats: Effects of deprivation state and nonreinforcement. *Physiology and Behavior, 56*(4), 701–707.

Druckman, D., & Bjork, R. A. (1994). *Learning, remembering, believing: Enhancing human performance.* Washington, DC: National Academy Press.

Drummond, S. P., Brown, G. G., Gillin, J. C., Stricker, J. L., Wong, E. C., & Buxton, R. B. (2000). Altered brain response to verbal learning following sleep deprivation. *Nature, 403,* 655–657.

Druss, B. G., Rosenheck, R. A., & Sledge, W. H. (2000). Health and disability costs of depressive illness in a major U.S. Corporation. *American Journal of Psychiatry, 157,* 1274–1278.

Dube, S. R., Felitti, V. J., Dong, M., Chapman, D. P., Giles, W. H., & Anda, R. F. (2003). Childhood abuse, neglect, and household dysfunction and the risk of illicit drug use: the adverse childhood experiences study. *Pediatrics, 111,* 564–572.

Dubertret, C., Hanoun, N., Ades, J., Hamon, M., & Gorwood, P. (2004). Family-based association studies between 5-HT-sub(5A) receptor gene and schizophrenia. Journal of Psychiatric Research, 38, 371–376.

Dubois, B. (2004). Amnestic MCI or prodromal Alzheimer's disease? *Lancet Neurology, 3*(4), 246–248.

DuBois, G. E. (2004). Unraveling the biochemistry of sweet and umami tastes. *Proceedings of the National Academy of Sciences, 101,* 13972–13973.

DuBreuil, S. C., Garry, M., & Loftus, E. F. (1998). Tales from the crib: Memories of infancy. In S. J. Lynn, & K. M. McConkey (Eds.), *Truth in memory* (pp. 137–160). New York: Guilford.

Dubrovsky, B. O. (2005). Steroids, neuroactive steroids and neurosteroids in psychopathology. *Progress in Neuropsychopharmacology and Biological Psychiatry, 29,* 169–192.

Ducharme, J. M., & Van Houten, R. (1994). Operant extinction in the treatment of severe maladaptive behavior: Adapting research to practice. *Behavior Modification, 18,* 139–170.

Duckitt, J. H. (1994). *The social psychology of prejudice.* Westport, CT: Praeger.

Duclos, S. E., & Laird, J. D. (2001). The deliberate control of emotional experience through control of expressions. *Cognition and Emotion, 15,* 27–56.

Dudai, Y. (2004). The neurobiology of consolidations, or, how stable is the engram? *Annual Review of Psychology, 55,* 51–86.

Dudley, N. M., Orvis, K. A., Lebeicki, J. E., & Cortina, J. M. (2006). A meta-analytic investigation of conscientiousness in the prediction of job performance: Examining the intercorrelations and the incremental validity of narrow traits. *Journal of Applied Psychology, 91,* 40–57.

Duffy, V. B., Fast, K., Cohen Z., Chodos, E., and Bartoshuk, L. M. (1999). Genetic taste status associates with fat food acceptance and body mass index in adults. *Chemical Senses.*

Duggan, A., Fuddy, L., Burrell, L., Higman, S. M., McFarlane, E., Windham, A., et al. (2004). Randomized trial of a statewide home visiting program to prevent child abuse: Impact in reducing parental risk factors. *Child Abuse and Neglect, 28,* 623–643.

Dujovne, V., & Houston, B. (1991). Hostility-related variables and plasma lipid levels. *Journal of Behavioral Medicine, 14,* 555–564.

Duke, C. R., & Carlson, L. (1994). Applying implicit memory measures: Word fragment completion in advertising tests. *Journal of Current Issues and Research in Advertising, 15,* 1–14.

Duncan, A. E., Scherrer, J., Fu, Q., Bucholz, K. K., Heath, A. C., et al. (2006). Exposure to paternal alcoholism does not predict development of alcohol-use disorders in offspring: Evidence from an offspring-of-twins study. Journal of Studies on Alcohol, 67, 649–656.

Duncan, B. L. (2002). The legacy of Saul Rosenwieg: The profundity of the dodo bird. *Journal of Psychotherapy Integration, 12*(1), 32–57.

Duncan, G. J., Brooks-Gunn, J., & Klebanov, P. K. (1994). Economic deprivation and early childhood development. *Child Development, 65,* 296–318.

Dunn, J., & Hughes, C. (2001). "I got some swords and you're dead!": Violent fantasy, antisocial behavior, friendship, and moral sensibility in young children. *Child Development, 72,* 491–505.

Dunne, E., & Fitzpatrick, A. C. (1999). The views of professionals on the role of self-help groups in the mental health area. *Irish Journal of Psychological Medicine, 16,* 84–89.

Dunning, D. (2001). On the motives underlying social cognition. In A. Tesser & N. Schwarz (Eds.), *Blackwell handbook of social psychology: Intraindividual processes* (pp. 348–374). Oxford, England: Blackwell.

Dunton, B. C., & Fazio, R. H. (1997). An individual difference measure of motivation to control prejudiced reactions. *Personality and Social Psychology Bulletin, 23,* 316–326.

Duran, B., Oetzel, J., Lucero, J., Jiang, Y., Novins, D.K., Manson, S., et al. (2005). Obstacles for rural American Indians seeking alcohol, drug, or mental health treatment. *Journal of Consulting and Clinical Psychology, 73,* 819–829.

Durand, M. V., & Barlow, D. H. (2006). Essentials of abnormal psychology. Belmont, CA: Thomson.

Durantini, M. R., Albarracín, D., Mitchell, A. L., Earl, A. N.,& Gillette, J. C. (2006). Conceptualizing the influence of social agents of behavior change: A meta-analysis of the effectiveness of HIV-prevention interventionists for different groups. *Psychological Bulletin, 132,* 212–248.

Durbin, C. E., & Klein, D. N. (2006). Ten-year stability of personality disorders among outpatients with mood disorders. Journal of Abnormal Psychology, 115, 75–84.

Durka, P. J., Malinowska, U., Szelenberger, W., Wakarow, A., & Blinowska, K. J. (2005). High resolution parametric description of slow wave sleep. *Journal of Neuroscience Methods, 147,* 15–21.

Durlak, J. A. (2006). Cognitive-behavioral treatments. In R. T. Ammerman (Ed.), *Comprehensive handbook of personality and psychopathology* (Vol. 3, pp. 438–447). New York: Wiley.

Durose, M. R., Harlow, C. W., Langan, P. A., Motivans, M., Rantala, R. R., & Smith, E. L. (2005). *Family violence statistics.* Washington, DC: Bureau of Justice Statistics.

Dutton, D. G., & Aron, A. P. (1974). Some evidence for heightened sexual attraction under conditions of high anxiety. *Journal of Personality and Social Psychology, 30,* 510–517.

Düzel, E., Vargha-Khamdem, F., Heinze, H. J., & Mishkin, M. (2001). Brain activity evidence for recognition without recollection after early hippocampal damage. *Proceedings of the National Academy of Science, 98,* 8101–8106.

Dweck, C. S. (1998). The development of early self-conceptions: Their relevance for motivational processes. In J. Heckhausen & C. S. Dweck (Eds.), *Motivation and self-regulation across the life span.* New York: Cambridge University Press.

Dwork, A. J., Arango, V., Underwood, M., Iievski, B., Rosoklija, G., Sackeim, H. A., et al. (2004). Absence of histological lesions in primate models of ECT and magnetic seizure therapy. *American Journal of Psychiatry, 161,* 576–578.

Dyche, L., & Zayas, L. H. (2001). Cross-cultural empathy and training the contemporary psychotherapist. *Clinical Social Work Journal, 29,* 245–258.

Dyck, E. (2005). Flashback: Psychiatric experimentation with LSD in historical perspective. *Canadian Journal of Psychiatry, 50,* 381–388.

d'Ydewalle, G., & Rosselle, H. (1978). Text expectations in text learning. In M. M. Gruneberg, P. E. Morris, & R. N. Sykes (Eds.), *Practical aspects of memory.* Orlando, FL: Academic Press.

Dyken, M. E., & Yamada, T. (2005). Narcolepsy and disorders of excessive somnolence. *Primary Care, 32,* 389–413.

Dzokoto, V. A., & Adams, G. (2005). Understanding genital-shrinking epidemics in West Africa: Koro, Juju, or mass psychogenic illness? Culture, Medicine, and Psychiatry, 29, 53–78.

Eagleman, D. M., Kagan, A. D., Nelson, S. S., Sagaram, D., & Sarma, A. K. (2007). A standardized test battery for the study of synesthesia. *Journal of Neuroscience Methods, 159,* 139–145.

Eagly, A. H. (1987). *Sex differences in social behavior: A social-role interpretation.* Hillsdale, NJ: Erlbaum.

Eagly, A. H. (1996). Differences between women and men: Their magnitude, practical importance, and political meaning. *American Psychologist, 51,* 158–159.

Eagly, A. H. (2005). Achieving relational authenticity in leadership: Does gender matter? *Leadership Quarterly, 16,* 459–474.

Eagly, A. H., Johannesen-Schmidt, M. C., & van Engen, M. L. (2003). Transformational, transactional, and laissez-faire leadership styles: A meta-analysis comparing women and men. *Psychological Bulletin, 129,* 569–591.

Eagly, A. H., & Karau, S. J. (1991). Gender and the emergence of leaders: A meta-analysis. *Journal of Personality and Social Psychology, 60,* 685–710.

Eagly, A. H., Karau, S. J., & Makhijani, M. G. (1995). Gender and the effectiveness of leaders: A meta-analysis. *Psychological Bulletin, 117,* 125–145.

Eagly, A. H., Makhijani, M. G., & Klonsky, B. G. (1992). Gender and evaluation of leaders: A meta-analysis. *Psychological Bulletin, 111,* 3–22.

Eagly, A. H., & Wood, W. (1999). The orgins of sex diffrences in human behavior: Evolved dispositions versus social roles. *American Psychologist, 54,* 408–423.

Eagly, A. H., Wood, W. & Johannesen-Schmidt, M. C. (2004). Social role theory of sex differences and similarities: Implications for the partner preferences of women and men. In A. H. Eagly, A. E. Beall, & R. J. Sternberg, (Eds), *The psychology of gender* (2nd ed., pp. 269–295). New York: Guilford Press.

East, P. L., & Jacobson, L. J. (2001). The younger siblings of teenage mothers: A follow-up of their pregnancy risk. *Developmental Psychology, 37,* 254–264.

Eaton, M. J., & Dembo, M. H. (1997). Differences in the motivational beliefs of Asian American and non-Asian students. *Journal of Educational Psychology, 89,* 433–440.

Ebert, S. A., Tucker, D. C., & Roth, D. L. (2002). Psychological resistance factors as predictors of general health status and physical symptom reporting. *Psychology Health & Medicine, 7,* 363–375.

Fahsing, I. A., Ask, K., & Granhag, P. A. (2004). The man behind the mask: Accuracy and predictors of eyewitness offender descriptions. *Journal of Applied Psychology, 89,* 722–729.

Falicov, C. J. (2003). Culture, society, and gender in depression. *Journal of Family Therapy, 25,* 371–387.

Fan, J., Ma, J., Li, X., Zhang, C., & Sun, W. (2006). Population-based and family-based association studies of an (AC)n dinucleotide repeat in an a-7 nicotinic receptor subunit gene and schizophrenia. *Schizophrenia Research, 84,* 222–227.

Farah, M. J. (1996). Is face recognition "special"? Evidence from neuropsychology. *Behavioral Brain Research, 76*(1–2), 181–189.

Farah, M. J. (2000). *The cognitive neuroscience of vision.* Malden, MA: Blackwell.

Farah, M. J., McMullen, P. A., & Meyer, M. M. (1991). Can recognition of living things be selectively impaired? *Neuropsychologia, 29*(2), 185–193.

Faraone, S. V., Doyle, A. E., Mick, E., Biederman, J. (2001). Meta-analysis of the association between the dopamine D4 gene 7-repeat allele and attention deficit hyperactivity disorder. *American Journal of Psychiatry, 158,* 1052–1057.

Faravelli, C., Rosi, S., Scarpato, M. A., Lampronti, L., et al. (2006). Threshold and subthreshold bipolar disorders in the Sesto Fiorentino Study. *Journal of Affective Disorders, 94,* 111–119.

Farha, B. (2005). Blundered predictions in 2004: A Sylvia Browne review. *Skeptical Inquirer, 29,* 8–9.

Farley, F (1986). The big T in personality. *Psychology Today, 20,* 44–52.

Farmer, J. D., Patelli, P., & Zovko, I. I. (2005). The predictive power of zero intelligence in financial markets. *Proceedings of the National Academy of Sciences of the USA, 102,* 2254–2259.

Farmer, R. F., & Nelson-Gray, R. (2005). *Personality-guided behavior therapy.* Washington, DC: American Psychological Association.

Farooqi, I. S., Jebb, S. A., Langmack, G., Lawrence, E., Cheetham, C. H., Prentice, A. M., et al. (1999). Effects of recombinant leptin therapy in a child with congenital leptin deficiency. *New England Journal of Medicine, 341,* 879–884.

Farooqi, I. S., Keogh, J. M., Kamath, S., Jones, S., Gibson, W. T., Trussel, R., et al. (2001). Metabolism: Partial leptin deficiency and human adiposity. *Nature, 414,* 34–35.

Farooqi, I. S., & O'Rahilly, S. (2004). Monogenic human obesity syndromes. *Recent Progress in Hormone Research, 59,* 409–424.

Farran, E., & Brown, J. (2006). Infants can organise visual information at just four months. *AlphaGalileo.* Retrieved August 13, 2007, from http://www.alphagalileo.org/index.cfm?fuseaction=readrelease&releaseid=511896.

Farrar, K. M., Krcmar, M., & Nowak, K. L. (2006). Contextual features of violent video games, mental models, and aggression. *Journal of Communication, 56,* 387–405.

Farrell, D., & Stamm, C. L. (1988). Meta-analysis of the correlates of employee absence. *Human Relations, 41,* 211–227.

Farroni, T., Csibra, G., Simion, F., & Johnson, M. H. (2002). Eye contact detection in humans from birth. *Proceedings of the National Academy of Science, 99,* 9602–9605.

Farroni, T., Johnson, M. H., Menon, E., Zulian, L., Faraguna, D., & Csibra, G. (2005). Newborns' preference for face-relevant stimuli: Effects of contrast polarity. *Proceedings of the National Academy of Sciences of the USA, 102,* 17245–17250.

Fassler, D. G., & Dumas, L. S. (1997). *Help me, I'm sad: Recognizing, treating, and preventing childhood depression.* New York: Viking Press.

Faulkner, D., & Foster, J. K. (2002). The decoupling of "explicit" and "implicit" processing in neuropsychological disorders: Insights into the neural basis of consciousness? *Psyche: An Interdisciplinary Journal of Research on Consciousness, 8,* NP. Retrieved December 7, 2004, from http://psyche.cs.monash.edu.au/v8/psyche-8-02-faulkner.html

Faulkner, M. (2001). The onset and alleviation of learned helplessness in older hospitalized people. *Aging & Mental Health, 5,* 379–386.

Faust, J., Olson, R., & Rodriguez, H. (1991). Same-day surgery preparation: Reduction of pediatric patient arousal and distress through participant modeling. *Journal of Consulting and Clinical Psychology, 59,* 475–478.

Feather, N. T., & Rauter, K. A. (2004). Organizational citizenship behaviours in relation to job status, job insecurity, organizational commitment and identification, job satisfaction and work values. *Journal of Occupational and Organizational Psychology, 77,* 81–94.

Feder, B. J. (2004, May 31). Technology strains to find menace in the crowd. *The New York Times,* p. C1.

Federal Bureau of Investigation. (2006). *Crime in the United States, 2005: Uniform crime reports.* Washington, DC: U.S. Department of Justice.

Feinberg, L., & Campbell, I. G. (1993). Total sleep deprivation in the rat transiently abolishes the delta amplitude response to darkness: Implications for the mechanism of the "negative delta rebound." *Journal of Neurophysiology, 70*(6), 2695–2699.

Feingold, A., & Mazzella, R. (1998). Gender differences in body image are increasing. *Psychological Science, 9,* 190–195.

Feingold, L., & Flamm, B. L. (2006). Magnet therapy: Extraordinary claims, but no proved benefits. *British Medical Journal, 332,* 4.

Feist, J., & Feist, G. J. (2002). *Theories of personality* (5th ed.). New York: McGraw-Hill.

Feit, R. (2003). LASEK results. *Ophthalmology Clinics of North America, 16*(1), 127–135.

Felder, R. M. & Brent, R. (2001). Effective strategies for cooperative learning. *Journal of Cooperation & Collaboration in College Teaching, 10,* 69–75.

Feldman, R. P., & Goodrich, J. T. (2001). Psychosurgery: A historical overview. *Neurosurgery, 48,* 647–657.

Felfe, J., & Goihl, K. (2002). Transformational leadership and commitment. In J. Felfe (Ed.), *Organizational development and leadership* (pp. 87–124). Frankfurt: Verlag Peter Lang.

Fellin, T., Pascual, O., Gobbo, S., Pozzan, T., Haydon, P. G., & Carmignoto, G. (2004). Neuronal synchrony mediated by astrocytic glutamate through activation of extrasynaptic NMDA receptors. *Neuron, 43,* 729–743.

Fellows, L. K., Heberlein, A. S., Morales, D. A., Shivde, G., Waller, S., & Wu, D. H. (2005). Method matters: An empirical study of impact in cognitive neuroscience. *Journal of Cognitive Neuroscience, 17,* 850–858.

Felten, D. L., Cohen, N., Ader, R., Felten, S. Y., Carlson, S. L., & Roszman, T. L. (1991). Central neural circuits involved in neural-immune interactions. In R. Ader (Ed.), *Psychoneuroimmunology* (2nd ed.). New York: Academic Press.

Felten, S. Y., Madden, K. S., Bellinger, D. L., Kruszewska, B., Moynihan, J. A., & Felten, D. L. (1998). The role of the sympathetic nervous system in the modulation of immune responses. *Advances in Pharmacology, 42,* 583–587.

Feltham, C. (2000). What are counselling and psychotherapy? In C. Feltham and I. Horton (Eds.), *Handbook of counselling and psychotherapy.* London: Sage.

Feng, R., Wang, H., Wang, J., Shrom, D., Zeng, X., & Tsien, J. Z. (2004). Forebrain degeneration and ventricle enlargement caused by double knockout of Alzheimer's presenilin-1 and presenilin-2. *Proceedings of the National Academy of Sciences, 101,* 8162–8167.

Fenn, K. M., Nusbaum, H. C., & Margoliash, D. (2003). Consolidation during sleep of perceptual learning of spoken language. *Nature, 425,* 614–616.

Fenson, L., Dale, P. S., Reznick, J. S., & Bates, E. (1994). Variability in early communicative development. *Monographs of the Society for Research in Child Development, 59,* 173.

Fenton, W. S., & McGlashan, T. H. (1991). Natural history of schizophrenia subtypes: 1. Longitudinal study of paranoid, hebephrenic, and undifferentiated schizophrenia. *Archives of General Psychiatry, 48,* 969–977.

Fenton, W. S., & McGlashan, T. H. (1994). Antecedent, symptoms progression, and long-term outcome of the deficit syndrome in schizophrenia. *American Journal of Psychiatry, 151,* 351–356.

Ferguson, C. J. (2002). Media violence: Miscast causality. *American Psychologist, 57,* 446–447.

Ferguson, C. J. (2007). Evidence for publication bias in video game violence effects literature: A meta-analytic review. *Aggression and Violent Behavior, 12,* 470–482.

Ferguson, M. J., & Bargh, J. A. (2004). How social perception can automatically influence behavior. *Trends in Cognitive Sciences, 8,* 33–39.

Fergusson, D., Glass, K. C., Waring, D., & Shapiro, S. (2004). Turning a blind eye: The success of blinding reported in a random sample of randomised, placebo controlled trials. *British Medical Journal, 328,* 432.

Fergusson, D. M., & Horwood, L. J. (1997). Early onset cannabis use and psychosocial adjustment in young adults. *Addiction, 92,* 279–296.

Fernández-Dols, J.-M. & Ruiz-Belda, M.-A. (1995). Are smiles a sign of happiness?: Gold medal winners at the Olympic Games. *Journal of Personality and Social Psychology, 69,* 1113–1119.

Ferraro, R., Lillioja, S., Fontvieille, A. M., Rising, R., Bogardus, C., & Ravussin, E. (1992). Lower sedentary metabolic rate in women compared with men. *Journal of Clinical Investigation, 90,* 780–784.

Ferris, G. R., Judge, T. A., Rowland, K. M., & Fitzgibbons, D. E. (1994). Subordinate influence and the performance evaluation process: Test of a model. *Organizational and Human Decision Processes, 58,* 101–135.

Ferro, J. M. (2001). Hyperacute cognitive stroke syndromes. *Journal of Neurology, 248*(10), 841–849.

Festinger, L. (1954). A theory of social comparison processes. *Human Relations, 7,* 117–140.

Festinger, L. (1957). *A theory of cognitive dissonance.* Evanston, IL: Row, Petersen.

Festinger, L., & Carlsmith, J. M. (1959). Cognitive consequences of forced compliance. *Journal of Abnormal and Social Psychology, 58,* 203–210.

Field, A. P. (2006). Is conditioning a useful framework for understanding the development and treatment of phobias? *Clinical Psychology Review, 26,* 857–875.

Field, T., Hernandez-Reif, M., Seligman, S., Krasnegor, J., Sunshine, W., Rivas-Chacon, R., et al. (1997). Juvenile rheumatoid arthritis: Benefits from massage therapy. *Journal of Pediatric Psychology, 22,* 607–617.

Field, T., Ironson, G., Scafidi, F., Nawrocki, T., Gonclaves, A., Burman, I., et al. (1996). Massage therapy reduces anxiety and enhances EEG pattern of alertness and math computations. *International Journal of Neuroscience, 86,* 197–205.

Fielder, W. R, Cohen, R. D., & Feeney, S. (1971). An attempt to replicate the teacher expectancy effect. *Psychological Reports, 29,* 1223–1228.

Fields, R. D. (2005). Making memories stick. *Scientific American, 292,* 74–81.

Fujita, F., & Diener, E. (2005). Life satisfaction set point: Stability and change. *Journal of Personality and Social Psychology, 88*, 158–164.

Fuligni, A. J., & Pedersen, S. (2002). Family obligation and the transition to young adulthood. *Developmental Psychology, 38*(5), 856–868.

Fuligni, A. J., Witknow, M., & Garcia, C. (2005). Ethnic identity and the academic adjustment of adolescents from Mexican, Chinese, and European backgrounds. *Developmental Psychology, 41*, 799–811.

Fuller, J. L., & Thompson, W. R. (1960). *Behavior genetics.* New York: Wiley.

Fullerton, C. S., Ursano, R. J., & Wang, L. (2004). Acute stress disorder, posttraumatic stress disorder, and depression in disaster or rescue workers. *American Journal of Psychiatry, 161*, 1370–1376.

Funder, D. C. (2004). *The personality puzzle* (3rd ed.). New York: Norton.

Funk, J. B., Flores, G., Buchman, D. D., & Germann, J. N. (1999). Rating electronic games: Violence is in the eye of the beholder. *Youth and Society, 30*, 283–312.

Funtowicz, M. N., & Widiger, T. A. (1999). Sex bias in the diagnosis of personality disorders: An evaluation of DSM-IV criteria. *Journal of Abnormal Psychology, 108*, 195–201.

Furey, M. L., Pietrini, P., & Haxby, J. V. (2000). Cholinergic enhancement and increased selectivity of perceptual processing during working memory. *Science, 290*, 2315–2319.

Furnham, A. (2001). Personality and individual differences in the workplace: Person-organization-outcome fit. In R. Hogan & B. Roberts (Eds.), *Personality psychology in the workplace* (pp. 223–251). Washington, DC: American Psychological Association.

Furstenberg, F. F., Brooks-Gunn, J., & Chase-Lansdale, L. (1989). Teenaged pregnancy and childbearing. *American Psychologist, 44*, 313–320.

Fyer, A. J., Hamilton, S. P., Durner, M., Haghighi, F., Heiman, G. A., Costa, R., et al. (2006). A third-pass genome scan in panic disorder: Evidence for multiple susceptibility loci. *Biological Psychiatry, 60*, 388–401.

Gabbard, G. O. (2004). *Long-term psychodynamic psychotherapy: A basic text.* Washington DC: American Psychiatric Association.

Gabrieli, J. D. E., Fleischman, D. A., Keane, M. M., Reminger, S. L., & Morrell, F. (1995). Double dissociation between memory systems underlying explicit and implicit memory in the human brain. *Psychological Science, 6*, 76–82.

Gaertner, S. L., & Dovidio, J. F. (1986). The aversive form of racism. In J. F. Dovidio & S. L. Gaertner (Eds.), *Prejudice, discrimination, and racism* (pp. 61–89). Orlando, FL: Academic Press.

Gagnon, J. F., Postuma, R. B., & Montplaisir, J. (2006). Update on the pharmacology of REM sleep behavior disorder. *Neurology, 67*, 742–747.

Gagnon, J. F., Postuma, R. B., Mazza, S., Doyon, J., & Montplaisir, J. (2006). Rapid-eye-movement sleep behaviour disorder and neurodegenerative diseases. *Lancet Neurology, 5*, 424–432.

Gaillard, R., Del Cul, A., Naccache, L., Vinckier, F., Cohen, L., & Dehaene, S. (2006). Nonconscious semantic processing of emotional words modulates conscious access. *Proceedings of the National Academy of Sciences of the USA, 103*, 7524–7529.

Gais, S., Lucas, B., & Born, J. (2006). Sleep after learning aids memory recall. *Learning & Memory, 13*, 259–262.

Galambos, N. L., Barker, E. T., & Krahn, H. J. (2006). Depression, self-esteem, and anger in emerging adulthood: Seven-year trajectories. *Developmental Psychology, 42*, 350–365.

Galanter, E. (1962). Contemporary psychophysics. In R. Brown (Ed.), *New directions in psychology* (Vol. 1). New York: Holt, Rinehart, Winston.

Galatzer-Levy, R. M., Bachrach, H., Skolnikoff, A., & Waldron, S., Jr. (2000). *Does psychoanalysis work?* New Haven, CT: Yale University Press.

Galea, S., Ahern, J., Resnick H., Kilpatrick D., Bucuvalas M., Gold, J., & Vlahov, D. (2002). Psychological sequelae of the September 11 terrorist attacks in New York City. *New England Journal of Medicine, 346*, 982–987.

Galea, S., Resnick, H., Ahern, J., Gold, J., Bucuvalas, M., Kilpatrick, D., et al. (2002). Posttraumatic stress disorder in Manhattan, New York City, after the September 11th terrorist attacks. *Journal of Urban Health, 79*, 340–353.

Galef, B. G., & Wright, T. J. (1995). Groups of naive rats learn to select nutritionally adequate foods faster than do isolated rats. *Animal Behaviour 49*(2), 403–409.

Galinsky, A. D., & Kray, L. J. (2004). From thinking about what might have been to sharing what we know: The effects of counterfactual mind-sets on information sharing in groups. *Journal of Experimental Social Psychology, 40*, 606–618.

Gallagher, M., & Chiba, A. A. (1996). The amygdala and emotion. *Current Opinions in Neurobiology, 6*(2), 221–227.

Gallagher, S., & Sørensen, J. B. (2006). Experimenting with phenomenology. *Consciousness and Cognition, 15*, 119–134.

Galloway, A. T., Addessi, E., Fragaszy, D. M., & Visalberghi, E. (2005). Social facilitation of eating familiar food in tufted capuchins (*Cebus appella*): Does it involve behavioral coordination? *International Journal of Primatology, 26*, 181–189.

Gallup. (1999, August 29). *American workers generally satisfied, but indicate their jobs leave much to be desired.* Princeton, NJ: Gallup Organization.

Galotti, K. M. (1999). *Cognitive psychology in and out of the laboratory* (2nd ed.). Belmont, CA: Brooks/Cole.

Galotti, K. M. (1999). Making a "major" real-life decision: College students choosing an academic major. *Journal of Educational Psychology, 91*, 379–387.

Galotti, K. M. (2007). Decision structuring in important real-life choices. *Psychological Science, 18*, 320–325.

Galton, F. (1883). *Inquiries into human faculty and its development.* London: Macmillan.

Gamer, M., Rill, H.-G., Vossel, G., & Godert, H. W. (2006). Psychophysiological and vocal measures in the detection of guilty knowledge. *International Journal of Psychophysiology, 60*, 76–87.

Gan, T. J., Jiao, K. R., Zenn, M., & Georgiade, G. (2004). A randomized controlled comparison of electro-acupoint stimulation or ondansetron versus placebo for the prevention of postoperative nausea and vomiting. *Anesthesia and Analgesia, 99*, 1070–1075.

Ganchrow, J. R., Steiner, J. E., & Daher, M. (1983). Neonatal facial expressions in response to different qualities and intensities of gustatory stimuli. *Infant Behavior and Development, 6*, 189–200.

Gangestad, S. W., Garver-Apgar, C. E., Simpson, J. A., & Cousins, A. J. (2007). Changes in women's mate preferences across the ovulatory cycle. *Journal of Personality and Social Psychology, 92*, 151–163.

Garb, H. N. (1997). Race bias, social class bias, and gender bias in clinical judgment. *Clinical Psychology: Science and Practice, 4*, 99–120.

Garb, H. N., Wood, J. M., Lilienfeld, S. O., & Nezworski, M. T. (2005). Roots of the Rorschach controversy. *Clinical Psychology Review, 25*, 97–118.

Garbarino, S., Nobili, L., Beelke, M., De Carli, F., & Ferrillo, F. (2001). The contributing role of sleepiness in highway vehicle accidents. *Sleep: Journal of Sleep Research and Sleep Medicine, 24*, 203–206.

Garber, J., Keiley, M. K., & Martin, N. C. (2002). Developmental trajectories of adolescents' depressive symptoms: Predictors of change. *Journal of Consulting and Clinical Psychology, 70*, 9–95.

Garber, R. J. (1992). Long-term effects of divorce on the self-esteem of young adults. *Journal of Divorce and Remarriage, 17*, 131–138.

Garbutt, J. C., Kranzler, H. R., O'Malley, S. S., Gastfriend, D. R., Pettinati, H. M., Silverman, B. L., et al. (2005). Efficacy and tolerability of long-acting injectable naltrexone for alcohol dependence: A randomized controlled trial. *Journal of the American Medical Association, 293*, 1617–1625.

Garcia, J., & Koelling, R. A. (1966). Relation of cue to consequences in avoidance learning. *Psychonomic Science, 4*, 123–124.

Garcia, J., Rusiniak, K. W., & Brett, L. P. (1977). Conditioning food-illness aversions in wild animals: Caveat Canonici. In H. Davis & H. M. B. Hurwitz (Eds.), *Operant-Pavlovian interactions*. Hillsdale, NJ: Erlbaum.

Garcia, S. M., Weaver, K., Moskowitz, G. B., & Darley, J. M. (2002). Crowded minds: The implicit bystander effect. *Journal of Personality and Social Psychology, 83*, 843–853.

Gardiner, H. W., & Kosmitzki, C. (2005). *Lives across cultures: Cross-cultural human development* (3rd ed.). Needham Heights, MA: Allyn & Bacon.

Gardner, H. (1991). Assessment in context: The alternative to standardized testing. In B. R. Gifford & M. C. O'Connor (Eds.), *Changing assessments: Alternative views of aptitude, achievement, and instruction* (pp. 77–120). Boston: Kluwer.

Gardner, H. (1993). *Multiple intelligences: The theory in practice.* New York: Basic Books.

Gardner, H. (1999). Are there additional intelligences? The case for naturalist, spiritual, and existential intelligences. In J. Kane (Ed.), *Education, information and transformation: Essays on learning and thinking* (pp. 111–131). Englewood Cliffs, NJ: Prentice Hall.

Gardner, H. (2002). *Learning from extraordinary minds.* Mahwah, NJ: Erlbaum.

Gardner, M. (1988). *The second Scientific American book of mathematical puzzles and diversions.* Chicago: University of Chicago Press.

Gardner, M., & Steinberg, L. (2005). Peer influence on risk taking, risk preference, and risky decision making in adolescence and adulthood: An experimental study. *Developmental Psychology, 41*, 625–635.

Gardner, R., Heward, W. L., & Grossi, T. A. (1994). Effects of response cards on student participation and academic achievement: A systematic replication with inner-city students during whole-class science instruction. *Journal of Applied Behavior Analysis, 27*, 63–71.

Gardner, R. A., & Gardner, B. T. (1978). Comparative psychology and language acquisition. *Annals of the New York Academy of Science, 309*, 37–76.

Garfield, S. L. (1998). Some comments on empirically supported treatments. *Journal of Consulting and Clinical Psychology, 66*, 121–125.

Garlick, D. (2002). Understanding the nature of general intelligence: The role of individual differences in neural plasticity as an explanatory mechanism. *Psychological Review, 109*, 116–136.

Garlick, D. (2003). Integrating brain science research with intelligence research. *Current Directions in Psychological Science, 12*, 185–188.

Garris, P. A., Kilpatrick, M., Bunin, M. A., Michael, D., Walker, Q. D., & Wightman, R. M. (1999). Dissociation of dopamine release in the nucleus accumbens from intracranial self-stimulation. *Nature, 398*, 67–69.

Garry, M., & Loftus, E. (1994). Pseudomemories without hypnosis. *International Journal of Clinical and Experimental Hypnosis, 42*(4), 363–373.

Garson, L. (2006). *Surviving Babylon: A journey through repressed memories of sexual abuse.* Atlanta, GA: Alexander Griffin Co.

Gatewood, R. D., & Feild, H. S. (2001). *Human resource selection* (5th ed.). Fort Worth, TX: Harcourt.

Gathercole, S. E., Pickering, S. J., Ambridge, B., & Wearing, H. (2004). The structure of working memory from 4 to 15 years of age. *Developmental Psychology, 40,* 177–190.

Gaudiano, B. A., & Dalrymple, K. L. (2005). EMDR variants, pseudoscience, and the demise of empirically supported treatments? *PsycCRITIQUES, 50,* 8.

Gauvain, M. (2001). *The social context of cognitive development.* New York: Guilford.

Gazzaley, A., Cooney, J. W., Rissman, J., & D'Esposito, M. (2005). Top-down suppression deficit underlies working memory impairment in normal aging. *Nature Neuroscience 8,* 1298–1300.

Gazzaley, A., Cooney, J. W., Rissman, J., & D'Esposito, M. (2005). Top-down suppression deficit underlies working memory impairment in normal aging. *Nature Neuroscience, 8,* 1298–1300.

Gazzaniga, M. S., & LeDoux, J. E. (1978). *The integrated mind.* New York: Plenum.

Ge, W. P., Yang, X. J., Zhang, Z., Wang, H. K., Shen, W., Deng, Q. D., et al. (2006). Long-term potentiation of neuron-glia synapses mediated by Ca2+-permeable AMPA receptors. *Science, 312,* 1533–1537.

Ge, X., Conger, R., & Elder, G. H. (2001). Pubertal transition, stressful life events, and the emergence of gender differences in adolescent depressive symptoms. *Developmental Psychology, 37,* 404–417.

Geary, D. C. (1999). Evolution and developmental sex differences. *Current Directions in Psychological Science, 8,* 115–120.

Geary, D. C. (2000). Evolution and proximate expression of human paternal investment. *Psychological Bulletin, 126,* 55–77.

Geddes, J. R., Burgess, S., Hawton, K., Jamison, K., & Goodwin, G. M. (2004). Long-term lithium therapy for bipolar disorder: Systematic review and meta-analysis of randomized controlled trials. *American Journal of Psychiatry, 161,* 217–222.

Geen, R. G. (1991). Social motivation. *Annual Review of Psychology, 42,* 377–399.

Geen, R. G. (1998). Aggression and antisocial behavior. In D. Gilbert, S. T. Fiske, & G. Lindzey (Eds.), *Handbook of social psychology* (4th ed., Vol. 2, pp. 317–356). Boston: McGraw-Hill.

Geen, R. G., & McCown, E. J. (1984). Effects of noise and attack on aggression and physiological arousal. *Motivation and Emotion, 8,* 231–241.

Gegenfurtner, K. R., & Kiper, D. C. (2003). Color vision. *Annual Review of Neuroscience, 26,* 181–206.

Geier, A. B., Rozin, P., & Doros, G. (2006). Unit bias: A new heuristic that helps explain the effect of portion size on food intake. *Psychological Science, 17,* 521–525.

Gelabert-Gonzalez, M., & Fernandez-Villa, J. (2001). Mutism after posterior fossa surgery: Review of the literature. *Clinical Neurology & Neurosurgery, 103,* 111–114.

Geldmacher, D. S., Provenzano, G., McRae, T., Mastey, V., & Ieni, J. R. (2003). Donepezil is associated with delayed nursing home placement in patients with Alzheimer's disease. *Journal of the American Geriatric Society, 51*(7), 937–944.

Gelfand, M. J., Nishii, L. H., & Raver, J. L. (2006). On the nature and importance of cultural tightness–looseness. *Journal of Applied Psychology, 91,* 1225–1244.

Gelhorn, H. L., Stallings, M. C., Young, S. E., Corley, R. P., Rhee, S. H., & Hewitt, J. K. (2005). Genetic and environmental influences on conduct disorder: symptom, domain and full-scale analyses. *Journal of Child Psychology and Psychiatry. 46,* 580–591.

Gelman, R., & Baillargeon, R. (1983). A review of some Piagetian concepts. In P. H. Mussen (Ed.), *Handbook of child psychology* (Vol. 3, pp. 167–230). New York: Wiley.

Gendle, M. H., White, T. L., Strawderman, M., Mactutus, C. F., Booze, R. M., Levitsky, D. A., & Strupp, B. J. (2004). Enduring effects of prenatal cocaine exposure on selective attention and reactivity to errors: Evidence from an animal model. *Behavioral Neuroscience, 118,* 290–297.

George, M. S., Anton, R. F., Bloomer, C., Teneback, C., Drobes, D. J., Lorberbaum, J. P., et al. (2001). Activation of prefrontal cortex and anterior thalamus in alcoholic subjects on exposure to alcohol-specific cues. *Archives of General Psychiatry, 58,* 345–352.

George, W. H., & Marlatt, G. A. (1986). The effects of alcohol and anger on interest in violence, erotica, and deviance. *Journal of Abnormal Psychology, 95,* 150–158.

Geraerts, E., Smeets, E., Jelicic, M., Merckelbach, H., & van Heerden, J. (2006). Retrieval inhibition of trauma-related words in women reporting repressed or recovered memories of childhood sexual abuse. *Behaviour Research and Therapy, 44,* 1129–1136.

Gerbner, G., Morgan, M., & Signorielli, N. (1994). *Television violence profile No. 16: The turning point.* Philadelphia: Annenberg School for Communication.

Gerhart, B. (2005). The (affective) dispositional approach to job satisfaction: Sorting out the policy implications. *Journal of Organizational Behavior, 26,* 79–97.

Gerin, W., Davidson, K. W., Christenfeld, N. J. S., Goyal, T., & Schwartz, J. E. (2006). The role of angry rumination and distraction in blood pressure recovery from emotional arousal. *Psychosomatic Medicine, 68,* 64–72.

Gerken, L. (1994). Child phonology: Past research, present questions, future directions. In M. A. Gernsbacher (Ed), *Handbook of psycholinguistics* (pp. 781–820). San Diego: Academic Press.

German, T. P., & Barrett, H. C. (2005). Functional fixedness in a technologically sparse culture. *Psychological Science, 16*(1), 1–5.

Gerschman, J. A., Reade, P. C., & Burrows, G. D. (1980). Hypnosis and dentistry. In G. D. Burrows & L. Dennerstein (Eds.), *Handbook of hypnosis and psychosomatic medicine.* Amsterdam: Elsevier.

Gershoff, E. T. (2002). Corporal punishment by parents and associated child behaviors and experiences: A meta-analytic and theoretical review. *Psychological Bulletin, 128,* 539–579.

Gerstner, C. R., & Day, D. V. (1997). Meta-analytic review of leader–member exchange theory: Correlates and construct issues. *Journal of Applied Psychology, 82,* 827–844.

Geschwind, N. (1968). Disconnexion syndromes in animals and man. *Brain, 88,* 237–294.

Geschwind, N. (1979). Specializations of the human brain. *Scientific American, 241,* 180–199.

Gessner, B. D., Ives, G. C., & Perham-Hester, K. A. (2001). Association between sudden infant death syndrome and prone sleep position, bed sharing, and sleeping outside an infant crib in Alaska. *Pediatrics, 108,* 923–927.

Getzfeld, A. R. (2006). *Essentials of abnormal psychology.* New York: Wiley.

Gfeller, J. D. (1994). Hypnotizability enhancement: Clinical implications of empirical findings. *American Journal of Clinical Hypnosis, 37*(2), 107–116.

Gianakos, I. (2002). Predictors of coping with work stress: The influences of sex, gender role, social desirability, and locus of control. *Sex Roles, 46,* 149–158.

Gianaros, P. J., May, J. C., Siegle, G. J., & Jennings, J. R. (2005). Is there a functional neural correlate of individual differences in cardiovascular reactivity? *Psychosomatic Medicine, 67,* 31–39.

Gibb, B. E., Alloy, L. B., Abramson, L. Y., Beevers, C. G., & Miller, I. W. (2004). Cognitive vulnerability to depression: A taxometric analysis. *Journal of Abnormal Psychology, 113,* 81–89.

Gibbons, R. D., Hur, K., Bhaumik, D. K., & Mann, J. J. (2005). The relationship between antidepressant use and rate of suicide. *Archives of General Psychiatry, 62,* 165–172.

Gibson, E. J., & Walk, R. D. (1960). The visual cliff. *Scientific American, 202,* 64–71.

Gibson, J. J. (1979). *The ecological approach to visual perception.* Boston: Houghton Mifflin.

Gifford, A. L., Bormann, J. E., Shively, M. J., Wright, B. C., Richman, D. D., & Bozzette, S. A. (2000). Predictors of self-reported adherence and plasma HIV concentrations in patients on multidrug antiretroviral regiments. *Journal of Acquired Immune Deficiency Syndromes, 23,* 386–395.

Gifford, R., & Hine, D. (1997). Toward cooperation in the commons dilemma. *Canadian Journal of Behavioural Science, 29,* 167–178.

Gifford-Smith, M., Dodge, K. A., Dishion, T. J., & McCord, J. (2005). Peer influence in children and adolescents: Crossing the bridge between developmental and intervention science. *Journal of Abnormal Child Psychology, 33,* 255–265.

Gigerenzer, G. (2004). Dread risk, September 11, and fatal traffic accidents. *Psychological Science, 15,* 286–287.

Gigerenzer, G., Todd, P. M., & ABC Research Group. (2000). *Simple heuristics that make us smart.* New York: Oxford University Press.

Gilbert, A. L., Regier, T., Kay, P., & Ivry, R. B. (2006). Whorf hypothesis is supported in the right visual field but not the left. *Proceedings of the National Academy of Sciences, 103,* 489–494.

Gilbert, C. D. (1992). Horizontal integration and cortical dynamics. *Neuron, 9,* 1–13.

Gilbert, D. T. (1998). Ordinary personology. In D. Gilbert, S. T. Fiske, & G. Lindzey (Eds.), *Handbook of social psychology* (Vol.2, 4th ed., pp. 89–150). Boston: McGraw-Hill.

Gilbert, D. T. (2006). *Stumbling on happiness.* New York: Knopf.

Gilbert, D. T., Morewedge, C. K., Risen, J. L., & Wilson, T. D. (2004). Looking forward to looking backward: The misprediction of regret. *Psychological Science, 15,* 346–350.

Gilbert, D. T., & Wilson, T. D. (1998). Miswanting: Some problems in the forecasting of future affective states. In J. P. Forgas (Ed.), *Feeling and thinking: The role of affect in social cognition* (pp. 178–197). New York: Cambridge University Press.

Gilbert, R., Salanti, G., Harden, M., & See, S. (2005). Infant sleeping position and the sudden infant death syndrome: A systematic review of observational studies and historical review of recommendations from 1940 to 2002. *International Journal of Epidemiology, 34,* 874–887.

Gilbert, R. M. (1984). Caffeine consumption. In G. A. Spiller (Ed.), *The methylxanthine beverages and foods: Chemistry, consumption, and health effects* (pp. 185–213). New York: Liss.

Gilbert, S. (1997, August 20). Two spanking studies indicate parents should be cautious. *New York Times Magazine.*

Gilboa-Schechtman, E., & Foa, E. B. (2001). Patterns of recovery from trauma: The use of intraindividual analysis. *Journal of Abnormal Psychology, 110,* 392–400.

Giles, L. C., Glonek, G. F., Luszcz, M. A., & Andrews, G. R. (2005). Effect of social networks on 10 year survival in very old Australians: The Australian longitudinal study of aging. *Journal of Epidemiology & Community Health, 59,* 574–579.

Giles, T. R. (1990). Bias against behavior therapy in outcome reviews: Who speaks for the patient? *The Behavior Therapist, 13,* 86–90.

Gillham, J. E. (Ed). (2000). *The science of optimism and hope: Research essays in honor of Martin E. P. Seligman.* Philadelphia: Templeton Foundation Press.

Gillham, J. E., Reivich, K. J., Freres, D. R., Chaplin, T. M., Shatté, A. J., Samuels, B., et al. (2007). School-based prevention of depressive symptoms: A randomized controlled study of the effectiveness and specificity of the Penn Resiliency Program. *Journal of Consulting and Clinical Psychology, 75,* 9–19.

Gilligan, C. (1982). *In a different voice: Psychological theory and women's development.* Cambridge, MA: Harvard University Press.

Gilligan, C. (1993). Adolescent development reconsidered. In A. Garrod (Ed.), *Approaches to moral development: New research and emerging themes.* New York: Teachers College Press.

Gilmore, G. C., Spinks, R. A., & Thomas, C. W. (2006). Age effects in coding tasks: Componential analysis and test of the sensory deficit hypothesis. *Psychology and Aging, 21,* 7–18.

Gilmore, M. M., & Murphy, C. (1989). Aging is associated with increased Weber ratios for caffeine, but not for sucrose. *Perception and Psychophysics, 46,* 555–559.

Gilmore, R. L., Heilman, K. M., Schmidt, R. P., Fennell, E. M., & Quisling, R. (1992). Anosognosia during Wada testing. *Neurology, 42*(4), 925–927.

Giltay, E. J., Geleijnse, J. M., Zitman, F. G., Hoekstra, T., & Schouten, E. G. (2004). Dispositional optimism and all-cause and cardiovascular mortality in a prospective cohort of elderly Dutch men and women. *Archives of General Psychiatry, 61,* 1126–1135.

Giltay, E. J., Kamphuis, M. H., Kalmijn, S., Zitman, F. G., & Kromhout, D. (2006). Dispositional optimism and the risk of cardiovascular death: The Zutphen elderly study. *Archives of Internal Medicine, 166,* 431–436.

Ginges, J., Atran, S., Medin, D., & Shikaki, K. (2007). Sacred bounds on rational resolution of violent political conflict. *Proceeedings of the National Academy of Sciences, 104,* 7357–7360.

Gingras, J. L., Mitchell, E. A., & Grattan, K. E. (2005). Fetal homologue of infant crying. *Archives of Disease in Childhood: Fetal and Neonatal Edition, 90,* F415–F418.

Ginsberg, D. L. (2006). Fatal agranulocytosis four years after clozapine discontinuation. *Primary Psychiatry, 13,* 32–33.

Giorgi-Guarnieri, D., Janofsky, J., Keram, E., Lawsky, S., Merideth, P., Mossman, D., et al. (2002). AAPL practice guideline for forensic psychiatric evaluation of defendants raising the insanity defense. *Journal of the American Academy of Psychiatry and the Law, 30*(Suppl. 2), S1–S40.

Givens, B. (1995). Low doses of ethanol impair spatial working memory and reduce hippocampal theta activity. *Alcoholism Clinical and Experimental Research, 19*(3), 763–767.

Gladwell, M. (2004, January 12). Big and bad. *New Yorker,* 28–33.

Gladwell, M. (2005). *Blink: The power of thinking without thinking.* New York: Little, Brown.

Glantz, K., Rizzo, A., & Graap, K. (2003). Virtual reality for psychotherapy: Current reality and future possibilities. *Psychotherapy: Theory, Research, Practice, and Training, 40,* 55–67.

Glanz, J. (1997). Sharpening the senses with neural "noise." *Science, 277,* 1759.

Glanzer, M., & Cunitz, A. (1966). Two storage mechanisms in free recall. *Journal of Verbal Learning and Verbal Behavior, 5,* 351–360.

Glasman, L. R., & Albarracín, D. (2006). Forming attitudes that predict future behavior: A meta-analysis of the attitude-behavior relation. *Psychological Bulletin, 132,* 778–822.

Glass, J. M., Adams, K. M., Nigg, J. T., Wong, M. M., Puttler, L. I., Buu, A., et al. (2006). Smoking is associated with neurocognitive deficits in alcoholism. *Drug and Alcohol Dependence, 82,* 119–126.

Glassbrenner, D. G. (2005). Driver cell phone use in 2005—Overall results. *National Occupant Protection Use Survey.* Washington, DC: National Highway Transportation Safety Board.

Glassop, L. I. (2002). The organizational benefits of teams. *Human Relations, 55,* 225–249.

Glazer, M., Baer, R. D., Weller, S., de Alba, J. E. G., & Liebowitz, S. W. (2004). Susto and soul loss in Mexicans and Mexican Americans. *Cross-Cultural Research: The Journal of Comparative Social Science, 38,* 270–288.

Gleaves, D. H., May, M. C., & Cardena, E. (2001). An examination of the diagnostic validity of dissociative identity disorder. *Clinical Psychology Review, 21,* 577–608.

Gleitman, L., & Landau, B. (1994). *The acquisition of the lexicon.* Cambridge: MIT Press.

Glenmullen, J. (2000). *Prozac backlash: Overcoming the dangers of Prozac, Zoloft, Paxil, and other antidepressants with safe, effective alternatives.* New York: Simon & Schuster.

Gleuckauf, R., & Quittner, A. (1992). Assertiveness training for disabled adults in wheelchairs: Self-report, role-play, and activity pattern outcomes. *Journal of Consulting and Clinical Psychology, 60,* 419–425.

Glick, P. T., & Fiske, S. (2001). Ambivalent sexism. In M. Zanna (Ed.), *Advances in experimental social psychology* (Vol. 33, pp. 115–188). New York: Academic Press.

Glover, J. A., Krug, D., Dietzer, M., George, B. W., & Hannon, M. (1990). "Advance" advance organizers. *Bulletin of the Psychonomic Society, 28,* 4–6.

Glynn, M., & Rhodes, P. (2005). *Estimated HIV prevalence in the United States at the end of 2003.* Paper presented at the National HIV Prevention Conference, Atlanta, GA, June.

Goebel, M. U., Trebst, A. E., Steiner, J., Xie, Y. F., Exton, M. S., Frede, S., et al. (2002). Behavioral conditioning of immunosuppression is possible in humans. *The FASEB Journal: Official Publication of the Federation of American Societies for Experimental Biology, 16,* 1869–1873.

Goenjian, A. K., Molina, L., Steinberg, A. M., Fairbanks, L. A., Alvarez, M. L., Goenjian, H. A., & Pynoos, R. S. (2001). Posttraumatic stress and depressive reactions among Nicaraguan adolescents after hurricane Mitch. *American Journal of Psychiatry, 158,* 788–794.

Gogtay, N., Giedd, J. N., Lusk, L., Hayashi, K. M., Greenstein, D., Vaituzis, A. C., Nugent, T. F., III, Herman, D. H., Clasen, L. S., Toga, A. W., Rapoport, J. L., & Thompson, P. M. (2004). Dynamic mapping of human cortical development during childhood through early adulthood. *Proceedings of the National Academy of Sciences, 101,* 8174–8179.

Gold, M. S. (1994). The epidemiology, attitudes, and pharmacology of LSD use in the 1990s. *Psychiatric Annals, 24*(3), 124–126.

Golden, R. N., Gaynes, B. N., Ekstrom, R. D., Hamer, R. M., Jacobsen, F. M., Suppes, T., et al. (2005). The efficacy of light therapy in the treatment of mood disorders: A review and meta-analysis of the evidence. *American Journal of Psychiatry, 162,* 656–662.

Goldenberg, J. L., Arndt, J., Hart, J., & Brown, M. (2005). Dying to be thin: The effects of mortality salience and body mass index on restricted eating among women. *Personality and Social Psychology Bulletin, 31,* 1400–1412.

Goldfried, M. R., & Davila, J. (2005). The role of relationship and technique in therapeutic change. *Psychotherapy: Theory, Research, Practice, Training, 42,* 421–430.

Golding, N. L., Staff, N. P., & Spruston, N. (2002). Dendritic spikes as a mechanism for cooperative long-term potentiation. *Nature, 418,* 326–331.

Goldman, M. S., Darkes, J., & Del Boca, F. K. (1999). Expectancy meditation of biopsychosocial risk for alcohol use and alcoholism. In I. Kirsch (Ed.), *How expectancies shape experience* (pp. 233–262). Washington, DC: American Psychological Association.

Goldstein, A. J., de Beurs, E., Chambless, D. L., & Wilson, K. A. (2000). EMDR for panic disorder with agoraphobia: Comparison with waiting list and credible attention-placebo control conditions. *Journal of Consulting and Clinical Psychology, 68,* 947–956.

Goldstein, E. B. (2002). *Sensation and perception* (6th ed.). Pacific Grove, CA: Wadsworth.

Goldstein, I., & Rosen, R. C. (Eds.). (2002). Guest editors' introduction: Female sexuality and sexual dysfunction. *Archives of Sexual Behavior, 31,* 391.

Goldstein, I. L. (1993). *Training in organizations: Needs assessment, development, and evaluation* (3rd ed.). Monterey, CA: Brooks/Cole.

Goldstein, J. (2001). *Does playing violent video games cause aggressive behavior?* Cultural Policy Center, University of Chicago http://culturalpolicy.uchicago.edu/conf-2001/papers/goldstein.html.

Goldstein, K. (1939). *The organism.* New York: American Book.

Goldstein, M. H., King, A. P., & West, M. J. (2003). Social interaction shapes babbling: Testing parallels between birdsong and speech. *Proceedings of the National Academy of Sciences, 100,* 8030–8035.

Goldstein, S. E., Davis-Kean, P. E., & Eccles, J. S. (2005). Parents, peers, and problem behavior: A longitudinal investigation of the impact of relationship perceptions and characteristics on the development of adolescent problem behavior. *Developmental Psychology, 41,* 401–413.

Golomb, J., Kluger, A., De Leon, M. J., Ferris, S. H., Mittelman, M., Cohen, J., & George, A. E. (1996). Hippocampal formation size predicts declining memory performance in normal aging. *Neurology, 47,* 810–813.

Goltz, H. C., DeSouza, J. F. X., Menon, R. S., Tweed, D. B., & Vilis, T. (2003). Interaction of retinal image and eye velocity in motion perception. *Neuron, 39,* 569–576.

Gomez, R. L., Bootzin, R. R., & Nadel, L. (2006). Naps promote abstraction in language–learning infants. *Psychological Science, 17,* 670–674.

Gone, J. (2004). Mental health services for Native Americans in the 21st century United States. *Professional Psychology: Theory and Practice, 35,* 10–18.

Gong, Y., & Fan, J. (2006). A longitudinal examination of the role of goal orientation in cross–cultural adjustment. *Journal of Applied Psychology, 91,* 176–184.

Gonsalves, B., & Paller, K. A. (2000). Neural events that underlie remembering something that never happened. *Nature Neuroscience, 3,* 1316–1321.

Gonsalves, B. D., Kahn, I., Curran, T., Norman, K. A., & Wagner, A. D. (2005). Memory strength and repetition suppression: Multimodal imaging of medial temporal cortical contributions to recognition. *Neuron, 47,* 751–761.

Gonzalez, J. S., Penedo, F. J., Antoni, M. H., Duran, R. E., McPherson-Baker, S., Ironson, G., et al. (2004). Social support, positive states of mind, and HIV treatment adherence in men and women living with HIV/AIDS. *Health Psychology, 23,* 413–418.

Goodenough, F. L. (1932). Expression of the emotions in a blind-deaf child. *Journal of Abnormal and Social Psychology, 27,* 328–333.

Goodglass, H., & Kaplan, E. (1982). *The assessment of aphasia and related disorders* (2nd ed.). Philadelphia: Lea & Febiger.

Goodman, G. S., Ghetti, S., Quas, J. A., Edelstein, R. S., Alexander, K. W., Redlich, A. D., et al. (2003). A prospective study of memory for child sexual abuse: New findings relevant to the repressed-memory controversy. *Psychological Science, 14,* 113–118.

Gooren, L. J., & Kruijver, F. P. (2002). Androgens and male behavior. *Molecular and Cellular Endocrinology, 198,* 31–40.

Gopnik, M., & Crago, M. B. (1991). Familial aggregation of developmental language disorder. *Cognition, 39,* 1–50.

Gordon, D. B., Dahl, J. L., Miaskowski, C., McCarberg, B., Todd, K. H., Paice, J. A., et al. (2005). American Pain Society recommendations for improving the quality of acute and cancer pain management: American Pain Society Quality of Care Task Force. *Archives of Internal Medicine, 165,* 1574–1580.

Gordon, P. (2004). Numerical cognition without words: Evidence from Amazonia. *Science, 306,* 496–499.

Gorman, J. M. (2002). Treatment of generalized anxiety disorder. *Journal of Clinical Psychiatry, 63,* 17–23.

Gorman, J. M. (2003). Treating generalized anxiety disorder. *Journal of Clinical Psychiatry, 64*(Suppl. 2), 24–29.

Gorman, J. M. (2005). Benzodiazepines: Taking the good with the bad and the ugly. *CNS Spectrums, 10,* 14–15.

Gorter, R. W., Butorac, M., Cobian, E. P., & van der Sluis, W. (2005). Medical use of cannabis in the Netherlands. *Neurology, 64,* 917–919.

Gosling, S. D. (2001). From mice to men: What can we learn about personality from animal research? *Psychological Bulletin, 127,* 45–86.

Gosling, S. D., Kwan, V. S. Y., & John, O. P. (2003). A dog's got personality: A cross-species comparative approach to personality judgments in dogs and humans. *Journal of Personality and Social Psychology, 85,* 1161–1169.

Gosling, S. D., Vazire, S., Srivastava, S., & John, O. P. (2004). Should we trust web-based studies? A comparative analysis of six preconceptions about Internet questionnaires. *American Psychologist, 59,* 93–104.

Goss Lucas, S., & Bernstein, D. A. (2005). *Teaching psychology: A step by step guide.* Mahwah, NJ: Erlbaum.

Gotlib, I. H., & Hammen, C. L. (1992). *Psychological aspects of depression: Toward cognitive interpersonal integration.* Chichester, England: Wiley.

Gotlib, I. H., Krasnoperova, E., Yue, D. N., & Joorman, J. (2004). Attentional biases for negative interpersonal stimuli in clinical depression. *Journal of Abnormal Psychology, 113,* 127–135.

Gottesman, I. I. (1991). *Schizophrenia genesis: The origins of madness.* New York: Freeman.

Gottfredson, L. S (1997). Why g matters: The complexity of everyday life. *Intelligence, 24,* 79–132.

Gottfredson, L. S. (2003). Dissecting practical intelligence theory: Its claims and evidence. *Intelligence, 31,* 343–397.

Gottfredson, L. S. (2004). Intelligence: Is it the epidemiologists' elusive "fundamental cause" of social class inequalities in health? *Journal of Personality and Social Psychology, 86,* 174–199.

Gottfredson, L. S., & Deary, I. J. (2004). Intelligence predicts health and longevity, but why? *Current Directions in Psychological Science, 13,* 1–4.

Gottfried, A. W. (1997, June). Parents' role is critical to children's learning. *APA Monitor,* p. 24.

Gottfried, J. A., & Dolan, R. J. (2003). The nose smells what the eye sees: Crossmodal visual facilitation of human olfactory perception. *Neuron, 39,* 375–386.

Gottfried, J. A., O'Doherty, J., & Dolan, R. J. (2003). Encoding predictive reward value in human amygdala and orbitofrontal cortex. *Science, 301,* 1104–1107.

Gottman, J. M., & Levenson, R. W. (2002). A two-factor model for predicting when a couple will divorce: Exploratory analyses using 14-year longitudinal data. *Family Process, 41,* 83–96.

Gottman, J. M., Driver, J., & Tabares, A. (2002). Building the sound marital house: An empirically derived couple therapy. In A. S. Gurman & N. S. Jacobson (Eds.), *Clinical handbook of couple therapy* (3rd ed., pp. 373–399). New York: Guilford Press.

Gottman, J. M., Gottman, J. S., & Declaire, J. (2006). *Ten lessons to transform your marriage.* New York: Crown Press.

Gould, E., Beylin, A., Tanapat, P., Reeves, A., & Schors, T. J. (1999). Learning enhances adult neurogenesis in the hippocampal formation. *Nature Neuroscience, 2,* 260–265.

Gould, R. A., Otto, M. W., Pollack, M. H., & Yap, L. (1997). Cognitive behavioral and pharmacological treatment of generalized anxiety disorder: A preliminary meta-analysis. *Behavior Therapy, 28,* 285–305.

Gow, A. J., Whiteman, M. C., Pattie, A., Whalley, L., Starr, J., & Deary, I. J. (2005). Lifetime intellectual function and satisfaction with life in old age: Longitudinal cohort study. *British Medical Journal, 331,* 141–142.

Grabe, H. J., Ruhrmann, S., Ettelt, S., Buhtz, F., Hochrein, A., Schulze-Rauschenbach, S., et al. (2006). Familiality of obsessive-compulsive disorder in nonclinical and clinical subjects. *American Journal of Psychiatry, 163,* 1986–1992.

Graeber, M. B., & Mehraein, P. (1999). Reanalysis of the first case of Alzheimer's disease. *European Archives of Psychiatry and Clinical Neuroscience, 249*(Suppl. 3), 10–13.

Graetz, K. A., Boyle, E. S., Kimble, C. E., Thompson, P., & Garloch, J. L. (1998). Information sharing in face-to-face, teleconferencing, and electronic chat groups. *Small Group Research, 29,* 714–743.

Graham, K., Osgood, D. W., Wells, S., & Stockwell, T. (2006). To what extent is intoxication associated with aggression in bars? A multilevel analysis. *Journal of Studies on Alcohol, 67,* 382–390.

Grammer, K., Fink, B., & Neave, N. (2005). Human pheromones and sexual attraction. *European Journal of Obstetrics, Gynecology, and Reproductive Biology, 118,* 135–142.

Grandey, A. A., Cordeiro, B., & Crouter, A. C. (2005). A longitudinal and multi-source test of the work-family conflict and job satisfaction relationship. *Journal of Occupational and Organizational Psychology, 78,* 305–323.

Grandin, T. (1996). *Thinking in pictures: And other reports from my life with autism.* New York: Vintage Press.

Granhag, P.-A. & Stromwall, L. (2004). *The detection of deception in forensic contexts.* New York: Cambridge University Press.

Grant, B. F., Dawson, D. A., Stinson, F. S., Chou, S. P., Dufour, M. C., & Pickering, R. P. (2004). The 12-month prevalence and trends in DSM-IV alcohol abuse and dependence: United States, 1991–1992 and 2001–2002. *Drug and Alcohol Dependence, 74,* 223–234.

Grant, H., & Dweck, C. S. (2003). Clarifying achievement goals and their impact. *Journal of Personality and Social Psychology, 85,* 541–553.

Grant, J. E., & Kim, S. W. (2002). *Stop me because I can't stop myself: Taking control of impulsive behavior.* New York: McGraw-Hill.

Graves, L., Pack, A., & Abel, T. (2001). Sleep and memory: A molecular perspective. *Trends in Neurosciences, 24,* 237–243.

Gray, J. A. (1991). Neural systems, emotions, and personality. In J. Madden IV (Ed.), *Neurobiology of learning, emotion, and affect* (pp. 272–306). New York: Raven Press.

Gray, J. A., & McNaughton, N. (2000). *The neuropsychology of anxiety: An enquiry into the functions of the septohippocampal system* (2nd ed.). New York: Oxford University Press.

Gray, J. R., Chabris, C. F., & Braver, T. S. (2003). Neural mechanisms of general fluid intelligence. *Nature Neuroscience, 6,* 316–322.

Gray, N., & Nye, P. S. (2001). American Indian and Alaska Native substance abuse: Co-morbidity and cultural issues. *American Indian and Alaska Native Mental Health Research, 10,* 67–84.

Gray, N. S., MacCulloch, M. J., Smith, J., Morris, M., & Snowden, R. J. (2003). Forensic psychology: Violence viewed by psychopathic murderers. *Nature, 423,* 497.

Gray, P. (2005). *The ego and analysis of defense.* Northvale, NJ: Aronson.

Graziano, M. S. A., Alisharan, S. E., Hu, X., & Gross, C. G. (2002). The clothing effect: Tactile neurons in the precentral gyrus do not respond to the touch of the familiar primate chair. *Proceedings of the New York Academy of Sciences, 99,* 11930–11933.

Graziano, M. S. A., Taylor, C. S., & Moore, T. (2002). Complex movements evoked by microstimulation of precentral cortex. *Neuron, 34,* 841–851.

Green, A. I., & Patel, J. K. (1996). The new pharmacology of schizophrenia. *Harvard Mental Health Letter, 13*(6), 5–7.

Green, C. S., & Bavelier, D. (2003). Action video game modifies visual selective attention. *Nature, 423,* 534–537.

Green, D. M., & Swets, J. A. (1966). *Signal detection theory and psychophysics.* New York: Wiley.

Green, J. T., & Woodruff-Pak, D. S. (2000). Eyeblink classical conditioning: Hippocampal formation is for neutral stimulus associations as cerebellum is for association response. *Psychological Bulletin, 126,* 138–158.

Green, R. A., Cross, A. J., & Goodwin, G. M. (1995). Review of the pharmacology and clinical pharmacology of 3,4-methylenedioxymethamphetamine (MDMA or "ecstacy"). *Psychopharmacology, 119,* 247–260.

Greenberg, J. (2002). Who stole the money and when? Individual and situational determinants of employee theft. *Organizational Behavior and Human Decision Processes, 89,* 985–1003.

Greenberg, J., Solomon, S., Pyszczynski, T., & Rosenblatt, A. (1992). Why do people need self-esteem? Converging evidence that self-esteem serves an anxiety-buffering function. *Journal of Personality and Social Psychology, 63,* 913–922.

Greenberg, R. M., & Kellner, C. H. (2005). Electroconvulsive therapy: A selected review. *American Journal of Geriatric Psychiatry, 13,* 268–281.

Greenberg, R. P., Constantino, M. J., & Bruce, N. (2006). Are patient expectations still relevant for psychotherapy process and outcome? *Clinical Psychology Review, 26,* 657–678.

Greene, E., & Loftus, E. F. (1998). Psycholegal research on jury damage awards. *Current Directions in Psychological Science, 7,* 50–54.

Greenfield, P. M. (1994). Video games as cultural artifacts. *Journal of Applied Developmental Psychology, 15,* 3–12.

Greenfield, P. M., & Childs, C. P. (1991). Developmental continuity in biocultural context. In R. Cohen & A. W. Siegel (Eds.), *Context and development* (pp. 135–159). Hillsdale, NJ: Erlbaum.

Greenfield, P. M., Suzuki, L. K., & Rothstein-Fisch, C. (2006). Cultural pathways through human development. In W. Damon & R. M. Lerner (Series Eds.) & K. A. Renninger & I. E. Sigel (Vol. Eds.), *Handbook of child psychology: Vol. 4. Child psychology in practice* (6th ed., pp. 655–699). New York: Wiley.

Greenhaus, J. H., Parasuraman, S., & Wormley, W. M. (1990). Effects of race on organizational experiences, job performance evaluations, and career outcomes. *Academy of Management Journal, 33,* 64–86.

Greenland, P., Knoll, M. D., Stamler, J., Neaton, J. D., Dyer, A. R., Garside, D. B., & Wilson, P. W. (2003). Major risk factors as antecedents of fatal and nonfatal coronary heart disease events. *Journal of the American Medical Association, 290,* 891–897.

Greenough, W. T., Black, J. E., & Wallace, C. S. (1987). Experience and brain development. *Child Development, 58,* 539–559.

Greenwald, A. G., & Banaji, M. R. (1995). Implicit social cognition: Attitudes, self-esteem, and stereotypes. *Psychological Review, 102,* 4–27.

Greenwald, A. G., Draine, S. C., & Abrams, R. L. (1996). Three cognitive markers of unconscious semantic activation. *Science, 273,* 1699–1702.

Greenwald, A. G., Klinger, M. R., & Schuh, E. S. (1995). Activation by marginally perceptible ("subliminal") stimuli: Dissociation of unconscious from conscious cognition. *Experimental Psychology: General, 124*(1), 22–42.

Greenwood, T. A., Schork, N. J., Eskin, E., & Kelsoe, J. R. (2006). Identification of additional variants within the human dopamine transporter gene provides further evidence for an association with bipolar disorder in two independent samples. *Molecular Psychiatry, 11,* 125–133.

Greer, A. E., & Buss, D. M. (1994). Tactics for promoting sexual encounters. *Journal of Sex Research, 31*(3), 185–201.

Gregg, V., Gibbs, J. C., & Basinger, K. S. (1994). Patterns of developmental delay in moral judgment by male and female delinquents. *Merrill-Palmer Quarterly, 40,* 538–553.

Gregory, R. L. (2005). Seeing after blindness. *Nature Neuroscience, 6,* 909–910.

Gregory, S. W., & Webster, S. (1996). A nonverbal signal in voices of interview partners effectively predicts communication accommodation and social status perceptions. *Journal of Personality and Social Psychology, 70,* 1231–1240.

Grewen, K. M., Girdler, S. S., Amico, J., & Light, K. C. (2005). Effects of partner support on resting oxytocin, cortisol, norepinephrine, and blood pressure before and after warm partner contact. *Psychosomatic Medicine, 67,* 531–538.

Griesinger, C. B., Richards, C. D., & Ashmore, J. F. (2005). Fast vesicle replenishment allows indefatigable signalling at the first auditory synapse. *Nature, 435,* 212–215.

Griffeth, R. W., Hom, P. W., & Gaertner, S. (2000). A meta-analysis of antecedents and correlates of employee turnover: Update, moderator tests, and research implications for the next millennium. *Journal of Management, 26,* 463–488.

Griffin, M. A., & Neal, A. (2000). Perceptions of safety at work: A framework for linking safety climate to safety performance, knowledge, and motivation. *Journal of Occupational Health Psychology, 5,* 347–358.

Griffitt, W. B., & Guay, P. (1969). "Object" evaluation and conditioned affect. *Journal of Experimental Research in Personality, 4,* 1–8.

Grigorenko, E. L. (2002). In search of the genetic engram of personality. In D. Cervone & W. Mischel (Eds.), *Advances in personality science* (pp. 29–82). New York: The Guilford Press.

Grimes, J. M., Ricci, L. A., & Melloni, R. H. (2006). Plasticity in anterior hypothalamic vasopressin correlates with aggression during anabolic-androgenic steroid withdrawal in hamsters. *Behavioral Neuroscience, 120,* 115–124.

Grinspoon, L. (1999). The future of medical marijuana. *Forsch Komplementarmed, 6,* 40–43.

Grinspoon, L., Bakalar, J. B., Zimmer, L., & Morgan, J. P. (1997). Marijuana addiction. *Science, 277,* 749, 750–752.

Grinspoon, S., Thomas, E., Pitts, S., Gross, E., Mickley, D., Killer, K., et al. (2000). Prevalence and predictive factors for regional osteopenia in women with anorexia nervosa. *Annals of Internal Medicine, 133,* 790–794.

Grisso, T., & Appelbaum, P. S. (1995). The MacArthur Treatment Competence Study: Vol. 3. Abilities of patients to consent to psychiatric and medical treatments. *Law and Human Behavior, 19,* 149–174.

Grob, C., & Dobkin-de-Rios, M. (1992). Adolescent drug use in cross-cultural perspective. *Journal of Drug Issues, 22*(1), 121–138.

Gronau, N., Ben-Shakhar, G., & Cohen, A. (2005). Behavioral and physiological measures in the detection of concealed information. *Journal of Applied Psychology, 90,* 147–158.

Groopman, J. (2000, January 24). Second opinion. *The New Yorker,* pp. 40–49.

Groopman, J. (2002, July 29). Hormones for men. *The New Yorker,* pp. 34–38.

Groopman, J. (2005, May 2). A model patient. *New Yorker,* 48–54.

Groopman, J. (2007). What's the trouble? *The New Yorker,* January 29, 36–41.

Gross, J. J. (2001). Emotion regulation in adulthood: Timing is everything. *Current Directions in Psychological Science, 10,* 214–219.

Grossman, M., & Ash, S. (2004). Primary progressive aphasia: A review. *Neurocase, 10*(1), 3–18.

Grosz, H. I., & Zimmerman, J. (1970). A second detailed case study of functional blindness: Further demonstration of the contribution of objective psychological data. *Behavior Therapy 1,* 115–123.

Grote, N. K., & Clark, M. S. (2001). Perceiving unfairness in the family: Cause or consequence of marital distress? *Journal of Personality and Social Psychology, 80,* 281–293.

Grotevant, H. D. (1998). Adolescent development in family contexts. In W. Damon & N. Eisenberg (Eds.), *Handbook of child psychology: Vol. 3. Social, emotional, and personality development* (5th ed., pp. 1097–1150). New York: Wiley.

Groth-Marnat, G. (1997). *Handbook of psychological assessment* (3rd ed.). New York: Wiley.

Groves, K. S. (2005). Linking leader skills, follower attitudes, and contextual variables via an integrated model of charismatic leadership. *Journal of Management, 31,* 255–277.

Grubb, P. L., Roberts, R. K., Swanson, N. G., Burnfield, J. L., & Childress, J. H. (2005). Organizational factors and psychological aggression: Results from a nationally representative sample of US companies. In V. Bowie, B. S. Fisher, & C. L. Cooper (Eds.), *Workplace violence: Issues, trends, strategies* (pp. 37–59). Portland, OR: Willan Publishing.

Grunberg, N. E. (1994). Overview: Biological processes relevant to drugs of dependence. *Addiction, 89*(11), 1443–1446.

Grusec, J. E., & Goodnow, J. J. (1994). Impact of parental discipline methods on the child's internalization of values. *Developmental Psychology, 30,* 4–19.

Grusec, J. E., Davidov, M., & Lundell, L. (2002). Prosocial and helping behavior. In P. K. Smith & C. H. Hart (Eds.), *Blackwell handbook of childhood social development* (pp. 457–474). Malden, MA: Blackwell.

Guadagno, R. E., Asher, T., Demaine, L. J., & Cialdini, R. B. (2001). When saying yes leads to saying no: Preference for consistency and the reverse foot-in-the-door effect. *Personality and Social Psychology Bulletin, 27,* 859–867.

Gualtieri, C. T., & Johnson, L. G. (2006). Antidepressant side effects in children and adolescents. *Journal of Child and Adolescent Psychopharmacology, 16,* 147–157.

Guerin, D. W., Gottfried, A. W., & Thomas, C. W. (1997). Difficult temperament and behaviour problems: A longitudinal study from 1.5 to 12 years. *International Journal of Behavioral Development, 21,* 71–90.

Guerlain, S. (1995). Using the critiquing approach to cope with brittle expert systems. *Proceedings of the Human Factors and Ergonomics Society 39th Annual Meeting, I* (pp. 233–237). Santa Monica, CA: Human Factors Society.

Guilford, J. P. (1959). Traits of creativity. In H. H. Anderson (Ed.), *Creativity and its cultivation* (pp. 142–161). New York: Harper & Row.

Guilleminault, C. (2004). Obstructive sleep apnea syndromes. *Medical Clinics of North America, 88,* 611–630.

Guilleminault, C., Palombini, L., Pelayo, R., & Chervin, R. D. (2003). Sleepwalking and sleep terrors in prepubertal children: What triggers them? *Pediatrics, 111,* 17–25.

Guimon, J. (2004). Evidence-based research studies on the results of group therapy: A critical review. *European Journal of Psychiatry, 18*(Suppl.), 49–60.

Gump, B. B., Reihman, J., Stewart, P., Lonky, E., & Darvill, T. (2005). Terrorism and cardiovascular responses to acute stress in children. *Health Psychology, 24,* 594–600.

Gunnoe, M. L., & Mariner, C. L. (1997). Toward a developmental-contextual model of the effects of parental spanking on children's aggressoin. *Archives of Pediatrics and Adolescent Medicine, 151,* 768–775.

Gupta, A. R., & State, M. W. (2007). Recent advances in the genetics of autism. *Biological Psychiatry, 61,* 429–437.

Gur, R. C., Mozley, L. H., Mozley, P. D., Resnick, S. M., Karp, J. S., Alavi, A., et al. (1995). Sex differences in regional cerebral glucose metabolism during a resting state. *Science, 267,* 528–531.

Gur, R. C., Skolnic, B. E., & Gur, R. E. (1994). Effects of emotional discrimination tasks on cerebral blood flow: Regional activation and its relation to performance. *Brain and Cognition, 25*(2), 271–286.

Gur, R. E., Cowell, P. E., Latshaw, A., Turetsky, B. I., Grossman, R. I., Arnold, S. E., et al. (2000). Reduced dorsal and orbital prefrontal gray matter volumes in schizophrenia. *Archives of General Psychiatry, 57,* 761–768.

Gura, T. (1999). Leptin not impressive in clinical trial. *Science, 286,* 881–882.

Gureje, O., Lasebikan, V. O., Kola, L., & Makanjuola, V. A. (2006). Lifetime and 12-month prevalence of mental disorders in the Nigerian Survey of Mental Health and Well-Being. *British Journal of Psychiatry, 188,* 465–471.

Gurman, A. S., & Jacobson, N. S. (2002). *Clinical handbook of couple therapy* (3rd ed.). New York: Guilford Press.

Gustafson, D., Rothenberg, E., Blennow, K., Steen, B., & Skoog, I. (2003). An 18-year follow-up of overweight and risk of Alzheimer disease. *Archives of Internal Medicine, 163,* 1524–1528.

Gustafsson, J. E., & Undheim, J. O. (1996). Individual differences in cognitive functions. In D. C. Berliner & R. C. Calfee (Eds.), *Handbook of educational psychology* (pp. 186–242). New York: Simon & Schuster Macmillan.

Guthrie, R. M., & Bryant, R. A. (2005). Auditory startle response in firefighters before and after trauma exposure. *American Journal of Psychiatry, 162,* 283–290.

Guyer, B., Freedman, M. A., Strobino, D. M., & Sondik, E. J. (2000). Annual summary of vital statistics: Trends in the health of Americans during the 20th century. *Pediatrics, 106,* 1307–1317.

Haaga, D. A. (2000). Introduction to the special section on stepped care models in psychotherapy. *Journal of Consulting and Clinical Psychology, 68,* 547–548.

Haber, R. N. (1979). Twenty years of haunting eidetic imagery: Where's the ghost? *The Behavioral and Brain Sciences, 2,* 583–629.

Haberlandt, K. (1999). *Human memory: Exploration and application.* Boston: Allyn & Bacon.

Haberstroh, J. (1995). *Ice cube sex: The truth about subliminal advertising.* South Bend, IN: Cross Cultural Publications/Crossroads.

Hackel, L. S., & Ruble, D. N. (1992). Changes in the marital relationship after the first baby is born: Predicting the impact of expectancy-disconfirmation. *Journal of Personality and Social Psychology, 62,* 944–957.

Hacking, I. (1995). *Rewriting the soul: Multiple personality and the sciences of memory.* Princeton, NJ: Princeton University Press.

Hackman, J. R. (1998). Why don't teams work? In R. S. Tindale, J. Edwards, & E. J. Posavac (Eds.), *Applications of theory and research on groups to social issues.* New York: Plenum.

Hackman, J. R., & Oldham, G. R. (1980). *Work redesign.* Reading, MA: Addison-Wesley.

Haddock, G., & Zanna, M. P. (1998). Authoritarianism, values, and the favorability and structure of antigay attitudes. In G. Herek (Ed.), *Stigma and sexual orientation: Understanding prejudice against lesbians, gay men, and bisexuals. Psychological perspectives on lesbian and gay issues.* Thousand Oaks, CA: Sage.

Hadjikhani, N., & de Gelder, B. (2003). Seeing fearful body expressions activates the fusiform cortex and amygdale. *Current Biology, 13,* 2201–2205.

Haefner, H., & Maurer, K. (2000). The early course of schizophrenia: New concepts for early intervention. In G. Andrews & S. Henderson (Eds.), *Unmet need in psychiatry: Problems, resources, responses* (p. 218–232). New York: Cambridge University Press.

Häfner, H. (2003). Gender differences in schizophrenia. *Psychoeuroendrocrinology, 28,* 17–54.

Hagen, E. P. (1980). *Identification of the gifted.* New York: Teachers College Press.

Hahdahl, K., Iversen, P. M., & Jonsen, B. H. (1993). Laterality for facial expressions: Does the sex of the subject interact with the sex of the stimulus face? *Cortex, 29*(2), 325–331.

Hahn, C.-S., & DiPietro, J. A. (2001). In vitro fertilization and the family: Quality of parenting, family functioning, and child psychosocial adjustment. *Developmental Psychology, 37,* 37–48.

Haidt, J. (2003). Elevation and the positive psychology of morality. In C. L. M. Keyes & J. Haidt (Eds.), *Flourishing: Positive psychology and the life well-lived* (pp. 275–289). Washington, DC: American Psychological Association.

Haier, R. J., White, N. S., & Alkire, M. T. (2003). Individual differences in general intelligence correlate with brain function during nonreasoning tasks. *Intelligence, 31,* 429–441.

Haldeman, D. C. (1994). The practice and ethics of sexual orientation-conversion therapy. *Consulting and Clinical Psychology, 62*(2), 221–227.

Halford, G. S., Baker, R., McCredden, J. E., & Bain, J. D. (2005). How many variables can humans process? *Psychological Science, 16*(1), 70–76.

Hall, C. S., Lindzey, G., & Campbell, J. P. (1998). *Theories of personality* (4th ed.). New York: Wiley.

Hall, G. (1991). *Perceptual and associative learning.* Oxford: Clarendon Press.

Hall, J. A. (1984). *Nonverbal sex differences.* Baltimore, MD: Johns-Hopkins University Press.

Hall, L. K., & Bahrick, H. P. (1998). The validity of metacognitive predictions of widespread learning and long-term retention. In G. Mazzoni & T. Nelson (Eds.), *Metacognition and cognitive neuropsychology: Monitoring and control processes* (pp. 23–36). Mahwah, NJ: Erlbaum.

Hall, W., & Degenhardt, L. (2003). Medical marijuana initiatives: Are they justified? How successful are they likely to be? *CNS Drugs, 17,* 689–697.

Halloran, M. J., & Kashima, E. S. (2004). Social identity and worldview validation: The effects of ingroup identity primes and mortality salience on value endorsement. *Personality and Social Psychology Bulletin, 30,* 915–925.

Halperin, D. (1992). *Sex differences in cognitive abilities.* Mahwah, NJ: Erlbaum.

Halpern, D. F. (1997). Sex differences in intelligence. *American Psychologist, 52,* 1091–1102.

Halpern, D. F. (2005). Psychology at the intersection of work and family: Recommendations for employers, working families, and policymakers. *American Psychologist, 60,* 397–409.

Halpern, D. F., & Hakel, M. D. (2003). *Applying the science of learning to university teaching and beyond: New directions for teaching and learning.* San Francisco: Jossey-Bass.

Hamad, G. G. (2004). The state of the art in bariatric surgery for weight loss in the morbidly obese patient. *Clinics in Plastic Surgery, 31,* 591–600.

Hamann, S., Herman, R. A., Nolan, C. L., & Wallen, K. (2004). Men and women differ in amygdala response to sexual stimuli. *Nature Neuroscience, 7,* 411–416.

Hamarat, E., Thompson, D., Steele, D., Matheny, K., & Simons, C. (2002). Age differences in coping resources and satisfaction with life among middle-aged, young-old, and oldest-old adults. *Journal of Genetic Psychology, 163*(3), 360–367.

Hamilton, D. L., & Sherman, J. (1994). Social stereotypes. In R. S. Wyer & T. K. Srull (Eds.), *Handbook of social cognition* (2nd ed.). Hillsdale, NJ: Erlbaum.

Hamilton, L. H., & Robson, B. (2006). Performing arts consultation: Developing expertise in this domain. *Professional Psychology: Research and Practice, 37,* 254–259.

Hamilton, W. D. (1964). The evolution of social behavior: Parts I and II. *Journal of Theoretical Biology 7,* 1–52.

Hamm, A. O., Vaitl, D., & Lang, P. J. (1989). Fear conditioning, meaning, and belongingness: A selective association analysis. *Journal of Abnormal Psychology, 98,* 395–406.

Hammad, T. A., Laughren, T., & Racoosin, J. (2006). Suicidality in pediatric patients treated with antidepressant drugs. *Archives of General Psychiatry, 63,* 332–339.

Hammen, C. (2005). Stress and depression. *Annual Review of Clinical Psychology, 1,* 293–319.

Hammer, E. (1968). Projective drawings. In A. I. Rabin (Ed.), *Projective techniques in personality assessment.* New York: Springer.

Hammerness, P., Basch, E., & Ulbricht, C. (2003). St. John's wort: A systematic review of adverse effects and drug interactions for the consultation psychiatrist. *Journal of Consultation Liaison Psychiatry, 44*(4), 271–282.

Hampson, S. E., & Goldberg, L. R. (2006). A first large cohort study of personality stability over the 40 years between elementary school and midlife. *Journal of Personality and Social Psychology, 91,* 763–779.

Hampson, S. E., Goldberg, L. R., Vogt, T. M., & Dubanoski, J. P. (2006). Forty years on: Teachers' assessments of children's personality traits predict self-reported health behaviors and outcomes at midlife. *Health Psychology, 25,* 57–64.

Hamrick, N., Cohen, S., & Rodriguez, M. S. (2002). Being popular can be healthy or unhealthy: Stress, social network diversity, and incidence of upper respiratory infection. *Health Psychology, 21,* 294–298.

Han, S., & Shavitt, S. (1994). Persuasion and culture: Advertising appeals in individualist and collectivist societies. *Journal of Experimental Social Psychology, 30,* 326–350.

Hancox, R. J., & Poulton, R. (2006). Watching television is associated with childhood obesity: But is it clinically important? *International Journal of Obesity, 30,* 171–175.

Handgraaf, M. J. J., & van Raaij, W. F. (2005). Fear and loathing no more: The emergence of collaboration between economists and psychologists. *Journal of Economic Psychology, 28,* 387–391.

Haney, M., Ward, A. S., Comer, S. D., Foltin, R. W., & Fischman, M. W. (1999). Abstinence symptoms following smoked marijuana in humans. *Psychopharmacology, 141,* 395–404.

Hanish, L. D., Martin, C. L., Fabes, R. A., Seonard, S., & Herzoh, M. (2005). Exposure to externalizing peers in early childhood: Homophily and peer contagion processes. *Journal of Abnormal Child Psychology, 33,* 267–281.

Hankin, B. L., & Abela, J. R. Z. (Eds.). (2005). *Development and psychopathology: A vulnerability-stress perspective.* Newberry Park, CA: Sage.

Hankin, B. L., & Abramson, L. Y. (2001). Development of gender differences in depression: An elaborated cognitive vulnerability-transactional stress theory. *Psychological Bulletin, 127,* 773–796.

Hankin, B. L., Fraley, R. C., & Abela, J. R. Z. (2005). Daily depression and cognitions about stress: Evidence for a traitlike depressogenic cognitive style and the prediction of depressive symptoms in a prospective daily diary study. *Journal of Personality and Social Psychology, 88,* 673–685.

Hanley, G. P., Piazza, C. C., Fisher, W. W., & Maglieri, K. A. (2005). On the effectiveness of and preference for punishment and extinction components of function-based interventions. *Journal of Applied Behavior Analysis, 38,* 51–65.

Hanson, G., & Venturelli, P. J. (1995). *Drugs and society* (4th ed.). Boston: Jones & Bartlett.

Hanson, S. J., & Burr, D. J. (1990). What connectionist models learn: Learning and representations in connectionist networks. *Behavioral and Brain Sciences, 13,* 471–518.

Happe, F. G. E., Winner, E., & Brownell, H. (1998). The getting of wisdom: Theory of mind in old age. *Developmental Psychology, 34,* 358–362.

Hara, K., Kubota, N., Tobe, K., Terauchi, Y., Miki, H., Komeda, K., et al. (2000). The role of PPARg as a thrifty gene both in mice and humans *British Journal of Nutrition, 84*(Suppl. 2), S235–S239.

Harasty, J., Double, K. L., Halliday, G. M., Kril, J. J., & McRitchie, D. A. (1997). Language-associated cortical regions are proportionally larger in the female brain. *Archives of Neurology, 54,* 171–176.

Hardesty, D. E., & Sackeim, H. A. (2007). Deep brain stimulation in movement and psychiatric disorders. *Biological Psychiatry, 61,* 831–835.

Hare, R. D. (1993). *Without conscience: The disturbing world of the psychopaths among us.* New York: Pocket Books.

Hariri, A. R., Drabant, E. M., Munoz, K. E., Kolachana, B. S., Mattay, V. S., Egan, M. F., et al. (2005). A susceptibility gene for affective disorders and the response of the human amygdala. *Archives of General Psychiatry, 62,* 146–152.

Harlow, H. F. (1949). The formation of learning sets. *Psychological Review, 56,* 51–65.

Harlow, H. F. (1959, June). Love in infant monkeys. *Scientific American,* pp. 68–74.

Harlow, T., Greaves, C., White, A., Brown, L., Hart, A., & Ernst, E. (2004). Randomised controlled trial of magnetic bracelets for relieving pain in osteoarthritis of the hip and knee. *British Medical Journal, 329,* 1450–1454.

Harman, W. S., Lee, T. W., Mitchell, T. R., Felps, W., & Ownes, B. P. (2007). The psychology of voluntary turnover. *Current Directions in Psychological Science, 16,* 51–54.

Harmison, R. J. (2006). Peak performance in sport: Identifying ideal performance states and developing athletes' psychological skills. *Professional Psychology: Research and Practice, 37,* 233–243.

Harmon, A. (2004, May 9). Neurodiversity forever: The disability movement turns to brains. *The New York Times,* p.1.

Harmon-Jones, E. (2004). On the relationship of frontal brain activity and anger: Examining the role of attitude toward anger. *Cognition and Emotion, 18,* 337–361.

Harmon-Jones, E., & Sigelman, J. (2001). State anger and prefrontal brain activity: Evidence that insult-related relative left prefrontal activation is associated with experienced anger and aggression. *Journal of Personality and Social Psychology, 80,* 797–804.

Harré, N., Brandt, T., & Houkamau, C. (2004). An examination of the actor-observer effect in young drivers' attributions for their own and their friends' risky driving. *Journal of Applied Social Psychology, 34,* 806–824.

Harris, G. C., & Aston-Jones, G. (1995). Involvement of D2 dopamine receptors in the nucleus acumbens in opiate withdrawal syndrome. *Nature, 371,* 155–157.

Harris, J. R. (1998). *The nurture assumption.* New York: Free Press.

Harris, J. R. (2000). Context-specific learning, personality, and birth order. *Current Directions in Psychological Science, 9,* 174–177.

Harrison, D. A., Newman, D. A., & Roth, P. L. (2006). How important are job attitudes? Meta-analytic comparisons of integrative behavioral outcomes and time sequences. *Academy of Management Journal, 49,* 305–325.

Harrison, D. A., Price, K. H., Gavin, J. H., & Florey, A. T. (2002). Time, teams, and task performance: Changing effects of surface- and deep-level diversity on group functioning. *Academy of Management Journal, 45,* 1029–1045.

Harrison, K. (2003). Fitness and excitation. In J. Bryant, & D. Roskos-Ewoldsen (Eds.), *Communication and emotion: Essays in honor of Dolf Zillmann* (pp. 473–489). Mahwah, NJ: Erlbaum.

Hart, A. J., Whalen, P. J., Shin, L. M., McInerney, S. C., Fischer, H., & Rauch, S. L. (2000). Differential response in the human amygdala to racial outgroup vs. ingroup face stimuli. *Neuroreport, 11,* 2351–2355.

Hart, C. L., Taylor, M. D., Smith, G. D., Whalley, L. J., Starr, J. M., Hole, D. J., et al. (2003). Childhood IQ, social class, deprivation, and their relationships with mortality and morbidity risk in later life: Prospective observational study linking the Scottish mental survey of 1932 and the midspan studies. *Psychosomatic Medicine, 65,* 877–883.

Hart, D., & Yates, M. (1997). The interrelation of self and identity in adolescence: A developmental account. In R. Vasta (Ed.), *Annals of child development: Vol. 12. A research annual* (pp. 207–243). London: Jessica Kingsley.

Harter, S. (2006). The self. In W. Damon & R. M. Lerner (Series Eds.) & N. Eisenberg (Vol. Ed.), *Handbook of child psychology: Vol. 3, Social, emotional, and personality development* (6th ed., pp. 505–570). New York: Wiley.

Hartmann, H. (1958). *Ego psychology and the problem of adaptation.* New York: International Universities Press.

Hartung, C. M., & Widiger, T. A. (1998). Gender differences in the diagnosis of mental disorders: Conclusions and controversies of *DSM-IV*. *Psychological Bulletin, 123,* 260–278.

Hartup, W. W., & Stevens, N. (1997). Friendships and adaptation in the life course. *Psychological Bulletin, 121,* 355–370.

Harvard Mental Health Letter. (2001). New treatments for cocaine addiction. *Harvard Mental Health Letter, 17,* 6–7.

Harvey, S. B., Stanton, B. R., & David, A. S. (2006). Conversion disorder: Towards a neurobiological understanding. *Neuropsychiatric Disease and Treatment, 2,* 13–20.

Harwood, K., McLean, N., & Durkin, K. (2007). First-time mothers' expectations of parenthood: What happens when optimistic expectations are not matched by later experiences? *Developmental Psychology, 43,* 1–12.

Hasin, D. S., Goodwin, R. D., Stinson, F. S., & Grant, B. F. (2005). Epidemiology of major depressive disorder: Results from the national epidemiologic survey on alcoholism and related conditions. *Archives of General Psychiatry, 62,* 1097–1106.

Haskett, M. E., Nears, K., Sabourin Ward, C., & McPherson, A. V. (2006). Diversity in adjustment of maltreated children: Factors associated with resilient functioning. *Clinical Psychology Review, 26,* 796–812.

Hastings, P. D., & Nuselovici, J. N. (2006). Development and psychopathology: A vulnerability-stress perspective (review). *Canadian Psychology, 47,* 143–145.

Hatcher, D., Brown, T., & Gariglietti, K. P. (2001). Critical thinking and rational emotive behavior therapy. *Inquiry: Critical Thinking Across the Disciplines, 20,* 6–18.

Hatfield, E., & Rapson, R. L. (2006). Passionate love, sexual desire, and mate selection: Cross-cultural and historical perspectives. In P. Noller & J. Feeney (Eds.), *Close relationships: Functions, forms and processes* (pp. 227–243). Hove, England: Psychology Press/Taylor & Francis.

Hatfield, J., Job, R. F. S., Hede, A. J., Carter, N. L., Peploe, P., Taylor, R., & Morrell, S. (2002). Human response to environmental noise: The role of perceived control. *International Journal of Behavioral Medicine, 9,* 341–359.

Hathaway, W. (2002, December 22). Henry M: The day one man's memory died. *Hartford Courant.*

Hattori, M., Fujiyama A., Taylor, T. D., Watanabe, H., Yada, T., Park, H. S., et al. (2000). The DNA sequence of human chromosome 21. *Nature, 405,* 311–319.

Hauptman, J., Lucas, C., Boldrin, M. N., Collins, H., & Segal, K. R. (2000). Orlistat in the long-term treatment of obesity in primary care settings. *Archives of Family Medicine, 9,* 160–167.

Hausknecht, J. P., Day, D. V., & Thomas, S. C. (2004). Applicant reactions to selection procedures: An updated model and meta-analysis. *Personnel Psychology, 57,* 639–683.

Haut, K. M., & Barch, D. M. (2006). Sex influences on material-sensitive functional lateralization in working and episodic memory: Men and women are not all that different. *NeuroImage, 32,* 411–422.

Haw, R. M., & Fisher, R. P. (2004). Effects of administrator-witness contact on eyewitness identification accuracy. *Journal of Applied Psychology, 89,* 1106–1112.

Hawkes, C. (2003). Olfaction in neurodegenerative disorders. *Movement Disorders, 18,* 364–372.

Hawkins, H. L., Kramer, A. R., & Capaldi, D. (1993). Aging, exercise, and attention. *Psychology and Aging, 7,* 643–653.

Haxby, J. V., Gobbini, M. I., Furey, M. L., Ishai, A., Schouten, J. L., & Pietrini, P. (2001). Distributed and overlapping representations of faces and objects in ventral temporal cortex. *Science, 293,* 2425–2430.

Hay, D. F., Pawlby, S., Angold, A., Harold, G. T., & Sharp, D. (2003). Pathways to violence in the children of mothers who were depressed postpartum. *Developmental Psychology, 39,* 1083–1094.

Hayden, E. P., & Nurnberger, J. I. (2006). Molecular genetics of bipolar disorder. *Genes, Brain & Behavior, 5,* 85–95.

Hayes, A. M., & Harris, M. S. (2000). The development of an integrative therapy for depression. In S. L. Johnson & A. M. Hayes (Eds.), *Stress, coping, and depression* (pp. 291–306). Mahwah, NJ: Erlbaum.

Hayes, R. A., Efron, L. A., Richman, G. S., Harrison, K. A., & Aguilera, E. L. (2000). The effects of behavioural contracting and preferred reinforcement on appointment keeping. *Behaviour Change, 17,* 90–96.

Haynes, J.-D., & Rees, G. (2005). Predicting the stream of consciousness from activity in human visual cortex. *Current Biology, 15,* 1301–1307.

Hays, K. F. (2006). Being fit: The ethics of practice diversification in performance psychology. *Professional Psychology: Research and Practice, 37,* 223–232.

Hays, P. A., & Iwamasa, G. Y. (Eds.). (2006). *Culturally responsive cognitive-behavioral therapy: Assessment, practice, and supervision.* Washington, DC: American Psychological Association.

He, L. F. (1987). Involvement of endogenous opioid peptides in acupuncture analgesia. *Pain, 31,* 99–121.

Hebb, D. O. (1949). *The organization of behavior.* New York: Wiley.

Hebb, D. O. (1955). Drives and the C. N. S. (conceptual nervous system). *Psychological Review, 62,* 243–254.

Hebert, L. E., Scherr, P. A., Bienias, J. I., Bennett, D. A., & Evans, D. A. (2003). Alzheimer disease in the U.S. population: Prevalence estimates using the 2000 Census. *Archives of Neurology, 60,* 1119–1122.

Hecker, J. E., Losee, M. C., Fritzler, B. K., & Fink, C. M. (1996). Self-directed versus therapist-directed cognitive behavioral treatment for panic disorder. *Journal of Anxiety Disorders, 10,* 253–265.

Hecker, J. E., & Thorpe, G. L. (1992). *Agoraphobia and panic: A guide to psychological treatment.* Boston: Allyn & Bacon.

Heckman, T. G., Anderson, E. S., Sikkema, K. J., Kochman, A., Kalichman, S., & Anderson, T. (2004). Emotional distress in nonmetropolitan persons living with HIV disease enrolled in a telephone-delivered, coping improvement group intervention. *Health Psychology, 23,* 94–100.

Hedge, A., & Yousif, Y. H. (1992). Effects of urban size, urgency, and cost of helpfulness: A cross-cultural comparison between the United Kingdom and the Sudan. *Journal of Cross-Cultural Psychology, 23,* 107–115.

Hedge, J. W., Borman, W. C., & Lammlein, S. E. (2006). *The aging workforce: Realities, myths, and implications for organizations.* Washington, DC: American Psychological Association.

Hedley, A. A., Ogden, C. L., Johnson, C. L., Carroll, M. D., Curtin, L. R., & Flegal, K. M. (2004). Prevalence of overweight and obesity among US children, adolescents, and adults, 1999–2002. *Journal of the American Medical Association, 291,* 2847–2850.

Heekeren, H. R., Wartenburger, I., Schmidt, H., Schwintowski, H.-P., & Villringer, A. (2003). An fMRI study of simple ethical decision-making. *Neuroreport, 14,* 1215–1219.

Hegarty, J. D., Baldessarini, R. J., Tohen, M., Waternaux, C., & Oepen, G. (1994). One hundred years of schizophrenia: A meta-analysis of the outcome literature. *American Journal of Psychiatry, 151,* 1409–1416.

Hegerl, U., Plattner, A., & Moller, H. J. (2004). Should combined pharmaco- and psychotherapy be offered to depressed patients? A qualitative review of randomized clinical trials from the 1990s. *European Archives of Psychiatry and Clinical Neuroscience, 254,* 99–107.

Heiby, E. M., DeLeon, P. H., & Anderson, T. (2004). A debate on prescription privileges for psychologists. *Professional Psychology: Research and Practice, 35,* 336–344.

Heider, E. (1972). Universals of color naming and memory. *Journal of Experimental Psychology, 93,* 10–20.

Heilman, K. M., Barrett, A. M., & Adair, J. C. (1998). Possible mechanisms of anosognosia: A defect in self-awareness. *Philosophical Transactions of the Royal Society of London: Series B. Biological Sciences, 353*(1377), 1903–1909.

Heilman, K. M., & Gonzalez-Rothi, L. (2003). Apraxia. In K. M. Heilman & E. Valenstein (Eds.), *Clinical neuropsychology* (4th ed.). New York: Oxford University Press.

Heilman, K. M., & Valenstein, E. (Eds.). (2003). *Clinical neuropsychology* (4th ed.). New York: Oxford University Press.

Heilman, K. M., Valenstein, E., & Watson, R. T. (2000). Neglect and related disorders. *Seminars in Neurology, 20*(4), 463–470.

Heilman, K. M., Watson, R. T., & Valenstein, E. (2003). Neglect and related disorders. In K. M. Heilman & E. Valenstein (Eds.), *Clinical neuropsychology* (4th ed.). New York: Oxford University Press.

Heiman, J. R. (2002). Sexual dysfunction: Overview of prevalence, etiological factors, and treatments. *Journal of Sex Research, 39,* 73–78.

Heine, S. J. (2003). Self-enhancement in Japan? A reply to Brown & Kobayashi. *Asian Journal of Social Psychology, 6,* 75–84.

Heine, S. J., Harihara, M., & Niiya, Y. (2002). Terror management in Japan. *Asian Journal of Social Psychology, 5,* 187–196.

Heiss, W. D., & Teasel, R. W. (2006). Brain recovery and rehabilitation. *Stroke, 37*(2), 314–316.

Hejmadi, A., Davidson, R. J., & Rozin, P. (2000). Exploring Hindu Indian emotion expressions: Evidence for accurate recognition by Americans and Indians. *Psychological Science, 11,* 183–187.

Heldt, E., Manfro, G. G., Kipper, L., Blaya, C., Isolan, L., & Otto, M. W. (2006). One-year follow-up of pharmacotherapy-resistant patients with panic disorder treated with cognitive-behavior therapy: Outcome and predictors of remission. *Behaviour Research and Therapy, 44,* 657–665.

Helgesen, S. (1998). *Everyday revolutionaries: Working women and the transformation of American life.* New York: Doubleday.

Heller, W. (1993). Neuropsychological mechanisms of individual differences in emotion, personality, and arousal. *NeuroPsychology, 7*(4), 486–489.

Heller, W., Nitschke, J. B., & Miller, G. A. (1998). Lateralization in emotion and emotional disorders. *Current Directions in Psychological Science, 7,* 26–32.

Helms, J. E. (1992). Why is there no study of cultural equivalence in standardized cognitive ability testing? *American Psychologist, 47,* 1083–1101.

Helms, J. E. (1997). The triple quandary of race, culture, and social class in standardized cognitive ability testing. In D. P. Flanagan, J. L. Genshaft, & P. L. Harrison (Eds.), *Contemporary intellectual assessment: Theories, tests, and issues.* New York: Guilford Press.

Helson, R., & Moane, G. (1987). Personality change in women from college to midlife. *Journal of Personality and Social Psychology, 53,* 176–186.

Helzer, J. E., Canino, G. J., Yeh, E., Bland, R. C., Lee, C. K., Hwu, H., & Newman, S. (1990). Alcoholism—North America and Asia: A comparison of population surveys with the diagnostic interview schedule. *Archives of General Psychiatry, 47,* 313–319.

Helzer, J. E., & Hudziak, J. J. (Eds.). (2002). *Defining psychopathology in the 21st century: DSM-V and beyond.* Washington DC: American Psychiatric Publishing, Inc.

Henderson, B., & Bernard, A. (Eds.). (1998). *Rotten reviews and rejections.* Wainscott, NY: Pushcart Press.

Hendrick, C., & Hendrick, S. S. (2003). Romantic love: Measuring cupid's arrow. In S. J. Lopez & C. R. Snyder (Eds.), *Positive psychological assessment: A handbook of models and measures* (pp. 235–249). Washington, DC: American Psychological Association.

Hendricks, P. S., & Thompson, J. K. (2005). An integration of cognitive-behavioral therapy and interpersonal psychotherapy for bulimia nervosa: A case study using the case formulation method. *International Journal of Eating Disorders, 37,* 171–174.

Henig, R. (2004, April 4). The quest to forget. *The New York Times,* p. 32.

Henker, B., & Whalen, C. K. (1989). Hyperactivity and attention deficits. *American Psychologist, 44,* 216–223.

Hennig, J., Reuter, M., Netter, P., Burk, C., & Landt, O. (2005). Two types of aggression are differentially related to serotonergic activity and the A779C TPH polymorphism. *Behavioral Neuroscience, 119,* 16–25.

Hensch, T. K. (2005). Critical period plasticity in local cortical circuits. *Nature Reviews. Neuroscience, 6,* 877–888.

Hense, R. L., Penner, L. A., & Nelson, D. L. (1995). Implicit memory for age stereotypes. *Social Cognition, 13,* 399–416.

Heppner, P. P., Heppner, M. J., Lee, D., Wang, Y.-W., Park, H., & Wang, L. (2006). Development and validation of a collectivist coping styles inventory. *Journal of Counseling Psychology, 53,* 107–125.

Hepworth, S. J., Schoemaker, M. J., Muir, K. R., Swerdlow, A. J., van Tongeren, M. J. A., & McKinney, P. A. (2006). Mobile phone use and risk of glioma in adults: Case control study. *British Medical Journal, 332,* 883–887.

Herbert, J. D., Lilienfeld, S. O., Lohr, J. M., Montgomery, R. W., O'Donohue, W. T., Rosen, G. M., & Tolin, D. F. (2000). Science and pseudoscience in the development of eye movement desensitization and reprocessing: Implications for clinical psychology. *Clinical Psychology Review, 20,* 945–971.

Heres, S., Davis, J., Maino, K., Jetzinger, E., Kissling, W., & Leucht, S. (2006). Why olanzapine beats risperidone, risperidone beats quetiapine, and quetiapine beats olanzapine: An exploratory analysis of head-to-head comparison studies of second-generation antipsychotics. *American Journal of Psychiatry, 163,* 185–194.

Hergenhahn, B. R., & Olson, M. (1997). *An introduction to theories of learning* (5th ed.). Upper Saddle River, NJ: Prentice-Hall.

Hergenhahn, B. R., & Olson, M. (2007). *Introduction to theories of personality* (7th ed.) Upper Saddle River, NJ: Prentice Hall.

Herman, C. P., Roth, D. A., & Polivy, J. (2003). Effects of the presence of others on food intake: A normative interpretation. *Psychological Bulletin, 129,* 873–886.

Herman, L. M., Richards, D. G., & Wolz, J. P. (1984). Comprehension of sentences by bottlenosed dolphins. *Cognition, 16,* 129–219.

Hermann, R. C., Dorwart, R. A., Hoover, C. W., & Brody, J. (1995). Variation in ECT use in the United States. *American Journal of Psychiatry, 152,* 869–875.

Hermans, D., Craske, M. G., Mineka, S., & Lovibond, P. F. (2006). Extinction in human fear conditioning. *Biological Psychiatry, 60,* 361–368.

Hernandez, D. J. (1997). Child development and the social demography of childhood. *Child Development, 68,* 149–169.

Herpertz, S. C., Werth, U., Lukas, G., Qunaibi, M., Schuerkens, A., Kunert, H.-J., et al. (2001). Emotion in criminal offenders with psychopathy and borderline personality disorder. *Archives of General Psychiatry, 58,* 737–745.

Herrenkohl, T., Hill, K., Chung, I.-J., Guo, J., Abbott, R. D., & Hawkins, D. J. (2004). Protective factors against serious violent behavior in adolescence: A prospective study of violent children. *Social Work Research, 27*(3), 179–191.

Herrmann, D. J., & Searleman, A. (1992). Memory improvement and memory theory in historical perspective. In D. Herrmann, H. Weingartner, A. Searlman, & C. McEvoy (Eds.), *Memory improvement: Implications for memory theory.* New York: Springer-Verlag.

Herrnstein, R. (1973). *I. Q. in the meritocracy.* Boston: Little, Brown.

Herrnstein, R. J., & Murray, C. (1994). *The bell curve: Intelligence and class structure in American Life.* New York: Free Press.

Hershcovis, M. S., Turner, N., Barling, J., Arnold, K. A., Dupré, K. E., Inness, M., LeBlanc, M. M., & Sivanathan, N. (2007). Predicting workplace aggression: A meta-analysis. *Journal of Applied Psychology, 92,* 228–238.

Hertlein, K., & Ricci, R. J. (2004). A systematic research synthesis of EMDR studies: Implementation of the platinum standard. *Trauma, Violence, and Abuse, 5,* 285–300.

Herz, R. S., & Cahill, E. D. (1997). Differential use of sensory information in sexual behavior as a function of gender. *Human Nature, 8,* 275–286.

Herzog, D. B. (1982). Bulimia: The secretive syndrome. *Psychosomatics, 22,* 481–487.

Herzog, D. B., Dorer, D. J., Keel, P. K., Selwyn, S. E., Ekeblad, E. R., Flores, A. T., et al. (1999). Recovery and relapse in anorexia and bulimia nervosa: A 7.5-year follow-up study. *Journal of the American Academy of Child and Adolescent Psychiatry, 38,* 829–837.

Herzog, T. A., & Blagg, C. O. (2007). Are most precontemplators contemplating smoking cessation? Assessing the validity of the stages of change. *Health Psychology, 26,* 222–231.

Hespos, S. J., & Baillargeon, R. (2001). Infants' knowledge about occlusion and containment events: A surprising discrepancy. *Psychological Science, 12,* 141–147.

Hespos, S. J., & Spelke, E. S. (2004). Conceptual precursors to language. *Nature, 430,* 453–456.

Hess, R. D., Chih-Mei, C., & McDevitt, T. M. (1987). Cultural variations in family beliefs about children's performance in mathematics: Comparisons among People's Republic of China, Chinese-American, and Caucasian-American families. *Journal of Educational Psychology, 79,* 179–188.

Hess, T. M., Hinson, J. T., & Statham, J. A. (2004). Explicit and implicit stereotype activation effects on memory: Do age and awareness moderate the impact of priming? *Psychology and Aging, 19,* 495–505.

Hesse, J., Mogelvang, B., & Simonsen, H. (1994). Acupuncture versus metropolol in migraine prophylaxis: A randomized trial of trigger point inactivation. *Journal of Internal Medicine, 235,* 451–456.

Heston, L. L. (1966). Psychiatric disorders in foster home-reared children of schizophrenic mothers. *British Journal of Psychiatry, 112,* 819–825.

Hetherington, E. M., & Stanley-Hagan, M. (2002). Parenting in divorced, single-parent, and stepfamilies. In M. H. Bornstein (Ed.), *Handbook of parenting* (2nd ed.). Mahwah, NJ: Erlbaum.

Hettema, J. M., Neale, M. C., & Kendler, K. S. (2001). A review and meta-analysis of the genetic epidemiology of anxiety disorders. *American Journal of Psychiatry, 158,* 1568–1578.

Hettema, J. M., Prescott, C. A., Myers, J. M., Neale, M. C., & Kendler, K. S. (2005). The structure of genetic and environmental risk factors for anxiety disorders in men and women. *Archives of General Psychiatry, 62,* 182–189.

Heymsfield, S. B., Greenberg, A. S., Fujioa, K., Dixon, R. M., Kushner, R., Hunt, T., et al. (1999). Recombinant leptin for weight loss in obese and lean adults. *Journal of the American Medical Association, 282*, 1568–1575.

Heywood, C. A., & Kentridge, R. W. (2003). Achromatopsia, color vision, and cortex. *Neurology Clinics, 21*, 483–500.

Hicks, B. M., Krueger, R. F., Iacono, W. G., McGue, M., & Patrick, C. J. (2004). Family transmission and heritability of externalizing disorders. *Archives of General Psychiatry, 61*, 922–928.

Hicks, R. A., Fernandez, C., & Pelligrini, R. J. (2001). The changing pattern of sleep habits of university students: An update. *Perceptual and Motor Skills, 93*, 648.

Highley, J. R., Walker, M. A., Crow, T. J., Esiri, M. M., & Harrison, P. J. (2003). Low medial and lateral right pulvinar volumes in schizophrenia: A postmortem study. *American Journal of Psychiatry, 160*, 1177–1179.

Hightower, J. R. R. (2005). Women and depression. In A. Barnes (Ed.), *The handbook of women, psychology, and the law* (pp. 192–211). New York: Wiley.

Higuchi, S., Matsushita, S., & Kashima, H. (2006). New findings on the genetic influences on alcohol use and dependence. *Current Opinion in Psychiatry, 19*, 253–265.

Hildebrandt, M. G., Steyerberg, E. W., Stage, K. B., Passchier, J., Kragh-Soerensen, P., and the Danish University Antidepressant Group. (2003). Are gender differences important for the clinical effects of antidepressants? *American Journal of Psychiatry, 160*, 1643–1650.

Hilgard, E. R. (1965). *Hypnotic susceptibility.* New York: Harcourt, Brace & World.

Hilgard, E. R. (1977). *Divided consciousness: Multiple controls in human thought and action.* New York: Wiley.

Hilgard, E. R. (1979). *Personality and hypnosis: A study of imaginative involvement.* Chicago: University of Chicago Press.

Hilgard, E. R. (1982). Hypnotic susceptibility and implications for measurement. International *Journal of Clinical and Experimental Hypnosis, 30*, 394–403.

Hilgard, E. R. (1992). Divided consciousness and dissociation. *Consciousness and Cognition, 1*, 16–31.

Hilgard, E. R., Morgan, A. H., & MacDonald, H. (1975). Pain and dissociation in the cold pressor test: A study of "hidden reports" through automatic key-pressing and automatic talking. *Journal of Abnormal Psychology, 84*, 280–289.

Hill, B. (1968). *Gates of horn and ivory.* New York: Taplinger.

Hill, C. (2005). Therapist techniques, client involvement, and the therapeutic relationship: Inextricably intertwined in the therapy process. *Psychotherapy: Theory, Research, Practice, Training, 42*, 431–442.

Hill, C. T., & Peplau, L. A. (1998). Premarital predictors of relationship outcomes: A 15-year follow-up of the Boston Couples Study. In T. N. Bradbury (Ed.), *The developmental course of marital dysfunction* (pp. 237–278). New York: Cambridge University Press.

Hill, D. L., & Mistretta, C. M. (1990). Developmental neurobiology of salt taste sensation. *Trends in Neuroscience, 13*, 188–195.

Hill, D. L., & Przekop, P. R., Jr. (1988). Influences of dietary sodium on functional taste receptor development: A sensitive period. *Science, 241*, 1826–1828.

Hill, J. O., & Peters, J. C. (1998). Environmental contributions to the obesity epidemic. *Science, 280*, 1371–1374.

Hill, R. A., & Barton, R. A. (2005). Psychology: Red enhances human performance in contests. *Nature, 435*, 293.

Hill, T., Lewicki, P., Czyzewska, M., & Boss, A. (1989). Self-perpetuating biases in person perception. *Journal of Personality and Social Psychology, 57*, 373–386.

Hiller, W., Leibbrand, R., Rief, W., & Fichter, M. M. (2006). Differentiating hypochondriasis from panic disorder. *Journal of Anxiety Disorders, 19*, 29–49.

Hilliard, R. B., Henry, W. P., & Strupp, H. H. (2000). An interpersonal model of psychotherapy: Linking patient and therapist developmental history, therapeutic process, and types of outcome. *Journal of Consulting and Clinical Psychology, 68*, 125–133.

Hilton, D. (2002). Thinking about causality: Pragmatic, social and scientific rationality. In P. E. Carruthers, S. Stich, & M. Siegal (Eds.), *The cognitive basis of science* (pp. 211–231). New York: Cambridge University Press.

Hilton, H. (1986). *The executive memory guide.* New York: Simon & Schuster.

Hinson, J. M., Jameson, T. L., & Whitney, P. (2002). Impulsive decision making and working memory. *Cognitive, Affective, & Behavioral Neuroscience, 2*, 341–353.

Hinton, J. (1967). *Dying.* Harmondsworth, England: Penguin.

Hintzman, D. L. (1978). *The psychology of learning and memory.* Freeman: San Francisco.

Hirota, K. (2006). Special cases: Ketamine, nitrous oxide and xenon. *Best Practice and Research: Clinical Anaesthesiology, 20*(1), 69–79.

Hiroto, D. S. (1974). Locus of control and learned helplessness. *Journal of Experimental Psychology, 102*, 187–193.

Hirschfeld, R. M., Allen, M. H., McEvoy, J. P., Keck, P. E., Jr, & Russell, J. M. (1999). Safety and tolerability of oral loading divalproex sodium in acutely manic bipolar patients. *Journal of Clinical Psychiatry, 60*, 815–818.

Hirschfeld, R. M. A., & Vornik, L. A. (2004). Newer antidepressants: Review of efficacy and safety of escitalopram and duloxetine. *Journal of Clinical Psychiatry, 65*(Suppl. 4), 46–52.

Hirsch-Pasek, K., Treiman, R., & Schneiderman, M. (1984). Brown and Hanlon revisited: Mothers' sensitivity to ungrammatical forms. *Journal of Child Language, 11*, 81–88.

Ho, B.-C., Andreasen, N. C., Nopoulos, P., Arndt, S., Magnotta, V., & Flaum M. (2003). Progressive structural brain abnormalities and their relationship to clinical outcome: A longitudinal magnetic resonance imaging study early in schizophrenia. *Archives of General Psychiatry, 60*, 585–594.

Ho, B.-C., Black, D. W., & Andreasen, N. C. (2003). Schizophrenia and other psychotic disorders. In R. E. Hales & S. C. Yudofsky (Eds.), *Textbook of clinical psychiatry* (4th ed., pp. 239–256). Washington, DC: American Psychiatric Publishing.

Ho, D. Y., & Chiu, C. (1998). Component ideas of individual, collectivism, and social organization. In U. Kim, C. Kagitcibasi, & H. C. Triandis (Eds.), *Individualism and collectivism: Theory, method, and applications.* Thousand Oaks, CA: Sage.

Ho, Y.-C., Cheung, M., & Chan, A. S. (2003). Music training improves verbal but not visual memory: Cross-sectional and longitudinal explorations in children. *Neuropsychology, 17*, 439–450.

Hobson, J. (1997). Dreaming as delirium: A mental status analysis of our nightly madness. *Seminar in Neurology, 17*, 121–128.

Hobson, J. A., Pace-Schott, E. F., Stickgold, R., & Kahn, D. (1998). To dream or not to dream? Relevant data from new neuroimaging and electrophysical studies. *Current Opinions in Neurobiology, 8*, 239–244.

Hobson, J. A., & Stickgold, R. (1994). Dreaming: A neurocognitive approach. *Consciousness and Cognition, 3*, 1–15.

Hochberg, L. R., Serruya, M. D., Friehs, G. M., Mukand, J. A., Saleh, M., Caplan, A. H., et al. (2006). Neuronal ensemble control of prosthetic devices by a human with tetraplegia. *Nature, 442*, 164–171.

Hochhalter, A., Sweeney, W., Bakke, B. L., Holub, R. J., & Overmier, J. B. (2001). Improving face recognition in alcohol dementia. *Clinical Gerontologist, 22*, 3–18.

Hodson, G., Dovidio, J. F., & Gaertner, S. L. (2004). The aversive form of racism. In J. L. Chin (Ed.), *The psychology of prejudice and discrimination: Racism in America* (Vol. 1, pp. 119–135). Westport, CT: Praeger Publishers/Greenwood Publishing Group.

Hoegl, M., & Parboteeah, K. P. (2006). Autonomy and teamwork in innovative projects. *Human Resource Management, 45*, 67–79.

Hoel, H., Faragher, B., & Cooper, C. L. (2004). Bullying is detrimental to health, but all bullying behaviors are not necessarily equally damaging. *British Journal of Guidance and Counseling, 32*, 367–387.

Hoffert, M. J. (1992). The neurophysiology of pain. In G. M. Aronoff (Ed.), *Evaluation and treatment of chronic pain.* Baltimore: Williams & Wilkins.

Hoffman, D. (1999, February 11). When the nuclear alarms went off, he guessed right. *International Herald Tribune,* p. 2.

Hoffman, H. G., Granhag, P. A., See, S. T. K., & Loftus, E. F. (2001). Social influences on reality-monitoring decisions. *Memory and Cognition, 29*, 394–404.

Hoffmann, J. P., & Cerbone, F. G. (2002). Parental substance use disorder and the risk of adolescent drug abuse: An event history analysis. *Drug and Alcohol Dependence, 66*, 255–264.

Hofmann, S. G., Meuret, A. E., Smits, J. A., Simon, N. M., Pollack, M. H., Eisenmenger, K., et al. (2006). Augmentation of exposure therapy with D-cycloserine for social anxiety disorder. *Archives of General Psychiatry, 63*, 298–304.

Hogan, R. (2005). In defense of personality measurement: New wine for old whiners. *Human Performance, 18*, 331–341.

Hogan, R., Curphy, G. J., & Hogan, J. (1994). What we know about leadership. *American Psychologist, 49*, 493–504.

Hogarth, R. M., & Einhorn, H. J. (1992). Order effects in belief updating: The belief adjustment model. *Cognitive Psychology, 24*, 1–55.

Hoglinger, G. U., Widmer, H. R., Spenger, C., Meyer, M., Seiler, R. W., Oertel, W. H., & Sautter, J. (2001). Influence of time in culture and BDNF pretreatment on survival and function of grafted embryonic rat ventral mesencephalon in the 6-OHDA rat model of Parkinson's disease. *Experimental Neurology, 167*, 148–157.

Hohman, A. A., & Shear, M. K. (2002). Community-based intervention research: Coping with the "noise" of real life in study design. *American Journal of Psychiatry, 159*, 201–207.

Hohmann, A. G., Syplita, R. L., Bolton, N. M., Neely, M. N., Fegley, D., Mangieri, R., et al. (2005). An endocannabinois mechanism for stress-pinduced analgesia. *Nature, 435*, 1108–1112.

Hohmann, G. W., (1966). Some effects of spinal cord lesions on experienced emotional feelings. *Psychophysiology, 3*, 143–156.

Holahan, C. K. (1994). Women's goal orientations across the life cycle: Findings from the Terman Study of the Gifted. In B. F. Turner & L. E. Troll (Eds.), *Women growing older* (pp. 35–67). Thousand Oaks, CA: Sage.

Holden, C. (1996). Small refugees suffer the effects of early neglect. *Science, 274*, 1076–1077.

Hollinger, R. C., Dabney, D. A., Lee, G., Hayes, R., Hunter, J., & Cummings, M. (1996). *1996 national retail security survey final report.* Gainesville: University of Florida.

Hollon, S. D., Jarrett, R. B., Nienbeg, A. A., Thase, M. E., Trivendi, M., et al. (2005). Psychotherapy and medication in the treatment of adult and geriatric depression: Which monotherapy or combined therapy? *Journal of Clinical Psychiatry, 66*, 455–468.

Hollon, S. D., Stewart, M. O., & Strunk, D. (2006).Enduring effects for cognitive behavior therapy in the treatment of depression and anxiety. *Annual Review of Psychology, 57,* 285–315.

Hollon, S. D., Thase, M. E., & Markowitz, J. C. (2002). Treatment and prevention of depression. *Psychological Science in the Public Interest, 3,* 39–77.

Holman, B. R. (1994). Biological effects of central nervous system stimulants. *Addiction, 89*(11), 1435–1441.

Holmes, D. S. (1991). *Abnormal psychology.* New York: HarperCollins.

Holmes, T. H., & Rahe, R. H. (1967). The Social Readjustment Rating Scale. *Journal of Psychosomatic Research, 11,* 213–218.

Holtmaat, A., Wilbrecht, L., Knott, G. W., Welker, E., & Svoboda, K. (2006). Experience-dependent and cell-type-specific spine growth in the neocortex. *Nature, 441,* 979–983.

Holway, A. H., & Boring, E. G. (1941). Determinants of apparent visual size with distance variant. *American Journal of Psychology, 54,* 21–37.

Hommer, D. W., Momenan, R., Kaiser, E., & Rawlings, R. R. (2001). Evidence for a gender-related effect of alcoholism on brain volumes. *American Journal of Psychiatry, 158,* 198–204.

Hong, Y., Morris, M. W., Chiu, C., & Benet-Martinez, V. (2000). Multicultural minds: A dynamic constructivist approach to culture and cognition. *American Psychologist, 55,* 709–720.

Honts, C. R., & Quick, B. D. (1995). The polygraph in 1996: Progress in science and the law. *North Dakota Law Review, 71,* 997–1020.

Hoobler, J. M., & Brass, D. J. (2006). Abusive supervision and family undermining as displaced aggression. *Journal of Applied Psychology, 91,* 1125–1133.

Hood, M. Y., Moore, L. L., Sundarajan-Ramamurti, A., Singer, M., Cupples, L. A., & Ellison, R. C. (2000). Parental eating attitudes and the development of obesity in children: The Framingham children's study. *International Journal of Obesity, 24,* 1319–1325.

Hooker, E. (1993). Reflections of a 40-year exploration: A scientific view on homosexuality. *American Psychologist, 48,* 450–453.

Hooley, J. M. (2004). Do psychiatric patients do better clinically if they live with certain kinds of families? *Current Directions in Psychological Science, 13,* 202–205.

Hopf, H. C., Muller, F. W., & Hopf, N. J. (1992). Localization of emotional and volitional facial paresis. *Neurology, 42*(10), 1918–1923.

Hopper, K., & Wanderling, J. (2000). Revisiting the developed versus developing country distinction in course and outcome in schizophrenia: Results from ISoS, the WHO Collaborative Followup Project. *Schizophrenia Bulletin, 26,* 835–846.

Horgan, J. (1996, December). Why Freud isn't dead. *Scientific American,* pp. 106–111.

Horne, J. A. (1988). *Why we sleep: The functions of sleep in humans.* Oxford: Oxford University Press.

Horner, P. J. & Gage, F. H. (2002). Regeneration in the adult and aging brain. *Archives of Neurology, 59,* 1717–1720.

Horney, K. (1937). *Neurotic personality of our times.* New York: Norton.

Horowitz, J. L., & Garber, J. (2006). The prevention of depressive symptoms in children and adolescents: A meta-analytic review. *Journal of Consulting and Clinical Psychology, 74,* 401–415.

Horton, J. E., Crawford, H. J., Harrington, G., & Downs, J. H., III. (2004). Increased anterior corpus callosum size associated positively with hypnotizability and the ability to control pain. *Brain, 127*(Pt. 8), 1741–1747.

Horvath, A. O. (2005). The therapeutic relationship: Research and theory: An introduction to the special issue. *Psychotherapy Research, 15,* 3–7.

Horwitz, A. V., Widom, C. S., McLaughlin, J., & White, H. R. (2001). The impact of childhood abuse and neglect on adult mental health: A prospective study. *Journal of Health and Social Behavior, 42,* 184–201.

Horwitz, B., Amunts, K., Bhattacharyya, R., Patkin, D., Jeffries, K., Zilles, K., et al. (2003). Activation of Broca's area during the production of spoken and signed language: A combined cytoarchitectonic mapping and PET analysis. *Neuropsychologia, 41,* 1868–1876.

Horwitz, P., & Christie, M. A. (2000). Computer-based manipulatives for teaching scientific reasoning: An example. In M. J. Jacobson & R. B. Kozuma (Eds.), *Innovations in science and mathematics education: Advanced designs for technologies of learning* (pp. 163–191). Mahwah, NJ: Erlbaum.

Hoshino-Browne, E., Zanna, A. S., Spencer, S. J., Zanna, M. P., Kitayama, S., & Lackenbauer, S. (2005). On the cultural guises of cognitive dissonance: The case of Easterners and Westerners. *Journal of Personality and Social Psychology, 89,* 294–310.

Hötting, K., & Röder, B. (2004). Hearing cheats touch, but less in congenitally blind than in sighted individuals. *Psychological Science, 15,* 60–64.

Houghton, G. (2005). *Connectionist models in cognitive psychology.* New York: Psychology Press.

Houpt, T. R. (1994). Gastric pressure in pigs during eating and drinking. *Physiology and Behavior, 56*(2), 311–317.

House, J. S., Landis, K. R., & Umberson, D. (1988). Structures and processes of social support. *Annual Review of Sociology, 14,* 293–318.

House, R. J., Hanges, P. J., Ruiz-Quintanilla, S. A., Dorfman, P. W., Javidan, M., Dickson, M., et al. (1999). Cultural influences on leadership and organizations: Project GLOBE. In W. H. Mobley, M. J. Gessner, & V. Arnold (Eds.), *Advances in global leadership* (Vol. 1, pp. 171–233). Stamford, CT: JAI.

Houston, B., & Vavac, C. (1991). Cynical hostility: Developmental factors, psychosocial correlates and health behaviors. *Health Psychology, 10,* 9–17.

Hoven, C. W., Duarte, C. S., Lucas, C. P., Wu, P., Mandell, D. J., Goodwin, R. D., et al. (2005). Psychopathology among New York city public school children 6 months after September 11. *Archives of General Psychiatry, 62,* 545–552.

Howard, D. V. (1983). *Cognitive psychology.* New York: Macmillan.

Howe, M. J. A., Davidson, J. W., & Sloboda, J. A. (1998). Innate talent: Reality or myth? *Behavioral and Brain Sciences, 21,* 399–442.

Howe, M. L. (2003). Memories from the cradle. *Current Directions in Psychological Science, 12,* 62–65.

Hoye, A., Rezvy, G., Hansen, V., & Olstad, R. (2006). The effect of gender in diagnosing early schizophrenia: An experimental case simulation study. *Social Psychiatry and Psychiatric Epidemiology, 41,* 549–555.

Hoyert, D. L., Kung, H.-C., & Smith, B. L. (2005). Deaths: Preliminary data for 2003. *National Vital Statistics Reports, 53,* 1–48.

Hoyle, R. H. (1993). Interpersonal attraction in the absence of explicit attitudinal information. *Social Cognition, 11,* 309–320.

Hoyle, R. H., Harris, M. J., & Judd, C. M. (2002). *Research methods in social relations.* Belmont, CA: Wadsworth.

Hoyt, M. F. (1995). Brief psychotherapies. In A. S. Gurman & S. B. Messer (Eds.), *Essential psychotherapies: Theory and practice* (pp. 441–487). New York: Guilford.

Hrdy, S. B. (1997). Raising Darwin's consciousness: Female sexuality and the prehominid origins of patriarchy. *Human Nature, 8,* 1–49.

Hrdy, S. B. (2003). The optimal number of fathers: Evolution, demography, and history in the shaping of female mate preferences. In S. J.Scher & F. Rauscher (Eds.), *Evolutionary psychology: Alternative approaches* (pp. 111–133). Dordrecht, Netherlands: Kluwer.

Hrobjartsson, A., & Gotzsche, P. C. (2001). Is the placebo powerless?: An analysis of clinical trials comparing placebo with no treatment. *The New England Journal of Medicine, 344,* 1594–1602.

Hu, F. B., Stampfer, M. J., Manson, J. E., Grodstein, F., Colditz, G. A., Speizer, F. E., & Willett, W. C. (2000). Trends in the incidence of coronary heart disease and changes in diet and lifestyle in women. *New England Journal of Medicine, 343,* 530–537.

Hu, P., Stylos-Allan, M., & Walker, M. P. (2006). Sleep facilitates consolidation of emotional declarative memory. *Psychological Science, 17,* 891–898.

Hu, S., Patatucci, A. M. L., Patterson, C., Li, L., Fulker, D. W., Cherny, S. S., et al. (1995). Linkage between sexual orientation and chromosome Xq28 in males but not females. *Nature Genetics, 11,* 248–256.

Hua, J. Y., & Smith, S. J. (2004). Neural activity and the dynamics of central nervous system development. *Nature Neuroscience, 7,* 327–332.

Hubbard, E. M., & Ramachandran, V. S. (2005). Neurocognitive mechanisms of synesthesia. *Neuron, 48,* 509–520.

Hubble, M. A., Duncan, B. L., & Miller, S. D. (Eds.). (1999). *The heart and soul of change: What works in psychotherapy.* Washington, DC: American Psychological Assocation.

Hubel, D. H., & Wiesel, T. N. (1979). Brain mechanisms of vision. *Scientific American, 241,* 150–162.

Hudson, W. (1960). Pictorial depth in perception in subcultural groups in Africa. *Journal of Social Psychology, 52,* 183–208.

Hudspeth, A. J. (1997). How hearing happens. *Neuron, 19,* 947–950.

Huesmann, L. R. (1995). *Screen violence and real violence: Understanding the link.* Auckland, NZ: Media Aware.

Huesmann, L. R. (1998). The role of social information processing and cognitive schema in the acquisition and maintenance of habitual aggressive behavior. In R. G. Geen & E. Donnerstein (Eds.), *Human aggression.* San Diego: Academic Press.

Huesmann, L. R., & Eron, L. D. (1986). *Television and the aggressive child: A cross-national comparison.* Hillsdale, NJ: Erlbaum.

Huesmann, L. R., Moise, J., Podolski, C., & Eron, L. (1997, April). *Longitudinal relations between early exposure to television violence and young adult aggression: 1977–1992.* Paper presented at the annual meeting of the Society for Research in Child Development, Washington, DC.

Huesmann, L. R., Moise-Titus, J., Podolski, C., & Eron, L. D. (2003). Longitudinal relations between children's exposure to TV violence and their aggressive and violent behavior in young adulthood: 1977–1992. *Developmental Psychology, 39,* 201–221.

Huestis, M. A., Gorelick, D. A., Heishman, S. J., Preston, K. L., Nelson, R. A., Moolchan, E. T., & Frank, R. A. (2001). Blockade of effects of smoked marijuana by the CB1-selective cannabinoid receptor antagonist SR141716. *Archives of General Psychiatry, 58,* 322–328.

Huffcutt, A. I., & Arthur, W. (1994). Hunter and Hunter (1984) revisited: Interview validity for entry-level jobs. *Journal of Applied Psychology, 79,* 184–190.

Huffcutt, A. I., Conway, J. M., Roth, P. L., & Stone, N. J. (2001). Identification and meta-analytic assessment of psychological constructs measured in employment interviews. *Journal of Applied Psychology, 86,* 897–913.

Hughes, B. M. (2006). Lies, damned lies, and pseudoscience: The selling of eye movement desensitization and reprocessing (EMDR). *PsycCritiques, 51,* 10.

Hughes, J. R., Higgins, S. T., & Bickel, W. K. (1994). Nicotine withdrawal versus other drug withdrawal syndromes: Similarities and dissimilarities. *Addiction, 89*(11), 1461–1470.

Hui, C., Lam, S. S. K., & Law, K. K. S. (2000). Instrumental values of organizational citizenship behavior for promotion: A field quasi-experiment. *Journal of Applied Psychology, 85,* 822–828.

Huizink, A. C., Mulder, E. J. H., & Buitelaar, J. K. (2004). Prenatal stress and risk for psychopathology. *Psychological Bulletin, 130,* 115–142.

Hull, C. L. (1943). *Principles of behavior.* New York: Appleton-Century-Crofts.

Humphreys, K. (2004). *Circles of recovery: Self-help organizations for addictions.* New York: Cambridge University Press.

Humphreys, L. G. (1984). General intelligence. In C. R. Reynolds & R. T. Brown (Eds.), *Perspectives on bias in mental testing.* New York: Plenum.

Hunsley, J., Lee, C. M., & Wood, J. M. (2003). Controversial and questionable assessment techniques. In S. O. Lilienfeld & S. J. Lynn (Eds.), *Science and pseudoscience in clinical psychology* (pp. 39–76). New York: Guilford Press.

Hunsley, J., & Rumstein-McKean, O. (1999). Improving psychotherapeutic services via randomized trials, treatment manuals, and component analysis designs. *Journal of Clinical Psychology, 55,* 1507–1517.

Hunt, C. B. (1980). Intelligence as an information processing concept. *British Journal of Psychology, 71,* 449–474.

Hunt, C. E., & Hauck, F. R. (2006). Sudden infant death syndrome. *Canadian Medical Association Journal, 174,* 1861–1869.

Hunt, D. M., Dulai, K. S., Bowmaker, J. K., & Mollon, J. D. (1995). The chemistry of John Dalton's color blindness. *Science, 267,* 984–988.

Hunt, E. (1983). On the nature of intelligence. *Science, 219,* 141–146.

Hunt, M. (1982). *The universe within.* New York: Simon & Schuster.

Hunt, M., & Forand, N. (2005). Cognitive vulnerability to depression in never depressed subjects. *Cognition and Emotion, 19,* 763–770.

Hunt, R., & Rouse, W. B. (1981). Problem solving skills of maintenance trainees in diagnosing faults in simulated power plants. *Human Factors, 23,* 317–328.

Hurt, H., Brodsky, N. L., Betancourt, L., & Braitman, L. E. (1995). Cocaine-exposed children: Follow-up through 30 months. *Journal of Developmental and Behavioral Pediatrics, 16*(1), 29–35.

Huston, A. C., & Wright, J. C. (1989). The forms of television and the child viewer. In G. Comstock (Ed.), *Public communication and behavior* (Vol. 2, pp. 103–159). San Diego: Academic Press.

Huston, T. L., Caughlin, J. P., Houts, R. M., Smith, S. E., & George, L. J. (2001). The connubial crucible: Newlywed years as predictors of marital delight, distress, and divorce. *Journal of Personality and Social Psychology, 80,* 237–252.

Huttenlocher, P. R. (1990). Morphometric study of human cerebral cortex development. *Neuropsychologia, 28,* 517–527.

Hwang, W.-C. (2006). The psychotherapy adaptation and modification framework: Application to Asian Americans. *American Psychologist, 61,* 702–715.

Hyde, J. S. (2005). The gender similarities hypothesis. *American Psychologist, 60,* 581–592.

Hyde, J. S., & Durik, A. M. (2000). Gender differences in erotic plasticity–Evolutionary or sociocultural forces? Comment on Baumeister (2000). *Psychological Bulletin, 126,* 375–379.

Hyde, K. L., & Peretz, I. (2004). Brains that are out of tune but in time. *Psychological Science, 15,* 356–360.

Hyde, K. L., Zatorre, R. J., Griffiths, T. D., Lerch, J. P., & Peretz, I. (2006). Morphometry of the amusic brain: A two-site study. *Brain, 129*(Pt. 10), 2562–2570.

Hyman, I. E., & Pentland, J. (1996). The role of mental imagery in the creation of false childhood memories. *Journal of Memory and Language, 35,* 101–117.

Hyman, I. E., Jr. (2000). The memory wars. In U. Neisser & I. E. Hyman Jr. (Eds.), *Memory observed* (2nd ed., pp. 374–379). New York: Worth.

Hyman, R. (2002). Why and when are smart people stupid? In R. J. Sternberg (Ed.), *Why smart people can be so stupid* (pp. 1–23). New Haven, CT: Yale University Press.

Hyman, S. E., Malenka, R. C., & Nestler, E. J. (2006). Neural mechanisms of addiction: The role of reward-related learning and memory. *Annual Review of Neuroscience, 29,* 565–598.

Hypericum Depression Trial Study Group. (2002). Effect of *Hypericum perforatum* (St. John's wort) in major depressive disorder: A randomized, controlled trial. *Journal of the American Medical Association, 287,* 1807–1814.

Iacono, W. G., & Patrick, C. J. (2006). Polygraph ("lie detector") testing: Current status and emerging trends. In I. B.Weiner & A. K. Hess (Eds.), *The handbook of forensic psychology* (3rd ed., pp. 552–588). Hoboken, NJ: Wiley.

Iancu, I., Poreh, A., Lehman, B., Shamir, E., & Kotler, M. (2005). The positive and negative symptoms questionnaire: A self-report in schizophrenia. *Comprehensive Psychiatry, 46,* 61–66.

Iani, C., Ricci, F., Ghem, E., & Rubichi, S. (2006). Hypnotic suggestion modulates cognitive conflict: The case of the flanker compatibility effect. *Psychological Science, 17,* 721–727.

Iervolino, A. C., Hines, M., Golombok, S. E., Rust, J., & Plomin, R. (2005). Genetic and environmental influences on sex-typed behavior during the preschool years. *Child Development, 76,* 826–840.

Igalens, J., & Roussel, P. (1999). A study of the relationships between compensation package, work motivation, and job satisfaction. *Journal of Organizational Behavior, 20,* 1003–1025.

Iijima, M., Arisaka, O., Minamoto, F., & Arai, Y. (2001). Sex differences in children's free drawings: A study on girls with congenital adrenal hyperplasia. *Hormones and Behavior, 40,* 99–104.

Ilgen, D. R., & Pulakos, E. D. (Eds.). (1999). *The changing nature of performance: Implications for staffing, motivation, and development.* San Francisco, CA: Jossey-Bass.

Ilies, R., & Judge, T. A. (2003). On the heritability of job satisfaction: The mediating role of personality. *Journal of Applied Psychology, 88,* 750–759.

Ilies, R., Scott, B. A., & Judge, T. A. (2006). The interactive effects of personal traits and experienced states on intraindividual patterns of citizenship behavior. *Academy of Management Journal, 49,* 561–575.

Imtiaz, K. E., Nirodi, G., & Khaleeli, A. A. (2001). Alexia without agraphia: A century later. *International Journal of Clinical Practice, 55*(3), 225–226.

Indovina, I., & Sanes, J. N. (2001). On somatotopic representation centers for finger movements in human primary motor cortex and supplementary motor area. *Neuroimage, 13,* 1027–1034.

Inness, M., Barling, J., & Turner, N. (2005). Understanding supervisor-targeted aggression: A within-person, between-jobs design. *Journal of Applied Psychology, 90,* 731–739.

Inoue-Nakamura, N., & Matsuzawa, T. (1997). Development of stone tool use by wild chimpanzees (Pan troglodytes). *Journal of Comparative Psychology, 111,* 159–173.

Insko, C. A., Schopler, J., Hoyle, R. H., Dardis, G. J., & Graetz, K. A. (1990). Individual-group discontinuity as a function of fear and greed. *Journal of Personality and Social Psychology, 58,* 68–79.

Institute of Medicine. (2006, April 5). *Sleep disorders and sleep deprivation: An unmet public health problem* [Press release]. Retrieved September 26, 2006, from http://www.iom.edu/CMS/3740/23160/33668.aspx.

International Association for the Evaluation of Education Achievement. (1999). *Trends in mathematics and science achievement around the world.* Boston: Lynch School of Education, Boston College.

International Human Genome Sequencing Consortium. (2001). Initial sequencing and analysis of the human genome. *Nature, 409,* 860–921.

International Human Genome Sequencing Consortium. (2004). Finishing the euchromatic sequence of the human genome. *Nature, 431,* 931–945.

Inzlicht, M., & Ben-Zeev, T. (2000). A threatening intellectual environment: Why females are susceptible to experiencing problem-solving deficits in the presence of males. *Psychological Science, 11,* 365–371.

Ironson, G., Freund, B., Strauss, J. L., & Williams J. (2002). Comparison of two treatments for traumatic stress: A community-based study of EMDR and prolonged exposure. *Journal of Clinical Psychology, 58,* 113–128.

Ironson, G., Wynings, C., Schneiderman, N., Baum, A., Rodriguez, M., Greenwood, D., et al. (1997). Posttraumatic stress symptoms, intrusive thoughts, loss, and immune function after Hurricane Andrew. *Psychosomatic Medicine, 59,* 128–141.

Ironson, G. H., Smith, P. C., Brannick, M. T., Gibson, W. M., & Paul, K. B. (1989). Constitution of a Job in General scale: A comparison of global, composite, and specific measures. *Journal of Applied Psychology, 74,* 193–200.

Irwin, M., Daniels, M., Smith, T., Bloom, E., & Weiner, H. (1987). Impaired natural killer cell activity during bereavement. *Brain, Behavior, and Immunity, 1,* 98–104.

Isaacowitz, D. M., Wadlinger, H. A., Goren, D., & Wilson, H. R. (2006). Selective preference in visual fixation away from negative images in old age? An eyei-tracking study. *Psychology and Again, 21,* 40–48.

Ishai, A., Ungerleider, L. G., & Haxby, J. V. (2000). Distributed neural systems for the generation of visual images. *Neuron, 28,* 979–990.

Ishikawa, A., Kanayama, Y., Matsumura, H., Tsuchimochi, H., Ishida, Y., & Nakamura, S. (2006). Selective rapid eye movement sleep deprivation impairs the maintenance of long-term potentiation in the rat hippocampus. *European Journal of Neuroscience, 24,* 243–248.

Ivanova, M. Y., & Israel, A. C. (2005). Family stability as a protective factor against the influences of pessimistic attributional style on depression. *Cognitive Therapy and Research, 29,* 243–251.

Iwahashi, K., Matsuo, Y., Suwaki, H., Nakamura, K., & Ichikawa, Y. (1995). CYP2E1 and ALDH2 genotypes and alcohol dependence in Japanese. *Alcoholism Clinical and Experimental Research, 19*(3), 564–566.

Iwamasa, G. Y., Sorocco, K. H., & Koonce, D. A. (2002). Ethnicity and clinical psychology: A content analysis of the literature. *Clinical Psychology Review, 22,* 932–944.

Iwamura, Y., Iriki, A., & Tanaka, M. (1994). Bilateral hand representation in the postcentral somatosensory cortex. *Nature, 369,* 554–556.

Izac, S. M., & Eeg, T. R. (2006). Basic anatomy and physiology of sleep. *American Journal of Electroneurodiagnostic Technology, 46*(1), 18–38.

Izard, C., Fine, S., Schultz, D. Mostow, A., Ackerman, B., & Youngstrom, E. (2001). Emotion knowledge as a predictor of social behavior and academic competence in children at risk. *Psychological Science, 12,* 18–23.

Izard, C. E. (1977). *Human emotions.* New York: Plenum.

Izard, C. E. (1993). Organizational and motivational functions of discrete emotions. In M. Lewis and J. M. Haviland (Eds.), *Handbook of emotions.* New York: Guilford.

Izumikawa, M., Minoda, R., Kawamoto, K., Abrashkin, K. A., Swiderski, D., L., Dolan, D. F., et al. (2005). Auditory hair cell replacement and hearing improvement by *Atoh1* gene therapy in deaf animals. *Nature, 11,* 271–276.

Jablensky, A. (2006). Subtyping schizophrenia: Implications for genetic research. *Molecular Psychiatry, 11,* 815–836.

Jaccard, J., Blanton, H., & Dodge, T. (2005). Peer influences on risk behavior: An analysis of the effects of a close friend. *Developmental Psychology, 41,* 135–147.

Jack, C. R. Jr., Petersen, R. C., Xu, Y. C., O'Brien, P. C., Smith, G. E., Ivnik, R. J., et al. (1999). Prediction of AD with MRI-based hippocampal volume in mild cognitive impairment. *Neurology, 52,* 1397–1403.

Jackson, B., Sellers, R. M., & Peterson, C. (2002). Pessimistic explanatory style moderates the effect of stress on physical illness. *Personality & Individual Differences, 32,* 567–573.

Jackson, J. W. (2002). The relationship between group identity and intergroup prejudice is moderated by sociostructural variation. *Journal of Applied Social Psychology, 32,* 908–933.

Jackson, L. A., von Eye, A., Biocca, F. A., Barbatsis, G., Zhao, Y., & Fitzgerald, H. E. (2006). Does home internet use influence the academic performance of low-income children? *Developmental Psychology, 42,* 429–435.

Jacob, S., Kinnunen, L. H., Metz, J., Cooper, M., & McClintock, M. K. (2001). Sustained human chemosignal unconsciously alters brain function. *Neuroreport, 12,* 2391–2394.

Jacob, S., & McClintock, M. K. (2000). Psychological state and mood effects of steroidal chemosignals in women and men. *Hormones and Behavior, 37,* 57–78.

Jacob, T., Waterman, B., Heath, A., True, W., Bucholz, K. K., Haber, R., et al. (2003). Genetic and environmental effects on offspring alcoholism: New insights using an offspring-of-twins design. *Archives of General Psychiatry, 60,* 1265–1272.

Jacobi, C., Hayward, C., de Zwaan, M., Kraemer, H. C., & Agras, W. S. (2004). Coming to terms with risk factors for eating disorders: Application of risk terminology and suggestions for a general taxonomy. *Psychological Bulletin, 130,* 19–65.

Jacobs, G. D., Pace-Schott, E. F., Stickgold, R., & Otto, M. W. (2004). Cognitive behavior therapy and pharmacotherapy for insomnia: A randomized controlled trial and direct comparison. *Archives of Internal Medicine, 164,* 1888–1896.

Jacobs, N., Kenis, G., Peeters, F., Derom, C., Vlietinck, R., & van Os, J. (2006). Stress-related negative affectivity and genetically altered serotonin transporter function: Evidence of synergism in shaping risk of depression. *Archives of General Psychiatry, 63,* 989–996.

Jacobson, E. (1938). *Progressive relaxation.* Chicago: University of Chicago Press.

Jacobson, J. W., Mulick, J. A., & Schwartz, A. A. (1995). A history of facilitated communication. *American Psychologist, 50,* 750–765.

Jacobson, K. (2002). ADHD in cross-cultural perspective: Some empirical results. *American Anthropologist, 104,* 283–286.

Jacobson, N. S., Christensen, A., Prince, S. E., Cordova, J., & Eldridge, K. (2000). Integrative behavioral couples therapy: An acceptance-based, promising new treatment for couple discord. *Journal of Consulting and Clinical Psychology, 68,* 351–355.

Jacoby, L. L., Marriott, M. J., & Collins, J. G. (1990). The specifics of memory and cognition. In T. K. Srull & R. S. Wyer (Eds.), *Advances in social cognition: Vol. 3. Content and process specificity in the effects of prior experiences.* Hillsdale, NJ: Erlbaum.

Jacoby, L. L., & Rhodes, M. G. (2006). False remembering in the aged. *Current Directions in Psychological Science, 15,* 49–53.

Jaffee, S., & Hyde, J. S. (2000). Gender differences in moral orientation: A meta-analysis. *Psychological Bulletin, 126,* 703–726.

Jaffee, S. R., Caspi, A., Moffitt, T. E., & Taylor, A. (2004). Physical maltreatment to antisocial child: Evidence of an environmentally mediated process. *Journal of Abnormal Psychology, 113,* 44–55.

Jago, R., Baranowski, T., Baranowski, J. C., Thompson, D., & Greaves, K. A. (2005). BMI from 3–6 y of age is predicted by TV viewing and physical activity, not diet. *International Journal of Obesity, 29,* 557–564.

Jahnke, J. C., & Nowaczyk, R. H. (1998). *Cognition.* Upper Saddle River, NJ: Prentice-Hall.

Jain, A. (2005). Treating obesity in individuals and populations. *British Medical Journal, 331,* 1387–1390.

Jakobsen, K. D., Frederiksen, J. N., Hansen, T., Jansson, L., et al. (2005). Reliability of clinical ICD-10 schizophrenia diagnoses. *Nordic Journal of Psychiatry, 59,* 209–212.

James, J. E. (2004). Critical review of dietary caffeine and blood pressure: A relationship that should be taken more seriously. *Psychosomatic Medicine, 66,* 63–71.

James, W. (1884). Some omissions of introspective psychology. *Mind, 9,* 1–26.

James, W. (1890). *Principles of psychology.* New York: Holt.

James, W. (1892). *Psychology: Briefer course.* New York: Holt.

Jameson, L. C., & Sloan, T. B. (2006). Using EEG to monitor anesthesia drug effects during surgery. *Journal of Clinical Monitoring and Computers, 20,* 445–472.

Jancke, L., & Kaufmann, N. (1994). Facial EMG responses to odors in solitude and with an audience. *Chemical Senses, 19(2),* 99–111.

Janik, V. M. (2000). Whistle matching in wild bottlenose dolphins. *Science, 289,* 1355–1357.

Janis, I. L. (1985). International crisis management in the nuclear age. *Applied Social Psychology Annual, 6,* 63–86.

Janis, I. L. (1989). *Crucial decisions: Leadership in policy making and crisis management.* New York: Free Press.

Janowiak, J. J., & Hackman, R. (1994). Meditation and college students' self-actualization and rated stress. *Psychological Reports, 75(2),* 1007–1010.

Janowitz, H. D. (1967). Role of gastrointestinal tract in the regulation of food intake. In C. F. Code (Ed.), *Handbook of physiology: Alimentary canal 1.* Washington, DC: American Physiological Society.

Jans, L. A. W., Riedel, W. J., Markus, C. R., & Blokland, A. (2007). Serotonergic vulnerability and depression: Assumptions, experimental evidence and implications. *Molecular Psychiatry, 12,* 522–543.

Jansen, P. G., & Vinkenburg, C. J. (2006). Predicting managerial career success from assessment center data: A longitudinal study. *Journal of Vocational Behavior, 68,* 253–266.

Janszky, J., Szucs, A., Halasz, P., Borbely, C., Hollo, A., Barsi, P., & Mirnics, Z. (2002). Orgasmic aura originates from the right hemisphere. *Neurology, 58,* 302–304.

Jefferis, B. M. J. H., Power, C., & Hertzman, C. (2002). Birth weight, childhood socioeconomic environment, and cognitive development in the 1958 British birth cohort study [Electronic version]. *British Medical Journal, 325,* 305.

Jeffries, K. J., Fritz, J. B., & Braun, A. R. (2003). Words in melody: An H(2)15O PET study of brain activation during singing and speaking. *Neuroreport, 14,* 749–754.

Jemal, A., Ward, E., Hao, Y., & Thun, M. (2005). Trends in the leading causes of death in the United States, 1970–2002. *Journal of the American Medical Association, 294,* 1255–1259.

Jencks, C., & Phillips, M. (Eds.). (1998). *The black-white test score gap.* Washington, DC: Brookings Institution Press.

Jenkins, H., & Barrett, J. (2003). *Schizophrenia, culture and subjectivity: The edge of experience.* West Nyack, NY: Cambridge University Press.

Jenkins, J. G., & Dallenbach, K. M. (1924). Oblivescence during sleep and waking. *American Journal of Psychology, 35,* 605–612.

Jenkins, M. R., & Culbertson, J. L. (1996). Prenatal exposure to alcohol. In R. L. Adams, O. A. Parsons, J. L. Culbertson, & S. J. Nixon (Eds.), *Neuropsychology for clinical practice: Etiology, assessment, and treatment of common neurological disorders* (pp. 409–452). Washington, DC: American Psychological Association.

Jenkins, R. O., & Sherbum, R. E. (2005). Growth and survival of bacteria implicated in sudden infant death syndrome on cot mattress materials. *Journal of Applied Microbiology, 99,* 573–579.

Jenner, P. (2001). Parkinson's disease, pesticides and mitochondrial dysfunction. *Trends in Neuroscience, 24,* 245–246.

Jensen, A. R. (1969). How much can we boost IQ and scholastic achievement? *Harvard Educational Review, 39,* 1–123.

Jensen, A. R. (1993). Why is reaction time correlated with psychometric g? *Current Directions in Psychological Science, 2,* 53–55.

Jensen, A. R. (1998). *The g factor: The science of mental ability.* Westport, CT: Praeger.

Jensen, A. R. (2006). *Clocking the mind: Mental chronometry and individual differences.* Cambridge, UK: Elsevier.

Jensen, M., & Karoly, P. (1991). Control beliefs, coping efforts, and adjustment to chronic pain. *Journal of Consulting and Clinical Psychology, 59,* 431–438.

Jeon, Y., & Polich, J. (2003). Meta-analysis of P300 and schizophrenia: Patients, paradigms, and practical implications. *Psychophysiology, 40,* 684–701.

Jevtovic-Todorovic, V., Wozniak, D. F., Benshoff, N. D., & Olney, J. W. (2001). A comparative evaluation of the neurotoxic properties of ketamine and nitrous oxide. *Brain Research, 895,* 264–267.

Jex, S. M., Adams, G. A., Elacqua, T. C., & Bachrach, D. G. (2002). Type A as a moderator of stressors and job complexity: A comparison of achievement strivings and impatience-irritability. *Journal of Applied Social Psychology, 32,* 977–996.

Johansen, J. P., Fields, H. L., & Manning, B. H. (2001). The affective component of pain in rodents: Direct evidence for a contribution of the anterior cingulate cortex. *Proceedings of the National Academy of Sciences, 98,* 8077–8082.

John, J. (2004). A theory of consciousness. *Current Directions in Psychological Science, 12,* 244–250.

John, O., & Srivastava, S. (1999). The big five taxonomy: History, measurement, and theoretical perspectives. In L. Pervin & O. John (Eds.), *Handbook of personality: Theory and research* (2nd ed., pp. 102–138). New York: Guilford.

Johnson, B. R. (2004). Involuntary commitment. In W. T. O'Donohue & E. R. Levensky (Eds.), *Handbook of forensic psychology: Resource for mental health and legal professionals* (pp. 767–780). New York: Elsevier Science.

Johnson, B. T., Maio, G. R., & Smith-McLallen, A. (2005). Communication and attitude change: Causes, processes, and effects. In D. Albarracín, B. T. Johnson, & M. P. Zanna (Eds.), *Handbook of attitudes* (pp. 617–669). Mahwah, NJ: Erlbaum.

Johnson, D. R., Westermeyer, J., Kattar, K., & Thuras, P. (2002). Daily charting of posttraumatic stress symptoms: A pilot study. *Journal of Nervous & Mental Disease*, 190, 683–692.

Johnson, E. O., Roth, T., Schultz, L., & Breslau, N. (2006). Epidemiology of DSM-IV insomnia in adolescence: Lifetime prevalence, chronicity, and an emergent gender different. *Pediatrics*, 117, 247–256.

Johnson, G. (2002). Comments on lithium toxicity. *Australian and New Zealand Journal of Psychiatry*, 36, 703.

Johnson, J., & Vickers, Z. (1993). Effects of flavor and macronutrient composition of food servings on liking, hunger and subsequent intake. *Appetite*, 21(1), 25–39.

Johnson, J. G., Cohen, P., Smailes, E. M., Kasen, S., & Brook, J. S. (2002). Television viewing and aggressive behavior during adolescence and adulthood. *Science*, 295, 2468–2471.

Johnson, J. M., & Endler, N. S. (2002). Coping with human immunodeficiency virus: Do optimists fare better? *Current Psychology: Developmental, Learning, Personality, Social*, 21, 3–16.

Johnson, J. S., & Newport, E. L. (1989). Critical period effects in second language learning. *Cognitive Psychology*, 21, 60–99.

Johnson, M. A., Dziurawiec, S., Ellis, H., & Morton, J. (1991). Newborns' preferential tracking of face-like stimuli and its subsequent decline. *Cognition*, 4, 1–19.

Johnson, S. L., McPhee, L., & Birch, L. L. (1991). Conditioned preferences: Young children prefer flavors associated with high dietary fat. *Physiology and Behavior*, 50, 1245–1251.

Johnson, S. L., Ruggero, C. J., & Carver, C. S. (2005). Cognitive, behavioral, and affective responses to reward: Links with hypomanic symptoms. *Journal of Social and Clinical Psychology*, 24, 894–906.

Johnson, S. P. (2004). Development of perceptual completion in infancy. *Psychological Science*, 15, 769–775.

Johnson, S. P., Amso, D., & Slemmer, J. A. (2003). Development of object concepts in infancy: Evidence for early learning in an eye-tracking paradigm. *Proceedings of the National Academy of Sciences*, 100, 10568–10573.

Johnson, W., Bouchard, T. J., Jr., Krueger, R. F., McGue, M., & Gottesman, I. I. (2004). Just one g: Consistent results form three test batteries. *Intelligence*, 32, 95–107.

Johnson, W. R., & Neal, D. (1998). Basic skills and the black-white earnings gap. In C. Jencks & M. Phillips (Eds.), *The black-white test score gap* (pp. 480–497). Washington, DC: Brookings Institute Press.

Johnson-Laird, P. N. (1983). *Mental models: Toward a cognitive science of language, inference, and consciousness*. Cambridge: Harvard University Press.

Johnson-Laird, P. N., Mancini, F., & Gangemi, A. (2006). A hyper-emotion theory of psychological illnesses. *Psychological Review*, 113, 822–841.

Johnston, L. D., O'Malley, P. M., Bachman, J. G., & Schulenberg, J. E. (2004). *Monitoring the Future national survey results on drug use, 1975–2003. Vol. I: Secondary school students* (NIH Publication No. 04-5507). Bethesda, MD: National Institute on Drug Abuse.

Jolij, J., & Lamme, V. A. (2005). Repression of unconscious information by conscious processing: Evidence from affective blindsight induced by transcranial magnetic stimulation. *Proceedings of the National Academy of Science of the USA*, 102, 10747–10751.

Jonas, E., Schimel, J., Greenberg, J., & Pyszczynski, T. (2002). The Scrooge effect: Evidence that mortality salience increases prosocial attitudes and behavior. *Personality and Social Psychology Bulletin*, 28, 1342–1353.

Jones, E. E. (1982). Psychotherapists' impressions of treatment outcome as a function of race. *Journal of Clinical Psychology*, 38, 722–731.

Jones, G. V. (1990). Misremembering a common object: When left is not right. *Memory & Cognition*, 18, 174–182.

Jones, H. E. (2006). Drug addiction during pregnancy. *Current Directions in Psychological Science*, 15, 126–130.

Jones, J. R., & Schaubroeck, J. (2004). Mediators of the relationship between race and organizational citizenship behavior. *Journal of Managerial Issues*, 16, 505–527.

Jones, L. V., & Appelbaum, M. I. (1989). Psychometric methods. *Annual Review of Psychology*, 40, 23–44.

Jones, M. A., Botsko, M., & Gorman, B. S. (2003). Predictors of psychotherapeutic benefit of lesbian, gay, and bisexual clients: The effects of sexual orientation matching and other factors. *Psychotherapy: Theory, Research, Practice, Training*, 40, 289–301.

Jones, W. H. S. (Ed. & Trans.). (1923). *Hippocrates* (Vol. 1). London: William Heinemann.

Jordan, N. C., Huttenlocher, J., & Levine, S. C. (1992). Differential calculation abilities in young children from middle- and low-income families. *Developmental Psychology*, 28, 644–653.

Josephson, W. L. (1987). Television violence and children's aggression: Testing the priming, social script, and disinhibition predictions. *Journal of Personality and Social Psychology*, 53, 882–890.

Joy, J. E., Watson, S. J., Jr., & Benson, J. A., Jr. (1999). *Marijuana and medicine: Assessing the science base*. Washington, DC: National Academy Press.

Judd, F. K., Jackson, H. J., Komiti, A., Murray, G., Hodgins, G., Fraser, C. (2002). High prevalence disorders in urban and rural communities. *Australian and New Zealand Journal of Psychiatry*, 36, 104–113.

Judge, T. A., Colbert, A. E., & Ilies, R. (2004). Intelligence and leadership: A quantitative review and test of theoretical propositions. *Journal of Applied Psychology*, 89, 542–552.

Judge, T. A., Piccolo, R. F., & Ilies, R. (2004). The forgotten ones? The validity of consideration and initiating structure in leadership research. *Journal of Applied Psychology*, 89, 36–51.

Judge, T. A., Thoresen, C. J., Bono, J. E., & Patton, G. K. (2001). The job satisfaction-job performance relationship: A qualitative and quantitative review. *Psychological Bulletin*, 127, 376–407.

Julien, R. M. (2005). *A primer of drug action* (10th ed.). New York: Worth.

Jung, C. G. (1916). *Analytical psychology*. New York: Moffat.

Jung, C. G. (1933). *Psychological types*. New York: Harcourt, Brace and World.

Jung, J., & Lee, S. (2006). Cross-cultural comparisons of appearance self-schema, body image, self-esteem, and dieting behavior between Korean and U.S. women. *Family & Consumer Sciences Research Journal*, 34, 350–365.

Jung, J., & Lennon, S. J. (2003). Body image, appearance self-schema, and media images. *Family & Consumer Sciences Research Journal*, 32, 27–51.

Juraska, J. M. (1998). Neural plasticity and the development of sex differences. *Annual Review of Sex Research*, 9, 20–38.

Jusczyk, P. W., Smith, L. B., & Murphy, C. (1981). The perceptual classification of speech. *Perception and Psychophysics*, 1, 10–23.

Jussim, L. (1989). Teacher expectations: Self-fulfilling prophecies, perceptual biases, and accuracy. *Journal of Personality and Social Psychology*, 57, 469–480.

Jussim, L., & Eccles, J. S. (1992). Teacher expectations: II. Construction and reflection of student achievement. *Journal of Personality and Social Psychology*, 63, 947–961.

Just, M. A., Carpenter, P. A., Keller, T. A., Emery, L., Zajac, H., & Thulborn, K. R. (2001). Interdependence of nonoverlapping cortical systems in dual cognitive tasks. *Neuroimage*, 14, 417–426.

Just, N., & Alloy, L. B. (1997). The response styles theory of depression: Tests and an extension of the theory. *Journal of Abnormal Psychology*, 106, 221–229.

Kadohisa, M., & Wilson, D.A. (2006). Separate encoding of identity and similarity of complex familiar odors in piriform cortex. *Proceedings of the National Academy of Sciences*, 103, 15206–15211.

Kagan, J. R., Snidman, N., Arcus, D., & Resnick, J. S. (1994). *Galen's prophecy: Temperament in human nature*. New York: Basic Books.

Kahn, E., & Rachman, A. W. (2000). Carl Rogers and Heinz Kohut: A historical perspective. *Psychoanalytic Psychology*, 17, 294–312.

Kahneman, D., Krueger, A. B., Schkade, D., Schwarz, N., & Stone, A. A. (2006). Would you be happier if you were richer? A focusing illusion. *Science*, 312, 1908–1910.

Kahneman, D., & Shane, F. (2005). A model of heuristic judgment. In K. Holyoak, & R.G. Morrison (Eds.), *The Cambridge handbook of thinking and reasoning* (pp. 267–293). New York: Cambridge University Press.

Kahneman, D., & Tversky, A. (1973). On the psychology of prediction. *Psychological Review*, 80, 237–251.

Kahneman, D., & Tversky, A. (1984). Choices, values, and frames. *American Psychologist*, 29, 341–356.

Kaitaro, T. (2001). Biological and epistemological models of localization in the nineteenth century: From Gall to Charcot. *Journal of Historical Neuroscience*, 10(3), 262–276.

Kajantie, E. J., & Phillips, D. I. W. (2006). The effects of sex and hormonal status on the physiological response to acute psychosocial stress. *Psychoneuroendocrinology*, 31, 151–178.

Kajiya, K., Inaki, K., Tanaka, M., Haga, T., Kataoka, H., & Touhara, K. (2001). Molecular bases of odor discrimination: Reconstitution of olfactory receptors that recognize overlapping sets of odorants. *Journal of Neuroscience*, 21, 6018–6025.

Kalb, L. M., & Loeber, R. (2003). Child disobedience and noncompliance: A review. *Pediatrics*, 111, 641–652.

Kalechstein, A. D., De La Garza, R., II, Mahoney, J. J., III, Fantegrossi, W. E., & Newton, T. F. (2007). MDMA use and neurocognition: A meta-analytic review. *Psychopharmacology* (Berlin), 189, 531–537.

Kales, A., & Kales, J. (1973). Recent advances in the diagnosis and treatment of sleep disorders. In G. Usdin (Ed.), *Sleep research and clinical practice*. New York: Brunner/Mazel.

Kales, H. C., DiNardo, A. R., Blow, F. C., McCarthy, J. F., et al. (2006). International medical graduates and the diagnosis and treatment of late-life depression. *Academic Medicine*, 81, 171–175.

Kales, H. C., Neighbors, H. W., Blow, F. C., Taylor, K. K., et al. (2005a). Race, gender, and psychiatrists' diagnosis and treatment of major depression among elderly patients. *Psychiatric Services*, 56, 721–728.

Kales, H. C., Neighbors, H. W., Valenstein, M., Blow, F. C., et al. (2005b). Effect of race and sex on primary care physicians' diagnosis and treatment of late-life depression. *Journal of the American Geriatrics Society*, 53, 777–784.

Kallgren, C. A., Reno, R. R., & Cialdini, R. B. (2000). A focus theory of normative conduct: When norms do and do not affect behavior. *Personality and Social Psychology Bulletin, 26,* 1002–1012.

Kalsbeek, A., Palm, I. F., La Fleur, S. E., Scheer, F. A., Perreau-Lenz, S., Ruiter, M, et al. (2006). SCN outputs and the hypothalamic balance of life. *Journal of Biological Rhythms, 21,* 458–469.

Kamdar, D., McAllister, D. J., & Turban, D. B. (2006). All in a day's work: How follower individual differences and justice perceptions predict OCB role definitions and behavior. *Journal of Applied Psychology, 91,* 841–855.

Kamin, L. J. (1969). Predictability, surprise, attention, and conditioning. In B. A. Campbell & R. M. Church (Eds.), *Punishment and aversive behavior* (pp. 279–296). New York: Appleton-Century-Crofts.

Kammeyer-Mueller, J. D., Wanberg, C. R., Glomb, T. M., & Ahlburg, D. (2005). The role of temporal shifts in turnover processes: It's about time. *Journal of Applied Psychology, 90,* 644–658.

Kammrath, L. K., Mendoza-Denton, R., & Mischel, W. (2005). Incorporating if . . . then . . . personality signatures in person perception: Beyond the person situation dichotomy. *Journal of Personality and Social Psychology, 88,* 605–618.

Kamp Dush, C. M., & Amato, P. R. (2005). Consequences of relationship status and quality for subjective well-being. *Journal of Social and Personal Relationships, 22,* 607–627.

Kamphuis, J. H., & Emmelkamp, P. M. (2001). Traumatic distress among support-seeking female victims of stalking. *American Journal of Psychiatry, 158,* 795–798.

Kanaya, T., Scullin, M. H., & Ceci, S. J. (2003). The Flynn effect and U.S. policies. *American Psychologist, 58,* 778–790.

Kanazawa, S. (2004). General intelligence as a domain-specific adaptation. *Psychological Review, 111,* 512–523.

Kancelbaum, B., Singer, B., & Wong, N. (2004). *Therapy in America 2004.* Retrieved June 14, 2004, from http://cms.psychologytoday.com/pto/press_release_050404.html

Kangas, M., Henry, J. L., & Bryant, R. A. (2005). Predictors of posttraumatic stress disorder following cancer. *Health Psychology, 24,* 579–585.

Kanki, B. J., & Foushee, H. C. (1990). Crew factors in the aerospace workplace. In S. Oskamp & S. Spacepan (Eds.), *People's reactions to technology* (pp. 18–31). Newbury Park, CA: Sage.

Kaplan, A. I. (2005). Therapist-patient privilege: Who owns the privilege? *Journal of Aggression, Maltreatment & Trauma, 11,* 135–143.

Kaplan, M. F., & Miller, C. E. (1987). Group decision making and normative vs. informational influence: Effects of type of issue and assigned decision rule. *Journal of Personality and Social Psychology, 53,* 306–313.

Kaptchuk, T. J., Stason, W. B., Legedza, A. R. T., Schnyer, R. N., Kerr, C. E., Stone, D. A., et al. (2006). Sham device vs. inert pill: Randomised controlled trial of two placebo treatments. *British Medical Journal, 332,* 391–397.

Kapur, N. (1999). Syndromes of retrograde amnesia: A conceptual and empirical synthesis. *Psychological Bulletin, 125,* 800–825.

Kapur, S., Sridhar, N., & Remington, G. (2004). The newer antipsychotics: Underlying mechanisms and the new clinical realities. *Current Opinion in Psychiatry, 17*(2), 115–121.

Karam, E. G., Mneimneh, Z. N. Karam, A. N., Fayyad, J. A., et al. (2006). Prevalence and treatment of mental disorders in Lebanon: A national epidemiological survey. *Lancet, 367,* 1000–1006.

Karasz, A. (2005). Cultural differences in conceptual models of depression. *Social Science and Medicine, 60,* 1625–1635.

Karau, S. J., & Williams, K. D. (1997). The effects of group cohesiveness on social loafing and social compensation. *Group Dynamics, 1,* 156–168.

Kareken, D. A., Mosnik, D. M., Doty, R. L., Dzemidzic, M., & Hutchins, G. D. (2003). Functional anatomy of human odor sensation, discrimination, and identification in health and aging. *Neuropsychology, 17,* 482–495.

Karni, A., Meyer, G., Adams, M., Turner, R., & Ungerleider, L. G. (1994). The acquisition and retention of a motor skill: A functional MRI study of long-term motor cortex plasticity. *Abstracts of the Society for Neuroscience, 20,* 1291.

Karon, B. P., & Widener, A. J. (1997). Repressed memories and World War II: Lest we forget. *Professional Psychology: Research and Practice, 28*(4), 338–340.

Karp, D. A. (1991). A decade of reminders: Changing age consciousness between fifty and sixty years old. In B. B. Hess & E. W. Markson (Eds.), *Growing old in America* (pp. 67–92). New Brunswick, NJ: Transaction.

Karver, M. S., Handelsman, J. B., Fields, S., & Bickman, L. (2006). Meta-analysis of therapeutic relationship variables in youth and family therapy: The evidence for different relationship variables in the child and adolescent treatment outcome literature. *Clinical Psychology Review, 26,* 50–65.

Kass, S. (1999). Frequent testing means better grades, studies find. *APA Monitor, 30,* 10.

Kasser, T., & Sharma, Y. S. (1999). Reproductive freedom, educational equality, and females' preference for resource-acquisition characteristics in mates. *Psychological Science, 10,* 374–377.

Kassin, S. M., Rigby, S., & Castillo, S. R. (1991). The accuracy-confidence correlation in eyewitness testimony: Limits and extensions of the retrospective self-awareness effect. *Journal of Personality and Social Psychology, 61,* 698–707.

Kastenbaum, R., Kastenbaum, B. K., & Morris, J. (1989). *Strengths and preferences of the terminally ill: Data from the National Hospice Demonstration Study.*

Kastin, A. J., & Pan, W. (2005). Targeting neurite growth inhibitors to induce CNS regeneration. *Current Pharmaceutical Design, 11,* 1247–1253.

Katkin, E. S., Wiens, S., & Öhman, A. (2001). Nonconscious fear conditioning, visceral perception, and the development of gut feelings. *Psychological Science, 12,* 366–370.

Kato, S., Wakasa, Y., & Yamagita, T. (1987). Relationship between minimum reinforcing doses and injection speed in cocaine and pentobarbital self-administration in crab-eating monkeys. *Pharmacology, Biochemistry, and Behavior, 28,* 407–410.

Katzell, R. A., & Thompson, D. E. (1990). Work motivation: Theory and practice. *American Psychologist, 45,* 144–153.

Kauffman, N. A., Herman, C. P., & Polivy, J. (1995). Hunger-induced finickiness in humans. *Appetite, 24,* 203–218.

Kaufman, J., & Charney, D. (2000). Comorbidity of mood and anxiety disorders. *Depression and Anxiety, 12*(Suppl. 1), 69–76.

Kaufman, J., Yang, B.-Z., Douglas-Palumberi, H., Crouse-Artus, M., Lipschitz, D., Krystal, J. H., & Gelernter, J. (2007). Genetic and environmental predictors of early alcohol use. *Biological Psychiatry, 61,* 1228–1234.

Kawakami, K., Dion, K. L., & Dovidio, J. F. (1998). Racial prejudice and stereotype activation. *Personality and Social Psychology Bulletin, 24,* 407–416.

Kawakami, K., Dovidio, J. F., & van Kamp, S. (2005). Kicking the habit: Effects of nonstereotypic association training and correction processes on hiring decisions. *Journal of Experimental Social Psychology, 41,* 68–75.

Kawakami, N., Takeshima, T., Ono, Y., Uda, H., et al. (2005). Twelve-month prevalence, severity and treatment of common mental disorders in communities in Japan: Preliminary findings from the World Mental Health Japan Survey 2002–2003. *Psychiatry and Clinical Neurosciences, 59,* 441–452.

Kawasaki, H., Adolphs, R., Kaufman, O., Damasio, H., Damasio, A. R., Granner, M., et al. (2001). Single-neuron responses to emotional visual stimuli recorded in human ventral prefrontal cortex. *Nature Neuroscience, 4,* 15–16.

Kay, P., & Regier, T. (2006). Language, thought and color: Recent developments. *Trends in Cognitive Science, 10,* 51–54.

Kaye, W. H., Klump, K. L., Frank, G. K., & Strober, M. (2000). Anorexia and bulimia nervosa. *Annual Review of Medicine, 51,* 299–313.

Kazanina, N., Phillips, C., & Idsardi, W. (2006). The influence of meaning on the perception of speech sounds. *Proceedings of the National Academy of Sciences, 103,* 11381–11386.

Kazantzis, N., Lampropoulos, G. K., & Deane, F. P. (2005). A national survey of practicing psychologists' use and attitudes toward homework in psychotherapy. *Journal of Consulting and Clinical Psychology, 73,* 742–748.

Kazarian, S. S., & Evans, D. R. (Eds.). (2001). *Handbook of cultural health psychology.* New York: Academic Press.

Kazdin, A. E. (1994a). *Behavior modification in applied settings* (5th ed.). Pacific Grove, CA: Brooks/Cole.

Kazdin, A. E. (1994b). Methodology, design, and evaluation in psychotherapy research. In A. E. Bergin & S. L. Garfield (Eds.), *Handbook of psychotherapy and behavior change* (4th ed., pp. 19–71). New York: Wiley.

Kazdin, A. E., & Weisz, J. R. (1998). Identifying and developing empirically supported child and adolescent treatments. *Journal of Consulting and Clinical Psychology, 66,* 19–36.

Kealy, E. M. (2005). Variations in the experience of schizophrenia: A cross-cultural review. *Journal of Social Work Research and Evaluation, 6,* 47–56.

Keating, D. P. (1990). Adolescent thinking. In S. S. Feldman & G. R. Elliott (Eds.), *At the threshold: The developing adolescent* (pp. 4–89). Cambridge, MA: Harvard University Press.

Kee, M., Hill, S. M., & Weist, M. D. (1999). School-based behavior management of cursing, hitting, and spitting in a girl with profound retardation. *Education and Treatment of Children, 22,* 171–178.

Keeling, L. J., & Hurink, J. F. (1996). Social facilitation acts more on the consummatory phase on feeding behaviour. *Animal Behaviour, 52,* 11–15.

Keen, R. E., & Berthier, N. E. (2004). Continuities and discontinuities in infants' representation of objects and events. In R. V. Kail (Ed.), *Advances in child development and behavior, Vol. 32* (pp. 243–279). San Diego: Elsevier Academic Press.

Keenan, K., & Wakschlag, L. S. (2004). Are oppositional defiant and conduct disorder symptoms normative behaviors in preschoolers? A comparison of referred and nonreferred children. *American Journal of Psychiatry, 161,* 356–358.

Keesey, R. E., & Powley, T. L. (1986). The regulation of body weight. *Annual Review of Psychology, 37,* 109–133.

Keil, F. (2006). Cognitive science and cognitive development. In W. Damon & R. M. Lerner (Series Eds.) & D. Kuhn & R. Siegler (Vol. Eds.), *Handbook of child psychology: Vol. 2, Cognition, perception, and language* (6th ed., pp. 609–635). New York: Wiley.

Keller, A., Ford, L. H., & Meacham, J. A. (1978). Dimensions of self-concept in preschool children. *Developmental Psychology, 14,* 483–489.

Keller, M. B., McCullough, J. P., Klein, D. N., Arnow, B., Dunner, D. L., Gelenberg, A. J., et al. (2000). A comparison of nefazodone, the cognitive behavioral-analysis system of psychotherapy, and their combination for the treatment of chronic depression. *New England Journal of Medicine, 342,* 1462–1470.

Keller, M. C., & Nesse, R. M. (2006). The evolutionary significance of depressive symptoms: Different adverse situations lead to different depressive symptom patterns. *Journal of Personality and Social Psychology, 91,* 316–330.

Keller, R. T. (2006). Transformational leadership, initiating structure, and substitutes for leadership: A longitudinal study of research and development project team performance. *Journal of Applied Psychology, 91,* 202–210.

Keller-Cohen, D., Toler, A., Miller, D., Fiori, K., & Bybee, D. (2004, August). *Social contact and communication in people over 85.* Paper presented at the convention of the American Psychological Association, Honolulu, HI.

Kelley, H. H. (1973). The processes of causal attribution. *American Psychologist, 28,* 107–128.

Kelley, K. W. (1985). Immunological consequences of changing environmental stimuli. In G. P. Moberg (Ed.), *Animal stress.* Bethesda, MD: American Physiological Society.

Kelley, W. M., Miezen, F. M., McDermott, K. B., Buckner, R. L., Raichle, M. E., Cohen, N. J., et al. (1998). Hemispheric asymmetry for verbal and nonverbal memory encoding in human dorsal frontal cortex. *Neuron, 20,* 927–936.

Kellman, P. J., & Arterberry, M. E. (2006). Infant visual perception. In W. Damon & R. M. Lerner (Series Eds.) & D. Kuhn & R. Siegler (Vol. Eds.), *Handbook of child psychology: Vol. 2. Cognition, perception, and language* (6th ed., pp. 109–160). New York: Wiley.

Kellner, C. H., Fink, M., Knapp, R., Petrides, G., Husain, M., Rummans, T., et al. (2005). Relief of expressed suicidal intent by ECT: A consortium for research in ECT study. *American Journal of Psychiatry, 162,* 977–982.

Kellner, C. H., Knapp, R. G., Petrides, G., Rummans, T. A., Husain, M. M., Rasmussen, K., et al. (2006). Continuation electroconvulsive therapy vs pharmacotherapy for relapse prevention in major depression. *Archives of General Psychiatry, 63,* 1337–1344.

Kellum, K. K., Carr, J. E., & Dozier, C. L. (2001). Response-card instruction and student learning in a college classroom. *Teaching of Psychology, 28,* 101–104.

Kelly, G. A. (1980). A psychology of the optimal man. In A. W. Landfield & L. M. Leitner (Eds.), *Personal construct psychology: Psychotherapy and personality.* New York: Wiley.

Kelly, J. F. (2003). Self-help for substance-use disorders: History, effectiveness, knowledge gaps and research opportunities. *Clinical Psychology Review, 23*(5), 639–663.

Kelly, T. H., Foltin, R. W., Emurian, C. S., & Fischman, M. W. (1990). Multidimensional behavioral effects of marijuana. *Progress in Neuro-Psychopharmacology and Biological Psychiatry, 14,* 885–902.

Kemeny, M. E. (2003). The psychobiology of stress. *Current Directions in Psychological Science, 12,* 124–129.

Kemper, S., Greiner, L. H., Marquis, J. G., Prenovost, K., & Mitzner, T. L. (2001). Language decline across the life span: Findings from the Nun Study. *Psychology and Aging, 16,* 227–239.

Kempermann, G., Gast, D., & Gage, F. H. (2002). Neuroplasticity in old age: Sustained fivefold induction of hippocampal neurogenesis by long-term environmental enrichment. *Annals of Neurology, 52,* 135–143.

Kendall, P. C., & Chambless, D. L. (Eds.). (1998). Special section: Empirically supported psychological therapies. *Journal of Consulting and Clinical Psychology, 66,* 3–167.

Kendall, P. C., & Sheldrick, R. C. (2000). Normative data for normative comparisons *Journal of Consulting and Clinical Psychology, 68,* 767–773.

Kendell, R., & Jablensky, A. (2003). Distinguishing between the validity and utility of psychiatric diagnoses. *American Journal of Psychiatry, 160,* 4–12.

Kendler, K. S. (2001). Twin studies of psychiatric illness: An update. *Archives of General Psychiatry, 58,* 1005–1014.

Kendler, K. S. (2005). "A gene for . . .": The nature of gene action in psychiatric disorders. *American Journal of Psychiatry, 162,* 1243–1252.

Kendler, K. S., Gardner, C. O., & Prescott, C. A. (2006). Toward a comprehensive developmental model for major depression in men. *American Journal of Psychiatry, 163,* 115–124.

Kendler, K. S., Gatz, M., Gardner, C. O., & Pedersen, N. L. (2006). A Swedish national twin study of lifetime major depression. *American Journal of Psychiatry, 163,* 109–114.

Kendler, K. S., Heath, A. C., Neale, M. C., Kessler, R. C., & Eaves, L. J. (1992). A population-based twin study of alcoholism in women. *Journal of the American Medical Association, 268,* 1877–1882.

Kendler, K. S., Hettema, J. M., Butera, F., Gardner, C. O., & Prescott, C. A. (2003). Life event dimensions of loss, humiliation, entrapment, and danger in the prediction of onsets of major depression and generalized anxiety. *Archives of General Psychiatry, 60,* 789–796.

Kendler, K. S., Jacobson, K. C., Myers, J., & Prescott, C. A. (2002). Sex differences in genetic and environmental risk factors for irrational fears and phobias. *Psychological Medicine, 32,* 209–217.

Kendler, K. S., Jacobson, K. C., Prescott, C. A., & Neale, M. C. (2003). Specificity of genetic and environmental risk factors for use and abuse/dependence of cannabis, cocaine, hallucinogens, sedatives, stimulants, and opiates in male twins. *American Journal of Psychiatry, 160,* 687–695.

Kendler, K. S., Kuhn, J. W., Vittum, J., Prescott, C. A., & Riley, B. (2005). The interaction of stressful life events and a serotonin transporter polymorphism in the prediction of episodes of major depression: A replication. *Archives of General Psychiatry, 62,* 529–535.

Kendler, K. S., Kuhn, J., & Prescott, C. A. (2004). The interrelationship of neuroticism, sex, and stressful life events in the prediction of episodes of major depression. *American Journal of Psychiatry, 161,* 631–636.

Kendler, K. S., Neale, M. C., Kessler, R. C., Heath, A. C., & Eaves, L. J. (1992). Major depression and generalized anxiety disorder: Same genes, (partly) different environments? *Archives of General Psychiatry, 49,* 716–722.

Kendler, K. S., Thornton, L. M., & Gardner, C. O. (2000). Stressful life events and previous episodes in the etiology of major depression in women: An evaluation of the "kindling" hypothesis. *American Journal of Psychiatry, 157,* 1243–1251.

Kendler, K. S., Thornton, L. M., & Gardner, C. O. (2001). Genetic risk, number of previous depressive episodes, and stressful life events in predicting onset of major depression. *American Journal of Psychiatry, 158,* 582–586.

Kendler, K. S., Thornton, L. M., Gilman, S. E., & Kessler, R. C. (2000). Sexual orientation in a U.S. national sample of twin and nontwin sibling pairs. *American Journal of Psychiatry, 157,* 1843–1846.

Kendzierski, D., & Costello, M. C. (2004). Healthy eating self-schema and nutrition behavior. *Journal of Applied Social Psychology, 34,* 2437–2451.

Kenrick, D. T. (1994). Evolutionary social psychology: From sexual selection to social cognition. In M. Zanna (Ed.), *Advances in experimental social psychology* (Vol. 26, pp. 75–122). San Diego: Academic Press.

Kenrick, D. T., Groth, G., Trost, M., & Sadalla, E. K. (1993). Integrating evolutionary and social exchange perspectives on relationships: Effects of gender, self-appraisal, and involvement level on mate selection. *Journal of Personality and Social Psychology, 64,* 951–969.

Kenrick, D. T., Keefe, R. C., Bryan, A. Barr, A., & Brown, S. (1995). Age preferences and mate choice among homosexuals and heterosexuals: A case for modular psychological mechanisms. *Journal of Personality and Social Psychology, 69,* 1166–1172.

Kenrick, D. T., Neuberg, S., & Cialdini, R. (2005). *Social psychology: Unraveling the mystery* (3rd ed). Boston, MA: Pearson.

Kensinger, E. A., & Corkin, S. (2004). Two routes to emotional memory: Distinct neural processes for valence and arousal. *Proceedings of the National Academy of Sciences, 101,* 3310–3315.

Kent, S., Rodriguez, F., Kelley, K. W., & Dantzer, R. (1994). Reduction in food and water intake induced by microinjection of interleukin-1b in the ventromedial hypothalamus of the rat. *Physiology and Behavior, 56*(5), 1031–1036.

Kenworthy, J. B., Turner, R. N., Hewstone, M., & Voci, A. (2006). Intergroup contact: When does it work, and why. In J. Dovidio, P. Glick, & L. Rudman (Eds.), *On the nature of prejudice: Fifty years after Allport.* Boston, MA: Blackwell.

Keogh, E., Bond, F. W., & Flaxman, P. E. (2006). Improving academic performance and mental health through a stress management intervention: Outcomes and mediators of change. *Behaviour Research and Therapy, 44,* 339–357.

Kepner, J. (2001). Touch in Gestalt body process psychotherapy: Purpose, practice, and ethics. *Gestalt Review, 5,* 97–114.

Kermer, D. A., Driver-Linn, E., Wilson, T. D., & Gilbert, D. T. (2006). Loss aversion is an affective forecasting error. *Psychological Science, 17,* 649–653.

Kernberg, O. (1984). *Severe personality disorders: Psychotherapeutic strategies.* New Haven/London: Yale University Press.

Kerr, N. L., & Tindale, R. S. (2004). Group performance and decision making. *Annual Review of Psychology, 55,* 623–655.

Kersting, K. (2004, September). Cross-cultural training: 30 years and going strong. *Monitor on Psychology,* 48–49.

Kertesz, A. (1993). Clinical forms of aphasia. *Acta Neurochirurgica. Supplementum (Wien), 56,* 52–58.

Keselman, H. J., Othman, A. R., Wilcox, R. R., & Fradette, K. (2004). The new and improved two-sample t test. *Psychological Science, 15,* 47–51.

Keshavan, M. S., Diwadkar, V. A., Montrose, D. M., Rajarethinam, R., & Sweeny, J. A. (2005). Premorbid indicators and risk for schizophrenia: A selective review and update. *Schizophrenia Research, 79,* 45–57.

Kessler R. C., Akiskal, H. S., Ames, M., Birnbaum, H., Greenberg, P., Hirschfeld, R. M. A., et al. (2006). Prevalence and effects of mood disorders on work performance in a nationally representative sample of U.S. workers. *American Journal of Psychiatry, 163,* 1561–1568.

Kessler, R. C., Adler, L., Barkley, R., Biederman, J., Conners, C. K., Demler, O., et al. (2006). The prevalence and correlates of adult ADHD in the United States: Results from the National Comorbidity Survey Replication. *American Journal of Psychiatry, 163,* 716–723.

Kessler, R. C., Berglund, P., Borges, G., Nock, M., & Wang, P. S. (2005). Trends in suicide ideation, plans, gestures, and attempts in the United States, 1990–1992 to 2001–2003. *Journal of the American Medical Association, 293,* 2487–2495.

Kessler, R. C., Berglund, P., Demler, O., Jin, R., & Walters, E. E. (2005). Lifetime prevalence and age of onset distributions of DSM-IV disorders in the national comorbidity survey replication. *Archives of General Psychiatry, 62,* 593–602.

Kessler, R. C., Berglund, P., Demler, O., Jin, R., Koretz, D., Merikangas, K. R., et al. (2003). The epidemiology of major depressive disorder: Results from the national comorbidity survey replication (NCS-R). *Journal of the American Medical Association, 289,* 3095–3105.

Kessler, R. C., Chiu, W. T., Demler, O., & Walters, E. E. (2005). Prevalence, severity, and comorbidity of 12-month DSM-IV disorders in the national comorbidity survey replication. *Archives of General Psychiatry, 62,* 617–627.

Kessler, R. C., Chiu, W. T., Jin, R., Ruscio, A. M., Shear, K., & Walters, E. E. (2006). The epidemiology of panic attacks, panic disorder, and agoraphobia in the National Comorbidity Survey Replication. *Archives of General Psychiatry, 63,* 415–424.

Kessler, R. C., Demler, O., Frank, R. G., Olfson, M., Pincus, H. A., et al. (2005). Prevalence and treatment of mental disorders, 1990 to 2003. *New England Journal of Medicine, 352,* 2515–2523.

Kessler, R. C., McGonagle, K. A., Zhao, S., Nelson, C. B., Hughes, M., Eshleman, S., et al. (1994). Lifetime and 12-month prevalence of DSM-III-R psychiatric disorders in the United States. *Archives of General Psychiatry, 51,* 8–19.

Kety, S. S., Wender, P. H., Jacobsen, B., Ingraham, L. J., Jansson, L., Faber, B., & Kinney, D. K. (1994). Mental illness in the biological and adoptive relatives of schizophrenic adoptees. *Archives of General Psychiatry, 51,* 442–455.

Keyes, C. L. M. (2007). Promoting and protecting mental health as flourishing: A complementary strategy for improving national mental health. *American Psychologist, 62,* 95–108.

Khan, A., Leventhal, R. M., Khan, S., & Brown, W. A. (2002). Suicide risk in patients with anxiety disorders: A meta-analysis of the FDA database. *Journal of Affective Disorders, 69,* 183–190.

Khan, J., Wei, J. S., Ringner, M., Saal, L. H., Ladanyi, M., Westermann, F., et al. (2001). Classification and diagnostic prediction of cancers using gene expression profiling and artificial neural networks. *Nature Medicine, 7,* 673–679.

Khot, U. N., Khot, M. B., Bajzer, C. T., Sapp, S. K., Ohman, E. M., Brener, S. J., et al. (2003). Prevalence of conventional risk factors in patients with coronary heart disease. *Journal of the American Medical Association, 290,* 898–904.

Kiecolt-Glaser, J. K., & Glaser, R. (1992). Psychoneuroimmunology: Can psychological interventions modulate immunity? *Journal of Consulting and Clinical Psychology, 60,* 569–575.

Kiecolt-Glaser, J. K., Loving, T. J., Stowell, J. R., Malarkey, W. B., Lemeshow, S., Dickinson, S. L., et al. (2005). Hostile marital interactions, proinflammatory cytokine production, and wound healing. *Archives of General Psychiatry, 62,* 1377–1384.

Kiecolt-Glaser, J. K., McGuire, L., Robles, T. F., & Glaser, R. (2002). Psychoneuroimmunology: Psychological influences on immune function and health. *Journal of Consulting & Clinical Psychology, 70,* 537–547.

Kiecolt-Glaser, J. K., & Newton, T. L. (2001). Marriage and health: His and hers. *Psychological Bulletin, 127,* 472–503.

Kiecolt-Glaser, J. K., Page, G. G., Marucha, P. T., MacCallum, R. C., & Glaser, R. (1998). Psychological influences on surgical recovery: Perspectives from psychoneuroimmunology. *American Psychologist, 11,* 1209–1218.

Kiecolt-Glaser, J. K., Preacher, K. J., MacCallum, R. C., Atkinson, C., Malarkey, W. B., & Glaser, R. (2003). Chronic stress and age-related increases in the proinflammatory cytokine IL-6. *Proceedings of the National Academy of Sciences, 100,* 9090–9095.

Kieffer, K. M., Schinka, J. A., & Curtiss, G. (2004). Person-environment congruence and personality domains in the prediction of job performance and work quality. *Journal of Counseling Psychology, 51,* 168–177.

Kiesler, D. J. (1996). *Contemporary interpersonal theory and research.* New York: Wiley.

Kiewra, K. A. (1989). A review of note-taking: The encoding storage paradigm and beyond. *Educational Psychology Review, 1,* 147–172.

Kihlstrom, J. F. (1999). The psychological unconscious. In L. Pervin & O. John (Eds.), *Handbook of personality* (pp. 424–442). New York: Guilford.

Kihlstrom, J. F. (2005). Dissociative disorders. *Annual Review of Clinical Psychology, 1,* 227–253.

Kilbourne, A. M., Haas, G. L., Musant, B. H., Bauer, M. S., & Picnus, H. A. (2004). Concurrent psychiatric diagnosis by age and race among persons with bipolar disorder. *Psychiatric Services, 55,* 931–933.

Kileen, P. R. (2005). An alternative to null-hypothesis significance tests. *Psychological Science, 16,* 345–353.

Kilgard, M. P., & Merzenich, M. M. (1998). Cortical map reorganization enabled by nucleus basalis activity. *Science, 279,* 1714–1718.

Kilgour, A. R., & Lederman, S. J. (2002). Face recognition by hand. *Perception and Psychophysics, 64,* 339–352.

Kilts, C. D., Schweitzer, J. B., Quinn, C. K., Gross, R. E., Faber, T. L., Muhammad, F., et al. (2001). Neural activity related to drug craving in cocaine addiction. *Archives of General Psychiatry, 58,* 334–341.

Kim, J., & Hatfield, E. (2004). Love types and subjective well-being: A cross-cultural study. *Social Behavior and Personality, 32,* 173–182.

Kim, N. S., & Ahn, W.-K. (2002). Clinical psychologists' theory-based representations of mental disorders predict their diagnostic reasoning and memory. *Journal of Experimental Psychology: General, 131,* 451–476.

Kimchi, R. (2003). Relative dominance of holistic and component properties in the perceptual organization of visual objects. In M. A. Peterson & G. Rhodes (Eds.), *Perception of faces, objects, and scenes* (pp. 235–268). New York: Oxford University Press.

Kimhy, D., Goetz, R., Yale, S., Corcoran, C., & Malaspina, D. (2005). Delusions in individuals with schizophrenia: Factor structure, clinical correlates, and putative neurobiology. *Psychopathology, 38,* 338–344.

Kimura, D. (1999). *Sex and cognition.* Cambridge: MIT Press.

King, J., & Pribram, K. H. (Eds.). (1995). *The scale of conscious experience: Is the brain too important to be left to specialists to study?* Mahwah, NJ: Erlbaum.

King, J. E., Weiss, A., & Farmer, K. H. (2005). A chimpanzee (*pan troglodytes*) analogue of cross-national generalization of personality structure: Zoological parks and an African sanctuary. *Journal of Personality, 73,* 389–410.

Kinney, H. C., Korein, J., Panigrahy, A., Dikkes, P., & Goode, R. (1994). Neuropathological findings in the brain of Karen Ann Quinlan: The role of the thalamus in the persistent vegetative state. *New England Journal of Medicine, 330*(21), 1469–1475.

Kinsey, A. C., Pomeroy, W. B., & Martin, C. E. (1948). *Sexual behavior in the human male.* Philadelphia: Saunders.

Kinsey, A. C., Pomeroy, W. B., Martin, C. E., & Gebhard, P. H. (1953). *Sexual behavior in the human female.* Philadelphia: Saunders.

Kircher, J. C., Horowitz, S. W., & Raskin, D. C. (1988). Meta-analysis of mock crime studies of the control question polygraph technique. *Law and Human Behavior, 12,* 79–90.

Kirchler, E., & Zani, B. (1995). Why don't they stay home? Prejudice against ethnic minorities in Italy. *Journal of Community and Applied Social Psychology, 5,* 59–65.

Kirkpatrick, B., Buchanan, R. W., Ross, D. E., & Carpenter, W. T., Jr. (2001). A separate disease within the syndrome of schizophrenia. *Archives of General Psychiatry, 58,* 165–171.

Kirsch, I. (1994a). Clinical hypnosis as a nondeceptive placebo: Empirically derived techniques. *American Journal of Clinical Hypnosis, 37*(2), 95–106.

Kirsch, I. (1994b). Defining hypnosis for the public. *Contemporary Hypnosis, 11*(3), 142–143.

Kirsch, I., & Braffman, W. (2001). Imaginative suggestibility and hypnotizability. *Psychological Science, 10,* 57–61.

Kirsch, I., Moore, T. J., Scoboria, A., & Nicholls, S. S. (2002). The emperor's new drugs: An analysis of antidepressant medication data submitted to the U.S. Food and Drug Administration [Electronic version]. *Prevention and Treatment, 5,* np.

Kirschenbaum, H., & Jourdan, A. (2005). The current status of Carl Rogers and the person-centered approach. *Psychotherapy: Theory, Research, Practice, Training, 42,* 37–51.

Kishi, T., & Elmquist, J. K. (2005). Body weight is regulated by the brain: A link between feeding and emotion. *Molecular Psychiatry, 10,* 132–146.

Kishioka, S., Miyamoto, Y., Fukunaga, Y., Nishida, S., & Yamamoto, H. (1994). Effects of a mixture of peptidase inhibitors (Amastatin, Captopril and Phosphoramidon) on met enkephalin, beta-endorphin, dynorphin (1–13) and electroacupuncture induced antinociception in rats. *Japanese Journal of Pharmacology, 66,* 337–345.

Kisilevsky, B. S., Hains, S. M. J., Lee, K., Xie, X., Huang, H., Ye, H. H., et al. (2003). Effects of experience on fetal voice recognition. *Psychological Science, 14,* 220–224.

Kitamura, C., & Burnham, D. (2003). Pitch and communicative intent in mother's speech: Adjustments for age and sex in the first year. *Infancy, 4,* 85–110.

Kitano, H., Chi, I., Rhee, S., Law, C., & Lubben, J. (1992). Norms and alcohol consumption: Japanese in Japan, Hawaii, and California. *Journal of Studies on Alcohol, 53,* 33–39.

Kitayama, N., Vaccarino, V., Kutner, M., Weiss, P., & Bremner, J.D. (2005). Magnetic resonance imaging (MRI) measurement of hippocampal volume in posttraumatic stress disorder: A meta-analysis. *Journal of Affective Disorders, 88,* 79–86.

Kitayama, S., & Markus, H. R (1992, May). *Construal of self as cultural frame: Implications for internationalizing psychology.* Paper presented to the Symposium on Internationalization and Higher Education, Ann Arbor.

Kitayama, S., Duffy, S., & Uchida, Y. (2007). Self as cultural mode of being. In S. Kitayama & D. Cohen (Eds.), *Handbook of cultural psychology.* New York: Guilford Press

Kitayama, S., Duffy, S., Kawamura, T., & Larsen, J. T. (2003). Perceiving an object and its context in different cultures: A cultural look at new look. *Psychological Science, 14,* 201–206.

Kitayama, S., Snibbe, A. C., Markus, H. R., & Suzuki, T. (2004). Is there any "free" choice?: Self and dissonance in two cultures. *Psychological Science, 15,* 527–533.

Kitayama, S., & Uchida, Y. (2003). Explicit self-criticism and implicit self-regard: Evaluating self and friend in two cultures. *Journal of Experimental Social Psychology, 39,* 476–482.

Kivimaki, M., Jussi, V., Elovainio, M., Helenius, H., Singh-Manoux, A., & Pentti, J. (2005). Optimism and pessimism as predictors of change in health after death or onset of severe illness in family. *Health Psychology, 24,* 413–421.

Kjaer, T. W., Bertelsen, C., Piccini, P., Brooks, D., Alving, J., & Lou, H. C. (2002). Increased dopamine tone during meditation-induced change of consciousness. *Cognitive Brain Research, 13,* 255–259.

Klahr, D., & Simon, H. (1999). Studies of scientific discovery: Complementary approaches and convergent findings. *Psychological Bulletin, 125,* 524–543.

Klaus, M. H., & Kennell, J. H. (1976). *Maternal infant bonding: The impact of early separation or loss on family development.* St. Louis: Mosby.

Klausner, H. A., & Lewandowski, C. (2002). Infrequent causes of stroke. *Emergency Medicine Clinics of North America, 20,* 657–670.

Kleemola, P., Jousilahti, P., Pietinen, P., Vartiainen, E., & Tuomilehto, J. (2000). Coffee consumption and the risk of coronary heart disease and death. *Archives of Internal Medicine, 160,* 3393–3400.

Klein, D. C., & Seligman, M. E. P. (1976). Reversal of performance deficits and perceptual deficits in learned helplessness and depression. *Journal of Abnormal Psychology, 85,* 11–26.

Klein, D. N. (1993). False suffocation alarms, spontaneous panics, and related conditions: An integrative hypothesis. *Archives of General Psychiatry, 50,* 306–316.

Klein, H. J., Wesson, M. J., Hollenbeck, J. R., & Alge, B. J. (1999). Goal commitment and the goal setting process: Conceptual clarification and empirical synthesis. *Journal of Applied Psychology, 84,* 885–896.

Klein, M. (1960). *The psychoanalysis of children.* New York: Grove Press.

Klein, M. (1975). *The writings of Melanie Klein: Vol. 3.* London: Hogarth Press.

Klein, M. (1991). The emotional life and ego-development of the infant with special reference to the depressive position. In P. King & R. Steiner (Eds.), *The Klein-Freud controversies: 1941–1945* (pp. 752–777). London: Tavistock/Routledge.

Kleinknecht, R. A. (1991). *Mastering anxiety: The nature and treatment of anxious conditions.* New York: Plenum.

Kleinknecht, R. A. (1994). Acquisition of blood, injury, and needle fears and phobias. *Behaviour Research and Therapy, 32,* 817–823.

Kleinknecht, R. A. (2000). Social phobia. In M. Hersen & M. K. Biaggio (Eds.), *Effective brief therapies: A clinician's guide.* New York: Academic Press.

Kleinman, A. (2004). Culture and depression. *New England Journal of Medicine, 351,* 951–953.

Kliewer, W., Parrish, K. A., Taylor, K. W., Jackson, K., Walker, J. M., & Shivy, V. A. (2006). Socialization of coping with community violence: Influences of caregiver coaching, modeling, and family context. *Child Development, 77,* 605–623.

Klin, A., Jones, W., Shultz, R., Volkmar, F., & Cohen, D. (2002). Defining and quantifying the social phenotype in autism. *American Journal of Psychiatry, 159,* 895–908.

Kline, D. A. (2005). Intuitive team decision making. In H. Montgomery, R. Lipshitz, & B. Brehmer (Eds.), *How professionals make decisions* (pp. 171–182). Mahwah, NJ: Erlbaum.

Kline, R. B. (2004). *Beyond significance testing: Reforming data analysis methods in behavioral research.* Washington, DC: APA.

Kline, S., & Groninger, L. D. (1991). The imagery bizarreness effect as a function of sentence complexity and presentation time. *Bulletin of the Psychonomic Society, 29,* 25–27.

Klinesmith, J., Kasser, T., & McAndrew, F. T. (2006). Guns, testosterone, and aggression: An experimental test of a mediational hypothesis. *Psychological Science, 17,* 568–571.

Kling, K. C., Hyde, J. S., Showers, C. J., & Buswell, B. N. (1999). Gender differences in self-esteem: A meta-analysis. *Psychological Bulletin, 125,* 470–500.

Klintsova, A. Y., & Greenough, W. T. (1999). Synaptic plasticity in cortical systems. *Current Opinion in Neurobiology, 9,* 203–208.

Klosko, J. S., Barlow, D. H., Tassinari, R., & Cerny, J. A. (1990). A comparison of alprazolam and behavior therapy in treatment of panic disorder. *Journal of Consulting and Clinical Psychology, 58,* 77–84.

Kluger, A. N., & DeNisi, A. (1998). Feedback interventions: Toward the understanding of a double-edged sword. *Current Directions in Psychological Science, 7,* 67–72.

Klump, K. L., & Culbert, K. M. (2007). Molecular genetic studies of eating disorders: Current status and future directions. *Current Directions in Psychological Science, 16,* 37–41.

Klunk, W. E., Engler, H., Nordberg, A., Wang, Y., Blomqvist, G., Holt, D. P., et al. (2004). Imaging brain amyloid in Alzheimer's disease with Pittsburgh Compound-B. *Annals of Neurology, 55,* 306–319.

Klunk, W. E., Lopresti, B. J., Ikonomovic, M. D., Lefterov, I. M., Koldamova, R. P., Abrahamson, E. E., et al. (2005). Binding of the positron emission tomography tracer Pittsburgh compound-B reflects the amount of amyloid-beta in Alzheimer's disease brain but not in transgenic mouse brain. *The Journal of Neuroscience: The Official Journal of the Society for Neuroscience, 25,* 10598–10606.

Knafo, A., Iervolino, A. C., & Plomin, R. (2005). Masculine girls and feminine boys: Genetic and environmental contributions to atypical gender development in early childhood. *Journal of Personality and Social Psychology, 88,* 400–412.

Knapp, S., & VandeCreek, L. (1997). Jaffee v. Redmond: The Supreme Court recognizes a psychotherapist-patient privilege in federal courts. *Professional Psychology: Research and Practice, 28,* 567–572.

Knecht, S., Floel, A., Drager, B., Breitenstein, C., Sommer, J., Henningsen, H., et al. (2002). Degree of language lateralization determines susceptibility to unilateral brain lesions. *Nature Neuroscience, 5,* 695–699.

Knopman, D., & Selnes, O. (2003). Neuropsychology of dementia. In K. M. Heilman & E. Valenstein (Eds.), *Clinical neuropsychology* (4th ed.). New York: Oxford University Press.

Knopman, D. S. (2006). Dementia and cerebrovascular disease. *Mayo Clinic Proceedings, 81*(2), 223–230.

Koch, C. (2003). *The quest for consciousness: A neurobiological approach.* Englewood, CO: Roberts.

Koch, C., & Davis, J. L. (Eds.). (1994). *Large-scale neuronal theories of the brain.* Cambridge: MIT Press.

Koelega, H. S. (1993). Stimulant drugs and vigilance performance: A review. *Psychopharmacology, 111*(1), 1–16.

Koger, S. M., Schettler, T., & Weiss, B. (2005). Environmental toxicants and developmental disabilities: A challenge for psychologists. *American Psychologist, 60,* 243–255.

Kohlberg, L., & Gilligan, C. (1971). The adolescent as a philosopher: The discovery of the self in a postconventional world. *Daedalus, 100,* 1051–1086.

Köhler, W. (1924). *The mentality of apes.* New York: Harcourt Brace.

Köhler, W. (1976). *The mentality of apes* (E. Winter, Trans.). Oxford, UK: Liveright.

Kohlmetz, C., Muller, S. V., Nager, W., Munte, T. F., & Altenmuller, E. (2003). Selective loss of timbre perception for keyboard and percussion instruments following a right temporal lesion. *Neurocase, 9*(1), 86–93.

Kohnert, K. (2004). Cognitive and cognate-based treatments for bilingual aphasia: A case study. *Brain and Language, 91,* 294–302.

Kohrt, B. A., Kunz, R. D., Baldwin, J. L., Koirala, N. R., et al. (2005). "Somatization" and "comorbidity": A study of Jhum-Jhum and depression in rural Nepal. *Ethos, 33,* 125–147.

Kohut, H. (1984). Selected problems of self-psychological theory. In J. D. Lichtenberg & S. Kaplan (Eds.), *Reflections on self psychology* (pp. 387–416). Hillsdale, NJ: Erlbaum.

Kolata, G. (2002, August 19.). Male hormone therapy popular but untested. *The New York Times.*

Kolata, G. (2003, April 22). Hormone studies: What went wrong? *The New York Times.*

Kolata, G., & Markel, H. (2001, April 29). Baby not crawling? Reason seems to be less tummy time. *New York Times.*

Kolb, B., Gorny, G., Li, Y., Samaha, A.-N., & Robinson, T. E. (2003). Amphetamine or cocaine limits the ability of later experience to promote structural plasticity in the neocortex and nucleus accumbens. *Proceedings of the National Academy of Sciences, 100,* 10523–10528.

Kolonin, M. G., Saha, P. K., Chan, L., Pasqualini, R., & Arap, W. (2004). Reversal of obesity by targeted ablation of adipose tissue. *Nature Medicine, 10,* 625–632.

Komatsu, S.-I., & Naito, M. (1992). Repetition priming with Japanese Kana scripts in word-fragment completion. *Memory & Cognition, 20,* 160–170.

Komorita, S. S. (1984). Coalition bargaining. In L. Berkowitz (Ed.), *Advances in experimental social psychology* (Vol. 18). New York: Academic Press.

Komorita, S. S., & Parks, C. D. (1996). *Social dilemmas.* Boulder, CO: Westview.

Konkol, R. J., Murphey, L. J., Ferriero, D. M., Dempsey, D. A., & Olsen, G. D. (1994). Cocaine metabolites in the neonate: Potential for toxicity. *Journal of Child Neurology, 9*(3), 242–248.

Konuk, E., Knipe, J., Eke, I., Yuksek, H., Yurtsever, A., & Ostep, S. (2006). The effects of eye movement desensitization and reprocessing (EMDR) therapy on posttraumatic stress disorder in survivors of the 1999 Marmara, Turkey, earthquake. *International Journal of Stress Management, 13,* 291–308.

Koob, G. F., & Bloom, F. E. (1988). Cellular and molecular mechanisms of drug dependence. *Science, 242,* 715–723.

Kop, W. J., Berman, D. S., Gransar, H., Wong, N. D., Miranda-Peats, R., White, M. D., et al. (2005). Social network and coronary artery calcification in asymptomatic individuals. *Psychosomatic Medicine, 67,* 343–352.

Koppenaal, L., & Glanzer, M. (1990). An examination of the continuous distractor task and the "long-term recency effect." *Memory & Cognition, 18,* 183–195.

Korchmaros, J. D., & Kenny, D. A. (2001). Emotional closeness as a mediator of the effect of genetic relatedness on altruism. *Psychological Science, 12,* 262–265.

Kordower, J. H., Emborg, M. E., Bloch, J., Ma, S. Y., Chu, Y., Leventhal, L., et al. (2000). Neurodegeneration prevented by lentiviral vector delivery of GDNF in primate models of Parkinson's disease. *Science, 290,* 767–773.

Koretz, D., Lynch, P. S., & Lynch, C. A. (2000, June). The impact of score differences on the admission of minority students: An illustration. *Statements of the National Board on Educational Testing and Public Policy, 1,* 1–15.

Korner, J., & Leibel, R. L. (2003). To eat or not to eat—How the gut talks to the brain. *The New England Journal of Medicine, 349,* 926–928.

Koshizuka, S., Okada, S., Okawa, A., Koda, M., Murasawa, M., Hashimoto, M., et al. (2004). Transplanted hematopoietic stem cells from bone marrow differentiate into neural lineage cells and promote functional recovery after spinal cord injury in mice. *Journal of Neuropathology and Experimental Neurology, 63,* 64–72.

Kosslyn, S. M. (1988). Aspects of a cognitive neuroscience of mental imagery. *Science, 240,* 1621–1626.

Kosslyn, S. M. (1994). *Image and mind*. Cambridge: Harvard University Press.

Kotani, N., Hashimoto, H., Sato, Y., Sessler, D. I., Yoshioka, H., Kitayama, M., et al. (2001). Preoperative intradermal acupuncture reduces postoperative pain, nausea and vomiting, analgesic requirement, and sympathoadrenal responses. *Anesthesiology, 95,* 349–356.

Kouider, S., & Dupoux, E. (2005). Subliminal speech priming. *Psychological Science, 16,* 617.

Kounios, J., Frymiare, J. L., Bowden, E. M., Fleck, J. I., Subramaniam, K., Parrish, T. B., & Jung-Beeman, M. (2006). The prepared mind: Neural activity prior to problem presentation predicts subsequent solution by sudden insight. *Psychological Science, 17,* 882–890.

Kouyoumdjian, H. (2004). Influence of unannounced quizzes and cumulative exams on attendance and study behavior. *Teaching of Psychology, 31,* 110–111.

Kozak, M. J., Liebowitz, M. R., & Foa, E. B. (2000). Cognitive behavior therapy and pharmacotherapy for obsessive-compulsive disorder: The NIMH-sponsored collaborative study. In W. K. Goodman, M. V. Rudorfer, & J. D. Maser (Eds.), *Obsessive-compulsive disorder: Contemporary issues in treatment* (pp. 501–530). Mahwah, NJ: Erlbaum.

Kozel, F. A., Padgett, T. M., & George, M. S. (2004). A replication study of the neural correlates of deception. *Behavioral Neuroscience, 118,* 852–856.

Kozlowski, S. W. J., & Ilgen, D. R. (2006). Enhancing the effectiveness of work groups and teams. *Psychological Science in the Public Interest, 7,* 77–124.

Kozorovitskiy, Y., Gross, C. G., Kopil, C., Battaglia, L., McBreen, M., Stranahan, A. M., et al. (2005). Experience induces structural and biochemical changes in the adult primate brain. *Proceedings of the National Academy of Sciences of the USA, 102,* 17478–17482.

Kraft, C. (1978). A psychophysical approach to air safety: Simulator studies of visual illusions in right approaches. In H. L. Picks, H. W. Leibowitz, J. E. Singer, A. Steinschneider, & H. W. Stevenson (Eds.), *Psychology: From research to practice.* New York: Plenum.

Krahn, L. E. (2003). Sleep disorders. *Seminars in Neurology, 23*(3), 307–314.

Krakauer, J. (1997). *Into thin air.* New York: Villard.

Krakow, B., Hollifield, M., Johnston, L., Koss, M., Schrader, R., Warner, T. D., et al. (2001). Imagery rehearsal therapy for chronic nightmares in sexual assault survivors with posttraumatic stress disorder: a randomized controlled trial. *Journal of the American Medical Association, 286,* 537–545.

Kramer, A. F., Larish, J., Weber, T., & Bardell, L. (1999). Training for executive control: Task coordination strategies and aging. In D. Gopher & A. Koriat (Eds.), *Attention and Performance XVII.* Cambridge: MIT Press.

Kramer, A. F., & Willis, S. (2002). Enhancing the cognitive vitality of older adults. *Current Directions in Psychological Science, 11,* 173–177.

Krantz, D., Contrada, R., Hill, D., & Friedler, E. (1988). Environmental stress and biobehavioral antecedents of coronary heart disease. *Journal of Consulting and Clinical Psychology, 56,* 333–341.

Krantz, D., & Durel, L. (1983). Psychobiological substrates of the Type A behavior pattern. *Health Psychology, 2,* 393–411.

Krantz, D. S., & McCeney, M. K. (2002). Effects of psychological and social factors on organic disease: A critical assessment of research on coronary heart disease. *Annual Review of Psychology, 53,* 341–369.

Kraus, W. E., Houmard, J. A., Duscha, B. D., Knetzger, K. J., Wharton, M. B., McCartney, J. S., et al. (2002). Effects of the amount and intensity of exercise on plasma lipoproteins. *The New England Journal of Medicine, 347,* 1483–1492.

Krause, M. S. (2005). How the psychotherapy research community must work toward measurement and why. *Journal of Clinical Psychology, 61,* 269–283.

Krause, M. S., & Lutz, W. (2006). How we really ought to be comparing treatments for clinical purposes. *Psychotherapy: Theory, Research, Practice, Training, 43,* 359–361.

Krause, N., & Shaw, B. A. (2000). Role-specific feelings of control and mortality. *Psychology and Aging, 15,* 617–626.

Kraut, R., Olson, J., Banaji, M., Bruckman, A., Cohen, J., & Couper, M. (2004). Psychological research online: Report of board of scientific affairs' advisory group on the conduct of research on the Internet. *American Psychologist, 59,* 105–117.

Krauzlis, R. J. (2002). Reaching for answers. *Neuron, 34,* 673–674.

Kray, L. J., & Galinsky, A. D. (2003). The debiasing effect of counterfactual mind-sets: Increasing the search for disconfirmatory information in group decisions. *Organizational Behavior and Human Decision Processes, 91,* 69–81.

Krebs, R. L. (1967). *Some relations between moral judgment, attention, and resistance to temptation.* Unpublished doctoral dissertation, University of Chicago, Chicago, IL.

Kreek, M. J., Nielsen, D. A., Butelman, E. R., & LaForge, K. S. (2005). Genetic influences on impulsivity, risk taking, stress responsivity and vulnerability to drug abuse and addiction. *Nature Neuroscience, 8,* 1450–1457.

Kress, J. S., & Elias, M. J. (2006). School-based social and emotional learning programs. In W. Damon & R. M. Lerner (Series Eds.) & K. A. Renninger & I. E. Sigel (Vol. Eds.), *Handbook of child psychology: Vol. 4, Child psychology in practice* (6th ed., pp. 592–618). New York: Wiley.

Kring, A. M., & Gordon, A. H. (1998). Sex differences in emotion: Expression, experience, and physiology. *Journal of Personality & Social Psychology, 74,* 686–703.

Kristof, N. D. (1997, August 17). Where children rule. *New York Times Magazine.*

Krohne, H. W., & Slangen, K. E. (2005). Influence of social support on adaptation to surgery. *Health Psychology, 24,* 101–105.

Kronfol, Z., & Remick, D. G. (2000). Cytokines and the brain: Implications for clinical psychiatry. *American Journal of Psychiatry, 157,* 683–694.

Krosnick, J. A., Betz, A. L., Jussim, L. J., & Lynn, A. R. (1992). Subliminal conditioning of attitude. *Personality and Social Psychology Bulletin, 18,* 152–162.

Krueger, J. (2001). Null hypothesis significance testing. *American Psychologist, 56,* 16–26.

Krueger, R. F., & Markon, K. E. (2006). Understanding psychopathology: Melding behavior genetics, personality, and quantitative psychology to develop an empirically based model. *Current Directions in Psychological Science 15,* 113–117.

Krueger, R. F., Hicks, B. M., Patrick, C. J., Carlson, S. R., Iacono, W. G., & McGue, M. (2002). Etiologic connections among substance dependence, antisocial behavior, and personality: Modeling the externalizing spectrum. *Journal of Abnormal Psychology, 111,* 411–424.

Krueger, R. F., Markon, K. E., & Bouchard, T. J., Jr. (2003). The extended genotype: The heritability of personality accounts for the heritability of recalled family environments in twins reared apart. *Journal of Personality, 71,* 809–833.

Kruger, D. J. (2003). Evolution and altruism: Combining psychological mediators with naturally selected tendencies. *Evolution and Human Behavior, 24,* 118–125.

Kruger, J., Wirtz, D., & Miller, D. T. (2005). Counterfactual thinking and the first instinct fallacy. *Journal of Personality and Social Psychology, 88,* 725–735.

Kryger, M. H., Roth, T., & Dement, W. C. (2000). *Principles and practice of sleep medicine* (3rd ed.). Philadelphia: Saunders.

Krykouli, S. E., Stanley, B. G., Seirafi, R. D., & Leibowitz, S. F (1990). Stimulation of feeding by galanin: Anatomical localization and behavioral specificity of this peptide's effects in the brain. *Peptides, 11*(5), 995–1001.

Kübler-Ross, E. (1975). *Death: The final stage of growth.* Englewood Cliffs, NJ: Prentice-Hall.

Kubzansky, L. D., Davidson, K. W., & Rozanski, A. (2005). The clinical impact of negative psychological states: Expanding the spectrum of risk for coronary artery disease. *Psychosomatic Medicine, 67*(S1), S10–S14.

Kuhn, D. (2006). Do cognitive changes accompany developments in the adolescent brain? *Perspectives on Psychological Science, 1,* 59–67.

Kuhn, D., & Franklin, S. (2006). The second decade: What develops (and how)? In W. Damon & R. M. Lerner (Series Eds.) & D. Kuhn & R. Siegler (Vol. Eds.), *Handbook of child psychology: Vol. 2. Cognition, perception, and language* (6th ed., pp. 953–994). New York: Wiley.

Kuhnen, C. M., & Knutson, B. (2005). The neural basis of financial risk taking. *Neuron, 47,* 763–770.

Kujala, T., Karma, K., Ceponiene, R., Belitz, S., Turkkila, P., Tervaniemi, M., & Naatanen, R. (2001). Plastic neural changes and reading improvement caused by audiovisual training in reading-impaired children. *Proceedings of the National Academy of Science, 98,* 10509–10514.

Kukull, W. A., Higdon, R., Bowen, J. D., McCormick, W. C., Teri, L., Schellenberg, G. D., et al. (2002). Dementia and Alzheimer disease incidence: A prospective cohort study. *Archives of Neurology, 59,* 1737–1746.

Kuncel, N. R., Hezlett, S. A., & Ones, D. (2004). Academic performance, career potential, creativity, and job performance: Can one construct predict them all? *Journal of Personality and Social Psychology, 86,* 148–161.

Kuncel, N. R., Hezlett, S. A., & Ones, D. S. (2001). A comprehensive meta-analysis of the predictive validity of the Graduate Records Examinations: Implications for graduate student selection and performance. *Psychological Bulletin, 127,* 162–181.

Kunen, S., Niederhauser, R., Smith, P. O., Morris, J. A., & Marx, B. D. (2005). Race disparities in psychiatric rates in emergency departments. *Journal of Consulting and Clinical Psychology, 73,* 116–126.

Kurbat, M. A. (1997). Can the recognition of living things really be selectively impaired? *Neuropsychologia, 35*(6), 813–827.

Kurdek, L. A. (2005). What do we know about gay and lesbian couples? *Current Directions in Psychological Science, 14,* 251–254.

Kurtz, L. F. (2004). Support and self-help groups. In C. D. Garvin, L. M. Gutiérrez, & M. J. Galinsky (Eds.), *Handbook of social work with groups* (pp. 139–159). New York: Guilford.

Kushner, M. G., Thuras, P., Kaminski, J., Anderson, N., Neumeyer, B., & Mackenzie, T. (2000). Expectancies for alcohol to affect tension and anxiety as a function of time. *Addictive Behaviors, 25,* 93–98.

Kusyszyn, I. (1990). Existence, effectance, esteem: From gambling to a new theory of human motivation. *International Journal of the Addictions, 25,* 159–177.

Kutchins, H., & Kirk, S. A. (1997). *Making us crazy: The psychiatric bible and the creation of mental disorders.* New York: Free Press.

Kvorning, N., Holmberg, C., Grennert, L., Aberg, A., & Akeson, J. (2004). Acupuncture relieves pelvic and low-back pain in late pregnancy. *Acta Obstetrics and Gynecology Scandinavia, 83,* 246–250.

Kwan, M., Greenleaf, W. J., Mann, J., Crapo, L., & Davidson, J. M. (1983). The nature of androgen action on male sexuality: A combined laboratory-self-report study on hypogonadal men. *Journal of Clinical Endocrinology and Metabolism, 57,* 557–562.

Kwate, N. O. A. (2001). Intelligence or misorientation? *Journal of Black Psychology, 27,* 221–238.

Kyllonen, P. C., & Christal, R. E. (1990). Reasoning ability is (little more than) working-memory capacity?! *Intelligence, 14,* 389–433.

Kymalainen, J. A., Weisman, A. G., Resales, G. A., & Armesto, J. C. (2006). Ethnicity, expressed emotion, and communication deviance in family members of patients with schizophrenia. *Journal of Nervous and Mental Disease, 194,* 391–396.

Laan, E., Everaerd, W., Van Aanhold, M. T., & Rebel, M. (1993). Performance demand and sexual arousal in woman. *Behavior Research and Therapy, 31,* 25–36.

LaBar, K. S., Gatenby, J. C., Gore, J. C., LeDoux, J. E., & Phelps, E. A. (1998). Human amygdala activation during conditioned fear acquisition and extinction: A mixed-trial fMRI study. *Neuron, 20,* 937–945.

Laboratory of Comparative Human Cognition. (1982). Culture and intelligence. In R. J. Sternberg (Ed.), *Handbook of intelligence* (pp. 642–722). New York: Cambridge University Press.

Labouvie-Vief, G. (1982). Discontinuities in development from childhood. In T. M. Field, A. Huston, H. C. Quay, L. Troll, & G. E. Finley (Eds.), *Review of human development.* New York: Wiley.

Labouvie-Vief, G. (1992). A new-Piagetian perspective on adult cognitive development. In R. J. Sternberg & C. A. Berg (Eds.), *Intellectual development.* New York: Cambridge University Press.

Lacayo, A. (1995). Neurologic and psychiatric complications of cocaine abuse. *Neuropsychiatry, Neuropsychology, and Behavioral Neurology, 8*(1), 53–60.

Lachman, M. E., & Andreoletti, C. (2006). Strategy use mediates the relationship between control beliefs and memory performance for middle-aged and older adults. *Journals of Gerontology: Psychological Sciences and Social Sciences, 61,* 88–94.

Ladd, G. (2005). *Peer relationships and social competence of children and youth.* New Haven, CT: Yale University Press.

Ladd, G. W., & Troop-Gordon, W. (2003). The role of chronic peer difficulties in the development of children's psychological adjustment problems. *Child Development, 74,* 1344–1367.

LaFrance, M., Hecht, M. A., & Paluck, E. L. (2003). The contingent smile: A meta-analysis of sex differences in smiling. *Psychological Bulletin, 129,* 305–334.

Lagerspetz, K. M. J., & Lagerspetz, K. Y. H. (1983). Genes and aggression. In E. C. Simmel, M. E. Hahn, & J. K. Walters (Eds.), *Aggressive behavior: Genetic and neural approaches.* Hillsdale, NJ: Erlbaum.

Lahey, B. B., Applegate, B., Waldman, I. D., Loft, J. D., Hankin, B. L., & Rick, J. (2004). The structure of child and adolescent psychopathology: Generating new hypotheses. *Journal of Abnormal Psychology, 113,* 358–385.

Lahey, B. B., Loeber, R., Hart, E. L., Frick, P. J., & Applegate, B. (1995). Four-year longitudinal study of conduct disorder in boys: Patterns and predictors of persistence. *Journal of Abnormal Psychology, 104,* 83–93.

Lai, C. S. L., Fisher, S. E., Hurst, J. A., Vargha-Khadem, F., & Monaco, A. P. (2001). A forkhead-domain gene is mutated in severe speech and language disorder. *Nature, 413,* 519–523.

Laird, R. D., Jordan, K. Y., Dodge, K. A., Pettit, G. S., & Gates, J. E. (2001). Peer rejection in childhood, involvement with antisocial peers in early adolescence, and the development of externalizing behavior problems. *Development and Psychopathology, 13,* 337–354.

Lakdawalla, D. N., Bhattacharya, J., & Goldman, D. P. (2004). Are the young becoming more disabled? *Health Affairs, 23,* 168–176.

Lakin, J. L., & Chartrand, T. L. (2003). Using nonconscious behavioral mimicry to create affiliation and rapport. *Psychological Science, 14,* 334–339.

Lalumière, M. L., Blanchard, R., & Zucker, K. J. (2000). Sexual orientation and handedness in men and women: A meta-analysis. *Psychological Bulletin, 126,* 575–592.

Lam, B., Sam, K., Mok, W. Y., Cheung, M., Fong, D. Y., Lam, J. C., et al. (2006). A randomised study of three non-surgical treatments in mild to moderate obstructive sleep apnoea. *Thorax, 62,* 354–359.

Lam, D. H., Watkins, E. R., Hayward, P., Bright, J., Wright, K., Kerr, N., Parr-Davis, G., & Sham, P. (2003). A randomized controlled study of cognitive therapy for relapse prevention for bipolar affective disorder: outcome of the first year. *Archives of General Psychiatry, 60,* 145–152.

Lamar, J. (2000). Suicides in Japan reach a record high. *British Medical Journal, 321,* 528.

Lamb, M. E. (1998). Assessments of children's credibility in forensic contexts. *Current Directions in Psychological Science, 7,* 43–46.

Lamb, M. E. (Ed.). (1997). *The role of the father in child development* (3rd ed.). New York: Wiley.

Lamb, M. E., & Ahnert, L. (2006). Nonparental child care. In W. Damon & R. M. Lerner (Series Eds.) & K. A. Renninger & I. E. Sigel (Vol. Eds.), *Handbook of child psychology: Vol. 4. Child psychology in practice* (6th ed., pp. 950–1016). New York: Wiley.

Lamberg, L. (2004). Impact of long working hours explored. *Journal of the American Medical Association, 292,* 25–26.

Lambert, M. J., & Barley, D. E. (2001). Research summary on the therapeutic relationship and psychotherapy outcome. *Psychotherapy, 38,* 357–361.

Lambert, M. J., & Bergin, A. E. (1994). The effectiveness of psychotherapy. In A. E. Bergin & S. L. Garfield (Eds.), *Handbook of psychotherapy and behavior change* (4th ed.). New York: Wiley.

Lambert, N. M. (1999). Developmental trajectories in psychology: Applications to education and training. *American Psychologist, 54,* 991–1002.

Lamm, C., Batson, C. D., & Decety, J. (2007). The neural basis of human empathy—Effects of perspective-taking and cognitive appraisal: An event-related fMRI study. *Journal of Cognitive Neuroscience, 19,* 42–58.

Lancaster, T. Hajek, P., Stead, L.F., West, R., & Jarvis, M.J. (2006). Prevention of relapse after quitting smoking: A systematic review of trials. *Archives of Internal Medicine, 166,* 828–835.

Landrigan, C. P., Rothschild, J. M., Cronin, J. W., Kaushal, R., Burdick, E., Katz, J. T., et al. (2004). Effect of reducing interns' work hours on serious medical errors in intensive care units. *New England Journal of Medicine, 351,* 1838–1848.

Landrine, H. (1991). Revising the framework of abnormal psychology. In P. Bronstein & K. Quina (Eds.), *Teaching a psychology of people.* Washington, DC: American Psychological Association.

Landsdale, M., & Laming, D. (1995). Evaluating the fragmentation hypothesis: The analysis of errors in cued recall. *Acta Psychologica, 88,* 33–77.

Lang, A. R., Goeckner, D. J., Adesso, V. J., & Marlatt, G. A. (1975). Effects of alcohol on aggression in male social drinkers. *Journal of Abnormal Psychology, 84,* 508–518.

Lang, C., Barco, A., Zablow, L., Kandel, E. R., Siegelbaum, S. A., & Zakharenko, S. S. (2004). Transient expansion of synaptically connected dendritic spines upon induction of hippocampal long-term potentiation. *Proceedings of the National Academy of Sciences of the USA, 101,* 16665–16670.

Lang, P. J. (1995). The emotion probe: Studies of motivation and attention. *American Psychologist, 50*(5), 372–385.

Lang, P. J., & Melamed, B. G. (1969). Avoidance conditioning therapy of an infant with chronic ruminative vomiting. *Journal of Abnormal Psychology, 74,* 1–8.

Langenberg, P., Ballesteros, M., Feldman, R., Damron, D., Anliker, J., Havas, S. (2000). Psychosocial factors and intervention-associated changes in those factors as correlates of change in fruit and vegetable consumption in the Maryland WIC 5 a day promotion program. *Annals of Behavioral Medicine, 22,* 307–315.

Langenbucher, J., & Nathan, P. E. (2006). Diagnosis and classification. In F. Andrasik (Ed.), *Comprehensive handbook of personality and psychopathology: Vol. 2: Adult psychopathology* (pp. 3–20). New York: Wiley.

Langens, T. A., & Schüler, J. (2007). Effects of written emotional expression: the role of positive expectancies. *Health Psychology, 26,* 174–182.

Langleben, D. D., Loughead, J. W., Bilker, W. B., Ruparel, K., Childress, A. R., Busch, S. I., & Gur, R. C. (2005). Telling truth from lie in individual subjects with fast event-related fMRI. *Human Brain Mapping, 26,* 262–272.

Langlois, J. H., Kalakanis, L., Rubenstein, A. J., Larson, A., Hallam, M., & Smoot, M. (2000). Maxims or myths of beauty: A meta-analytic and theoretical review. *Psychological Bulletin, 126,* 390–423.

Lansford, J. E., Chang, L., Dodge, K. A., Malone, P. S., Oburu, P., Palmérus, K., et al. (2005). Physical discipline and children's adjustment: Cultural normativeness as a moderator. *Child Development, 76,* 1234–1246.

Lantz, J. (2004). Research and evaluation issues in existential psychotherapy. *Journal of Contemporary Psychotherapy, 34,* 331–340.

Lanzenberger, R. R., Mitterhauser, M., Spindelegger, C., Wadsak, W., Klein, N., Mien, L. K., et al. (2007). Reduced serotonin-1a receptor binding in social anxiety disorder. *Biological Psychiatry, 61,* 1081–1089.

Lapierre, L. M., & Allen, T. D. (2006). Work-supportive family, family-supportive supervision, use of organizational benefits, and problem-focused coping: Implications for work-family conflict and employee well-being. *Journal of Occupational Health Psychology, 11,* 169–181.

Lapointe, L. (1990). *Aphasia and related neurogenic language disorders.* New York: Thieme Medical.

Larimer, M. E., Turner, A. P., Mallett, K. A., & Geisner, I. M. (2004). Predicting drinking behavior and alcohol-related problems among fraternity and sorority members: Examining the role of descriptive and injunctive norms. *Journal of Addictive Behaviors, 18,* 203–212.

Larsen, J. T., McGraw, A. P., Mellers, B. A., & Cacioppo, J. T. (2004). The agony of victory and thrill of defeat: Mixed emotional reactions to disappointing wins and relieving losses. *Psychological Science, 15,* 325–330.

Larsen, R., & Buss, D. M. (2005). *Personality psychology: Domains of knowledge about human nature* (2nd ed.). New York: McGraw-Hill.

Larson, E. B., Wang, L., Bowen, J. D., McCormick, W. C., Teri, L., Crane, P., & Kukull, W. (2006). Exercise is associated with reduced risk of incident dementia among persons 65 years of age and older. *Annals of Internal Medicine, 144,* 73–81.

Larson, G. E., & Saccuzzo, D. P. (1989). Cognitive correlates of general intelligence: Toward a process theory of g. *Intelligence, 13,* 5–32.

Larson, J. R., Jr., Christensen, C., Franz, T. M., & Abbott, A. S. (1998). Diagnosing groups: The pooling, management, and impact of shared and unshared case information in team-based medical decision making. *Journal of Personality and Social Psychology, 75,* 93–108.

Larson, M. C., Gunnar, M. R., & Hertsgaard, L. (1991). The effects of morning naps, car trips, and maternal separation on adrenocortical activity in human infants. *Child Development, 62,* 362–372.

Larzelere, R. E. (1996). A review of the outcomes of parental use of nonabusive or customary physical punishment. *Pediatrics, 98,* 824–828.

Lashley, K. S. (1950). In search of the engram. *Society of Experimental Biology, Symposium 4,* 454–482.

Latané, B. (1981). The psychology of social impact. *American Psychologist, 36,* 343–356.

Latané, B., & Rodin, J. (1969). A lady in distress: Inhibiting effects of friends and strangers on bystander intervention. *Journal of Experimental Social Psychology, 5,* 189–202.

Latham, G. P. (2004). Motivate employee performance through goal-setting. In E. A. Locke (Ed.), *Handbook of principles of organizational behavior* (pp. 107–119). Malden, MA: Blackwell.

Latham, G. P., Skarlicki, D., Irvine, D., & Siegel, J. P. (1993). The increasing importance of performance appraisals to employee effectiveness in organizational settings in North America. In C. L. Cooper & I. T. Robertson (Eds.), *International review of industrial and organizational psychology 1993* (pp. 87–132). Chichester, UK: Wiley.

Lau, I. Y.-M., Lee, S., & Chiu, C. (2004). Language, cognition, and reality: Constructing shared meanings through communication. In M. Schaller & C. S. Crandall (Eds.), *The psychological foundations of culture* (pp. 77–97). Mahwah, NJ: Erlbaum.

Laughery, K. R. (1999). Modeling human performance during system design. In E. Salas (Ed.), *Human/technology interaction in complex systems* (Vol. 9, pp. 147–174). Stamford, CT: JAI Press.

Laughlin, P. L. (1999). Collective induction: Twelve postulates. *Organizational Behavior and Human Decision Processes, 80,* 50–69.

Laumann, E. O., Gagnon, J. H., Michael, R. T., & Michaels, S. (1994). *The social organization of sexuality: Sexual practices in the United States.* Chicago: University of Chicago Press.

Laumann, E. O., & Michael, R. T. (Eds.). (2000). *Sex, love, and health in America: Private choices and public policies.* Chicago: University of Chicago Press.

Laumann, E. O., Paik, A., & Rosen, R. C. (1999). Sexual dysfunction in the United States: Prevalence and predictors. *Journal of the American Medical Association, 281,* 537–544.

Laumann, E. O., Paik, A., Glasser, D. B., Kang, J.-H., Wang, T., Levinson, B., et al. (2006). A cross-national study of subjective sexual well-being among older women and men: Findings from the global study of sexual attitudes and behaviors. *Archives of Sexual Behavior, 35,* 145–161.

Laurenceau, J.-P., Hayes, A. M., & Feldman, G. C. (2007). Some methodological and statistical issues in the study of change processes in psychotherapy. *Clinical Psychology Review, 27,* 682–695.

Laurenceau, J.-P., Stanley, S. M., Olmos-Gallo, A., Baucom, B., & Markman, H. J. (2004). Community-based prevention of marital dysfunction: Multilevel modeling of a randomized effectiveness study. *Journal of Consulting and Clinical Psychology, 72,* 933–943.

Laureys, S. (2004). Functional neuroimaging in the vegetative state. *NeuroRehabilitation, 19*(4), 335–341.

Lavoie, M. E., Dupuis, F., Johnston, K. M., Leclerc, S., & Lassonde, M. (2004). Visual P300 effects beyond symptoms in concussed college athletes. *Journal of Clinical and Experimental Neuropsychology, 26,* 55–73.

Law, D. J., Pellegrino, J. W., & Hunt, E. B. (1993). Comparing the tortoise and the hare: Gender differences and experience in dynamic spatial reasoning tasks. *Psychological Science, 4,* 35–40.

Law, K. L., Stroud, L. R., LaGasse, L. L., Niaura, R., Liu, J., & Lester, B. M. (2003). Smoking during pregnancy and newborn neurobehavior. *Pediatrics, 111,* 1318–1323.

Law, M. H., Cotton, R. G. H., & Berger, G. E. (2006). The role of phospholipases A2 in schizophrenia. *Molecular Psychiatry, 11,* 547–556.

Lawford, B. R., Young, R. M., Rowell, J. A., Qualichefski, J., Fletcher, B. H., Syndulko, et al. (1995). Bromocriptine in the treatment of alcoholics with the D2 dopamine receptor A1 allele. *Nature Medicine, 1*(4), 337–341.

Lawless, H. T., & Engen, T. (1977). Associations to odors: Interference, memories and verbal learning. *Journal of Experimental Psychology, 3,* 52–59.

Lawrie, S. M., Whalley, H. C., Abukmeil, S. S., Kestelman, J., Donnelly, L., Miller, P., et al. (2001). Brain structure, genetic liability, and psychotic symptoms in subjects at high risk of developing schizophrenia. *Biological Psychiatry, 49,* 811–823.

Lazar, S. W., Kerr, C. E., Wasserman, R. H., Gray, J. R., Greve, D. N., Treadway, M. T., et al. (2005). Meditation experience is associated with increased cortical thickness. *Neuroreport, 16,* 1893–1897.

Lazarus, A. A. (1971). *Behavior therapy and beyond.* New York: McGraw-Hill.

Lazarus, R. S. (1966). *Psychological stress and the coping process.* New York: McGraw-Hill.

Lazarus, R. S. (1991). *Emotion and adaptation.* New York: Oxford University Press.

Lazarus, R. S. (1999). *Stress and emotion: A new synthesis.* New York: Springer.

Lazarus, R. S., & Folkman, S. (1984). *Stress, appraisal, and coping.* New York: Springer-Verlag.

Lazarus, R. S., Opton, E. M., Nomikos, M. S., & Rankin, M. O. (1965). The principle of short-circuiting of threat: Further evidence. *Journal of Personality, 33,* 622–635.

Lea, M., Spears, R., & de Groot, D. (2001). Knowing me, knowing you: Anonymity effects on social identity processes within groups. *Personality and Social Psychology Bulletin, 27,* 526–537.

Leahy, R. L., McGinn, L. K., Busch, F. N., & Milrod, B. L. (2005). Anxiety disorders. In G. O. Gabbard, J. S. Beck, & J. Holmes (Eds.), *Oxford textbook of psychotherapy* (pp. 137–161). London: Oxford University Press.

Leaper, C., Anderson, K. J., & Sanders, P. (1998). Moderators of gender effects on parents' talk to their children: A meta-analysis. *Developmental Psychology, 34,* 3–27.

Leary, M. R. (2004). The function of self-esteem in terror management theory and sociometer theory: Comment on Pyszczynski et al. (2004). *Psychological Bulletin, 130,* 478–482.

LeBlanc, M. M., & Barling, J. (2004). Workplace aggression. *Current Directions in Psychological Science, 13,* 9–12.

LeBlanc, M. M., Dupre, K. E., & Barling, J. (2006). Public-initiated violence. In K. E. Kelloway, J. Barling, & J. J. Hurrell (Eds.), *Handbook of workplace violence* (pp. 261–280). Thousand Oaks, CA: Sage.

Leckman, J. F., & Kim, Y. (2006). A primary candidate gene for obsessive-compulsive disorder. Archives of *General Psychiatry, 63,* 717–720.

LeDoux, J. E. (1995). Emotion: Clues from the brain. *Annual Review of Psychology, 46,* 209–235.

Lee, H. S., Nelms, J. L., Nguyen, M., Silver, R., & Lehman, M. N. (2003). The eye is necessary for a circadian rhythm in the suprachiasmatic nucleus. *Nature Neuroscience, 6,* 111–112.

Lee, J. L. C., Everitt, B. J., & Thomas, K. L. (2004). Independent cellular processes for hippocampal memory consolidation and reconsolidation. *Science, 304,* 839–843.

Lee, K., Ogunfowora, B., & Ashton, M. C. (2005). Personality traits beyond the big five: Are they within the HEXACO space? *Journal of Personality, 73,* 1437–1463.

Lee, K., Williams, L. M., Breakspear, M., & Gordon, E. (2003). Synchronous gamma activity: A review and contribution to an integrative neuroscience model of schizophrenia. *Brain Research Reviews, 41,* 57–78.

Lee, R. M., & Yoo, H. C. (2004). Structure and measurement of ethnic identity for Asian American college students. *Journal of Counseling Psychology, 51,* 263–269.

Lee, S., Colditz, G., Berkman, L., & Kawachi, I. (2003). Caregiving to children and grandchildren and risk of coronary heart disease in women. *American Journal of Public Health, 93,* 1939–1944.

Lee, V. E., Brooks-Gunn, J., & Schnur, E. (1988). Does Head Start work? A 1-year follow-up comparison of disadvantaged children attending Head Start, no preschool, and other preschool programs. *Developmental Psychology, 24,* 210–222.

Leeb, R. T., & Rejskind, F. G. (2004). Here's looking at you kid! A longitudinal study of perceived gender differences in mutual gaze behavior in young infants. *Sex Roles, 50*(1–2), 1–5.

Leff, J. (2006). Whose life is it anyway? Quality of life for long-stay patients discharged from psychiatric hospitals. In H. Katschnig, H. Freeman, & N. Sartorius (Eds.), *Quality of life in mental disorders* (2nd ed., pp. 247–255). New York: Wiley.

Legerstee, M., Anderson, D., & Schaffer, A. (1998). Five- and eight-month-old infants recognize their faces and voices as familiar and social stimuli. *Child Development, 69,* 37–50.

Lehman, D. R., Chiu, C., & Schaller, M. (2004). Psychology and culture. *Annual Review of Psychology, 55,* 689–714.

Lehman, H. E. (1967). Schizophrenia: IV. Clinical features. In A. M. Freedman, H. I. Kaplan, & H. S. Kaplan (Eds.), *Comprehensive textbook of psychiatry.* Baltimore: Williams & Wilkins.

Leibel, R. L., Rosenbaum, M., & Hirsch, J. (1995). Changes in energy expenditure resulting from altered body weight. *New England Journal of Medicine, 332*(10), 621–628.

Leibowitz, H. W., Brislin, R., Perlmutter, L., & Hennessy, R. (1969). Ponzo perspective illusion as a manifestation of space perception. *Science, 166,* 1174–1176.

Leibowitz, S. F. (1992). Neurochemical-neuroendocrine systems in the brain controlling macronutrient intake and metabolism. *TINS, 15,* 491–497.

Leichsenring, F., Rabung, S., & Leibing, E. (2004). The efficacy of short-term psychodynamic psychotherapy in specific psychiatric disorders: A meta-analysis. *Archives of General Psychiatry, 61,* 1208–1216.

Leigh, B. C., & Stacy, A. W. (2004). Alcohol expectancies and drinking in different age groups. *Addiction, 99,* 215–227.

Leiner, H. C., Leiner, A. L., & Dow, R. S. (1993). Cognitive and language functions of the human cerebellum. *Trends in Neuroscience, 16,* 444–447.

Leippe, M. R., Manion, A. P., & Romanczyk, A. (1992). Eyewitness persuasion: How and how well do fact finders judge the accuracy of adults' and children's memory reports? *Journal of Personality and Social Psychology, 63,* 181–197.

Lejuez, C. W., Hopko, D. R., Levine, S., Gholkar, R., & Collins, L. (2005). The therapeutic alliance in behavior therapy. *Psychotherapy: Theory, Research, Practice, and Training, 42,* 456–468.

Lemere, C. A., Maier, M., Jiang, L., Peng, Y., & Seabrook, T. J. (2006). Amyloid-beta immunotherapy for the prevention and treatment of Alzheimer disease: Lessons from mice, monkeys, and humans. *Rejuvenation Res., 9,* 77–84.

Lemmer, B., Kern, R. I., Nold, G., & Lohrer, H. (2002). Jet lag in athletes after eastward and westward time-zone transition. *Chronobiology International, 19,* 743–764.

Lemoine, P., Kermadi, I., Garcia-Acosta, S., Garay, R. P., & Dib, M. (2006). Double-blind, comparative study of cyamemazine vs. bromazepam in the benzodiazepine withdrawal syndrome. *Progress in Neuro-Psychopharmacology & Biological Psychiatry, 30,* 131–137.

Lenneberg, E. H. (1967). *Biological foundations of language.* New York: Wiley.

Lent, R. W., Brown, S. D., Talleyrand, R., McPartland, E. B., Davis, T., & Chopra, S. B. et al. (2002). Career choice barriers, supports, and coping strategies: College students' experiences. *Journal of Vocational Behavior, 60,* 61–72.

Lenzenweger, M. F., McLachlan, G., & Rubin, D. B. (2007). Resolving the latent structure of schizophrenia endophenotypes using expectation-maximization-based finite mixture modeling. *Journal of Abnormal Psychology, 116,* 16–29.

Leonard, B. E. (1992). *Fundamentals of psychopharmacology.* New York: Wiley.

Leonhardt, D. (2000, May 24). Makes sense to test for common sense. Yes? No? *New York Times.*

Leopold, D. (2002). Distortion of olfactory perception: Diagnosis and treatment. *Chemical Senses, 27,* 611–615.

LePage, J. P., DelBen, K., Pollard, S., McGhee, S., Vanhorn, L., Murphy, J., et al. (2003). Reducing assaults on an acute psychiatric unit using a token economy: A 2-year follow-up. *Behavioral Interventions, 18,* 179–190.

Lepore, L., & Brown, R. (1997). Category and stereotype activation: Is prejudice inevitable? *Journal of Personality and Social Psychology, 72,* 275–287.

Lepore, S. J. (1995). Cynicism, social support, and cardiovascular reactivity. *Health Psychology, 14,* 210–216.

Lepore, S. J., Evans, G., & Schneider, M. (1991). Dynamic role of social support in the link between chronic stress and psychological distress. *Journal of Personality and Social Psychology, 61,* 899–909.

Leppel, K., Williams, M. L., & Waldauer, C. (2001). The impact of parental occupation and socioeconomic status on choice of college major. *Journal of Family and Economic Issues, 22,* 373–394.

Lerner, J. S., Gonzalez, R. M., Small, D. A., & Fischhoff, B. (2003). Effects of fear and anger on perceived risks of terrorism: A national field experiment. *Psychological Science, 14,* 144–150.

Lettvin, J. Y., Maturana, H. R., McCulloch, W. S., & Pitts, W. H. (1959). What the frog's eye tells the frog's brain. *Proceedings of the Institute of Radio Engineers, 47,* 1940–1951.

Levant, R. F. (2005). Evidence-based practice in psychology. *Monitor on Psychology, 36,* 5.

LeVay, S. (1991). A difference in hypothalamic structure between heterosexual and homosexual men. *Science, 253,* 1034–1037.

Leve, L. D., Kim, H. K., & Pears, K. C. (2005). Childhood temperament and family environment as predictors of internalizing and externalizing trajectories from ages 5 to 17. *Journal of Abnormal Child Psychology, 33,* 505–520.

Levenson, H. (2003). Time-limited dynamic psychotherapy: An integrationist perspective. *Journal of Psychotherapy Integration, 13,* 300–333.

Levenson, R. W., Ekman, P., & Friesen, W. V. (1990). Voluntary facial action generates emotion-specific autonomic nervous system activity. *Psychophysiology, 27(4),* 363–384.

Levenson, R. W., Ekman, P., Heider, K., & Friesen, W. V. (1992). Emotion and autonomic nervous system activity in the Minangkabau of West Sumatra. *Journal of Personality and Social Psychology, 62(6),* 972–988.

Levenston, G. K., Patrick, C. J., Bradley, M. M., & Lang, P. J. (2000). The psychopath as observer: Emotion and attention in picture processing. *Journal of Abnormal Psychology, 109,* 373–385.

Levine, R. V., Martinez, T. M., Brase, G., & Sorenson, K. (1994). Helping in 36 U.S. cities. *Journal of Personality and Social Psychology, 67,* 69–82.

Levine, R., Sato, S., Hashimoto, T., & Verna, J. (1995). Love and marriage in eleven cultures. *Journal of Cross-Cultural Psychology, 26,* 554–571.

Levine, S. (1999, February 1). In a loud and noisy world, baby boomers pay the consequences. *International Herald Tribune.*

Levinson, D. F. (2006). The genetics of depression: A review. *Biological Psychiatry, 60,* 84–92.

Levinson, D. F., Evgrafov, O. V., Knowles, J. A., Potash, J. B., Weissman, M. M., Scheftner, W. A., et al. (2007). Genetics of recurrent early-onset major depression (GenRED): Significant linkage on chromosome 15q25-q26 after fine mapping with single nucleotide polymorphism markers. *American Journal of Psychiatry, 164,* 259–264.

Levinson, S. C. (1996). Language and space. *Annual Review of Anthropology, 25,* 353–382.

Levinthal, C. F. (2001). *Drugs, behavior, and modern society* (3rd ed.). Boston: Allyn & Bacon.

Levitt, P., Ebert, P., Mirnics, K., Nimgaonkar, V. L., & Lewis, D. A. (2006). Making the case for a candidate vulnerability gene in schizophrenia: Convergent evidence for regulator of g-protein signaling 4 (RGS4). *Biological Psychiatry, 60,* 534–537.

Levy, B. R., Slade, M. D., Kunkel, S. R., & Kasl, S. V. (2002). Longevity increased by positive self-perceptions of aging. *Journal of Personality & Social Psychology, 83(2),* 261–270.

Levy, D. A., Bayley, P. J., & Squire L. R. (2004). The anatomy of semantic knowledge: Medial vs. lateral temporal lobe. *Proceedings of the National Academies of Science, 101,* 6710–6715.

Levy, F., Hay, D. A., & Bennett, K. S. (2006). Genetics of attention deficit hyperactivity disorder: A current review and future prospectus. *International Journal of Disability, Development, and Education, 53,* 5–20.

Levy, G. D., Taylor, M. G., & Gelman, S. A. (1995). Traditional and evaluative aspects of flexibility in gender roles, social conventions, moral rules, and physical laws. *Child Development, 66,* 515–531.

Levy, K. N., Clarkin, J. F., Yeomans, F. E., Scott, L. N., Wasserman, R. H., & Kernberg, O. (2006). The mechanisms of change in the treatment of borderline personality disorder with transference focused psychotherapy. *Journal of Clinical Psychology, 62,* 481–501.

Levy-Shiff, R. (1994). Individual and contextual correlates of marital change across the transition to parenthood. *Developmental Psychology, 30,* 591–601.

Lewicki, P. (1992). Nonconscious acquisition of information. *American Psychologist, 47,* 796–801.

Lewin, T. (2003, October 29). A growing number of video viewers watch from crib. *New York Times,* p. 1.

Lewinsohn, P. M., Joiner, T. E., & Rohde, P. (2001). Evaluation of cognitive diathesis-stress models in precicting Major Depressive Disorder in adolescents. *Journal of Abnormal Psychology, 110,* 203–215.

Lewinsohn, P. M., & Rosenbaum, M. (1987). Recall of parental behavior by acute depressives, remitted depressives, and nondepressives. *Journal of Personality and Social Psychology, 52,* 611–619.

Lewis Claar, R., & Blumenthal, J. A. (2003). The value of stress-management interventions in life-threatening medical conditions. *Current Directions in Psychological Science, 12,* 133–137.

Lewis, J. W., Brefczynski, J. A., Phinney, R. E., Janik, J. J., & DeYoe, E. A. (2005). Distinct cortical pathways for processing tool versus animal sounds. *Journal of Neuroscience, 25(21),* 5148–5158.

Lewis, T. T., Everson-Rose, S. A., Powell, L. H., Matthews, K. A., Brown, C., Karavolos, K., et al. (2006). Chronic exposure to everyday discrimination and coronary artery calcification in African-American women: The SWAN heart study. *Psychosomatic Medicine, 68,* 362–368.

Lewontin, R. (1976). Race and intelligence. In N. J. Block & G. Dworkin (Eds.), *The IQ controversy: Critical readings.* New York: Pantheon.

Lewy, A. J., Lefler, B. J., Emens, J. S., & Bauer, V. K. (2006). The circadian basis of winter depression. *Proceedings of the National Academy of Sciences of the USA, 103,* 7414–7419.

Lezak, M. D., Loring, D. W., & Howieson, D. B. (2004). *Neuropsychological assessment* (4th ed.). New York: Oxford University Press.

Li, D-K., Petitti, D. B., Willinger, M., McMahon, R., Odouli, R., Vu, H., & Hoffman, H. J. (2003). Infant sleeping position and the risk of sudden infant death syndrome in California, 1997–2000. *American Journal of Epidemiology, 157,* 446–455.

Li, D.-K., Willinger, M., Petitti, D. B., Odouli, R., Liu, L., & Hoffman, H. J. (2006). Use of a dummy (pacifier) during sleep and risk of sudden infant death syndrome (SIDS): Population based case-control study. *British Medical Journal, 332,* 18–22.

Li, F., Harmer, P., McAuley, E., Duncan, T., Duncan, S. C., Chaumeton, N., & Fisher, K. J. (2001). An evaluation of the effects of Tai Chi exercise on physical function among older persons: A randomized controlled trial. *Annals of Behavioral Medicine, 23,* 139–146.

Li, G., Jack, C. R., Jr., & Yang, E. S. (2006). An fMRI study of somatosensory-implicated acupuncture points in stable somatosensory stroke patients. *Journal of Magnetic Resonance Imaging, 24,* 1018–1024.

Li, J. (2005). Mind or virtue: Western and Chinese beliefs about learning. *Current Directions in Psychological Science, 14,* 190–194.

Li, L. C., & Kim, B. S. K. (2004). Effects of counseling style and client adherence to Asian cultural values on counseling process with Asian American college students. *Journal of Counseling Psychology, 51,* 158–167.

Li, M. D. (2006). The genetics of nicotine dependence. *Current Psychiatry Reports, 8,* 158–164.

Li, N. P., & Kenrick, D. T. (2006). Sex similarities and differences in preferences for short-term mates: What, whether, and why. *Journal of Personality and Social Psychology, 90,* 468–489.

Li, S., Cullen, W., Anwyl, R., & Rowan, M. J. (2003). Dopamine-dependent facilitation of LTP induction in hippocampal CA1 by exposure to spatial novelty. *Nature Neuroscience, 6,* 526–531.

Li, S. C., Lindenberger, U., Hommel, B., Aschersleben, G., Prinz, W., & Baltes, P. B. (2004). Transformations in the couplings among intellectual abilities and constituent cognitive processes across the life span. *Psychological Science, 15,* 155–163.

Li, W., Piëch, V., & Gilbert, C. D. (2004). Perceptual learning and top-down influences in primary visual cortex. *Nature Neuroscience, 7,* 651–657.

Liao, H., & Rupp, D. E. (2005). The impact of justice climate and justice orientation on work outcomes: A cross-level multifoci framework. *Journal of Applied Psychology, 90,* 242–256.

Liben, L. (1978). Perspective-taking skills in young children: Seeing the world through rose-colored glasses. *Developmental Psychology, 14,* 87–92.

Liben-Nowell, D., Novak, J., Kumar, R., Raghaven, P., & Tomkins, A. (2005). Geographic routing in social networks. *Proceedings of the National Academy of Sciences of the USA, 102,* 11623–11628.

Lickey, M., & Gordon, B. (1991). *Medicine and mental illness: The use of drugs in psychiatry.* San Francisco: Freeman.

Lieberman, J. A., Stroup, T. S., McEvoy, J. P., Swartz, M. S., Rosenheck, R. A., Perkins, D. O., et al. (2005). Effectiveness of antipsychotic drugs in patients with chronic schizophrenia. *New England Journal of Medicine, 353,* 1209–1223.

Lieberman, J. A., Stroup, T. S., McEvoy, J. P., Swartz, M. S., Rosenheck, R. A., Perkins, D. O., et al. (2005). Effectiveness of antipsychotic drugs in patients with chronic schizophrenia. *New England Journal of Medicine, 353,* 1209–1223.

Lieberman, M. A. (1996). Perspective on adult life crises. In V. L. Bengtson (Ed.), *Adulthood and aging: Research on continuities and discontinuities* (pp. 146–168). New York: Springer.

Lieberman, M. A., & Tobin, S. (1983). *The experience of old age.* New York: Basic Books.

Lieberman, M. D., Ochsner, K. N., Gilbert, D. T., & Schacter, D. L. (2001). Do amnesics exhibit cognitive dissonance reduction? The role of explicit memory and attention in attitude change. *Psychological Science, 121,* 135–140.

Lieberman, P. (1991). *Uniquely human.* Cambridge: Harvard University Press.

Liechti, M. E., Gamma, A., & Vollenweider, F. X. (2001). Gender differences in the subjective effects of MDMA. *Psychopharmacology, 154,* 161–168.

Liepert, J., Bauder, H., Miltner, W. H. R., Taub, E., & Weiller, C. (2000). Treatment-induced cortical reorganization after stroke in humans. *Stroke, 31,* 1210.

Lievens, F., Harris, M. M., Van Keer, E., & Bisqueret, C. (2003). Predicting cross-cultural training performance: The validity of personality, cognitive ability, and dimensions measured by an assessment center and a behavior description interview. *Journal of Applied Psychology, 88,* 476–489.

Light, K. C., Girdler, S. S., Sherwood, A., Bragdon, E. E., Brownley, K. A., West, S. G., & Hinderliter, A. L. (1999). High stress responsivity predicts later blood pressure only in combination with positive family history and high life stress. *Hypertension, 33,* 1458–1464.

Light, L. L. (1991). Memory and aging: Four hypotheses in search of data. *Annual Review of Psychology, 42,* 333–376.

Lilienfeld, S. O. (2007). Psychological treatments that cause harm. *Perspectives on Psychological Science, 2,* 53–70.

Lilienfeld, S., Wood, J., & Garb, H. N. (2000). The scientific status of projective tests. *Psychological Science in the Public Interest, 1,* 27–66.

Lilienfeld, S. O., & Lynn, S. J. (2003). Dissociative identity disorder: Multiple personalities, multiple controversies. In S. O. Lilienfeld & S. J. Lynn (Eds.), *Science and pseudoscience in clinical psychology* (pp. 109–142). New York: Guilford.

Lilienfeld, S. O., Lynn, S. J., Kirsch, I., Chaves, J. F., Sarbin, T. R., Ganaway, G. K., & Powell, R. A. (1999). Dissociative identity disorder and the sociocognitive model: Recalling the lessons of the past. *Psychological Bulletin, 125,* 507–523.

Lim, B.-C., & Ployhart, R. E. (2004). Transformational leadership: Relations to the five-factor model and team performance in typical and maximum contexts. *Journal of Applied Psychology, 89,* 610–621.

Lim, R. F. (Ed.). (2006). *Clinical manual of cultural psychiatry.* Washington, DC: American Psychiatric Publishing, Inc.

Lim, S.-L., & Kim, J.-H. (2005). Cognitive processing of emotional information in depression, panic, and somatoform disorder. *Journal of Abnormal Psychology, 114,* 50–61.

Lim, V. K. G., Teo, T. S. H., & Loo, G. L. (2003). Sex, financial hardship and locus of control: An empirical study of attitudes towards money among Singaporean Chinese. *Personality and Individual Differences, 34,* 411–429.

Lin, K.-M. & Poland, R. E. (1995). Ethnicity, culture, and psychopharmacology. In F. E. Bloom & D. J. Kupfer (Eds.), *Psychopharmacology: The fourth generation of progress.* New York: Raven Press.

Lin, L., Umahara, M., York, D. A., & Bray, G. A. (1998). Beta-casomorphins stimulate and enterostatin inhibits the intake of dietary fat in rats. *Peptides, 19,* 325–331.

Lin, S., Thomas, T. C., Storlien, L. H., & Huang, X. F. (2000). Development of high fat diet-induced obesity and leptin resistance in C57Bl/6J mice. *International Journal of Obesity Related Metabolic Disorders, 24,* 639–646.

Lin, Y., & Raghubir, P. (2005). Gender differences in unrealistic optimism about marriage and divorce: Are men more optimistic and women more realistic? *Personality and Social Psychology Bulletin, 31,* 198–207.

Lindberg, N., Tani, P., Virkkunen, M., Porkka-Heiskanen, T., Appelberg, B., et al. (2005). Quantitative electroencephalographic measures in homicidal men with antisocial personality disorder. *Psychiatry Research, 136,* 7–15.

Linde, K., Streng, A., Jurgens, S., Hoppe, A., Brinkhaus, B., Witt, C., et al. (2005). Acupuncture for patients with migraine: A randomized controlled trial. *Journal of the American Medical Association, 293,* 2118–2125.

Lindsay, D. S., Hagen, L., Read, J. D., Wade, K., & Gary, M. (2004). True photographs and false memories. *Psychological Science, 15,* 149–154.

Lindsey, D. T., & Brown, A. M. (2006). Universality of color names. *Proceedings of the National Academy of Sciences, 103,* 16608–16613.

Lindvall, O., & Hagell, P. (2001). Cell therapy and transplantation in Parkinson's disease. *Clinical Chemistry and Laboratory Medicine, 39,* 356–361.

Linley, P. A., & Joseph, S. (Eds.). (2004). *Positive psychology in practice.* Hoboken, NJ: Wiley.

Linn, R. L., & Gronlund, N. E. (2000). *Measurement and assessment in teaching* (8th ed.). Upper Saddle River, NJ: Merrill/Prentice-Hall.

Linnet, K. M., Dalsgaard, S., Obel, C., Wisborg, K., Henriksen, T. B., Rodriguez, A., et al. (2003). Maternal lifestyle factors in pregnancy risk of attention deficit hyperactivity disorder and associated behaviors: Review of the current evidence. *American Journal of Psychiatry, 160,* 1028–1040.

Linnet, K. M., Wisborg, K., Obel, C., Secher, N. J., Thomsen, P. H, Agerbo, E., & Henriksen, T. B. (2005). Smoking during pregnancy and the risk for hyperkinetic disorder in offspring. *Pediatrics, 116,* 462–467.

Lippa, R. A. (2003). Are 2D:4D finger-length ratios related to sexual orientation?: Yes for men, no for women. *Journal of Personality and Social Psychology, 85,* 179–188.

Lira, A., Zhou, M., Castanon, N., Ansorge, M. S., Gordon, J. A., Francis, J. H., et al. (2003). Altered depression-related behaviors and functional changes in the dorsal raphe nucleus of serotonin transporter-deficient mice. *Biological Psychiatry, 54,* 960–971.

Lisanby, S. H. (Ed.). (2004). *Brain stimulation in psychiatric treatment.* Washington, DC: American Psychiatric Association.

Lisspers, J., Sundin, Ö., Öhman, A., Hofman-Bang, C., Rydén, L., & Nygren, Å. (2005). Long-term effects of lifestyle behavior change in coronary artery disease: Effects on recurrent coronary events after percutaneous coronary intervention. *Health Psychology, 24,* 41–48.

Littlewood, R. (1992). Psychiatric diagnosis and racial bias: Empirical and interpretative approaches. *Social Science & Medicine, 34,* 141–149.

Liu, J., Raine, A., Venables, P. H.,& Mednick, S. A. (2004). Malnutrition at age 3 years and externalizing behavior problems at ages 8, 11, and 17 years. *American Journal of Psychiatry, 161,* 2005–2013.

Liu, S., Prince, M., Blizard, B., & Mann, A. (2002). The prevalence of psychiatric morbidity and its associated factors in general health care in Taiwan. *Psychological Medicine, 32,* 629–637.

Liu, Y., Gao, J.-H., Liu, H.-L., & Fox, P. (2000). The temporal response of the brain after eating revealed by functional MRI. *Nature, 405,* 1058–1062.

Lively, W. M. (2001). Syncope and neurologic deficits in a track athlete: A case report. *Medicine and Science in Sports and Exercise, 33,* 345–347.

Livesley, W. J. (2005). Behavioral and molecular genetic contributions to a dimensional classification of personality disorders. *Journal of Personality Disorders, 19,* 131–155.

Livingstone, M. S., & Hubel, D. H. (1987). Psychological evidence for separate channels for the perception of form, color, movement and depth. *Journal of Neuroscience, 7,* 3416–3468.

Lleras, A., & Moore, C. M. (2006). What you see is what you get: Functional equivalence of a perceptually filled-in surface and a physically presented stimulus. *Psychological Science, 17,* 876–881.

Lochman, J. E., & Wells, K.,C. (2004). The coping power program for preadolescent aggressive boys and their parents: Outcome effects at 1-year follow-up. *Journal of Consulting and Clinical Psychology, 72,* 571–578.

Locke, E. A. (2000). Motivation, cognition, and action: An analysis of studies of task goals and knowledge. *Applied Psychology: An International Review, 49,* 408–429.

Locke, E. A., & Latham G. P. (1990). *A theory of goal setting & task performance.* Englewood Cliffs, NJ: Prentice Hall.

Locke, E. A., & Latham, G. P. (2002). Building a practically useful theory of goal setting and task motivation: A 35-year odyssey. *American Psychologist, 57,* 705–717.

Locurto, C. (1991). Beyond IQ in preschool programs? *Intelligence, 15,* 295–312.

Loeber, R., & Stouthamer-Loeber, M. (1998). Development of juvenile aggression and violence. Some common misconceptions and controversies. *American Psychologist, 53,* 242–259.

Loehlin, J. C. (1989). Partitioning environmental and genetic contributions to behavioral development. *American Psychologist, 44,* 1285–1292.

Loehlin, J. C. (1992). *Genes and environment in personality development.* Newbury Park, CA: Sage.

Loehlin, J. C., Neiderhiser, J. M., & Reiss, D. (2003). The behavior genetics of personality and the NEAD study. *Journal of Research in Personality, 37,* 373–387.

McDougall, S. J. P., de Bruijn, O., & Curry, M. B. (2000). Exploring the effects of icon characteristics on user performance: The role of icon concreteness, complexity, and distinctiveness. *Journal of Experimental Psychology: Applied, 6,* 291–306.

McDougall, W. (1908). *An introduction to social psychology.* London: Methuen.

McEvoy, G. M., & Beatty, R. W. (1989). Assessment centers and subordinate appraisals of managers: A seven-year examination of predictive validity. *Personnel Psychology, 42,* 37–52.

McEvoy, S. P., Stevenson, M. R., McCartt, A. T., Woodward, M., Haworth, C., Palamara, P., & Cercarelli, R. (2005). Role of mobile phones in motor vehicle crashes resulting in hospital attendance: A case-crossover study. *British Medical Journal, 331,* 428.

McFadden, D., & Pasanen, E. G. (1998). Comparison of the auditory systems of heterosexuals and homosexuals: Click-evoked otoacoustic emissions. *Proceedings of the National Academy of Science USA, 95,* 2709–2713.

McGarvey, C., McDonnell, M., Hamilton, K., O'Regan, M., & Matthews, T. (2006). An 8-year study of risk factors for SIDS: Bed-sharing versus non-bed-sharing. *Archives of Disease in Childhood, 91,* 318–323.

McGaugh, J. L. (2003). *Memory and emotion.* New York: Columbia University Press.

McGechan, A., & Wellington, K. (2005). Ramelteon. *CNS Drugs, 19,* 1057–1065.

McGehee, D. S., Heath, M. J. S., Gelber, S., Devay, P., & Role, L. W. (1995). Nicotine enhancement of fast excitatory synaptic transmissions in CNS by presynaptic receptors. *Science, 269,* 1692–1696.

McGlashan, T. H., & Hoffman, R. E. (2000). Schizophrenia as a disorder of reduced synaptic connectivity. *Archives of General Psychiatry, 57,* 637–648.

McGlone, J. (1980). Sex differences in human brain asymmetry: A critical survey. *The Behavioral and Brain Sciences, 3,* 215–263.

McGlynn, F. D., Smitherman, T. A., & Gothard, K. D. (2004). Comment on the status of systematic desensitization. *Behavior Modification, 28,* 194–205.

McGlynn, S. M. & Schacter, D. L. (1989). Unawareness of deficits in neuropsychological syndromes. *Journal of Clinical and Experimental Neuropsychology, 11*(2), 143–205.

McGorry, P. D., Yung, A. R., Phillips, L. J., Yuen, H. P., Francey, S., Cosgrave, E. M., et al. (2002). Randomized controlled trial of interventions designed to reduce the risk of progression to first-episode psychosis in a clinical sample with subthreshold symptoms. *Archives of General Psychiatry, 59,* 921–928.

McGowan, E., Eriksen, J., & Hutton, M. (2006). A decade of modeling Alzheimer's disease in transgenic mice. *Trends in Genetics: TIG, 22,* 281–289.

McGue, M. (1992). When assessing twin concordance, use the probandwise not the pairwise rate. *Schizophrenia Bulletin, 18,* 171–176.

McGue, M. (1999). The behavioral genetics of alcoholism. *Current Directions in Psychological Science, 8,* 109–115.

McGue, M., Bouchard, T. J., Jr., Iacono, W. G., & Lykken, D. T. (1993). Behavioral genetics of cognitive ability: A life-span perspective. In R. Plomin & G. E. McClearn (Eds.), *Nature, nurture and psychology* (pp. 59–76). Washington, DC: American Psychological Association.

McGue, M., Elkins, I., Walden, B., & Iacono, W. G. (2005). Perceptions of the parent-adolescent relationship: A longitudinal investigation. *Developmental Psychology, 41,* 971–984.

McGuffin, P., Rijsdijk, F., Andrew, M., Sham, P., Katz, R., & Cardno, A. (2003). The heritability of bipolar affective disorder and the genetic relationship to unipolar depression. *Archives of General Psychiatry, 60,* 497–502.

McIntosh, J. L. (2003). U.S.A. Suicide: 2003 official final data. American Association of Suicidology website. Retrieved August 21, 2006, from http://www.suicidology.org/displaycommon.cfm?an=1&subarticlenbr=21.

McLendon, D., McLendon, T, & Petr, C. G. (2005). Family-directed structural therapy. *Journal of Marital & Family Therapy, 31,* 327–339.

McLeod, J. D., Kessler, R. C., & Landis, K. R. (1992). Speed of recovery from major depressive episodes in a community sample of married men and women. *Journal of Abnormal Psychology, 101,* 277–286.

McLeod, P., Reed, N., & Dienes, Z. (2003). Psychophysics: How fielders arrive in time to catch the ball. *Nature, 426,* 244–245.

McLoyd, V. C. (1998). Socioeconomic disadvantage and child development. *American Psychologist, 53,* 185–204.

McMahon, P. (2000, January 31). Oregon man leads life without frills, leaves $9 million to charities, children. *USA Today,* p. 4A.

McNally, R. J. (2003). Recovering memories of trauma: A view from the laboratory. *Current Directions in Psychological Science, 12,* 32–35.

McNally, R. J. (2007). Mechanisms of exposure therapy: How neuroscience can improve psychological treatments for anxiety disorders. *Clinical Psychology Review, 27,* 750–759.

McNally, R. J., & Amir, N. (1996). Perceptual implicit memory for trauma-related information in post-traumatic stress disorder. *Cognition & Emotion, 10,* 551–556.

McNally, R. J., Clancy, S. A., Barrett, H. M., & Parker, H. A. (2005). Reality monitoring in adults reporting repressed, recovered, or continuous memories of childhood sexual abuse. *Journal of Abnormal Psychology, 114,* 147–152.

McNally, R. J., Clancy, S. A., & Schacter, D. L. (2001). Directed forgetting of trauma cues in adults reporting repressed or recovered memories of childhood sexual abuse. *Journal of Abnormal Psychology, 110,* 151–156.

McNally, R. J., Clancy, S. A., Schacter, D. L., & Pittman, R. K. (2000a). Cognitive processing of trauma cues in adults reporting repressed, recovered, or continuous memories of childhood sexual abuse. *Journal of Abnormal Psychology, 109,* 355–359.

McNally, R. J., Clancy, S. A., Schacter, D. L., & Pittman, R. K. (2000b). Personality profiles, dissociation, and absorption in women reporting repressed, recovered, or continuous memories of childhood sexual abuse. *Journal of Consulting and Clinical Psychology, 68,* 1033–1037.

McNay, E. C., McCarty, R. C., & Gold, P. E. (2001). Fluctuations in brain glucose concentration during behavioral testing: Dissociations between brain areas and between brain and blood. *Neurobiology of Learning and Memory, 75,* 325–337.

McNeil, D. W., & Zvolensky, M. J. (2000). Systematic desensitization. In A. E. Kazdin (Ed.), *Encyclopedia of psychology* (Vol.7, pp. 533–535). Washington, DC: American Psychological Association.

McNeil, J. E., & Warrington, E. K. (1993). Prosopagnosia: A face-specific disorder. *Quarterly Journal of Experimental Psychology: Human Experimental Psychology, 46A*(1), 1–10.

McNelis, P. D. (2004). *Neural networks in finance: Gaining predictive edge in the market.* New York: Academic Press.

McNulty, J. K., & Karney, B. R. (2004). Positive expectations in the early years of marriage: Should couples expect the best or brace for the worst? *Journal of Personality and Social Psychology, 86,* 729–743.

McPhail, T. L., & Penner, L. A. (1995, August). *Can similarity moderate the effects of aversive racism?* Paper presented at the 103rd annual meeting of the American Psychological Association, New York.

McQuaid, J. R., Granholm, E., McClure, F. S., Roepke, S., Pedrelli, P., Patterson, T. L., et al. (2000). Development of an integrated cognitive-behavioral and social skills training intervention for older patients with schizophrenia. *Journal of Psychotherapy Practice and Research, 9,* 149–156.

McQuaid, J. R., Monroe, S. M., Roberts, J. E., Kupfer, D. J., & Frank, E. (2000). A comparison of two life stress assessment approaches: Prospective prediction of treatment outcome in recurrent depression. *Journal of Abnormal Psychology, 109,* 787–791.

McTigue, K. M., Harris, R., Hemphill, B., Lux, L., Sutton, S., Bunton, A. J., & Lohr, K. N. (2003). Screening and interventions for obesity in adults: Summary of the evidence for the U.S. Preventive Services Task Force. *Annals of Internal Medicine, 139,* 933–949.

Medin, D. L., Ross, B. H., & Markman, A. B. (2001). *Cognitive psychology* (3rd ed.). Fort Worth, TX: Harcourt.

Medina-Mora, M. E, Borges, G., Lara, C., Benjet, C., Blanco, J., et al. (2005). Prevalence, service use, and demographic correlates of 12-month DSM-IV psychiatric disorders in Mexico: Results from the Mexican National Comorbidity Study. *Psychological Medicine, 35,* 1773–1783.

Medsker, G. J., Katkowski, D. A., & Furr, D. (2003). Income and employment survey results for the Society of Industrial and Organizational Psychology. *Industrial Psychologist, 43,* 36–54.

Mehl, M. R. & Pennebaker, J. W. (2003). The social dynamics of a cultural upheaval: Social interactions surrounding September 11, 2001. *Psychological Science, 14,* 579–585.

Meichenbaum, D. (1977). *Cognitive behavior modification: An integrative approach.* New York: Plenum.

Meichenbaum, D. H. (1995). Cognitive-behavioral therapy in historical perspective. In B. Bongar & L. E. Beutler (Eds.), *Comprehensive textbook of psychotherapy: Theory and practice* (pp. 140–158). New York: Oxford University Press.

Melamed, S. Fried, Y., & Froom, P. (2001). The interactive effect of chronic exposure to noise and job complexity on changes in blood pressure and job satisfaction: A longitudinal study of industrial employees. *Journal of Occupational Health Psychology, 6,* 182–195.

Melamed, S., Shirom, A., Toker, S., Berliner, S., & Shapira, I. (2006). Burnout and risk of cardiovascular disease: Evidence, possible causal paths, and promising research directions. *Psychological Bulletin, 132,* 327–353.

Melander, H., Ahlqvist-Rastad, J., Meijer, G., & Beerman, B. (2003). Evidence b(i)ased medicine—selective reporting from studies sponsored by pharmaceutical industry: Review of studies in new drug applications. *British Medical Journal, 326,* 1171–1173.

Melchart, D., Streng, A., Hoppe, A., Brinkhaus, B., Witt, C., Wagenpfeil, S., et al. (2005). Acupuncture in patients with tension-type headache: Randomised controlled trial. *British Medical Journal, 331,* 376–382.

Melchior, C. L. (1990). Conditioned tolerance provides protection against ethanol lethality. *Pharmacology, Biochemistry and Behavior, 37,* 205–206.

Melzack, R., & Wall, P. D. (1965). Pain mechanisms: A new theory. *Science, 150,* 971–979.

Memon, A., Vrij, A., & Bull, R. (2004). *Psychology and law: Truthfulness, accuracy and credibility* (2nd ed.). New York: Wiley.

Menaker, M., & Vogelbaum, M. A. (1993). Mutant circadian period as a marker of suprachiasmatic nucleus function. *Journal of Biological Rhythms, 8,* 93–98.

Mendez, I., Sanchez-Pernaute, R., Cooper, O., Vinuela, A., Ferrari, D., Bjorklund, L., et al. (2005). Cell type analysis of functional fetal dopamine cell suspension transplants in the striatum and substantia nigra of patients with Parkinson's disease. *Brain, 128,* 1498–1510.

Mendlowicz, M. V., Rapaport, M. H., Thompson, P., Kelsoe, J. R., Golshan, S., Judd, L. L., et al. (1998). A comparison of descriptive characteristics of male outpatients and inpatients with affective disorders. *International Clinical Psychopharmacology, 13,* 245–252.

Meng, C. F., Wang, D., Ngeow, J., Lao, L., Peterson, M., & Paget, S. (2003). Acupuncture for chronic low back pain in older patients: A randomized, controlled trial. *Rheumatology (Oxford), 42,* 1508–1517.

Mennella, J. A., & Beauchamp, G. K. (1996). The human infant's response to vanilla flavors in mother's milk and formula. *Infant Behavior and Development, 19,* 13–19.

Menon, G. J., Rahman, I., Menon, S. J., & Dutton, G. N. (2003). Complex visual hallucinations in the visually impaired: The Charles Bonnet syndrome. *Survey Ophthalmology, 48,* 58–72.

Menzies, D., Nair, A., Williamson, P. A., Schembri, S., Al-Khairalla, M. Z., Barnes, M., et al. (2006). Respiratory symptoms, pulmonary function, and markers of inflammation among bar workers before and after a legislative ban on smoking in public places. *Journal of the American Medical Association, 296,* 1742–1748.

Mercer, C. H., Fenton, K. A., Johnson, A. M., Wellings, K., Macdowall, W., McManus, et al. (2003). Sexual function problems and help seeking behaviour in Britain: National probability sample survey. *British Medical Journal, 327,* 426–427.

Merchant, J. A., & Lundell, J. A. (2001). *Workplace violence: A report to the nation.* Iowa City: University of Iowa.

Merckelbach, H., Devilly, G. J., & Rassin, E. (2002). Alters in dissociative identity disorder: Metaphors or genuine entities? *Clinical Psychology Review, 22,* 481–497.

Merikangas, K. R., Akiskal, H. S., Angst, J., Greenberg, P. E., Hirschfeld, R. M. A., Petukhova, M., & Kessler, R. C. (2007). Lifetime and 12-month prevalence of bipolar spectrum disorder in the national comorbidity survey replication. *Archives of General Psychiatry, 64,* 543–552.

Merritt, M. M., Bennett, G. G., Jr, Williams, R. B., Edwards, C. L., & Sollers, J. J., III. (2006). Perceived racism and cardiovascular reactivity and recovery to personally relevant stress. *Health Psychology, 25,* 364–369.

Mesman, J., & Koot, H. M. (2000). Common and specific correlates of preadolescent internalizing externalizing psychopathology. *Journal of Abnormal Psychology, 109,* 428–437.

Mesquita, B., & Frijda, N. H. (1992). Cultural variations in emotions: A review. *Psychological Bulletin, 112,* 179–204.

Messer, S. B. (2004). Evidence-based practice: Beyond empirically supported treatments. *Professional Psychology: Research and Practice, 35,* 580–588.

Messer, S. B., & Kaplan, A. H. (2004). Outcomes and factors related to efficacy of brief psychodynamic therapy. In D. P. Charman (Ed.), *Core processes in brief psychodynamic psychotherapy: Advancing effective practice* (pp. 103–118). Mahwah, NJ: Erlbaum.

Messick, S. (1989). Validity. In R. Linn (Ed.), *Educational measurement* (3rd ed., pp. 13–103). New York: American Council on Education/Macmillan.

Messinger, A., Squire, L. R., Zola, S. M., & Albright, T. D. (2001). Neuronal representations of stimulus associations develop in the temporal lobe during learning. *Proceedings of the National Academy of Science, 98,* 12239–12244.

Messinger, D. S., Bauer, C. R., Das, A., Seifer, R., Lester, B. M., Lagasse, L. L., et al. (2004). The maternal lifestyle study: Cognitive, motor, and behavioral outcomes of cocaine-exposed and opiate-exposed infants through three years of age. *Pediatrics, 113,* 1677–1685.

Mesulam, M. M. (1990). Large-scale neurocognitive networks and distributed processing for attention, language, and memory. *Annals of Neurology, 28*(5), 597–613.

Mesulam, M. M. (2001). Primary progressive aphasia. *Annals of Neurolology, 49*(4), 425–423.

Metzinger, T. (Ed.). (2000). *Neural correlates of consciousness: Empirical and conceptual questions.* Cambridge: MIT Press.

Meyer, B. H. F. L., Ehrhardt, A. A., Rosen, L. R., & Gruen, R. S. (1995). Prenatal estrogens and the development of homosexual orientation. *Developmental Psychology, 31*(1), 12–21.

Meyer, G. J., Finn, S. E., Eyde, L. D., Kay, G. G., Moreland, K. L., Dies, R. R., et al. (2001). Psychological testing and psychological assessment: A review of evidence and issues. *American Psychologist, 56,* 128–165.

Meyer, G. J., Mihura, J. L., & Smith, B. L. (2005). The interclinician reliability of Rorschach interpretation in four data sets. *Journal of Personality Assessment, 84,* 296–314.

Meyer, I. H. (2003). Prejudice, social stress, and mental health in lesbian, gay, and bisexual populations: Conceptual issues and research evidence. *Psychological Bulletin, 129,* 674–697.

Meyer, J. D., & Salovey, P. (1997). What is emotional intelligence? In P. Salovey & D. Sluyter (Eds.), *Emotional development and emotional intelligence* (pp. 3–31). New York: Basic Books.

Meyer, R. G. (1975). A behavioral treatment of sleepwalking associated with test anxiety. *Behavior Therapy and Experimental Psychiatry, 6,* 167–168.

Meyer, U., Feldon, J., Schedlowski, M., & Yee, B. K. (2005). Toward and immuno-precipitated neurodevelopmental animal model of schizophrenia. *Neuroscience & Biobehavioral Reviews, 29,* 913–947.

Mezey, E., Key, S., Vogelsang, G., Szalayova, I., Lange, G. D., & Crain, B. (2003). Transplanted bone marrow generates new neurons in human brains. *Proceedings of the National Academy of Sciences, 100,* 1364–1369.

Mezulis, A. H., Abramson, L. Y., Hyde, J. S., & Hankin, B. L. (2004). Is there a universal positivity bias in attributions? A meta-analytic review of individual, developmental, and cultural differences in the self-serving attributional bias. *Psychological Bulletin, 130,* 711–747.

Mezzacappa, E. S., Katkin, E. S. & Palmer, S. N. (1999). Epinephrine, arousal and emotion: A new look at two-factor theory. *Cognition and Emotion, 13,* 181–199.

Michael, R. T., Wadsworth, J., Feinleib, J., Johnson, A. M., Laumann, E. O., & Wellings, K. (1998). Private sexual behavior, public opinion, and public health policy related to sexually transmitted diseases: A US-British comparison. *American Journal of Public Health, 88,* 749–754.

Michel, C., Rossion, B., Han, J., Chung, C.-S., & Caldara, R. (2006). Holistic processing is finely tuned for faces of one's own race. *Psychological Science, 17,* 608–615.

Mick, E., Biederman, J., Prince, J., Fischer, M. J., & Faraone, S. V. (2002). Impact of low birth weight on attention-deficit hyperactivity disorder. *Journal of Developmental and Behavioral Pediatrics, 23,* 16–22.

Middeldorp, C. M., Cath, D. C., Van Dyck, R., & Boomsma, D. I., (2005). The co-morbidity of anxiety and depression in the perspective of genetic epidemiology: A review of twin and family studies. *Psychological Medicine, 35,* 611–6224.

Midlarsky, E., Jones, S., & Corley, R. (2005). Personality correlates of heroic rescue during the holocaust. *Journal of Personality, 73,* 907–934.

Miklowitz, D. J., & Alloy, L. B. (1999). Psychosocial factors in the course and treatment of bipolar disorder: Introduction to the special section. *Journal of Abnormal Psychology, 108,* 555–557.

Miklowitz, D. J., Otto, M. W., Frank, E., Reilly Harrington, N. A., Wisniewski, S. R., Kogan, J. N., et al. (2007). Psychosocial treatments for bipolar depression. *Archives of General Psychiatry, 64,* 419–426.

Mikulincer, M. & Shaver, P. R. (2005). Mental representations of attachment security: Theoretical foundation for a positive social psychology. In M. W.Baldwin (Ed.), *Interpersonal cognition* (pp. 233–266). New York: Guilford Press.

Milak, M. S., Parsey, R. V., Keilp, J., Oquendo, M. A., Malone, K. M., & Mann, J. J. (2005). Neuroanatomic correlates of psychopathologic components of major depressive disorder. *Archives of General Psychiatry, 62,* 397–408.

Milev, P., Ho, B. C., Arndt, S., & Andreasen, N. C. (2005). Predictive values of neurocognition and negative symptoms on functional outcome in schizophrenia: A longitudinal first-episode study with 7-year follow-up. *American Journal of Psychiatry, 162,* 495–506.

Milgram, N. W., Siwak-Tapp, C. T., Araujo, J., & Head, E. (2006). Neuroprotective effects of cognitive enrichment. *Ageing Research Reviews, 5,* 354–369.

Milgram, S. (1963). Behavioral study of obedience. *Journal of Abnormal and Social Psychology, 67,* 371–378.

Milgram, S. (1965). Some conditions of obedience and disobedience to authority. *Human Relations, 18,* 57–76.

Milgram, S. (1974). *Obedience to authority.* New York: Harper & Row.

Milgram, S. (1977, October). Subject reaction: The neglected factor in the ethics of experimentation. *Hastings Center Report* (pp. 19–23).

Milisen, K., Braes, T., Fick, D. M., & Foreman, M. D. (2006). Cognitive assessment and differentiating the 3 Ds (dementia, depression, delirium). *Nursing Clinics of North America, 41*(1), 1–22.

Millar, H. R., Wardell, F., Vyvyan, J. P., Naji, S. A., Prescott, G. J., & Eagles, J. M. (2005). Anorexia nervosa mortality in Northeast Scotland, 1965–1999. *American Journal of Psychiatry, 162,* 753–757.

Miller, C. L., Miceli, P. J., Whitman, T. L., & Borkowski, J. G. (1996). Cognitive readiness to parent and intellectual-emotional development in children of adolescent mothers. *Developmental Psychology, 32,* 533–541.

Miller, D. D., McEvoy, J. P., Davis, S. M., Caroff, S. N., Saltz, B. L., Chakos, M. H., et al. (2005). Clinical correlates of tardive dyskinesia in schizophrenia: Baseline data from the CATIE schizophrenia trial. *Schizophrenia Research, 80,* 33–43.

Miller, G. (1956). The magical number seven, plus or minus two: Some limits on our capacity to process information. *Psychological Review, 63,* 81–97.

Miller, G. (2003). Spying on the brain, one neuron at a time. *Science, 300,* 78.

Miller, G. (2006). The unseen: Mental illness's global toll. *Science, 311,* 458–461.

Miller, G. A. (1991). *The science of words.* New York: Scientific American Library.

Miller, G. A., Heise, G. A., & Lichten, W. (1951). The intelligibility of speech as a function of the context of the test materials. *Journal of Experimental Psychology, 41,* 329–335.

Miller, J. (2001). The cultural grounding of social psychological theory. In A. Tesser & N. Schwarz (Eds.), *Blackwell handbook of social psychology: Intraindividual processes* (pp. 22–43). Oxford, UK: Blackwell.

Miller, J. D., Lynam, D., Zimmerman, R. S., Logan, T. K., Leukefeld, C., & Clayton, R. (2004). The utility of the Five Factor Model in understanding risky sexual behavior. *Personality and Individual Differences, 36,* 1611–1626.

Miller, J. G. (1994). Cultural diversity in the morality of caring: Individually oriented versus duty-based interpersonal moral codes. *Cross-cultural Research, 28,* 3–39.

Miller, J. G. (2002). Bringing culture to basic psychological theory—Beyond individualism and collectivism: Comment on Oyserman et al. *Psychological Bulletin, 128,* 97–109.

Miller, J. G., & Bersoff, D. M. (1994). Cultural influences on the moral status of reciprocity and the discounting of endogenous motivation. *Personality and Social Psychology Bulletin, 20,* 592–607.

Miller, K. F., Smith, C. M., Zhu, J., & Zhang, H. (1995). Preschool origins of cross-national differences in mathematical competence: The role of number-naming systems. *Psychological Science, 6,* 56–60.

Miller, L. A., Taber, K. H., Gabbard, G. O., & Hurley, R. A. (2005). Neural underpinnings of fear and its modulation: Implications for anxiety disorders. *Journal of Neuropsychiatry & Clinical Neuroscience, 17,* 1–6.

Miller, L. C., Putcha-Bhagavatula, A., & Pedersen, W. C. (2002). Men's and women's mating preferences: Distinct evolutionary mechanisms? *Current Directions in Psychological Science, 11,* 88–93.

Miller, L. K. (1999). The savant syndrome: Intellectual impairment and exceptional skill. *Psychological Bulletin, 125,* 31–46.

Miller, L. T., & Vernon, P. A. (1992). The general factor in short-term memory, intelligence, and reaction time. *Intelligence, 16,* 5–29.

Miller, M. M., & McEwen, B. S. (2006). Establishing an agenda for translational research on PTSD. *Annals of the New York Academy of Sciences, 1071,* 294–312.

Miller, N. E. (1959). Liberalization of basic S-R concepts: Extensions to conflict behavior, motivation, and social learning. In S. Koch (Ed.), *Psychology: A study of science* (Vol. 2, pp. 196–292). New York: McGraw-Hill.

Miller, P., Slawinski, J., Blessing, J., & Schwartz, S. (2006). Gender differences in high-school students' views about science. *International Journal of Science Education, 28,* 363–381.

Miller, T. Q., Heath, L., Molcan, J. R., & Dugoni, B. L. (1991). Imitative violence in the real world: A reanalysis of homicide rates following championship prize fights. *Aggressive Behavior, 17,* 121–134.

Miller, W. R., & Rollnick, S. (2002). *Motivational interviewing: Preparing people for change* (2nd ed.). New York: Guilford.

Millon, T., & Davis, R. D. (1996). *Disorders of personality. DSM-IV and beyond* (2nd ed.). New York: Wiley.

Milner, B. (1965). Visually-guided maze learning in man: Effects of bilateral hippocampal, bilateral frontal, and unilateral cerebral lesions. *Neuropsychologia, 3,* 317–338.

Milner, B. (1966). Amnesia following operation on temporal lobes. In C. W. M. Whitty & O. L. Zangwill (Eds.), *Amnesia.* London: Butterworth.

Milner, B. (2005). The medial temporal-lobe amnesic syndrome. *Psychiatric Clinics of North America, 28*(3), 599–611.

Milner, D. (1983). *Children and race.* Beverly Hills, CA: Sage.

Miltenberger, R. G. (2003). *Behavior modification: Principles and procedures* (3rd ed.). Pacific Grove, CA: Wadsworth.

Mineka, S., & Zinbarg, R. (2006). A contemporary learning theory perspective on the etiology of anxiety disorders: It's not what you thought it was. *American Psychologist, 61,* 10–26.

Ming, E. E., Adler, G. K., Kessler, R. C., Fogg, L. F., Matthews, K. A., Herd, J. A., & Rose, R. M. (2004). Cardiovascular reactivity to work stress predicts subsequent onset of hypertension: The air traffic controller health change study. *Psychosomatic Medicine, 66,* 459–465.

Minsky, S., Vega, W., Miskimen, T., Gara, M., & Escobar, J. (2003). Diagnostic patterns in Latino, African American, and European American psychiatric patients. *Archives of General Psychiatry, 60,* 637–644.

Minuzzi, L., Nomikos, G. G., Wade, M. R., Jensen, S. B., Olsen, A. K., & Cumming, P. (2005). Interaction between LSD and dopamine D2/3 binding sites in pig brain. *Synapse, 56,* 198–204.

Miotto, K., Darakjian, J., Basch, J., Murray, S., Zogg, J., & Rawson, R. (2001). Gamma-hydroxybutyric acid: Patterns of use, effects and withdrawal. *American Journal on Addictions, 10,* 232–241.

Miranda, J., & Green, B. L. (1999). The need for mental health services research focusing on poor young women. *Journal of Mental Health Policy and Economics, 2,* 73–89.

Mischel, W. (2004a). *Introduction to personality: Toward an integration.* Hoboken, NJ: Wiley.

Mischel, W. (2004b). Toward an integrative science of the person. *Annual Review of Psychology, 55,* 1–22.

Mitchell, D. B. (1991). Implicit memory, explicit theories. *Contemporary Psychology, 36,* 1060–1061.

Mitchell, D. B. (2006). Nonconscious priming after 17 years: Invulnerable implicit memory? *Psychological Science, 17,* 925–929.

Mitchell, J. T., & Nelson-Gray, R. O. (2006). Attention-deficit/hyperactivity disorder symptoms in adults: Relationship to Gray's Behavioral Approach System. *Personality and Individual Differences, 40,* 749–760.

Mitchell, K. J., & Zaragoza, M. S. (1996). Repeated exposure to suggestion and false memory: The role of contextual variability. *Journal of Memory and Learning, 35,* 246–260.

Mitra, M., Wilber, N., Allen, D., & Walker, D. K. (2005). Prevalence and correlates of depression as a secondary condition among disabilities. *American Journal of Orthopsychiatry, 75,* 76–85.

Mitte, K. (2005a). A meta-analysis of the efficacy of psycho- and pharmacotherapy in panic disorder with and without agoraphobia. *Journal of Affective Disorders, 88,* 27–45.

Mitte, K. (2005b). Meta-analysis of cognitive-behavioral treatments for generalized anxiety disorder: A comparison with pharmacotherapy. *Psychological Bulletin, 131,* 785–795.

Miura, I. T., Okomoto, Y., Kim, C. C., Steere, M., & Fayol, M. (1993). First graders' cognitive representation of number and understanding of place value. *Journal of Educational Psychology, 81,* 109–114.

Miyamoto, Y., & Kitayama, S. (2002). Cultural variation in correspondence bias: The critical role of attitude diagnosticity of socially constrained behavior. *Journal of Personality and Social Psychology, 83,* 1239–1248.

Miyamoto, Y., Nisbett, R. E., & Masuda, T. (2006). Culture and the physical environment: Holistic versus analytic perceptual affordances. *Psychological Science, 17,* 113–119.

Moen, P., Erickson, W. A., Agarwal, M., Fields, V., & Todd, L. (2000). *The Cornell Retirement and Well-Being Study. Final Report.* Ithaca, NY: Cornell University.

Moffitt, T. E. (2002). Teen-aged mothers in contemporary Britain. *Journal of Child Psychology & Psychiatry & Allied Disciplines, 43,* 727–742.

Moffitt, T. E., Caspi, A., & Rutter, M. (2005). Strategy for investigating interactions between measured genes and measured environments. *Archives of General Psychiatry, 62,* 473–481.

Mogenson, G. J. (1976). Neural mechanisms of hunger: Current status and future prospects. In D. Novin, W. Wyrwicka, & G. Bray (Eds.), *Hunger: Basic mechanisms and clinical applications.* New York: Raven.

Mohr, C., Binkofski, F., Erdmann, C., Buchel, C., & Helmchen, C. (2005). The anterior cingulate cortex contains distinct areas dissociating external from self-administered painful stimulation: A parametric fMRI study. *Pain, 114,* 347–357.

Mohr, C., Rohrenbach, C. M., Landis, T., & Regard, M. (2001). Associations to smell are more pleasant than to sound. *Journal of Clinical and Experimental Neuropsychology, 23,* 484–489.

Mohr, D. C., Hart, S. L., Julian, L., Catledge, C., Honos-Webb, L., Vella, L., et al. (2005). Telephone-administered psychotherapy for depression. *Archives of General Psychiatry, 62,* 1007–1014.

Mokdad, A. H., Marks, J. S., Stroup, D. F., & Gerberding, J. L. (2004). Actual causes of death in the United States, 2000. *Journal of the American Medical Association, 291,* 1238–1245.

Molden, D. C., & Dweck, C. S. (2000). Meaning and motivation. In C. Sansone & J. M. Harackiewicz (Eds.), *Intrinsic and extrinsic motivation: The search for optimal motivation and performance.* San Diego, CA: Academic Press.

Molsa, P. K., Marttila, R. J., & Rinne, U. K. (1995). Long-term survival and predictors of mortality in Alzheimer's disease and multi-infarct dementia. *Acta Neurologica Scandinavica, 91,* 159–164.

Molteni, R., Zheng, J.-Q., Ying, Z., Gómez-Pinilla, F., & Twiss, J. (2004). Voluntary exercise increases axonal regeneration from sensory neurons. *Proceedings of the National Academies of Science, 101,* 8473–8478.

Monane, M., Leichter, D., & Lewis, O. (1984). Physical abuse in psychiatrically hospitalized children and adolescents. *Journal of the American Academy of Child and Adolescent Psychiatry, 23,* 653–658.

Moncrief, W. C., Babakus, E., Cravens, D. W., & Johnston, M. W. (2000). Examining gender differences in field sales organizations. *Journal of Business Research, 49,* 245–257.

Moncrieff, J., & Kirsch, I. (2005). Efficacy of antidepressants in adults. *British Medical Journal, 331,* 155–157.

Moniz, E (1948). How I came to perform prefrontal leucotomy. *Proceedings of the first international congress of psychosurgery* (pp. 7–18). Lisbon: Edicoes Atica.

Monroe, S., Thase, M., & Simons, A. (1992). Social factors and psychobiology of depression: Relations between life stress and rapid eye movement sleep latency. *Journal of Abnormal Psychology, 101,* 528–537.

Montague, P. R., Hyman, S. E., & Cohen, J. D. (2004). Computational roles for dopamine in behavioural control. *Nature, 431,* 760–767.

Monteith, M. J., Sherman, J. W., & Devine, P. G. (1998). Suppression as a stereotype control strategy. *Personality & Social Psychology Review, 2,* 63–82.

Monteith, M. J., Zuwerink, J. R., & Devine, P. G. (1994). Prejudice and prejudice reduction: Classic challenges and contemporary approaches. In P. G. Devine, D. L. Hamilton, & T. M. Ostrom (Eds.), *Social cognition: Impact on social psychology* (pp. 324–346). San Diego, CA: Academic Press.

Monterosso, J., Ainslie, R., Mullen, P. A., & Gault, B. (2002). The fragility of cooperation: A false feedback study of a sequential iterated prisoner's dilemma. *Journal of Economic Psychology, 23,* 437–448.

Montmayeur, J. P., Liberles, S. D., Matsunami, H., & Buck, L. B. (2001). A candidate taste receptor gene near a sweet taste locus. *Nature Neuroscience, 4,* 492–498.

Montoya, I. D., Gorelick, D. A., Preston, K. L., Schroeder, J. R., Umbricht, A., Cheskin, L. J., et al. (2004). Randomized trial of buprenorphine for treatment of concurrent opiate and cocaine dependence. *Clinical and Pharmacological Therapeutics, 75,* 34–48.

Mookadam, F., & Arthur, H. M. (2004). Social support and its relationship to morbidity and mortality after acute myocardial infarction: Systematic overview. *Archives of Internal Medicine, 164,* 1514–1518.

Moon, Y. (2003). Don't blame the computer: When self-disclosure moderates the self-serving bias. *Journal of Consumer Psychology, 13,* 125–137.

Moore, J. W., Tingstom, D. H., Doggett, R. A., & Carlyon, W. D. (2001). Restructuring an existing token economy in a psychiatric facility for children. *Child & Family Behavior Therapy, 23,* 53–60.

Moore, K. A. (2005). *Family strengths: Often overlooked, but real.* Washington, DC: Child Trends.

Moorman, R. H., & Byrne, Z. S. (2005). How does organizational justice affect organizational citizenship behavior? In J. Greenberg & J. A. Colquitt (Eds.), *Handbook of organizational justice* (pp. 355–380). Mahwah, NJ: Erlbaum.

Moos, R., Schaefer, J., Andrassy, J., & Moos, B. (2001). Outpatient mental health care, self-help groups, and patients' one-year treatment outcomes. *Journal of Clinical Psychology, 57,* 273–287.

Moradi, B., Dirks, D., & Matteson, A. V. (2005). Roles of sexual objectification experiences and internalization of standards of beauty in eating disorder symptomatology: A test and extension of objectification theory. *Journal of Counseling Psychology, 52,* 420–428.

Moran, C. C. (2002). Humor as a moderator of compassion fatigue. In C. R. Figley (Ed.), *Treating compassion fatigue* (pp. 139–154). New York: Brunner-Routledge.

Moran, D. R. (2000, June). *Is active learning for me?* Poster presented at APS Preconvention Teaching Institute, Denver.

Moran, R. (2006). Learning in high-tech and multimedia environments. *Current Directions in Psychological Science, 15,* 63–67.

Moreland, R. L., & Beach, S. R. (1992). Exposure effects in the classroom: The development of affinity among students. *Journal of Experimental Social Psychology, 28,* 255–276.

Morewedge, C. K., Gilbert, D. T., & Wilson, T. D. (2005). The least likely of times: How remembering the past biases forecasts of the future. *Psychological Science, 16*(8), 626–630.

Morgan, C. A., Doran, A., Steffian, G., Hazlett, G., & Southwick, S. M. (2006). Stress-induced deficits in working memory and visuo-constructive abilities in special operations soldiers. *Biological Psychiatry, 60,* 722–729.

Morgan, C. D., & Murray, H. A. (1935). A method for investigating fantasy: The Thematic Apperception Test. *Archives of Neurology and Psychiatry, 34,* 289–306.

Morgan, C., Isaac, J. D., & Sansone, C. (2001). The role of interest in understanding the career choices of female and male college students. *Sex Roles, 44,* 295–320.

Morgan, D., Diamond, D. M., Gottschall, P. E., Ugen, K. E., Dickey, C., Hardy, J., et al. (2000). A beta peptide vaccination prevents memory loss in an animal model of Alzheimer's disease. *Nature, 408,* 982–985.

Morgeson, F. P., Johnson, M. D., Campion, M. A., Medsker, G. J., & Mumford, T. V. (2006). Understanding reactions to job redesign: A quasi-experimental investigation of the moderating effects of organizational context on perceptions of performance behavior. *Personnel Psychology, 59,* 333–363.

Morin, A. (2006). Levels of consciousness and self-awareness: A comparison and integration of various neurocognitive views. *Consciousness and Cognition, 15,* 358–371.

Morisky, D. E., Stein, J. A., Chiao, C., Ksobiech, K., & Malow, R. (2006). Impact of a social influence intervention on condom use and sexually transmitted infections among establishment-based female sex workers in the Philippines: A multilevel analysis. *Health Psychology, 25,* 595–603.

Morris, J. S., DeGelder, B., Weiskrantz, L., & Dolan, R. J. (2001). Differential extrageniculostriate and amygdala responses to presentation of emotional faces in a cortically blind field. *Brain, 124,* 1241–1252.

Morris, J. S., Friston, K. J., Buchel, C., Frith, C. D., Young, A. W., Calder, A. J., et al. (1998). A neuromodulatory role for the human amygdala in processing emotional facial expressions. *Brain, 121,* 47–57.

Morris, L. (2000, December 5). Hold the anaesthetic. I'll hypnotise myself instead. *Daily Mail,* p. 25.

Morris, M. C., Evans, D. A., Tangney, C. C., Bienias, J. L., & Wilson, R. S. (2006). Associations of vegetable and fruit consumption with age-related cognitive change. *Neurology, 67,* 1370–1376.

Morrison, K. H., Bradley, R., & Westen, D. (2003). The external validity of controlled clinical trials of psychotherapy for depression and anxiety: A naturalistic study. *Psychology and Psychotherapy: Theory, Research & Practice, 76*(2), 109–132.

Morrongiello, B. A., & Hogg, K. (2004). Mothers' reactions to children misbehaving in ways that can lead to injury: Implications for gender differences in children's risk taking and injuries. *Sex Roles, 50*(1–2), 103–118.

Mortimer, J. A., Snowdon, D. A., & Markesbery, W. R. (2003). Head circumference, education, and risk of dementia: Findings from the nun study. *Journal of Clinical and Experimental Neuropsychology, 25,* 671–679.

Mortimer, R. G., Goldsteen, K., Armstrong, R. W., & Macrina, D. (1988). *Effects of enforcement, incentives, and publicity on seat belt use in Illinois.* University of Illinois, Dept. of Health & Safety Studies, Final Report to Illinois Dept. of Transportation (Safety Research Report 88–11).

Morton, B. E., & Rafto, S. E. (2006). Corpus callosum size is linked to dichotic deafness and hemisphericity, not sex or handedness. *Brain and Cognition, 62,* 1–8.

Morton, G. J., Cummings, D. E., Baskin, D. G., Barsh, G. S., & Schwartz, M. W. (2006). Central nervous system control of food intake and body weight. *Nature, 443,* 289–295.

Moscovici, S. (1985). Social influence and conformity. In G. Lindzey & E. Aronson (Eds.), *The handbook of social psychology* (Vol. 2, 3rd ed.). New York: Random House.

Moses, E. B., & Barlow, D. H. (2006). A new unified treatment approach for emotional disorders based on emotion science. *Current Directions in Psychological Science, 15,* 146–150.

Moskowitz, G. B. (2005). *Social cognition: Understanding self and others.* New York: Guilford Press.

Moss, E., Bureau, J.-F., Cyr, C., Mongeau, C., & St.-Laurent, D. (2004). Correlates of attachment at age 3: Construct validity of the preschool attachment classification system. *Developmental Psychology, 40,* 323–334.

Mostert, M. P. (2001). Facilitated communication since 1995: A review of published studies. *Journal of Autism and Developmental Disorders, 31,* 287–313.

Mroczek, D. K., & Spiro, A., III. (2005). Changing life satisfaction during adulthood: Findings from the Veterans Affairs normative aging study. *Journal of Personality and Social Psychology, 88,* 189–202.

Muchinsky, P. M. (2003). *Psychology applied to work* (7th ed.). Belmont, CA: Thomson.

Mueller, K. L., Hoon, M. A., Erlenbach, I., Chandrashekar, J., Zuker, C. S., & Ryba, N. J. (2005). The receptors and coding logic for bitter taste. *Nature, 434,* 225–229.

Mufson, L., Polack, D., & Moreau, D. (2004). *Interpersonal psychotherapy for depressed adolescents* (2nd ed.). New York: Guilford.

Muir, J. L. (1997). Acetylcholine, aging, and Alzheimer's disease. *Pharmacological and Biochemical Behavior, 56*(4), 687–696.

Mullen, B. (1986). Atrocity as a function of lynch mob composition: A self-attention perspective. *Personality and Social Psychology Bulletin, 12,* 187–197.

Mumford, M. D., Connelly, M. S., Helton, W. B., Strange, J. M., & Osburn, H. K. (2001). On the construct validity of integrity tests: Individual and situational factors as predictors of test performance. *International Journal of Selection and Assessment, 9,* 240–257.

Mumme, D. L., & Fernald, A. (2003). The infant as onlooker: Learning from emotional reactions observed in a television scenario. *Child Development, 74,* 221–237.

Munakata, Y. (2006). Information processing approaches to development. In W. Damon & R. M. Lerner (Series Eds.) & D. Kuhn & R. Siegler (Vol. Eds.), *Handbook of child psychology: Vol. 2. Cognition, perception, and language* (6th ed., pp. 426–463). New York: Wiley.

Munley, P. H. (2002). Comparability of MMPI-2 scales and profiles over time. *Journal of Personality Assessment, 78,* 145–160.

Muñoz, R. F., & Mendelson, T. (2005). Toward evidence-based interventions for diverse populations: The San Francisco General Hospital prevention and treatment manuals. *Journal of Consulting and Clinical Psychology, 73,* 790–799.

Munte, T. F., Altenmuller, E., & Jancke, L. (2002). The musician's brain as a model of neuroplasticity. *Nature Reviews Neuroscience, 3,* 473–478.

Murray, B. (2000). Learning from real life. *APA Monitor, 31,* 72–73.

Murray, C. (2003). *Human accomplishment: The pursuit of excellence in the arts and sciences, 800 BC to 1950.* New York: HarperCollins.

Murray, E. A., & Mishkin, M. (1985). Amygdalectomy impairs crossmodal association in monkeys. *Science, 228,* 604–606.

Murray, H. A. (1938). *Explorations in personality.* New York: Oxford University Press.

Murray, J. A., & Terry, D. (1999). Parental reactions to infant death: The effects of resources and coping strategies. *Journal of Social and Clinical Psychology, 18,* 341–369.

Mussweiler, T. (2003). "Everything is relative": Comparison processes in social judgment: The 2002 Jaspars Lecture. *European Journal of Social Psychology, 33,* 719–733.

Myers, B. J. (1987). Mother-infant bonding as a critical period. In M. H. Bornstein (Ed.), *Sensitive periods in development: Interdisciplinary perspectives.* Hillsdale, NJ: Erlbaum.

Myers, D. G. (2000). The funds, friends, and faith of happy people. *American Psychologist, 55,* 56–57.

Myers, D. G. (2004). *Intuition: Its powers and perils.* New Haven, CT: Yale University Press.

Myers, K. M., & Davis, M. (2007). Mechanisms of fear extinction. *Molecular Psychiatry, 12,* 120–150.

Myers, K. P., & Sclafani, A. (2006). Development of learned flavor preferences. *Developmental Psychobiology, 48,* 380–388.

Myers, P. I., & Hammill, D. D. (1990). *Learning disabilities: Basic concepts, assessment practices, and instructional strategies.* Austin, TX: Pro-Ed.

Nabeshima, T., & Yamada, K. (2000). Neurotrophic factor strategies for the treatment of Alzheimer disease. *Alzheimer Disease & Associated Disorders, 14*(Suppl. 1), S39–46.

Nadeau, S., & Crosson, B. (1995). A guide to the functional imaging of cognitive processes. *Neuropsychiatry, Neuropsychology, and Behavioral Neurology, 8,* 143–162.

Nader, K., Bechara, A., & Van der Kooy, D. (1997). Neurobiological constraints on behavioral models of motivation. *Annual Review of Psychology, 48,* 85–114.

Nader, K., Schafe, G. E., & Le Doux, J. E. (2000). Fear memories require protein synthesis in the amygdala for reconsolidation after retrieval. *Nature, 406,* 722–726.

Naëgelé, B., Launois, S. H., Mazza, S., Feuerstein, C., Pepin, J. L., & Levy, P. (2006). Which memory processes are affected in patients with obstructive sleep apnea? An evaluation of 3 types of memory. *Sleep, 29,* 533–544.

Nagy, T. F. (1999). *Ethics in plain English: An illustrative casebook for psychologists.* Washington, DC: American Psychological Association.

Nairne, J. S. (2003). Sensory and working memory. In A. F. P. Healy, R. W. Proctor, & I. B. Weiner (Eds.), *Handbook of psychology: Vol. 4. Experimental psychology* (pp. 423–444). New York: Wiley.

Naito, M., & Miura, H. (2001). Japanese children's numerical competencies: Age-and schooling-related influences on the development of number concepts and addition skills. *Developmental Psychology, 37,* 217–230.

Nakamura, J., & Csikszentmihalyi, M. (2001). Catalytic creativity. *American Psychologist, 56,* 337–341.

Nakano, K., & Kitamura, T. (2001). The relation of the anger subcomponent of Type A behavior to psychological symptoms in Japanese and foreign students. *Japanese Psychological Research, 43,* 50–54.

Nakao, M., & Yano, E. (2006). Prediction of major depression in Japanese adults: Somatic manifestations of depression in annual health examinations. *Journal of Affective Disorders, 90,* 29–35.

Nakayama, K. (1994). James J. Gibson: An appreciation. *Psychological Review, 101,* 329–335.

Nanchahal, K., Morris, J. N., Sullivan, L. M., & Wilson, P. W. (2005). Coronary heart disease risk in men and the epidemic of overweight and obesity. *International Journal of Obesity, 29,* 317–323.

Nater, U. M., Gaab, J., Rief, W., & Ehlert, U. (2006). Recent trends in behavioral medicine. *Current Opinion in Psychiatry, 19,* 180–183.

Nathan, P. E., & Langenbucher, J. W. (1999). Psychopathology: Description and classification. *Annual Review of Psychology, 50,* 79–107.

Nathan, P. E., Stuart, S. P., & Dolan, S. L. (2000). Research on psychotherapy efficacy and effectiveness: Between Scylla and Charybdis? *Psychological Bulletin, 126,* 964–981.

Nathan, P. E., Stuart, S. P., & Dolan, S. L. (2003). Research on psychotherapy efficacy and effectiveness: Between Scylla and Charybdis? In A. E. Kazdin (Ed.), *Methodological issues & strategies in clinical research* (3rd ed., pp. 505–546). Washington, DC: American Psychological Association.

Nathanson, M., Bergman, P. S., & Gordon, G. G. (1952). Denial of illness: Its occurrence in one hundred consecutive cases of hemiplegia. *Archives of Neurology and Psychiatry, 68,* 380–397.

National Association of Anorexia Nervosa and Associated Disorders. (2002). *Facts about eating disorders.* Retrieved August 26, 2003, from http://www.altrue.net/site/anadweb/content.php?type=1&id=6982.

National Center for Chronic Disease Prevention and Health Promotion. (2002). Trends in sexual risk behaviors among high school students—United States, 1991–2001. *Morbidity and Mortality Weekly Report, 51,* 856–859.

National Center for Education Statistics. (2002). *Digest of education statistics, 2001.* Washington, DC: Office of Educational Research & Improvement, U.S. Dept. of Education.

National Center for Education Statistics. (2003). *Postsecondary institutions in the United States: Fall 2002 and degrees and other awards conferred: 2001–02.* Washington, DC: U.S. Department of Education.

National Center for Health Statistics. (2000). *Trends in pregnancies and pregnancy rates by outcome: Estimates for the United States, 1976–1996.* Washington, DC: Centers for Disease Control and Prevention.

National Center for Health Statistics. (2001). *Births, marriages, divorces, and deaths: Provisional data for January–December 2000.* Hyattsville, Maryland: Public Health Service.

National Center for Injury Prevention and Control. (2002). *Ten leading causes of death, United States.* Washington, DC: Centers for Disease Control.

National Center on Addiction and Substance Abuse. (2004). *National Survey of American Attitudes on Substance Abuse: IX. Teen dating practices and sexual activity.* New York: Author.

National Computer Systems. (1992). *Catalog of assessment instruments, reports, and services.* Minneapolis: National Computer Systems.

National Highway Traffic Safety Administration. (2005). *Traffic safety facts.* Washington, DC: National Center for Statistics and Analysis.

National Information Center for Children and Youth with Disabilities. (2000, June 18). *NICHCY Fact Sheet #7.* Retrieved December 13, 2004, from http://www.ldonline.org/ld_indepth/general_info/gen-2.html

National Institute for Clinical Excellence. (2004). *Depression: Management of depression in primary and secondary care* (Clinical Practice Guideline No. 23). Retrieved August 11, 2005, from http://www.nice.org.uk/page.aspx?o=cg023.

National Institute for Occupational Safety and Health. (1999). *Stress at work.* Washington, DC: NIOSH Publication No. 99–101.

National Institute of Mental Health. (1995). *Medications.* Washington, DC: U.S. Department of Health and Human Services.

National Institute of Mental Health. (2004, April 23). *Statement on antidepressant medications for children: Information for parents and caregivers.* Retrieved April 24, 2004, from www.nimh.nih.gov/press/StmntAntidepmeds.cfm

National Institute of Mental Health. (2006). *The numbers count: Mental disorders in America.* Retrieved August 8, 2006, from http://www.nimh.nih.gov.publicat/-numbers.cfm.

National Institute on Alcohol Abuse and Alcoholism. (2000). *Tenth special report to the U.S. Congress on alcohol and health* (Publication No. 00–1583). Washington, DC: National Institutes of Health.

National Institute on Alcohol Abuse and Alcoholism. (2001). *Alcoholism: Getting the facts.* Bethesda, MD: Author.

National Institute on Drug Abuse. (2000). Facts about MDMA (Ecstasy). *NIDA Notes, 14.* Retrieved December 13, 2004, from http://drugabuse.gov/NIDA_Notes/NNVol14N4/tearoff.html.

National Institute on Drug Abuse. (2004). Marijuana. *NIDA Info Facts.* Retrieved April 29, 2004, from http://www.nida.nih.gov/Infofax/marijuana.html.

National Institutes of Health. (2001). *Eating disorders: Facts about eating disorders and the search for solutions* (NIH Publication No. 01–4901). Washington, DC: U.S. Department of Health and Human Services.

National Institutes of Health Consensus Conference. (1998). Acupuncture. *Journal of the American Medical Association, 280,* 1518–1524.

National Joint Committee on Learning Disabilities. (1994). *Collective perspective on issues affecting learning disabilities.* Austin, TX: Pro-Ed.

National Safety Council. (2004). *Reports on injuries in America, 2003.* Itasca, IL: Author.

National Science Foundation. (2004a). *Doctoral scientists and engineers: 2001 profile tables.* Arlington, VA: Author.

National Science Foundation. (2004b). *Women, minorities, and persons with disabilities in science and engineering.* Arlington, VA: Author.

National Task Force on the Prevention and Treatment of Obesity. (2000). Dieting and the development of eating disorders in overweight and obese adults. *Archives of Internal Medicine, 160,* 2581–2589.

Navarrete-Palacios, E., Hudson, R., Reyes-Guerrero, G., & Guevara-Guzman, R. (2003). Lower olfactory threshold during the ovulatory phase of the menstrual cycle. *Biological Psychology, 63,* 269–279.

Neary, D., & Snowden, J. (1996). Fronto-temporal dementia: Nosology, neuropsychology, and neuropathology. *Brain and Cognition, 31*(2), 176–187.

Neary, D., Snowden, J. S., & Mann, D. M. (1993). The clinical pathological correlates of lobar atrophy. *Dementia, 4*(3–4), 154–159.

Needham, A., & Baillargeon, R. (1999). Effects of prior experience on 4.5 month-old infants' object segregation. *Infant Behavior & Development, 21,* 1–24.

Neff, L. A., & Karney, B. R. (2005). To know you is to love you: The implications of global adoration and specific accuracy for marital relationships. *Journal of Personality and Social Psychology, 88,* 480–497.

Neher, A. (1991). Maslow's theory of motivation: A critique. *Journal of Humanistic Psychology, 31,* 89–112.

Neighbors, H. W., Caldwell, C., Williams, D. R., Nesse, R., Taylor, R. J., Bullard, K. M., et al. (2007). Race, ethnicity, and the use of services for mental disorders. *Archives of General Psychiatry, 64,* 485–494.

Neighbors, H. W., Trierweiler, S. J., Fort, B. C., & Muroff, J. R. (2003). Racial differences in DSM diagnosis using a semi-structured instrument: The importance of clinical judgment in the diagnosis of African Americans. *Journal of Health and Social Behavior, 44,* 237–256.

Neisser, U. (1997). Never a dull moment. *American Psychologist, 52,* 79–81.

Neisser, U. (2000). Memorists. In U. Neisser & I. E. Hyman, Jr. (Eds.), *Memory observed* (2nd ed., pp. 475–478). New York: Worth.

Neisser, U., Boodoo, G., Bouchard, T. J., Boykin, A. W., Brody, N., Ceci, S. J., et al. (1996). Intelligence: Knowns and unknowns. *American Psychologist, 51,* 77–101.

Neisser, U., & Harsch, N. (1992). Phantom flashbulbs: False recollections of hearing the news about *Challenger.* In E. Winograd & U. Neisser (Eds.), *Affect and accuracy in recall: Studies of "flashbulb" memories* (pp. 9–31). New York: Cambridge University Press.

Nelson, C. A. (1999). Neural plasticity and human development. *Current Directions in Psychological Science, 8,* 42–45.

Nelson, C. A. (2006). Of eggshells and thin-skulls: A consideration of racism-related mental illness impacting Black women. *International Journal of Law and Psychiatry, 29,* 112–136.

Nelson, C. A., Thomas, K. M., & de Haan, M. (2006). Neural bases of cognitive development. In W. Damon & R. M. Lerner (Series Eds.) & D. Kuhn & R. Siegler (Vol. Eds.), *Handbook of child psychology: Vol. 2, Cognition, perception, and language* (6th ed., pp. 3–57). New York: Wiley.

Nelson, D. L. (1999). Implicit memory. In D. E. Morris & M. Gruneberg (Eds.), *Theoretical aspects of memory.* London: Routledge.

Nelson, D. L., McKinney, V. M., & Bennett, D. J. (1999). Conscious and automatic uses of memory in cued recall and recognition. In B. H. Challis & B. M. Velichkovsky (Eds.), *Stratification in cognition and consciousness* (p. 173–202). Amsterdam: John Benjamins.

Nelson, D. L., McKinney, V. M., Gee, N. R., & Janczura, G. A. (1998). Interpreting the influence of implicitly activated memories on recall and recognition. *Psychological Review, 105,* 299–324.

Nelson, G., & Prilleltensky, I. (2004). *Community psychology: In pursuit of liberation and well-being.* New York: Palgrave Macmillan.

Nelson, K. (1986). Event knowledge and cognitive development. In K. Nelson (Ed.), *Event knowledge: Structure and function in development* (pp. 1–19). Hillsdale, NJ: Erlbaum.

Nelson, K. (1993). The psychological and social origins of autobiographical memory. *Psychological Science, 4,* 7–14.

Nelson, K., & Fivush, R. (2004). The emergence of autobiographical memory: A social cultural developmental theory. *Psychological Review, 111,* 486–511.

Nelson, T. D., & Steele, R. G. (2006). Beyond efficacy and effectiveness: A multifaceted approach to treatment evaluation. *Professional Psychology: Research and Practice, 37,* 389–397.

Nelson-LeGall, S., & Resnick, L. (1998). Help seeking, achievement motivation, and the social practice of intelligence in school. In S. A. Karabenick (Ed.), *Strategic help seeking* (pp. 39–60). Mahwah, NJ: Erlbaum.

Nemeroff, C. B., Heim, C. M., Thase, M. E., Klein, D. N., Rush, A. J., Schatzberg, A. F., et al. (2003). Differential responses to psychotherapy versus pharmacotherapy in patients with chronic forms of major depression and childhood trauma. *Proceedings of the National Academy of Science, 100,* 14293–14296.

Nestadt, G., Hsu, F.-C., Samuels, J., Bienvenu, O. J., Reti, I. Costa, P. T., Jr., et al. (2005). Latent structure of the *Diagnostic and Statistical Manual of Mental Disorders, Fourth Edition,* personality disorder criteria. *Comprehensive Psychiatry, 47,* 54–62.

Nestler, E. J. (2001). Molecular basis of long-term plasticity underlying addiction. *National Review of Neuroscience, 2,* 119–128.

Netter, P. (2006). Dopamine challenge tests as an indicator of psychological traits. *Human Psychopharmacology: Clinical and Experimental, 21,* 91–99.

Neugarten, B. L. (1977). Personality and aging. In J. E. Birren & K. W. Schaie (Eds.), *Handbook of the psychology of aging.* New York: Van Nostrand Reinhold.

Neumann, C. S., Grimes, K., Walker, E. F., & Baum, K. (1995). Developmental pathways to schizophrenia: Behavioral subtypes. *Journal of Abnormal Psychology, 104,* 558–566.

Neumeister, A., Bain, E., Nugent, A. C., Carson, R. E., Bonne, O., Luckenbaugh, D. A., et al. (2004). Reduced serotonin type 1A receptor binding in panic disorder. *Journal of Neuroscience, 24,* 589–591.

Neuwelt, E. A. (2004). Mechanisms of disease: The blood-brain barrier. *Neurosurgery, 54,* 131–140.

Neves-Pereira, M., Cheung, J. K., Pasdar, A., Zhang, F., Breen, G., Yates, P., et al. (2005). BDNF gene is a risk factor for schizophrenia in a Scottish population. *Molecular Psychiatry, 10,* 208–212.

Neville, H. J., Bavelier, D., Corina, D., Rauschecker, J., Karni, A., Lalwani, A., et al. (1998). Cerebral organization for language in deaf and hearing subjects: Biological constraints and effects of experience. *Proceedings of the National Academy of Science USA, 95,* 922–929.

Newberg, A., Alavi, A., Baime, M., Pourdehnad, M., Santanna, J., & d'Aquili, E. (2001). The measurement of regional cerebral blood flow during the complex cognitive task of meditation: A preliminary SPECT study. *Psychiatry Research, 106,* 113–122.

Newcombe, N. S., Drummey, A. B., Fox, N. A., Lie, E., & Ottinger-Alberts, W. (2000). Remembering early childhood: How much, how, and why (or why not). *Current Directions in Psychological Science, 9,* 55–58.

Newcombe, N. S., & Fox, N. A. (1994). Infantile amnesia: Through a glass darkly. *Child Development, 65,* 31–40.

Newell, A., & Simon, H. A. (1972). *Human problem solving.* Englewood Cliffs, NJ: Prentice-Hall.

Newsome, J. T. (1999). Another side to caregiving: Negative reactions to being helped. *Current Directions in Psychological Science, 8,* 183–187.

Newsome, J. T., & Schulz, R. (1998). Caregiving from the recipient's perspective: Negative reactions to being helped. *Health Psychology, 17,* 172–181.

Neziroglu, F., McKay, D., & Yaryura-Tobias, J. A. (2000). Overlapping and distinctive features of hypochondriasis and obsessive-compulsive disorder. *Journal of Anxiety Disorders, 14,* 603–614.

Ng, B.-Y. (2000). Phenomenology of trance states seen at a psychiatric hospital in Singapore: A cross-cultural perspective. *Transcultural Psychiatry, 37,* 560–579.

Niaura, R., & Abrams, D. B. (2002). Smoking cessation: Progress, priorities, and prospectus. *Journal of Consulting and Clinical Psychology, 70,* 494–509.

Nicassio, P. M., Meyerowitz, B. E., & Kerns, R. D. (2004). The future of health psychology interventions. *Health Psychology, 23,* 132–137.

NICHD Early Child Care Research Network. (2005a). *Child care and child development: Results from the NICHD Study of Early Child Care and Youth Development.* New York: Guilford.

NICHD Early Child Care Research Network. (2005b). Duration and developmental timing of poverty and children's cognitive and social development from birth to first grade. *Child Development, 76,* 795–810.

NICHD Early Child Care Research Network. (2006). Infant-mother attachment classification: Risk and protection in relation to changing maternal caregiving quality. *Developmental Psychology, 42,* 38–58.

NICHD Early Child Care Research Network (2007). Are there long-term effects of early child care? *Child Development, 78,* 681–701.

Nichols, D. F. (2006). Tell me a story: MMPI responses and personal biography in the case of a serial killer. *Journal of Personality Assessment, 86,* 242–262.

Nichols, R. (1978). Twin studies of ability, personality, and interests. *Homo, 29,* 158–173.

Nicholson, A., Fuhrer, R., & Marmot, M. (2005). Psychological distress as a predictor of CHD events in men: The effect of persistence and components of risk. *Psychosomatic Medicine, 67,* 522–530.

Nicholson, I. R., & Neufeld, R. W. J. (1993). Classification of the schizophrenias according to symptomatology: A two factor model. *Journal of Abnormal Psychology, 102,* 259–270.

Nickell, J. (1997, January/February). Sleuthing a psychic sleuth. *Skeptical Inquirer, 21,* 18–19.

Nickell, J. (2001). Exorcism! Driving out the nonsense. *Skeptical Inquirer, 25,* 20–24.

Nickerson, C., Schwarz, N., Diener, E., & Kahneman, D. (2003). Zeroing in on the dark side of the American dream: A closer look at the negative consequences of the goal for financial success. *Psychological Science, 14,* 531–536.

Nickerson, R. A., & Adams, M. J. (1979). Long-term memory for a common object. *Cognitive Psychology, 11,* 287–307.

Nicoll, J., & Kieffer, K. M. (2005, August). *Violence in video games: A review of the empirical research.* Presented at the meeting for the American Psychological Association, Washington, DC.

Nicotra, A., Critchley, H. D., Mathias, C. J., & Dolan, R. J. (2006). Emotional and autonomic consequences of spinal cord injury explored using functional brain imaging. *Brain, 129,* 718–728.

Niederhoffer, K. G., & Pennebaker, J. W. (2002). Sharing one's story: On the benefits of writing or talking about emotional experience. In C. R. Snyder & S. J. Lopez (Eds.), *Handbook of positive psychology* (pp. 573–583). London: Oxford University Press.

Niederman, R., & Richards, D. (2005). Evidence-based dentistry: Concepts and implementation. *Journal of the American College of Dentistry, 72,* 37–41.

Niemela, M., & Saarinen, J. (2000). Visual search for grouped versus ungrouped icons in a computer interface. *Human Factors, 42,* 630–635.

Nienhuys, J. W. (2001). Spontaneous human combustion: Requiem for Phyllis. *Skeptical Inquirer, 25,* 28–34.

Nietzel, M. T. (1999). Psychology applied to the legal system. In A. M. Stec & D. A. Bernstein (Eds.), *Psychology: Fields of application.* Boston: Houghton Mifflin.

Nietzel, M. T., & Bernstein, D. A. (1987). *Introduction to clinical psychology* (2nd ed.). New York: Prentice-Hall.

Nigg, J. T. (2000). On inhibition/disinhibition in developmental psychopathology: Views from cognitive and personality psychology and a working inhibition taxonomy. *Psychological Bulletin, 126,* 220–246.

Nigg, J. T. (2001). Is ADHD a disinhibitory disorder? *Psychological Bulletin, 127,* 571–598.

Niiya, Y., Crocker, J., & Bartmess, E. N. (2004). From vulnerability to resilience: Learning orientations buffer contingent self-esteem from failure. *Psychological Science, 15,* 801–805.

Nijhawan, R. (1997). Visual decomposition of colour through motion extrapolation. *Nature, 386,* 66–69.

Nijstad, B. A., Stroebe, W., & Lodewijkx, H. F. M. (2003). Production blocking and idea generation: Does blocking interfere with cognitive processes? *Journal of Experimental Social Psychology, 39,* 531–548.

Nilsson, G. (1996, November). Some forms of memory improve as people age. *APA Monitor,* p. 27.

Nisbett, R. E., & Masuda, T. (2003). Culture and point of view. *Proceedings of the National Academy of Sciences, 100,* 11163–11170.

Nishimura, T., Mikami, A., Suzuki, J., & Matsuzawa, T. (2003). Descent of the larynx in chimpanzee infants. *Proceedings of the National Academy of Science, 100*, 6930–6933.

Niznikiewicz, M. A., O'Donnell, B. F., Nestor, P. G., Smith, L., Law, S., Karapelou, M., et al. (1997). ERP assessment of visual and auditory language processing in schizophrenia. *Journal of Abnormal Psychology, 106*, 85–94.

Noble, H. B. (2000, January 25). Outgrowth of new field of tissue engineering. *New York Times*.

Noblett, K. L., & Coccaro, E. F. (2005). Molecular genetics of personality. *Current Psychiatry Reports, 7*, 73–80.

Nock, M. K., & Kessler, R. C. (2006). Prevalence of and risk factors for suicide attempts versus suicide gestures: Analysis of the National Comorbidity Survey. *Journal of Abnormal Psychology, 115*, 616–623.

Nock, M. K., Kazdin, A. E., Hirpi, E., & Kessler, R. C. (2006). Prevalence, subtypes and correlates of DSM-IV conduct disorder in the National Comorbidity Survey Replication. *Psychological Medicine, 36*, 699–710.

Noftle, E.E. & Shaver, P.R. (2006). Attachment dimensions and the big five personality traits: Associations and comparative ability to predict relationship quality. *Journal of Research in Personality, 40*, 179–208.

Noland, V. J., Liller, K. D., McDermott, R. J., Coulter, M. L., & Seraphine, A. E. (2004). Is adolescent sibling violence a precursor to college dating violence? *American Journal of Health Behavior, 28*, 13–22.

Nolen-Hoeksema, S. (1990). *Sex differences in depression.* Stanford, CA: Stanford University Press.

Nolen-Hoeksema, S. (2001). Gender differences in depression. *Current Directions in Psychological Science, 10*, 173–176.

Nolen-Hoeksema, S. (2006). The etiology of gender differences in depression. In C. M. Mazure & G. P. Keita (Eds.), *Understanding depression in women: Applying empirical research to practice and policy* (pp. 9–43). Washington, DC: American Psychological Association.

Nolen-Hoeksma, S., Morrow, J., & Fredrickson, N. (1993). Response styles and the duration of episodes of depressed mood. *Journal of Abnormal Psychology, 102*, 20–28.

Noll, R. B. (1994). Hypnotherapy for warts in children and adolescents. *Journal of Developmental and Behavioral Pediatrics, 15*(3), 170–173.

Nomura, H., Inoue, S., Kamimura, N., Shimodera, S., Mino, Y., et al. (2005). A cross-cultural study on expressed emotion in careers of people with dementia and schizophrenia: Japan and England. *Social Psychiatry and Psychiatric Epidemiology, 40*, 564–570.

Norcross, J. C. (2002). *Psychotherapy relationships that work: Therapist contributions and responsiveness to patients.* London: Oxford University Press.

Norcross, J. C., Beutler, L. E., & Levant, R. F. (2005). *Evidence-based practices in mental health: Debate and dialogue on the fundamental questions.* Washington, DC: American Psychological Association.

Norcross, J. C., Hedges, M., & Castle, P. H. (2002). Psychologists conducting psychotherapy in 2001: A study of Division 29 membership. *Psychotherapy: Theory, Research, Practice, Training, 39*, 97–102.

Norcross, J. C., Santrock, J. W., Campbell, L. F., Smith, T. P., Sommer, R., & Zuckerman, E. L. (2000). *Authoritative guide to self-help resources in mental health.* New York: Guilford.

Norman, D. A. (1988). *The psychology of everyday things.* New York: Basic Books.

Norman, T., & Olver, J. S. (2004). New formulations of existing antidepressants: Advantages in the management of depression. *CNS Drugs, 18*, 505–520.

Nourkova, V. V., Bernstein, D. M., & Loftus, E. F. (2004). Biography becomes autobiography: Distorting the subjective past. *American Journal of Psychology, 117*, 65–80.

Novick, K. K., & Novick, J. (2005). *Working with parents makes therapy work.* Northvale, NJ: Aronson.

Nowak, M. A., Komarova, N. L., & Niyogi, P. (2001). Evolution of universal grammar. *Science, 291*, 114–118.

Nowak, M. A., May, R. M., & Sigmund, K. (1995). The arithmetics of mutual help. *Scientific American, 272*, 76–81.

Noyes, R., & Hoehn-Saric, R. (2006). *The anxiety disorders.* London: Cambridge University Press.

Nunn, J. A., Gregory, L. J., Brammer, M., Williams, S. C., Parslow, D. M., Morgan, M. J., et al. (2002). Functional magnetic resonance imaging of synesthesia: Activation of V4/V8 by spoken words. *Nature Neuroscience, 5*, 371–375.

Nutt, D. J. (2005a). Death by tricyclic: The real antidepressant scandal? *Journal of Psychopharmacology, 19*, 123–124.

Nutt, D. J. (2005b). Overview of diagnosis and drug treatments of anxiety disorders. *CNS Spectrums, 10*, 49–56.

Nyberg, L., Petersson, K. M., Nilsson, L. G., Sandblom, J., Aberg, C., & Ingvar, M. (2001). Reactivation of motor brain areas during explicit memory for actions. *Neuroimage, 14*, 521–528.

Oatley, K. (1993). Those to whom evil is done. In R. S. Wyer & T. K. Srull (Eds.), *Toward a general theory of anger and emotional aggression: Advances in social cognition* (Vol. 6). Hillsdale, NJ: Erlbaum.

Oberman, L. M., & Ramachandran, V. S. (2007). The simulating social mind: The role of the mirror neuron system and simulation in the social and communicative deficits of autism spectrum disorders. *Psychological Bulletin, 133*, 310–327.

O'Brien, J. T. (2006). Depression and comorbidity. *American Journal of Psychiatry, 14*, 187–190.

O'Brien, T. L. (1991, September 2). Computers help thwart "groupthink" that plagues meetings. *Chicago Sun Times*.

O'Connor, T. G., Ben-Shlomo, Y., Heron, J., Golding, J., Adams, D., & Glover, V. (2005). Prenatal anxiety predicts individual differences in cortisol in pre-adolescent children. *Biological Psychiatry, 58*, 211–217.

Oden, M. H. (1968). The fulfillment of promise: 40-year follow-up of the Terman gifted group. *Genetic Psychology Monographs, 17*, 3–93.

O'Donohue, W. T., Hayes, S. C., & Fisher, J. E. (2003). *Cognitive behavior therapy: Applying empirically supported techniques in your practice.* New York: Wiley.

O'Donohue, W., Fisher, J. E., & Hayes, S. C. (Eds.). (2003). *Cognitive behavior therapy: Applying empirically supported techniques in your practice.* New York: Wiley.

O'Driscoll, M., Brough, P., & Kalliath, T. (2006). Work-family conflict and facilitation. In F. Jones, R. J. Burke, & M. Westman (Eds.), *Work-life balance: A psychological perspective* (pp. 117–142). New York: Psychology Press.

Oettingen, G., Pak, H., & Schnetter, K. (2001). Self-regulation of goal setting: Turning free fantasies about the future into binding goals. *Journal of Personality and Social Psychology, 80*, 736–753.

O'Farrell, T. J. (1995). Marital and family therapy. In R. K. Hester & W. R. Miller (Eds.), *Handbook of alcoholism treatment approaches* (2nd ed., pp. 195–220). Boston: Allyn & Bacon.

Ogden, C. L., Carroll, M. D., Curtin, L. R., McDowell, M. A., Tabak, C. J., & Flegal, K. M. (2006). Prevalence of overweight and obesity in the United States, 1999–2004. *Journal of the American Medical Association, 295*, 1549–1555.

O'Hare, D., & Roscoe, S. (1991). *Flight deck performance: The human factor.* Ames: Iowa University Press.

Ohayon, M. M., & Roth, T. (2003). Place of chronic insomnia in the course of depressive and anxiety disorders. *Journal of Psychiatric Research, 37*, 9–15.

Ohira, H., & Kurono, K. (1993). Facial feedback effects on impression formation. *Perceptual and Motor Skills, 77*(3, Pt. 2), 1251–1258.

Öhman, A., Dimberg, U., & Öst, L. G. (1985). Animal and social phobias: A laboratory model. In S. Reiss & R. R. Bootzin (Eds.), *Theoretical issues in behavior therapy.* Orlando, FL: Academic Press.

Öhman, A., & Mineka, S. (2001). Fears, phobias, and preparedness: Toward an evolved module of fear and fear learning. *Psychological Review, 108*, 483–522.

Öhman, A., & Mineka, S. (2003). The malicious serpent: Snakes as a prototypical stimulus for an evolved module of fear. *Current Directions in Psychological Science, 12*, 5–9.

Öhman, A., & Soares, J. F. (1994). "Unconscious anxiety": Phobic responses to masked stimuli. *Journal of Abnormal Psychology, 103*(2), 231–240.

Ohring, R., Graber, J. A., & Brooks-Gunn, J. (2002). Girls' recurrent and concurrent body dissatisfaction: Correlates and consequences over 8 years. *International Journal of Eating Disorders, 31*(4), 404–415.

Okie, S. (2005). Medical marijuana and the Supreme Court. *New England Journal of Medicine, 353*, 648–651.

Olds, J. (1973). Commentary on positive reinforcement produced by electrical stimulation of septal areas and other regions of rat brain. In E. S. Valenstein (Ed.), *Brain stimulation and motivation: Research and commentary.* Glenview, IL: Scott, Foresman.

Olds, J., & Milner, P. (1954). Positive reinforcement produced by electrical stimulation of septal areas and other regions of the rat brain. *Journal of Comparative and Physiological Psychology, 47*, 419–427.

O'Leary, D. S., Block, R. I., Koeppel, J. A., Flaum, M., Schulz, S. K., Andreason, N. C., et al. (2002). Effects of smoking marijuana on brain perfusion and cognition. *Neuropsychopharmacology, 26*, 802–816.

Olfson, M., Blanco, C., Liu, L., Moreno, C., & Laje, G. (2006). National trends in the outpatient treatment of children and adolescents with antipsychotic drugs. *Archives of General Psychiatry, 63*, 679–685.

Olfson, M., Marcus, S. C., & Shaffer, D. (2006). Antidepressant drug therapy and suicide in depressed children and adolescents: A case-control study. *Archives of General Psychiatry, 63*, 865–872.

Olfson, M., Marcus, S. C., Druss, B., Elinson, L., Tanielian, T., & Pincus, H. A. (2002). National trends in the outpatient treatment of depression. *Journal of the American Medical Association, 287*, 203–209.

Olfson, M., Mechanic, D., Hansell, S., Boyer, C. A., & Walkup, J. (1999). Prediction of homelessness within three months of discharge among inpatients with schizophrenia. *Psychiatric Services, 50*, 667–673.

Oliner, S. P., & Oliner, P. M. (1988). *The altruistic personality: Rescuers of Jews in Nazi Europe.* New York: Free Press.

Olio, K. A. (1994). Truth in memory. *American Psychologist, 49*, 442–443.

Olivares, R., Michalland, S., & Aboitiz, F. (2000). Cross-species and intraspecies morphometric analysis of the corpus callosum. *Brain and Behavior and Evolution, 55,* 37–43.

Ollendick, T. H., & Prinz, R. J. (2002). Editors' comment: International consensus statement on attention deficit hyperactivity disorder (ADHD). *Clinical Child and Family Psychology Review, 5,* 87.

Olshansky, S. J., Passaro, D. J., Hershow, R. C., Layden, J., Carnes, B. A., Brody, J., et al. (2005). A potential decline in life expectancy in the United States in the 21st century. *New England Journal of Medicine, 352,* 1138–1145.

Olson, I. R., Rao, H., Moore, K. S., Wang, J., Detre, J. A., & Aguirre, G. K. (2006). Using perfusion fMRI to measure continuous changes in neural activity with learning. *Brain and Cognition, 60,* 262–271.

Olson, J. M., & Stone, J. (2005). The influence of behavior on attitudes. In D. Albarracín, B. T. Johnson, & M. P. Zanna (Eds.), *Handbook of attitudes* (pp. 223–271). Mahwah, NJ: Erlbaum.

Olson, L. (1997). Regeneration in the adult central nervous system. *Nature Medicine, 3,* 1329–1335.

Olson, M. A., & Fazio, R. H. (2001). Implicit attitude formation through classical conditioning. *Psychological Science, 12,* 413–417.

Olson, M. B., Krantz, D. S., Kelsey, S. F., Pepine, C. J., Sopko, G., Handberg, E., et al. (2005). Hostility scores are associated with increased risk of cardiovascular events in women undergoing coronary angiography: A report from the NHLBI-sponsored WISE study. *Psychosomatic Medicine, 67,* 546–552.

Olsson, A., Ebert, J. P., Banaji, M. R., & Phelps, E. A. (2005). The role of social groups in the persistence of learned fear. *Science, 309,* 785–787.

Oman, D., Hedberg, J., & Thoreson, C. E. (2006). Passage meditation reduces perceived stress in health professionals: A randomized controlled trial. *Journal of Consulting and Clinical Psychology, 74,* 714–719.

Onaivi, E. S., Leonard, C. M., Ishiguro, H., Zhang, P. W., Lin, Z., Akinshola, B. E., & Uhl, G. R. (2002). Endocannabinoids and cannabinoid receptor genetics. *Progress in Neurobiology, 66,* 307–344.

O'Neill, H. (2000, September 24). After rape, jail—a friendship forms. *St. Petersburg Times,* pp. 1A, 14A.

Ones, D., & Viswesvaran, C. (2001). Personality at work: Criterion focused occupational personality scales used in personnel selection. In R. Hogan & B. Roberts (Eds.), *Personality psychology in the workplace* (pp. 63–92). Washington, DC: American Psychological Association.

Ong, A. D., Bergeman, C. S., Bisconti, T. L., & Wallace, K. A. (2006). Psychological resilience, positive emotions, and successful adaptation to stress in later life. *Journal of Personality & Social Psychology, 91,* 730–749.

Oommen, B.S., & Stahl, J. S. (2005). Inhibited head movements: A risk of combining phoning with other activities? *Neurology, 65,* 754–756.

Operario, D., & Fiske, S. T. (2001). Stereotypes: Processes, structures, content, and context. In R. Brown & S. Gaertner (Eds.), *Blackwell handbook in social psychology: Intergroup processes* (pp. 22–44). Oxford, UK: Blackwell.

Oppel, S. (2000, March 5). Managing ABCs like a CEO. *St. Petersburg Times,* 1A, 12–13A.

Oquendo, M. A., Ellis, S. P., Greenwald, S., Malone, K. M., Weissman, M. M., & Mann, J. J. (2001). Ethnic and sex differences in suicide rates relative to major depression in the United States. *American Journal of Psychiatry, 158,* 1652–1658.

Oquendo, M. A., & Mann, J. J. (2000). The biology of impulsivity and suicidality. *Psychiatric Clinics of North America, 23,* 11–25.

Oquendo, M. A., & Mann, J. J. (2001). Identifying and managing suicide risk in bipolar patients. *Journal of Clinical Psychiatry, 62,* 31–34.

Orbell, J. M., van de Kragt, A. J. C., & Dawes, R. M. (1988). Explaining discussion induced cooperation. *Journal of Personality and Social Psychology, 54,* 811–819.

O'Reilly, R.C. (2006). Biologically based computational models of high-level cognition. *Science, 314,* 91–94.

Orme-Johnson, D. W., Schneider, R. H., Son, Y. D., Nidich, S., & Cho, Z. H. (2006). Neuroimaging of meditation's effect on brain reactivity to pain. *Neuroreport, 17,* 1359–1363.

Orne, M. T., & Evans, F. J. (1965). Social control in the psychological experiment: Antisocial behavior and hypnosis. *Journal of Personality and Social Psychology, 1,* 189–200.

Orne, M. T., Sheehan, P. W., & Evans, F. J. (1968). Occurrence of posthypnotic behavior outside the experimental setting. *Journal of Personality and Social Psychology, 9,* 189–196.

Ortiz-Walters, R., & Gilson, L. L. (2005). Mentoring in academia: An examination of the experiences of protégés of color. *Journal of Vocational Behavior, 67,* 459–475.

Osherson, D., Perani, D., Cappa, S., Schnur, T., Grassi, F., & Fazio, F. (1998). Distinct brain loci in deductive versus probabilistic reasoning. *Neuropsychologia, 36,* 369–376.

Oskamp, S., & Schultz, P. W. (1998). *Applied social psychology* (2nd ed.). Upper Saddle River, NJ: Prentice-Hall.

Öst, L.-G. (1978). Behavioral treatment of thunder and lightning phobia. *Behavior Research and Therapy, 16,* 197–207.

Öst, L.-G. (1992). Blood and injection phobia: Background and cognitive, physiological and behavioral variables. *Journal of Abnormal Psychology, 101,* 68–74.

Öst, L.-G., Hellström, K., & Kåver, A. (1992). One- versus five-session exposure in the treatment of needle phobia. *Behavior Therapy, 23,* 263–282.

Öst, L.-G., Salkovskis, P. M., & Hellström, K. (1991). One-session therapist-directed exposure vs. self-exposure in the treatment of spider phobia. *Behavior Theapy, 22,* 407–422.

Ostfeld, B. M., Perl, H., Esposito, L., Hempstead, K., Hinnen, R., Sandler, A., et al. (2006). Sleep environment, positional, lifestyle, and demographic characteristics associated with bed sharing in sudden infant death syndrome cases: A population-based study. *Pediatrics, 118,* 2051–2059.

Ostir, G. V., Berges, I. M., Markides, K. S., & Ottenbacher, K. J. (2006). Hypertension in older adults and the role of positive emotions. *Psychosomatic Medicine, 68,* 727–733.

Ostrov, J. M. (2006). Deception and subtypes of aggression during early childhood. *Journal of Experimental Child Psychology, 93,* 322–336.

Ott, J. (2005). Level and inequality of happiness in nations: Does greater happiness of a greater number imply greater inequality in happiness? *Journal of Happiness Studies, 6,* 397–420.

Otto, M. W., Pollack, M. H., Gould, R. A., Worthington, J. J., III, McArdle, E. T., Rosenbaum, J. F., & Heimberg, R. G. (2000). A comparison of the efficacy of clonazepam and cognitive-behavioral group therapy for the treatment of social phobia. *Journal of Anxiety Disorders, 14,* 345–358.

Otto, M. W., Smits, J. A. J., & Reese, H. E. (2005). Combined psychotherapy and pharmacotherapy for mood and anxiety disorders in adults: Review and analysis. *Clinical Psychology: Science and Practice, 12,* 72–86.

Overmier, J. B. (2002). On learned helplessness. *Integrative Physiological & Behavioral Science, 37,* 4–8.

Overmier, J. B., & Seligman, M. E. P. (1967). Effects of inescapable shock upon subsequent escape and avoidance learning. *Journal of Comparative and Physiological Psychology, 63,* 23–33.

Ovsiew, F. (2006). An overview of the psychiatric approach to conversion disorder. In M. Hallet et al. (Eds.), *Psychogenic movement disorders: Neurology and neuropsychiatry* (pp. 112–121). New York: Lippincott Williams & Wilkins.

Owsley, C., Ball, K., McGwin, G., Pulley, L., Sloane, M. E., Roenker, D. L., et al. (1998). Visual processing impairment and risk of motor vehicle crashes among older adults. *Journal of the American Medical Association, 279,* 1083–1088.

Oyserman, D., Coon, H. M., & Kemmelmeier, M. (2002). Rethinking individualism and collectivism: Evaluation of theoretical assumptions and meta-analyses. *Psychological Bulletin, 128,* 3–72.

Özgen, E. (2004). Language, learning, and color perception. *Current Directions in Psychological Science, 13,* 95–98.

Özgen, E., & Davies, I. R. L. (2002). Acquisition of categorical color perception: A perceptual learning approach to the linguistic relativity hypothesis. *Journal of Experimental Psychology: General, 131,* 477–493.

Pacher, P., Batkai, S., & Kunos, G. (2006). The endocannabinoid system as an emerging target of pharmacotherapy. *Pharmacological Reviews, 58,* 389–462.

Paik, H., & Comstock, G. (1994). The effects of television violence on antisocial behavior: A meta-analysis. *Communication Research, 21,* 516–546.

Paivio, A. (1986). *Mental representations: A dual coding approach.* New York: Oxford University Press.

Paivio, S. C., & Greenberg, L. S. (1995). Resolving "unfinished business": Efficacy of experiential therapy using empty-chair dialogue. *Journal of Consulting and Clinical Psychology, 63,* 419–425.

Palkovitz, R., Copes, M. A., & Woolfolk, T. N. (2001). It's like . . . you discover a new sense of being: Involved fathering as an evoker of adult development. *Men & Masculinities, 4*(1), 49–69.

Palmer, S. E. (1999). *Vision science: Photons to phenomenology.* Cambridge, MA: MIT Press.

Palmeri, T. J., Blake, R., Marois, R., Flanery, M. A., & Whetsell, W. Jr. (2002). The perceptual reality of synesthetic colors. *Proceedings of the National Academy of Sciences, 99,* 4127–4131.

Palmisano, M., & Herrmann, D. (1991). The facilitation of memory performance. *Bulletin of the Psychonomic Society, 29,* 557–559.

Paloski, W. H. (1998). Vestibulospinal adaptation to microgravity. *Otolaryngol Head and Neck Surgery, 118,* S39–S44.

Paluszynska, D. A., Harris, K. A., & Thach, B. T. (2004). Influence of sleep position experience on ability of prone-sleeping infants to escape from asphyxiating microenvironments by changing head position. *Pediatrics, 114,* 1634–1639.

Paoletti, M. G. (1995). Biodiversity, traditional landscapes and agroecosystem management. *Landscape and Urban Planning, 31*(1–3), 117–128.

Pape, H. C., Munsch, T., & Budde, T. (2004). Novel vistas of calcium-mediated signalling in the thalamus. *Pflugers Archives, 448,* 131–138.

Pardini, D. A., & Lochman, J. E. (2003). Treatment of oppositional defiant disorder. In M. A. Reinecke, F. M. Dattilio, & A. Freeman (Eds.), *Cognitive therapy with children and adolescents.* New York: Guilford Press.

Smith, S., & Donnerstein, E. (1998). Harmful effects of exposure to media violence: Learning of aggression, emotional desensitization, and fear. In R. Geen & E. Donnerstein (Eds.), *Human aggression: Theories, research, and implications for policy.* New York: Academic Press.

Smith, S., & Freedman, D. G. (1983, April). *Mother-toddler interaction and maternal perception of child temperament in two ethnic groups: Chinese-American and European-American.* Paper presented at the meeting of the Society for Research in Child Development, Detroit, MI.

Smith, S. M., & Vela, E. (2001). Environmental context-dependent memory: A review and meta-analysis. *Psychonomic Bulletin & Review, 8,* 203–220.

Smith, S. S., O'Hara, B. F., Persico, A. M., Gorelick, D. A., Newlin, D. B., Vlahov, D., et al. (1992). Genetic vulnerability to drug abuse: The D2 dopamine receptor Taq i B1 restriction fragment length polymorphism appears more frequently in polysubstance abusers. *Archives of General Psychiatry, 49,* 723–727.

Smith, T. B., Constantine, M. G., Dunn, T. W., Dinehart, J. M., & Montoya, J. A. (2006). Multicultural education in the mental health professions: A meta-analytic review. *Journal of Counseling Psychology, 53,* 132–145.

Smith, T. W., & Suls, J. (2004). Introduction to the special section on the future of health psychology. *Health Psychology, 23,* 115–118.

Smith, T. W., Orleans, C. T., & Jenkins, C. D. (2004). Prevention and health promotion: Decades of progress, new challenges, and an emerging agenda. *Health Psychology, 23,* 126–131.

Smith, V. L. (1991). Prototypes in the courtroom: Lay representations of legal concepts. *Journal of Personality and Social Psychology, 44,* 787–797.

Smith-Crowe, K., Burke, M. J., & Landis, R. S. (2003). Organizational climate as a moderator of safety knowledge–safety performance relationships. *Journal of Organizational Behavior, 24,* 861–876.

Smither, J. W., London, M., & Reilly, R. R. (2005). Does performance improve following multisource feedback? A theoretical model, meta-analysis, and review of empirical findings. *Personnel Psychology, 58,* 33–66.

Smits, J. A. J., O'Cleirigh, C. M., & Otto, M. W. (2006). Combining cognitive-behavioral therapy and pharmacotherapy for the treatment of panic disorder. *Journal of Cognitive Psychotherapy, 20,* 75–84.

Smyth, C. L., & MacLachlan, M. (2005). Confirmatory factor analysis of the Trinity Inventory of Precursors to Suicide (TIPS) and its relationship to hopelessness and depression. *Death Studies, 29,* 333–350.

Snarey, J. (1987). A question of morality. *Psychological Bulletin, 97,* 202–232.

Snellingen, T., Evans, J. R., Ravilla, T., & Foster, A. (2002). Surgical interventions for age-related cataract. *Cochrane Database System Review, 2,* CD001323.

Snodgrass, S. R. (1994). Cocaine babies: A result of multiple teratogenic influences. *Journal of Child Neurology, 9*(3), 227–233.

Snow, R. E. (1995). Pygmalion and intelligence? *Current Directions in Psychological Science, 4,* 169–171.

Snowden, L. R., & Cheung, F. (1990). Use of inpatient mental health services by members of ethnic minority groups. *American Psychologist, 45,* 347–355.

Snyder, C. R., & Lopez, S. J. (2006). *Handbook of positive psychology.* New York: Oxford University Press.

Snyder, C. R., & Lopez, S. J. (2007). *Positive psychology: The scientific and practical explorations of human strengths.* New York: Sage.

Snyder, M., & Haugen, J. A. (1995). Why does behavioral confirmation occur? A functional perspective on the role of the target. *Personality and Social Psychology Bulletin, 21,* 963–974.

Snyderman, M., & Rothman, S. (1987). Survey of expert opinion on intelligence and aptitude testing. *American Psychologist, 42,* 137–144.

Sobel, D. M., & Kirkham, N. Z. (2006). Blickets and babies: The development of causal reasoning in toddlers and infants. *Developmental Psychology, 42,* 1103–1115.

Society for Industrial and Organizational Psychology. (2007). *Graduate training programs.* Retrieved February 10, 2007, from http://www.siop.org/gtp/gtplookup.asp.

Soenens, B., Vansteenkiste, M., Luyckx, K., & Goossens, L. (2006). Parenting and adolescent problem behavior: An integrated model with adolescent self-disclosure and perceived parental knowledge as intervening variables. *Developmental Psychology, 42,* 305–318.

Soetens, E., Casaer, S., D'Hooge, R., & Hueting, J. E. (1995). Effect of amphetamine on long-term retention of verbal material. *Psychopharmacology, 119,* 155–162.

Sohlberg, S., & Jansson, B. (2002). Unconscious responses to "mommy and I are one": Does gender matter? In R. F. Bornstein & J. M. Masling (Eds.), *The psychodynamics of gender and gender role. Vol. 10: Empirical studies in psychoanalytic theories* (pp. 165–201). Washington, DC, US: American Psychological Association.

Sohler, N., & Bromet, E. J. (2003). Does racial bias influence psychiatric diagnoses assigned at first hospitalization? *Social Psychiatry and Psychiatric Epidemiology, 38,* 463–472.

Soken, N. H., & Pick, A. D. (1992). Intermodal perception of happy and angry expressive behaviors by seven-month-old infants. *Child Development, 63,* 787–795.

Sokoloff, L. (1981). Localization of functional activity in the central nervous system by measurement of glucose utilization with radioactive deoxyglucose. *Journal of Cerebral Blood Flow and Metabolism, 1,* 7–36.

Sokolowska, M., Siegel, S., & Kim, J. A. (2002). Intraadministration associations: Conditional hyperalgesia elicited by morphine onset cues. *Journal of Experimental Psychology: Animal Behavior Processes, 28,* 309–20.

Solomon, R. L. (1980). The opponent-process theory of acquired motivation: The costs of pleasure and the benefits of pain. *American Psychologist, 35,* 691–712.

Solomon, R. L., Kamin, L. J., & Wynne, L. C. (1953). Traumatic avoidance learning: The outcomes of several extinction procedures with dogs. *Journal of Abnormal and Social Psychology, 48,* 291–302.

Solomon, S., Greenberg, J., Pyszczynski, T. (2004). The cultural animal: Twenty years of terror management theory and research. In J. Greenberg, S. Koole, & T. Pyszczynski (Eds.), *Handbook of experimental existential psychology* (pp. 13–34). New York: Guilford Press.

Solomonson, A. L., & Lance, C. E. (1997). Examination of the relationship between true halo and halo error in performance ratings. *Journal of Applied Psychology, 82,* 665–674.

Solowij, N., Stephens, R. S., Roffman, R. A., Babor, T., Kadden, R., Miller, M., et al. (2002). Cognitive functioning of long-term heavy cannabis users seeking treatment. *Journal of American Medical Association, 287,* 1123–1131.

Sommer, R. (1999). Applying environmental psychology. In D. A. Bernstein & A. M. Stec (Eds.), *The psychology of everyday life.* Boston: Houghton Mifflin.

Sorce, J., Emde, R., Campos, J., & Klinnert, M. (1981, April). *Maternal emotional signaling: Its effect on the visual cliff behavior of one-year-olds.* Paper presented at the meeting of the Society for Research in Child Development, Boston, MA.

Sørensen, H. J., Mortensen, E. L., Reinisch, J. M., & Mednick, S. A. (2003). Do hypertension and diuretic treatment in pregnancy increase the risk of schizophrenia in offspring? *American Journal of Psychiatry, 160,* 464–468.

Sorrentino, R. M., & Roney, C. J. R. (2000). *The uncertain mind: Individual differences in facing the unknown.* Philadelphia: Psychology Press.

Sowdon, J. (2001). Is depression more prevalent in old age? *Australian & New Zealand Journal of Psychiatry, 35,* 782–787.

Sowell, E. R., Peterson, B. S., Thompson, P. M., Welcome, S. E., Henkenius, A. L., & Toga, A. W. (2003). Mapping cortical change across the human life span. *Nature Neuroscience, 6,* 309–315.

Sowell, T. (2005). *Black rednecks and white liberals.* San Francisco: Encounter Books

Spangler, G., Fremmer-Bombik, E., & Grossman, K. (1996). Social and individual determinants of infant attachment security and disorganization. *Infant Mental Health Journal, 17,* 127–139.

Spanier, C., Frank, E., McEachran, A. B., Grochocinski, V. J., & Kupfer, D. J. (1996). The prophylaxis of depressive episodes in recurrent depression following discontinuation of drug therapy: Integrating psychological and biological factors. *Psychological Medicine, 26,* 461–475.

Spano, M. S., Ellgren, M., Wang, X., & Hurd, Y. L. (2007). Prenatal cannabis exposure increases heroin seeking with allostatic changes in limbic enkephalin systems in adulthood. *Biological Psychiatry, 61,* 554–563.

Spanos, N. P. (1994). Multiple identity enactments and multiple personality disorder: A sociocognitive perspective. *Psychological Bulletin, 116,* 143–165.

Spanos, N. P. (1996). *Multiple identities and false memories: A sociocognitive perspective.* Washington, DC: American Psychological Association.

Spanos, N. P., Burnley, M. C. E., & Cross, P. A. (1993). Response expectancies and interpretations as determinants of hypnotic responding. *Journal of Personality and Social Psychology, 65*(6), 1237–1242.

Sparks, K., Cooper, C., Fried, Y., & Shirom, A. (1997). The effects of hours of work on health: A meta-analytic review. *Journal of Occupational and Organizational Psychology, 70,* 391–408.

Sparks, K., Faragher, B., & Cooper, C. L. (2001). Well-being and occupational health in the 21st century workplace. *Journal of Occupational and Organizational Psychology, 74,* 489–509.

Spear, L. P. (2000). Neurobiological changes in adolescence. *Current Directions in Psychological Science, 9,* 111–114.

Spearman, C. E. (1904). General intelligence objectively determined and measured. *American Journal of Psychology, 15,* 201–293.

Spearman, C. E. (1927). *The abilities of man.* New York: Macmillan.

Speckhard, A. (2002). Voices from the inside: Psychological responses to toxic disasters. In J. M. Havenaar & J. G. Cwikel (Eds.), *Toxic turmoil: Psychological and societal consequences of ecological disasters* (pp. 217–236). New York: Plenum.

Spector, P. E. (1985). Measurement of human service staff satisfaction: Development of the Job Satisfaction Survey. *American Journal of Community Psychology, 13,* 693–713.

Spector, P. E. (2002). Employee control and occupational stress. *Current Directions in Psychological Science, 11,* 133–136.

Spector, P. E. (2003). *Industrial & organizational psychology: Research and practice* (3rd ed.). New York: Wiley.

Spector, P. E., Fox, S., & Domalgaski, T. (2006). Emotions, violence, and counterproductive work behavior. In E. K. Kelloway, J. Barling, & J. J. Hurrell (Eds.), *Handbook of workplace violence* (pp. 29–46). Thousand Oaks, CA: Sage.

Spelke, E. S., Breinlinger, K., Macomber, J., & Jacobson, K. (1992). Origins of knowledge. *Psychological Review, 99*, 605–632.

Spence, C., & Read, L. (2003). Speech shadowing while driving: On the difficulty of splitting attention between eye and ear. *Psychological Science, 14*, 251–256.

Spence, S. H. (2003). Social skills training with children and young people: Theory, evidence, and practice. *Child and Adolescent Mental Health, 8*, 84–96.

Spence, S. H., Donovan, C., Brechman-Toussaint, M. (2000). The treatment of childhood social phobia: The effectiveness of a social skills training-based, cognitive-behavioral intervention, with and without parental involvement. *Journal of Child Psychology and Psychiatry and Allied Disciplines, 41*, 713–726.

Spence, S. H., Sheffield, J. K., & Donovan, C. L. (2005). Long-term outcome of a school-based, universal approach to prevention of depression in adolescents. *Journal of Consulting and Clinical Psychology, 73*, 160–167.

Spencer, S., Steele, C. M., & Quinn, D. (1997). *Under suspicion on inability: Stereotype threats and women's math performance.* Unpublished manuscript.

Spencer, T. J. (2002). Attention-deficit/hyperactivity disorder. *Archives of Neurology, 59*, 314–316.

Sperry, R. W. (1968). Hemisphere deconnection and unity in conscious awareness. *American Psychologist, 23*, 723–733.

Sperry, R. W. (1974). Lateral specialization in the surgically separated hemispheres. In F. O. Schmitt & F. G. Wordon (Eds.), *The neurosciences third study program.* Cambridge: MIT Press.

Spiegel, D. (Ed.). (1994). *Dissociation: Culture, mind, and body.* Washington, DC: American Psychiatric Press.

Spiegel, D. A., & Bruce, T. J. (1997). Benzodiazepines and and exposure-based cognitive behavior therapies for panic disorder: Conclusions from combined treatment trials. *American Journal of Psychiatry, 151*, 876–881.

Spillmann, L., Otte, T., Hamburger, K., & Magnussen, S. (2006). Perceptual filling-in from the edge of the blind spot. *Vision Research, 46*, 4252–4257.

Spinath, F. M., Harlaar, N., Ronald, A., & Plomin, R. (2004). Substantial genetic influence on mild mental impairment in early childhood. *American Journal of Mental Retardation, 109*, 34–43.

Spinath, F. M., Price, T. S., Dale, P. S., & Plomin, R. (2004). Genetic and environmental origins of language disability and ability. *Child Development, 75*, 445–454.

Spinhoven, P., Kuile, M., Kole-Snijders, A. M., Mansfeld, H. M., Ouden, D. L., & Vlaeyen, J. W. (2005). Catastrophizing and internal pain control as mediators of outcome in the multidisciplinary treatment of chronic low back pain. *European Journal of Pain, 8*, 211–219.

Spinrad, T. L., Eisenberg, N.,Cumberland, A., Fabes, R. A., Valiente, C., Shepard, S. A., et al. (2006). Relation of emotion-related regulation to children's social competence: A longitudinal study. *Emotion, 6*, 498–510.

Spira, J. L. (2001). Study design casts doubt on value of St. John's wort in treating depression. *British Medical Journal, 322*, 493.

Spitz, H. H. (1991). Commentary on Locurto's "Beyond IQ in preschool programs?" *Intelligence, 15*, 327–333.

Spitz, H. H. (1997). *Nonconscious movements: From mystical messages to facilitated communication.* Hillsdale, NJ: Erlbaum.

Spitzer, R. L., Gibbon, M., Skodol, A. E., & Williams, J. B. W., & First, M. B. (Eds.). (1994). *DSM-IV casebook: A learning companion to the Diagnostic and Statistical Manual of Mental Disorders* (4th ed.). Washington, DC: American Psychiatric Association.

Spitzer, R. L., Skodol, A. E., Gibbon, M., & Williams, J. B. W. (1983). *Psychopathology: A casebook.* New York: McGraw-Hill.

Sprecher, S., Hatfield, E., Anthony, C., & Potapova, E. (1994). Token resistance to sexual intercourse and consent to unwanted sexual intercourse: College students' dating experiences in three countries. *Journal of Sex Research, 31*(2), 125–132.

Springer, K., & Belk, A. (1994). The role of physical contact and association in early contamination sensitivity. *Developmental Psychology, 30*(6), 864–868.

Springer, M. V., McIntosh, A. R., Winocur, G., & Grady, C. L. (2005). The relation between brain activity during memory tasks and years of education in young and older adults. *Neuropsychology, 19*, 181–192.

Springer, S. P., & Deutsch, G. (1989). *Left brain, right brain.* San Francisco: Freeman.

Spychalski, A. C., Quinones, M. A., Gaugler, B. B., & Pohley, K. (1997). A survey of assessment center practices in organizations in the U.S. *Personnel Psychology, 50*, 71–90.

Squire, L. (1987). *Memory and brain.* New York: Oxford University Press.

Squire, L. R. (1986). Mechanisms of memory. *Science, 232*, 1612–1619.

Squire, L. R. (1992). Memory and the hippocampus: A synthesis from findings with rats, monkeys, and humans. *Psychological Review, 99*, 195–231.

Squire, L. R., Amara, D. G., & Press, G. A. (1992). Magnetic resonance imaging of the hippocampal formation and mamillary nuclei distinguish medial temporal lobe and diencephalic amnesia. *Journal of Neuroscience, 10*, 3106–3117.

Squire, L. R., & McKee, R. (1992). The influence of prior events on cognitive judgments in amnesia. *Journal of Experimental Psychology: Learning, Memory, and Cognition, 18*, 106–115.

Srinivas, K. (1993). Perceptual specificity in nonverbal priming. *Journal of Experimental Psychology: Learning, Memory, and Cognition 19*, 582–602.

Srivastava, S., John, O. P., Gosling, S. D., & Potter, J. (2003). Development of personality in early and middle adulthood: Set like plaster or persistent change? *Journal of Personality and Social Psychology, 84*, 1041–1053.

Sroka, J. J., & Braida, L. D. (2005). Human and machine consonant recognition. *Speech Communication, 45*, 401–423.

Sroufe, L. A., Fox, N. E., & Pancake, V. R. (1983). Attachment and dependency in developmental perspective. *Child Development, 54*, 1615–1627.

Stacey, J., & Biblarz, T. J. (2001). (How) Does the sexual orientation of parents matter? *American Sociological Review, 66*, 159–183.

Staddon, J. E. R., & Ettinger, R. H. (1989). *Learning: An introduction to the principles of adaptive behavior.* San Diego: Harcourt Brace Jovanovich.

Stafford, R. S., & Radley, D. C. (2003). National trends in antiobesity medication use. *Archives of Internal Medicine, 163*, 1046–1050.

Stahl, S. M. (2002). Selective actions on sleep or anxiety by exploiting GABA-A/benzodiazepine receptor subtypes. *Journal of Clinical Psychiatry, 63*, 179–180.

Staley, J. K., Sanacora, G., Tamagnan, G., Maciejewski, P. K., Malison, R. T., Berman, R. M., et al. (2006). Sex differences in diencephalon serotonin transporter availability in major depression. *Biological Psychiatry, 59*, 40–47.

Standing, L., Conezio, J., & Haber, R. N. (1970). Perception and memory for pictures: Single-trial learning of 2500 visual stimuli. *Psychonomic Science, 19*, 73–74.

Stanhope, N., Cohen, G., & Conway, M. A. (1993). Very long-term retention of a novel. *Applied Cognitive Psychology, 7*, 239–256.

Stankov, L. (1989). Attentional resources and intelligence: A disappearing link. *Personality and Individual Differences, 10*, 957–968.

Stanley, B. G., Willett, V. L., Donias, H. W., & Ha-Lyen, H. (1993). The lateral hypothalamus: A primary site mediating excitatory aminoacid-elicited eating. *Brain Research, 63*(1–2), 41–49.

Stanovich, K. E. (2004). *How to think straight about psychology* (7th ed.). Boston: Allyn Bacon.

Stanovich, K. E., & West, R. F. (2002). Individual differences in reasoning: Implications for the rationality debate? In T. Gilovich, D. Griffin, & D. Kahneman (Eds.), *Heuristics and biases: The psychology of intuitive judgment* (pp. 421–440). New York: Cambridge University Press.

Stansfeld, S. A., & Marmot, M. G. (Eds.). (2002). *Stress and the heart: Psychosocial pathways to coronary heart disease.* London: BMJ Books.

Stanton-Hicks, M., & Salamon, J. (1997). Stimulation of the central and peripheral nervous system for the control of pain. *Journal of Clinical Neurophysiology, 14*, 46–62.

Starkman, N., & Rajani, N. (2002). The case for comprehensive sex education. *AIDS Patient Care & STDs, 16*, 313–318.

Starkstein, S. E., Fedoroff, J. P., Price, T. R., Leigguarda, R., & Robinson, R. G. (1992). Anosognosia in patients with cerebrovascular lesions: A study of causative factors. *Stroke, 23*, 1446–1453.

Stasser, G. (1991). Pooling of unshared information during group discussion. In S. Worchel, W. Wood, & J. Simpson (Eds.), *Group processes and productivity.* Beverly Hills, CA: Sage.

Stasser, G., Stewart, D., & Wittenbaum, G. M. (1995). Expert roles and information exchange during discussion: The importance of knowing who knows what. *Journal of Experimental Social Psychology, 31*, 244–265.

Staudt, M., Grodd, W., Niemann, G., Wildgruber, D., Erb, M., & Krageloh-Mann, I. (2001). Early left periventricular brain lesions induce right hemispheric organization of speech. *Neurology 2001, 57*, 122–125.

Stauffer, J. M., & Buckley, M. R. (2005). The existence and nature of racial bias in supervisory ratings. *Journal of Applied Psychology, 90*, 586–591.

Staw, B. M., Bell, N. E., & Clausen, J. A. (1986). The dispositional approach to job attitudes: A lifetime longitudinal test. *Administrative Science Quarterly, 31*, 56–77.

Staw, B. M., & Cohen-Charash, Y. (2005). The dispositional approach to job satisfaction: More than a mirage, but not yet an oasis. *Journal of Organizational Behavior, 26*, 59–78.

Steadman, H. J. (1993). *Reforming the insanity defense: An evaluation of pre- and post-Hinckley reforms.* New York: Guilford.

Stec, A. M., & Bernstein, D. A. (Eds.). (1999). *Psychology: Fields of application.* Boston: Houghton Mifflin.

Steele, C. M. (1997). A threat in the air: How stereotypes shape intellectual identity and performance. *American Psychologist, 52*, 613–629.

Steele, C. M., & Aronson, J. (2000). Stereotype threat and the intellectual test performance of African Americans. In C. Stangor (Ed.), *Stereotypes and prejudice: Essential readings* (pp. 369–389). Philadelphia: Psychology Press/Taylor & Francis.

Steele, C. M., Spencer, S. J., & Lynch, M. (1993). Self-image resilience and dissonance: The role of affirmational resources. *Journal of Personality and Social Psychology, 64*, 885–896.

Steele, T. D., McCann, U. D., & Ricaurte, G. A. (1994). 3,4-methylenedioxymethamphetamine (MDMA, ecstacy): Pharmacology and toxicology in animals and humans. *Addiction, 89*(5), 539–551.

Stefanacci, L., Buffalo, E. A., Schmolck, H., & Squire, L. R. (2000). Profound amnesia after damage to the medial temporal lobe: A neuroanatomical and neuropsychological profile of patient E. P. *Journal of Neuroscience, 20*(18), 7024–7036.

Steffen, P. R., McNeilly, M., Anderson, N., & Sherwood, A. (2003). Effects of perceived racism and anger inhibition on ambulatory blood pressure in African Americans. *Psychosomatic Medicine, 65,* 746–750.

Stein, D. M., & Lambert, M. J. (1995). Graduate training in psychotherapy: Are therapy outcomes enhanced? *Journal of Consulting and Clinical Psychology, 63,* 182–196.

Stein, E. (1999). *The mismeasure of desire: The science, theory and ethics of sexual orientation.* New York: Oxford University Press.

Stein, M. A. (1993, November 30). Spacewalking repair team to work on Hubble flaws; shower head inspires a device to improve focusing ability. *Los Angeles Times,* A1, A5.

Stein, M. B., Chavira, D. A., & Jang, K. L. (2001). Bringing up bashful baby: Developmental pathways to social phobia. *Psychiatric Clinics of North America, 24,* 661–675.

Steinberg, L. (1990). Autonomy, conflict, and harmony in the family relationship. In S. S. Feldman & G. R. Elliott (Eds.), *At the threshold: The developing adolescent* (pp. 255–276). Cambridge, MA: Harvard University Press.

Steinberg, L., Dornbusch, S. M., & Brown, B. B. (1992). Ethnic differences in adolescent achievement: An ecological perspective. *American Psychologist, 47,* 723–729.

Steinberg, L. (2007). Risk taking in adolescence: New perspectives from brain and behavioral science. *Current Directions in Psychological Science, 16,* 55–59.

Steindler, D. A. & Pincus, D. W. (2002). Stem cells and neuropoiesis in the adult human brain. *Lancet, 359,* 1047–1054.

Steiner, J. E., Glaser, D., Hawilo, M. E., & Berridge, K. C. (2001). Comparative expression of hedonic impact: Affective reactions to taste by human infants and other primates. *Neuroscience and Biobehavioral Reviews, 25,* 53–74.

Steiner, J. M., & Fahrenberg, J. (2000). Authoritarianism and social status of former members of the Waffen-SS and SS and of the Wehrmacht: An extension and reanalysis of the study published in 1970. *Koelner Zeitschrift fuer Soziologie und Sozialpsychologie, 52,* 329–348.

Stephan, K. E., Marshall, J. C., Friston, K. J., Rowe, J. B., Ritzl, A., Zilles, K., & Fink, G. R. (2003). Lateralized cognitive processes and lateralized task control in the human brain. *Science, 301,* 384–386.

Stephens, R. S., Roffman, R. A., & Simpson, E. E. (1994). Treating adult marijuana dependence: A test of the relapse prevention model. *Journal of Consulting and Clinical Psychology, 62*(1), 92–99.

Steptoe, A., Peacey, V., & Wardle, J. (2006). Sleep duration and health in young adults. *Archives of Internal Medicine, 166,* 1689–1692.

Steptoe, A., Wardle, J., & Marmot, M. (2005). Positive affect and health-related neuroendocrine, cardiovascular, and inflammatory processes. *Proceedings of the National Academy of Sciences of the USA, 102,* 6508–6512.

Steriade, M., & McCarley, R. W. (1990). *Brainstem control of wakefulness and sleep.* New York: Plenum.

Stern, K., & McClintock, M. K. (1998). Regulation of ovulation by human pheromones. *Nature, 392,* 177–179.

Stern, W. L. (1912). Über die psychologishen Methoden der Intelligenzpurfüng. *Ber. V. Kongress Exp. Psychol., 16,* 1–160. American translation by G. M. Whipple (1913). The psychological methods of testing intelligence. *Educational Psychology Monographs, 13.* Baltimore: Warwick & York.

Sternberg, R. J. (1985). *Beyond IQ: A triarchic theory of human intelligence.* Cambridge, England: Cambridge University Press.

Sternberg, R. J. (1988a). Triangulating love. In R. J. Sternberg & M. L. Barnes (Eds.), *The psychology of love* (pp. 500–520). New Haven: Yale University Press.

Sternberg, R. J. (1988b). *The triarchic mind.* New York: Cambridge Press.

Sternberg, R. J. (1989). Domain generality versus domain specificity: The life and impending death of a false dichotomy. *Merrill-Palmer Quarterly, 35,* 115–130.

Sternberg, R. J. (1996). *Successful intelligence.* New York: Simon & Schuster.

Sternberg, R. J. (1997a). Construct validation of a triangular love scale. *European Journal of Social Psychology, 27,* 313–335.

Sternberg, R. J. (1997a). Construct validation of a triangular love scale. *European Journal of Social Psychology, 27,* 313–335.

Sternberg, R. J. (1997b). The triarchic theory of intelligence. In D. P. Flanagan, J. L. Genshaft, & P. L. Harrison (Eds.), *Contemporary intellectual assessment: Theories, tests, and issues* (pp. 92–104). New York: Guilford Press.

Sternberg, R. J. (1999). Ability and expertise: It's time ot replace the current model of intelligence. *American Educator Spring 1999,* pp. 10–51.

Sternberg, R. J. (2001). What is the common thread of creativity?: Its dialectical relation to intelligence and wisdom. *American Psychologist, 56,* 360–362.

Sternberg, R. J. (2004). Culture and intelligence. *American Psychologist, 59,* 325–338.

Sternberg, R. J. (Ed.). (2000). *Handbook of human intelligence* (2nd ed.). Cambridge, MA: Cambridge University Press.

Sternberg, R. J., & Dess, N. K. (2001). Creativity for the new millennium. *American Psychologist, 56,* 332.

Sternberg, R. J., & Grigorenko, E. L. (Eds.). (2004a). *Creativity: From potential to realization.* Washington, DC: APA Books.

Sternberg, R. J., & Grigorenko, E. L. (Eds.). (2004b). *Culture and competence: Contexts of life success.* Washington, DC: APA Books.

Sternberg, R. J., Hojjat, M., & Barnes, M. L. (2001). Empirical tests of aspects of a theory of love as a story. *European Journal of Personality, 15,* 199–218.

Sternberg, R. J., & Kaufman, J. C. (1998). Human abilities. *Annual Review of Psychology, 49,* 479–502.

Sternberg, R. J., Lautrey, J., & Lubart, T. I. (2003). Where are we in the field of intelligence, how did we get here, and where are we going? In R. J. Sternberg, J. Lautrey, et al. (Eds.), *Models of intelligence: International perspectives* (pp. 3–25). Washington, DC: American Psychological Association.

Sternberg, R. J., & Lubart, T. I. (1992). Buy low and sell high: An investment approach to creativity. *Current Directions in Psychological Science, 1*(1), 1–5.

Sternberg, R. J., & O'Hara, L. A. (1999). Creativity and intelligence. In R. J. Sternberg, et al. (Eds.), *Handbook of creativity* (pp. 251–272). New York: Cambridge University Press.

Sternberg, R. J., & The Rainbow Project Coordinators. (2006). The Rainbow Project: Enhancing the SAT through assessments of analytical, practical, and creative skills. *Intelligence, 34,* 321–350.

Sternberg, R. J., & Williams, W. M. (1997). Does the graduate record examination predict meaningful success of graduate training of psychologists? A Case Study. *American Psychologist, 52,* 630–641.

Sternberg, R. J., Wagner, R. K., Williams, W. M., & Horvath, J. A. (1995). Testing common sense. *American Psychologist, 50,* 912–927.

Stettler, D. D., Yamahachi, H., Li, W., Denk, W., & Gilbert, C. D. (2006). Axons and synaptic boutons are highly dynamic in adult visual cortex. *Neuron, 49,* 877–887.

Steunenberg, B., Beekman, A. T. F., Deeg, D. J. H., & Kerkhof, A. J. F. M. (2006). Personality and the onset of depression in late life. *Journal of Affective Disorders, 92,* 243–251.

Steven, M. S., Hansen, P. C., & Blakemore, C. (2006). Activation of color-selective areas of the visual cortex in a blind synesthete. *Cortex, 42,* 304–308.

Stevens, A. (1996). *Private myths: Dreams and dreaming.* Cambridge, MA: Harvard University Press.

Stevens, C., Sanders, L., & Neville, H. (2006). Neurophysiological evidence for selective auditory attention deficits in children with specific language impairment. *Brain Research, 1111,* 143–152.

Stevens, J. C., & Hooper, J. E. (1982). How skin and object temperature influence touch sensation. *Perception and Psychophysics, 32,* 282–285.

Stevens, J. C., & Pollack, M. H. (2005). Benzodiazepines in clinical practice: Consideration of their long-term use and alternative agents. *Journal of Clinical Psychiatry, 66*(Suppl. 2), 21–27.

Stevens, R. D., & Bhardwaj, A. (2006). Approach to the comatose patient. *Critical Care Medicine, 34*(1), 31–41.

Stevenson, H. (1992). *A long way from being number one: What we can learn from East Asia.* Washington, DC: Federation of Behavior, Psychological and Cognitive Sciences.

Stevenson, R. J., & Boakes, R. A. (2003). A mnemonic theory of odor perception. *Psychological Review, 110,* 340–364.

Stewart, G. L. (2006). A meta-analytic review of relationships between team design features and team performance. *Journal of Management, 32,* 29–55.

Stewart, J. H. (2005). Hypnosis in contemporary medicine. *Mayo Clinic Proceedings, 80,* 511–524.

Stewart, R., & Przyborski, S. (2002). Non-neural adult stem cells: Tools for brain repair? *Bioessays, 24,* 708–713.

Stewart, S. E., Platko, J., Fagerness, J., Birns, J., Jenike, E., Smoller, J. W., et al. (2007). A genetic family-based association study of OLIG2 in obsessive-compulsive disorder. *Archives of General Psychiatry, 64,* 209–214.

Stewart, W. F., Ricci, J. A., Chee, E., Hahn, S. R., & Morganstein, D. (2003). Cost of lost productive work time among US workers with depression. *Journal of the American Medical Association, 289,* 3135–3144.

Stice, E., & Fairburn, C. G. (2003). Dietary and dietary-depressive subtypes of bulimia nervosa show differential symptom presentation, social impairment, comorbidity, and course of illness. *Journal of Consulting and Clinical Psychology, 71,* 1090–1094.

Stice, E., Ragan, J., & Randall, P. (2004). Prospective relations between social support and depression: Differential direction of effects for parent and peer support? *Journal of Abnormal Psychology, 113,* 155–159.

Stice, E., & Shaw, H. (2004). Eating disorder prevention programs: A meta-analytic review. *Psychological Bulletin, 130,* 206–227.

Stice, E., Shaw, H., & Nathan, C. (2006). A meta-analytic review of obesity prevention programs for children and adolescents: The skinny on interventions that work. *Psychological Bulletin, 132,* 667–691.

Stickgold, R., Malia, A., Maguire, D., Roddenberry, D., & O'Connor, M. (2000). Replaying the game: Hypnagogic images in normals and amnesics. *Science, 290,* 350–353.

Stickgold, R., Rittenhouse, C. D., & Hobson, J. A. (1994). Dream splicing: A new technique for assessing thematic coherence in subjective reports of mental activity. *Consciousness and Cognition, 3*(1), 114–128.

Stiles, W. B., Barkham, M., Twigg, E., Mellor-Clark, J., & Cooper, M. (2006). Effectiveness of cognitive-behavioural, person-centered and psychodynamic therapies as practised in UK national health service settings. *Psychological Medicine, 36,* 555–566.

Stillman, J. A. (2002). Gustation: Intersensory experience par excellence. *Perception, 31,* 1491–1500.

Stillwell, M. E. (2002). Drug-facilitated sexual assault involving gamma-hydroxybutyric acid. *Journal of Forensic Science, 47,* 1133–1134.

Stipek, D. J., & Ryan, R. H. (1997). Economically disadvantaged preschoolers: Ready to learn but further to go. *Developmental Psychology, 33,* 711–723.

Stoff, D. M., Breiling, J., & Maser, J. D. (Eds.). (1997). *Handbook of antisocial behavior.* New York: Wiley.

Stone, A., & Valentine, T. (2003). Perspectives on prosopagnosia and models of face recognition. *Cortex, 39,* 31–40.

Stone, J. (2003). Self-consistency for low self-esteem in dissonance processes: The role of self-standards. *Personality and Social Psychology Bulletin, 29,* 846–858.

Stone, J., & Cooper, J. (2001). A self-standards model of cognitive dissonance. *Journal of Experimental Social Psychology, 37,* 228–243.

Stone, L. D., & Pennebaker, J. W. (2002). Trauma in real time: Talking and avoiding online conversations about the death of Princess Diana. *Basic and Applied Social Psychology, 24,* 173–183.

Stone, S. P., Halligan, P. W., & Greenwood, R. J. (1993). The incidence of neglect phenomena and related disorders in patients with acute left or right hemisphere stroke. *Age and Ageing, 22,* 46–52.

Stoney, C. M., & Engebretson, T. O. (1994). Anger and hostility: Potential mediators of the sex differences in coronary heart disease. In T. Smith, A. Siegman (Eds.), *Anger, hostility, and the heart* (pp. 215–237). Mahwah, NJ: Erlbaum.

Stoney, C. M., & Finney, M. L. (2000). Social support and stress: Influences on lipid reactivity. *International Journal of Behavioral Medicine, 7,* 111–126.

Stoney, C. M., & Hughes, J. W. (1999). Lipid reactivity among men with a parental history of myocardial infarction. *Psychophysiology, 36,* 484–490.

Stoney, C. M., Hughes, J. W., Kuntz, K. K., West, S. G., & Thornton, L. M. (2002). Cardiovascular stress responses among Asian Indian and European American women and men. *Annals of Behavioral Medicine, 24,* 113–121.

Stoney, C. M., Matthews, K. A., McDonald, R. H., & Johnson, C. A. (1988). Sex differences in lipid, lipoprotein, cardiovascular, and neuroendocrine responses to acute stress. *Psychophysiology, 25,* 646–656.

Strahan, E. J., Spencer, S. J., & Zanna, M. P. (2005). Subliminal priming and persuasion: How motivation affects the activation of goals and the persuasiveness of messages. In F. R.Kardes, P. Herr, & J. Nantel (Eds.), *Applying social cognition to consumer-focused strategy* (pp. 267–280). Mahwah, NJ: Erlbaum.

Strain, E. C., Mumford, G. K., Silverman, K., & Griffiths, R. R. (1994). Caffeine dependence syndrome: Evidence from case histories and experimental evaluations. *Journal of the American Medical Association, 272*(13), 1043–1048.

Strakowski, S. M., DelBello, M. P., & Adler, C. M. (2005). The functional neuroanatomy of bipolar disorder: A review of neuroimaging findings. *Molecular Psychiatry, 10,* 105–116.

Strathearn, L., Gray, P. H., O'Callaghan, M. J., & Wood, D. O. (2001). Childhood neglect and cognitive development in extremely low birth weight infants: A prospective study. *Pediatrics, 108,* 142–151.

Strauss, E., & Wada, J. (1983). Lateral preferences and cerebral speech dominance. *Cortex, 19*(2), 165–177.

Strauss, R. S., & Pollack, H. A. (2001). Epidemic increases in childhood overweight: 1986–1998. *Journal of the American Medical Association, 286,* 2845–2848.

Strayer, D. L., & Drews, F. A. (2006). Multi-tasking in the automobile. In A. Kramer, D. Wiegmann, & A. Kirlik (Eds.), *Applied attention: From theory to practice* (pp. 121–133). New York: Oxford University Press.

Strayer, D. L., Drews, F. A., & Crouch, D. J. (2003). Fatal distraction? A comparison of the cell-phone driver and the drunk driver. In D. V. McGehee, J. D. Lee, & M. Rizzo (Eds.), *Driving Assessment 2003: International symposium on human factors in driver assessment, training, and vehicle design* (pp. 25–30). Iowa City, IA: University of Iowa Public Policy Center,

Strayer, D. L., Drews, F. A., Crouch, D. J., & Johnston, W. A. (2004). Why do cell phone conversations interfere with driving? In W. R. Walker & D. Herrmann (Eds.), *Cognitive technology: Transforming thought and society.* Jefferson, NC: McFarland.

Strayer, D. L., Drews, F. A., & Johnston, W. A. (2003). Cell phone-induced failures of visual attention during simulated driving. *Journal of Experimental Psychology: Applied, 9,* 23–32.

Stricker, G. (2006). Assimilative psychodynamic psychotherapy integration. In G. Stricker & J. Gold (Eds.), *A casebook of psychotherapy integration* (pp. 55–63). Washington, DC: American Psychological Association.

Strickland, T., Ranganath, V., Lin, K.-M., Poland, R., Mendoza, R., & Smith, M. (1991). Psychopharmacologic considerations in the treatment of Black American populations. *Psychopharmacology Bulletin, 27,* 441–448.

Strohmetz, D. B., Rind, B., Fisher, R., & Lynn, M. (2002). Sweetening the till: The use of candy to increase restaurant tipping. *Journal of Applied Social Psychology, 32,* 300–309.

Strohschein, L. (2005). Household income histories and child mental health trajectories. *Journal of Health and Social Behavior, 46,* 359–375.

Stromberg, C. D., Haggarty, D. J., Leibenluft, R. F., McMillian, M. H., Mishkin, B., et al. (1988). *The psychologist's legal handbook.* Washington, DC: Council for the National Register of Health Service Providers in Psychology.

Stromberg, C., Schneider, J., & Joondeph, B. (1993, August). Dealing with potentially dangerous patients. *The Psychologist's Legal Update,* No. 2, pp. 3–12.

Stroop, J. R. (1935). Studies of interference in serial verbal reactions. *Journal of Experimental Psychology, 18,* 643–662.

Strümpfer, D. J. W. (2005). Standing on the shoulders of giants: Notes on early positive psychology (psychofortology). *South African Journal of Psychology, 35,* 21–45.

Strunk, D. R., Lopez, H., & DeRubeis, R. J. (2006). Depressive symptoms are associated with unrealistic negative predictions of future life events. *Behaviour Research and Therapy, 44,* 875–896.

Strupp, H. H., & Hadley, S. W. (1979). Specific versus non-specific factors in psychotherapy. *Archives of General Psychiatry, 36,* 1125–1136.

Stuart, R. B. (2004). Twelve practical suggestions for achieving multicultural competence. *Professional Psychology: Theory and Practice, 35,* 3–9.

Stuart, S., & Robertson, M. (2003). *Interpersonal psychotherapy: A clinician's guide.* London: Arnold Publishers.

Stunkard, A. J., Allison, K. C., & O'Reardon, J. P. (2005). The night eating syndrome: A progress report. *Appetite, 45,* 182–186.

Stürmer, T., Hasselbach, P., & Amelang, M. (2006). Personality, lifestyle, and risk of cardiovascular disease and cancer: Follow-up of population based cohort. *British Medical Journal, 332,* 1359.

Subotnik, K. L., Nuechterlein, K. H., Green, M. F., Horan, W. P., et al. (2006). Neurocognitive and social cognitive correlates of formal thought disorder in schizophrenia patients. *Schizophrenia Research, 85,* 84–95.

Subrahmanyam, K., David, S., & Greenfield, P. (2006). Connecting developmental constructions to the internet: Identity presentation and sexual exploration in online teen chat rooms. *Developmental Psychology, 42,* 395–406.

Subrahmanyam, K., & Greenfield, P. M. (1994). Effect of video game practice on spatial skills in girls and boys. *Journal of Applied Developmental Psychology, 15,* 13–32.

Subrahmanyam, K., Greenfield, P M., & Tynes, B. (2004). Constructing sexuality and identity in an Internet teen chatroom. *Journal of Applied Developmental Psychology, 25,* 651–666.

Suddath, R. L., Christison, G. W., Torrey, E. F., Casanova, M. F., & Weinberger, D. R. (1990). Anatomical abnormalities in the brains of monopsychotic twins discordant for schizophrenia. *New England Journal of Medicine, 322,* 789–794.

Sue, D. (1992). *Asian and Caucasian subjects' preference for different counseling styles.* Unpublished manuscript, Western Washington University.

Sue, S., & Okazaki, S. (1990). Asian-American educational achievements: A phenomenon in search of an explanation. *American Psychologist, 45,* 913–920.

Suedfeld, P., & Tetlock, P. (2001). Individual differences in information processing. In A. Tesser & N. Schwarz (Eds.), *Blackwell handbook of social psychology: Intraindividual processes* (pp. 284–304). Oxford, England: Blackwell.

Sufka, K. J. & Price, D. D. (2002). Gate control theory reconsidered. *Brain and Mind, 3,* 277–290.

Suh, E., Diener, E., & Fujita, F. (1996). Events and subjective well-being: Only recent events matter. *Journal of Personality and Social Psychology, 70,* 1091–1102.

Suinn, R. M. (2001). The terrible twos: Anger and anxiety. *American Psychologist, 56,* 27–36.

Sullivan, H. S. (1954). *The psychiatric interview.* New York: Norton.

Sullivan, P. F., Kendler, K. S., & Neale, M. C. (2003). Schizophrenia as a complex trait: Evidence from a meta-analysis of twin studies. *Archives of General Psychiatry, 60,* 1187–1192.

Suls, J., & Bunde, J. (2005). Anger, anxiety, and depression as risk factors for cardiovascular disease: The problems and implications of overlapping affective dispositions. *Psychological Bulletin, 131,* 260–300.

Suls, J., & Fletcher, B. (1985). The relative efficacy of avoidant and nonavoidant coping strategies: A meta-analysis. *Health Psychology, 4,* 249–288.

Suls, J., & Rothman, A. (2004). Evolution of the biopsychosocial model: Prospects and challenges for health psychology. *Health Psychology, 23,* 119–125.

Suls, J., & Wan, C. K. (1993). The relationship between trait hostility and cardiovascular reactivity: A quantitative review and analysis. *Psychophysiology, 30,* 1–12.

Sundberg, N., & Sue, S. (1989). Research and research hypotheses about effectiveness in intercultural counseling. In P. Pederson, J. Draguns, W. Lonner, & J. Trimble (Eds.), *Counseling across cultures* (3rd ed.). Honolulu: University of Hawaii Press.

Suomi, S. (1999). Attachment in rhesus monkeys. In J. Cassidy & P. Shaver (Eds.), *Handbook of attachment* (pp. 181–197). New York: Guilford.

Suomi, S. (2004). Aggression, serotonin, and gene-environment interactions in rhesus monkeys. In J. T. Cacioppo & G. G. Berntson (Eds.), *Essays in social neuroscience* (pp. 15–27). Cambridge, MA: MIT Press.

Super, C. M., & Super, D. E. (2001). *Opportunities in psychology careers.* Chicago: VGM Career Books.

Surtees, P. G., Wainwright, N. W., Luben, R., Khaw, K. T., & Day, N. E. (2006). Mastery, sense of coherence, and mortality: Evidence of independent associations from the EPIC–Norfolk Prospective Cohort Study. *Health Psychology, 25*(1), 102–110.

Suslow, T., Ohrmann, P., Bauer, J., Rauch, A. V., Schwindt, W., Arolt, V., et al. (2006). Amygdala activation during masked presentation of emotional faces predicts conscious detection of threat-related faces. *Brain and Cognition, 61,* 243–248.

Süss, H. M., Oberauer, K., Wittmann, W. W., Wilhelm, O., & Schulze, R. (2002). Working memory explains reasoning ability—and a little bit more. *Intelligence, 30,* 261–288.

Suzdak, P. D., Glowa, J. R., Crawley, J. N., Schwartz, R. D., Skolnick, P., & Paul, S. M. (1986). A selective imidazobenzodiazepine antagonist of ethanol in the rat. *Science, 234,* 1243–1247.

Suzuki, L. A., & Valencia, R. R. (1997). Race-ethnicity and measured intelligence. *American Psychologist, 52,* 1103–1114.

Svartberg, M., Stiles, T. C., & Seltzer, M. H. (2004). Randomized, controlled trial of the effectiveness of short-term dynamic psychotherapy and cognitive therapy for cluster C personality disorders. *American Journal of Psychiatry, 161,* 810–817.

Swaab, D. E., & Hofman, M. A. (1995). Sexual differentiation of the human hypothalamus in relation to gender and sexual orientation. *Trends in Neuroscience, 18*(6) 264–270.

Swaab, D. F., Chung, W. C., Kruijver, F. P., Hofman, M. A., & Ishunina, T. A. (2001). Structural and functional sex differences in the human hypothalamus. *Hormones and Behavior, 40,* 93–98.

Swan, G. E., & Carmelli, D. (1996). Curiosity and mortality in aging adults: A 5-year follow-up of the Western Collaborative Group Study. *Psychology and Aging, 11,* 449–453.

Swann, W. B., Jr., De La Ronde, C., & Hixon, J. G. (1994). Authenticity and positivity strivings in marriage and courtship. *Journal of Personality and Social Psychology, 66,* 857–869.

Swarte, N. B., van der Lee, M. L., van der Bom, J. G., van den Bout, J., & Heintz, A. P. M. (2003). Effects of euthanasia on the bereaved family and friends: A cross sectional study. *British Medical Journal, 327,* 189.

Swartz, M. S., Perkins, D. O., Stroup, T. S., Davis, S. M., Capuano, G., Rosenheck, R. A., et al. (2007). Effects of antipsychotic medications on psychosocial functioning in patients with chronic schizophrenia: Findings from the NIMH CATIE study. *American Journal of Psychiatry, 164,* 428–436.

Sweller, J., & Gee, W. (1978). Einstellung: The sequence effect and hypothesis theory. *Journal of Experimental Psychology: Human Learning and Memory, 4,* 513–526.

Swets, J. A. (1996). *Signal detection theory and ROC analysis in psychology and diagnostics.* New Jersey: Erlbaum.

Swets, J. A., Dawes, R. M., & Monahan, J. (2000). Psychological science can improve diagnostic decisions. *Psychological Science in the Public Interest, 1,* 1–26.

Swindle, R., Jr., Heller, K., Pescosolido, B., & Kikuzawa, S. (2000). Responses to nervous breakdowns in America over a 40-year period: Mental health policy implications. *American Psychologist, 55,* 740–749.

Swithers, S. E., & Hall, W. G. (1994). Does oral experience terminate ingestion? *Appetite, 23*(2), 113–138.

Symons, D. (1979). *The evolution of human sexuality.* Oxford, UK: Oxford University Press.

Symons, D. (1995). Beauty is in the adaptations of the beholder: The evolutionary psychology of human female sexual attractiveness. In P. R. Abramson & S. D. Pinkerton (Eds.), *Sexual nature, sexual culture* (pp. 80–118). Chicago: University of Chicago Press.

Szasz, T. (2003). The psychiatric protection order for the "battered mental patient." *British Medical Journal, 327,* 1449–1451.

Szegedi, A., Kohnen, R., Dienel, A., & Kieser, M. (2005). Acute treatment of moderate to severe depression with hypericum extract WS 5570 (St John's wort): Randomised controlled double blind non-inferiority trial versus paroxetine. *British Medical Journal, 330,* 503.

Tabbarah, M., Crimmins, E. M., & Seeman, T. E. (2002). The relationship between cognitive and physical performance: MacArthur studies of successful aging. *Journals of Gerontology: Series A: Biological Sciences and Medical Sciences, 57,* 228–235.

Tabert, M. H., Manly, J. J., Liu, X., Pelton, G. H., Rosenbaum, S., Jacobs, M., et al. (2006). Neuropsychological prediction of conversion to Alzheimer disease in patients with mild cognitive impairment. *Archives of General Psychiatry, 63,* 916–924.

Taggar, S., Hackett, R., & Saha, S. (1999). Leadership emergence in autonomous work teams: Antecedents and outcomes. *Personnel Psychology, 52,* 899–926.

Taggart, M. (2004, May 3). My little (twin) sister. *Daily Mail,* p. 25.

Tagliabue, J. (1999, January 28). Devil gets his due, but Catholic church updates exorcism rites. *International Herald Tribune,* p. 6.

Tailby, C., Wright, L. L., Metha, A. B., & Calford, M. B. (2005). Activity-dependent maintenance and growth of dendrites in adult cortex. *Proceedings of the National Academy of Sciences of the USA, 102,* 4631–4636.

Takashima, A., Petersson, K.M., Rutters, F., Tendolkar, I., Jensen, O., Zwarts, M. J., et al. (2006). Declarative memory consolidation in humans: A prospective functional magnetic resonance imaging study. *Proceedings of the National Academy of Sciences of the USA, 103,* 756–761.

Takayama, Y., Sugishita, M., Kido, T., Ogawa, M., & Akiguchi, I. (1993). A case of foreign accent syndrome without aphasia caused by a lesion of the left precentral gyrus. *Neurology, 43,* 1361–1363.

Takeuchi, A. H., & Hulse, S. H. (1993). Absolute pitch. *Psychological Bulletin, 113,* 345–361.

Talarico, J. F., & Rubin, D. C. (2003). Confidence, not consistency, characterizes flashbulb memories. *Psychological Science, 14,* 455–461.

Talmi, D., Grady, C. L., Goshen-Gottstein, Y., & Moscovitch, M. (2005). Neuroimaging the serial position curve: A test of single-store versus dual-store models. *Psychological Science, 16,* 716–723.

Tamminga, C. A., & Holcomb, H. H. (2005). Phenotype of schizophrenia: A review and formulation. *Molecular Psychiatry, 10,* 27–39.

Tan, G., Hammond, D. C., & Joseph, G. (2005). Hypnosis and irritable bowel syndrome: A review of efficacy and mechanism of action. *American Journal of Clinical Hypnosis, 47,* 161–178.

Tanaka, H., Taira, K., Arakawa, M., Toguti, H., Urasaki, C., Yamamoto, Y., et al. (2001). Effects of short nap and exercise on elderly people having difficulty sleeping. *Psychiatry and Clinical Neurosciences, 55,* 173–174.

Tankersley, D., Stowe, C. J., & Huettel, S. A. (2007). Altruism is associated with an increased neural response to agency. *Nature Neuroscience, 10,* 150–151.

Tan-Laxa, M. A., Sison-Switala, C., Rintelman, W., & Ostrea, E. M. (2004). Abnormal auditory brainstem response among infants with prenatal cocaine exposure. *Pediatrics, 113,* 357–360.

Tannen, D. (1994). *Gender and discourse.* New York: Oxford University Press.

Tanner, J. M. (1978). *Foetus into man: Physical growth from conception to maturity.* London: Open Books.

Tanner, J. M. (1992). Growth as a measure of nutritional and hygienic status of a population. *Hormone Research, 38,* 106–115.

Tarabar, A. F. & Nelson, L. S. (2004). The gamma-hydroxybutyrate withdrawal syndrome. *Toxicological Reviews, 23,* 45–49.

Tarr, S. J., & Pyfer, J. L. (1996). Physical and motor development of neonates/infants prenatally exposed to drugs in utero: A meta-analysis. *Adapted Physical Activity Quarterly, 13,* 269–287.

Task Force on Promotion and Dissemination of Psychological Procedures. (1995). Training in and dissemination of empirically validated psychological treatments: Report and recommendations. *Clinical Psychologist, 48,* 3–23.

Tasker, F., & Golombok, S. (1995). Adults raised as children in lesbian families. *American Journal of Orthopsychiatry, 65*(2), 203–215.

Tassi, P., & Muzet, A. (2001). Defining states of consciousness. *Neuroscience and Biobehavioral Reviews, 25,* 175–191.

Taub, E. (2004). Harnessing brain plasticity through behavioral techniques to produce new treatments in neurorehabilitation. *American Psychologist, 59,* 692–704.

Taubenfeld, S. M., Milekic, M. H., Monti, B., & Alberini, C. M. (2001). The consolidation of new but not reactivated memory requires hippocampal C/EBPb. *Nature Neuroscience, 4,* 813–818.

Tavris, C. (2002). The high cost of skepticism. *Skeptical Inquirer, 26*(4), 41–44.

Tavris, C. (2003). Mind games: Psychological warfare between therapists and scientists. *The Chronicle of Higher Education, 49,* B7–B9.

Tavris, C. (2004, January 3). *From Dora to Jane Doe: The use and abuse of case studies.* Paper presented at the 26th Annual National Institute on the Teaching of Psychology, St. Petersburg, Florida.

Taylor, H. (2001, August 8). *The Harris Poll #38.* Retrieved April 12, 2005, from http://harrisinteractive.com/harris_poll.

Taylor, H. A., & Tversky, B. (1992). Spatial mental models derived from survey and route descriptions. *Journal of Memory and Language, 31,* 261–292.

Taylor, J. G. (2002). Paying attention to consciousness. *Trends in Cognitive Science, 6,* 206–210.

Taylor, M. J., Freemantle, N., Geddes, J. R., & Bhagwagar, Z. (2006). Early onset of selective serotonin reuptake inhibitor antidepressant action. *Archives of General Psychiatry, 63,* 1217–1223.

Taylor, R. L., & Richards, S. B. (1991). Patterns of intellectual differences of Black, Hispanic, and White children. *Psychology in the Schools, 28,* 5–8.

Taylor, S. (2003). Outcome predictors for three PTSD treatments: Exposure therapy, EMDR, and relaxation training. *Journal of Cognitive Psychotherapy, 17,* 149–161.

Taylor, S. (2004). Efficacy and outcome predictors for three PTSD treatments: Exposure therapy, EMDR, and relaxation training. In S. Taylor (Ed.), *Advances in the treatment of posttraumatic stress disorder: Cognitive-behavioral perspectives* (pp. 13–37). New York: Springer.

Taylor, S., Peplau, A., & Sears, D. (2006). *Social psychology* (12th ed.). Upper Saddle River, NJ: Pearson/Prentice Hall.

Taylor, S., Thordarson, D. S., Maxfield, L., Fedoroff, I. C., Lovell, K., & Ogrodniczuk, J. (2003). Comparative efficacy, speed, and adverse effects of three PTSD treatments: Exposure therapy, EMDR, and relaxation training. *Journal of Consulting and Clinical Psychology, 71,* 330–338.

Taylor, S. E. (2002). *Health psychology* (5th ed.). New York: McGraw-Hill.

Taylor, S. E., Dickerson, S. S., & Klein, L. C. (2002). Toward a biology of social support. In C. R. Snyder & S. L. Lopez (Eds.), *Handbook of positive psychology* (pp. 556–569). London: Oxford University Press.

Taylor, S. E., Gonzaga, G. C., Klein, L. C., Hu, P., Greendale, G. A., & Seeman, T. E. (2006). Relation of oxytocin to psychological stress responses and hypothalamic-pituitary-adrenocortical axis activity in older women. *Psychosomatic Medicine, 68,* 238–245.

Taylor, S. E., Kemeny, M. E., Aspinwall, L. G., Schneider, S. G., Rodriguez, R., & Herbert, M. (1992). Optimism, coping, psychological distress, and high-risk sexual behavior among men at risk for acquired immunodeficiency syndrome (AIDS). *Journal of Personality and Social Psychology, 63,* 460–473.

Taylor, S. E., Kemeny, M. E., Reed, G. M., Bower, J. E., & Gruenewald, T. L. (2000). Psychological resources, positive illusions, and health. *American Psychologist, 55,* 99–109.

Taylor, S. E., Klein, L. C., Lewis, B. P., Gruenewald, T. L., Gurung, R. A. R., & Updegraff, J. A. (2000). Biobehavioral responses to stress in females: Tend-and-befriend, not fight-or-flight. *Psychological Review, 107,* 411–429.

Taylor, S. E., Lerner, J. S., Sherman, K. D., Sage, R. M., & McDowell, N. K. (2003). Are self-enhancing cognitions associated with health or unhealthy biological profiles? *Journal of Personality and Social Psychology, 85,* 605–615.

Taylor, S. P., & Hulsizer, M. R. (1998). Psychoactive drugs and human aggression. In R. G. Geen & E. Donnerstein (Eds.), *Human aggression* (pp. 139–167). San Diego: Academic Press.

Tecott, L. H., Sun, L. M., Akana, S. F., Strack, A. M., Lowenstein, D. H., Dallman, M. F., & Julius, D. (1995). Eating disorder and epilepsy in mice lacking 5–HT2C serotonin receptors. *Nature, 374,* 542–546.

Teghtsoonian, R. (1992). In defense of the pineal gland. *Behavioral and Brain Sciences, 15,* 224–225.

Teigen, K. H. (1994). Yerkes-Dodson: A law for all seasons. *Theory and Psychology, 4*(4), 525–547.

Tellegen, A., Lykken, D. T., Bouchard, T. J., Wilcox, K. J., Segal, N. L., & Rich, S. (1988). Personality similarity in twins reared apart and together. *Journal of Personality and Social Psychology, 54,* 1031–1039.

Tenenbaum, H. R., & Leaper, C. (2003). Parent-child conversations about science: The socializations of gender inequities? *Developmental Psychology, 39,* 34–47.

Teng, Y. D., Lavik, E. B., Qu, X., Park, K. I., Ourednik, J., Zurakowski, D., et al. (2002). Functional recovery following traumatic spinal cord injury mediated by a unique polymer scaffold seeded with neural stem cells. *Proceedings of the National Academy of Science, 99,* 3024–3029.

Teplin, L. A., McClelland, G. M., Abram, K. M., & Weiner, D. A. (2005). Crime victimization in adults with severe mental illness. *Archives of General Psychiatry, 62,* 911–921.

Ter Riet, G., Kleijnen, J., & Knipschild, P. (1990). Acupuncture and chronic pain: A criteria-based meta-analysis. *Journal of Clinical Epidemiology, 43,* 1191–1199.

Terman, L. M. (1916). *The measurement of intelligence.* Boston: Houghton Mifflin.

Terman, L. M., & Oden, M. H. (1947). *The gifted child grows up: Vol. 4. Genetic studies of genius.* Stanford, CA: Stanford University Press.

Terman, L. M., & Oden, M. H. (1959). *The gifted group at midlife.* Stanford, CA: Stanford University Press.

Terman, M., & Terman, J. S. (2005). Light therapy for seasonal and nonseasonal depression: Efficacy, protocol, safety, and side effects. *CNS Spectrums, 10,* 647–663.

Terrace, H. S., Petitto, L. A., Sanders, D. L., & Bever, J. G. (1979). Can an ape create a sentence? *Science, 206,* 891–902.

Tesser, A. (2001). Self-esteem: The frequency of temporal-self and social comparisons in people's personal appraisals. In A. Tesser & N. Schwarz (Eds.), *Blackwell handbook of social psychology: Intraindividual processes* (pp. 479–498). Oxford, UK: Blackwell.

Tetlock, P. E. (2006). *Expert political judgment: How good is it? How can we know?* Princeton, NJ: Princeton University Press.

Thakkar, R. R., Garrison, M. M., & Christakis, D. A. (2006). A systematic review for the effects of television viewing by infants and preschoolers. *Pediatrics, 118,* 2025–2031.

Thaler, E. R., Kennedy, D. W., & Hanson, C.W. (2001). Medical applications of electronic nose technology: Review of current status. *American Journal of Rhinology, 15,* 291–295.

Thanos, P. K., Volkow, N. D., Freimuth, P., Umegaki, H., Ikari, H., Roth, G., et al. (2001). Overexpression of dopamine D2 receptors reduces alcohol self-administration. *Journal of Neurochemistry, 78,* 1094–1103.

Thase, M. E. (2002). Antidepressant effects: The suit may be small, but the fabric is real. *Prevention & Treatment, 5,* Article 32. Retrieved December 13, 2004, from http://www.journals.apa.org/prevention/volume5/pre0050032c.html

Thase, M. E., Friedman, E. S., Biggs, M. M., Wisniewski, S. R., Trivedi, M. H., Luther, J. F., et al. (2007). Cognitive therapy versus medication in augmentation and switch strategies as second-step treatments: A STAR*D report. *American Journal of Psychiatry, 164,* 739–752.

Theeuwes, J., Godijn, R., & Pratt, J. (2004). A new estimation of the duration of attentional dwell time. *Psychonomic Bulletin and Review, 11,* 60–64.

Thelen, E. (1995). Motor development: A new synthesis. *American Psychologist, 50,* 79–95.

Theofilopoulos, S., Goggi, J., Riaz, S. S., Jauniaux, E., Stern, G. M., & Bradford, H. F. (2001). Parallel induction of the formation of dopamine and its metabolites with induction of tyrosine hydroxylase expression in foetal rat and human cerebral cortical cells by brain-derived neurotrophic factor and glial-cell derived neurotrophic factor. *Brain Research: Developmental Brain Research, 127,* 111–122.

Thiessen, E. D., Hill, E. A., & Saffran, J. R. (2005). Infant-directed speech facilitates word segmentation. *Infancy, 7,* 53–71.

Thom, A., Sartory, G., & Jöhren, P. (2000). Comparison between one-session psychological treatment and benzodiazepine in dental phobia. *Journal of Consulting and Clinical Psychology, 68,* 378–387.

Thomas, A., & Chess, S. (1977). *Temperament and development.* New York: Brunner/Mazel.

Thomas, E. L., & Robinson, H. A. (1972). *Improving reading in every class: A sourcebook for teachers.* Boston: Allyn & Bacon.

Thomas, J. A., & Walton, D. (2007). Measuring perceived risk: Self-reported and actual hand positions of SUV and car drivers. *Traffic Psychoogy and Behavior, 10,* 201–207.

Thomas, K. W., & Schmidt, W. H. (1976). A survey of managerial interests with respect to conflict. *Academy of Management Journal, 19,* 315–318.

Thompson, C., Koon, E., Woodwell, W., Jr., & Beauvais, J. (2002). *Training for the next economy: An ASTD state of the industry report on trend in employer-provided training in the United States.* Washington, DC: American Society for Training and Development.

Thompson, D. S., & Pollack, B. G. (2001, August 26). Psychotropic metabolism: Gender-related issues. *Psychiatric Times, 14.* Available: http://www.mhsource.com/pt/p010147.html

Thompson, J. K. (1996). Introduction: Assessment and treatment of binge eating disorder. In J. K. Thompson (Ed.), *Body image, eating disorders, and obesity* (pp. 1–22). Washington, DC: American Psychological Association.

Thompson, P. M., Giedd, J. N., Woods, R. P., Macdonald, D., Evans, A. C., & Toga, A. W. (2000). Growth patterns in the developing brain detected by using continuum mechanical tensor maps. *Nature, 404,* 190–193.

Thompson, P. M., Hayashi, K. M., Simon, S. L., Geaga, J. A., Hong, M. S., Sui, Y., et al. (2004). Structural abnormalities in the brains of human subjects who use methamphetamine. *Journal of Neuroscience, 24,* 6028–6036.

Thompson, R. A. (2006). The development of the person: Social understanding, relationships, self, conscience. In W. Damon & R. M. Lerner (Series Eds.) & N. Eisenberg (Vol. Ed.), *Handbook of child psychology: Vol. 3. Social, emotional, and personality development* (6th ed., pp. 24–98). New York: Wiley.

Thompson-Brenner, H., Glass, S., & Westen, D. (2003). A multidimensional meta-analysis of psychotherapy for bulimia nervosa. *Clinical Psychology: Science and Practice, 10,* 269–287.

Thomson, C. P. (1982). Memory for unique personal events: The roommate study. *Memory & Cognition, 10,* 324–332.

Thoresen, C. J., Kaplan, S. A., Barsky, A. P., Warren, C. R., & deChermont, K. (2003). The affective underpinnings of job perceptions and attitudes: A meta-analytic review and integration. *Psychological Bulletin, 129,* 914–945.

Thorndike, E. L. (1898). Animal intelligence: An experienced study of the associative process in animals. *Psychological Monographs, 2*(Whole No. 8).

Thorndike, E. L. (1905). *The elements of psychology.* New York: Seiler.

Thorndike, R. L. (1968). [Review of the book *Pygmalion in the classroom*]. *American Educational Research Journal, 5,* 708–711.

Thorndike, R. L., & Hagen, E. P. (1996). *Form 5 CogAT interpretive guide of school administrators: All levels.* Chicago: Riverside.

Thorndike, R. M. & Dinnel, D. L. (2001). *Basic statistics for the behavioral sciences.* Upper Saddle River, NJ: Prentice-Hall.

Thorngren, J. M., & Kleist, D. M. (2002). Multiple family group therapy: An interpersonal/postmodern approach. *Family Journal–Counseling and Therapy for Couples and Families, 10,* 167–176.

Thurstone, L. L. (1938). *Primary mental abilities.* Chicago: University of Chicago Press.

Tian, H.-G., Nan, Y., Hu, G., Dong, Q.-N., Yang, X.-L., Pietinen, P., & Nissinen, A. (1995). Dietary survey in a Chinese population. *European Journal of Clinical Nutrition, 49,* 27–32.

Tienari, P., Wynne, L. C., Läksy, K., Moring, J., Nieminen, P., et al. (2003). Genetic boundaries of the schizophrenia spectrum: Evidence from the Finnish Adoptive Family Study of Schizophrenia. *American Journal of Psychiatry, 160,* 1587–1594.

Tiihonen, J., Kuikka, J., Bergstrom, K., Hakola, P., Karhu, J., Ryynänen, O.-P., & Föhr, J. (1995). Altered striatal dopamine re-uptake site densities in habitually violent and non-violent alcoholics. *Nature Medicine, 1(7),* 654–657.

Timberlake, W., & Farmer-Dougan, V. A. (1991). Reinforcement in applied settings: Figuring out ahead of time what will work. *Psychological Bulletin, 110(3),* 379–391.

Timko, C., Finney, J. W., & Moos, R. H. (2005). The 8-year course of alcohol abuse: Gender differences in social context and coping. *Alcoholism: Clinical and Experimental Research, 29,* 612–621.

Timms, P. (2005). Is there still a problem with homelessness and schizophrenia? *International Journal of Mental Health, 34,* 57–75.

Tinbergen, N. (1989). *The study of instinct.* Oxford, UK: Clarendon.

Tindale, R. S., & Kameda, T. (2000). "Social sharedness" as a unifying theme for information processing in groups. *Group Processes and Intergroup Relations, 3,* 123–140.

Tippmann-Piekert, M., Park, J. G., Boeve, B. F., Shepard, J. W., & Silber, M. H. (2007). Pathologic gambling in patients with restless legs syndrome treated with dopaminergic agonists. *Neurology, 68,* 301–303.

Tobler, P. N., Fiorillo, C. D., & Schultz, W. (2005). Adaptive coding of reward value by dopamine neurons. *Science, 307,* 1642–1645.

Tohen, M., Zarate, C. A., Jr., Hennen, J., Khalsa, H.-M. K., Strakowski, S. M., Gebre-Medhin, P., et al. (2003). The McLean-Harvard first-episode mania study: Prediction of recovery and first recurrence. *American Journal of Psychiatry, 160,* 2099–2107.

Tolman, D. L., Impett, E. A., Tracy, A. J., & Michael, A. (2006). Looking good, sounding good: Femininity ideology and adolescent girls' mental health. *Psychology of Women Quarterly, 30,* 85–95.

Tolman, E. C., & Honzik, C. H. (1930). Introduction and removal of reward and maze performance in rats. *University of California Publication in Psychology, 4,* 257–265.

Toni, N., Buchs, P. A., Nikonenko, I., Bron, C. R., & Muller, D. (1999). LTP promotes formation of multiple spine synapses between a single axon terminal and a dendrite. *Nature, 402,* 421–425.

Torasdotter, M., Metsis, M., Henriksson, B. G., Winblad, B., & Mohammed, A. H. (1998). Environmental enrichment results in higher levels of nerve growth factor mRNA in the rat visual cortex and hippocampus. *Behavior and Brain Research, 93,* 83–90.

Törnros, J. E., & Bolling, A. K. (2005). Mobile phone use: Effects of handheld and hands-free phones on driving performance. *Accident Analysis and Prevention, 37,* 902–909.

Törnros, J. E., & Bolling, A. K. (2006). Mobile phone use: Effects of conversation on mental workload and driving speed in rural and urban environments. *Transportation Research Part F: Traffic Psychology and Behaviour, 9,* 298–306.

Tougas, F., Rinfret, N., Beaton, A. M., & de la Sablonnière, R. (2005). Policewomen acting in self-defense: Can psychological disengagement protect self-esteem from the negative outcomes of relative deprivation? *Journal of Personality and Social Psychology, 88,* 790–800.

Tourangeau, R., Rips, L. J., & Rasinski, K. (2000). *The psychology of the survey response.* Cambridge, England: Cambridge University Press.

Touzani, K., Puthanveettil, S. V., & Kandel, E. R. (2007). Consolidation of learning strategies during spatial working memory taks requires protein synthesis in the prefrontal cortex. *Proceedings of the National Academy of Sciences, 104,* 5632–5637.

Townsend, J. M., Kline, J., & Wasserman, T. H. (1995). Low-investment copulation: Sex differences in motivational and emotional reactions. *Ethology and Sociobiology, 16(1),* 25–51.

Trabasso, T. R., & Bower, G. H. (1968). *Attention in learning.* New York: Wiley.

Tracey, I. (2005). Nociceptive processing in the human brain. *Current Opinion in Neurobiology, 15,* 478–487.

Tramer, M. R., Carroll, D., Campbell, F. A., Reynolds, D. J., Moore, R. A., & McQuay, H. J. (2001). Cannabinoids for control of chemotherapy induced nausea and vomiting: quantitative systematic review. *British Medical Journal, 323,* 16–21.

Treboux, D., Crowell, J. A., & Waters, E. (2004). When "new" meets "old": Configurations of adult attachment representations and their implications for marital functioning. *Developmental Psychology, 40,* 295–314.

Treiber, F. A., Musante, L., Kapuku, G., Davis, C., Litaker, M., & Davis, H. (2001). Cardiovascular (CV) responsivity and recovery to acute stress and future CV functioning in youth with family histories of CV disease: A 4-year longitudinal study. *International Journal of Psychophysiology, 41,* 65–74.

Treisman, A. (1988). Features and objects: The 14th Bartlett memorial lecture. *Quarterly Journal of Experimental Psychology, 40,* 201–237.

Treisman, A. (1999). Feature binding, attention, and object perception. In G. W. Humphreys, J. Duncan., & A. Treisman (Eds.), *Attention, space, and action* (pp. 91–111). New York: Oxford University Press.

Tremblay, A., & Bueman, B. (1995). Exercise-training, macronutrient balance and body weight control. *International Journal of Obesity, 19(2),* 79–86.

Tremblay, R. E., Pihl, R. O., Vitaro, F., & Dobkin, P. (1994). Predicting early onset of male antisocial behavior from preschool behavior. *Archives of General Psychiatry, 51,* 732–739.

Trevor, C. O. (2001). Interactions among actual ease-of-movement determinants and job satisfaction in the prediction of voluntary turnover. *Academy of Management Journal, 44,* 621–638.

Triandis, H. C. (1998). Vertical and horizontal individualism and collectivism: Theory and research implications for international management. In J. L. C. Cheng, R. B. Peterson, et al. (Eds.), *Advances in international comparative management* (Vol. 12, pp. 7–35). Stamford, CT: JAI Press.

Triandis, H. C., & Trafimow, D. (2001). Cross-national prevalence of collectivism. In C. Sedikides & M. B. Brewer (Eds.), *Individual self, relational self, collective self* (pp. 259–276). New York: Psychology Press.

Trierweiler, S. J., Muroff, J. R., Jackson, M. S., Neighbors, H. W., & Munday, C. (2005). Clinician race, situational attributions, and diagnoses of mood versus schizophrenia disorders. *Cultural Diversity & Ethnic Minority Psychology, 11,* 351–364.

Trierweiler, S. J., Neighbors, H. W., Munday, C., Thompson, E. E., Binion, V. J., & Gomez, J. P. (2000). Clinician attributions associated with the diagnosis of schizophrenia in African American and non-African American patients. *Journal of Consulting and Clinical Psychology, 68,* 171–175.

Trifiletti, L. B., Shields, W., McDonald, E., Reynaud, F., & Gielen, A. (2006). Tipping the scales: Obese children and child safety seats. *Pediatrics, 117,* 1197–1202.

Trillin, A. S. (2001, January 29). Betting your life. *New Yorker,* pp. 38–41.

Tronick, E. Z. (1989). Emotions and emotional communication in infants. *American Psychologist, 44,* 112–119.

Tronick, E. Z., Messinger, D. S., Weinberg, M. K., Lester, B. M., LaGasse, L., Seifer, R., et al. (2005). Cocaine exposure is associated with subtle compromises of infants' and mothers' social-emotional behavior and dyadic features of their interaction in the face-to-face still-face paradigm. *Developmental Psychology, 41,* 711–722.

Trope, Y., Cohen, O., & Alfieri, T. (1991). Behavior identification as a mediator of dispositional inference. *Journal of Personality and Social Psychology, 61,* 873–883.

Tropp, L. R., & Pettigrew, T. F. (2005). Relationships between intergroup contact and prejudice among minority and majority status groups. *Psychological Science, 16,* 951–957.

Trower, P. (1995). Adult social skills: State of the art and future directions. In W. O'Donohue & L. Krasner (Eds.), *Handbook of psychological skills training: Clinical techniques and applications* (pp. 54–80). Boston: Allyn & Bacon.

Trujillo, C. M. (1986). A comparative evaluation of classroom interactions between professors and minority and non-minority college students. *American Educational Research Journal, 23,* 629–642.

Trujillo, K. A., & Akil, H. (1991). Inhibition of morphine tolerance and dependence by the NMDA receptor antagonist MK-801. *Science, 251,* 85–87.

Trull, T. J., & Sher, K. J. (1994). Relationship between the five-factor model of personality and Axis I disorders in a nonclinical sample. *Journal of Personality and Social Psychology, 103,* 350–360.

Trunzo, J. J., & Pinto, B. M. (2003). Social support as a mediator of optimisim and distress in breast cancer survivors. *Journal of Consulting and Clinical Psychology, 71,* 805–811.

Tryon, W. W. (2005). Possible mechanisms for why desensitization and exposure therapy work. *Clinical Psychology Review, 25,* 67–95.

Tsai, J. L., Knutson, B., & Fung, H. H. (2006). Cultural variation in affect evaluation. *Journal of Personality and Social Psychology, 90,* 288–307.

Tsai, J. L., Levenson, R. W., & McCoy, K. (2006). Cultural and temperamental variation in emotional response. *Emotion, 6,* 484–497.

Tsakiris, M., & Haggard, P. (2005). The rubber hand illusion revisited: Visuotactile integration and self-attribution. *Journal of Experimental Psychology: Human Perception and Performance, 31,* 80–91.

Tseng, W., Kan-Ming, M., Li-Shuen, L., Guo-Qian, C., Li-Wah, O., & Hong-Bo, Z. (1992). Koro epidemics in Guangdong China. *Journal of Nervous and Mental Disease, 180,* 117–123.

Tsuang, M. T., Stone, W. S., & Faraone, S. V. (2000). Toward reformulating the diagnosis of schizophrenia. *American Journal of Psychiatry, 157,* 1041–1950.

Tuch, S. A., & Martin, J. K. (1991). Race in the workplace: Black/white differences in the sources of job satisfaction. *The Sociological Quarterly, 32,* 103–116.

Tucker, C. M., & Herman, K. C. (2002). Using culturally sensitive theories and research to meet the academic needs of low-income African American children. *American Psychologist, 57,* 762–773.

Tuckman, B. W. (2003). The effect of learning and motivation strategies training on college students' achievement. *Journal of College Student Development, 4,* 430–437.

Tuller, D. (2004, January 27). Britain poised to approve medicine derived from marijuana. *The New York Times,* p. F5.

Tulving, E. (1983). *Elements of episodic memory.* New York: Oxford University Press.

Tulving, E. (1993). Self-knowledge of an amnesic individual is represented abstractly. In T. K. Srull & R. S. Wyer (Eds.), *The mental representation of trait and autobiographical knowledge about the self: Advances in social cognition* (Vol. 5). Hillsdale, NJ: Erlbaum.

Tulving, E. (2000). Introduction to memory. In M. S. Gazzaniga (Ed.), *The new cognitive neurosciences* (pp. 727–732). Cambridge, MA: MIT Press.

Tulving, E. (2005). Episodic memory and autonoesis: Uniquely human? In H. S. Terrace and J. Metcalfe (Eds.), *The missing link in cognition: Origins of self-reflective consciousness* (pp. 3–56). New York: Oxford University Press.

Tulving, E., Hayman, C. A. G., & Macdonald, C. A. (1991). Long-lasting perceptual priming and semantic learning in amnesia: A case experiment. *Journal of Experimental Psychology: Learning, Memory, and Cognition, 17,* 595–617.

Tulving, E., & Psotka, J. (1971). Retroactive inhibition in free recall: Inaccessibility of information available in the memory store. *Journal of Experimental Psychology, 87,* 1–8.

Tulving, E., & Schacter, D. L. (1990). Priming and human memory systems. *Science, 247,* 301–306.

Tulving, E., Schacter, D. L., & Stark, H. (1982). Priming effects in word-fragment completion are independent of recognition memory. *Journal of Experimental Psychology: Learning, Memory, and Cognition, 8,* 336–342.

Tuomilehto, J., Lindstrom, J., Eriksson, J. G., Valle, T. T., Hamalainen, H., Ilanne-Parikka, P., et al. (2001). Prevention of type 2 diabetes mellitus by changes in lifestyle among subjects with impaired glucose tolerance. *New England Journal of Medicine, 344,* 1343–1350.

Turiel, E. (2006). The development of morality. In W. Damon & R. M. Lerner (Series Eds.) & N. Eisenberg (Vol. Ed.), *Handbook of child psychology: Vol. 3. Social, emotional, and personality development* (6th ed., pp. 789–859). New York: Wiley.

Turkheimer, E., Haley, A., Waldron, M., D'Onofrio, B., & Gottesman, I. I. (2003). Socioeconomic status modifies heritability of IQ in young children. *Psychological Science, 14,* 623–628.

Turkheimer, E., & Waldron, M. (2000). Nonshared environment: A theoretical, methodological, and quantitative review. *Psychological Bulletin, 126,* 78–108.

Turkington, C. (1987). Special talents. *Psychology Today,* pp. 42–46.

Turner, B. G., Beidel, D. C., Hughes, S., & Turner, M. W. (1993). Test anxiety in African-American school children. *School Psychology Quarterly, 8,* 140–152.

Turner, J. C. (1991). *Social influence.* Pacific Grove, CA: Brooks/Cole.

Turner, R. J., & Lloyd, D. A. (2004). Stress burden and the lifetime incidence of psychiatric disorder in young adults: Racial and ethnic contrasts. *Archives of General Psychiatry, 61,* 481–488.

Turner, S. M., DeMers, S. T., Fox, H. R., & Reed, G. M. (2001). APA's guidelines for test user qualifications: An executive summary. *American Psychologist, 56,* 1099–1113.

Tuszynski, M. H., Thal, L., Pay, M., Salmon, D. P., U, H. S., Bakay, R., et al. (2005). A phase 1 clinical trial of nerve growth factor gene therapy for Alzheimer disease. *Nature Medicine, 11,* 551–555.

Tversky, A. (1972). Elimination by aspects: A theory of choice. *Psychological Review, 79,* 281–299.

Tversky, A., & Kahneman, D. (1974). Judgment under uncertainty: Heuristics and biases. *Science, 185,* 1124–1131.

Tversky, A., & Kahneman, D. (1981). The framing of decisions and the psychology of choice. *Science, 211,* 453–458.

Tversky, A., & Kahneman, D. (1991). Loss aversion in riskless choice: A reference dependent model. *Quarterly Journal of Economics, 106,* 1039–1061.

Tversky, A., & Kahneman, D. (1993). Probabilistic reasoning. In A. Goldman (Ed.), *Readings in philosophy and cognitive science* (pp. 43–68). Cambridge: MIT Press.

Tversky, B., & Tuchin, M. (1989). A reconciliation of the evidence on eyewitness testimony: Comments on McCloskey and Zaragoza. *Journal of Experimental Psychology: General, 118,* 86–91.

Tyler, K. L., & Malessa, R. (2000). The Goltz-Ferrier debates and the triumph of cerebral localizationalist theory. *Neurology, 55,* 1015–1024.

Tziner, A., Murphy, K. R., & Cleveland, J. N. (2005). Contextual and rater factors affecting rating behavior. *Group and Organization Management, 30,* 89–98.

Uchida, Y., Kitayama, S., Mesquita, B., & Reyes, J. A. (2001, June). *Interpersonal sources of happiness: The relative significance in Japan, the Philippines, and the United States.* Paper presented at Annual Convention of American Psychological Society, Toronto, Canada.

Uchino, B. N., Cacioppo, J. T. & Kiecolt-Glaser, J. K. (1996). The relationship between social support and physiological process: A review with emphasis on underlying mechanisms and implications for health. *Psychological Bulletin, 119,* 488–531.

Udry, J. R., & Chantala, K. (2003). Masculinity-femininity guides sexual union formation in adolescents. *Personality and Social Psychology Bulletin, 30,* 44–55.

Ugajin, T., Hozawa, A., Ohkubo, T., Asayama, K., Kikuya, M., Obara, T., et al. (2005). White-coat hypertension as a risk factor for the development of home hypertension: The Ohasama study. *Archives of Internal Medicine, 165,* 1541–1546

U.K. Statistical Bulletin. (1999). *Electro convulsive therapy: Survey covering the period from January 1999 to March 1999, England.* London: Department of Health.

Ulett, G. A. (2003). Acupuncture, magic, and make-believe. *The Skeptical Inquirer, 27*(2), 47–50.

Ullian, E. M., Sapperstein, S. K., Christopherson, K. S., & Barres, B. A. (2001). Control of synapse number by glia. *Science, 291,* 657–661.

Ullmann, L. P., & Krasner, L. (1965). *Case studies in behavior modification.* New York: Holt, Rinehart & Winston.

Umbreit, J., Ferro, J., Liaupsin, C. J., & Lane, K. L. (2006). *Functional behavioral assessment and function-based intervention: An effective, practical approach.* Upper Saddle River, NJ: Prentice Hall.

Ungerleider, L. G., & Mishkin, M. (1982). Two cortical visual systems. In D. J. Ingle, M. A. Goodale, & R. J. W. Mansfield (Eds.), *Analysis of visual behavior.* Cambridge, MA: MIT Press.

Ungless, M. A., Whistler, J. L., Malenka, R. C., & Bonci, A. (2001). Single cocaine exposure in vivo induces long-term potentiation in dopamine neurons. *Nature, 411,* 583–587.

United States Bureau of the Census. (2006). *Income, poverty, and health insurance coverage in the United States: 2005.* Washington, DC: U.S. Government Printing Office.

United States Food and Drug Administration. (2005, April 11). *FDA public health advisory: Deaths with antipsychotics in elderly patients with behavioral disturbances.* Washington, DC: U.S. Department of Health and Human Services.

Uno, K., Katagiri, H., Yamada, T., Ishigaki, Y., Ogihara, T., Imai, J., et al. (2006). Neuronal pathway from the liver modulates energy expenditure and systemic insulin sensitivity. *Science, 312,* 1656–1659.

Urban, N. N. (2002). Lateral inhibition in the olfactory bulb and in olfaction. *Physiology and Behavior, 77,* 607–612.

Urry, H. L., Nitschke, J. B., Dolski, I., Jackson, D. C., Dalton, K. M., Mueller, C. J., et al. (2004). Making a life worth living: Neural correlates of well-being. *Psychological Science, 15,* 367–372.

U.S. Bureau of Labor Statistics (2007). *Injuries, illnesses, and fatalities, 2005.* Washington, D.C.: U.S. Department of Labor. Retrieved May 9, 2007, from http://www.bls.gov/iif/home.htm#tables.

U.S. Bureau of Labor Statistics. (2004). *American Time Use Survey.* Washington, DC: U.S. Department of Labor.

U.S. Census Bureau. (2006). *2005 American community survey.* Washington, DC: U.S. Government Printing Office.

U.S. Department of Health and Human Services Office of Applied Studies. (2003). *Results from the 2002 National Survey on Drug Use and Health: Summary of national finding* (DHHS Publication No. SMA 03-3836, NHSDA Series H-22). Rockville, MD: Substance Abuse and Mental Health Services Administration.

U.S. Department of Health and Human Services. (2001a). *Alzheimer's disease fact sheet.* Washington, DC: U.S. Public Health Service (NIH Publication No. 01-3431).

U.S. Department of Health and Human Services. (2001b). *Women and smoking: A report of the Surgeon General.* Atlanta: Centers for Disease Control and Prevention.

U.S. Department of Justice. (1999). *Eyewitness evidence: A guide for law enforcement.* Washington, DC: National Institute of Justice.

U.S. Department of Justice. (2007). *Crime characteristics.* Retrieved January 31, 2007, from http://www.ojp.usdoj.gov/bjs/cvict_c.htm#relate.

U.S. Department of Labor. (2004). Occupational employment. *Occupational Outlook Quarterly, 47*(4), 14.

U.S. Surgeon General. (1999). *Mental health: A report of the surgeon general.* Rockville, MD: U.S. Department of Health and Human Services.

U.S. Surgeon General. (2004). *The health consequences of smoking: A report of the Surgeon General.* Washington, DC: Centers for Disease Control and Prevention, Office on Smoking and Health.

Uttal, W. R. (2003). *The new phrenology: The limits of localizing cognitive processes in the brain.* Cambridge, MA: MIT Press.

Uvnas-Moberg, K., Arn, I., & Magnusson, D. (2005). The psychobiology of emotion: The role of the oxytocinergic system. *International Journal of Behavioral Medicine, 12,* 59–65.

Uwe, H. (2005). Therapeutic alliance: The best synthesizer of social influences on the therapeutic situation? On links to other constructs, determinants of its effectiveness, and its role for research in psychotherapy in general. *Psychotherapy Research, 15,* 9–23.

Valencia-Flores, M., Castano, V. A., Campos, R. M., Rosenthal, L., Resendiz, M., Vergara, P., et al. (1998). The siesta culture concept is not supported by the sleep habits of urban Mexican students. *Journal of Sleep Research, 7,* 21–29.

Valenstein, E. S. (Ed.). (1980). *The psychosurgery debate.* San Francisco: Freeman.

Valent, F., Brusaferro, S., & Barbone, F. (2001). A case-crossover study of sleep and childhood injury. *Pediatrics, 107,* e23.

Valenza, E., Simion, F., Assia, V. M., & Umilta, C. (1996). Face preference at birth. *Journal of Experimental Psychology: Human Perception and Performance, 22,* 892–903.

Valli, K., Revonsuo, A., Pälkäs, O., & Punamäki, R.-L. (2006). The effect of trauma on dream content—A field study of Palestinian children. *Dreaming, 16,* 63–87.

Van Bezooijen, R., Otto, S. A., & Heenan, T. A (1983). Recognition of vocal expression of emotion: A three-nation study to identify universal characteristics. *Journal of Cross-Cultural Psychology, 14,* 387–406.

van Bokhoven, I., van Goozen, S. H. M., van Engeland, H., Schaal, B., Arseneault, L., Séguin, J. R., et al. (2006). Salivary testosterone and aggression, delinquency, and social dominance in a population-based longitudinal study of adolescent males. *Hormones and Behavior, 50,* 118–125.

Van den Bergh, B. R., & Marcoen, A. (2004). High antenatal maternal anxiety is related to ADHD symptoms, externalizing problems, and anxiety in 8- and 9-year-olds. *Child Development, 75,* 1085–1097.

Van der Lely, H. K. J. (1994). Canonical linking rules: Forward versus reverse linking in normally developing and specifically language-impaired children. *Cognition, 51,* 29–72.

van der Maas, H. L. J., Dolan, C. V., Grasman, R. P. P., Wicherts, J. M,, Huizenga, H. & M., Raijmakers, M. E. J. (2006). A dynamical model of general intelligence: The positive manifold of intelligence by mutualism. *Psychological Review, 113,* 842–861.

Van der Molen, J. H. W. (2004). Violence and suffering in television news: Toward a broader conception of harmful television content for children. *Pediatrics, 113,* 1771–1775.

Van Duiji, M., Cardena, E., & de Jong, J. (2005). The validity of DSM-IV dissociative disorder categories in South-West Uganda. *Transcultural Psychiatry, 42,* 219–241.

Van Eerde, W., & Thierry, H. (1996). Vrooms's expectancy models and work-related criteria: A meta-analysis. *Journal of Applied Psychology, 81,* 575–586.

Van Essen, D. C., Anderson, C. H., & Felleman, D. J. (1992). Information processing in the primate visual system: An integrated systems perspective. *Science, 255,* 419–423.

van Goozen, S. H. M., Fairchild, G., Snoek, H., & Harold, G. T. (2007). The evidence for a neurobiological model of childhood antisocial behavior. *Psychological Bulletin, 133,* 149–182.

van Griensven, F., Chakkradband, S., Thienkrua, W., Pengjuntr, W., Cardozo, B. L., Tantipiwatanaskul, P., et al. (2006). Mental health problems among adults in tsunami-affected areas in southern Thailand. *Journal of the American Medical Association, 296,* 537–548.

Van Hoesen, G. W., Hyman, B. T., & Damasio, A. R. (1991). Entorhinal cortex pathology in Alzheimer's disease. *Hippocampus, 1*(1), 1–8.

van IJzendoorn, M. H. (1995). Adult attachment representations, parental responsiveness, and infant attachment: A meta-analysis on the predictive validity of the Adult Attachment Interview. *Psychological Bulletin, 117,* 387–403.

van IJzendoom, M. H., & Juffer, F. (2005). Adoption as a successful natural intervention enhancing adopted children's IQ and school performance. *Current Directions in Psychological Science, 14,* 326–330.

Van Knippenberg, D., De Dreu, C., & Homan, A. (2004). Work group diversity and group performance: An integrative model and research agenda. *Journal of Applied Psychology, 89,* 1108–1022.

Van Lange, P. A. M., & Sedikides, C. (1998). Being more honest but not necessarily more intelligent than others: Generality and explanations for the Muhammad Ali effect. *European Journal of Social Psychology, 28,* 675–680.

van Praag, H., Christie, B. R., Sejnowski, T. J., & Gage, F. H. (1999). Running enhances neurogenesis, learning, and long-term potentiation in mice. *Proceedings of the National Academy of Sciences, 96,* 13427–13431.

Van Sickel, A. D. (1992). Clinical hypnosis in the practice of anesthesia. *Nurse Anesthesiologist, 3,* 67–74.

van Wassenhove, V., Grant, K. W., & Poeppel, D. (2005). Visual speech speeds up the neural processing of auditory speech. *Proceedings of the National Academy of Sciences of the USA, 102,* 1181–1186.

van Wel, F., ter Bogt, T., & Raaijmakers, Q. (2002). Changes in the parental bond and the well-being of adolescents and young adults. *Adolescence, 37*(146), 317–333.

Vance, D. E., Roenker, D. L., Cissell, G. M., Edwards, J. D., Wadley, V. G., & Ball, K. K. (2006). Predictors of driving exposure and avoidance in a field study of older drivers from the state of Maryland. *Accident Analysis and Prevention, 38,* 823–831.

VandeCreek, L., Janus, M.-D., Pennebaker, J. W., & Binau, B. (2002). Praying about difficult experiences as self-disclosure to God. *International Journal for the Psychology of Religion, 12,* 29–39.

Vandewater, E. A., Rideout, V. J., Wartella, E. A., Huang, X., Lee, J. H., & Shim, M. S. (2007). Digital childhood: Electronic media and technology use among infants, toddlers, and preschoolers. *Pediatrics, 119,* 1006–1015.

Vanheule, S., Desmet, M., Rosseel, Y., & Meganck, R. (2006). Core transference themes in depression. *Journal of Affective Disorders, 91,* 71–75.

Vanman, E. J., Saltz, J. L., Nathan, L. R., & Warren, J. A. (2004). Racial discrimination by low-prejudiced whites. *Psychological Science, 15,* 711–714.

Vasan, R. S., Pencina, M. J., Cobain, M., Freiberg, M. S., & D'Agostino, R. B. (2005). Estimated risks for developing obesity in the Framingham heart study. *Annals of Internal Medicine, 143,* 473–480.

Vattano, F. (2000). *The mind: Video teaching modules* (2nd ed.). Fort Collins, CO: Colorado State University and Annenberg/CPB.

Vaughan, S. C. (1998). *The talking cure: The science behind psychotherapy.* New York: Henry Holt.

Vazza, G., Bertolin, C., Scudellaro, E., Vettori, A., Boaretto, F., Rampinelli, S., et al. (2007). Genome-wide scan supports the existence of a susceptibility locus for schizophrenia and bipolar disorder on chromosome 15q26. *Molecular Psychiatry, 12,* 87–93.

Vecera, S. P., Vogel, E. K., & Woodman, G. F. (2002). Lower region: A new cue for figure-ground assignment. *Journal of Experimental Psychology: General, 131,* 194–205.

Veenstra-VanderWeele, J., & Cook, E. H., Jr. (2004). Molecular genetics of autism spectrum disorder. *Molecular Psychiatry, 9,* 819–832.

Velakoulis, D., Wood, S. J., Wong, M. T., McGorry, P. D., Yung, A., Phillips, L., et al. (2006). Hippocampal and amygdala volumes according to psychosis stage and diagnosis: A magnetic resonance imaging study of chronic schizophrenia, first-episode psychosis, and ultra-high-risk individuals. *Archives of General Psychiatry, 63,* 139–149.

Velicer, C. M, Heckbert, S. R., Lampe, J. W., Potter, J. D., Robertson, C. A., & Taplin, S. H. (2004). Antibiotic use in relation to the risk of breast cancer. *Journal of the American Medical Association, 291,* 827–835.

Velligan, D. I., Bow-Thomas, C. C., Huntzinger, C., Ritch, J., Ledbetter, N., Prihoda, T. J., & Miller, A. L. (2000). Randomized controlled trial of the use of compensatory strategies to enhance adaptive functioning in outpatients with schizophrenia. *American Journal of Psychiatry, 157,* 1317–1328.

Verghese, J., Lipton, R. B., Katz, M. J., Hall, C. B., Derby, C. A., Kuslansky, G., et al. (2003). Leisure activities and the risk of dementia in the elderly. *New England Journal of Medicine, 348,* 2508–2516.

Verhagen, J. V. (2006). The neurocognitive bases of human multimodal food perception: Consciousness. *Brain Research Reviews, 53,* 271–286.

Vernacchio, L., Corwin, M. J., Lesko, S. M., Vezina, R. M., Hunt, C. E., Hoffman, H. J., et al. (2003). Sleep position of low birth weight infants. *Pediatrics, 111,* 633–640.

Verster, J. C., & Volkerts, E. R. (2004). Clinical pharmacology, clinical efficacy, and behavioral toxicity of alprazolam: A review of the literature. *CNS Drug Reviews, 10,* 45–76.

Vierikko, E., Pulkkinen, L., Kaprio, J., & Rose, R. J. (2006). Genetic and environmental sources of continuity and change in teacher–rated aggression during early adolescence. *Aggressive Behavior, 32,* 308–320.

Vigano, D., Rubino, T., & Parolaro, D. (2005). Molecular and cellular basis of cannabinoid and opioid interactions. *Pharmacology, Biochemistry, and Behavior, 81,* 360–368.

Vignoles, V. L., Regalia, C., Manzi, C., Golledge, J., & Scabini, E. (2006). Beyond self-esteem: Influence of multiple motives on identity construction. *Journal of Personality and Social Psychology, 90,* 308–333.

Villalta-Gil, V., Vilaplana, M., Ochoa, S., Dolz, M., Usall, J., Haro, J. M., et al. (2006). Four symptom dimensions in outpatients with schizophrenia. *Comprehensive Psychiatry, 47,* 384–388.

Vineis, P., Airoldi, L., Veglia, P., Olgiati, L., Pastorelli, R., Autrup, H., et al. (2005). Environmental tobacco smoke and risk of respiratory cancer and chronic obstructive pulmonary disease in former smokers and never smokers in the EPIC prospective study. *British Medical Journal, 330,* 277.

Vingerhoets, G., Berckmoes, C., & Stroobant, N. (2003). Cerebral hemodynamics during discrimination of prosodic and semantic emotion in speech studied by transcranial Doppler ultrasonography. *Neuropsychology, 17,* 93–99.

Vinod, K. Y., Yalamanchili, R., Xie, S., Cooper, T. B., & Hungund, B. L. (2006). Effect of chronic ethanol exposure and its withdrawal on the endocannabinoid system. *Neurochemistry International, 49,* 619–625.

Visser, B. A., Ashton, M. C., & Vernon, P. A. (2006). Beyond g: Putting multiple intelligences theory to the test. *Intelligence, 34,* 487–502.

Visser, P. J., Krabbendam, L., Verhey, F. R., Hofman, P. A., Verhoeven, W. M., Tuinier, S., et al. (1999). Brain correlates of memory dysfunction in alcoholic Korsakoff's syndrome. *Journal of Neurology, Neurosurgery, and Psychiatry, 67*(6), 774–778.

Viswesvaran, C., & Ones, D. S. (2000). Measurement error in "Big Five factors" personality assessment: Reliability generalization across studies and measures. *Educational and Psychological Measurement, 60,* 224–235.

Vitaliano, P. P., Zhang, J. M., & Scanlan, J. M. (2003). Is caregiving hazardous to one's physical health? A meta-analysis. *Psychological Bulletin, 129,* 946–972.

Vocisano, C., Klein, D. N., Arnow, B., Rivera, C., Blalock, J. A., Rothbaum, B., et al. (2004). Therapist variables that predict symptom change in psychotherapy with chronically depressed outpatients. *Psychotherapy: Theory, Research, Training, Practice, 41,* 255–265.

Vokey, J. R. (2002). Subliminal messages. In J. R. Vokey & S. W. Allen (Eds.), *Psychological sketches* (6th ed., pp. 223–246). Lethbridge, Alberta, Canada: Psyence Ink.

Vokey, J. R., & Read, J. D. (1985). Subliminal messages: Between the devil and the media. *American Psychologist, 40,* 1231–1239.

Volkow, N. D., Chang, L., Wang, G. J., Fowler, J. S., Franceschi, D., Sedler, M. J., et al. (2001). Higher cortical and lower subcortical metabolism in detoxified methamphetamine abusers. *American Journal of Psychiatry, 158,* 383–389.

Vollebergh, W. A. M., Iedema, J., Bijl, R. V., de Graaf, R., Smit, F., & Ormel, J. (2001). The structure and stability of common mental disorders: The NEMESIS study. *Archives of General Psychiatry, 58,* 597–603.

Vollset, S. E., Tverdal, A., & Gjessing, H. K. (2006). Smoking and deaths between 40 and 70 years of age in women and men. *Annals of Internal Medicine, 144,* 381–389.

Volpicelli, J. R., Ulm, R. R., Altenor, A., & Seligman, M. E. P. (1983). Learned mastery in the rat. *Learning and Motivation, 14,* 204–222.

Volz, J. (2000). Successful aging. The second 50. *APA Monitor, 31,* 24–28.

von Bekesy, G. (1960). *Experiments in hearing.* New York: McGraw-Hill.

Von Wright, J. M., Anderson, K., & Stenman, U. (1975). Generalization of conditioned GSRs in dichotic listening. In P. M. A. Rabbitt & S. Dornic (Eds.), *Attention and performance V*. New York: Academic Press.

Voracek, M., & Fisher, M. L. (2002). Shapely centrefolds? Temporal change in body measures: trend analysis. *British Medical Journal, 325*, 1447–1448.

Vorel, S. R., Liu, X., Hayes, R. J., Spector, J. A., & Gardner, E. L. (2001). Relapse to cocaine-seeking after hippocampal theta burst stimulation. *Science, 292*, 1175–1178.

Vroom, V. (1964). *Work and motivation*. New York: Wiley.

Vyse, S. A. (2000). *Believing in magic: The psychology of superstition* (reprint ed.). New York: Oxford University Press.

Wachtel, S. R., ElSohly, M. A., Ross, S. A., Ambre, J., & de Wit, H. (2002). Comparison of the subjective effects of Delta-sup-9-tetrahydrocannabinol and marijuana in humans. *Psychopharmacology, 161*, 331–339.

Wacker, J., Chavanon, M.-L., & Stemmler, G. (2006). Investigating the dopaminergic basis of extraversion in humans: A multilevel approach. *Journal of Personality and Social Psychology, 91*, 171–187.

Wadden, T. A., Berkowitz, R. I., Sarwer, D. B., Prus-Wisniewski, R., & Steinberg, C. (2001). Benefits of lifestyle modification in the pharmacologic treatment of obesity: A randomized trial. *Archives of Internal Medicine, 161*, 218–227.

Wadden, T. A., Berkowitz, R. I., Womble, L. G., Sarwer, D. B., Phelan, S., Cato, R. K., et al. (2005). Randomized trial of lifestyle modification and pharmacotherapy for obesity. *New England Journal of Medicine, 353*, 2111–2120.

Wade, C. (1988, April). *Thinking critically about critical thinking in psychology*. Paper presented at the annual meeting of the Western Psychological Association, San Francisco, CA.

Wade, J. B. (2004). Neuropsychologists diagnose traumatic brain injury. *Brain Injury, 18*(7), 629–643.

Wade, W. A., Treat, T. A., & Stuart, G. L. (1998). Transporting an empirically supported treatment for panic disorder to a service clinic setting: A benchmarking strategy. *Journal of Consulting and Clinical Psychology, 66*, 231–239.

Wadsworth, S. (1994). School achievement. In J. C. DeFries, R. Pomin, & D. W. Fulker (Eds.), *Nature and nurture during middle childhood* (pp. 86–101). Cambridge, MA: Blackwell.

Wadsworth, S. J., Olson, R. K., Pennington, B. F., & DeFries, J. C. (2000). Differential genetic etiology of reading disability as a function of IQ. *Journal of Learning Disabilities, 33*, 192–200.

Waelti, P., Dickinson, A., & Schultz, W. (2001). Dopamine responses comply with basic assumptions of formal learning theory. *Nature, 412*, 43–48.

Wager, T. D., Rilling, J. K., Smith, E. E., Sokolik, A., Casey, K. L., Davidson, R. J., et al. (2004). Placebo-induced changes in fMRI in the anticipation and experience of pain. *Science, 303*, 1162–1167.

Wagner, A. D. (1999). Working memory contributions to human learning and remembering. *Neuron, 22*, 19–22.

Wagner, A. D., Schacter, D. L., & Rotte, M. (1998). Building memories: Remembering and forgetting of verbal experiences as predicted by brain activity. *Science, 281*, 1188–1191.

Wagner, K. D., Ambrosini, P., Rynn, M., Wohlberg, C., Yang, R., Greenbaum, M. S., et al. (2003). Efficacy of sertraline in the treatment of children and adolescents with major depressive disorder: Two randomized controlled trials. *Journal of the American Medical Association, 290*, 1033–1041.

Wagner, U., Hallschmid, M., Rasch, B., & Born, J. (2006). Brief sleep after learning keeps emotional memories alive for years. *Biological Psychiatry, 60*, 788–790.

Wahlsten, D. (1999). Single-gene influences on brain and behavior. *Annual Review of Psychology, 50*, 599–624.

Wai, J., Lubinski, D., & Benbow, C. P. (2005). Creativity and occupational accomplishments among intellectually precocious youths: An age 13 to age 33 longitudinal study. *Journal of Educational Psychology, 97*, 484–492.

Wakefield, J. C. (1992). The concept of mental disorder: On the boundary between biological facts and social values. *American Psychologist, 47*, 373–388.

Wakefield, J. C. (1999). Evolutionary versus prototype analyses of the concept of disorder. *Journal of Abnormal Psychology, 108*, 374–399.

Wakschlag, L. S., Leventhal, B. L., Pine, D. S., Pickett, K. E., & Carter, A. S. (2006). Elucidating early mechanisms of developmental psychopathology: The case of prenatal smoking and disruptive behavior. *Child Development, 77*, 893–906.

Walberg, H. J. (1987). Studies show curricula efficiency can be attained. *NASSP Bulletin, 71*, 15–21.

Waldman, I. D., & Gizer, I. R. (2006). The genetics of attention deficit hyperactivity disorder. *Clinical Psychology Review, 26*, 396–432.

Walker, E. F., & Diforio, D. (1998). Schizophrenia: A neural diathesis-stress model. *Psychological Review, 104*, 667–685.

Walker, L. (1991). The feminization of psychology. *Psychology of Women Newsletter of Division, 35*, 1, 4.

Walker, L. J. (1989). A longitudinal study of moral reasoning. *Child Development, 60*, 157–166.

Walker, L. J. (1995). Sexism in Kohlberg's moral psychology? In W. M. Kurtines & J. L. Gewirtz (Eds.), *Moral development: An introduction* (pp. 83–107). Boston: Allyn & Bacon.

Walker, M. P., & Stickgold, R. (2006). Sleep, memory, and plasticity. *Annual Review of Psychology, 57*, 139–166.

Walker, M. P., Brakefield, T., Hobson, J. A., & Stickgold, R. (2003). Dissociable stages of human memory consolidation and reconsolidation. *Nature, 425*, 616–620.

Walker-Andrews, A. S., Bahrick, L. E., Raglioni, S. S., & Dias, I. (1991). Infants' bimodal perception of gender. *Ecological Psychology, 3*, 55–75.

Wall, T. L., Shea, S. H., Chan, K. K., & Carr, L. G. (2001). A genetic association with the development of alcohol and other substance use behavior in Asian Americans. *Journal of Abnormal Psychology, 110*, 173–178.

Wallace, B. A., & Shapiro, S. (2006). Mental balance and well-being: Building bridges between Buddhism and western psychology. *American Psychologist, 61*, 690–701.

Wallace, J. C., Popp, E., & Mondore, S. (2006). Safety climate as a mediator between foundation climates and occupational accidents: A group-level investigation. *Journal of Applied Psychology, 91*, 681–688.

Wallace, R. K., & Benson, H. (1972). The physiology of meditation. *Scientific American, 226*, 84–90.

Wallen, K., & Lovejoy, J. (1993). Sexual behavior: Endocrine function and therapy. In J. Shulkin (Ed.), *Hormonal pathways to mind and brain*. New York: Academic Press.

Waller, D. (2000). Individual differences in spatial learning from computer-simulated environments. *Journal of Experimental Psychology: Applied, 6*, 307–321.

Wallerstein, R. S. (2002). The growth and transformation of American ego psychology. *Journal of the American Psychoanalytic Association, 50*, 135–169.

Wallis, G., & Bülthoff, H. H. (2001). Effects of temporal association on recognition memory. *Proceedings of the National Academy of Sciences, 98*(8), 4800–4804.

Wallis, J. D., Anderson, K. C., & Miller, E. K. (2001). Single neurons in prefrontal cortex encode abstract rules. *Nature, 411*, 953–956.

Wallman, J., Gottlieb, M. D., Rajaram, V., & Fugate-Wentzek, L. A. (1987). Local retinal regions control local eye growth and myopia. *Science, 237*, 73–76.

Walsh, D. (2000). Interactive violence and children: Testimony submitted to the Committee on Commerce, Science, and Transportation, United States Senate, March 21, 2000 [On-line]. Retrieved January 9, 2007, from http://www.mediaandthefamily.org/press/senateviolence.shtml.

Walsh, R., & Shapiro, S. L. (2006). The meeting of meditative disciplines and Western psychology: A mutually enriching dialogue. *American Psychologist, 61*, 227–239.

Walton, G. E., Bower, N. J. A., & Bower, T. G. R. (1992). Recognition of familiar faces by newborns. *Infant Behavior and Development, 15*, 265–269.

Wampold, B. E. (2005). Estimating variability in outcomes attributable to therapists: A naturalistic study of outcomes in managed care. *Journal of Consulting and Clinical Psychology, 73*, 914–923.

Wampold, B. E., Ahn, H. & Coleman, H. L. K. (2001). Medical model as metaphor: Old habits die hard. *Journal of Counseling Psychology, 48*, 263–273.

Wampold, B. E., Lichtenberg, J. W., & Waehler, C. A. (2002). Principles of empirically supported interventions in counseling psychology. *Counseling Psychologist, 30*, 197–217.

Wampold, B. E., Minami, T., Tierney, S. C., Baskin, T. W., & Bhati, K. S. (2005). The placebo is powerful: Estimating placebo effects in medicine and psychotherapy from randomized clinical trials. *Journal of Clinical Psychology, 61*, 835–854.

Wampold, B. E., Mondin, G. W., Moody, M., Stich, F., Benson, K., & Ahn, H. (1997). A meta-analysis of outcome studies comparing bona fide psychotherapies: Empirically, "All must have prizes." *Psychological Bulletin, 122*, 203–215.

Wanek, J. E., Sackett, P. R., & Ones, D. S. (2003). Towards an understanding of integrity test similarities and differences: An item-level analysis of seven tests. *Personnel Psychology, 56*, 873–894.

Wang, C., Collet, J. P., & Lau, J. (2004). The effect of Tai Chi on health outcomes in patients with chronic conditions: A systematic review. *Archives of Internal Medicine, 164*, 493–501.

Wang, O. (2006). Earliest recollections of self and others in European American and Taiwanese young adults. *Psychological Science, 17*, 708–714.

Wang, P. S., Demler, O., Olfson, M., Pincus, H. A., Wells, K. B., & Kessler, R. C. (2006). Changing profiles of service sectors used in mental health care in the United States. *American Journal of Psychiatry, 163*, 1187–1198.

Wang, P. S., Lane, M., Olfson, M., Pincus, H. A., Wells, K. B., & Kessler, R. C. (2005). Twelve-month use of mental health services in the United States: Results from the National Comorbidity Survey Replication. *Archives of General Psychiatry, 62*, 629–640.

Wang, P. S., Schneeweiss, S., Avorn, J., Fischer, M. A., Mogun, H., Solomon, D. H., et al. (2005). Risk of death in elderly users of conventional vs. atypical antipsychotic medications. *New England Journal of Medicine, 353*, 2335–2341.

Wang, S.-H., & Baillargeon, R. (2005). Inducing infants to detect a physical violation in a single trial. *Psychological Science, 16*, 542–549.

Wang, X., Merzenich, M. M., Sameshima, K., & Jenkins, W. M. (1995). Remodelling of hand representation in adult cortex determined by timing of tactile stimulation. *Nature, 378,* 71–75.

Wang, Y., & Lobstein, T. (2006). Worldwide trends in childhood overweight and obesity. *International Journal of Pediatric Obesity, 1,* 11–25.

Wang, Y., Mi, J., Shan, X. Y., Wang, Q. J., & Ge, K. Y. (2007). Is China facing an obesity epidemic and the consequences? The trends in obesity and chronic disease in China. *International Journal of Obesity, 31,* 177–188.

Warburton, D. M. (1995). Effects of caffeine on cognition and mood without caffeine abstinence. *Psychopharmacology, 119,* 66–70.

Ward, C. (1994). Culture and altered states of consciousness. In W. J. Lonner & R. S. Malpass (Eds.), *Psychology and culture.* Boston: Allyn & Bacon.

Ward, J., & Mattingley, J. B. (2006). Synaesthesia: an overview of contemporary findings and controversies. *Cortex, 42,* 129–136.

Warneken, F., & Tomasello, M. (2006). Altruistic helping in human infants and young chimpanzees. *Science, 311,* 1301–1303.

Warner, L., Kessler, R., Hughes, M., Anthony, J., & Nelson, C. (1995). Prevalence and correlates of drug use and dependence in the United States. *Archives of General Psychiatry, 52,* 219–229.

Warren, J. I., & South, S. C. (2006). Comparing the constructs of antisocial personality disorder and psychopathy in a sample of incarcerated women. *Behavioral Sciences and the Law, 24,* 1–20.

Warrington, E. K., & Weiskrantz, L. (1970). The amnesic syndrome: Consolidation of retrieval? *Nature, 228,* 626–630.

Watanabe, K., & Shimojo, S. (2001). When sound affects vision: Effects of auditory grouping on visual motion perception. *Psychological Science, 12,* 109–116.

Watanabe, S., Sakamoto, J., & Wakita, M. (1995). Pigeons' discrimination of paintings by Monet and Picasso. *Journal of Experimental Analysis of Behavior, 63,* 165–174.

Watanabe, T., Náñez, J. E., & Sasaki, Y. (2001). Perceptual learning without perception. *Nature, 413,* 844–848.

Waterman, A. S. (1982). Identity development from adolescence to adulthood: An extension of theory and a review of research. *Developmental Psychology, 18,* 341–358.

Watkins, L. R., & Maier, S. F. (2003). When good pain turns bad. *Current Directions in Psychological Science, 12,* 232–235.

Watson, D. (2005). Rethinking the mood and anxiety disorders: A quantitative hierarchical model for DSM-V. *Journal of Abnormal Psychology, 114,* 522–536.

Watson, J. B. (1913). Psychology as the behaviorist views it. *Psychological Review, 20,* 158–177.

Watson, J. B. (1919). *Psychology from the standpoint of a behaviorist.* Philadelphia: Lippincott.

Watson, J. B. (1925). *Behaviorism.* London: Kegan Paul, Trench, Trubner.

Watson, R. T., & Heilman, K. M. (1979). Thalamic neglect. *Neurology, 29*(5), 690–694.

Wearden, A. J., Tarrier, N., Barrowclough, C., Zastowny, T. R., & Rahill, A. A. (2000). A review of expressed emotion research in health care. *Clinical Psychology Review, 20,* 633–666.

Webb, T. L., & Sheeran, P. (2006). Does changing behavioral intentions engender behavior change? A meta-analysis of the experimental evidence. *Psychological Bulletin, 132,* 249–268.

Weber, J. M., Kopelman, S., & Messick, D. M. (2004). A conceptual review of decision making in social dilemmas: Applying a logic of appropriateness. *Personality and Social Psychology Review, 8,* 281–307.

Weber, R., Ritterfeld, U., & Mathiak, K. (2006). Does playing violent video games induce aggression? Empirical evidence of a functional magnetic resonance imaging study. *Media Psychology, 8,* 39–60.

Wechsler, D. (1939). *The measurement of adult intelligence.* Baltimore: Williams & Wilkins.

Wechsler, D. (1949). *The Wechsler Intelligence Scale for Children.* New York: Psychological Corporation.

Wechsler, D. (2003). *Wechsler Intelligence Scale for Children* (4th ed.). San Antonio, TX: Psychological Corporation.

Wecker, N. S., Kramer, J. H., Hallam, B. J., & Delis, D. C. (2005). Mental flexibility: Age effects on switching. *Neuropsychology, 19,* 345–352.

Wegge, J., & Haslam, S. A. (2005). Improving work motivation and performance in brainstorming groups: The effects of three group goal-setting strategies. *European Journal of Work and Organizational Psychology, 14,* 400–430.

Wegner, D. M., Fuller, V. A. & Sparrow, B. (2003). Clever hands: Uncontrolled intelligence in facilitated communication. *Journal of Personality and Social Psychology, 85,* 5–19.

Wegner, D. M., Wenzlaff, R. M., & Kozak, M. (2004). Dream rebound: The return of suppressed thoughts in dreams. *Psychological Science, 15,* 232–236.

Weiler, B. L., & Widom, C. S. (1996). Psychopathy and violent behavior in abused and neglected young adults. *Criminal Behaviour and Mental Health, 6,* 253–271.

Weinberg, J., & Levine, S. (1980). Psychobiology of coping in animals: The effects of predictability. In S. Levine & H. Ursin (Eds.), *Coping and health.* New York: Plenum.

Weinberg, R. A. (1989). Intelligence and IQ: Landmark issues and great debates. *American Psychologist, 44,* 98–104.

Weinberg, R. A., Scarr, S., & Waldman, I. D. (1992). The Minnesota transracial adoption study: A follow-up of IQ test performance at adolescence. *Intelligence, 16,* 117–135.

Weiner, B. (1993). On sin versus sickness: A theory of perceived responsibility and social motivation. *American Psychologist, 48*(9), 957–965.

Weingarten, H. P. (1983). Conditioned cues elicit feeding in sated rats: A role for learning in meal initiation. *Science, 220,* 431–433.

Weinraub, M., Horvath, D. L., & Gringlas, M. B. (2002). Single parenthood. In M. H. Bornstein (Ed.), *Handbook of parenting: Vol. 3. Being and becoming a parent* (2nd ed., pp. 109–140). Mahwah, NJ: Erlbaum.

Weinstein, D. (1999, July 24). Who are you? *Sunday Telegraph Magazine,* pp. 24–26.

Weinstein, E. A., & Kahn, R. L. (1955). *Denial of illness: Symbolic and physiological aspects.* Springfield, IL: Thomas.

Weiss, A., King, J. E., & Perkins, L. (2006). Personality and subjective well-being in orangutans (*pongo pygmaeus and pongo abelii*). *Journal of Personality and Social Psychology, 90,* 501–511.

Weiss, B., & Weisz, J. R. (1995). Relative effectiveness of behavioral versus nonbehavioral child psychotherapy. *Journal of Consulting and Clinical Psychology, 63,* 317–320.

Weissberg, R. P., Kumpfer, K. L., & Seligman, M. E. P. (2003). Prevention that works for children and youth. *American Psychologist, 58,* 425–432.

Weissman, D. H., Roberts, K. C., Visscher, K. M., & Woldorff, M. G. (2006). The neural basis of momentary lapses of attention. *Nature Neuroscience, 9,* 971–978.

Weissman, M. M., Bland, R., Joyce, P. R., Newman, S., Wells, J. E., & Wittchen, H. U. (1993). Sex differences in rates of depression: Cross-national perspectives. *Journal of Affective Disorders, 29,* 77–84.

Weisstein, N., & Harris, C. S. (1974). Visual detection of line segments: An object superiority effect. *Science, 186,* 752–755.

Weisz, J. R., & Jensen, P. S. (1999). Efficacy and effectiveness of psychotherapy and pharmacotherapy with children and adolescents. *Mental Health Services Research, 1,* 125–157.

Weisz, J. R., McCarty, C. A., & Valeri, S. M. (2006). Effects of psychotherapy for depression in children and adolescents: A meta-analysis. *Psychological Bulletin, 132,* 132–149.

Weisz, J. R., Weersing, V. R., & Henggeler, S. W. (2005). Jousting at straw men: Comment on Westen, Novotry, and Thompson-Brenner (2004). *Psychological Bulletin, 131,* 418–426.

Weisz, J. R., Weiss, B., Han, S. S., Granger, D. A., & Morton, T. (1995). Effects of psychotherapy with children and adolescents revisited: A meta-analysis of treatment outcome studies. *Psychological Bulletin, 117,* 450–468.

Wells, A., & Matthews, G. (2006). Cognitive vulnerability to anxiety disorders: An integration. In L. B. Alloy & J. H. Ruskind (Eds.), *Cognitive vulnerability to emotional disorders* (pp. 303–325). New York: Erlbaum.

Wells, G. L., & Bradfield, A. L. (1999). Distortions in eyewitness' recollections: Can the postidentification-feedback effect be moderated? *Psychological Science, 10,* 138–144.

Wells, G. L., Malpass, R. S., Lindsay, R. C. L., Fisher, R. P., Turtle, J. W., & Fulero, S. M. (2000). From the lab to the police station: A successful application of eyewitness research. *American Psychologist, 55,* 581–598.

Wells, G. L., Memon, A., & Penrod, S. D. (2006). Eyewitness evidence: Improving its probative value. *Psychological Science in the Public Interest, 7,* 45–75.

Wells, G. L., & Olson, E. A. (2003). Eyewitness testimony. *Annual Review of Psychology, 54,* 277–295.

Wells, G. L., Olson, E. A., & Charman, S. D. (2002). The confidence of eyewitnesses in their identifications from lineups. *Current Directions in Psychological Science, 11,* 151–154.

Wells, G. L., Olson, E. A., & Charman, S. D. (2003). Distorted retrospective eyewitness reports as functions of feedback and delay. *Journal of Experimental Psychology: Applied, 9,* 42–52.

Wells, S., Graham, K., & West, P. (2000). Alcohol-related aggression in the general population. *Journal of Studies on Alcohol, 61,* 626–632.

Weltzin, T. E., Bulik, C. M., McConaha, C. W., & Kaye, W. H. (1995). Laxative withdrawal and anxiety in bulimia nervosa. *International Journal of Eating Disorders, 17*(2), 141–146.

Wen, W., Shu, X. O., Gao, T., Yang, G., Li, Q., Li, H., & Zheng, W. (2006). Environmental tobacco smoke and mortality in Chinese women who have never smoked: Prospective cohort study. *British Medical Journal, 333,* 333–376.

Wenzel, A., Sharp, I. R., Brown, G. K., Greenberg, R. L., & Beck, A. T. (2006). Dysfunctional beliefs in panic disorder: The Panic Belief Inventory. *Behaviour Research and Therapy, 44,* 819–833.

Werker, J. F., Lloyd, V. L., Pegg, J. E., & Polka, L. (1996). Putting the baby in the bootstraps: Toward a more complete understanding of the role of input in infant speech processing. In J. L. Morgan & K. Demuth (Eds.), *Signal to syntax* (pp. 427–447). Mahwah, NJ: Erlbaum.

Werner, E. (2003, January 28). Police: Sons kill mom, dismember her after seeing it done on "The Sopranos." *Naples Daily News.*

Wertheimer, M. (2000). *A brief history of psychology* (4th ed.). Belmont, CA: Wadsworth.

West, M. A., Borrill, C. S., & Unsworth, K. L. (1998). Team effectiveness in organizations. In C. L. Cooper & I. T. Robertson (Eds.), *International review of industrial and organizational psychology 1998* (pp. 1–48). Chichester, UK: Wiley.

West, R., & Sohal, T. (2006). "Catastrophic" pathways to smoking cessation: Findings from national survey. *British Medical Journal, 332,* 458–460.

Westall, F. C. (2006). Molecular mimicry revisited: Gut bacteria and multiple sclerosis. *Journal of Clinical Microbiology, 44,* 2099–2104.

Westen, D. (1998). The scientific legacy of Sigmund Freud: Toward a psychodynamically informed psychological science. *Psychological Bulletin, 124,* 333–371.

Westen, D. (2005). Implications of research in cognitive neuroscience for psychodynamic psychotherapy. In G. Gabbard, J. Beck, & J. Holmes (Eds.), *Oxford textbook of psychotherapy* (pp. 447–454). Oxford: Oxford University Press.

Westen, D., & Bradley, R. (2005). Empirically supported complexity. *Current Directions in Psychological Science, 14,* 266–271.

Westen, D., & Gabbard, G. O. (1999). Psychoanalytic approaches to personality. In L. Pervin & O. John (Eds), *Handbook of personality: Theory and research* (2nd ed., pp. 57–101). New York: Guilford.

Westen, D., & Morrison, K. (2001). A multidimensional meta-analysis of treatments for depression, panic, and generalized anxiety disorder: An empirical examination of the status of empirically supported therapies. *Journal of Consulting and Clinical Psychology, 69,* 875–899.

Westen, D., Novotny, C. M., & Thompson-Brenner, H. (2004). The empirical status of empirically supported psychotherapies: Assumptions, findings, and reporting in controlled clinical trials. *Psychological Bulletin, 130,* 631–663.

Westen, D., Shedler, J., & Bradley, R. (2006). A prototype approach to personality disorder diagnosis. *American Journal of Psychiatry, 163,* 846–856.

Westerterp-Plantenga, M. S., Smeets, A., & Lejeune, M. P. (2005). Sensory and gastrointestinal satiety effects of capsaicin on food intake. *International Journal of Obesity, 29,* 682–688.

Weston, C., & Went, F. (1999). Speaking up for yourself: Description and evaluation of an assertiveness training program for people with learning disabilities. *Mental Handicap, 27,* 110–115.

Weuve, J., Kang, J. H., Manson, J. E., Breteler, M. M. B., Ware, J. H., & Grodstein, F. (2004). Physical activity, including walking, and cognitive function in older women. *Journal of the American Medical Association, 292,* 1454–1461.

Whaley, A. L. (2001). Cultural mistrust: An important psychological construct for diagnosis and treatment of African-Americans. *Professional Psychology: Research and Practice, 32,* 555–562.

Whalley, L. J., & Deary, I. J. (2001). Longitudinal cohort study of childhood IQ up to age 76. *British Medical Journal, 322,* 819.

Whalley, L. J., Starr, J. M., Athawes, R., Hunter, D., Pattie, A., & Deary, I. J. (2000). Childhood mental ability and dementia. *Neurology, 55,* 1455–1459.

Wharton, C. M., Grafman, J., Flitman, S. S., Hansen, E. K., Brauner, J., Marks, A., & Honda, M. (2000). Toward neuroanatomical models of analogy: A positron emission tomography study of analogical mapping. *Cognitive Psychology, 40,* 173–197.

Wheeler, M. E., & Fiske, S. T. (2005). Controlling racial prejudice. *Psychological Science, 16,* 56–63.

Wheeler, S. C., & Petty, R. E. (2001). The effects of stereotype activation on behavior: A review of possible mechanisms. *Psychological Bulletin, 127,* 797–826.

Whimbey, A. (1976). *Intelligence can be taught.* New York: Bantam.

Whitaker, D. J., Morrison, S., Lindquist, C., Hawkins, S. R., O'Neil, J. A., Nesius, A. M., et al. (2006). A critical review of interventions for the primary prevention of perpetration of partner violence. *Aggression and Violent Behavior, 11,* 151–166.

Whitam, F. L., Diamond, M., & Martin, J. (1993). Homosexual orientation in twins: A report on 61 pairs and three triplet sets. *Archives of Sexual Behavior, 22*(3), 187–206.

Whitbourne, S. K., Zuschlag, M. K., Elliot, L. B., & Waterman, A. D. (1992). Psychosocial development in adulthood: A 22-year sequential study. *Journal of Personality and Social Psychology, 63,* 260–271.

White, A. T., & Spector, P. E. (1987). An investigation of age-related factors in the age-job satisfaction relationship. *Psychology and Aging, 2,* 261–265.

White, D. E., & Glick, J. (1978). *Competence and the context of performance.* Paper presented at the meeting of the Jean Piaget Society, Philadelphia.

White, F. J. (1998). Nicotine addiction and the lure of reward. *Nature Medicine, 4,* 659–660.

White, J. H., & Litovitz, G. (1998). A comparison of inpatient and outpatient women with eating disorders. *Archives of Psychiatric Nursing, 12,* 181–194.

White, K. S., Brown, T. A., Somers, T. J., & Barlow, D. H. (2006). Avoidance behavior in panic disorder: The moderating influences of perceived control. *Behaviour Research and Therapy, 44,* 147–157.

White, R. W. (1959). Motivation reconsidered: The concept of competence. *Psychological Review, 66,* 297–333.

White, S. M. (2006). Talking genes. *Advances in Speech Language Pathology, 8,* 2–6.

Whitlock, J. L., Powers, J. L., & Eckenrode, J. (2006). The virtual cutting edge: The internet and adolescent self-injury. *Developmental Psychology, 42,* 407–417.

Whitlock, J. R., Heynen, A. J., Shuler, M. G., & Bear, M. F. (2006). Learning induces long-term potentiation in the hippocampus. *Science, 313,* 1093–1097.

Whitman, T. L., Borkowski, J. G., Keogh, D. A., & Week, K. (2001). *Interwoven lives: Adolescent mothers and their children.* Mahwah, NJ: Lawrence Erlbaum.

Whitney, P. (2001). Schemas, frames, and scripts in cognitive psychology. In N. J. Smelser & P. B. Baltes (Eds.), *International encyclopedia of the social and behavioral sciences.* The Netherlands: Elsevier.

Whittington, C. J., Kendall, T., & Pilling, S. (2005). Are SSRIs and atypical antidepressants safe and effective for children and adolescents? *Current Opinion in Psychiatry, 18,* 21–25.

Whorf, B. L. (1956). *Language, thought, and reality.* Cambridge/New York: MIT Press/Wiley.

Wible, C. G., Anderson, J., Shenton, M. E., Kricun, A., Hirayasu, Y., Tanaka, S., et al. (2001). Prefrontal cortex, negative symptoms, and schizophrenia: An MRI study. *Psychiatry Research, 108,* 65–78.

Wickens, C. D. (1989). Attention and skilled performance. In D. Holding (Ed.), *Human skills* (pp. 71–105). New York: Wiley.

Wickens, C. D. (1992). *Engineering psychology and human performance* (2nd ed.). New York: HarperCollins.

Wickens, C. D. (2002). Situation awareness and workload in aviation. *Current Directions in Psychological Science, 11,* 128–133.

Wickens, C. D., & Carswell, C. M. (2006). Information processing. In G. Salvendy (Ed.), *Handbook of human factors and ergonomics* (3rd ed.). Hoboken, NJ: Wiley Interscience.

Wickens, C. D., Gordon-Becker, S., & Liu, Y. (2004). *Introduction to human factors engineering* (2nd ed.). Upper Saddle River, NJ: Prentice Hall.

Wickens, C. D., Lee, J. D., Liu, Y., & Gordon-Becker, S. (2004). *Introduction to human factors engineering* (2nd ed.). Upper Saddle River, NJ: Prentice Hall.

Wickens, C. D., Stokes, A., Barnett, B., & Hyman, F. (1992). The effects of stress on pilot judgment in a MIDIS simulator. In O. Svenson & J. Maule (Eds.), *Time pressure and stress in human judgment and decision making* (pp. 271–292). New York: Plenum.

Wicker, B., Keysers, C., Plailly, J., Royet, J. P., Gallese, V., & Rizzolatti, G. (2003). Both of us disgusted in My insula: The common neural basis of seeing and feeling disgust. *Neuron, 40,* 655–664.

Wickham, D. (2001, September 3). Castration often fails to halt offenders. *USA Today.*

Wicks, S., Hjern, A., Gunnell, D., Lewis, G., & Dalman, C. (2005). Social adversity in childhood and the risk of developing psychosis: A national cohort study. *American Journal of Psychiatry, 162,* 1652–1657.

Widiger, T. A. (1997). The construct of mental disorder. *Clinical Psychology: Science and Practice, 4,* 262–266.

Widiger, T. A., & Clark, L. A. (2000). Toward *DSM-V* and the classification of psychopathology. *Psychological Bulletin, 126,* 946–963.

Widiger, T. A., & Sanderson, C. J. (1995). Assessing personality disorders. In J. N. Butcher (Ed.), *Clinical personality assessment: Practical approaches* (pp. 380–394). New York: Oxford University Press.

Widiger, T. A., & Sankis, L. M. (2000). Adult psychopathology: Issues and controversies. *Annual Review of Psychology, 51,* 377–404.

Widiger, T. A., & Simonsen, E. (2005). Introduction to Part Two of the Special Section on the Research Agenda for the Development of Dimensional Classification of Personality Disorder. *Journal of Personality Disorders, 19,* 211.

Widiger, T. A., Simonsen, E., Sirovatka, P., & Reiger, D. A. (2006). *Dimensional models of personality disorders: Refining the research agenda for DSM-V.* Washington, DC: American Psychiatric Publishing.

Widiger, T. A., & Trull, T. J. (2007). Plate tectonics in the classification of personality disorder: Shifting to a dimensional model. *American Psychologist, 62,* 71–83.

Widom, C. S. (1989). The cycle of violence. *Science, 244,* 160–166.

Widom, C. S. (2000). Childhood victimization: Early adversity, later psychopathology. *National Insitute of Justice Journal, 19,* 2–9.

Wiedenfeld, S., O'Leary, A., Bandura, A., Brown, S., Levine, S., & Raska, K. (1990). Impact of perceived self-efficacy in coping with stressors on components of the immune system. *Journal of Personality and Social Psychology, 59,* 1082–1094.

Wiederhold, B. K., & Wiederhold, M. D. (2005). *Virtual reality therapy for anxiety disorders: Advances in evaluation and treatment.* Washington, DC: American Psychological Association.

Wiens, S., Mezzacappa, E. S., & Katkin, E. S. (2000). Heartbeat detection and the experience of emotions. *Cognition & Emotion, 14,* 417–427.

Wiertelak, E. P., Maier, S. F., & Watkins, L. R. (1992). Cholecystokinin antianalgesia: Safety cues abolish morphine analgesia. *Science, 256,* 830–833.

Wigfield, A., & Eccles, J. S. (2000). Expectancy-value theory of achievement motivation. *Contemporary Educational Psychology, 25,* 68–81.

Wilcoxon, H. C., Dragoin, W. B., & Kral, P. A. (1971). Illness-induced aversions in rat and quail: Relative salience of visual and gustatory cues. *Science, 171,* 826–828.

Wilhelm, K., Mitchell, P. B., Niven, H., Finch, A., Wedgwood, L., et al. (2006). Life events, first depression onset, and the serotonin transporter gene. *British Journal of Psychiatry, 188,* 210–215.

Willford, J. A., Leech, S. L., & Day, N. L. (2006). Moderate prenatal alcohol exposure and cognitive status of children at age 10. *Alcoholism: Clinical and Experimental Research, 30,* 1051–1059.

Williams, G. V., & Goldman-Rakic, P. S. (1995). Modulation of memory fields by dopamine D1 receptors in prefrontal cortex. *Nature, 376,* 572–575.

Williams, J. E., & Best, D. L. (1990). *Measuring stereotypes: A multination study* (Rev. ed.). Newbury Park, CA: Sage.

Williams, J. H. G., Waiter, G. D., Gilchrist, A., Perrett, D. I., Murray, A. D., et al. (2006). Neural mechanisms of imitation and 'mirror neuron' functioning in autistic spectrum disorder. *Neuropsychologia, 44,* 610–621.

Williams, K. D., Jackson, J. M., & Karau, S. J. (1995). In D. Schroeder (Ed.), *Social dilemmas: Perspectives on individuals and groups* (pp. 117–142). Westport, CT: Praeger.

Williams, K. D., & Sommer, K. L. (1997). Social ostracism by coworkers: Does rejection lead to loafing or compensation? *Personality and Social Psychology Bulletin, 23,* 693–706.

Williams, L. M. (1994). What does it mean to forget child sexual abuse? A reply to Loftus, Garry, and Feldman (1994). *Journal of Consulting and Clinical Psychology, 62,* 1182–1186.

Williams, N. L., Reardon, J. M., Murray, K. T., & Cole, T. M. (2005). Anxiety disorders: A developmental vulnerability-stress perspective. In B. L. Hankin & J. R. Z. Abela (Eds.), *Development of psychopathology: A vulnerability-stress perspective* (pp. 289–327). Newberry Park, CA: Sage.

Williams, R. A. (2005). A short course in family therapy: Translating research into practice. *Family Journal: Counseling and Therapy for Couples and Families 13,* 188–194.

Williams, R. B. (2001). Hostility and heart disease: Williams et al. (1980). *Advances in Mind-Body Medicine, 17,* 52–55.

Williams, R. J., & Connolly, D. (2006). Does learning about the mathematics of gambling change gambling behavior? *Psychology of Addictive Behavior, 20,* 62–68.

Williams, T. J., Pepitone, M. E., Christensen, S. E., Cooke, B. M., Huberman, A. D., Breedlove, N. J., et al. (2000). Finger-length ratios and sexual orientation. *Nature, 404,* 455–456.

Williams-Piehota, P., Pizarro, J., Schneider, T. R., Mowad, L., & Salovey, P. (2005). Matching health messages to monitor-blunter coping styles to motivate screening mammography. *Health Psychology, 24,* 58–67.

Willis, J., & Todorov, A. (2006). First impressions: Making up your mind after a 100-ms exposure to a face. *Psychological Science, 17,* 592–598.

Willis, S. L., & Schaie, K. W. (1999). Intellectual functioning in midlife. In S. L. Willis & J. D. Reid (Eds.), *Life in the middle: Psychological and social development in middle age* (pp. 233–247). San Diego, CA: Academic Press.

Willis, W. D., Jr. (1988). Dorsal horn neurophysiology of pain. *Annals of the New York Academy of Science, 531,* 76–89.

Wills, T. A., Sandy, J. M., Yaeger, A., & Shinar, O. (2001). Family risk factors and adolescent substance use: Moderation effects oft temperament dimension. *Developmental Psychology, 37,* 283–297.

Wilson, E. J., MacLeod, C., Matthews, A., & Rutherford, E. M. (2006). The causal role of interpretive bias in anxiety reactivity. *Journal of Abnormal Psychology, 115,* 103–111.

Wilson, G. T. (1997). Dissemination of cognitive behavioral treatments: Commentary. *Behavior Therapy, 28,* 473–475.

Wilson, G. T., Nathan, P. E., O'Leary, K. D., & Clark, L. A. (1996). *Abnormal psychology.* Boston: Allyn & Bacon.

Wilson, K., & French, C. C. (2006). The relationship between susceptibility to false memories, dissociativity, and paranormal belief and experience. *Personality and Individual Differences, 41,* 1493–1502.

Wilson, R. S., Beck, T. L., Bienias, J. L., & Bennett, D. A. (2007). Terminal cognitive decline: Accelerated loss of cognition in the last years of life. *Psychosomatic Medicine, 69,* 131–137.

Wilson, T. D., & Gilbert, D. T. (2005). Affective forecasting: Knowing what to want. *Current Directions in Psychological Science, 14,* 131–134.

Wilson, W. J. (1997). *When work disappears: The world of the new urban poor.* New York: Vintage Books.

Wimo, A., & Winblad, B. (2001). Health economical aspects of Alzheimer disease and its treatment. *Psychogeriatrics, 1,* 189–193.

Winawer, J., Witthoft, N., Frank, M. C., Wu, L., Wade, A. R., & Boroditsky, L. (2007). Russian blues reveal effects of language on color discrimination. *Proceedings of the National Academy of Sciences, 104,* 7780–7785.

Winemiller, M. H., Billow, R. G., Laskowski, E. R., & Harmsen, W. S. (2003). Effect of magnetic vs sham-magnetic insoles on plantar heel pain: A randomized controlled trial. *Journal of the American Medical Association, 290,* 1474–1478.

Winer, G. A., Cottrell, J. E., Gregg, V., Fournier, J. S., & Bica, L. A. (2002). Fundamentally misunderstanding visual perception: Adults' belief in visual emissions. *American Psychologist, 57,* 417–424.

Winkelmayer, W. C., Stampfer, M. J., Willett, W. C., & Curhan, G. C. (2005). Habitual caffeine intake and the risk of hypertension in women. *Journal of the American Medical Association, 294,* 2330–2335.

Winkielman, P., & Berridge, K. C. (2004). Unconscious emotion. *Current Directions in Psychological Science, 13,* 120–123.

Winkielman, P., & Cacioppo J. T. (2004). Mind at ease puts a smile on the face: Psychophysiological evidence that processing facilitation elicits positive affect. *Journal of Personality and Social Psychology, 81,* 989–1000.

Winn, P. (1995). The lateral hypothalamus and motivated behavior: An old syndrome reassessed and a new perspective gained. *Current Directions in Psychological Science, 4,* 182–187.

Winner, E. (2000). Giftedness: Current theory and research. *Current Directions in Psychological Science, 9,* 153–156.

Winson, J. (1990, November). The meaning of dreams. *Scientific American,* pp. 86–96.

Winston, A., Been, H., & Serby, M. (2005). Psychotherapy and psychopharmacology: Different universes or an integrated future? *Journal of Psychotherapy Integration, 15,* 213–223.

Winter, D. G. (1996). *Personality: Analysis and interpretation of lives.* New York: McGraw-Hill.

Winterer, G. (2006). Cortical microcircuits in schizophrenia—The dopamine hypothesis revisited. *Pharmacopsychiatry, 39,* S68–S71.

Wintersteen, M. B., Mensinger, J. L., & Diamond, G. S. (2005). Do gender and racial differences between patient and therapist affect therapeutic alliance and treatment retention in adolescents? *Professional Psychology: Research and Practice, 36,* 400–408.

Wisborg, K., Kesmodel, U., Bech, B. H., Hedegaard, M., & Henriksen, T. B. (2003). Maternal consumption of coffee during pregnancy and stillbirth and infant death in first year of life: Prospective study. *British Medical Journal, 326,* 420.

Wise, R. A., & Rompre, P. P. (1989). Brain dopamine and reward. *Annual Review of Psychology, 40,* 191–225.

Wiseman, R., West, D., & Stemman, R. (1996, January/February). Psychic crime detectives: A new test for measuring their successes and failures. *Skeptical Inquirer, 21,* 38–58.

Wismer Fries, A. B., Ziegler, T. E., Kurian, J. R., Jacoris, S., & Pollak, S. D. (2005). Early experience in humans is associated with changes in neuropeptides critical for regulating social behavior. *Proceedings of the National Academy of Sciences of the USA, 102,* 17237–17240.

Witt, C., Brinkhaus, B., Jena, S., Linde, K., Streng, A., Wagenpfeil, S., et al. (2005). Acupuncture in patients with osteoarthritis of the knee: A randomised trial. *Lancet, 366,* 136–143.

Witt, L. A., & Ferris, G. R. (2003). Social skills as a moderator of the conscientiousness-performance relationship: Convergent results across four studies. *Journal of Applied Psychology, 88,* 809–821.

Witt, M., & Wozniak, W.(2006). Structure and function of the vomeronasal organ. *Advances in Otorhinolaryngology, 63,* 70–83.

Wittchen, H. U., & Hoyer, J. (2001). Generalized anxiety disorder: Nature and course. *Journal of Clinical Psychiatry, 62,* 15–19.

Wixted, J. T. (2004). The psychology and neuroscience of forgetting. *Annual Review of Psychology, 55,* 235–269.

Wohlfarth, T., Storosum, J. G., Elferink, A. J. A., van Zweiten, B. J., Fouwels, A., & van den Brink, W. (2004). Response to tricyclic antidepressants: Independent of gender? *American Journal of Psychiatry, 161,* 370–372.

Wolak, J., Mitchell, K., & Finkelhor, D. (2007). Unwanted and wanted exposure to online pornography in a national sample of youth internet users. *Pediatrics, 119,* 247–257.

Woldt, A. L., & Toman, S. M. (Eds.). (2005). *Gestalt therapy: History, theory, and practice.* Newbury Park, CA: Sage.

Wolf, M., Sander van Doorn, G., Leimar, O., & Weissing, F. J. (2007). Life-history trade-offs favour the evolution of animal personalities. *Nature, 447,* 581–584.

Wolf, S. L., Winstein, C. J., Miller, J. P., Taub, E., Uswatte, G., Morris, D., et al. (2006). Effect of constraint-induced movement therapy on upper extremity function 3 to 9 months after stroke. *Journal of the American Medical Association, 296,* 2095–2104.

Wolfe, J. M. (1998). What can 1 million trials tell us about visual search? *Psychological Science, 9,* 33–39.

Wolfe, J. M., Alvarez, G. A., & Horowitz, T. S. (2000). Attention is fast but volition is slow. *Nature, 406,* 691.

Wolman, C., van den Broek, P., & Lorch, R. F. (1997). Effects of causal structure and delayed story recall by children with mild mental retardation, children with learning disabilities, and children without disabilities. *Journal of Special Education.*

Wolpaw, J. R., & Chen, X. Y. (2006). The cerebellum in maintenance of a motor skill: A hierarchy of brain and spinal cord plasticity underlies H-reflex conditioning. *Learning & Memory, 13,* 208–215.

Wolpe, J. (1958). *Psychotherapy by reciprocal inhibition.* Stanford, CA: Stanford University Press.

Wolpert, I. (1924). Die Simultanagnosie: Störung der Gesamtauffassung. *Archiv für Psychiatrie und Nervenkrankheiten, vereinigt mit Zeitschrift für die gesamte Neurologie und Psychiatrie, 93,* 397–413.

Wong, K. F. E., & Kwong, J. Y. Y. (2005). Between-individual comparisons in performance evaluation: A perspective from prospect theory. *Journal of Applied Psychology, 90,* 284–294.

Wood, J. M., Tyrrell, R. A., & Carberry, T. P. (2005). Limitations in drivers' ability to recognize pedestrians at night. *Human Factors, 47,* 644–653.

Wood, W., & Eagly, A. H. (2002). A cross-cultural analysis of the behavior of women and men: Implications for the origins of sex differences. *Psychological Bulletin, 128,* 699–727.

Wood, W., Wong, F. Y., & Chachere, G. (1991). Effects of media violence on viewers' aggression in unconstrained social interaction. *Psychological Bulletin, 109,* 371–383.

Woodcock, R. W., McGrew, K. S., & Mather, N. (2001). *Woodcock-Johnson III Tests of Cognitive Abilities.* Itasca, IL: Riverside.

Woodhead, M. (1988). When psychology informs public policy: The case of early childhood intervention. *American Psychologist, 43,* 443–454.

Woods, S. C., Schwartz, M. W., Baskin, D. G., & Seeley, R. J. (2000). Food intake and the regulation of body weight. *Annual Review of Psychology, 51,* 255–277.

Woods, S. C., Seeley, R. J., Porte, D., Jr., & Schwartz, M. W. (1998). Signals that regulate food intake and energy homeostasis. *Science, 280,* 1378–1383.

Woodward, T. S., Moritz, S., Cuttler, C., & Whitman, J. C. (2006). The contribution of a cognitive bias against disconfirmatory evidence (BADE) to delusions in schizophrenia. *Journal of Clinical and Experimental Neuropsychology, 28,* 605–617.

Woolley, J. D. (1997). Thinking about fantasy: Are children fundamentally different thinkers and believers from adults? *Child Development, 68,* 991–1011.

Worchel, S., Cooper, J., Goethals, G. R., & Olson, J. (2000). *Social psychology.* Belmont, CA: Wadsworth.

Workman, M. (2005). Expert decision support system use, disuse, and misuse: A study using the theory of planned behavior. *Computers in Human Behavior, 21,* 211–231.

World Health Organization Mental Health Survey Consortium. (2004). Prevalence, severity, and unmet need for treatment of mental disorders in the World Health Organization World Mental Health Surveys. *Journal of the American Medical Association, 291,* 2581–2590.

World Health Organization. (2001). *The world health report 2001—mental health: New understanding, new hope.* Retrieved August 6, 2006, from http://www.who.int/whr/2001/en/index.html.

World Health Organization. (2003). *AIDS epidemic update.* Geneva, Switzerland: WHO.

Wren, C. S. (1999, February 24). U.N. drug board urges research on marijuana as medicine. *New York Times.* Retrieved December 13, 2004, from http://query.nytimes.com/gst/abstract.html?res=F10A13F83A590C778EDDAB0894D1494D81

Wright, B. A., & Fitzgerald, M. B. (2001). Different patterns of human discrimination learning for two interaural cues to sound location. *Proceedings of the National Academy of Science, 98,* 12307–12312.

Wright, B. A., & Zecker, S. G. (2004). Learning problems, delayed development, and puberty. *Proceedings of the National Academy of Sciences, 101,* 9942–9946.

Wright, D. B. (1993). Recall of the Hillsborough disaster over time: Systematic biases of "flashbulb" memories. *Applied Cognitive Psychology, 7,* 129–138.

Wright, E. F., Voyer, D., Wright, R. D., & Roney, C. (1995). Supporting audiences and performance under pressure: The home-ice disadvantage in hockey championships. *Journal of Sport Behavior, 18,* 21–28.

Wright, R. (1994). *The moral animal: The new science of evolutionary psychology.* New York: Random House.

Wright, T. A. (2003). Positive organizational behavior: An idea whose time has truly come. *Journal of Organizational Behavior, 24,* 437–442.

Wupperman, P., & Neumann, C. S. (2006) Depressive symptoms as a function of sex-role, rumination, and neuroticism. *Personality and Individual Differences, 40,* 189–201.

Wurtman, R. J. (2006). Narcolepsy and the hypocretins. *Metabolism, 55*(10 Suppl. 2), S36–S39.

Wurtman, R. J., & Wurtman, J. J. (1995). Brain serotonin, carbohydrate-craving, obesity and depression. *Obesity Research, 3*(Suppl. 4), 477S–480S.

Wyer, R. S., Jr. (2004). The cognitive organization and use of general knowledge. In J. T. Jost & M. R. Banaji (Eds.), *Perspectivism in social psychology: The yin and yang of scientific progress* (pp. 97–112). Washington, DC: American Psychological Association.Yaffe, K., Barnes, D., Nevitt, M., Lui, L.-Y., & Covinsky, K. (2001). A prospective study of physical activity and cognitive decline in elderly women. *Archives of Internal Medicine, 161,* 1703–1708.

Wynne, C. L. (2004). *Do animals think?* Princeton, NJ: Princeton University Press.

Wynne, K., Park, A. J., Small, C. J., Patterson, M., Ellis, S. M., Murphy, K. G., et al. (2005). Subcutaneous oxyntomodulin reduces body weight in overweight and obese subjects: A double-blind, randomized, controlled trial. *Diabetes, 54,* 2390–2395.

Xu, D., Liu, T., Ashe, J., & Bushara, K. O. (2006). Role of the olivo-cerebellar system in timing. *The Journal of Neuroscience: The Official Journal of the Society for Neuroscience, 26,* 5990–5995.

Xue, Y., Leventhal, T., Brooks-Gunn, J., & Earls, F. J. (2005). Neighborhood residence and mental health problems of 5- to 11-year-olds. *Archives of General Psychiatry, 62,* 554–563.

Yaffe, K., Barnes, D., Nevitt, M., Lui, L.-Y., & Covinsky, K. (2001). A prospective study of physical activity and cognitive decline in elderly women. *Archives of Internal Medicine, 161,* 1703–1708.

Yahr, P., & Jacobsen, C. H. (1994). Hypothalamic knife cuts that disrupt mating in male gerbils sever efferents and forebrain afferents of the sexually dimorphic area. *Behavioral Neuroscience, 108*(4), 735–742.

Yakeley, J., Shoenberg, P., & Heady, A. (2004). Who wants to do psychiatry? the influence of a student psychotherapy scheme: A 10-year retrospective study. *Psychiatric Bulletin, 28,* 208–212.

Yakimovich, D., & Saltz, E. (1971). Helping behavior: The cry for help. *Psychonomic Science, 23,* 427–428.

Yalom, I. D. (1980). *Existential psychotherapy.* New York: Basic Books.

Yalom, I. D. (1995). Stimulus-driven attentional capture. *Current Directions in Psychological Science, 2,* 156–161.

Yalom, I. D. (2002). *The gift of therapy.* New York: HarperCollins.

Yamagata, S., Suzuki, A., Ando, J., Ono, Y., Kijima, N., Yoshimura, K., et al. (2006). Is the genetic structure of human personality universal? a cross-cultural twin study from North America, Europe, and Asia. *Journal of Personality and Social Psychology, 90,* 987–998.

Yamaguchi, S., Isejima, H., Matsuo, T., Okura, R., Yagita, K., Kobayashi, M., & Okamura, H. (2003). Synchronization of cellular clocks in the suprachiasmatic nucleus. *Science, 302,* 1408–1412.

Yan, B., Li, K., Xu, J., Wang, W., Li, K., Liu, H., et al. (2005). Acupoint-specific fMRI patterns in human brain. *Neuroscience Letters, 383,* 236–240.

Yang, C. M., Spielman, A. J., & Glovinsky, P. (2006). Nonpharmacologic strategies in the management of insomnia. *Psychiatric Clinics of North America, 29,* 895–919.

Yantis, S. (1993). Stimulus-driven attentional capture. *Current Directions in Psychological Science, 2,* 156–161.

Yarkoni, T., Braver, T. S., Gray, J. R., & Green, L. (2005). Prefrontal brain activity predicts temporally extended decision making. *Journal of the Experimental Analysis of Behavior, 84,* 537–554.

Yehuda, R., Bryant, R., Marmar, C., & Zohar, J. (2005). Pathological responses to terrorism. *Neuropsychopharmacology, 30,* 1793–1805.

Yela, C., & Sangrador, J. L. (2001). Perception of physical attractiveness throughout loving relationships. *Current Research in Social Psychology, 6,* 57–75.

Yeomans, M. R., & Mobini, S. (2006). Hunger alters the expression of acquired hedonic but not sensory qualities of food-paired odors in humans. *Journal of Experimental Psychology: Animal Behavior Processes, 32,* 460–466.

Yerkes, R. M. (Ed.). (1921). Psychological examining in the U.S. Army. *Memoirs of the National Academy of Sciences,* No. 15.

Yesavage, J. A., Leirer, V. O., Denari, M., & Hollister, L. E. (1985). Carry-over effects of marijuana intoxication on aircraft pilot performance: A preliminary report. *American Journal of Psychiatry, 142,* 1325–1329.

Yeung, L. M., Linver, M. R., & Brooks-Gunn, J. (2002). How money matters for young children's development: Parental investment and family processes. *Child Development, 73,* 1861–1879.

Yonas, A., Arterberry, M. E., & Granrud, C. D. (1987). Space perception in infancy. In R. Vasta (Ed.), *Annals of child development* (Vol. 4, pp. 1–34). Greenwich, CT: JAI Press.

Yongxia, R. (2006). Acupuncture treatment of Jacksonian epilepsy—A report of 98 cases. *Journal of Traditional Chinese Medicine, 26*(3), 177–178.

Yonkers, K., Kando, J., Cole, J., & Blumenthal, S. (1992). Gender differences in pharmacokinetics and pharmacodynamics of psychotropic medication. *American Journal of Psychiatry, 149,* 587–595.

Yoo, S.-S., Hu, P. T., Gujar, N., Jolesz, F. A., & Walker, M. P. (2007). A deficit in the ability to form new human memories without sleep. *Nature Neuroscience, 10,* 385–392.

York, J. L., & Welte, J. W. (1994). Gender comparisons of alcohol consumption in alcoholic and nonalcoholic populations. *Journal of Studies on Alcohol, 55*(6), 743–750.

Yoshimasu, K., Washio, M., Tokunaga, S., Tanaka, K., Liu, Y., Kodama, H., et al. (2002). Relation between Type A behavior pattern and the extent of coronary atherosclerosis in Japanese women. *International Journal of Behavioral Medicine, 9,* 77–93.

Youm, Y., & Laumann, E. O. (2002). Social network effects on the transmission of sexually transmitted diseases. *Sexually Transmitted Diseases, 29,* 689–697.

Young, M. (1971). Age and sex differences in problem solving. *Journal of Gerontology, 26,* 331–336.

Young, M. S., Turner, J., Denny, G., & Young, M. (2004). Examining external and internal poverty as antecedents of teen pregnancy *American Journal of Health Behavior, 28,* 361–373.

Youniss, J., & Yates, M. (1997). *Community service and social responsibility in youth.* Chicago: University of Chicago Press.

Younkin, S. G. (2001). Amyloid beta vaccination: reduced plaques and improved cognition. *Nature Medicine, 7,* 18–19.

Yousif, Y., & Korte, C. (1995). Urbanization, culture, and helpfulness: Cross-cultural studies in England and the Sudan. *Journal of Cross-Cultural Psychology, 26,* 474–489.

Yovel, I., & Mineka, S. (2005). Emotion-congruent attentional biases: The perspective of hierarchical models of emotional disorders. *Personality and Individual Differences, 38,* 785–795.

Yufik, A. (2005). Revisiting the Tarasoff decision: Risk assessment and liability in clinical and forensic practice. *American Journal of Forensic Psychology, 23*(4), 5–21.

Yukl, G., & Van Fleet, D. D. (1992). Theory and research on leadership in organizations. In M. D. Dunnette & L. M. Hough (Eds.), *Handbook of industrial and organizational psychology* (Vol. 3, 2nd ed., pp. 147–198). Palo Alto, CA: Consulting Psychologists Press.

Yun, S., Faraj, S., & Sims, H. P. (2005). Contingent leadership and effectiveness of trauma resuscitation teams. *Journal of Applied Psychology, 90,* 1288–1296.

Zaccarco, S. J. (2007). Trait-based perspectives of leadership. *American Psychologist, 62,* 6–16.

Zachar, P., & Kendler, K. S. (2007). Psychiatric disorders: A conceptual taxonomy. *American Journal of Psychiatry, 164,* 557–565.

Zadnik, K. (2001). Association between night lights and myopia: True blue or a red herring? *Archives of Ophthalmology, 119,* 146.

Zagefka, H., & Brown, R. (2005). Comparisons and perceived deprivation in ethnic minority settings. *Personality and Social Psychology Bulletin, 31,* 467–482.

Zahn-Waxler, C., Friedman, R. J., Cole, P. M., Mizuta, I., & Hiruma, N. (1996). Japanese and United States preschool children's responses to conflict and distress. *Child Development, 67,* 2462–2477.

Zahn-Waxler, C., Radke-Yarrow, M., Wagner, E., & Chapman, M. (1992). Development of concern for others. *Developmental Psychology, 28,* 1038–1047.

Zahrani, S. S., & Kaplowitz, S. A. (1993). Attributional biases in individualistic and collectivist cultures: A comparison of Americans with Saudis. *Social Psychology Quarterly, 56*(3), 223–233.

Zajonc, R. B. (1965). Social facilitation. *Science, 149,* 269–274.

Zajonc, R. B. (1998). Emotions. In D. Gilbert, S. T. Fiske, & G. Lindzey (Eds.), *Handbook of social psychology* (Vol. 1, 4th ed., pp. 591–634). Boston: McGraw-Hill.

Zakriski, A. L., Wright, J. C., & Underwood, M. K. (2005). Gender similarities and differences in children's social behavior: Finding personality in contextualized patterns of adaptation. *Journal of Personality and Social Psychology, 88,* 844–855.

Zalta, A. K., & Keel, P. K. (2006). Peer influence on bulimic symptoms in college students. *Journal of Abnormal Psychology, 115,* 185–189.

Zambelis, T., Paparrigopoulos, T., & Soldatos, C. R. (2002). REM sleep behaviour disorder associated with a neurinoma of the left pontocerebral angle. *Journal of Neurology, Neurosurgery, and Psychiatry, 72,* 821–822.

Zammit, S., Allebeck, P., Andreasson, S., Lundberg, I., & Lewis, G. (2002). Self reported cannabis use as a risk factor for schizophrenia in Swedish conscripts of 1969: Historical cohort study. *British Medical Journal, 325,* 1199.

Zanarini, M. C., Skodol, A. E., Bender, D., Dolan, R., Sanislow, C., Schaefer, E., et al. (2000). The collaborative longitudinal personality disorders study: Reliability of axis I and II diagnoses. *Journal of Personality Disorders, 14,* 291–299.

Zatorre, R. J. (2003). Music and the brain. *Annals of the New York Academy of Sciences, 999,* 4–14.

Zeanah, C. H., Smyke, A. T., Koga, S. F., & Carlson, E. (2005). Attachment in institutionalized and community children in Romania. *Child Development, 76,* 1015–1028.

Zeki, S. (1992). The visual image in mind and brain. *Scientific American, 267,* 68–76.

Zelenski, J. M., & Larsen, R. J. (1999). Susceptibility to affect: A comparison of three taxonomies. *Journal of Personality, 67,* 761–791.

Zeman, A. (2001). Consciousness. *Brain, 124,* 1263–1289.

Zeman, A., Britton, T., Douglas, N., Hansen, A., Hicks, J., Howard, R., et al. (2004). Narcolepsy and excessive daytime sleepiness. *British Medical Journal, 329,* 724–728.

Zenderland, L. (1998). *Measuring minds: Henry Herbert Goddard and the origins of American intelligence testing.* New York: Cambridge University Press.

Zeng, F. G. (2005). Trends in cochlear implants. *Trends in Amplification, 8,* 1–34.

Zernike, K. (2000, October 3). Colleges shift emphasis on drinking. *New York Times.*

Zhang, G., & Simon, H. A. (1985). STM capacity for Chinese words and idioms: Chunking and acoustical loop hypothesis. *Memory & Cognition, 13,* 193–201.

Zhang, Y., Hoon, M. A., Chandrashekar, J., Mueller, K. L., Cook, B., Wu, D., et al. (2003). Coding of sweet, bitter, and umami tastes: Different receptor cells sharing similar signaling pathways. *Cell, 112,* 293–301.

Zhang, Y., Proenca, R., Maffei, M., Barone, M., Leopold, L., & Friedman, J. M. (1994). Positional cloning of the mouse obese gene and its human homologue. *Nature, 372,* 425–432.

Zhao, H., & Seibert, S. E. (2006). The big five personality dimensions and entrepreneurial status: A meta-analytical review. *Journal of Applied Psychology, 91,* 259–271.

Zhao, M., Momma, S., Delfani, K., Carlen, M., Cassidy, R. M., Johansson, C. B., et al. (2003). Evidence for neurogenesis in the adult mammalian substantia nigra. *Proceedings of the National Academy of Sciences, 100,* 7925–7930.

Zhou, J.-N., Hofman, M. A., Gooren, L. J. G., & Swaab, D. F. (1995). A sex difference in the human brain and its relation to transsexuality. *Nature, 378,* 68–70.

Zhou, Q., Eisenberg, N., Wang, Y., & Reiser, M. (2004). Chinese children's effortful control and dispositional anger/frustration relations to parenting styles and children's social functioning. *Developmental Psychology, 40,* 352–366.

Zigler, E. F., & Muenchow, S. (1992). *Head Start: The inside story of America's most successful educational experiment.* New York: Basic Books.

Zigler, E., & Seitz, V. (1982). Social policy and intelligence. In R. J. Sternberg (Ed.), *Handbook of human intelligence* (pp. 586–641). Cambridge, UK: Cambridge University Press.

Zillmann, D. (1988). Cognition-excitation interdependencies in aggressive behavior. *Aggressive Behavior, 14,* 51–64.

Zillmann, D. (1998). *Connections between sexuality and aggression* (2nd ed.). Hillsdale, NJ: Erlbaum.

Zillmann, D. (2003). Theory of affective dynamics: Emotions and moods. In J. Bryant & D. Roskos-Ewoldsen (Eds.), *Communication and emotion: Essays in honor of Dolf Zillmann* (pp. 533–567). Mahwah, NJ: Erlbaum.

Zillmann, D., Katcher, A. H., & Milavsky, B. (1972). Excitation transfer from physical exercise to subsequent aggressive behavior. *Journal of Experimental Social Psychology, 8,* 247–259.

Zimbardo, P. G. (1973). The psychological power and pathology of imprisonment. In E. Aronson & R. Helmreich (Eds.), *Social psychology.* New York: Van Nostrand.

Zimmerman, B. J., & Schunk, D. H. (2003). Albert Bandura: The scholar and his contributions to educational psychology. In B. J. Zimmerman (Ed.), *Educational psychology: A century of contributions* (pp. 431–457). Mahwah, NJ: Erlbaum.

Zimmerman, F. J., Glew, G. M., Christakis, D. A., & Katon, W. (2005). Early cognitive stimulation, emotional support, and television watching as predictors of subsequent bullying among grade-school children. *Archives of Pediatric Adolescent Medicine, 159,* 384–388.

Zimmerman, M. A. (1990). Toward a theory of learned hopefulness: A structural model analysis of participation and empowerment. *Journal of Research in Personality, 24,* 71–86.

Zimmerman, M., McDermut, W., & Mattia, J. I. (2000). Frequency of anxiety disorders in psychiatric outpatients with major depressive disorder. *American Journal of Psychiatry, 157,* 1337–1340.

Zimmerman, M., Posternak, M. A., Attiullah, N., Freidman, M., Michael, R. J., et al. (2005). Why isn't bupropion the most frequently prescribed antidepressant? *Journal of Clinical Psychiatry, 66,* 603–610.

Zinbarg, R. E., & Barlow, D. H. (1996). Structure of anxiety and the anxiety disorders: A hierarchical model. *Journal of Abnormal Psychology, 105,* 181–193.

Zinbarg, R. E., & Mineka, S. (1991). Animal models of psychopathology: II. Simple phobia. *The Behavior Therapist, 14,* 61–65.

Zoellner, L. A., Foa, E. B., Brigidi, B. D., & Przeworski, A. (2000). Are trauma victims susceptible to "false memories"? *Journal of Abnormal Psychology, 109,* 517–524.

Zoellner, T., & Maercker, A. (2006). Posttraumatic growth in clinical psychology: A critical review and introduction of a two component model. *Clinical Psychology Review, 26,* 626–653.

Zola-Morgan, S. (1995). Localization of brain function: The legacy of Franz Joseph Gall (1758–1828). *Annual Review of Neuroscience, 18,* 359–383.

Zou, Z., & Buck, L. B. (2006). Combinatorial effects of odorant mixes in olfactory cortex. *Science, 311,* 1477–1481.

Zou, Z., Horowitz, L. F., Montmayeur, J.-P., Snapper, S., & Buck, L. B. (2001). Genetic tracing reveals a stereotyped sensory map in the olfactory cortex. *Nature, 414,* 173–179.

Zsambok, C. E., & Klein, G. (1997). *Naturalistic decision making.* Hillsdale, NJ: Erlbaum.

Zuberbühler, K. (2005). The phylogenetic roots of language. *Current Directions in Psychological Science, 14,* 126–130.

Zubieta, J.-K., Bueller, J. A., Jackson, L. R., Scott, D. J., Xu, Y., Koeppe, R. A., et al. (2005). Placebo effects mediated by endogenous opioid activity on μ-opioid receptors. *Journal of Neuroscience, 25,* 7754–7762.

Zucker, A. N., Ostrove, J. M., & Stewart, A. J. (2002). College-educated women's personality development in adulthood: Perceptions and age differences. *Psychology & Aging, 17*(2), 236–244.

Zuckerman, M. (1979). *Sensation seeking: Beyond the optimal level of arousal.* Hillsdale, NJ: Erlbaum.

Zuckerman, M. (1984). Sensation seeking: A comparative approach to a human approach. *Behavioral and Brain Sciences, 7,* 413–471.

Zuckerman, M. (1990). Some dubious premises in research and theory on racial differences. *American Psychologist, 45,* 1297–1303.

Zuckerman, M. (1996). "Conceptual clarification" or confusion in "The study of sensation seeking" by J. S. H. Jackson and M. Maraun. *Personality and Individual Differences, 21,* 111–114.

Zuckerman, M. (2004). The shaping of personality: Genes, environments, and chance encounters. *Journal of Personality Assessment, 82,* 11–22.

Zuroff, D. C., & Blatt, S. J. (2006). The therapeutic relationship in the brief treatment of depression: Contributions to clinical improvement and enhanced adaptive capacities. *Journal of Consulting and Clinical Psychology, 74,* 130–140.

Zuvekas, S. H., Vitiello, B., & Nordquist, G. S. (2006). Recent trends in stimulant medication use among U.S. children. *American Journal of Psychiatry, 163,* 579–585.

CREDITS

PHOTOGRAPHS

Chapter 1: p. 1: ©Paul Hardy/CORBIS. p. 4: Shaywitz et al., 1995. NMR Research/Yale Medical School. p. 5: Photographs courtesy of Baddesigns.Com. p. 6: ©Tom Stewart/Corbis. p. 7: Courtesy of eHARMONY.com. p. 8: Michael Hewes/Getty Images. p. 11: Photofest. p. 14: Psychology Archives—The Univ. of Akron. p. 15: Harvard University Archives. p. 18: Jose Luis Pelaez, Inc./CORBIS. p. 19: Photodisc. p. 20: Mary Kate Denny/PhotoEdit. p. 21: ©Richard T. Nowitz/CORBIS. p. 22: Courtesy of Wellesley College Archives, photo by Partridge. p. 23: Archives and Special Collections, Rembert E. Stokes Learning Resources Center, Wilberforce University. p. 25: ©Deanpictures/The Image Works.

Chapter 2: p. 27: ©Royalty-Free/CORBIS. p. 31: Jack Hollingsworth/Getty Images. p. 32: Mason Morfitt/Getty Images. p. 33: Keith Brofsky/Getty Images. p. 35 (top): Eric Bean/Getty Images. p. 35 (bottom): David Young-Wolff/PhotoEdit. p. 36: Everett Collection. p. 37: Mark Richards/PhotoEdit. p. 42 (top): AP IMAGES. p. 42 (bottom): Photodisc. p. 43: Christopher Bissell/Getty Images. p. 46: ©Joel Gordon 1998. p. 48: ©George Shelley/CORBIS. p. 51: Bob Daemmrich/Stock, Boston, LLC. p. 54: Robin Nelson/PhotoEdit. p. 55: ©Holger Winkler/zefa/Corbis.

Chapter 3: p. 58: ©Howard Sochurek/The Medical File. p. 64: ©Dennis Kunkel/PHOTOTAKE. p. 66: ©Ariel Skelley/CORBIS. p. 69: Don Fawcett/Photo Researchers. p. 72: From Levin DN, Xiaoping H, et al. The Brain: Integrated three-dimensional display of MR and PET images. Radiology 1989; 172:783–789. Radiological Society of North America. p. 73: From "New findings of the correlation between acupoints and corresponding brain cortices using functional MRI," by Cho et al, Proceedings of the National Academy of Sciences, vol. 95, pp. 2670–2673, March 1998. ©1998 National Academy of Sciences, USA. p. 75: Professor Bradley P. Sutton, University of Illinois at Urbana-Champagne. p. 78: ©Bachmann/The Image Works. p. 81: © Dr. D. Dickson/Peter Arnold, Inc. p. 82: By permission of John Wiley & Sons. p. 87: Cleveland FES Center, Cleveland VA Medical Center, Case Western Reserve University, Cleveland, Ohio. p. 88: Jose Luis Pelaez, Inc./Getty Images. p. 90: Dan McCoy/Rainbow. p. 101: ©Tom Brakefiled/CORBIS. p. 100: Terry Wild Stock.

Chapter 4: p. 106: Darren Robb/Getty Images. p. 110: ©Ed Bock/CORBIS. p. 111: Bonnie Kamin/PhotoEdit. p. 113: Ed Roy. p. 114: Dr. Joseph E. Hawkins, Kresge Hearing Research Institute, University of Michigan. p. 115: Yellow Dog Productions/Getty Images. p. 116: David Young-Wolff/PhotoEdit. p. 121: Dr. Frank Schaeffel. p. 122: Omikron/Photo Researchers. p. 129: Fritz Goro/Getty Images. p. 132: Dr. Francoise Vienot. p. 135: Gary Braasch. p. 137 (top): Omikron/Photo Researchers. p. 137 (bottom): L.M. Bartoshuk and U.B. Duffy. p. 141: AP IMAGES. p. 143 (top): Alain Evrard/Photo Researchers, Inc. p. 143 (bottom): J.D. Sloane/Index Stock Imagery. p. 144: AP IMAGES. p. 145: Bob Daemmrich/The Image Works. p. 147: Alain Evrard/Photo Researchers.

Chapter 5: p. 152: Nicholas Parfitt/Getty Images. p. 155: Stephen R. Swinburne/Stock Boston, LLC. p. 159: Bill Aron/PhotoEdit. p. 161: Farrell Grehan/Photo Researchers. p. 165: Frank Whitney/Rainbow. p. 166: Dies Irae, 1987, Italy, artwork by Kurt Wenner. p. 167 (top): AP IMAGES. p. 167 (bottom): Ira Kirschenbaum/Stock, Boston, LLC. p. 169: ©PictureNet/CORBIS. p. 170: George Eastman House. p. 172: Phillip Kent/www.anamorphosis.com. p. 175: John Chiasson/Getty Images. p. 176: ©2001 Mark D. Phillips/markdphillips.com, All Rights Reserved. p. 177: Shannon Fagan/Getty images. p. 181: Mark Richards/PhotoEdit. p. 185: Professor Ron Rensink. p. 188: Larry Mulvehill/Rainbow. p. 189: Kayte M. Deloma/PhotoEdit.

Chapter 6: p. 193: Rayman/Getty Images. p. 195: Jonathan Nourok/PhotoEdit. p. 196: Photofest. p. 201: Bonnie Kamin/PhotoEdit. p. 202: ©Steven Needham/Envision. p. 203: ©Herb Lingl/aerialarchives.com. p. 204:

©Gerard Lacz/Peter Arnold, Inc. p. 206 (left): Archives of the History of American Psychology. p. 206 (right): Nina Leen/Getty Images. p. 209: Frank Lotz/Black Star. p. 210: ©Bob Daemmrich/The Image Works. p. 211: Dynamic Graphics Group/Creatas/Alamy. p. 212: Courtesy of the Lincoln Electric Company. p. 214: AP IMAGES. p. 217: Source: Lang & Melamed, 1969. p. 218: ImageState/Alamy. p. 225: From *The Mentality of Apes* by W. Kohler, 1976, published by Routledge and Kegan Paul. p. 226: Paul Chesley/Getty Images. p. 227: Alfred Bandura. p. 230: Charles Gupton/Stock Boston, LLC. p. 231: M. Ferguson/PhotoEdit. p. 232 (top): Hank Morgan/Rainbow. p. 232 (bottom): Jim Cummins/Getty Images.

Chapter 7: p. 236: Image Etc Ltd/Alamy. p. 239: Mary Kate Denny/Getty Images. p. 240: ©Jeff Greenberg/The Image Works. p. 242: Frank Siteman, Stock, Boston, LLC. p. 248: AP IMAGES. p. 251: Photo of painting by Susan Schwartzenberg, ©Franco Magnani. Photo of Pontito by Susan Schwartzenberg, ©Exploratorium, www.exploratrium.edu. p. 253: Mary Kate Denny/PhotoEdit. p. 256: Professor William F. Brewer. p. 258: AP IMAGES. p. 262: Laurence Monneret/Stone/Getty Images. p. 266: Courtesy of Elizabeth Loftus. p. 269: Courtesy of Dominique Muller, M.D., Ph.D. p. 271: Paul Gilham/Getty Images. p. 274: Mark Lewis/Getty Images.

Chapter 8: p. 279: Eyewire. p. 283 (top): AP IMAGES. p. 283 (bottom): Bob Daemmrich/Stock, Boston, LLC. p. 285: From *Cognitive Psychology and Its Implications* by John R. Anderson ©2000, 1995, 1985, 1980, by Worth Publishers and W.H. Freeman and Company. p. 286 (left): NASA. p. 286 (right): Joe Sohm/Stock, Boston, LLC. p. 287: Jeff Greenberg/PhotoEdit. p. 291: Paul Howell/Getty Images. p. 294: Jason Homa/Getty Images. p. 295: AP IMAGES. p. 296: AP IMAGES. p. 297: National Institute of Neurological Disorders and Stroke. p. 304: ©Laurence Kesterson/CORBIS SYGMA. p. 307: AP IMAGES. p. 308: ©Joh Feingersh/zefa/Corbis. p. 312: Eastcott/Momatiuk/The Image Works. p. 314: Joe McNally. p. 317: Don Smetzer/PhotoEdit. p. 319: Susan Kuklin/Photo Researchers, Inc.

Chapter 9: p. 325: Dex Image/Getty Images. p. 326: David Welling/Animals Animals. p. 332: AP IMAGES. p. 335 (left): Jacques Jangoux/Photo Researchers. p. 335 (right): Nathan Benn/National Geographic Image Collection. p. 336: Will & Deni McIntyre/Photo Researchers. p. 340: Colin Young-Wolff/PhotoEdit. p. 341: David Young-Wolff/PhotoEdit. p. 342: Jodi Cobb/National Geographic/Getty Images. p. 343: Patrick Ward/Stock, Boston, LLC. p. 347: Tony Freeman/PhotoEdit. p. 348: Grant Mason/Manni Mason's Pictures. p. 354 (top): Photo by Jules Asher at NIMH. p. 354 (bottom): Jeff Greenberg/PhotoEdit. p. 356: ©Geiger Kraig/CORBIS SYGMA. p. 357: ©Larry Mulvehill/The Image Works. p. 358: ©1994 Joel Gordon. p. 360: A. Ramey/Stock, Boston, LLC.

Chapter 10: p. 365: ©John Birdsall/The Image Works. p. 369: Records of the Public Health Service, National Archives. p. 370: Copyright ©2004 by The Riverside Publishing Company. Photograph from the Woodcock-Johnson® III (WJ III ®) reproduced with permission of the publisher. All rights reserved. p. 375: Jeff Greenberg/The Image Works. p. 381: Andy Sacks/Getty Images. p. 383: Bob Daemmrich. p. 389: Stephen Collins/Photo Researchers. p. 391: Comstock Images/Alamy. p. 395: Skjold/The Image Works. p. 398: Fraser Hale/St. Petersburg Times. p. 399: Edison National Historic Site.

Chapter 11: p. 403: ©Mark Gamba/CORBIS. p. 405: Shawn Thew/Getty Images. p. 406: ©Dwight Kuhn. p. 407: AP IMAGES. p. 409: Andrew Shennan/Getty Images. p. 413: Richard Howard. p. 415: Peter Menzel/Stock, Boston, LLC. p. 418: ©Petre Buzoianu/CORBIS. p. 423: Mary Kate Denny/PhotoEdit. p. 425: Bob Daemmrich/The Image Works. p. 429: Mary Kate Denny/PhotoEdit. p. 431: David Joel/Getty Images. p. 435: Myrleen Ferguson/PhotoEdit. p. 437: Joe Hoyle/The Daily Illini. p. 439: From *The Neurological Examination*, 4th ed., by R.N. Dejong, New York: Lippincott/Harper & Row, 1979. Reproduced by permission of Lippincott

Williams & Wilkins. **p. 445:** Bob Daemmrich. **p. 447:** Bob Daemmrich/Stock, Boston, LLC. **p. 450 (top):** AP IMAGES. **p. 450 (bottom left):** Eastcott/Momatiuk/Woodfin Camp. **p. 450 (bottom right):** Rick Smolan/Stock, Boston, LLC.

Chapter 12: p. 456: ©Myrleen Cate/Index Stock Imagery. **p. 459 (top):** B. Anderson/Photo Researchers. **p. 459 (bottom):** ©Christina Salvador/Sygma/Corbis. **p. 460:** Lennart Nilson/Bonnierforlagen AB. **p. 462:** Charles A. Nelson, Ph.D., Institute of Child Development, University of Minnesota. **p. 463:** Petit Format/J. DaCunha/Photo Researchers. **p. 466:** ©George S. Zimbel 2007. **p. 467:** Courtesy of Carolyn Rovee-Collier. **p. 471:** ©Pedrick/The Image Works. **p. 476:** Robert Brenner/PhotoEdit. **p. 477:** ©Joe Polleross/The Image Works. **p. 478:** Dynamic Graphics Group/Creatas/Alamy. **p. 479:** Peter Correz/Getty Images. **p. 481:** Martin Rogers/Stock, Boston, LLC. **p. 483:** Michael Newman/PhotoEdit. **p. 484:** Lawrence Migdale/Getty Images. **p. 486:** David Young-Wolff/PhotoEdit. **p. 488:** David Grossman/Photo Researchers. **p. 490:** Michelle Bridwell/PhotoEdit. **p. 493:** AP IMAGES. **p. 496:** ©L. Clarke/CORBIS. **p. 498:** Mary Kate Denny/PhotoEdit. **p. 502:** David Young-Wolff/PhotoEdit. **p. 506:** Steve Liss/Getty Images. **p. 509:** Michael Newman/PhotoEdit. **p. 510:** ©Reuters/CORBIS.

Chapter 13: p. 516: Christina Kennedy/Getty Images. **p. 518:** Lori Adamski Peek/Getty Images. **p. 520:** AP IMAGES. **p. 521:** Piet van Lier. **p. 525:** AP IMAGES. **p. 526:** Photofest. **p. 528:** ©Reuters/CORBIS. **p. 532:** ©Lauren Greenfield/VII. **p. 537:** Lennart Nilson/Bonnierforlagen AB. **p. 539 (top):** Bruce Ayres/Getty Images. **p. 539 (bottom):** ©Esbin-Anderson/The Image Works. **p. 543:** ©Gustavo Gilabert/Corbis. **p. 545:** Dr. Raymond Fowler. **p. 546:** Copyright 2007 B.S.I.P./. Custom Medical Stock - Custom Medical Stock Photo, All Rights Reserved.

Chapter 14: p. 550: ©Andersen Ross/Blend Images/Corbis. **p. 552:** Mary Evans Picture Library. **p. 555:** Bob Daemmrich/Stock, Boston, LLC. **p. 556:** ©Bettmann/CORBIS. **p. 559:** John Neubauer/PhotoEdit. **p. 562:** Robert Caputo/Aurora. **p. 564:** Rosanne Olson/Getty Images. **p. 570 (left):** ©Michael Childers/CORBIS SYGMA. **p. 570 (right):** AP IMAGES. **p. 571:** Chris Graythen/Getty Images. **p. 572:** ©Andrew Holbrooke/Corbis. **p. 574:** Steve Kagan/Getty Images. **p. 577:** AP IMAGES. **p. 583:** Charlotte Miller.

Chapter 15: p. 587: Janis Christie/Getty Images. **p. 590:** ©Jim Cornfield/CORBIS. **p. 591:** Mark A. Johnson/Alamy. **p. 592:** ©J.L. Dugast/Peter Arnold, Inc. **p. 593:** ©Burstein Collection/CORBIS. **p. 604:** ©Louis Psihoyos/Corbis. **p. 605:** Michael Banka/Getty Images. **p. 606:** ©Abe Rezny/The Image Works. **p. 608:** Photodisc. **p. 609:** Dr. Susan Mineka. **p. 612:** Photofest. **p. 619:** Pascal Goetgheluck/Photo Researchers, Inc. **p. 623:** D. Silbersweig/E. Stern, Cornell Medical Center. **p. 625:** Grunnitus/Photo Researchers. **p. 626:** National Institutes of Mental Health. **p. 630:** Hillsboro County Sheriff, Tampa, Florida. **p. 634:** Juan Silva/Getty Images. **p. 639:** AP IMAGES.

Chapter 16: p. 643: ©John Lund/CORBIS. **p. 645:** Stock Montage. **p. 646:** Bill Aron/PhotoEdit. **p. 647:** ©Edmund Engelman. **p. 649:** M. Grecco/Stock, Boston, LLC. **p. 651:** Michael Rougier/Getty Images. **p. 652:** Zigy Kaluzny/Getty Images. **p. 655:** Georgia Tech Photo by Gary Meek. **p. 656:** Rick Friedman/Black Star. **p. 659:** Institute for Rational-Emotive Therapy. **p. 661:** James Wilson/Woodfin Camp. **p. 672:** Spencer Grant/PhotoEdit. **p. 674:** AP IMAGES. **p. 675:** The Medical History Museum of the University of Zurich. **p. 676:** Will & Deni McIntyre/Photo Researchers. **p. 678:** Mario Tama/Getty Images. **p. 685:** ©Andrew Holbrooke/Corbis.

Chapter 17: p. 688: ©Charles Gupton/CORBIS. **p. 690:** AP IMAGES. **p. 692:** ©Bob Daemmrich/The Image Works. **p. 694:** Michael Newman/PhotoEdit. **p. 696:** ©Tom McCarthy/Rainbow. **p. 698:** Peter Ginter. **p. 699:** ©Bob Daemmrich/The Image Works. **p. 702:** David Woo/Stock, Boston, LLC. **p. 708 (top, bottom):** Photo by Joshua Correll. **p. 709:** Bonnie Kamin/PhotoEdit. **p. 710:** Robert Brenner/PhotoEdit. **p. 713:** John Lund/Sam Diephuis/Getty Images. **p. 716:** ©D.P.A./The Image Works. **p. 718:** Myrleen Ferguson/PhotoEdit.

Chapter 18: p. 721: AP IMAGES. **p. 724 (left):** AP IMAGES. **p. 724 (right):** ©David Leeson/The Image Works. **p. 725:** AP IMAGES. **p. 726 (left):** Nabeel Turner/Getty Images. **p. 726 (right):** ©Bettmann/CORBIS. **p. 730 (top):** Amy Etra/PhotoEdit. **p. 730 (bottom):** ©Ariel Skelley/CORBIS. **p. 731:** By permission of Alexandra Milgram. **p. 733:** John Chiasson/Getty Images. **p. 734:** AP IMAGES. **p. 735:** AP IMAGES. **p. 739:** Sky Bonillo/PhotoEdit. **p. 744:** Eduardo Citrinblum. **p. 745:** Courtesy North Carolina State University. **p. 746:** ©Ellen Senisi/The Image Works. **p. 747:** Benali/Getty Images. **p. 749:** Mark C. Burnett/Photo Researchers. **p. 752:** CBS/Monty Brinton/Landov. **p. 757:** Jeff Haynes/Getty Images.

Chapter 19: p. 761: CNRI/Photo Researchers, Inc. **p. 765:** Musee Dupuytren, Paris. **p. 771:** Dr. Suzanne Corkin, Massachusetts Institute of Technology. **p. 780:** Science Photo Library/Photo Researchers, Inc. **p. 784:** Science Photo Library/Photo Researchers, Inc.

Chapter 20: p. 789: Digital Vision/Getty Images. **p. 791:** David Young-Wolff/PhotoEdit. **p. 793:** ©Norbert von der Groeben/The Image Works. **p. 800:** Paul Conklin/PhotoEdit. **p. 802:** John Neubauer/PhotoEdit. **p. 808:** ©Esbin-Anderson/The Image Works. **p. 813:** Mark Richards/PhotoEdit. **p. 815:** ©Ralf Finn Hestoft/CORBIS. **p. 816:** ©Lester Lefkowitz/CORBIS. **p. 819:** ©UPPA/Topham/The Image Works.

TABLES AND ILLUSTRATIONS

Figure 1.2, p. 4: From *Developmental Psychology: Theory, Research, and Applications*, first edition by Shaffer. ©1985. Reprinted with permission of Wadsworth, a division of Thomson Learning: www.thomsonrights.com. Fax 800 730-2215. **Figure 1.3, p. 5:** From *American Journal of Psychology*. Copyright 1961 by the Board of Trustees of the University of Illinois. Used with permission of the University of Illinois Press. **Table 1.3, p. 12:** From P. Rozin, S. Dow, M. Moscovitch, and S. Rajaram, "The role of memory for recent eating experiences in onset and cessation of meals. Evidence from the amnesic syndrome," *Psychological Science*, 9, 1998, pp. 392–396. Reprinted by permission of Blackwell Publishing, www.Blackwell-synergy.com.

Figure 3.11, p. 73: *Source:* Cho, Z. H., Chung, S. C., Jones, J. P., Park, J. B., Park, H. J., Lee, H. J., Wong, E. K., & Min, B. I. (1998). New findings of the correlation between acupoints and corresponding brain cortices using functional MRI. *Proceedings of the National Academy of Science, USA, 95,* 5, pp. 2670–2573. Copyright 1998 National Academy of Sciences, U.S.A. **Figure 3.17, p. 85:** From *The Cerebral Cortex of Man*, by Penfield/Rasmussen, Macmillan, 1950. Reprinted with permission of Gale, a division of Thompson Learning: www.thomsonrights.com. Fax 800 730-2215. **Figure 3.18, p. 88:** From Hubel, D., *Eye, Brain, and Vision*, American Scientific Library, 1988, pp. 138–139. Reprinted by permission of the illustrator, Carol Donner, S. A. **Figure 3.21, p. 94:** Reprinted by permission of the publisher from *The Postnatal Development of the Human Cerebral Cortex*, Vols. I–VIII by Jesse LeRoy Conel, Cambridge, Mass: Harvard University Press, Copyright © 1939, 1975 by the President and Fellows of Harvard College.

Table 4.1, p. 112: *Fundamentals of Sensation and Perception* by M. W. Levine and J. M. Shefner. Addison Wesley, 1981. Reprinted by permission of the author. **Figure 4.5, p. 117:** G.L. Rasmussen and W.F. Windle, Neural Mechanisms of the Auditory and Vestibular Systems, 1960. Courtesy of Charles C. Thomas, Publisher, Springfield, Illinois. **Figure 4.12, p. 124:** From *Sensation and Perception*, Fourth Edition by Stanley Coren, Lawrence M. Ward, and James T. Enns, p. 275; Copyright © 1994. Reprinted with permission of John Wiley & Sons, Inc. **Figure 4.22, p. 134:** Ramachandran, V.S. & Hubbard, E.M. (2001), Psychophysical Investigations into the Neural Basis of Synaesthesia," from *Proceeding of the Royal Society of London B Biological Sciences*, 268, 979–983 (figure #3).

Figure 5.5, p. 162: From J.P. Frisby, *Seeing: Illusion, Brain, and Mind*, 1979, p. 14. By permission of Oxford University Press. **Figure 5.14, p. 174:** From *Sensation and Perception*, Fourth Edition by Stanley Coren, Lawrence

NAME INDEX

Entries that appear in blue refer to the Neuropsychology or Industrial/Organizational Psychology chapters or the appendixes.

Helgesen, S., 510
Heller, W., 90, 439
Hellström, K., 656, 657
Helmholtz, H. von, 13, 117, 129
Helms, J. E., 385
Helson, R., 507, 509
Helzer, J. E., 594, 597, 599
Henderson, B., 302
Hendrick, C., 715
Hendrick, S. S., 715
Hendricks, P. S., 660, 670
Henggeler, S. W., 664
Henig, R., 267
Henker, B., 633
Hennessey, B. A., 396
Hennig, J., 737
Henrich, C. C., 497
Henry, J. L., 527
Henry, M. E., 676
Henry, W. P., 670
Hensch, T. K., 94
Hense, R. L., 331, 712
Heppner, P. P., 531
Hepworth, S. J., 31
Herbert, J. D., 33
Herbert, T. B., 532, 538
Heres, S., 682
Hergenhahn, B. R., 215, 268, 553, 556, 572
Hering, E., 130, 131
Herman, C. P., 415, 416, 545
Herman, K. C., 685
Herman, L. M., 319
Hermann, J. H., 345
Hermans, D., 655
Hernandez, D. J., 508
Hernandez-Reif, M., 140, 461
Herpetz, S. C., 630
Herrenkohl, T., 497
Herrmann, D., 274
Herrmann, D. J., 275
Herrnstein, R. J., 379, A-3, A-4
Hershcovis, M. S., 812
Hertlein, K., 31
Hertsgaard, L., 482
Hertz, H., 111
Hertzman, C., 461
Herz, R. S., 423
Herzog, D. B., 419
Herzog, T. A., 545
Hespos, S. J., 463, 468
Hess, R. D., 430
Hess, T. M., 504, 506
Hesse, J., 145
Heston, L. L., A-3
Hetherington, E. M., 508
Hettema, J. M., 607, 619
Heuper, W. C., 302
Heward, W. L., 231
Hewstone, M., 693, 729
Heydens-Gahir, H. A., 807
Heymsfield, S. B., 413
Heywood, C. A., 131
Hezlett, S. A., 371, 375
Hicks, B. M., 633
Hicks, R. A., 338
Higgins, D. M., 566

Higgins, S. T., 357
Highley, J. R., 625
Hightower, J. R. R., 594
Higuchi, S., 636
Hildebrandt, M. G., 681
Hilgard, E. R., 346, 347, 348
Hill, B., 345
Hill, C., 670, 671
Hill, C. T., 715, 716
Hill, D. L., 137
Hill, E. A., 463
Hill, J. O., 412
Hill, R. A., 39
Hill, S. M., 657
Hill, T., 694
Hiller, W., 610
Hiller-Sturmhofel, S., 772
Hilliard, R. B., 670
Hillis, A. E., 87
Hillyard, S. A., 132
Hilton, D., 293
Hilton, H., 274
Hinckley, J., Jr., 639, 640
Hine, D., 754
Hines, M., 90, 491
Hinson, J. M., 292
Hinson, J. T., 506
Hinton, J., 511
Hintzman, D. L., 208
Hippocrates, 559, 674–675
Hirota, K., 358
Hiroto, D. S., 221, 222
Hirsch, J., 417
Hirsch, L. J., 358
Hirsch-Pasek, K., 316
Hirschfeld, R. M., 679
Hirschfeld, R. M. A., 617, 678
Hitch, G. J., 246
Hitler, A., A-3
Hittner, J. B., 568
Hixon, J. G., 716
Ho, B.-C., 622, 626
Ho, D. Y., 576
Ho, H., 389
Ho, Y.-C., 479
Hobson, J. A., 344, 345, 346
Hochberg, L. R., 87
Hochhalter, A., 219
Hodges, L. F., 655
Hodson, G., 711
Hoeger, R., 529
Hoegl, M., 817
Hoehn-Saric, R., 604, 606
Hoel, H., 815
Hofer, S. M., 512
Hoffert, M. J., 143
Hoffman, D., 36, 300
Hoffman, H. G., 260, 727
Hoffman, R. E., 627
Hoffmann, J. P., 636, 638
Hofman, M. A., 425
Hofmann, A., 358
Hofmann, S. G., 683
Hogan, H. P., 258
Hogan, J., 817
Hogan, R., 551, 817
Hogarth, R. M., 293

Höge, A., 812
Hogg, K., 491
Hoglinger, G. U., 92
Hohman, A. A., 670
Hohmann, A. G., 143
Hohmann, G. W., 443
Holahan, C. J., 510
Holcomb, H. H., 625
Holden, C., 481
Holland, C. R., 374
Hollander, E., 607
Hollinger, R. C., 811
Hollon, S. D., 665, 670, 678, 682, 683
Holloway, R. L., 90
Holman, B. R., 355
Holmes, D. S., 610
Holmes, T. H., 520–521
Holstein, J. E., 56
Holtmaat, A., 95
Holtz, A., 661
Holway, A. H., 171
Hommer, D. W., 636
Hong, Y., 317
Honts, C. R., 445
Honzik, C. H., 223
Hoobler, J. M., 527
Hood, K. E., 737
Hood, M. Y., 417
Hooker, E., 424
Hooley, J. M., 627
Hooper, J. E., 140
Hopf, H. C., 439
Hopf, N. J., 439
Hopkins, R. O., 272
Hopmeyer, A., 488
Hopper, K., 594, 595
Horan, J. J., 659
Horgan, J., 648
Horne, J. A., 337
Horner, P. J., 92
Horney, K., 556, 558, 585
Horowitz, J. L., 685
Horowitz, S. W., 445
Horowitz, T. S., 183
Horrobin, J., 399
Horton, J. E., 347
Horvath, A. O., 671
Horvath, D. L., 508, 807
Horwitz, A. V., 632
Horwitz, B., 89
Horwitz, P., 232
Horwood, L. J., 361
Hoshino-Browne, E., 705
Hötting, K., 132
Houghton, G., 220
Houkamau, C., 699
Houpt, T. R., 412
House, J. S., 532
House, R. J., 817
Houston, B., 540, 541
Hoven, C. W., 528, 607
Howard, D. V., 246
Howe, M. J. A., 232
Howe, M. L., 475

Howieson, D. B., 762, 763, 771
Hoye, A., 601
Hoyer, J., 605
Hoyert, D. L., 534
Hoyle, R. H., 34, 38, 695
Hoyt, M. F., 648
Hrdy, S. B., 408
Hrobjartsson, A., 42
Hu, F. B., 540
Hu, P., 344
Hu, S., 424
Hua, J. Y., 94
Huang, X., 478
Hubbard, E. M., 133
Hubble, M. A., 666
Hubel, D. H., 125, 126, 175
Huckabee, J. C., 521
Hudson, W., 179
Hudspeth, A. J., 116
Hudziak, J. J., 597, 599
Huesmann, L. R., 227, 228, 229, 739, 741
Huestis, M. A., 359
Huettel, S. A., 707
Huffcutt, A. I., 793, 794, 796
Huffman, A. H., 811
Hughes, B. M., 31
Hughes, C., 488
Hughes, J. R., 357
Hughes, J. W., 540
Hui, C., 810
Huizink, A. C., 461
Hull, C. L., 408
Hulse, S. H., 113
Hulsizer, M. R., 738
Hume, D., 13
Humedian, M., 672
Humphreys, K., 662
Humphreys, L. G., 379
Hunsberger, B., 708
Hunsley, J., 583, 668
Hunt, C. B., 388
Hunt, C. E., 340
Hunt, D. M., 132
Hunt, E., 387, 388
Hunt, E. B., 491
Hunt, M., 237, 620
Hunt, R., 300
Hunter, J., 375
Hurink, J. F., 415
Hurt, H., 356
Hurtley, S. M., 537
Huster, G., 544
Huston, A. C., 227
Huston, T. L., 717
Huttenlocher, J., 379
Huttenlocher, P. R., 93
Hutton, M., 82
Hwang, W.-C., 672
Hyde, J. S., 423, 491, 493, 500
Hyde, K. L., 113
Hyde, T. M., 781
Hyman, B. T., 772
Hyman, I. A., 97
Hyman, I. E., 265, 266
Hyman, R., 300
Hyman, S. E., 215

SUBJECT INDEX/GLOSSARY

Key terms, which appear in **boldface**, are followed by their definitions. Entries that appear in blue refer to the Neuropsychology or Industrial/Organizational Psychology chapters or the appendixes.

AA. *See* Affirmative action (AA)
Abecedarian Project, 382
Abilify, 677, 680
Abnormal behavior, 589, 590
Absenteeism, 808, 811
Absolute threshold *The minimum amount of stimulus energy that can be detected 50 percent of the time,* 155–156
Abstract thought, 472, 499
Abuse, child. *See* Child abuse
Acceptance, 650–651
Accessory structures *Structures, such as the lens of the eye, that modify a stimulus,* 108
   auditory, 108, 118
   olfactory, 134
   visual, 120
Accidental reinforcement, 214
Accidents, workplace, 814–815
Accommodation (in cognitive development) *The process of modifying schemas when familiar schemas do not work,* 466
Accommodation (in eye structure) *The ability of the lens to change its shape and bend light rays so that objects are in focus,* 120, 168, 181
Acetylcholine *A neurotransmitter used by neurons in the peripheral and central nervous systems in the control of functions ranging from muscle contraction and heart rate to digestion and memory,* 96, 99, 268, 357, 440, 784
Achievement motivation, 428–433, 582
Achievement test *A measure of what a person has accomplished or learned in a particular area,* 372, 375
Acoustic encoding *The mental representation of information as a sequence of sounds,* 238, 246
Acquired immune deficiency syndrome (AIDS), 102, 423, 517, 519, 533–534, 537, 538, 542, 588, 637, 813
Acquisition, in classical conditioning, 199, 203
Acronyms, 273, 276
Acrophobia, 604
ACTH. *See* Adrenocorticotropic hormone (ACTH)
Action potential *An abrupt wave of electrochemical changes traveling down an axon when a neuron becomes depolarized,* 62–64, 63–67, 70, 109, 110, 123, 139
Action tendency, 437
Activation-synthesis theory, 346
Active learning, 231–232
Active listening, 651
Actor-observer bias *The tendency to attribute other people's behavior to internal causes while attributing one's own behavior (especially errors and failures) to external causes,* 699–700
Actual criterion, for job performance, 795
Actualizing tendency *According to Rogers, an innate inclination toward growth that motivates all people,* 572
Acuity *Visual clarity, which is greatest in the fovea because of its large concentration of cones,* 121, 181

Acupuncture, 73, 144–146
Adaptation *The process through which responsiveness to an unchanging stimulus decreases over time*
   to changing environments, 194, 195, 200
   in sensory systems, 109, 121, 140
Addiction *Development of a physical need for a psychoactive drug. See also* Physical dependence
   dependence and, 352, 355, 357, 361, 635–638
   opponent-process theory and, 196
   research on, 83
Additive color mixing, 128
A-delta fibers, 141, 142
ADHD. *See* Attention deficit hyperactivity disorder (ADHD)
Adjustment disorders, 598
Adolescence, 494–503
   AIDS in, 496
   cognitive development in, 499–501, 511
   identity in, 498–499
   moral reasoning in, 500, 501
   parenting and, 496, 497
   puberty and, 494, 497–498, 511
   sexual activity in, 496–497
   sleep patterns in, 339
   suicide in, 495, 616
   violent behavior in, 457, 497–498
Adoption studies, 48, 378, 380, 381, 425, 565, 625, A-3, A-7
Adrenal cortex, 100, 537
Adrenal glands, 102, 144, 425, 523, 524, 538, 540
Adrenaline, 96, 524, 540
Adrenal medulla, 100, 441
Adrenocorticotropic hormone (ACTH), 101, 524
Adulthood, 339, 501–503. *See also* Late adulthood
   career choice, 502–503
   cognitive changes in, 503–507
   identity crisis, 501–502
   physical changes in, 503
   social changes in, 507–511
Affect, 614
Affection, in intimate relationships, 715–716
Affective disorders, 598, 614, 618. *See also* Mood disorders
Afferent neurons, 70
Affirmative action (AA), 800
Afterimages, 130
Age-graded test items, 367
Age regression, 347–349
Aggression *An act that is intended to cause harm to another person,* 18, 20, 38, 567, 569, 736–744
   alcohol and, 738
   arousal and, 489
   biological factors in, 737–738
   in childhood, 497, 512
   circumstances for, 742–744
   cognitive factors in, 20
   cultural factors in, 738–739
   defensive, 737
   emotional factors in, 742
   environmental influences on, 743–744
   frustration and, 742

   gender differences in, 491, 497
   generalized arousal and, 742–743
   genetic factors in, 406, 737–738
   instrumental, 811, 812
   observational learning of, 226, 227
   parenting style and, 486
   pornography and, 742, 743
   punishment and, 216
   reasons for, 737–739
   serotonin and, 97
   stress and, 526
   television and, 227–229
   temperature and, 739, 743
   testosterone and, 97, 738
   video games and, 740–741
   in workplace, 811
Aggressive pornography, 742, 743
Agonist *Drug that mimics the effects of the neurotransmitter that normally binds to a neural receptor,* 351, 353, 357, 358
Agoraphobia *An anxiety disorder involving strong fear of being alone or away from the security of home,* 603, 605, 606, 653, 656, 669, 679, 680
Agranulocytosis, 677
Agreeableness, 561, 581, 756
AI. *See* Artificial intelligence (AI)
AIDS. *See* Acquired immune deficiency syndrome (AIDS)
Alarm reactions, 523–524
Alcohol, 59, 66, 78, 97, 497, A-6
   aggression and, 738
   anxiolytics and, 679
   as depressant, 353–355, 359
   illness and, 518, 539
   medications and, 678, 679
   memory and, 353, 636
   prenatal risks and, 398, 461, 636
   sleeping pills and, 339
   stress and, 526, 531, 546
   in substance-related disorder, 635–637
Alcohol abuse, 635–637, 669, 696, 723
Alcohol dependence, 635–637, 669
Alcoholism *A pattern of drinking that may lead to addiction and almost always causes severe social, physical, and other problems,* 272, 635–638, 683
Alexia without agraphia, 765–766
Algorithm *A systematic procedure that cannot fail to produce a correct solution to a problem, if a solution exists,* 290, 292
ALI. *See* American Law Institute (ALI)
Alpha waves, 336, 337, 349
Alprazolam, 679, 680
Altered state of consciousness *A condition in which changes in mental processes are extensive enough that a person or others notice significant differences in psychological and behavioral functioning,* 335, 346, 347, 349–350
Altruism *An unselfish concern for another's welfare,* 744–752
Alzheimer's disease, 49, 61, 394, 506–507
   background of, 80–81
   chemistry of, 96, 269
   dementia and, 80, 593, 784–785

Attachment *A deep and enduring relationship with the person with whom a baby has shared many experiences,* 481–484, 507, 508
 day care and, 483–484
 object relations and, 556–557, 593, 649
Attention deficit disorders, 78, 400, 593
Attention deficit hyperactivity disorder (ADHD), 78, 633–634, 680
Attention *The process of directing and focusing psychological resources to enhance perception, performance, and mental experience,* 181–187, 335, 355
 aging and, 395, 504–505
 anxiety and, 437
 automatic processing and, 186–187
 brain and, 187
 brain function and, 74, 77, 78, 90, 95
 characteristics of, 182
 in childhood, 473
 in classical conditioning, 201
 cognitive ability and, 388
 covert, 182–183
 directing, 184
 dissociation and, 266
 divided, 185–186, 185–186, 189, 506
 hypnosis and, 346–347, 349
 ignoring information and, 184
 intelligence and, 388
 schizophrenia and, 623, 627
 selective, 184, 245, 246
 stress and, 525
 thought and, 282, 284
Attitude *A predisposition toward a particular cognitive, emotional, or behavioral reaction to objects,* 708–710, 714, 716, 805
 changing, 703–706
 forming, 702–703
 structure of, 701–707
Attraction, 713–714
 physical attractiveness and, 714
 similar attitudes and, 714
Attributes, in decision making, 305
Attributional biases, 699–700
Attributional style, 620
Attribution *The process of explaining the causes of people's behavior, including one's own*
 biases in, 699–700
 cultural factors in, 698
 emotions and, 447, 449
 interpersonal conflict and, 755
 sources of, 697–698
Atypical neuroleptics, 677
Audition. *See* Hearing
Auditory cortex, 84, 86, 90, 110, 115, 118, 133, 272
Auditory nerve *The bundle of axons that carries stimuli from the hair cells of the cochlea to the brain,* 109, 110, 113–115, 117, 118, 146
Authoritarianism, 708, 734
Authoritarian parents *Firm, punitive, and unsympathetic parents who value obedience from the child and authority for themselves,* 381, 485–487
Authoritative parents *Parents who reason with the child, encourage give and take, and are firm but understanding,* 486–487, 493

Authority figures, 734–736
Autism, 593, 634, 657
Autistic disorder, 598, 634
Autistic spectrum disorders, 634
Auto accidents, 354
Autoimmune disorders *Physical problems caused when cells of the body's immune system attack normal body cells as if they were foreign invaders,* 102
Autokinetic phenomenon, 727
Automatic processing, 186–187
Autonomic nervous system (ANS) *The subsystem of the peripheral nervous system that carries messages between the central nervous system and the heart, lungs, and other organs and glands,* 68–69, 102, 630
 amphetamines and, 356
 consciousness and, 333
 emotions and, 438, 439–441, 443–446
 nicotine and, 357
 stress and, 523–524, 537–538, 607
 vestibular sense and, 146
Autonomic reactivity, 540
Autonomous work teams (AWTs) *Self-managed employee groups that do not report to anyone for routine daily supervision,* 816–817
Availability heuristic *A mental shortcut through which judgments are based on information that is most easily brought to mind,* 294–295, 303, 306
Aversion conditioning *A method that uses classical conditioning to create a negative response to a particular stimulus,* 654, 655
Aversion therapy, 655, 657–658
Aversive racism, 711–713
Aviation psychology, 187–188
Avoidance-avoidance conflicts, 435
Avoidance conditioning *A type of learning in which an organism responds to a signal in a way that prevents exposure to an aversive stimulus,* 207–209, 218
Avoidant attachment, 482
Avoidant personality disorder, 629
Axes, 597, 598
Axon *A neuron fiber that carries signals from the body of a neuron out to where communication occurs with other neurons,* 62, 63, 65–67, 69–71, 73, 78, 91, 92, 96, 97, 109, 110, 113, 115, 122–125, 135, 138, 139, 141, 269, 440
Babbling *The first sounds infants make that resemble speech,* 314
Baby talk, 463, 479
Backward conditioning, 200
Baclofen, 356
Balance, sense of, 146, 147
Balanced bilinguals, 317
Balanced relationships, 714, 716
Barbiturates, 355, 359, 635, 679
Bargaining, 755
Bariatric surgery, 417
BAS. *See* Behavioral approach system (BAS)
Basal ganglia, 438
Basal nucleus, 85

Basilar membrane *The floor of the fluid-filled duct that runs through the cochlea,* 113, 114, 117
B-cells, 102, 537, 538
Bed nucleus of the stria terminalis (BnST), 422
Bed-wetting, 598
Behavioral approach *An approach to psychology emphasizing that human behavior is determined mainly by what a person has learned, especially from rewards and punishments,* 19–20, 22
 to learning, 220, 223
 to personality, 567, 570
 to psychology, 653–660
 to treatment, 661, 664
Behavioral approach system (BAS), 563
Behavioral coping strategies, 546, 547
Behavioral dependence, 635
Behavioral family therapy, 669
Behavioral genetics *The study of the effect of genes on behavior,* 46–49, 426, 563–566, 625, A-1–A-8
Behavioral inhibition system (BIS), 563
Behavioral marital intervention, 663
Behavioral marital therapy, 669
Behavioral medicine, 517
Behavioral signatures, 569
Behavioral stress responses, 526
Behavior-focused rating forms, 797
Behaviorism, 16, 17, 19, 220, 327, A-3
Behavior modification *Treatments that use operant conditioning methods to change behavior,* 654
Behavior therapy *Treatments that use classical conditioning principles to change behavior,* 653–660, 669, 670
 cognitive-behavior therapy as, 658–660
 techniques of, 654–658
Belief bias, 291
The Bell Curve (Herrnstein & Murray), A-4
Belongingness, 433, 434, 574
Benzedrine, 355
Benzodiazepines, 679–682, 684
Beta-amyloid, 81–83
Beta-endorphin, 523
Bias
 attributional, 699–701
 confirmation, 32, 291–292, 300–301
 in decision making, 306–307
 employee selection interviews and, 794
 experimenter, 41, 43, 43–44, 319–320, 631
 in heuristics, 294
 in IQ tests, 372, 375–376, 384–386
 in job performance appraisals, 797
 in perceptual recognition, 176–177
 in problem solving, 300–301
 in psychological diagnoses, 600–603
 in social perception, 694
Biased sample *A group of research participants selected from a population each of whose members did not have an equal chance of being chosen,* 45
Big-five model, of personality, 560–561, 566, 578, 580, 581, 583, 756
Bilingualism, 280, 317
Binge drinking, 636, 637

Coverage of Behavioral Genetics, Evolutionary Psychology, and Sociocultural Variables in *Psychology*, Eighth Edition

Indicates material in optional Chapters 19, Neuropsychology, and 20, Industrial/Organizational Psychology— available for inclusion in your textbook upon request. Please consult your sales representative for details.

Behavioral Genetics

- Reference to genetics and neuroscience (Ch. 1, p. 10)
- Genetics appendix reference (Ch. 1, p. 18)
- In Review chart reference to genetics as characteristic of biological approach (Ch. 1, p. 22)
- Linkages: Psychological Research Methods and Behavioral Genetics (Ch. 2, pp. 46–49)
- End-of-chapter Linkages diagram shows connection between behavioral genetics and other subfields of psychology (Ch. 2, p. 56)
- Experience-dependent gene expression; influence of genetics on height (Ch. 3, p. 59)
- Focus on Research Methods: Manipulating Genes in Animal Models of Human Disease (Ch. 3, pp. 81–83)
- Linkages: Human Development and the Changing Brain (Ch. 3, pp. 93–94)
- Pitch-recognition abilities (Ch. 4, p. 116)
- Near-sightedness (Ch. 4, p. 120)
- Genetically determined differences in ability to taste (Ch. 4, p. 137)
- Genetics and attention to novel stimuli (Ch. 6, p. 195)
- Biopreparedness for learning and taste aversions (Ch. 6, pp. 201–202)
- Role of genetics in language acquisition (Ch. 8, pp. 316–317)
- Genetic predisposition for sleep apnea and for SIDS (Ch. 9, p. 340)
- In Review chart reference to genetic role in sleep apnea and SIDS (Ch. 9, p. 345)
- Biochemical effects of alcohol (Ch. 9, p. 355)
- Influence of genetics on intelligence and individual differences in intelligence (Ch. 10, pp. 377–379)
- Genetics and group differences in IQ scores (Ch. 10, pp. 379–380)
- In Review chart reference to influence of genetics on IQ Scores (differences among people on intelligence test performance) (Ch. 10, p. 384)
- Mental retardation and genetics (Ch. 10, p. 398)
- Genetics and instincts (Ch. 11, pp. 406–407)
- Genetic predisposition toward obesity or anorexia nervosa (Ch. 11, pp. 416–418)
- Thinking Critically: What Shapes Sexual Orientation? (Ch. 11, pp. 424–427)
- Genetics and sexual dysfunctions (Ch. 11, p. 427)
- Influence of genetics on happiness (individual differences in happiness and inherited personality factors) (Ch. 11, p. 433)
- Genetics and emotional expression (Ch. 11, p. 449)
- Developmental psychology—how development throughout the life span is affected by both genetics and the environment (Ch. 12, p. 457)
- Genetics and the nature–nurture debate (Ch. 12, p. 459)
- Genetics and prenatal development (Ch. 12, pp. 460–461)
- Motor development and nature–nurture influences (Ch. 12, p. 464)
- Temperament and genetic predispositions (Ch. 12, p. 480)
- Biology and gender roles (Ch. 12, p. 491)
- Violence in adolescence and genetics (Ch. 12, p. 497)
- Decline of cognitive abilities and genetics (Ch. 12, p. 505)
- Genetically determined autonomic reactivity and the relationship between hostility and heart disease (Ch. 13, p. 541)
- Thinking Critically: Are Personality Traits Inherited?—the genetics of traits (Ch. 14, pp. 563–566)
- Genetic influences as part of biopsychosocial model (Ch. 15, pp. 592–593, and in Table 15.1 on p. 596)
- Genetic influences as part of the diathesis-stress model (Ch. 15, pp. 594–596, and in Table 15.1 on p. 596)
- Genetic influences and anxiety disorders (Ch. 15, pp. 606–607)
- The role of genetics in mood disorders (Ch. 15, pp. 618–619, 625)
- Research in schizophrenia and behavioral genetics (Ch. 15, pp. 625–627)
- In Review chart: Schizophrenia (Ch. 15, p. 627)
- Genetics and Vulnerability Theory (Ch. 15, p. 628)
- Genetic predisposition for antisocial personality disorder (Ch. 15, pp. 630–631)
- Genetic predisposition toward externalizing disorders (Ch. 15, pp. 633–634)
- Genetics and internalizing disorders (Ch. 15, p. 634)
- Genetics and addiction (Ch. 15, p. 636)
- Genetic differences in drug metabolism (Ch. 16, p. 681)
- Linkages: Biological and Social Psychology (Ch. 17, pp. 706–707)
- Genetic mechanisms in aggression (Ch. 18, pp. 737–738)
- Genetics and helping behavior (Ch. 18, p. 749)
- Focus on Research Methods: Does Family Matter? (Ch. 18, pp. 750–751)
- *Neurodegeneration and genetics (Ch. 19, p. 770)
- *Thinking Critically: Is Job Satisfaction Genetic? (Ch. 20, pp. 808–810)
- What behavioral genetics is (behavioral genetics appendix, p. A-1)
- The Biology of Genetics and Heredity (behavioral genetics appendix, p. A-1)
- History of Genetic Research (behavioral genetics appendix, pp. A-3–A-4)
- The Focus on Research in Behavioral Genetics (behavioral genetics appendix, p. A-4)
- Genetic Factors in Psychology (behavioral genetics appendix, pp. A-5–A-7)
- Behavioral Genetics and Environmental Influences (behavioral genetics appendix, pp. A-7–A-8)

Evolutionary Psychology

- The Evolutionary Approach (Ch. 1, p. 18)
- In Review chart: Approaches to Psychology (Ch. 1, p. 22)
- Linkages: Perception and Human Development (researchers who take an evolutionary approach) (Ch. 5, pp. 180–181)
- Evolutionary approach to psychology and individual variability in the capacity to adapt (Ch. 6, p. 194)
- Evolution and biopreparedness (association of pain with external stimuli, taste aversion) (Ch. 6, p. 202)
- Evolutionary approach and instincts (behavioral predispositions, choice of marriage partner, and genetic fitness) (Ch. 11, pp. 406–408)
- Evolution and obesity (Ch. 11, p. 417)
- Gender differences and the evolutionary approach (Ch. 12, p. 492)
- Predisposition for fear and evolution (Ch. 15, p. 609)
- Intimate relationships and love (Ch. 17, p. 715)
- Why are People Aggressive? (Ch. 18, pp. 737–738)
- Evolutionary approach to social psychology—explaining helping (Ch. 18, p. 749)
- Focus on Research Methods: Does Family Matter?—evolutionary explanation of helping and altruism (Ch. 18, pp. 750–751)
- In Review chart: Theories of Helping Behaviors (Ch. 18, p. 752)